The Book of Video Lists

About the Author

Tom Wiener's articles and reviews have appeared in *USA Today*, the *Washington Post*, *TV Guide, Entertainment Weekly*, and *Library Journal*. He is a former senior editor of *American Film* magazine and a former editor of publications for a national video store chain. He lives in a two-VCR house in Washington, D.C.

Tom Wiener

The Book of Video Lists

More than 700 Categories of Movies You Can See on Video
Cross-referenced with 7,500 Capsule Reviews

Andrews and McMeel
A Universal Press Syndicate Company
Kansas City

The Book of Video Lists
copyright © 1988, 1989, 1991, 1992, 1993 by Tom Wiener.
All rights reserved.
Printed in the United States of America.
No part of this book may be used or reproduced
in any manner whatsoever without written permission
except in the case of reprints in the context of reviews.
For information write Andrews and McMeel,
a Universal Press Syndicate Company,
4900 Main Street, Kansas City, Missouri 64112.

Designed by Cameron Poulter.

Library of Congress Cataloging-in-Publication Data

Wiener, Tom.
    The book of video lists / by Tom Wiener.
      p. cm. Includes indexes.
    ISBN 0-8362-8031-8 (ppb) : $16.95
    1. Video recordings—Catalogs. 2. Motion pictures—Catalogs.
I. Title.
PN1992.95.W55 1992
016.79143'75—dc20   92-31591
                                      CIP

Attention: Schools and Businesses

Andrews and McMeel books are available at quantity discounts
with bulk purchase for educational, business, or sales promotional use.
For information, please write to:
Special Sales Department, Andrews and McMeel, 4900 Main Street,
Kansas City, Missouri 64112.

Contents

Introduction

You know the feeling:

You're in a video store, standing in front of a shelf full of tapes. Some of the films you've seen, a few titles sound familiar, and most you've never heard of. You know what kind of a movie you want to rent, but how do you find it? Your hands are sweating, the titles blur together, you're thinking about all the time you've been standing there looking for a movie when you could be home watching one . . .

That's where *The Book of Video Lists* comes in. This book will make you a smarter video renter because it provides you with hundreds of suggestions tailored to your tastes in movies, whether you're a fan of sentimental love stories, gangster dramas, Broadway musicals, or gory horror stories, whether your favorite screen performer is Tom Cruise or Joan Crawford, whether you're looking for a film directed by Spike Lee or David Lean.

Think of this book as a video matchmaker, designed to get you and the right movie together for an evening's entertainment. *The Book of Video Lists,* unlike any other video or movie guide, is organized by subjects and stars and directors, the way most people shop for movies on tape. It's a guide you can use every time you make a trip to the video store.

First, a few words on the contents of this book.

There are two types of lists in this book. The subject lists (for example, World War II, Romantic Comedies, Musical Films About Show Biz) are selective. To list every World War II drama, romantic comedy, or backstage musical available on video would make this book longer than the Manhattan Yellow Pages and a lot less useful. The second type of lists, the Check Lists, attempt to be inclusive. More on those under "How to Use This Book."

There is no way this or any other video guide, no matter how large, can be comprehensive. Each month dozens of new releases arrive on the market. An increasing number of them are direct-to-video films that have never played in theaters, plus children's, music, exercise, and other special-interest programs. This book doesn't try to cover the entire video waterfront; it concentrates on theatrical films, still the most popular form of home entertainment. I have included a selection of comedy and music performance tapes, movies originally made for TV, and TV miniseries if they are of sufficient interest to merit a look on home video.

I'll leave the laserdisc listings to other guides. Presently, laserdiscs serve mainly serious collectors, not casual renters, since few stores, even in the largest metropolitan areas, carry a selection of them for rent. Once you watch a film on laser—especially those special-edition discs with extra audio tracks and footage—it's not easy to go back to videocassettes. But for now, the economics of discs are prohibitive for most of us.

Every film in this book has been carefully checked for its availability on home video. However, some titles have been "discontinued" by their distributors. When a home video title is discontinued, rental copies may stay in circulation but cannot be replaced once they are defective. If you're looking to find a discontinued movie for purchase, you'll have a lot of problems, unless a video retailer is willing to sell you a used rental copy. Chapter 20 lists several hundred titles unavailable on videocassette and a shorter list of discontinued titles. In including some of the latter titles on the lists in this book, I've made some judgment calls; if a title was only recently discontinued, there may still be enough rental copies in circulation to justify including the film here.

Don't be disappointed if your video store doesn't carry all 7,500 titles in this guide. Most video stores, even the largest ones, can be ruthless about their inventory of "catalog" titles, i.e., tapes that have been in circulation more than a year or so. Home video, it is clear, is a "hits-driven" business; the latest releases are what stores stock in great numbers because that's what most renters look for.

Looking for titles more than a year or two old and especially those from the 1930s, '40s, '50s, and '60s (not to mention the silent era, which most stores treat as though it never happened) can be a frustrating experience. Here's some advice on what to do when you can't find a tape you want:

- •Be persistent. Ask someone at the store for help. It may be shelved in a location you haven't checked, or the store may carry it but it's out on a rental.

- •If you want to purchase the tape, you should be able to order it. A good video store operates the way a full-service book or record store does: They'll obtain a title from their distributor and hold it for you. If your video store can't or won't provide this service, look for a store that will.

- •Most stores won't order a title if you only want to rent. After all, there's no guarantee that, after *you* take that wonderful but obscure movie home for a night, anyone else will rent it. Check out other stores in your area; finding that special tape may be worth the extra time. And in the process you may discover a video store that carries films more suited to your interests.

- •Try mail-order sources. There are dozens of them, catering to all tastes. Some even offer rentals by mail. For a very good list, check out Leonard Maltin's annual (and invaluable) *TV Movies and Video Guide*. It's a book anyone with a mildly serious interest in movies should own anyway.

How to Use This Book

The first portion of the book contains chapters on categories common to most video stores:

Action/Adventure (AC)
Classics (CL)
Comedy (CO)
Cult Films (CU)
Drama (DR)
Family/Children's (FA)
Foreign Films (FF)
Horror (HO)
Musicals (MU)
Mystery/Suspense (MY)
Science Fiction (SF)
Westerns (WE)

The two-letter codes after each category are used in the general index. More on that in a moment.

Each of these chapters contains lists of titles arranged by topic; the lists are numbered in sequence. For example, the first list in the Action/Adventure chapter lists a selection of World War II films **(AC1)**. In the Comedy chapter, the seventh list is a collection of movie spoofs **(CO7)**. Fans of British mysteries can begin their investigations with the fifteenth list under Mystery/Suspense **(MY15).**

To these broad category chapters, I've added several other chapters of lists:

Director Check Lists (DT)
Historical/Fictional Characters Check Lists (HF)
Star Check Lists (ST)
Writer Check Lists (WR)
Video Extra (XT)

The **Director** chapter contains 144 filmmakers, from Woody Allen to William Wyler, from Frank Capra to Oliver Stone. In **Historical/Fictional Characters,** you'll find movies portraying the high (Jesus Christ) and the mighty (Tarzan). The **Star** chapter lists 234 of your favorite players, from Abbott and Costello to James Woods and Joanne Woodward. **Writer Check Lists** embrace the art of William Shakespeare and the craft of Stephen King; it's a guide mainly to writers whose works have been adapted to the screen. The **Video Extra** chapter contains miscellaneous collections of films not confined to one category. Looking for the winners of the major Oscars? Or anti-war, road, or wedding movies? They're all in Video Extra.

For this Fifth Edition, two new lists in the Video Extra chapter may need some explanation. **XT28** is titled Oscar Justice, my personal revision of the major Academy Awards from the recent and distant past. Shortly after I came up with this (by no means original) idea, I learned of Danny Peary's provocative and entertaining book, *Alternate Oscars*. My choices occasionally coincide with Peary's, but while Peary considered all films released in a given year, I made my choices only from the nominated films and performances. If I haven't picked an alternate, it means 1. I'm satisfied with the Academy's decision, 2. The quality difference between the winner and a runner-up is too slight, or 3. I haven't seen all the nominees and can't make an informed decision.

XT29 is a list of movies currently not on videocassette that I'd like to see made available. Again, this is a personal selection, drawn from the lengthy list in Chapter 20. I have included descriptions of these films in the Title Index as a way of making my case for their release on home video. In each instance, I've indicated that the film is Unavailable on Video to avoid any confusion.

The **Check Lists** are more inclusive than the subject lists. In a few cases, where the prodigious output of some stars (and the limited availability of some of their more obscure titles) warrants, I've been selective. The Star Check Lists include titles where the performer may have appeared only briefly. I have tried to indicate where a player's appearance is very brief by using the designation (bit) after the title of the film. (This isn't the place to distinguish between a cameo appearance and a bit role; I'll just let the shorter word work for both.) If you're unsure about a title featuring a star you're interested in, please check the film's entry in the Title Index before you rent. There, I've noted whether that actor is featured or plays a bit part. You may, for example, want to rent *Young Frankenstein* to see Gene Hackman's brief but hilarious cameo as the blind hermit, but you may not necessarily want to sit all the way through the 1979 version of *Invasion of the Body Snatchers* just to see Robert Duvall as a priest. (Hint: If you miss the first five minutes, you've missed him.)

I've also included chapters titled **Essential Viewing** and **Highly Recommended/Recommended.** The nearly 400 films listed under Essential Viewing are intended as a guide to movies of enduring interest. If you want a capsule history of the movies from 1915 to 1980, this is a good place to start. If you want to consider yourself a well-informed movie person, I would modestly suggest you start with this list. For convenience, I have divided this chapter into historical sections, in chronological order. And because I can't yet presume to know this soon which films of the 1980s are Essential Viewing, the list ends at 1980.

The nearly 2,000 titles in the Highly Recommended/Recommended chapter are a matter of my personal taste, which is eclectic enough to include *The Silence of the Lambs, Tootsie, Pandora's Box,* and *The Last Waltz.* Should none of those films be to your liking, you may still agree with some of my other recommendations. If you think in terms of a star rating system, a Highly Recommended title is ****, a Recommended title is ***. Again, if you're unsure of a title, read the discription in the Title Index before you rent.

I have included brief commentary on as many titles as possible to give you an idea of what I admired and disliked about each film. There are many films in this book I enjoyed, but they also possessed too many flaws for me to recommend. A short list of recent such titles—which I'd give the equivalent of a **½ rating—would include *Sneakers, A River Runs Through It, Enchanted April, Rush, A Midnight Clear,* and *Scent of a Woman.* You may disagree with my personal assessment of those or other titles in this book, and that's fine. *The Book of Video Lists* is not organized around my ratings or opinions. There are plenty of bad and ugly films mixed in with the good ones in this book, as you'll discover from some of my comments in the Title Index. In those cases, all I can say is *Caveat Renter.*

If you're unsure about a film, read my description and comments, talk to a friend whose opinions you trust who's seen the film, or talk to someone at your favorite video store who knows your tastes. Ultimately, the only video guide that can perfectly match your taste in movies is the one you'd write, if only you had the time and some nice publisher who would agree to publish it.

And finally, Chapter 20 is a long but by no means inclusive list of movies still unavailable on videocassette. If you can't find a certain title in this book or in your favorite video store, check this list. Like all lists in this book, it is accurate as of our press time. The list includes many surprisingly popular films, cult favorites that video stores get requests for regularly, films by major directors or featuring important stars. It's my hope that publishing this list will stir distributors to make some of these titles available; I'd like nothing better than to shorten this list for the next edition.

Every film in this book (except titles in Chapter 20) is listed alphabetically in the **Title Index.** Each index entry contains the year of release, color (C) or black and white (B&W), running time, and MPAA rating. Also included are a short description of the film and, on selected titles, personal comments on the merits of the film. This is not a critical guide to films on video, so I've kept my comments brief. Following that are the code designations for the list or lists that film appears on. For example, *Bram Stoker's Dracula* is coded **DT29** (Francis Ford Coppola Check List), **HF7** (Dracula Check List), **HO4** (Vampires), **HO25** (Sexy Horror), **MU12** (Pop Stars in Non-Musical Roles—for Tom Waits), and **ST109** (Anthony Hopkins Check List). After the list codes, I've indicated if the title is *Essential Viewing*, and if I consider it *Highly Recommended* or *Recommended*.

The **Title Index** can be used in several ways. If you're browsing one of the lists in the first portion of the book and a title is unfamiliar, look it up in the Index. Or, you may want to start in the Index with a title you already know, to check out others on the same subject, or with the same star, by the same director, with the same historical or fictional character, or based on the same author's work.

Some notes on dates, running times, and ratings.

On the lists, you'll notice that a title may be designated by a date. Where a date appears alone, it indicates that the same title has been used for more than one film. For instance, there are two movies named *Frantic*, a 1958 Jeanne Moreau drama and a 1988 thriller starring Harrison Ford. Where a date appears with the word "version," it's to show that the same story has been filmed more than once. *Henry V* was filmed in 1945 with Laurence Olivier and in 1989 with Kenneth Branagh. In some cases, I've indicated "version" even if a remake (or original) is not available on video, for the sake of clarity.

The dates reflect the film's original theatrical release (if it's a foreign film, release in its country of origin), its original TV air date, or its release to home video if it never showed in theaters or on TV.

Running times apply to the home video version of the film. Some films have been shortened or lengthened for release on home video, and I've tried to reflect that as faithfully as possible. (See List **CU10** in the Cult Chapter for a collection of movies which have added footage for home video release.)

MPAA ratings are to be used as guidelines, especially by parents. Any entry designated NR has not been rated by the MPAA. This includes most films released before 1968, movies made for broadcast or cable TV, and music performance videos. Some movies are available in two versions, one rated (usually "R"), another unrated. I've tried to indicate dual availability wherever possible.

This book may have one name below the title but, like a film, it was really a collaboration. Chuck Lean and Ron Castell were present at the creation; their love for good books and good movies nurtured the project. Mike Clark and Stephen Zito, two gentlemen whose writing and love of movies have inspired me, contributed enormously to this book. Pat Dowell, Patrick Sheehan, and Scott Simmon graciously lent advice on various lists; Mr. Sheehan has always been quick to check on the smallest details about individual titles for me.

I want to acknowledge several invaluable sources of published information: Leonard Maltin's *TV Movies and Video Guide* (still the best single volume movie reference at any price), National Video Clearinghouse's *The Video Source Book*, Video Hound's *Golden Movie Retriever* (I'm flattered by the Hound's own attempts at list-making), *Video Movie Guide* by Mick Martin and Marsha Porter, *The Encyclopedia of Film* by James Monaco and the editors of *Baseline* and Ephraim Katz's *The Film Encyclopedia*, The Phantom's *Ultimate Video Guide* and Michael Weldon's *Psychotronic Encyclopedia of Film* (the latter two especially helpful for off-the-beaten-track titles), and Roy Pickard's *Who Played Who on the Screen.*

These people helped make this project happen: Jed Lyons; Rafe Sagalyn, who found it a new home; Lauren Malnati, Rich Swope, and Liz Godin, who provided important research assistance in the very beginning; Lori Shimabukuro and Rich Swope for ongoing bulletins on the release of classic titles; Ray Heinrich of One to One Communications for unsurpassed expertise in all matters technical; Janet Huffman, Carlos Aguilar, Bill Nuhn, Michael James, Terri Nyman, Michelle Lewis, Al Hollin, Mark Miller, Rosemary Prillaman, Tonda Hernandez, Pam Uhl, Roxanne Kavounis, and Jennifer Wyckoff—all members in good standing of the Erol's Alumni Association; Bruce Eder for information on letterboxed titles; Ty Burr for the kind words when they really counted; Joe Goluski for giving me lots of air time in Syracuse; Lori Shimabukuro and Joyce Woodward, lovely dinner companions and very reliable sources; Maureen Humphrys and Louise Millikan for ongoing culinary support; Bill Kenly and Jackie Sigmund for longtime moral support; Heidi Diamond, the maven of marketing, for fighting the good fight; J.P. Faber, wherever you are now; and Mort Zedd, a man whose knack for marrying into a good family is matched only by his skills as a movie extra.

Finally, to Barbara Humphrys, thanks for her insightful suggestions and proofreading; for her patience, her humor, her love, and her willingness to stay home Saturday nights to watch tapes, I am always grateful.

I welcome comments and corrections from readers. Please address them to me at Andrews and McMeel, 4900 Main Street, Kansas City, Missouri 64112.

—Tom Wiener

1 Action/Adventure (AC)

AC1	World War II	**AC14**	Romantic Adventure
AC2	World War I	**AC15**	Costume Adventure
AC3	Korean War	**AC16**	Historical Adventure
AC4	Vietnam War (and aftermath)	**AC17**	Super Heroes
AC5	Civil War	**AC18**	Sword and Sorcery Fantasies
AC6	Other Conflicts	**AC19**	Tales of Revenge
AC7	Prisoners of War	**AC20**	Mercenaries and Other Combatants
AC8	Urban Action	**AC21**	Soldiers of Fortune
AC9	Cops and Robbers	**AC22**	Gangster Sagas
AC10	Hot Wheels	**AC23**	Disaster Stories
AC11	The Wild Blue Yonder	**AC24**	Stories of Survival
AC12	Adventure in the Great Outdoors	**AC25**	One-Man Armies
AC13	Adventure Classics	**AC26**	Martial Arts Action

See also: Fictional Character Check List HF2 James Bond; Star Check Lists ST20 Charles Bronson, ST36 Sean Connery, ST64 Clint Eastwood, ST69 Errol Flynn, ST128 Alan Ladd, ST134 Bruce Lee, ST146 Steve McQueen, ST165 Chuck Norris, ST183 Burt Reynolds, ST195 Arnold Schwarzenegger, ST204 Sylvester Stallone

---

AC1 World War II
Across the Pacific
Action in the North Atlantic
Air Force
The Americanization of Emily
Anzio
Armored Command
Attack Force Z
Back to Bataan
Bataan
Battle Cry
Battle Force
Battle of Britain
Battle of the Bulge
Battleground
Betrayed (1954)
Between Heaven and Hell
The Big Red One
Bombardier
Breakthrough (1978)
The Bridge at Remagen
A Bridge Too Far
China Sky
Command Decision
Commandos
The Counterfeit Traitor
Cross of Iron
The Cruel Sea
D-Day the Sixth of June
Dangerous Moonlight
Das Boot

The Day Will Dawn
Days of Glory
December 7th
The Deep Six
The Desert Fox
The Desert Rats
Desperate Journey
Destination Tokyo
Destroyer
The Devil's Brigade
The Dirty Dozen
The Dirty Dozen: The Next Mission
The Eagle Has Landed
The Enemy Below
Farewell to the King
The Fighting Seabees
The Fighting Sullivans
Fires on the Plain
Flying Leathernecks
Flying Tigers
Force 10 From Navarone
The 49th Parallel
From Here to Eternity
The Gallant Hours
Guadalcanal Diary
Gung Ho! (1943)
The Guns of Navarone
Halls of Montezuma
Hell in the Pacific
Home of the Brave
The Immortal Battalion

The Immortal Sergeant
In Harm's Way
In Which We Serve
Is Paris Burning?
Joan of Paris
Kings Go Forth
The Lion Has Wings
The Longest Day
The Malta Story
The Man Who Never Was
Marine Raiders
Memphis Belle (1990 version)
A Midnight Clear
Midway
Morituri
The Mountain Road
Murphy's War
The Naked and the Dead
Never So Few
None but the Brave
The North Star
Objective, Burma!
One of Our Aircraft Is Missing
Operation Crossbow
Operation Pacific
Patton
The Purple Heart
Pursuit of the *Graf Spee*
Raid on Rommel
Run Silent, Run Deep
Sahara
Sands of Iwo Jima
The Sea Chase
The Sea Shall Not Have Them
The Sea Wolves
Sink the Bismarck!
633 Squadron
Soldier of Orange
Sundown
They Were Expendable
13 Rue Madeleine
Thirty Seconds Over Tokyo
This Is Korea/December 7th
To Hell and Back
To the Shores of Tripoli
Tobruk
Tora! Tora! Tora!
The Train
Twelve O'Clock High
A Walk in the Sun
The War Lover
Where Eagles Dare
Wing and a Prayer
A Yank in the R.A.F.
The Young Lions

AC2 World War I
All Quiet on the Western Front
The Big Parade
The Blue Max

Crimson Romance
The Dawn Patrol (1938 version)
A Farewell to Arms (1932 and 1957 versions)
Forty Thousand Horsemen
Gallipoli
Hearts of the World
Hell's Angels
The Iron Major
The Lighthorsemen
Men of Bronze
Paths of Glory
Sergeant York
Suzy
What Price Glory?
Wings
Zeppelin

AC3 Korean War
All the Young Men
Battle Circus
The Bridges at Toko-Ri
Field of Honor
M*A*S*H
Men in War
One Minute to Zero
Pork Chop Hill
Retreat, Hell!
Sergeant Ryker
The Steel Helmet
This Is Korea/December 7th
Torpedo Alley

AC4 Vietnam War (and aftermath)
Air America
Apocalypse Now
Bat 21
Born on the Fourth of July
The Boys in Company C
Braddock: Missing in Action III
Casualties of War
China Gate
Dear America: Letters Home From Vietnam
The Deer Hunter
84 Charlie Mopic
Fighting Mad (1977)
Flight of the Intruder
Full Metal Jacket
Go Tell the Spartans
Good Morning, Vietnam
The Green Berets
Hamburger Hill
The Iron Triangle
Missing in Action
Missing in Action 2: The Beginning
Platoon
Purple Hearts
Rambo: First Blood II
Saigon: Year of the Cat
The Siege of Firebase Gloria
Tornado
Uncommon Valor

AC5 Civil War
See also: WE6 Civil War Westerns
The Birth of a Nation
The Blue and the Gray
Friendly Persuasion
Glory
Gone With the Wind
Mosby's Marauders
The Red Badge of Courage
She Wore a Yellow Ribbon
Shenandoah

AC6 Other Conflicts
Allegheny Uprising
The Battle of Algiers
The Buccaneer
Captain Horatio Hornblower
The Charge of the Light Brigade (1936 version)
Damn the Defiant!
Drums Along the Mohawk
The Four Feathers
Heartbreak Ridge
The Last of the Mohicans (1936 and 1992 versions)
Lost Command
Mutiny
The Real Glory
Revolution
The Sand Pebbles
Soldiers of Fortune
Zulu
Zulu Dawn

AC7 Prisoners of War
The Bridge on the River Kwai
The Dunera Boys
Escape to Athena
Grand Illusion
The Great Escape
The Hanoi Hilton
King Rat
Merry Christmas, Mr. Lawrence
Missing in Action 2: The Beginning
P.O.W.: The Escape
Prisoners of the Sun
Stalag 17
Von Ryan's Express
Women of Valor

AC8 Urban Action
See also: AC9 Cops and Robbers, AC22 Gangster Sagas
Above the Law
Action Jackson
American Me
Angel
Armed Response
Assault on Precinct 13
Avenging Angel
Backdraft
Band of the Hand

China Girl
Cold Sweat
Darkman
Defiance
Detroit 9000
Die Hard
The Driver
8 Million Ways to Die
Enemy Territory
Fear City
Getting Even
Gloria
Gordon's War
Hard Times
Harley Davidson & the Marlboro Man
The Hidden
The Hunter
The Killer Elite
King of New York
Knights of the City
The Last Boy Scout
The Last of the Finest
The Mack
Marked for Death
Point Blank
Predator 2
Rapid Fire
The Return of Superfly
Savage Streets
Shaft
Shaft's Big Score!
Short Fuse
Streets of Fire
Superfly
Sweet Sweetback's Baadasssss Song
Switchblade Sisters
Thief
Tougher Than Leather
Trespass
The Warriors (1979)

AC9 Cops and Robbers
See also: AC8 Urban Action, AC22 Gangster Sagas
Across 110th Street
The Anderson Tapes
Another 48 HRS
Badge of the Assassin
Badge 373
Black Rain (U.S.)
The Blue Knight
Bullitt
City in Fear
Cobra
Code of Silence
Colors
Coogan's Bluff
Dead-Bang
Dead Heat
The Dead Pool

Deep Cover
The Detective (1968)
Dick Tracy
Dirty Harry
Downtown
Electra Glide in Blue
The Enforcer (1976)
The FBI Story
Fatal Beauty
The First Deadly Sin
48 HRS
The French Connection
The French Connection II
The Gauntlet
The Getaway
The Glitter Dome
The Hard Way
The Hitman
Hollywood Vice Squad
Homicide
The Hot Rock
Hustle
Jackie Chan's Police Force
The January Man
King of New York
Kinjite: Forbidden Subjects
Kuffs
The Laughing Policeman
Lethal Weapon
Lethal Weapon 2
Lethal Weapon 3
McQ
Madigan
Magnum Force
Maximum Force
Miami Blues
The Naked City
The New Centurions
New Jack City
Nighthawks
Off Limits (1988)
One Good Cop
The Organization
Point Break
The Presidio
Quiet Cool
Red Heat (1988)
Renegades
Report to the Commissioner
Ricochet
RoboCop
RoboCop 2
The Rookie
Running Scared
The Seven-ups
Shakedown
Sharky's Machine
Stark
State of Grace
Stick

The Stone Killer
Strike Force
Sudden Impact
The Taking of Pelham One Two Three
Tango and Cash
They Call Me MISTER Tibbs!
Thunderbolt and Lightfoot
Tightrope
To Live and Die in L.A.
Under Cover
Under the Gun
Vice Squad
Walking Tall (series)
Year of the Dragon

AC10 Hot Wheels
Black Moon Rising
Cannonball
The Cannonball Run
Cannonball Run II
Convoy
Days of Thunder
Death Race 2000
Deathsport
Eat My Dust!
Electra Glide in Blue
Flatbed Annie
Gone in 60 Seconds
Grand Prix
Grand Theft Auto
The Gumball Rally
King of the Mountain
The Last Chase
Le Mans
Mad Max
Mad Max Beyond Thunderdome
Race With the Devil
The Racers
Rad
Red Line 7000
Return to Macon County
The Road Warrior
Rolling Vengeance
Safari 3000
Thunder Road
Vanishing Point
Wheels of Fire
The Wild Angels
The Wraith

AC11 The Wild Blue Yonder
Aces: Iron Eagle III
Air America
The Aviator
Battle of Britain
The Blue Max
Blue Thunder
The Bridges at Toko-Ri
Chain Lightning
Choke Canyon

The Dawn Patrol (1938 version)
Dive Bomber
Fire Birds
Firefox
Flight of the Intruder
Flying Tigers
A Gathering of Eagles
The Great Waldo Pepper
Hell's Angels
High Road to China
Hot Shots!
Into the Sun
Iron Eagle
Iron Eagle II
Jet Pilot
Memphis Belle (1990 version)
Only Angels Have Wings
Passenger 57
The Right Stuff
633 Squadron
The Spirit of St. Louis
Strategic Air Command
Test Pilot
Top Gun
Twelve O'Clock High
The War Lover
Wings
The Wings of Eagles
Zeppelin

AC12 Adventure in the Great Outdoors

See also: HF22 Fictional Character Check
   List: Tarzan
The Abyss
The African Queen
Alive
Amazon
Baby . . . Secret of the Lost Legend
The Bear
Beneath the 12 Mile Reef
The Big Blue
The Bounty
A Breed Apart
The Call of the Wild
China Seas
Clan of the Cave Bear
Crusoe
Death Hunt
The Deep
The Dove
The Eiger Sanction
The Emerald Forest
The Flight of the Eagle
Flight of the Phoenix
Hatari!
Ivory Hunters
K-2
King Solomon's Mines (1937, 1950, and 1985
   versions)
The Last of the Mohicans (1992 version)

Legend of the Lost
The Legend of Wolf Mountain
Leviathan
The Light at the End of the World
Lord of the Flies (1963 and 1990 versions)
The Man From Snowy River
The Man Who Would Be King
March or Die
Mogambo
The Mountain
Mountains of the Moon
Mutiny on the Bounty (1935 and 1962
   versions)
The Naked Jungle
The Naked Prey
Never Cry Wolf
Point Break
Quest for Fire
Raise the Titanic!
Reap the Wild Wind
The Red Tent
Return to Snowy River, Part II
Shark!
Shoot to Kill
Shout at the Devil
Skullduggery
Sorcerer
Stanley and Livingstone
Thunderball
The Treasure of the Sierra Madre
Undersea Kingdom
We of the Never Never
White Dawn
Wind
The Wind and the Lion
The Wreck of the *Mary Deare*

AC13 Adventure Classics

See also: AC14 Romantic Adventure, AC15
   Costume Adventure, Historical/Fictional
   Character Check List HF22 Tarzan
The Adventures of Robin Hood
Beau Brummel (1954 version)
Beau Geste (1939 version)
The Black Arrow (1948)
The Black Pirate
Captain Blood
Captain Horatio Hornblower
Captains Courageous
The Charge of the Light Brigade (1936 version)
The Corsican Brothers
The Crimson Pirate
Don Juan
Don Q: Son of Zorro
Drums
The Flame and the Arrow
The Four Feathers
Gunga Din
The Hurricane (1937 version)
The Iron Mask

Ivanhoe (1952 version)
Kim
King Solomon's Mines (1937 and 1950 versions)
Knights of the Round Table
The Last of the Mohicans
The Lives of a Bengal Lancer
The Lost Patrol
The Lost World (1925 version)
The Mark of Zorro (1920 and 1940 versions)
The Most Dangerous Game
Mutiny on the Bounty (1935 version)
Only Angels Have Wings
The Prisoner of Zenda (1937 and 1952 versions)
Reap the Wild Wind
Red Dust
San Francisco
Scaramouche
The Scarlet Pimpernel (1934 version)
The Sea Hawk
The Sea Wolf
The Seven Samurai
The Thief of Bagdad (1924 and 1940 versions)
The Three Musketeers (1948 version)
Treasure Island (1934 version)
The Treasure of the Sierra Madre
The Vikings
The Wages of Fear
Yojimbo

AC14 Romantic Adventure

See also: AC13 Adventure Classics
The African Queen
American Dreamer
The Aviator
Bird of Paradise (1932 version)
Brenda Starr
The Great Race
High Road to China
Into the Night
Jewel of the Nile
Ladyhawke
Lassiter
The Last of the Mohicans (1992 version)
Mogambo
The Princess Bride
Raiders of the Lost Ark
Red Dust
Robin and Marian
Romancing the Stone
Time After Time
The Wind and the Lion
Year of the Comet

AC15 Costume Adventure

See also: AC13 Adventure Classics
The Adventures of Captain Fabian
Against All Flags
At Sword's Point
The Beloved Rogue

Blackbeard, the Pirate
Captain Kidd
Captain Sinbad
The Elusive Pimpernel
The Fifth Musketeer
The Four Musketeers
His Majesty O'Keefe
Journey of Honor
The Man in the Iron Mask (1939 and 1977 versions)
The Mark of Zorro (1920 and 1940 versions)
The Master of Ballantrae
Moonfleet
Nate and Hayes
The Pirate Warrior
Pirates
Prince Valiant
The Princess Bride
Robin and Marian
Robin Hood (1991)
Robin Hood, Prince of Thieves
Sinbad the Sailor
Son of Sinbad
The Spanish Main
Swashbuckler (1976)
Swashbuckler (1984)
Sword of Sherwood Forest
The Three Musketeers (1974 version)

AC16 Historical Adventure

See also: AC1-7 War Movies
Alexander the Great
Botany Bay
The Bounty
The Buccaneer
The Charge of the Light Brigade (1936 version)
The Conqueror
El Cid
The Flight of the Eagle
The Hindenburg
Lionheart (1987)
Mountains of the Moon
Mutiny on the Bounty (1935 and 1962 versions)
One Million B.C.
The Sicilian
The War Lord
The Wind and the Lion

AC17 Super Heroes

The Adventures of Buckaroo Banzai Across the Eighth Dimension
The Adventures of Hercules
Batman (1966)
Batman (1989)
Batman Returns
Captain America
Conan the Barbarian
Conan the Destroyer

Condorman
Doc Savage: The Man of Bronze
Masters of the Universe
The Rocketeer
Sheena
Supergirl
Superman (series)
Teenage Mutant Ninja Turtles
Teenage Mutant Ninja Turtles II: The Secret
   of the Ooze
Teenage Mutant Ninja Turtles III: The Turtles
   Are Back . . . in Time

AC18 Sword & Sorcery Fantasies
The Beastmaster
Beastmaster 2: Through the Portals of Time
The Blade Master
Conan the Barbarian
Conan the Destroyer
Deathstalker
Deathstalker II
Dragonslayer
Excalibur
Fire and Ice
Flesh and Blood (1985)
Jason and the Argonauts
Krull
Ladyhawke
Legend
The Magic Sword
Metalstorm: The Destruction of Jared-Syn
Red Sonja
Robin Hood and the Sorcerer
The 7th Voyage of Sinbad
She (1985 version)
Ulysses (1955)
Warriors of the Wind
Willow
Wizards of the Lost Kingdom

AC19 Tales of Revenge
The Bounty Hunter
Darkman
Death Wish (series)
Dixie Dynamite
The Exterminator
The Exterminator 2
An Eye for an Eye
Eye of the Tiger
F/X
The Family
52 Pick-up
Fighting Back
Fighting Mad (1976)
The Final Mission
Firepower
Fleshburn
Hard to Kill
Instant Justice
The Killer Elite

The Ladies Club
The Last Boy Scout
The Mean Machine
Miller's Crossing
Ms. 45
Next of Kin
No Mercy
Out for Justice
Payoff
Point Blank
Revenge (1990)
Ricochet
Rolling Thunder
Rolling Vengeance
Savage Streets
Slaughter
Stacy's Knights
Steele Justice
Sudden Impact
Underworld, U.S.A.
Vigilante
White Lightning

AC20 Mercenaries and Other Combatants
American Commandos
The Annihilators
Code Name: Wild Geese
Death Before Dishonor
The Delta Force
Delta Force 2
The Dirty Dozen
The Dirty Dozen: The Next Mission
The Dogs of War
The Final Option
Gold Raiders
Gordon's War
High Velocity
Invasion U.S.A.
Let's Get Harry
Navy SEALS
Nightforce
Opposing Force
Red Dawn
Red Scorpion
The Rescue
Sniper
Terror Squad
Toy Soldiers (1984)
Toy Soldiers (1991)
Uncommon Valor
Universal Soldier
The Wild Geese
Wild Geese II

AC21 Soldiers of Fortune
Allan Quatermain and the Lost City of Gold
Big Trouble in Little China
Escape From New York
Firewalker
High Road to China

Indiana Jones and the Last Crusade
Indiana Jones and the Temple of Doom
Jake Speed
Jewel of the Nile
Jungle Raiders
King Solomon's Mines (1937, 1950, and 1985)
McBain
The Mines of Kilimanjaro
Raiders of the Lost Ark
Romancing the Stone
Shanghai Surprise
Soldier of Fortune
Soldiers of Fortune
Treasure of the Four Crowns

AC22 Gangster Sagas

See also: AC8 Urban Action, AC9 Cops and
   Robbers
Al Capone
American Me
Angels With Dirty Faces
The Big Heat
Billy Bathgate
Black Caesar
Black Rain (U.S.)
Bloody Mama
Brighton Rock
Brother Orchid
Bugsy
Bullets or Ballots
The Cotton Club
Dick Tracy
Dillinger
"G" Men
The Gangster
The Godfather
The Godfather, Part II
The Godfather, Part III
The Godfather: The Complete Epic, 1902–1958
The Godfather Trilogy, 1901–1980
GoodFellas
The Gunrunner
Hell on Frisco Bay
Hell Up in Harlem
High Sierra
I Died a Thousand Times
I, Mobster
Johnny Apollo
King of New York
King of the Roaring 20's—The Story of
   Arnold Rothstein
Kiss of Death
The Krays
Lady Killer
Lepke
Little Caesar
The Long Good Friday
Lucky Luciano
Machine Gun Kelly
Mean Frank and Crazy Tony

Men of Respect
Miller's Crossing
Mobsters
Once Upon a Time in America
Party Girl
Prime Cut
The Public Enemy
The Rise and Fall of Legs Diamond
The Roaring Twenties
The St. Valentine's Day Massacre
Scarface (1932 and 1983 versions)
Show Them No Mercy!
Squizzy Taylor
The Street With No Name
The Underworld Story
The Untouchables
White Heat
The Yakuza

AC23 Disaster Stories

Airport
Airport 1975
Airport '77
Avalanche
Beyond the Poseidon Adventure
The Cassandra Crossing
City on Fire
The Concorde—Airport '79
The Devil at 4 O'Clock
Earthquake
Flood!
The Hindenburg
Hurricane
The Hurricane
Juggernaut (1974)
The Last Voyage
Meteor
A Night to Remember (1958)
The Poseidon Adventure
Rollercoaster
San Francisco
The Towering Inferno
When Time Ran Out

AC24 Stories of Survival

The Abyss
Alive
Avenging Force
Back From Eternity
The Blood of Heroes
Bridge to Nowhere
The Call of the Wild
Certain Fury
Crusoe
Cut and Run
Cyborg
Deadlock
Death Valley
Deliverance
Flight of the Phoenix

Goliath Awaits
Gray Lady Down
Hunter's Blood
The Island (1980)
Lifeboat
Lord of the Flies (1963 and 1990 versions)
Mad Max Beyond Thunderdome
Man Friday
Man in the Wilderness
The Most Dangerous Game
Mountains of the Moon
The Naked Jungle
The Naked Prey
Never Cry Wolf
Nowhere To Hide
Opposing Force
Out of Control
Papillon
Predator
Quest for Fire
Quigley Down Under
The Red Tent
The Road Warrior
Runaway Train
The Savage Is Loose
The Sea Shall Not Have Them
Sea Wife
Sorcerer
Southern Comfort
The Treasure of the Sierra Madre
Trespass
Under Siege
White Dawn

AC25 One-Man Armies

Above the Law
The Bounty Hunter
Bulletproof
Bullies
Commando
Die Hard
Die Hard 2: Die Harder
Equalizer 2000
An Eye for an Eye
Eye of the Tiger
First Blood
A Force of One
Forced Vengeance
Ghost Warrior
Hard to Kill
Instant Justice
The Killer
Mad Max
Mad Max Beyond Thunderdome
Malone
Man on Fire
Marked for Death
Nowhere To Hide
Nowhere To Run
One Man Force

Out for Justice
Passenger 57
Point Blank
Point of No Return
Predator
Rambo: First Blood II
Rambo III
Raw Deal
Red Scorpion
Road House
The Road Warrior
RoboCop
RoboCop 2
The Soldier
Stone Cold
Streets of Fire
The Terminator
Terminator 2: Judgment Day
Total Recall
Under Siege
Universal Soldier
Walking Tall
Walking Tall, Part Two
Walking Tall: The Final Chapter
Wanted: Dead or Alive

AC26 Martial Arts Action

See also: Star Check Lists ST134 Bruce Lee,
    ST165 Chuck Norris
American Ninja
American Ninja 2: The Confrontation
American Ninja 3: Blood Hunt
Best of the Best
Best of the Best II
The Big Brawl
Big Trouble in Little China
Billy Jack
Bloodfist (series)
Bloodsport
Circle of Iron
Cleopatra Jones
Cleopatra Jones and the Casino of Gold
Cyborg
Double Impact
Hard to Kill
Jackie Chan's Police Force
Kickboxer
Kill and Kill Again
Kill or Be Killed
The Last Dragon
Legend of the Seven Golden Vampires
Lionheart (1990)
Mission of Justice
No Retreat, No Surrender
The Perfect Weapon
Pray for Death
The Protector
Rapid Fire
T.N.T. Jackson
3 Ninjas

2 Classics (CL)

CL1	Classics Illustrated: Literary Adaptations	**CL13**	Religious Stories
CL2	Screen Biographies	**CL14**	Delayed Classics: Movies Unappreciated in Their Own Times
CL3	Historical Drama	**CL15**	Memorable Screen Teams
CL4	Classic Love Stories		Katharine Hepburn and Spencer Tracy
CL5	Women's Pictures		Humphrey Bogart and Lauren Bacall
CL6	Classic Tear Jerkers		Fred Astaire and Ginger Rogers
CL7	Show Business Stories		William Powell and Myrna Loy
CL8	Social Problem Dramas		Richard Burton and Elizabeth Taylor
CL9	Great Color Films		Nelson Eddy and Jeanette MacDonald
CL10	Classic Sound Comedies		Mickey Rooney and Judy Garland
CL11	Classic Silent Comedies		Bob Hope and Bing Crosby
CL12	Classic Silent Dramas		Dean Martin and Jerry Lewis

CL1 Classics Illustrated: Literary Adaptations

See also: DR19 Modern Fiction on Film;
  Writer Check Lists WR4 Noel Coward,
  WR5 Charles Dickens, WR7 William
  Faulkner, WR8 F. Scott Fitzgerald, WR9
  E.M. Forster, WR13 Ernest Hemingway,
  WR14 Henry James, WR17 D.H. Lawrence,
  WR20 Sinclair Lewis, WR23 W. Somerset
  Maugham, WR24 John O'Hara, WR25
  Eugene O'Neill, WR28 William Shake-
  speare, WR29 George Bernard Shaw, WR32
  John Steinbeck, WR33 Robert Louis
  Stevenson, WR35 Mark Twain

Alice Adams
Anna Karenina (1935 and 1948 versions)
Barry Lyndon
Becky Sharp
Billy Budd
The Brothers Karamazov
Caesar and Cleopatra
Camille
Captains Courageous
Carrie (1952)
Decameron Nights
Far From the Madding Crowd
Greed
The Guardsman
The Heiress
Hunchback
The Hunchback of Notre Dame
The Importance of Being Earnest
Jane Eyre (1944 version)
The Last of the Mohicans (1936 and 1992
  versions)
Les Misérables (1935 and 1978 versions)
Little Women (1933 and 1949 versions)
Madame Bovary (1934, 1949, and 1991 versions)
The Mill on the Floss
Moby Dick
The Picture of Dorian Gray
Pride and Prejudice
The Private Affairs of Bel Ami
Pygmalion
The Red Badge of Courage
Romola
The Sea Wolf
Tom Jones
Vanity Fair
War and Peace (1956 and 1968 versions)
Wuthering Heights (1939 and 1954 versions)

CL2 Screen Biographies

See also: DR4 The Famous and Notorious,
  MU5 Musical Life Stories
Abe Lincoln in Illinois
Abraham Lincoln
The Babe Ruth Story
The Barretts of Wimpole Street
Carbine Williams
Christopher Columbus
Citizen Kane
Cleopatra (1934, 1963)
Courageous Mr. Penn
The Diary of Anne Frank
Disraeli
Edison, the Man
The Gallant Hours
Gentleman Jim
The Great Moment

Houdini
I'll Cry Tomorrow
The Iron Major
Jack London
Jim Thorpe—All American
Joan of Arc
Juarez
Knute Rockne, All American
Lawrence of Arabia
The Life of Emile Zola
Lust for Life
The McConnell Story
Madame Curie
Man of a Thousand Faces
Marie Antoinette
Mata Hari (1932)
Moulin Rouge
Napoleon (1927)
The Pride of St. Louis
Pride of the Yankees
The Private Life of Henry VIII
The Private Lives of Elizabeth and Essex
Rembrandt
Sergeant York
Sister Kenny
Song of Love
The Spirit of St. Louis
To Hell and Back
The Toast of New York
Viva Villa!
Wilson
Young Mr. Lincoln

CL3 Historical Drama
See also: DR5 Historical Drama
Anastasia
Beau Brummel (1924 version)
The Birth of a Nation
Black Magic (1949)
Caesar and Cleopatra
Cleopatra (1934 and 1963 versions)
Conquest
Demetrius and the Gladiators
Desiree
The Devil's Disciple
Dr. Zhivago
The Egyptian
The FBI Story
The Fall of the Roman Empire
55 Days at Peking
Fire Over England
The Four Horsemen of the Apocalypse (1961
   version)
Gone With the Wind
The Gorgeous Hussy
Jezebel
Julius Caesar (1953 version)
Land of the Pharaohs
The Long Gray Line
Mary of Scotland

Mayerling (1936 version)
Mutiny on the Bounty (1935 version)
A Night to Remember (1958)
Northwest Passage
The Private Lives of Elizabeth and Essex
Queen Christina
Raintree County
Rasputin and the Empress
San Francisco
Scott of the Antarctic
Stanley and Livingstone
A Tale of Two Cities (1935 and 1958 versions)
Tempest (1928)
That Hamilton Woman
Tower of London (1939 version)
The Virgin Queen
War and Peace (1956 and 1968 versions)

CL4 Classic Love Stories
See also: DR1 Romantic Drama
The African Queen
Algiers
Anna Karenina (1935 version)
Back Street
Brief Encounter (1945 version)
Camille
Casablanca
The Clock
Dark Victory
Dr. Zhivago
The Enchanted Cottage
A Farewell to Arms (1932 and 1957 versions)
Flesh and the Devil
Gilda
Gone With the Wind
The Heiress
History Is Made at Night
Intermezzo (1939 version)
Letter From an Unknown Woman
Love Affair
Love in the Afternoon
Love Is a Many Splendored Thing
Marty
Mayerling (1936 version)
Mr. Skeffington
Notorious
Now, Voyager
The Philadelphia Story
A Place in the Sun
Portrait of Jennie
Queen Christina
The Rainmaker
Random Harvest
The Rose Tattoo
Sabrina
The Sheik
The Shop Around the Corner
Summertime
Tabu
That Hamilton Woman

Waterloo Bridge
The White Cliffs of Dover
Without Love
Wuthering Heights (1939 version)

CL5 Women's Pictures
See also: DR10 Today's Woman
Alice Adams
Autumn Leaves
The Bride Wore Red
By Love Possessed
Camille
Chained
Christopher Strong
Craig's Wife
Dance, Girl, Dance
The Divorcee
Female
Four Daughters
Humoresque
I Love My Life
I'll Cry Tomorrow
In This Our Life
Kitty Foyle
The Letter
Madame Bovary (1934 and 1949 versions)
Madame X (1966 version)
Mannequin (1937)
Mildred Pierce
Morning Glory
Mr. Skeffington
Now, Voyager
The Old Maid
Possessed (1931)
Possessed (1947)
Prix de Beauté
Sadie McKee
The Sin of Madelon Claudet
Since You Went Away
The Sisters
Stella Dallas
Susan Lennox: Her Fall and Rise
That Certain Woman
Three on a Match
Until They Sail
When Ladies Meet (1941 version)
When Love Has Gone
The Wind
A Woman Rebels
A Woman's Face (1941 version)
The Women (1939)

CL6 Classic Tear Jerkers
See also: DR2 For a Good Cry
Applause
Back Street (1961 version)
Blonde Venus
Blossoms in the Dust
Brief Encounter (1945 version)
Carrie (1952)

Casablanca
The Champ (1931)
City Lights
Dark Victory
Going My Way
The Heiress
How Green Was My Valley
Imitation of Life (1959 version)
In Name Only
It's a Wonderful Life
Johnny Belinda
Journey for Margaret
King's Row
Kitty Foyle
Letter From an Unknown Woman
Limelight
Madame X (1966 version)
Made for Each Other (1939)
Magnificent Obsession (1954 version)
Mildred Pierce
Penny Serenade
A Place in the Sun
The Red Shoes
The Sin of Madelon Claudet
Since You Went Away
Stella Dallas
Summertime
Tomorrow Is Forever
Written on the Wind
Wuthering Heights (1939 version)

CL7 Show Business Stories
See also: DR12 Backstage Dramas, MU4
    Musical Films About Show Biz
Adorable Julia
All About Eve
Applause
The Bad and the Beautiful
Blessed Event
Bombshell
Career
The Carpetbaggers
Circus World
The Country Girl (1954 version)
Dance, Girl, Dance
Dancing Lady
A Double Life
A Face in the Crowd
Free and Easy
The Great Gabbo
The Greatest Show on Earth
Hollywood Canteen
Humoresque
I Dream Too Much
In Person
Inside Daisy Clover
It's a Great Feeling
Lady Killer
The Last Command
Limelight

The Lost Squadron
Main Street to Broadway
Man of a Thousand Faces
The Moon's Our Home
Reckless (1935)
The Red Shoes
The Seven Little Foys
Show People
Sidewalks of London
Smash-Up, The Story of a Woman
Speak Easily
Stage Door
Stage Struck (1958)
Stand-In
The Star
A Star Is Born (1937 and 1954 versions)
Sunset Boulevard
Sweet Smell of Success
Sweethearts
Swing High, Swing Low
Torch Song
Trapeze
Twentieth Century
Two Weeks in Another Town
What Price Hollywood?
The Wings of Eagles
A Woman's Secret
Young and Willing

CL8 Social Problem Dramas
See also: DR7 Modern Problems
Bad Day at Black Rock
The Best Years of Our Lives
Black Fury
Blackboard Jungle
The Boy With Green Hair
Boys Town
Crossfire
The Crowd
Dead End
The Defiant Ones (1958 version)
Fury
Gentleman's Agreement
The Grapes of Wrath
Heroes for Sale
Home of the Brave
How Green Was My Valley
I Am a Fugitive From a Chain Gang
Inherit the Wind
Intruder in the Dust
Judgment at Nuremberg
Knock on Any Door
The Last Angry Man
The Lost Weekend
The Man With the Golden Arm
The Men
Men of Boys Town
Mr. Deeds Goes to Town
Mrs. Miniver
The Next Voice You Hear

On the Waterfront
Our Daily Bread
The Pearl
Pinky
A Place in the Sun
The Prisoner
Raisin in the Sun
Rebel Without a Cause
The Snake Pit
So Ends Our Night
Street Scene
Tender Comrade
They Drive By Night
They Won't Forget
Three Comrades
Till the End of Time
To Kill a Mockingbird
12 Angry Men

CL9 Great Color Films
The Adventures of Robin Hood
The Barefoot Contessa
Becky Sharp
Black Narcissus
Black Orpheus
Cover Girl
DuBarry Was a Lady
Duel in the Sun
The Far Country
The Four Feathers
Funny Face
The Garden of Allah
The Golden Coach
Heller in Pink Tights
Henry V (1945 version)
Lust for Life
Moulin Rouge
Pal Joey
The Phantom of the Opera (1943
  version)
The Pirate
The Quiet Man
The Red Shoes
The River (1951)
Summer Holiday
Tales of Hoffmann
The Ten Commandments (1956 version)
The Thief of Bagdad (1940 version)
The Yearling
Yolanda and the Thief

CL10 Classic Sound Comedies
See also: Star Check Lists ST1 Abbott and
  Costello, ST67 W.C. Fields, ST120 Danny
  Kaye, ST138 Laurel and Hardy, ST152 The
  Marx Brothers, ST226 Mae West
Adam's Rib
Arsenic and Old Lace
Artists and Models
The Awful Truth

Bachelor Apartment
Ball of Fire
Born Yesterday (1950 version)
Bringing Up Baby
A Connecticut Yankee
The Court Jester
The Devil and Miss Jones
Dinner at Eight
Doubting Thomas
Duck Soup
The Front Page (1931 version)
Hail the Conquering Hero
The Great Dictator
Harvey
Heaven Can Wait (1943)
His Girl Friday
Holiday
The Horn Blows at Midnight
It Happened One Night
It's a Gift
It's a Great Feeling
It's in the Bag
Kind Hearts and Coronets
The Lady Eve
The Ladykillers
The Matchmaker
The Milky Way (1936)
Mister Roberts
Monkey Business (1931)
Monkey Business (1952)
The More the Merrier
Mr. Blandings Builds His Dream
   House
Mr. Lucky
My Favorite Wife
My Little Chickadee
My Man Godfrey
Ninotchka
Nothing Sacred
One, Two, Three
The Palm Beach Story
Pat and Mike
The Philadelphia Story
Platinum Blonde
Private Lives
The Senator Was Indiscreet
The Seven Year Itch
Some Like It Hot
Sons of the Desert
Sullivan's Travels
The Talk of the Town
The Thin Man
To Be or Not to Be (1942 version)
Twentieth Century
Unfaithfully Yours (1948 version)
Woman of the Year
The Yellow Cab Man
You Can't Cheat an Honest Man
You Can't Take It With You (1938
   version)

CL11 Classic Silent Comedies

See also: Director Check Lists DT24 Charlie
   Chaplin, DT66 Buster Keaton
The Circus
City Lights
College
The Freshman (1925)
The General
The Gold Rush
Harold Lloyd's World of Comedy
It
It's the Old Army Game
Modern Times
My Best Girl
Our Hospitality
Running Wild
Safety Last
Show People
So This Is Paris
Spite Marriage
Steamboat Bill, Jr.
The Strong Man
The Three Ages
When Comedy Was King

CL12 Classic Silent Dramas

See also: Director Check Lists DT52 D.W.
   Griffith, DT129 Erich Von Stroheim
Battleship Potemkin
Beau Brummel (1924 version)
The Beloved Rogue
Ben-Hur: A Tale of the Christ
The Big Parade
The Birth of a Nation
Blind Husbands
Blood and Sand (1922 version)
Broken Blossoms
The Covered Wagon
The Crowd
Diary of a Lost Girl
The Docks of New York
Don Juan
Earth
Flesh and the Devil
Foolish Wives
Greed
Intolerance
The Iron Mask
Judith of Bethulia
The King of Kings (1927 version)
The Kiss (1929)
The Last Command
The Last Laugh
The Mark of Zorro
Metropolis (1925 edition)
Mysterious Lady
Napoleon (1927)
Old Ironsides
Our Dancing Daughters
Pandora's Box

Passion (1918)
The Passion of Joan of Arc
Queen Kelly
Romola
Sadie Thompson
The Sheik
The Single Standard
Sparrows
The Student Prince of Old Heidelberg
The Ten Commandments (1923 version)
The Thief of Bagdad (1926 version)
Too Hot To Handle
Variety
Way Down East
The Wedding March
The Wind
Wings
A Woman of Affairs
A Woman of Paris

CL13 Religious Stories
Barabbas
Ben-Hur
Ben-Hur: A Tale of the Christ
The Bible
David and Bathsheba
The Greatest Story Ever Told
The Green Pastures
Jesus of Nazareth
Judith of Bethulia
King David
The King of Kings (1927 and 1961
   versions)
Moses
The Nativity
Peter and Paul
The Robe
Salome
Samson and Delilah
The Silver Chalice
Sodom and Gomorrah
Solomon and Sheba
Song of Bernadette
The Story of Ruth
The Ten Commandments (1923 and 1956
   versions)

CL14 Delayed Classics: Movies Unappreciated in Their Own Times
Beat the Devil
Come and Get It
The Devil and Daniel Webster
Fantasia
The Golden Coach
Intolerance
It's a Wonderful Life
Lola Montes
The Magnificent Ambersons
The Nutty Professor
Once Upon a Time in the West

Petulia
Rio Bravo
The Searchers
Sylvia Scarlett
To Be or Not to Be (1942 version)
Touch of Evil
The Trouble With Harry
Vertigo

CL15 Memorable Screen Teams
See also: Star Check Lists ST1 Abbott and
   Costello, ST113 Laurel and Hardy

Katharine Hepburn and Spencer Tracy
Adam's Rib
Desk Set
Guess Who's Coming to Dinner
Keeper of the Flame
Pat and Mike
The Sea of Grass
State of the Union
Without Love
Woman of the Year

Humphrey Bogart and Lauren Bacall
The Big Sleep
Dark Passage
Key Largo
To Have and Have Not

Fred Astaire and Ginger Rogers
The Barkleys of Broadway
Carefree
Flying Down to Rio
Follow the Fleet
The Gay Divorcee
Roberta
Shall We Dance
The Story of Vernon and Irene Castle
Swing Time
Top Hat

William Powell and Myrna Loy
After the Thin Man
Another Thin Man
The Great Ziegfeld
Love Crazy
Manhattan Melodrama
The Shadow of the Thin Man
Song of the Thin Man
The Thin Man
The Thin Man Goes Home

Richard Burton and Elizabeth Taylor
Cleopatra (1963)
The Comedians
Divorce His, Divorce Hers
Doctor Faustus
Hammersmith Is Out
The Sandpiper
The Taming of the Shrew

Under Milk Wood
The V.I.P.s
Who's Afraid of Virginia Woolf?

Nelson Eddy and Jeanette MacDonald
Bitter Sweet
The Girl of the Golden West
I Married an Angel
Maytime
Naughty Marietta
New Moon
Rose Marie (1936 version)
Sweethearts

Mickey Rooney and Judy Garland
Andy Hardy Meets Debutante
Babes in Arms
Babes on Broadway
Girl Crazy
Life Begins for Andy Hardy
Love Finds Andy Hardy

Strike up the Band
Thoroughbreds Don't Cry
Words and Music

Bob Hope and Bing Crosby
Road to Bali
The Road to Hong Kong
Road to Morocco
Road to Rio
Road to Singapore
Road to Utopia
Road to Zanzibar

Dean Martin and Jerry Lewis
Artists and Models
At War with the Army
The Caddy
Hollywood or Bust
Jumping Jacks
My Friend Irma
Scared Stiff

3 Comedy (CO)

CO1 Romantic Comedies
CO2 Comedies for Modern Times
CO3 Contemporary Comedy Teams
CO4 Growing Up
CO5 Funny Families
CO6 Nutty Nostalgia
CO7 Movie Spoofs
CO8 The Lighter Side of Show Biz
CO9 Action Comedies
CO10 Crime and Suspense Comedies
CO11 Special Effects for Laughs
CO12 Offbeat Comedy
CO13 The Alumni of "Saturday Night Live"
    Dan Aykroyd
    Jim Belushi
    John Belushi
    Chevy Chase
    Billy Crystal
    Jane Curtin
    Eddie Murphy
    Bill Murray
    Gilda Radner

CO14 The Alumni of "SCTV"
    John Candy
    Joe Flaherty
    Eugene Levy
    Andrea Martin
    Rick Moranis
    Catherine O'Hara
    Harold Ramis
    Martin Short
    Dave Thomas
CO15 The Alumni of "Monty Python's
    Flying Circus"
    The Troupe
    Individually
CO16 Performance Comics
CO17 Classic and Contemporary British
    Comedy
CO18 Campus Comedy
CO19 Sports for Laughs
CO20 Fish Out Of Water: Funny Tales of
    Misplaced Persons
CO21 Uniformly Funny: Service Comedies

See Also: Director Check Lists DT1 Woody Allen, DT17 Mel Brooks, DT24 Charlie Chaplin, DT66 Buster Keaton, DT121 Preston Sturges; Star Check Lists ST1 Abbott and Costello, ST28 Cheech and Chong, ST67 W.C. Fields, ST99 Goldie Hawn, ST107 Judy Holliday, ST108 Bob Hope, ST120 Danny Kaye, ST133 Laurel and Hardy, ST139 Jerry Lewis, ST150 Steve Martin, ST152 The Marx Brothers, ST160 Dudley Moore, ST180 Richard Pryor, ST198 Peter Sellers, ST226 Mae West; Writer Check List WR30 Neil Simon

---

CO1 Romantic Comedies

All Night Long
Almost You
American Dreamer
Annie Hall
Arthur
Arthur 2: On the Rocks
Barefoot in the Park
Best Friends
Blind Date (1987)
Blume in Love
Boeing Boeing
Boomerang
Born Yesterday
    (1950 and 1993 versions)
Broadcast News
The Buddy System
Bull Durham
The Butcher's Wife
Cactus Flower
Chances Are
Continental Divide
Cousins
Crocodile Dundee
Crocodile Dundee II
Cross My Heart
Crossing Delancey
The Cutting Edge
Defending Your Life
Designing Woman
The Electric Horseman
Forty Carats
The Four Seasons
Frozen Assets
Funny About Love
The Goodbye Girl
Green Card
Groundhog Day

Hard Promises
He Said, She Said
The Heartbreak Kid
Heartburn
Honeymoon in Vegas
HouseSitter
House Calls
I Will, I Will . . . for Now
It Takes Two
It's My Turn
Joe Vs. the Volcano
L.A. Story
The Linguini Incident
Living on Tokyo Time
Lost and Found
Love at Large
Love Potion No. 1
Loverboy
Lovesick
Man Trouble
Manhattan
Married to It
The Marrying Man
Meeting Venus
Micki & Maude
A Midsummer Night's Sex Comedy
Modern Love
Modern Romance
The Moon Is Blue
Moonstruck
Murphy's Romance
Never on Sunday
A New Life
Night Shift
Once Around
Only the Lonely
The Opposite Sex . . . And How To Live With
   Them
The Owl and the Pussycat
Paternity
Period of Adjustment
Pete 'n' Tillie
Pillow Talk
Play It Again, Sam
Pretty Woman
Quackser Fortune Has a Cousin in the Bronx
Reuben, Reuben
Romantic Comedy
Roxanne
Samantha
Say Anything . . .
Sex and the Single Girl
Shampoo
She's Gotta Have It
She's Having a Baby
Shirley Valentine
Singles
Skin Deep
Someone to Love
Something Short of Paradise

Splash
Star Spangled Girl
Starting Over
The Sure Thing
Surrender
Surviving Desire
Sweet Hearts Dance
Switching Channels
Tall Story
10
The Tender Trap
That Lucky Touch
That Touch of Mink
A Touch of Class
True Love
Tune in Tomorrow . . .
Victor/Victoria
The War of the Roses
What's New, Pussycat?
When Harry Met Sally . . .
Who Am I This Time?
The Woman in Red
Working Girl
Worth Winning
Year of the Comet

CO2 Comedies for Modern Times
After Hours
Air America
Alice
Amos & Andrew
Annie Hall
Antonia and Jane
Baby Boom
Bebe's Kids
Being There
Between the Lines
Bob & Carol & Ted & Alice
Bob Roberts
Boomerang
Born Yesterday (1993 version)
Britannia Hospital
Broadcast News
Carbon Copy
Chan Is Missing
Citizens Band
City Slickers
The Coca-Cola Kid
Cold Turkey
Confessions of a Peeping John
Crazy People
Creator
D.C. Cab
Deal of the Century
Desk Set
Desperately Seeking Susan
The Distinguished Gentleman
Down and Out in Beverly Hills
Dr. Strangelove or; How I Learned to Stop
   Worrying and Love the Bomb

Earth Girls Are Easy
The Experts
First Monday in October
For Richer, For Poorer
The Fortune Cookie
Fun With Dick and Jane
Gas-s-s-s
The Gods Must Be Crazy
The Graduate
The Grass Is Always Greener Over the Septic
   Tank
Gremlins 2: The New Batch
Gung Ho (1986)
Heartburn
Hero
High Hopes
Honky Tonk Freeway
How to Get Ahead in Advertising
I Love You, Alice B. Toklas
In the Spirit
It's My Turn
King of Comedy
L.A. Story
Life Stinks
Little Murders
Livin' Large
Living on Tokyo Time
Local Hero
The Lonely Guy
Lost in America
Making Mr. Right
Manhaatan
Max Headroom
Melvin and Howard
Metropolitan
The Milagro Beanfield War
The Money Pit
Moon Over Parador
Mother, Jugs and Speed
Mr. Mom
My Blue Heaven
Mystery Train
A New Life
New York Stories
Night on Earth
Night Shift
North Dallas Forty
One, Two, Three
One Woman or Two
Other People's Money
The Out-of-Towners
Patti Rocks
Perfect!
Planes, Trains, and Automobiles
The Pope Must Diet
The President's Analyst
The Prisoner of Second Avenue
Private Benjamin
Putney Swope
Rancho Deluxe

Real Genius
Repo Man
Rosalie Goes Shopping
The Russians Are Coming! The Russians Are
   Coming!
Scenes From a Mall
Scenes From the Class Struggle in Beverly
   Hills
School Daze
Scrooged
The Secret of My Success
Semi-Tough
Serial
Sex and the Single Girl
Shampoo
She-Devil
She's Gotta Have It
A Shock to the System
Sidewalk Stories
Singles
Smile
Something Wild
Soul Man
Stars and Bars
Stay Hungry
Stay Tuned
Steel Magnolias
Steelyard Blues
Straight Talk
Strictly Business
The Super
The Survivors
Take This Job and Shove It
Tanner
Three Men and a Baby
Three Men and a Little Lady
Tootsie
Toys
Trust
29th Street
Valley Girl
Vibes
The War of the Roses
What About Bob?
Where the Buffalo Roam
Where the Heart Is
Where Were You When the Lights Went
   Out?
White Men Can't Jump
Whoops Apocalypse
Wild in the Streets
Working Girl
Wrong Is Right

CO3 Contemporary Comedy Teams
See also: Star Check List ST28 Cheech and
   Chong
All of Me
Amos & Andrew
Another You

Armed and Dangerous
Bedazzled
Bedtime Story
The Best of Times
Big Business
The Blues Brothers
Brain Donors
Brewster's Millions
Buddy Buddy
City Heat
Dirty Rotten Scoundrels
The Dream Team
Feds
A Fine Mess
The Fortune Cookie
The Front Page (1974)
The In-Laws
Ishtar
Macaroni
Nine to Five
The Odd Couple
Outrageous Fortune
Planes, Trains, and Automobiles
Pure Luck
Running Scared
Scenes From a Mall
See No Evil, Hear No Evil
Silver Streak
Stir Crazy
The Sunshine Boys
The Survivors
Three Amigos
Throw Momma from the Train
Tin Men
Tough Guys
Trading Places
Twins
Vibes
Volunteers
What About Bob?
White Men Can't Jump
Wise Guys

CO4 Growing Up
American Graffiti
Auntie Mame
Back to the Future
The Bad News Bears
Big
Big Girls Don't Cry . . . They Get Even
Big Shots
Billie
Breaking Away
Cooley High
Don't Tell Mom the Babysitter's Dead
Dutch
Fandango
Fast Times at Ridgemont High
Ferris Bueller's Day Off
The Flamingo Kid

Footloose
For Keeps
French Postcards
The Graduate
Gregory's Girl
Happy Birthday, Gemini
Heathers
Heaven Help Us
Home Alone
Home Alone 2: Lost in New York
Hope and Glory
House Party
Johnny Be Good
The Joy of Sex
Little Darlings
A Little Romance
Matinee
Mermaids
Metropolitan
My Bodyguard
My Life as a Dog
Mystery Date
National Lampoon's Animal House
The Night Before
A Night in the Life of Jimmy Reardon
Porky's (series)
Queen of Hearts
Real Genius
Revenge of the Nerds
Rich Kids
Risky Business
Rita, Sue and Bob Too
Samantha
Say Anything . . .
Singles
Sixteen Candles
Some Kind of Wonderful
Teen Wolf
Valley Girl
Wayne's World
With Six You Get Eggroll
The World of Henry Orient
You're a Big Boy Now
You Can't Hurry Love

CO5 Funny Families
The Addams Family
The Applegates
Auntie Mame
Author! Author!
Back to the Future, Part II
Beethoven
Betsy's Wedding
Big Business
Big Girls Don't Cry . . . They Get Even
Brighton Beach Memoirs
A Christmas Story
Come Blow Your Horn
Cookie
Coupe de Ville

Crimes of the Heart
Daddy's Dyin' . . . Who's Got the Will?
Don't Tell Mom the Babysitter's Dead
Drop Dead Fred
18 Again!
Family Business
Father of the Bride (1991 version)
First Family
Folks!
For Richer, For Poorer
Garbo Talks
Ghost Dad
The Great Outdoors
Hannah and Her Sisters
Honey, I Blew Up the Kid
Honey, I Shrunk the Kids
Hope and Glory
The Hotel New Hampshire
I Ought to Be in Pictures
Irreconcilable Differences
Life With Father
Like Father, Like Son
Look Who's Talking
Look Who's Talking Too
Lovers and Other Strangers
Max Dugan Returns
Mermaids
Morgan Stewart's Coming Home
Mr. Hobbs Takes a Vacation
Mr. Mom
National Lampoon's Christmas Vacation
National Lampoon's European Vacation
National Lampoon's Vacation
Only the Lonely
Over the Brooklyn Bridge
Overboard
Papa's Delicate Condition
Paradise Alley
Parenthood
Parents
Passed Away
The Plot Against Harry
Portnoy's Complaint
Postcards From the Edge
The Prince of Pennsylvania
Problem Child
Queen of Hearts
Radio Days
Raising Arizona
She's Out of Control
Sibling Rivalry
Stop! Or My Mom Will Shoot
Suburban Commando
This Is My Life
A Thousand Clowns
Too Much Sun
The Toy
True Love
Trust
Tune in Tomorrow . .

29th Street
Twins
Twister
Uncle Buck
Vice Versa
Waiting for the Light
A Wedding
What About Bob?
Where the Heart Is
Where's Poppa?
Yours, Mine and Ours

CO6 Nutty Nostalgia
American Graffiti
Back to the Future
Back to the Future, Part II
Back to the Future, Part III
Barton Fink
Biloxi Blues
Bloodhounds of Broadway
Brighton Beach Memoirs
A Christmas Story
Cooley High
Coupe de Ville
Cry-Baby
Diner
The Flamingo Kid
Good Morning, Vietnam
The Great Race
Hairspray
Harlem Nights
Harry and Walter Go to New York
Heartbreak Hotel
Hearts of the West
History of the World—Part I
Hope and Glory
How I Won the War
I Wanna Hold Your Hand
Impromptu
In the Mood
A League of Their Own
The Lords of Flatbush
Love at Stake
M*A*S*H
Matinee
Mermaids
Monsieur Beaucaire
More American Graffiti
Mr. North
My Favorite Year
Nadine
The Night They Raided Minsky's
1941
Papa's Delicate Condition
Paper Moon
Parents
Peggy Sue Got Married
A Private Function
Privates on Parade
Radio Days

Royal Flash
The Secret Diary of Sigmund Freud
Shag
The Skin Game (1971)
Start the Revolution Without Me
The Sting
Sunset
Those Daring Young Men in Their Jaunty
   Jalopies
Those Lips, Those Eyes
Those Magnificent Men in Their Flying
   Machines
Tin Men
The Twelve Chairs
The World's Greatest Lover

CO7 Movie Spoofs
The Adventures of Sherlock Holmes' Smarter
   Brother
Airplane!
Airplane II: The Sequel
Amazon Women on the Moon
The Big Bus
Blazing Saddles
Bullshot
Casino Royale
Cat Ballou
The Cheap Detective
City Heat
Cry-Baby
Dark Star
Dead Men Don't Wear Plaid
11 Harrowhouse
Erik the Viking
The Feud
High Anxiety
Hot Shots!
I'm Gonna Git You Sucka!
In Like Flint
The Jet Benny Show
Johnny Dangerously
The Last Polka
The Last Remake of Beau Geste
Loose Shoes
Love at First Bite
Lust in the Dust
The Man With Two Brains
Matinee
Monty Python and the Holy Grail
Monty Python's Life of Brian
Movie Movie
Murder by Death
The Naked Gun
The Naked Gun 2½: The Smell of Fear
National Lampoon's Loaded Weapon 1
Our Man Flint
The Prisoner of Zenda (1979 version)
Repossessed
Robin and the Seven Hoods
Rock 'n' Roll High School

The Rocky Horror Picture Show
Rustler's Rhapsody
Silent Movie
Sleeper
Spaceballs
Take the Money and Run
There's Nothing Out There
This Is Spinal Tap
Top Secret!
Transylvania 6–5000
What's Up, Tiger Lily?
Yellowbeard
Young Frankenstein
Zelig

CO8 The Lighter Side of Show Biz
After the Fox
All You Need Is Cash
Barton Fink
The Big Picture
Broadway Danny Rose
CB4
Champagne for Caesar
A Chorus of Disapproval
The Commitments
Crimes and Misdemeanors
Delirious
Enter Laughing
FM
Gentlemen Prefer Blondes
Ginger and Fred
The Groove Tube
The Hard Way
Hearts of the West
Hollywood Boulevard
Hollywood or Bust
Hollywood Shuffle
Home Movies
Hooper
Irreconcilable Differences
Ishtar
Kiss Me, Stupid
The Loved One
Matinee
Meeting Venus
Mistress
Modern Romance
Moon Over Parador
Movers and Shakers
Mr. Saturday Night
My Favorite Year
My Geisha
Noises Off
Postcards From the Edge
The Producers
The Purple Rose of Cairo
Radio Days
The Ratings Game
Real Life
Rhinestone

Roadie
Romantic Comedy
Room Service
S.O.B.
Smile
Soapdish
Songwriter
Stardust Memories
Stay Tuned
Sunset
The Sunshine Boys
Sweet Liberty
The Tall Guy
Tapeheads
That's Adequate
This Is My Life
Those Lips, Those Eyes
Tootsie
Tune in Tomorrow . . .
Tunnelvision
UHF
Under the Rainbow
Wayne's World
Who Framed Roger Rabbit
The World's Greatest Lover
You Can't Take It With You (1984 version)

CO9 Action Comedies
See also: CO10 Crime and Suspense
    Comedies
Air America
The Ambushers
Any Which Way You Can
Beverly Hills Cop
Beverly Hills Cop II
Bird on a Wire
The Cannonball Run
Cannonball Run II
The Cheap Detective
Cold Feet
Crocodile Dundee
Crocodile Dundee II
Donovan's Reef
Every Which Way But Loose
Fuzz
Ghostbusters
Ghostbusters II
The Golden Child
The Grissom Gang
The Gumball Rally
The Hard Way
Howard the Duck
Hudson Hawk
If Looks Could Kill
Innerspace
Into the Sun
It's a Mad Mad Mad Mad World
Kuffs
Midnight Run
Murderer's Row

Raising Arizona
Running Scared
Scavenger Hunt
See No Evil, Hear No Evil
Short Time
Smokey and the Bandit (series)
Speed Zone
Stop! Or My Mom Will Shoot
Think Big
Those Daring Young Men in Their Jaunty
    Jalopies
Those Magnificent Men in Their Flying
    Machines
3 Ninjas
Weekend at Bernie's

CO10 Crime and Suspense Comedies
See also: CO9 Action Comedies, MY17 Comic
    Mysteries, Star Check List ST198 Peter
    Sellers (for *Pink Panther* titles)
The Adventures of Sherlock Holmes' Smarter
    Brother
Another You
Bank Shot
Big Trouble
The Black Marble
Boris and Natasha
The Brain
Breaking In
Bull'seye!
Burglar
Cadillac Man
Career Opportunities
The Cheap Detective
The Choirboys
Clue
Compromising Positions
Cookie
Crackers
Crazy Mama
Curly Sue
Curse of the Pink Panther
Desire and Hell at the Sunset Motel
Disorganized Crime
$ (Dollars)
Dragnet (1987)
The Dumb Waiter
11 Harrowhouse
Ernest Goes to Jail
Family Business
Finders Keepers
A Fish Called Wanda
Flashback
Fletch
Fletch Lives
The Flim Flam Man
Foul Play
The Freshman (1990)
Fun With Dick and Jane
The Gun in Betty Lou's Handbag

Heart Condition
Hexed
Hopscotch
The Hot Rock
How to Murder Your Wife
Hudson Hawk
I Love You to Death
The In-Laws
Johnny Dangerously
Jumpin' Jack Flash
K-9
The Ladykillers
The Lavender Hill Mob
Let's Do It Again
Little Vegas
Loose Cannons
The Man With One Red Shoe
Married to the Mob
Men at Work
Mo' Money
Moonlighting (1985)
Murder by Death
My Blue Heaven
Mystery Date
The Naked Gun
The Naked Gun 2½: The Smell of Fear
National Lampoon's Loaded Weapon 1
Once Upon a Crime
Opportunity Knocks
Oscar
A Piece of the Action
Pink Cadillac
The Plot Against Harry
Pocket Money
The Pope Must Diet
Pure Luck
Quick Change
Raising Arizona
Rancho Deluxe
Rough Cut
Ruthless People
Second Sight
See No Evil, Hear No Evil
Silver Streak
Slither
Some Like It Hot
Special Delivery
Stakeout
The Sting
Stir Crazy
Take the Money and Run
They All Laughed
The Thief Who Came to Dinner
Things Change
Three Fugitives
Throw Momma from the Train
Tough Guys
The Trouble With Harry
True Identity
Turner and Hooch

Two Way Stretch
Who Framed Roger Rabbit
Who's Harry Crumb?
Win, Place or Steal
Wise Guys

CO11 Special Effects for Laughs
Arachnophobia
Back to the Future
Back to the Future, Part II
Back to the Future, Part III
Beetlejuice
Big Top Pee-wee
Death Becomes Her
Explorers
Ghost Dad
Ghostbusters
Ghostbusters II
The Golden Child
Gremlins
Gremlins 2: The New Batch
High Spirits
Honey, I Blew Up the Kid
Honey, I Shrunk the Kids
Howard the Duck
The Incredible Shrinking Woman
Innerspace
Jekyll & Hyde . . . Together Again
Little Monsters
Max Headroom
Modern Problems
Mom and Dad Save the World
My Demon Lover
My Science Project
My Stepmother Is an Alien
Pee-wee's Big Adventure
Second Sight
Short Circuit
Short Circuit 2
Teen Wolf
Weird Science
Who Framed Roger Rabbit

CO12 Offbeat Comedy
See also: CU5 Cult Comedy
The Adventures of Buckaroo Banzai Across
   the Eighth Dimension
After Hours
The Applegates
Bagdad Cafe
Barton Fink
Being There
Big Top Pee-wee
Bliss
Brewster McCloud
The Cars That Ate Paris
Catch-22
The Coca-Cola Kid
Cold Feet
Consuming Passions

A Day in the Death of Joe Egg
Death Becomes Her
Delicatessen
Desire and Hell at the Sunset Motel
Down by Law
Dr. Strangelove or; How I Learned to Stop
  Worrying and Love the Bomb
The End
Entertaining Mr. Sloane
Eversmile, New Jersey
The Freshman (1990)
Grace Quigley
Harold and Maude
Heathers
The Hospital
How I Won the War
I Love You to Death
In the Spirit
I've Heard the Mermaids Singing
King of Comedy
Little Murders
Lolita
Loot
The Loved One
M*A*S*H
The Magic Christian
Malcolm
Me and Him
Miss Firecracker
Monster in a Box
Mr. Sycamore
My Dinner With Andre
My New Gun
Nasty Habits
Neighbors
A New Leaf
92 in the Shade
The Object of Beauty
Oh Dad, Poor Dad, Mama's Hung You in the
  Closet and I'm Feeling So Sad
Outrageous
Parents
Passed Away
Pee-wee's Big Adventure
Private Parts
Pulp
Putney Swope
Repo Man
The Return of Captain Invincible
Riders of the Storm
The Rocky Horror Picture Show
Rosencrantz and Guildenstern Are Dead
Salvation
Shakes the Clown
A Shock to the System
Short Time
Silent Movie
Something Wild
Stranger Than Paradise
Swimming to Cambodia

Toys
The Trouble With Harry
Trust
UFOria
The Unbelievable Truth
Used Cars
Where's Poppa?
Young Einstein
You're a Big Boy Now
Zelig

CO13 The Alumni of "Saturday Night Live"

Dan Aykroyd (1952–)
All You Need Is Cash (bit)
The Best of Chevy Chase
The Best of Dan Aykroyd
The Best of Gilda Radner
The Best of John Belushi
The Blues Brothers
Caddyshack II
Chaplin
The Couch Trip
Doctor Detroit
Dragnet (1987)
Driving Miss Daisy
Ghostbusters
Ghostbusterr II
The Great Outdoors
Into the Night (bit)
It Came From Hollywood
Loose Cannons
Love at First Sight
My Girl
My Stepmother Is an Alien
Neighbors
1941
Nothing but Trouble (1991) (also director)
Sneakers
Spies Like Us
This Is My Life
Trading Places
Twilight Zone—The Movie

Jim Belushi (1954–)
About Last Night
Curly Sue
Diary of a Hitman
Homer and Eddie
Jumpin' Jack Flash
K-9
Little Shop of Horrors
The Man With One Red Shoe
Mr. Destiny
Once Upon a Crime
Only the Lonely
The Palermo Connection
Pinocchio (1984 version)
The Principal

Real Men
Red Heat
Salvador
Taking Care of Business
Thief
Traces of Red
Trading Places (bit)

John Belushi (1949–1982)
All You Need Is Cash (bit)
The Best of Chevy Chase
The Best of Dan Aykroyd
The Best of Gilda Radner
The Best of John Belushi
The Blues Brothers
Continental Divide
Goin' South
National Lampoon's Animal House
Neighbors
1941
Old Boyfriends

Chevy Chase (1944–)
The Best of Chevy Chase
The Best of Dan Aykroyd
The Best of Gilda Radner
The Best of John Belushi
Caddyshack
Caddyshack II
Deal of the Century
Fletch
Fletch Lives
Follow That Bird
Foul Play
Funny Farm
The Groove Tube
Hero
Memoirs of an Invisible Man
Modern Problems
National Lampoon's Christmas Vacation
National Lampoon's European Vacation
National Lampoon's Vacation
Nothing but Trouble (1991)
Oh, Heavenly Dog!
Seems Like Old Times
Spies Like Us
Three Amigos
Tunnelvision
Under the Rainbow

Billy Crystal (1947–)
An All-Star Salute to the Improv
Animalympics (character voice)
The Best of Comic Relief
The Best of Comic Relief '90
Billy Crystal: A Comic's Line
Billy Crystal: Don't Get Me Started
Billy Crystal: Night Train to Moscow
Breaking Up Is Hard To Do
City Slickers

Comic Relief 2
Comic Relief III
Enola Gay: The Men, the Mission, the
    Atomic Bomb
Memories of Me
Mr. Saturday Night
The Princess Bride
Rabbit Test
Richard Lewis: "I'm in Pain"
Running Scared
This Is Spinal Tap
The Three Little Pigs
Throw Momma From the Train
When Harry Met Sally . . .
Your Favorite Laughs From an Evening at the
    Improv

Jane Curtin (1947–)
The Best of Dan Aykroyd
The Best of Chevy Chase
The Best of Gilda Radner
The Best of John Belushi
How to Beat the High Cost of Living
O.C. & Stiggs
Suspicion (1987 version)

Eddie Murphy (1961–)
Another 48 HRS
Best Defense
The Best of Eddie Murphy: "Saturday Night
    Live"
Beverly Hills Cop
Beverly Hills Cop II
Boomerang
Coming to America
The Distinguished Gentleman
Eddie Murphy: Delirious
Eddie Murphy Raw
48 HRS
The Golden Child
Harlem Nights (also director)
Trading Places

Bill Murray (1950–)
The Best of Dan Aykroyd
The Best of Gilda Radner
The Best of John Belushi
Caddyshack
Ghostbusters
Ghostbusters II
Groundhog Day
Little Shop of Horrors (1986 version)
Loose Shoes
Mad Dog and Glory
Meatballs
Quick Change (also co-director)
The Razor's Edge (1984 version)
Scrooged
Stripes
Tootsie

What About Bob?
Where the Buffalo Roam

Gilda Radner (1946–1989)
All You Need Is Cash (bit)
Animalympics (character voice)
The Best of Chevy Chase
The Best of Dan Aykroyd
The Best of Gilda Radner
The Best of John Belushi
First Family
Gilda Live
Hanky Panky
Haunted Honeymoon
It Came From Hollywood
The Last Detail (bit)
Movers and Shakers
The Woman in Red

CO14 The Alumni of "SCTV"

John Candy (1950–)
Armed and Dangerous
The Blues Brothers (bit)
Boris and Natasha (bit)
Brewster's Millions
The Clown Murders
Delirious
Find the Lady
Follow That Bird
Going Berserk
The Great Outdoors
Home Alone (bit)
It Came From Hollywood
JFK
The Last Polka
Little Shop of Horrors (1986 version)
Lost and Found (bit)
National Lampoon's Vacation
1941
Nothing but Trouble (1991)
Once Upon a Crime
Only the Lonely
Planes, Trains, and Automobiles
Really Weird Tales
The Rescuers Down Under (character voice)
The Silent Partner
Spaceballs
Speed Zone
Splash
Stripes
Summer Rental
Uncle Buck
Volunteers
Who's Harry Crumb?

Joe Flaherty (1950–)
Back to the Future, Part II
Blue Monkey
Follow That Bird

Going Berserk
One Crazy Summer
Really Weird Tales
Speed Zone
Stripes (bit)
Used Cars

Eugene Levy (1946–)
Armed and Dangerous
Billy Crystal: Don't Get Me Started
Club Paradise
Father of the Bride (1991 version) (bit)
Going Berserk
The Last Polka
National Lampoon's Vacation
Once Upon a Crime (director only)
Speed Zone
Splash
Stay Tuned

Andrea Martin (1947–)
Black Christmas
Boris and Natasha
Club Paradise
Comic Relief 2
Rude Awakening
Stepping Out
Too Much Sun
Worth Winning

Rick Moranis (1954–)
Club Paradise
Ghostbusters
Ghostbusters II
Head Office
Honey, I Blew Up the Kid
Honey, I Shrunk the Kids
The Last Polka
Little Shop of Horrors (1986 version)
My Blue Heaven
Parenthood
Spaceballs
Strange Brew
Streets of Fire
The Wild Life

Catherine O'Hara (1954–)
After Hours
Beetlejuice
Betsy's Wedding
Comic Relief 2
Heartburn
Home Alone
Home Alone 2: Lost in New York
The Last Polka
Little Vegas
Really Weird Tales

Harold Ramis (1944–)
Baby Boom

The Best of Comic Relief
Caddyshack (director only)
Club Paradise (director only)
Ghostbusters
Ghostbusters II
Groundhog Day (also director)
National Lampoon's Vacation (director only)
Richard Lewis: "I'm in Pain"
Stealing Home
Stripes

Martin Short (1951–)
The Best of Comic Relief
The Big Picture
Captain Ron
Cross My Heart
Father of the Bride (1991 version)
Innerspace
Lost and Found (bit)
Pure Luck
Really Weird Tales
Sunset Limousine
Three Amigos
Three Fugitives

Dave Thomas (1949–)
Boris and Natasha
The Experts (director only)
Follow That Bird
Love at Stake
Moving
My Man Adam
Strange Brew (also director)
Stripes (bit)

CO15 The Alumni of "Monty Python's Flying Circus"

The Troupe
And Now for Something Completely Different
Life of Python
Monty Python and the Holy Grail
Monty Python Live at the Hollywood Bowl
Monty Python's Flying Circus, Volumes 1–22
Monty Python's Life of Brian
Monty Python's The Meaning of Life
Parrot Sketch Not Included

Individually (but sometimes together)
Graham Chapman (1941–1989)
The Magic Christian
The Odd Job
The Secret Policeman's Other Ball
Yellowbeard

John Cleese (1939–)
An American Tale: Fievel Goes West
  (character voice)
The Big Picture
The Bliss of Mrs. Blossom (bit)

Bull'seye!
Clockwise
Erik the Viking
Fawlty Towers, Volumes 1–4
A Fish Called Wanda
The Great Muppet Caper
The Magic Christian
Privates on Parade
The Secret Policeman's Other Ball
The Secret Policeman's Private Parts
Silverado
The Statue (bit)
Time Bandits
Whoops Apocalypse
Yellowbeard

Terry Gilliam (1940–)
Director only, unless noted.
The Adventures of Baron Münchausen
Brazil
The Fisher King
Jabberwocky
The Secret Policeman's Private Parts (actor)
Spies Like Us (bit, actor)
Time Bandits

Eric Idle (1943–)
The Adventures of Baron Münchausen
All You Need Is Cash
The Mikado (1987 version)
Mom and Dad Save the World
National Lampoon's European Vacation
Nuns on the Run
The Pied Piper of Hamelin
Too Much Sun
Yellowbeard

Terry Jones (1942–)
Erik the Viking (also director)
Labyrinth
Personal Services (director only)
Ripping Yarns
The Secret Policeman's Other Ball
The Secret Policeman's Private Parts

Michael Palin (1943–)
Brazil
A Fish Called Wanda
Jabberwocky
The Missionary
A Private Function
Ripping Yarns
The Secret Policeman's Other Ball
The Secret Policeman's Private Parts
Time Bandits

CO16 Performance Comics
See also: ST180 Richard Pryor Check List
An All-Star Salute to the Improv
The Andy Kaufman Sound Stage Special

An Audience With Mel Brooks
Bette Midler's Mondo Beyondo
The Best of Benny Hill, vols. 1–5
The Best of Comic Relief
Best of Comic Relief '90
The Best of Spike Jones, vols. 1–3
Bill Cosby: 49
Bill Cosby: Himself
Billy Crystal: A Comic's Line
Billy Crystal: Don't Get Me Started
Billy Crystal: Night Train to Moscow
Carlin at Carnegie
Comic Relief 2
Comic Relief III
The Complete "Weird Al" Yankovic
Eddie Murphy: Delirious
Eddie Murphy Raw
Eric Bogosian: Funhouse
The Ernest Film Festival
An Evening With Bobcat Goldthwait: Share
    the Warmth
An Evening With Robin Williams
The First Howie Mandel Special
Gallagher: The Bookkeeper
Gallagher: The Maddest
Gallagher: Melon Crazy
Gallagher: Over Your Head
Gallagher: Stuck in the '60s
Garry Shandling: Alone in Vegas
Garry Shandling Show, 25th Anniversary
    Special
George Carlin on Campus
Gilda Live
HBO Comedy Club
Jackie Mason on Broadway
Joe Bob Briggs Dead in Concert
The Joe Piscopo New Jersey Special
The Joe Piscopo Video
Jonathan Winters: On the Ledge
The Lenny Bruce Performance Film
Monster in a Box
Richard Lewis: "I'm in Pain"
Robert Klein: Child of the '60s, Man of the
    '80s
Robert Klein on Broadway
Robin Williams Live!
Sam Kinison Live!
The Search for Signs of Intelligent Life in the
    Universe
Spalding Gray: Terrors of Pleasure
Steve Martin Live
Steven Wright Live
Swimming to Cambodia
Ten From Your Show of Shows
Whoopi Goldberg: Fontaine . . . Why Am I
    Straight?
Whoopi Goldberg Live
Without You I'm Nothing
Your Favorite Laughs From an Evening at the
    Improv

CO17 Classic & Contemporary British Comedy

See also: CO15 The Alumni of "Monty
    Python's Flying Circus"
Alfie
Antonia and Jane
The Belles of St. Trinians
Billy Liar
Blame It on the Bellboy
The Bliss of Mrs. Blossom
Britannia Hospital
Bullshot
The Captain's Paradise
Carry On Doctor
A Chorus of Disapproval
Comfort and Joy
The Commitments
Consuming Passions
A Day in the Death of Joe Egg
The Demi-Paradise
Doctor at Large
Doctor at Sea
Doctor in Distress
Doctor in the House
Eat the Peach
Educating Rita
Entertaining Mr. Sloane
The Favor, the Watch, and the Very Big Fish
A Fish Called Wanda
Georgy Girl
Getting It Right
The Goon Show Movie
The Gospel According to Vic
Green Grow the Rushes
Gregory's Girl
Gumshoe
High Hopes
Hobson's Choice (1954 version)
Hope and Glory
The Horse's Mouth
How I Won the War
How to Get Ahead in Advertising
I'm All Right, Jack
Kind Hearts and Coronets
The Ladykillers
Last Holiday
The Lavender Hill Mob
Letter to Brezhnev
Local Hero
Loot
The Magic Christian
Make Mine Mink
The Man in the White Suit
The Millionairess
Morgan: A Suitable Case for Treatment
The Mouse That Roared
The Naked Truth
No Surrender
Nuns on the Run
Only Two Can Play

Personal Services
Peter's Friends
The Pope Must Diet
A Private Function
The Promoter
Queen of Hearts
Rita, Sue and Bob Too
The Ruling Class
Shirley Valentine
The Smallest Show on Earth
Stars and Bars
The Statue
Storm in a Teacup
Strike It Rich
The Tall Guy
That Sinking Feeling
30 Is a Dangerous Age, Cynthia
Tom Jones
Two Way Stretch
Waltz of the Toreadors
We Think the World of You
Whisky Galore
Whoops Apocalypse
Wish You Were Here
Withnail & I
The Wrong Arm of the Law
The Wrong Box

CO18 Campus Comedy

See also: DR25 School Days
Bedtime for Bonzo
The Belles of St. Trinians
Class of Nuke 'Em High
College
College Swing
The Computer Wore Tennis Shoes
Cooley High
Encino Man
Fast Times at Ridgemont High
The Freshman (1925)
The Freshman (1990)
Getting Straight
The Gospel According to Vic
Gregory's Girl
Gross Anatomy
Heathers
Heaven Help Us
Horse Feathers
House Party 2
How I Got Into College
Kindergarten Cop
The Ladies' Man
My Bodyguard
My Science Project
National Lampoon's Animal House
National Lampoon's Class Reunion
Necessary Roughness
The Nutty Professor
Porky's (series)
Real Genius

Revenge of the Nerds
Rock 'n' Roll High School
School Daze
Soul Man
Star Spangled Girl
Summer School
Teacher's Pet
The Trouble With Angels
A Woman of Distinction
Zero for Conduct

CO19 Sports for Laughs

See also: DR22 For Sports Fans
All the Marbles
The Bad News Bears
The Best of Times
The Bingo Long Traveling All-Stars and
　Motor Kings
Bull Durham
The Caddy
Class Act
The Cutting Edge
Fast Break
Johnny Be Good
The Kid From Brooklyn
Ladybugs
A League of Their Own
Let It Ride
The Longest Yard
The Main Event
Major League
Man's Favorite Sport?
Matilda
Mr. Baseball
Necessary Roughness
No Holds Barred
North Dallas Forty
Paper Lion
Paradise Alley
Pat and Mike
Semi-Tough
Ski Patrol
Slap Shot
Stroker Ace
Tall Story
White Men Can't Jump
Wildcats

CO20 Fish Out of Water: Funny Tales of Misplaced Persons

Adventures in Babysitting
After Hours
All of Me
Back to the Future
Back to the Future, Part II
Back to the Future, Part III
Bagdad Cafe
Beverly Hills Cop
Beverly Hills Cop II
Big

Bill and Ted's Bogus Journey
Bill and Ted's Excellent Adventure
Chances Are
City Slickers
Class Act
The Coca-Cola Kid
Coming to America
The Couch Trip
Critical Condition
Crocodile Dundee
Crocodile Dundee II
Daisy Miller
Delirious
Desperately Seeking Susan
The Distinguished Gentleman
Doc Hollywood
Down and Out in Beverly Hills
Dream a Little Dream
The Dream Team
Easy Money
18 Again!
Encino Man
The Errand Boy
The Experts
The Flamingo Kid
Flashback
Freaky Friday
George Washington Slept Here
Good Neighbor Sam
The Great McGinty
Groundhog Day
Hail the Conquering Hero
The Hard Way
Heart Condition
Heaven Can Wait (1978)
Hercules Goes Bananas
Here Comes Mr. Jordan
Howard the Duck
Identity Crisis
If Looks Could Kill
Ishtar
Kindergarten Cop
A King in New York
King Ralph
Late for Dinner
Life Stinks
Like Father, Like Son
Livin' Large
Local Hero
The Loved One
Maxie
Mom and Dad Save the World
Moon Over Parador
Morgan: A Suitable Case for Treatment
Moscow on the Hudson
Mr. Baseball
Mr. Mom
Mr. Winkle Goes to War
My Cousin Vinny
My Man Godfrey

Never a Dull Moment (1950)
Nuns on the Run
The Out-of-Towners
Out on a Limb
Overboard
Paper Lion
Peggy Sue Got Married
Pretty Woman
The Ritz
Rude Awakening
The Secret of My Success
Simon
Sister Act
Soul Man
Splash
Stay Tuned
Straight Talk
Strictly Business
Sullivan's Travels
The Super
Switch
Taking Care of Business
Things Change
Tough Guys
Trading Places
Troop Beverly Hills
True Identity
Vice Versa
Walk, Don't Run
We're No Angels (1989 version)
Yentl

CO21 Uniformly Funny: Service Comedies

At War with the Army
Biloxi Blues
Buck Privates
Captain Newman, M.D.
Catch-22
Caught in the Draft
The Chaplin Revue (Shoulder Arms and The Pilgrim)
Doughboys
Ensign Pulver
Good Morning, Vietnam
Great Guns
Hot Shots!
How I Won the War
In the Navy
Jumping Jacks
Keep 'em Flying
Kelly's Heroes
The Last Detail
M*A*S*H
Mr. Winkle Goes to War
Never Wave at a WAC
Off Limits (1953)
Operation Petticoat
Pack Up Your Troubles
The Perfect Furlough

Private Benjamin
Privates on Parade
The Sad Sack
The Secret War of Harry Frigg
She's in the Army Now
Soldier in the Rain
Stripes

Teahouse of the August Moon
Up in Arms
Up the Creek (1958)
The Wackiest Ship in the Army
What Did You Do in the War, Daddy?
Which Way to the Front?

4 Cult Films (CU)

CU1 Midnight Movies
CU2 Camp Cult
CU3 "Head" Movies
CU4 Cult Horror and Science Fiction
CU5 Cult Comedy
CU6 Notoriously Sexy
CU7 Famous for Gore and Violence
CU8 Censored or Banned Movies
CU9 Political Statements
CU10 Footage Added for Video
CU11 "Bad" Movies
CU12 Bad Taste? You Be the Judge
CU13 Cult Movies by Famous Directors
CU14 Directors Who Got Their Starts With Roger Corman
CU15 Cult Movies by One-Shot Directors
CU16 Documentaries
CU17 Cult Casting
CU18 Remakes of Famous Movies
CU19 Letterboxed Movies
CU20 Widescreen Movies That Should Be Letterboxed

See also: Director Check Lists DT3 Pedro Almodóvar, DT4 Robert Altman, DT6 Allan Arkush, DT8 Paul Bartel, DT15 John Boorman, DT23 John Carpenter, DT26 Jean Cocteau, DT27 Joel Coen, DT28 Larry Cohen, DT33 Joe Dante, DT34 Brian De Palma, DT37 Jonathan Demme, DT46 Bill Forsyth, DT49 Samuel Fuller, DT51 Peter Greenaway, DT56 Walter Hill, DT62 Jim Jarmusch, DT64 Philip Kaufman, DT74 Richard Lester, DT79 David Lynch, DT81 Terrence Malick, DT89 Errol Morris, DT90 Paul Morrissey, DT93 Max Ophuls, DT99 Michael Powell, DT101 Nicholas Ray, DT106 Nicolas Roeg, DT110 Alan Rudolph, DT111 Ken Russell, DT115 Ridley Scott, DT117 Douglas Sirk, DT132 John Waters, DT141 Ed Wood, Jr.

CU1 Midnight Movies
Angel Heart
Bad Lieutenant
Blue Velvet
A Clockwork Orange
Dawn of the Dead
Eraserhead
Frankenhooker
Greaser's Palace
The Harder They Come
Hardware
Harold and Maude
King of Hearts
Magical Mystery Tour
Myra Breckenridge
Night of the Living Dead (1968 version)
Outrageous!
Performance
Pink Flamingos
Reefer Madness
Rock 'n' Roll High School
The Rocky Horror Picture Show
Rude Boy
Santa Sangre
Sid & Nancy
Something Wild
Stranger Than Paradise
Tetsuo: The Iron Man
The Texas Chainsaw Massacre
200 Motels
Wild at Heart
Zentropa

CU2 Camp Cult
Beyond the Valley of the Dolls
Bride of the Gorilla
The Conqueror
The Cool and the Crazy
Female on the Beach
Forbidden Zone
The Fountainhead
Heat (1972)
High School Confidential
Hush . . . Hush Sweet Charlotte
Jet Pilot
The Killers (1964 version)
Land of the Pharaohs
The Lonely Lady
Mommie Dearest
Myra Breckenridge
The Private Files of J. Edgar Hoover
Sextette
Shack Out on 101
Sincerely Yours
Strait-Jacket
Valley of the Dolls (1967 version)

What Ever Happened to Baby Jane?
The Wicked Lady
The Wild One
The Women (1939)

CU3 "Head" Movies
Altered States
Cocaine Cowboys
Easy Rider
Fantasia
Head
More
Naked Lunch
Performance
The Trip
200 Motels
2001: A Space Odyssey
Up in Smoke
Yellow Submarine
Zabriskie Point

CU4 Cult Horror and Science Fiction
The Abominable Dr. Phibes
Altered States
Android
Andy Warhol's Dracula
Andy Warhol's Frankenstein
Barbarella
Basket Case
Blood Couple
A Boy and His Dog
Brazil
The Bride of Frankenstein
The Brood
Carnival of Souls
A Clockwork Orange
The Conqueror Worm
Dance of the Damned
Dark Star
Daughters of Darkness
Dawn of the Dead
The Day the Earth Stood Still
Death Race 2000
Fahrenheit 451
Forbidden Planet
Frankenhooker
Freaks
Glen and Randa
Halloween
The Hills Have Eyes
I Walked with a Zombie
The Incredible Shrinking Man
The Incredibly Strange Creatures Who
    Stopped Living and Became Crazy
    Mixed-Up Zombies
Invasion of the Bee Girls
Invasion of the Body Snatchers (1956 and
    1978 versions)
King Kong (1933 version)
Liquid Sky

The Little Shop of Horrors (1960 version)
The Man Who Fell to Earth
Martin
Night of the Living Dead (1968 version)
Night Tide
Piranha
Re-Animator
The Reflecting Skin
Scanners
Slaughterhouse Five
The Sorcerers
Suspiria
The Texas Chainsaw Massacre
Theatre of Blood
Them
The Thing (From Another World)
2001: A Space Odyssey
The Wicker Man
Zardoz

CU5 Cult Comedy
The Adventures of Buckaroo Banzai Across
    the Eighth Dimension
After Hours
Angels Over Broadway
Beat the Devil
Bedazzled
Bedtime for Bonzo
Brewster McCloud
Eating Raoul
Get Crazy
Greetings
Harold and Maude
The Heartbreak Kid
Heathers
Hollywood Boulevard
The Horn Blows at Midnight
It's a Gift
King of Comedy
King of Hearts
Kiss Me, Stupid
La Cage aux Folles
The Ladykillers
Little Murders
Matador
Morgan: A Suitable Case for
    Treatment
My Dinner With Andre
Pee-wee's Big Adventure
Rancho Deluxe
Repo Man
The Rocky Horror Picture Show
The Ruling Class
Shakes the Clown
Slither
Something for Everyone
To Be or Not to Be (1942 version)
Used Cars
Where the Heart Is
Where's Poppa?

CU6 Notoriously Sexy

Angel Heart
Baby Doll
Bad Lieutenant
Barbarella
Basic Instinct
Betty Blue
Beyond the Valley of the Dolls
Big Bad Mama
Body Heat
Body of Evidence
Butterfly
Caligula
The Cook, The Thief, His Wife and Her Lover
Crimes of Passion
Damage
Dark Obsession
Daughters of Darkness
Devil in the Flesh
Ecstasy
The Fourth Man
The Girl in a Swing
Henry & June
In the Realm of the Senses
Kiss Me, Stupid
L'Année des Meduses
Last Tango in Paris
Liquid Sky
The Lover
Lovers
Maitresse
The Night Porter
9½ Weeks
Pandora's Box
Rendez-vous
She's Gotta Have It
Something for Everyone
Summer Lovers
Sweet Movie
Tales of Ordinary Madness
Thief of Hearts
Tie Me Up! Tie Me Down!
Two Moon Junction
The Unbearable Lightness of Being
Wild Orchid
Wild Orchid II: Two Shades of Blue
Zandalee

CU7 Famous for Gore and Violence

Across 110th Street
Akira
Basket Case
Bride of Re-Animator
The Brood
Caligula
The Cook, The Thief, His Wife and
  Her Lover
Dawn of the Dead
Enter the Dragon
The Evil Dead

Fingers
The Fly (1986 version)
Frankenhooker
From Beyond
Hardware
Henry: Portrait of a Serial Killer
The Killer
King of New York
Mad Max
Maniac
Mother's Day
Ms. 45
Night of the Living Dead (1968 and 1990
  versions)
Point Blank
Re-Animator
Reservoir Dogs
Santa Sangre
Scanners
Scarface (1983 version)
Shogun Assassin
Taxi Driver
Tetsuo: The Iron Man
The Texas Chainsaw Massacre
Twitch of the Death Nerve
2000 Maniacs
The Warriors
The Wild Bunch

CU8 Censored or Banned Movies

Baby Doll
Bad Lieutenant
Carnal Knowledge
A Clockwork Orange
The Commissar
Ecstasy
Freaks
Hail Mary
In the Realm of the Senses
J'Accuse
Ju Dou
Kiss Me, Stupid
The Lovers (1959)
The Miracle (1948)
The North Star
Oliver Twist (1948 version)
Ossessione
The Outlaw
Peeping Tom
Viridiana
The War Game
Witchcraft Through the Ages

CU9 Political Statements

See also: DR21 Political Dramas
The Battle of Algiers
Billy Jack
Burn!
The Harder They Come
JFK

The Manchurian Candidate
The Parallax View
Potemkin
Salt of the Earth
Strike!
Sympathy for the Devil
Ten Days That Shook the World/October
The War Game
Winter Kills

CU10 Footage Added for Video
This list includes films with footage restored
    from early theatrical versions, as well as
    titles with never-seen-before scenes. Check
    the Title Index for details on each film.
And God Created Woman (1988 version)
Angel Heart
Another Pair of Aces: Three of a Kind
Backtrack
The Bad Sleep Well
Basic Instinct
Blade Runner
Body of Evidence
The Bullfighter and the Lady
Captain Blood
Cat Chaser
Cheyenne Autumn
Colors
Crimes of Passion
Damage
Dr. Jekyll and Mr. Hyde (1932 version)
The Executioner's Song
Fatal Attraction
The Fearless Vampire Killers
Frankenstein (1931 version)
The Godfather, Part III
The Godfather Trilogy, 1901–1980
Hawaii
Hellbound: Hellraiser II
The Hidden Fortress
Is Paris Burning?
Isadora
It's a Mad Mad Mad Mad World
JFK
Johnny Be Good
The Lawnmower Man
Lawrence of Arabia
Liebestraum
Lost Horizon
Love Crimes
The Lover
Macbeth (1948 version)
Mr. Skeffington
New York, New York
Oliver Twist (1948 version)
Pat Garrett and Billy the Kid
Red River
Richard III
Rocco and His Brothers
Salem's Lot

Santa Sangre
Scandal
The Sea Hawk
The Sicilian
Star Trek—The Motion Picture
Stealing Heaven
Stop Making Sense
Stromboli
The Sun Shines Bright
Suspiria
Sweet Charity
Tales of Hoffmann
Tarzan and His Mate
Thief of Hearts
This Is Elvis
Touch of Evil
Twin Peaks
Two English Girls
The Wedding March
When Time Ran Out
Whore
Wild Orchid
Wild Orchid II: Two Shades of Blue
Wild Rovers
The Wizard of Oz
Zandalee

CU11 "Bad" Movies
Attack of the Killer Tomatoes
Cocaine Fiends
The Creeping Terror
Frankenstein Island
Glen or Glenda?
Manos, the Hands of Fate
Night of the Bloody Apes
Plan 9 From Outer Space
Queen of Outer Space
Reefer Madness
Revenge of the Dead
Robot Monster
Tarzan, the Ape Man (1981 version)
Terror of Tiny Town
They Saved Hitler's Brain
Zombie Island Massacre

CU12 Bad Taste? You Be the Judge
Andy Warhol's Bad
Blue Velvet
Desperate Living
Eraserhead
Female Trouble
Flesh
Heat (1972)
The Loved One
Mondo Trasho
Multiple Maniacs
Pink Flamingos
Polyester
Shakes the Clown
Suburbia

Trash
Where's Poppa?

CU13 Cult Movies by Famous Directors
Beat the Devil (John Huston)
The Collector (William Wyler)
Fahrenheit 451 (François Truffaut)
Last Tango in Paris (Bernardo Bertolucci)
Rio Bravo (Howard Hawks)
The Searchers (John Ford)
Vertigo (Alfred Hitchcock)

CU14 Directors Who Got Their Starts With Roger Corman
Boxcar Bertha (Martin Scorsese)
Caged Heat (Jonathan Demme)
Dementia 13 (Francis Ford Coppola)
Grand Theft Auto (Ron Howard)
Hollywood Boulevard (Joe Dante and Allan Arkush)
Night Call Nurses (Jonathan Kaplan)
Targets (Peter Bogdanovich)

CU15 Cult Movies by One-Shot Directors
Carnival of Souls (Herk Harvey)
Deadline at Dawn (Harold Clurman)
The Honeymoon Killers (Leonard Kastle)
The Night of the Hunter (Charles Laughton)
One-Eyed Jacks (Marlon Brando)
The Senator Was Indiscreet (George S. Kaufman)

CU16 Documentaries
See also: MU10 Rock Concert Films, MU11 Rock Documentaries
BIOGRAPHIES
Arruza
The Eleanor Roosevelt Story
Elmore Leonard's Criminal Records
General Idi Amin Dada
The James Dean Story
Let's Get Lost
Listen Up: The Lives of Quincy Jones
Marjoe
Notebook on Cities and Clothes
Superstar: The Life and Times of Andy Warhol
Vincent: The Life and Death of Vincent van Gogh
CURRENT AFFAIRS
American Dream (1991)
Blood in the Face
Chicken Ranch
Common Threads: Stories From the Quilt
Down and Out in America
Feed
Harlan County, U.S.A.
Incident at Oglala
Roger and Me

A Sense of Loss
Streetwise
The Thin Blue Line
The Times of Harvey Milk
Underground
HISTORY
The Atomic Cafe
Berkeley in the Sixties
Brother, Can You Spare a Dime?
The Civil War
The Day After Trinity
Dear America: Letters Home From Vietnam
December 7th
Hearts and Minds
Heavy Petting
Hotel Terminus
Let There Be Light
Louisiana Story
Men of Bronze
Millhouse: A White Comedy
Night and Fog
Shoah
The Sorrow and the Pity
Ten Days That Shook the World/October
This Is Korea/December 7
Triumph of the Will
Vietnam: In the Year of the Pig
MOVIES
America at the Movies
Burden of Dreams
Buster Keaton: A Hard Act to Follow
The Epic That Never Was
George Stevens: A Filmmaker's Journey
Harold Lloyd: The Third Genius
Hearts of Darkness: A Filmmaker's Apocalypse
I'm Almost Not Crazy: John Cassavetes—The Man and His Work
Lightning Over Water
Lulu in Berlin
Making of a Legend—Gone With the Wind
Marlene
Marlon Brando
Montgomery Clift
Roger Corman: Hollywood's Wild Angel
Unknown Chaplin
MUSIC
Always for Pleasure
Athens, GA
Celebrating Bird: The Triumph of Charlie Parker
Hot Pepper
Jazz on a Summer's Day
Mingus
Ornette Coleman—Made in America
Say Amen, Somebody
Thelonius Monk: Straight, No Chaser
PEOPLES AND CULTURES
Herdsmen of the Sun
Land Without Bread

Man of Aran
Mississippi Blues
Mondo Cane
Nanook of the North
Paris Is Burning
Salesman
The Sky Above, the Mud Below
PERFORMING ARTS
The Children of Theatre Street
The Lenny Bruce Performance Film
Voices of Sarafina!
Wisecracks
PERSONAL DOCUMENTS
Best Boy
The Big Bang
Cousin Bobby
Garlic Is As Good As Ten Mothers
Gates of Heaven
Grey Gardens
Heaven
Koyaanisqatsi
Sherman's March
Tokyo-Ga
Vernon, Florida
SCIENCE
A Brief History of Time
For All Mankind
Gizmo!
The Hellstrom Chronicle
SPORTS
Derby
Olympia
On Any Sunday
Pumping Iron
Pumping Iron II: The Women
Tokyo Olympiad
When It Was a Game

CU17 Cult Casting

American Graffiti
The Balcony
Candy Mountain
Casino Royale
Catch-22
The Chase (1966)
Dancing Lady
Dinner at Eight
Forever and a Day
Grand Hotel
Harold and Maude
Into the Night
It's a Mad Mad Mad Mad World
Johnny Guitar
The Last Tycoon
The Loved One
The Magnificent Seven
The Outsiders
The Player
Shadows and Fog
Spies Like Us

A Wedding
Winter Kills

CU18 Remakes of Famous Movies

See also: FF8 Foreign Films and Their
    American Remakes; MU14 Musical
    Remakes of Non-Musical Films
Note: Remake title is listed first; original title,
    if different, follows in parentheses. Titles
    are listed only if both remake and original
    are on tape.
An Affair to Remember (Love Affair)
Against All Odds (1984) (Out of the Past)
Always (A Guy Named Joe)
And God Created Woman
The Bride (The Bride of Frankenstein)
Body and Soul
Born Yesterday
Brief Encounter
Cape Fear
Cat People
The Champ
The Children's Hour (These Three)
Circle of Love (La Ronde)
The Corn Is Green
The Country Girl
D.O.A.
Desperate Hours (The Desperate Hours)
Diary of a Chambermaid
Dirty Rotten Scoundrels (Bedtime Story)
Fancy Pants (Ruggles of Red Gap)
Farewell, My Lovely (Murder, My Sweet)
Father of the Bride
The Fly
The Front Page
Guncrazy (Gun Crazy)
Heaven Can Wait (Here Comes Mr. Jordan)
Hobson's Choice
House of Wax (Mystery of the Wax Museum)
Hurricane (The Hurricane)
I Died a Thousand Times (High Sierra)
Invaders From Mars
Invasion of the Body Snatchers
Jamaica Inn
The Jazz Singer
Journey Into Fear
King Kong
The Lady Vanishes
Lord of the Flies
The Man Who Knew Too Much
Mogambo (Red Dust)
Narrow Margin (The Narrow Margin)
Never Say Never Again (Thunderball)
Night of the Living Dead
The Phantom of the Opera
A Pocketful of Miracles (Lady for a Day)
The Postman Always Rings Twice
Scarface
Silk Stockings (Ninotchka)
Stage Struck (1958) (Morning Glory)

A Star Is Born
Stella (Stella Dallas)
The Sun Shines Bright (Judge Priest)
Suspicion
Switching Channels (His Girl Friday)
The Thing (The Thing [From Another World])
The 39 Steps
To Be or Not to Be
Unfaithfully Yours
Walk, Don't Run (The More the Merrier)
We're No Angels

CU19 Letterboxed Movies

Note: Many of these titles are reissues of films originally released on home video in standard format. Always check the tape box or ask your video retailer before renting or buying, to make sure you have the format you want.

Akira Kurosawa's Dreams
The Alamo
All the Vermeers in New York
Always
Apocalypse Now
Backdraft
Basic Instinct
Ben Hur (chariot race only)
Blade Runner
Can-Can (musical numbers only)
The Color Purple
The Cook, The Thief, His Wife and Her Lover
Glory
The Graduate
Guys and Dolls (final number only)
Henry V (1989 version)
High and Low
Hit the Deck (final number only)
Indiana Jones and the Last Crusade
Indiana Jones and the Temple of Doom
Inner Space
It's a Mad Mad Mad Mad World (modified)
Jaws
King of Hearts
Kwaidan
The Last of the Mohicans (1992 version)
L'Avventura
Lawrence of Arabia
A League of Their Own
L'Innocente
Lola Montes
Manhattan
Mystery Train
The Naked Kiss
New York, New York
Night on Earth
Picnic
Raiders of the Lost Ark
Red Beard
Rendez-vous

Satyricon
Shock Corridor
Shoot the Piano Player
Spartacus (restored version)
The Ten Commandments (1956 version)
Thelma & Louise
Tokyo Olympiad
Truth or Dare
2001: A Space Odyssey
When a Woman Ascends the Stairs
Woodstock (some sequences)

CU20 Widescreen Movies That Should Be Letterboxed

Advise and Consent
All the President's Men
American Graffiti
Around the World in 80 Days
The Arrangement
The Big Country
Bonjour Tristesse
Brewster McCloud
The Bridge on the River Kwai
Butch Cassidy and the Sundance Kid
Cape Fear (1991 version)*
Carnal Knowledge
Cheyenne Autumn
Chinatown*
Cool Hand Luke
Cry in the Dark
Day of the Locust
The Doors*
Dune
East of Eden (1955 version)*
El Cid
Finian's Rainbow*
Flaming Star
Flight of the Phoenix
A Funny Thing Happened on the Way to the Forum*
The Girl Can't Help It
The Good, the Bad & the Ugly*
Grand Prix*
The Guns of Navarone
The Haunting
How To Marry a Millionaire*
Hud
The Hustler*
In Cold Blood
In Harm's Way
It's Always Fair Weather*
Junior Bonner
Klute
Lady and the Tramp
The Long Gray Line
McCabe and Mrs. Miller*
McLintock!
Madigan
The Man From Laramie
Man of the West

The Man Who Knew Too Much (1956 version)
Mister Roberts
The Molly Maguires
Nashville
1941
On a Clear Day You Can See Forever
Once Upon a Time in the West
One-Eyed Jacks
The Outlaw Josey Wales
The Parallax View
Plenty
Point Blank*
Raintree County
Ran
Rebel Without a Cause*
Ride Lonesome
Ride the High Country*
The Right Stuff*
River of No Return
Roxanne
The Russia House*
The Seven Year Itch
Sleeping Beauty (1959 version)
The Spirit of St. Louis
A Star Is Born (1954 version)
The Sugarland Express*
Superman II
10
A Time to Love and a Time to Die
To Catch a Thief
Trapeze
Tron
Vertigo
The War Lord
A Wedding
West Side Story*
The Wild Bunch
Zabriskie Point
*letterboxed on laser disc

5 Drama (DR)

DR1 Romantic Drama
See also: CL4 Classic Love Stories
About Last Night
The Accidental Tourist
Always
The Americanization of Emily
Atlantic City
Baby, It's You
Benny & Joon
The Bodyguard
Breakfast at Tiffany's
Breathless (1983 version)
Chapter Two
Children of a Lesser God
Chilly Scenes of Winter
Choose Me
Close My Eyes
Cocktail
Cold Sassy Tree
The Cook, The Thief, His Wife and Her Lover
Crazy From the Heart
Crazy in Love
The Crying Game
Damage
Dangerous Liaisons
Days of Heaven
Dirty Dancing
Dogfight
Dying Young
Elvira Madigan
Endless Love
Enemies, A Love Story
Ethan Frome
Everybody's All American

The Fabulous Baker Boys
Fanny (1932 and 1961 versions)
Far and Away
Far From the Madding Crowd
The Far Pavilions
Fools
Forever Young
Frankie and Johnny (1991)
The French Lieutenant's Woman
Fresh Horses
Ghost
The Girl From Petrovka
The Go-Between
Goodbye, Columbus
Griffin and Phoenix: A Love Story
A Handful of Dust
Hanover Street
Hard Choices
Havana
I Know Where I'm Going
In a Shallow Grave
Independence Day
Last Tango in Paris
Liar's Moon
Love Among the Ruins
Love at Large
Love Letters
Love Story
Love With the Proper Stranger
The Lover
Lovespell
Mad Dog and Glory
Made in Heaven
Mahogany

A Man in Love
The Miracle (1991)
Mississippi Masala
Mrs. Soffel
More
A Night Full of Rain
An Officer and a Gentleman
Old Gringo
Once Around
Out of Africa
The Passion of Anna
Pete 'n' Tillie
Petulia
The Pick-up Artist
The Playboys
Prelude to a Kiss
The Rachel Papers
Racing With the Moon
The Rainbow
Robin and Marian
The Roman Spring of Mrs. Stone
Romance on the Orient Express
The Romantic Englishwoman
Rome Adventure
A Room With a View
sex, lies, and videotape
Silent Night, Lonely Night
The Slugger's Wife
Somewhere in Time
Sommersby
Sophie's Choice
Splendor in the Grass
Stanley & Iris
Starman
The Sterile Cuckoo
Strangers When We Meet
A Summer Place
Tender Mercies
Tequila Sunrise
The Thorn Birds
Trouble in Mind
Truly, Madly, Deeply
Turtle Diary
Two for the Road
Two for the Seesaw
The Unbearable Lightness of Being
Untamed Heart
Until September
Used People
Valmont
Verboten!
Violets Are Blue . . .
The Virgin and the Gypsy
A Walk in the Spring Rain
The Way We Were
White Palace
Who's that Knocking at My Door
Willie and Phil
Winter People
Women & Men: Stories of Seduction

Women & Men: Stories of Seduction, Part 2
Women in Love
Yanks

DR2 For a Good Cry
See also: CL6 Classic Tear Jerkers
Awakenings
Beaches
Brian's Song
Careful, He Might Hear You
Clara's Heart
Curly Sue
The Doctor
Dominick and Eugene
Duet for One
Dying Young
Field of Dreams
For the Boys
Forever Young
Gaby—A True Story
Ghost
Griffin and Phoenix: A Love Story
The Heart Is a Lonely Hunter
Imitation of Life (1959 version)
Jack the Bear
Lorenzo's Oil
Love Story
Madame X (1966 version)
Mask
Men Don't Leave
Miles To Go
The Natural
Of Mice and Men (1992 version)
On Golden Pond
Ordinary People
The Other Side of Midnight
Paradise
Places in the Heart
Project X
Rage of Angels
Regarding Henry
Resurrection
Silence Like Glass
Six Weeks
Sommersby
Sophie's Choice
Steel Magnolias
Stella
Sweet Dreams
Table for Five
Tea and Sympathy
Tender Mercies
Terms of Endearment
Untamed Heart
Wild Hearts Can't Be Broken

DR3 Forbidden Love
American Gigolo
Basic Instinct
Betrayal (1983)

Betrayed
Body Heat
Body of Evidence
The Boys in the Band
Cal
Close My Eyes
The Collection
The Collector
Coming Home
Crimes of Passion
The Crying Game
Damage
Desert Hearts
Edward II
Every Time We Say Goodbye
Falling in Love
The Far Pavilions
Fatal Attraction
Five Days One Summer
Fool for Love
Fortune and Men's Eyes
Georgy Girl
Hanna K.
Hard Choices
Henry & June
The Hot Spot
Island in the Sun
Jagged Edge
Jungle Fever
The Killing of Sister George
Lady Chatterly's Lover (1955 and 1981 versions)
Last Exit to Brooklyn
Last Tango in Paris
Lianna
Liebestraum
Lilith
Lola
Longtime Companion
Looking for Mr. Goodbar
Love Letters
Lovespell
Making Love
Maurice
Mayerling (1936 version)
Mississippi Masala
Murmur of the Heart
My Beautiful Laundrette
My Own Private Idaho
Nijinsky
9½ Weeks
Out of Season
A Patch of Blue
Personal Best
Poison ("Homo" segment)
The Postman Always Rings Twice (1946 and 1981 versions)
Pretty Baby
Prick Up Your Ears
Reflections in a Golden Eye
Return Engagement

Romeo and Juliet (1936 and 1968 versions)
The Runner Stumbles
Ryan's Daughter
The Sandpiper
The Savage Is Loose
Shadows
Someone To Watch Over Me
Stealing Heaven
The Stripper
Summer Lovers
Sunday Bloody Sunday
Swing Shift
Swoon
A Taste of Honey
Tea and Sympathy
Ten Days Wonder
The Thorn Birds
Torch Song Trilogy
Two Moon Junction
Verboten!
Victim
Wild Orchid
Wonderland
X, Y, and Zee
Zandalee
Zebrahead

DR4 The Famous and Notorious

See also: CL2 Screen Biographies, MU5 Musical Life Stories

All Creatures Great and Small (James Herriot)
Amadeus
The Amazing Howard Hughes
Anastasia: The Mystery of Anna (Anna Anderson)
An Angel at My Table (Janet Frame)
The Babe (Babe Ruth)
Barnum
Becoming Colette
Birdman of Alcatraz (Robert Stroud)
Blaze (Blaze Starr)
Born on the Fourth of July (Ron Kovic)
Bound for Glory
Bugsy (Benjamin Siegel)
Cast a Giant Shadow (Mickey Marcus)
Chaplin
Citizen Cohn (Roy Cohn)
Clarence Darrow
Cross Creek (Marjorie Kinan Rawlings)
Dante's Inferno (Dante Gabriel Rosetti)
Edward II
84 Charing Cross Road (Helen Hanff)
The Elephant Man (John Merrick)
Ernie Kovacs: Between the Laughter
Fear Strikes Out (Jimmy Piersall)
For Us, the Living (Medgar Evers)
Frances (Frances Farmer)
Gandhi
Gathering Storm (Winston Churchill)
The Great White Hope (Jack Johnson)

The Greatest (Muhammad Ali)
Harlow (Baker version) (Jean Harlow)
Heart Beat (Jack Kerouac, Neal and Carolyn
 Cassady)
Heart Like a Wheel (Shirley Muldowney)
Henry & June (Henry and June Miller)
Hitler
Hoffa
Ike: The War Years (Dwight Eisenhower)
The Incredible Sarah (Sarah Bernhardt)
Isadora (Isadora Duncan)
The Jackie Robinson Story
The Jayne Mansfield Story
The Josephine Baker Story
Julia (Lillian Hellman)
Kafka
King (Martin Luther King, Jr.)
The Krays (Reggie and Ronnie Kray)
The Last Days of Patton
The Last Emperor (Pu Yi)
The Last Four Days (Adolf Hitler)
Lenny (Lenny Bruce)
MacArthur (Douglas MacArthur)
Malcolm X
A Man Called Peter (Peter Marshall)
The Man Who Broke 1,000 Chains (Robert
 Elliot Burns)
Mandela (Nelson Mandela)
The Miracle Worker (Helen Keller and Anne
 Sullivan)
Mobsters (Lucky Luciano, Frank Costello,
 Benjamin "Bugsy" Siegel, Meyer Lansky)
Mountains of the Moon (Richard Burton and
 John Hanning Speke)
Mussolini and I
My Left Foot (Christy Brown)
My Wicked, Wicked Ways (Errol Flynn)
The Naked Civil Servant (Quentin Crisp)
Nijinsky
One Man's War (Joel Filartiga)
Out of Africa (Isak Dinesen)
Patton
The Pistol: The Birth of a Legend (Pete
 Maravich)
Pope John Paul II
Prick Up Your Ears (Joe Orton)
Priest of Love (D.H. Lawrence)
The Private Files of J. Edgar Hoover
Raging Bull (Jake LaMotta)
Reds (John Reed)
Romero (Oscar Romero)
Saint Joan (Joan of Arc)
Salome's Last Dance (Oscar Wilde)
Somebody Up There Likes Me (Rocky
 Graziano)
The Song of Bernadette (Bernadette of
 Lourdes)
Sophia Loren: Her Own Story
Stalin
Stevie (Stevie Smith)

Sunrise at Campobello (Franklin Roosevelt)
Sweet Dreams (Patsy Cline)
This Boy's Life (Tobias Wolff)
Tucker: The Man and His Dream (Preston
 Tucker)
Vincent & Theo (Vincent and Theo van
 Gogh)
Viva Knievel! (Evel Knievel)
Wilma (Wilma Rudolph)
Wired (John Belushi)
Wolf at the Door (Paul Gauguin)
A Woman Called Golda (Golda Meir)
Young Catherine (Catherine the Great)
Young Winston (Winston Churchill)

DR5 Historical Drama
See also: CL3 Historical Drama
Alan and Naomi
Anne of the Thousand Days
The Assassination of Trotsky
The Assisi Underground
Barry Lyndon
Beautiful Dreamers
Becket
Belizaire the Cajun
Billy Bathgate
Black Robe
Bleak House
The Blue and the Gray
Bonnie and Clyde
Burke and Wills
Burn!
Caligula
Christopher Columbus: The Discovery
Come See the Paradise
The Cotton Club
Crisis at Central High
Cromwell
The Damned
Dance With a Stranger
Dangerous Liaisons
Daniel
The Deadly Tower
The Devils
The Draughtsman's Contract
Dreamchild
Eight Men Out
Ellis Island
Empire of the Sun
Enemies, A Love Story
Enola Gay: The Men, the Mission, the
 Atomic Bomb
The Execution of Private Slovik
Exodus
Far and Away
Fat Man and Little Boy
Fortunes of War
1492: Conquest of Paradise
The Front
Glory

The Godfather
The Godfather, Part II
The Godfather: The Complete Epic, 1902–1958
The Godfather Trilogy, 1901–1980
Good Morning, Babylon
Guilty by Suspicion
Hannah's War
Haunted Summer
Havana
Hawaii
Henry V (1945 and 1989 versions)
Hester Street
Holocaust
The Inner Circle
Inside the Third Reich
JFK
Jenny's War
Julius Caesar (1970 version)
Khartoum
The Kitchen Toto
Lady Jane
Lady Caroline Lamb
Let Him Have It
The Lindbergh Kidnapping Case
The Lion in Winter
Lion of the Desert
Little Gloria . . . Happy at Last
The Long Walk Home
Love Field
A Man for All Seasons (1966 and 1988 versions)
Mandingo
Marat/Sade
Masala
Matewan
The Mission
Mississippi Burning
Mister Johnson
The Moderns
The Molly Maguires
The Murder of Mary Phagan
Nicholas and Alexandra
A Night to Remember (1958)
1918
Old Gringo
On Valentine's Day
One Against the Wind
The Orphan Train
Picnic at Hanging Rock
Places in the Heart
Playing for Time
Pretty Baby
Prisoner of Honor
Prisoners of the Sun
Ragtime
The Return of the Soldier
Revolution
Ruby
Scandal
Separate but Equal
Shaka Zulu

Ship of Fools
Shogun
The Sicilian
Sommersby
Spartacus
Swing Kids
Swing Shift
Swoon
Tai-Pan
Three Sovereigns for Sarah
A Town Like Alice
Triumph of the Spirit
Valmont
Voyage of the Damned
War and Remembrance
Waterloo
White Mischief
The Winds of War
Yanks
Zoot Suit

DR6 True-Life Contemporary Drama
Act of Vengeance
Afterburn
Alive
All the President's Men
American Me
At Close Range
Awakenings
Badge of the Assassin
Betrayal (1978)
Bill
Bill: On His Own
The Burning Bed
Buster
Castaway
Casualties of War
Chattahoochee
Communion
Conrack
Courage (1986)
Cry Freedom
A Cry in the Dark
Death of a Centerfold
The Deliberate Stranger
Dog Day Afternoon
84 Charing Cross Road
Eleni
The Entity
The Execution of Raymond Graham
The Executioner's Song
The Falcon and the Snowman
Fatal Vision
Final Warning
Fire in the Sky
Gaby—A True Story
Gideon's Trumpet
GoodFellas
Gorillas in the Mist
Guyana Tragedy: The Story of Jim Jones

Heat Wave
Helter Skelter
I'm Dancing as Fast as I Can
Iron and Silk
Kent State
The Killing Fields
The Killing of Randy Webster
Lean on Me
Leave 'Em Laughing
Lorenzo's Oil
Manhunt for Claude Dallas
Marie
Mask
Midnight Express
Missing
Murder or Mercy
Not Without My Daughter
On Wings of Eagles
The Onion Field
Operation Thunderbolt
Patty Hearst
Prince of the City
The Pursuit of D.B. Cooper
Raid on Entebbe
Rape and Marriage: The Rideout Case
Reversal of Fortune
The Right Stuff
Rush
Sakharov
The Search for Bridey Murphy
Serpico
A Shining Season
Sid & Nancy
Silkwood
Skokie
Stand and Deliver
STAR 80
The Sugarland Express
Sybil
Talk Radio
The Terry Fox Story
The Three Faces of Eve
21 Hours at Munich
Unnatural Causes
The Waterdance
Weeds
A World Apart

DR7 Modern Problems
See also: CL8 Social Problem Dramas
About Last Night
Absence of Malice
The Adjuster
Alamo Bay
Alice's Restaurant
All the Vermeers in New York
Amazing Grace and Chuck
Amazon
Amber Waves
American Me

Angel City
And Nothing but the Truth
Article 99
The Baby Maker
The Big Chill
Birdy
Blue Collar
Bob Roberts
The Bonfire of the Vanities
The Boost
The Border
Born on the Fourth of July
Boyz N the Hood
Cadence
Cal
Carnal Knowledge
The China Syndrome
City of Hope
City of Joy
Clean and Sober
Cocaine: One Man's Seduction
Coming Home
The Conversation
Country
Cry, the Beloved Country
Cutter's Way
The Day After
The Days of Wine and Roses
The Deer Hunter
Distant Thunder (1988)
Do the Right Thing
The Doctor
Dogfight
Double Edge
Drugstore Cowboy
A Dry White Season
Dudes
Easy Rider
El Norte
End of the Line
End of the Road
Executive Suite
F.I.S.T.
Falling Down
The Fisher King
Flatliners
For Queen and Country
For Us, the Living
Four Friends
Gardens of Stone
Grand Canyon
Guess Who's Coming to Dinner
Hail, Hero!
The Handmaid's Tale
Hanna K.
Hardcore
Heart of Dixie
A Hero Ain't Nothin' But a Sandwich
Homicide
Husbands and Wives

Iceman
The Image
In Country
Iron Maze
Jacknife
Jacob's Ladder
Joe
Johnny Got His Gun
Jungle Fever
Katherine
Keeping On
King
License to Kill (1984)
Light Sleeper
Listen to Me
Longtime Companion
Looking for Mr. Goodbar
Mandela
Medicine Man
Medium Cool
The Men's Club
Miles From Home
Mindwalk
Mississippi Burning
Murder or Mercy
Music Box
My Beautiful Laundrette
My Little Girl
Network
Nightbreaker
Out
Out of the Rain
Over the Edge
The Panic in Needle Park
Petulia
The Ploughman's Lunch
The Poppy Is Also a Flower
Power (1986)
The Power of One
Powwow Highway
Project X
Promised a Miracle
Promised Land
Queens Logic
Return of the Secaucus Seven
Rage
The Rapture
The River (1984)
River's Edge
Romero
Running on Empty
Salvador
Sarafina!
School Ties
Sex, Drugs, Rock & Roll
The Shadow Box
Shame (1961)
Skokie
Some Kind of Hero
South Central

Special Bulletin
Split Image
St. Elmo's Fire
Straight Out of Brooklyn
Streamers
Street Smart
Talk Radio
Testament
Texasville
Thunderheart
True Colors
Turtle Beach
Twilight's Last Gleaming
The Ugly American
The Unbearable Lightness of Being
Under Fire
Unnatural Causes
Wall Street
WarGames
Welcome Home
When He's Not a Stranger
Where the Day Takes You
Who'll Stop the Rain?
Whose Life Is it, Anyway?
Windy City
A World Apart
Zabriskie Point

DR8 Family Crises
The Accidental Tourist
All My Sons
American Dream (1981)
At Close Range
Autumn Sonata
Avalon
The Baby Maker
Bed & Breakfast
Bloodbrothers
Bonjour Tristesse
Born on the Fourth of July
Boyz N the Hood
Brideshead Revisited
Cat on a Hot Tin Roof (1958 and 1984
    versions)
Cavalcade
Clara's Heart
Class Action
Close My Eyes
The Color Purple
Country
Crimes and Misdemeanors
Criss Cross (1992)
Crooked Hearts
Da
Dad
The Dead
Dead Ringers
Death of a Salesman (1985 version)
Descending Angel
Desert Bloom

Desire Under the Elms
Distant Thunder (1988)
Distant Voices, Still Lives
The Doctor
Dominick and Eugene
The Dressmaker
Driving Miss Daisy
East of Eden (1955 and 1982 versions)
The Fabulous Baker Boys
Falling From Grace
Family Secrets
Far North
Field of Dreams
Firstborn
Five Easy Pieces
Forever and a Day
Gas, Food, Lodging
The Good Father
The Good Mother
The Great Santini
Grown-Ups
Hail, Hero!
Hard Frame
Harry and Son
High Tide
Home for the Holidays
Home from the Hill
Hot Spell
Howards End
I Never Sang for My Father
I Remember Mama
Immediate Family
In Celebration
In Country
The Indian Runner
Interiors
Irreconcilable Differences
Islands in the Stream
Jack the Bear
Joshua Then and Now
Jungle Fever
Junior Bonner
King of the Gypsies
Kramer vs. Kramer
The Last Days of Chez Nous
Light of Day
Long Day's Journey Into Night (1962 and 1987 versions)
Lorenzo's Oil
Love Streams
The Mambo Kings
Mask
Memories of Me
Men Don't Leave
Miles To Go
Misunderstood
The Mosquito Coast
Mr. and Mrs. Bridge
Music Box
My Heroes Have Always Been Cowboys

My Old Man
'night, Mother
Nothing in Common
The Oldest Living Graduate
On Golden Pond
Once Around
One Good Cop
Only When I Laugh
Ordinary People
Out of the Blue
Paradise
Paris, Texas
Places in the Heart
Poison Ivy
Postcards From the Edge
The Prince of Pennsylvania
The Prince of Tides
Promised a Miracle
Providence
Radio Flyer
Rambling Rose
Rain Man
A Raisin in the Sun (1961 and 1989 versions)
Regarding Henry
Reversal of Fortune
Rich in Love
The River Niger
A River Runs Through It
Rocket Gibraltar
Running on Empty
Sarah, Plain and Tall
See You in the Morning
September
Shoot the Moon
Shy People
Sometimes a Great Notion
Square Dance
Staying Together
The Stone Boy
Strangers: The Story of a Mother and Daughter
Suddenly, Last Summer
Summertree
Table for Five
Tank
Tell Me a Riddle
Terms of Endearment
This Boy's Life
To Sleep With Anger
Toys in the Attic
Tribute
Twice in a Lifetime
An Unremarkable Life
Used People
A Voyage 'Round My Father
Wait Until Spring, Bandini
Wedding in White
The Whales of August
Who's Afraid of Virginia Woolf?
A Woman Under the Influence

The World According to Garp
A World Apart

DR9 Troubled Youth
Afraid of the Dark
Alan and Naomi
All the Right Moves
Bad Boys
Billy Bathgate
The Best Little Girl in the World
Beverly Hills, 90210
The Boy Who Could Fly
The Boys Next Door
The Breakfast Club
A Child Is Waiting
The Chocolate War
Criss Cross (1992)
D.A.R.Y.L.
David and Lisa
Dead Poets Society
Desert Bloom
Empire of the Sun
The Escape Artist
Flirting
Footloose
Foxes
Gas, Food, Lodging
Grandview, U.S.A.
The Heart Is a Lonely Hunter
A Hero Ain't Nothin' But a Sandwich
Housekeeping
if . . .
Jack the Bear
Juice
Just Another Girl on the IRT
The Karate Kid
The Karate Kid, Part II
The Karate Kid, Part III
The Kitchen Toto
Last Summer
The Legend of Billie Jean
Less Than Zero
Little Man Tate
Lord of the Flies (1963 and 1990
   versions)
Lost Angels
Lucas
The Man in the Moon
The Manhattan Project
Mask
The Member of the Wedding
My Girl
My Little Girl
The New Kids
New York Stories
Ordinary People
The Outsiders
Over the Edge
Paperhouse
Permanent Record

Pretty in Pink
Pump Up the Volume
The Quiet One
Radio Flyer
Rebel Without a Cause
Reckless (1984)
Rich in Love
River's Edge
The Rocking Horse Winner
Roll of Thunder, Hear My Cry
Rumble Fish
Scent of a Woman
School Ties
A Separate Peace
Shout
Simple Men
Smooth Talk
Splendor in the Grass
Split Image
Square Dance
Stacking
Stand by Me
Suburbia
Swing Kids
Taps
Tex
That Was Then, This Is Now
This Boy's Life
Ticket to Heaven
Tuff Turf
Twin Peaks: Fire Walk With Me
Vision Quest
Welcome Home, Roxy Carmichael
Where the Day Takes You
Where the River Runs Black
Wildflower
The Wizard of Loneliness
The Year My Voice Broke
Zebrahead
Zelly and Me

DR10 Today's Woman
See also: CL5 Women's Pictures
The Accused
Alice
Alice Doesn't Live Here Anymore
An Angel at My Table
Anna
Another Woman
Antonia and Jane
Beaches
Bed & Breakfast
The Bell Jar
Between Friends
The Burning Bed
Business as Usual
Callie and Son
The Cemetery Club
Cold Heaven
The Color Purple

Come Along With Me
Courage (1986)
Crazy in Love
Cries and Whispers
Crimes of the Heart
Crossing Delancey
Darling
Desert Hearts
Diary of a Mad Housewife
The Dollmaker
Duet for One
The End of Innocence
Enormous Changes
Entre Nous
The Execution
Extremities
Family Secrets
The Far North
First Monday in October
Fried Green Tomatoes
Gas, Food, Lodging
The Girls of Huntington House
Gloria
The Good Mother
The Good Woman of Bangkok
Gorillas in the Mist
Grand Isle
The Group
The Handmaid's Tale
Hanna K.
Heart Like a Wheel
Heat and Dust
High Tide
Hold the Dream
Housekeeping
Hustling
I'm Dancing as Fast as I Can
Independence Day
Intimate Strangers
Just Between Friends
The Last Days of Chez Nous
Leaving Normal
Lianna
Little Man Tate
Lumiere
Mahogany
Marie
Men Don't Leave
Mortal Thoughts
Mystic Pizza
Norma Rae
Not Without My Daughter
The Nun's Story
Nuts
Old Boyfriends
Passion Fish
Personal Best
Plenty
Rachel, Rachel
Rachel River

Raggedy Man
The Rain People
Rape of Love
The Rapture
Resurrection
Rich and Famous
Say Goodbye, Maggie Cole
See How She Runs
sex, lies, and videotape
She-Devil
Shirley Valentine
Shy People
Siesta
The Silence of the Lambs
The Slender Thread
Steel Magnolias
Stella
Strapless
Summer Wishes, Winter Dreams
Swing Shift
Testament
Thelma & Louiie
The Three Faces of Eve
The Turning Point
Twenty-One
An Unmarried Woman
Up the Sandbox
Vagabond
When He's Not a Stranger
Whore
The Witches of Eastwick
A Woman of Substance
A Woman Under the Influence
Working Girl
Working Girls

DR11 Golden Oldsters

Amos
The Christmas Wife
Cocoon
Cocoon: The Return
Dad
Dreamchild
Driving Miss Daisy
A Family Upside Down
Fried Green Tomatoes
The Gin Game
Going in Style
Grace Quigley
The Grey Fox
Harry and Tonto
Home To Stay
I Never Sang for My Father
Kotch
Love Among the Ruins
Mr. Halpern and Mr. Johnson
No Surrender
On Golden Pond
A Piano for Ms. Cimino
Reunion

Right of Way
Summer Solstice
Tell Me a Riddle
Tough Guys
The Trip to Bountiful
The Whales of August
White Mama
A Woman's Tale

DR12 Backstage Dramas

See also: CL7 Show Business Stories, MU4
    Musical Films About Show Biz
Barnum
Bird
The Bodyguard
Carny
The Competition
The Country Girl (1982 version)
Crossroads
Dancers
Dingo
The Dresser
Eddie and the Cruisers
Eddie and the Cruisers II: Eddie Lives!
The Entertainer
The Fabulous Baker Boys
Fast Forward
The Five Heartbeats
Flashdance
For the Boys
The Front
The Gig
Graffiti Bridge
Great Balls of Fire
Hear My Song
Hearts of Fire
Honeysuckle Rose
Honky Tonk Man
I Could Go On Singing
The Idolmaker
The Image
The Incredible Sarah
Jane Austen in Manhattan
Jo Jo Dancer: Your Life Is Calling
Light of Day
The Love Machine
The Mambo Kings
Mo' Better Blues
Nashville
Network
New York, New York
Nijinsky
One-Trick Pony
Payday
Pete Kelly's Blues
The Playboys
Punchline
Pure Country
Purple Rain
The Rose

'Round Midnight
Rude Boy
Shakespeare Wallah
Sid & Nancy
Sing
Sparkle
Staying Alive
Stepping Out
Sweet Dreams
Talk Radio
Tap
Tender Mercies
The Turning Point
Valley of the Dolls (1967 version)
Wired

DR13 Inside the Movie Business

An Almost Perfect Affair
Anna
The Barefoot Contessa
Blow Out
Chaplin
The Comic
Day for Night
The Day of the Locust
Death of a Centerfold
8½
F/X
F/X 2: The Deadly Art of Illusion
Fade-In
Frances
The French Lieutenant's Woman
The Goddess
Good Morning, Babylon
Guilty by Suspicion
Harlow (Baker version)
Inserts
The Last Movie
The Last Tycoon
Malice in Wonderland
A Man in Love
Mommie Dearest
My Wicked, Wicked Ways
The Oscar
The Player
Postcards From the Edge
Queenie
STAR 80
A Star Is Born (1937 and 1954 versions)
The State of Things
Strangers Kiss
The Stunt Man
Stunts
Sunset Boulevard
Targets
The Users
The Way We Were
What Ever Happened to Baby Jane?
White Hunter, Black Heart
The Wild Party

DR14 Black Life

Aaron Loves Angela
The Autobiography of Miss Jane Pittman
Bebe's Kids
Blue Collar
Boyz N the Hood
The Brother from Another Planet
Brother John
The Color Purple
Cooley High
Cornbread, Earl and Me
The Cotton Club
Cry Freedom
Cry, the Beloved Country
Def by Temptation
Do the Right Thing
A Dream for Christmas
A Dry White Season
The Emperor Jones
The Final Comedown
The Five Heartbeats
For Love of Ivy
For Queen and Country
For Us, the Living
Glory
The Great White Hope
The Greatest
Heat Wave
A Hero Ain't Nothin' But a Sandwich
Jo Jo Dancer: Your Life Is Calling
The Josephine Baker Story
Juice
Jungle Fever
Just Another Girl on the IRT
The Kid Who Loved Christmas
King
The Kitchen Toto
The Klansman
Lady Sings the Blues
The Learning Tree
The Liberation of L.B. Jones
The Long Walk Home
Lost in the Stars
Mahogany
Malcolm X
Mandela
The Mark of the Hawk
Marvin and Tige
Men of Bronze
Mississippi Masala
Mo' Better Blues
Murder on the Bayou
Native Son
New Jack City
Pinky
The Power of One
Purlie Victorious
The Quiet One
A Rage in Harlem
A Raisin in the Sun (1961 and 1989 versions)

The Return of Superfly
The River Niger
Roll of Thunder, Hear My Cry
Sarafina!
School Daze
Shadows
She's Gotta Have It
The Sky Is Gray
A Soldier's Story
Something of Value
Sounder
South Central
Sparkle
Straight Out of Brooklyn
Strictly Business
Superfly
Sweet Sweetback's Baadasssss Song
To Sleep With Anger
Zebrahead

DR15 Life in the Big City

Aaron Loves Angela
Addict
Alphabet City
All the Vermeers in New York
American Dream (1981)
. . . And Justice for All
Avalon
Backdraft
Barfly
The Big Town
The Bonfire of the Vanities
Boyz N the Hood
Breakfast at Tiffany's
Bright Lights, Big City
The Brother from Another Planet
Candyman
Chan Is Missing
The Chosen (1981)
City of Hope
City of Joy
Colors
Cornbread, Earl and Me
The Cotton Club
Crossing Delancey
Dim Sum: a little bit of heart
Do the Right Thing
Echo Park
Enormous Changes
Falling Down
Fear City
The Fisher King
Five Corners
Flashdance
Fort Apache, The Bronx
Frankie and Johnny (1991)
Grand Canyon
Hangin' With the Homeboys
Heat Wave
A Hero Ain't Nothin' But a Sandwich

Hester Street
Homicide
House of Games
Husbands and Wives
Hustling
The Incident (1967)
Jacob's Ladder
Juice
Jungle Fever
Just Another Girl on the IRT
The Last Angry Man
Last Exit to Brooklyn
Light Sleeper
London Kills Me
Mad Dog and Glory
Marvin and Tige
Mean Streets
Medium Cool
Midnight Cowboy
Moscow on the Hudson
My Own Private Idaho
New Jack City
New York Stories
Night and the City (1950 and
    1992 versions)
Night on Earth
On the Nickel
One Good Cop
The Panic in Needle Park
The Pawnbroker
Petulia
The Pope of Greenwich Village
Q & A
Queens Logic
A Rage in Harlem
Roseland
Saturday Night Fever
Scent of a Woman
Signal 7
Slaves of New York
Smithereens
Someone to Watch Over Me
South Central
Stand and Deliver
State of Grace
Straight Out of Brooklyn
A Stranger Among Us
Street Smart
The Streets of L.A.
Studs Lonigan
Taxi Driver
Times Square
Turk 182
Urban Cowboy
The Wanderers
The Warriors
Where the Day Takes You
Who's That Knocking on
    My Door?
Zoot Suit

DR16 Lives of Crime

See also: Action/Adventure, Mystery/Suspense
    Chapters
Against All Odds (1984)
American Me
At Close Range
Atlantic City
Bad Lieutenant
Badlands
Billy Bathgate
Blood Simple
Bonnie and Clyde
The Brotherhood
Bugsy
Buster
Chicago Joe and the Showgirl
Chiefs
Cop
Criminal Law
Cruising
The Crying Game
Dance With a Stranger
Diary of a Hitman
Diggstown
Drugstore Cowboy
The Executioner's Song
The Falcon and the Snowman
Fatal Vision
Fingers
GoodFellas
The Grifters
Guncrazy
Helter Skelter
The Honeymoon Killers
In Cold Blood
Internal Affairs
Johnny Handsome
Joyride
Kansas
The Krays
Last Rites
Light Sleeper
Mean Streets
The Mechanic
Mikey and Nicky
Miles From Home
Miller's Crossing
Mona Lisa
Mrs. Soffel
The Onion Field
Patty Hearst
Performance
Point Blank
A Prayer for the Dying
Prince of the City
Prizzi's Honor
Q & A
A Rage in Harlem
Reservoir Dogs
The Return of Superfly

Rush
Serpico
Star Chamber
State of Grace
Straight Time
Suddenly
Superfly
10 Rillington Place
Thelma & Louise
Thief
True Confessions
Wisdom
Witness

DR17 Court's in Session
The Accused
Anatomy of a Murder
. . . And Justice for All
Body of Evidence
The Bonfire of the Vanities
Class Action
The Court-Martial of Billy
 Mitchell
Criminal Law
A Cry in the Dark
Defenseless
A Few Good Men
Illegal
The Incident (1990)
Inherit the Wind
Irreconcilable Differences
Jagged Edge
Judgment at Nuremberg
Kramer vs. Kramer
The Lady in Question
Let Him Have It
The Lindbergh Kidnapping Case
Love Among the Ruins
Music Box
Nuts
QB VII
The Paradine Case
Paris Trout
Presumed Innocent
Prisoners of the Sun
Promised a Miracle
The Pursuit of Happiness
Rape and Marriage: The Rideout
 Case
Reversal of Fortune
The Rose Garden
Sergeant Rutledge
Sergeant Ryker
Storyville
Suspect
They Won't Believe Me
They Won't Forget
To Kill a Mockingbird
12 Angry Men
Until They Sail

The Verdict
Witness for the Prosecution
 (1957 version)
The Wreck of the *Mary Deare*

DR18 Prison Dramas
American Me
Bad Boys
Birdman of Alcatraz
Brubaker
Cadence
Caged Heat
Chattahoochee
Convicts Four
Cool Hand Luke
Crashout
The Criminal Code
Dead Man Out
Deadlock
Each Dawn I Die
Escape From Alcatraz
Fast-Walking
Fortune and Men's Eyes
The Glass House
I Want to Live! (1958 version)
An Innocent Man
Kiss of the Spider Woman
Ladies They Talk About
Lock Up
The Longest Yard
Midnight Express
On the Yard
Papillon
Passage to Marseilles
Poison ("Homo" segment)
Pressure Point
Riot in Cell Block 11
Seven Miles From Alcatraz
Short Eyes
There Was a Crooked Man
Weeds

DR19 Modern Fiction on Film
See also: CL1 Classics Illustrated: Literary
 Adaptations; Writer Check Lists WR7
 William Faulkner, WR8 F. Scott Fitzgerald,
 WR9 E.M. Forster, WR11 Graham Greene,
 WR13 Ernest Hemingway, WR14 Henry
 James, WR17 D.H. Lawrence, WR20 Sinclair
 Lewis, WR23 W. Somerset Maugham,
 WR24 John O'Hara, WR32 John Steinbeck

Thomas Berger
The Feud
Little Big Man
Neighbors

E.L. Doctorow
Billy Bathgate
Daniel

Thomas Hardy
Far From the Madding Crowd
Tess

S.E. Hinton
The Outsiders
Rumble Fish
Tex

John Irving
The Hotel New Hampshire
The World According to Garp

James Jones
From Here to Eternity
Some Came Running

James Joyce
The Dead
Portrait of the Artist as a Young
   Man
Ulysses (1967)

Ken Kesey
One Flew Over the Cuckoo's
   Nest
Sometimes a Great Notion

Carson McCullers
The Ballad of the Sad Cafe
The Heart Is a Lonely Hunter
Reflections in a Golden Eye

Thomas McGuane
Keep the Change
92 in the Shade

Larry McMurtry
Hud
The Last Picture Show
Lonesome Dove
Terms of Endearment
Texasville

Vladimir Nabokov
Despair
Lolita

John Nichols
The Milagro Beanfield War
The Sterile Cuckoo
The Wizard of Loneliness

Philip Roth
Goodbye, Columbus
Portnoy's Complaint

Kurt Vonnegut
Slapstick (Of Another Kind)
Slaughterhouse Five

Evelyn Waugh
A Handful of Dust
The Loved One

Nathanael West
Day of the Locust
Lonelyhearts

Herman Wouk
The Caine Mutiny
Marjorie Morningstar
War and Remembrance
The Winds of War

Other Authors
The Accidental Tourist
The Adventurers
All the King's Men
Anthony Adverse
At Play in the Fields of the Lord
The Bell Jar
Birdy
Bloodhounds of Broadway
The Bonfire of the Vanities
Brideshead Revisited
Bright Lights, Big City
The Carpetbaggers
Catch-22
Charly
Chilly Scenes of Winter
A Clockwork Orange
Cold Heaven
The Color Purple
The Comfort of Strangers
Crooked Hearts
Cry, the Beloved Country
Damage
Death in Venice
Deliverance
The Ebony Tower
End of the Road
Endless Love
Enemies, A Love Story
Enormous Changes
Ethan Frome
Exodus
Fahrenheit 451
Fat City
Fortunes of War
God's Little Acre
The Good Earth
Grand Isle
The Group
The Handmaid's Tale
The Horse's Mouth
Housekeeping
The Human Comedy
In Country
Ironweed
Johnny Got His Gun

Joshua Then and Now
Justine
Last Exit to Brooklyn
The Last Temptation of Christ
Less Than Zero
The Lonely Passion of Judith Hearne
Lord Jim
Lord of the Flies (1963 and 1990 versions)
The Lover
The Magician of Lublin
The Mambo Kings
The Man With the Golden Arm
The Manchurian Candidate
Manhunter
The Men's Club
A Midnight Clear
The Mosquito Coast
Mr. and Mrs. Bridge
Mister Johnson
Mr. North
Myra Breckenridge
Naked Lunch
The Name of the Rose
Native Son
The Natural
1984
Old Gringo
Ordinary People
Paris Trout
A Place in the Sun
Presumed Innocent
The Prince of Tides
QB VII
Quartet (1981)
Reuben, Reuben
Rich in Love
A River Runs Through It
Seize the Day
A Separate Peace
The Sheltering Sky
Ship of Fools
Shogun
The Silence of the Lambs
Slaves of New York
Sophie's Choice
Steppenwolf
Studs Lonigan
Swann in Love
Tell Me a Riddle
That Forsyte Woman
They Shoot Horses, Don't They?
The Tin Drum
The Trial
Twister
The Unbearable Lightness of Being
Under the Volcano
Valley of the Dolls (1967 version)
Voyager
Wait Until Spring, Bandini
Walk on the Wild Side

The War Lover
Waterland
Who'll Stop the Rain?
Winter Kills
Wise Blood
The Witches of Eastwick
A Woman of Affairs
Women & Men: Stories of Seduction
Women & Men: Stories of Seduction,
    Part 2
The Young Lions

DR20 Plays on Film

See also: Writer Check Lists WR4 Noel
    Coward, WR25 Eugene O'Neill, WR26
    Harold Pinter, WR28 William Shakespeare,
    WR29 George Bernard Shaw, WR30 Neil
    Simon, WR38 Tennessee Williams
Agnes of God
All My Sons
Arsenic and Old Lace
The Balcony
The Boys in the Band
Bus Stop
The Cemetery Club
The Chalk Garden
Children of a Lesser God
The Children's Hour
A Chorus of Disapproval
Clarence Darrow
The Collection
Come Back, Little Sheba
Come Back to the Five & Dime, Jimmy Dean,
    Jimmy Dean
Command Decision
Crimes of the Heart
Cyrano de Bergerac (1950 and 1990 versions)
Da
Dangerous Liaisons
A Day in the Death of Joe Egg
Dead End
Death of a Salesman (1985 version)
Deathtrap
A Doll's House (Bloom and Fonda versions)
Driving Miss Daisy
Edward II
84 Charing Cross Road
An Enemy of the People
The Entertainer
Equus
Extremities
A Few Good Men
Frankie and Johnny (1991)
The Front Page (1931 version)
George Washington Slept Here
The Gin Game
The Glass Menagerie
Glengarry Glen Ross
The Great White Hope
The Green Pastures

Grown-Ups
The Guardsman
Happy Birthday, Gemini
Harvey
Hedda
I Am a Camera
I Never Sang for My Father
In Celebration
Inherit the Wind
K-2
La Tartuffe
Life With Father
The Little Foxes
Look Back in Anger
Love Streams
Luv
The Madwoman of Chaillot
Male and Female
The Man Who Came to Dinner
Marat/Sade
The Matchmaker
The Member of the Wedding
The Millionairess
The Miracle Worker
Miss Firecracker
The Moon Is Blue
'night, Mother
Noises Off
Nuts
On Dad, Poor Dad, Mama's Hung You in the
   Closet and I'm Feeling So Sad
The Oldest Living Graduate
On Borrowed Time
On Golden Pond
Orphans
Other People's Money
Our Town
The Petrified Forest
The Philadelphia Story
Picnic
Please Don't Eat the Daisies
Plenty
Prelude to a Kiss
A Raisin in the Sun (1961 and 1989
   versions)
The River Niger
Rosencrantz and Guildenstern Are Dead
Sarafina!
Separate Tables (1958 and 1983 versions)
Sex, Drugs, Rock & Roll
The Shadow Box
Shirley Valentine
Sleuth
A Soldier's Story
Stage Door
Steel Magnolias
Streamers
Susan and God
The Swan
Talk Radio

Tall Story
A Taste of Honey
Tea and Sympathy
That Championship Season
These Three
The Time of Your Life
Torch Song Trilogy
Toys in the Attic
The Trojan Women
True West
Two for the Seesaw
Volpone
Watch on the Rhine
When Ladies Meet
Who's Afraid of Virginia Woolf?
Whose Life Is It Anyway?
The Wild Duck
You Can't Take It With You (1938 and 1984
   versions)
Young and Willing

DR21 Political Dramas
See also: CU9 Political Statements
Advise and Consent
All the King's Men
All the President's Men
Being There
The Best Man
Blaze
Bob Roberts
The Candidate
Closet Land
Gabriel Over the White House
Guilty by Suspicion
Hometown Story
JFK
The Last Hurrah
A Lion Is in the Streets
The Manchurian Candidate
Marie
1984
No Way Out
The Parallax View
Power (1986)
Power Play
Primary Motive
Scandal
The Seduction of Joe Tynan
Seven Days in May
The Shoes of the Fisherman
Storyville
Ten North Frederick
True Colors
The Ugly American
Under Fire
White Nights (1985)
The Wilby Conspiracy
Wilson
Winter Kills
The Year of Living Dangerously

DR22 For Sports Fans
See also: CO18 Sports for Laughs
ARM WRESTLING
Over the Top
BASEBALL
The Babe
The Babe Ruth Story
Bang the Drum Slowly
Chasing Dreams
Eight Men Out
Fear Strikes Out
Field of Dreams
It's Good to be Alive
The Jackie Robinson Story
Long Gone
The Natural
The Pride of St. Louis
Pride of the Yankees
Talent for the Game
Tiger Town
The Winning Team
BASKETBALL
Heaven Is a Playground
Hoosiers
Inside Moves
One on One
The Pistol: The Birth of a Legend
That Championship Season
BOXING
Body and Soul (1947 and 1981 versions)
The Champ (1931 and 1979 versions)
Champion
City for Conquest
Diggstown
Fat City
Gentleman Jim
Gladiator
Golden Boy
The Great White Hope
The Harder They Fall
Homeboy
Kid Galahad (1937 and 1962 versions)
The Power of One
Raging Bull
Rocky (series)
The Set-Up
Somebody Up There Likes Me
Split Decisions
Streets of Gold
Tough Enough
CYCLING
American Flyers
Breaking Away
The Dirt Bike Kid
Rad
FOOTBALL
All the Right Moves
Brian's Song
Easy Living
Everybody's All American

Knute Rockne, All American
Trouble Along the Way
GYMNASTICS
American Anthem
HOCKEY
The Mighty Ducks
Youngblood
HORSE RACING/SHOWING
Phar Lap
Sylvester
MARTIAL ARTS
Best of the Best
The Karate Kid
The Karate Kid, Part II
The Karate Kid, Part III
MOTOR SPORTS
Bobby Deerfield
Days of Thunder
Fast Company
Grand Prix
Greased Lightning
Heart Like a Wheel
The Last American Hero
The Racers
Red Line 7000
Winning
POOL
The Color of Money
The Hustler
ROWING
The Boy in Blue
Oxford Blues
RUGBY
This Sporting Life
RUNNING
Chariots of Fire
The Loneliness of the Long Distance
   Runner
On the Edge
Personal Best
Running Brave
A Shining Season
Wilma
SAILING
Wind
SKATEBOARDING
Thrashin'
SKIING
Aspen Extreme
Downhill Racer
SOCCER
Hot Shot
Victory
SURFING
Big Wednesday
North Shore
SWIMMING
Dawn!
VOLLEYBALL
Side Out

WRESTLING
Vision Quest

DR23 British Drama
Accident
And Nothing But the Truth
Anna Karenina (1948 version)
Another Country
The Beachcomber
The Belly of an Architect
Betrayal (1983)
Billy Liar
Bleak House
Blithe Spirit
Brideshead Revisited
Brighton Rock
Brimstone and Treacle
Business as Usual
Cal
The Chalk Garden
Chariots of Fire
Chicago Joe and the Showgirl
Close My Eyes
The Collection
The Cook, The Thief, His Wife and Her Lover
Courageous Mr. Penn
The Cruel Sea
Cry, the Beloved Country
The Crying Game
Damage
Dance With a Stranger
Dante's Inferno
Dark Obsession
Darling
Decameron Nights
Distant Voices, Still Lives
The Draughtsman's Contract
The Dresser
The Dressmaker
Edward II
Encore
The Entertainer
The Fallen Idol
The Field
Fools of Fortune
For Queen and Country
Forever and a Day
Fortunes of War
Gandhi
The Good Father
A Handful of Dust
Hear My Song
Heat and Dust
Hedda
Henry V (1945 and 1989 versions)
Hidden Agenda
Howards End
I See a Dark Stranger
if . . .
The Immortal Battalion

In Celebration
Java Head
A Kid for Two Farthings
A Kind of Loving
King Lear
Knights and Emeralds
The Krays
Lady Jane
The Last Days of Dolwyn
Let Him Have It
Little Dorrit
London Kills Me
The Loneliness of the Long Distance Runner
The Lonely Passion of Judith Hearne
The Long Good Friday
Look Back in Anger
Lord of the Flies (1963 version)
Love on the Dole
Major Barbara
The Man in Grey
Marat/Sade
A Married Man
Memphis Belle (1990)
Mona Lisa
The Miracle (1991)
My Beautiful Laundrette
My Left Foot
Negatives
Nicholas Nickleby
The Night My Number Came Up
No Surrender
O Lucky Man!
Paperhouse
Pascali's Island
Pickwick Papers
The Playboys
The Ploughman's Lunch
A Prayer for the Dying
Prick Up Your Ears
Priest of Love
The Prisoner
Prospero's Books
Pygmalion
Quartet (1949)
The Rainbow
The Romantic Englishwoman
A Room With a View
Sammy and Rosie Get Laid
Scandal
Séance on a Wet Afternoon
Separate Tables (1983 version)
The Servant
Shakespeare Wallah
Shattered (1972)
The Shooting Party
Sidewalks of London
The Singer Not the Song
The Sleeping Tiger
The Spanish Gardener
Steaming

Stevie
Stormy Monday
Strapless
Sunday Bloody Sunday
A Taste of Honey
This Happy Breed
This Sporting Life
Thunder in the City
Trio
The Triple Echo
Truly, Madly, Deeply
Turtle Diary
Ulysses (1967)
Victim
A Voyage 'Round My Father
The War Game
Waterland
Wetherby
When the Whales Came
Where Angels Fear To Tread
White Mischief
Women in Love
Wonderland
Young Winston

DR24 The World of Business
Agency
The Amazing Howard Hughes
The Arrangement
The Betsy
The Bonfire of the Vanities
Bugsy
The Carpetbaggers
Citizen Kane
Employees Entrance
Executive Suite
F.I.S.T.
Female
The Formula
Giant
Glengarry Glen Ross
The Godfather
The Godfather, Part II
The Godfather, Part III
The Godfather: The Complete Epic,
   1902–1958
The Godfather Trilogy, 1901–1980
Great Guy
Hoffa
House of Strangers
The Hucksters
Limit Up
The Man in the Gray Flannel Suit
Mr. Arkadin
Nothing in Common
Once Upon a Time in America
Other People's Money
Patterns
Rollover
Save the Tiger

Skyscraper Souls
The Temp
Tucker: The Man and His Dream
Wall Street

DR25 School Days
See also: CO18 Campus Comedy
Absolution
All-American Murder
An Annapolis Story
Au Revoir, les Enfants
Beverly Hills, 90210
Blackboard Jungle
The Breakfast Club
Carrie (1976)
The Chocolate War
The Class of Miss MacMichael
Class of 1984
Class of 1999
Conrack
The Corn Is Green (1945 version)
Crisis at Central High
Dangerously Close
Dead Poets Society
The Devil's Playground
Fame
Flirting
The Girls of Huntington House
Goodbye, Mr. Chips (1939 and 1969
   versions)
Heart of Dixie
High School Confidential
if . . .
The Imposter
Lean on Me
Listen to Me
Little Man Tate
The Loneliness of the Long Distance Runner
Mazes and Monsters
One on One
The Paper Chase
Permanent Record
The Prime of Miss Jean Brodie
The Principal
Pump Up the Volume
Scent of a Woman
School Ties
A Separate Peace
Shout
Sing
Stand and Deliver
Taps
Teachers
To Sir, With Love
Toy Soldiers (1991)
Vital Signs
Waterland
When He's Not a Stranger
Why Shoot the Teacher?
Zebrahead

DR26 Small Town Life
Ah, Wilderness
All the Right Moves
Amber Waves
Americana
Anatomy of a Murder
Arachnophobia
As Summers Die
The Best Years of Our Lives
Blue City
Blue Velvet
Breaking Away
Bus Stop
The Chase (1966)
Chiefs
Cold Sassy Tree
Come Back to the Five & Dime, Jimmy Dean, Jimmy Dean
Crazy From the Heart
The Deer Hunter
East of Eden (1955)
Endangered Species
Falling From Grace
The Feud
Flamingo Road
Footloose
Four Daughters
Fried Green Tomatoes
Fury
Gas, Food, Lodging
Grandview, U.S.A.
The Heart Is a Lonely Hunter
High Noon
Hoosiers
The Human Comedy
The Incident (1990)
Independence Day
Iron Maze
Johnny Come Lately
Judge Priest
King's Row
The Klansman
The Last Picture Show
Leap of Faith
A Letter to Three Wives
The Liberation of L.B. Jones
The Lost Boys
Magic Town
The Magnificent Ambersons
The Man in the Moon
Maria's Lovers
The Milagro Beanfield War
Murphy's Romance
Mystic Pizza
The Naked Kiss
1918
One False Move
Our Town
Out of the Rain
Paris Trout

Peyton Place
Picnic
The Playboys
Pollyanna
Promised Land
Rachel River
Racing With the Moon
Raggedy Man
Rambling Rose
Shadow of a Doubt
Shame (1988)
She Couldn't Say No
Shout
Signs of Life
Some Came Running
Splendor in the Grass
Stand by Me
Staying Together
Steel Magnolias
The Sun Shines Bright
Testament
Texasville
They Won't Forget
This Boy's Life
A Tiger Walks
To Kill a Mockingbird
Tortilla Flat
Tough Guys Don't Dance
Twin Peaks
Twin Peaks: Fire Walk With Me
Two Moon Junction
The Unbelievable Truth
The Underworld Story
Vernon, Florida
Welcome Home, Roxy Carmichael
Why Shoot the Teacher?
The Wild One
The Witches of Eastwick
The Wizard of Loneliness
Young at Heart

DR27 Strangers in Strange Lands: Tales of Culture Clash
At Play in the Fields of the Lord
The Barbarian and the Geisha
The Belly of an Architect
Beyond the Limit
Black Robe
Bombay Talkie
The Brother from Another Planet
Burn!
Cabaret
The Challenge
City of Joy
The Comedians
The Comfort of Strangers
Conrack
Cool World
Deliverance
Double Edge

El Norte
The Emerald Forest
The Europeans
A Far Off Place
Footloose
Forever Young
Gorillas in the Mist
Greystoke
Guns at Batasi
Heat and Dust
Hell in the Pacific
I Am a Camera
In the Heat of the Night
Iron and Silk
Keys of the Kingdom
Lawrence of Arabia
The Left Hand of God
The Man Who Fell to Earth
Midnight Express
The Mission
Mississippi Masala
Mister Johnson
Moonlighting (1982)
Moscow on the Hudson
The Naked Prey
Night and the City (1950 version)
Not Without My Daughter
Old Gringo

Passage to India
The Passenger
Quigley Down Under
Rebel (1986)
'Round Midnight
Salvador
Shakespeare Wallah
The Sheltering Sky
Shogun
Shy People
Simba
Southern Comfort
Starman
A Stranger Among Us
Stroszek
Tarzan's New York Adventure
Thunderheart
The Treasure of the Sierra Madre
The Ugly American
Voyager
The White Dawn
Witness
The World of Suzy Wong
The Yakuza
Yanks
Year of the Gun
Zentropa
Zorba the Greek

6 Director Check Lists (DT)

DT1	Robert Aldrich	**DT51**	Peter Greenaway
DT2	Woody Allen	**DT52**	D.W. Griffith
DT3	Pedro Almodóvar	**DT53**	Howard Hawks
DT4	Robert Altman	**DT54**	Werner Herzog
DT5	Michelangelo Antonioni	**DT55**	George Roy Hill
DT6	Allan Arkush	**DT56**	Walter Hill
DT7	Gillian Armstrong	**DT57**	Alfred Hitchcock
DT8	Paul Bartel	**DT58**	Ron Howard
DT9	Robert Benton	**DT59**	John Hughes
DT10	Bruce Beresford	**DT60**	John Huston
DT11	Ingmar Bergman	**DT61**	James Ivory
DT12	Busby Berkeley	**DT62**	Jim Jarmusch
DT13	Bernardo Bertolucci	**DT63**	Norman Jewison
DT14	Budd Boetticher	**DT64**	Philip Kaufman
DT15	John Boorman	**DT65**	Elia Kazan
DT16	Albert Brooks	**DT66**	Buster Keaton
DT17	Mel Brooks	**DT67**	Stanley Kramer
DT18	Tod Browning	**DT68**	Stanley Kubrick
DT19	Luis Buñuel	**DT69**	Akira Kurosawa
DT20	Tim Burton	**DT70**	Fritz Lang
DT21	James Cameron	**DT71**	David Lean
DT22	Frank Capra	**DT72**	Spike Lee
DT23	John Carpenter	**DT73**	Sergio Leone
DT24	Charlie Chaplin	**DT74**	Richard Lester
DT25	René Clair	**DT75**	Barry Levinson
DT26	Jean Cocteau	**DT76**	Ernst Lubitsch
DT27	Joel Coen	**DT77**	George Lucas
DT28	Larry Cohn	**DT78**	Sidney Lumet
DT29	Francis Ford Coppola	**DT79**	David Lynch
DT30	Roger Corman	**DT80**	Leo McCarey
DT31	David Cronenberg	**DT81**	Terrence Malick
DT32	George Cukor	**DT82**	Louis Malle
DT33	Joe Dante	**DT83**	Rouben Mamoulian
DT34	Cecil B. DeMille	**DT84**	Joseph L. Mankiewicz
DT35	Jonathan Demme	**DT85**	Anthony Mann
DT36	Brian De Palma	**DT86**	Elaine May
DT37	Vittorio De Sica	**DT87**	Paul Mazursky
DT38	Stanley Donen	**DT88**	Vincente Minnelli
DT39	Carl Dreyer	**DT89**	Errol Morris
DT40	Blake Edwards	**DT90**	Paul Morrissey
DT41	Sergei Eisenstein	**DT91**	Mike Nichols
DT42	Rainer Werner Fassbinder	**DT92**	Marcel Ophuls
DT43	Federico Fellini	**DT93**	Max Ophuls
DT44	John Ford	**DT94**	Alan J. Pakula
DT45	Milos Forman	**DT95**	Sam Peckinpah
DT46	Bill Forsyth	**DT96**	Arthur Penn
DT47	Bob Fosse	**DT97**	Roman Polanski
DT48	Stephen Frears	**DT98**	Sydney Pollack
DT49	Samuel Fuller	**DT99**	Michael Powell
DT50	Jean-Luc Godard	**DT100**	Otto Preminger

DT101 Nicholas Ray	**DT123** Bertrand Tavernier
DT102 Satyajit Ray	**DT124** Jacques Tourneur
DT103 Rob Reiner	**DT125** François Truffaut
DT104 Jean Renoir	**DT126** King Vidor
DT105 Martin Ritt	**DT127** Luchino Visconti
DT106 Nicolas Roeg	**DT128** Josef Von Sternberg
DT107 Eric Rohmer	**DT129** Erich Von Stroheim
DT108 George Romero	**DT130** Andrzej Wajda
DT109 Roberto Rossellini	**DT131** Raoul Walsh
DT110 Alan Rudolph	**DT132** John Waters
DT111 Ken Russell	**DT133** Peter Weir
DT112 John Sayles	**DT134** Orson Welles
DT113 John Schlesinger	**DT135** William Wellman
DT114 Martin Scorsese	**DT136** Wim Wenders
DT115 Ridley Scott	**DT137** Lina Wertmuller
DT116 Don Siegel	**DT138** James Whale
DT117 Douglas Sirk	**DT139** Billy Wilder
DT118 Steven Spielberg	**DT140** Robert Wise
DT119 George Stevens	**DT141** Ed Wood, Jr.
DT120 Oliver Stone	**DT142** William Wyler
DT121 Preston Sturges	**DT143** Robert Zemeckis
DT122 Jacques Tati	**DT144** Fred Zinnemann

DT1 Robert Aldrich (1918–1983)
All the Marbles
Apache
Autumn Leaves
The Choirboys
The Dirty Dozen
Flight of the Phoenix
Four for Texas
The Frisco Kid
The Grissom Gang
Hush . . . Hush, Sweet Charlotte
Hustle
The Killing of Sister George
Kiss Me Deadly
The Longest Yard
Sodom and Gomorrah
Too Late the Hero
Twilight's Last Gleaming
Ulzana's Raid
Vera Cruz
What Ever Happened to Baby Jane?

DT2 Woody Allen (1935–)
See also: XT30 He Directs, She Acts
All films writer-director-actor, unless noted.
Annie Hall
Bananas
Broadway Danny Rose
Crimes and Misdemeanors
Everything You Always Wanted to Know
    About Sex But Were Afraid to Ask
Hannah and Her Sisters
Husbands and Wives
Love and Death
Manhattan
A Midsummer Night's Sex Comedy

New York Stories (co-director)
Shadows and Fog
Sleeper
Stardust Memories
Take the Money and Run
What's Up, Tiger Lily?
Zelig
WRITER-DIRECTOR ONLY
Alice
Another Woman
Interiors
The Purple Rose of Cairo
Radio Days*
September
*also narrator
WRITER-ACTOR ONLY
Play It Again, Sam
What's New, Pussycat?
ACTOR ONLY
Casino Royale
The Front
King Lear (1987 version)
Scenes From a Mall

DT3 Pedro Almodóvar (1951–)
Dark Habits
Labyrinth of Passion
Law of Desire
Matador
Pepi, Luci, Bom
Tie Me Up! Tie Me Down!
What Have I Done to Deserve This?
Women on the Verge of a Nervous Breakdown

DT4 Robert Altman (1925–)
Aria (co-director)

Beyond Therapy
Brewster McCloud
Buffalo Bill & the Indians
Come Back to the Five & Dime, Jimmy Dean,
  Jimmy Dean
Countdown
The Dumb Waiter
Fool for Love
The James Dean Story (co-director)
The Long Goodbye
M*A*S*H
McCabe and Mrs. Miller
Nashville
O.C. & Stiggs
The Player
Popeye
Quintet
The Room
Secret Honor
Streamers
Tanner
That Cold Day in the Park
Vincent & Theo
A Wedding

DT5 Michelangelo Antonioni (1912–)
Blow-Up
The Eclipse
Il Grido
The Lady Without Camelias
L'Avventura
Love in the City (co-director)
The Passenger
Red Desert
Zabriskie Point

DT6 Allan Arkush (1948–)
Caddyshack II
Deathsport
Get Crazy
Heartbeeps
Hollywood Boulevard (co-director)
Rock 'n' Roll High School
ACTOR ONLY
Roger Corman: Hollywood's Wild Angel

DT7 Gillian Armstrong (1950–)
Fires Within
High Tide
The Last Days of Chez Nous
Mrs. Soffel
My Brilliant Career
Starstruck

DT8 Paul Bartel (1938–)
Cannonball
Death Race 2000
Eating Raoul*
The Longshot
Lust in the Dust

Not for Publication
Private Parts
Scenes From the Class Struggle in Beverly
  Hills*
*also actor
ACTOR ONLY
Amazon Women on the Moon
Caddyshack II
Chopping Mall
Desire and Hell at the Sunset Motel
Gremlins 2: The New Batch (bit)
Hollywood Boulevard
Killer Party
The Pope Must Diet
Rock 'n' Roll High School

DT9 Robert Benton (1932–)
Bad Company
Billy Bathgate
Kramer vs. Kramer
The Late Show
Nadine
Places in the Heart
Still of the Night

DT10 Bruce Beresford (1940–)
Aria (co-director)
Barry McKenzie Holds His Own
Black Robe
Breaker Morant
The Club
Crimes of the Heart
Don's Party
Driving Miss Daisy
The Fringe Dwellers
The Getting of Wisdom
Her Alibi
King David
Mister Johnson
Puberty Blues
Tender Mercies

DT11 Ingmar Bergman (1918–)
See also: XT30 He Directs, She Acts
After the Rehearsal
Autumn Sonata
Brink of Life
Cries and Whispers
The Devil's Eye
The Devil's Wanton
Dreams
Fanny and Alexander
From the Life of Marionettes
Hour of the Wolf
A Lesson in Love
The Magic Flute
The Magician
Night Is My Future
The Passion of Anna
Persona

Port of Call
Sawdust and Tinsel (The Naked Night)
Scenes From a Marriage
Secrets of Women
The Serpent's Egg
The Seventh Seal
Shame (1968)
The Silence
Smiles of a Summer Night
Summer Interlude
Summer With Monika
Three Strange Loves
Through a Glass, Darkly
To Joy
The Virgin Spring
Wild Strawberries
Winter Light
SCREENPLAY ONLY
The Best Intentions

DT12 Busby Berkeley (1895–1976)
Babes in Arms
Babes on Broadway
Dames*
Easy to Love*
Footlight Parade*
For Me and My Gal
42nd Street*
Girl Crazy*
Gold Diggers of 1933*
Gold Diggers of 1935
Jumbo*
Million Dollar Mermaid*
Roman Scandals*
Small Town Girl*
Stage Struck (1936)
Strike Up the Band
Take Me Out to the Ball Game
Ziegfeld Girl*
NON-MUSIC
They Made Me a Criminal
*choreography only

DT13 Bernardo Bertolucci (1940–)
Before the Revolution
The Conformist
The Last Emperor
Last Tango in Paris
1900
Partner
The Sheltering Sky
The Spider's Strategem
Tragedy of a Ridiculous Man

DT14 Budd Boetticher (1916–)
Arruza
The Bullfighter and the Lady
The Human Gorilla
The Magnificent Matador
The Rise and Fall of Legs Diamond

WESTERNS
Decision at Sundown
Horizons West
The Man From the Alamo
Ride Lonesome
The Tall T
A Time for Dying
ACTOR ONLY
Tequila Sunrise (bit)

DT15 John Boorman (1933–)
Deliverance
The Emerald Forest
Excalibur
Exorcist II: The Heretic
Hell in the Pacific
Hope and Glory
Point Blank
Where the Heart Is
Zardoz

DT16 Albert Brooks (1947–)
All films director-actor, unless noted.
Defending Your Life
Lost in America
Modern Romance
Real Life
ACTOR ONLY
Broadcast News
Private Benjamin
Taxi Driver
Twilight Zone—The Movie
Unfaithfully Yours

DT17 Mel Brooks (1926–)
All films writer-director-actor, unless noted.
An Audience With Mel Brooks
Blazing Saddles
High Anxiety
The History of the World: Part I
Life Stinks
The Producers
Silent Movie
Spaceballs
The Twelve Chairs
Young Frankenstein
ACTOR ONLY
The Muppet Movie
Putney Swope
To Be or Not to Be (1983 version)
CHARACTER VOICE
Look Who's Talking Too

DT18 Tod Browning (1882–1962)
The Devil Doll
Dracula (1931 version)
Freaks
Mark of the Vampire
Outside the Law
The Unholy Three (1925 version)

The Unknown
West of Zanzibar

DT19 Luis Buñuel (1900–1983)
The Brute
The Criminal Life of Archibaldo de la Cruz
Diary of a Chambermaid (1964 version)
The Discreet Charm of the Bourgeosie
El: This Strange Passion
The Exterminating Angel
Fever Mounts in El Pao
Illusion Travels by Streetcar
L'Age d'Or
Land Without Bread
Los Olvidados
Mexican Bus Ride
The Milky Way (1970)
Nazarin
The Phantom of Liberty
Simon of the Desert
Susana
That Obscure Object of Desire
Tristana
Un Chien Andalou (co-director)
Viridiana
A Woman Without Love
Wuthering Heights (1954 version)

DT20 Tim Burton (1960–)
Aladdin and His Wonderful Lamp
Batman (1989)
Batman Returns
Beetlejuice
Edward Scissorhands
Frankenweenie
Pee-wee's Big Adventure
ACTOR ONLY
Singles (bit)

DT21 James Cameron (1954–)
The Abyss
Aliens
Piranha II: The Spawning
The Terminator
Terminator 2: Judgment Day

DT22 Frank Capra (1897–1991)
Arsenic and Old Lace
Broadway Bill
Here Comes the Groom
A Hole in the Head
It Happened One Night
It's a Wonderful Life
Lady for a Day
Lost Horizon
Meet John Doe
Mr. Deeds Goes to Town
Mr. Smith Goes to Washington
Platinum Blonde
Pocketful of Miracles

State of the Union
The Strong Man
That Certain Thing
You Can't Take It With You

DT23 John Carpenter (1948–)
Assault on Precinct 13
Big Trouble in Little China
Christine
Dark Star
Elvis: The Movie
Escape From New York
The Fog
Halloween
Memoirs of an Invisible Man
Prince of Darkness
Starman
They Live
The Thing

DT24 Charlie Chaplin (1889–1977)
*Numerous anthologies of Chaplin's short films are
    available. The list below is a broad selection.*
SHORT FILMS
The Chaplin Essanay Book I
The Chaplin Revue
Charlie Chaplin Carnival
Charlie Chaplin Cavalcade
Charlie Chaplin Festival
Charlie Chaplin—The Early Years, Vols. I–IV
Charlie Chaplin's Keystone Comedies 1–5
The Kid/The Idle Class
Kid's Auto Race/Mabel's Married Life
The Knockout/Dough and Dynamite
The Rink/The Immigrant
The Tramp/A Woman
Work/Police
FEATURE FILMS
The Circus
City Lights
The Gold Rush
The Great Dictator
A King in New York
Limelight
Modern Times
Monsieur Verdoux
Show People*
Tillie's Punctured Romance
A Woman of Paris
SUBJECT ONLY
Chaplin
DOCUMENTARY SUBJECT
Unknown Chaplin
When Comedy Was King
*actor only

DT25 René Clair (1898–1981)
A Nous la Liberte
And Then There Were None
The Crazy Ray

Entr'acte
Forever and a Day (co-director)
The Ghost Goes West
I Married a Witch
The Italian Straw Hat
Le Million
Love and the Frenchwoman
Under the Roofs of Paris

DT26 Jean Cocteau (1889–1963)
Beauty and the Beast (1946 version)
Blood of a Poet
Orpheus
Testament of Orpheus (also actor)

DT27 Joel Coen (1955–)
*Coen's brother Ethan produces their films, which
they co-write.*
Barton Fink
Blood Simple
Miller's Crossing
Raising Arizona
ACTOR ONLY
Spies (bit)

DT28 Larry Cohen (1941–)
Black Caesar
Deadly Illusion (co-director)
God Told Me To
Hell Up in Harlem
Housewife
It Lives Again
It's Alive!
It's Alive III: Island of the Alive
Perfect Strangers
The Private Files of J. Edgar Hoover
Q
Return to Salem's Lot
Special Effects
The Stuff
Wicked Stepmother

DT29 Francis Ford Coppola (1939–)
Apocalypse Now
The Bellboy and the Playgirls
Bram Stoker's Dracula
The Conversation
The Cotton Club
Dementia 13
Finian's Rainbow
Gardens of Stone
The Godfather
The Godfather, Part II
The Godfather, Part III
The Godfather: The Complete Epic,
   1902–1958
The Godfather Trilogy, 1901–1980
New York Stories (co-director)
One From the Heart
The Outsiders

Peggy Sue Got Married
The Rain People
Rip Van Winkle
Rumble Fish
Tonight for Sure
Tucker: The Man and His Dream
You're a Big Boy Now
DOCUMENTARY SUBJECT
Hearts of Darkness: A Filmmaker's
   Apocalypse

DT30 Roger Corman (1926–)
*Corman has produced and "presented" scores of
   films too numerous to mention here.*
Apache Woman
Attack of the Crab Monsters
Bloody Mama
A Bucket of Blood
Carnival Rock
Creature from the Haunted Sea
The Fall of the House of Usher
Frankenstein Unbound
Gas-s-s-s
The Gunslinger
The Haunted Palace
I, Mobster
It Conquered the World
The Last Woman on Earth
The Little Shop of Horrors (1960 version)
Machine Gun Kelly
The Masque of the Red Death (1964 version)
The Pit and the Pendulum
Premature Burial
The Raven (1963)
Rock All Night
The St. Valentine's Day Massacre
Shame (1961)
She-Gods of Shark Reef
Swamp Diamonds
Tales of Terror
The Terror
Tomb of Ligeia
Tower of London (1962 version)
The Trip
The Undead
The Wasp Woman
The Wild Angels
X: The Man With X-Ray Eyes
ACTOR ONLY
Cannonball
The Godfather, Part II
The Godfather: The Complete Epic,
   1902–1958
The Godfather Trilogy, 1901–1980
The Howling (bit)
The Silence of the Lambs
The State of Things
Swing Shift
DOCUMENTARY SUBJECT
Roger Corman: Hollywood's Wild Angel

DT31 David Cronenberg (1943–)
The Brood
Dead Ringers
The Dead Zone
Fast Company
The Fly (1986 version)
Naked Lunch
Rabid
Scanners
They Came From Within
Videodrome
ACTOR ONLY
Into the Night
Nightbreed

DT32 George Cukor (1889–1983)
Adam's Rib
Bhowani Junction
A Bill of Divorcement
Born Yesterday (1950 version)
Camille
The Corn Is Green (1979 version)
David Copperfield
Dinner at Eight
A Double Life
Gaslight
Heller in Pink Tights
Holiday
It Should Happen to You
Justine
Keeper of the Flame
Les Girls
Let's Make Love
Little Women (1933 version)
Love Among the Ruins
My Fair Lady
Pat and Mike
The Philadelphia Story
Rich and Famous
Romeo and Juliet (1936 version)
Song Without End (co-director)
A Star Is Born (1954 version)
Susan and God
Sylvia Scarlett
Two-Faced Woman
What Price Hollywood?
A Woman's Face (1941 version)
The Women (1939)

DT33 Joe Dante (1944–)
Amazon Women on the Moon
  (co-director)
The 'Burbs
Explorers
Gremlins
Gremlins 2: The New Batch
Hollywood Boulevard (co-director)
The Howling
Innerspace
Matinee

Piranha
Twilight Zone—The Movie
  (co-director)
ACTOR ONLY
Roger Corman: Hollywood's Wild Angel
Sleepwalkers

DT34 Cecil B. DeMille (1881–1959)
Cleopatra (1934)
The Greatest Show on Earth
The King of Kings (1927 version)
Madam Satan
The Plainsman
Reap the Wild Wind
The Road to Yesterday
Samson and Delilah
The Ten Commandments (1923 and 1956
  versions)
ACTOR ONLY
Free and Easy (bit)
Sunset Boulevard

DT35 Jonathan Demme (1944–)
Caged Heat
Citizens Band
Cousin Bobby
Crazy Mama
Fighting Mad (1976)
Last Embrace
Married to the Mob
Melvin and Howard
The Silence of the Lambs
Something Wild
Stop Making Sense
Swimming to Cambodia
Swing Shift
Who Am I This Time?
ACTOR ONLY
Into the Night
Roger Corman: Hollywood's Wild Angel

DT36 Brian De Palma (1940–)
Blow Out
Body Double
The Bonfire of the Vanities
Carrie (1976)
Casualties of War
Confessions of a Peeping John
Dressed to Kill (1980)
The Fury
Greetings
Home Movies
Obsession
Phantom of the Paradise
Raising Cain
Scarface (1983 version)
Sisters
The Untouchables
The Wedding Party (co-director)
Wise Guys

DT37 Vittorio De Sica (1902–1974)
All films director-actor, unless noted.
After the Fox
The Bandits of Orgosolo*
The Bicycle Thief*
Bocaccio '70 (co-director)*
The Children Are Watching Us
The Garden of the Finzi-Continis*
The Gold of Naples
Indiscretion of an American Wife*
Miracle in Milan*
The Roof*
Shoeshine*
Teresa Venerdi
Two Women*
Umberto D.*
Woman Times Seven*
Yesterday, Today & Tomorrow*
*director only
ACTOR ONLY
Andy Warhol's Dracula
The Battle of Austerlitz
The Earrings of Madame de . . .
A Farewell to Arms (1957 version)
General Della Rovere
If It's Tuesday, This Must Be Belgium
It Started in Naples
The Millionairess
Shoes of the Fisherman
SUBJECT ONLY
Sophia Loren: Her Own Story

DT38 Stanley Donen (1924–)
Arabesque
Bedazzled
Blame It on Rio
Charade
The Grass Is Greener
Indiscreet (1958)
Saturn 3
Two for the Road
MUSICALS
Damn Yankees*
Deep in My Heart
Funny Face
Give a Girl a Break
It's Always Fair Weather**
The Little Prince
Love Is Better Than Ever
Movie, Movie
On the Town**
The Pajama Game*
Royal Wedding
Seven Brides for Seven Brothers
Singin' in the Rain**
*with George Abbott
**with Gene Kelly

DT39 Carl Dreyer (1889–1968)
Day of Wrath

Gertrud
Leaves From Satan's Book
Master of the House
Ordet
The Passion of Joan of Arc
Vampyr

DT40 Blake Edwards (1922–)
See also: XT30 He Directs, She Acts
Blind Date (1987)
Breakfast at Tiffany's
Curse of the Pink Panther
The Days of Wine and Roses
Experiment in Terror
A Fine Mess
The Great Race
The Man Who Loved Women (1983 version)
Micki & Maude
Operation Petticoat
The Party
The Perfect Furlough
The Pink Panther
The Pink Panther Strikes Again
Return of the Pink Panther
The Revenge of the Pink Panther
S.O.B.
A Shot in the Dark
Skin Deep
Sunset
Switch
The Tamarind Seed
10
That's Life!
This Happy Feeling
The Trail of the Pink Panther
Victor/Victoria
What Did You Do in the War, Daddy?
Wild Rovers

DT41 Sergei Eisenstein (1898–1948)
Alexander Nevsky
The General Line
Ivan the Terrible, Parts I and II
Potemkin
Que Viva Mexico!
Strike
Ten Days That Shook the World/
    October

DT42 Rainer Werner Fassbinder
(1945–1982)
Ali—Fear Eats the Soul*
The American Soldier*
Berlin Alexanderplatz
The Bitter Tears of Petra Van Kant
Chinese Roulette
Despair
Fox and His Friends*
Gods of the Plague*
The Marriage of Maria Braun

The Merchant of Four Seasons
Mother Kusters Goes to Heaven
Querelle
Veronika Voss
*also actor
SUBJECT ONLY
A Man Like Eva
ACTOR ONLY
Kamikaze '89

DT43 Federico Fellini (1920–)
See also: XT30 He Directs, She Acts
Amarcord
And the Ship Sails On
Bocaccio '70 (co-director)
City of Women
The Clowns
8½
Fellini's Roma
Ginger and Fred
I Vitelloni
Il Bidone
Juliet of the Spirits
La Dolce Vita
La Strada
Love in the City (co-director)
Nights of Cabiria
Satyricon
Variety Lights (co-director)
The White Sheik
ACTOR ONLY
The Flowers of St. Francis
The Miracle (1948)
We All Loved Each Other So Much

DT44 John Ford (1895–1973)
Arrowsmith
December 7th
Donovan's Reef
Drums Along the Mohawk
The Fugitive
The Grapes of Wrath
How Green Was My Valley
The Hurricane
The Informer
Judge Priest
The Last Hurrah
The Long Gray Line
The Long Voyage Home
The Lost Patrol
Mary of Scotland
Mister Roberts (co-director)
Mogambo
The Quiet Man
The Sun Shines Bright
They Were Expendable
This Is Korea/December 7th
Wee Willie Winkie
What Price Glory?
  (1952 version)

The Wings of Eagles
Young Mr. Lincoln
WESTERNS
Cheyenne Autumn
Fort Apache
The Horse Soldiers
How the West Was Won (co-director)
The Man Who Shot Liberty Valance
My Darling Clementine
Rio Grande
The Searchers
Sergeant Rutledge
She Wore a Yellow Ribbon
Stagecoach
Straight Shootin'
3 Godfathers
Two Rode Together
Wagonmaster

DT45 Milos Forman (1932–)
Amadeus
The Firemen's Ball
Hair
Loves of a Blonde
One Flew Over the Cuckoo's Nest
Ragtime
Valmont
ACTOR ONLY
Heartburn

DT46 Bill Forsyth (1946–)
Breaking In
Comfort and Joy
Gregory's Girl
Housekeeping
Local Hero
That Sinking Feeling

DT47 Bob Fosse (1927–1987)
All films director-choreographer, unless noted.
All That Jazz
Cabaret
Damn Yankees*
Give a Girl a Break**
Kiss Me Kate**
The Little Prince*
My Sister Eileen (1955 version)*
The Pajama Game (choreographer only)
Pippin (choreographer only)
Sweet Charity
*actor, choreographer only
**actor only
NON-MUSIC
Lenny
STAR 80

DT48 Stephen Frears (1941–)
Dangerous Liaisons
The Grifters
Gumshoe

Hero
The Hit
My Beautiful Laundrette
Prick Up Your Ears
Saigon: Year of the Cat
Sammy and Rosie Get Laid

DT49 Samuel Fuller (1911–)
The Baron of Arizona
The Big Red One
China Gate
I Shot Jesse James
The Naked Kiss
Pickup on South Street
Run of the Arrow
Shark!
Shock Corridor
The Steel Helmet
Underworld, U.S.A.
Verboten!
ACTOR ONLY
The American Friend
Hammett
The Last Movie
Pierrot le Fou
Return to Salem's Lot
Slapstick (Of Another Kind)
The State of Things

Terry Gilliam see CO15 The Alumni of
"Monty Python's Flying Circus"

DT50 Jean-Luc Godard (1930–)
Alphaville
Aria (co-director)
Band of Outsiders
Breathless (1959 version)
Contempt
First Name: Carmen*
Hail, Mary
King Lear (1987 version)
Le Gai Savior
Les Carabiniers
A Married Woman
Masculine-Feminine
My Life to Live
The Oldest Profession (co-director)
Pierrot le Fou
Sympathy for the Devil
Weekend
A Woman Is a Woman
*also actor

DT51 Peter Greenaway (1942–)
The Belly of an Architect
The Cook, The Thief, His Wife and Her Lover
The Draughtsman's Contract
Drowning by Numbers
Prospero's Books
A Zed and Two Naughts

DT52 D.W. Griffith (1875–1948)
Abraham Lincoln
The Avenging Conscience
The Birth of a Nation
Broken Blossoms
D.W. Griffith Triple Feature
Dream Street
Hearts of the World
Home, Sweet Home
Intolerance
Isn't Life Wonderful
Judith of Bethulia
The Love Flower
Orphans of the Storm
Sally of the Sawdust
The Short Films of D.W. Griffith, Vols. I–II
The Sorrows of Satan
True Heart Susie
Way Down East
The White Rose (1923)

DT53 Howard Hawks (1896–1977)
Air Force
Ball of Fire
Barbary Coast
The Big Sleep (1946 version)
Bringing Up Baby
Come and Get It (co-director)
The Criminal Code
Gentlemen Prefer Blondes
Hatari!
His Girl Friday
Land of the Pharaohs
Man's Favorite Sport?
Monkey Business (1952)
Only Angels Have Wings
Red Line 7000
Scarface (1932 version)
Sergeant York
A Song Is Born
To Have and Have Not
Twentieth Century
WESTERNS
The Big Sky
El Dorado
The Outlaw (co-director)
Red River
Rio Bravo
Rio Lobo

DT54 Werner Herzog (1942–)
Aguirre: The Wrath of God
Every Man for Himself and God Against All
Fitzcarraldo
Heart of Glass
Herdsmen of the Sun
Stroszek
Where the Green Ants Dream
ACTOR ONLY
Burden of Dreams

Man of Flowers
Werner Herzog Eats His Shoe

DT55 George Roy Hill (1922–)
Butch Cassidy and the Sundance Kid
Funny Farm
The Great Waldo Pepper
Hawaii
The Little Drummer Girl
A Little Romance
Period of Adjustment
Slap Shot
Slaughterhouse Five
The Sting
Thoroughly Modern Millie
Toys in the Attic
The World According to Garp
The World of Henry Orient

DT56 Walter Hill (1942–)
Another 48 HRS
Brewster's Millions
Crossroads
The Driver
Extreme Prejudice
48 HRS
Hard Times
Johnny Handsome
The Long Riders
Red Heat
Southern Comfort
Streets of Fire
Tales From the Crypt (1989; co-director)
Trespass
The Warriors

DT57 Alfred Hitchcock (1899–1980)
The Birds
Blackmail
Champagne
Dial M for Murder
Easy Virtue
Family Plot
Foreign Correspondent
Frenzy
I Confess
Jamaica Inn (1939 version)
Juno and the Paycock
The Lady Vanishes (1938 version)
Lifeboat
The Lodger
The Man Who Knew Too Much (1934 and
  1956 versions)
The Manxman
Marnie
Mr. and Mrs. Smith
Murder!
North by Northwest
Notorious
Number 17

The Paradine Case
Psycho
Rear Window
Rebecca
Rich and Strange
The Ring
Rope
Sabotage
Saboteur
The Secret Agent
Shadow of a Doubt
The Skin Game (1931)
Spellbound
Stage Fright
Strangers on a Train
Suspicion
The 39 Steps (1935 version)
To Catch a Thief
Topaz
Torn Curtain
The Trouble With Harry
Under Capricorn
Vertigo
The Wrong Man
Young and Innocent

DT58 Ron Howard (1954–)
Backdraft
Cocoon
Far and Away
Grand Theft Auto*
Gung Ho (1986)
Night Shift
Parenthood
Splash
Willow
*also actor
ACTOR ONLY
American Graffiti
Bitter Harvest
The Courtship of Eddie's Father
Eat My Dust!
More American Graffiti
The Music Man
The Shootist
Village of the Giants
The Wild Country

DT59 John Hughes (1950–)
All films writer-director, unless noted.
The Breakfast Club
Curly Sue
Ferris Bueller's Day Off
Planes, Trains, and Automobiles
She's Having a Baby
Sixteen Candles
Uncle Buck
Weird Science
PRODUCER-WRITER
Career Opportunities

The Great Outdoors
Home Alone
Home Alone 2: Lost in New York
National Lampoon's Christmas Vacation
Pretty in Pink
Some Kind of Wonderful
PRODUCER ONLY
Only the Lonely
WRITER ONLY
Dutch
Mr. Mom
Nate and Hayes
National Lampoon's Class Reunion
National Lampoon's European Vacation
National Lampoon's Vacation

DT60 John Huston (1906–1987)
Across the Pacific
The African Queen
Annie
The Asphalt Jungle
The Barbarian and the Geisha
Beat the Devil
The Bible*
Casino Royale (co-director)
The Dead
Fat City
In This Our Life
Key Largo
Let There Be Light
The Life and Times of Judge Roy Bean*
The List of Adrian Messenger*
The Mackintosh Man
The Maltese Falcon
The Man Who Would Be King
The Misfits
Moby Dick
Moulin Rouge
The Night of the Iguana
Phobia
Prizzi's Honor
The Red Badge of Courage
Reflections in a Golden Eye
The Treasure of the Sierra Madre*
Under the Volcano
The Unforgiven
Victory
Wise Blood
*also actor
ACTOR ONLY
Angela
Battle for the Planet of the Apes
Battle Force
Breakout
Cannery Row (narrator)
The Cardinal
Chinatown
Lovesick
Man in the Wilderness
Myra Breckenridge

Tentacles
The Visitor
The Wind and the Lion
Winter Kills

DT61 James Ivory (1928–)
Bombay Talkie
The Bostonians
The Europeans
Heat and Dust
The Householder
Howards End
Hullabaloo Over George and Bonnie's Pictures
Jane Austen in Manhattan
Maurice
Mr. and Mrs. Bridge
Quartet (1981)
A Room With a View
Roseland
Savages (1972)
Shakespeare Wallah
Slaves of New York
The Wild Party (1975)

DT62 Jim Jarmusch (1953–)
Down by Law
Mystery Train
Night on Earth
Stranger Than Paradise
ACTOR ONLY
American Autobahn
Straight to Hell

DT63 Norman Jewison (1926–)
Agnes of God
. . . And Justice for All
Best Friends
The Cincinnati Kid
F.I.S.T.
Fiddler on the Roof
In Country
In the Heat of the Night
Jesus Christ Superstar
Moonstruck
Other People's Money
Rollerball
The Russians Are Coming! The Russians Are
  Coming!
Send Me No Flowers
A Soldier's Story
The Thomas Crown Affair
The Thrill of It All

DT64 Philip Kaufman (1936–)
Henry & June
Invasion of the Body Snatchers (1979 version)
The Right Stuff
The Unbearable Lightness of Being
The Wanderers
The White Dawn

DT65 Elia Kazan (1909–)
The Arrangement
Baby Doll
East of Eden (1955)
A Face in the Crowd
Gentleman's Agreement
The Last Tycoon
On the Waterfront
Panic in the Streets
Pinky
The Sea of Grass
Splendor in the Grass
A Streetcar Named Desire
A Tree Grows in Brooklyn
Viva Zapata!
ACTOR ONLY
City for Conquest

DT66 Buster Keaton (1895–1966)
*Many compilations of Keaton's short films are
available on video; this list represents a
generous selection. Keaton's career as an actor
for hire in sound films was marked by a
number of low-budget entries. The selection
below (marked *actor only) reflects the most
easily available and those of most interest.*
SHORT FILMS/COMPILATIONS
The Balloonatic/One Week
The Blacksmith/The Balloonatic
Buster Keaton Festival Vols. I–III
Buster Keaton Rides Again/The Railrodder
Buster Keaton: The Golden Years
Buster Keaton: The Great Stone Face
FEATURE FILMS
The Adventures of Huckleberry Finn (1960
    version)
Around the World in 80 Days (bit)*
The Cameraman
College
Doughboys*
Forever and a Day (bit)*
Free and Easy*
A Funny Thing Happened on the Way to the
    Forum*
The General
It's a Mad Mad Mad Mad World
    (bit)
Limelight*
MGM's Big Parade of Comedy*
Our Hospitality
Speak Easily*
Spite Marriage
Steamboat Bill, Jr.
Sunset Boulevard*
The Three Ages
What! No Beer*
*actor only
DOCUMENTARY SUBJECT
Buster Keaton: A Hard Act to Follow
When Comedy Was King

DT67 Stanley Kramer (1913–)
Bless the Beasts and Children
The Defiant Ones
The Domino Principle
Guess Who's Coming to Dinner
Inherit the Wind
It's a Mad Mad Mad Mad World
Judgment at Nuremberg
Not as a Stranger
On the Beach
The Pride and the Passion
R.P.M.
The Runner Stumbles
Ship of Fools

DT68 Stanley Kubrick (1928–)
Barry Lyndon
A Clockwork Orange
Dr. Strangelove or; How I Learned to Stop
    Worrying and Love the Bomb
Full Metal Jacket
Killer's Kiss
The Killing
Lolita
Paths of Glory
The Shining
Spartacus
2001: A Space Odyssey

DT69 Akira Kurosawa (1910–)
Akira Kurosawa's Dreams
The Bad Sleep Well
Dersu Uzala
Dodes'ka-den
Drunken Angel
The Hidden Fortress
High and Low
The Idiot
Ikiru
Kagemusha
The Lower Depths (1957
    version)
The Men Who Tread on the Tiger's
    Tail
No Regrets for Our Youth
Ran
Rashomon
Red Beard
Sanjuro
SanShiro Sugata
The Seven Samurai
Stray Dog
Throne of Blood
Yojimbo

DT70 Fritz Lang (1890–1976)
Beyond a Reasonable Doubt
The Big Heat
Clash by Night
Cloak and Dagger (1946)

Destiny
Dr. Mabuse, the Gambler
Fury
The House by the River
Human Desire
Journey to the Lost City
Kriemhilde's Revenge
Liliom
M (1931 version)
Metropolis
Moonfleet
Rancho Notorious
The Return of Frank James
Scarlet Street
Secret Beyond the Door
Siegfried
Spiders
Spies
The Testament of Dr. Mabuse
The Thousand Eyes of Dr. Mabuse
Western Union
While the City Sleeps
The Woman in the Moon
You Only Live Once
ACTOR ONLY
Contempt

DT71　David Lean (1908–1991)
Blithe Spirit
The Bridge on the River Kwai
Brief Encounter (1945 version)
Dr. Zhivago
Great Expectations
Hobson's Choice
In Which We Serve (co-director)
Lawrence of Arabia
Madeleine
Oliver Twist (1948 version)
A Passage to India
Ryan's Daughter
Summertime
This Happy Breed

DT72　Spike Lee (1956–)
All films director-writer-actor.
Do the Right Thing
Jungle Fever
Malcolm X
Mo' Better Blues
School Daze
She's Gotta Have It

DT73　Sergio Leone (1921–1989)
A Fistful of Dollars
A Fistful of Dynamite
For a Few Dollars More
The Good, the Bad, and the Ugly
Once Upon a Time in the West
NON-WESTERN
Once Upon a Time in America

DT74　Richard Lester (1932–)
Butch and Sundance: The Early Days
Cuba
Finders Keepers
The Four Musketeers
A Funny Thing Happened on the Way to the
　Forum
Get Back
A Hard Day's Night
Help!
How I Won the War
Juggernaut (1974)
Petulia
The Ritz
Robin and Marian
Superman II
Superman III
The Three Musketeers (1974 version)

DT75　Barry Levinson (1932–)
Avalon
Bugsy
Diner
Good Morning, Vietnam
The Natural
Rain Man*
Tin Men
Toys
Young Sherlock Holmes
*also actor
ACTOR ONLY
High Anxiety

DT76　Ernst Lubitsch (1892–1947)
Gypsy Blood
Heaven Can Wait (1943)
Lady Windermere's Fan
The Marriage Circle
The Merry Widow
Ninotchka
One Arabian Night*
Passion (1918)
The Shop Around the Corner
So This Is Paris
The Student Prince of Old Heidelberg
That Uncertain Feeling
To Be or Not To Be (1942 version)
*also actor

DT77　George Lucas (1944–)
American Graffiti
Star Wars
THX-1138
ACTOR ONLY
Hearts of Darkness: A Filmmaker's
　Apocalypse

DT78　Sidney Lumet (1924–)
The Anderson Tapes
Daniel

Deathtrap
Dog Day Afternoon
Equus
Fail-Safe
Family Business
The Fugitive Kind
Garbo Talks
The Group
Just Tell Me What You Want
Long Day's Journey Into Night (1962 version)
The Morning After
Murder on the Orient Express
Network
The Pawnbroker
Power (1986)
Prince of the City
Q & A
Running on Empty
Serpico
Stage Struck
A Stranger Among Us
12 Angry Men
The Verdict
The Wiz
ACTOR ONLY
Listen Up: The Lives of Quincy Jones

DT79 David Lynch (1946–)
Blue Velvet
Dune
The Elephant Man
Eraserhead
Industrial Symphony No. 1—The Dream of
    the Broken Hearted
Twin Peaks
Twin Peaks: Fire Walk With Me (also actor)
Wild at Heart
ACTOR ONLY
Zelly and Me

DT80 Leo McCarey (1898–1969)
An Affair to Remember
The Awful Truth
The Bells of St. Mary's
Duck Soup
Going My Way
Good Sam
Indiscreet (1931)
Love Affair
The Milky Way (1936)
Once Upon a Honeymoon
Ruggles of Red Gap

DT81 Terrence Malick (1942–)
Badlands
Days of Heaven

DT82 Louis Malle (1932–)
Alamo Bay
Atlantic City

Au Revoir, les Enfants
Crackers
Damage
Frantic (1958)
The Lovers
May Fools
Murmur of the Heaat
My Dinner With André
Pretty Baby
A Very Private Affair
Zazie dans le Metro

DT83 Rouben Mamoulian (1897–1987)
Applause
Becky Sharp
Blood and Sand (1941 version)
Dr. Jekyll and Mr. Hyde (1932
    version)
Golden Boy
The Mark of Zorro (1940 version)
Queen Christina
Silk Stockings
Summer Holiday

DT84 Joseph L. Mankiewicz
(1909–1993)
All About Eve
The Barefoot Contessa
Cleopatra (1963)
5 Fingers
The Ghost and Mrs. Muir
Guys and Dolls
The Honey Pot
House of Strangers
Julius Caesar (1953 version)
A Letter to Three Wives
Sleuth
Suddenly, Last Summer
There Was a Crooked Man

DT85 Anthony Mann (1906–1967)
A Dandy in Aspic
Desperate
El Cid
The Fall of the Roman Empire
The Glenn Miller Story
God's Little Acre
The Great Flamarion
He Walked by Night (co-director)
Men in War
Railroaded
Strategic Air Command
T-Men
Thunder Bay
WESTERNS
Bend of the River
The Far Country
The Man From Laramie
Man of the West
The Naked Spur

The Tin Star
Winchester '73

DT86 Elaine May (1932–)
The Heartbreak Kid
Ishtar
Mikey and Nicky
A New Leaf*
*also actress
ACTRESS ONLY
California Suite
Enter Laughing
In the Spirit
Luv

DT87 Paul Mazursky (1930–)
*Mazursky appears in his films in small
supporting roles.*
Blume in Love
Bob & Carol & Ted & Alice
Down and Out in Beverly Hills
Enemies, A Love Story
Harry and Tonto
Moon Over Parador
Moscow on the Hudson
Scenes From a Mall
Tempest (1982)
An Unmarried Woman
Willie and Phil
ACTOR ONLY
Blackboard Jungle
The History of the World: Part I
I Love You, Alice B. Toklas
Into the Night
A Man, a Woman and a Bank
Man Trouble
Punchline
Scenes From the Class Struggle in Beverly Hills
A Star Is Born (1976 version)

DT88 Vincente Minnelli (1910–1986)
See also: XT30 He Directs, She Acts
The Bad and the Beautiful
The Clock
The Courtship of Eddie's Father
Designing Woman
Father of the Bride (1950 version)
Father's Little Dividend
The Four Horsemen of the Apocalypse (1961
version)
Home from the Hill
I Dood It
The Long, Long Trailer
Lust for Life
Madame Bovary (1949 version)
A Matter of Time
The Reluctant Debutante
The Sandpiper
Some Came Running
Tea and Sympathy

Two Weeks in Another Town
Undercurrent
MUSICALS
An American in Paris
The Band Wagon
Bells Are Ringing
Brigadoon
Cabin in the Sky
Gigi
Kismet
Meet Me in St. Louis
On a Clear Day You Can See Forever
The Pirate
Yolanda and the Thief
Ziegfeld Follies

DT89 Errol Morris (1948–)
A Brief History of Time
Gates of Heaven
The Thin Blue Line
Vernon, Florida

DT90 Paul Morrissey (1939–)
Andy Warhol's Dracula
Andy Warhol's Frankenstein
Beethoven's Nephew
Flesh
Heat (1972)
The Hound of the Baskervilles (1977 version)
Mixed Blood
Spike of Bensonhurst
Trash
ACTOR ONLY
Superstar: The Life and Times of Andy Warhol

DT91 Mike Nichols (1931–)
Biloxi Blues
Carnal Knowledge
Catch-22
The Day of the Dolphin
Gilda Live
The Gin Game
The Graduate
Heartburn
Postcards From the Edge
Regarding Henry
Silkwood
Whoopi Goldberg Live
Who's Afraid of Virginia Woolf?
Working Girl

DT92 Marcel Ophuls (1927–)
Hotel Terminus
A Sense of Loss
The Sorrow and the Pity

DT93 Max Ophuls (1902–1957)
Caught
The Earrings of Madame De . . .
La Ronde

La Signora di Tutti
Le Plaisir
Letter From an Unknown Woman
Liebelei
Lola Montes
The Reckless Moment

DT94 Alan J. Pakula (1928–)
All the President's Men
Comes a Horseman
Consenting Adults
Dream Lover
Klute
Orphans
The Parallax View
Presumed Innocent
Rollover
See You in the Morning
Sophie's Choice
Starting Over
The Sterile Cuckoo

DT95 Sam Peckinpah (1925–1984)
Bring Me the Head of Alfredo Garcia
Convoy
Cross of Iron
The Getaway
The Killer Elite
The Osterman Weekend
Straw Dogs
WESTERNS
The Ballad of Cable Hogue
The Deadly Companions
Junior Bonner
Major Dundee
Pat Garrett and Billy the Kid*
Ride the High Country
The Wild Bunch
*also actor
ACTOR ONLY
Invasion of the Body Snatchers (1956 version)
The Visitor

DT96 Arthur Penn (1922–)
Alice's Restaurant
Bonnie and Clyde
The Chase (1966)
Dead of Winter
Four Friends
The Left-Handed Gun
Little Big Man
The Miracle Worker
The Missouri Breaks
Night Moves
Penn & Teller Get Killed
Target

DT97 Roman Polanski (1933–)
Chinatown*
Diary of Forbidden Dreams*

The Fearless Vampire Killers*
Frantic (1988)
Knife in the Water
Macbeth (1971 version)
Pirates
Repulsion
Rosemary's Baby
The Tenant*
Tess
*also actor
ACTOR ONLY
The Magic Christian

DT98 Sydney Pollack (1934–)
Absence of Malice
Bobby Deerfield
The Electric Horseman
Havana
Jeremiah Johnson
Out of Africa
The Scalphunters
The Slender Thread
They Shoot Horses, Don't They?
This Property Is Condemned
Three Days of the Condor
Tootsie*
The Way We Were
The Yakuza
*also actor
ACTOR ONLY
Death Becomes Her
Husbands and Wives
The Player (bit)

DT99 Michael Powell (1905–1990)
All co-directed with Emeric Pressburger, except *
Black Narcissus
A Canterbury Tale
The Elusive Pimpernel
The 49th Parallel
I Know Where I'm Going
Ill Met by Moonlight
The Life and Death of Colonel Blimp
The Lion Has Wings*
One of Our Aircraft Is Missing
Peeping Tom*
Pursuit of the *Graf Spee*
The Red Shoes
The Small Back Room
The Spy in Black*
Tales of Hoffmann
Thief of Bagdad (1940 version)*

DT100 Otto Preminger (1906–1986)
Advise and Consent
Anatomy of a Murder
Bonjour Tristesse
The Cardinal
The Court-Martial of Billy Mitchell
Exodus

In Harm's Way
Laura
The Man With the Golden Arm
The Moon Is Blue
River of No Return
Saint Joan
ACTOR ONLY
Stalag 17
They Got Me Covered

DT101 Nicholas Ray (1911–1979)
Born To Be Bad
55 Days at Peking
Flying Leathernecks
In a Lonely Place
Johnny Guitar
King of Kings
Knock on Any Door
The Lusty Men
On Dangerous Ground
Party Girl
Rebel Without a Cause
They Live by Night
A Woman's Secret
DOCUMENTARY SUBJECT
Lightning Over Water
ACTOR ONLY
The American Friend

DT102 Satyajit Ray (1921–1992)
The Adversary
Aparajito
Devi
Distant Thunder (1973)
The Home and the World
Pather Panchali
Two Daughters
The World of Apu

DT103 Rob Reiner (1945–)
A Few Good Men
Misery
The Princess Bride
Stand by Me
The Sure Thing
This Is Spinal Tap*
When Harry Met Sally . . .
*also actor
ACTOR ONLY
Billy Crystal: Don't Get Me Started
Enter Laughing
Postcards From the Edge
Richard Lewis: "I'm in Pain"
Where's Poppa?

DT104 Jean Renoir (1894–1979)
Boudu Saved From Drowning
The Crime of Monsieur Lange
A Day in the Country*
Diary of a Chambermaid (1946 version)

Elena and Her Men
The Elusive Corporal
French Cancan
The Golden Coach
Grand Illusion
La Bête Humaine*
La Chienne
La Marseillaise
The Little Theatre of Jean Renoir
The Lower Depths (1936 version)
Madame Bovary (1934 version)
Picnic on the Grass
The River (1951)
Rules of the Game*
The Southerner
The Testament of Dr. Cordelier
This Land Is Mine
Toni
Tournament
*also actor

DT105 Martin Ritt (1914–1990)
Back Roads
The Black Orchid
The Brotherhood
Casey's Shadow
Conrack
Cross Creek
The Front
The Great White Hope
Hombre
Hud
The Long Hot Summer (1958 version)
The Molly Maguires
Murphy's Romance
Norma Rae
Nuts
Paris Blues
Pete 'n' Tillie
Sounder
The Spy Who Came in From the Cold
Stanley & Iris
ACTOR ONLY
The Slugger's Wife

DT106 Nicolas Roeg (1928–)
See also: XT30 He Directs, She Acts
Castaway
Cold Heaven
Don't Look Now
Eureka
Insignificance
The Man Who Fell to Earth
Performance (co-director)
Track 29
The Witches

DT107 Eric Rohmer (1920–)
The Aviator's Wife
Boyfriends and Girlfriends

Chloe in the Afternoon
Claire's Knee
Four Adventures of Reinette and Mirabelle
Full Moon in Paris
Le Beau Mariage
My Night at Maud's
Pauline at the Beach
Summer

DT108 George Romero (1940–)
The Crazies
Creepshow
Creepshow 2
Dawn of the Dead
Day of the Dead
Knightriders
Martin
Monkey Shines: An Experiment in Fear
Night of the Living Dead (1968 version)
Season of the Witch
Two Evil Eyes
ACTOR ONLY
The Silence of the Lambs

DT109 Roberto Rossellini (1906–1977)
See also: XT30 He Directs, She Acts
Augustine of Hippo
Blaise Pascal
Europa '51
Fear
The Flowers of St. Francis
General Della Rovere
Germany Year Zero
The Messiah
The Miracle (1948)
Open City
Paisan
The Rise of Louis XIV
Stromboli
Vanina Vanini
Voyage to Italy

DT110 Alan Rudolph (1943–)
Choose Me
Endangered Species
Love at Large
Made in Heaven
The Moderns
Mortal Thoughts
Nightmare Circus
Premonition
Roadie
Songwriter
Trouble in Mind
Welcome to L.A.
ACTOR ONLY
The Player (bit)

DT111 Ken Russell (1927–)
Altered States
Aria (co-director)
The Boy Friend
Crimes of Passion
Dante's Inferno
The Devils
Gothic
Lair of the White Worm
Lisztomania
Mahler
The Music Lovers
Prisoner of Honor
The Rainbow
Salome's Last Dance
Tommy
Whore*
Women & Men: Stories of Seduction (co-director)
Women in Love
*also actor
ACTOR ONLY
The Russia House

DT112 John Sayles (1950–)
All films writer-director-actor, unless noted.
Baby, It's You*
The Brother from Another Planet
City of Hope
Eight Men Out
Lianna
Matewan
Passion Fish*
The Return of the Secaucus Seven
*writer-director only
WRITER ONLY
Breaking In
Enormous Changes
The Howling
Piranha
WRITER-ACTOR ONLY
Alligator
Unnatural Causes
ACTOR ONLY
Hard Choices
Little Vegas
Matinee
Something Wild
Straight Talk

DT113 John Schlesinger (1926–)
The Believers
Billy Liar
Darling
The Day of the Locust
The Falcon and the Snowman
Far From the Madding Crowd
Honky Tonk Freeway
A Kind of Loving
Madame Sousatzka
Marathon Man
Midnight Cowboy

Pacific Heights
Separate Tables (1983 version)
Sunday Bloody Sunday
Yanks

DT114 Martin Scorsese (1942–)
After Hours
Alice Doesn't Live Here Anymore
Boxcar Bertha
Cape Fear (1991 version)
The Color of Money
GoodFellas
King of Comedy
The Last Temptation of Christ
The Last Waltz
Mean Streets
New York, New York
New York Stories (co-director)
Raging Bull
Taxi Driver*
Two by Scorsese
Who's That Knocking at My Door?
*also actor
ACTOR ONLY
Akira Kurosawa's Dreams
Cannonball
Guilty by Suspicion
Roger Corman: Hollywood's Wild Angel
'Round Midnight

DT115 Ridley Scott (1939–)
Alien
Black Rain (U.S.)
Blade Runner
The Duellists
1492: Conquest of Paradise
Legend
Someone To Watch Over Me
Thelma & Louise

DT116 Don Siegel (1912–1991)
An Annapolis Story
The Beguiled
The Big Steal
The Black Windmill
Charley Varrick
Coogan's Bluff
Dirty Harry
Escape From Alcatraz
Flaming Star
Hell Is for Heroes
Invasion of the Body Snatchers (1956 version)
Jinxed!
The Killers (1964 version)
Madigan
Private Hell 36
Riot in Cell Block 11
Rough Cut
The Shootist

Telefon
Two Mules for Sister Sara
ACTOR ONLY
Into the Night
Invasion of the Body Snatchers (1979 version)
Play Misty for Me

DT117 Douglas Sirk (1900–1987)
The First Legion
Imitation of Life (1959 version)
Magnificent Obsession
A Time to Live and a Time to Die
Written on the Wind

DT118 Steven Spielberg (1947–)
Always
Close Encounters of the Third Kind
The Color Purple
Duel
E.T.—The Extra-Terrestrial
Empire of the Sun
Hook
Indiana Jones and the Last Crusade
Indiana Jones and the Temple of Doom
Jaws
Night Gallery (co-director)
1941
Raiders of the Lost Ark
The Sugarland Express
Twilight Zone—The Movie (co-director)
ACTOR ONLY
Listen Up: The Lives of Quincy Jones

DT119 George Stevens (1904–1975)
Alice Adams
Annie Oakley
A Damsel in Distress
The Diary of Anne Frank
Giant
The Greatest Story Ever Told
Gunga Din
I Remember Mama
Kentucky Kernels
The More the Merrier
The Only Game in Town
Penny Serenade
A Place in the Sun
Quality Street
Shane
Swing Time
The Talk of the Town
Vivacious Lady
Woman of the Year
DOCUMENTARY SUBJECT
George Stevens: A Filmmaker's Journey

DT120 Oliver Stone (1946–)
Born on the Fourth of July
The Doors
The Hand

JFK
Platoon
Salvador
Seizure
Talk Radio
Wall Street

DT121 Preston Sturges (1898–1959)
The Beautiful Blonde From Bashful Bend
Christmas in July
The Great McGinty
The Great Moment
Hail the Conquering Hero
The Lady Eve
The Miracle of Morgan's Creek
The Palm Beach Story
The Sin of Harold Diddlebock
Sullivan's Travels
Unfaithfully Yours (1948 version)
ACTOR ONLY
Paris Holiday

DT122 Jacques Tati (1908–1982)
Jour de Fête
Mr. Hulot's Holiday
My Uncle
Playtime
ACTOR ONLY
Sylvia and the Phantom

DT123 Bertrand Tavernier (1941–)
Beatrice
Clean Slate
The Clockmaker
Daddy Nostalgia
Deathwatch
The Judge and the Assassin
Life and Nothing But
Mississippi Blues (co-director)
'Round Midnight
A Sunday in the Country

DT124 Jacques Tourneur (1904–1977)
Appointment in Honduras
Berlin Express
Cat People (1942 version)
Comedy of Terrors
Curse of the Demon
Days of Glory
Easy Living
Experiment Perilous
The Flame and the Arrow
Great Day in the Morning
I Walked with a Zombie
The Leopard Man
Out of the Past
Wichita

DT125 François Truffaut (1932–1984)
The Bride Wore Black

Confidentially Yours
Day for Night*
Farenheit 451
The 400 Blows
The Green Room*
Jules and Jim
The Last Metro
Love on the Run
The Man Who Loved Women (1977 version)
Mississippi Mermaid
Shoot the Piano Player
Small Change
The Soft Skin
Stolen Kisses
The Story of Adele H.
Two English Girls
The Wild Child*
The Woman Next Door
*also actor
ACTOR ONLY
Close Encounters of the Third Kind

DT126 King Vidor (1894–1982)
Beyond the Forest
The Big Parade
Bird of Paradise
The Champ (1931 version)
The Citadel
The Crowd
Duel in the Sun
The Fountainhead
Hallelujah
Man Without a Star
Northwest Passage
Our Daily Bread
Ruby Gentry
Show People
Solomon and Sheba
Stella Dallas
Street Scene
War and Peace (1956 version)
ACTOR ONLY
It's a Great Feeling (bit)
Love and Money

DT127 Luchino Visconti (1906–1976)
Bellissima
Bocaccio '70 (co-director)
Conversation Piece
The Damned
Death in Venice
La Terra Trema
L'Innocente
Ossessione
Rocco and His Brothers
Senso
White Nights (1957)

DT128 Josef von Sternberg (1894–1969)
Blonde Venus

The Blue Angel
The Docks of New York
Jet Pilot
The Last Command
Macao
Morocco
The Shanghai Gesture
ACTOR ONLY
The Epic That Never Was

DT129 Erich Von Stroheim (1885–1957)
All films director-actor, unless noted.
Blind Husbands
Foolish Wives
Greed*
Queen Kelly
The Wedding March
*director only
ACTOR ONLY
As You Desire Me
Crimson Romance
Grand Illusion
The Great Flamarion
The Great Gabbo
Hearts of the World
Intolerance
Lost Squadron
Napoleon (1955 version)
The North Star
So Ends Our Night
Sunset Boulevard

DT130 Andrzej Wajda (1927–)
Ashes and Diamonds
Birch Wood
Danton
Kanal
A Love in Germany
Man of Iron
Man of Marble

DT131 Raoul Walsh (1887–1981)
Along the Great Divide
Background to Danger
Battle Cry
The Big Trail
Blackbeard, The Pirate
Captain Horatio Hornblower
Dark Command
Desperate Journey
Distant Drums
Gentleman Jim
Going Hollywood
Gun Fury
High Sierra
The Horn Blows at Midnight
The King and Four Queens
A Lion Is in the Streets
The Naked and the Dead
Northern Pursuit

Objective, Burma!
Pursued
The Roaring Twenties
Sadie Thompson*
Sea Devils
The Sheriff of Fractured Jaw
Silver River
The Strawberry Blonde
The Tall Men
They Died With Their Boots On
They Drive By Night
The Thief of Bagdad (1924 version)
White Heat
*also actor
ACTOR ONLY
The Birth of a Nation
It's a Great Feeling (bit)

DT132 John Waters (1946–)
Cry-Baby
Desperate Living
Divine
Female Trouble
Hairspray*
Mondo Trasho
Multiple Maniacs
Pink Flamingos
Polyester
*also actor
ACTOR ONLY
Something Wild

DT133 Peter Weir (1944–)
The Cars That Ate Paris
Dead Poets Society
Gallipoli
Green Card
The Last Wave
The Mosquito Coast
Picnic at Hanging Rock
The Plumber
Witness
The Year of Living Dangerously

DT134 Orson Welles (1915–1985)
All films director-actor, unless noted.
Chimes at Midnight
Citizen Kane
The Lady From Shanghai
Macbeth (1948 version)
The Magnificent Ambersons*
Mr. Arkadin
Othello (1952 version)
The Stranger
Touch of Evil
The Trial
*director-narrator only
ACTOR ONLY
Battle Force (narrator)
The Battle of Austerlitz

Black Magic (1949)
Butterfly
Casino Royale
Catch-22
Is Paris Burning?
Jane Eyre (1944 version)
Journey Into Fear
The Long, Hot Summer (1958 version)
A Man for All Seasons (1966 version)
The Man Who Saw Tomorrow (narrator)
Moby Dick
The Muppet Movie
Napoleon (1955 version)
Necromancy
Someone to Love
Start the Revolution Without Me (narrator)
Ten Days Wonder
The Third Man
Tomorrow Is Forever
Transformers, The Movie (character voice)
The VIPs
The Vikings (narrator)
Voyage of the Damned
Waterloo

DT135 William Wellman (1896–1975)
Across the Wide Missouri
Battleground
Beau Geste (1939 version)
Blood Alley
Buffalo Bill
Goodbye, My Lady
Heroes for Sale
Lady of Burlesque
Magic Town
The Next Voice You Hear
Night Nurse
Nothing Sacred
The Ox-Bow Incident
Public Enemy
A Star Is Born (1937 version)
Wings

DT136 Wim Wenders (1945–)
Alice in the Cities
The American Friend
The Goalie's Anxiety at the Penalty Kick
Hammett
Kings of the Road
Lightning Over Water
Notebook on Cities and Clothes
Paris, Texas
The Scarlet Letter (1980 version)
The State of Things
Tokyo-Ga
Wings of Desire
Wrong Move

DT137 Lina Wertmuller (1928–)
All Screwed Up

Blood Feud
Camorra
Joke of Destiny
Love and Anarchy
A Night Full of Rain
The Seduction of Mimi
Seven Beauties
Sotto . . . Sotto
Summer Night
Swept Away

DT138 James Whale (1896–1957)
The Bride of Frankenstein
Frankenstein (1931 version)
Hell's Angels (uncredited)
The Invisible Man
The Man in the Iron Mask (1939 version)
Show Boat (1936 version)
Sinners in Paradise
Wives Under Suspicion

DT139 Billy Wilder (1906–)
The Apartment
Buddy Buddy
Double Indemnity
Fedora
The Fortune Cookie
The Front Page (1974 version)
Irma La Douce
Kiss Me, Stupid
The Lost Weekend
Love in the Afternoon
One, Two, Three
The Private Life of Sherlock Holmes
Sabrina
The Seven Year Itch
Some Like It Hot
The Spirit of St. Louis
Stalag 17
Sunset Boulevard
Witness for the Prosecution (1957 version)

DT140 Robert Wise (1914–)
The Andromeda Strain
Audrey Rose
Blood on the Moon
The Body Snatcher
Born To Kill
Criminal Court
The Curse of the Cat People
The Day the Earth Stood Still
The Desert Rats
Executive Suite
The Haunting
The Hindenburg
I Want to Live!
Mademoiselle Fifi
Rooftops
Run Silent, Run Deep
The Sand Pebbles

The Set-Up
Somebody Up There Likes Me
The Sound of Music
Star Trek—The Motion Picture
Two for the Seesaw
West Side Story (co-director)

DT141 Ed Wood, Jr. (1922–1978)
Bride of the Monster
Glen or Glenda?
Jail Bait
Plan 9 from Outer Space
Revenge of the Dead
The Sinister Urge
The Violent Years

DT142 William Wyler (1902–1981)
Ben-Hur
The Best Years of Our Lives
The Big Country
Carrie (1952)
The Children's Hour
The Collector
Come and Get It (co-director)
Dead End
The Desperate Hours
Dodsworth
Friendly Persuasion
Funny Girl
The Heiress
Jezebel
The Letter
The Liberation of L.B. Jones

The Little Foxes
Mrs. Miniver
Roman Holiday
These Three
The Westerner
Wuthering Heights (1939 version)

DT143 Robert Zemeckis (1952–)
Back to the Future
Back to the Future, Part II
Back to the Future, Part III
Death Becomes Her
I Wanna Hold Your Hand
Romancing the Stone
Tales From the Crypt (1989; co-director)
Used Cars
Who Framed Roger Rabbit

DT144 Fred Zinnemann (1907–)
Behold a Pale Horse
The Day of the Jackal
Five Days One Summer
From Here to Eternity
High Noon
Julia
A Man for All Seasons (1966 version)
Member of the Wedding
The Men
The Nun's Story
Oklahoma!
The Search
The Seventh Cross
The Sundowners

7 Family/Children's (FA)

FA1 Disney Live Action Features
  Action/Adventure
    Comedy
    Documentary
    Drama
    Horror/Mystery/Suspense
    Musical
    Science Fiction/Fantasy
    Western
FA2 Disney Animated Features
FA3 Classic Literature
FA4 Family Adventure

FA5 Animal Stories
FA6 Comedy
FA7 Dramas About Contemporary Kids
FA8 Science Fiction/Fantasy
FA9 Musicals
FA10 Non-Disney Animated Features
FA11 Warner Brothers Cartoon Collections
FA12 Faerie Tale Theatre Check List
FA13 Christmas Stories
FA14 The Muppets Check List
FA15 Kids in Jeopardy

FA1 Disney Live Action Features

ACTION/ADVENTURE
Benji the Hunted
Black Arrow (1984 version)
Cheetah
Condorman
Davy Crockett
Davy Crockett and the River Pirates
A Far Off Place
The Fighting Prince of Donegal
The Great Locomotive Chase
Homeward Bound: The Incredible Journey
In Search of the Castaways
The Incredible Journey
Island at the Top of the World
The Journey of Natty Gann
Kidnapped (1960 version)
King of the Grizzlies
The Last Flight of Noah's Ark
The Light in the Forest
Lightning: The White Stallion
Miracle of the White Stallions
Nikki, Wild Dog of the North
The Rocketeer
Shipwrecked
Swiss Family Robinson
The Sword and the Rose
Ten Who Dared
Third Man on the Mountain
Toby Tyler
Treasure Island (1950 version)
20,000 Leagues Under the Sea
White Fang
The Wild Country
COMEDY
The Absent-Minded Professor

The Barefoot Executive
The Billion Dollar Hobo
Blackbeard's Ghost
The Boatniks
Bon Voyage!
Candleshoe
The Cat from Outer Space
The Computer Wore Tennis Shoes
The Devil and Max Devlin
Freaky Friday
Gus
Herbie Goes Bananas
Herbie Goes to Monte Carlo
Herbie Rides Again
The Horse in the Gray Flannel Suit
Lt. Robin Crusoe, USN
Lots of Luck
The Love Bug
The Million Dollar Duck
The Misadventures of Merlin Jones
Monkeys Go Home!
The Monkey's Uncle
Moon Pilot
Never a Dull Moment (1968)
No Deposit, No Return
The North Avenue Irregulars
Now You See Him, Now You Don't
The One and Only Genuine Original Family
  Band
The Parent Trap
The Shaggy D.A.
The Shaggy Dog
Snowball Express
Son of Flubber
Superdad
That Darn Cat

The Trouble With Angels
The World's Greatest Athlete
DOCUMENTARY
The Living Desert
Secrets of Life
The Vanishing Prairie
White Wilderness
DRAMA
Almost Angels
Amy
The Blue Yonder
Charley and the Angel
Child of Glass
Follow Me, Boys!
The Girl Who Spelled Freedom
Greyfriars Bobby
Johnny Tremain
The Littlest Horse Thieves
The Littlest Outlaw
Napoleon and Samantha
Night Crossing
Pollyanna
So Dear to My Heart
Summer Magic
Those Calloways
A Tiger Walks
Wild Hearts Can't Be Broken
HORROR/MYSTERY/SUSPENSE
Emil and the Detectives
Escape from Witch Mountain
The Moon-Spinners
Return to Witch Mountain
The Watcher in the Woods
MUSICAL
Babes in Toyland
The Happiest Millionaire
Mary Poppins
Pete's Dragon
SCIENCE FICTION/FANTASY
Bedknobs and Broomsticks
The Black Hole
Darby O'Gill and the Little People
The Gnome-Mobile
The Three Lives of Thomasina
Tron
Unidentified Flying Oddball
WESTERN
The Adventures of Bullwwip Griffin
The Apple Dumpling Gang
The Apple Dumpling Gang Rides Again
The Castaway Cowboy
Hot Lead and Cold Feet
Old Yeller
One Little Indian
Savage Sam
Smith!

FA2 Disney Animated Features
Aladdin
Alice in Wonderland (1951 version)
Bambi
Beauty and the Beast (1991 version)
The Brave Little Toaster
Cinderella (1950 version)
Duck Tales: The Movie—Treasure of the Lost
   Lamp
Dumbo
Fantasia
The Great Mouse Detective
The Jungle Book (1967 version)
Lady and the Tramp
The Legend of Sleepy Hollow
The Little Mermaid (1989 version)
101 Dalmatians
Peter Pan (1953 version)
Pinocchio (1940 version)
The Rescuers
The Rescuers Down Under
Robin Hood (1973)
Sleeping Beauty (1959 version)
The Sword in the Stone
The Three Caballeros
The Wind in the Willows

FA3 Classic Literature
The Adventures of Huckleberry Finn (1939,
   1960, and 1985 versions)
The Adventures of Tom Sawyer (1938 and
   1973 versions)
Alice in Wonderland (1951 version)
Alice's Adventures in Wonderland
Anne of Green Gables
Captains Courageous
Casey at the Bat
A Connecticut Yankee in King Arthur's Court
   (1949 version)
David Copperfield
Great Expectations
Heidi (1937 version)
Huckleberry Finn
The Legend of Sleepy Hollow (1980 version)
Little Lord Fauntleroy (1936 and 1980
   versions)
Mysterious Island
Oliver Twist (1922, 1933, and 1948 versions)
The Prince and the Pauper (1937 and 1978
   versions)
The Secret Garden (1949 version)
Tom Brown's School Days (1940 version)
Tom Sawyer
Treasure Island (1934, 1950, and 1990
   versions)
20,000 Leagues Under the Sea

FA4 Family Adventure
Across the Great Divide
The Adventures of Robin Hood
The Adventures of the Wilderness Family
The Amazing Mr. Blunden

Any Friend of Nicholas Nickleby Is a Friend
  of Mine
Archer's Adventure
Around the World in 80 Days
Around the World Under the Sea
At the Earth's Core
The Black Pirate
Brighty of the Grand Canyon
Captain Sinbad
Clarence, the Cross-Eyed Lion
Cold River
Courage Mountain
The Crimson Pirate
The Dove
Five Weeks in a Balloon
Freddie as F.R.O.7.
Gunga Din
Hatari!
Hook
Island of the Blue Dolphins
Ivanhoe
Jack the Giant Killer
The Journey of Natty Gann
Journey to the Center of the Earth (1959 and
  1989 versions)
The Jungle Book (1942 version)
Kim
King Solomon's Mines (1950 version)
The Legend of Wolf Mountain
The Life and Times of Grizzly Adams
Lionheart (1987)
Lives of a Bengal Lancer
The Man in the Iron Mask (1939 and 1977
  versions)
The Mark of Zorro (1920 and 1940 versions)
Mountain Family Robinson
My Pet Monster
My Side of the Mountain
Mysterious Island
Never Cry Wolf
The New Adventures of Pippi Longstocking
Olly, Olly, Oxen Free
Orphan Train
Pippi Longstocking (series)
Prince Valiant
The Prisoner of Zenda (1937 version)
The Quest
The Railway Children
Return to Oz
Scaramouche
The Scarlet Pimpernel
The Sea Gypsies
Superman (series)
Sword of the Valiant
Tarzan and His Mate
Tarzan and the Trappers
Tarzan Escapes
Tarzan Finds a Son!
Tarzan, the Ape Man (1932 version)
Tarzan, the Fearless

Tarzan's New York Adventure
Tarzan's Revenge
Tarzan's Secret Treasure
Teenage Mutant Ninja Turtles
Teenage Mutant Ninja Turtles II: The Secret
  of the Ooze
Teenage Mutant Ninja Turtles III: The Turtles
  Are Back—in Time
The Thief of Bagdad (1940 version)
Treasure Island (1934, 1950, and 1990
  versions)
Wee Willie Winkie
When the North Wind Blows
The Wilderness Family, Part 2
Young Sherlock Holmes

FA5 Animal Stories
All Creatures Great and Small
The Amazing Dobermans
The Bear
Beethoven
Benji
Benji Takes a Dive at Marineland
Benji the Hunted
Big Red
Bingo
Black Beauty (1946 and 1971 versions)
The Black Stallion
The Black Stallion Returns
Blue Fire Lady
Born Free
Brighty of the Grand Canyon
Casey's Shadow
Challenge to Lassie
Charlie, the Lonesome Cougar
Cheetah
Christian the Lion
Clarence, the Cross-Eyed Lion
Courage of Lassie
The Day of the Dolphin
A Dog of Flanders
Flipper
Flipper's New Adventure
For the Love of Benji
The Golden Seal
Goldy: The Last of the Golden Bears
Goodbye, My Lady
Hambone and Hillie
Homeward Bound: The Incredible Journey
The Incredible Journey
International Velvet
It's a Dog's Life
Lassie Come Home
The Legend of Lobo
Lightning: The White Stallion
Living Free
The Magic of Lassie
Mighty Joe Young
The Miracle of the White Stallions
Misty

National Velvet
Nikki, Wild Dog of the North
Oh, Heavenly Dog!
Old Yeller
Phar Lap
The Red Pony (1949 and 1973 versions)
Ring of Bright Water
Son of Lassie
The Story of Seabiscuit
Sylvester
Where the Red Fern Grows
Where the Red Fern Grows, Part Two
White Fang
Wild Hearts Can't Be Broken
The Yearling
Zebra in the Kitchen

FA6 Comedy
See also: Director Check Lists DT24 Charlie
    Chaplin, DT66 Buster Keaton; Star Check
    Lists ST1 Abbott and Costello, ST120
    Danny Kaye, ST133 Laurel and Hardy,
    ST152 The Marx Brothers
Almost an Angel
Beethoven
Big Girls Don't Cry . . . They Get Even
Big Top Pee-wee
Billie
C.H.O.M.P.S.
A Christmas Story
Cinderfella
The Courtship of Eddie's Father
Ernest Goes to Camp
Ernest Goes to Jail
Ernest Saves Christmas
Ernest Scared Stupid
General Spanky
The Great Race
Hawmps!
Hollywood or Bust
Home Alone
Home Alone 2: Lost in New York
Honey, I Blew Up the Kid
Honey, I Shrunk the Kids
If It's Tuesday, This Must Be Belgium
It's a Mad Mad Mad Mad World
Little Miss Marker (1980 version)
The Long, Long Trailer
Matilda
Matinee
Mom and Dad Save the World
Oh God!
Oh God! Book II
Oh God! You Devil
On the Right Track
The Peanut Butter Solution
Pee-wee's Big Adventure
Please Don't Eat the Daisies
The Prize Fighter
Purple People Eater

Short Circuit
Short Circuit 2
Suburban Commando
They Went That-a-Way and That-a-Way
Those Daring Young Men in Their Jaunty
    Jalopies
Those Magnificent Men in Their Flying
    Machines
Three Men and Baby
Three Men and a Little Lady
3 Ninjas
The Young Magician
Who Framed Roger Rabbit
With Six You Get Eggroll
Yours, Mine and Ours

FA7 Dramas About Contemporary Kids
Amazing Grace and Chuck
Big Shots
Birch Interval
Bless the Beasts and Children
Blue Fin
The Boy Who Could Fly
Casey's Shadow
The Champ (1979 version)
D.A.R.Y.L.
The Dirt Bike Kid
The Double McGuffin
The Earthling
The Escape Artist
Fast Talking
From the Mixed-Up Files of Mrs. Basil E.
    Frankweiler
The Girl Who Spelled Freedom
Gregory's Girl
A Hero Ain't Nothin' But a Sandwich
Hot Shot
I Am the Cheese
Jimmy the Kid
The Karate Kid
The Karate Kid, Part II
The Karate Kid, Part III
A Kid for Two Farthings
Little Man Tate
Lucas
The Mighty Ducks
My Girl
My Side of the Mountain
Paradise
The Peanut Butter Solution
The Pistol: The Birth of a Legend
Rad
Savannah Smiles
Somewhere Tomorrow
Tiger Bay
Tiger Town
Where the Lilies Bloom
Where the River Runs Black
Whistle Down the Wind
The Wizard

FA8 Science Fiction/Fantasy
See also: SF13 Family Fantasy/Sci-Fi
The Adventures of Baron Münchausen
Aladdin
*batteries not included
Battle for the Planet of the Apes
Beneath the Planet of the Apes
The Brothers Lionheart
The Canterville Ghost (1968 version)
Clarence
Close Encounters of the Third Kind
Conquest of the Planet of the Apes
The Dark Crystal
The Day the Earth Stood Still
E.T.—The Extra-Terrestrial
The Empire Strikes Back
The Enchanted Forest
Escape From the Planet of the Apes
Explorers
The 5,000 Fingers of Dr. T
Flight of the Navigator
From the Earth to the Moon
The Golden Voyage of Sinbad
Heartbeeps
The Hobbit
The Incredible Mr. Limpet
The Incredible Shrinking Man
Jason and the Argonauts
King Kong (1933 version)
Labyrinth
The Land of Faraway
Little Monsters
Little Nemo: Adventures in Slumberland
Lord of the Rings
Masters of the Universe
The NeverEnding Story
The NeverEnding Story II: The Next Chapter
Once Upon a Midnight Scary
The Phantom Tollbooth
Planet of the Apes
Return of the Jedi
The 7 Faces of Dr. Lao
The 7th Voyage of Sinbad
Sinbad and the Eye of the Tiger
Something Wicked This Way Comes
Spaced Invaders
Star Trek (series)
Star Wars
Thief of Bagdad (1940 version)
Time Bandits
The Time Machine
tom thumb
Tuck Everlasting
The War of the Worlds
The Watcher in the Woods
The Water Babies
Willie Wonka and the Chocolate Factory
Willow
The Witches
The Wonderful World of the Brothers Grimm

FA9 Musicals
Annie
Bugsy Malone
Camelot
Carousel
Chitty Chitty Bang Bang
Cinderella (1964 version)
A Connecticut Yankee in King Arthur's Court
   (1949 version)
Doctor Dolittle
Fiddler on the Roof
Follow That Bird
The Glass Slipper
Half a Sixpence
Hans Christian Andersen
A Hard Day's Night
Help!
Jesus Christ Superstar
The King and I
Li'l Abner
March of the Wooden Soldiers
Mary Poppins
Meet Me in St. Louis
The Music Man
My Fair Lady
Newsies
Oklahoma!
Oliver!
The Pirates of Penzance
Popeye
1776
Singin' in the Rain
The Sound of Music
South Pacific
State Fair (1945 and 1962 versions)
West Side Story
Willie Wonka and the Chocolate Factory
The Wiz
The Wizard of Oz (1939 version)
Yankee Doodle Dandy

FA10 Non-Disney Animated Features
The Adventures of an American Rabbit
The Adventures of Mark Twain
Alakazam the Great
All Dogs Go to Heaven
An American Tail
An American Tail: Fievel Goes West
Animalympics
Babar: The Movie
Bon Voyage, Charlie Brown
A Boy Named Charlie Brown
The Care Bears Movie
Charlotte's Web
The Chipmunk Adventure
Dorothy in the Land of Oz
The Dragon That Wasn't (Or Was He?)
Ferngully . . . The Last Rainforest
The Flight of the Dragons
Freddie as F.R.O.7.

Gnomes, Vol. 1
Gulliver's Travels (1939 version)
Here Come the Littles
Hey There, It's Yogi Bear
The Hobbit
It's an Adventure, Charlie Brown
Jetsons: The Movie
Journey Back to Oz
Journey Through Fairyland
The Land Before Time
The Last Unicorn
The Lion, the Witch and the Wardrobe
Little Nemo: Adventures in Slumberland
Lord of the Rings
Mad Monster Party?
A Man Called Flintstone
My Little Pony: The Movie
The Nutcracker Prince
Pinocchio and the Emperor of Night
Puff the Magic Dragon
Quackbusters
Rock-a-Doodle
Scruffy
The Secret of NIMH
Shinbone Alley
Snoopy Come Home
Starchaser: The Legend of Orin
Teddy Ruxpin: Teddy Outsmarts M.A.V.O.
Transformers: The Movie
Watership Down
The Wizard of Oz (1982 version)

FA11 Warner Brothers Cartoon Collections

The Best of Bugs Bunny and Friends
Bugs and Daffy: The Wartime Cartoons
Bugs and Daffy's Carnival of the Animals
Bugs Bunny and Elmer Fudd Cartoon Festival
Bugs Bunny Cartoon Festival
Bugs Bunny Classics
Bugs Bunny in King Arthur's Court
The Bugs Bunny/Road Runner Movie
Bugs Bunny Superstar
Bugs Bunny's 3rd Movie: 1001 Rabbit Tales
Bugs Bunny's Wacky Adventures
Cartoon Movietstars: Bugs!
Cartoon Movietstars: Daffy!
Cartoon Movietstars: Elmer!
Cartoon Movietstars: Porky!
Daffy Duck Cartoon Festival
Daffy Duck: The Nuttiness Continues
Daffy Duck's Movie: Fantastic Island
Elmer Fudd Cartoon Festival
Elmer Fudd's Comedy Capers
Foghorn Leghorn's Fractured Funnies
The Golden Age of Looney Tunes
The Looney, Looney, Looney Bugs Bunny
  Movie
Pepe LePew's Skunk Tales
Porky Pig and Daffy Duck Cartoon Festival

Road Runner vs. Wile E. Coyote: The Classic
  Chase
A Salute to Chuck Jones
A Salute to Friz Freleng
A Salute to Mel Blanc

FA12 Faerie Tale Theatre Check List

Aladdin and His Wonderful Lamp
Beauty and the Beast (1984 version)
The Boy Who Left Home to Find Out About
  the Shivers
Cinderella (1984 version)
The Dancing Princesses
The Emperor's New Clothes
Goldilocks and the Three Bears
Hansel and Gretel
Jack and the Beanstalk (1983 version)
The Little Mermaid (1984 version)
Little Red Riding Hood
The Nightingale
The Pied Piper of Hamelin
Pinocchio (1984 version)
The Princess and the Pea
The Princess Who Never Laughed
Puss In Boots
Rapunzel
Rip Van Winkle
Rumpelstiltskin
Sleeping Beauty (1985 version)
Snow Queen
Snow White and the Seven Dwarfs (1983
  version)
The Tale of the Frog Prince
The Three Little Pigs
Thumbelina

FA13 Christmas Stories

All I Want for Christmas
Beyond Tomorrow
The Bishop's Wife
A Christmas Carol (1938 and 1951 versions)
The Christmas Coal Mine Miracle
Christmas in Connecticut
Christmas Lilies of the Field
A Christmas Story
A Christmas to Remember
The Christmas Tree
Comfort and Joy
A Dream for Christmas
Ernest Saves Christmas
Holiday Affair
Home Alone
It Came Upon a Midnight Clear
It's a Wonderful Life
The Kid Who Loved Christmas
The Man in the Santa Claus Suit
Miracle Down Under
Miracle on 34th Street
The Muppet Christmas Carol
National Lampoon's Christmas Vacation

The Nutcracker Prince
Nutcracker, the Motion Picture
One Magic Christmas
Prancer
Santa Claus—The Movie
Scrooge (1935 and 1970 versions)
Scrooged

FA14 The Muppets Check List
Children's Songs and Stories With the
   Muppets
Country Music with the Muppets
Fozzie's Muppet Scrapbook
The Great Muppet Caper
The Kermit and Piggy Story
The Muppet Christmas Carol
Muppet Moments
The Muppet Movie
The Muppet Revue
Muppet Treasures
The Muppets Take Manhattan
Rock Music With the Muppets
Rowlf's Rhapsodies With the Muppets

FA15 Kids in Jeopardy
Adventures in Babysitting
Courage Mountain
D.A.R.Y.L.

E.T.—The Extra-Terrestrial
The Earthling
Empire of the Sun
The Escape Artist
Escape to Witch Mountain
Explorers
A Far Off Place
The 5,000 Fingers of Dr. T
Flight of the Navigator
The Goonies
Home Alone
Home Alone 2: Lost in New York
Honey, I Shrunk the Kids
Hook
Journey for Margaret
Labyrinth
The Legend of Wolf Mountain
On the Right Track
The Orphan Train
Paper Tiger
Return from Witch Mountain
Shipwrecked
Time Bandits
Treasure Island (1934, 1950, and 1990
   versions)
Where the Lilies Bloom
Wildflower
The Wizard

8 Foreign Films (FF)

FF1 France
  Action/Adventure
  Comedy
  Drama
  Horror
  Musicals
  Mystery/Suspense
  Science Fiction/Fantasy
FF2 Italy
  Action/Adventure
  Comedy
  Drama
  Horror
  Mystery/Suspense
  Science Fiction/Fantasy
FF3 Germany
  Action/Adventure
  Comedy
  Drama
  Horror
  Musical
  Mystery/Suspense
  Science Fiction/Fantasy
FF4 Japan
  Action/Adventure
  Drama
  Horror
  Science Fiction/Fantasy
FF5 Australia/New Zealand
  Action/Adventure

  Comedy
  Drama
  Musical
  Mystery/Suspense
  Science Fiction/Fantasy
FF6 Latin America
  Argentina
  Brazil
  Cuba
  Mexico
  Nicaragua
FF7 Other Countries of the World
  Canada
  (Peoples' Republic of) China
  Czechoslovakia
  Denmark
  Finland
  Greece
  Holland
  Hungary
  India
  Poland
  Soviet Union
  Spain
  Sweden
  Switzerland
  Yugoslavia
FF8 Foreign Films & Their American
  Remakes

FF1 France
See also: Director Check Lists DT50 Jean-Luc
  Godard, DT104 Jean Renoir, DT107 Eric
  Rohmer, DT122 Jacques Tati, DT123 Ber-
  trand Tavernier, DT125 François Truffaut
ACTION/ADVENTURE
The Bear
Bob le Flambeur
L'Addition
La Balance
La Femme Nikita
Quest for Fire
Swashbuckler (1984)
COMEDY
A Nous la Liberte
The Baker's Wife
Black and White in Color
Buffet Froid
César
Cousin, Cousine
The Crazy Ray
Delicatessen
Donkey Skin
Fanny (1932 version)
Get Out Your Handkerchiefs
Happy New Year (1973 version)
High Heels
Italian Straw Hat
La Cage aux Folles
La Cage aux Folles II
La Cage aux Folles III: The Wedding
La Chevre
Le Bourgeois Gentilhomme
Le Million
Le Sex Shop
Les Compères

Lovers Like Us
Marius
May Fools
Mon Oncle d'Amerique
Murmur of the Heart
My New Partner
Next Year, If All Goes Well
A Pain in the A—
Pardon Mon Affaire
Princess Tam-Tam
Robert et Robert
Salut l'Artiste
The Tall Blonde Man With One Black Shoe
Three Men and a Cradle
Too Beautiful for You
Under the Roofs of Paris
A Very Curious Girl
Zazie dans le Metro
Zero for Conduct
DRAMA
A Coeur Joie
A Nos Amours
Act of Aggression
And Now, My Love
Au Revoir, Les Enfants
Bad Girls
Beau Pere
Betty Blue
Camille Claudel
Cesar and Rosalie
Children of Paradise
Chocolat
Choice of Arms
Cyrano de Bergerac (1990 version)
Diary of a Chambermaid (1964 version)
Diary of a Country Priest
The Double Life of Veronique
Entre Nous
The Eternal Return
Forbidden Games
The Game Is Over
Going Places
The Grand Highway
Heart of a Nation
Heat of Desire
Hiroshima, Mon Amour
I Love All of You
I Sent a Letter to My Love
Indochine
J'Accuse
Jean de Florette
L'Année des Meduses
L'Atalante
La Boum
La Passante
La Ronde
La Truite
La Vie Continue
Le Jour Se Lève
Les Liaisons Dangereuses

The Lacemaker
Last Year at Marienbad
The Little Thief
Lola (1961)
Loulou
Love and the Frenchwoman
Love Songs
The Lover
Lumière
Madame Bovary (1991 version)
Madame Rosa
Maitresse
A Man and a Woman
A Man and a Woman: 20 Years Later
Manon of the Spring
Melo
Mr. Klein
The Moon in the Gutter
My Father's Glory
My Mother's Castle
Mysteries
Nana (1955 version)
Napoleon (1927)
The Passion of Joan of Arc
Police
Providence
Ramparts of Clay
Rape of Love
Rendez-vous
The Return of Martin Guerre
The Rise of Louis XIV
A Simple Story
State of Siege
Stavisky
Sugar Cane Alley
Sundays and Cybèle
Swann in Love
Therese
Toto le Heros
Tous les Matins du Monde
Under Satan's Sun
Uranus
Vagabond
Vincent, François, Paul and the
   Others
Volpone
HORROR
Eyes Without a Face
MUSICALS
Le Bal
The Umbrellas of Cherbourg
Zou Zou
MYSTERY/SUSPENSE
The Bride Wore Black
Cat and Mouse
Dear Detective
Diabolically Yours
Diabolique
Diva
Investigation

Jupiter's Thigh
Le Doulos
Melodie en Sous-Sol
Monsieur Hire
Rider on the Rain
Rififi
Scene of the Crime
Sincerely, Charlotte
Sois Belle et Tais-Toi
This Man Must Die
The Wages of Fear
Wedding in Blood
Z
SCIENCE FICTION/FANTASY
Beauty and the Beast (1946 version)
Blood of a Poet
Fantastic Planet
Le Dernier Combat

FF2 Italy

See also: Director Check Lists DT5 Michelangelo Antonioni, DT13 Bernardo Bertolucci, DT35 Vittorio De Sica, DT43 Federico Fellini, DT109 Roberto Rossellini, DT127 Luchino Visconti, DT137 Lina Wertmuller
ACTION/ADVENTURE
Hercules
Mean Frank and Crazy Tony
COMEDY
All the Way, Boys
Big Deal on Madonna Street
Divorce—Italian Style
Down and Dirty
General Della Rovere
The Icicle Thief
The Immortal Bachelor
Lady of the Evening
Lovers and Liars
Lunatics and Lovers
Macaroni
Madigan's Millions
Malicious
Mediterraneo
Seduced and Abandoned
Sex With a Smile
Shoot Loud, Louder . . . I Don't Understand
We All Loved Each Other So Much
Where's Picone?
Wifemistress
DRAMA
Allonsanfan
The Battle of Algiers
Brother Sun, Sister Moon
Burn!
China Is Near
Christ Stopped at Eboli
Cinema Paradiso
Dark Eyes
Devil in the Flesh
The Eyes, The Mouth

The Family (1987)
The Gospel According to St. Matthew
Henry IV
The Inheritance
Kaos
La Grande Bourgeoise
La Nuit de Varennes
Massacre in Rome
The Night of the Shooting Stars
1900
Open City
Padre Padrone
Paisan
Passion of Love
Sacco and Vanzetti
A Special Day
Stromboli
Teorema
Three Brothers
Time of Indifference
The Tree of the Wooden Clogs
HORROR
Beyond the Door
Beyond the Door 2
Twitch of the Death Nerve
MYSTERY/SUSPENSE
The Bird with the Crystal Plumage
SCIENCE FICTION/FANTASY
The Tenth Victim

FF3 Germany

See also: Director Check Lists DT42 Rainer Werner Fassbinder, DT54 Werner Herzog, DT136 Wim Wenders
ACTION/ADVENTURE
Das Boot
The Testament of Dr. Mabuse
The Thousand Eyes of Dr. Mabuse
COMEDY
Men . . .
Sugarbaby
DRAMA
The Blue Angel
Christiane F.
Coup de Grace
Diary of a Lost Girl
Europa, Europa
Faust
The Inheritors
Joyless Street
Kameradschaft
Kamikaze '89
Kriemhilde's Revenge
The Last Laugh
The Lost Honor of Katharina Blum
M (1931 version)
Maedchen in Uniform (1931 version)
A Man Like Eva
The Nasty Girl
Pandora's Box

Passion (1918)
Siegfried
Spies
The Tin Drum
Tonio Kroger
Variety
The Wannsee Conference
The White Rose
Westfront 1918
Woman in Flames
Zentropa
HORROR
The Cabinet of Dr. Caligari
The Golem
MUSICAL
The Threepenny Opera
MYSTERY/SUSPENSE
Spiders
SCIENCE FICTION/FANTASY
Destiny
Metropolis
The NeverEnding Story
The NeverEnding Story II: The Next
   Chapter

FF4 Japan
See also: Director Check List DT69 Akira
   Kurosawa
ACTION/ADVENTURE
The Gambling Samurai
Kojiro
The One-Eyed Swordsman
Samurai Saga
The Samurai Trilogy
Shogun Assassin
Sword of Doom
Zatoichi Vs. Yojimbo
COMEDY
The Family Game
Tampopo
A Taxing Woman
DRAMA
The Ballad of Narayama
Black Rain (Jap.)
Double Suicide
Early Summer
Fires on the Plain
Floating Weeds
The Forty-seven Ronin, Part One
The Forty-seven Ronin, Part Two
Gate of Hell
The Go Masters
The Golden Demon
Himatsuri
The Human Condition
In the Realm of the Senses
Irezumi
The Island (1962)
Late Chrysanthemums
The Life of Oharu

MacArthur's Children
The Makioka Sisters
Merry Christmas, Mr. Lawrence
Mishima
Mother
Odd Obsession
Rikisha-Man
Saga of the Vagabonds
Sansho the Bailiff
Street of Shame
Tokyo Story
Ugetsu
When a Woman Ascends the Stairs
Woman in the Dunes
HORROR
The Ghost of Yotsuya
Kwaidan
SCIENCE FICTION/FANTASY
Akira
Ghidrah, the Three-Headed
   Monster
Godzilla, King of the Monsters
Godzilla 1985
Godzilla on Monster Island
Godzilla vs. Megalon
Godzilla vs. Monster Zero
Godzilla vs. Mothra
Gorath
The H-Man
The Human Vapor
The Last War
Mothra
The Mysterians
Robot Carnival
Rodan
Terror of Mechagodzilla
Tetsuo: The Iron Man

FF5 Australia/New Zealand
ACTION/ADVENTURE
Escape 2000
Fortress
Forty Thousand Horsemen
The Lighthorsemen
Mad Dog Morgan
Mad Max
Mad Max Beyond Thunderdome
The Man From Snowy River
The Odd Angry Shot
The Quest
Razorback
Return to Snowy River, Part II
The Road Warrior
Walk Into Hell
We of the Never Never
COMEDY
Barry McKenzie Holds His Own
Bliss
The Cars That Ate Paris
Crocodile Dundee

Crocodile Dundee II
Don's Party
Malcolm
Norman Loves Rose
Rikky and Pete
Spotswood
Touch and Go (1980)
Young Einstein
DRAMA
An Angel at My Table
Breaker Morant
Burke and Wills
Cactus
Caddie
Careful, He Might Hear You
Chain Reaction
The Club
A Cry in the Dark
A Dangerous Summer
Dawn!
The Devil's Playground
Dingo
Flirting
The Fringe Dwellers
The Getting of Wisdom
The Good Woman of Bangkok
Ground Zero
Heatwave
High Rolling
High Tide
Kangaroo
The Killing of Angel Street
Kitty and the Bagman
The Last Days of Chez Nous
The Last Wave
Lonely Hearts
Man of Flowers
The Mango Tree
Miracle Down Under
My Brilliant Career
My First Wife
Newsfront
Now and Forever
Picnic at Hanging Rock
Prisoners of the Sun
Proof
Puberty Blues
Rebel (1986)
Shame (1988)
Sleeping Dogs
Squizzy Taylor
Storm Boy
Summer City
Tim
A Town Like Alice
Traveling North
Turtle Beach
Warm Nights on a Slow-Moving
  Train
Weekend of Shadows

Who Killed Baby Azaria
The Wild Duck
Winter of Our Dreams
A Woman's Tale
The Year My Voice Broke
MUSICAL
Dogs in Space
Starstruck
MYSTERY/SUSPENSE
Dead Calm
Patrick
SCIENCE FICTION/FANTASY
The Time Guardian

FF6 Latin America
See also: Director Check List DT19 Luis
  Buñuel
ARGENTINA
Antonio das Mortes
Apartment Zero
Camila
Man Facing Southeast
Miss Mary
The Official Story
Subway to the Stars
BRAZIL
Black Orpheus
Bye Bye Brazil
Dona Flor and Her Two Husbands
Gabriela
Hour of the Star
I Love You
Kiss of the Spider Woman
Lady on the Bus
Pixote
CUBA
Memories of Underdevelopment
MEXICO
Erendira
NICARAGUA
Alsino and the Condor

FF7 Other Countries of the World
See also: Director Check Lists DT3 Pedro
  Almodóvar, DT11 Ingmar Bergman,
  DT19 Luis Buñuel, DT41 Sergei Eisenstein,
  DT102 Satyajit Ray, DT130 Andrzej Wajda
CANADA
The Decline of the American Empire
Jesus of Montreal
Mon Oncle
(PEOPLE'S REPUBLIC OF) CHINA
Ju Dou
Raise the Red Lantern
CZECHOSLOVAKIA
Closely Watched Trains
Ecstasy
The Firemen's Ball
Loves of a Blonde
The Shop on Main Street

DENMARK
Babette's Feast
Pelle the Conqueror
FINLAND
Ariel
GREECE
Iphigenia
HOLLAND
The Assault
The Fourth Man
A Question of Silence
Spetters
Turkish Delight
The Vanishing (1988 version)
HONG KONG
The Killer
HUNGARY
Colonel Redl
Father
Mephisto
My Twentieth Century
The Revolt of Job
Time Stands Still
INDIA
Salaam Bombay!
POLAND
The Double Life of Veronique
Knife in the Water
Moonlighting (1982)
Year of the Quiet Sun
(THE FORMER) SOVIET UNION
Arsenal
The Commissar
Earth
The End of St. Petersburg
Little Vera
Moscow Does Not Believe in
    Tears
The Overcoat
Repentance
Shadows of Forgotten Ancestors
A Slave of Love
Storm Over Asia
Taxi Blues
War and Peace (1968 version)
SPAIN
Carmen
El Amor Brujo
Half of Heaven
Holy Innocents
Lovers
The Spirit of the Beehive

SWEDEN
The Best Intentions
Elvira Madigan
The Flight of the Eagle
Intermezzo (1936 version)
June Night
My Life as a Dog
The Sacrifice
Swedenhielms
Witchcraft Through the Ages
SWITZERLAND
The Boat Is Full
Journey of Hope
(THE FORMER) YUGOSLAVIA
Hey Babu Riba
Montenegro
WR—Mysteries of the Organism
When Father Was Away on Business

FF8 Foreign Films and their American Remakes

Boudou Saved From Drowning/Down and
    Out in Beverly Hills
Breathless (1959)/Breathless (1983)
Cousin, Cousine/Cousins
Diabolique/Reflections of Murder
Doña Flor and Her Two Husbands/Kiss Me
    Goodbye
The Grand Highway/Paradise
Happy New Year (1973)/Happy New Year
    (1987)
Intermezzo (1936)/Intermezzo (1939)
Jules and Jim/Willie and Phil
La Bête Humaine/Human Desire
La Chevre/Pure Luck
La Chienne/Scarlet Street
La Femme Nikita/Point of No Return
La Vie Continue/Men Don't Leave
The Man Who Loved Women (1977)/The
    Man Who Loved Women (1983)
A Pain in the A—/Buddy Buddy
Pardon Mon Affaire/The Woman in Red
The Return of Martin Guerre/Sommersby
The Seduction of Mimi/Which Way Is Up?
The Seven Samurai/The Magnificent Seven
The Tall Blonde Man With One Black Shoe/
    The Man With One Red Shoe
Three Men and a Cradle/Three Men and a
    Baby
The Vanishing (1988)/The Vanishing (1993)
The Virgin Spring/Last House on the Left
Wages of Fear/Sorcerer
Yojimbo/A Fistful of Dollars

9 Historical/Fictional Character (HF)

HF1	Billy the Kid (William Bonney)	**HF12**	Adolf Hitler
HF2	James Bond	**HF13**	Doc Holliday
HF3	Buffalo Bill (William F. Cody)	**HF14**	Sherlock Holmes
HF4	Charlie Chan	**HF15**	Robin Hood
HF5	Nick and Nora Charles	**HF16**	Jesse James
HF6	George Armstrong Custer	**HF17**	Jesus Christ
HF7	Dracula	**HF18**	Abraham Lincoln
HF8	Bulldog Drummond	**HF19**	Napoleon (Bonaparte)
HF9	Wyatt Earp	**HF20**	Annie Oakley
HF10	The Frankenstein Monster	**HF21**	The Saint
HF11	Wild Bill Hickok	**HF22**	Tarzan

HF1 Billy the Kid (William Bonney)
(1859–1881)
Bill and Ted's Excellent Adventure
Billy the Kid Returns
Gore Vidal's Billy the Kid
The Left-Handed Gun
The Outlaw
Pat Garrett and Billy the Kid
Return of the Badmen
Young Guns
Young Guns II

HF2 James Bond (created 1953 by Ian
Fleming)
Casino Royale
Diamonds Are Forever
Dr. No
For Your Eyes Only
From Russia With Love
Goldfinger
Happy Anniversary 007: 25 Years of James Bond
Licence to Kill
Live and Let Die
The Living Daylights
The Man With the Golden Gun
Moonraker
Never Say Never Again
Octopussy
On Her Majesty's Secret Service
The Spy Who Loved Me
Thunderball
A View to a Kill
You Only Live Twice

HF3 Buffalo Bill (William F. Cody)
(1846–1917)
Annie Oakley

Buffalo Bill
Buffalo Bill and the Indians
The Plainsman (1936)
Pony Express
Young Buffalo Bill

HF4 Charlie Chan (created 1925 by Earl
Derr Biggers)
Castle in the Desert
Charlie Chan and the Curse of the Dragon
  Queen
Charlie Chan at the Opera
Charlie Chan at the Wax Museum
Charlie Chan in Paris
Charlie Chan in Rio
Charlie Chan's Secret
The Chinese Cat
The Jade Mask
Meeting at Midnight
Murder by Death
Murder Over New York
The Scarlet Clue
The Secret Service
The Shanghai Cobra

HF5 Nick and Nora Charles (created 1932
by Dashiell Hammett)
After the Thin Man
Another Thin Man
Shadow of the Thin Man
Song of the Thin Man
The Thin Man
The Thin Man Goes Home

HF6 George Armstrong Custer
(1839–1876)
Little Big Man
The Plainsman (1936)

Santa Fe Trail
Son of the Morning Star
They Died With Their Boots On

HF7 Dracula (created 1897 by Bram Stoker)
Abbott and Costello Meet Frankenstein
Andy Warhol's Dracula
Blacula
Bram Stoker's Dracula
The Brides of Dracula
Count Dracula
Count Dracula and His Vampire Bride
Dr. Terror's Gallery of Horrors
Dracula (1931, 1973, and 1979 versions)
Dracula (1931 Spanish version)
Dracula and Son
Dracula vs. Frankenstein
Dracula's Daughter
The Horror of Dracula
House of Frankenstein
Legend of the Seven Golden Vampires
Love at First Bite
The Magic Christian
The Monster Club
Nosferatu
Scars of Dracula
The Seven Brothers Meet Dracula
Son of Dracula

HF8 Bulldog Drummond (created 1920
by H.C. Melleile)
Bulldog Drummond
Bulldog Drummond at Bay
Bulldog Drummond Comes Back
Bulldog Drummond Escapes
Bulldog Drummond in Africa
Bulldog Drummond Strikes Back
Bulldog Drummond's Bride
Bulldog Drummond's Peril
Bulldog Drummond's Revenge
Bulldog Drummond's Secret Police

HF9 Wyatt Earp (1848–1929)
Cheyenne Autumn
Gunfight at the O.K. Corral
Hour of the Gun
My Darling Clementine
Wichita
Winchester '73

HF10 The Frankenstein Monster
(created 1818 by Baron Frankenstein and
Mary Shelley)
Abbott and Costello Meet Frankenstein
Andy Warhol's Frankenstein
The Bride
The Bride of Frankenstein
The Curse of Frankenstein
Dracula vs. Frankenstein
The Evil of Frankenstein

Frankenstein (1931, 1973, and 1982 versions)
Frankenstein and the Monster From Hell
Frankenstein Meets the Wolf Man
Frankenstein—1970
Frankenstein Unbound
Frankenweenie
The Horror of Frankenstein
House of Frankenstein
The Monster Club
Robot Carnival
Son of Frankenstein
The Spirit of the Beehive
Transylvania 6-5000
Young Frankenstein

HF11 Wild Bill Hickok (1837–1876)
Calamity Jane
Little Big Man
The Plainsman (1936)
Pony Express
The White Buffalo
Young Bill Hickok

HF12 Adolf Hitler (1869–1945)
Battle of Britain
The Desert Fox
The Great Dictator
Highway to Hell
Hitler
Hitler—Dead or Alive
Hitler: The Last Ten Days
Inside the Third Reich
The Miracle of Morgan's Creek
To Be or Not To Be (1942 and 1983 versions)
Which Way to the Front?
Zelig

HF13 Doc Holliday (1849–1885)
Cheyenne Autumn
Gunfight at the O.K. Corral
Hour of the Gun
My Darling Clementine
The Outlaw

HF14 Sherlock Holmes (created 1889 by
Arthur Conan Doyle)
The Adventures of Sherlock Holmes
Dressed to Kill (1946)
The Hound of the Baskervilles (1938, 1959,
and 1977 versions)
House of Fear
Masks of Death
Murder by Decree
Pearl of Death
The Private Life of Sherlock Holmes
Pursuit to Algiers
The Scarlet Claw
The Seven Percent Solution
Sherlock Holmes and the Incident at Victoria
Falls

Sherlock Holmes and the Secret Weapon
Sherlock Holmes and the Voice of Terror
Sherlock Holmes Faces Death
Sherlock Holmes in Washington
The Silver Blaze
The Speckled Band
Spider Woman
A Study in Scarlet
A Study in Terror
Terror by Night
They Might Be Giants
The Triumph of Sherlock Holmes
Without a Clue
The Woman in Green
Young Sherlock Holmes

HF15 Robin Hood (legendary character of
medieval song and story)
The Adventures of Robin Hood
Ivanhoe
Robin and Marian
Robin Hood (1973)
Robin Hood (1991)
Robin Hood and the Sorcerer
Robin Hood: Prince of Thieves
Sword of Sherwood Forest
Time Bandits

HF16 Jesse James (1847–1882)
Best of the Badmen
Days of Jesse James
The Great Northfield, Minnesota Raid
I Shot Jesse James
Jesse James
Jesse James at Bay
The Long Riders

HF17 Jesus Christ
Bad Lieutenant
Barabbas
Ben-Hur
Ben-Hur: A Tale of Christ
The Favor, the Watch, and the Very Big Fish
The Gospel According to St. Matthew
Greaser's Palace
The Greatest Story Ever Told
The History of the World, Part I
Intolerance
Jesus Christ Superstar
Jesus of Nazareth
The King of Kings (1927 and 1961 versions)
The Last Temptation of Christ
The Messiah
The Milky Way (1970)
The Nativity
The Ruling Class
Whistle Down the Wind

HF18 Abraham Lincoln (1809–1865)
Abe Lincoln in Illinois
Abraham Lincoln
Anthony Adverse
Bill and Ted's Excellent Adventure
The Birth of a Nation
The Blue and the Gray
How the West Was Won
The Littlest Rebel
The Plainsman
Santa Fe Trail
They Died With Their Boots On
Young Mr. Lincoln

HF19 Napoleon (1769–1821)
Anthony Adverse
The Battle of Austerlitz
Bill and Ted's Excellent Adventure
Conquest
Desiree
Love and Death
Napoleon (1927 and 1955 versions)
Time Bandits
War and Peace (1956 and 1968 versions)
Waterloo

HF20 Annie Oakley (1860–1926)
Annie Oakley
Buffalo Bill and the Indians
The Plainsman (1936)

HF21 The Saint (created 1929 by Leslie
Chartens)
The Saint in London
The Saint in New York
The Saint Strikes Back
The Saint Takes Over
The Saint's Vacation

HF22 Tarzan (created 1914 by Edgar Rice
Burroughs)
Greystoke: The Legend of Tarzan, Lord of the
  Apes
Tarzan and His Mate
Tarzan and the Green Goddess
Tarzan and the Trappers
Tarzan Escapes
Tarzan Finds a Son!
Tarzan of the Apes
Tarzan, the Ape Man (1932 and 1981
  versions)
Tarzan the Fearless
Tarzan's New York Adventure
Tarzan's Revenge
Tarzan's Secret Treasure

10 Horror (HO)

See also: Writer Check Lists WR12 Stephen King, WR21 Edgar Allan Poe

---

HO1 Classic Horror
The Beast With Five Fingers
The Black Cat
The Body Snatcher
The Bride of Frankenstein
The Cabinet of Dr. Caligari
Cat People (1942 version)
Curse of the Demon
Dead of Night (1945)
The Devil Doll
Dr. Jekyll and Mr. Hyde (1920, 1932, and
    1941 versions)
Doctor X
Dracula (1931 version)
Eyes Without a Face
Frankenstein (1931 version)
Frankenstein Meets the Wolf Man
Freaks
The Golem
The Haunting
The Horror of Dracula
House of Wax
I Walked with a Zombie
The Invisible Man (1933 version)
King Kong (1933 version)
M
Mad Love
The Mask of Fu Manchu
The Masque of the Red Death (1964 version)
The Mummy (1932 version)
The Mummy's Hand

The Mystery of the Wax Museum
Nosferatu
The Phantom of the Opera (1925 version)
The Picture of Dorian Gray (1945 version)
Psycho
The Raven (1935)
Son of Dracula
Son of Frankenstein
The Uninvited
Werewolf of London
White Zombie
The Wolf Man

HO2 Ghost Stories
The Changeling
The Curse of the Cat People
Dark Places
Dead of Night (1945)
The Fog
The Ghost Breakers
Ghost Story
The Haunting
The Haunting of Julia
Lady in White
Legend of Hell House
Poltergeist
Poltergeist II
Poltergeist III
Scared Stiff
The Shining
Sole Survivor

The Supernaturals
13 Ghosts
Turn of the Screw
The Uninvited
The Watcher in the Woods

HO3 Haunted Houses
The Amityville Horror
Amityville II: The Possession
Amityville 3-D
The Bat
Burnt Offerings
Castle of Blood
The Evil
The Ghost Breakers
The Haunted Palace
The Haunting
The Haunting of Julia
House
House on Haunted Hill
House II: The Second Story
The House Where Evil Dwells
Legend of Hell House
The People Under the Stairs
Poltergeist
Poltergeist II
Scared Stiff
The Shining
13 Ghosts
Twice Dead
The Watcher in the Woods
Witchtrap
You'll Find Out

HO4 Werewolves
An American Werewolf in London
The Beast Must Die
The Beast Within
The Company of Wolves
The Curse of the Werewolf
The Howling
The Howling II
Howling III: The Marsupials
The Howling IV
Legend of the Werewolf
Mad at the Moon
Silver Bullet
Teen Wolf
Werewolf of London
The Werewolf of Washington
The Wolf Man
Wolfen

HO5 Vampires
See also: Fictional Character Check List HF7
    Dracula
Andy Warhol's Dracula
Blacula
Blood Couple
The Bloodsuckers

Bram Stoker's Dracula
The Brides of Dracula
Buffy the Vampire Slayer
Captain Kronos: Vampire Hunter
Children of the Night
Count Dracula
Count Dracula and His Vampire Bride
Count Yorga, Vampire
Dance of the Damned
Daughters of Darkness
Dracula (1931, 1973, and 1979 versions)
Dracula (1931 Spanish version)
Dracula and Son
Dracula's Daughter
The Fearless Vampire Killers
Fright Night
Fright Night II
Graveyard Shift (1987)
The Horror of Dracula
The Hunger
Innocent Blood
Lair of the White Worm
Legend of the Seven Golden Vampires
Lifeforce
The Lost Boys
Love at First Bite
Lust for a Vampire
Mark of the Vampire
Martin
Near Dark
Nosferatu
The Reflecting Skin
A Return to Salem's Lot
The Return of the Vampire
Rockula
Salem's Lot
Scars of Dracula
The Seven Brothers Meet Dracula
Son of Dracula
To Sleep with a Vampire
Vamp
The Vampire Lovers
Vampire Over London
Vampire's Kiss
Vampyr

HO6 Zombies
Carnival of Souls
Children Shouldn't Play With Dead Things
Dawn of the Dead
Day of the Dead
Dead and Buried
Dead Heat
Deathdream
Hard Rock Zombies
I Walked with a Zombie
Isle of the Dead
Night of the Living Dead (1968 and 1990
    versions)
Pet Sematary Two

Psychomania
The Return of the Living Dead
Revenge of the Zombies
The Serpent and the Rainbow
Sometimes They Come Back
The White Zombie
Zombie
Zombie Island Massacre

HO7 People With Psychic Powers
Black Rainbow
Cameron's Closet
Carrie (1976)
Creepers
Dark Forces
The Dead Zone
The Evil Mind
The Eyes of Laura Mars
The Fury
The Initiation of Sarah
Jennifer
The Medusa Touch
Patrick
Scanners
Scanners II: The New Order
The Shout
Sweet 16

HO8 Tales of Possession
The Awakening
Beyond the Door
Beyond the Door 2
The Boogeyman
Child's Play
Child's Play 2
Child's Play 3
Dark Places
Diary of a Madman
The Evil Dead
The Evil Dead 2: Dead by Dawn
The Exorcist
Exorcist II: The Heretic
Exorcist III: Legion
The Haunted Palace
The Haunting of Morella
Horror Express
I'm Dangerous Tonight
Magic
Mausoleum
Nightbreed
Nothing But the Night
The Possession of Joel Delaney
Repossessed

HO9 Psycho Killers
Alone in the Dark
The Bird With the Crystal Plumage
Blood and Black Lace
The Brute Man
Chamber of Horrors

Daughter of Horror
Deep Red
Don't Answer the Phone
Exorcist III: Legion
Eyeball
Eyes of a Stranger
Fade to Black
The First Power
Halloween
Halloween II
Halloween 4: The Return of Michael Myers
Halloween 5: The Revenge of Michael Myers
Happy Birthday to Me
He Knows You're Alone
The Hitcher
Honeymoon
The Human Monster
Jack the Ripper
The Love Butcher
Myers
The Night Visitor
The Phantom of the Opera (1925, 1943, and
    1989 versions)
Popcorn
Psycho
Psycho II
Psycho III
Schizoid
Shocker
Silent Night, Deadly Night
Slumber Party Massacre
Twitch of the Death Nerve

HO10 Deal With the Devil
Angel Heart
Angel on My Shoulder (1946 and 1980
    versions)
Bedazzled
Black Sunday (1961)
Blood on Satan's Claw
The Chosen (1978)
Damien: Omen II
Damn Yankees
Def by Temptation
The Devil and Daniel Webster
The Devil and Max Devlin
The Devil's Nightmare
The Devil's Partner
The Devil's Rain
Faust
The Final Conflict
The First Power
The Gate
Heaven Can Wait (1943)
Highway to Hell
Horror Hotel
Leonor
Limit Up
The Mephisto Waltz
Mister Frost

The Omen
Rosemary's Baby
The Seventh Victim
The Sorrows of Satan
Stay Tuned
To the Devil, a Daughter
The Unholy
The Visitor

HO11 Cults
Because of the Cats
The Believers
The Bloodsuckers
Brotherhood of Satan
Children of the Corn
Children of the Corn II: The Final Sacrifice
Curse of the Demon
The Dark Secret of Harvest Home
Deadly Blessing
The Devils
The Devil's Rain
The Devil's Undead
The Legacy
Legend of the Minotaur
Manos, The Hands of Fate
The Mephisto Waltz
Necromancy
Nomads
Nothing But the Night
Race With the Devil
Rosemary's Baby
Season of the Witch
The Seventh Victim
Videodrome
The Wicker Man

HO12 Teens in Trouble
April Fool's Day
Black Christmas
Brain Damage
Buffy the Vampire Slayer
Carrie (1976)
The Final Terror
Friday the 13th (series)
The Funhouse
Gate II
Graduation Day
Hell Night
The Initiation of Sarah
Killer Party
Last House on the Left
The Mutilator
A Nightmare on Elm Street (series)
Popcorn
Prom Night
Sleepaway Camp
Sleepwalkers
Sorority House Massacre
Summer Camp Nightmare
Suspiria

Terror Train
The Texas Chainsaw Massacre
There's Nothing Out There
Zombie High

HO13 Scary Kids
Audrey Rose
The Baby
The Bad Seed
The Beast Within
The Brood
Cameron's Closet
Children of the Corn
Children of the Corn II: The Final
  Sacrifice
Children of the Damned
Damien: Omen II
Evilspeak
The Exorcist
Exorcist II: The Heretic
Firestarter
The Godsend
It Lives Again
It's Alive
It's Alive III: Island of the Alive
Jennifer
The Kindred
The Little Girl Who Lives Down the Lane
The Lost Boys
The Omen
Village of the Damned

HO14 Bad Blood: Horror Stories About Families
See also: HO15 Evil Twins
Arnold
The Beast in the Cellar
Children of the Night
Crucible of Horror
The Curse
The Curse of the Cat People
Daughter of Dr. Jekyll
Dementia 13
Don't Look Now
Eraserhead
Flowers in the Attic
The Guardian
Hellbound: Hellraiser II
Hellraiser
The Hills Have Eyes
The Kiss (1988)
Near Dark
The Oblong Box
The Possession of Joel Delaney
Psycho Sisters
Pumpkinhead
The Reflecting Skin
Seizure
Severed Ties
Sister, Sister (1987)

Sleepwalkers
The Texas Chainsaw Massacre
The Texas Chainsaw Massacre 2
What Ever Happened to Baby Jane?

HO15 Evil Twins
Basket Case
Basket Case II
Basket Case 3: The Progeny
The Black Room
Blood Link
Dead Men Walk
Dead Ringers
The Man Who Haunted Himself
The Other
Raising Cain
Sisters
Twins of Evil

HO16 Animals and Other Creepy Creatures
Alligator
Ants!
Arachnophobia
Ben
The Birds
Bug
Child's Play
Child's Play 2
Child's Play 3
Creature from Black Lake
Creepers
Critters
Critters 2: The Main Course
Cujo
Deepstar Six
Dogs of Hell
Dolls
Dolly Dearest
Eaten Alive
Frogs
Ghoulies
Graveyard Shift (1990)
Gremlins
Gremlins 2: The New Batch
Humanoids from the Deep
In the Shadow of Kilimanjaro
Jaws (series)
King Kong (1933 and 1976 versions)
The Leopard Man
The Leprechaun
Link
Monkey Shines: An Experiment in Fear
The Nest
Nightwing
Of Unknown Origin
Orca
The Pack
Pet Sematary

Pin
Piranha
Piranha II: The Spawning
Puppet Master
Q
Razorback
The Runestone
Squirm
Swamp Thing
The Swarm
Tremors
Trolls
The Uncanny
Venom
Willard
Wolfen

HO17 Memorable Transformations
An American Werewolf in London
The Company of Wolves
Demons
Dr. Jekyll and Mr. Hyde (1932 version)
The Fly (1986 version)
The Howling
Tetsuo: The Iron Man
The Thing
The Wolf Man

HO18 Gory Horror
Basket Case
Basket Case 2
Basket Case 3: The Progeny
Blood Feast
Bride of Re-Animator
Dawn of the Dead
Day of the Dead
Dr. Butcher, M.D.
The Evil Dead
The Evil Dead 2: Dead by Dawn
Frankenhooker
Friday the 13th (series)
Maniac (1980)
Mother's Day
Night of the Living Dead (1968 and 1990 versions)
Nightbreed
A Nightmare on Elm Street (series)
Rabid
Re-Animator
The Return of the Living Dead
Zombie

HO19 Scary But Not Bloody
See also: HO1 Classic Horror
The Amityville Horror
The Beast With Five Fingers
The Body Snatcher
The Cat People (1942 version)
The Changeling
Coma

Curse of the Demon
The Dead Zone
Don't Look Now
Dracula (1979 version)
Freaks
Fright Night
The Ghost Breakers
Ghost Story
The Haunting
The Haunting of Julia
House
House of the Long Shadows
House of Wax
House on Haunted Hill
Lady in White
Link
Mad Love
Magic
The Mask of Fu Manchu
The Mummy's Hand
Poltergeist
Rosemary's Baby
Scared Stiff
Something Wicked This Way Comes
Strait-Jacket
13 Ghosts
Turn of the Screw
The Uninvited

HO20 Science Runs Amok
See also: Fictional Character Check List HF10
   The Frankenstein Monster; SF5 Science
   Gone Wrong
The Abominable Dr. Phibes
Andy Warhol's Frankenstein
The Ape
Atom Age Vampire
Body Parts
The Brain That Wouldn't Die
The Bride
The Bride of Frankenstein
Bride of Re-Animator
Circus of Horrors
The Curse of Frankenstein
Darkman
Daughter of Dr. Jekyll
Deadly Friend
Dr. Giggles
Dr. Jekyll and Mr. Hyde (1920, 1932, 1941,
   and 1973 versions)
Dr. Phibes Rises Again
Eyes Without a Face
Fiend Without a Face
Flatliners
The Fly (1958 and 1986 versions)
The Fly II
Frankenhooker
Frankenstein (1931, 1973, and 1982 versions)
Frankenstein Unbound
From Beyond

Halloween III: Season of the Witch
The Happiness Cage
House of Frankenstein
The Invisible Man
The Island of Dr. Moreau
The Lawnmower Man
Link
Mad Love
The Man They Could Not Hang
The Man Who Lived Again
Mania
Murders in the Rue Morgue
Nightmare Weekend
Re-Animator
The Return of the Fly
Scream and Scream Again
Screamers
Severed Ties
Son of Frankenstein
The Sorcerers
Terminal Choice
The Terminal Man
The Vampire Bat
Watchers
Werewolf of London

HO21 Mutant Monsters
C.H.U.D.
City of the Walking Dead
Class of Nuke 'Em High
The Crazies
The Curse
The Cyclops
The Invisible Ray
Mutant
Night of the Creeps
Severed Ties
Slithis
The Toxic Avenger
Transmutations
Tremors
The Wasp Woman

HO22 Mad Machinery
Chopping Mall
Christine
Demon Seed
The Lift
Maximum Overdrive
Tetsuo: The Iron Man
Videodrome

HO23 Horror Anthologies
Asylum
Black Sabbath
Cat's Eye
Creepshow
Creepshow 2
Dead of Night (1945)
Dr. Terror's House of Horrors

Escapes
From Beyond the Grave
Grim Prairie Tales
The House That Dripped Blood
The Monster Club
Night Gallery
Nightmares
The Offspring
Once Upon a Midnight Scary
Tales From the Crypt (1972)
Tales From the Crypt (1989)
Tales From the Darkside: The Movie
Tales of Terror
Torture Garden
Trilogy of Terror
Twice-Told Tales
Twilight Zone—The Movie
The Uncanny

HO24 Horror For Laughs
The Addams Family
An American Werewolf in London
Andy Warhol's Dracula
Andy Warhol's Frankenstein
Arnold
Basket Case II
Buffy the Vampire Slayer
Comedy of Terrors
Critters
Critters 2: The Main Course
Dr. Giggles
The Fearless Vampire Killers
The Ghost Breakers
Ghosts on the Loose
Gremlins
Gremlins 2: The New Batch
Highway to Hell
Hillbillys in a Haunted House
The Little Shop of Horrors (1960 version)
Love at First Bite
Microwave Massacre
The Monster Squad
Motel Hell
Piranha
The Plumber
Psychos in Love
Repossessed
Return of the Living Dead
Scared Stiff
Slaughterhouse
The Stuff
Terror at Red Wolf Inn
Theatre of Blood
There's Nothing Out There
The Toxic Avenger
Transylvania Twist
Tremors
Vamp
Witches' Brew
You'll Find Out

HO25 Sexy Horror
Because of the Cats
Bram Stoker's Dracula
Cat People (1982 version)
Def by Temptation
Demon Seed
The Entity
From Beyond
Gothic
The Haunting of Morella
Humanoids from the Deep
Innocent Blood
Lair of the White Worm
Lust for a Vampire
The Vampire Lovers

HO26 Horror With a British Accent
The Abominable Dr. Phibes
And Now the Screaming Starts
Asylum
The Beast in the Cellar
Bloodbath at the House of Death
The Brides of Dracula
Captain Kronos: Vampire Hunter
Children of the Damned
Circus of Horrors
The Conqueror Worm
Count Dracula and His Vampire Bride
The Creeping Flesh
The Curse of Frankenstein
The Curse of the Werewolf
Dead of Night (1945)
The Doctor and the Devils
Dr. Phibes Rises Again
Dr. Terror's House of Horrors
The Evil of Frankenstein
Frankenstein and the Monster From Hell
From Beyond the Grave
The Ghoul (1933)
The Ghoul (1975)
The Gorgon
The Haunting of Julia
Horror of Dracula
The Horror of Frankenstein
Legend of the Seven Golden Vampires
Lust for a Vampire
The Man Who Lived Again
Mania
The Mummy (1959 version)
Nothing But the Night
The Picture of Dorian Gray (1945 version)
Scars of Dracula
Scream and Scream Again
The Seven Brothers Meet Dracula
The Skull
Tales From the Crypt (1972)
Terror in the Wax Museum
Theatre of Blood
To the Devil, a Daughter
Turn of the Screw

Vampire Over London
Village of the Damned
The Watcher in the Woods

HO27 Val Lewton Check List
Bedlam
The Body Snatcher

Cat People (1942 version)
The Curse of the Cat People
I Walked with a Zombie
Isle of the Dead
The Leopard Man
Mademoiselle Fifi
The Seventh Victim

11 Musicals (MU)

MU1 MGM Musicals	**MU10** Rock Concert Films
MU2 The Best of Broadway	**MU11** Rock Documentaries
MU3 Great Dancing Musicals	**MU12** Films With Pop Stars in Non-Musical Roles
MU4 Musical Films About Show Biz	**MU13** All Black Musicals
MU5 Musical Life Stories	**MU14** Musical Remakes of Non-Musical Films
MU6 Musical Americana	**MU15** Musical Revues
MU7 Musicals That Won Major Oscars	**MU16** Strangest Musicals
MU8 Fantasies and Fairy Tales	**MU17** Non-Singing Actors in Musical Roles
MU9 Rock Musicals	

MU1 MGM Musicals

An American in Paris
Anchors Aweigh
Athena
Babes in Arms
Babes on Broadway
The Band Wagon
The Barkleys of Broadway
Bathing Beauty
Because You're Mine
Bells Are Ringing
Born To Dance
Brigadoon
Broadway Melody of 1936
Broadway Melody of 1938
Broadway Melody of 1940
Broadway Rhythm
Broadway Serenade
The Cat and the Fiddle
Cover Girl
Dangerous When Wet
Duchess of Idaho
Easter Parade
Easy To Love
The Firefly
Gigi
Girl Crazy
Going Hollywood
Good News
The Great Caruso
The Harvey Girls
High Society
Hit the Deck
Holiday in Mexico
Honolulu
I Dood It
In the Good Old Summertime
Invitation to the Dance
It's Always Fair Weather

Jupiter's Darling
Kismet
Kiss Me Kate
Les Girls
Lili
Love Is Better Than Ever
Meet Me in St. Louis
The Merry Widow (1952 version)
Million Dollar Mermaid
My Dream Is Yours
Nancy Goes to Rio
Neptune's Daughter
On an Island With You
On the Town
The Opposite Sex
Pagan Love Song
Panama Hattie
The Pirate
Rich, Young and Pretty
Romance on the High Seas
Rose Marie
Royal Wedding
Seven Brides for Seven Brothers
Show Boat (1951 version)
Ship Ahoy
Silk Stockings
Singin' in the Rain
Skirts Ahoy!
Small Town Girl
Strike Up the Band
The Student Prince
Summer Stock
Sweet Adeline
Take Me Out to the Ball Game
Texas Carnival
That Midnight Kiss
That's Entertainment!
That's Entertainment, Part 2
Three Little Words

Thrill of a Romance
Till the Clouds Roll By
Two Girls and a Sailor
Two Weeks With Love
The Unsinkable Molly Brown
The Wizard of Oz
Words and Music
Ziegfeld Follies
Ziegfeld Girl

MU2 The Best of Broadway
Annie
The Best Little Whorehouse in Texas
Brigadoon
Bye Bye Birdie
Cabaret
Camelot
Can-Can
Carousel
A Chorus Line
Damn Yankees
Fiddler on the Roof
Finian's Rainbow
Flower Drum Song
42nd Street
Funny Girl
A Funny Thing Happened on the Way to the
    Forum
Grease
Guys and Dolls
Hair
Hello, Dolly!
How to Succeed in Business Without Really
    Trying
Jesus Christ, Superstar
The King and I
Kismet
Kiss Me Kate
Li'l Abner
A Little Night Music
Mame
Man of La Mancha
The Music Man
My Fair Lady
Oh! Calcutta!
Oklahoma!
Oliver!
One Touch of Venus
Paint Your Wagon
The Pajama Game
Pal Joey
Panama Hattie
Pippin
Purlie Victorious
Rio Rita
1776
Show Boat (1936 and 1951 versions)
The Sound of Music
South Pacific
Sweeney Todd

Sweet Charity
West Side Story
The Wiz

MU3 Great Dancing Musicals
See also: Director Check List DT8 Busby
    Berkeley; Star Check Lists ST2 Fred Astaire,
    ST123 Gene Kelly
All That Jazz
Best Foot Forward
The Boy Friend
Carmen
A Chorus Line
Dirty Dancing
Flashdance
Footloose
Good News
Invitation to the Dance
Pennies From Heaven
The Red Shoes
Saturday Night Fever
Seven Brides for Seven Brothers
Stormy Weather
Sweet Charity
Tap
That's Dancing!
West Side Story

MU4 Musical Films About Show Biz
See also: CL7 Show Business Stories, DR12
    Backstage Dramas
All That Jazz
Babes in Arms
Babes on Broadway
The Band Wagon
The Barkleys of Broadway
The Boy Friend
Breaking Glass
Broadway Melody
Broadway Melody of 1936
Broadway Melody of 1938
Broadway Melody of 1940
Broadway Rhythm
Broadway Serenade
Bye Bye Birdie
Carmen
A Chorus Line
Crossover Dreams
Dames
Eddie and the Cruisers
Eddie and the Cruisers II: Eddie Lives!
Fame
Footlight Parade
For Me and My Gal
42nd Street
Give My Regards to Broad Street
Going Hollywood
Gold Diggers of 1933
Gold Diggers of 1935
Give a Girl a Break

Holiday Inn
The Idolmaker
It Happened in Brooklyn
It's a Date
The Jazz Singer (1927 and 1980 versions)
Jumbo
Les Girls
Light of Day
Love Is Better Than Ever
Lucky Me
Lullaby of Broadway
Mr. Music
My Dream Is Yours
Nancy Goes to Rio
New York, New York
One Night of Love
Orchestra Wives
Phantom of the Paradise
Presenting Lily Mars
The Rose
Show Boat (1936 and 1951 versions)
Singin' in the Rain
Sparkle
Springtime in the Rockies
A Star Is Born (1954 and 1976 versions)
Starstruck
Staying Alive
Step Lively
Stormy Weather
The Story of Vernon and Irene Castle
Strike Up the Band
Summer Stock
Sun Valley Serenade
Swing Time
That Midnight Kiss
That'll Be the Day
There's No Business Like Show Business
Tonight and Every Night
Wasn't That a Time!
White Christmas
Wonder Man
You'll Never Get Rich
Young Man With a Horn
Ziegfeld Follies

MU5 Musical Life Stories
Amadeus (Mozart)
The Benny Goodman Story
Bird (Charlie Parker)
Bound for Glory (Woody Guthrie)
The Buddy Holly Story
Coal Miner's Daughter (Loretta Lynn)
Deep in My Heart (Sigmund Romberg)
The Doors
The Fabulous Dorseys
The Eddy Duchin Story
Elvis: The Movie
The Five Pennies (Red Nichols)
Funny Girl (Fanny Brice)
Funny Lady (Fanny Brice)

The Glenn Miller Story
Great Balls of Fire (Jerry Lee Lewis)
The Great Caruso
The Great Waltz (Johann Strauss)
The Great Ziegfeld
Gypsy (Gypsy Rose Lee)
Hear My Song (Josef Locke)
I'll See You in My Dreams (Gus Kahn)
Jolson Sings Again
The Jolson Story
La Bamba (Ritchie Valens)
Lady Sings the Blues (Billie Holiday)
Lizstomania
Love Me or Leave Me (Ruth Etting)
Mahler
The Music Lovers (Petr Tchaikovsky)
Night and Day (Cole Porter)
Rhapsody in Blue (George Gershwin)
Seven Little Foys (Eddie Foy)
Sinatra
The Singing Nun (Soeur Sourire)
Song of Love (Robert and Clara Schumann)
Song of Norway (Edvard Grieg)
A Song to Remember (Frederic Chopin)
Song Without End (Franz Liszt)
The Sound of Music (Maria von Trapp)
Stars and Stripes Forever (John Philip Sousa)
The Story of Vernon and Irene Castle
Sweet Dreams (Patsy Cline)
This Is Elvis
Three Little Words (Bert Kalmar and Harry
    Ruby)
Yankee Doodle Dandy (George M. Cohan)
Till the Clouds Roll By (Jerome Kern)
Wagner
Words and Music (Richard Rodgers and
    Lorenz Hart)

MU6 Musical Americana
By the Light of the Silvery Moon
Bye Bye Birdie
Calamity Jane (1953)
Carousel
Damn Yankees
Easter Parade
Flower Drum Song
Good News
Guys and Dolls
The Harvey Girls
Holiday Inn
Li'l Abner
Louisiana Purchase
Meet Me in St. Louis
The Music Man
Nashville
New York, New York
Newsies
Oklahoma!
On Moonlight Bay
On the Town

Paint Your Wagon
Seven Brides for Seven Brothers
Show Boat (1936 and 1951 versions)
Stars and Stripes Forever
State Fair (1945 and 1962 versions)
Take Me out to the Ball Game
Texas Carnival
Thoroughly Modern Millie
The Unsinkable Molly Brown
The West Point Story
West Side Story
White Christmas
Yankee Doodle Dandy
Zoot Suit

MU7 Musicals That Won Major Oscars
An American in Paris
Broadway Melody
Cabaret
Funny Girl
Gigi
The Great Ziegfeld
The King and I
Mary Poppins
My Fair Lady
Oliver!
The Sound of Music
West Side Story
Yankee Doodle Dandy

MU8 Fantasies and Fairy Tales
Beauty and the Beast (1991 version)
Brigadoon
Cabin in the Sky
Camelot
Cinderella (1964 version)
A Connecticut Yankee in King Arthur's Court
Doctor Dolittle
Finian's Rainbow
The Glass Slipper
Kismet
Little Shop of Horrors (1986 version)
Mary Poppins
On a Clear Day You Can See Forever
Sergeant Pepper's Lonely Hearts Club Band
Tales of Hoffmann
Tommy
The Wiz
The Wizard of Oz
Xanadu
Yellow Submarine
Yolanda and the Thief

MU9 Rock Musicals
See also: Star Check List ST178 Elvis Presley
Absolute Beginners
Beat Street
The Blues Brothers
Body Rock
Breakin'

Breakin' 2: Electric Boogaloo
Breaking Glass
Bye Bye Birdie
Can't Stop the Music
The Commitments
Dogs in Space
Fame
Get Crazy
The Girl Can't Help It
Give My Regards to Broad Street
Graffiti Bridge
Grease
Grease 2
Hair
A Hard Day's Night
The Harder They Come
Head
Help!
The Idolmaker
Jesus Christ, Superstar
Magical Mystery Tour
One-Trick Pony
Phantom of the Paradise
Pink Floyd: The Wall
Purple Rain
Quadrophenia
Roadie
Rock 'n' Roll High Schol
Rock, Pretty Baby
Rock, Rock, Rock
The Rocky Horror Picture Show
The Rose
Running Out of Luck
Shake, Rattle and Rock
Shout
A Star Is Born (1976 version)
Starstruck
Tapeheads
Thank God, It's Friday
That'll Be the Day
Times Square
Tommy
200 Motels
Wild Style
Yellow Submarine

MU10 Rock Concert Films
The Concert for Bangladesh
Delicate Sound of Thunder
Divine Madness
Elvis—The 1968 Comeback Special
Get Back
Gimme Shelter
The Grateful Dead Movie
Heartland Reggae
Jimi Plays Berkeley
Joe Cocker: Mad Dogs and Englishmen
The Last Waltz
Let's Spend the Night Together
The MUSE Concert: No Nukes

Monterey Pop
Motown 25: Yesterday, Today, Forever
Nelson Mandela, 70th Birthday Tribute
Rust Never Sleeps
Sign O' the Times
Simon and Garfunkel: The Concert in
  Central Park
Soul to Soul
Stop Making Sense
That Was Rock
U2 Live at Red Rocks "Under a Blood Red Sky"
Woodstock
Ziggy Stardust and the Spiders From Mars

MU11 Rock Documentaries
The Beatles: The First U.S. Visit
Bring on the Night
Chuck Berry: Hail! Hail! Rock 'n' Roll
The Compleat Beatles
The Decline of Western Civilization
The Decline of Western Civilization II: The
  Metal Years
Don't Look Back
Elvis '56
Elvis on Tour
Elvis: That's the Way It Is
Imagine: John Lennon
Janis
Jimi Hendrix
The Kids Are Alright
Let It Be
The Song Remains the Same
This Is Elvis
This Is Spinal Tap
25 x 5: The Continuing History of the
  Rolling Stones
U2: Rattle and Hum
X, The Unheard Music

**MU12 Films with Pop Stars in Non-
Musical Roles**
See also: Star Check Lists ST4 Fred Astaire,
  ST29 Cher, ST40 Bing Crosby, ST81 Judy
  Garland, ST123 Gene Kelly, ST156 Bette
  Midler, ST178 Elvis Presley, ST199 Frank
  Sinatra, ST211 Barbra Streisand

Ruben Blades
Crazy From the Heart
Critical Condition
Dead Man Out
Disorganized Crime
Fatal Beauty
Homeboy
The Milagro Beanfield War
Mo' Better Blues
One Man's War
Predator 2
The Super
The Two Jakes

David Bowie
The Hunger
Into the Night
Just a Gigolo
Labyrinth
The Last Temptation of Christ
The Linguini Incident
The Man Who Fell to Earth
Merry Christmas, Mr. Lawrence
Twin Peaks: Fire Walk With Me

Kris Kristofferson
Alice Doesn't Live Here Anymore
Big Top Pee-wee
Blume in Love
Bring Me the Head of Alfredo Garcia
Convoy
Flashpoint
Heaven's Gate
The Last Movie
Millennium
Pat Garrett and Billy the Kid
Rollover
Semi-Tough
Another Pair of Aces: Three of a Kind
Trouble in Mind
Welcome Home

Sting
The Bride
Brimstone and Treacle
Dune
Julia and Julia
Plenty
Stormy Monday

Others
The Alamo (Frankie Avalon)
Another Pair of Aces: Three of a Kind (Willie
  Nelson)
At Play in the Fields of the Lord (Tom Waits)
Awakenings (Dexter Gordon)
Backtrack (Bob Dylan)
Barbarosa (Willie Nelson)
Basket Case 2 (Annie Ross)
Basket Case 3: The Progeny (Annie Ross)
Best Revenge (Levon Helm)
The Black Stallion (Hoyt Axton)
Bloodhounds of Broadway (Madonna)
Body of Evidence (Madonna)
Boomerang (Eartha Kitt)
Boyz N the Hood (Ice Cube)
Bram Stoker's Dracula (Tom Waits)
Buried Alive (1990-TV) (Hoyt Axton)
Buster (Phil Collins)
Captain Newman, M.D. (Bobby Darin)
Carnal Knowledge (Art Garfunkel)
Carny (Robbie Robertson)
Catch-22 (Art Garfunkel)
Caveman (Ringo Starr)
Certain Fury (Irene Cara)

China Gate (Nat King Cole)
Clue (Lee Ving)
Coal Miner's Daughter (Levon Helm)
Cold Feet (Tom Waits)
Conan the Destroyer (Grace Jones)
Corrupt (John Lydon)
Cry-Baby (Iggy Pop)
The Death Squad (Michelle Phillips)
Desire and Hell at the Sunset Motel (David
    Johansen)
Desperately Seeking Susan (Madonna)
Dillinger (Michelle Phillips)
The Dollmaker (Levon Helm)
Down by Law (John Lurie, Tom Waits)
Dudes (Lee Ving)
The Electric Horseman (Willie Nelson)
End of the Line (Levon Helm)
Enemy Territory (Ray Parker, Jr.)
Ernest Scared Stupid (Eartha Kitt)
Escape From New York (Isaac Hayes)
Escape to Athena (Sonny Bono)
Foxes (Cherie Curie)
Frankenstein Unbound (Michael Hutchence)
Freejack (Mick Jagger, David Johansen)
Goldilocks and the Three Bears (Carole King)
Gremlins (Hoyt Axton)
A Gunfight (Johnny Cash)
Hairspray (Ruth Brown, Debby Harry, and
    Sonny Bono)
Hamlet (1969 version) (Marianne Faithfull)
The Happy Ending (Robert [Bobby] Darin)
The Hard Way (LL Cool J)
Hardware (Iggy Pop)
Harry Tracy, Desperado (Gordon Lightfoot)
Heart Like a Wheel (Hoyt Axton)
Hook (Phil Collins, David Crosby)
How I Won the War (John Lennon)
Huckleberry Finn (Merle Haggard)
I'm Gonna Git You Sucka! (Isaac Hayes)
Into the Night (Carl Perkins)
Ironweed (Tom Waits)
Jo Jo Dancer, Your Life Is Calling (Carmen
    McRae and Billy Eckstine)
Juice (Cindy Herron)
The Krays (Gary and Martin Kemp)
A League of Their Own (Madonna)
Leap of Faith (Meat Loaf)
Let It Ride (David Johansen)
Lethal Weapon (Darlene Love)
Let's Get Harry (Glenn Frey)
Liar's Moon (Hoyt Axton)
Little Man Tate (Harry Connick, Jr.)
Lost Angels (Adam Horovitz)
Love at Large (Neil Young)
Mad Max Beyond Thunderdome (Tina
    Turner)
McVicar (Roger Daltrey)
The Magic Christian (Ringo Starr)
Memphis Belle (Harry Connick, Jr.)
The Milagro Beanfield War (Freddy Fender)

Modern Love (Frankie Valli)
Murder on the Bayou (Papa John Creach)
Mystery Train (Screamin' Jay Hawkins, Rufus
    Thomas, Joe Strummer, Tom Waits,
    and Sy Richardson)
Ned Kelly (Mick Jagger)
New Jack City (Ice-T)
The Nightingale (Mick Jagger)
Nine to Five (Dolly Parton)
Nomads (Adam Ant)
None But the Brave (Tommy Sands)
North Dallas Forty (Mac Davis)
North to Alaska (Fabian)
Oh, God! (John Denver)
One Trick Pony (Lou Reed)
Pat Garrett and Billy the Kid (Bob Dylan and
    Rita Coolidge)
The Player (Lyle Lovett)
Pressure Point (Bobby Darin)
Pump Up the Volume (Annie Ross)
Queens Logic (Tom Waits)
The Red-Headed Stranger (Willie Nelson)
The Right Stuff (Levon Helm)
Rio Bravo (Rick Nelson)
Roadie (Meat Loaf)
Roadside Prophets (John Doe, Adam
    Horovitz, Arlo Guthrie)
The Room (Annie Lennox)
Rumble Fish (Tom Waits)
Runaway (Gene Simmons)
The Running Man (Mick Fleetwood)
Rush (Gregg Allman)
Salvador (John Doe)
Sarafina! (Miriam Makeba)
Scrooged (David Johansen)
Shadows and Fog (Madonna)
Shanghai Surprise (Madonna)
Short Fuse (Art Garfunkel)
Siesta (Grace Jones)
Smooth Talk (Levon Helm)
Staying Together (Levon Helm)
Steel Magnolias (Dolly Parton)
Straight Talk (Dolly Parton)
Straight to Hell (Elvis Costello, Dick Rude,
    Joe Strummer, and Grace Jones)
Stranger Than Paradise (John Lurie)
Tales From the Darkside: The Movie
    (Deborah Harry and David Johansen)
Thief (Willie Nelson)
To Sir, With Love (Lulu, Michael Des Barres)
Toys (LL Cool J)
Tremors (Reba McIntire)
Trespass (Ice Cube, Ice-T)
True Grit (Glen Campbell)
Twin Peaks: Fire Walk With Me (Chris Isaak)
The Two Jakes (Tom Waits)
Union City (Deborah Harry)
Unnatural Causes (Patti LaBelle)
Vamp (Grace Jones)
Vibes (Cyndi Lauper)

Videodrome (Deborah Harry)
A View to a Kill (Grace Jones)
Voyage to the Bottom of the Sea (Frankie Avalon)
The Wackiest Ship in the Army (Rick Nelson)
Wanted: Dead or Alive (Gene Simmons)
Wayne's World (Meat Loaf)
Where the Day Takes You (Will Smith)
Who's That Girl (Madonna)
Zandalee (Aaron Neville)

MU13 All Black Musicals
Cabin in the Sky
The Duke Is Tops
Hallelujah
Lost in the Stars
Stormy Weather
The Wiz

MU14 Musical Remakes of Non-Musical Films
Bundle of Joy
Cabaret
Daddy Long Legs
The Farmer Takes a Wife (1953 version)
Goodbye, Mr. Chips (1969 version)
Hello, Dolly!
High Society
In the Good Old Summertime
Kid Galahad
Kiss Me Kate
A Little Night Music
Little Shop of Horrors (1986 version)
Mame
Miss Sadie Thompson
My Fair Lady
My Sister Eileen (1955 version)
The Old Curiosity Shop (1975 version)
Oliver!
The Opposite Sex
Phantom of the Paradise
Scrooge (1970 version)
Silk Stockings
A Song Is Born
A Star Is Born (1954 version)
Step Lively
Summer Holiday
Sweet Charity
Young at Heart

MU15 Musical Revues
Glorifying the American Girl
The King of Jazz
Stage Door Canteen
Thank Your Lucky Stars
That's Dancing!
That's Entertainment!
That's Entertainment, Part 2
Thousands Cheer

MU16 Strangest Musicals
Absolute Beginners
Aria
Bugsy Malone
The Fastest Guitar Alive
Forbidden Zone
Industrial Symphony No. 1—The Dream of the Broken Hearted
The Last Dragon
The Little Prince
Le Bal
Little Shop of Horrors (1986 version)
Murder at the Vanities
Never Steal Anything Small
One From the Heart
Pennies From Heaven
Pink Floyd: The Wall
The Rocky Horror Picture Show
Sergeant Pepper's Lonely Hearts Club Band
1776
The Umbrellas of Cherbourg

MU17 Non-Singing Actors in Musical Roles
The Best Little Whorehouse in Texas (Burt Reynolds)
Camelot (Richard Harris and Vanessa Redgrave)
Doctor Dolittle (Rex Harrison)
Goodbye, Mr. Chips (1969 version) (Peter O'Toole)
Guys and Dolls (Marlon Brando)
Honkytonk Man (Clint Eastwood)
Idiot's Delight (Clark Gable)
A Little Night Music (Elizabeth Taylor)
Man of La Mancha (Peter O'Toole and Sophia Loren)
My Fair Lady (Rex Harrison)
Paint Your Wagon (Clint Eastwood and Lee Marvin)
Yankee Doodle Dandy (James Cagney)

12 Mystery/Suspense (MY)

MY1	Classic Film Noir	**MY11**	Amateur Sleuths
MY2	Contemporary Film Noir	**MY12**	Whodunits
MY3	Women in Danger	**MY13**	Crazy Killers
MY4	Tough Dames	**MY14**	Suspense in the Family Way
MY5	Suspense and Romance	**MY15**	British Mystery/Suspense
MY6	Political Intrigue	**MY16**	Suspense in Other Foreign Settings
MY7	Wrong Man Thrillers	**MY17**	Comic Mysteries
MY8	True-Life Suspense	**MY18**	Heists
MY9	Cat and Mouse Games	**MY19**	The _____ From Hell
MY10	Private Eyes and Other Detectives		

MY1 Classic Film Noir

The Asphalt Jungle
The Big Combo
The Big Heat
The Big Sleep (1946 version)
Born to be Bad
Born To Kill
Cat People (1942 version)
Caught
The Chase (1946)
City That Never Sleeps
Cornered
Criss Cross (1949)
Crossfire
Cry Danger
D.O.A. (1949 version)
The Dark Mirror
Dark Passage
Dead Reckoning
Deadline at Dawn
Desperate
Detour
Double Indemnity
Fear in the Night (1947)
Follow Me Quietly
Force of Evil
The Gangster
Gilda
The Glass Key
Gun Crazy
He Walked by Night
High Sierra
His Kind of Woman
The Hitch-Hiker
The Human Gorilla
I Died a Thousand Times
I Wake Up Screaming
In a Lonely Place

Journey Into Fear (1943 version)
Kansas City Confidential
Key Largo
Killer Bait
Killer's Kiss
The Killing
Kiss Me Deadly
Kiss of Death
Knock on any Door
The Lady From Shanghai
Lady in the Lake
Laura (1944)
The Maltese Falcon
Mildred Pierce
Moonrise
Murder My Sweet
The Naked City
The Narrow Margin
Niagara
Night and the City (1950 version)
The Night of the Hunter
On Dangerous Ground
Out of the Past
Panic in the Streets
Pickup on South Street
The Pitfall
The Postman Always Rings Twice (1946 version)
Private Hell 36
The Racket
The Reckless Moment
Road House (1948)
Scarlet Street
The Set-Up
Shack Out on 101
Slightly Scarlet
Sorry, Wrong Number
Split Second (1953)

The Strange Love of Martha Ivers
The Stranger (1946)
The Street With No Name
Suddenly
Sunset Boulevard
Sweet Smell of Success
T-Men
They Live by Night
They Won't Believe Me
This Gun for Hire
Touch of Evil
Try and Get Me
Undercurrent
Union Station
While the City Sleeps
White Heat
The Window
You Only Live Once

The Public Eye
Reservoir Dogs
Shattered (1991)
The Silence of the Lambs
Stormy Monday
Taxi Driver
Tequila Sunrise
To Live and Die in L.A.
Tough Guys Don't Dance
True Believer
True Confessions
Twin Peaks
Twin Peaks: Fire Walk With Me
The Two Jakes
Union City
White Sands
Who'll Stop the Rain
Wild at Heart

MY2 Contemporary Film Noir

After Dark, My Sweet
Against All Odds (1984)
The American Friend
Angel Heart
Basic Instinct
The Big Easy
Blade Runner
Blood Simple
Blue Velvet
Body Heat
Body of Evidence
Bring Me the Head of Alfredo Garcia
Cape Fear (1962 and 1991 versions)
Chinatown
Cutter's Way
D.O.A. (1988 version)
Dance With a Stranger
Deep Cover
The Driver
Experiment in Terror
Eyes of Laura Mars
52 Pick-Up
Final Analysis
The Grifters
Hammett
The Hot Spot
Hustle
Jennifer Eight
Kill Me Again
The Long Goodbye
The Manchurian Candidate
Manhunter
Marlowe
Narrow Margin
Night and the City (1992 version)
Night Moves
No Way Out (1987)
One False Move
Performance
Pretty Poison

MY3 Women in Danger

Apology
Backtrack
Berserk
Beware, My Lovely
Black Rainbow
Blue Steel
Born to Kill
Candles at Nine
Cape Fear (1962 and 1991 versions)
Caught
Charade
The Collector
Coma
Conflict
The Cradle Will Fall
Dead Again
Deadbolt
Dead of Winter
Death Sentence
Deceived
Defenseless
Dial M for Murder
Diary of a Hitman
Double Vision
Dream Lover
The Entity
Experiment Perilous
Eyes of Laura Mars
The Fan
Frenzy
Gaslight
Ghost
Glitz
The Hand That Rocks the Cradle
He Knows You're Alone
Hear No Evil
Heart of Midnight
Honeymoon
The House on Carroll Street
Impulse

Jack the Ripper (1988)
Jack's Back
Jagged Edge
Jamaica Inn (1939 and 1985 versions)
Jane Doe
Jennifer Eight
A Kiss Before Dying
Klute
Lady in a Cage
Laura
Love Crimes
Love From a Stranger
Masquerade
Midnight Lace
The Morning After
Mortal Thoughts
Ms. 45
The Naked Edge
Narrow Margin
The Narrow Margin
Night Watch
No Way To Treat a Lady
Notorious
Paris Trout
The Plumber
Positive I.D.
The Reckless Moment
Rent-a-Cop
Rider on the Rain
Scream of Fear
Secret Beyond the Door
See No Evil
Shining Through
Sidney Sheldon's Bloodline
The Silence of the Lambs
Silhouette
Single White Female
Sleeping With the Enemy
Someone to Watch Over Me
Sorry, Wrong Number
The Spiral Staircase
Stakeout
A Stranger Among Us
A Stranger Is Watching
Suspicion (1941 and 1987 versions)
The Two Mrs. Carrolls
Undercurrent
Unlawful Entry
The Vanishing (1988 and 1993
    versions)
The Very Edge
Wait Until Dark
When Michael Calls
Whispers
Whispers in the Dark

MY4 Tough Dames
Alligator Eyes
Basic Instinct
Body Heat

Body of Evidence
Born to be Bad
The Bride Wore Black
Buried Alive (1990-TV)
The Dark Mirror
Dead Reckoning
Dead Ringer
Detour
Double Indemnity
Easy Virtue
Final Analysis
Gilda
The Grifters
Guncrazy
Gun Crazy
The Hand That Rocks the
    Cradle
The Hot Spot
Kill Me Again
Killer Bait
Kiss Me Deadly
Last Embrace
Madame Sin
Ms. 45
Niagara
The Pitfall
Poison Ivy
Pretty Poison
Proof
The Public Eye
Scarlet Street
Sea of Love
Shattered (1991)
The Temp
To Have and Have Not
Tough Guys Don't Dance
V.I. Warshawski
What's the Matter With Helen?

MY5 Suspense and Romance
Against All Odds (1984)
Backtrack
Basic Instinct
Betrayed (1988)
The Big Easy
Blood Money
Body Double
Body Heat
Cat Chaser
Dead Again
Deja Vu
Double Indemnity
Dressed to Kill (1980)
Eye of the Needle
Eyewitness
Final Analysis
The Fourth Man
Gun Crazy
The Hot Spot
Jagged Edge

Klute
Laura (1944)
Marnie
Masquerade
The Morning After
The Next Man
No Mercy
No Way Out (1987)
Notorious
Obsession
Out of the Past
The Postman Always Rings Twice (1946 and
    1981 versions)
Sea of Love
Shattered
Shining Through
Someone to Watch Over Me
Spellbound
Still of the Night
Suspicion (1941 and 1987 versions)
The Tamarind Seed
They're Playing With Fire
Thief of Hearts
The Thomas Crown Affair
To Catch a Thief
Vertigo

MY6 Political Intrigue

See also Fictional Character Check List: HF2
    James Bond
All the President's Men
All Through the Night
The Amateur
Another Country
Arabesque
Background to Danger
Berlin Express
Black Sunday (1977)
The Black Windmill
Blow Out
The Boys From Brazil
The Brotherhood of the Rose
By Dawn's Early Night
The Comedians
Cornered
A Dandy in Aspic
Dark Journey
The Day of the Jackal
Deadline
Defence of the Realm
Diplomatic Courier
The Domino Principle
The Eagle Has Landed
The Eiger Sanction
Executive Action
Eye of the Needle
The Falcon and the Snowman
Flashpoint
5 Fingers
Foreign Correspondent

The Formula
The Fourth Protocol
The Fourth War
Funeral in Berlin
The General Died at Dawn
Gorky Park
Half Moon Street
Hidden Agenda
The Holcroft Covenant
Hot Line
Hotel Reserve
The House on Carroll Street
The Hunt for Red October
Ice Station Zebra
The Ipcress File
JFK
The Jigsaw Man
Journey Into Fear
Keeping Track
The Kidnapping of the President
The Killer Elite
Knight Without Armour
Last Embrace
The Little Drummer Girl
Little Nikita
The Looking Glass War
The Mackintosh Man
Madame Sin
The Man Who Knew Too Much (1934 and
    1955 versions)
The Manchurian Candidate
Memoirs of an Invisible Man
Miracle Mile
The Next Man
Night Flight From Moscow
No Way Out (1987)
Notorious
The Odessa File
The Osterman Weekend
The Package
The Palermo Connection
The Parallax View
Patriot Games
Permission to Kill
The Philadelphia Experiment
Philby, Burgess and Maclean: Spy Scandal of
    the Century
The President's Plane Is Missing
The Prize
The Quiller Memorandum
Ruby
The Russia House
Sabotage
Saboteur
The Salamander
Scorpio
Sebastian
The Secret Agent
Shining Through
A Show of Force

Spy in Black
The Spy Who Came in From the Cold
St. Ives
The Stranger (1946)
The Tamarind Seed
Target
Telefon
The Third Man
The 39 Steps (1935 and 1978 versions)
Three Days of the Condor
Topaz
Torn Curtain
The Whistle Blower
Winter Kills
World War III
Year of the Gun
The Yin and Yang of Mr. Go

MY7 Wrong Man Thrillers
All-American Murder
The Bedroom Window
Consenting Adults
Criminal Court
Cry Danger
Frenzy
Hit and Run
I Confess
I Wake Up Screaming
An Innocent Man
Jack's Back
Jennifer Eight
Madhouse (1974)
The Man Who Knew Too Much (1934 and
   1955 versions)
Marathon Man
Mirage
North by Northwest
Out of Bounds
The Paris Express
Pendulum
Physical Evidence
Presumed Innocent
Run
Saboteur
Slamdance
Star of Midnight
The Stranger on the Third Floor
10 Rillington Place
They Made Me a Criminal
They Won't Believe Me
The 39 Steps (1935 and 1978 versions)
Three Days of the Condor
Under Suspicion
The Wrong Man
Year of the Gun
Young and Innocent

MY8 True-Life Suspense
See also: DR6 True-Life Contemporary Drama
Adam

Agatha
Beyond a Reasonable Doubt
The Boston Strangler
The Brink's Job
Buster
Desperate Hours
The Desperate Hours
Dance With a Stranger
Fatal Vision
Hammett
Hide in Plain Sight
The Honeymoon Killers
In Cold Blood
JFK
Jack the Ripper (1988)
Lovers
Philby, Burgess and Maclean: Spy Scandal of
   the Century
Robbery
Swoon
10 Rillington Place
The Thin Blue Line
Without a Trace

MY9 Cat and Mouse Games
Ambition
Apartment Zero
Bad Influence
Best Seller
Black Widow
Cape Fear (1962 and 1991 versions)
Charley Varrick
Consenting Adults
Criminal Law
Deathtrap
Duel
F/X
F/X 2: The Deadly Art of Illusion
The Formula
The Hand That Rocks the Cradle
Highpoint
House of Games
Internal Affairs
Into the Fire
The Last of Sheila
Manhunter
Miami Blues
Misery
Pacific Heights
Ricochet
Rope
The Silence of the Lambs
The Silent Partner
Single White Female
Sleuth
Strangers on a Train
Unlawful Entry
The Vanishing (1988 and 1993 versions)
Where Sleeping Dogs Lie
White Sands

MY10 Private Eyes and Other Detectives

See also: Fictional Character Check Lists HF4 Charlie Chan, HF5 Nick and Nora Charles, HF8 Bulldog Drummond, HF14 Sherlock Holmes, HF21 The Saint; Writer Check Lists WR2 Raymond Chandler, WR3 Agatha Christie, WR12 Dashiell Hammett, WR22 Ross MacDonald, WR31 Mickey Spillane

The Adventures of Ford Fairlane
Angel Heart
The Art of Crime
The Big Fix
Chinatown
Columbo: Prescription Murder
Dead Again
The Drowning Pool
Everybody Wins
From Hollywood to Deadwood
Gotham
In the Heat of the Night
The Kennel Murder Case
Kill Me Again
Klute
Lady in Cement
Laguna Heat
The Late Show
Love at Large
Moonlighting (1985)
Night Moves
One Shoe Makes It Murder
Satan Met a Lady
Shaft
Shaft's Big Score!
Shamus
Shattered
Smile Jenny, You're Dead
Sunburn
Tony Rome
The Two Jakes
Under Suspicion
An Unsuitable Job for a Woman
V.I. Warshawski

MY11 Amateur Sleuths

Blind Date (1984)
Blow Out
Blow-Up
Blue Velvet
Coma
Compromising Positions
The Conversation
Deadline at Dawn
Deceived
The Detective (1954)
Double Vision
Dressed to Kill (1980)
Gleaming the Cube
Gumshoe
Her Alibi

The Mean Season
Mike's Murder
Murder Ahoy
Murder at the Gallop
A Murder Is Announced
Murder Most Foul
Murder, She Said
The Murri Affair
The Naked Edge
The Naked Face
The Name of the Rose
A Night to Remember (1942)
Ordeal by Innocence
The Parallax View
The Public Eye
Rear Window
Rope
Sisters
The Squeeze (1987)
Stunts
True Believer
The Velvet Touch
Why Didn't They Ask Evans?

MY12 Whodunits

The Alphabet Murders
And Then There Were None
Appointment With Death
The Body in the Library
Death on the Nile
Evil Under the Sun
Green for Danger
Killjoy
The Last of Sheila
The List of Adrian Messenger
Murder Ahoy
Murder at the Gallop
Murder at the Vanities
A Murder Is Announced
Murder on the Orient Express
Murder, She Said
A Pocketful of Rye
Rehearsal for Murder
The Seven Dials Mystery
Ten Little Indians (1975 version)
They Only Kill Their Masters
The Thirteenth Guest
Traces of Red

MY13 Crazy Killers

Basic Instinct
Blue Steel
The Boston Strangler
City in Fear
Criminal Law
Dressed to Kill (1980)
Fatal Attraction
Follow Me Quietly
Frenzy
Glitz

Henry: Portrait of a Serial Killer
The Housekeeper
Jack the Ripper (1988)
Jack's Back
The Killer Inside Me
The Lodger
M (1931 version)
Manhunter
The Mean Season
Mister Frost
Murder by Decree
No Way To Treat a Lady
Play Misty for Me
Raising Cain
Relentless
The Silence of the Lambs
Sisters
The Stepfather
Stepfather II
Strangers on a Train
Targets
Ten to Midnight
White of the Eye

MY14 Suspense in the Family Way
Afraid of the Dark
The Bad Seed
The Brotherhood of the Rose
The Cold Room
The Dark Mirror
Don't Look Now
Eye of the Storm
Fatal Attraction
Final Analysis
The Grifters
The Hand That Rocks the Cradle
Little Nikita
Murder by Natural Causes
Party Line
Patriot Games
Perfect Strangers
Persecution
Raising Cain
Reflections of Murder
Road to Salina
Scalpel
Secret Ceremony
Shadow of a Doubt
The Stepfather
Stepfather II
Torment
True Confessions
Where Are the Children?
White of the Eye
Winter Kills
Without a Trace

MY15 British Mystery/Suspense
See also: Fictional Character Check List HF14
    Sherlock Holmes

Afraid of the Dark
The Alphabet Murders
And Then There Were None
Bellman and True
The Blue Lamp
Bulldog Jack
Candles at Nine
The Cat and the Canary (1978 version)
Clouds Over Europe
Dance With a Stranger
The Dark Corner
The Detective (1954)
Endless Night
The Evil Mind
Green for Danger
Gumshoe
Hotel Reserve
Kind Hearts and Coronets
The Lady Vanishes (1938 version)
The Ladykillers
The Lavender Hill Mob
The League of Gentlemen
The Long Dark Hall
Madeleine
Madhouse (1974)
The Man Who Never Was
Murder Ahoy
Murder at the Gallop
A Murder Is Announced
Murder, She Said
The Night Has Eyes
Number 17
Odd Man Out
Persecution
Philby, Burgess and Maclean: Spy Scandal of
    the Century
Psycho-Circus
Robbery
Sabotage
Scream of Fear
Seance on a Wet Afternoon
The Secret Agent
The Seven Dials Mystery
Sleuth
The Spy in Black
Stormy Monday
10 Rillington Place
Theatre of Death
The 39 Steps (1935 version)
Tiger Bay
Under Suspicion
An Unsuitable Job for a Woman
The Whistle Blower
Why Didn't They Ask Evans?
Young and Innocent

MY16 Suspense In Other Foreign Settings
The American Friend
And Hope to Die

Cat Chaser
Clean Slate (Coup de Torchon)
Club Extinction
Confidentially Yours
Dear Detective
Deathwatch
Diabolique
Diva
Five Golden Dragons
The Fourth Man
Frantic (1958)
Frantic (1988)
Gorky Park
Heatwave
High and Low
The Hostage Tower
Hotel Colonial
The Italian Job
The Man on the Eiffel Tower
The Master Touch
The Mighty Quinn
The Name of the Rose
The Night of the Generals
Off Limits (1988)
One Deadly Summer
The Plumber
Proof of the Man
Rififi
Road Games
The Russia House
Sincerely, Charlotte
Topkapi
Wedding in Blood
Year of the Gun
Z

MY17 Comic Mysteries

See also: CO10 Crime and Suspense
    Comedies
Arsenic and Old Lace
Bullshot
Catch Me a Spy
Clue
Dead Men Don't Wear Plaid
The Ex-Mrs. Bradford
The Gorilla
Hanky Panky
Her Alibi
The January Man
Kind Hearts and Coronets
Lady of Burlesque
The Ladykillers
The Lavender Hill Mob
The League of Gentlemen
Legal Eagles
The Mad Miss Manton
The Man With Bogart's Face
Mr. and Mrs. North
Murder by Death
My Favorite Blonde

My Favorite Brunette
A Night to Remember (1942)
One Body Too Many
Penn & Teller Get Killed
Scandalous
The Squeeze (1987)
Star of Midnight
Sunset
The Thin Man (series)
The Trouble With Harry
Whistling in Brooklyn
Whistling in the Dark
Who Done It?
Without a Clue

MY18 Heists

The Anderson Tapes
The Asphalt Jungle
Bank Shot
Bellman and True
Big Deal on Madonna Street
The Big Steal
Bob le Flambeur
The Brain
The Brink's Job
Buster
Charley Varrick
Crackers
Criss Cross (1949)
Dead Heat on a Merry-Go-Round
Diamonds
Disorganized Crime
$ (Dollars)
11 Harrowhouse
Escape to Athena
A Fish Called Wanda
Gambit
The Getaway
Going in Style
The Great Train Robbery
Happy New Year (1973 and 1987 versions)
Honor Among Thieves
The Hot Rock
How to Beat the High Co$t of Living
Hudson Hawk
The Italian Job
Kelly's Heroes
The Killing
Lady Ice
The Lavender Hill Mob
The League of Gentlemen
Loophole
Malcolm
A Man, a Woman and a Bank
Ocean's Eleven
Reservoir Dogs
Rififi
Robbery
Seven Thieves
Sneakers

The Thomas Crown Affair
Thunderbolt and Lightfoot
Topkapi

MY19 The _____ From Hell
BUDDY
Bad Influence
Strangers on a Train
COP
Internal Affairs
Unlawful Entry
DOMESTIC WORKER
The Guardian
The Hand That Rocks the Cradle
The Housekeeper
The Servant
FAN
The Fan
King of Comedy
Misery

NEIGHBOR
Consenting Adults
Neighbors
OFFICE WORKER
The Temp
ONE-NIGHT STAND
Fatal Attraction
Hexed
Play Misty for Me
PSYCHIATRIST
Dressed To Kill (1980)
Whispers in the Dark
RELATIVE
Shadow of a Doubt
ROOMMATE
Apartment Zero
Deadbolt
Single White Female
TENANT
Pacific Heights

13 Science Fiction/Fantasy (SF)

SF1 Classic '50s Sci-Fi
The Beast From 20,000 Fathoms
The Blob
The Brain From Planet Arous
The Crawling Eye
Creature From the Black Lagoon
The Day the Earth Stood Still
Destination Moon
Earth vs. the Flying Saucers
Fiend Without a Face
The Fly (1958 version)
Forbidden Planet
4D Man
I Married a Monster from Outer Space
The Incredible Shrinking Man
Invaders From Mars (1953 version)
Invasion of the Body Snatchers (1956 version)
It Came From Outer Space
Journey to the Center of the Earth (1959 version)
Kronos
On the Beach
Rocket Ship X-M
The Thing (From Another World)
Them!
This Island Earth
War of the Worlds
When Worlds Collide

SF2 Classic Pre-'50s Sci-Fi/Fantasy
Angel on My Shoulder (1946 version)
Beauty and the Beast (1946 version)
The Bishop's Wife
Blood of a Poet
The Canterville Ghost

The Devil and Daniel Webster
Dr. Cyclops
Frankenstein (1931 version)
Gabriel Over the White House
The Ghost and Mrs. Muir
The Ghost Goes West
A Guy Named Joe
Here Comes Mr. Jordan
I Married a Witch
King Kong (1933 version)
Lost Horizon
Metropolis (1926 edition)
On Borrowed Time
The Testament of Dr. Mabuse
The Thief of Bagdad (1924 and 1940 versions)
Things to Come
Topper

SF3 Outer (and Inner) Space Travel
Alien
Aliens
Alien³
The Angry Red Planet
At the Earth's Core
Beyond the Stars
The Black Hole
Destination Moon
Explorers
Fantastic Voyage
First Men In the Moon
Flight to Mars
Innerspace
Journey to the Center of the Earth (1959 and 1989 versions)
Journey to the Far Side of the Sun
Marooned

Rocket Ship X-M
Saturn 3
Silent Running
SpaceCamp
Spacehunter: Adventures in the Forbidden Zone
Star Trek (series)
This Island Earth
20,000 Leagues Under the Sea
2001: A Space Odyssey
2010: The Year We Make Contact
Voyage to the Bottom of the Sea

SF4 Time Travel
Army of Darkness: Evil Dead 3
Back to the Future
Back to the Future, Part II
Back to the Future, Part III
Beastmaster 2: Through the Portals of Time
Biggles: Adventures in Time
Bill and Ted's Bogus Journey
Bill and Ted's Excellent Adventure
A Connecticut Yankee
A Connecticut Yankee in King Arthur's Court
Daleks: Invasion Earth 2150 A.D.
Dinosaurus!
Escapes
The Final Countdown
Forever Young
Frankenstein Unbound
Freejack
Highlander
Highlander II: The Quickening
The Land That Time Forgot
Late for Dinner
Light Years
The Lost World (1925 version)
Millennium
The People That Time Forgot
Peggy Sue Got Married
The Philadelphia Experiment
Slaughterhouse Five
Sleeper
Somewhere in Time
Star Trek IV: The Voyage Home
Teenage Mutant Ninja Turtles III: The Turtles
    Are Back . . . in Time
The Terminator
Terminator 2: Judgment Day
Time After Time
Time Bandits
The Time Guardian
The Time Machine
Timerider
The Undead
Where Time Began

SF5 Science Gone Wrong
See also: HO20 Science Runs Amok
Altered States
Android

The Andromeda Strain
The Asphyx
Brainstorm
Coma
Deathwatch
Dr. Cyclops
Dreamscape
Edward Scissorhands
Embryo
Eve of Destruction
The Fly (1958 and 1986 versions)
The Fly II
4D Man
Island of Terror
Looker
Metropolis
Spontaneous Combustion
The Terminal Man
WarGames
X: The Man With the X-Ray Eyes

SF6 Mad Machines
Colossus: The Forbin Project
Demon Seed
Eve of Destruction
Futureworld
Hardware
Robot Carnival
Runaway
Saturn 3
The Terminator
Terminator 2: Judgment Day
Tetsuo: The Iron Man
2001: A Space Odyssey
Westworld

SF7 Sci-Fi Disaster
The Andromeda Strain
The Day of the Triffids
The Day the Earth Caught Fire
Island of the Burning Doomed
Meteor
The Swarm
War of the Worlds
When Worlds Collide

SF8 Survival Adventures
After the Fall of New York
The Andromeda Strain
Cherry 2000
Endgame
Enemy Mine
Escape From New York
Exterminators of the Year 3000
Firebird 2015 A.D.
Future-Kill
The Last Starfighter
Logan's Run
Planet of the Apes (series)
Quintet

Soylent Green
W
Warlords of the 21st Century
Warriors of the Wasteland
Zardoz

SF9 Alien Visitors
Bad Channels
The Blob
The Brain From Planet Arous
The Brother from Another Planet
Close Encounters of the Third Kind
Cocoon
Cocoon: The Return
Communion
The Crawling Eye
The Day the Earth Stood Still
The Day Time Ended
E.T.—The Extra-Terrestrial
Earth Girls Are Easy
Earth vs. the Flying Saucers
Fire in the Sky
I Married a Monster from Outer Space
Invaders From Mars (1953 and 1985 versions)
Invasion of the Body Snatchers (1956 and
    1978 versions)
It Came From Outer Space
It Conquered the World
The Man Who Fell to Earth
Starman
Strange Invaders
Suburban Commando
They Live
The Thing
The Thing (From Another World)
This Island Earth
Village of the Damned
War of the Worlds
Wavelength

SF10 Mutant Monsters
Creature From the Black Lagoon
Empire of the Ants
Food of the Gods
Godzilla (series)
Gorgo
The Hideous Sun Demon
It Came from Beneath the Sea
King Kong
Mysterious Island
Prophecy
Them!

SF11 Future Wars Against Dictators
Brazil
Dune
The Empire Strikes Back
Escape 2000
Fahrenheit 451
The Last Chase

1984
Return of the Jedi
Rollerball
Running Man
Star Wars
THX 1138
Total Recall
Tron

SF12 After the Holocaust
After the Fall of New York
Aftermath
Akira
A Boy and His Dog
City Limits
Creation of the Humanoids
Cyborg
Damnation Alley
The Day After
Glen and Randa
Hardware
The Last Man on Earth
The Last Woman on Earth
Lord of the Flies
Night of the Comet
On the Beach
Planet of the Apes (series)
The Quiet Earth
Testament
Things to Come
Threads
Virus

SF13 Family Sci-Fi/Fantasy
See also: FA8 Family Sci-Fi/Fantasy
The Adventures of Baron Münchausen
Aurora Encounter
Battle for the Planet of the Apes
Beneath the Planet of the Apes
The Black Hole
The Blue Bird (1940 version)
The Brothers Lionheart
Clash of the Titans
Conquest of the Planet of the Apes
Creature From the Black Lagoon
The Dark Crystal
The Day the Earth Stood Still
E.T.—The Extra-Terrestrial
Edward Scissorhands
The Empire Strikes Back
Escape From the Planet of the Apes
Explorers
From the Earth to the Moon
The Hobbit
Journey to the Center of the Earth (1959 and
    1989 versions)
King Kong (1933 version)
The Land of Faraway
Labyrinth
Laserblast

The Last Starfighter
Legend
Lord of the Rings
Making Contact
The Man Who Could Work Miracles
Masters of the Universe
The NeverEnding Story
The NeverEnding Story II: The Next Chapter
Planet of the Apes
Return of the Jedi
Return to Oz
The 7 Faces of Dr. Lao
The 7th Voyage of Sinbad
Something Wicked This Way Comes
Space Raiders
Spaced Invaders
Spacehunter: Adventures in the Forbidden
  Zone
Star Trek (series)
Star Wars
Starchaser: The Legend of Orion
The Time Machine
Transformers
Tron
20,000 Leagues Under the Sea
The War of the Worlds
The Watcher in the Woods
Willow
The Wizard of Oz
Wizards

SF14 Spectacular Sets
The Adventures of Baron Münchausen
Batman (1989)
Batman Returns
The Black Hole
Blade Runner
Brazil
Legend
Metropolis
Things to Come
Transatlantic Tunnel

SF15 Oscar-Winning Special Effects
Alien
Death Becomes Her
Destination Moon
Dr. Cyclops
E.T.—The Extra-Terrestrial
The Empire Strikes Back
Fantastic Voyage
Logan's Run
Marooned
Reap the Wild Wind
Star Wars
Superman
Terminator 2: Judgment Day
The Time Machine
tom thumb
Total Recall

20,000 Leagues Under the Sea
2001: A Space Odyssey
When Worlds Collide

SF16 Special Effects Milestones
An American Werewolf in London
Close Encounters of the Third Kind
King Kong (1933 version)
The Lost World (1925 version)
Metropolis (1926 edition)
Star Wars
Them!
Tron
2001: A Space Odyssey

SF17 Future Cops and Robbers
Alien Nation
Blade Runner
A Clockwork Orange
Crime Zone
The Hidden
I Come in Peace
The Killings at Outpost Zeta
Outland
Runaway
Slipstream
Space Rage
Split Second (1992)
Trancers

SF18 Japanese Sci-Fi
Akira
Dagora, the Space Monster
Ghidrah, the Three-Headed Monster
Godzilla, King of the Monsters
Godzilla 1985
Godzilla on Monster Island
Godzilla vs. Megalon
Godzilla vs. Monster Zero
Godzilla vs. Mothra
Gorath
The H-Man
The Human Vapor
The Last War
Mothra
The Mysterians
Robot Carnival
Rodan
Terror of Mechagodzilla
Virus

SF19 Science Fiction With a Foreign Accent
See also: SF18 Japanese Sci-Fi
Alphaville
The Asphyx
Attack of the Robots
Barbarella
Biggles: Adventures in Time
Daleks: Invasion Earth 2150 A.D.

The Day of the Triffids
The Day the Earth Caught Fire
Deathwatch
Dr. Who and the Daleks
The Fantastic Planet
Island of Terror
Island of the Burning Doomed
Journey to the Far Side of the Sun
The Last Days of Man on Earth
Le Dernier Combat
Man Facing Southeast
The Quatermass Conclusion
Threads
Village of the Damned
Zardoz

SF20 Sci-Fi Horror
Alien
Alien Predators
Alien³
Aliens
Altered States
Creature
The Fly (1986 version)
The Fly II
Galaxy of Terror
Hardware
The Island of Dr. Moreau
Lifeforce
Phase IV
Planet of Blood
Star Crystal
Terror Vision
The Thing
Xtro

SF21 Sci-Fi Spoofs
The Adventures of Buckaroo Banzai Across
    the Eighth Dimension
Dark Star
Death Race 2000
Earth Girls Are Easy
Flash Gordon
Galaxina

Heartbeeps
The Ice Pirates
The Incredible Shrinking Woman
Innerspace
The Jet Benny Show
The Last Days of Man on Earth
The Man With Two Brains
Mom and Dad Save the World
Monster in the Closet
Night of the Comet
Really Weird Tales
Simon
Sleeper
Spaceballs
Strange Invaders
The Tenth Victim

SF22 Sexy Sci-Fi/Fantasy
Barbarella
A Boy and His Dog
Demon Seed
Galaxina
The Invasion of the Bee Girls
Liquid Sky

SF23 Sci-Fi Check List: Classic Series
PLANET OF THE APES
Battle for the Planet of the Apes
Beneath the Planet of the Apes
Conquest of the Planet of the Apes
Escape From the Planet of the Apes
Planet of the Apes
STAR TREK
The Motion Picture
II: The Wrath of Khan
III: The Search for Spock
IV: The Voyage Home
V: The Final Frontier
VI: The Undiscovered Country
STAR WARS
Star Wars
The Empire Strikes Back
Return of the Jedi

14 Star Check Lists (ST)

ST1	Abbott and Costello	**ST51**	Robert De Niro
ST2	Julie Andrews	**ST52**	Gérard Depardieu
ST3	Jean Arthur	**ST53**	Laura Dern
ST4	Fred Astaire	**ST54**	Danny DeVito
ST5	Gene Autry	**ST55**	Marlene Dietrich
ST6	Brigitte Bardot	**ST56**	Matt Dillon
ST7	Ellen Barkin	**ST57**	Kirk Douglas
ST8	John Barrymore	**ST58**	Melvyn Douglas
ST9	Alan Bates	**ST59**	Michael Douglas
ST10	Warren Beatty	**ST60**	Richard Dreyfuss
ST11	Jean-Paul Belmondo	**ST61**	Faye Dunaway
ST12	Annette Bening	**ST62**	Irene Dunne
ST13	Ingrid Bergman	**ST63**	Robert Duvall
ST14	Dirk Bogarde	**ST64**	Clint Eastwood
ST15	Humphrey Bogart	**ST65**	Mia Farrow
ST16	Charles Boyer	**ST66**	Sally Field
ST17	Sonia Braga	**ST67**	W.C. Fields
ST18	Marlon Brando	**ST68**	Albert Finney
ST19	Jeff Bridges	**ST69**	Errol Flynn
ST20	Charles Bronson	**ST70**	Bridget Fonda
ST21	Louise Brooks	**ST71**	Henry Fonda
ST22	Richard Burton	**ST72**	Jane Fonda
ST23	Nicolas Cage	**ST73**	Joan Fontaine
ST24	James Cagney	**ST74**	Harrison Ford
ST25	Michael Caine	**ST75**	Jodie Foster
ST26	Lon Chaney, Sr.	**ST76**	Morgan Freeman
ST27	Lon Chaney, Jr.	**ST77**	Clark Gable
ST28	Cheech and Chong	**ST78**	Greta Garbo
ST29	Cher	**ST79**	Ava Gardner
ST30	Julie Christie	**ST80**	John Garfield
ST31	Jill Clayburgh	**ST81**	Judy Garland
ST32	Montgomery Clift	**ST82**	James Garner
ST33	Glenn Close	**ST83**	Greer Garson
ST34	Claudette Colbert	**ST84**	Richard Gere
ST35	Ronald Colman	**ST85**	Mel Gibson
ST36	Sean Connery	**ST86**	John Gielgud
ST37	Gary Cooper	**ST87**	Lillian Gish
ST38	Kevin Costner	**ST88**	Danny Glover
ST39	Joan Crawford	**ST89**	Whoopi Goldberg
ST40	Bing Crosby	**ST90**	Jeff Goldblum
ST41	Tom Cruise	**ST91**	Betty Grable
ST42	Jamie Lee Curtis	**ST92**	Cary Grant
ST43	Peter Cushing	**ST93**	Melanie Griffith
ST44	Bette Davis	**ST94**	Charles Grodin
ST45	Geena Davis	**ST95**	Alec Guinness
ST46	Judy Davis	**ST96**	Gene Hackman
ST47	Doris Day	**ST97**	Tom Hanks
ST48	Daniel Day-Lewis	**ST98**	Jean Harlow
ST49	Olivia de Havilland	**ST99**	Goldie Hawn
ST50	Catherine Deneuve	**ST100**	Susan Hayward

ST101 Rita Hayworth	**ST161** Jeanne Moreau
ST102 Audrey Hepburn	**ST162** Paul Newman
ST103 Katharine Hepburn	**ST163** Jack Nicholson
ST104 Barbara Hershey	**ST164** Nick Nolte
ST105 Dustin Hoffman	**ST165** Chuck Norris
ST106 William Holden	**ST166** Warren Oates
ST107 Judy Holliday	**ST167** Maureen O'Hara
ST108 Bob Hope	**ST168** Laurence Olivier
ST109 Anthony Hopkins	**ST169** Peter O'Toole
ST110 Dennis Hopper	**ST170** Al Pacino
ST111 Bob Hoskins	**ST171** Gregory Peck
ST112 Rock Hudson	**ST172** Joe Pesci
ST113 Holly Hunter	**ST173** Michelle Pfeiffer
ST114 William Hurt	**ST174** Sidney Poitier
ST115 Anjelica Huston	**ST175** Dick Powell
ST116 Jeremy Irons	**ST176** William Powell
ST117 Glenda Jackson	**ST177** Tyrone Power
ST118 James Earl Jones	**ST178** Elvis Presley
ST119 Boris Karloff	**ST179** Vincent Price
ST120 Danny Kaye	**ST180** Richard Pryor
ST121 Diane Keaton	**ST181** Robert Redford
ST122 Michael Keaton	**ST182** Vanessa Redgrave
ST123 Gene Kelly	**ST183** Burt Reynolds
ST124 Grace Kelly	**ST184** Ralph Richardson
ST125 Deborah Kerr	**ST185** Jason Robards
ST126 Klaus Kinski	**ST186** Edward G. Robinson
ST127 Kevin Kline	**ST187** Ginger Rogers
ST128 Alan Ladd	**ST188** Roy Rogers
ST129 Burt Lancaster	**ST189** Mickey Rooney
ST130 Jessica Lange	**ST190** Mickey Rourke
ST131 Angela Lansbury	**ST191** Kurt Russell
ST132 Charles Laughton	**ST192** Rosalind Russell
ST133 Laurel and Hardy	**ST193** Robert Ryan
ST134 Bruce Lee	**ST194** Susan Sarandon
ST135 Christopher Lee	**ST195** Arnold Schwarzenegger
ST136 Jennifer Jason Leigh	**ST196** George C. Scott
ST137 Vivien Leigh	**ST197** Randolph Scott
ST138 Jack Lemmon	**ST198** Peter Sellers
ST139 Jerry Lewis	**ST199** Frank Sinatra
ST140 Carole Lombard	**ST200** Christian Slater
ST141 Sophia Loren	**ST201** Wesley Snipes
ST142 Myrna Loy	**ST202** Sissy Spacek
ST143 Bela Lugosi	**ST203** James Spader
ST144 Joel McCrea	**ST204** Sylvester Stallone
ST145 Shirley MacLaine	**ST205** Harry Dean Stanton
ST146 Steve McQueen	**ST206** Barbara Stanwyck
ST147 John Malkovich	**ST207** James Stewart
ST148 Fredric March	**ST208** Dean Stockwell
ST149 Dean Martin	**ST209** Madeleine Stowe
ST150 Steve Martin	**ST210** Meryl Streep
ST151 Lee Marvin	**ST211** Barbra Streisand
ST152 The Marx Brothers	**ST212** Elizabeth Taylor
ST153 James Mason	**ST213** Shirley Temple
ST154 Marcello Mastroianni	**ST214** Gene Tierney
ST155 Walter Matthau	**ST215** Lily Tomlin
ST156 Bette Midler	**ST216** Rip Torn
ST157 Toshiro Mifune	**ST217** Spencer Tracy
ST158 Robert Mitchum	**ST218** Kathleen Turner
ST159 Marilyn Monroe	**ST219** Lana Turner
ST160 Dudley Moore	**ST220** Liv Ullmann

ST221 Lee Van Cleef
ST222 Christopher Walken
ST223 Denzel Washington
ST224 John Wayne
ST225 Sigourney Weaver
ST226 Mae West
ST227 Billy Dee Williams

ST228 Robin Williams
ST229 Bruce Willis
ST230 Paul Winfield
ST231 Debra Winger
ST232 Shelley Winters
ST233 James Woods
ST234 Joanne Woodward

ST1 Abbott (1895–1974) **and Costello**
(1906–1959)
Abbott and Costello in Hollywood
Abbott and Costello Meet Captain Kidd
Abbott and Costello Meet Dr. Jekyll and
  Mr. Hyde
Abbott and Costello Meet Frankenstein
Abbott and Costello Meet the Invisible Man
Abbott and Costello Meet the Killer, Boris
  Karloff
Africa Screams
Buck Privates
Buck Privates Come Home
Dance with Me Henry
Hit the Ice
Hold That Ghost
In the Navy
Jack and the Beanstalk (1952 version)
Keep 'em Flying
Lost in a Harem
Mexican Hayride
MGM's Big Parade of Comedy
The Naughty Nineties
The Noose Hangs High
Pardon My Sarong
Ride 'em Cowboy
Rio Rita
The Time of Their Lives
Who Done It?
The Wistful Widow of Wagon Gap

Woody Allen
See: Director Check List: DT2 Woody Allen

ST2 Julie Andrews (1935–)
See also: XT30 He Directs, She Acts
The Americanization of Emily
Children's Songs and Stories With the Muppets
Duet for One
Hawaii
Little Miss Marker (1980 version)
The Man Who Loved Women (1983 version)
Mary Poppins
S.O.B.
The Sound of Music
The Tamarind Seed
10
That's Life!
Thoroughly Modern Millie
Torn Curtain
Victor/Victoria

ST3 Jean Arthur (1908–1991)
Danger Lights
The Devil and Miss Jones
The Ex-Mrs. Bradford
History Is Made at Night
A Lady Takes a Chance
The Making of a Legend—Gone With the Wind
The More the Merrier
Mr. Deeds Goes to Town
Mr. Smith Goes to Washington
Only Angels Have Wings
The Plainsman
Shane
The Talk of the Town
You Can't Take It With You (1938 version)

ST4 Fred Astaire (1899–1987)
See also: CL15 Memorable Screen Teams—
  Fred Astaire and Ginger Rogers
The Amazing Dobermans
A Family Upside Down
George Stevens: A Filmmaker's Journey
Ghost Story
The Man in the Santa Claus Suit
On the Beach
Paris When It Sizzles (bit)
The Purple Taxi
The Towering Inferno
MUSICALS
The Band Wagon
The Barkleys of Broadway
The Belle of New York
Broadway Melody of 1940
Carefree
Daddy Long Legs
A Damsel in Distress
Dancing Lady
Easter Parade
Finian's Rainbow
Flying Down to Rio
Follow the Fleet
Funny Face
The Gay Divorcee
Holiday Inn
Let's Dance
Roberta
Royal Wedding
Second Chorus
Shall We Dance
Silk Stockings
The Sky's the Limit

The Story of Vernon and Irene Castle
Swing Time
That's Dancing!
That's Entertainment!
That's Entertainment, Part 2
Three Little Words
Top Hat
Yolanda and the Thief
You Were Never Lovelier
You'll Never Get Rich
Ziegfeld Follies (with Gene Kelly)

ST5 Gene Autry (1907–)
The Big Show
The Big Sombrero
Blue Canadian Rockies
Boots and Saddles
Call of the Canyon
Colorado Sunset
Cow Town
Down Mexico Way
Git Along, Little Dogies
Heart of the Rio Grande
The Hills of Utah
In Old Santa Fe
Last of the Pony Riders
Loaded Pistols
The Man From Music Mountain
Man of the Frontier
Melody Ranch
Melody Trail
Mexicali Rose
Mystery Mountain
Night Stage to Galveston
Oh Susannah
The Old Barn Dance
The Old Corral
On Top of Old Smoky
Phantom Empire (serial)
Prairie Moon
Public Cowboy No. 1
Radio Ranch (condensed version of
   Phantom Empire serial)
Ride, Ranger, Ride
Riders of the Whistling Pines
Ridin' on a Rainbow
Rim of the Canyon
Robin Hood of Texas
Rootin' Tootin' Rhythm
Round-Up Time in Texas
Saginaw Trail
Sioux City Sue
South of the Border
Springtime in the Rockies (1937)
Valley of Fire
Twilight on the Rio Grande
Winning of the West
Yodelin' Kid From Pine Ridge
NON-WESTERN
Manhattan Merry-Go-Round

Dan Aykroyd
See: CO13 The Alumni of "Saturday Night
   Live"

Lauren Bacall
See: CL15 Memorable Screen Teams—
   Humphrey Bogart and Lauren Bacall

ST6 Brigitte Bardot (1934–)
A Coeur Joie
And God Created Woman (1957 version)
The Bride Is Much Too Beautiful
Contempt
Crazy for Love
Dear Brigitte (bit)
Doctor at Sea
Le Repos du Guerrier
The Legend of Frenchie King
Mademoiselle Striptease
Ms. Don Juan
Ravishing Idiot
Shalako
Testament of Orpheus
That Naughty Girl
A Very Private Affair
Voulez-Vous Danser Avec Moi?
The Women (1969)

ST7 Ellen Barkin (1954–)
Act of Vengeance
The Adventures of Buckaroo Banzai Across
   the Eighth Dimension
The Big Easy
Blood Money
Daniel
Desert Bloom
Diner
Down by Law
Eddie and the Cruisers
Enormous Changes
Harry and Son
Johnny Handsome
Kent State
Made in Heaven (bit)
Man Trouble
The Princess Who Had Never Laughed
Sea of Love
Siesta
Switch
Tender Mercies
Terminal Choice
This Boy's Life

ST8 John Barrymore (1882–1942)
Beau Brummel (1924 version)
The Beloved Rogue
A Bill of Divorcement
Bulldog Drummond Comes Back
Bulldog Drummond's Peril
Bulldog Drummond's Revenge

Dinner at Eight
Don Juan
Dr. Jekyll and Mr. Hyde (1920 version)
Grand Hotel
The Great Man Votes
Marie Antoinette
Maytime
Playmates
Rasputin and the Empress
Romeo and Juliet (1936 version)
State's Attorney
Svengali (1931 version)
Tempest (1928)
Topaze
Twentieth Century

ST9 Alan Bates (1934–)
Britannia Hospital
Club Extinction
The Collection
A Day in the Death of Joe Egg
Duet for One
The Entertainer
Far From the Madding Crowd
Georgy Girl
The Go-Between
Hamlet (1990 version)
In Celebration
A Kind of Loving
King of Hearts
Mister Frost
Nijinsky
A Prayer for the Dying
Quartet (1981)
Return of the Soldier
The Rose
Royal Flash
Separate Tables (1983 version)
The Shout
Story of a Love Story
The Trespasser
An Unmarried Woman
A Voyage 'Round My Father
We Think the World of You
Whistle Down the Wind
The Wicked Lady
Women in Love
Zorba the Greek

ST10 Warren Beatty (1937–)
All Fall Down
Bonnie and Clyde
Bugsy
Dick Tracy*
$ (Dollars)
George Stevens: A Filmmaker's Journey
Heaven Can Wait**
Ishtar
Lilith
McCabe and Mrs. Miller

The Only Game in Town
The Parallax View
Promise Her Anything
Reds*
The Roman Spring of Mrs. Stone
Shampoo
Splendor in the Grass
Truth or Dare
*also director
**also co-director

ST11 Jean-Paul Belmondo (1933–)
The Brain
Breathless (1959 version)
Casino Royale
High Heels
Is Paris Burning?
Le Doulos
Le Magnifique
Love and the Frenchwoman
Pierrot le Fou
Scoumoune
Sois Belle et Tais-Toi
Stavisky
Stuntwoman
Swashbuckler (1984)
Two Women
Un Singe En Hiver
A Woman Is a Woman

Jim Belushi
See: CO13 The Alumni of "Saturday Night
   Live"

John Belushi
See: CO13 The Alumni of "Saturday Night
   Live"

ST12 Annette Bening (1958–)
Bugsy
The Great Outdoors
The Grifters
Guilty by Suspicion
Postcards From the Edge
Regarding Henry
Valmont

ST13 Ingrid Bergman (1915–1982)
See also: XT30 He Directs, She Acts
Adam Had Four Sons
Anastasia
Arch of Triumph
Autumn Sonata
The Bells of St. Mary's
Cactus Flower
Casablanca
The Count of the Old Town
Dollar
Dr. Jekyll and Mr. Hyde (1941 version)
Elena and Her Men

Europa '51
Fear
From The Mixed-Up Files of Mrs. Basil E.
　Frankweiler
Gaslight
Goodbye Again
Indiscreet (1958)
The Inn of the Sixth Happiness
Intermezzo (1936 and 1939 versions)
Joan of Arc
June Night
A Matter of Time
Murder on the Orient Express
Notorious
Only One Night
Spellbound
Stromboli
Swedenhielms
Under Capricorn
Voyage to Italy
A Walk in the Spring Rain
Walpurgis Night
A Woman Called Golda
A Woman's Face (1938 version)

ST14 Dirk Bogarde (1921–)
Accident
The Blue Lamp
A Bridge Too Far
Daddy Nostalgia
Damn the Defiant!
The Damned
Darling
Death in Venice
Despair
Doctor at Large
Doctor at Sea
Doctor in Distress
Doctor in the House
The Epic That Never Was
I Could Go on Singing
Ill Met by Moonlight
Justine
McGuire, Go Home!
Night Flight From Moscow
The Night Porter
Permission to Kill
Providence
Quartet (1949)
The Sea Shall Not Have Them
Sebastian
The Servant
Simba
The Singer Not the Song
The Sleeping Tiger
Song Without End
The Spanish Gardener
A Tale of Two Cities (1958 version)
Victim
The Vision

ST15 Humphrey Bogart (1899–1957)
See also CL15 Memorable Screen Teams—
　Humphrey Bogart and Lauren Bacall
Across the Pacific
Action in the North Atlantic
The African Queen
All Through the Night
Angels With Dirty Faces
The Barefoot Contessa
Battle Circus
Beat the Devil
The Big Sleep (1946)
Brother Orchid
Bullets or Ballots
The Caine Mutiny
Call It Murder
Casablanca
Chain Lightning
Conflict
Dark Passage
Dark Victory
Dead End
Dead Reckoning
The Desperate Hours
The Enforcer (1951)
The Harder They Fall
High Sierra
In a Lonely Place
Key Largo
Kid Galahad (1937 version)
Knock on Any Door
The Left Hand of God
The Maltese Falcon
Marked Woman
The Oklahoma Kid
Passage to Marseilles
The Petrified Forest
The Roaring Twenties
Sabrina
Sahara
Sirocco
Stand-In
Thank Your Lucky Stars
They Drive By Night
Three on a Match
To Have and Have Not
Tokyo Joe
The Treasure of the Sierra Madre
The Two Mrs. Carrolls
Virginia City
We're No Angels (1955 version)
SUBJECT ONLY
The Man With Bogart's Face
Play It Again, Sam

ST16 Charles Boyer (1897–1978)
Adorable Julia
Algiers
All This and Heaven Too
The April Fools

Arch of Triumph
Around the World in 80 Days (bit)
Barefoot in the Park
Break of Hearts
The Buccaneer
Casino Royale
Conquest
The Earrings of Madame de . . .
Fanny (1961 version)
The Four Horsemen of the Apocalypse
  (1961 version)
The Garden of Allah
Gaslight
Heart of a Nation (narrator)
History Is Made at Night
Is Paris Burning?
Liliom
Love Affair
The Madwoman of Chaillot
A Matter of Time
Mayerling (1936 version)
Nana (1955 version)
Red-Headed Woman
Stavisky

ST17 Sonia Braga (1951–)
Doña Flor and Her Two Husbands
Gabriela
I Love You
Kiss of the Spider Woman
Lady on the Bus
The Last Prostitute
The Man Who Broke 1,000 Chains
The Milagro Beanfield War
Moon Over Parador
The Rookie

ST18 Marlon Brando (1924–)
Apocalypse Now
The Appaloosa
Bedtime Story
Burn!
The Chase (1966)
Christopher Columbus: The Discovery
Desiree
A Dry White Season
The Formula
The Freshman (1990)
The Fugitive Kind
The Godfather
The Godfather: The Complete Epic,
  1902–1958
The Godfather Trilogy, 1901–1980
Guys and Dolls
Hearts of Darkness: A Filmmaker's Apocalypse
Julius Caesar (1953 version)
Last Tango in Paris
The Men
The Missouri Breaks
Morituri

Mutiny on the Bounty (1962 version)
The Nightcomers
On the Waterfront
One-Eyed Jacks
Reflections in a Golden Eye
Sayonara
A Streetcar Named Desire
Superman
Teahouse of the August Moon
The Ugly American
Viva Zapata!
The Wild One
The Young Lions
DOCUMENTARY SUBJECT
Marlon Brando

ST19 Jeff Bridges (1949–)
Against All Odds (1984)
Bad Company
Cold Feet
Cutter's Way
Eight Million Ways to Die
The Fabulous Baker Boys
Fat City
The Fisher King
Hearts of the West
Heaven's Gate
Jagged Edge
King Kong (1976 version)
Kiss Me Goodbye
The Last American Hero
The Last Picture Show
The Last Unicorn (character voice)
The Morning After
Nadine
Rancho Deluxe
Rapunzel
See You in the Morning
Silent Night, Lonely Night (bit)
Starman
Stay Hungry
Texasville
Thunderbolt and Lightfoot
Tron
Tucker: The Man and His Dream
The Vanishing (1993 version)
Winter Kills
The Yin and Yang of Mr. Go

ST20 Charles Bronson (1921–)
Act of Vengeance
Apache*
Assassination
Borderline
Breakheart Pass
Breakout
Caboblanco
Chato's Land
Chino
Cold Sweat

Death Hunt
Death Wish (series)
Diplomatic Courier (bit)
The Dirty Dozen
Drum Beat
The Evil That Men Do
The Family (1970)
Four for Texas
The Great Escape
Hard Times
Honor Among Thieves
House of Wax*
The Indian Runner
Jubal
Kid Galahad (1962 version)
Kinjite: Forbidden Subjects
Lola (1969)
Love and Bullets
Machine Gun Kelly
The Magnificent Seven
Master of the World
The Mechanic
Messenger of Death
Miss Sadie Thompson*
Mr. Majestyk
Murphy's Law
Never So Few
Once Upon a Time in the West
Pat and Mike*
Raid on Entebbe
Red Sun
Rider on the Rain
Run of the Arrow
The Sandpiper
Showdown at Boot Hill
Soldiers of Fortune
Someone Behind the Door
St. Ives
The Stone Killer
Telefon
10 to Midnight
This Property Is Condemned
Vera Cruz*
Villa Rides!
The White Buffalo
*billed as Charles Buchinski or Charles
  Buchinsky

ST21 Louise Brooks (1900–1985)
Diary of a Lost Girl
It's the Old Army Game
Love 'Em and Leave 'Em
Overland Stage Riders
Pandora's Box
Prix de Beaute
DOCUMENTARY SUBJECT
Lulu in Berlin

Mel Brooks
See: Director Check List: DT17 Mel Brooks

ST22 Richard Burton (1925–1984)
See also: CL15 Memorable Screen Teams—
  Richard Burton and Elizabeth Taylor
Absolution
Alexander the Great
Anne of the Thousand Days
The Assassination of Trotsky
Becket
Bluebeard
Breakthrough
Brief Encounter (1974 version)
Circle of Two
Cleopatra (1963)
The Comedians
The Desert Rats
Divorce His, Divorce Hers
Doctor Faustus
Ellis Island
Equus
Exorcist II: The Heretic
Gathering Storm
Green Grow the Rushes
Hammersmith Is Out
Ice Palace
The Klansman
The Last Days of Dolwyn
The Longest Day
Look Back in Anger
Lovespell
Massacre in Rome
The Medusa Touch
The Night of the Iguana
1984
Raid on Rommel
The Robe
The Sandpiper
Sea Wife
The Spy Who Came in From the Cold
The Taming of the Shrew
The Tempest (1963 version)
Under Milk Wood
The VIPs
Wagner
Where Eagles Dare
Who's Afraid of Virginia Woolf?
The Wild Geese

ST23 Nicolas Cage (1964–)
Amos & Andrew
Birdy
The Boy in Blue
The Cotton Club
Fire Birds
Honeymoon in Vegas
Industrial Symphony No. 1: The Dream of
  the Broken Hearted
Moonstruck
Peggy Sue Got Married
Racing With the Moon
Raising Arizona

Time to Kill
Valley Girl
Vampire's Kiss
Wild at Heart
Zandalee

ST24 James Cagney (1899–1986)
Angels With Dirty Faces
Blonde Crazy
Blood on the Sun
The Bride Came C.O.D.
City for Conquest
Each Dawn I Die
Footlight Parade
"G" Men
The Gallant Hours
Great Guy
Johnny Come Lately
Kiss Tomorrow Goodbye
Lady Killer
A Lion Is in the Streets
Love Me or Leave Me
Man of a Thousand Faces
A Midsummer Night's Dream (1935 version)
Mister Roberts
Never Steal Anything Small
The Oklahoma Kid
One, Two, Three
The Public Enemy
Ragtime
The Roaring Twenties
The Seven Little Foys
Something to Sing About
The Strawberry Blonde
13 Rue Madeleine
The Time of Your Life
The West Point Story
What Price Glory? (1952 version)
White Heat
Yankee Doodle Dandy

ST25 Michael Caine (1933–)
Alfie
Ashanti
Battle of Britain
Beyond the Limit
Beyond the Poseidon Adventure
Billion Dollar Brain
The Black Windmill
Blame It on Rio
A Bridge Too Far
Bull'seye!
California Suite
Deathtrap
The Destructors
Dirty Rotten Scoundrels
Dressed to Kill (1980)
The Eagle Has Landed
Educating Rita
The Fourth Protocol

Funeral in Berlin
Gambit
Half Moon Street
The Hand
Hannah and Her Sisters
Harry and Walter Go to New York
The Holcroft Covenant
The Ipcress File
The Island
The Italian Job
Jack the Ripper (1988)
Jaws the Revenge
The Jigsaw Man
The Last Valley
The Man Who Would Be King
Mona Lisa
Mr. Destiny
The Muppet Christmas Carol
Noises Off
Pulp
The Romantic Englishwoman
A Shock to the System
Silver Bears
Sleuth
Surrender
The Swarm
Sweet Liberty
Too Late the Hero
Victory
Water
The Whistle Blower
The Wilby Conspiracy
Without a Clue
Woman Times Seven
The Wrong Box
X, Y and Zee
Zulu

John Candy
See: CO14 The Alumni of "SCTV"

ST26 Lon Chaney, Sr. (1883–1930)
Flesh and Blood (1922)
The Hunchback of Notre Dame (1923 version)
Nomads of the North
Oliver Twist (1922 version)
Outside the Law
The Phantom of the Opera (1925 version)
The Scarlet Car
Shadows
The Shock
The Unholy Three (1925 and 1930 versions)
The Unknown
West of Zanzibar
SUBJECT ONLY
Man of a Thousand Faces

ST27 Lon Chaney, Jr. (1906–1973)
Abbott and Costello Meet Frankenstein
Behave Yourself!

The Black Castle
The Black Sleep
Bird of Paradise (1932)
Bride of the Gorilla
The Bushwackers
Casanova's Big Night
The Cyclops
Daniel Boone, Trail Blazer
The Defiant Ones (1958 version)
Dr. Terror's Gallery of Horrors
Dracula vs. Frankenstein
Frankenstein Meets the Wolf Man
The Haunted Palace
High Noon
Hillbillys in a Haunted House
House of Frankenstein
I Died a Thousand Times
The Indestructible Man
The Indian Fighter
A Lion Is in the Streets
Manfish
My Favorite Brunette
Not as a Stranger
Of Mice and Men
The Old Corral
One Million B.C.
Only the Valiant
Passion (1954)
Riders of Death Valley
Sixteen Fathoms Deep
Son of Dracula
Spider Baby
Undersea Kingdom
The Wolf Man
SUBJECT ONLY
Man of a Thousand Faces

Charlie Chaplin
See: Director Check List: DT24 Charlie Chaplin

Graham Chapman
See: CO15 The Alumni of "Monty Python's
Flying Circus"

Chevy Chase
See: CO13 The Alumni of "Saturday Night Live"

ST28 Cheech (1946–) **and Chong** (1938–)
After Hours
Born in East L.A.*
Cheech and Chong's Next Movie
Cheech and Chong's The Corsican Brothers
Echo Park*
Far Out Man
Ferngully . . . The Last Rainforest (character
voices)
Get Out of My Room
Ghostbusters II*
It Came From Hollywood
Nice Dreams
Rude Awakening*

Still Smokin'
Things Are Tough All Over
Up in Smoke
Yellowbeard
*Cheech only

ST29 Cher (1946–)
Come Back to the Five & Dime, Jimmy Dean,
Jimmy Dean
Mask
Mermaids
Moonstruck
The Player (bit)
Silkwood
Suspect
The Witches of Eastwick

ST30 Julie Christie (1941–)
Billy Liar
Darling
Demon Seed
Don't Look Now
Dr. Zhivago
Fahrenheit 451
Far From the Madding Crowd
Fools of Fortune
The Go-Between
Heat and Dust
Heaven Can Wait (1978)
McCabe and Mrs. Miller
Miss Mary
Nashville
Petulia
Power (1986)
Return of the Soldier
Secret Obsessions
Separate Tables (1983 version)
Shampoo

ST31 Jill Clayburgh (1944–)
The Art of Crime
The Best of Chevy Chase
First Monday in October
Griffin and Phoenix: A Love Story
Hanna K
Hustling
I'm Dancing as Fast as I Can
It's My Turn
Miles to Go
Portnoy's Complaint
Rich in Love
Semi-Tough
Shy People
Silver Streak
Starting Over
The Terminal Man
The Thief Who Came to Dinner
An Unmarried Woman
The Wedding Party
Where Are the Children?
Whispers in the Dark

John Cleese
See: CO15 The Alumni of "Monty Python's
　Flying Circus"

ST32　Montgomery Clift
(1920–1966)
The Big Lift
From Here to Eternity
The Heiress
I Confess
Indiscretion of an American Wife
Judgment at Nuremberg
Lonelyhearts
The Misfits
A Place in the Sun
Raintree County
Red River
The Search
Suddenly Last Summer
The Young Lions
DOCUMENTARY SUBJECT
Montgomery Clift

ST33　Glenn Close (1947–)
The Big Chill
Dangerous Liaisons
Fatal Attraction
Hamlet (1990 version)
Hook (bit)
Immediate Family
Jagged Edge
Light Years (character voice)
Maxie
Meeting Venus
The Natural
Orphan Train
Reversal of Fortune
Sarah, Plain and Tall
The Stone Boy
The World According to Garp

ST34　Claudette Colbert (1905–)
Boom Town
Cleopatra (1934 version)
Drums Along the Mohawk
The Egg and I
Guest Wife
I Cover the Waterfront
It Happened One Night
Let's Make It Legal
The Palm Beach Story
Since You Went Away
Texas Lady
Three Came Home
Tomorrow Is Forever
Without Reservations

ST35　Ronald Colman (1891–1958)
Around the World in 80 Days (bit)
Arrowsmith

Bulldog Drummond
Champagne for Caesar
A Double Life
Lady Windermere's Fan
Lost Horizon (1937 version)
Lucky Partners
The Prisoner of Zenda (1937
　version)
Random Harvest
Romola
A Tale of Two Cities (1935 version)
The Talk of the Town
The White Sister

ST36　Sean Connery (1930–)
The Anderson Tapes
Another Time, Another Place
A Bridge Too Far
Cuba
Darby O'Gill and the Little People
Diamonds Are Forever
Dr. No
Family Business
A Fine Madness
Five Days One Summer
From Russia With Love
Goldfinger
The Great Train Robbery
Happy Anniversary 007: 25 Years of
　James Bond
Highlander
Highlander II: The Quickening
The Hunt for Red October
Indiana Jones and the Last Crusade
The Longest Day
The Man Who Would Be King
Marnie
Medicine Man
Meteor
The Molly Maguires
Murder on the Orient Express
The Name of the Rose
Never Say Never Again
The Next Man
Outland
The Presidio
The Red Tent
Robin and Marian
Robin Hood: Prince of Thieves (bit)
The Russia House
Shalako
Sword of the Valiant
The Terrorists
Thunderball
Time Bandits
The Untouchables
The Wind and the Lion
Wrong Is Right
You Only Live Twice
Zardoz

ST37 Gary Cooper (1901–1961)
Ball of Fire
Beau Geste (1939 version)
Blowing Wild
Cloak and Dagger (1946)
The Court-Martial of Billy Mitchell
A Farewell to Arms (1932 version)
The Fountainhead
Friendly Persuasion
The General Died at Dawn
Good Sam
It
It's a Great Feeling (bit)
Lives of a Bengal Lancer
Love in the Afternoon
Meet John Doe
Morocco
Mr. Deeds Goes to Town
The Naked Edge
Pride of the Yankees
The Real Glory
Sergeant York
Ten North Frederick
Wings
The Wreck of the *Mary Deare*
WESTERNS
Along Came Jones
The Cowboy and the Lady
Distant Drums
Fighting Caravans
The Hanging Tree
High Noon
Man of the West
The Plainsman
They Came to Cordura
Vera Cruz
The Virginian
The Westerner

ST38 Kevin Costner (1955–)
American Flyers
The Bodyguard
Bull Durham
Chasing Dreams (bit)
Dances With Wolves*
Fandango
Field of Dreams
Frances (bit)
The Gunrunner
JFK
No Way Out
Revenge (1990)
Robin Hood: Prince of Thieves
Silverado
Stacy's Knights
Table for Five (bit)
Testament
Truth or Dare (bit)
The Untouchables
*also director

ST39 Joan Crawford (1904–1977)
Above Suspicion
Autumn Leaves
Berserk
The Bride Wore Red
Chained
Dance, Fools, Dance
Dancing Lady
Female on the Beach
Flamingo Road
Forsaking All Others
The Gorgeous Hussy
Grand Hotel
Hollywood Canteen (bit)
Humoresque
I Live My Life
It's a Great Feeling (bit)
Johnny Guitar
The Last of Mrs. Cheyney
Mannequin (1937)
MGM's Big Parade of Comedy
Mildred Pierce
Night Gallery
Our Dancing Daughters
Our Modern Maidens
Possessed (1931)
Possessed (1947)
Rain
Reunion in France
Sadie McKee
The Shining Hour
Strait-Jacket
Strange Cargo
Susan and God
Torch Song
What Ever Happened to Baby Jane?
When Ladies Meet
A Woman's Face (1941 version)
The Women (1939)

ST40 Bing Crosby (1904–1977)
See Also: CL15 Memorable Screen Teams—
   Bob Hope and Bing Crosby
The Bells of St. Mary's
The Country Girl (1954 version)
Going Hollywood
Going My Way
The Legend of Sleepy Hollow (narration and
   songs)
Little Boy Lost
My Favorite Brunette (bit)
The Princess and the Pirate (bit)
Reaching for the Moon (bit)
MUSICALS
A Connecticut Yankee in King Arthur's Court
   (1948 version)
Here Comes the Groom
High Society
Holiday Inn
The King of Jazz

Let's Make Love
Mr. Music
Road to Bali
The Road to Hong Kong
Road to Morocco
Road to Rio
Road to Singapore
Road to Utopia
Road to Zanzibar
Robin and the Seven Hoods
That's Entertainment!
That's Entertainment, Part II
White Christmas

ST41 Tom Cruise (1962–)
All the Right Moves
Born on the Fourth of July
Cocktail
The Color of Money
Days of Thunder
Endless Love (bit)
Far and Away
A Few Good Men
Legend
Losin' It
The Outsiders
Rain Man
Risky Business
Taps
Top Gun

Billy Crystal
See: CO13 The Alumni of "Saturday Night
   Live"

Jane Curtin
See: CO13 The Alumni of "Saturday Night Live"

ST42 Jamie Lee Curtis (1958–)
Amazing Grace and Chuck
As Summers Die
Blue Steel
Death of a Centerfold
Dominick and Eugene
A Fish Called Wanda
The Fog
Forever Young
Grandview, U.S.A.
Halloween
Halloween 2
Love Letters
A Man in Love
My Girl
Perfect!
Prom Night
Queens Logic
Road Games
She's in the Army Now
Terror Train
Trading Places

ST43 Peter Cushing (1913–)
Alexander the Great
And Now the Screaming Starts
Asylum
At the Earth's Core
The Beast Must Die
Biggles: Adventures in Time
The Blood Beast Terror
The Bloodsuckers
The Brides of Dracula
Call Him Mr. Shatter
A Choice of Weapons
A Chump at Oxford
Count Dracula and His Vampire Bride
The Creeping Flesh
The Curse of Frankenstein
Daleks: Invasion Earth 2150 A.D.
The Devil's Undead
Dr. Phibes Rises Again
Dr. Terror's House of Horrors
Dr. Who and the Daleks
Dynasty of Fear
The Evil of Frankenstein
Fear in the Night (1972)
Frankenstein and the Monster from Hell
From Beyond the Grave
The Ghoul (1975)
The Gorgon
Hamlet (1948 version)
Horror Express
Horror of Dracula
The Hound of the Baskervilles (1959
   version)
House of the Long Shadows
The House That Dripped Blood
Island of Terror
Island of the Burning Doomed
Land of the Minotaur
Legend of the Seven Golden Vampires
Legend of the Werewolf
Madhouse (1974)
Mania
Masks of Death
Moulin Rouge
The Mummy (1959 version)
Nothing But the Night
Scream and Scream Again
The Seven Brothers Meet Dracula
Shock Waves
Silent Scream (1984)
The Skull
Star Wars
Sword of Sherwood Forest
Sword of the Valiant
Tales from the Crypt
Top Secret!
Torture Garden
Twins of Evil
The Uncanny
The Vampire Lovers

ST44 Bette Davis (1908–1989)
All About Eve
All This and Heaven, Too
As Summers Die
Beyond the Forest
The Bride Came C.O.D.
Bureau of Missing Persons
Burnt Offerings
Cabin in the Cotton
The Catered Affair
The Corn Is Green (1945 version)
Dangerous
The Dark Secret of Harvest Home
Dark Victory
Dead Ringer
Death on the Nile
Deception
The Disappearance of Aimee
The Empty Canvas
Ex-Lady
Fashions of 1934
The Great Lie
Hell's House
Hollywood Canteen
Hush . . . Hush, Sweet Charlotte
In This Our Life
Jezebel
Juarez
June Bride
Kid Galahad (1937 version)
The Letter
The Little Foxes
Little Gloria . . . Happy at Last
Madame Sin
The Man Who Came to Dinner
Marked Woman
Mr. Skeffington
Now, Voyager
Of Human Bondage (1934 version)
The Old Maid
The Petrified Forest
Phone Call From a Stranger
A Piano for Mrs. Cimino
Pocketful of Miracles
The Private Lives of Elizabeth and Essex
Return from Witch Mountain
Right of Way
Satan Met a Lady
The Sisters
The Star
A Stolen Life
Strangers: The Story of a Mother and
    Daughter
Thank Your Lucky Stars
That Certain Woman
Three on a Match
The Virgin Queen
Watch on the Rhine
The Watcher in the Woods
Way Back Home

The Whales of August
What Ever Happened to Baby Jane?
Where Love Has Gone
White Mama
Wicked Stepmother
Winter Meeting

ST45 Geena Davis (1957–)
The Accidental Tourist
Beetlejuice
Earth Girls Are Easy
Fletch
The Fly (1986 version)
Hero
A League of Their Own
Quick Change
Secret Weapons
Thelma & Louise
Tootsie (bit)
Transylvania 6-5000

ST46 Judy Davis (1956–)
Alice
Barton Fink
The Final Option
Heatwave
High Rolling
High Tide
Husbands and Wives
Impromptu
Kangaroo
My Brilliant Career
Naked Lunch
One Against the Wind
A Passage to India
Rocket to the Moon
Where Angels Fear to Tread
Winter of Our Dreams
A Woman Called Golda

ST47 Doris Day (1924–)
April in Paris
By the Light of the Silvery Moon
Calamity Jane (1953)
The Glass Bottom Boat
I'll See You in My Dreams
It's a Great Feeling
Jumbo
Love Me or Leave Me
Lover Come Back
Lucky Me
Lullaby of Broadway
The Man Who Knew Too Much (1956
    version)
Midnight Lace
My Dream Is Yours
On Moonlight Bay
The Pajama Game
Pillow Talk
Please Don't Eat the Daisies

Romance on the High Seas
Send Me No Flowers
Tea for Two
Teacher's Pet
That Touch of Mink
The Thrill of It All
The Tunnel of Love
The West Point Story
Where Were You When the Lights Went
   Out?
The Winning Team
With Six You Get Eggroll
Young at Heart
Young Man With a Horn

ST48 Daniel Day-Lewis (1958–)
The Bounty (bit)
Eversmile, New Jersey
Gandhi (bit)
How Many Miles to Babylon?
The Last of the Mohicans (1992 version)
My Beautiful Laundrette
My Left Foot
A Room With a View
Stars and Bars
Sunday, Bloody Sunday (bit)
The Unbearable Lightness of Being

ST49 Olivia de Havilland (1916–)
The Adventurers
Airport '77
The Ambassador's Daughter
Anastasia: The Mystery of Anna
Anthony Adverse
Captain Blood
The Charge of the Light Brigade (1936 version)
The Dark Mirror
Dodge City
The Fifth Musketeer
Gone With the Wind
The Heiress
Hollywood Canteen
Hush . . . Hush, Sweet Charlotte
In This Our Life
Lady in a Cage
Making of a Legend—Gone With the Wind
A Midsummer Night's Dream
Not as a Stranger
The Private Lives of Elizabeth and Essex
The Proud Rebel
Santa Fe Trail
The Snake Pit
The Strawberry Blonde
The Swarm
Thank Your Lucky Stars
They Died With Their Boots On

ST50 Catherine Deneuve (1943–)
Act of Aggression
The April Fools

A Choice of Arms
Donkey Skin
The Hunger
Hustle
I Love All of You
Indochine
La Grande Bourgeoise
The Last Metro
Love Songs
Lovers Like Us
March or Die
The Murri Affair
Repulsion
Scene of the Crime
A Slightly Pregnant Man
Tristana
The Umbrellas of Cherbourg

ST51 Robert De Niro (1943–)
Addict
Angel Heart
Awakenings
Backdraft
Bang the Drum Slowly
Bloody Mama
Brazil
Cape Fear (1991 version)
Confessions of a Peeping John
Dear America: Letters Home From Vietnam
   (narrator)
The Deer Hunter
Falling in Love
The Godfather, Part II
The Godfather: The Complete Epic,
   1902–1958
The Godfather Trilogy, 1901–1980
GoodFellas
Greetings
Guilty by Suspicion
Jacknife
King of Comedy
The Last Tycoon
Mad Dog and Glory
Mean Streets
Midnight Run
The Mission
Mistress
New York, New York
Night and the City (1992 version)
1900
Once Upon a Time in America
Raging Bull
Stanley & Iris
The Swap
Taxi Driver
This Boy's Life
True Confessions
The Untouchables
The Wedding Party
We're No Angels (1989 version)

ST52 Gérard Depardieu (1948–)
Buffet Froid
Camille Claudel
A Choice of Arms
Cyrano de Bergerac (1990 version)
Danton
1492: Conquest of Paradise
Get Out Your Handkerchiefs
Going Places
Green Card
I Love All of You
Jean de Florette
La Chevre
Le Tartuffe*
Les Compères
The Last Metro
Loulou
Maitresse
Mon Oncle d'Amerique
The Moon in the Gutter
1900
One Woman or Two
Police
The Return of Martin Guerre
Stavisky (bit)
Too Beautiful for You
Under Satan's Sun
Uranus
Vincent, Francois, Paul and the Others
The Woman Next Door
*also director

ST53 Laura Dern (1966–)
Afterburn
Blue Velvet
Fat Man and Little Boy
Haunted Summer
Industrial Symphony No. 1: The Dream of
    the Broken Hearted
Mask
Rambling Rose
Smooth Talk
Strange Case of Dr. Jekyll & Mr. Hyde
Teachers (bit)
Wild at Heart

ST54 Danny DeVito (1944–)
Batman Returns
Goin' South
Going Ape
Head Office
Hoffa*
Hurry Up, or I'll Be 30
Jack the Bear
Jewel of the Nile
Joe Piscopo New Jersey Special
Johnny Dangerously
My Little Pony (character voice)
One Flew Over the Cuckoo's Nest
Other People's Money

The Ratings Game*
Romancing the Stone
Ruthless People
Terms of Endearment
Throw Momma from the Train*
Tin Men
Twins
The Van
The War of the Roses*
Wise Guys
*also director

ST55 Marlene Dietrich (1901–1992)
Around the World in 80 Days (bit)
Blonde Venus
The Blue Angel
Destry Rides Again
The Garden of Allah
Judgment at Nuremberg
Just a Gigolo
Knight Without Armour
Morocco
Paris When It Sizzles
Rancho Notorious
Seven Sinners
The Spoilers (1942 version)
Stage Fright
Touch of Evil
Witness for the Prosecution (1957 version)
DOCUMENTARY SUBJECT
Marlene

ST56 Matt Dillon (1964–)
The Big Town
Bloodhounds of Broadway
Drugstore Cowboy
The Flamingo Kid
Kansas
A Kiss Before Dying (1991 version)
Liar's Moon
Little Darlings
My Bodyguard
Native Son
The Outsiders
Over the Edge
Rebel (1986)
Rumble Fish
Singles
Target
Tex
Women and Men: Stories of Seduction, Part 2

ST57 Kirk Douglas (1916–)
Along the Great Divide
Amos
The Arrangement
The Bad and the Beautiful
The Big Sky
The Big Trees
The Brotherhood

Cast a Giant Shadow
Catch Me a Spy
Champion
The Chosen (1978)
The Devil's Disciple
Dr. Jekyll and Mr. Hyde (1973 version)
Draw!
Eddie Macon's Run
The Final Countdown
For Love or Money
The Fury
A Gunfight
Gunfight at the O.K. Corral
Holocaust Survivors: Remembrance of Love
Home Movies
In Harm's Way
The Indian Fighter
Is Paris Burning?
Last Train From Gun Hill
The Light at the Edge of the World
The List of Adrian Messenger
Lonely Are the Brave
Lust for Life
The Man From Snowy River
Man Without a Star
The Master Touch
My Dear Secretary
Once Is Not Enough
Oscar (bit)
Out of the Past
Paths of Glory
Posse*
Queenie
The Racers
Saturn 3
Seven Days in May
Spartacus
The Strange Love of Martha Ivers
Strangers When We Meet
There Was a Crooked Man
Tough Guys
20,000 Leagues Under the Sea
Two Weeks in Another Town
Ulysses (1955)
The Vikings
The Villain
The War Wagon
The Way West
Young Man With a Horn
*also director

ST58 Melvyn Douglas (1902–1981)
The Americanization of Emily
Annie Oakley
As You Desire Me
Being There
Billy Budd
Captains Courageous
The Changeling
The Death Squad

The Gorgeous Hussy
Ghost Story
Hard Frame
Hotel
Hud
I Never Sang for My Father
Intimate Strangers
MGM's Big Parade of Comedy
Making of a Legend—Gone With the Wind
Mr. Blandings Builds His Dream House
Murder or Mercy
My Forbidden Past
Ninotchka
The Sea of Grass
The Seduction of Joe Tynan
The Shining Hour
Tell Me a Riddle
The Tenant
That Uncertain Feeling
Twilight's Last Gleaming
Two-Faced Woman
The Vampire Bat
Woman in the Shadows
A Woman's Secret

ST59 Michael Douglas (1944–)
Adam at 6 A.M.
Basic Instinct
Black Rain (U.S.)
The China Syndrome
A Chorus Line
Coma
Falling Down
Fatal Attraction
Hail, Hero!
It's My Turn
Jewel of the Nile
Napoleon and Samantha
Romancing the Stone
Shining Through
The Star Chamber
Summertree
Wall Street
The War of the Roses
When Michael Calls

ST60 Richard Dreyfuss (1947–)
Always
American Graffiti
The Apprenticeship of Duddy Kravitz
The Big Fix
The Buddy System
Close Encounters of the Third Kind
The Competition
Dillinger
Down and Out in Beverly Hills
The Goodbye Girl
Inserts
Jaws
Let It Ride

Moon Over Parador
Nuts
Once Again
Postcards From the Edge
Prisoner of Honor
Rosencrantz and Guildenstern Are Dead
The Second Coming of Suzanne
Stakeout
Stand by Me (narrator)
Tin Men
Valley of the Dolls (1967 version) (bit)
What About Bob?
Whose Life Is It, Anyway?

ST61 Faye Dunaway (1941–)
The Arrangement
Barfly
Beverly Hills Madam
Bonnie and Clyde
Burning Secret
The Champ (1979 version)
Chinatown
Cold Sassy Tree
The Country Girl (1982 version)
The Deadly Trap
The Disappearance of Aimee
Double Edge
Ellis Island
Eyes of Laura Mars
The First Deadly Sin
The Four Musketeers
The Gamble
The Handmaid's Tale
Little Big Man
Midnight Crossing
Mommie Dearest
Network
Ordeal by Innocence
Silhouette
Supergirl
The Temp
The Thomas Crown Affair
Three Days of the Condor
The Three Musketeers (1974 version)
The Towering Inferno
The Two Jakes (character voice)
Voyage of the Damned
Wait Until Spring, Bandini
The Wicked Lady

ST62 Irene Dunne (1901–1990)
Ann Vickers
The Awful Truth
Bachelor Apartment
Cimarron
Consolation Marriage
A Guy Named Joe
I Remember Mama
Joy of Living
Life With Father

Love Affair
My Favorite Wife
Never a Dull Moment (1950)
Penny Serenade
Roberta
Show Boat (1936 version)
Sweet Adeline
The White Cliffs of Dover

ST63 Robert Duvall (1931–)
Apocalypse Now
Badge 373
Belizaire the Cajun (bit)
The Betsy
Breakout
Bullitt
Captain Newman, M.D. (bit)
The Chase (1966)
Colors
The Conversation
Countdown
Days of Thunder
The Detective (1968) (bit)
The Eagle Has Landed
Falling Down
The Godfather
The Godfather, Part II
The Godfather: The Complete Epic,
   1902–1958
The Godfather Trilogy, 1901–1980
The Great Northfield, Minnesota, Raid
The Great Santini
The Greatest
The Handmaid's Tale
Hearts of Darkness: A Filmmaker's
   Apocalypse
Hotel Colonial
Ike: The War Years
Invasion of the Body Snatchers (1978
   version) (bit)
Joe Kidd
The Killer Elite
Lady Ice
Let's Get Harry
The Lightship
Lonesome Dove
M*A*S*H
The Natural
Network
Newsies
The Pursuit of D.B. Cooper
The Rain People
Rambling Rose
The Seven Percent Solution
A Show of Force (bit)
Stalin
The Stone Boy
THX 1138
Tender Mercies
The Terry Fox Story

To Kill a Mockingbird
Tomorrow
True Confessions
True Grit
DIRECTOR ONLY
Angelo, My Love

ST64 Clint Eastwood (1930–)
Any Which Way You Can
City Heat
Coogan's Bluff
The Dead Pool
Dirty Harry
The Eiger Sanction*
The Enforcer (1976)
Escape From Alcatraz
Every Which Way But Loose
Firefox*
The Gauntlet*
Heartbreak Ridge*
Honkytonk Man*
Kelly's Heroes
Magnum Force
Paint Your Wagon
Pink Cadillac
Play Misty for Me*
The Rookie*
Sudden Impact*
Thunderbolt and Lightfoot
Tightrope
Where Eagles Dare
White Hunter, Black Heart*
WESTERNS
The Beguiled
Bronco Billy*
A Fistful of Dollars
For a Few Dollars More
The Good, the Bad, and the Ugly
Hang 'em High
High Plains Drifter*
Joe Kidd
The Outlaw Josey Wales*
Pale Rider*
Two Mules for Sister Sara
Unforgiven*
*also director
DIRECTOR ONLY
Bird

Nelson Eddy
See: CL15 Memorable Screen Teams—Nelson
  Eddy and Jeanette MacDonald

ST65 Mia Farrow (1945–)
See also: XT30 He Directs, She Acts
Alice
Another Woman
Avalanche
Broadway Danny Rose
Crimes and Misdemeanors

A Dandy in Aspic
Death on the Nile
The Great Gatsby
Guns at Batasi
Hannah and Her Sisters
The Haunting of Julia
High Heels
Hurricane
Husbands and Wives
The Last Unicorn (character voice)
A Midsummer Night's Sex Comedy
New York Stories
The Purple Rose of Cairo
Radio Days
Rosemary's Baby
Secret Ceremony
See No Evil
September
Shadows and Fog
Supergirl
A Wedding
Zelig

ST66 Sally Field (1946–)
Absence of Malice
Back Roads
Beyond the Poseidon Adventure
The End
Heroes
Home for the Holidays
Homeward Bound: The Incredible Journey
  (character voice)
Hooper
Kiss Me Goodbye
Murphy's Romance
Norma Rae
Not Without My Daughter
Places in the Heart
Punchline
Smokey and the Bandit
Smokey and the Bandit II
Soapdish
Stay Hungry
Steel Magnolias
Surrender
Sybil
The Way West

ST67 W.C. Fields (1879–1946)
The Bank Dick
The Barber Shop
The Best of W.C. Fields
David Copperfield
The Dentist
A Fatal Glass of Beer/The Pool Sharks
A Flask of Fields
International House
It's a Gift
MGM's Big Parade of Comedy
Mrs. Wiggs of the Cabbage Patch

My Little Chickadee
Never Give a Sucker an Even Break
Running Wild
Sally of the Sawdust
W.C. Fields Comedy Bag
W.C. Fields Festival
You Can't Cheat an Honest Man

ST68 Albert Finney (1936–)
Alpha Beta
Annie
The Dresser
The Duellists
The Entertainer (bit)
Gumshoe
The Image
Looker
Loophole
Miller's Crossing
Murder on the Orient Express
Orphans
The Playboys
Pope John Paul II
Rich in Love
Scrooge (1970 version)
Shoot the Moon
Tom Jones
Two for the Road
Under the Volcano
Wolfen

Joe Flaherty
See: CO14 The Alumni of "SCTV"

ST69 Errol Flynn (1909–1959)
Adventures of Captain Fabian
The Adventures of Don Juan
The Adventures of Robin Hood
Against All Flags
Assault of the Rebel Girls (Cuban Rebel Girls)
Captain Blood
The Charge of the Light Brigade (1936
   version)
The Dawn Patrol (1938 version)
Desperate Journey
Dive Bomber
Dodge City
Edge of Darkness
Escape Me Never
Gentleman Jim
Kim
The Master of Ballantrae
Northern Pursuit
Objective, Burma!
The Prince and the Pauper (1937 version)
The Private Lives of Elizabeth and Essex
San Antonio
Santa Fe Trail
The Sea Hawk
Silver River

The Sisters
Thank Your Lucky Stars
That Forsyte Woman
They Died With Their Boots On
Virginia City
The Warriors (1955)
SUBJECT ONLY
My Wicked, Wicked Ways

ST70 Bridget Fonda (1964–)
Aria
Army of Darkness: Evil Dead 3 (bit)
Doc Hollywood
Frankenstein Unbound
The Godfather, Part III
The Godfather Trilogy, 1901–1980
Iron Maze
Leather Jackets
Light Years
Out of the Rain
Point of No Return
Scandal
Shag
Single White Female
Singles
Strapless
You Can't Hurry Love

ST71 Henry Fonda (1905–1982)
Advise and Consent
Ash Wednesday
Battle Force
Battle of the Bulge
The Best Man
A Big Hand for the Little Lady
The Big Street
The Boston Strangler
The Cheyenne Social Club
City on Fire
Clarence Darrow
Drums Along the Mohawk
Fail-Safe
The Farmer Takes a Wife (1935 version)
Fedora
Fort Apache
The Fugitive
Gideon's Trumpet
The Grapes of Wrath
The Great Smokey Roadblock
Home to Stay
How the West Was Won
I Dream Too Much
The Immortal Sergeant
In Harm's Way
Jesse James
Jezebel
The Lady Eve
The Last Four Days
The Longest Day
The Mad Miss Manton

Madigan
The Magnificent Dope
Main Street to Broadway (bit)
Meteor
Midway
Mister Roberts
The Moon's Our Home
My Darling Clementine
My Name Is Nobody
Night Flight From Moscow
The Oldest Living Graduate
On Golden Pond
Once Upon a Time in the West
The Ox-Bow Incident
The Red Pony (1973 version)
The Return of Frank James
Rollercoaster
Sex and the Single Girl
Sometimes a Great Notion
Stage Struck
Summer Solstice
The Swarm
Tentacles
That Certain Woman
There Was a Crooked Man
The Tin Star
Too Late the Hero
12 Angry Men
Wanda Nevada
War and Peace (1956 version)
Warlock (1959)
Wings of the Morning
The Wrong Man
You Only Live Once
Young Mr. Lincoln
Yours, Mine and Ours

ST72 Jane Fonda (1937–)
Agnes of God
Any Wednesday
Barbarella
Barefoot in the Park
California Suite
Cat Ballou
The Chase (1966)
The China Syndrome
Circle of Love
Comes a Horseman
Coming Home
The Dollmaker
A Doll's House (Fonda version)
The Electric Horseman
Fun With Dick and Jane
The Game Is Over
Joy House
Julia
Klute
The Morning After
Nine to Five
Old Gringo

On Golden Pond
Period of Adjustment
Rollover
Stanley & Iris
Steelyard Blues
Tall Story
They Shoot Horses, Don't They?
A Walk on the Wild Side

ST73 Joan Fontaine (1917–)
Beyond a Reasonable Doubt
The Bigamist
Born To Be Bad
Casanova's Big Night
A Damsel in Distress
Decameron Nights
Gunga Din
Island in the Sun
Ivanhoe
Jane Eyre (1944 version)
Letter From an Unknown Woman
Maid's Night Out
A Million to One
Quality Street
Rebecca
September Affair
Suspicion (1941 version)
Until They Sail
The Users
Voyage to the Bottom of the Sea
The Women (1939)

ST74 Harrison Ford (1942–)
American Graffiti
Apocalypse Now
Blade Runner
The Conversation
Dead Heat on a Merry-Go-Round (bit)
The Empire Strikes Back
Force 10 From Navarone
Frantic (1988)
The Frisco Kid
Getting Straight (bit)
Hanover Street
Heroes
Indiana Jones and the Last Crusade
Indiana Jones and the Temple of Doom
Luv (bit)
More American Graffiti (bit)
The Mosquito Coast
Patriot Games
Presumed Innocent
Raiders of the Lost Ark
Regarding Henry
Return of the Jedi
Star Wars
Witness
Working Girl
Zabriskie Point

ST75 Jodie Foster (1962–)
The Accused
Alice Doesn't Live Here Anymore
Backtrack
The Blood of Others
Bugsy Malone
Candleshoe
Carny
Five Corners
Foxes
Freaky Friday
The Hotel New Hampshire
The Little Girl Who Lives Down the Lane
Little Man Tate*
Napoleon and Samantha
O'Hara's Wife
One Little Indian
Shadows and Fog
Siesta
The Silence of the Lambs
Smile Jenny, You're Dead
Sommersby
Stealing Home
Svengali (1983 version)
Taxi Driver
Tom Sawyer
*also director

ST76 Morgan Freeman (1937–)
Blood Money
The Bonfire of the Vanities
Brubaker
Clean and Sober
Driving Miss Daisy
The Execution of Raymond Graham
Eyewitness
Glory
Harry and Son
Johnny Handsome
Lean on Me
Marie
The Power of One
Robin Hood: Prince of Thieves
Roll of Thunder, Hear My Cry
Street Smart
That Was Then . . . This is Now
Unforgiven

ST77 Clark Gable (1901–1960)
Across the Wide Missouri
Betrayed (1954)
Boom Town
But Not for Me
Chained
China Seas
Command Decision
Dance, Fools, Dance
Dancing Lady
Forsaking All Others
A Free Soul

Gone With the Wind
Hold Your Man
Honky Tonk
The Hucksters
Idiot's Delight
It Happened One Night
It Started in Naples
The King and Four Queens
The Making of a Legend—Gone With the Wind
Manhattan Melodrama
The Misfits
Mogambo
Mutiny on the Bounty (1935 version)
Night Nurse
No Man of Her Own
The Painted Desert
Possessed (1931)
Red Dust
Run Silent, Run Deep
San Francisco
Saratoga
Soldier of Fortune
Strange Cargo
Susan Lennox: Her Fall and Rise
The Tall Men
Teacher's Pet
Test Pilot
That's Entertainment!
That's Entertainment, Part 2
Too Hot to Handle
Wife vs. Secretary

ST78 Greta Garbo (1905–1990)
Anna Christie
Anna Karenina (1935 version)
As You Desire Me
Camille
Conquest
Flesh and the Devil
Gosta Berling's Saga
Grand Hotel
Inspiration
Joyless Street
The Kiss (1929)
Mata Hari (1932)
MGM's Big Parade of Comedy
Mysterious Lady
Ninotchka
The Painted Veil
Queen Christina
Romance
The Single Standard
Susan Lennox: Her Fall and Rise
Two-Faced Woman
Wild Orchids
A Woman of Affairs

ST79 Ava Gardner (1924–1990)
The Barefoot Contessa
Bhowani Junction

The Bible
The Cassandra Crossing
City on Fire
Earthquake
East Side, West Side
55 Days at Peking
Ghosts on the Loose
The Hucksters
The Kidnapping of the President
The Knights of the Round Table
The Life and Times of Judge Roy Bean
The Long Hot Summer (1986 version)
Mogambo
My Forbidden Past
The Night of the Iguana
On the Beach
One Touch of Venus
Permission to Kill
Priest of Love
Regina
Reunion in France
The Sentinel
Seven Days in May
Show Boat (1951 version)
The Snows of Kilimanjaro
Whistle Stop
SUBJECT ONLY
Sinatra

ST80 John Garfield (1913–1952)
Air Force
Body and Soul (1947 version)
Destination Tokyo
The Fallen Sparrow
Force of Evil
Four Daughters
Gentleman's Agreement
Hollywood Canteen (bit)
Humoresque
Juarez
The Postman Always Rings Twice (1946 version)
The Sea Wolf
Thank Your Lucky Stars
They Made Me a Criminal
Tortilla Flat

ST81 Judy Garland (1922–1969)
See also: CL15 Memorable Screen Teams—
   Mickey Rooney and Judy Garland; XT30
   He Directs, She Acts
Andy Hardy Meets Debutante
A Child Is Waiting
The Clock
Judgment at Nuremberg
Life Begins for Andy Hardy
Listen, Darling
Love Finds Andy Hardy
Thoroughbreds Don't Cry
MUSICALS
Babes in Arms

Babes on Broadway
Broadway Melody of 1938
Easter Parade
Everybody Sing
For Me and My Gal
Girl Crazy
The Harvey Girls
I Could Go On Singing
In the Good Old Summertime
Little Nellie Kelly
Meet Me in St. Louis
The Pirate
Presenting Lily Mars
A Star Is Born (1954 version)
Strike Up the Band
Summer Stock
That's Entertainment!
That's Entertainment, Part 2
Thousands Cheer
Till the Clouds Roll By
The Wizard of Oz
Words and Music
Ziegfeld Follies
Ziegfeld Girl

ST82 James Garner (1928–)
The Americanization of Emily
The Castaway Cowboy
The Children's Hour
Decoration Day
The Distinguished Gentleman (bit)
Duel at Diablo
The Fan
Fire in the Sky
The Glitter Dome
Grand Prix
The Great Escape
Hour of the Gun
How Sweet It Is
A Man Called Sledge
Marlowe
Murphy's Romance
One Little Indian
Sayonara
The Skin Game (1971)
Sunset
Support Your Local Sheriff
Tank
They Only Kill Their Masters
The Thrill of It All
Victor/Victoria
The Wheeler Dealers

ST83 Greer Garson (1908–)
Blossoms in the Dust
Goodbye, Mr. Chips (1939 version)
The Happiest Millionaire
Invincible Mr. Disraeli
Julia Misbehaves
Madame Curie

Mrs. Miniver
Pride and Prejudice
Random Harvest
The Singing Nun
Sunrise at Campobello
That Forsyte Woman
When Ladies Meet

ST84 Richard Gere (1949–)
American Gigolo
Beyond the Limit
Bloodbrothers
Breathless (1983 version)
The Cotton Club
Days of Heaven
Final Analysis
Internal Affairs
King David
Looking for Mr. Goodbar
Miles From Home
No Mercy
An Officer and a Gentleman
Power (1986)
Pretty Woman
Report to the Commissioner (bit)
Sommersby
Strike Force
Yanks

ST85 Mel Gibson (1956–)
Air America
Attack Force Z
Bird on a Wire
The Bounty
Forever Young
Gallipoli
Hamlet (1990 version)
Lethal Weapon
Lethal Weapon 2
Lethal Weapon 3
Mad Max
Mad Max Beyond Thunderdome
Mrs. Soffel
The River (1984)
The Road Warrior
Summer City
Tequila Sunrise
Tim
The Year of Living Dangerously

ST86 John Gielgud (1904–)
Appointment With Death
Around the World in 80 Days (bit)
Arthur
Arthur 2: On the Rocks
Becket
Brideshead Revisited
Caligula
The Canterville Ghost (1986 version)
Chariots of Fire
Chimes at Midnight

The Elephant Man
11 Harrowhouse
The Formula
Frankenstein (1982 version)
Gandhi
Getting It Right
Hunchback
Inside the Third Reich
Invitation to the Wedding
Julius Caesar (1953 and 1970 versions)
Laurence Olivier—A Life
Les Miserables (1978 version)
Lion of the Desert
The Loved One
A Man for All Seasons (1988 version)
Murder by Decree
Murder on the Orient Express
Plenty
Portrait of the Artist as a Young Man
The Power of One
The Priest of Love
Probe
Prospero's Books
Providence
Richard II
Richard III
Romeo and Juliet (1954 version, introducer)
Romeo and Juliet (1979 version)
Romance on the Orient Express
Saint Joan
Scandalous
The Scarlet and the Black
Sebastian
The Secret Agent
The Seven Dials Mystery
Shining Through
The Shoes of the Fisherman
The Shooting Party
Sphinx
Strike It Rich
Wagner
War and Remembrance
The Whistle Blower
Why Didn't They Ask Evans?
The Wicked Lady

Terry Gilliam
See: CO15 The Alumni of "Monty Python's
    Flying Circus"

ST87 Lillian Gish (1896–1993)
The Adventures of Huckleberry Finn (1985
    version)
The Birth of a Nation
Broken Blossoms
The Comedians
Commandos Strike at Dawn
D.W. Griffith Triple Feature
Duel in the Sun
Follow Me, Boys!

Hambone and Hillie
Hearts of the World
His Double Life
Hobson's Choice (1983 version)
Home, Sweet Home
Intolerance
Judith of Bethulia
The Night of the Hunter
Orphans of the Storm
Portrait of Jennie
Romola
The Short Films of D.W. Griffith,
 Vols. I–II
Sweet Liberty
True Heart Susie
The Unforgiven
Way Down East
A Wedding
The Whales of August
The White Sister
The Wind

ST88 Danny Glover (1947–)
Bat 21
The Color Purple
Dead Man Out
Flight of the Intruder
Grand Canyon
Keeping On
Lethal Weapon
Lethal Weapon 2
Lethal Weapon 3
Lonesome Dove
Mandela
Memorial Day
Out
Places in the Heart
Predator 2
Pure Luck
A Rage in Harlem
A Raisin in the Sun (1989 version)
Silverado
To Sleep With Anger
Witness

ST89 Whoopi Goldberg (1949–)
The Best of Comic Relief
The Best of Comic Relief '90
Burglar
Clara's Heart
The Color Purple
Comic Relief 2
Comic Relief 3
Fatal Beauty
Ghost
Homer and Eddie
Jumpin' Jack Flash
The Long Walk Home
National Lampoon's Loaded Weapon 1
 (bit)

Nelson Mandela, 70th Birthday Tribute
The Player
Sarafina!
Sister Act
Soapdish
The Telephone
Whoopi Goldberg: Fontaine . . . Why Am I
 Straight
Whoopi Goldberg Live
Wisecracks

ST90 Jeff Goldblum (1950–)
The Adventures of Buckaroo Banzai Across the
 Eighth Dimension
Between the Lines
Beyond Therapy
The Big Chill
Death Wish
Deep Cover
Earth Girls Are Easy
Ernie Kovacs: Between the Laughter
The Favor, The Watch, and the Very Big Fish
The Fly (1986 version)
Framed
Into the Night
Invasion of the Body Snatchers (1979
 version)
The Legend of Sleepy Hollow (1990 version)
Nashville
The Player (bit)
Rehearsal for Murder
The Right Stuff
The Sentinel
Shooting Elizabeth
Silverado
Special Delivery
The Tall Guy
Thank God It's Friday (bit)
The Three Little Pigs
Threshold
Transylvania 6–5000
Twisted Obsession
Vibes

ST91 Betty Grable (1916–1973)
The Beautiful Blonde From Bashful Bend
College Swing
Down Argentine Way
The Farmer Takes a Wife (1953 version)
Follow the Fleet (bit)
Footlight Serenade
The Gay Divorcee (bit)
How To Marry a Millionaire
I Wake Up Screaming
Moon Over Miami
Pin-Up Girl
Song of the Islands
Springtime in the Rockies
Three Broadway Girls (bit)
A Yank in the RAF

ST92 Cary Grant (1904–1986)
An Affair to Remember
Amazing Adventure
Arsenic and Old Lace
The Awful Truth
The Bachelor and the Bobby Soxer
The Bishop's Wife
Blonde Venus
Bringing Up Baby
Charade
Destination Tokyo
Every Girl Should Be Married
Father Goose
The Grass Is Greener
Gunga Din
His Girl Friday
Holiday
Houseboat
The Howards of Virginia
In Name Only
Indiscreet (1958)
MGM's Big Parade of Comedy
Monkey Business (1952)
Mr. Blandings Builds His Dream House
Mr. Lucky
My Favorite Wife
Night and Day
None but the Lonely Heart
North by Northwest
Notorious
Once Upon a Honeymoon
Only Angels Have Wings
Operation Petticoat
Penny Serenade
The Philadelphia Story
The Pride and the Passion
She Done Him Wrong
Suspicion (1941 version)
Suzy
Sylvia Scarlett
The Talk of the Town
That Touch of Mink
To Catch a Thief
The Toast of New York
Topper
Walk, Don't Run
Without Reservations (bit)

ST93 Melanie Griffith (1957–)
Body Double
The Bonfire of the Vanities
Born Yesterday (1993 version)
Cherry 2000
The Drowning Pool
Fear City
In the Spirit
Joyride
The Milagro Beanfield War
Night Moves
One on One (bit)

Pacific Heights
Paradise
She's in the Army Now
Shining Through
Smile
Something Wild
Stormy Monday
A Stranger Among Us
Underground Aces
Women and Men: Stories of Seduction
Working Girl

ST94 Charles Grodin (1935–)
Beethoven
Catch-22
The Couch Trip
11 Harrowhouse
The Grass Is Always Greener Over the
    Septic Tank
The Great Muppet Caper
Grown-Ups
The Heartbreak Kid
Heaven Can Wait (1978)
The Incredible Shrinking Woman
Ishtar
It's My Turn
Just Me and You
King Kong (1976 version)
Last Resort
The Lonely Guy
Midnight Run
Movers and Shakers
Real Life
Rosemary's Baby
Seems Like Old Times
Sex and the College Girl
Sunburn
Taking Care of Business
The Woman in Red
You Can't Hurry Love (bit)

ST95 Alec Guinness (1914–)
The Bridge on the River Kwai
Brother Sun, Sister Moon
The Captain's Paradise
The Comedians
Cromwell
Damn the Defiant!
The Detective (1954)
Dr. Zhivago
The Empire Strikes Back
The Fall of the Roman Empire
Great Expectations
A Handful of Dust
Hitler: The Last Ten Days
The Horse's Mouth
Kafka
Kind Hearts and Coronets
The Ladykillers
Last Holiday

The Lavender Hill Mob
Lawrence of Arabia
Little Dorrit
Little Lord Fauntleroy (1980 version)
Lovesick
The Malta Story
The Man in the White Suit
Murder by Death
Oliver Twist (1948 version)
A Passage to India
The Prisoner
The Promoter
The Quiller Memorandum
Raise the Titanic!
Return of the Jedi
Scrooge (1970 version)
Star Wars
The Swan
To Paris With Love
Tunes of Glory

ST96 Gene Hackman (1930–)
All Night Long
Another Woman
Bat 21
Bite the Bullet
Bonnie and Clyde
A Bridge Too Far
Class Action
The Conversation
Doctors' Wives
The Domino Principle
Downhill Racer
Eureka
The French Connection
The French Connection II
Full Moon in Blue Water
Hawaii
Hoosiers
I Never Sang for My Father
Lilith
Loose Cannons
March or Die
Marooned
Mississippi Burning
Misunderstood
Narrow Margin
Night Moves
No Way Out
The Package
The Poseidon Adventure
Postcards From the Edge
Power (1986)
Prime Cut
Reds
Scarecrow
Split Decisions
Superman
Superman II
Superman IV: The Quest for Peace

Target
Twice in a Lifetime
Uncommon Valor
Under Fire
Unforgiven
Young Frankenstein
Zandy's Bride

ST97 Tom Hanks (1956–)
Bachelor Party
Big
The Bonfire of the Vanities
The 'Burbs
Dragnet (1987)
Every Time We Say Goodbye
He Knows You're Alone
Joe Vs. the Volcano
A League of Their Own
The Man With One Red Shoe
Mazes and Monsters
The Money Pit
Nothing in Common
Punchline
Radio Flyer (narrator)
Splash
Turner and Hooch
Volunteers

Oliver Hardy
See: Star Check List ST113 Laurel
    and Hardy

ST98 Jean Harlow (1911–1937)
Bombshell
China Seas
Dinner at Eight
The Girl From Missouri
Hell's Angels (1930)
Hold Your Man
Libeled Lady
MGM's Big Parade of Comedy
Personal Property
Platinum Blonde
Public Enemy
Reckless (1935)
Red Dust
Red-Headed Woman
Riff Raff
Saratoga
Suzy
Wife vs. Secretary

ST99 Goldie Hawn (1945–)
Best Friends
Bird on a Wire
Butterflies Are Free
Cactus Flower
Criss Cross (1992)
Death Becomes Her
Deceived

$ (Dollars)
The Duchess and the Dirtwater Fox
Foul Play
The Girl From Petrovka
HouseSitter
Lovers and Liars
The One and Only, Genuine, Original Family
   Band (bit)
Overboard
Private Benjamin
Protocol
Seems Like Old Times
Shampoo
The Sugarland Express
Swing Shift
There's a Girl in My Soup
Wildcats

ST100 Susan Hayward (1918–1975)
Adam Had Four Sons
Back Street (1961 version)
Beau Geste (1939 version)
The Conqueror
David and Bathsheba
Deadline at Dawn
Demetrius and the Gladiators
The Fighting Seabees
The Hairy Ape
The Honey Pot
House of Strangers
I Married a Witch
I Want To Live!
I'll Cry Tomorrow
Jack London
The Lost Moment
The Lusty Men
Rawhide
Reap the Wild Wind
Say Goodbye, Maggie Cole
Smash-up: The Story of a Woman
The Snows of Kilimanjaro
Soldier of Fortune
They Won't Believe Me
Tulsa
Valley of the Dolls (1967 version)
Young and Willing

ST101 Rita Hayworth (1918–1987)
Affair in Trinidad
Angels Over Broadway
Blood and Sand (1941 version)
Circus World
Cover Girl
Fire Down Below
Gilda
The Lady From Shanghai
The Lady in Question
The Loves of Carmen
Miss Sadie Thompson
Only Angels Have Wings

Pal Joey
The Poppy Is Also a Flower
Renegade Ranger
Road to Salina
Salome
Separate Tables (1958 version)
The Strawberry Blonde
Susan and God
They Came to Cordura
Tonight and Every Night
Trouble in Texas (as Rita Cansino)
You Were Never Lovelier
You'll Never Get Rich

ST102 Audrey Hepburn (1929–1993)
Always
Breakfast at Tiffany's
Charade
The Children's Hour
Funny Face
The Lavender Hill Mob (bit)
Love in the Afternoon
My Fair Lady
The Nun's Story
Paris When It Sizzles
Robin and Marian
Roman Holiday
Sabrina
Sidney Sheldon's Bloodline
They All Laughed
Two for the Road
The Unforgiven
Wait Until Dark
War and Peace (1956 version)

ST103 Katharine Hepburn (1907–)
See also: CL15 Memorable Screen Teams—
   Katharine Hepburn and Spencer Tracy
Adam's Rib
The African Queen
Alice Adams
A Bill of Divorcement
Break of Hearts
Bringing Up Baby
Christopher Strong
The Corn Is Green (1979 version)
Desk Set
Dragon Seed
George Stevens: A Filmmaker's Journey
Grace Quigley
Guess Who's Coming to Dinner
Holiday
Keeper of the Flame
The Lion in Winter
The Little Minister
Little Women (1933 version)
Long Day's Journey Into Night
   (1962 version)
Love Among the Ruins
The Madwoman of Chaillot

Mary of Scotland
MGM's Big Parade of Comedy
Morning Glory
Olly, Olly, Oxen Free
On Golden Pond
Pat and Mike
The Philadelphia Story
Quality Street
The Rainmaker
Rooster Cogburn
The Sea of Grass
Song of Love
Spitfire (1934)
Stage Door
Stage Door Canteen
State of the Union
Suddenly, Last Summer
Summertime
Sylvia Scarlett
That's Entertainment, Part 2
The Trojan Women
Undercurrent
Without Love
Woman of the Year
A Woman Rebels

ST104 Barbara Hershey (1948–)
Americana
Angel on My Shoulder (1980 version)
The Baby Maker
Beaches
Boxcar Bertha
A Choice of Weapons
Defenseless
Diamonds*
The Entity
Falling Down
Flood!
Hannah and Her Sisters
Hoosiers
Last Summer
The Last Temptation of Christ
The Liberation of L.B. Jones
My Wicked, Wicked Ways
The Natural
The Nightingale
Paris Trout
Passion Flower
The Public Eye
The Pursuit of Happiness
The Right Stuff
Shy People
The Stunt Man
Swing Kids
Take This Job and Shove It
Tin Men
Tune in Tomorrow . . .
A World Apart
With Six You Get Eggroll
*billed as Barbara Seagull

ST105 Dustin Hoffman (1937–)
Agatha
All the President's Men
Billy Bathgate
Common Threads: Stories From the Quilt
    (narrator)
Death of a Salesman (1985 version)
Dick Tracy
Family Business
The Graduate
Hero
Hook
Ishtar
Kramer vs. Kramer
Lenny
Little Big Man
Madigan's Millions
Marathon Man
Midnight Cowboy
Papillon
Rain Man
Straight Time
Straw Dogs
Tootsie

ST106 William Holden (1918–1981)
Alvarez Kelly
Ashanti, Land of No Mercy
The Blue Knight
Born Yesterday (1950 version)
The Bridge on the River Kwai
The Bridges at Toko-Ri
Casino Royale
The Christmas Tree
The Counterfeit Traitor
The Country Girl (1954 version)
Damien: Omen II
The Dark Past
Dear Wife
The Devil's Brigade
The Earthling
Escape to Athena (bit)
Executive Suite
Fedora
Golden Boy
The Horse Soldiers
The Key
Love Is a Many Splendored Thing
The Man From Colorado
Miss Grant Takes Richmond
The Moon Is Blue
Network
Our Town
Paris When It Sizzles
Picnic
Rachel and the Stranger
S.O.B.
Sabrina
Stalag 17
Sunset Boulevard

Texas
The Towering Inferno
21 Hours at Munich
Union Station
When Time Ran Out
The Wild Bunch
Wild Rovers
The World of Suzie Wong
Young and Willing

ST107 Judy Holliday (1922-1965)
Adam's Rib
Bells Are Ringing
Born Yesterday (1950 version)
It Should Happen to You
The Solid Gold Cadillac

ST108 Bob Hope (1903–)
See also: CL15 Memorable Screen Teams—
   Bob Hope and Bing Crosby
Boy, Did I Get a Wrong Number!
Cancel My Reservation
Casanova's Big Night
Caught in the Draft
College Swing
Fancy Pants
The Ghost Breakers
The Great Lover
Here Come the Girls
The Lemon Drop Kid
Louisiana Purchase
Monsieur Beaucaire
The Muppet Movie (bit)
My Favorite Blonde
My Favorite Brunette
Off Limits (1953)
The Paleface
Paris Holiday
The Princess and the Pirate
Road to Bali
The Road to Hong Kong
Road to Morocco
Road to Rio
Road to Singapore
Road to Utopia
Road to Zanzibar
The Seven Little Foys
Son of Paleface
Sorrowful Jones
Spies Like Us (bit)
They Got Me Covered

ST109 Anthony Hopkins (1937–)
All Creatures Great and Small
Audrey Rose
The Bounty
A Bridge Too Far
Bram Stoker's Dracula
A Change of Seasons
Chaplin

A Chorus of Disapproval
Desperate Hours
A Doll's House (Claire Bloom)
84 Charing Cross Road
The Elephant Man
Freejack
The Girl From Petrovka
The Good Father
Hamlet (1969 version)
Howards End
Hunchback
International Velvet
Juggernaut
The Lindbergh Kidnapping Case
The Lion in Winter
The Looking Glass War
Magic
A Married Man
Mussolini and I
One Man's War
Othello (1982 version)
Peter and Paul
QB VII
The Silence of the Lambs
Spotswood
Young Winston

ST110 Dennis Hopper (1936–)
The American Friend
Apocalypse Now
Backtrack
Black Widow
Blood Red
Blue Velvet
Chattahoochee
Cool Hand Luke
Double-Crossed
Easy Rider*
Eye of the Storm
Flashback
Giant
The Glory Stompers
Gunfight at the O.K. Corral
Hang 'em High
Hearts of Darkness: A Filmmaker's
   Apocalypse
Hoosiers
The Indian Runner
The Inside Man
King of the Mountain
The Last Movie*
Mad Dog Morgan
My Science Project
Night Tide
O.C. & Stiggs
The Osterman Weekend
Out of the Blue*
Paris Trout
The Pick-up Artist
Planet of Blood

Rebel Without a Cause
Riders of the Storm
River's Edge
Rumble Fish
Running Out of Luck
The Sons of Katie Elder
Stark
Straight to Hell
Superstar: The Life and Times of Andy
  Warhol
The Texas Chainsaw Massacre II
Tracks
The Trip
True Grit
Wild Times
*also director
DIRECTOR ONLY
Colors
The Hot Spot

ST111 Bob Hoskins (1942–)
Beyond the Limit
Brazil
The Cotton Club
The Dunera Boys
The Favor, The Watch, and the Very Big Fish
Heart Condition
The Inner Circle
Inserts
Lassiter
The Lonely Passion of Judith Hearne
The Long Good Friday
Mermaids
Mona Lisa
Mussolini and I
Othello (1982 version)
Passed Away
Pink Floyd: The Wall
A Prayer for the Dying
The Raggedy Rawney*
Royal Flash (bit)
Shattered (1991)
Sweet Liberty
Who Framed Roger Rabbit
*also director

ST112 Rock Hudson (1925–1985)
The Ambassador
Avalanche
Bend of the River
Embryo
A Farewell to Arms (1957 version)
A Gathering of Eagles
Giant
Gun Fury
Horizons West
Ice Station Zebra
Lover Come Back
Magnificent Obsession
Man's Favorite Sport?

The Mirror Crack'd
Pillow Talk
Sea Devils
Send Me No Flowers
Showdown
Something of Value
Tobruk
The Undefeated
The Vegas Strip Wars
Winchester 73
World War III
Written on the Wind

ST113 Holly Hunter (1958–)
Always
Animal Behavior
Broadcast News
Crazy in Love
End of the Line
Miss Firecracker
Murder on the Bayou
Once Around
Raising Arizona
Roe vs. Wade
Svengali (1983 version) (bit)
Swing Shift
Urge to Kill

ST114 William Hurt (1950–)
The Accidental Tourist
Alice
Altered States
The Big Chill
Body Heat
Broadcast News
Children of a Lesser God
The Doctor
Eyewitness
Gorky Park
I Love You to Death
Kiss of the Spider Woman
A Time of Destiny

ST115 Anjelica Huston (1951–)
The Addams Family
The Cowboy and the Ballerina
Crimes and Misdemeanors
The Dead
Enemies, A Love Story
Gardens of Stone
The Grifters
A Handful of Dust
Ice Pirates
The Last Tycoon (bit)
Lonesome Dove
Mr. North
The Player (bit)
The Postman Always Rings Twice (1981
  version)
Prizzi's Honor

Swashbuckler (1976) (bit)
The Witches

Eric Idle
See: CO15 The Alumni of "Monty Python's
Flying Circus"

ST116 Jeremy Irons (1948–)
Betrayal (1983)
Brideshead Revisited
A Chorus of Disapproval
Damage
Dead Ringers
The French Lieutenant's Woman
Kafka
The Mission
Moonlighting (1982)
Nijinsky
Reversal of Fortune
Swann in Love
Waterland
The Wild Duck

ST117 Glenda Jackson (1936–)
And Nothing But the Truth
Beyond Therapy
The Boyfriend (bit)
Business as Usual
The Class of Miss MacMichael
Hedda
Hopscotch
House Calls
The Incredible Sarah
Lost and Found
Marat/Sade
The Music Lovers
Nasty Habits
Negatives
The Rainbow
Return of the Soldier
The Romantic Englishwoman
Sakharov
Salome's Last Dance
Stevie
Strange Interlude
Sunday Bloody Sunday
A Touch of Class
Triple Echo
Turtle Diary
Women in Love

ST118 James Earl Jones (1931–)
Aladdin and His Wonderful Lamp
Allan Quatermain and the Lost City of Gold
Best of the Best
The Bingo Long Traveling All-Stars and
    Motor Kings
Blood Tide
The Bushido Blade
By Dawn's Early Light
City Limits (narrator)

The Comedians
Coming to America
Conan the Barbarian
Deadly Hero
Dr. Strangelove or; How I Learned to Stop
    Worrying and Love the Bomb
The Empire Strikes Back (character voice)
End of the Road
Exorcist II: The Heretic
Field of Dreams
Gardens of Stone
The Great White Hope
The Greatest
Grim Prairie Tales
Guyana Tragedy: The Story of Jim Jones
Heat Wave
The Hunt for Red October
Ivory Hunters
The Last Remake of Beau Geste
Matewan
My Little Girl
Patriot Games
A Piece of the Action
Pinocchio and the Emperor of Night
    (character voice)
Return of the Jedi (character voice)
The River Niger
Sneakers
Sommersby
Soul Man
Star Wars (character voice)
Swashbuckler (1976)
Three Fugitives
The Vegas Strip Wars

Terry Jones
See: CO15 The Alumni of "Monty Python's
Flying Circus"

ST119 Boris Karloff (1887–1969)
Abbott and Costello Meet Dr. Jekyll and Mr.
    Hyde
Abbott and Costello Meet the Killer, Boris
    Karloff
The Ape
Bedlam
Before I Hang
The Bells
The Black Castle
The Black Cat
The Black Room
Black Sabbath
The Body Snatcher
The Bride of Frankenstein
British Intelligence
Cauldron of Blood
Chamber of Fear
Charlie Chan at the Opera
Comedy of Terrors
Corridors of Blood
The Criminal Code

The Daydreamer (voice only)
Dick Tracy Meets Gruesome
Die, Monster, Die!
Doomed to Die
The Fatal Hour
Frankenstein (1931 version)
Frankenstein—1970
The Ghoul (1933)
The Haunted Strangler
House of Frankenstein
The Invisible Ray
Island Monster
Isle of the Dead
Juggernaut (1937)
The King of the Kongo
The Lost Patrol
Macabre Serenade
Mad Monster Party? (voice only)
The Man They Could Not Hang
The Man Who Lived Again
The Mask of Fu Manchu
Mr. Wong, Detective
Mr. Wong in Chinatown
The Mummy (1932 version)
Mystery of Mr. Wong
Old Ironsides
The Raven (1935 and 1963 versions)
Sabaka
Scarface (1932 version)
The Secret Life of Walter Mitty
Sinister Invasion
Snake People
Son of Frankenstein
The Sorcerers
Targets
The Terror
Tower of London (1939 version)
Transylvania Twist
You'll Find Out

ST120 Danny Kaye (1913–1987)
The Court Jester
The Five Pennies
Hans Christian Andersen
The Inspector General
The Kid From Brooklyn
The Madwoman of Chaillot
The Secret Life of Walter Mitty
Skokie
A Song Is Born
Up in Arms
White Christmas
Wonder Man

Buster Keaton
See: Director Check List DT66

ST121 Diane Keaton (1946–)
See also: XT30 He Directs, She Acts
Annie Hall

Baby Boom
Crimes of the Heart
Father of the Bride (1991 version)
The Godfather
The Godfather, Part II
The Godfather, Part III
The Godfather: The Complete Epic,
   1902–1958
The Godfather Trilogy, 1901–1980
The Good Mother
Harry and Walter Go to New York
I Will, I Will . . . For Now
Interiors
The Lemon Sisters
The Little Drummer Girl
Looking for Mr. Goodbar
Love and Death
Lovers and Other Strangers
Manhattan
Mrs. Soffel
Play It Again, Sam
Radio Days
Reds
Shoot the Moon
Sleeper
DIRECTOR ONLY
Heaven
Wildflower

ST122 Michael Keaton (1951–)
Batman (1989)
Batman Returns
Beetlejuice
Clean and Sober
The Dream Team
Gung Ho (1986)
Johnny Dangerously
Mr. Mom
Night Shift
One Good Cop
Pacific Heights
The Squeeze
Touch and Go (1986)
Your Favorite Laughs From an Evening at
   the Improv

ST123 Gene Kelly (1912–)
The Black Hand
Forty Carats
Inherit the Wind
Marjorie Morningstar
The Three Musketeers (1948 version)
Viva Knievel!
MUSICALS
An American in Paris
Anchors Aweigh
Brigadoon
Cover Girl
Deep in My Heart
DuBarry Was a Lady

For Me and My Gal
Invitation to the Dance
It's Always Fair Weather*
Les Girls
Let's Make Love
Love Is Better Than Ever (bit)
On the Town*
The Pirate
Singin' in the Rain*
Summer Stock
Take Me Out to the Ball Game
That's Dancing!
That's Entertainment!
That's Entertainment, Part 2
Thousands Cheer
Words and Music
Xanadu
Ziegfeld Follies (with Fred Astaire)
*also co-director with Stanley Donen
DIRECTOR ONLY
The Cheyenne Social Club
A Guide for the Married Man
Hello, Dolly!

ST124 Grace Kelly (1928–1982)
The Bridges at Toko-Ri
The Children of Theatre Street (narrator)
The Country Girl (1954 version)
Dial M for Murder
High Noon
High Society
Mogambo
Rear Window
The Swan
To Catch a Thief

ST125 Deborah Kerr (1921–)
An Affair to Remember
The Arrangement
Black Narcissus
Bonjour Tristesse
Casino Royale
The Chalk Garden
Courageous Mr. Penn
The Day Will Dawn
From Here to Eternity
The Grass Is Greener
Hold the Dream
The Hucksters
I See a Dark Stranger
Julius Caesar (1953 version)
The King and I
King Solomon's Mines
The Life and Death of Colonel Blimp
Major Barbara
The Naked Edge
The Night of the Iguana
The Prisoner of Zenda (1952 version)
Quo Vadis?
Separate Tables (1958 version)

The Sundowners
Tea and Sympathy
A Woman of Substance

ST126 Klaus Kinski (1926–1991)
Aguirre: The Wrath of God
Android
Beauty and the Beast (1984 version)
Buddy Buddy
A Bullet for the General
Burden of Dreams
Code Name: Wild Geese
Count Dracula
Crawlspace
Creature
Deadly Sanctuary
Fitzcarraldo
For a Few Dollars More
Jack the Ripper (1980)
The Little Drummer Girl
Operation Thunderbolt
The Ruthless Four
Schizoid
The Secret Diary of Sigmund Freud
Shoot the Living, Pray for the Dead
The Soldier
A Time to Love and a Time to Die
Venom
Woyzeck

ST127 Kevin Kline (1947–)
The Big Chill
Chaplin
Consenting Adults
Cry Freedom
A Fish Called Wanda
Grand Canyon
I Love You to Death
The January Man
The Pirates of Penzance
Silverado
Soapdish
Sophie's Choice
Violets Are Blue

ST128 Alan Ladd (1913–1964)
All the Young Men
The Badlanders
Botany Bay
Branded
Citizen Kane (bit)
The Carpetbaggers
The Deep Six
Drum Beat
Duel of Champions
Gangs Inc.*
The Glass Key
Hell on Frisco Bay
The Howards of Virginia (bit)
Joan of Paris

The McConnell Story
The Proud Rebel
Shane
This Gun for Hire
*billed as Allan Ladd

ST129 Burt Lancaster (1913–)
Airport
Apache
Atlantic City
Barnum
Birdman of Alcatraz
Buffalo Bill and the Indians
The Cassandra Crossing
A Child Is Waiting
Come Back, Little Sheba
Control
Conversation Piece
The Crimson Pirate
Criss Cross (1949)
The Devil's Disciple
Elmer Gantry
Executive Action
Field of Dreams
The Flame and the Arrow
From Here to Eternity
Go Tell the Spartans
Gunfight at the O.K. Corral
His Majesty O'Keefe
The Island of Dr. Moreau
Jim Thorpe—All American
Judgment at Nuremberg
The Kentuckian*
The List of Adrian Messenger
Little Treasure
Local Hero
Moses
1900
On Wings of Eagles
The Osterman Weekend
The Professionals
The Rainmaker
Rocket Gibraltar
The Rose Tattoo
Run Silent, Run Deep
The Scalphunters
Scorpio
Separate but Equal
Separate Tables (1958 version)
Seven Days in May
Sorry, Wrong Number
Sweet Smell of Success
The Swimmer
Tough Guys
The Train
Trapeze
Twilight's Last Gleaming
Ulzana's Raid
The Unforgiven
Vengeance Valley

Vera Cruz
Zulu Dawn
*also director

ST130 Jessica Lange (1949–)
All That Jazz
Cape Fear (1991 version)
Cat on a Hot Tin Roof (1984 version)
Country
Crimes of the Heart
Everybody's All American
Far North
Frances
How to Beat the High Co$t of Living
King Kong (1976 version)
Men Don't Leave
Music Box
Night and the City (1992 version)
The Postman Always Rings Twice (1981
   version)
Sweet Dreams
Tootsie

ST131 Angela Lansbury (1925–)
All Fall Down
Beauty and the Beast (1991; character voice)
Bedknobs and Broomsticks
Blue Hawaii
A Breath of Scandal
The Company of Wolves
The Court Jester
Death on the Nile
Gaslight
The Greatest Story Ever Told (bit)
Harlow (Carroll Baker version)
The Harvey Girls
The Lady Vanishes (1979 version)
A Lawless Street
Little Gloria . . . Happy at Last
The Long Hot Summer (1958 version)
The Manchurian Candidate
The Mirror Crack'd
Mutiny
National Velvet
The Picture of Dorian Gray
The Pirates of Penzance
The Private Affairs of Bel Ami
The Reluctant Debutante
Samson and Delilah
Something for Everyone
State of the Union
Sweeney Todd
The Three Musketeers (1948 version)
Till the Clouds Roll By
The World of Henry Orient

ST132 Charles Laughton (1899–1962)
Abbott and Costello Meet Captain Kidd
Advise and Consent
Arch of Triumph

The Barretts of Wimpole Street (1934 version)
The Beachcomber
The Canterville Ghost
Captain Kidd
The Epic That Never Was
Forever and a Day
Hobson's Choice
The Hunchback of Notre Dame (1939 version)
Jamaica Inn
Les Miserables (1935 version)
The Man on the Eiffel Tower
Mutiny on the Bounty
The Paradine Case
The Private Life of Henry VIII
Rembrandt
Ruggles of Red Gap
Salome
Sidewalks of London
Spartacus
They Knew What They Wanted
This Land Is Mine
The Tuttles of Tahiti
Witness for the Prosecution
DIRECTOR ONLY
The Night of the Hunter

ST133 Laurel (1890–1965)
and Hardy (1892–1957)
Air Raid Wardens
Atoll K
Block-Heads
The Bohemian Girl
Bonnie Scotland
The Bullfighters
A Chump at Oxford
The Devil's Brother
The Fighting Kentuckian*
The Flying Deuces
Great Guns
Hollywood Party
Laurel and Hardy at Work
Laurel and Hardy Comedy Classics, Vols. I–IX
Laurel and Hardy's Laughing 20's
Laurel and Hardy On the Lam
Laurel and Hardy: Stan "Helps" Ollie
March of the Wooden Soldiers
MGM's Big Parade of Comedy
Movie Struck
Nothing But Trouble (1944)
The Music Box/Helpmates
Our Relations
Pack Up Your Troubles
Pardon Us
Saps at Sea
Sons of the Desert
Swiss Miss
Way Out West
When Comedy Was King
The Wizard of Oz (1925 version)*
*Hardy only

ST134 Bruce Lee (1941–1973)
Bruce Lee: The Legend
Bruce Lee: The Man/The Myth
The Chinese Connection
Enter the Dragon
Fist of Fear, Touch of Death
Fists of Fury
Game of Death
Marlowe
The Real Bruce Lee
Return of the Dragon

ST135 Christopher Lee (1922–)
Against All Odds (1969)
Airport '77
Albino
Bear Island
The Boy Who Left Home to Find Out About
   the Shivers
Captain Horatio Hornblower
Caravans
Castle of Fu Manchu
Castle of the Living Dead
Circle of Iron
Corridors of Blood
Count Dracula
Count Dracula and His Vampire Bride
The Creeping Flesh
The Crimson Pirate
The Curse of Frankenstein
Dark Places
The Devil's Undead
Doctor Terror's House of Horrors
Double Vision
Dracula and Son
End of the World
An Eye for an Eye
The Face of Fu Manchu
The Far Pavilions
Five Golden Dragons
The Four Musketeers
The Girl
Goliath Awaits
The Gorgon
Gremlins 2: The New Batch
The Hands of Orlac
Hannie Caulder (bit)
Hercules in the Haunted World
Horror Castle
Horror Express
Horror Hotel
Horror of Dracula
The Hound of the Baskervilles (1959 version)
House of the Long Shadows
The House That Dripped Blood
The Howling II
Ill Met by Moonlight
Island of the Burning Doomed
Jaguar Lives!
Jocks

Journey of Honor
Julius Caesar (1970 version)
The Keeper
Killer Force
The Land of Faraway
The Magic Christian
The Man With the Golden Gun
Moulin Rouge
The Mummy (1959 version)
Murder Story
1941
Nothing But the Night
The Oblong Box
The Private Life of Sherlock Holmes
Psycho-Circus
Pursuit of the *Graf Spee*
Return from Witch Mountain
The Return of Captain Invincible
The Rosebud Beach Hotel
Safari 3000
The Salamander
Scars of Dracula
Scott of the Antarctic
Scream and Scream Again
Scream of Fear
Serial
Shaka Zulu
Sherlock Holmes and the Incident at
   Victoria Falls
The Skull
A Tale of Two Cities (1958 version)
Theatre of Death
The Three Musketeers (1974 version)
To the Devil a Daughter
The Torture Chamber of Dr. Sadism
Treasure Island (1990 version)
The Warriors (1955)
The Wicker Man
Wild for Kicks

ST136 Jennifer Jason Leigh (1958–)
Angel City
Backdraft
The Best Little Girl in the World
The Big Picture
Buried Alive (1990, TV)
Crooked Hearts
Easy Money
Eyes of a Stranger
Fast Times at Ridgemont High
Flesh + Blood
Girls of the White Orchid
Grandview, USA
Heart of Midnight
The Hitcher
The Killing of Randy Webster
Last Exit to Brooklyn
The Men's Club
Miami Blues
Rush

Single White Female
Sister, Sister (1987)
Under Cover
Wrong Is Right (bit)

ST137 Vivien Leigh (1913–1967)
Anna Karenina (1948 version)
Caesar and Cleopatra
Dark Journey
Fire Over England
Gone With the Wind
Making of a Legend—Gone With the Wind
The Roman Spring of Mrs. Stone
Ship of Fools
Sidewalks of London
Storm in a Teacup
A Streetcar Named Desire
That Hamilton Woman
Waterloo Bridge

ST138 Jack Lemmon (1925–)
Airport '77
The Apartment
The April Fools
Bell, Book and Candle
Buddy Buddy
The China Syndrome
Dad
The Days of Wine and Roses
Fire Down Below
For Richer, for Poorer
The Fortune Cookie
The Front Page (1974 version)
Glengarry Glen Ross
Good Neighbor Sam
The Great Race
Harold Lloyd: The Third Genius
How to Murder Your Wife
Irma La Douce
It Should Happen to You
JFK
Kotch
Long Day's Journey Into Night (1987 version)
Luv
Macaroni
Mass Appeal
Missing
Mister Roberts
The Murder of Mary Phagan
My Sister Eileen (1955 version)
The Odd Couple
The Out-of-Towners
The Player (bit)
The Prisoner of Second Avenue
Save the Tiger
Some Like It Hot
That's Life!
Tribute
The Wackiest Ship in the Army

Eugene Levy
See: CO14 The Alumni of "SCTV"

ST139 Jerry Lewis (1926–)
See also: CL15 Memorable Screen Teams—
    Dean Martin and Jerry Lewis
Artists and Models
At War with the Army
The Bellboy*
The Best of Comic Relief
The Big Mouth*
Boeing Boeing
The Caddy
Cinderfella
Cookie
Cracking Up
The Delicate Delinquent
The Disorderly Orderly
Don't Raise the Bridge, Lower the River
The Errand Boy*
The Family Jewels
The Geisha Boy
Hardly Working*
Hollywood or Bust
It's a Mad Mad Mad Mad World (bit)
Jerry Lewis Live
Jumping Jacks
King of Comedy
The Ladies' Man
Mr. Saturday Night (bit)
My Friend Irma
The Nutty Professor*
The Patsy*
The Sad Sack
Scared Stiff
Slapstick (Of Another Kind)
Which Way to the Front?*
*also director

ST140 Carole Lombard (1908–1942)
High Voltage
In Name Only
Lady by Choice
Made for Each Other (1939)
Making of a Legend—Gone With the Wind
MGM's Big Parade of Comedy
Mr. and Mrs. Smith
My Man Godfrey
No Man of Her Own
Nothing Sacred
Power (1928)
Racketeer
Swing High, Swing Low
They Knew What They Wanted
To Be or Not to Be (1942 version)
Twentieth Century

ST141 Sophia Loren (1934–)
Aida
Angela

Arabesque
The Black Orchid
Blood Feud
Bocaccio '70
Brass Target
A Breath of Scandal
Brief Encounter (1974 version)
The Cassandra Crossing
Courage (1986)
Desire Under the Elms
El Cid
The Fall of the Roman Empire
Firepower
The Gold of Naples
Heller in Pink Tights
Houseboat
It Started in Naples
The Key
La Favorita
Lady of the Evening
Legend of the Lost
Man of La Mancha
The Millionairess
Operation Crossbow
The Pride and the Passion
Running Away
Sophia Loren: Her Own Story
A Special Day
Two Women
Yesterday, Today and Tomorrow

ST142 Myrna Loy (1905–)
See also: CL15 Memorable Screen Teams—
    William Powell and Myrna Loy
After the Thin Man
Airport 1975
The Ambassador's Daughter
The Animal Kingdom
Another Thin Man
Ants!
The April Fools
Arrowsmith
The Bachelor and the Bobby Soxer
The Best Years of Our Lives
Broadway Bill
A Connecticut Yankee
Consolation Marriage
Don Juan
The End
From the Terrace
The Great Ziegfeld
The Jazz Singer (1927 version) (bit)
Just Tell Me What You Want
Libeled Lady
Lonelyhearts
Love Crazy
Manhattan Melodrama
The Mask of Fu Manchu
MGM's Big Parade of Comedy
Midnight Lace

Mr. Blandings Builds His Dream House
The Red Pony (1949 version)
Shadow of the Thin Man
So This Is Paris
Song of the Thin Man
Summer Solstice
Test Pilot
The Thin Man
The Thin Man Goes Home
Too Hot to Handle
Topaze
Vanity Fair
Wife vs. Secretary

ST143 Bela Lugosi (1882–1956)
Abbott and Costello Meet Frankenstein
The Ape Man
Bela Lugosi Meets a Brooklyn Gorilla (The
  Boys From Brooklyn)
The Black Cat
Black Dragons
The Black Sleep
The Body Snatcher
Bowery at Midnight
Bride of the Monster
Chandu on the Magic Island
The Corpse Vanishes
The Death Kiss
Dracula (1931 version)
Frankenstein Meets the Wolf Man
Ghosts on the Loose
Glen or Glenda?
The Gorilla
The Human Monster
International House
Invisible Ghost
The Invisible Ray
Killer Bats (The Devil Bat)
Mark of the Vampire
The Midnight Girl
Murder by Television
Murders in the Rue Morgue (1932 version)
Mysterious Mr. Wong
The Mystery of the Mary Celeste: The
  Phantom Ship
Ninotchka
One Body Too Many
The Phantom Creeps
Plan 9 From Outer Space
The Raven (1935)
The Return of Chandu
Return of the Ape Man
Return of the Vampire
S.O.S. Coastguard
Scared to Death
Son of Frankenstein
Spooks Run Wild
Vampire Over London
White Zombie
The Wolf Man

You'll Find Out
Zombies on Broadway

Jeanette MacDonald
See: CL15 Memorable Screen Teams—
  Nelson Eddy and Jeanette MacDonald

ST144 Joel McCrea (1905–1990)
Barbary Coast
Bird of Paradise
Buffalo Bill
Come and Get It
Cry Blood Apache (bit)
Dead End
Foreign Correspondent
Four Faces West
George Stevens: A Filmmaker's Journey
The Great American Cowboy (narrator)
The Great Moment
Lost Squadron
The More the Merrier
The Most Dangerous Game
The Oklahoman
Our Little Girl
The Palm Beach Story
Primrose Path
Ramrod
Ride the High Country
South of St. Louis
Sullivan's Travels
These Three
They Shall Have Music
Wichita

ST145 Shirley MacLaine (1934–)
All in a Night's Work
The Apartment
Around the World in 80 Days
Artists and Models
Ask Any Girl
Being There
The Bliss of Mrs. Blossom
Can-Can
Cannonball Run II
Career
A Change of Seasons
The Children's Hour
Defending Your Life (bit)
Gambit
Hot Spell
Irma La Douce
Loving Couples
Madame Sousatzka
The Matchmaker
My Geisha
The Possession of Joel Delaney
Postcards From the Edge
Some Came Running
Steel Magnolias
Sweet Charity

Terms of Endearment
The Trouble With Harry
The Turning Point
Two for the Seesaw
Two Mules for Sister Sara
Used People
Waiting for the Light
Woman Times Seven

ST146 Steve McQueen (1930–1980)
Baby, the Rain Must Fall
The Blob (1958 version)
Bruce Lee: The Legend
Bullitt
The Cincinnati Kid
An Enemy of the People
The Getaway
The Great Escape
Hell Is for Heroes
The Honeymoon Machine
The Hunter
Junior Bonner
Le Mans
Love With the Proper Stranger
The Magnificent Seven
Nevada Smith
Never Love a Stranger
Never So Few
On Any Sunday
Papillon
The Reivers
The Sand Pebbles
Soldier in the Rain
Somebody Up There Likes Me
The Thomas Crown Affair
Tom Horn
The Towering Inferno
The War Lover

ST147 John Malkovich (1953–)
American Dream (1981)
Dangerous Liaisons
Death of a Salesman (1985 version)
Eleni
Empire of the Sun
The Glass Menagerie (1987 version)
Jennifer Eight
Making Mr. Right
Miles From Home
The Object of Beauty
Places in the Heart
Queens Logic
Rocket to the Moon
Shadows and Fog
The Sheltering Sky
True West

ST148 Fredric March (1897–1975)
Alexander the Great
Anna Karenina (1935 version)

Anthony Adverse
The Barretts of Wimpole Street
The Best Years of Our Lives
The Bridges at Toko-ri
Christopher Columbus
The Desperate Hours
Dr. Jekyll and Mr. Hyde (1930 version)
Executive Suite
Hombre
I Married a Witch
Inherit the Wind
Les Miserables (1935 version)
The Man in the Grey Flannel Suit
Mary of Scotland
Nothing Sacred
Seven Days in May
So Ends Our Night
A Star Is Born (1937 version)
Susan and God
The Wild Party (1929)

Andrea Martin
See: CO14 The Alumni of "SCTV"

ST149 Dean Martin (1917–)
See also: CL15 Memorable Screen Teams—
    Dean Martin and Jerry Lewis
Airport
All in a Night's Work
The Ambushers
Artists and Models
At War With the Army
Bandolero!
Bells Are Ringing
The Caddy
Cannonball Run
Cannonball Run 2
Career
Five Card Stud
Four for Texas
Hollywood or Bust
Jumping Jacks
Kiss Me, Stupid
Murderers' Row
My Friend Irma
Ocean's Eleven
Rio Bravo
Robin and the Seven Hoods
Scared Stiff
Some Came Running
The Sons of Katie Elder
Toys in the Attic
The Young Lions

ST150 Steve Martin (1945–)
All of Me
The Best of Dan Aykroyd
The Best of Gilda Radner
Dead Men Don't Wear Plaid
Dirty Rotten Scoundrels

Father of the Bride (1991 version)
Grand Canyon
HouseSitter
The Jerk
The Kids Are Alright
L.A. Story
Leap of Faith
Little Shop of Horrors (1986 version)
The Lonely Guy
The Man With Two Brains
Movers and Shakers
The Muppet Movie
My Blue Heaven
Parenthood
Pennies From Heaven
Planes, Trains, and Automobiles
Rowlf's Rhapsodies With the Muppets
Roxanne
Sergeant Pepper's Lonely Hearts Club
   Band
Steve Martin Live
Three Amigos

ST151 Lee Marvin (1924–1987)
Bad Day at Black Rock
The Big Heat
The Big Red One
The Caine Mutiny
Cat Ballou
The Comancheros
Death Hunt
The Delta Force
Diplomatic Courier (bit)
The Dirty Dozen
The Dirty Dozen: The Next Mission
Dog Day
Donovan's Reef
Gorky Park
Great Scout and Cathouse Thursday
Gun Fury
Hangman's Knot
Hell in the Pacific
I Died a Thousand Times
The Killers (1964 version)
The Klansman
The Man Who Shot Liberty Valance
The Missouri Traveler
Monte Walsh
Not as a Stranger
Paint Your Wagon
Pete Kelly's Blues
Pocket Money
Point Blank
Prime Cut
The Professionals
Raintree County
Sergeant Ryker
Shack Out on 101
Ship of Fools
Shout at the Devil

The Stranger Wore a Gun
The Wild One

ST152 The Marx Brothers
Chico (1886–1961), **Groucho** (1890–1971),
Harpo (1898–1964), **Zeppo** (1901–1979)
Animal Crackers
At the Circus
The Big Store
The Cocoanuts
Copacabana*
A Day at the Races
Double Dynamite*
Duck Soup
A Girl in Every Port*
Go West
Horse Feathers
Love Happy
MGM's Big Parade of Comedy
Monkey Business (1931)
Mr. Music*
A Night at the Opera
A Night in Casablanca
Room Service
Stage Door Canteen**
That's Entertainment, Part 2
*Groucho only
**Harpo only

ST153 James Mason (1909–1984)
The Assisi Underground
Bad Man's River
The Blue Max
Botany Bay
The Boys From Brazil
Caught
Cold Sweat
Cross of Iron
A Dangerous Summer
The Desert Fox
The Desert Rats
The Destructors
East Side, West Side
11 Harrowhouse
Evil Under the Sun
The Fall of the Roman Empire
5 Fingers
ffolkes
Fire Over England
Forever Darling
Georgy Girl
Heaven Can Wait (1978)
The High Command
Hotel Reserve
Inside Out
Island in the Sun
Ivanhoe
Jesus of Nazareth
Journey to the Center of the Earth (1959
   version)

Julius Caesar (1953 version)
The Kidnap Syndicate
The Last of Sheila
Lolita
Lord Jim
The Mackintosh Man
Madame Bovary (1949 version)
The Man in Grey
Mandingo
The Mill on the Floss (bit)
Murder by Decree
The Night Has Eyes
North by Northwest
Odd Man Out
Prince Valiant
The Prisoner of Zenda (1952 version)
The Reckless Moment
Salem's Lot: The Movie
The Seventh Veil
The Shooting Party
Sidney Sheldon's Bloodline
A Star Is Born (1954 version)
20,000 Leagues Under the Sea
The Verdict
Voyage of the Damned
Water Babies
The Wicked Lady
Yellowbeard
The Yin and the Yang of Mr. Go

ST154 Marcello Mastroianni (1923–)
Allonsanfan
Beyond Obsession
Big Deal on Madonna Street
Blood Feud
City of Women
Dark Eyes
Diary of Forbidden Dreams
The Divine Nymph
8½
Gabriela
Ginger and Fred
Henry IV
La Dolce Vita
La Nuit de Varennes
Lady of the Evening
Lunatics and Lovers
Macaroni
Massacre in Rome
The Poppy Is Also a Flower
Salut l'Artiste
Shoot Loud, Louder, I Don't Understand
A Slightly Pregnant Man
A Special Day
Stay as You Are
The Tenth Victim
Used People
A Very Private Affair
We All Loved Each Other So Much
Where the Hot Wind Blows

White Nights (1957)
Wifemistress
Yesterday, Today and Tomorrow

ST155 Walter Matthau (1920–)
The Bad News Bears
Buddy Buddy
Cactus Flower
California Suite
Casey's Shadow
Charade
Charley Varrick
The Couch Trip
Earthquake
Ensign Pulver
A Face in the Crowd
Fail-Safe
First Monday in October
The Fortune Cookie
The Front Page (1974 version)
A Guide for the Married Man
Hello Dolly!
Hopscotch
House Calls
I Ought to Be in Pictures
The Incident (1990)
The Indian Fighter
JFK
The Kentuckian
King Creole
Kotch
The Laughing Policeman
Little Miss Marker (1980 version)
Lonely Are the Brave
Mirage
Movers and Shakers
A New Leaf
The Odd Couple
Pete 'n' Tillie
Pirates
Plaza Suite
The Secret Life of an American Wife
Strangers When We Meet
The Sunshine Boys
The Survivors
The Taking of Pelham One Two Three

ST156 Bette Midler (1945–)
Beaches
Bette Midler—Art or Bust
Bette Midler's Mondo Beyondo
Big Business
Divine Madness
Down and Out in Beverly Hills
For the Boys
Hawaii (bit)
Jinxed!
Outrageous Fortune
The Rose
Ruthless People

Scenes From a Mall
Stella

ST157 Toshiro Mifune (1920–)
The Bad Sleep Well
The Bushido Blade
The Challenge (1982)
Drunken Angel
The Gambling Samurai
Grand Prix
Hell in the Pacific
The Hidden Fortress
High and Low
The Idiot
Journey of Honor (bit)
The Life of Oharu
The Lower Depths (1957 version)
Midway
1941
Paper Tiger
Proof of the Man
Rashomon
Red Beard
Red Lion
Red Sun
Rikisha-Man
The Saga of the Vagabonds
Samurai Saga
The Samurai Trilogy
Sanjuro
The Seven Samurai
Shogun
Stray Dog
Sword of Doom
Throne of Blood
Winter Kills
Yojimbo
Zatoichi vs. Yojimbo

ST158 Robert Mitchum (1917–)
Agency
The Ambassador
The Amsterdam Kill
Anzio
The Big Sleep (1978 version)
The Big Steal
Blood on the Moon
Border Patrol
Breakthrough
The Brotherhood of the Rose
Cape Fear (1962 and 1991 versions)
Crossfire
El Dorado
The Enemy Below
Farewell, My Lovely
Fire Down Below
Five Card Stud
The Grass Is Greener
Gung Ho! (1943)
His Kind of Woman

Holiday Affair
Home from the Hill
The Human Comedy (bit)
The Hunters
The Last Tycoon
The List of Adrian Messenger
The Longest Day
The Lusty Men
Macao
Maria's Lovers
Matilda
Midway
Mr. North
My Forbidden Past
The Night of the Hunter
Not as a Stranger
One Minute to Zero
One Shoe Makes It Murder
Out of the Past
Pursued
Rachel and the Stranger
The Racket
The Red Pony (1949 version)
River of No Return
Ryan's Daughter
Scrooged
Second Chance
Secret Ceremony
She Couldn't Say No
The Sundowners
That Championship Season
Thirty Seconds Over Tokyo
Thompson's Last Run
Thunder Road
Till the End of Time
Two for the Seesaw
Undercurrent
Villa Rides!
War and Remembrance
The Way West
The Winds of War
The Yakuza

ST159 Marilyn Monroe (1926–1962)
All About Eve
The Asphalt Jungle
Bus Stop
Clash by Night
Don't Bother To Knock
Gentlemen Prefer Blondes
Hometown Story
How to Marry a Millionaire
Let's Make It Legal
Let's Make Love
Love Happy
Love Nest
The Misfits
Monkey Business (1952)
Niagara
The Prince and the Showgirl

River of No Return
The Seven Year Itch
Some Like It Hot
There's No Business Like Show Business
We're Not Married

Monty Python's Flying Circus
See: CO15

ST160 Dudley Moore (1935–)
Alice's Adventures in Wonderland
Arthur
Arthur 2: On the Rocks
Bedazzled
Best Defense
Blame It on the Bellboy
Comic Relief 2
Crazy People
Foul Play
The Hound of the Baskervilles (1977 version)
Like Father, Like Son
Lovesick
Micki & Maude
Romantic Comedy
Santa Claus—The Movie
Six Weeks
10
30 Is a Dangerous Age, Cynthia
Those Daring Young Men in Their Jaunty
   Jalopies
Unfaithfully Yours (1984 version)
Wholly Moses
The Wrong Box

Rick Moranis
See: CO14 The Alumni of "SCTV"

ST161 Jeanne Moreau (1928–)
The Bride Wore Black
Chimes at Midnight
Diary of a Chambermaid (1964 version)
Frantic (1958)
Going Places
Heat of Desire
Jules and Jim
La Femme Nikita
The Last Tycoon
Les Liaisons Dangereuses
The Little Theatre of Jean Renoir
The Lovers
Lumiere*
Monte Walsh
Mr. Klein
The Oldest Profession
Querelle
The Train
The Trial
A Woman Is a Woman
Your Ticket Is No Longer Valid
*also director

Eddie Murphy
See: CO13 The Alumni of "Saturday Night
Live"

Bill Murray
See: CO13 The Alumni of "Saturday Night
Live"

ST162 Paul Newman (1925–)
See also: XT30 He Directs, She Acts
Absence of Malice
Blaze
Buffalo Bill and the Indians
Butch Cassidy and the Sundance Kid
Cat on a Hot Tin Roof (1958 version)
The Color of Money
Come Along With Me (character voice)
Cool Hand Luke
The Drowning Pool+
Exodus
Fat Man and Little Boy
Fort Apache, The Bronx
From the Terrace+
Harper
Harry and Son*+
Hombre
Hud
The Hustler
The Left-Handed Gun
The Life and Times of Judge Roy Bean
The Long Hot Summer (1958 version)+
The Mackintosh Man
Mr. and Mrs. Bridge+
A New Kind of Love+
Paris Blues+
Pocket Money
The Prize
Quintet
The Secret War of Harry Frigg
Silent Movie (bit)
The Silver Chalice
Slap Shot
Somebody Up There Likes Me
Sometimes a Great Notion*
The Sting
Sweet Bird of Youth
Torn Curtain
The Towering Inferno
Until They Sail
The Verdict
When Time Ran Out
Winning
The Young Philadelphians
*also director
+with Joanne Woodward
DIRECTOR ONLY
The Glass Menagerie
Rachel, Rachel
The Shadow Box

ST163 Jack Nicholson (1937–)
Batman (1989)
The Border
Broadcast News
Carnal Knowledge
Chinatown
Easy Rider
Ensign Pulver (bit)
A Few Good Men
Five Easy Pieces
Flight to Fury
Goin' South*
Heartburn
Hell's Angels on Wheels
Hoffa
Ironweed
The Last Detail
The Last Tycoon
The Little Shop of Horrors (1960 version)
Man Trouble
The Missouri Breaks
On a Clear Day You Can See Forever
One Flew Over the Cuckoo's Nest
The Passenger
The Postman Always Rings Twice (1981 version)
Prizzi's Honor
Psych-Out
The Raven (1963)
Rebel Rousers
Reds
Ride in the Whirlwind
The Shining
The Shooting
Studs Lonigan
Terms of Endearment
The Terror
Tommy
The Two Jakes*
The Wild Ride
The Witches of Eastwick
*also director

ST164 Nick Nolte (1941–)
Another 48 HRS
Cannery Row
Cape Fear (1991 version)
Death Sentence
The Deep
Down and Out in Beverly Hills
Everybody Wins
Extreme Prejudice
Farewell to the King
48 HRS
Grace Quigley
Heart Beat
Lorenzo's Oil
New York Stories
North Dallas Forty
The Player (bit)

The Prince of Tides
Q & A
Return to Macon County
The Runaway Barge
Teachers
Three Fugitives
Under Fire
Weeds
Who'll Stop the Rain?

ST165 Chuck Norris (1939–)
Braddock: Missing in Action III
Breaker! Breaker!
Code of Silence
The Delta Force
Delta Force 2
An Eye for an Eye
Firewalker
A Force of One
Forced Vengeance
Game of Death
Good Guys Wear Black
Hero and the Terror
The Hitman
Invasion U.S.A.
Lone Wolf McQuade
Missing in Action
Missing in Action 2: The Beginning
The Octagon
Return of the Dragon
Silent Rage
Slaughter in San Francisco

ST166 Warren Oates (1928–1982)
And Baby Makes Six
Badlands
The Blue and the Gray
Blue Thunder
The Border
Bring Me the Head of Alfredo Garcia
The Brink's Job
Cockfighter
Crooks and Coronets
Dillinger
Dixie Dynamite
Drum
East of Eden (1982 version)
The Hired Hand
In the Heat of the Night
Major Dundee
My Old Man
1941
92 in the Shade
Race With the Devil
Return of the Seven
Ride the High Country
The Rise and Fall of Legs Diamond
The Shooting
Sleeping Dogs
Smith!

Stripes
There Was a Crooked Man
The Thief Who Came to Dinner
Tom Sawyer
Tough Enough
The White Dawn
The Wild Bunch

Catherine O'Hara
See: CO14 The Alumni of "SCTV"

ST167 Maureen O'Hara (1920–)
Against All Flags
At Sword's Point
Big Jake
Buffalo Bill
Dance, Girl, Dance
The Deadly Companions
The Fallen Sparrow
How Green Was My Valley
The Hunchback of Notre Dame (1939
   version)
The Immortal Sergeant
Jamaica Inn
Lisbon
McLintock!
Magnificent Matador
Miracle on 34th Street
Mr. Hobbs Takes a Vacation
Only the Lonely
The Parent Trap
The Quiet Man
The Rare Breed
The Red Pony (1973 version)
Rio Grande
Sinbad the Sailor
The Spanish Main
This Land Is Mine
To the Shores of Tripoli
The Wings of Eagles
A Woman's Secret

ST168 Laurence Olivier (1907–1989)
As You Like It
Battle of Britain
The Betsy
The Bounty
The Boys From Brazil
Brideshead Revisited
A Bridge Too Far
Carrie (1952)
Clash of the Titans
Clouds Over Europe
The Collection
The Demi-Paradise
The Devil's Disciple
The Divorce of Lady X
Dracula (1979 version)
The Ebony Tower
The Entertainer

Fire Over England
The 49th Parallel
Hamlet (1948 version)*
Henry V (1945 version)*
I Stand Condemned
The Jazz Singer (1980 version)
Jesus of Nazareth
The Jigsaw Man
Khartoum
Lady Caroline Lamb
A Little Romance
Love Among the Ruins
Marathon Man
Mr. Halpern and Mr. Johnson
Nicholas and Alexandra
Pride and Prejudice
The Prince and the Showgirl*
Rebecca
Richard III*
The Seven Percent Solution
The Shoes of the Fisherman
Sleuth
Spartacus
That Hamilton Woman
A Voyage 'Round My Father
Wagner
Wild Geese II
Wuthering Heights (1939 version)
*also director
DOCUMENTARY SUBJECT
Laurence Olivier—A Life

ST169 Peter O'Toole (1932–)
Becket
The Bible
Caligula
Club Paradise
Creator
Foxtrot
Goodbye, Mr. Chips (1969 version)
High Spirits
Kidnapped
King Ralph
The Last Emperor
Lawrence of Arabia
The Lion in Winter
Lord Jim
Man Friday
Man of La Mancha
Masada
Murphy's War
My Favorite Year
The Night of the Generals
The Nutcracker Prince (character voice)
Power Play
The Ruling Class
The Stunt Man
Supergirl
Svengali (1983 version)
Under Milk Wood

What's New, Pussycat?
Zulu Dawn

ST170 Al Pacino (1940–)
. . . And Justice for All
Author! Author!
Bobby Deerfield
Cruising
Dick Tracy
Dog Day Afternoon
Frankie and Johnny (1991)
Glengarry Glen Ross
The Godfather
The Godfather, Part II
The Godfather, Part III
The Godfather: The Complete Epic, 1902–1958
The Godfather Trilogy, 1901–1980
The Panic in Needle Park
Revolution
Scarecrow
Scarface
Scent of a Woman
Sea of Love
Serpico

Michael Palin
See: CO15 The Alumni of "Monty Python's
   Flying Circus"

ST171 Gregory Peck (1916–)
Amazing Grace and Chuck
Arabesque
Behold a Pale Horse
The Big Country
The Blue and the Gray
The Boys From Brazil
The Bravados
Cape Fear (1962 and 1991 versions)
Captain Horatio Hornblower
Captain Newman, M.D.
David and Bathsheba
Days of Glory
Designing Woman
Duel in the Sun
Gentleman's Agreement
The Gunfighter
The Guns of Navarone
How the West Was Won
Keys of the Kingdom
MacArthur
Mackenna's Gold
The Man in the Gray Flannel Suit
Marooned
Mirage
Moby Dick
Old Gringo
The Omen
On the Beach
Only the Valiant
Other People's Money

The Paradine Case
Pork Chop Hill
Roman Holiday
The Scarlet and the Black
The Sea Wolves
The Snows of Kilimanjaro
Spellbound
The Stalking Moon
To Kill a Mockingbird
Twelve O'Clock High
The Yearling

ST172 Joe Pesci (1943–)
Backtrack
Betsy's Wedding
Easy Money
The Enforcer (1975)
Eureka
GoodFellas
Home Alone
Home Alone 2: Lost in New York
JFK
I'm Dancing as Fast as I Can
Lethal Weapon 2
Lethal Weapon 3
Man on Fire (1987)
My Cousin Vinny
Once Upon a Time in America
The Public Eye
Raging Bull
The Super

ST173 Michelle Pfeiffer (1957–)
Amazon Women on the Moon
Batman Returns
Callie and Son
Charlie Chan and the Curse of the Dragon
   Queen
Dangerous Liaisons
The Fabulous Baker Boys
Falling in Love Again
Frankie and Johnny (1991)
Grease 2
Into the Night
Ladyhawke
Love Field
Married to the Mob
The Russia House
Scarface (1983 version)
Sweet Liberty
Tequila Sunrise
The Witches of Eastwick

ST174 Sidney Poitier (1924–)
All the Young Men
The Bedford Incident
Blackboard Jungle
Brother John
Buck and the Preacher*
Cry, the Beloved Country

The Defiant Ones (1958 version)
Duel at Diablo
For Love of Ivy
Goodbye, My Lady
The Greatest Story Ever Told (bit)
Guess Who's Coming to Dinner
In the Heat of the Night
Let's Do It Again*
Lilies of the Field
Little Nikita
The Mark of the Hawk
The Organization
Paris Blues
A Patch of Blue
A Piece of the Action*
Pressure Point
A Raisin in the Sun (1961 version)
Separate but Equal
Shoot to Kill
The Slender Thread
Sneakers
Something of Value
They Call Me MISTER Tibbs!
To Sir, With Love
Uptown Saturday Night*
The Wilby Conspiracy
*also director
DIRECTOR ONLY
Fast Forward
Ghost Dad
Hanky Panky
Stir Crazy

ST175 Dick Powell (1904–1963)
The Bad and the Beautiful
Blessed Event
Christmas in July
Cornered
Cry Danger
Dames
Footlight Parade
42nd Street
Gold Diggers of 1933
Gold Diggers of 1935
Hollywood Hotel
In the Navy
A Midsummer Night's Dream
Murder, My Sweet
Stage Struck (1936)
Station West
Susan Slept Here
DIRECTOR ONLY
The Conqueror
The Enemy Below
The Hunters
Split Second (1953)

ST176 William Powell (1892–1984)
See also: CL15 Memorable Screen Teams—
   William Powell and Myrna Loy

After the Thin Man
Another Thin Man
The Ex-Mrs. Bradford
Fashions of 1934
Feel My Pulse
The Great Ziegfeld
How to Marry a Millionaire
The Kennel Murder Case
The Last Command
Libeled Lady
Life With Father
Love Crazy
Manhattan Melodrama
Mister Roberts
Mr. Peabody and the Mermaid
My Man Godfrey
Reckless (1935)
The Senator Was Indiscreet
Shadow of the Thin Man
Song of the Thin Man
Star of Midnight
The Thin Man
The Thin Man Goes Home
Ziegfeld Follies

ST177 Tyrone Power (1913–1958)
Blood and Sand (1941 version)
Diplomatic Courier
The Eddy Duchin Story
Jesse James
Johnny Apollo
The Long Gray Line
Marie Antoinette
The Mark of Zorro
Rawhide
The Razor's Edge (1946 version)
Witness for the Prosecution (1957 version)
A Yank in the RAF

ST178 Elvis Presley (1935–1977)
Blue Hawaii
Clambake
Double Trouble
Flaming Star
Follow That Dream
Frankie and Johnny (1966)
Fun in Acapulco
G.I. Blues
Girl Happy
Girls! Girls! Girls!
Harum Scarum
It Happened at the World's Fair
Jailhouse Rock
Kid Galahad (1962 version)
King Creole
Kissin' Cousins
Live a Little, Love a Little
Loving You
Paradise, Hawaiian Style
Roustabout

Speedway
Spinout
Stay Away, Joe
Tickle Me
The Trouble With Girls
Viva Las Vegas
Wild in the Country
NON-MUSIC
Change of Habit
Charro!
Love Me Tender
DOCUMENTARY SUBJECT
Elvis '56
Elvis 1968 Comeback Special
Elvis on Tour
Elvis: That's the Way It Is
This Is Elvis
SUBJECT ONLY
Elvis: The Movie
Heartbreak Hotel

ST179 Vincent Price (1911–)
Abbott and Costello Meet Frankenstein
The Abominable Dr. Phibes
Adventures of Captain Fabian
Backtrack
The Baron of Arizona
The Bat
Bloodbath at the House of Death
The Boy Who Left Home to Find Out About
  the Shivers
Casanova's Big Night
Champagne for Caesar
Comedy of Terrors
The Conqueror Worm
Convicts Four
Cry of the Banshee
Dangerous Mission
Dead Heat
The Devil's Triangle (narrator)
Diary of a Madman
Dr. Goldfoot and the Bikini Machine
Dr. Phibes Rises Again
Edward Scissorhands
Escapes
The Fall of the House of Usher
The Fly (1958 version)
The Great Mouse Detective (character voice)
The Haunted Palace
His Kind of Woman
House of 1,000 Dolls
House of the Long Shadows
House of Wax
House on Haunted Hill
The Invisible Man Returns
Journey Into Fear (1975 version)
Keys of the Kingdom
The Last Man on Earth
Laura
Madhouse (1974)

The Masque of the Red Death (1964 version)
Master of the World
The Monster Club
The Oblong Box
The Offspring
Once Upon a Midnight Scary (narrator)
Pirate Warrior
The Pit and the Pendulum
The Private Lives of Elizabeth and Essex
The Raven (1963)
The Return of the Fly
Scavenger Hunt
Scream and Scream Again
Shock
Snow White and the Seven Dwarfs (1983
  version)
Son of Sinbad
Song of Bernadette
Tales of Terror
The Ten Commandments (1956 version)
Theatre of Blood
The Three Musketeers (1948 version)
The Tingler
Tomb of Ligeia
Tower of London (1939 and 1962 version)
The Trouble With Girls
Twice Told Tales
The Whales of August
While the City Sleeps
Wilson

ST180 Richard Pryor (1940–)
Adios Amigo
Another You
The Best of Chevy Chase
The Bingo Long Traveling All-Stars and
  Motor Kings
Blue Collar
Brewster's Millions
Bustin' Loose
California Suite
Car Wash
Critical Condition
Greased Lightning
Harlem Nights
Jo Jo Dancer, Your Life Is Calling*
Lady Sings the Blues
The Mack
Moving
The Muppet Movie
Richard Pryor: Here and Now
Richard Pryor: Live and Smokin'
Richard Pryor: Live in Concert
Richard Pryor Live on the Sunset Strip
See No Evil, Hear No Evil
Silver Streak
Some Call It Loving
Some Kind of Hero
Stir Crazy
Superman III

The Toy
Uptown Saturday Night
Which Way Is Up?
Wholly Moses
Wild in the Streets
The Wiz
*also director

Gilda Radner
See: CO13 The Alumni of "Saturday Night
Live"

Harold Ramis
See: CO14 The Alumni of "SCTV"

ST181 Robert Redford (1937–)
All the President's Men
Barefoot in the Park
A Bridge Too Far
Brubaker
Butch Cassidy and the Sundance Kid
The Candidate
The Chase (1966)
Downhill Racer
The Electric Horseman
The Great Gatsby
The Great Waldo Pepper
Havana
The Hot Rock
Incident at Oglala (narrator)
Inside Daisy Clover
Jeremiah Johnson
Legal Eagles
The Natural
Out of Africa
Sneakers
The Sting
Tell Them Willie Boy Is Here
This Property Is Condemned
Three Days of the Condor
The Way We Were
DIRECTOR ONLY
The Milagro Beanfield War
Ordinary People
A River Runs Through It (also narrator)

ST182 Vanessa Redgrave (1937–)
Agatha
Bear Island
Blow-Up
The Bostonians
Camelot
Consuming Passions
The Devils
Howards End
Isadora
Julia
A Man for All Seasons (1966 and 1988
   versions)
Morgan: A Suitable Case for Treatment

Murder on the Orient Express
Orpheus Descending
Out of Season
Playing for Time
Prick Up Your Ears
The Seven Percent Solution
Snow White and the Seven Dwarfs (1983
   version)
Steaming
Three Sovereigns for Sarah
The Trojan Women
Wagner
Wetherby
Yanks
Young Catherine

ST183 Burt Reynolds (1936–)
All Dogs Go to Heaven (character voice)
Angel Baby (bit)
Armored Command
Best Friends
The Best Little Whorehouse in Texas
Breaking In
The Cannonball Run
Cannnonball Run II
City Heat
Deliverance
The End*
Everything You Always Wanted To Know
   About Sex (But Were Afraid to Ask)
Fade-In
Fuzz
Gator*
Hard Frame
Heat
Hooper
Hustle
The Longest Yard
Malone
The Man Who Loved Cat Dancing
The Man Who Loved Women (1983 version)
Modern Love
Navajo Joe
100 Rifles
Operation C.I.A.
Paternity
Physical Evidence
The Player (bit)
Rent-a-Cop
Rough Cut
Semi-Tough
Shamus
Shark!
Sharky's Machine*
Silent Movie (bit)
Skullduggery
Smokey and the Bandit
Smokey and the Bandit II
Smokey and the Bandit 3 (bit)
Starting Over

Stick*
Stroker Ace
Switching Channels
White Lightning
*also director

ST184 Ralph Richardson (1902–1983)
Alice's Adventures in Wonderland
Anna Karenina (1948 version)
The Battle of Britain
Bulldog Jack
Chimes at Midnight (narrator)
The Citadel
Clouds Over Europe
The Day Will Dawn
The Divorce of Lady X
A Doll's House (Bloom)
Dr. Zhivago
Dragonslayer
Exodus
The Fallen Idol
The Four Feathers
The Ghoul (1933)
Give My Regards to Broad Street (bit)
Greystoke: The Legend of Tarzan, Lord of the
  Apes
The Heiress
Invitation to the Wedding
Java Head
Khartoum
Lady Caroline Lamb
Laurence Olivier—A Life
Long Day's Journey Into Night (1962 version)
The Looking Glass War
The Man in the Iron Mask (1977 version)
The Man Who Could Work Miracles
O Lucky Man!
Richard III
Rollerball
Tales From the Crypt (1972)
Things To Come
Thunder in the City
Time Bandits
Wagner
Who Slew Auntie Roo?
Witness for the Prosecution (1982 version)
The Wrong Box

ST185 Jason Robards (1922–)
All the President's Men
Any Wednesday
The Ballad of Cable Hogue
Black Rainbow
A Big Hand for the Little Lady
A Boy and His Dog
Bright Lights, Big City
Burden of Dreams
By Love Possessed
Caboblanco
A Christmas to Remember

The Christmas Wife
Comes a Horseman
The Day After
Dream a Little Dream
Final Warning
Fools
The Good Mother
Hour of the Gun
Hurricane
Isadora
Johnny Got His Gun
Julia
Julius Caesar (1970 version)
Laguna Heat
The Legend of the Lone Ranger
Long Day's Journey Into Night (1962 version)
The Long Hot Summer (1985 version)
Max Dugan Returns
Melvin and Howard
Mr. Sycamore
Murders in the Rue Morgue (1971 version)
The Night They Raided Minsky's
Once Upon a Time in the West
Parenthood
Pat Garrett and Billy the Kid
Quick Change
Raise the Titanic!
Reunion
The St. Valentine's Day Massacre
Sakharov
Something Wicked This Way Comes
Square Dance
Storyville
A Thousand Clowns
Tora! Tora! Tora!
You Can't Take It With You (1984 version)

ST186 Edward G. Robinson (1893–1973)
Barbary Coast
Brother Orchid
Bullets or Ballots
Cheyenne Autumn
The Cincinnati Kid
Destroyer
Double Indemnity
Good Neighbor Sam
Hell on Frisco Bay
A Hole in the Head
House of Strangers
I Am the Law
It's a Great Feeling (bit)
Illegal
Key Largo
Kid Galahad (1937 version)
Little Caesar
Mackenna's Gold
Mr. Winkle Goes to War
My Geisha
Never a Dull Moment (1968)
Our Vines Have Tender Grapes

The Prize
The Red House
Robin and the Seven Hoods
Scarlet Street
The Sea Wolf
Seven Thieves
Song of Norway
Soylent Green
The Stranger
The Ten Commandments (1956 version)
Thunder in the City
Two Weeks in Another Town
The Violent Men

ST187 Ginger Rogers (1911–)
See also: CL15 Memorable Screen Teams—
   Fred Astaire and Ginger Rogers
Bachelor Mother
The Barkleys of Broadway
Carefree
Cinderella (1964 version)
Fifth Avenue Girl
Finishing School
Flying Down to Rio
Follow the Fleet
42nd Street
The Gay Divorcee
George Stevens: A Filmmaker's Journey
Gold Diggers of 1933
Having Wonderful Time
In Person
Kitty Foyle
Lucky Partners
Monkey Business (1952)
Once Upon a Honeymoon
Primrose Path
Quick, Let's Get Married
Roberta
Romance in Manhattan
Shall We Dance
A Shriek in the Night
Stage Door
Star of Midnight
The Story of Vernon and Irene Castle
Swing Time
Tender Comrade
That's Dancing!
The Thirteenth Guest
The Tip Off
Tom, Dick and Harry
Top Hat
Vivacious Lady
We're Not Married

ST188 Roy Rogers (1912–)
Along the Navajo Trail
Apache Rose
The Arizona Kid
Bad Man of Deadwood
Bells of Coronado

Bells of Rosarita
Bells of San Angelo
The Big Show (with The Sons of the Pioneers,
   billed as Leonard Slye)
Billy the Kid Returns
Carson City Kid
Colorado
Come on, Rangers
The Cowboy and the Senorita
Dark Command
Days of Jesse James
Don't Fence Me In
Down Dakota Way
Eyes of Texas
The Far Frontier
Frontier Pony Express
The Gay Ranchero
The Golden Stallion
Grand Canyon Trail
Hands Across the Border
Heart of the Golden West
Heart of the Rockies
Helldorado
Home in Oklahoma
Idaho
In Old Amarillo
In Old Caliente
In Old Cheyenne
Jesse James at Bay
King of the Cowboys
Lights of Old Santa Fe
Man From Cheyenne
My Pal Trigger
Nevada City
Night Time in Nevada
North of the Great Divide
Old Barn Dance (billed as Dick Weston)
The Old Corral
On the Old Spanish Trail
The Ranger and the Lady
Ridin' Down the Canyon
Robinhood of the Pecos
Roll on Texas Moon
Romance on the Range
Rough Riders Roundup
Saga of Death Valley
San Fernando Valley
Sheriff of Tombstone
Shine on Harvest Moon
Silver Spurs
Son of Paleface
Song of Arizona
Song of Nevada
Song of Texas
Sons of the Pioneers
South of Santa Fe
Southward Ho!
Springtime in the Sierras
Sunset in El Dorado
Sunset in the West

Sunset on the Desert
Sunset Serenade
Susanna Pass
Texas Legionnaires
Texas Lightning
Trail of Robin Hood
Trigger, Jr.
Twilight in the Sierras
Under California Stars
Under Nevada Skies
Under Western Stars
Utah
Wall Street Cowboy
The Yellow Rose of Texas
Young Bill Hickok
Young Buffalo Bill
NON-WESTERN
Hollywood Canteen (bit)

ST189 Mickey Rooney (1920–)
See also: CL15 Memorable Screen Teams—
    Mickey Rooney and Judy Garland
The Adventures of Huckleberry Finn (1939
    version)
Ah, Wilderness
Andy Hardy Gets Spring Fever
Andy Hardy Meets Debutante
Andy Hardy's Double Life
Andy Hardy's Private Secretary
The Atomic Kid
Babes in Arms
Babes on Broadway
The Big Wheel
Bill
Bill: On His Own
The Black Stallion
Boys Town
Breakfast at Tiffany's
The Bridges at Toko-Ri
Captains Courageous
The Care Bears Movie (character voice)
Chained
The Comic
The Domino Principle
Erik the Viking
Find the Lady
Girl Crazy
Hide-Out
The Human Comedy
It Came Upon a Midnight Clear
It's a Mad Mad Mad Mad World
Journey Back to Oz
    (character voice)
King of the Roaring 20's—
    The Story of Arnold Rothstein
Leave 'em Laughing
The Legend of Wolf Mountain
Life Begins for Andy Hardy
Lightning: The White Stallion
Little Lord Fauntleroy (1936 version)

Little Nemo: Adventures in Slumberland
    (character voice)
Love Finds Andy Hardy
Love Laughs at Andy Hardy
The Magic of Lassie
Manhattan Melodrama
Manipulator
Maximum Force
Men of Boys Town
A Midsummmr Night's Dream
My Heroes Have Always Been Cowboys
My Outlaw Brother
National Velvet
Off Limits (1953)
Pete's Dragon
Pulp
Reckless (1935)
Riffraff
Senior Trip
Silent Night, Deadly Night 5: The Toymaker
Strike Up the Band
Summer Holiday
Thousands Cheer
Words and Music

ST190 Mickey Rourke (1950–)
Angel Heart
Barfly
Body Heat
City in Fear
Desperate Hours
Diner
Eureka
Harley Davidson and the Marlboro Man
Heaven's Gate (bit)
Homeboy
Johnny Handsome
9½ Weeks
The Pope of Greenwich Village
A Prayer for the Dying
Rape and Marriage: The Rideout Case
Rumble Fish
White Sands
Wild Orchid
The Year of the Dragon

ST191 Kurt Russell (1951–)
Amber Waves
Backdraft
The Barefoot Executive
The Best of Times
Big Trouble in Little China
Captain Ron
Charley and the Angel
The Christmas Coal Mine Miracle
The Computer Wore Tennis Shoes
The Deadly Tower
Elvis: The Movie
Escape From New York
Follow Me, Boys!

The Horse in the Gray Flannel Suit
It Happened at the World's Fair (bit)
The Mean Season
Mosby's Marauders
Now You See Him, Now You Don't
The One and Only, Genuine, Original Family
   Band
Overboard
Silkwood
Superdad
Swing Shift'
Tango & Cash
Tequila Sunrise
The Thing
Unlawful Entry
Used Cars
Winter People

ST192 Rosalind Russell (1908–1976)
Auntie Mame
The Citadel
China Seas
Craig's Wife
Forsaking All Others
Gypsy
His Girl Friday
Never Wave at a WAC
Oh Dad, Poor Dad—Mama's Hung You in the
   Closet and I'm Feeling So Sad
Picnic
Reckless (1935)
Sister Kenny
The Trouble With Angels
The Velvet Touch
A Woman of Distinction
The Women (1939)

ST193 Robert Ryan (1909–1973)
And Hope to Die
Anzio
Back From Eternity
Bad Day at Black Rock
Battle of the Bulge
Behind the Rising Sun
Berlin Express
Best of the Badmen
Beware, My Lovely
Billy Budd
Bombardier
Born To Be Bad
The Boy With Green Hair
Caught
Clash by Night
Crossfire
The Dirty Dozen
Escape to Burma
Executive Action
Flying Leathernecks
God's Little Acre
Horizons West

Hour of the Gun
Ice Palace
The Iron Major
King of Kings
Lonelyhearts
The Longest Day
The Love Machine
Marine Raiders
Men in War
A Minute to Pray, A Second to Die
The Naked Spur
On Dangerous Ground
The Professionals
The Racket
Return of the Badmen
The Set-Up
The Sky's the Limit
The Tall Men
Tender Comrade
Trail Street
The Wild Bunch

ST194 Susan Sarandon (1946–)
Atlantic City
Beauty and the Beast (1984 version)
Bob Roberts (bit)
The Buddy System
Bull Durham
Compromising Positions
A Dry White Season
The Front Page (1974 version)
The Great Smokey Roadblock
The Great Waldo Pepper
The Hunger
The January Man
Joe
King of the Gypsies
Light Sleeper
Lorenzo's Oil
Loving Couples
Mussolini and I
The Other Side of Midnight
The Player (bit)
Pretty Baby
The Rocky Horror Picture Show
Something Short of Paradise
Sweet Hearts Dance
Tempest
Thelma & Louise
White Palace
Who Am I This Time?
The Witches of Eastwick
Women of Valor

ST195 Arnold Schwarzenegger (1947–)
Commando
Conan the Barbarian
Conan the Destroyer
Hercules Goes Bananas
The Jayne Mansfield Story

Kindergarten Cop
The Long Goodbye (bit)
Predator
Pumping Iron
Raw Deal
Red Heat
Red Sonja
Running Man
Scavenger Hunt (bit)
Stay Hungry
The Terminator
Terminator 2: Judgment Day
Total Recall
Twins
The Villain

ST196 George C. Scott (1927-)
Anatomy of a Murder
Bank Shot
The Bible
The Changeling
The Day of the Dolphin
Descending Angel*
Dr. Strangelove or; How I Learned to Stop
  Worrying and Love the Bomb
Exorcist III: Legion
Firestarter
The Flim Flam Man
The Formula
The Hanging Tree
Hardcore
The Hindenburg
The Hospital
The Hustler
Islands in the Stream
The Last Days of Patton
The List of Adrian Messenger
Movie, Movie
The Murders in the Rue Morgue
The New Centurions
Patton
Petulia
The Prince and the Pauper (1978 version)
Rage (1972)*
The Rescuers Down Under (character voice)
The Savage Is Loose*
Taps
They Might Be Giants
*also director

ST197 Randolph Scott (1898–1987)
Bombardier
Captain Kidd
China Sky
Follow the Fleet
Gung Ho! (1943)
My Favorite Wife
Rebecca of Sunnybrook Farm
Roberta
Susannah of the Mounties
To the Shores of Tripoli

WESTERNS
Abilene Town
Badman's Territory
Buffalo Stampede
Cariboo Trail
Coroner Creek
Decision at Sundown
The Doolins of Oklahoma
Hangman's Knot
Jesse James
The Last of the Mohicans (1936 version)
A Lawless Street
Man in the Saddle
Man of the Forest
The Nevadan
Rage at Dawn
Return of the Badmen
Ride Lonesome
Ride the High Country
Rocky Mountain Mystery
Seventh Cavalry
The Spoilers (1942 version)
The Stranger Wore a Gun
The Tall T
Ten Wanted Men
To the Last Man
Trail Street
Virginia City
Wagon Wheels
Western Union

ST198 Peter Sellers (1925–1980)
After the Fox
Alice's Adventures in Wonderland
The Battle of the Sexes
Being There
The Blockhouse
The Bobo
Carlton-Browne of the F.O.
Casino Royale
Down Among the Z-Men
Dr. Strangelove or; How I Learned to Stop
  Worrying and Love the Bomb
The Fiendish Plot of Dr. Fu Manchu
Ghost in the Noonday Sun
The Goon Show Movie
The Great McGonagall
Heavens Above
I Love You, Alice B. Toklas
I'm All Right, Jack
The Ladykillers
Lolita
The Magic Christian
The Millionairess
The Mouse That Roared
Muppet Treasures
Murder by Death
The Naked Truth
Never Let Go
Only Two Can Play

The Party
The Pink Panther
The Pink Panther Strikes Again
The Prisoner of Zenda (1979 version)
Return of the Pink Panther
The Revenge of the Pink Panther
The Road to Hong Kong (bit)
Rowlf's Rhapsodies With the Muppets
A Shot in the Dark
The Smallest Show on Earth
There's a Girl in My Soup
tom thumb
Trail of the Pink Panther
Two Way Stretch
Up the Creek (1958)
Waltz of the Toreadors
What's New Pussycat?
Woman Times Seven
The World of Henry Orient
The Wrong Arm of the Law
The Wrong Box

Martin Short
See: CO14 The Alumni of "SCTV"

ST199 Frank Sinatra (1915–)
Around the World in 80 Days (bit)
Cannonball Run II (bit)
Cast a Giant Shadow
Come Blow Your Horn
The Detective (1968)
The Devil at 4 O'Clock
Double Dynamite
The First Deadly Sin
Four for Texas
From Here to Eternity
A Hole in the Head
Kings Go Forth
Lady in Cement
The List of Adrian Messenger
Listen Up: The Lives of Quincy Jones
The Man With the Golden Arm
The Manchurian Candidate
The Miracle of the Bells
Never So Few
None But the Brave*
Not as a Stranger
Ocean's Eleven
Paris When It Sizzles (bit)
The Pride and the Passion
Some Came Running
Suddenly
The Tender Trap
Tony Rome
Von Ryan's Express
MUSICALS
Anchors Aweigh
Can-Can
Guys and Dolls
High Society

Higher and Higher
It Happened in Brooklyn
On the Town
Pal Joey
Robin and the Seven Hoods
Ship Ahoy
Step Lively
Take Me Out to the Ball Game
That's Entertainment!
That's Entertainment, Part 2
Till the Clouds Roll By
Young at Heart
*also director
SUBJECT ONLY
Sinatra

ST200 Christian Slater (1969–)
Beyond the Stars
Ferngully . . . The Last Rainforest (character
    voice)
Gleaming the Cube
Heathers
Kuffs
The Legend of Billie Jean
Mobsters
The Name of the Rose
Pump Up the Volume
Robin Hood: Prince of Thieves
Star Trek VI: The Undiscovered Country (bit)
Tales From the Darkside: The Movie
Tucker: The Man and His Dream
Twisted
Untamed Heart
Where the Day Takes You (bit)
The Wizard
Young Guns II

ST201 Wesley Snipes (1963–)
Jungle Fever
King of New York
Major League
Mo' Better Blues
New Jack City
Passenger 57
Streets of Gold
The Waterdance
White Men Can't Jump

ST202 Sissy Spacek (1949–)
Badlands
Carrie (1976)
Coal Miner's Daughter
Crimes of the Heart
Ginger in the Morning
The Girls of Huntington House
Hard Promises
Heart Beat
JFK
Katherine
The Long Walk Home

The Man With Two Brains (character voice)
Marie
Missing
'night, Mother
Prime Cut
Raggedy Man
The River (1984)
Violets Are Blue . . .
Welcome to L.A.

ST203 James Spader (1960–)
Baby Boom
Bad Influence
Bob Roberts
Cocaine: One Man's Seduction
Endless Love
Family Secrets
Jack's Back
Less Than Zero
Mannequin (1987)
The New Kids
Pretty in Pink
The Rachel Papers
sex, lies and videotape
Storyville
True Colors
Tuff Turf
Wall Street
White Palace

ST204 Sylvester Stallone (1946–)
Bananas (bit)
Cannonball
Cobra
Death Race 2000
F.I.S.T.
Farewell, My Lovely
First Blood
Lock Up
The Lords of Flatbush
Nighthawks
Oscar
Over the Top
Paradise Alley*
Rambo: First Blood II
Rambo III
Rebel (1973)
Rhinestone
Rocky
Rocky II*
Rocky III*
Rocky IV*
Rocky V
Stop! Or My Mom Will Shoot
Tango & Cash
Victory
*also director
DIRECTOR ONLY
Staying Alive

ST205 Harry Dean Stanton (1926–)
Alien
The Black Marble
Christine
Cockfighter
Cool Hand Luke
Deathwatch
Dillinger
Dream a Little Dream
Escape From New York
Farewell, My Lovely
Flatbed Annie
Fool for Love
The Fourth War
The Godfather, Part II
The Godfather: The Complete Epic,
    1902–1958
The Godfather Triology, 1901–1980
Kelly's Heroes
The Last Temptation of Christ
Man Trouble
The Missouri Breaks
Mr. North
92 in the Shade
The Oldest Living Graduate
One From the Heart
One Magic Christmas
Paris, Texas
Pat Garrett and Billy the Kid
Payoff
Pretty in Pink
Private Benjamin
The Proud Rebel*
Rafferty and the Gold Dust Twins
Rancho Deluxe
Rebel Rousers*
Red Dawn
Repo Man
Ride in the Whirlwind
Rip Van Winkle
The Rose
Slamdance
Stars and Bars
Straight Time
Twin Peaks: Fire Walk With Me
Twister
UFOria
Where the Lilies Bloom
Wild at Heart
Wise Blood
Young Doctors in Love
Zandy's Bride
*billed as Dean Stanton

ST206 Barbara Stanwyck (1907–1990)
Annie Oakley
Baby Face
Ball of Fire
Blowing Wild
The Bride Walks Out

Cattle Queen of Montana
Christmas in Connecticut
Clash by Night
Double Indemnity
East Side, West Side
Escape to Burma
Executive Suite
Golden Boy
Hollywood Canteen (bit)
Ladies They Talk About
The Lady Eve
Lady of Burlesque
The Mad Miss Manton
The Maverick Queen
Meet John Doe
Night Nurse
Roustabout
Sorry, Wrong Number
Stella Dallas
The Strange Love of Martha Ivers
The Thorn Birds
The Two Mrs. Carrolls
The Violent Men
Walk on the Wild Side

ST207 James Stewart (1908–)
After the Thin Man
Airport '77
An Amerrcan Tale: Fievel Goes West
  (character voice)
Anatomy of a Murder
Bandolero!
Bell, Book and Candle
Bend of the River
The Big Sleep (1978 version)
Born To Dance
Broken Arrow
Carbine Williams
Cheyenne Autumn
The Cheyenne Social Club
Dear Brigitte
Destry Rides Again
The FBI Story
The Far Country
Flight of the Phoenix
The Glenn Miller Story
The Gorgeous Hussy (bit)
The Greatest Show on Earth
Harvey
How the West Was Won
It's a Wonderful Life
Made for Each Other (1939)
The Magic of Lassie
Magic Town
The Man From Laramie
The Man Who Knew Too Much (1956
  version)
The Man Who Shot Liberty Valance
The Mountain Road
Mr. Hobbs Takes a Vacation

Mr. Smith Goes to Washington
The Naked Spur
The Philadelphia Story
Pot o' Gold
The Rare Breed
Rear Window
Right of Way
Rope
Rose Marie
Shenandoah
The Shootist
The Shop Around the Corner
The Spirit of St. Louis
Strategic Air Command
Thunder Bay
Two Rode Together
Vertigo
Vivacious Lady
Wife vs. Secretary
Winchester '73
You Can't Take It With You (1938 version)
Ziegfeld Girl

ST208 Dean Stockwell (1936–)
Alsino and the Condor
Anchors Aweigh
Backtrack
Beverly Hills Cop II
Blue Velvet
The Boy With Green Hair
Buying Time
Dune
The Dunwich Horror
Gardens of Stone
Gentleman's Agreement
Kim
The Last Movie
The Legend of Billie Jean
Limit Up
The Loners
Long Day's Journey Into Night (1962 version)
Married to the Mob
Paris, Texas
Psych-Out
The Secret Garden (1949 version)
Smokescreen
Son of the Morning Star
Song of the Thin Man
The Time Guardian
To Live and Die in L.A.
Tracks
Tucker: The Man and His Dream
Werewolf of Washington
Win, Place or Steal
Wrong Is Right

ST209 Madeleine Stowe (1958–)
The Amazons
Closet Land
The Last of the Mohicans (1992 version)

The Nativity
Revenge (1990)
Stakeout
Tropical Snow
The Two Jakes
Unlawful Entry
Worth Winning

ST210 Meryl Streep (1949–)
A Cry in the Dark
Death Becomes Her
The Deer Hunter
Defending Your Life
Falling in Love
The French Lieutenant's Woman
Heartburn
Holocaust
Ironweed
Julia
Kramer vs. Kramer
Manhattan
Out of Africa
Plenty
Postcards From the Edge
The Seduction of Joe Tynan
She-Devil
Silkwood
Sophie's Choice
Still of the Night

ST211 Barbra Streisand (1942–)
All Night Long
For Pete's Sake
Listen Up: The Lives of Quincy Jones
The Main Event
Nuts
The Owl and the Pussycat
The Prince of Tides*
Up the Sandbox
The Way We Were
What's Up, Doc?
MUSICALS
Funny Girl
Funny Lady
Hello, Dolly!
On a Clear Day You Can See Forever
A Star Is Born (1976 version)
Yentl*
*also director

ST212 Elizabeth Taylor (1932–)
See also: CL15 Memorable Screen Teams—
   Richard Burton and Elizabeth Taylor
Ash Wednesday
Beau Brummel (1954 version)
Between Friends
The Big Hangover
Butterfield 8
Cat on a Hot Tin Roof (1958 version)
Cleopatra (1963)

The Comedians
Conspirator
Courage of Lassie
A Date With Judy
Divorce His, Divorce Hers
Doctor Faustus
The Driver's Seat
Elephant Walk
Father of the Bride (1950 version)
Father's Little Dividend
Giant
The Girl Who Had Everything
Hammersmith Is Out
Ivanhoe
Jane Eyre (1944 version) (bit)
Julia Misbehaves
Lassie Come Home
The Last Time I Saw Paris
Life With Father
A Little Night Music
Little Women (1949 version)
Love Is Better Than Ever
Malice in Wonderland
The Mirror Crack'd
National Velvet
Night Watch
The Only Game in Town
A Place in the Sun
Poker Alice
Raintree County
Reflections in a Golden Eye
Return Engagement
Rhapsody
The Sandpiper
Secret Ceremony
Suddenly, Last Summer
The Taming of the Shrew
Under Milk Wood
The VIPs
Who's Afraid of Virginia Woolf?
Winter Kills
X, Y and Zee

ST213 Shirley Temple (1928–)
Baby Take a Bow
The Bachelor and the Bobby Soxer
The Blue Bird
Bright Eyes
Captain January
Curly Top
Dimples
Fort Apache
Heidi (1937 version)
Just Around the Corner
The Little Colonel
Little Miss Broadway
The Little Princess
The Littlest Rebel
Miss Annie Rooney
Our Little Girl

Poor Little Rich Girl
Rebecca of Sunnybrook Farm
Since You Went Away
Stand Up and Cheer
The Story of Seabiscuit
Stowaway
Susannah of the Mounties
To the Last Man
Wee Willie Winkie

Dave Thomas
See: CO14 The Alumni of "SCTV"

ST214 Gene Tierney (1920-1991)
Advise and Consent
The Egyptian
The Ghost and Mrs. Muir
Heaven Can Wait (1943)
Laura
The Left Hand of God
Night and the City (1950 version)
The Razor's Edge (1946 version)
The Return of Frank James
The Shanghai Gesture
Sundown (1941)
Toys in the Attic

ST215 Lily Tomlin (1939–)
All of Me
Big Business
The Incredible Shrinking Woman
The Late Show
Nashville
Nine to Five
The Player (bit)
The Search for Signs of Intelligent Life in
   the Universe
Shadows and Fog

ST216 Rip Torn (1931–)
Airplane II: The Sequel (bit)
Another Pair of Aces: Three of a Kind
Baby Doll
The Beastmaster
Beautiful Dreamers
Beer
Betrayal (1978)
Birch Interval
The Blue and the Gray
By Dawn's Early Light
Cat on a Hot Tin Roof (1984 version)
The Cincinnati Kid
City Heat
Cold Feet
Coma
Cotter
Cross Creek
Defending Your Life
Dolly Dearest
The Execution

Extreme Prejudice
First Family
Flashpoint
Heartland
Hit List
Jinxed
King of Kings
Laguna Heat
The Man Who Fell to Earth
Manhunt for Claude Dallas
Misunderstood
Nadine
Nasty Habits
One-Trick Pony
Payday
Pork Chop Hill
The President's Plane Is Missing
The Private Files of J. Edgar Hoover
Rape and Marriage: The Rideout Case
The Seduction of Joe Tynan
A Shining Season
Silence Like Glass
Slaughter
Songwriter
Sophia Loren: Her Own Story
Steel Cowboy
A Stranger Is Watching
Summer Rental
Sweet Bird of Youth
You're a Big Boy Now
DIRECTOR ONLY
The Telephone

ST217 Spencer Tracy (1900–1967)
See also: CL15 Memorable Screen Teams—
   Katharine Hepburn and Spencer Tracy
Adam's Rib
Bad Day at Black Rock
Boom Town
Boys Town
Broken Lance
Captains Courageous
Desk Set
The Devil at 4 O'Clock
Dr. Jekyll and Mr. Hyde (1941 version)
Edison, the Man
Father of the Bride (1950 version)
Father's Little Dividend
Fury
Guess Who's Coming to Dinner
A Guy Named Joe
How the West Was Won*
Inherit the Wind
It's a Mad Mad Mad Mad World
Judgment at Nuremberg
Keeper of the Flame
The Last Hurrah
Libeled Lady
Mannequin (1937)
Men of Boys Town

The Mountain
Northwest Passage
Pat and Mike
Riffraff (1935)
San Francisco
The Sea of Grass
The Seventh Cross
Stanley and Livingstone
State of the Union
Test Pilot
That's Entertainment, Part 2
Thirty Seconds Over Tokyo
Tortilla Flat
Without Love
Woman of the Year
*narrator only

ST218 Kathleen Turner (1954–)
The Accidental Tourist
Body Heat
A Breed Apart
Crimes of Passion
Dear America: Letters Home From Vietnam
   (narrator)
Jewel of the Nile
Julia and Julia
The Man With Two Brains
Peggy Sue Got Married
Prizzi's Honor
Romancing the Stone
Switching Channels
V.I. Warshawski
The War of the Roses
Who Framed Roger Rabbit (character voice)

ST219 Lana Turner (1920–)
Another Time, Another Place
The Bad and the Beautiful
Betrayed (1954)
Bittersweet Love
By Love Possessed
Dr. Jekyll and Mr. Hyde (1941 version)
Green Dolphin Street
Honky Tonk
Imitation of Life
Love Finds Andy Hardy
Madame X (1966 version)
Making of a Legend—Gone With the Wind
Persecution
Peyton Place
The Postman Always Rings Twice (1946 version)
The Sea Chase
They Won't Forget
The Three Musketeers (1948 version)
Witches' Brew
Ziegfeld Girl

ST220 Liv Ullmann (1939–)
See also: XT30 He Directs, She Acts
Autumn Sonata

The Bay Boy
A Bridge Too Far
Cold Sweat
Cries and Whispers
Dangerous Moves
Forty Carats
Gaby—A True Story
Hour of the Wolf
Leonor
Mindwalk
The Night Visitor
The Passion of Anna
Persona
Richard's Things
The Rose Garden
Scenes From a Marriage
The Serpent's Egg
Shame (1968)
The Wild Duck
Zandy's Bride

ST221 Lee Van Cleef (1925–1989)
Armed Response
Bad Man's River
Beyond the Law
The Big Combo
The Bravados
Captain Apache
China Gate
Code Name: Wild Geese
Commandos
The Conqueror
Death Rides a Horse
El Condor
Escape From New York
For a Few Dollars More
The Good, the Bad and the
   Ugly
Gunfight at the O.K.
   Corral
The Hard Way (1979)
High Noon
It Conquered the World
Jungle Raiders
Kansas City Confidential
Kid Vengeance
The Lonely Man
A Man Alone
The Man Who Shot Liberty Valance
Mean Frank and Crazy Tony
The Octagon
Ride Lonesome
Speed Zone
The Squeeze (1980)
The Stranger and the Gunfighter
Take a Hard Ride
Ten Wanted Men
Thieves of Fortune
The Tin Star
The Young Lions

ST222 Christopher Walken (1943–)
All-American Murder
The Anderson Tapes
Annie Hall
At Close Range
Batman Returns
Biloxi Blues
Brainstorm
The Comfort of Strangers
Communion
The Dead Zone
Deadline
The Deer Hunter
The Dogs of War
The Happiness Cage
Heaven's Gate
Homeboy
King of New York
Last Embrace
McBain
The Milagro Beanfield War
The Mind Snatchers
Mistress (bit)
Pennies From Heaven
Roseland
Sarah, Plain and Tall
The Sentinel
Shoot the Sun Down
A View to a Kill
Who Am I This Time?

ST223 Denzel Washington (1954–)
Carbon Copy
Cry Freedom
For Queen and Country
Glory
Heart Condition
Licence to Kill
Malcolm X
The Mighty Quinn
Mississippi Masala
Mo' Better Blues
Power (1986)
Ricochet
A Soldier's Story
Wilma

ST224 John Wayne (1907–1979)
Note: Numerous B Westerns with Wayne are
   on tape but are not widely available.
Baby Face (bit)
Back to Bataan
The Barbarian and the Geisha
Big Jim McLain
Blood Alley
Brannigan
Cast a Giant Shadow
Circus World
The Conqueror
Donovan's Reef

The Fighting Seabees
Flying Leathernecks
Flying Tigers
The Greatest Story Ever Told (bit)
The Green Berets*
Hatari!
The Hell Fighters
In Harm's Way
Jet Pilot
Lady for a Night
The Lady From Louisiana
Legend of the Lost
The Long Voyage Home
The Longest Day
McQ
Operation Pacific
The Quiet Man
Reap the Wild Wind
Reunion in France
The Sands of Iwo Jima
The Sea Chase
Seven Sinners
They Were Expendable
Trouble Along the Way
Tycoon
Wake of the Red Witch
Wheel of Fortune
The Wings of Eagles
Without Reservations
WESTERNS
The Alamo**
Allegheny Uprising
Angel and the Badman
Big Jake
The Big Trail
Cahill: U.S. Marshal
Chisum
The Comancheros
The Cowboys
Dakota
Dark Command
El Dorado
The Fighting Kentuckian
Flame of the Barbary Coast
Fort Apache
The Horse Soldiers
How the West Was Won
In Old California
A Lady Takes a Chance
McLintock!
The Man Who Shot Liberty Valance
North to Alaska
Overland Stage Raiders
Red River
Rio Bravo
Rio Grande
Rio Lobo
Rooster Cogburn
The Searchers
She Wore a Yellow Ribbon

The Shootist
The Sons of Katie Elder
The Spoilers (1942 version)
Stagecoach
Three Faces West
3 Godfathers
The Train Robbers
True Grit
The Undefeated
War of the Wildcats
The War Wagon
*also co-director
**also director

ST225 Sigourney Weaver (1949–)
Alien
Alien^3
Aliens
Annie Hall (bit)
Deal of the Century
Eyewitness
1492: Conquest of Paradise
Ghostbusters
Ghostbusters II
Gorillas in the Mist
Half Moon Street
Madman
One Man or Two
Working Girl
The Year of Living Dangerously

Orson Welles
See: Director Check List DT112 Orson Welles

ST226 Mae West (1892–1980)
My Little Chickadee
Myra Breckenridge
Sextette
She Done Him Wrong

ST227 Billy Dee Williams (1937–)
Batman (1989)
The Bingo Long Traveling All-Stars and
  Motor Kings
Brian's Song
Chiefs
Christmas Lilies of the Field
Courage (1986)
Deadly Illusion
Driving Me Crazy
The Empire Strikes Back
Fear City
The Final Comedown
The Glass House
Hostage Tower
The Imposter
Lady Sings the Blues
The Last Angry Man
Mahogany
Marvin and Tige

Nighthawks
Number One With a Bullet
Oceans of Fire
The Out-of-Towners (bit)
Return of the Jedi

ST228 Robin Williams (1952–)
The Adventures of Baron Münchausen (billed
  as Ray Tutto)
Aladdin (character voice)
An All-Star Salute to the Improv
Awakenings
The Best of Comic Relief
Best of Comic Relief '90
The Best of Times
Cadillac Man
Club Paradise
Comic Relief 2
Comic Relief III
Dead Again
Dead Poets Society
Dear America: Letters Home From Vietnam
  (narrator)
An Evening With Robin Williams
Ferngully . . . The Last Rainforest (character
  voice)
The Fisher King
Good Morning, Vietnam
HBO Comedy Club: Tenth Anniversary
  Young Comedians Special
Hook
Jonathan Winters: On the Ledge
Moscow on the Hudson
Popeye
Richard Lewis: "I'm in Pain"
Robin Williams Live!
Seize the Day
Shakes the Clown (bit)
The Survivors
The Tale of the Frog Prince
Toys
The World According to Garp

ST229 Bruce Willis (1955–)
Billy Bathgate
Blind Date (1987)
The Bonfire of the Vanities
Death Becomes Her
Die Hard
Die Hard 2: Die Harder
Hudson Hawk
In Country
The Last Boy Scout
Look Who's Talking (character voice)
Look Who's Talking Too (character voice)
Moonlighting (1985)
Mortal Thoughts
National Lampoon's Loaded Weapon 1
  (bit)
The Player (bit)

Sunset
That's Adequate

ST230 Paul Winfield (1940–)
Angel City
Big Shots
The Blue and the Gray
Blue City
Brother John
Carbon Copy
Conrack
Damnation Alley
Death Before Dishonor
For Us, the Living
Gordon's War
Green Eyes
A Hero Ain't Nothin' But a Sandwich
High Velocity
Hustle
It's Good To Be Alive
King
Mike's Murder
R.P.M.
The Serpent and the Rainbow
Sounder
The Terminator
Twilight's Last Gleaming

ST231 Debra Winger (1955–)
Betrayed (1988)
Black Widow
Cannery Row
Everybody Wins
French Postcards
Leap of Faith
Legal Eagles
Made in Heaven
Mike's Murder
An Officer and a Gentleman
The Sheltering Sky
Slumber Party '57
Terms of Endearment
Thank God, It's Friday (bit)
Urban Cowboy

ST232 Shelley Winters (1922–)
Alfie
The Balcony
Behave Yourself!
Bloody Mama
Blume in Love
City on Fire
Cleopatra Jones
Deja Vu
The Delta Force
Diamonds
The Diary of Anne Frank
A Double Life
Elvis: The Movie
Enter Laughing

Executive Suite
The Gangster
The Greatest Story Ever Told (bit)
Harper
I Am a Camera
I Died a Thousand Times
The Initiation of Sarah
Journey Into Fear (1975 version)
King of the Gypsies
Knickerbocker Holiday
Lolita
The Magician of Lublin
Mambo
The Night of the Hunter
Over the Brooklyn Bridge
A Patch of Blue
Pete's Dragon
Phone Call From a Stranger
A Place in the Sun
The Poseidon Adventure
Purple People Eater
Revenge (1971)
S.O.B.
The Scalphunters
Shattered (1972)
Stepping Out
The Tenant
Tentacles
That Lucky Touch
Time of Indifference
Treasure of Pancho Villa
An Unremarkable Life
The Visitor
What's the Matter With Helen?
Who Slew Auntie Roo?
Wild in the Streets
Wildfire
Winchester '73

ST233 James Woods (1947–)
Against All Odds (1984)
Badge of the Assassin
The Black Marble
Best Seller
The Boost
Cat's Eye
Chaplin
The Choirboys
Citizen Cohn
Cop
Diggstown
The Disappearance of Aimee
Eyewitness
Fast-Walking
The Hard Way
Holocaust
Immediate Family
Joshua Then and Now
Night Moves
Once Upon a Time in America

The Onion Field
Salvador
Split Image
Straight Talk
True Believer
Videodrome
The Way We Were
Women and Men: Stories of Seduction

ST234 Joanne Woodward (1930–)
See also: XT30 He Directs, She Acts
A Big Hand for the Little Lady
A Christmas to Remember
Crisis at Central High
The Drowning Pool*
The End
A Fine Madness
From the Terrace*
The Fugitive Kind

The Glass Menagerie (1987 version)
Harry and Son*
The Long Hot Summer (1958 version)*
Mr. and Mrs. Bridge*
A New Kind of Love*
Paris Blues*
Rachel, Rachel
See How She Runs
The Shadow Box
The Streets of L.A.
The Stripper
Summer Wishes, Winter Dreams
Sybil
They Might Be Giants
The Three Faces of Eve
Winning
*with Paul Newman
DIRECTOR ONLY
Come Along With Me

15 Westerns (WE)

WE1 Western Epics
WE2 Lone Gunfighters
WE3 Sympathetic Outlaws
WE4 Cavalry Stories
WE5 Revenge in the Old West
WE6 Civil War Westerns
WE7 Indians as Heroes
WE8 Women of the West

WE9 South of the Border
WE10 North of the Border
WE11 Last Days of the Frontier
WE12 The Contemporary West
WE13 Spaghetti Westerns
WE14 Western Comedies/Spoofs
WE15 Cult Westerns

See also: Historical/Fictional Character Check Lists HF1 Billy the Kid (William Bonney), HF3 Buffalo Bill (William F. Cody), HF6 George Armstrong Custer, HF9 Wyatt Earp, HF11 Wild Bill Hickok, HF13 Doc Holliday, HF16 Jesse James, HF20 Annie Oakley

WE1 Western Epics
The Alamo
The Big Country
The Big Sky
The Big Trail
Bite the Bullet
Cheyenne Autumn
Cimarron
The Covered Wagon
Dances With Wolves
Duel in the Sun
The Good, the Bad, and the Ugly
Heaven's Gate
How the West Was Won
Little Big Man
Lonesome Dove
Mackenna's Gold
The Magnificent Seven
Once Upon a Time in the West
The Plainsman
Red River
Silverado
Son of the Morning Star
The Unforgiven
The Way West

WE2 Lone Gunfighters
Annie Oakley
A Fistful of Dollars
For a Few Dollars More
The Gunfighter
High Noon
High Noon, Part Two: The Return of Will
  Kane
The Legend of the Lone Ranger
The Lonely Man

Man Without a Star
My Name Is Nobody
Pale Rider
The Red-Headed Stranger
Rooster Cogburn
Shane
The Shootist
The Tin Star
True Grit
Warlock (1959)
The Westerner
The White Buffalo

WE3 Sympathetic Outlaws
Bad Jim
The Badlanders
Barbarosa
The Ballad of Gregorio Cortez
Best of the Badmen
Branded
Butch and Sundance: The Early Days
Butch Cassidy and the Sundance Kid
Charro!
The Doolins of Oklahoma
The Good, the Bad, and the Ugly
Gore Vidal's Billy the Kid
The Grey Fox
Harry Tracy, Desperado
Jesse James
The Law and Jake Wade
The Left-Handed Gun
The Long Riders
Mad Dog Morgan
A Man Alone
Man of the West
A Minute to Pray, A Second to Die

The Missouri Breaks
Ned Kelly
Nevada Smith
The Outlaw
The Outlaw Josey Wales
Pat Garrett and Billy the Kid
Stagecoach
The Stranger Wore a Gun
Tell Them Willie Boy Is Here
There Was a Crooked Man
3 Godfathers
Tom Horn
Unforgiven
The Wild Bunch

WE4 Cavalry Stories
Dances With Wolves
Duel at Diablo
Fort Apache
The Horse Soldiers
Rio Grande
Sergeant Rutledge
She Wore a Yellow Ribbon
Soldier Blue
Son of the Morning Star
They Died With Their Boots On
Ulzana's Raid

WE5 Revenge in the Old West
Best of the Badmen
The Bravados
Cattle Queen of Montana
Coroner Creek
The Deadly Trackers
Death Rides a Horse
Decision at Sundown
Django Shoots First
Hannie Caulder
High Plains Drifter
Kid Vengeance
Macho Callahan
The Man From Laramie
Man in the Wilderness
My Darling Clementine
Navajo Joe
Nevada Smith
Once Upon a Time in the
   West
One-Eyed Jacks
The Outlaw Josey Wales
The Ox-Bow Incident
Pursued
Quigley Down Under
Rancho Notorious
The Red-Headed Stranger
The Return of Frank James
Ride Lonesome
The Searchers
The Sons of Katie Elder
Unforgiven

Young Guns
Young Guns II

WE6 Civil War Westerns
See also: AC5 War Movies—Civil War
Alvarez Kelly
Bad Company
The Beguiled
The Comancheros
Dark Command
The Fastest Guitar Alive
The Good, the Bad, and the
   Ugly
Hangman's Knot
The Horse Soldiers
How the West Was Won (one
   segment)
The Jayhawkers
Love Me Tender
Macho Callahan
Major Dundee
Massacre at Fort Holman
The Outlaw Josey Wales
Run of the Arrow
Santa Fe Trail
Shenandoah
The Skin Game (1971)
South of St. Louis
The Undefeated
Virginia City

WE7 Indians As Heroes
Apache
Broken Arrow
Chato's Land
Cheyenne Autumn
Chino
Dances With Wolves
Eagle's Wing
Flaming Star
Geronimo
Hombre
I Will Fight No More Forever
Little Big Man
A Man Called Horse
Mohawk
Naked in the Sun
Navajo Joe
100 Rifles
Return of a Man Called Horse
Run of the Arrow
The Searchers
Smith!
Soldier Blue
Tell Them Willie Boy Is Here
Triumphs of a Man Called Horse
Ulzana's Raid
The Unforgiven
The Vanishing American
War Party

When the Legends Die
Windwalker

WE8 Women of the West
Angel and the Badman
Annie Oakley
Apache Woman
Bad Man's River
The Ballad of Cable Hogue
Barbary Coast
The Beautiful Blonde From Bashful Bend
A Big Hand for the Little Lady
Calamity Jane
Cat Ballou
Cattle Queen of Montana
Comes a Horseman
Destry Rides Again
Duel in the Sun
Fancy Pants
The Girl of the Golden West
The Gunslinger
The Hanging Tree
Hannie Caulder
Heartland
Heller in Pink Tights
Honky Tonk
Johnny Guitar
Jubilee Trail
The King and Four Queens
Lonesome Dove
McCabe and Mrs. Miller
Mad at the Moon
The Man Who Loved Cat Dancing
The Maverick Queen
The Misfits
My Darling Clementine
Once Upon a Time in the West
The Plainsman (1936)
Poker Alice
Rachel and the Stranger
Ramrod
Rancho Notorious
The Rare Breed
Renegade Ranger
River of No Return
Rooster Cogburn
San Antonio
The Stalking Moon
Texas Lady
Thousand Pieces of Gold
Two Mules for Sister Sara
The Unforgiven
The Violent Men
Virginia City
Zandy's Bride

WE9 South of the Border
The Americano
The Appaloosa
Bandolero!

Barbarosa
A Bullet for Sandoval
The Deadly Trackers
Django
El Condor
A Fistful of Dynamite
Goin' South
My Outlaw Brother
100 Rifles
Pancho Villa
The Professionals
Take a Hard Ride
They Came to Cordura
The Treasure of Pancho Villa
Vera Cruz
Villa Rides
Viva Villa!
Viva Zapata!
The Wild Bunch
Young Guns II

WE10 North of the Border
Blue Canadian Rockies
The Far Country
The Grey Fox
Harry Tracy, Desperado
McCabe and Mrs. Miller
North of the Great Divide
North to Alaska
The Spoilers (1942 version)

WE11 Last Days of the Frontier
The Ballad of Cable Hogue
Buffalo Bill and the Indians
Butch Cassidy and the Sundance Kid
The Grey Fox
McCabe and Mrs. Miller
The Man Who Shot Liberty Valance
Monte Walsh
Ride the High Country
The Shootist
Tell Them Willie Boy Is Here
Tom Horn
The Wild Bunch
Wild Times

WE12 The Contemporary West
Another Pair of Aces: Three of a Kind
Bad Day at Black Rock
Bronco Billy
City Slickers
Comes a Horseman
Coogan's Bluff
Cotter
The Cowboy and the Lady
The Electric Horseman
Giant
Goldenrod
The Great American Cowboy
Hud

In Old Cheyenne
Junior Bonner
Keep the Change
A Lady Takes a Chance
Last Night at the Alamo
Lonely Are the Brave
The Lusty Men
The Misfits
My Heroes Have Always Been Cowboys
Pocket Money
Rancho Deluxe
Three Faces West
Urban Cowboy
War Party
When the Legends Die

WE13 Spaghetti Westerns
Beyond the Law
Django
Django Shoots First
A Fistful of Dollars
A Fistful of Dynamite
For a Few Dollars More
The Good, the Bad, and the Ugly
Hang 'Em High
A Minute to Pray, A Second to Die
My Name Is Nobody
The Stranger and the Gunfighter
They Call Me Trinity
Trinity Is Still My Name

WE14 Western Comedies/Spoofs
Adios Amigo
Along Came Jones
Back to the Future, Part III
Bad Man's River
The Beautiful Blonde From Bashful Bend
A Big Hand for the Little Lady
Blazing Saddles
The Brothers O'Toole
Butch and Sundance: The Early Days
Butch Cassidy and the Sundance Kid
Cat Ballou
The Cheyenne Social Club
Destry Rides Again
Draw!
The Duchess and the Dirtwater Fox
Fancy Pants
Four for Texas
The Frisco Kid
Go West (1940)
Goin' South
Great Scout and Cathouse Thursday
A Lady Takes a Chance
The Last Ride of the Dalton Gang

Lust in the Dust
McLintock!
My Little Chickadee
The Paleface
Pocket Money
Rancho Deluxe
Ride 'Em Cowboy
Ruggles of Red Gap
Rustler's Rhapsody
The Scalphunters
The Sheriff of Fractured Jaw
Son of Paleface
Straight to Hell
Support Your Local Sheriff
There Was a Crooked Man
They Call Me Trinity
Trinity Is Still My Name
The Villain
The War Wagon
Waterhole #3
Way Out West
The Wistful Widow of Wagon Gap

WE15 Cult Westerns
Bad Company
The Culpepper Cattle Company
Duel in the Sun
Greaser's Palace
The Great Northfield, Minnesota, Raid
The Hired Hand
Jeremiah Johnson
Johnny Guitar
The Life and Times of Judge Roy Bean
McCabe and Mrs. Miller
Man of the West
The Missouri Breaks
Ned Kelly
The Oklahoma Kid
Once Upon a Time in the West
One-Eyed Jacks
The Outlaw
Pat Garrett and Billy the Kid
Rancho Notorious
Ride in the Whirlwind
Rio Bravo
The Searchers
The Shooting
The Skin Game (1971)
The Tall T
The Terror of Tiny Town
There Was a Crooked Man
3:10 to Yuma
Ulzana's Raid
Wild Rovers
Will Penny

16 Writer Check Lists (WR)

WR1 James M. Cain	**WR21** Robert Ludlum
WR2 Raymond Chandler	**WR22** Ross MacDonald
WR3 Agatha Christie	**WR23** W. Somerset Maugham
WR4 Noel Coward	**WR24** John O'Hara
WR5 Charles Dickens	**WR25** Eugene O'Neill
WR6 Daphne du Maurier	**WR26** Harold Pinter
WR7 William Faulkner	**WR27** Edgar Allan Poe
WR8 F. Scott Fitzgerald	**WR28** William Shakespeare
WR9 E.M. Forster	**WR29** George Bernard Shaw
WR10 Frederick Forsyth	**WR30** Neil Simon
WR11 Graham Greene	**WR31** Mickey Spillane
WR12 Dashiell Hammett	**WR32** John Steinbeck
WR13 Ernest Hemingway	**WR33** Robert Louis Stevenson
WR14 Henry James	**WR34** Jim Thompson
WR15 Stephen King	**WR35** Mark Twain
WR16 Louis L'Amour	**WR36** Jules Verne
WR17 D.H. Lawrence	**WR37** H.G. Wells
WR18 John Le Carré	**WR38** Tennessee Williams
WR19 Elmore Leonard	**WR39** Cornell Woolrich (William Irish)
WR20 Sinclair Lewis	

WR1 James M. Cain (1892–1977)
Butterfly
Double Indemnity
Mildred Pierce
Ossessione
The Postman Always Rings Twice (1946 and
1981 versions)
Slightly Scarlet

WR2 Raymond Chandler (1888–1959)
The Big Sleep (1946 and 1978 versions)
The Brasher Doubloon
The Falcon Takes Over
Farewell, My Lovely
Lady in the Lake
The Long Goodbye
Marlowe
Murder My Sweet

WR3 Agatha Christie (1891–1976)
The Alphabet Murders
And Then There Were None
Appointment With Death
The Body in the Library
Death on the Nile
Endless Night
Evil Under the Sun
Love From a Stranger

The Mirror Crack'd
Murder Ahoy
Murder at the Gallop
Murder Most Foul
A Murder Is Announced
Murder on the Orient Express
Murder, She Said
Ordeal by Innocence
A Pocketful of Rye
The Seven Dials Mystery
Ten Little Indians
Why Didn't They Ask Evans
Witness for the Prosecution (1957
version)
SUBJECT ONLY
Agatha

WR4 Noel Coward (1899–1973)
Bitter Sweet
Blithe Spirit
Brief Encounter (1945 and 1974 versions)
Cavalcade
Private Lives
This Happy Breed
ACTOR ONLY
In Which We Serve (also co-director)
The Italian Job
Paris When It Sizzles

WR5 Charles Dickens (1812–1870)
Bleak House
A Christmas Carol (1938 and 1951 versions)
David Copperfield
Great Expectations (1946 version)
Little Dorrit
Miracle Down Under
The Muppet Christmas Carol
Nicholas Nickleby
The Old Curiosity Shop (1935 and 1975
    versions)
Oliver!
Oliver Twist (1922, 1933, and 1948 versions)
Pickwick Papers
Scrooge (1935 and 1970 versions)
Scrooged
A Tale of Two Cities (1935 and 1958 versions)

WR6 Daphne du Maurier (1907–1989)
The Birds
Don't Look Now
Jamaica Inn (1939 and 1985 versions)
Rebecca

WR7 William Faulkner (1897–1962)
Barn Burning
Intruder in the Dust
Land of the Pharaohs
The Long Hot Summer (1958 and 1985
    versions)
The Reivers
Tomorrow

WR8 F. Scott Fitzgerald (1896–1940)
The Great Gatsby
The Last Time I Saw Paris
The Last Tycoon
Three Comrades

WR9 E.M. Forster (1879–1970)
Howards End
Maurice
A Passage to India
A Room With a View
Where Angels Fear to Tread

WR10 Frederick Forsyth (1938–)
The Day of the Jackal
The Dogs of War
The Fourth Protocol
The Odessa File

WR11 Graham Greene (1904–1991)
Beyond the Limit
The Comedians
The Fallen Idol
The Fugitive
Saint Joan
Strike It Rich
The Third Man
This Gun for Hire

WR12 Dashiell Hammett (1894–1961)
After the Thin Man
Another Thin Man
The Dain Curse
The Glass Key
The Maltese Falcon
Satan Met a Lady
Shadow of the Thin Man
Song of the Thin Man
The Thin Man
The Thin Man Goes Home
Watch on the Rhine
Woman in the Shadows
SUBJECT ONLY
Hammett
Julia

WR13 Ernest Hemingway (1899–1961)
A Farewell to Arms (1932 and 1957 versions)
Islands in the Stream
The Killers (1964 version)
My Old Man
The Snows of Kilimanjaro
To Have and Have Not
Women and Men: Stories of Seduction
SUBJECT ONLY
The Moderns

WR14 Henry James (1843–1916)
The Bostonians
Daisy Miller
The Europeans
The Green Room
The Heiress
The Lost Moment
The Nightcomers
Turn of the Screw

WR15 Stephen King (1948–)
BASED ON WORKS BY KING
Carrie (1976)
Children of the Corn
Children of the Corn II: The Final Sacrifice
Christine
Cujo
The Dead Zone
Firestarter
Graveyard Shift (1990)
The Lawnmower Man
Maximum Overdrive*
Misery
Pet Sematary**
Salem's Lot
Return to Salem's Lot
The Shining
Silver Bullet
Sleepwalkers**
Sometimes They Come Back
Stand by Me
Stephen King's Golden Years

Stephen King's It
Tales From the Darkside: The Movie
ORIGINAL SCREENPLAYS
Cat's Eye
Creepshow**
Creepshow 2
*also director
**also actor

WR16 Louis L'Amour (1908–1988)
Cancel My Reservation
Heller in Pink Tights
The Quick and the Dead
The Sacketts

WR17 D.H. Lawrence (1885–1930)
Kangaroo
Lady Chatterly's Lover (1955 and 1981 versions)
The Rainbow
The Rocking Horse Winner
The Trespasser
The Virgin and the Gypsy
Women in Love
SUBJECT ONLY
Priest of Love

WR18 John Le Carré (1931–)
The Little Drummer Girl
The Looking Glass War
The Russia House
The Spy Who Came in From the Cold

WR19 Elmore Leonard (1925–)
The Ambassador
Cat Chaser
52 Pick-Up
Glitz
Hombre
Joe Kidd
Mr. Majestyk
Stick
The Tall T
3:10 to Yuma
DOCUMENTARY SUBJECT
Elmore Leonard's Criminal Records

WR20 Sinclair Lewis (1885–1931)
Ann Vickers
Arrowsmith
Dodsworth
Elmer Gantry

WR21 Robert Ludlum (1927–)
The Holcroft Covenant
The Osterman Weekend

WR22 Ross MacDonald (1915–1983)
Blue City
The Drowning Pool
Harper

WR23 W. Somerset Maugham
(1874–1965)
Adorable Julia
Beachcomber
Encore
The Letter
Of Human Bondage (1934 version)
The Painted Veil
Quartet (1949)
Rain
The Razor's Edge (1946 and 1984 versions)
Sadie Thompson
Secret Agent
Trio

WR24 John O'Hara (1905–1970)
Butterfield 8
From the Terrace
Pal Joey
Ten North Frederick

WR25 Eugene O'Neill (1883–1953)
Ah, Wilderness
Anna Christie
Desire Under the Elms
The Emperor Jones
The Hairy Ape
Long Day's Journey Into Night (1962 and
  1987 versions)
The Long Voyage Home
Strange Interlude (1932 and 1988 versions)
Summer Holiday
SUBJECT ONLY
Reds

WR26 Harold Pinter (1930–)
Accident
Betrayal (1983)
The Comfort of Strangers
The Dumb Waiter
The French Lieutenant's Woman
The Go-Between
The Handmaid's Tale
The Last Tycoon
The Quiller Memorandum
Reunion
The Room
The Servant
Turtle Diary (also actor)
ACTOR ONLY
The Tamarind Seed

WR27 Edgar Allan Poe (1809–1849)
The Avenging Conscience
Buried Alive
Castle of Blood
Fall of the House of Usher
The Fall of the House of Usher (1949 and
  1980 versions)
The Haunting of Morella

Manfish
The Masque of the Red Death (1964 and
1989 versions)
Murders in the Rue Morgue (1932 and 1971
versions)
The Murders in the Rue Morgue (1986)
The Oblong Box
The Pit and the Pendulum
The Premature Burial
The Raven (1935 and 1963 versions)
Tales of Terror
The Tomb of Ligeia
The Torture Chamber of Dr. Sadism
Two Evil Eyes

WR28 William Shakespeare (1564–1616)
As You Like It (1936 version)
Chimes at Midnight
Forbidden Planet
Hamlet (1948, 1969, and 1990 versions)
Henry V (1945 and 1989 versions)
Jubal
Julius Caesar (1953 and 1970 versions)
King Lear (1971 and 1987 versions)
Kiss Me Kate
Macbeth (1948 and 1971 versions)
Men of Respect
A Midsummer Night's Dream (1935 version)
My Own Private Idaho
Othello (1952 version)
Prospero's Books
Ran
Richard II
Richard III
Romeo and Juliet (1936, 1954, 1968, and
1979 versions)
Rosencrantz and Guildenstern Are Dead
The Taming of the Shrew
Tempest (1982 version)
The Tempest (1963 version)
Throne of Blood

WR29 George Bernard Shaw (1856–
1950)
Androcles and the Lion
Caesar and Cleopatra
The Devil's Disciple
Major Barbara
The Millionairess
My Fair Lady
Pygmalion
Saint Joan

WR30 Neil Simon (1927–)
*Based on Simon plays, or original screenplays by
Simon, unless noted*
After the Fox
Barefoot in the Park
Biloxi Blues
Brighton Beach Memoirs

California Suite
Chapter Two
The Cheap Detective
Come Blow Your Horn
The Goodbye Girl
The Heartbreak Kid*
I Ought to Be in Pictures
Last of the Red Hot Lovers
The Marrying Man
Max Dugan Returns
Murder by Death
The Odd Couple
Only When I Laugh
The Out of Towners
Plaza Suite
The Prisoner of Second Avenue
Seems Like Old Times
The Slugger's Wife
Star Spangled Girl
The Sunshine Boys
*Simon screenplay, based on Bruce Jay
Friedman story

WR31 Mickey Spillane (1918–)
The Girl Hunters
I, the Jury (1982 version)
Kiss Me Deadly

WR32 John Steinbeck (1902–1968)
Cannery Row
East of Eden (1955 and 1982 versions)
The Grapes of Wrath
Of Mice and Men (1939 and 1992 versions)
The Pearl
The Red Pony (1949 and 1973 versions)
Tortilla Flat
Viva Zapata!

WR33 Robert Louis Stevenson (1850–1894)
Abbott and Costello Meet Dr. Jekyll and Mr.
Hyde
Black Arrow
The Black Arrow
The Body Snatcher
Dr. Jekyll and Mr. Hyde (1920, 1932, 1941,
and 1973 versions)
Jekyll and Hyde . . . Together Again
Kidnapped
Strange Case of Dr. Jekyll and Mr. Hyde
Treasure Island (1934, 1950 and 1990 versions)
The Wrong Box

WR34 Jim Thompson (1908–1977)
After Dark, My Sweet
Clean Slate (Coup de Torchon)
The Getaway
The Grifters
The Killer Inside Me
The Killing
Paths of Glory

WR35 Mark Twain (1835–1910)
The Adventures of Huckleberry Finn (1939, 1960, and 1985 versions)
The Adventures of Mark Twain
The Adventures of Tom Sawyer (1938 and 1973 versions)
Bugs Bunny in King Arthur's Court
A Connecticut Yankee
A Connecticut Yankee in King Arthur's Court
Huckleberry Finn
The Prince and the Pauper (1937 and 1978 versions)
Pudd'nhead Wilson
Tom Sawyer
Unidentified Flying Oddball

WR36 Jules Verne (1828–1905)
Around the World in 80 Days
Five Weeks in a Balloon
From the Earth to the Moon
In Search of the Castaways
Journey to the Center of the Earth (1959 and 1989 versions)
The Light at the Edge of the World
Master of the World
Mysterious Island
20,000 Leagues Under the Sea
Where Time Began

WR37 H.G. Wells (1866–1946)
Empire of the Ants
First Men In the Moon
Food of the Gods
Half a Sixpence
The Invisible Man
The Island of Dr. Moreau
The Man Who Could Work Miracles

Things to Come
The Time Machine
Village of the Giants
The War of the Worlds
SUBJECT ONLY
Time After Time

WR38 Tennessee Williams (1912–1983)
Baby Doll
Cat on a Hot Tin Roof (1958 and 1984 versions)
The Fugitive Kind
The Glass Menagerie (1987 version)
The Night of the Iguana
Orpheus Descending
Period of Adjustment
The Roman Spring of Mrs. Stone
The Rose Tattoo
A Streetcar Named Desire
Suddenly, Last Summer
Summer and Smoke
Sweet Bird of Youth
This Property Is Condemned

WR39 Cornell Woolrich (1903–1968)
Woolrich often wrote under the name William Irish, the source author for some of these films.
The Bride Wore Black
The Chase (1946)
Deadline at Dawn
Fear in the Night (1947)
I'm Dangerous Tonight
The Leopard Man
Mississippi Mermaid
Rear Window
The Window

17 Video Extra (XT)

XT1 Academy Award: Best Picture
XT2 Academy Award: Best Actor
XT3 Academy Award: Best Actress
XT4 Academy Award: Best Supporting Actor
XT5 Academy Award: Best Supporting Actress
XT6 Academy Award: Best Director
XT7 Academy Award: Best Foreign Language Film
XT8 All in the Family: Movies Featuring Real-Life Mothers, Fathers, Sons, Daughters, Sisters, Brothers
On Location
Movies That Make Good Use of Major Cities
XT9 New York
XT10 Los Angeles
XT11 Chicago
XT12 Washington, D.C.
XT13 San Francisco
XT14 New Orleans
XT15 London
XT16 Paris
XT17 Rome
XT18 Movin' On: Road Movies

XT19 All Aboard: Train Movies
XT20 Here Comes the Bride: Memorable Wedding Scenes and Wedding Movies
XT21 Stunning Debuts: Legendary First Starring Roles
XT22 Fond Farewells: Memorable Final Performances
XT23 What I Really Want To Do: Actors Turned Directors
XT24 Life After Death
XT25 Anti-War Movies
XT26 Fifty Double Bills of Recommended Movies
XT27 The More the Merrier: Actors in Multiple Roles
XT28 Oscar Justice: Nominated Movies and Performances That Should Have Won
XT29 Movies That Should Be on Video— Now
XT30 He Directs, She Acts: Famous Offscreen Spouses/Lovers
XT31 Movie Mad: Stories of People Obsessed With Films or Filmmaking

---

XT1 Academy Award: Best Picture

1927–28	Wings	1950	All About Eve
1928–29	Broadway Melody	1951	An American in Paris
1929–30	All Quiet on the Western Front	1952	The Greatest Show on Earth
1930–31	Cimarron	1953	From Here to Eternity
1931–32	Grand Hotel	1954	On the Waterfront
1933	Cavalcade	1955	Marty
1934	It Happened One Night	1956	Around the World in 80 Days
1935	Mutiny on the Bounty	1957	The Bridge on the River Kwai
1936	The Great Ziegfeld	1958	Gigi
1937	The Life of Emile Zola	1959	Ben-Hur
1938	You Can't Take It With You	1960	The Apartment
1939	Gone With the Wind	1961	West Side Story
1940	Rebecca	1962	Lawrence of Arabia
1941	How Green Was My Valley	1963	Tom Jones
1942	Mrs. Miniver	1964	My Fair Lady
1943	Casablanca	1965	The Sound of Music
1944	Going My Way	1966	A Man for All Seasons
1945	The Lost Weekend	1967	In the Heat of the Night
1946	The Best Years of Our Lives	1968	Oliver!
1947	Gentleman's Agreement	1969	Midnight Cowboy
1948	Hamlet	1970	Patton
1949	All the King's Men	1971	The French Connection
		1972	The Godfather

1973	The Sting
1974	The Godfather, Part II
1975	One Flew Over the Cuckoo's Nest
1976	Rocky
1977	Annie Hall
1978	The Deer Hunter
1979	Kramer vs. Kramer
1980	Ordinary People
1981	Chariots of Fire
1982	Gandhi
1983	Terms of Endearment
1984	Amadeus
1985	Out of Africa
1986	Platoon
1987	The Last Emperor
1988	Rain Man
1989	Driving Miss Daisy
1990	Dances With Wolves
1991	The Silence of the Lambs
1992	Unforgiven

XT2 Academy Award: Best Actor

1927–28	The Last Command (Emil Jannings)
1929–30	Disraeli (George Arliss)
1930–31	A Free Soul (Lionel Barrymore)
1931–32	(tie) The Champ (Wallace Beery) Dr. Jekyll and Mr. Hyde (Fredric March)
1932–33	The Private Life of Henry VIII (Charles Laughton)
1934	It Happened One Night (Clark Gable)
1935	The Informer (Victor McLaglen)
1937	Captains Courageous (Spencer Tracy)
1938	Boys Town (Spencer Tracy)
1939	Goodbye, Mr. Chips (Robert Donat)
1940	The Philadelphia Story (James Stewart)
1941	Sergeant York (Gary Cooper)
1942	Yankee Doodle Dandy (James Cagney)
1943	Watch on the Rhine (Paul Lukas)
1944	Going My Way (Bing Crosby)
1945	The Lost Weekend (Ray Milland)
1946	The Best Years of Our Lives (Fredric March)
1947	A Double Life (Ronald Colman)
1948	Hamlet (Laurence Olivier)
1949	All The King's Men (Broderick Crawford)
1950	Cyrano de Bergerac (Jose Ferrer)
1951	The African Queen (Humphrey Bogart)
1952	High Noon (Gary Cooper)
1953	Stalag 17 (William Holden)
1954	On the Waterfront (Marlon Brando)

1955	Marty (Ernest Borgnine)
1956	The King and I (Yul Brynner)
1957	The Bridge on the River Kwai (Alec Guinness)
1958	Separate Tables (David Niven)
1959	Ben-Hur (Charlton Heston)
1960	Elmer Gantry (Burt Lancaster)
1961	Judgment at Nuremberg (Maximilian Schell)
1962	To Kill a Mockingbird (Gregory Peck)
1963	Lilies of the Field (Sidney Poitier)
1964	My Fair Lady (Rex Harrison)
1965	Cat Ballou (Lee Marvin)
1966	A Man for all Seasons (Paul Scofield)
1967	In the Heat of the Night (Rod Steiger)
1968	Charly (Cliff Robertson)
1969	True Grit (John Wayne)
1970	Patton (George C. Scott)
1971	The French Connection (Gene Hackman)
1972	The Godfather (Marlon Brando)
1973	Save the Tiger (Jack Lemmon)
1974	Harry and Tonto (Art Carney)
1975	One Flew Over the Cuckoo's Nest (Jack Nicholson)
1976	Network (Peter Finch)
1977	The Goodbye Girl (Richard Dreyfuss)
1978	Coming Home (Jon Voight)
1979	Kramer vs. Kramer (Dustin Hoffman)
1980	Raging Bull (Robert De Niro)
1981	On Golden Pond (Henry Fonda)
1982	Gandhi (Ben Kingsley)
1983	Tender Mercies (Robert Duvall)
1984	Amadeus (F. Murray Abraham)
1985	Kiss of the Spider Woman (William Hurt)
1986	The Color of Money (Paul Newman)
1987	Wall Street (Michael Douglas)
1988	Rain Man (Dustin Hoffman)
1989	My Left Foot (Daniel Day-Lewis)
1990	Reversal of Fortune (Jeremy Irons)
1991	The Silence of the Lambs (Anthony Hopkins)
1992	Scent of a Woman (Al Pacino)

XT3 Academy Award: Best Actress

1928–29	Coquette (Mary Pickford)
1929–30	The Divorcee (Norma Shearer)
1930–31	The Sin of Madelon Claudet (Helen Hayes)
1932–33	Morning Glory (Katharine Hepburn)
1934	It Happened One Night (Claudette Colbert)
1935	Dangerous (Bette Davis)

1936	The Great Ziegfeld (Luise Rainer)
1937	The Good Earth (Luise Rainer)
1938	Jezebel (Bette Davis)
1939	Gone With the Wind (Vivien Leigh)
1940	Kitty Foyle (Ginger Rogers)
1941	Suspicion (Joan Fontaine)
1942	Mrs. Miniver (Greer Garson)
1943	The Song of Bernadette (Jennifer Jones)
1944	Gaslight (Ingrid Bergman)
1945	Mildred Pierce (Joan Crawford)
1947	The Farmer's Daughter (Loretta Young)
1948	Johnny Belinda (Jane Wyman)
1949	The Heiress (Olivia de Havilland)
1950	Born Yesterday (Judy Holliday)
1951	A Streetcar Named Desire (Vivien Leigh)
1952	Come Back, Little Sheba (Shirley Booth)
1953	Roman Holiday (Audrey Hepburn)
1954	The Country Girl (Grace Kelly)
1955	The Rose Tattoo (Anna Magnani)
1956	Anastasia (Ingrid Bergman)
1957	The Three Faces of Eve (Joanne Woodward)
1958	I Want to Live! (Susan Hayward)
1960	Butterfield 8 (Elizabeth Taylor)
1961	Two Women (Sophia Loren)
1962	The Miracle Worker (Anne Bancroft)
1963	Hud (Patricia Neal)
1964	Mary Poppins (Julie Andrews)
1965	Darling (Julie Christie)
1966	Who's Afraid of Virginia Woolf? (Elizabeth Taylor)
1967	Guess Who's Coming to Dinner (Katharine Hepburn)
1968	(tie) The Lion in Winter (Katharine Hepburn)
	Funny Girl (Barbra Streisand)
1969	The Prime of Miss Jean Brodie (Maggie Smith)
1970	Women in Love (Glenda Jackson)
1971	Klute (Jane Fonda)
1972	Cabaret (Liza Minnelli)
1973	A Touch of Class (Glenda Jackson)
1974	Alice Doesn't Live Here Anymore (Ellen Burstyn)
1975	One Flew over the Cuckoo's Nest (Louise Fletcher)
1976	Network (Faye Dunaway)
1977	Annie Hall (Diane Keaton)
1978	Coming Home (Jane Fonda)
1979	Norma Rae (Sally Field)
1980	Coal Miner's Daughter (Sissy Spacek)
1981	On Golden Pond (Katharine Hepburn)

1982	Sophie's Choice (Meryl Streep)
1983	Terms of Endearment (Shirley MacLaine)
1984	Places in the Heart (Sally Field)
1985	The Trip to Bountiful (Geraldine Page)
1986	Children of a Lesser God (Marlee Matlin)
1987	Moonstruck (Cher)
1988	The Accused (Jodie Foster)
1989	Driving Miss Daisy (Jessica Tandy)
1990	Misery (Kathy Bates)
1991	The Silence of the Lambs (Jodie Foster)
1992	Howards End (Emma Thompson)

Note: *Room at the Top* (Simone Signoret), the 1959 winner, has been discontinued; copies on videocassette are difficult to find.

XT4 Academy Award: Best Supporting Actor
Note: Award debuted in 1936.

1936	Come and Get It (Walter Brennan)
1937	The Life of Emile Zola (Joseph Schildkraut)
1939	Stagecoach (Thomas Mitchell)
1940	The Westerner (Walter Brennan)
1941	How Green Was My Valley (Donald Crisp)
1943	The More the Merrier (Charles Coburn)
1944	Going My Way (Barry Fitzgerald)
1945	A Tree Grows in Brooklyn (James Dunn)
1946	The Best Years of Our Lives (Harold Russell)
1947	Miracle on 34th Street (Edmund Gwenn)
1948	The Treasure of the Sierra Madre (Walter Huston)
1949	Twelve O'Clock High (Dean Jagger)
1950	All About Eve (George Sanders)
1951	A Streetcar Named Desire (Karl Malden)
1952	Viva Zapata! (Anthony Quinn)
1953	From Here to Eternity (Frank Sinatra)
1954	The Barefoot Contessa (Edmond O'Brien)
1955	Mister Roberts (Jack Lemmon)
1956	Lust for Life (Anthony Quinn)
1957	Sayonara (Red Buttons)
1958	The Big Country (Burl Ives)
1959	Ben-Hur (Hugh Griffith)
1960	Spartacus (Peter Ustinov)
1961	West Side Story (George Chakiris)
1962	Sweet Bird of Youth (Ed Begley)
1963	Hud (Melvyn Douglas)

1964	Topkapi (Peter Ustinov)	1947	Gentleman's Agreement (Celeste Holm)
1965	A Thousand Clowns (Martin Balsam)	1948	Key Largo (Claire Trevor)
1966	The Fortune Cookie (Walter Matthau)	1949	All the King's Men (Mercedes McCambridge)
1967	Cool Hand Luke (George Kennedy)	1950	Harvey (Josephine Hull)
1969	They Shoot Horses, Don't They? (Gig Young)	1951	A Streetcar Named Desire (Kim Hunter)
1970	Ryan's Daughter (John Mills)	1952	The Bad and the Beautiful (Gloria Grahame)
1971	The Last Picture Show (Ben Johnson)	1953	From Here to Eternity (Donna Reed)
1972	Cabaret (Joel Grey)	1954	On the Waterfront (Eva Marie Saint)
1973	The Paper Chase (John Houseman)	1955	East of Eden (Jo Van Fleet)
1974	The Godfather, Part II (Robert DeNiro)	1956	Written on the Wind (Dorothy Malone)
1975	The Sunshine Boys (George Burns)	1957	Sayonara (Miyoshi Umeki)
1976	All the President's Men (Jason Robards)	1958	Separate Tables (Wendy Hiller)
1977	Julia (Jason Robards)	1959	The Diary of Anne Frank (Shelley Winters)
1978	The Deer Hunter (Christopher Walken)	1960	Elmer Gantry (Shirley Jones)
1979	Being There (Melvyn Douglas)	1961	West Side Story (Rita Moreno)
1980	Ordinary People (Timothy Hutton)	1962	The Miracle Worker (Patty Duke)
1981	Arthur (John Gielgud)	1963	The VIPs (Margaret Rutherford)
1982	An Officer and a Gentleman (Louis Gossett, Jr.)	1964	Zorba the Greek (Lila Kedrova)
1983	Terms of Endearment (Jack Nicholson)	1965	A Patch of Blue (Shelley Winters)
1984	The Killing Fields (Haing S. Ngor)	1966	Who's Afraid of Virginia Woolf? (Sandy Dennis)
1985	Cocoon (Don Ameche)	1967	Bonnie and Clyde (Estelle Parsons)
1986	Hannah and Her Sisters (Michael Caine)	1968	Rosemary's Baby (Ruth Gordon)
1987	The Untouchables (Sean Connery)	1969	Cactus Flower (Goldie Hawn)
1988	A Fish Called Wanda (Kevin Kline)	1970	Airport (Helen Hayes)
1989	Glory (Denzel Washington)	1971	The Last Picture Show (Cloris Leachman)
1990	GoodFellas (Joe Pesci)	1972	Butterflies Are Free (Eileen Heckart)
1991	City Slickers (Jack Palance)	1973	Paper Moon (Tatum O'Neal)
1992	Unforgiven (Gene Hackman)	1974	Murder on the Orient Express (Ingrid Bergman)

XT5 Academy Award: Best Supporting Actress

Note: Award debuted in 1936.

1936	Anthony Adverse (Gale Sondergaard)	1975	Shampoo (Lee Grant)
		1976	Network (Beatrice Straight)
		1977	Julia (Vanessa Redgrave)
1938	Jezebel (Fay Bainter)	1978	California Suite (Maggie Smith)
1939	Gone With the Wind (Hattie McDaniel)	1979	Kramer vs. Kramer (Meryl Streep)
1940	The Grapes of Wrath (Jane Darwell)	1980	Melvin and Howard (Mary Steenburgen)
1941	The Great Lie (Mary Astor)	1981	Reds (Maureen Stapleton)
1942	Mrs. Miniver (Teresa Wright)	1982	Tootsie (Jessica Lange)
1944	None but the Lonely Heart (Ethel Barrymore)	1983	The Year of Living Dangerously (Linda Hunt)
		1984	A Passage to India (Peggy Ashcroft)
1945	National Velvet (Anne Revere)	1985	Prizzi's Honor (Anjelica Huston)
1946	The Razor's Edge (Anne Baxter)	1986	Hannah and Her Sisters (Dianne Wiest)
		1987	Moonstruck (Olympia Dukakis)
		1988	The Accidental Tourist (Geena Davis)

1989	My Left Foot (Brenda Fricker)
1990	Ghost (Whoopi Goldberg)
1991	The Fisher King (Mercedes Ruehl)
1992	My Cousin Vinny (Marisa Tomei)

XT6 Academy Award: Best Director

1929–30	All Quiet on the Western Front (Lewis Milestone)
1933	Cavalcade (Frank Lloyd)
1934	It Happened One Night (Frank Capra)
1935	The Informer (John Ford)
1936	Mr. Deeds Goes to Town (Frank Capra)
1937	The Awful Truth (Leo McCarey)
1938	You Can't Take It With You (Frank Capra)
1939	Gone With the Wind (Victor Fleming)
1940	The Grapes of Wrath (John Ford)
1941	How Green Was My Valley (John Ford)
1942	Mrs. Miniver (William Wyler)
1943	Casablanca (Michael Curtiz)
1944	Going My Way (Leo McCarey)
1945	The Lost Weekend (Billy Wilder)
1946	The Best Years of Our Lives (William Wyler)
1947	Gentleman's Agreement (Elia Kazan)
1948	The Treasure of the Sierra Madre (John Huston)
1949	A Letter to Three Wives (Joseph L. Mankiewicz)
1950	All About Eve (Joseph L. Mankiewicz)
1951	A Place in the Sun (George Stevens)
1952	The Quiet Man (John Ford)
1953	From Here to Eternity (Fred Zinnemann)
1954	On the Waterfront (Elia Kazan)
1955	Marty (Delbert Mann)
1956	Giant (George Stevens)
1957	The Bridge on the River Kwai (David Lean)
1958	Gigi (Vincente Minnelli)
1959	Ben-Hur (William Wyler)
1960	The Apartment (Billy Wilder)
1961	West Side Story (Robert Wise)*
1962	Lawrence of Arabia (David Lean)
1963	Tom Jones (Tony Richardson)
1964	My Fair Lady (George Cukor)
1965	The Sound of Music (Robert Wise)
1966	A Man for All Seasons (Fred Zinnemann)
1967	The Graduate (Mike Nichols)
1968	Oliver! (Carol Reed)
1969	Midnight Cowboy (John Schlesinger)
1970	Patton (Franklin J. Schaffner)

1971	The French Connection (William Friedkin)
1972	Cabaret (Bob Fosse)
1973	The Sting (George Roy Hill)
1974	The Godfather, Part II (Francis Ford Coppola)
1975	One Flew Over the Cuckoo's Nest (Milos Forman)
1976	Rocky (John G. Avildsen)
1977	Annie Hall (Woody Allen)
1978	The Deer Hunter (Michael Cimino)
1979	Kramer vs. Kramer (Robert Benton)
1980	Ordinary People (Robert Redford)
1981	Reds (Warren Beatty)
1982	Gandhi (Richard Attenborough)
1983	Terms of Endearment (James L. Brooks)
1984	Amadeus (Milos Forman)
1985	Out of Africa (Sydney Pollack)
1986	Platoon (Oliver Stone)
1987	The Last Emperor (Bernardo Bertolucci)
1988	Rain Man (Barry Levinson)
1989	Born on the Fourth of July (Oliver Stone)
1990	Dances With Wolves (Kevin Costner)
1991	The Silence of the Lambs (Jonathan Demme)
1992	Unforgiven (Clint Eastwood)

*Wise and choreographer Jerome Robbins shared screen credit for directing; Robbins won a special Oscar for his contribution to the film.

XT7 Academy Award: Best Foreign Language Film

1949	The Bicycle Thief (Italy)
1951	Rashomon (Japan)
1952	Forbidden Games (France)
1954	Gate of Hell (Japan)
1955	Samurai (The Seven Samurai) (Japan)
1956	La Strada (Italy)
1957	Nights of Cabiria (Italy)
1958	My Uncle (France)
1959	Black Orpheus (Brazil)
1960	The Virgin Spring (Sweden)
1961	Through a Glass, Darkly (Sweden)
1962	Sundays and Cybéle (France)
1963	8½ (Italy)
1964	Yesterday, Today and Tomorrow (Italy)
1965	The Shop on Main Street (Czechoslovakia)
1966	A Man and a Woman (France)
1967	Closely Watched Trains (Czechoslovakia)

1968	War and Peace (Soviet Union)
1969	Z (France)
1971	The Garden of the Finzi-Continis (Italy)
1972	The Discreet Charm of the Bourgeoisie (France)
1973	Day for Night (France)
1974	Amarcord (Italy)
1975	Dersu Uzala (Japan)
1976	Black and White in Color (France)
1977	Madame Rosa (France)
1978	Get Out Your Handkerchiefs (France)
1979	The Tin Drum (Germany)
1980	Moscow Does Not Believe in Tears (Soviet Union)
1981	Mephisto (Hungary)
1983	Fanny and Alexander (Sweden)
1984	Dangerous Moves (Switzerland)
1985	The Official Story (Argentina)
1986	The Assault (Holland)
1987	Babette's Feast (Denmark)
1988	Pelle the Conqueror (Denmark)
1989	Cinema Paradiso (Italy)
1990	Journey of Hope (Switzerland)
1991	Mediterraneo (Italy)
1992	Indochine (France)

XT8 All in the Family: Real-life Mothers, Fathers, Sons, Daughters, Sisters, Brothers

At Close Range (Sean and Christopher Penn)
Big Jake (John and Patrick Wayne)
Big Wednesday (Barbara Hale and William Katt)
Boxcar Bertha (David and John Carradine)
Bull'seye! (Roger Moore and Deborah Barrymore)
Cadence (Martin and Charlie Sheen)
The Chalk Garden (John and Hayley Mills)
The Chase (1966) (Marlon and Jocelyn Brando)
Cheech and Chong's The Corsican Brothers (Tommy, Rae Dawn, and Robbi Chong; Cheech and Rikki Marin)
Cry Blood Apache (Jody and Joel McCrea)
Do the Right Thing (Spike and Joie Lee)
Double Edge (Amos and Teddy Kollek)
Dying Young (Colleen Dewhurst and Campbell Scott)
Ellis Island (Richard and Kate Burton)
The Fabulous Baker Boys (Beau and Jeff Bridges)
Far and Away (Rance and Clint Howard)
Far Out Man (Tommy and Paris Chong)
The Fifth Musketeer (Lloyd and Beau Bridges)
The Fog (Jamie Lee Curtis and Janet Leigh)
Four Daughters (Rosemary, Priscilla, and Lola Lane)
Gas Food Lodging (Ione Skye and Donovan Leitch)

Groundhog Day (Bill Murray and Brian Doyle-Murray)
Hannah and Her Sisters (Maureen O'Sullivan and Mia Farrow)
Hearts of the World (Lillian and Dorothy Gish)
Home, Sweet Home (Lillian and Dorothy Gish)
Honkytonk Man (Clint and Kyle Eastwood)
Howards End (Vanessa and Jemma Redgrave)
Identity Crisis (Melvin and Mario Van Peebles)
In the Spirit (Elaine May and Jeannie Berlin)
Journey of Honor (Sho and Kane Kosugi)
Judith of Bethalia (Lillian and Dorothy Gish)
The Krays (Gary and Martin Kemp)
A Lion Is in the Streets (James and Jeanne Cagney)
The Long Riders (David, Keith and Robert Carradine; Christopher and Nicholas Guest; Stacy and James Keach; Dennis and Randy Quaid)
McLintock! (John and Patrick Wayne)
Main Street to Broadway (Lionel and Ethel Barrymore)
Men at Work (Emilio Estevez and Charlie Sheen)
Mo' Better Blues (John and Nicholas Turturro; Spike and Joie Lee)
Mo' Money (Damon and Marlon Wayans)
National Lampoon's Loaded Weapon 1 (Emilio Estevez and Charlie Sheen)
Nightbreaker (Martin Sheen and Emilio Estevez)
On Golden Pond (Henry and Jane Fonda)
Orphans of the Storm (Lillian and Dorothy Gish)
Our Hospitality (Buster and Joseph Keaton, and Buster Keaton, Jr.)
Pacific Heights (Tippi Hedren and Melanie Griffith)
Paper Moon (Ryan and Tatum O'Neal)
The Player (Michael and Stephen Tolkin)
The Prince of Tides (Barbra Streisand and Jason Gould)
The Proud Rebel (Alan and David Ladd)
Rambling Rose (Diane Ladd and Laura Dern)
Rasputin and the Empress (John, Ethel, and Lionel Barrymore)
Red River (Harry Carey, Sr., and Harry Carey, Jr.)
Rocky V (Sylvester and Sage Stallone)
Romola (Lillian and Dorothy Gish)
Say Anything (Joan and John Cusack)
School Daze (Spike and Joie Lee)
The Searchers (Natalie and Lana Wood)
See How She Runs (Joanne Woodward and Lissy Newman)
The Short Films of D.W. Griffith: Volume 2 (The Musketeers of Pig Alley) (Lillian and Dorothy Gish)

Silent Night, Lonely Night (Lloyd and Jeff
   Bridges)
Sixteen Candles (Joan and John Cusack)
That's Life! (Jack and Chris Lemmon; Julie
   Andrews and Emma Walton)
Think Big (Peter and David Paul)
Thunder Road (Robert and Jim Mitchum)
Tightrope (Clint and Alison Eastwood)
Tous les Matins du Monde (Gerard and
   Guillaume Depardieu)
The Treasure of the Sierra Madre (Walter and
   John Huston)
Tucker: The Man and His Dream (Lloyd and
   Jeff Bridges)
Wall Street (Martin and Charlie Sheen)
Wanda Nevada (Henry and Peter Fonda)
Wild at Heart (Diane Ladd and Laura Dern)
The Wild Country (Ronny and Clint
   Howard)
A Woman Under the Influence (Gena and
   Lady Rowlands)
Yankee Doodle Dandy (James and Jeanne
   Cagney)
Young Guns (Emilio Estevez and Charlie
   Sheen)
A Zed and Two Noughts (Brian and Eric
   Deacon)

XT9 On Location: New York
Across 110th Street ·
Addict
After Hours
Alice
All the Vermeers in New York
The Anderson Tapes
Annie Hall
Arthur
Arthur 2: On the Rocks
Barefoot in the Park
The Believers
The Bonfire of the Vanities
Breakfast at Tiffany's
Bright Lights, Big City
Broadway Danny Rose
The Butcher's Wife
The Cameraman
China Girl
The Clock
Coming to Ameeica
Coogan's Bluff
Crocodile Dundee
Crocodile Dundee II
Crossing Delancey
The Crowd
Death Wish
Desperately Seeking Susan
Do the Right Thing
Dog Day Afternoon
The Dream Team
Enormous Changes

Eyewitness
Falling in Love
Fame
The Fisher King
Fort Apache, The Bronx
Frankie and Johnny (1991)
The French Connection
The Freshman (1990)
Funny Girl
Garbo Talks
Ghostbusters
Ghostbusters II
Green Card
Greetings
Hair
Hangin' With the Homeboys
Hannah and Her Sisters
Highlander
Home Alone 2: Lost in New York
Husbands and Wives
Hustling
It Should Happen to You
It's My Turn
Jacob's Ladder
Juice
Jungle Fever
Just Tell Me What You Want
Killer's Kiss
King Kong (1933 and 1976 versions)
King of Comedy
King of New York
Legal Eagles
Light Sleeper
Liquid Sky
Love With the Proper Stranger
Madigan
Manhattan
Marathon Man
Married to the Mob
Mean Streets
Metropolitan
Midnight Cowboy
Moscow on the Hudson
The Muppets Take Manhattan
The Naked City
New Jack City
New York Stories
Night on Earth
Nighthawks
North by Northwest
The Odd Couple
On the Town
The Out-of-Towners
The Palermo Connection
The Pawnbroker
The Pick-up Artist
Prince of the City
Q
Q & A
Queens Logic

Quick Change
Radio Days
Raging Bull
Rich Kids
Rooftops
Roseland
Rosemary's Baby
Saboteur
Saturday Night Fever
Scent of a Woman
Senior Trip
Serpico
Single White Female
Slaves of New York
Smithereens
Someone to Watch Over Me
Sophie's Choice
Splash
State of Grace
Straight Out of Brooklyn
A Stranger Among Us
A Stranger Is Watching
Street Smart
The Taking of Pelham One Two
   Three
Taxi Driver
They All Laughed
A Thousand Clowns
Times Square
Turk 182
An Unmarried Woman
Wall Street
The Warriors
West Side Story
When Harry Met Sally . . .
Where the Heart Is
Where Were You When the Lights Went
   Out?
Who's that Knocking at My Door?
Without a Trace
Wolfen
Working Girl
The World of Henry Orient
You're a Big Boy Now

XT10 On Location: Los Angeles
Against All Odds (1984)
Annie Hall
Beastmaster 2: Through the Portals of Time
Beverly Hills Cop
Beverly Hills Cop II
Beverly Hills, 90210
Blue Thunder
Boyz N the Hood
California Suite
Chinatown
Colors
The Day of the Locust
Down and Out in Beverly Hills
Echo Park

Falling Down
Grand Canyon
Internal Affairs
Killer Bait
L.A. Story
Lost Angels
The Loved One
Night of the Comet
Night on Earth
Point Blank
Pretty Woman
Repo Man
Scenes From a Mall
Shampoo
Slamdance
The Streets of L.A.
To Live and Die in L.A.
True Confessions
The Two Jakes
Vice Squad
Welcome to L.A.
Where the Day Takes You
White Men Can't Jump
Zabriskie Point

XT11 On Location: Chicago
About Last Night
Adventures in Babysitting
Backdraft
Big Shots
The Blues Brothers
Candyman
City That Never Sleeps
Code of Silence
Continental Divide
Cooley High
Ferris Bueller's Day Off
Heaven Is a Playground
Henry: Portrait of a Serial
   Killer
The Hunter
Mad Dog and Glory
Medium Cool
Music Box
Nothing in Common
Red Heat
Risky Business
Running Scared
Straight Talk
V.I. Warshawski
Windy City

XT12 On Location: Washington, D.C.
Advise and Consent
All the President's Men
Being There
Born Yesterday (1950 and 1993 versions)
Broadcast News
Chances Are
D.C. Cab

The Day the Earth Stood Still
The Distinguished Gentleman
Earth vs. the Flying Saucers
The Exorcist
Exorcist II: The Heretic
Exorcist III: Legion
First Family
First Monday in October
Heartburn
Houseboat
In Country
JFK
The Last Detail
Mr. Smith Goes to Washington
No Way Out
Point of No Return
Power (1986)
The President's Analyst
Protocol
Scorpio
The Seduction of Joe Tynan
Sherlock Holmes in Washington
Short Fuse
St. Elmo's Fire
Suspect
True Colors

XT13 On Location: San Francisco

Basic Instinct
Bullitt
Chan Is Missing
The Conversation
The Dead Pool
Dim Sum: a little bit of heart
Dirty Harry
The Enforcer (1976)
Experiment in Terror
Final Analysis
Fools
48 HRS
Foul Play
Invasion of the Body Snatchers (1979
   version)
The Killer Elite
Kuffs
The Laughing Policeman
Magnum Force
Memoirs of an Invisible Man
Pacific Heights
Petulia
Point Blank
The Presidio
Psych-Out
Shattered
Signal 7
Sneakers
Time After Time
Vertigo
A View to a Kill
What's Up, Doc?

XT14 On Location: New Orleans

Angel Heart
The Big Easy
The Cat People (1982 version)
The Drowning Pool
Easy Rider
Hard Times
JFK
Johnny Handsome
Obsession
Panic in the Streets
Pretty Baby
Storyville
Tightrope
Tune in Tomorrow . . .

XT15 On Location: London

Absolute Beginners
An American Werewolf in London
Blow-Up
Brannigan
Darling
Frenzy
Georgy Girl
Gorgo
A Hard Day's Night
The Krays
London Kills Me
The Long Good Friday
Look Back in Anger
Midnight Lace
Mona Lisa
My Beautiful Laundrette
Night and the City (1950 version)
Sammy and Rosie Get Laid
The Tall Guy
Turtle Diary

XT16 On Location: Paris

American Dreamer
Bob le Flambeur
Breathless (1959 version)
Charade
The Day of the Jackal
The Destructors
Dingo
Diva
The 400 Blows
Frantic (1988)
French Postcards
Funny Face
If Looks Could Kill
Is Paris Burning?
La Balance
Last Tango in Paris
A Little Romance
The Man on the Eiffel Tower
Masculine-Feminine
Night on Earth
Paris Blues

'Round Midnight
Shoot the Piano Player
The Testament of Dr. Cordelier
Zazie dans le Métro

XT17 On Location: Rome
After the Fox
The Belly of an Architect
The Eclipse
Fellini's Roma
La Dolce Vita
Love in the City
Night on Earth
Open City
Roman Holiday
The Roman Spring of Mrs. Stone
Rome Adventure
The Roof
The White Sheik

XT18 Movin' On: Road Movies
Alice Doesn't Live Here Anymore
Alligator Eyes
American Autobahn
Around the World in 80 Days
Back Roads
Backtrack
Badlands
The Big Steal
Bird on a Wire
Bonnie and Clyde
Bring Me the Head of Alfredo Garcia
Bustin' Loose
Cold Feet
Convoy
Coupe de Ville
Crazy Mama
Duel
Dutch
Easy Rider
Eddie Macon's Run
Fandango
Five Easy Pieces
Flashback
The Gauntlet
The Getaway
Going Places
The Great Race
The Great Smokey Roadblock
Harry and Tonto
Heroes
Highway to Hell
The Hit
Hollywood or Bust
Homer and Eddie
If It's Tuesday, This Must Be Belgium
It Happened One Night
It's a Mad Mad Mad Mad World
The Journey of Natty Gann
Joyride

Just Me and You
Kings of the Road
The Last Detail
Leaving Normal
The Loners
The Long, Long Trailer
Lost in America
Love Field
Mad Max
Midnight Run
Moving
National Lampoon's European Vacation
National Lampoon's Vacation
Near Dark
North by Northwest
Out
Outrageous Fortune
Paper Moon
Paris, Texas
Payday
Pee-wee's Big Adventure
Pierrot le Fou
Planes, Trains, and Automobiles
Powwow Highway
Rafferty and the Gold Dust Twins
Rain Man
The Rain People
Road Games
The Road Warrior
Roadie
Roadside Prophets
Saboteur
Scarecrow
Sherman's March
Slither
Smokey and the Bandit (series)
Something Wild
The Sugarland Express
Sullivan's Travels
The Sure Thing
Tanner
Thelma & Louise
They Live by Night
Think Big
The 39 Steps (1935 and 1978 versions)
Three Fugitives
Two for the Road
Weekend
Wild at Heart
The Wizard
You Only Live Once

XT19 All Aboard: Train Movies
Breakheart Pass
Closely Watched Trains
Finders Keepers
Flashback
From Russia With Love
The General
Go West

The Great Locomotive Chase
The Great Train Robbery
The Grey Fox
Horror Express
How the West Was Won
The Incident (1967)
The Journey of Natty Gann
The Lady Vanishes (1939 and 1979 versions)
Murder on the Orient Express
Narrow Margin
The Narrow Margin
Orphan Train
The Palm Beach Story
Planes, Trains, and Automobiles
Romance on the Orient Express
Runaway Train
Silver Streak
Strangers on a Train
The Taking of Pelham One Two Three
Terror Train
Tracks
The Train
The Train Robbers
Twentieth Century
Warm Nights on a Slow Moving Train
Zentropa

XT20 Here Comes the Bride: Memorable Wedding Scenes and Wedding Movies

Betsy's Wedding
Blind Date (1987)
The Bride Wore Black
The Catered Affair
Cousin, Cousine
Cousins
The Deer Hunter
Father of the Bride (1950 and 1991 versions)
The Godfather
Goodbye, Columbus
The Graduate
Greed
Hard Promises
The Heartbreak Kid
Heartburn
Here Comes the Groom
High Society
Invitation to the Wedding
La Cage aux Folles III: The
    Wedding
Lovers and Other Strangers
Modern Love
The Philadelphia Story
Prelude to a Kiss
Prizzi's Honor
Seven Brides for Seven Brothers
Sixteen Candles
Three Men and a Little Lady
True Love
A Wedding

Wedding in White
The Wedding March
The Wedding Party

XT21 Stunning Debuts: Legendary First Starring Roles

Adam's Rib (Judy Holliday)
Body Heat (Kathleen Turner)
Breathless (1959 version) (Jean-Paul
    Belmondo)
Citizen Kane (Orson Welles)
Come Back, Little Sheba (Shirley Booth)
East of Eden (James Dean)
48 HRS (Eddie Murphy)
Funny Girl (Barbra Streisand)
Golden Boy (William Holden)
Goodbye, Mr. Chips (1939 version) (Greer
    Garson)
Great Expectations (Alec Guinness)
The Invisible Man (Claude Rains)
Journey for Margaret (Margaret O'Brien)
Lawrence of Arabia (Peter O'Toole)
Mary Poppins (Julie Andrews)
The Men (Marlon Brando)
On the Waterfront (Eva Marie Saint)
The Outlaw (Jane Russell)
Roman Holiday (Audrey Hepburn)
Romance on the High Seas (Doris Day)
Splendor in the Grass (Warren Beatty)
This Gun for Hire (Alan Ladd)
To Have and Have Not (Lauren Bacall)
The Trouble With Harry (Shirley
    MacLaine)

XT22 Fond Farewells: Memorable Final Performances

Advise and Consent (Charles Laughton)
Bells Are Ringing (Judy Holliday)
The Carpetbaggers (Alan Ladd)
Enter the Dragon (Bruce Lee)
Giant (James Dean)
Guess Who's Coming to Dinner (Spencer
    Tracy)
The Harder They Fall (Humphrey Bogart)
The Killers (1964 version) (Ronald
    Reagan)
The Misfits (Clark Gable and Marilyn
    Monroe)
Mister Roberts (William Powell)
Network (Peter Finch)
On Golden Pond (Henry Fonda)
Ride the High Country (Randolph
    Scott)
S.O.B. (William Holden)
Saratoga (Jean Harlow)
Shane (Jean Arthur)
The Shootist (John Wayne)
To Be or Not to Be (1942 version) (Carole
    Lombard)

The Unholy Three (1930 version) (Lon
Chaney, Sr.)
Walk, Don't Run (Cary Grant)

XT23 What I Really Want to Do: Actors Turned Directors

See also CO13 Star Check Lists: Dan Aykroyd,
Eddie Murphy; CO14 Harold Ramis, Dave
Thomas; ST10 Warren Beatty; ST18 Marlon
Brando; ST38 Kevin Costner; ST54 Danny
DeVito; ST57 Kirk Douglas; ST63 Robert
Duvall; ST64 Clint Eastwood; ST75 Jodie
Foster; ST110 Dennis Hopper; ST121 Diane
Keaton; ST123 Gene Kelly; ST129 Burt
Lancaster; ST132 Charles Laughton; ST138
Jack Lemmon; ST139 Jerry Lewis; ST161
Jeanne Moreau; ST162 Paul Newman;
ST163 Jack Nicholson; ST168 Laurence
Olivier; ST174 Sidney Poitier; ST175 Dick
Powell; ST180 Richard Pryor; ST181 Robert
Redford; ST183 Burt Reynolds; ST196
George C. Scott; ST199 Frank Sinatra;
ST204 Sylvester Stallone; ST211 Barbra
Streisand; ST216 Rip Torn, ST234 Joanne
Woodward

Alan Arkin
Little Murders

Richard Attenborough
A Bridge Too Far
A Chorus Line
Cry Freedom
Gandhi
Magic
Young Winston

Tony Bill
Crazy People
Five Corners
My Bodyguard
Six Weeks
Untamed Heart

Kenneth Branagh
Dead Again
Henry V (1989 version)

James Caan
Hide in Plain Sight

Dyan Cannon
The End of Innocence

David Carradine
Americana

John Cassavetes
Big Trouble
A Child Is Waiting
Gloria

Love Streams
A Woman Under the Influence

Martin Donovan
Apartment Zero
Mad at the Moon

Emilio Estevez
Men at Work

Peter Fonda
The Hired Hand
Wanda Nevada

Paul Michael Glaser
The Cutting Edge

Bobcat Goldthwait
Shakes the Clown

Keith Gordon
The Chocolate War
A Midnight Clear

Lee Grant
Down and Out in America
Staying Together
Tell Me a Riddle

Paul Henreid
Dead Ringer

Sondra Locke
Impulse

Ida Lupino
The Bigamist
The Hitch-Hiker
The Trouble With Angels

Penny Marshall
Awakenings
Big
Jumpin' Jack Flash
A League of Their Own

John Cougar Mellencamp
Falling From Grace

Burgess Meredith
The Man on the Eiffel Tower

Ray Milland
Lisbon

Robert Montgomery
Lady in the Lake

Vic Morrow
A Man Called Sledge

Leonard Nimoy
Funny About Love
The Good Mother
Star Trek III: The Search for Spock
Star Trek IV: The Voyage Home
Three Men and a Baby

James Edward Olmos
American Me

Sean Penn
The Indian Runner

Anthony Perkins
Psycho III

Prince
Graffiti Bridge
Under the Cherry Moon

Anthony Quinn
The Buccaneer

Tim Robbins
Bob Roberts

William Shatner
Star Trek V: The Final Frontier

Gary Sinise
Of Mice and Men (1992 version)

Peter Ustinov
Billy Budd

Ralph Waite
On the Nickel

Gene Wilder
The Adventures of Sherlock Holmes'
   Smarter Brother
Haunted Honeymoon
The Woman in Red
The World's Greatest Lover

Fred Williamson
Adios Amigo

XT24 Life After Death
All of Me
Almost an Angel
Always
Angel on My Shoulder (1946 and 1980
   versions)
Arthur 2: On the Rocks
Beetlejuice
Blithe Spirit
Candyman
The Canterville Ghost (1944 and 1986
   versions)

Carnival of Souls
Chances Are
Charley and the Angel
Death Becomes Her
Defending Your Life
Doña Flor and Her Two Husbands
18 Again!
Flatliners
Ghost
Ghost Dad
A Guy Named Joe
Heart Condition
Heaven Can Wait (1943)
Heaven Can Wait (1978)
Hellbound: Hellraiser II
Hello Again
Hellraiser
Hellraiser III: Hell on Earth
Here Comes Mr. Jordan
High Spirits
The Horn Blows at Midnight
I Married a Witch
Identity Crisis
The Indestructible Man
Jacob's Ladder
Julia and Julia
Kiss Me Goodbye
Liliom
Made in Heaven
Mannequin (1987)
Maxie
Oh, Heavenly Dog!
O'Hara's Wife
Switch
The Time of Their Lives
Truly, Madly, Deeply
Wings of Desire

XT25 Give Peace a Chance: Anti-War Movies
All Quiet on the Western Front
The Americanization of Emily
The Big Parade
Born on the Fourth of July
Catch-22
Dr. Strangelove or; How I Learned to Stop
   Worrying and Love the Bomb
Fires on the Plain
Gallipoli
Grand Illusion
How I Won the War
The Human Condition
J'Accuse
Johnny Got His Gun
Les Carabiniers
M*A*S*H
A Midnight Clear
Paths of Glory
Platoon
The Red Badge of Courage

The War Game
Westfront 1918

XT26 Fifty Double Bills of Recommended Movies

About Last Night *and* Singles
Alice Doesn't Live Here Anymore *and* Men Don't Leave
All Fall Down *and* Hud
All You Need Is Cash *and* This Is Spinal Tap
An American Werewolf in London *and* The Howling
Android *and* Making Mr. Right
Apocalypse Now *and* Platoon
Being There *and* The Great McGinty
Brazil *and* Delicatessen
Burden of Dreams *and* Hearts of Darkness: A Filmmaker's Apocalypse
The Buddy Holly Story *and* La Bamba
The Candidate *and* Tanner
Cinema Paradiso *and* Radio Days
Coal Miner's Daughter *and* Sweet Dreams
Lulu in Berlin *and* Marlene
The Coca Cola Kid *and* Local Hero
Contempt *and* Barton Fink
The Crying Game *and* Mona Lisa
Deliverance *and* Southern Comfort
Don't Look Back *and* Truth or Dare
Easy Rider *and* Lost in America
8½ *and* Stardust Memories
His Girl Friday *and* Broadcast News
Jules and Jim *and* Two English Girls
Killer's Kiss *and* Strangers Kiss
The Late Show *and* Miami Blues
Lulu in Berlin *and* Marlene
Midnight Cowboy *and* The Fisher King
The Mission *and* Black Robe
Norma Rae *and* Silkwood
North Dallas Forty *and* Bull Durham
Los Olvidados *and* Pixote
Over the Edge *and* Streetwise
The Owl and the Pussycat *and* Night Shift
Payday *and* One Trick Pony
Rancho Deluxe *and* 92 in the Shade
Rear Window *and* The Conversation
Red Dust *and* Only Angels Have Wings
Rififi *and* Topkapi
Serpico *and* Prince of the City
A Shot in the Dark *and* The Naked Gun
Some Like It Hot *and* Tootsie
The Stunt Man *and* White Hunter, Black Heart
Sunset Boulevard *and* S.O.B.
Taxi Driver *and* Light Sleeper
Treasure of the Sierra Madre *and* Trespass
The War Game *and* Special Bulletin
Wolfen *and* Candyman
Woodstock *and* Gimme Shelter
You Only Live Once *and* Bonnie and Clyde

XT27 The More the Merrier: Actors in Multiple Roles

Big Business (Bette Midler and Lily Tomlin)
Bull'seye (Michael Caine and Roger Moore)
Cat Ballou (Lee Martin)
Chaplin (Moira Kelly)
Cheech and Chong's The Corsican Brothers (Cheech and Chong)
Come and Get It (Frances Farmer)
The Dark Mirror (Olivia de Havilland)
Dead Ringer (Bette Davis)
Dead Ringers (Jeremy Irons)
Deja Vu (Jaclyn Smith and Nigel Terry)
Double Impact (Jean-Claude Van Damme)
The Double Life of Veronique (Irene Jacob)
Double Vision (Kim Cattrall)
Dr. Strangelove or; How I Learned to Stop Worrying and Love the Bomb (Peter Sellers)
The End of the World (Christopher Lee)
The Family Jewels (Jerry Lewis)
The Great Dictator (Charlie Chaplin)
Hellraiser III: Hell on Earth (Doug Bradley)
Joe Vs. the Volcano (Meg Ryan)
Kind Hearts and Coronets (Alec Guinness)
A Kiss Before Dying (1991 version) (Sean Young)
Kissin' Cousins (Elvis Presley)
The Life and Death of Colonel Blimp (Deborah Kerr)
The Loved One (Jonathan Winters)
The Man From Snowy River (Kirk Douglas)
Moon Over Parador (Richard Dreyfuss)
The Mouse That Roared (Peter Sellers)
My Twentieth Century (Dorothea Segda)
No Way to Treat a Lady (Rod Steiger)
Nothing but Trouble (Dan Aykroyd)
Out on a Limb (Jeffrey Jones)
The Parent Trap (Hayley Mills)
The Prize (Edward G. Robinson)
Raising Cain (John Lithgow)
The 7 Faces of Dr. Lao (Tony Randall)
Sisters (Margot Kidder)
Start the Revolution Without Me (Gene Wilder and Donald Sutherland)
Used Cars (Jack Warden)
Vertigo (Kim Novak)
Which Way Is Up? (Richard Pryor)
Woman Times Seven (Shirley MacLaine)

XT28 Oscar Justice: Nominees Who Should Have Won

Note: See XT1–7 for the actual winners
BEST PICTURE
1937   The Awful Truth
1938   Grand Illusion
1941   Citizen Kane

1942	The Magnificent Ambersons
1944	Double Indemnity
1952	The Quiet Man
1956	The Ten Commandments
1959	Anatomy of a Murder
1961	The Hustler
1964	Dr. Strangelove or; How I Learned to Stop Worring and Love the Bomb
1965	Darling
1967	Bonnie and Clyde
1973	Cries and Whispers
1976	Network
1978	An Unmarried Woman
1979	Apocalypse Now
1980	Raging Bull
1981	Reds
1990	GoodFellas

BEST ACTOR

1935	Mutiny on the Bounty (Charles Laughton)
1941	Citizen Kane (Orson Welles)
1943	Casablanca (Humphrey Bogart)
1951	A Streetcar Named Desire (Marlon Brando)
1955	The Man With the Golden Arm (Frank Sinatra)
1959	Anatomy of a Murder (James Stewart)
1962	Lawrence of Arabia (Peter O'Toole)
1964	Dr. Strangelove or; How I Learned to Stop Worrying and Love the Bomb (Peter Sellers)
1965	The Spy Who Came in From the Cold (Richard Burton)
1967	The Graduate (Dustin Hoffman)
1968	The Heart Is a Lonely Hunter (Alan Arkin)
1969	Midnight Cowboy (Jon Voight)
1973	Last Tango in Paris (Marlon Brando)
1974	The Godfather, Part II (Al Pacino)
1979	The China Syndrome (Jack Lemmon)
1988	Mississippi Burning (Gene Hackman)

BEST ACTRESS

1941	Ball of Fire (Barbara Stanwyck)
1943	The More the Merrier (Jean Arthur)
1960	The Sundowners (Deborah Kerr)
1962	Long Day's Journey Into Night (Katharine Hepburn)
1967	Wait Until Dark (Audrey Hepburn)
1978	An Unmarried Woman (Jill Clayburgh)
1981	The French Lieutenant's Woman (Meryl Streep)
1983	The Bostonians (Vanessa Redgrave)

BEST SUPPORTING ACTOR

1944	Laura (Clifton Webb)
1946	Notorious (Claude Rains)
1947	Crossfire (Robert Ryan)
1949	The Heiress (Ralph Richardson)
1956	Written on the Wind (Robert Stack)

1961	The Hustler (George C. Scott)
1968	The Producers (Gene Wilder)
1969	Easy Rider (Jack Nicholson)
1970	I Never Sang for My Father (Gene Hackman)

BEST SUPPORTING ACTRESS

1950	All About Eve (Thelma Ritter)
1957	Witness for the Prosecution (Elsa Lanchester)
1963	Lilies of the Field (Lilia Skala)
1966	A Man for All Seasons (Wendy Hiller)
1969	Bob & Carol & Ted & Alice (Dyan Cannon)
1970	Five Easy Pieces (Karen Black)
1974	Blazing Saddles (Madeline Kahn)
1981	Only When I Laugh (Joan Hackett)

BEST DIRECTOR

1941	Citizen Kane (Orson Welles)
1944	Double Indemnity (Billy Wilder)
1955	East of Eden (Elia Kazan)
1959	Some Like It Hot (Billy Wilder)
1961	The Hustler (Robert Roseen)
1964	Dr. Strangelove or; How I Learned to Stop Worrying and Love the Bomb (Stanley Kubrick)
1965	Darling (John Schlesinger)
1968	The Battle of Algiers (Gillo Pontecorvo)
1972	The Godfather (Francis Ford Coppola)
1973	Cries and Whispers (Ingmar Bergman)
1976	All the President's Men (Alan J. Pakula)
1978	Coming Home (Hal Ashby)
1979	Apocalypse Now (Francis Ford Coppola)
1980	Raging Bull (Martin Scorsese)
1982	Tootsie (Sydney Pollack)
1989	Henry V (Kenneth Branagh)
1990	GoodFellas (Martin Scorsese)

BEST FOREIGN LANGUAGE FILM

1964	Woman in the Dunes (Japan)
1966	The Battle of Algiers (Italy)
1970	Tristana (Spain)
1977	That Obscure Object of Desire (Spain)
1982	Clean Slate (Coup de Torchon) (France)

XT29 Films That Should Be on Videotape—Now

Note: See Chapter 20 for a lengthy list of titles unavailable on videotape.

American Madness
Attack!
Belle de Jour
The Big Carnival (Ace in the Hole)
The Big Clock
The Big Knife

Bluebeard's Eighth Wife
Design for Living
Drive, He Said
Faces
Hot Tomorrows
How to Steal a Million
I Was a Male War Bride
The Iceman Cometh
Images
The Innocents
Lacombe, Lucien
The Landlord
Lord Love a Duck
Loving
Made for Each Other (1971)
Midnight (1939)
The Navigator
No Way Out (1950)
Out of It
Play It As It Lays
Point of Order
The Scarlet Empress
Seconds
Seven Chances
The Stranger (1967)
Such Good Friends
Thieves Like Us
Walkabout
Wild Boys of the Road
You're Telling Me

XT30 He Directs, She Acts: Famous Offscreen Spouses/Lovers

Woody Allen and Mia Farrow
Alice
Another Woman
Broadway Danny Rose
Crimes and Misdemeanors
Hannah and Her Sisters
Husbands and Wives
A Midsummer Night's Sex Comedy
New York Stories
The Purple Rose of Cairo
Radio Days
September
Shadows and Fog
Zelig

Woody Allen and Diane Keaton
Annie Hall
Interiors
Love and Death
Manhattan
Radio Days
Sleeper

Ingmar Bergman and Liv Ullmann
Autumn Sonata
Cries and Whispers

Hour of the Wolf
The Passion of Anna
Persona
Scenes From a Marriage
The Serpent's Egg
Shame (1968)

John Cassavetes and Gena Rowlands
Gloria
Love Streams
A Woman Under the Influence

Blake Edwards and Julie Andrews
The Man Who Loved Women (1983 version)
S.O.B.
The Tamarind Seed
10
That's Life!
Victor/Victoria

Federico Fellini and Giulietta Massina
Juliet of the Spirits
La Strada
Nights of Cabiria
Variety Lights
The White Sheik

Vincente Minnelli and Judy Garland
Meet Me in St. Louis
The Pirate
Ziegfeld Follies

Paul Newman and Joanne Woodward
The Glass Menagerie (1987 version)
Harry and Son
Rachel, Rachel
The Shadow Box

Nicolas Roeg and Theresa Russell
Cold Heaven
Eureka
Insignificance
Track 29

Roberto Rossellini and Ingrid Bergman
Europa '51
Fear
Stromboli
Voyage to Italy

XT31 Movie Mad: Stories of People Obsessed with Films or Filmmaking

Annie Hall
Apartment Zero
Cinema Paradiso
David Holtzman's Diary
Day for Night
8½
Hearts of Darkness: A Filmmaker's Apocalypse

Home Movies
The Last Tycoon
Matinee
Peeping Tom
Play It Again, Sam
Real Life

Sherman's March
S.O.B.
Something Short of Paradise
Stardust Memories
The Stunt Man

18 Essential Viewing Lists

As explained in "How to Use This Book," this is a check list of films that have made their mark on film history, usually for better, sometimes for worse. If you're looking to become a better educated person about the history of film, I suggest you start with this list.

The lists are broken down by half-decades, except for the silent film era and the first talkies. I feel this organization is especially useful for viewers looking for historical currents and trends as reflected in movies. It also gives a sense of the evolution (some would say devolution) of the art of film.

The numbers after each title indicate the date of its original release.

1915–30
All Quiet on the Western Front 30
Ben-Hur: A Tale of the Christ 26
The Big Parade 25
The Birth of a Nation 15
The Blue Angel 30
Broken Blossoms 19
The Cabinet of Dr. Caligari 19
The Chaplin Revue 18–22
Charlie Chaplin Cavalcade 16
The Circus 28
The Crowd 28
Don Juan 26
Dr. Mabuse, the Gambler 22–23
The Freshman 25
The General 27
The Gold Rush 25
Greed 24
Hell's Angels 30
Intolerance 16
It 27
The Jazz Singer 27
The Kid 21
L'Age d'Or 30
The Last Command 28
The Last Laugh 24
The Mark of Zorro 20
Metropolis 26
Nanook of the North 22
Napoleon 27
Nosferatu 22
Pandora's Box 28
The Passion of Joan of Arc 28
Potemkin 25
The Sheik 21
Show People 28
Steamboat Bill, Jr. 28
The Ten Commandments 23
Ten Days That Shook the World/October 27
The Thief of Bagdad 24

Un Chien Andalou 28
Way Down East 20
The Wind 28
Wings 27

1931–35
A Nous la Liberte 31
Blonde Venus 32
The Bride of Frankenstein 35
City Lights 31
Dr. Jekyll and Mr. Hyde 32
Dracula 31
Duck Soup 33
Footlight Parade 33
42nd Street 33
Frankenstein 31
Freaks 32
Grand Hotel 32
I Am a Fugitive From a Chain
   Gang 32
It Happened One Night 34
It's a Gift 34
King Kong 33
L'Atalante 34
Little Caesar 31
M 31
Man of Aran 34
Mutiny on the Bounty 35
A Night at the Opera 35
The Public Enemy 31
Queen Christina 33
Scarface 32
Sons of the Desert 33
Tarzan, the Ape Man 32
The Thin Man 35
The 39 Steps 35
Top Hat 35
Triumph of the Will 35
Twentieth Century 34
Zero for Conduct 33

1936–40
The Adventures of Robin Hood 38
Alexander Nevsky 38
Angels With Dirty Faces 38
The Awful Truth 37
Bringing Up Baby 38
Dark Victory 39
Dead End 37
Destry Rides Again 39
Dodsworth 36
Fantasia 40
Fury 36
Gone With the Wind 39
Grand Illusion 37
The Grapes of Wrath 40
The Great Dictator 40
The Great McGinty 40
Gunga Din 39
His Girl Friday 40
Holiday 37
The Lady Vanishes 38
Lost Horizon 37
Mr. Deeds Goes to Town 36
Mr. Smith Goes to Washington 39
Modern Times 36
My Man Godfrey 36
Ninotchka 39
Olympia 38
Only Angels Have Wings 39
The Philadelphia Story 40
Pinocchio 40
Rebecca 40
Rules of the Game 39
The Shop Around the Corner 40
Stagecoach 39
Stella Dallas 37
Swing Time 36
The Thief of Bagdad 40
The Wizard of Oz 39
The Women 39
Wuthering Heights 39
You Only Live Once 37
Young Mr. Lincoln 39

1941–45
Bambi 42
Brief Encounter 45
Casablanca 43
Cat People 42
Children of Paradise 44
Citizen Kane 41
Double Indemnity 44
Going My Way 44
Henry V 45
High Sierra 41
Ivan the Terrible, Part
  One 43
King's Row 42
The Lady Eve 41
Laura 44

The Lost Weekend 45
The Magnificent Ambersons 42
The Maltese Falcon 41
Meet John Doe 41
Meet Me in St. Louis 44
Mildred Pierce 45
Mrs. Miniver 42
Ossessione 42
The Ox-Bow Incident 43
Shadow of a Doubt 43
Sullivan's Travels 41
To Be or Not To Be 42
A Tree Grows in Brooklyn 45
Woman of the Year 42
Yankee Doodle Dandy 42

1946–50
Adam's Rib 49
All About Eve 50
All the King's Men 49
The Asphalt Jungle 50
Beauty and the Beast 46
The Best Years of Our Lives 46
The Bicycle Thief 49
The Big Sleep 46
Born Yesterday 50
Diary of a Country Priest 50
Duel in the Sun 46
Father of the Bride 50
Force of Evil 48
Fort Apache 48
Great Expectations 46
Hamlet 48
Home of the Brave 49
It's a Wonderful Life 46
Ivan the Terrible, Part Two 46
Kind Hearts and Coronets 49
La Terra Trema 47
Los Olvidados 50
The Louisiana Story 48
My Darling Clementine 46
The Naked City 48
Notorious 46
On the Town 49
Open City 46
Out of the Past 47
The Postman Always Rings
  Twice 46
Red River 48
The Set-Up 49
She Wore a Yellow Ribbon 49
Shoeshine 46
Sorry, Wrong Number 48
Sunset Boulevard 50
They Live by Night 49
The Third Man 49
The Treasure of the Sierra
  Madre 48
White Heat 49
Winchester '73 50

1951–55
The African Queen 51
An American in Paris 51
The Bad and the Beautiful 52
Bad Day at Black Rock 55
The Band Wagon 53
Beat the Devil 54
The Big Heat 53
Blackboard Jungle 55
The Crimson Pirate 52
The Day the Earth Stood Still 51
Diabolique 55
East of Eden 55
Forbidden Games 51
From Here to Eternity 53
High Noon 52
Ikiru 52
Kiss Me Deadly 55
La Strada 54
The Lavender Hill Mob 51
Limelight 52
The Man With the Golden Arm 55
Marty 55
Mr. Hulot's Holiday 53
Night and Fog 55
On the Waterfront 54
A Place in the Sun 51
The Quiet Man 52
Rashomon 51
Rear Window 54
Rebel Without a Cause 55
The Seven Samurai 54
Shane 53
Singin' in the Rain 52
Smiles of a Summer Night 55
Stalag 17 53
A Star Is Born 54
Strangers on a Train 51
A Streetcar Named Desire 51
The Thing (From Another World) 51
Tokyo Story 53
Ugetsu 53
Umberto D 55
The Wages of Fear 52
The Wild One 54

1956–60
Anatomy of a Murder 59
Aparajito 57
The Apartment 60
Ashes and Diamonds 58
Ben-Hur 59
Breathless 59
The Bridge on the River Kwai 57
Forbidden Planet 56
The 400 Blows 59
Giant 56
Hiroshima, Mon Amour 60
The Incredible Shrinking Man 57
Invasion of the Body Snatchers 56

La Dolce Vita 60
L'Avventura 60
Look Back in Anger 58
North by Northwest 59
Pather Panchali 56
Paths of Glory 57
Pillow Talk 59
Psycho 60
Rio Bravo 59
The Searchers 56
The Seventh Seal 56
Some Like It Hot 59
Sweet Smell of Success 57
The Ten Commandments 56
Touch of Evil 58
12 Angry Men 57
Vertigo 58
Wild Strawberries 57
The World of Apu 59

1961–65
The Battle of Algiers 65
Cleopatra 63
Contempt 63
Darling 65
Divorce—Italian Style 62
Dr. Strangelove or; How I Learned to Stop
    Worrying and Love the Bomb 64
8½ 63
The Exterminating Angel 62
Goldfinger 64
A Hard Day's Night 64
The Hustler 61
Jules and Jim 61
Knife in the Water 62
Last Year at Marienbad 62
Lawrence of Arabia 62
The Loneliness of the Long Distance Runner
    62
The Man Who Shot Liberty Valance 62
The Manchurian Candidate 62
Ride the High Country 62
The Servant 63
Shoot the Piano Player 62
A Shot in the Dark 64
The Silence 63
The Sound of Music 65
This Sporting Life 63
Tom Jones 63
Viridiana 61
West Side Story 61
What Ever Happened to Baby Jane? 62
Yojimbo 61

1966–70
The Battle of Algiers 66
Blow-Up 66
Bonnie and Clyde 67
Butch Cassidy and the Sundance Kid 69
The Dirty Dozen 67

Don't Look Back 67
Easy Rider 69
Five Easy Pieces 70
Funny Girl 68
Gimme Shelter 70
The Good, the Bad and the Ugly 67
The Graduate 67
if . . . 69
In the Heat of the Night 67
Love Story 70
M*A*S*H 70
Medium Cool 69
Midnight Cowboy 69
My Night at Maud's 70
Night of the Living Dead 69
Once Upon a Time in the West 68
Patton 70
Persona 66
Petulia 68
Point Blank 67
The Producers 68
Rosemary's Baby 68
Salesman 69
The Sorrow and the Pity 70
Tokyo Olympiad 66
2001: A Space Odyssey 68
The War Game 67
Weekend 67
Who's Afraid of Virginia Woolf? 66
The Wild Bunch 69
Woodstock 70
Z 69
Zabriskie Point 70

1971–75
Aguirre: The Wrath of God 72
Amarcord 74
American Graffiti 73
Badlands 73
Cabaret 72
Chinatown 74
A Clockwork Orange 71
The Conformist 71
The Conversation 74
Cries and Whispers 72
Day for Night 73
Death Wish 74
Dirty Harry 71
The Discreet Charm of the Bourgeoisie 72
Enter the Dragon 73
The Exorcist 73

The French Connection 71
The Godfather 72
The Godfather, Part II 74
Jaws 75
The Last Picture Show 71
Last Tango in Paris 73
Mean Streets 73
Nashville 75
One Flew Over the Cuckoo's Nest 75
Shampoo 75
Straw Dogs 71
The Texas Chainsaw Massacre 74
The Towering Inferno 74
The Way We Were 73
Young Frankenstein 74

1976–80
Alien 79
All the President's Men 76
Annie Hall 77
Apocalpyse Now 79
Carrie 76
The China Syndrome 79
Close Encounters of the Third Kind 77
Coming Home 78
Days of Heaven 78
The Deer Hunter 78
The Elephant Man 80
The Empire Strikes Back 80
Friday the 13th 80
Halloween 78
Heaven's Gate 80
Kramer vs. Kramer 79
The Last Waltz 78
Man of Iron 80
Man of Marble 77
Manhattan 78
The Marriage of Maria Braun 78
Network 76
Ordinary People 80
Raging Bull 80
Rocky 76
Saturday Night Fever 77
Seven Beauties 76
Star Wars 77
Superman 78
Taxi Driver 76
10 79
The Tin Drum 79
The Turning Point 77
The Warriors 79

19 Highly Recommended and Recommended Titles

As noted in "How to Use This Book," these titles are my personal recommendations. My taste is pretty eclectic; however, discerning readers may note some trends toward certain genres or styles of filmmaking.

I will admit to one very broad prejudice. Because so many films are imitations, homages, ripoffs, sequels, and remakes, I prize originality above all other virtues. If a movie can't easily be compared to any other film, my interest is piqued. This doesn't mean I treasure only the weird and offbeat; there are plenty of those films that lack originality, too.

If a title on these lists is unfamiliar to you, check out the description in the Title Index before you rent. Your taste and mine are bound to intersect somewhere, but not at every point on the broad map of film history.

Highly Recommended

Adam's Rib
The African Queen
All About Eve
All of Me
All Quiet on the Western Front (1930 version)
All the President's Men
Amarcord
American Dream (1991)
Anatomy of a Murder
Annie Hall
Apocalypse Now
Babette's Feast
Bad Company
The Ballad of Cable Hogue
The Band Wagon
The Birth of a Nation
The Black Stallion
Bonnie and Clyde
Brazil
The Bride of Frankenstein
The Bridge on the River Kwai
Burden of Dreams
Cape Fear (1991 version)
Casablanca
Children of Paradise
Chinatown
Chuck Berry: Hail! Hail! Rock 'n' Roll
Citizen Kane
City Lights
The Civil War
The Conversation
Cool Hand Luke
The Crimson Pirate
The Crowd
The Crying Game
The Day the Earth Stood Still
Days of Heaven
Diner
The Discreet Charm of the Bourgeoisie
Do the Right Thing
Don't Look Back
Double Indemnity
Dr. Strangelove or; How I Learned to Stop Worrying and Love the Bomb
Duck Soup
Dumbo
8½
Eight Men Out
Elvis '56
Elvis—1968 Comeback Special
Enter the Dragon
The Exterminating Angel
Fawlty Towers, Volumes 1–4
Five Easy Pieces
The 400 Blows
The Four Musketeers
From Here to Eternity
From Russia With Love
The General
Ghostbusters
The Godfather
The Godfather, Part II
The Godfather: The Complete Epic, 1902–1958
The Gold Rush
The Golden Age of Looney Tunes
Goldfinger
Gone With the Wind
The Good, the Bad, and the Ugly
GoodFellas
The Graduate
Grand Hotel

Grand Illusion
The Great Escape
Greed
Gunga Din
A Hard Day's Night
The Heartbreak Kid
Hearts of Darkness: A Filmmaker's
    Apocalypse
Help!
His Girl Friday
Hope and Glory
Howards End
The Hustler
Intolerance
Invasion of the Body Snatchers (1956 and
    1978 versions)
It Happened One Night
It's a Gift
Ivan the Terrible, Part One
Ivan the Terrible, Part Two
Jaws
Juggernaut
Jules and Jim
The Kid/The Idle Class
King Kong (1933 version)
Kiss Me Deadly
Lady and the Tramp
The Lady Eve
The Lady Vanishes (1938 version)
The Last Waltz
Lawrence of Arabia
Little Caesar
Local Hero
Lonesome Dove
Long Day's Journey Into Night
The Long Good Friday
Los Olvidados
Lost in America
M
M*A*S*H
McCabe and Mrs. Miller
Mad Max
The Maltese Falcon
The Man Who Fell to Earth
The Manchurian Candidate
Mean Streets
Medium Cool
Melvin and Howard
Metropolis (1926 and 1984 editions)
Miller's Crossing
Modern Times
Monterey Pop
Monty Python's Flying Circus, Volumes 1–22
My Darling Clementine
Napoleon (1927)
Network
Night Moves
Night of the Living Dead
Ninotchka
North by Northwest

North Dallas Forty
Notorious
Olympia
On the Waterfront
Once Upon a Time in America
Once Upon a Time in the West
One-Eyed Jacks
One Flew Over the Cuckoo's Nest
One, Two, Three
Only Angels Have Wings
Out of the Past
The Palm Beach Story
Pandora's Box
The Passion of Anna
Paths of Glory
Petulia
The Phantom of the Opera (1925 version)
The Philadelphia Story
Pinocchio
Pixote
The Player
Point Blank
Potemkin
Psycho
The Public Enemy
Radio Days
Raging Bull
Ran
Rancho Deluxe
Rear Window
Rebel Without a Cause
Red Dust
Ride the High Country
Risky Business
The Road Warrior
Robin and Marian
Robin Williams Live!
Rosemary's Baby
S.O.B.
A Salute to Chuck Jones
Scarface (1932 version)
The Seven Samurai
The 7th Voyage of Sinbad
Shame (1968)
Shoeshine
A Shot in the Dark
The Silence of the Lambs
Singin' in the Rain
Some Like It Hot
Something Wild
Sons of the Desert
The Sorrow and the Pity
Southern Comfort
Stalag 17
A Star Is Born (1954 version)
Stop Making Sense
Strangers on a Train
A Streetcar Named Desire
Sullivan's Travels
Sunset Boulevard

Sweet Smell of Success
Swing Time
Sylvia Scarlett
Taxi Driver
The Ten Commandments (1956 version)
Ten From Your Show of Shows
Terms of Endearment
The Thin Blue Line
The Thin Man
The Third Man
The 39 Steps (1935 version)
The Three Musketeers (1974 version)
Throne of Blood
To Be or Not To Be (1943 version)
Tootsie
Top Hat
Touch of Evil
The Treasure of the Sierra Madre
Twentieth Century
Unknown Chaplin
Vertigo
Viridiana
The Wages of Fear
When It Was a Game
White Heat
Who Am I This Time?
Who Framed Roger Rabbit
Who'll Stop the Rain?
The Wild Bunch
The Wild Child
The Wizard of Oz
Woman of the Year
The Women
Woodstock
Young Frankenstein
Zero for Conduct

Recommended

A Nos Amours
About Last Night
Absolute Beginners
Accident
The Adventures of Baron Münchausen
The Adventures of Buckaroo Banzai Across
   the Eighth Dimension
The Adventures of Robin Hood
Advise and Consent
Afraid of the Dark
After Hours
Aguirre: The Wrath of God
Airplane!
Aladdin
Alexander Nevsky
Alfie
Alice Doesn't Live Here Anymore
Alice in Wonderland
Alien
Aliens
All Fall Down
All That Jazz

All the King's Men
All the Right Moves
All You Need Is Cash
Always
Amadeus
American Graffiti
An American in Paris
American Me
An American Werewolf in London
And Now for Something Completely
   Different
The Anderson Tapes
Android
An Angel at My Table
Angels With Dirty Faces
The Apartment
Arruza
Arsenic and Old Lace
Arthur
Ashes and Diamonds
The Asphalt Jungle
Assault on Precinct 13
Atlantic City
The Atomic Cafe
Au Revoir, les Enfants
Avalon
The Awful Truth
The Bachelor and the Bobby-Soxer
Back to the Future
Bad Day at Black Rock
The Bad News Bears
The Bad Sleep Well
Badlands
Ball of Fire
Bambi
Bananas
Band of Outsiders
The Bank Dick
Barfly
Barry Lyndon
Barton Fink
Basket Case
Batman (1989 version)
The Battle of Algiers
The Beatles: The First U.S. Visit
Beauty and the Beast (1946 and 1991
   versions)
Bedazzled
Beetlejuice
The Beguiled
Being There
The Bellboy
Bellman and True
Berkeley in the Sixties
The Best of Comic Relief
The Best of Eddie Murphy: "Saturday Night
   Live"
The Best Years of Our Lives
Betrayal (1983)
Between the Lines

Big
The Big Bang
The Big Combo
Big Deal on Madonna Street
The Big Heat
The Big Parade
The Big Red One
The Big Sleep (1946 version)
The Big Steal
Billy Budd
Bird
Birdman of Alcatraz
The Black Cat
Black Orpheus
Black Robe
The Blackboard Jungle
Blacksmith/The Balloonatic
Blade Runner
Blaze
Blazing Saddles
Blonde Venus
Blow-Up
The Blue Angel (1930 version)
Blue Collar
Blue Velvet
Blume in Love
Bob & Carol & Ted & Alice
Bob le Flambeur
Body Heat
Bombshell
Bonjour Tristesse
Born to Kill
Born Yesterday
Bound for Glory
Boyz N the Hood
Bram Stoker's Dracula
Breakfast at Tiffany's
Breaking Away
Breaking In
Breathless (1959 version)
Brewster McCloud
Brideshead Revisited
Brief Encounter (1945)
A Brief History of Time
Bringing Up Baby
Broadcast News
Broadway Danny Rose
Broken Blossoms
The Brood
The Buddy Holly Story
Buffalo Bill and the Indians
Bugs and Daffy's Carnival of the Animals
Bugsy
Bull Durham
The Bullfighter and the Lady
Bullitt
Burn!
Buster Keaton: A Hard Act to Follow
Buster Keaton Festival Vol. I
Buster Keaton Festival Vol. II

Buster Keaton Rides Again/The Railrodder
Cabaret
The Cabinet of Dr. Caligari
The Cameraman
Camille
The Candidate
Candyman
Cannery Row
Cape Fear (1962 version)
Careful, He Might Hear You
Carmen (1983)
Carnival of Souls
Carny
Carrie (1952)
Carrie (1976)
Cat People (1942 version)
Catch-22
Caught
César and Rosalie
Champion
The Chaplin Essanay Book I
The Chaplin Revue
Charade
Charley Varrick
Charlie Chaplin Carnival
Charlie Chaplin Cavalcade
Charlie Chaplin Festival
Charlie Chaplin—The Early Years, Volumes
    I–IV
Charlie Chaplin's Keystone Comedies 1–5
The Chase (1966)
Children of a Lesser God
The China Syndrome
The Chocolate War
A Christmas Story
Cinderella (1950)
Cinema Paradiso
The Circus
Clean and Sober
Clean Slate
A Clockwork Orange
Close Encounters of the Third Kind
Coal Miner's Daughter
The Coca-Cola Kid
Cocoon
The Collector
The Color of Money
Come and Get It
Comes a Horseman
Comfort and Joy
The Commitments
Common Threads: Stories From the Quilt
The Compleat Beatles
The Concert for Bangladesh
The Conformist
Contempt
Coogan's Bluff
The Cook, The Thief, His Wife and Her Lover
Cousins
Cries and Whispers

The Criminal Code
Criss Cross (1949)
Crossfire
Crossing Delancey
Crusoe
A Cry in the Dark
Cuba
Cutter's Way
Damn Yankees
Dance With a Stranger
Dances With Wolves
Dancing Lady
Dangerous Liaisons
Darling
Das Boot
David Copperfield
Dawn of the Dead
The Dawn Patrol (1938 version)
The Day After Trinity
Day for Night
A Day in the Country
The Day of the Jackal
The Day of the Locust
The Days of Wine and Roses
The Dead
Dead End
Dead Ringers
The Dead Zone
Dear America: Letters Home From Vietnam
Defending Your Life
Delicatessen
Deliverance
Derby
Dersu Uzala
Desert Bloom
Desperate Journey
Desperately Seeking Susan
Destry Rides Again
Detour
The Devil's Playground
Diabolique
Diary of a Lost Girl
Die Hard
Dillinger
Dinner at Eight
The Dirty Dozen
Dirty Harry
Diva
Divorice—Italian Style
The Doctor
Dodes'ka-den
Dodsworth
Dog Day Afternoon
Dogfight
The Dollmaker
Donovan's Reef
Don's Party
Don't Look Now
Down and Out in Beverly Hills
Downhill Racer

Dracula (1931 version)
Dreamchild
Driving Miss Daisy
Dr. Jekyll and Mr. Hyde (1932 version)
Dr. No
A Dry, White Season
Duel
Duel in the Sun
The Duellists
Earth vs. the Flying Saucers
East of Eden (1955 version)
Easy Rider
Eat the Peach
84 Charing Cross Road
84 Charlie Mopic
The Elephant Man
El Norte
El: This Strange Passion
Elmer Fudd's Comedy Capers
The Empire Strikes Back
Employees Entrance
Enemies, A Love Story
Entre Nous
The Epic That Never Was
The Escape Artist
Escape From Alcatraz
Europa, Europa
Every Man for Himself and God Against All
Everything You Always Wanted to Know
    About Sex (But Were Afraid to Ask)
The Execution of Private Slovik
The Exorcist
Eyewitness
The Fabulous Baker Boys
A Face in the Crowd
Family Plot
Fanny and Alexander
Fantasia
Far From the Madding Crowd
Fast Times at Ridgemont High
Fast-Walking
Fat City
Fatal Vision
Father of the Bride (1950 version)
Feed
The Feud
A Few Good Men
Fiddler on the Roof
52 Pick-Up
Final Analysis
Finian's Rainbow
Firstborn
A Fish Called Wanda
The Fisher King
A Fistful of Dollars
Fitzcarraldo
The Flamingo Kid
Flight of the Phoenix
The Fly (1986 version)
Footlight Parade

For a Few Dollars More
Forbidden Games
Forbidden Planet
Force of Evil
Fort Apache
42nd Street
The Fourth Man
Frances
Frankenstein (1931)
Frankie and Johnny (1991)
Frantic (1988)
Freaks
The French Connection
The French Lieutenant's Woman
Frenzy
The Freshman (1990)
Full Metal Jacket
Fury
Gabriel Over the White House
Gallipoli
Gandhi
Gates of Heaven
George Stevens: A Filmmaker's Journey
Get Crazy
The Getaway
Gimme Shelter
The Girl Can't Help It
Glengarry Glen Ross
Glory
The Go-Between
Going in Style
Good Morning, Vietnam
Goodbye, Columbus
The Goodbye Girl
The Grapes of Wrath
The Great Dictator
Great Expectations
The Great McGinty
The Great Northfield, Minnesota, Raid
Green for Danger
Grey Gardens
The Grifters
Groundhog Day
Gumshoe
Gun Crazy
Gunfight at the O.K. Corral
Gung Ho (1986)
Hairspray
Halloween
Hamlet (1948 version)
Hammett
A Handful of Dust
Hannah and Her Sisters
Hardcore
The Harder They Come
Harold Lloyd's World of Comedy
Harold Lloyd: The Third Genius
Harry and Tonto
The Heart Is a Lonely Hunter
Heart Like a Wheel

Heartland
Hearts and Minds
Hearts of the West
Heathers
Heaven Help Us
The Heiress
Hell in the Pacific
Hell Is for Heroes
Heller in Pink Tights
Hell's Angels (1930)
Helter Skelter
Henry V (1945 and 1989 versions)
Henry: Portrait of a Serial Killer
Heroes for Sale
High and Low
High Hopes
High Plains Drifter
High Sierra
High Society
High Tide
Holiday
Holocaust
The Honeymoon Killers
Hoosiers
Horse Feathers
House Calls
House of Games
Housekeeping
How I Won the War
The Howling
Hud
Humanoids from the Deep
The Hunchback of Notre Dame (1939 version)
The Hunt for Red October
Husbands and Wives
Hustle
I Know Where I'm Going
I Married a Monster from Outer Space
I Never Sang For My Father
I Walked With a Zombie
I Wanna Hold Your Hand
if . . .
Ikiru
I'm Gonna Git You Sucka
In Cold Blood
In Name Only
In the Heat of the Night
In Which We Serve
The Incredible Shrinking Man
Inherit the Wind
The In-Laws
Internal Affairs
Intruder in the Dust
The Invivsble Man
Isadora
It Came From Outer Space
JFK
Jackie Mason on Broadway
Jack's Back

Jailhouse Rock
Jazz on a Summer's Day
Jean de Florette
Jennifer Eight
Jeremiah Johnson
Jimi Hendrix
Johnny Guitar
Judgment at Nuremberg
Julia
Julius Caesar (1953 version)
Jungle Fever
Junior Bonner
Kagemusha
Kanal
Key Largo
The Killer
Killer's Kiss
The Killing
The Killing Fields
Kind Hearts and Coronets
King of Comedy
King Rat
Kiss of Death
Klute
Knife in the Water
Kramer vs. Kramer
The Krays
La Balance
La Bamba
La Bête Humaine
La Dolce Vita
La Ronde
The Lady From Shanghai
The Ladykillers
L'Age d'Or
The Last Command
The Last Days of Chez Nous
The Last Detail
Last Embrace
The Last Emperor
The Last Laugh
The Last of the Mohicans (1992 version)
The Last Picture Show
The Last Polka
Last Tango in Paris
The Last Temptation of Christ
The Last Tycoon
The Late Show
Laura
Laurel and Hardy Comedy Classics
The Lavender Hill Mob
Le Jour se Leve
A League of Their Own
The Lenny Bruce Performance Film
Let's Get Lost
Letter From an Unknown Woman
A Letter to Three Wives
Libeled Lady
Light Sleeper
Lightning Over Water

Lilith
Liquid Sky
Little Big Man
The Little Drummer Girl
Little Man Tate
The Little Mermaid
The Lodger
Lolita
The Loneliness of the Long Distance Runner
The Long Goodbye
The Longest Day
Longtime Companion
Look Back in Anger
Lorenzo's Oil
The Lost Patrol
The Lost Weekend
Love Among the Ruins
The Lower Depths (1957 version)
Lulu in Berlin
Mad Dog and Glory
Mad Love
Madigan
The Magnificent Ambersons
The Magnificent Seven
Making Mr. Right
Making of a Legend—Gone With the Wind
The Makioka Sisters
Malcolm X
A Man for All Seasons (1966 version)
The Man Who Shot Liberty Valance
The Man Who Would Be King
The Man With the Golden Arm
Manhattan
Manhunter
Manon of the Spring
Marat/Sade
The Mark of Zorro (1920 version)
Marlene
The Marriage of Maria Braun
Married to the Mob
Martin
Mask
Matewan
Matinee
Max Headroom
Mediterraneo
Meet Me in St. Louis
Meeting Venus
The Men
Men Don't Leave
Men of Bronze
Metropolitan
Miami Blues
Midnight Cowboy
Midnight Run
The Misfits
Mishima
Missing
The Mission
Mississippi Masala

Mississippi Mermaid
Mister Johnson
Mister Roberts
The Molly Maguires
Mona Lisa
Moonlighting (1985)
Moonstruck
The More the Merrier
The Most Dangerous Game
Motown 25: Yesterday, Today and Tomorrow
Mountains of the Moon
Mr. Blandings Builds His Dream House
Mr. Hulot's Holiday
Mr. Lucky
Mrs. Soffel
The Mummy (1932 version)
Murmur of the Heart
The Music Man
The Mutiny on the Bounty (1935 version)
My Beautiful Laundrette
My Brilliant Career
My Fair Lady
My Favorite Year
My Left Foot
My Man Godfrey
Mystery Train
Nadine
The Naked Gun
The Naked Kiss
The Naked Prey
Nanook of the North
The Narrow Margin
National Lampoon's Animal House
Near Dark
New Jack City
A New Leaf
New York Stories
Newsfront
Night and Fog
Night and the City (1950 version)
A Night at the Opera
The Night My Number Came Up
Night of the Comet
The Night of the Hunter
The Night of the Shooting Stars
Night Shift
1900
92 in the Shade
No Way Out
None but the Lonely Heart
Norma Rae
Nothing in Common
O Lucky Man!
Objective, Burma!
Oliver Twist (1948 version)
On the Town
Once Around
One False Move
101 Dalmatians
The Onion Field

Open Doors
Ordinary People
Out of Africa
The Outlaw Josey Wales
Over the Edge
The Owl and the Pussycat
The Ox-Bow Incident
The Pajama Game
Panic in the Streets
The Paper Chase
The Parallax View
Paris Is Burning
Paris Trout
Passion Fish
The Passion of Joan of Arc
Pat and Mike
Pat Garrett and Billy the Kid
Patterns
Patton
Peeping Tom
Pee-wee's Big Adventure
Pennies From Heaven
Performance
Persona
Peter Pan (1953 version)
Phase IV
Pickup on South Street
Pierrot le Fou
A Place in the Sun
Platoon
Play Misty for Me
The Playboys
Point Break
Postcards From the Edge
The Postman Always Rings Twice (1946 version)
Pretty Poison
Prime Cut
Prince of the City
The Prisoner of Zenda (1937 version)
Prizzi's Honor
The Producers
The Professionals
Proof
Providence
The Public Eye
Pulp
Pump Up the Volume
Q & A
Quadrophenia
Queen Christina
Queen of Hearts
Que Viva Mexico!
The Quiet Man
Rain Man
The Rain People
Raise the Red Lantern
The Rapture
Rashomon
Real Genius

Real Life
Red River
Reds
Repo Man
Repulsion
Reservoir Dogs
The Return of the Living Dead
The Return of the Secaucus Seven
Reuben, Reuben
Reversal of Fortune
Ride Lonesome
The Right Stuff
River's Edge
Road Runner vs. Wile E. Coyote: The Classic
   Chase
Roadie
The Roaring Twenties
Rocco and His Brothers
Roger Corman: Hollywood's Wild Angel
Romancing the Stone
A Room With a View
'Round Midnight
Roxanne
Sabrina
Salesman
A Salute to Mel Blanc
Salvador
The Sand Pebbles
SanShiro Sugata
Say Amen, Somebody
Say Anything
Scandal
Scarlet Street
School Daze
The Searchers
The Secret Policeman's Other Ball
Seize the Day
Serpico
The Servant
The Seven Percent Solution
The Seventh Seal
The Seventh Victim
sex, lies, and videotape
Shack Out on 101
The Shadow Box
Shadow of a Doubt
Shall We Dance
Shampoo
Shane
Shanghai Express
She Wore a Yellow Ribbon
Sherman's March
She's Gotta Have It
Shoah
Shock Corridor
Short Eyes
Show People
Sid & Nancy
The Silent Partner
Silkwood

Silver Streak
Simon of the Desert
Since You Went Away
Singles
Sisters
The Skin Game (1971)
Skyscraper Souls
Slap Shot
Slaughterhouse Five
Sleuth
Slither
Small Change
Smile
Smiles of a Summer Night
So This Is Paris
Sommersby
Song of the Thin Man
Songwriter
Sorcerer
Sorry, Wrong Number
Sounder
Spartacus
Special Bulletin
Splash
Splendor in the Grass
The Spy Who Came In From the Cold
The Spy Who Loved Me
Stagecoach (1939 version)
Star Wars
Stardust Memories
Start the Revolution Without Me
Starting Over
Stay Hungry
Steamboat Bill, Jr.
The Stepfather
The Stone Boy
Stormy Monday
Straight Time
The Stranger (1946)
Stray Dog
Streetwise
The Stunt Man
Suburbia
The Sugarland Express
Sunday, Bloody Sunday
Superstar: The Life and Times of Andy
   Warhol
The Sure Thing
Sweet Dreams
Swimming to Cambodia
The Tall Guy
The Tall T
The Taming of the Shrew
Tampopo
Tanner '88
Tapeheads
The Tenant
Tequila Sunrise
The Terminator
That Hamilton Woman

Thelma & Louise
Thelonius Monk: Straight, No Chaser
Them!
There Was a Crooked Man
They All Laughed
They Shoot Horses, Don't They?
They Won't Believe Me
The Thing (From Another World)
Things Change
This Gun for Hire
This Is Elvis
This Is Spinal Tap
This Sporting Life
A Thousand Clowns
The Three Caballeros
This Boy's Life
3:10 to Yuma
Till the End of Time
Time After Time
Time Bandits
The Times of Harvey Milk
The Tin Drum
To Kill a Mockingbird
To Live and Die in L.A.
Tokyo Olympiad
Topkapi
The Tramp/A Woman
Trespass
Triumph of the Will
Trouble in Mind
True Confessions
True West
Truth or Dare
Tucker: The Man and His Dream
Turtle Diary
12 Angry Men
25 x 5: The Continuing History of the
    Rolling Stones
20,000 Leagues Under the Sea
Twin Peaks
Two by Scorsese
Two English Girls
Two for the Road
The Two Jakes
2001: A Space Odyssey
Ugetsu
Ulzana's Raid
Un Chien Andalou
Under Fire
Under Siege
Unforgiven
An Unmarried Woman
Used Cars
Vagabond
Valley Girl
The Vanishing (1988 version)
Variety Lights

Vera Cruz
The Verdict
Vernon, Florida
Wait Until Dark
Walk Softly, Stranger
The Wanderers
The Wannsee Conference
The War Game
The Warriors (1979)
Way Down East
Wayne's World
A Wedding
The Wedding March
Weekend
West Side Story
What Price Hollywood?
What's Up, Tiger Lily?
Where Angels Fear To Tread
Where the Heart Is
Where the Lilies Bloom
While the City Sleeps
White Men Can't Jump
White of the Eye
Who's Afraid of Virginia Woolf?
Who's That Knocking at My Door?
Wild Strawberries
Will Penny
Winchester '73
The Wind
Wings of Desire
Wise Blood
Wisecracks
The Witches
Witness for the Prosecution
The Wolf Man
Wolfen
A Woman's Tale
A Woman Under the Influence
Women in Love
Women on the Verge of a Nervous
    Breakdown
Working Girl
Working Girls
A World Apart
The Wrong Box
Wuthering Heights (1939 version)
The Yakuza
Yankee Doodle Dandy
Yellow Submarine
Yojimbo
Young and Innocent
The Young Lions
Young Mr. Lincoln
Z
Zabriskie Point
Zelig
Zentropa

20 Unavailable on Videocassette

The following is a list of frequently requested titles, films by major directors or featuring important stars, or movies of historical interest that are still not on videocassette as of Summer 1993.

Some of the more popular titles are available in unauthorized, pirated cassettes, whose quality is nearly always suspect.

A few titles are available on laser disc only; they are indicated (disc).

A special thanks to Mike Clark and Lori Shimabukuro for helping me to compile this list.

The Actress
The Adventures of Robinson Crusoe
The Affairs of Dobie Gillis
Alex in Wonderland
Alexander's Ragtime Band
All the Way Home
All That Heaven Allows
America, America
American Hot Wax
American Madness
American Pop
An American Tragedy
Anna and the King of Siam
Annie Get Your Gun
Antonia: A Portrait of the
    Woman
At Long Last Love
Attack!
Bad Timing: A Sensual Obsession
Beast of the City
The Bedsitting Room
The Beggar's Opera
Belle de Jour
Belle of the Nineties
The Big Carnival (Ace in the Hole)
The Big Clock
The Big House
The Big Knife (disc)
Bigger Than Life
Billion Dollar Brain
Bird of Paradise (1951 version)
The Bitter Tea of General Yen
The Black Cauldron
Black Legion
The Black Rose
Blue Skies
The Blue Veil
Bluebeard's Eighth Wife
Boccaccio '70
Boom!
Boomerang (1947)
The Brave Bulls

Bread and Chocolate
The Breaking Point (1950)
Breezy
Bright Road
Bright Victory
Brute Force
Bunny Lake Is Missing
Caged
Call Me Madam
Call Northside 777
Captain From Castile
Carmen Jones (disc)
Cattle Annie and Little Britches
Céline and Julie Go Boating
The Chant of Jimmie Blacksmith
The Chapman Report
The Charge of the Light Brigade
    (1966 version)
Cheaper by the Dozen
Christmas Holiday
Claudine
Cluny Brown
The Cobweb (disc)
A Cold Wind in August
Colorado Territory
Comanche Station
Come Fill the Cup
Coming Apart
Crime Without Passion
The Crusades
Cul-de-sac
The Dark Angel
The Dark at the Top of the Stairs
Darling Lili
Deadhead Miles
Deadline, U.S.A.
Death of a Salesman
    (1951 version)
Death Takes a Holiday
    (1934 version)
Decision Before Dawn
Deep End

Design for Living
The Devil Is a Woman
Dishonored
Drive, He Said
Dutchman
Easy Living (1937)
The Effect of Gamma Rays on Man-in-the-
　Moon Marigolds
El Topo
The Emigrants
Emma
Emperor of the North
Every Day's a Holiday
Faces
Fellini's Casanova
Five Graves to Cairo
Five Million Years to Earth
Five Star Final
Fixed Bayonets
For Whom the Bell Tolls
Foreign Affair
Forever Amber
The Fortune
Forty Guns
The Four Poster
Fourteen Hours
Frenchman's Creek
The Furies
The Gang's All Here
The Glass Menagerie (1950 version)
Go, Man, Go!
Godspell
Goin' to Town
Gorilla at Large
The Great Gatsby (1949 version)
The Great Man
The Green Years
The Gypsy Moths
Hangover Square
The Hard Way (1942)
The Hasty Heart
A Hatful of Rain
Having a Wild Weekend
He Ran All the Way
He Who Gets Slapped
Heaven Knows, Mr. Allison
Heavy Metal
Helen of Troy
Here Come the Nelsons
The High and the Mighty
The Hill
Hitler's Madmen
Hold Back the Dawn
Hondo
Hot Tomorrows
The House on 92nd St.
How to Steal a Million
I Walk Alone
I Walk the Line
I Was a Male War Bride

The Iceman Cometh
I'm No Angel
Images
The Innocents
Island in the Sky
It Happens Every Spring
The Joker Is Wild
The Killers (1946 version)
The Killing of a Chinese Bookie
The King of Marvin Gardens
A Kiss Before Dying (1956 version)
The Knack, and How to Get It
Knock on Wood
La Chinoise
La Guerre est Finie
Lacombe, Lucien
The Landlord
L'Atalante
Leave Her to Heaven
The Legend of Lylah Clare
Leo the Last
The Leopard
Let the Good Times Roll
Little Man, What Now?
Living It Up
The Lodger (1944 version)
London After Midnight
Lord Love a Duck
Lost Boundaries
Love Me Tonight
Loving
Lucky Lady
M (1951 version)
Made for Each Other (1971)
The Magnificent Yankee
The Major and the Minor
Make Way for Tomorrow
The Man Between
The Man I Love
Man on a Tightrope
The Man on the Flying Trapeze
Man's Castle
The Marquise of O
The Marrying Kind
Meet Danny Wilson
The Merry Widow (1925 version)
Mickey One
Midnight (1939)
The Miracle Woman
Modesty Blaise
The Mortal Storm
The Mother and the Whore
Mother Wore Tights
Mourning Becomes Electra
Movie Crazy
Muriel
My Cousin Rachel
My Foolish Heart
My Gal Sal
My Son John

The Nanny
The Navigator
The New Land
Nightmare Alley
No Highway in the Sky
No Way Out (1950)
The Northwest Mounted Police
Nosferatu the Vampyre
Nothing but a Man
O'Henry's Full House
The Old Dark House
The Old-Fashioned Way
The Old Man and the Sea
One Foot in Heaven
One Hour With You
One-Way Passage
Opening Night
Our Man in Havana
Out of It
Outcast of the Islands
Pandora and the Flying Dutchman
People Will Talk
Peppermint Soda
Phantom of the Rue Morgue
The Phenix City Story
The Pied Piper
Pinky
Play It As It Lays
Point of Order
Porgy and Bess
The Power and the Glory
Private Worlds
The Pumpkin Eater
Purple Noon
The Rains Came
The Revolutionary
Roxie Hart
The Royal Family of Broadway
Saturday Night and Sunday Morning
Saturday's Hero
The Savage Innocents
The Scarlet Empress
The Scoundrel
Seconds
Seven Chances
Seven Men From Now
Seven Women (disc)
Shepherd of the Hills
Sherlock Jr.
The Sign of the Cross
Six of a Kind
The Sniper
Snow White and the Seven Dwarfs
Song of the South
Sons and Lovers
Spirits of the Dead
Station Six Sahara
Steamboat 'Round the Bend
Storm Warning
The Story of Three Loves

The Stranger (1967)
Such Good Friends
Sudden Fear
Sunrise
The Suspect
Take Care of My Little Girl
The Tarnished Angels
Tell Me That You Love Me, Junie
    Moon
Tender Is the Night
Teresa
That Man From Rio
These Are the Damned
Thieves Like Us
Three Coins in the Fountain (disc)
Three Smart Girls
3 Women
Thunderbolt
Titanic
To Die in Madrid
To Each His Own
Tobacco Road
Track of the Cat
Trader Horn
Trouble in Paradise
20,000 Years in Sing Sing
Two-Lane Blacktop
Unconquered
Union Pacific
Up the Down Staircase
Valentino (1951 and 1977 versions)
The Valley of Decision
Victoria the Great
A View From the Bridge
Walkabout
Wanda
The Way of All Flesh
We Were Strangers
Welcome to Hard Times
Where's Charley?
White Dog
Wild Boys of the Road
Wild Is the Wind
Wild River
Will Success Spoil Rock Hunter?
The Woman in the Window
Woman's World
Wonder Bar (disc)
Young Girls of Rochefort
You're Telling Me

Discontinued Movies
These titles were made available on
    videocassette at one time but have been
    withdrawn from manufacture. Thus, copies
    are difficult to find. See "How to Use This
    Book" for further explanation.
Autumn Sonata
Beauty and the Beast (1991 version)
Bedazzled

The Detective
Diva
Fantasia*
The Great Mouse Detective
The Haunting
The Killing of Sister George
Lady and the Tramp
Medium Cool
101 Dalmatians
The Rescurers

The Rescuers Down Under
Room at the Top
Seven Days in May
Sleeping Beauty (1959)
They Shoot Horses, Don't They?
Three Coins in the Fountain
*Fantasia was made available to retailers for fifty days beginning November 1, 1991. Replacement copies cannot be ordered until it is re-released.

Title Index

A Coeur Joie (1967, B&W, 89m, NR)
Brigitte Bardot plays a bored housewife who resumes her career, only to fall in love with another man. **ST6**

A Nos Amours (1984, C, 102m, R)
From France, a drama of a teen-aged girl (Sandrine Bonnaire) with a string of lovers and family problems. Directed by Maurice Pialat, who also plays the girl's father. **FF1,** *Recommended*

A Nous la Liberté (1931, B&W, 87m, NR)
French director René Clair's comic look at how machinery takes over people's lives. **DT25, FF1,** *Essential*

Aaron Loves Angela (1975, C, 98m, R)
New York romance between a black Harlem youth (Kevin Hooks) and a Puerto Rican girl (Irene Cara). Moses Gunn costars. **DR14, DR15**

Abbott and Costello in Hollywood (1945, B&W, 83m, NR)
Bud and Lou invade the MGM lot and run into plenty of surprise guest stars. **ST1**

Abbott and Costello Meet Captain Kidd (1952, C, 70m, NR)
Charles Laughton hams it up as the notorious pirate in this A&C comedy. **ST1, ST112**

Abbott and Costello Meet Dr. Jekyll and Mr. Hyde (1953, B&W, 77m, NR)
Bud and Lou are in London where Lou is accidentally injected with the Mr. Hyde serum. Boris Karloff costars. **ST1, ST100, WR33**

Abbott and Costello Meet Frankenstein (1948, B&W, 83m, NR)
Dracula (Bela Lugosi) wants to use Lou's brain in the Frankenstein monster (Glenn Strange) and the Wolfman (Lon Chaney, Jr.) tries to warn him that he's in danger. Vincent Price has a bit at the end as the Invisible Man. **HF7, HF10, ST1, ST27, ST143, ST179**

Abbott and Costello Meet the Invisible Man (1951, B&W, 82m, NR)
With the help of a little invisibility, A&C come to the rescue of a boxer who's fighting a gangster. With Nancy Guild, Arthur Franz, and Adele Jergens. **ST1**

Abbott and Costello Meet the Killer, Boris Karloff (1949, B&W, 84m, NR)
Karloff tries to do away with Lou in this A&C comic mystery. **ST1, ST100**

Abe Lincoln in Illinois (1939, B&W, 110m, NR)
Raymond Massey stars as the small-town lawyer who would eventually become our sixteenth President. **CL2, HF18**

Abilene Town (1946, B&W, 89m, NR)
Randolph Scott Western set in post–Civil War Kansas, where the townspeople are feuding over land rights. **ST197**

Abominable Dr. Phibes, The (1971, C, 93m, PG)
Vincent Price hams it up in this tongue-in-cheek horror film about a disfigured doctor seeking revenge. **CU4, HO20, HO26, ST179**

About Last Night (1986, C, 116m, R)
Comedy-drama about four young Chicago singles, two of whom think they've found love but aren't sure. Rob Lowe, Demi Moore, Jim Belushi, and Elizabeth Perkins star. Underrated film with some pointed observations about modern romance. **CO13, DR1, DR7, XT11,** *Recommended*

Above Suspicion (1943, B&W, 90m, NR)
Joan Crawford and Fred MacMurray play newlyweds asked by the Allies to play spies while on their honeymoon in Europe. **ST39**

Above the Law (1988, C, 97m, R)
Steven Seagal plays a superagent (martial arts training, multilingual, weapons expert) with friends in the Mob. He's on the trail of a CIA-sponsored drug ring. **AC8, AC25**

Abraham Lincoln (1930, B&W, 97m, NR)
Walter Huston stars in director D.W. Griffith's account of the sixteenth president's life. This is a restored version, with slavery sequences once thought lost. **CL2, DT52, HF18**

Absence of Malice (1981, C, 116m, PG)
Newspaper reporter (Sally Field) tries for big scoop on Miami construction boss (Paul Newman) and his involvement with crime, only to find out her target is innocent. Writ-

ten by ex-journalist Kurt Luedtke; Sydney Pollack directed. **DR7, DT98, ST66, ST162**

Absent-Minded Professor, The
(1961, B&W, 97m, G)
Fred MacMurray plays the forgetful inventor who discovers flubber—an amazing substance that raises his Model T and basketball team to new heights in this classic Disney comedy. **FA1**

Absolute Beginners
(1986, C, 107m, PG-13)
Stylized musical look at London in the late 1950s, when rock 'n' roll was about to break through and the teenager would become king. Patsy Kensit and Eddie O'Connell star; David Bowie, Ray Davies, and Sade perform musical numbers. Director Julien Temple offers a swirling, densely textured look at the city and its people. **MU9, MU16, XT15,** *Recommended*

Absolution (1981, C, 105m, NR)
Richard Burton stars in this drama of a priest at a boys' school who's the victim of a cruel practical joke. Written by Anthony Shaffer. **DR25, ST22**

Abyss, The (1989, C, 140m, PG-13)
Undersea spectacular, with rescue mission trying to free a nuclear submarine from a precarious position. Ed Harris and Mary Elizabeth Mastrantonio star. Directed by James Cameron with his usual verve, but a disappointing ending mars the film's impact. **AC12, AC24, DT21**

Accident (1967, C, 105m, NR)
Drama set at a British university, centering on a professor's affair with a lovely young student. Dirk Bogarde, Stanley Baker, Jacqueline Sassard, Delphine Seyrig, and Michael York star. Written by Harold Pinter, who also has a small role; directed by Joseph Losey. Contemporary British decadence at its ripest. **DR23, ST14, WR26,** *Recommended*

Accidental Tourist, The
(1988, C, 121m, PG)
Anne Tyler's novel, set in Baltimore, about a guidebook writer who hates to travel, his estranged wife, and a loopy dog trainer. William Hurt, Kathleen Turner, and Oscar winner Geena Davis star, with Amy Wright, Ed Begley, Jr., David Ogden Stiers, and Bill Pullman. Lawrence Kasdan directed. Good on particulars, but somehow misses the author's quirky sensibility. **DR1, DR8, DR19, ST45, ST114, ST218, XT5**

Accused, The (1988, C, 110m, R)
Oscar winner Jodie Foster stars as a woman who's been brutally assaulted in a bar. A de-termined prosecutor (Kelly McGillis) presses charges against the onlookers at the scene of the crime. Directed by Jonathan Kaplan. Worth seeing for Foster, but none of the other characters (especially McGillis) are as fully realized. **DR10, DR17, ST61, XT3**

Ace in the Hole see *Big Carnival, The*

Aces: Iron Eagle III (1992, C, 93m, R)
Louis Gossett, Jr., returns to the unfriendly skies, recruiting veteran pilots to bomb a cocaine-producing factory in Peru. The twist: he and his men are on an unauthorized mission using vintage planes. With Rachel Mc-Lish, Horst Bucholz, Sonny Chiba, and Fred Dalton Thompson. **AC11**

Across 110th Street (1972, C, 102m, R)
Violent crime thriller, with New York police and the Mob in a race to catch freelance robbers who made off with $300,000 of Mob money. Anthony Quinn, Yaphet Kotto, and Anthony Franciosa star. **AC9, CU7, XT9**

Across the Great Divide
(1977, C, 100m, G)
Family adventure about two orphaned children making the trek over dangerous Rocky Mountain terrain to earn their inherited land in frontier Oregon. **FA4**

Across the Pacific (1942, B&W, 97m, NR)
Humphrey Bogart spy yarn set during World War II, with several of his *Maltese Falcon* cohorts along (Mary Astor, Sydney Greenstreet, director John Huston). **AC1, DT60, ST15**

Across the Wide Missouri
(1951, C, 78m, NR)
Clark Gable stars in this colorful tale of exploration in the frontier West. With Ricardo Montalban, John Hodiak, and Adolphe Menjou. Directed by William Wellman. **DT135, ST77**

Act of Aggression (1973, C, 100m, R)
French drama of a man who takes the law into his own hands to avenge his wife and daughter's murders. Jean-Louis Trintignant and Catherine Deneuve star. **FF1, ST50**

Act of Vengeance (1986, C, 96m, NR)
Charles Bronson plays real-life union leader Jock Yablonski in this story of his murder at the hands of corrupt United Mine Workers officials. Wilford Brimley costars as Tony Boyle, with Ellen Burstyn, Hoyt Axton, Ellen Barkin, and Keanu Reeves. Originally made for cable TV. **DR6, ST7, ST20**

Action in the North Atlantic
(1943, B&W, 127m, NR)
Humphrey Bogart sets sail with the merchant marine during World War II. With Raymond

Massey, Alan Hale, and Sam Levene. **AC1, ST15**

Action Jackson (1988, C, 95m, R)
Carl Weathers plays Detroit's most determined police sergeant, Jericho "Action" Jackson. He keeps his cool as a ruthless auto tycoon, a scheming mistress, and his own police force cross his path in this thriller. Craig T. Nelson and Vanity costar. **AC8**

Adam (1983, C, 100m, NR)
JoBeth Williams and Daniel J. Travanti play the real-life couple whose missing son case stirred controversy and congressional debate. Originally made for TV. **MY8**

Adam at 6 A.M. (1970, C, 100m, PG)
Michael Douglas is a college professor who takes a laborer's job for the summer. With Lee Purcell, Joe Don Baker, and Meg Foster. **ST59**

Adam Had Four Sons
(1941, B&W, 81m, NR)
Family drama starring Ingrid Bergman as a French governess for a widower (Warner Baxter) with four boys. With Susan Hayward, Fay Wray, Richard Denning, and June Lockhart. **ST13, ST100**

Adam's Rib (1949, B&W, 101m, NR)
Katharine Hepburn and Spencer Tracy are husband and wife lawyers who wind up on opposing sides of a marital dispute in court. Judy Holliday, in her film debut, is hilarious as the dizzy defendant. Written by Ruth Gordon and Garson Kanin; directed by George Cukor. Perhaps the funniest courtroom movie ever. **CL10, CL15, DT32, ST103, ST107, ST217, XT21,** *Essential, Highly Recommended*

Addams Family, The
(1991, C, 99m, PG-13)
Charles Addams's ghoulish cartoon characters make the leap from the pages of *The New Yorker* to the screen in this comedy starring Raul Julia and Anjelica Huston. With Christopher Lloyd, Dan Hedaya, Elizabeth Wilson, Christina Ricci, and Jimmy Workman. **CO5, HO24, ST96**

Addict (1971, C, 90m, R)
The life and very hard times of a New York City heroin addict, an ex-hairdresser, played by George Segal. Karen Black costars; Robert De Niro has a small part. Directed by Ivan Passer. Original title: *Born To Win*. **DR15, ST51, XT9**

Adios Amigo (1975, C, 87m, PG)
In this Western comedy, Fred Williamson (who also wrote and directed) costars with

Richard Pryor as a very hip pair of gunslingers. **ST180, WE14, XT23**

Adjuster, The (1991, C, 102m, R)
Canadian-produced drama of an insurance adjuster, who uses his job as a front for his voyeurism, and his wife, a censor who is secretly taping licentious material. Elias Koteas, Arsinee Khanjian, and Maury Chaykin star. **DR7**

Adorable Julia (1962, C, 94m, NR)
Lilli Palmer stars as an aging actress involved with a young man (Jean Sorel), unbeknownst to her director-producer husband (Charles Boyer). Based on W. Somerset Maugham's novel and play, *Theatre*. **CL7, ST16, WR23**

Adventure for Two see *Demi-Paradise, The*

Adventurers, The (1970, C, 171m, PG)
Harold Robbins tale of a South American country convulsed by revolution and characters convulsed by greed and lust. Candice Bergen and Bekim Fehmiu star, with Ernest Borgnine, Olivia de Havilland, Leigh Taylor-Young, Rossano Brazzi, and Jaclyn Smith. Originally rated R; edited to get a PG. **DR19, ST49**

Adventures in Babysitting
(1987, C, 99m, PG-13)
Shaggy dog tale of teen babysitter dragging her charges off to downtown Chicago to help a stranded friend. Elisabeth Shue stars. **CO20, FA15, XT11**

Adventures of an American Rabbit, The (1986, C, 85m, G)
Feature cartoon about Rob Rabbit, a normal bunny transformed into a superhero. **FA10**

Adventures of Baron Münchausen, The
(1989, C, 126m, PG)
Spectacular adventure fantasy, based on real German nobleman with a penchant for spinning fabulous and less than credible tales. John Neville stars, with Sarah Polley as his young companion, and Eric Idle, Robin Williams (billed as "Ray Tutto"), Oliver Reed, and Uma Thurman. Directed with great flair by Terry Gilliam. **CO15, FA8, SF13, SF14, ST228,** *Recommended*

Adventures of Buckaroo Banzai Across the Eighth Dimension, The
(1984, C, 103m, PG)
Adventure comedy about a superhero who's a brain surgeon, race car driver, and rock singer—among other talents. Peter Weller stars, with Ellen Barkin, Jeff Goldblum, and John Lithgow. Almost too hip for its own good, but full of quirky and amusing characters. **AC17, CO12, CU5, SF21, ST7, ST90,** *Recommended*

Adventures of Bullwhip Griffin, The
(1967, C, 110m, NR)
Disney Western comedy, with a novice Bostonian who thinks he can make a bundle during the gold rush days. Roddy McDowall, Suzanne Pleshette, and Karl Malden star. **FA1**

Adventures of Captain Fabian
(1951, B&W, 100m, NR)
Errol Flynn swashbuckler as the hero defending Micheline Presle from murder charge. Agnes Moorehead and Vincent Price costar. **AC15, ST69, ST179**

Adventures of Don Juan, The
(1948, C, 110m, NR)
Costume adventure about history's roguish lover, starring Errol Flynn. Viveca Lindfors and Ann Rutherford costar as his conquests. **ST69**

Adventures of Ford Fairlane, The
(1990, C, 100m, R)
Controversial stand-up comic Andrew Dice Clay plays a "rock 'n' roll detective"—a private dick who's assigned to music industry cases. With Wayne Newton as a slimy executive and Priscilla Presley, Morris Day, and Lauren Holly. **MY10**

Adventures of Hercules, The
(1984, C, 89m, NR)
Lou Ferrigno plays the well-muscled hero of mythology in this adventure saga. **AC17**

Adventures of Huckleberry Finn, The
(1939, B&W, 89m, NR)
Mark Twain's classic of a boy and a runaway slave in a thrilling raft trip down the Mississippi. Mickey Rooney stars. **FA3, WR35**

Adventures of Huckleberry Finn, The
(1960, C, 107m, NR)
Eddie Hodges plays Twain's famed rascal, with boxer Archie Moore as Jim. In support: Tony Randall, Patty McCormack, Neville Brand, and Buster Keaton. **DT66, FA3, WR35**

Adventures of Huckleberry Finn, The
(1985, C, 121m, NR)
The Mark Twain classic about adventurous Huck (Patrick Day) rafting down the Mississippi with his runaway friend Jim (Samm-Art Williams). With Sada Thompson, Lillian Gish, Richard Kiley, and Butterfly McQueen. Originally made for public TV; shown at 240 minutes. **FA3, ST71, WR35**

Adventures of Mark Twain, The
(1985, C, 90m, G)
The art of claymation is used to capture the likeness of Mark Twain's literary characters (Tom Sawyer, Huck Finn, and Becky

Thatcher) in this animated adventure story. **FA10, WR35**

Adventures of Milo in the Phantom Tollbooth, The see *Phantom Tollbooth, The*

Adventures of Robin Hood, The
(1938, C, 102m, NR)
Errol Flynn plays the dashing Sherwood Forest outlaw. Olivia de Havilland, Basil Rathbone, and Claude Rains costar in this classic adventure romp. **AC13, CL9, FA4, HF15, ST49, ST69,** *Essential, Recommended*

Adventures of Sherlock Holmes, The
(1939, B&W, 83m, NR)
Sherlock Holmes and Dr. Watson outsmart their arch-rival Professor Moriarity in the first Holmes movie to star Basil Rathbone and Nigel Bruce. **HF14**

Adventures of Sherlock Holmes' Smarter Brother, The (1978, C, 91m, PG)
Gene Wilder plays the title role in this spoof of Holmesiana. With Madeline Kahn, Marty Feldman, and Dom DeLuise. Wilder directed. **CO7, CO10, XT23**

Adventures of the Wilderness Family, The (1975, C, 100m, G)
A modern-day family trades in their big-city lifestyle for pioneer life in the West. **FA4**

Adventures of Tom Sawyer, The
(1938, C, 93m, NR)
Mark Twain's classic about the Missouri boy whose endless curiosity gets him into all sorts of mischief. Tommy Kelly, Jackie Moran, Walter Brennan, and Victor Jory star. **FA3, WR35**

Adventures of Tom Sawyer, The
(1973, C, 78m, NR)
Mark Twain's classic of a boyhood in Hannibal, Missouri, starring Josh Albee, with Jeff Tyler, Jane Wyatt, Buddy Ebsen, John McGiver, and as Injun Joe, Vic Morrow. **FA3, WR35**

Adventuress, The see *I See a Dark Stranger*

Adversary, The (1971, B&W, 110m, NR)
Indian director Satyajit Ray's story of a college graduate who can't find work, starring Dhritiman Chatterjee. **DT102**

Advise and Consent
(1962, B&W, 139m, NR)
Director Otto Preminger offers a first-rate drama of Washington political wheeling and dealing over the controversial nomination of a left-wing senator to become Secretary of State. Henry Fonda stars, with Don Murray, Charles Laughton (in his last film), Walter Pidgeon, Peter Lawford, and Gene Tierney.

Based on a novel by Allen Drury. Widescreen cinematography will be lost on video. **CU20, DR21, DT100, ST71, ST132, ST214, XT12, XT22,** *Recommended*

Affair in Trinidad (1952, B&W, 98m, NR)
Rita Hayworth and Glenn Ford star in this thriller of a cabaret singer and her brother-in-law tracking her husband's killer. **ST101**

Affair To Remember, An
(1957, C, 115m, NR)
Shipboard romance between Cary Grant and Deborah Kerr turns tragic. Directed by Leo McCarey; a remake of his 1939 film, *Love Affair.* **CL4, CL6, CU18, DT80, ST92, ST125**

Afraid of the Dark (1991, C, 91m, R)
British psychological thriller about a young boy (Ben Keyworth) who's fascinated with the world of the blind. With James Fox and Fanny Ardant. Cowriter and director Mark Peploe creates a genuinely unsettling atmosphere, is especially good at understanding the fantasy world of children. **DR9, MY14, MY15,** *Recommended*

Africa Screams (1949, B&W, 79m, NR)
Abbott and Costello go on safari with big-game hunter Frank Buck. **ST1**

African Queen, The (1951, C, 105m, NR)
Romantic adventure teaming Humphrey Bogart (an Oscar winner) with Katharine Hepburn as the hard-drinking pilot and the uptight spinster who cruise treacherous waters to thwart the Germans in World War I. Directed by John Huston; written by James Agee. **AC12, AC14, CL4, DT60, ST15, ST103, XT2,** *Essential, Highly Recommended*

After Dark, My Sweet (1990, C, 114m, R)
A punch-drunk fighter, a shiftless dame, and a sleazy con man are the trio of would-be kidnappers in this adaptation of Jim Thompson's novel. Jason Patric, Rachel Ward, and Bruce Dern star. The setting, the Palm Springs area, steals the show. Directed and cowritten by James Foley. **MY2, WR34**

After Hours (1985, C, 96m, R)
Ordinary guy finds himself stranded in the middle of the night in an unfriendly New York neighborhood. Offbeat comedy directed by Martin Scorsese stars Griffin Dunne, with John Heard, Rosanna Arquette, Catherine O'Hara, Thomas Chong, Teri Garr, Verna Bloom, and Linda Fiorentino. **CO2, CO12, CO14, CO20, CU5, DT114, ST28, XT9,** *Recommended*

After the Fall of New York
(1985, C, 95m, R)
Adventure saga set in post-holocaust America, where only the strong survive. Michael Sopkiw stars. **SF8, SF12**

After the Fox (1966, C, 103m, NR)
Peter Sellers stars in a comedy about a frustrated film director on location in Rome. Victor Mature chews the scenery as a fading star. Directed by Vittorio De Sica; written by Neil Simon. **CO8, DT37, ST198, WR30, XT17**

After the Rehearsal (1984, C, 72m, R)
Swedish drama from director Ingmar Bergman about the intricate relationships of a theater director and his actresses. Erland Josephson, Ingrid Thulin, and Lena Olin star. **DT11**

After the Thin Man
(1936, B&W, 113m, NR)
More parties, more hangovers, and more crime for the high-society detective couple Nick and Nora Charles (William Powell, Myrna Loy) in their second screen adventure. James Stewart costars as one of their suspects. **CL15, HF5, MY17, ST142, ST176, ST207, WR12**

Afterburn (1992, C, 103m, R)
True-life drama of military pilot's wife pressing for an explanation of her spouse's death in an air crash. Laura Dern stars, with Robert Loggia, Vincent Spano, and Michael Rooker. Originally made for TV. **DR6, ST53**

Aftermath (1985, C, 96m, NR)
A trio of astronauts returns to Earth after a long journey to find a nuclear holocaust has ravaged the planet. **SF12**

Against All Flags (1952, C, 83m, NR)
Errol Flynn plays a British soldier who finds his way into a pirate stronghold—and into Maureen O'Hara's heart. Anthony Quinn costars. **AC15, ST69, ST167**

Against All Odds (1969, C, 93m, R)
The dastardly Fu Manchu plans to murder several world leaders by sending them slave girls saturated in poison which will kill anyone who kisses them. Christopher Lee stars. Original title: *The Blood of Fu Manchu.* Also known as *Kiss and Kill.* **ST135**

Against All Odds (1984, C, 128m, R)
An ex-jock (Jeff Bridges), hired to track down the runaway wife of a shady nightclub owner (James Woods), finds her and falls in love with her. Rachel Ward costars in this remake of the classic thriller, *Out of the Past,* set in contemporary Los Angeles. Jane Greer, the female star of the original, plays Ward's mother. Attractive leads can't save story whose convolutions worked better in original. **CU18, DR16, MY2, MY5, ST19, ST233, XT10**

Agatha (1979, C, 98m, PG)
Vanessa Redgrave portrays mystery writer Agatha Christie in this dramatic account of her eleven-day disappearance in 1926. Dustin Hoffman costars as an inquisitive reporter who tracks Christie down. **MY8, ST105, ST182, WR3**

Agency (1981, C, 94m, R)
Robert Mitchum stars in this drama about a politician gaining power through subliminal television advertising. With Lee Majors, Valerie Perrine, and Alexandra Stewart. **DR24, ST158**

Agnes of God (1985, C, 98m, PG-13)
A young nun is the center of controversy over a murdered newborn infant. Jane Fonda, Anne Bancroft, and Meg Tilly star in this version of John Pielmeyer's play directed by Norman Jewison. **DR20, DT63, ST72**

Aguirre: The Wrath of God (1972, C, 90m, NR)
Vivid, gripping adventure tale of mad conquistador (Klaus Kinski) driving his men to destruction in the jungles of South America. Werner Herzog directed on stunning locations. One of the breakthrough films of the New German Cinema movement. **DT54, ST126,** *Essential, Recommended*

Ah, Wilderness (1935, B&W, 101m, NR)
Eugene O'Neill's comedy-drama of a small town adolescent's coming of age. Lionel Barrymore and Wallace Beery head the cast, with Aline MacMahon, Eric Linden, and Mickey Rooney. **DR26, ST189, WR25**

Aida (1953, C, 96m, NR)
Screen version of the famed opera, starring Sophia Loren (with her singing voice dubbed). **ST141**

Air America (1990, C, 112m, R)
Mel Gibson and Robert Downey, Jr., are pilots involved in CIA-sponsored smuggling in Laos during the Vietnam War. Action comedy scores some political points about America's covert activities during the war. **AC4, AC11, CO2, CO9, ST85**

Air Force (1943, B&W, 124m, NR)
Howard Hawks's World War II drama about bomber crew action in Pearl Harbor, Manila, and the Coral Sea. John Garfield, John Ridgely, Gig Young, and Arthur Kennedy star. **AC1, DT53, ST80**

Air Raid Wardens (1943, B&W, 67m, NR)
Laurel and Hardy homefront comedy, with Edgar Kennedy, Jacqueline White, and Horace (Stephen) McNally. **ST133**

Airplane! (1980, C, 88m, PG)
Spoof of disaster movies (and the *Airport* series in particular), with a joke every four seconds, most of them quite funny. Robert Hays and Julie Hagerty star, with Lloyd Bridges, Peter Graves, Robert Stack, Leslie Nielsen, Kareem Abdul-Jabbar, and many guests. **CO7,** *Recommended*

Airplane II: The Sequel (1982, C, 85m, PG)
Follow-up to *Airplane!* with same joke ratio, plus Robert Hays, Julie Hagerty, Lloyd Bridges, Peter Graves, William Shatner, and Rip Torn in a small role. **CO7, ST216**

Airport (1970, C, 137m, G)
Original Disaster in the Sky adventure, with snowed-in runways, bomb-crippled planes, cute stowaways, and an all-star cast: Burt Lancaster, Dean Martin, George Kennedy, Helen Hayes (an Oscar winner), Van Heflin, Jacqueline Bisset, and Jean Seberg. **AC23, ST129, ST149, XT5**

Airport 1975 (1974, C, 106m, PG)
Second *Airport* film has Charlton Heston at the controls, Karen Black as a stewardess, and a passenger list including Helen Reddy (as a singing nun), Gloria Swanson (as herself), Myrna Loy, and Linda Blair. **AC23, ST142**

Airport '79 see *Concorde, The—Airport '79*

Airport '77 (1977, C, 113m, PG)
The third edition of the Unfriendly Skies finds James Stewart's luxury jetliner in the ocean with pilot Jack Lemmon attempting a rescue. Lee Grant, Brenda Vaccaro, George Kennedy, Joseph Cotten, Olivia de Havilland, Christopher Lee, and many more appear. **AC23, ST49, ST135, ST138, ST207**

Akira (1988, C, 124m, NR)
Japanese animated film follows the exploits of motorcycle-riding teen-aged gangs in a post-apocalypse Tokyo. Cult following for its violence. Strictly for fans of the genre. **CU7, FF4, SF12, SF18**

Akira Kurosawa's Dreams (1990, C, 120m, PG)
Japan's master director offers eight episodes drawn from his own nighttime musings. Akira Terao, Mitsunori Isaki, and Martin Scorsese (as Vincent Van Gogh) are among the actors. Available in letterboxed format. **CU19, DT69, DT114**

Al Capone (1959, B&W, 105m, NR)
Rod Steiger plays Scarface in this bullet-riddled film biography. With Fay Spain, James Gregory, and Martin Balsam. **AC22**

Aladdin (1987, C, 95m, NR)
An updated version of the magic lamp tale, with Bud Spencer starring as the genie summoned by a boy who finds the lamp in a junk shop. **FA8**

Aladdin (1992, C, 90m, G)
Spectacular Disney animation and Robin Williams's show-stealing voice characterizations as the Genie enliven this familiar tale of the young thief and his bottled servant. Scott Weinger and Brad Kane provide the voice of Aladdin, Linda Larkin and Lea Salonga the Princess Jasmine. **FA2, ST228,** *Recommended*

Aladdin and His Wonderful Lamp
(1985, C, 60m, NR)
Robert Carradine is the young man at odds with a wicked magician (Leonard Nimoy) until a powerful genie (James Earl Jones) and a beautiful princess appear before him. From the Faerie Tale Theatre series. Directed by Tim Burton. **FA12, DT20, ST118**

Alakazam the Great (1961, C, 84m, NR)
Animated adventure of a monkey who's made King of the Animals. Voices by Jonathan Winters, Frankie Avalon, Arnold Stang, and Sterling Holloway. **FA10**

Alamo, The (1960, C, 161m, NR)
The legendary battle of a small band of Texans against the Mexican army, directed by and starring John Wayne as Davy Crockett. With Richard Widmark, Laurence Harvey, Chill Wills, and Frankie Avalon. Now available in a letterboxed edition on two cassettes, with overture and entr'acte music by Dimitri Tiomkin. **CU19, MU12, ST224, WE1**

Alamo Bay (1985, C, 98m, R)
Texas fishermen clash with Vietnamese immigrants trying to make a living in the same waters. Amy Madigan and Ed Harris star in this topical drama directed by Louis Malle. Music by Ry Cooder. **DR7, DT82**

Alan & Naomi (1992, C, 96m, PG)
Gentle drama set in 1944 Brooklyn of a young Jewish boy befriending an immigrant girl traumatized after seeing her parents murdered by the Nazis. Lukas Haas and Vanessa Zaoui star, with Michael Gross and Amy Aquino. **DR5, DR9**

Albino (1976, C, 85m, NR)
A murderous albino stalks beautiful women. Christopher Lee and Trevor Howard star. **ST135**

Alexander Nevsky (1938, B&W, 107m, NR)
Stirring historical drama about Russia's defense in the thirteenth century against German forces. Directed by Sergei Eisenstein;

music by Sergei Prokofiev. The battle on the ice is one of the great speactacles of all film history. **DT41,** *Essential, Recommended*

Alexander the Great (1956, C, 141m, NR)
Richard Burton plays the great conqueror in this adventure drama. Fredric March, Claire Bloom, and Peter Cushing costar. Directed by Robert Rossen. **AC16, ST22, ST43, ST148**

Alfie (1966, C, 114m, NR)
Michael Caine, in his breakthrough role, is a roguish ladies' man in this British comedy with Jane Asher, Shelley Winters, and Millicent Martin. **CO17, ST25, ST232,** *Recommended*

Algiers (1938, B&W, 95m, NR)
Classic romance stars Charles Boyer as Pepe Le Moko, who falls for a spoiled little rich girl (Hedy Lamarr) on her visit to the Casbah district of Algiers. **CL4, ST16**

Ali—Fear Eats the Soul
(1974, C, 94m, NR)
A German widow in her sixties marries an Arab man thirty years younger. Rainer Werner Fassbinder directed this drama; he also plays a small role. **DT42**

Alias Bulldog Drummond see *Bulldog Jack*

Alice (1990, C, 106m, PG-13)
Mia Farrow is a lapsed Catholic, the wife of a wealthy Manhattan lawyer (William Hurt), a woman whose empty life needs something. At first she thinks that means taking a lover (Joe Mantegna). Woody Allen wrote and directed this very loose remake of Fellini's *Juliet of the Spirits,* and like most of his recent films, it has its moments—but not many. With Alec Baldwin, Blythe Danner, Judy Davis, Keye Luke (as a medicine man), Bernadette Peters, and Cybill Shepherd. **CO2, DR10, DT2, ST46, ST65, ST114, XT9, XT30**

Alice Adams (1935, B&W, 99m, NR)
Booth Tarkington's comedy features Katharine Hepburn as a social climber who finds true happiness with a modest young man (Fred MacMurray). Directed by George Stevens. **CL1, CL5, DT119, ST103**

Alice Doesn't Live Here Anymore
(1974, C, 113m, PG)
A New Mexico housewife, suddenly widowed, decides to move with her adolescent son to California, where she can pursue her ambition to be a professional singer. Oscar winner Ellen Burstyn stars in this superbly crafted comedy-drama, with Kris Kristofferson, Diane Ladd, Alfred Lutter, and Jodie Foster. Written by Robert Getchell; directed by

Martin Scorsese. **DR10, DT114, MU12, ST75, XT3, XT18,** *Recommended*

Alice in the Cities (1974, B&W, 110m, NR)
Drama of the friendship between an American journalist and an abandoned nine-year-old German girl. Directed by Wim Wenders. **DT136**

Alice in Wonderland (1951, C, 75m, G)
Disney animation brings Lewis Carroll's enchanting classic to life as Alice ventures through the looking glass to discover a world of colorful and frightening characters. **FA2, FA3,** *Recommended*

Alice's Adventures in Wonderland (1973, C, 97m, G)
Live-action version of the Lewis Carroll story, filmed in England with a cast that features Peter Sellers, Dudley Moore, Ralph Richardson, and Spike Milligan. **FA3, ST160, ST184, ST198**

Alice's Restaurant (1969, C, 111m, PG)
Arlo Guthrie's famed song about a disastrous Thanksgiving Day and his problems with the draft is the basis for this amiable comedy-drama. Guthrie stars, with Pat Quinn and James Broderick. Directed by Arthur Penn. Some good moments, but pace flags too often. **DR7, DT96**

Alien (1979, C, 116m, R)
Science fiction horror classic about life form invading spaceship and destroying the crew one by one. Sigourney Weaver stars, with Yaphet Kotto, Ian Holm, Veronica Cartwright, Harry Dean Stanton, and John Hurt. Directed by Ridley Scott; Oscar winner for special effects. As scary as movies get. **DT115, SF3, SF15, SF20, ST205, ST225,** *Essential, Recommended*

Alien Massacre see *Dr. Terror's Gallery of Horrors*

Alien Nation (1988, C, 96m, R)
In Los Angeles in the near future, a race of aliens resembling humans have become the new minority immigrant problem. An alien cop (Mandy Patinkin) and his human partner (James Caan) team up to uncover a criminal conspiracy within the alien community. **SF17**

Alien Predators (1987, C, 92m, R)
A trio of Americans visiting Spain help a scientist control an alien invasion which has taken over a small town. Martin Hewitt, Dennis Christopher, and Lynn-Holly Johnson star. **SF20**

Alien³ (1992, C, 115m, R)
Third in the sci-fi/horror tale of the baddest

alien creature of them all has Sigourney Weaver back as Ripley, battling her nemesis on a penal colony planet. With Charles S. Dutton, Charles Dance, Paul McGann, and Lance Henriksen. Directed by David Fincher. Dark, brooding, the least appealing of the trilogy. **SF3, SF20, ST225**

Aliens (1986, C, 135m, R)
Smashing sequel to *Alien*, with survivor Sigourney Weaver returning to hunt down queen mother of creature from first film. Superb blend of action and suspense from director James Cameron. With Michael Biehn, Lance Henriksen, and Paul Reiser. **DT21, SF3, SF20, ST225,** *Recommended*

Alive (1993, C, 127m, R)
True story of 1972 Andes air crash of a plane carrying members of an Uruguayan rugby club and how some survived, resorting to cannibalizing the corpses. Ethan Hawke, Vincent Spano, and Josh Hamilton star, with John Malkovich in a bit part. Based on Piers Paul Read's outstanding book. Directed by Frank Marshall. **AC12, AC24, DR6**

All About Eve (1950, B&W, 138m, NR)
Witty, Oscar-winning look at life in the theater, with ambitious ingenue (Anne Baxter) trying to upstage aging but still formidable veteran (Bette Davis). With Oscar winner George Sanders, Gary Merrill, Celeste Holm, Thelma Ritter, and Marilyn Monroe. Joseph L. Mankiewicz won Oscars for both his direction and original screenplay. Ritter should have won an Oscar. **CL7, DT84, ST44, ST159, XT1, XT4, XT6, XT28** *Essential, Highly Recommended*

All-American Murder (1992, C, 93m, R)
Mystery, laced with dark humor, of college student (Charlie Schlatter) accused of killing a coed, given a chance to investigate the case by a strange cop (Christopher Walken). With Josie Bissett, Richard Kind, and Joanna Cassidy. Wirtten by Barry Sandler. **DR25, MY7, ST222**

All Creatures Great and Small (1974, C, 92m, NR)
Drama adapted from James Herriot's autobiography, following the veterinarian's career from his apprenticeship to an established practice in England's lush countryside. Simon Ward and Anthony Hopkins star. Originally made for TV. **DR4, FA5, ST109**

All Dogs Go to Heaven (1989, C, 87m, G)
A junkyard dog gets a second chance at life with a new owner, a little girl who can predict the outcome of horse races. Among the character voices in this animated feature are

Burt Reynolds, Dom DeLuise, and Judith Barsi. **FA10, ST183**

All Fall Down (1962, B&W, 110m, NR)
Intense drama of self-absorbed young man (Warren Beatty) and his effect on his family and the woman who loves him. With Eva Marie Saint, Brandon de Wilde, Karl Malden, and Angela Lansbury. Written by William Inge, directed by John Frankenheimer. Early Beatty, already revealing his charismatic screen presence. **DR8, ST10, ST131,** *Recommended*

All I Want for Christmas
(1991, C, 92m, G)
A thirteen-year-old boy (Ethan Randall) and his seven-year-old sister (Thora Birch) try to reunite their divorced parents (Harley Jane Kozak and Jamey Sheridan) for the holidays. **FA13**

All in a Night's Work (1961, C, 94m, NR)
An office worker is victimized by a misunderstanding involving a respectable businessman. Comedy starring Shirley MacLaine and Dean Martin. **ST145. ST149**

All My Sons (1986, C, 122m, NR)
Adaptation of Arthur Miller's play about a family trying to deal with the loss of a son in World War II. James Whitmore, Aidan Quinn, Joan Allen, and Michael Learned star. Originally made for TV. **DR8, DR20**

All Night Long (1981, C, 88m, R)
A middle-aged manager of an all-night drug store falls in love with his neighbor's wife in this romantic comedy starring Gene Hackman, Barbra Streisand, and Dennis Quaid. **CO1, ST96, ST211**

All of Me (1984, C, 93m, PG-13)
A swinging lawyer finds half his body possessed by a ditsy spinster in this frantic and consistently enjoyable comedy. Steve Martin (never better) and Lily Tomlin star, with Victoria Tennant, Richard Libertini, Selma Diamond, and Jason Bernard. **CO3, CO20, ST150, ST215, XT24,** *Highly Recommended*

All Quiet on the Western Front
(1930, B&W, 130m, NR)
Harrowing, moving drama of German youth and his disillusionment during World War I combat. Lew Ayres stars. Oscar winner Lewis Milestone directed. An antiwar classic that won the Academy Award for Best Picture. **AC2, XT1, XT6, XT25,** *Essential, Highly Recommended*

All Screwed Up (1976, C, 105m, PG)
Comedy-drama of two Italian farmers who move to the city and have problems adjusting to urban life. Directed by Lina Wertmuller. **DT137**

All-Star Salute to the Improv
(1988, C, 60m, NR)
Robert Klein hosts this collection of bits from fellow comics who got career boosts from appearances at the famed Hollywood club. Among the stars: Billy Crystal, Robin Williams, Richard Lewis, and Martin Mull. Originally made for cable TV. **CO13, CO16, ST228**

All That Jazz (1979, C, 123m, R)
Bob Fosse's autobiographical musical drama about a director-choreographer juggling too many balls in his professional and personal life. Roy Scheider stars, with Ann Reinking, Jessica Lange, Leland Palmer, Cliff Gorman, and Ben Vereen. Sensational dance numbers. **DT47, MU3, MU4, ST130,** *Recommended*

All the King's Men (1949, B&W, 109m, NR)
Superbly drawn portrait of a Southern politician whose idealism is corrupted into demagoguery. Oscar winner for Best Picture, Actor (Broderick Crawford), Supporting Actress (Mercedes McCambridge, in her film debut), and Screenplay Adaptation (by director Robert Rossen). Based on Robert Penn Warren's novel, which mirrored the career of Louisiana's Huey Long. **DR19, DR21, XT1, XT2, XT5,** *Essential, Recommended*

All the Marbles (1981, C, 113m, R)
Raucous comedy set in the world of ladies' professional wrestling, featuring a lovely tag team (Laurene Landon and Vicki Frederick) and their unscrupulous manager (Peter Falk). Robert Aldrich directed. **CO19, DT1**

All the President's Men
(1976, C, 138m, PG)
Robert Redford and Dustin Hoffman play the real-life *Washington Post* reporters who uncovered the Watergate scandal. With Martin Balsam, Jack Warden, Jane Alexander, Hal Holbrook, and Oscar winner Jason Robards as Ben Bradlee. Directed by Alan J. Pakula; adapted by William Goldman. As gripping an experience as if you've never heard a word about Watergate. Pakula should have won the Oscar. Widescreen cinematography by Gordon Willis will be lost on video. **CU20, DR6, DR21, DT94, MY6, ST105, ST181, ST185, XT4, XT12, XT28,** *Essential, Highly Recommended*

All the Right Moves (1983, C, 91m, R)
In a small town in Pennsylvania, a high school football star breaks with his coach and finds that he's being shut out of a college scholarship—his only way out of the

depressed town. Tom Cruise, Craig T. Nelson, and Lea Thompson star. **DR9, DR22, DR26, ST41,** *Recommended*

All the Vermeers in New York
(1992, C, 87m, NR)
Drama of stockbroker and a French woman, set against the art and financial worlds of Manhattan. Stephen Lack and Emmanuelle Chaulet star. Directed by Jon Jost. Available in letterboxed edition. **CU19, DR7, DR15, XT9**

All the Way, Boys (1973, C, 105m, PG)
Terence Hill and Bud Spencer star in this Italian comedy about two go-for-broke adventurers flying a decrepit airplane through the Andes. **FF2**

All the Young Men (1960, B&W, 87m, NR)
Standard-issue Korean War drama starring Alan Ladd, Sidney Poitier, James Darren, and Mort Sahl. **AC3, ST128, ST174**

All This and Heaven Too
(1940, B&W, 143m, NR)
Drama set in nineteenth-century France finds Bette Davis as a governess involved in a scandalous relationship with her aristocrat employer (Charles Boyer). **ST16, ST44**

All Through the Night
(1942, B&W, 107m, NR)
Humphrey Bogart's a New York gangster playing the right side of the law when he and his men take on Nazi spies. Conrad Veidt, Peter Lorre, and Judith Anderson play Bogie's foes; also in the cast are Jane Darwell, Frank McHugh, Jackie Gleason, and Phil Silvers, the latter duo supplying some comic moments. **MY6, ST15**

All You Need Is Cash (1978, C, 70m, NR)
The Beatles are spoofed in this rockumentary about a popular British rock group called The Rutles. Monty Python's Eric Idle heads the cast of loonies; watch for Dan Aykroyd, John Belushi, and Gilda Radner among the bit players. Also known as *The Rutles;* originally made for TV. **CO8, CO13, CO15, XT26,** *Recommended*

Allan Quatermain and the Lost City of Gold (1986, C, 100m, PG)
Sequel to the latest version of *King Solomon's Mines* has title hero (Richard Chamberlain) on the trail of a legendary city, battling restless natives, hungry crocodiles, and other obstacles. With Sharon Stone and James Earl Jones. **AC21, ST118**

Allegheny Uprising (1939, B&W, 81m, NR)
This action saga of colonial America teams John Wayne with Claire Trevor against a British Army officer. **AC6, ST224**

Alligator (1980, C, 94m, R)
A pet alligator is flushed down the toilet; in the sewer system he grows into a monster and begins to terrorize the city. Tongue-in-cheek horror written by John Sayles, who also has a small role. Robert Forster stars, with Robin Riker, Michael Gazzo, Dean Jagger, and Jack Carter. Sayles's script is the star; worth a look for genre fans. **DT112, HO16**

Alligator Eyes (1990, C, 101m, R)
Moody thriller about three friends traveling from New York to North Carolina, picking up a mysterious hitchhiking woman (Annabelle Larsen) who is blind. Written and directed by John Feldman. **MY4, XT18**

Allonsanfan (1974, C, 117m, NR)
Comedy set in early nineteenth-century Italy about a group of idealists living in the not-so-distant past. Marcello Mastroianni stars; directed by Paolo and Vittorio Taviani. **FF2, ST154**

Almost an Angel (1990, C, 97m, PG)
Paul Hogan wrote this family comedy in which he plays an ex-con who saves a man's life only to be killed; he's sent back to Earth as an angel. With Linda Kozlowski and, as God, Charlton Heston. **FA6, XT24**

Almost Angels (1962, C, 93m, G)
Disney drama of young singer in the Vienna Boys' Choir whose voice is beginning to change. **FA1**

Almost Perfect Affair, An
(1979, C, 93m, PG)
A young American filmmaker, on his first trip to the Cannes Film Festival, has a fling with the bored wife of an Italian producer. Keith Carradine and Monica Vitti star, with Raf Vallone. Directed by Michael Ritchie. **DR13**

Almost You (1984, C, 96m, R)
Romantic comedy, with a New York woman questioning her marriage after she's injured in an auto accident. Brooke Adams and Griffin Dunne star. **CO1**

Alone in the Dark (1982, C, 92m, R)
Three psychopaths escape from an asylum and seek revenge on their psychiatrist. Jack Palance, Donald Pleasence, and Martin Landau star. **HO9**

Along Came Jones (1945, B&W, 90m, NR)
A Western comedy with Gary Cooper as a cowboy who's the victim of mistaken identity. Loretta Young costars. **ST37, WE14**

Along the Great Divide
(1951, B&W, 88m, NR)
Kirk Douglas is a Western lawman trying to

bring in a fugitive through a blinding sand-storm. Directed by Raoul Walsh. **DT131, ST57**

Along the Navajo Trail
(1945, B&W, 66m, NR)
Roy Rogers and Gabby Hayes ride to protect innocent ranchers. With Dale Evans. **ST188**

Alpha Beta (1973, C, 67m, NR)
Albert Finney and Rachel Roberts play a couple whose marriage is slowly disintegrating. **ST68**

Alphabet City (1984, C, 98m, R)
Drama of life on New York's Lower East Side, where the mean streets are lettered—thus, the title. Vincent Spano stars. **DR15**

Alphabet Murders, The
(1966, B&W, 90m, NR)
Tony Randall plays Agatha Christie's sleuth Hercule Poirot; he's on the trail of a killer with a victim list that reveals he is working his way through the alphabet. Frank Tashlin wrote this comic mystery. Margaret Rutherford appears briefly as Miss Marple. **MY12, MY15, WR3**

Alphaville (1965, B&W, 100m, NR)
French science fiction thriller, with Eddie Constantine as a detective trying to rescue a kidnapped scientist. Directed by Jean-Luc Godard. **DT50, SF19**

Alsino and the Condor (1982, C, 89m, R)
From Nicaragua, a drama of a young crippled boy who finds self-esteem fighting with a guerrilla band. Directed by Miguel Littin. Dean Stockwell stars. **FF6, ST208**

Altered States (1980, C, 103m, R)
Scientist lets his experiments in primal research overwhelm him. William Hurt stars, with Blair Brown, Charles Haid, and Bob Balaban. Science fiction film packed with dazzling imagery from director Ken Russell. Paddy Chayevsky scripted but had his name removed in dispute with director. The writer's penchant for bombast does remain. Worth a look for followers of the principals. **CU3, CU4, DT111, SF5, SF20, ST114**

Alvarez Kelly (1966, C, 116m, NR)
In this Civil War Western, William Holden and Richard Widmark are on opposite sides of the conflict. **ST106, WE6**

Always (1989, C, 121m, PG)
Remake of *A Guy Named Joe*, updating that fantasy-drama's setting to contemporary Montana. A fire-fighting pilot (Richard Dreyfuss) returns after his death to encourage a young pilot (Brad Johnson) who begins romancing the dead man's girl (Holly Hunter). With John Goodman and Audrey Hepburn. Directed by Steven Spielberg. Available only in letterboxed format. Heartfelt moments, although the director can't resist smothering them in production values. **CU18, CU19, DR1, DT118, ST60, ST102, ST113, XT24**, *Recommended*

Always for Pleasure (1979, C, 58m, NR)
Documentary portrait of New Orleans' Mardi Gras scene, with emphasis on the music; directed by Les Blank. **CU16**

Amadeus (1984, C, 158m, PG)
Oscar-winning film portrait of Wolfgang Amadeus Mozart, the brilliant and irritatingly immature composer, as told by his arch-rival Antonio Salieri. Thomas Hulce and F. Murray Abraham star under Milos Forman's direction. Abraham and Forman also won Oscars. Glorious use of Mozart music. **DT45, MU5, XT1, XT2, XT6**, *Recommended*

Amarcord (1974, C, 127m, PG)
Federico Fellini's comic memoir of his youth in a seaside village is full of memorable characters and classic moments. Oscar winner for Best Foreign Language Film; arguably Fellini's best work. **DT43, XT7**, *Essential, Highly Recommended*

Amateur, The (1982, C, 111m, R)
A computer operator (John Savage) swears revenge on the terrorists who murdered his girlfriend. **MY6**

Amazing Adventure
(1936, B&W, 70m, NR)
On a bet, a wealthy man joins the working class to prove that his skills are worthy of a real job. Cary Grant stars in this British comedy. Original title: *The Amazing Quest of Ernest Bliss*. Released in the U.S. as *Romance and Riches*. **ST92**

Amazing Dobermans, The
(1976, C, 94m, PG)
Fred Astaire plays a former con man whose trained Dobermans help stop a gang of racketeers. **FA5, ST4**

Amazing Grace and Chuck
(1987, C, 115m, PG)
A young boy gains international fame when he refuses to pitch in his Little League games to protest the arms race. Joshua Zuehlke stars, with Gregory Peck, Jamie Lee Curtis, and pro basketball player Alex English. **DR7, FA7, ST42, ST171**

Amazing Howard Hughes, The
(1977, C, 119m, NR)
Dramatization of the life of the aviation pioneer/movie producer/casino owner/legendary lover, starring Tommy Lee Jones, with Ed Flanders as Noah Dietrich and Tovah Feld-

shuh as Katharine Hepburn. Originally made for TV; shown at 215 minutes. **DR4, DR24**

Amazing Mr. Blunden, The
(1972, C, 100m, PG)
Two children travel in time with the help of a friendly ghost. Lynne Frederick and Garry Miller star in this family adventure with Laurence Naismith. **FA4**

Amazing Quest of Ernest Bliss, The
see *Amazing Adventure*

Amazon (1992, C, 88m, R)
Adventure tale, with pro–rain forest message, about a Finnish businessman and his daughter stranded in the Brazil backcountry, rescued by a bush pilot. Kari Väänänen, Robert Davi, and Rae Dawn Chong star. Widescreen photography will be lost on video unless letterboxed. **AC12, DR7**

Amazon Women on the Moon
(1987, C, 85m, R)
Catch-all parody of late-night TV movies and commercials, with series of skits featuring lots of stars (Rosanna Arquette, Michelle Pfeiffer, Griffin Dunne, Steve Allen, Henny Youngman, Arsenio Hall, Carrie Fisher, and Paul Bartel). Joe Dante, Carl Gottlieb, Peter Horton, John Landis, and Robert K. Weiss directed. **C07, DT8, DT33, ST173**

Amazons, The (1984, C, 100m, NR)
A woman doctor uncovers an underground organization of females out to topple the male power structure. Tamara Dobson stars, with Jack Scalia, Stella Stevens, Madeleine Stowe, and Jennifer Warren. Originally made for TV. **ST209**

Ambassador, The (1984, C, 97m, R)
Robert Mitchum plays an American diplomat in Israel caught up in the Palestinian problem. With Rock Hudson, Ellen Burstyn, and Donald Pleasence. Loosely based on Elmore Leonard's crime novel, *52 Pick-Up*. **ST112, ST158, WR19**

Ambassador's Daughter, The
(1956, C, 100m, NR)
Romance of title character wooed by soldier in Paris, starring Olivia de Havilland and John Forsythe. With Myrna Loy, Adolphe Menjou, and Edward Arnold. **ST49, ST142**

Amber Waves (1980, C, 105m, NR)
Drama of a farmer (Dennis Weaver) and male model (Kurt Russell) stuck in a small town, exchanging views of the state of the nation. Mare Winningham won an Emmy for her supporting performance in this made-for-TV film. **DR7, DR26, ST191**

Ambition (1991, C, 100m, R)
A writer plays a deadly game of cat-and-mouse with a recently paroled killer. Lou Diamond Phillips and Clancy Brown star; Phillips wrote the screenplay. **MY9**

Ambushers, The (1968, C, 102m, NR)
Third in the *Matt Helm* spy spoof series, with Dean Martin out to protect the first U.S. flying saucer from sabotage. With Senta Berger, Janice Rule, James Gregory, and Albert Salmi. **C09, ST149**

America at the Movies
(1976, C/B&W, 116m, NR)
Compilation of scenes from over eighty movie classics, produced by the American Film Institute. **CU16**

American Anthem (1986, C, 100m, PG-13)
Gymnast Mitch Gaylord stars in this flashy drama about the triumphs and heartbreak of competitive gymnastics. **DR22**

American Autobahn (1984, C, 90m, NR)
A journalist uncovers a story on a weapons ring and takes to the road with the baddies in hot pursuit. Jan Jalanek, Michael von der Goltz, and Jim Jarmusch star. **DT62, XT18**

American Commandos (1985, C, 88m, R)
An ex-Green Beret returns to Southeast Asia to carry on the war against deadly drug dealers. Christopher Mitchum stars. **AC20**

American Dream (1981, C, 74m, NR)
Pilot film for TV series about a family who moves from a wealthy Chicago suburb to a racially mixed city neighborhood. Stephen Macht and Karen Carlson star, with Michael Hershewe, Hans Conried, John McIntire, and John Malkovich. **DR8, DR15, ST147**

American Dream (1992, C, 100m, PG-13)
Oscar-winning documentary about a mid-1980s strike against a Minnesota meat-packing plant. Brilliantly shows how workers were squeezed by both the company and the national union leadership, which both wanted a quick solution to the dispute. A sobering portrait of life for the working man in Reagan-era America. Directed by Barbara Kopple. **CU16,** *Highly Recommended*

American Dreamer (1984, C, 105m, PG)
New Jersey housewife wins trip to Paris, finds herself involved in international intrigue and with a dashing Englishman. JoBeth Williams and Tom Conti star. **AC14, CO1, XT16**

American Flyers (1985, C, 113m, PG-13)
Two estranged brothers are reunited when they enter a grueling bicycle race, only to have one of them fall critically ill. Kevin Costner and David Grant star, with Alex-

andra Paul and Rae Dawn Chong. **DR22, ST38**

American Friend, The
(1977, C, 127m, NR)
From director Wim Wenders comes this suspense story about an innocent German picture framer hired to kill a gangster. Bruno Ganz and Dennis Hopper star; film directors Nicholas Ray and Samuel Fuller have small roles. Based on a novel by Patricia Highsmith. A film that seems to be more about filmmaking than telling a story. **DT49, DT101, DT136, MY2, MY16, ST110**

American Gigolo (1980, C, 117m, R)
Hollywood hustler is set up for murder, turns to the woman he really loves for help. Richard Gere and Lauren Hutton star. Paul Schrader directed. Cold, heartless, but a real starmaker for Gere. **DR3, ST84**

American Graffiti (1973, C, 112m, PG)
Cruising in a small California town, 1962; a nostalgic comedy with a cast full of future stars. Ron Howard, Richard Dreyfuss, Cindy Williams, Charles Martin Smith, Paul LeMat, and Candy Clark star, with Mackenzie Phillips, Harrison Ford, Bo Hopkins, Suzanne Somers, and Wolfman Jack. George Lucas directed. Wall-to-wall rock soundtrack almost steals the show. Widescreen cinematography will be lost on video. **C04, C06, CU17, CU20, DT58, DT77, ST60, ST74,** *Essential, Recommended*

American in Paris, An
(1951, C, 113m, NR)
Artist Gene Kelly goes to the City of Light for inspiration and meets a young Parisian dancer (Leslie Caron). Winner of seven Academy Awards, including Best Picture, features an all-Gershwin score. Directed by Vincente Minnelli. **DT88, MU1, MU7, ST123, XT1,** *Essential, Recommended*

American Madness (1932, B&W, 81m, NR)
Melodramatic but effective drama of Depression-era bank scandal that leads to depositor run and near disaster. Walter Huston stars, with Pat O'Brien, Kay Johnson, and Constance Cummings. Directed by Frank Capra. One of his unjustly neglected films, with a dynamic performance by Walter Huston. UNAVAILABLE ON VIDEO. **XT29**

American Me (1992, C, 125m, R)
Edward James Olmos plays a crime boss in L.A.'s Mexican Mafia in this true story. With William Forsythe, Pepe Serna, Danny De La Paz, Daniel Villareal, and Evelina Fernandez. Large portion of story shot in Folsom Prison. Olmos directed. Brutal cautionary story

doesn't pull punches or glamorize its characters. **AC8, AC22, DR6, DR7, DR16, DR18, XT23,** *Recommended*

American Ninja (1985, C, 95m, R)
Michael Dudikoff stars in this martial arts adventure about an American battling an international arms dealer and his renegade army. Steve James costars. **AC26**

American Ninja 2: The Confrontation
(1987, C, 90m, R)
More martial arts action with Michael Dudikoff and Steve James up against an army of warriors programmed by a madman. **AC26**

American Ninja 3: Blood Hunt
(1989, C, 90m, R)
David Bradley takes over from Michael Dudikoff in this popular martial arts series. This chapter once again takes place at a tournament on a tropical island controlled by a madman (Marjoe Gortner). Steve James costars. **AC26**

American Soldier, The (1970, C, 80m, NR)
Early film from German director Rainer Werner Fassbinder about a hit man stars Karl Scheydt and Elga Sorbas. The director has a small role. **DT42**

American Tail, An (1986, C, 80m, G)
Fievel the mouse emigrates with his family from the Old World to a new life in America. He encounters many adventures along the way in this animated production. **FA10**

American Tail: Fievel Goes West, An
(1991, C, 74m, G)
Sequel has the resourceful rodent journeying to the frontier. Philip Glasser provides the voice of Fievel, with James Stewart as Wyatt Burp, plus Amy Irving and John Cleese. **C015, FA10, ST207**

American Werewolf in London, An
(1981, C, 95m, R)
Two Americans backpacking across the English moors are attacked by a werewolf; one is killed and one becomes a werewolf, in a series of elaborate transformation scenes. David Naughton, Griffin Dunne, and Jenny Agutter star. Directed by John Landis, who gives the story unexpected jolts of dark humor. Ground-breaking makeup effects by Rick Baker. **HO4, HO24, SF16, XT15, XT26,** *Recommended*

Americana (1981, C, 91m, PG)
David Carradine directed this moody tale of a Vietnam vet rebuilding a small town's merry-go-round. The director stars with Barbara Hershey. Filmed in 1973. **DR26, ST104, XT23**

Americanization of Emily, The
(1964, B&W, 117m, NR)
Acidic comedy-drama of the U.S. Army's attempts to ensure that an American (James Garner) is the first man to hit the Normandy beaches on D-Day. Meanwhile, he's involved in an up-and-down affair with a British woman (Julie Andrews). With Melvyn Douglas and James Coburn. Written by Paddy Chayefsky. **AC1, DR1, ST2, ST58, ST82, XT25**

Americano, The (1955, C, 85m, NR)
A cowboy (Glenn Ford) travels to Brazil with a herd of cattle, unaware that the rancher he's delivering them to has been murdered. **WE9**

Amityville Horror, The (1979, C, 117m, R)
A family moves into their dream house, which turns out to be haunted. Based on an allegedly true story. James Brolin, Margot Kidder, and Rod Steiger star. **HO3, HO19**

Amityville II: The Possession
(1982, C, 104m, R)
A prequel to *The Amityville Horror* chronicles the events leading to the possession of the eldest son and his slaughter of the rest of the family. Burt Young and Rutanya Alda star. **HO3**

Amityville 3-D (1983, C, 105m, PG)
Two journalists and a parapsychologist inhabit the Amityville house to find out once and for all if the house is haunted. Tony Roberts, Candy Clark, and Tess Harper star. **HO3**

Amos (1985, C, 100m, NR)
A seventy-year-old man in a nursing home and a nurse engage in a clash of wills. Kirk Douglas and Elizabeth Montgomery star in this drama originally shown on TV. **DR11, ST57**

Amos & Andrew (1993, C, 94m, PG-13)
Comedy of black intellectual moving in to exclusive community, mistakenly arousing concern from neighbors, getting mixed up with petty criminal. Samuel L. Jackson and Nicolas Cage star, with Dabney Coleman, Michael Lerner, Margaret Colin, Brad Dourif, and Giancarlo Esposito. **CO2, CO3, ST23**

Amsterdam Kill, The (1977, C, 90m, R)
Thriller about the international drug trade stars Robert Mitchum as a retired agent back on the job. With Bradford Dillman, Richard Egan, and Leslie Nielsen. **ST158**

Amy (1981, C, 100m, G)
In the early 1900s, a headstrong woman decides to leave her husband and embark on a career of teaching handicapped children. Jenny Agutter stars in this Disney drama, with Barry Newman, Kathleen Nolan, and Nanette Fabray. **FA1**

Anastasia (1956, C, 105m, NR)
Ingrid Bergman won an Oscar for her performance as an amnesiac chosen to impersonate the long-lost daughter of Czar Nicholas of Russia. With Yul Brynner, Helen Hayes, and Akim Tamiroff. **CL3, ST13, XT3**

Anastasia: The Mystery of Anna
(1986, C, 190m, NR)
TV miniseries examines the claim by Anna Anderson to be the daughter of Czar Nicholas and Alexandra, a survivor of the Russian Revolution. Amy Irving stars, with Olivia de Havilland, Omar Sharif and Claire Bloom (as Nicholas and Alexandra), Elke Sommer, Susan Lucci, and Rex Harrison. **DR4, ST49**

Anatomy of a Murder
(1959, B&W, 160m, NR)
James Stewart is a small-town lawyer who defends an Army officer (Ben Gazzara) on charges that he murdered the man who raped his wife (Lee Remick). Memorable courtroom drama, with George C. Scott, Eve Arden, Kathryn Grant, Arthur O'Connell, and Joseph Welch. Directed by Otto Preminger (perhaps his best film). Music by Duke Ellington, who appears briefly as a pianist in a tavern band. Stewart and Preminger should have won Oscars. **DR17, DR26, DT100, ST196, ST207,** *Essential, Highly Recommended*

Anchors Aweigh (1945, C, 140m, NR)
Gene Kelly joins Frank Sinatra in a rousing musical about two sailor friends who fall for the same girl (Kathryn Grayson). With a very young Dean Stockwell. **MU1, ST123, ST199, ST208**

And Baby Makes Six (1979, C, 104m, NR)
A middle-aged couple (Warren Oates, Colleen Dewhurst) have mixed feelings when they learn they're about to have their fourth child. Originally made for TV. **ST166**

And God Created Woman
(1957, C, 92m, NR)
Brigitte Bardot's signature role: the Temptress of St. Tropez. Directed by Roger Vadim. Scandalous in its time, relatively tame now. **ST6**

And God Created Woman
(1988, C, 100m, R)
Director Roger Vadim offers a remake (in name only) of his erotic drama, this time with Rebecca De Mornay as the free-spirited young woman. Also available in a re-edited, unrated version, with additional sexy footage

added; running time: 98 minutes. **CU10, CU18**

And Hope to Die (1972, C, 99m, R)
Thriller with international cast (Robert Ryan, Tisa Farrow, Jean-Louis Trintignant, Lea Massari, and Aldo Ray) about a kidnap gang and their already dead target. Directed by René Clement. **MY16, ST193**

... And Justice for All (1979, C, 117m, R)
A Baltimore lawyer is asked to defend a corrupt judge on charges that he murdered a prostitute. Al Pacino and John Forsythe star, with Jack Warden and Christine Lahti. Directed by Norman Jewison; cowritten by Barry Levinson. Melodramatic to a fault. **DR15, DR17, DT63, ST170**

And Nothing But the Truth
(1982, C, 102m, NR)
British drama of TV journalists (Glenda Jackson, Jon Finch) at work on a big exposé about a multinational corporation. **DR7, DR23, ST117**

And Now for Something Completely Different (1972, C, 89m, PG)
Collection of classic bits by the Monty Python troupe. **CO15, Recommended**

And Now, My Love
(1975, C/B&W, 121m, PG)
French romantic drama about a wealthy woman (Marthe Keller) and rascal (André Dussolier) who manage to come together from widely different backgrounds. **FF1**

And Now the Screaming Starts
(1973, C, 87m, R)
An aristocratic family is cursed by a disembodied hand which is avenging the rape of a virgin servant girl. Peter Cushing, Ian Ogilvy, and Stephanie Beacham star. **HO26, ST43**

And the Ship Sails On
(1984, C, 138m, PG)
Federico Fellini parable set on a luxury liner cruise on the eve of World War I, with the usual assortment of Fellini grotesques and outrageous behavior. **DT43**

And Then There Were None
(1945, B&W, 98m, NR)
Ten visitors to a lonely island begin to disappear one by one. Barry Fitzgerald and Walter Huston star in this version of the Agatha Christie tale. Directed by René Clair. **DT25, MY15, WR3**

Anderson Tapes, The (1972, C, 98m, PG)
Thieves plan to rob apartments in a New York building over a summer holiday weekend. Sean Connery and Dyan Cannon star,

with Martin Balsam, Christopher Walken (his first film), and Garrett Morris. Directed by Sidney Lumet. Solid suspense, good use of locations. **AC9, DT78, MY18, ST36, ST222, XT9, Recommended**

Androcles and the Lion
(1952, B&W, 98m, NR)
George Bernard Shaw's fable of a Christian in ancient Rome who befriends a lion. Jean Simmons, Alan Young, Victor Mature, Elsa Lanchester, and Robert Newton star. **WR29**

Android (1982, C, 80m, PG)
Low-budget, resourceful, amusing science fiction drama starring Klaus Kinski as a mad scientist and Don Opper as the title creation. Many references to classic film *Metropolis*; directed by Aaron Lipstadt. **CU4, SF5, ST126, XT26, Recommended**

Andromeda Strain, The
(1971, C, 130m, G)
Deadly virus threatens to trigger nuclear disaster in this science fiction adventure from director Robert Wise. Arthur Hill, David Wayne, James Olson, and Kate Reid star. Based on a novel by Michael Crichton. Exciting, but not especially memorable. **DT140, SF5, SF7, SF8**

Andy Hardy Gets Spring Fever
(1939, B&W, 85m, NR)
Mickey Rooney plays that all-American boy who's up to his ears in trouble when he decides to produce his high school's annual play. **ST189**

Andy Hardy Meets Debutante
(1940, B&W, 89m, NR)
Mickey Rooney and Judy Garland star in this ninth installment of the long-running series. Andy takes on a Manhattan socialite. Judy sings two numbers. **CL15, ST81, ST189**

Andy Hardy's Double Life
(1942, B&W, 92m, NR)
More trouble for Andy (Mickey Rooney), as his romantic complications include Esther Williams. **ST189**

Andy Hardy's Private Secretary
(1940, B&W, 101m, NR)
Mickey Rooney's affable lad mixes it up with Kathryn Grayson. **ST189**

Andy Kaufman Sound Stage Special, The (1983, C, 60m, NR)
An hour of offbeat humor with the very unpredictable comedian, assisted by comic Elayne Boosler. **CO16**

Andy Warhol's Bad (1971, C, 100m, R)
Suburban housewife runs a hit man squad out of her home—and that's just for starters

in this movie that strives for outrageousness and bad taste at every turn. Carroll Baker, Perry King, Susan Tyrrell star. **CU12**

Andy Warhol's Dracula (1974, C, 93m, R) Campy horror film from producer Warhol and director Paul Morrissey about vampire who needs virgins to survive. Udo Kier and Joe Dallesandro star, with Vittorio De Sica. **CU4, DT37, DT90, HF7, HO5, HO24**

Andy Warhol's Frankenstein (1974, C, 94m, R) Gory update of the mad doctor story, produced by Warhol and directed by Paul Morrissey, originally shown in 3-D to disbelieving audiences. Not for viewers with weak stomachs. **CU4, DT90, HF10, HO20, HO24**

Angel (1984, C, 92m, R) Orphaned teen-ager goes to high school by day, but cruises Hollywood Boulevard as a prostitute at night, where she's befriended by a colorful collection of street characters. Donna Wilkes, Cliff Gorman, Susan Tyrrell, Dick Shawn, and Rory Calhoun star. **AC8**

Angel and the Badman (1947, B&W, 100m, NR) Western action and romance as a notorious gunslinger (John Wayne) mends his ways for the affections of a Quaker girl. **ST224**

Angel at My Table, An (1990, C, 158m, NR) True-life story of New Zealand writer Janet Frame, mistakenly diagnosed as a schizophrenic and institutionalized for eight years. Kerry Fox stars in this film originally shown in three parts on New Zealand TV. Directed by Jane Campion. Sometimes harrowing, always absorbing tale. **DR4, DR10, FF5,** *Recommended*

Angel Baby (1961, B&W, 97m, NR) Drama of traveling evangelist (Salome Jens), her promoter (George Hamilton), and his overbearing wife (Mercedes McCambridge). Burt Reynolds's film debut. **ST183**

Angel City (1980, C, 100m, NR) Drama of horrible conditions a family encounters in a migrant workers' camp. Ralph Waite and Paul Winfield star, with Jennifer Warren and Jennifer Jason Leigh. Originally made for TV. **DR7, ST136, ST230**

Angel Heart (1987, C, 113m, R) Detective thriller stars Mickey Rourke as a private eye hired to track down a missing singer, getting involved in a New Orleans voodoo cult. Robert De Niro and Lisa Bonet costar. An unrated version is also available, containing a few seconds of footage that

nearly got the film an "X" rating. Cheesy adaptation of William Hjortsberg's classy novel. **CU1, CU6, CU10, HO10, MY2, MY10, ST51, ST190, XT14**

Angel on My Shoulder (1946, B&W, 101m, NR) Fantasy story of dead criminal sent to Earth as a judge and his battles with Satan. Paul Muni stars. **HO10, SF2, XT24**

Angel on My Shoulder (1980, C, 100m, NR) Remake of classic fantasy stars Peter Strauss as a Chicago gangster, with Richard Kiley, Barbara Hershey, and Janis Paige. **HO10, ST104, XT24**

Angela (1977, C, 100m, NR) A middle-aged woman and younger man are attracted to one another, unaware that they're mother and son. Sophia Loren and Steve Railsback star, with John Huston. **DT60, ST141**

Angelo, My Love (1983, C, 115m, R) Robert Duvall directed this drama about a young gypsy hustler (Angelo Evans) which mixes staged scenes with real-life moments. **ST63**

Angels Over Broadway (1940, B&W, 80m, NR) Offbeat comedy from writer Ben Hecht and cinematographer Lee Garmes (they codirected). Douglas Fairbanks, Jr., plays a hustler trying to redeem himself. With Rita Hayworth, Thomas Mitchell, and John Qualen. **CU5, ST101**

Angels With Dirty Faces (1938, B&W, 97m, NR) Two childhood friends grow apart when one joins the clergy and the other becomes a gangster. James Cagney and Pat O'Brien star, with Humphrey Bogart, Ann Sheridan, and the Dead End Kids. Quintessential Warner Brothers 1930s blend of social realism and entertainment. Hokey but lots of fun; the Cagney death-row walk is not to be missed. **AC22, ST15, ST24,** *Essential, Recommended*

Angry Red Planet, The (1959, C, 83m, NR) Science fiction drama of trip to Mars, starring Gerald Mohr and Nora Hayden. **SF3**

Animal Behavior (1989, C, 90m, PG) A researcher and composer find love in this romantic drama starring Karen Allen and Armand Assante, with Holly Hunter. **ST113**

Animal Crackers (1930, B&W, 98m, NR) The Marx Brothers crash a party. Groucho sings "Hooray for Captain Spaulding." Margaret Dumont is appalled. **ST152**

Animal House see *National Lampoon's Animal House*

Animal Kingdom, The
(1932, B&W, 85m, NR)
Leslie Howard plays an artist who has to choose between two women: a free spirit and a conventional lady. With Ann Harding and Myrna Loy. **ST142**

Animalympics (1979, C, 80m, NR)
Feature cartoon with various members of the animal kingdom competing in sporting events. Billy Crystal, Gilda Radner, and Harry Shearer are among the actors supplying the voices. **CO13, FA10**

Ann Vickers (1933, B&W, 72m, NR)
Drama based on the Sinclair Lewis novel of a woman who becomes pregnant by a cad and is redeemed by a judge. Irene Dunne, Walter Huston, and Bruce Cabot star. **ST62, WR20**

Anna (1987, C, 101m, PG-13)
Drama of the relationship (à la *All About Eve*) between an aging Czech film star and her young protégée, both living in New York. Oscar nominee Sally Kirkland and Paulina Porizkova star. **DR10, DR13**

Anna Christie (1930, B&W, 90m, NR)
Adaptation of Eugene O'Neill's classic play finds Greta Garbo as a former prostitute whose past begins to haunt her when she falls for a sailor (Charles Bickford). **ST78, WR25**

Anna Karenina (1935, B&W, 95m, NR)
Greta Garbo stars in Tolstoy's tragic love story of a forbidden affair. With Fredric March and Freddie Bartholomew. **CL1, CL4, ST78, ST148**

Anna Karenina (1948, B&W, 123m, NR)
Vivien Leigh plays Tolstoy's doomed heroine in this British-produced film. With Ralph Richardson and Kieron Moore. **CL1, DR23, ST137, ST184**

Annapolis Story, An (1955, C, 81m, NR)
John Derek and Kevin McCarthy play rival midshipmen, both in love with Diana Lynn. Directed by Don Siegel. **DR25, DT116**

Anne of Green Gables
(1985, C, 195m, NR)
Adaptation of the children's classic about an orphan girl who brings joy to the older couple who adopt her. Megan Follows stars, with Colleen Dewhurst. Originally made for TV. **FA3**

Anne of the Thousand Days
(1969, C, 145m, PG)
Historical drama of Henry VIII (Richard Burton) and his wife Anne Boleyn (Genevieve Bujold), who bore him an heir but was still executed. **DR5, ST22**

Annie (1982, C, 128m, PG)
Lavish musical, based on the Broadway smash, about comic strip characters—a frizzy-haired orphan and her rich guardian, Daddy Warbucks. Aileen Quinn and Albert Finney star, with support from Carol Burnett, Ann Reinking, Bernadette Peters, and Tim Curry. Directed by John Huston. **DT60, FA9, MU2, ST68**

Annie Hall (1977, C, 95m, PG)
Woody Allen's brilliant romantic comedy about an anxious New York comedian and a daffy singer from the Midwest finding—and losing—love. Oscar winner for Best Picture, Director, Actress (Diane Keaton), and Original Screenplay (Allen and Marshall Brickman). With Tony Roberts, Christopher Walken, Colleen Dewhurst, Carol Kane, Shelley Duvall, Paul Simon, and (if you look fast in the last scene) Sigourney Weaver. Among other attributes, one of the best movies about life in both New York and Los Angeles. **CO1, CO2, DT2, ST121, ST222, ST225, XT1, XT3, XT6, XT9, XT10, XT30, XT31,** *Essential, Highly Recommended*

Annie Oakley (1935, B&W, 88m, NR)
Barbara Stanwyck plays the legendary sharpshooter. Preston Foster and Melvyn Douglas costar, with Moroni Olsen as Buffalo Bill. Directed by George Stevens. **DT119, HF3, HF20, ST58, ST206, WE2, WE8**

Annihilators, The (1985, C, 87m, R)
A synchronized fighting unit just back from overseas gets some stateside action in a small Southern town overrun with sleazy criminals. Christopher Stone, Andy Wood, and Lawrence Hilton-Jacobs star. **AC20**

Another Country (1984, C, 90m, NR)
Drama set in 1930s Britain about two boarding school chums who eventually became spies for the Soviets. Based on the lives of Guy Burgess and Donald Maclean. Rupert Everett and Colin Firth star. **DR23, MY6**

Another 48 HRS (1990, C, 102m, R)
Nick Nolte and Eddie Murphy reprise their white cop/black con roles for more interracial insults, gunplay, and above all, car chases. Walter Hill directed. **AC9, CO13, DT56, ST164**

Another Pair of Aces: Three of a Kind
(1991, C, 93m, NR)
Comedy starring Willie Nelson and Kris Kristofferson as a safecracker and Texas Ranger who team to help out a pal (Rip Torn) accused of murder. With Joan Severance. Originally made for TV; sexy footage added for video. **CO10, CU10, MY12, ST216, WE12**

Another Thin Man
(1939, B&W, 105m, NR)
William Powell and Myrna Loy return as detectives Nick and Nora Charles in their third adventure, in which they not only solve another crime, but start a family with the birth of Nick, Jr. **CL15, HF5, MY17, ST142, ST176, WR12**

Another Time, Another Place
(1958, B&W, 98m, NR)
Lana Turner melodrama of wartime widow's nervous breakdown. Sean Connery has a small role. **ST36, ST219**

Another Woman (1988, C, 81m, PG)
Drama starring Gena Rowlands as a New York academic who becomes involved with the problems of a troubled younger woman (Mia Farrow). Woody Allen wrote and directed. With Gene Hackman, John Houseman, Ian Holm, Martha Plimpton, Blythe Danner, and Sandy Dennis. **DR10, DT2, ST65, ST96, XT30**

Another You (1991, C, 98m, R)
Comedy of a street hustler (Richard Pryor) and compulsive liar (Gene Wilder) teaming up for a scam. With Mercedes Ruehl, Stephen Lang, and Vanessa Williams. **CO3, CO10, ST180**

Anthony Adverse (1936, B&W, 141m, NR)
Epic saga, based on bestselling novel, of young man's adventures in nineteenth-century America, including an encounter with Abraham Lincoln. Fredric March stars, with Olivia de Havilland, Claude Rains, and Oscar winner Gale Sondergaard. **DR19, HF18, ST49, ST148, XT5**

Antonia and Jane (1991, C, 69m, NR)
British comedy-drama of two women friends unwittingly telling their secrets to the same shrink. Saskia Reeves and Imelda Stauton star. Originally made for BBC-TV. **CO2, CO17, DR10**

Antonio das Mortes (1970, C, 100m, NR)
True-life drama from Argentina about a bounty hunter, hired in 1939 to kill leftist rebels, who turns on his employers. Directed by Glauber Rocha. **FF6**

Ants! (1977, C, 88m, NR)
An army of killer ants terrorizes a resort. Suzanne Somers, Myrna Loy, and Lynda Day George star. **HO16, ST142**

Any Friend of Nicholas Nickleby Is a Friend of Mine (1981, C, 55m, NR)
Period family adventure set in small town, where a strange man (Fred Gwynne) takes a young boy into his confidence. Written by Ray Bradbury. **FA4**

Any Number Can Win see *Melodie en Sous-Sol*

Any Wednesday (1966, C, 109m, NR)
A New York executive tries to write off his mistress's apartment as a business expense in this comedy starring Jason Robards and Jane Fonda. **ST72, ST185**

Any Which Way You Can
(1980, C, 116m, PG)
Sequel to *Every Which Way But Loose* has street brawler Clint Eastwood and his orangutan Clyde mixing it up with comic baddies. Sondra Locke, Geoffrey Lewis, and William Smith costar. **CO9, ST64**

Anzio (1968, C, 117m, PG)
Drama centering on the Allied invasion of a significant Italian beachhead in World War II. Robert Mitchum, Peter Falk, and Robert Ryan star. **AC1, ST158, ST193**

Apache (1954, C, 91m, NR)
Burt Lancaster stars in this historical account of the bitter battle between the Indians and the U.S. Cavalry. Directed by Robert Aldrich. Watch for Charles Buchinski (Bronson) in the supporting cast. **DT1, ST20, ST129, WE7**

Apache Rose (1947, C, 75m, NR)
Roy Rogers Western set on a gambling ship. Dale Evans pilots a tugboat, and Bob Nolan and the Sons of the Pioneers provide the harmonies. **ST188**

Apache Woman (1955, C, 83m, NR)
Early effort from director Roger Corman, a Western starring Lloyd Bridges as a government agent caught between Indians and whites, romancing a half-breed. With Joan Taylor, Lance Fuller, and Corman's favorite supporting player, Dick Miller. **DT30, WE8**

Aparajito (1957, B&W, 108m, NR)
Indian director Satyajit Ray's classic *Apu* trilogy continues with this second chapter in which Apu grows up and is brought to Benares to begin his education. Pinaki Sen Gupta and Kanu Banerji star. **DT102, *Essential***

Apartment, The (1960, B&W, 125m, NR)
Writer-director Billy Wilder's Oscar-winning
comedy about a schnook (Jack Lemmon)
who lets his bosses borrow his pad for their
little one-night stands. Shirley MacLaine and
Fred MacMurray costar. Devastating look at
conformity in the world of big business.
DT139, ST138, ST145, XT1, XT6, *Essential,*
Recommended

Apartment Zero (1989, C, 116m, R)
Offbeat thriller from Argentina (shot in English) concerning a Buenos Aires film buff
(Colin Firth) who takes in a strange boarder
(Hart Bochner). Directed by Martin Donovan, who cut film from its original 124 minutes for video. Creepy, if not always plausi-
ble. Film fans will want to check it out. **FF6,**
MY9, MY19, XT23, XT31

Ape, The (1940, B&W, 61m, NR)
A kindly doctor becomes obsessed with his
experiments after the death of his wife and
child. He soon resorts to murder disguised as
an ape. Boris Karloff stars. **HO20, ST119**

Ape Man, The (1943, B&W, 64m, NR)
Bela Lugosi experiments with a serum derived from ape blood to give humans the
power of a gorilla. **ST143**

Apocalypse Now (1979, C, 139m, R)
Director Francis Ford Coppola's nightmarish
vision of the Vietnam War, starring Martin
Sheen, Marlon Brando, and Robert Duvall,
with Harrison Ford, Dennis Hopper, Frederic
Forrest, Sam Bottoms, G.D. Spradlin, and
Larry Fishburne. Effective use of rock music,
brilliant imagery. Film and director should
have won Oscars. Available in letterboxed
format. Behind-the-scenes documentary:
Hearts of Darkness: A Filmmaker's Apocalypse.
AC4, CU19, DT29, ST18, ST63, ST74,
ST110, XT26, XT28, *Essential, Highly*
Recommended

Apology (1986, C, 98m, NR)
Thriller about an artist (Lesley Ann Warren)
who solicits confessions by phone, until a
serial killer calls for her forgiveness. Peter
Weller and John Glover costar. **MY3**

Appaloosa, The (1966, C, 98m, NR)
Western drama starring Marlon Brando as a
cowboy who journeys to Mexico to retrieve
his stolen horse. John Saxon and Anjanette
Comer costar. Sluggish; even Brando fans will
find this a tough ride. **ST18, WE9**

Applause (1929, B&W, 78m, NR)
Early talkie focuses on burlesque star (Helen
Morgan) whose better days are behind her
but has hopes for her young daughter.

Directed by Rouben Mamoulian. **CL6, CL7,**
DT83

Apple Dumpling Gang, The
(1975, C, 100m, G)
Three frisky kids strike it rich and trigger a
wild bank robbery in the gold-mad West. Bill
Bixby, Susan Clark, Don Knotts, and Tim
Conway star in this Disney Western. **FA1**

Apple Dumpling Gang Rides Again,
The (1979, C, 88m, G)
Two bumbling outlaws try to go straight, but
they can't even seem to get that right. Disney Western stars Tim Conway, Don Knotts,
and Tim Matheson. **FA1**

Applegates, The (1991, C, 90m, R)
Offbeat comedy about giant Brazilian cock-
roaches disguised as typical suburban family.
Ed Begley, Jr., and Stockard Channing star,
with Cami Cooper, Bobby Jacoby, and Dab-
ney Coleman. Cowritten and directed by
Michael Lehmann. Also known as *Meet the*
Applegates. **CO5, CO12**

Appointment in Honduras
(1953, C, 79m, NR)
An American and his pals help out a Latin
American country. Glenn Ford, Ann Sher-
idan, and Zachary Scott star. Directed by
Jacques Tourneur. **DT124**

Appointment With Death
(1988, C, 102m, PG)
Hercule Poirot (Peter Ustinov) solves a mur-
der in 1937 Jerusalem. The suspects in this
Agatha Christie whodunit include Lauren
Bacall, Piper Laurie, John Gielgud, and Carrie
Fisher. **MY12, ST86, WR3**

Apprenticeship of Duddy Kravitz, The
(1974, C, 121m, PG)
Richard Dreyfuss plays a Jewish hustler in
this comedy-drama set in 1940s Montreal,
based on Mordecai Richler's novel. With Micheline Lanctot, Jack Warden, Randy Quaid,
Joseph Wiseman, and Denholm Elliott. Star-
making performance by Dreyfuss; film has its
moments but rambles. **ST60**

April Fools, The (1969, C, 95m, PG)
A married man decides to start his life all
over again by running off with a lovely
French girl. Jack Lemmon and Catherine
Deneuve star, with Charles Boyer and Myrna
Loy. **ST16, ST50, ST138, ST142**

April Fool's Day (1986, C, 90m, R)
A rich college girl throws a party at her family's home on an island and her guests begin
to disappear. Deborah Foreman stars. **HO12**

April in Paris (1952, C, 101m, NR)
Doris Day musical, set aboard a ship bound

for Paris. She's a showgirl; Ray Bolger plays a diplomat. **ST47**

Arab Conspiracy, The see *Next Man, The*

Arabesque (1966, C, 105m, NR)
Espionage thriller about a college professor (Gregory Peck) lured into political intrigue by a beautiful woman (Sophia Loren). Directed by Stanley Donen. **DT38, MY6, ST141, ST171**

Arachnophobia (1990, C, 103m, PG-13)
Small-town move proves almost disastrous for family when they discover their barn is home to a deadly South American spider and its offspring. Jeff Daniels stars as man with title affliction (fear of you-know-what). With Harley Jane Kozak, John Goodman, Julian Sands, and Henry Jones. Mixes comedy with its thrills, not always successfully. **CO11, DR26, HO16**

Arch of Triumph (1948, B&W, 120m, NR)
Wartime drama stars Ingrid Bergman as a woman in love with an Austrian refugee (Charles Boyer). Charles Laughton costars. **ST13, ST16, ST132**

Archer's Adventure (1985, C, 120m, NR)
Family adventure, set in nineteenth century, about a young man and his horse crossing the trackless wastes of Australia. **FA4**

Aria (1988, C, 90m, R)
Ten directors concoct short films built around opera arias. Among the filmmakers: Jean-Luc Godard, Ken Russell, Robert Altman, Bruce Beresford, and Julien Temple. The stars include Theresa Russell, Bridget Fonda, Buck Henry, John Hurt, and Beverly D'Angelo. Wildly uneven, but worth a look for followers of the directors. **DT4, DT10, DT50, DT111, MU16, ST70**

Ariel (1990, C, 74m, NR)
Finnish comedy of a mine worker (Turo Pajala) who loses his job and takes to the road. Directed by Aki Kaurismaki. **FF7**

Arizona Kid, The (1939, B&W, 61m, NR)
Early Roy Rogers Western has him singing and dispensing justice, with Gabby Hayes and Dale Evans along to help. **ST161**

Armed and Dangerous
(1986, C, 88m, PG-13)
John Candy and Eugene Levy star in this comedy about pair of inept security guards. With Robert Loggia and Meg Ryan. **CO3, CO14**

Armed Response (1986, C, 95m, R)
Chinatown gang war erupts in this drama starring David Carradine and Lee Van Cleef, with Mako and Dick Miller. **AC8, ST189**

Armored Attack see *North Star, The*

Armored Command
(1961, B&W, 99m, NR)
World War II action, starring Howard Keel, with Tina Louise and Burt Reynolds. **AC1, ST157**

Army of Darkness: Evil Dead 3
(1993, C, 95m, R)
Director Sam Raimi's *The Dead Have Risen* series continues with this time-travel tale, set in the days of King Arthur. Bruce Campbell is back, now battling an army of skeletons. Look fast for Bridget Fonda. **SF4, ST70**

Arnold (1973, C, 100m, PG)
A rich old man dies but his fiancée goes through with the wedding so she and his family can spend his fortune. Then the members of the family begin to die in strange ways. Stella Stevens, Roddy McDowall, and Elsa Lanchester star in this comic horror story. **HO14, HO24**

Around the World in 80 Days
(1956, C, 175m, G)
Jules Verne tale of an outrageous wager—at least for the late nineteenth century. David Niven and Cantinflas play the champion travelers; Shirley MacLaine costars, with dozens of familiar faces in bit parts, including Ronald Colman, Charles Boyer, John Gielgud, Frank Sinatra, Marlene Dietrich, and Buster Keaton. Oscar winner for Best Picture and Musical Score. Widescreen will be lost on video. **CU20, DT66, FA4, ST16, ST35, ST55, ST86, ST145, ST199, WR36, XT1, XT18**

Around the World Under the Sea
(1966, C, 117m, NR)
Family adventure of special submarine and its record-setting voyage. Lloyd Bridges stars, with Shirley Eaton, David McCallum, and Keenan Wynn. **FA4**

Arrangement, The (1969, C, 120m, R)
Business executive reexamines his life after a failed suicide attempt. Kirk Douglas stars, with Faye Dunaway, Deborah Kerr, and Richard Boone. Drama from director Elia Kazan, based on his novel. Widescreen will be lost on video. An interesting failure; Kazan doesn't hold back, which is to his credit as an artist. **DR24, DT65, ST57, ST125**

Arrowsmith (1931, B&W, 99m, NR)
Director John Ford's film of the Sinclair Lewis novel about a country doctor who travels to the West Indies to study tropical ailments. Ronald Colman and Helen Hayes star, with Myrna Loy. **DT44, ST142, WR20**

Arruza (1972, C, 75m, NR)
A documentary portrait of Carlos Arruza, one of Mexico's great bullfighters. Directed by Budd Boetticher. **CU16, DT14,** *Recommended*

Arsenal (1929, B&W, 70m, NR)
Classic silent antiwar drama from Soviet director Alexander Dovzhenko, set in the waning days of World War I and the early days of the Revolution. **FF7**

Arsenic and Old Lace
(1944, B&W, 118m, NR)
Frantic mystery-comedy, based on the hit play about a couple of sweet, innocent-looking maiden aunts who poison their gentlemen callers. Cary Grant, Raymond Massey, and Peter Lorre star. Directed by Frank Capra. Its once daring qualities have dated badly. Grant certainly expends a lot of energy. **CL10, DR20, DT22, MY17, ST92,** *Recommended*

Art of Crime, The (1975, C, 92m, NR)
Offbeat mystery has a gypsy gumshoe investigating a murder charge brought against a fellow antique dealer. Ron Leibman stars, with José Ferrer, David Hedison, and Jill Clayburgh. Originally produced as a pilot for TV series. **MY10, ST31**

Arthur (1981, C, 97m, PG)
A tipsy Manhattan millionaire playboy falls in love with a kooky shoplifter, although he's engaged to a socialite. Dudley Moore, Liza Minnelli, and Oscar winner John Gielgud star in this romantic comedy. **CO1, ST86, ST160, XT4, XT9,** *Recommended*

Arthur 2: On the Rocks
(1988, C, 113m, PG)
Sequel to *Arthur* finds the tipsy millionaire married to his true love, about to lose his fortune. Dudley Moore, Liza Minnelli, and John Gielgud (in ghostly form) reprise their roles from the first film. **CO1, ST86, ST160, XT9, XT24**

Article 99 (1992, C, 100m, R)
Drama set in a Veterans Administration hospital, as an experienced doctor (Ray Liotta) shows a new physician (Kiefer Sutherland) how to cut through the absurdly tangled red tape. With Forest Whitaker, Lea Thompson, John C. McGinley, John Mahoney, Keith David, Kathy Baker, and Eli Wallach. **DR7**

Artists and Models (1955, C, 109m, NR)
Dean Martin and Jerry Lewis comedy, written and directed by Frank Tashlin, about a painter and his telepathic chum. With Shirley MacLaine, Dorothy Malone, Eva Gabor, and Anita Ekberg. **CL10, CL15, ST139, ST145, ST149**

As Summers Die (1986, C, 87m, NR)
Drama set in small town in 1959 has a lawyer determined to help a poor black woman fight the ruling family who is trying to force her off her property. Scott Glenn, Bette Davis, and Jamie Lee Curtis star. Originally made for TV. **DR26, ST42, ST44**

As You Desire Me (1932, B&W, 71m, NR)
Greta Garbo plays an amnesiac struggling to work out matters with her husband. With Melvyn Douglas, Erich Von Stroheim, and Hedda Hopper. Based on a play by Luigi Pirandello. **DT129, ST58, ST78**

As You Like It (1936, B&W, 96m, NR)
William Shakespeare's comedy explores the many facets of love. Laurence Olivier and Elisabeth Bergner star. **ST168, WR28**

Ash Wednesday (1973, C, 99m, R)
Elizabeth Taylor plays a woman who undergoes plastic surgery in this drama costarring Henry Fonda. **ST71, ST212**

Ashanti (1979, C, 117m, R)
The wife of a British doctor (Michael Caine) is kidnapped by a slave trader (Peter Ustinov). William Holden costars in this adventure set in the Middle East. **ST25, ST106**

Ashes and Diamonds
(1958, B&W, 96m, NR)
Polish drama set in the immediate aftermath of World War II, when a Resistance youth (Zbigniew Cybulski) assassinates the wrong man. Directed by Andrzej Wajda; the third in his famed wartime trilogy. **DT130,** *Essential, Recommended*

Ask Any Girl (1959, C, 101m, NR)
Early Shirley MacLaine vehicle has her playing a naive young woman seeking her fortune in New York. With David Niven, Gig Young, Rod Taylor, and Jim Backus. **ST145**

Aspen Extreme (1993, C, 117m, PG-13)
Two buddies abandon the Rust Belt life in Detroit to become ski instructors and enjoy the high life on the Colorado slopes. Paul Gross and Peter Berg star, with Finola Hughes, Teri Polo, and William Russ. Plenty of ski footage. **DR22**

Asphalt Jungle, The
(1950, B&W, 112m, NR)
An aging criminal returns from prison to recruit his old gang for one final heist. Sterling Hayden and Sam Jaffe star, with Jean Hagen and Marilyn Monroe. Directed by John Huston, at the top of his form. **DT60, MY1, MY18, ST159,** *Essential, Recommended*

Asphyx, The (1972, C, 99m, PG)
British science fiction drama, set in the
1870s, with a scientist isolating the spirit of
death and achieving immortality in the process. Robert Stephens, Robert Powell, and
Jane Lapotaire star. **SF5, SF19**

Assassination (1987, C, 88m, PG-13)
A Secret Service agent (Charles Bronson) has
reason to believe that the new First Lady (Jill
Ireland) is in danger. **ST20**

Assassination of Trotsky, The
(1972, C, 103m, R)
Brooding account of the final days of the
Soviet leader, living in exile in Mexico. Rich-
ard Burton stars, with Alain Delon and Romy
Schneider. Directed by Joseph Losey.
DR5, ST22

Assault, The (1986, C, 149m, NR)
During the closing days of World War II, a
young boy witnesses his family's betrayal to
the Nazis and their deportation to the death
camps. Oscar-winning drama from Holland.
FF7, XT7

Assault of the Rebel Girls
(1959, C, 68m, NR)
In Errol Flynn's last film, he plays himself in
the fight to aid Fidel Castro's revolution. Also
known as *Cuban Rebel Girls.* **ST69**

Assault on Precinct 13 (1976, C, 90m, R)
Isolated police station is besieged by vengeful
street gangs in this low-budget thriller from
director John Carpenter. Loose remake of *Rio
Bravo.* Emphasis is on suspense rather than
violence. **AC8, DT23,** *Recommended*

Assisi Underground, The
(1985, C, 115m, PG)
A young cleric hides Jews from the Nazis in
World War II Italy. Based on a true story, this
drama stars Ben Cross, James Mason, Irene
Papas, and Maximilian Schell. **DR5, ST153**

Asylum (1972, C, 92m, PG)
Four scary stories by Robert Bloch are linked
together by the conclusion of the fourth
story. Peter Cushing stars, with Barbara Parkins, Britt Ekland, and Charlotte Rampling.
HO23, HO26, ST43

At Close Range (1986, C, 115m, R)
A criminal tries to involve his young sons in
his line of work, in this drama based on a
true story. Sean and Christopher Penn star,
with Christopher Walken and Mary Stuart
Masterson. Directed by James Foley. Sean
Penn doesn't grab sympathy for his character's plight. **DR6, DR8, DR16, ST222,
XT8**

At Play in the Fields of the Lord
(1991, C, 187m, R)
Drama based on Peter Matthiessen novel set
in Amazon jungle, with two missionary cou-
ples and a soldier of fortune hired to push
Indians off their land, all clashing. Tom
Berenger, Aidan Quinn, Kathy Bates, John
Lithgow, and Daryl Hannah star, with Tom
Waits. Directed by Hector Babenco. **DR19,
DR27, MU12**

At Sword's Point (1952, C, 81m, NR)
Swashbuckler stars Cornell Wilde as hero,
Maureen O'Hara as his lady fair. **AC15,
ST167**

At the Circus (1939, B&W, 87m, NR)
The Marx Brothers take over the big top.
Groucho sings "Lydia the Tattooed Lady."
Margaret Dumont is not amused. **ST152**

At the Earth's Core (1976, C, 90m, PG)
Science fiction adventure, based on Edgar
Rice Burroughs story, about scientists burrow-
ing from England into subterranean kingdom
of monsters. Peter Cushing, Doug McClure,
and Caroline Munro star. **FA4, SF3, ST43**

At War with the Army
(1950, B&W, 93m, NR)
Dean Martin and Jerry Lewis join the paratroopers in their first starring feature. **CL15,
CO21, ST139, ST149**

Athena (1954, C, 96m, NR)
MGM musical of two Boston sisters (Jane
Powell, Debbie Reynolds) wooed by a lawyer
(Edmund Purdom) and singer (Vic Damone).
MU1

Athens, GA (1987, C, 82m, NR)
Documentary of rock music scene in title
town, focusing on R.E.M. and other local
bands. **CU16**

Atlantic City (1980, C, 104m, R)
An aging gangster and an aspiring casino
dealer are the improbable romantic couple
in this offbeat and satisfyingly melancholy
drama set in Atlantic City. Burt Lancaster
and Susan Sarandon star. Written by John
Guare; directed by Louis Malle. **DR1, DR16,
DT82, ST129, ST194,** *Recommended*

Atoll K (1950, B&W, 80m, NR)
Laurel and Hardy inherit an island but don't
realize they're sitting on top of a uranium
mine. Their last film together. Also known as
Utopia. **ST133**

Atom Age Vampire (1961, B&W, 87m, NR)
A mad doctor fixes a dancer's disfigured face,
becomes obsessed with keeping her beautiful,
and kills other women for their cells so he
can preserve the dancer's looks. **HO20**

Atomic Cafe, The (1982, C/B&W, 88m, NR)
Collection of propaganda film clips from the 1950s about the dangers of nuclear war and how to survive one. Funny and chilling at the same time. **CU16,** *Recommended*

Atomic Kid, The (1954, B&W, 86m, NR)
An innocent man wanders into an atomic test site and emerges alive but with extraordinary powers. Mickey Rooney stars in this comedy. **ST189**

Atonement of Gosta Berling, The see *Gosta Berling's Saga*

Attack! (1956, B&W, 107m, NR)
Superb antiwar film from director Robert Aldrich, with Jack Palance as weary soldier correctly suspecting his commanding officer (Eddie Albert) is a coward whose timidity will cost his men their lives. With Lee Marvin, Robert Strauss, Richard Jaeckel, and Buddy Ebsen. UNAVAILABLE ON VIDEO. **XT29**

Attack Force Z (1981, C, 84m, NR)
Australian-produced World War II drama of commandos on a rescue mission. John Phillip Law, Sam Neill, and Mel Gibson star. **AC1, ST85**

Attack of the Crab Monsters
(1957, B&W, 68m, NR)
Director Roger Corman's no-budget horror tale of brain-eating crabs attacking visitors to a desert island. Richard Garland and Pamela Duncan try to dodge the claws. **DT30**

Attack of the Killer Tomatoes
(1980, C, 87m, PG)
Cult "bad" movie that tries to spoof science fiction films about marauding giant vegetables and winds up being just plain awful. **CU11**

Attack of the Robots
(1967, B&W, 85m, NR)
Combination of science fiction drama and spy thriller, with secret agent out to stop terrorists from programming robots for political assassinations. Shot in France; dubbed into English. Eddie Constantine stars. **SF19**

Au Revoir, les Enfants
(1988, C, 103m, PG)
French director Louis Malle's heartfelt, autobiographical drama about a schoolboy befriending a Jewish classmate during the Occupation. **DR25, DT82, FF1,** *Recommended*

Audience With Mel Brooks, An
(1984, C, 55m, NR)
In London, Brooks performs in several sketches with his wife, Anne Bancroft, and Ronny Graham. He also answers questions from the audience. **CO16, DT17**

Audrey Rose (1977, C, 113m, PG)
A twelve-year-old girl begins having nightmares about being in a fire and an investigation reveals that she is the reincarnation of Audrey Rose, a girl who died in a fiery car crash. Marsha Mason, Anthony Hopkins, and John Beck star. Robert Wise directed. **DT140, HO13, ST109**

Augustine of Hippo (1972, C, 120m, NR)
Another in the series of films by director Roberto Rossellini on famous figures in history, this one about the later years of the saint and his wrestling with matters of church and state. Made for Italian TV. **DT109**

Auntie Mame (1958, C, 143m, NR)
Rosalind Russell is the colorful title character in this lavish adaptation of Patrick Dennis's memoir of his eccentric relative. With Forrest Tucker, Coral Browne, Fred Clark, Roger Smith, Patric Knowles, and Peggy Cass. Russell overacts; a big hit in its day, this film has dated badly. **CO4, CO5, ST192**

Aurora Encounter (1985, C, 90m, PG)
A Texas town is the site for a friendly alien's visit in this humorous science fiction tale. Jack Elam stars. **SF13**

Author! Author! (1982, C, 110m, PG)
Domestic comedy starring Al Pacino as a playwright whose wife (Tuesday Weld) leaves him with a brood of children (most of them from her previous marriages). Dyan Cannon costars. **CO5, ST170**

Autobiography of Miss Jane Pittman, The (1974, C, 110m, NR)
Epic story of a black woman's journey from slavery to equality in the modern South, starring Cicely Tyson. Winner of nine Emmys; originally made for TV. **DR14**

Autumn Afternoon, An
(1962, B&W, 112m, NR)
Drama from Japanese director Yasujiro Ozu, about a widower (Chishu Ryu) who pushes his daughter into marriage so she won't be forced to care for him in his old age. **FF4**

Autumn Leaves (1956, B&W, 108m, NR)
Joan Crawford is the middle-aged woman who finds romance with a man (Cliff Robertson) half her age. Their happiness turns sour when his secret past catches up with him. Directed by Robert Aldrich. **CL5, DT1, ST39**

Autumn Sonata (1978, C, 97m, PG)
Ingrid Bergman and Liv Ullmann star in this drama of a mother and daughter reunited after seven years, with old wounds opened. Directed by Ingmar Bergman; dialogue in

Swedish and English. **DR8, DT11, ST13, ST220, XT30**

Avalanche (1978, C, 91m, PG)
A new ski resort is about to get more powder than the weather forecast predicted. Rock Hudson, Mia Farrow, Robert Forster, and Jeanette Nolan star in this disaster adventure. **AC23, ST65, ST112**

Avalon (1990, C, 126m, PG)
Acutely observed, affecting saga of Baltimore family, beginning with immigration in first quarter of the century, ending with dissolution of clan to the suburbs and the numbing effects of television. Writer-director Barry Levinson's third Baltimore film (after *Diner* and *Tin Men*) stars Armin Mueller-Stahl as the patriarch, Aidan Quinn as his son, Elijah Wood as his grandson; with Kevin Pollak, Elizabeth Perkins, Lou Jacobi, and Joan Plowright. Music by Randy Newman. **DR8, DR15, DT75,** *Recommended*

Avengers, The see *Day Will Dawn, The*

Avenging Angel (1985, C, 93m, R)
Sequel to *Angel*, with prostitute, now in college, gunning for killer of cop who befriended her. Betsy Russell stars, with Rory Calhoun and Susan Tyrrell returning from first film. **AC8**

Avenging Conscience, The
(1914, B&W, 78m, NR)
This early horror film from D.W. Griffith is based on Edgar Allan Poe's *The Tell-Tale Heart*. **DT52, WR27**

Avenging Force (1986, C, 104m, R)
A terrorist group dumps a special agent in the midst of a swamp and forces him to fight for his life. Michael Dudikoff stars. **AC24**

Aviator, The (1985, C, 98m, PG)
Grounded pilot agrees to fly spunky young woman through treacherous territory, and romance develops. Christopher Reeve and Rosanna Arquette star. **AC11, AC14**

Aviator's Wife, The (1981, C, 104m, NR)
French comedy about a young man's disillusionment with his current lover and a chance encounter with a new possibility. Directed by Eric Rohmer. **DT107**

Awakening, The (1980, C, 102m, R)
An Egyptologist defies a curse and releases the spirit of an evil queen, who then possesses his daughter. Based on a novel by Bram Stoker. Charlton Heston, Susannah York, and Stephanie Zimbalist star. **HO8**

Awakenings (1990, C, 121m, PG-13)
True story of New York doctor uncovering what he thinks is a cure for group of patients in coma-life state. Robin Williams and Robert De Niro star, with Julie Kavner, Ruth Nelson, John Heard, Penelope Ann Miller, Max von Sydow, and Dexter Gordon. Based on Oliver Sacks's book; directed by Penny Marshall. Music by Randy Newman. Occasionally affecting but seems too often to miss full impact of the material. **DR2, DR6, MU12, ST51, ST228, XT23**

Awful Truth, The (1937, B&W, 92m, NR)
Comedy classic pairs Irene Dunne and Cary Grant as a screwy divorced couple who interfere with one another's love life. Ralph Bellamy costars. Oscar-winning direction by Leo McCarey; film also should have won. **CL10, DT80, ST62, ST92, XT6, XT28,** *Essential, Recommended*

Babar: The Movie (1989, C, 79m, G)
Animated feature starring the beloved children's storybook favorite, the gentle elephant, plus all his friends. **FA10**

Babe, The (1992, C, 115m, PG)
Bio of George Herman Ruth, the greatest ballplayer ever to wear the New York Yankee pinstripes. John Goodman stars, with Kelly McGillis, Trini Alvarado, Bruce Boxleitner, and James Cromwell. Written by John Fusco, directed by Arthur Hiller. **DR4, DR22**

Babe Ruth Story, The
(1948, B&W, 106m, NR)
William Bendix plays the Sultan of Swat, as he bats and pitches his way out of a Baltimore orphanage to become the greatest New York Yankee of them all. **CL2, DR22**

Babes in Arms (1939, B&W, 96m, NR)
Judy Garland and Mickey Rooney put on a show to raise money for their vaudevillian parents. Directed by Busby Berkeley. **CL15, DT12, MU1, MU4, ST81, ST189**

Babes in Toyland (1934) see *March of the Wooden Soldiers*

Babes in Toyland (1961, C, 105m, NR)
Victor Herbert's music is featured in this Disney fantasy set in the make-believe world of Mother Goose. Annette Funicello, Ray Bolger, Ed Wynn, and Tommy Sands star. **FA1**

Babes on Broadway (1941, B&W, 118m, NR)
Mickey Rooney-Judy Garland musical extravaganza, in which the stars put on a show for poor kids. Busby Berkeley directed. **CL15, DT12, MU1, MU4, ST81, ST189**

Babette's Feast (1987, C, 102m, PG)
Remarkably subtle and rich drama, based on a story by Isak Dinesen. A pair of unmarried sisters in a Danish village take in a French

woman as a cook and she unexpectedly enriches their lives. Oscar winner as Best Foreign Language Film. Gabriel Axel wrote and directed. **FF7, XT7,** *Highly Recommended*

Baby, The (1973, C, 102m, R)
A retarded man is babied by his overprotective mother and sister. When a social worker gets involved with the case, murder soon follows. Anjanette Comer and Ruth Roman star. **HO13**

Baby Boom (1987, C, 110m, PG)
A Manhattan business executive has her single life turned upside-down when she inherits an infant from a relative. Diane Keaton stars in this comedy, with Harold Ramis, Sam Shepard, and James Spader. **CO2, CO14, ST121, ST203**

Baby Doll (1956, B&W, 114m, NR)
Tennessee Williams's play about a poor Southern farmer who can't keep his teen-aged wife happy. Eli Wallach, Carroll Baker, and Karl Malden star, with Rip Torn. Directed by Elia Kazan. Condemned by the Catholic Church and banned in some cities on its original release. **CU6, CU8, DT65, ST216, WR38**

Baby Face (1933, B&W, 70m, NR)
Barbara Stanwyck plays a barmaid with ambitions to marry into money—and isn't afraid to use her sexuality. Remarkably candid drama with George Brent, Donald Cook, Margaret Lindsay, and in a bit role, John Wayne. **ST206, ST224**

Baby, It's You (1983, C, 105m, R)
Romantic drama involving a Jewish girl and an Italian guy, starting in a New Jersey high school. Rosanna Arquette and Vincent Spano star. John Sayles wrote and directed. Four period rock 'n' roll songs from the film's original soundtrack were replaced for video version. **DR1, DT112**

Baby Maker, The (1970, C, 109m, R)
An infertile couple hire a free spirit (Barbara Hershey) as a surrogate mother, with predictably complicated results. Written and directed by James Bridges. **DR7, DR8, ST104**

Baby . . . Secret of the Lost Legend (1985, C, 95m, PG)
On an expedition in the jungles of Africa, a young couple stumble onto an infant dinosaur and wind up protecting it from a greedy scientist. William Katt and Sean Young star. **AC12**

Baby Take a Bow (1934, B&W, 76m, NR)
Shirley Temple's first starring role has her helping her ex-con dad (James Dunn) to go straight. **ST213**

Baby, the Rain Must Fall
(1965, B&W, 100m, NR)
Just out of prison, a drifter tries to settle down with his wife and child but soon becomes restless. Steve McQueen stars, with Lee Remick and Don Murray. **ST146**

Bachelor and the Bobby-Soxer, The
(1947, B&W, 95m, NR)
A playboy (Cary Grant), hauled in for disturbing the peace, is sentenced by a judge (Myrna Loy) to court her younger sister (Shirley Temple). Written by Sidney Sheldon. Only stars of Grant's and Loy's magnitude could make this kind of material work—and they do. **ST92, ST142, ST213,** *Recommended*

Bachelor Apartment
(1931, B&W, 77m, NR)
Title says it all in this naughty film from the days before Hollywood's Production Code had any teeth in it. Director Lowell Sherman stars as a roue; his ladies include Irene Dunne, Mae Murray, and Claudia Dell. **CL10, ST62**

Bachelor Mother (1939, B&W, 81m, NR)
Ginger Rogers comedy has her a single woman mothering an abandoned infant. With David Niven and Charles Coburn. **ST187**

Bachelor Party (1984, C, 100m, R)
Tom Hanks stars as a soon-to-be-married man whose buddies throw him the party of his life. **ST97**

Back From Eternity (1956, B&W, 97m, NR)
Adventure drama of survivors of jungle plane crash, starring Robert Ryan, Anita Ekberg, Rod Steiger, and Phyllis Kirk. **AC24, ST193**

Back Roads (1981, C, 94m, R)
Romantic comedy about a pair of drifters who fall in love while traveling the South together. Sally Field and Tommy Lee Jones star; directed by Martin Ritt. **DT105, ST66, XT18**

Back Street (1961, C, 107m, NR)
The classic Fannie Hurst soaper about a fashion designer (Susan Hayward) who is hopelessly in love with a married man (John Gavin). **CL4, CL6, ST100**

Back to Bataan (1945, B&W, 95m, NR)
John Wayne leads American troops into the Philippines to battle the Japanese. Anthony Quinn costars. **AC1, ST224**

Back to the Future (1985, C, 116m, PG)
A teen-ager is transported back in time to the 1950s, where he plays matchmaker for his future parents. Michael J. Fox stars, with Christopher Lloyd, Lea Thompson, and Crispin Glover. Robert Zemeckis directed. An enjoyable idea unfortunately stretched

through two sequels. **CO4, CO6, CO11, CO20, DT143, SF4,** *Recommended*

Back to the Future, Part II
(1989, C, 108m, PG)
Follow-up to the time-travel comedy, with Michael J. Fox moving from the present to the future and back to the past. Emphasis is on saving his family—and town—from awful fate. Christopher Lloyd costars, with Lea Thompson, Thomas F. Wilson, and Joe Flaherty in a brief role. **CO5, CO6, CO11, CO14, CO20, DT143, SF4**

Back to the Future, Part III
(1990, C, 120m, PG)
Marty McFly and his pal Doc Brown take a long, strange trip to the Old West. Michael J. Fox and Christopher Lloyd star, with Thomas F. Wilson, Lea Thompson, and Elisabeth Shue from the first two BTTF films, and Mary Steenburgen, Pat Buttram, Dub Taylor, Harry Carey, Jr., and ZZ Top. Directed by Robert Zemeckis. **CO6, CO11, CO20, DT143, SF4, WE14**

Backdraft (1991, C, 135m, R)
Drama of the lives and loves of Chicago firefighters, focusing on a pair of brothers (Kurt Russell, William Baldwin). With Robert De Niro, Donald Sutherland, Jennifer Jason Leigh, Scott Glenn, and Rebecca De Mornay. Directed by Ron Howard. Available in letterboxed edition. The special effects are the star. **AC8, CU19, DR15, DT58, ST51, ST136, ST191, XT11**

Background to Danger
(1943, B&W, 80m, NR)
World War II intrigue in Turkey, starring George Raft, with Brenda Marshall, Sydney Greenstreet, and Peter Lorre. Directed by Raoul Walsh. **DT131, MY6**

Backtrack (1992, C, 102m, R)
Quirky thriller of hit man (Dennis Hopper, who also directed) hit by Cupid's arrow, falling in love with his intended victim (Jodie Foster). With Dean Stockwell, Vincent Price, John Turturro, Fred Ward, Joe Pesci, and in small roles, Charlie Sheen and Bob Dylan. Produced by Dick Clark. Filmed in 1989; when originally released as *Catchfire* with running time of 98 minutes, Hopper refused directorial credit (it was changed to commonly used pseudonym Alan Smithee); video version is "director's cut" which restores footage. Flawed by Hopper's mannered direction and performance; in fact, only performer not doing a shtick is Foster. Undoubtedly destined for cult status. **CU10, MU12, MY3, MY5, ST75, ST110, ST172, ST179, ST208, XT18**

Bad see *Andy Warhol's Bad*

Bad and the Beautiful, The
(1952, B&W, 118m, NR)
Quintessential Hollywood tale of a tough producer (Kirk Douglas) and those who work under his thumb. With Lana Turner, Dick Powell, Gloria Grahame (an Oscar winner), and Barry Sullivan. Directed by Vincente Minnelli. **CL7, DT88, ST57, ST175, ST219, XT5,** *Essential*

Bad Boys (1983, C, 123m, R)
Prison drama, set in facility for youth offenders, with the new loner taking on the established king of the cell block. Sean Penn and Esai Morales star, with Reni Santoni and Ally Sheedy. **DR9, DR18**

Bad Channels (1992, C, 88m, R)
Science fiction comedy-drama has an alien taking over a rock radio station, enlivening the format, but also shrinking women to take back home. Paul Hipp and MTV's Martha Quinn star. **SF9**

Bad Company (1972, C, 93m, PG)
Jeff Bridges and Barry Brown play a couple of drifters set loose on the frontier during the Civil War. With Jim Davis, David Huddleston, and Ed Lauter. Written by Robert Benton and David Newman; directed by Benton. Quiet, well observed, and very rewarding portrait of less than heroic nineteenth-century America. **DT9, ST19, WE6, WE15,** *Highly Recommended*

Bad Day at Black Rock
(1955, C, 81m, NR)
Riveting mystery-drama of a one-armed stranger (Spencer Tracy) in a contemporary Western town to uncover a mystery. Great supporting cast includes Robert Ryan, Lee Marvin, Ernest Borgnine (as good a trio of villains as you'll see), Anne Francis, and Dean Jagger. Use of widescreen will be lost on video. **CL8, ST151, ST193, ST217, WE12,** *Recommended*

Bad Girls (1968, C, 97m, R)
French romantic triangle involving an aging courtesan, a dissipated playboy, and a lovely street waif. Stephane Audran, Jean-Louis Trintignant, and Jacqueline Sassard star. Claude Chabrol directed. Originally released as *Les Biches* at 104 minutes. **FF1**

Bad Influence (1990, C, 99m, R)
Cat-and-mouse thriller of a callow young man (James Spader) and his new, hedonistic, blackmailing pal (Rob Lowe). Lowe is genuinely scary, but the Spader character isn't believable. **MY9, MY19, ST203**

Bad Jim (1990, C, 90m, PG)
A trio of Western outlaws pull off a string of

robberies, claiming to be Billy the Kid's gang. James Brolin, John Clark Gable, and Richard Roundtree star, with Harry Carey, Jr., Rory Calhoun, and Ty Hardin. **WE3**

Bad Lieutenant (1992, C, 96m, NC-17)
Harvey Keitel plays a New York cop gone over the edge from the stress of his job, his gambling debts, and a king-sized case of Catholic guilt. His latest case: investigating the rape of a nun in a church. With Frankie Thorn, Zoe Lund, and Paul Hipp as Jesus Christ. Written by Lund, directed by Abel Ferrara. Banned in its original release in Ireland. Also available in a 91-minute, R-rated version. **CU1, CU6, CU8, DR16, HF17**

Bad Man of Deadwood
(1941, B&W, 54m, NR)
Roy Rogers Western has him playing a man with a secret past who joins a circus as a sharpshooter. **ST188**

Bad Man's River (1972, C, 89m, PG)
Comic Western starring Lee Van Cleef as an outlaw whose gang is harassed by a feisty woman (Gina Lollobrigida). With James Mason. **ST153, ST221, WE8, WE14**

Bad News Bears, The (1976, C, 102m, PG)
An inept Little League team and their beer-guzzling coach are saved from humiliation by a talented young pitcher, who just happens to be a girl. Walter Matthau and Tatum O'Neal star. Michael Ritchie directed. A most cheerfully profane comedy. **CO4, CO19, ST155,** *Recommended*

Bad Seed, The (1956, B&W, 129m, NR)
An innocent-looking little girl (Patty McCormack) holds the terrible secret to a rash of mysterious deaths. **HO13, MY14**

Bad Sleep Well, The
(1960, B&W, 152m, NR)
Japanese drama of corporate corruption, directed by Akira Kurosawa, starring Toshiro Mifune. New video version restores edited footage to the original theatrical running time. Rewards patient viewer with stunning set-pieces, especially opening scene. **CU10, DT69, ST157,** *Recommended*

Badge of the Assassin (1985, C, 100m, NR)
Real-life drama of New York district attorney looking for a pair of cop killers. James Woods stars, with Yaphet Kotto, Alex Rocco, and Pam Grier. Originally made for TV. **AC9, DR6, ST233**

Badge 373 (1973, C, 116m, R)
Sequel of sorts to *The French Connection* starring Robert Duvall as a New York lawman fighting a lone battle against the Mob. **AC9, ST63**

Badlanders, The (1958, C, 83m, NR)
Alan Ladd and Ernest Borgnine star in a Western drama of feuding gold robbers, set in Arizona. **ST128, WE3**

Badlands (1973, C, 95m, PG)
Cult drama about a young couple's murder spree in the 1950s Midwest, loosely based on the Charles Starkweather-Caril Fugate case. Martin Sheen and Sissy Spacek star, with Warren Oates. Terrence Malick wrote and directed; his deadpan approach to horrific events has influenced a number of contemporary filmmakers. **DR16, DT81, ST166, ST202, XT18,** *Essential, Recommended*

Badman's Territory
(1946, B&W, 97m, NR)
Randolph Scott is a sheriff clashing with outlaws who are out of his jurisdiction. **ST197**

Bagdad Cafe (1988, C, 91m, PG)
Off-center comedy about a German woman stranded in the California desert, and her relationship with a black woman who runs a greasy spoon. Marianne Sagebrecht and CCH Pounder star. **CO12, CO20**

Baker's Wife, The (1938, B&W, 124m, NR)
Classic French comedy, directed by Marcel Pagnol, of forlorn baker abandoned by his spouse. **FF1**

Balcony, The (1963, B&W, 84m, NR)
The Jean Genet play about life in a bordello during a revolution, with Shelley Winters as the madam and a jaw-dropping supporting cast: Peter Falk, Lee Grant, Ruby Dee, and Leonard Nimoy. **CU17, DR20, ST232**

Ball of Fire (1941, B&W, 111m, NR)
To further his research, a language professor (Gary Cooper) and his seven colleagues consult a stripper (Barbara Stanwyck) for her interpretations of slang in this classic comedy. Directed by Howard Hawks; written by Billy Wilder and Charles Brackett. Stanwyck deserved an Oscar. **CL10, DT53, ST37, ST206, XT28,** *Recommended*

Ballad of Cable Hogue, The
(1970, C, 121m, R)
From director Sam Peckinpah comes this gentle, comic tale of an old prospector (Jason Robards), his lady friend (Stella Stevens), and their misadventures in the desert. With David Warner, Strother Martin, L.Q. Jones, R.G. Armstrong, and Slim Pickens. Genial, mellow stuff from a filmmaker unfairly known only for his skill at portraying violence. **DT95, ST185, WE8, WE11,** *Highly Recommended*

Ballad of Gregorio Cortez, The
(1982, C, 99m, NR)
Drama based on the famous 1901 manhunt
for a Mexican cowhand who, in self-defense,
killed a Texas sheriff and became a folk hero
when he tried to escape. Edward James
Olmos stars. Originally made for public TV.
WE3

Balloonatic, The/One Week
(1923/1920, B&W, 48m, NR)
A Buster Keaton double feature on one tape.
In the first short, he's caught in a runaway
hot-air balloon. In the second, Buster and his
new bride buy a pre-fab home. **DT66**

Bambi (1942, C, 69m, G)
Classic Disney animated feature about a
kind-hearted fawn and his forest friends.
FA2, *Essential, Recommended*

Bananas (1971, C, 82m, PG)
Wild Woody Allen comedy, basically a se-
ries of sketches starring Woody as Fielding
Melish, product tester. Sight gags, puns,
in-jokes, political humor—they're all here.
With Louise Lasser and Howard Cosell; Syl-
vester Stallone has a bit part. **DT2, ST204,**
Recommended

Band of Outsiders (1964, B&W, 97m, NR)
French director Jean-Luc Godard at his playful, provocative best, in a tale of theft that
turns into a running political and cultural
commentary. Anna Karina, Sami Frey, and
Claude Brasseur star. **DT50,** *Recommended*

Band of the Hand (1986, C, 109m, R)
Five buddies try to stay straight on the mean
streets of Miami in this urban action thriller.
James Remar and Stephen Lang star. **AC8**

Band Wagon, The (1953, C, 112m, NR)
Fred Astaire plays a fading movie star
whose songwriting pals want him for their
new Broadway show. Cyd Charisse, Jack Buchanan, Oscar Levant, and Nanette Fabray
costar. Among the many highlights: the Girl
Hunt Ballet. Directed by Vincente Minnelli;
written by Betty Comden and Adolph
Green. As good as Hollywood musicals get.
DT88, MU1, MU4, ST4, *Essential, Highly
Recommended*

Bandits of Orgosolo, The
(1961, B&W, 98m, NR)
Italian drama, directed by Vittorio De Sica,
of a shepherd giving shelter to a band of
thieves. **DT37**

Bandolero! (1968, C, 106m, PG)
James Stewart and Dean Martin are two fugitive brothers who take Raquel Welch hostage
from Texas to Mexico. **ST149, ST207, WE9**

Bang the Drum Slowly
(1973, C, 97m, PG)
A star pitcher tries to help his roommate, a
third-string catcher, face up to a fatal illness.
Michael Moriarty and Robert De Niro star in
this drama. Overrated, especially as a baseball
film. **DR22, ST51**

Bank Dick, The (1940, B&W, 74m, NR)
W.C. Fields gets a job as a bank guard, and
a robber decides to make his move. With
Grady Sutton and Franklin Pangborn. Contains one of the greatest comic car rides of
them all. **ST67,** *Recommended*

Bank Shot (1974, C, 83m, PG)
Comic heist by Donald Westlake stars George
C. Scott as head of gang planning to steal an
entire bank. With Joanna Cassidy, Sorrell
Booke, G. Wood, and Clifton James. **CO10,
MY18, ST196**

Bar Sinister see *It's a Dog's Life*

Barabbas (1962, C, 134m, NR)
Anthony Quinn plays the robber whose free-
dom spelled doom for Jesus Christ in this
biblical epic. With Silvana Mangano, Arthur
Kennedy, Jack Palance, and Ernest Borgnine.
CL13, HF17

Barbarella (1968, C, 98m, PG)
Science fiction spoof, with spacey heroine
(Jane Fonda) experiencing all kinds of adven-
tures. Considered sexy at the time of its
release, but check the rating. **CU4, CU6,
SF19, SF22, ST72**

Barbarian and the Geisha, The
(1958, C, 105m, NR)
Historical drama starring John Wayne as
a diplomat who helps open 19th-century
Japan to the West. Directed by John Huston.
DR27, DT60, ST224

Barbarosa (1982, C, 90m, PG)
Willie Nelson plays an aging outlaw who
teaches a naive farm boy survival skills to
carry on his legend along the Tex-Mex bor-
der. With Gary Busey and Gilbert Roland.
Written by William Witliff; directed by Fred
Schepisi on magnificent locations in Texas's
Big Bend country. **MU12, WE3, WE9**

Barbary Coast (1935, B&W, 90m, NR)
Miriam Hopkins plays a saloon singer in the
Gold Rush days of San Francisco, fending off
the advances of her ruthless boss (Edward G.
Robinson). With Joel McCrea. Howard Hawks
directed. **DT53, ST144, ST186, WE8**

Barber Shop, The (1933, B&W, 21m, NR)
Classic W.C. Fields short, with Bill playing a
barber with a very sharp razor. **ST67**

Barefoot Contessa, The
(1954, C, 128m, NR)
Humphrey Bogart stars as a manipulative director who promotes his protégée (Ava Gardner) into stardom, with the help of a cynical press agent (Oscar winner Edmond O'Brien). Striking color photography; directed by Joseph L. Mankiewicz. **CL9, DR13, DT84, ST15, ST79, XT4**

Barefoot Executive, The
(1971, C, 95m, G)
Disney comedy finds Kurt Russell as a young employee at a struggling TV network; with the help of a clever chimpanzee, he goes from the mailroom to executive row in no time. **FA1, ST191**

Barefoot in the Park (1967, C, 105m, NR)
Neil Simon's romantic comedy about a young couple's struggles to make a life in New York, starring Jane Fonda and Robert Redford. Charles Boyer and Mildred Natwick offer fine support. **CO1, ST16, ST72, ST181, WR30, XT9**

Barfly (1987, C, 99m, R)
Two skid-row alcoholics strike up a friendship of sorts, based on their mutual love of the bottle. Mickey Rourke and Faye Dunaway star in this wry and intoxicating comedy-drama based on the writings of Charles Bukowski. **DR15, ST61, ST190,** *Recommended*

Barkleys of Broadway, The
(1949, C, 109m, NR)
Fred Astaire and Ginger Rogers play famous dancing partners who marry, separate, and then reunite. **CL15, MU1, MU4, ST4, ST187**

Barn Burning (1980, C, 40m, NR)
Adaptation of William Faulkner short story about the infamous Snopes family, starring Tommy Lee Jones. Written by Horton Foote; originally made for public TV. **WR6**

Barn of the Living Dead see *Nightmare Circus*

Barnum (1986, C, 100m, NR)
Burt Lancaster plays the famed nineteenth-century showman in this biographical drama. With Hanna Schygula. Originally made for TV. **DR4, DR12, ST129**

Baron of Arizona, The
(1950, B&W, 90m, NR)
Vincent Price stars as a landgrabbing villain in nineteenth-century Arizona. Directed by Samuel Fuller. **DT49, ST179**

Barretts of Wimpole Street, The
(1934, B&W, 110m, NR)
Story of romance between nineteenth-century poets Elizabeth Barrett and Robert Browning. Norma Shearer and Fredric March star, with Charles Laughton and Maureen O'Sullivan. Also known as *Forbidden Alliance.* 1957 remake by same director, Sidney Franklin, not available on video. **CL2, ST132, ST148**

Barry Lyndon (1975, C, 183m, PG)
Stanley Kubrick's epic about an eighteenth-century Irish scoundrel. Based on William Makepeace Thackeray's classic novel. Exquisitely photographed by John Alcott. Ryan O'Neal and Marisa Berenson star. Deliberately paced, ultimately rewarding, although best seen on the big screen. **CL1, DR5, DT68,** *Recommended*

Barry McKenzie Holds His Own
(1974, C, 93m, NR)
Australian comedy from director Bruce Beresford about twin brothers (both played by Barry Crocker) and a woman who is mistaken for the queen of England. **DT10, FF5**

Barton Fink (1991, C, 116m, R)
Dark comedy of idealistic playwright (John Turturro) who comes to 1941 Hollywood to become a screenwriter and ends up with writer's block. With John Goodman (sensational), Judy Davis, John Mahoney, Michael Lerner, and Jon Polito. Directed by Joel Coen; he and his brother Ethan wrote the screenplay. Evocative production design by Dennis Gassner. **CO6, CO8, CO12, DT27, ST46, XT26,** *Recommended*

Basic Instinct (1992, C, 127m, R)
Thriller, set in San Francisco, of a bisexual woman writer suspected of being an ice-pick killer by a cop—who then falls into bed with her. Michael Douglas and Sharon Stone (a star-making role) are the leads, with George Dzundza, Jeanne Tripplehorn, and Dorothy Malone in support. Screenplay by Joe Eszterhas, directed by Paul Verhoeven. Available in letterboxed edition. Also available in an unrated director's cut with about a minute of extra footage that nearly earned the film an NC-17 rating, plus interviews with Douglas, Stone, and Verhoeven; running time: 150 minutes. Not without virtues, but ultimately a prime example of the director's penchant for overkill; particularly offensive is its portrayal of women in general. **CU6, CU10, CU19, DR3, MY2, MY4, MY5, MY13, ST59, XT13**

Basket Case (1982, C, 89m, NR)
Horror story of separated Siamese twins, one a deformed monster, both seeking revenge on the doctors who separated them. Has well-deserved cult reputation. Frank

Henenlotter wrote and directed; Kevin Van Hentenryck stars. **CU4, CU7, HO15, HO18,** *Recommended*

Basket Case II (1990, C, 89m, R)
Gruesome follow-up to the Siamese twins horror tale, with same star and writer-director. Annie Ross heads the supporting cast. **HO15, HO18, HO24, MU12**

Basket Case 3: The Progeny
(1992, C, 90m, R)
As title suggests, this entry in the Siamese twins horror series concentrates on the off-spring between the monster Belial (the deformed twin) and his "mate," Eve. Kevin Van Hentenryck returns as the "good" twin; Annie Ross is back as the mother figure from Chapter 2. **HO15, HO18, MU12**

Bat, The (1959, B&W, 80m, NR)
Haunted house tale from Mary Roberts Rine-hart stars Vincent Price, Agnes Moorehead, and Gavin Gordon. **HO3, ST179**

Bat 21 (1988, C, 88m, R)
An American soldier, stranded behind enemy lines during the Vietnam War, has as his only hope a courageous chopper pilot. Gene Hackman and Danny Glover star. **AC4, AC24, ST88, ST96**

Bataan (1943, B&W, 114m, NR)
Classic World War II drama of brave Americans holding out against impossible odds. Robert Taylor, George Murphy, and Thomas Mitchell star. **AC1**

Bathing Beauty (1944, C, 101m, NR)
Esther Williams's first starring role has her playing a swim coach; Red Skelton is her ex-husband trying to win her back. With Basil Rathbone, Ethel Smith, Xavier Cugat, and Harry James and His Orchestra. **MU1**

Batman (1966, C, 105m, NR)
Adventure starring the Caped Crusader from the comics, spun off from the popular TV series of the mid-1960s. Adam West and Burt Ward repeat their roles as Batman and Robin; comic villains are played by Burgess Meredith, Cesar Romero, and Lee Meriwether. **AC17**

Batman (1989, C, 126m, PG-13)
Michael Keaton is the Caped Crusader, Jack Nicholson is the Joker in this extravagantly produced adventure of the comic book hero. With Kim Basinger, Robert Wuhl, Jack Palance, Billy Dee Williams, and Pat Hingle. Eye-popping production design by Anton Furst; Tim Burton directed. More the Joker's movie than Batman's but Burton's weird sensibility helps. **AC17, DT20, SF14, ST122, ST163, ST227,** *Recommended*

Batman Returns (1992, C, 126m, PG-13)
Michael Keaton's second outing as the Caped Crusader; he squares off against three foes: the Penguin (Danny DeVito), Catwoman (Michelle Pfeiffer), and evil industrialist Max Schreck (Christopher Walken). With Michael Gough (as Alfred), Michael Murphy, Pat Hingle, and Paul Reubens (as the Penguin's father). Written by Daniel Waters and directed by Tim Burton; they color this story a shade too darkly, especially in the gross-out antics of the Penguin. Pfeiffer's terrific, but the real star is the production design by Bo Welch. **AC17, DT20, SF14, ST54, ST122, ST173, ST222**

*batteries not included
(1987, C, 107m, PG)
A group of tenants in a New York slum apartment house scheduled for demolition get some unusual help from an army of tiny aliens. Jessica Tandy and Hume Cronyn head the cast of this family fantasy drama. **FA8**

Battle Circus (1953, B&W, 90m, NR)
Humphrey Bogart drama of a surgeon's trials during the Korean War. With June Allyson and Keenan Wynn. Directed by Richard Brooks. **AC3, DT15**

Battle Cry (1955, C, 149m, NR)
World War II drama, taking Marine outfit through training and into combat. Based on Leon Uris's novel; directed by Raoul Walsh. Van Heflin, Tab Hunter, and Dorothy Malone star. **AC1, DT131**

Battle for the Planet of the Apes
(1973, C, 92m, PG)
Fifth and final in the Apes series, featuring clips from earlier installments. Roddy McDowall, Paul Williams, and John Huston star. **DT60, FA8, SF8, SF13, SF23**

Battle Force (1978, C, 97m, NR)
Drama traces the lives of two families, one German and the other American, up to World War II. Helmut Berger and Samantha Eggar star, with John Huston, Henry Fonda, and Stacy Keach. Newsreel footage narrated by Orson Welles. Also known as *The Great Battle.* **AC1, DT60, DT134, ST71**

Battle of Algiers, The
(1965, B&W, 123m, NR)
Documentary-style drama of Algerian resistance to French colonialism during the 1950s. Powerful political film directed by Gillo Pontecorvo in unnervingly vivid fashion. Should have won Best Foreign Language Film Oscar; director also should have been tapped when he was nominated

in 1968. **AC6, CU9, FF2, XT28,** *Essential, Recommended*

Battle of Austerlitz, The
(1960, C, 123m, NR)
Drama of Napoleon's final battle features international cast: Claudia Cardinale, Martine Carol, Leslie Caron, Vittorio De Sica, Jean Marais, Jack Palance, Orson Welles, and Pierre Mondy as Bonaparte. Directed by Abel Gance. Original running running time: 166 minutes. **DT37, DT134, HF19**

Battle of Britain (1969, C, 132m, G)
All-star British cast enlivens this account of aerial combat over British soil during World War II. Michael Caine, Christopher Plummer, Laurence Olivier, Ralph Richardson, Harry Andrews, and Trevor Howard appear, with Rolf Stiefel as Hitler. **AC1, AC11, HF12, ST25, ST168, ST184**

Battle of the Bulge, The
(1965, C, 141m, NR)
Henry Fonda, Robert Shaw, Robert Ryan, and Dana Andrews star in this account of the 1944 battle for Belgium against desperate German forces. Original running time: 163 minutes. **AC1, ST71, ST193**

Battle of the Sexes, The
(1960, B&W, 88m, NR)
Peter Sellers plays an auld Scot with murder in his heart in this British comedy. **ST198**

Battleground (1949, B&W, 118m, NR)
World War II drama centering on the Battle of the Bulge, starring Van Johnson, John Hodiak, Ricardo Montalban, and George Murphy. Directed by William Wellman. **AC1, DT135**

Battleship Potemkin see *Potemkin*

Bay Boy, The (1984, C, 107m, R)
Coming-of-age drama set in rural Canada during the Depression, starring Kiefer Sutherland, Liv Ullmann, and Peter Donat. **ST220**

Beachcomber, The (1938, B&W, 92m, NR)
British drama from W. Somerset Maugham story of beach bum's encounter with a missionary, featuring real-life husband and wife stars Charles Laughton and Elsa Lanchester. **DR23, ST132, WR23**

Beaches (1988, C, 123m, PG-13)
The lifelong friendship of two women (Bette Midler, Barbara Hershey) is put to the test when one falls fatally ill. An unabashedly sentimental drama directed by Garry Marshall. Midler performs several songs. **DR2, DR10, ST104, ST156**

Bear, The (1988, C, 90m, PG)
French adventure tale of a bear cub's learning survival skills in the face of hunters and the vagaries of Mother Nature. **AC12, FA5, FF1**

Bear Island (1980, C, 118m, PG)
Adaptation of the Alistair MacLean novel about the race for a Nazi submarine loaded with gold, trapped under the Arctic ice. Donald Sutherland, Vanessa Redgrave, and Christopher Lee star. **ST135, ST182**

Beast From 20,000 Fathoms, The
(1953, B&W, 80m, NR)
Classic 1950s sci-fi story of prehistoric creature set free by atomic testing to run rampant. Special effects by Ray Harryhausen. Costarring with the Beast are Paul Christian and Paula Raymond. **SF1**

Beast in the Cellar, The (1970, C, 87m, R)
Two spinster sisters hide their maniacal brother in the basement in this British horror story. Beryl Reid and Flora Robson star. **HO14, HO26**

Beast Must Die, The (1974, C, 93m, PG)
A wealthy man believes his friend is a werewolf. He installs surveillance cameras throughout his home, then invites his friends for the weekend. Peter Cushing stars. **HO4, ST43**

Beast With Five Fingers, The
(1946, B&W, 88m, NR)
Classic horror tale of a dead pianist whose severed hand returns for revenge. Robert Alda stars, with Andrea King and the peerless Peter Lorre. **HO1, HO19**

Beast Within, The (1982, C, 90m, R)
A woman, raped on her wedding night by a deformed fiend, gives birth to a son who never misbehaves, until his seventeenth birthday. Ronny Cox, Bibi Besch, and Paul Clemens star. **HO4, HO13**

Beastmaster, The (1982, C, 118m, PG)
Sword and sorcery adventure, featuring a hero who communicates with animals, a lovely slave girl, and an evil priest. Marc Singer, Tanya Roberts, and Rip Torn star. **AC18, ST216**

Beastmaster 2: Through the Portals of Time (1990, C, 90m, PG-13)
Second Beastmaster saga has Marc Singer leaping through time warp into present-day Los Angeles to pursue villains Wings Hauser and Sarah Douglas. **AC18, SF4, XT10**

Beat Street (1984, C, 106m, PG)
Inner-city kids put on a show in this breakdancing musical, starring Rae Dawn Chong and Guy Davis. **MU9**

Beat the Devil (1954, B&W, 89m, NR)
Humphrey Bogart and Jennifer Jones head

the cast of this unusual spoof of spy films. Written by Truman Capote and John Huston (who also directed). Gina Lollobrigida, Robert Morley, and Peter Lorre costar. Misunderstood on its initial release, now a cult classic for its groundbreaking spoofing of the international thriller genre. **CL14, CU5, CU13, DT60, ST15,** *Essential*

Beatles, The: The First U.S. Visit
(1991, B&W, 90m, NR)
Documentary of Fab Four's 1964 invasion of America, with familiar clips from Ed Sullivan shows and lots of rare offstage footage. Directed by Albert and David Maysles. **MU11,** *Recommended*

Beatrice (1988, C, 132m, R)
French drama, set during the Hundred Years' War, of a warrior who comes home to bully his son and embark on an incestuous relationship with his daughter. Directed by Bertrand Tavernier. Also known as *The Passion of Beatrice.* **DT123**

Beau Brummel (1924, B&W, 92m, NR)
Silent historical drama of the famed ladies' man who led a life of dissolution after seeing his true love married off to a nobleman he despised. John Barrymore stars, with Mary Astor and Willard Louis. **CL3, CL12, ST8**

Beau Brummel (1954, C, 113m, NR)
Swashbuckler classic features Stewart Granger as the nineteenth-century British lover and swordsman. With Elizabeth Taylor, Peter Ustinov, and Robert Morley. **AC13, ST212**

Beau Geste (1939, B&W, 114m, NR)
Classic Foreign Legion tale of three brothers surviving desert hardships, tribal warfare. Gary Cooper, Ray Milland, Robert Preston, and Brian Donlevy star, with Susan Hayward. Directed by William Wellman. **AC13, DT135, ST37, ST100**

Beau Pere (1981, C, 120m, NR)
French comedy-drama about a man's relationship with his teen-aged stepdaughter blossoming into romance after the death of her mother. Patrick Dewaere and Ariel Besse star. Bertrand Blier directed. **FF1**

Beautiful Blonde From Bashful Bend, The (1949, C, 77m, NR)
Comic western about a woman gunslinger who's mistaken for a proper lady. Betty Grable stars, with Cesar Romero, Rudy Vallee, and Sterling Holloway. Directed by Preston Sturges. **DT121, ST91, WE8, WE14**

Beautiful Dreamers
(1992, C, 107m, PG-13)
Rip Torn plays Walt Whitman in this historical drama about the writer's friendship with a physician (Colm Theore) trying to treat the retarded. **DR5, ST216**

Beauty and the Beast
(1946, B&W, 92m, NR)
From French director Jean Cocteau, the classic fable of an impossible romance. Jean Marais and Josette Day star. **DT26, FF1, SF2,** *Essential, Recommended*

Beauty and the Beast (1984, C, 60m, NR)
Love is in the eye of the beholder—as the beauty (Susan Sarandon) brings out the best in the beast (Klaus Kinski) in a romantic fantasy from Faerie Tale Theatre. **FA12, ST126, ST194**

Beauty and the Beast (1991, C, 85m, G)
Animated version of the legend with first-rate songs. Voices by Paige O'Hara, Robby Benson, Jerry Orbach, and Angela Lansbury. Discontinued from manufacture as of April 1993; copies may be hard to find. **FA2, MU8, ST131,** *Recommended.*

Bebe's Kids (1992, C, 73m, PG-13)
Animated story based on characters created by comic Robin Harris, his girlfriend's impossible children. Faizon Love provides the voice of the late comic. As the rating suggests, parents might want to pre-screen before letting younger kids view. **CO2, DR14**

Because of the Cats (1973, C, 95m, R)
A gang of wealthy kids fall into a bizarre murder cult. Sylvia Kristel stars. **HO11, HO25**

Because You're Mine (1952, C, 103m, NR)
MGM musical of opera star (Mario Lanza) who's drafted, falls in love with an officer's daughter (Doretta Morrow). **MU1**

Becket (1964, C, 148m, NR)
Historical drama of clash between England's King Henry II (Peter O'Toole) and the Archbishop of Canterbury, Thomas à Becket (Richard Burton). With John Gielgud. **DR5, ST22, ST86, ST169**

Becky Sharp (1935, C, 83m, NR)
Adaptation of Thackeray's classic novel of social climbing, *Vanity Fair*, with Miriam Hopkins in title role. Important as first full-length film shot in 3-color Technicolor. Directed by Rouben Mamoulian. **CL1, CL9, DT83**

Becoming Colette (1992, C, 97m, R)
Drama of early career of French writer and her turn-of-the-century marriage to a man who forced her to write erotica under his pseudonym. Mathilda May stars, with Klaus

Maria Brandauer, Virginia Madsen, and Paul Rhys. **DR4**

Bed & Breakfast (1992, C, 98m, PG-13)
Three women from different generations of the same family who run a B&B on the coast of Maine must deal with the arrival of a handsome amnesiac—who's really a con man. Roger Moore, Talia Shire, Colleen Dewhurst, and Nina Siemaszko star. **DR8, DR10**

Bedazzled (1967, C, 107m, NR)
Comedy of nerdy man who makes several deals with the Devil to be near the woman he loves. Dudley Moore and Peter Cook star; Stanley Donen directed. Cook and Moore are delightful. **CO3, CU5, DT38, HO10, ST160,** *Recommended*

Bedford Incident, The
(1965, B&W, 102m, NR)
An aggressive U.S. naval captain tries to attack a Soviet submarine in international waters. Richard Widmark stars, with Sidney Poitier and Martin Balsam. **ST174**

Bedknobs and Broomsticks
(1971, C, 117m, G)
An amateur witch (Angela Lansbury) helps the British win a few World War II battles in this Disney fantasy. **FA1, ST131**

Bedlam (1946, B&W, 79m, NR)
Val Lewton produced this psychological thriller about a young lady (Anna Lee) in eighteenth-century England who tries to reform conditions at an insane asylum and finds herself being committed. Boris Karloff stars as her tormentor. **HO27, ST119**

Bedroom Window, The (1987, C, 112m, R)
Wrong-man thriller in the Hitchcock mold has an innocent man (Steve Guttenberg) accused of murder when he covers for the witness—his lover and his boss's wife. Isabelle Huppert and Elizabeth McGovern costar. **MY7**

Bedtime for Bonzo (1951, B&W, 83m, NR)
Comedy about a professor who takes a chimp into his house as an experiment. Ronald Reagan's name at the top of the cast has made this a cult comedy. **CO18, CU5**

Bedtime Story (1963, C, 99m, NR)
Comedy of two rival seducers plying their trade on the French Riviera. Marlon Brando and David Niven costar. Remade as *Dirty Rotten Scoundrels*. **CO3, ST18**

Beer (1985, C, 82m, R)
A female ad executive comes up with a tasteless campaign to sell suds—and, of course, it works. Satire starring Loretta Swit, with Rip Torn, Kenneth Mars, and Dick Shawn. **ST216**

Beethoven (1992, C, 88m, PG)
Family comedy of a lovable, slobbering St. Bernard who disrupts a suburban neighborhood. Charles Grodin stars, with Bonnie Hunt and Dean Jones (as a villain!). **CO5, FA5, FA6, ST94**

Beethoven's Nephew (1985, C, 103m, NR)
Historical comedy about the composer's relationship with his only nephew. Wolfgang Reichmann stars, with Dietmar Prinz, Jane Birkin, and Nathalie Baye. Directed by Paul Morrissey. **DT90**

Beetlejuice (1988, C, 92m, PG)
A pair of friendly ghosts can't scare away the obnoxious family that's moved into their house, so they call on a legendary "bio-exorcist" for help. Alec Baldwin, Geena Davis, and Michael Keaton (at his manic best) star, with Catherine O'Hara, Winona Ryder, and Jeffrey Jones in this comedy packed with wild special effects. Directed by Tim Burton, who stamps the material with his own brand of original humor. **CO11, CO14, DT20, ST45, ST122, XT24,** *Recommended*

Before I Hang (1940, B&W, 71m, NR)
A doctor working on a rejuvenation serum becomes a killer when he uses the blood of a murderer. Boris Karloff, Evelyn Keyes star. **ST119**

Before the Revolution
(1964, C, 115m, NR)
Director Bernardo Bertolucci's second feature is an intense drama of a youth trying to decide between commitment to political activism and a marriage into a bourgeois family. **DT13**

Beguiled, The (1971, C, 109m, R)
Clint Eastwood plays a wounded Confederate soldier who seeks shelter in a girls' school, with disastrous results. With Geraldine Page and Elizabeth Hartman. Directed by Don Siegel. Creepy, unsettling, with one of Eastwood's best performances. **DT116, ST64, WE6,** *Recommended*

Behave Yourself! (1951, B&W, 81m, NR)
A couple is chased by a criminal gang after witnessing a crime. Farley Granger and Shelley Winters star, with Lon Chaney, Jr., in this thriller played for laughs. **ST27, ST232**

Behind Locked Doors see *Human Gorilla, The*

Behind the Rising Sun
(1943, B&W, 89m, NR)
Drama of Japanese man (J. Carrol Naish) who gets his Americanized son involved in

1930s Sino-Japanese conflict. With Margo, Tom Neal, and Robert Ryan. **ST193**

Behold a Pale Horse
(1964, B&W, 118m, NR)
Drama of post–Civil War Spain, with exiled guerrilla Gregory Peck deciding to return to his homeland, in the face of certain death at the hands of an old enemy (Anthony Quinn). Fred Zinnemann directed. **DT144, ST171**

Being There (1980, C, 124m, PG)
A reclusive gardener is set loose on the world when his boss dies, and his cryptic remarks are mistaken for profound political observations. Peter Sellers stars in this poker-faced, brilliantly played satire, adapted from Jerzy Kosinski's novel. With Shirley MacLaine, Oscar winner Melvyn Douglas, Jack Warden, and Richard Dysart. Directed by Hal Ashby; photographed by Caleb Deschcanel. Shot in Washington, D.C., and at the Biltmore Estate in Asheville, N.C. **CO2, CO12, DR21, ST58, ST145, ST198, XT4, XT12, XT26,** *Recommended*

Bela Lugosi Meets a Brooklyn Gorilla
(1952, B&W, 74m, NR)
Duke Mitchell and Sammy Petrillo (the poor man's Martin and Lewis) are shipwrecked on an island where a mad doctor (Bela Lugosi) is conducting bizarre experiments. Also known as *The Boys From Brooklyn.* **ST143**

Believers, The (1987, C, 114m, R)
A widowed police psychiatrist discovers his son has been chosen as the next sacrifice to a religious cult operating out of Harlem. Martin Sheen stars, with Helen Shaver, Robert Loggia, and Harley Cross. Directed by John Schlesinger. **DT113, HO11, XT9**

Belizaire the Cajun (1986, C, 100m, PG)
The swamps of nineteenth-century Louisiana are the setting for this drama of an herbal dealer with eyes for the Cajun wife of an Anglo man. Armand Assante stars, with Gail Youngs, Michael Schoeffling, and Stephen McHattie. Watch for Robert Duvall in a bit part as a preacher. **DR5, ST63**

Bell, Book, and Candle
(1958, C, 103m, NR)
Kim Novak plays a contemporary witch who casts a love spell on her next-door neighbor (James Stewart) in this comedy. With Jack Lemmon, Elsa Lanchester, Ernie Kovacs, and Hermione Gingold. **ST138, ST207**

Bell Jar, The (1979, C, 107m, R)
Drama set in the early 1950s about a sensitive college student's breakdown, based on the autobiographical novel by poet Sylvia Plath. Marilyn Hasset stars, with Julie Harris,

Anne Jackson, and Barbara Barrie. **DR10, DR19**

Bellboy, The (1960, B&W, 72m, NR)
Jerry Lewis stars in this series of comic sketches set in a plush Miami Beach hotel. Lewis's character never speaks; this was his first film as a director and still may be his best. **ST139,** *Recommended*

Bellboy and the Playgirls, The
(1962, B&W/C, 94m, NR)
A 1958 German film, shot in B&W, about a bellboy/Peeping Tom spying on lingerie models, had color sequences added, directed in the U.S. by a young Francis Ford Coppola. It's a long way from here to *The Godfather.* Also known as *The Playgirls and the Bellboy.* **DT29**

Belle de Jour (1967, C, 100m, R)
Catherine Deneuve stars in this disturbing portrait of a French housewife drawn to a second life as a prostitute. One of director Luis Buñuel's greatest films. UNAVAILABLE ON VIDEO. **XT29**

Belle of New York, The
(1952, C, 82m, NR)
Gay '90s musical has Fred Astaire as a playboy pursuing a missionary, played by Vera-Ellen. **ST4**

Belles of St. Trinians, The
(1955, B&W, 90m, NR)
Classic British comedy set in a girls' school run by a zany headmistress, whose bookie brother would like to use the students as part of his operation. Alastair Sim stars (in two roles), with Joyce Grenfell, George Cole, and Hermione Baddeley. **CO17, CO18**

Bellissima (1951, B&W, 112m, NR)
An overbearing mother pushes her daughter into a stage career in this Italian drama starring Anna Magnani. Luchino Visconti directed. **DT127**

Bellman and True (1988, C, 112m, R)
Bank robbers enlist the aid of a mild-mannered computer expert, threatening his son if he doesn't cooperate. Bernard Hill stars in this first-rate British thriller that concentrates more on character than action. **MY15, MY18,** *Recommended*

Bells, The (1926, B&W, 108m, NR)
Silent drama of an innkeeper who murders a traveler and is tormented by his conscience. Lionel Barrymore stars, with Boris Karloff. **ST119**

Bells Are Ringing (1960, C, 127m, NR)
Musical comedy about an answering service operator and a ladies' man. Judy Holliday (in

her last film) stars with Dean Martin. Vincente Minnelli directed. Songs include "Just in Time" and "The Party's Over." **DT88, MU1, ST107, ST149, XT22**

Bells of Coronado (1950, B&W, 67m, NR)
Roy Rogers stars in this contemporary Western about an insurance agent out to thwart a uranium deal with foreign agents. **ST188**

Bells of Rosarita (1945, B&W, 68m, NR)
Roy Rogers gallops to the rescue of a young girl. **ST188**

Bells of St. Mary's, The
(1945, B&W, 126m, NR)
Sequel to *Going My Way,* with Father O'Malley (Bing Crosby) in a new parish with a wise Sister Superior (Ingrid Bergman). Directed by Leo McCarey. **DT80, ST13, ST40**

Bells of San Angelo (1947, B&W, 54m, NR)
Roy Rogers takes on evildoers who want to snatch a young girl's ranch. With Dale Evans. **ST188**

Belly of an Architect, The
(1987, C, 108m, R)
An American architect visits Rome to oversee an exhibit honoring his hero, eighteenth-century designer Etienne-Louis Boullee. Brian Dennehy and Chloe Webb star in this typically reflective film from British director Peter Greenaway. **DR23, DR27, DT51, XT17**

Beloved Rogue, The
(1927, B&W, 99m, NR)
Silent drama of poet-adventurer François Villon, a costume tale that plays fast and loose with history. John Barrymore stars, with Conrad Veidt and Marceline Day. **AC15, CL12, ST8**

Ben (1972, C, 94m, PG)
A sequel to *Willard* has the lead rat, Ben, befriend a sick young boy. Lee Harcourt Montgomery and Joseph Campanella star. Michael Jackson sings the title song. **HO16**

Ben-Hur (1959, C, 217m, G)
Charlton Heston and Stephen Boyd star in this religious epic which won a record eleven Academy Awards, including statues for Heston, director William Wyler, and supporting actor Hugh Griffith. New edition has chariot race presented in letterboxed format. It shouldn't be considered sacrilegious to state that this hasn't worn well, though the action scenes still pack a punch. **CL13, CU19, DT142, HF17, XT1, XT2, XT4, XT6**

Ben-Hur: A Tale of the Christ
(1926, B&W/C, 148m, NR)
Silent classic, shot with then-record budget, about rival charioteers in the time of Christ.

Ramon Novarro and Francis X. Bushman star. Video version includes original tinted and Technicolor sequences. **CL12, CL13, HF17,** *Essential*

Bend of the River (1952, C, 91m, G)
Wagon train saga set in 1840s Oregon, starring James Stewart, Arthur Kennedy, and Rock Hudson. Directed by Anthony Mann. **DT85, ST112, ST207**

Beneath the Planet of the Apes
(1970, C, 95m, PG)
Second *Planet of the Apes* story features the simian heroes battling human mutants who somehow survived the holocaust. James Franciscus, Kim Hunter, and Charlton Heston star. **FA8, SF8, SF13, SF23**

Beneath the 12 Mile Reef
(1953, C, 102m, NR)
The scenery's the star in this adventure of a Florida family of sponge divers. Robert Wagner and Terry Moore star. **AC12**

Benji (1980, C, 87m, G)
Benji, the Laurence Olivier of the dog world, stars in his first adventure story. **FA5**

Benji Takes a Dive at Marineland
(1984, C, 60m, NR)
America's canine hero takes a tour of Marineland—and comes up swimming in this family adventure. **FA5**

Benji the Hunted (1987, C, 88m, G)
The lovable mutt uses his wits in the wilderness to protect some lion cubs in this adventure from the Disney studios. **FA1, FA5**

Benny & Joon (1993, C, 98m, PG)
Romantic story involving mentally ill young woman and her unlikely suitor, an eccentric young man. Mary Stuart Masterson and Johnny Depp star, with Aidan Quinn, Julianne Moore, Oliver Moore, and C.C.H. Pounder. **DR1**

Benny Goodman Story, The
(1955, C, 116m, G)
Film bio of America's premier jazz clarinetist, with Steve Allen as the King of Swing. Benny's great sidemen, Gene Krupa, Lionel Hampton, and Teddy Wilson, appear as themselves. **MU5**

Berkeley in the Sixties
(1990, C/B&W, 117m, NR)
Oscar-nominated documentary provides look back at student protest on the University of California campus, plus perspective from recent interviews with many of the participants. Produced and directed by Mark Kitchell. Originally made for public TV. A first-rate work of history. **CU16,** *Recommended*

Berlin Alexanderplatz
(1980, C, 931m, NR)
Epic portrait of Berlin during the 1920s from director Rainer Werner Fassbinder, adapted from novel by Alfred Doblin. Originally produced for German TV in thirteen episodes. Gunter Lamprecht, Hanna Schygulla, and Barbara Sukowa star. **DT42**

Berlin Express (1948, B&W, 86m, NR)
In Berlin after World War II, several Allied agents attempt to free a German government offical kidnapped by members of the Nazi underground. Merle Oberon, Robert Ryan, and Paul Lukas star. Directed by Jacques Tourneur. **DT124, MY6, ST193**

Berserk (1967, C, 96m, NR)
A circus owner (Joan Crawford) becomes frantic when a series of murders occur under her big top. **MY3, ST39**

Best Boy (1980, C, 111m, NR)
Oscar-winning documentary about filmmaker Ira Wohl's retarded cousin, a fifty-two-year-old man named Philly. **CU16**

Best Defense (1984, C, 94m, R)
Comedy about the arms race, featuring two related stories. In one, Dudley Moore bumbles through the development of a super tank, and in the other, Eddie Murphy plays a soldier stationed in the Middle East who has to employ the weapon. **CO13, ST160**

Best Foot Forward (1943, C, 95m, NR)
Big Broadway star decides to pay a visit to a small town in this musical comedy featuring outstanding dance numbers. Lucille Ball stars. **MU3**

Best Friends (1982, C, 116m, PG)
When a screenwriting team changes their status from Living Together to Married, their love life suffers. Burt Reynolds and Goldie Hawn star, with Ron Silver and Richard Libertini. Directed by Norman Jewison. **CO1, DT63, ST99, ST183**

Best Intentions, The (1992, C, 180m, NR)
Swedish drama written by Ingmar Bergman, based on the courtship and early married days of his parents, a theology student and daughter of wealthy parents. Samuel Fröler, Pernilla August, and Max von Sydow star. Directed by Bille August (husband of the co-star). Originally a six-hour presentation on Swedish TV. **DT11, FF7**

Best Little Girl in the World, The
(1981, C, 100m, NR)
Jennifer Jason Leigh plays a teen afflicted with anorexia nervosa. With Charles Durning, Eva Marie Saint, Melanie Mayron, Viveca

Lindfors, Jason Miller, and Ally Sheedy. Originally made for TV. **DR9, ST136**

Best Little Whorehouse in Texas, The
(1982, C, 114m, R)
The hit Broadway musical about a sheriff (Burt Reynolds) who tries to close down the infamous Chicken Ranch, run by his girlfriend (Dolly Parton). **MU2, MU17, ST183**

Best Man, The (1964, B&W, 102m, NR)
Gore Vidal adapted his own play about dirty-and double-dealing at a political convention. Henry Fonda and Cliff Robertson star, with Edie Adams and Shelley Berman. **DR21, ST71**

Best of Benny Hill Show, Volumes 1–5, The (1981–85, C, 517m, NR)
Five tapes of highlights from the risqué British comedian's popular TV program. **CO16**

Best of Bugs Bunny and Friends, The
(1986, C, 53m, NR)
Collection of Warner Brothers classic cartoon stars features *Duck Soup to Nuts*, *A Feud There Was*, and *Tweetie Pie*. Bugs's costars include Daffy Duck, Tweetie Pie, and Porky Pig. **FA11**

Best of Chevy Chase, The
(1987, C, 60m, NR)
Chevy's brief stint on "Saturday Night Live" yields this hour of comedy, featuring his Gerald Ford impression and his "Weekend Update" bits. With Richard Pryor and Jill Clayburgh. **CO13, ST31, ST180**

Best of Comic Relief, The
(1986, C, 120m, NR)
Highlights of a benefit show to help homeless people, hosted by Robin Williams, Billy Crystal, and Whoopi Goldberg. Among the comics featured are Jay Leno, Garry Shandling, Howie Mandel, Bobcat Goldthwait, Jerry Lewis, Harold Ramis, and Martin Short. **CO13, CO14, CO16, ST89, ST139, ST228,** *Recommended*

Best of Comic Relief '90
(1990, C, 120m, NR)
Whoopi Goldberg, Robin Williams, and Billy Crystal host this edition of the annual comedians' benefit to aid the homeless. With Bobcat Goldthwait, Elayne Boosler, George Carlin, and the Simpsons. **CO13, CO16, ST89, ST228**

Best of Dan Aykroyd, The
(1986, C, 60m, NR)
Classic Aykroyd bits from "Saturday Night Live," including the Bass-o-matic salesman, Richard Nixon, and the Coneheads. With Steve Martin. **CO13, ST150**

Best of Eddie Murphy: "Saturday Night Live," The (1989, C, 79m, NR)
Eddie's memorable bits from Saturdays gone by, including Mr. Robinson's Neighborhood, Little Richard Simmons, James Brown, Bill Cosby, and Buckwheat. **CO13**, *Recommended*

Best of Gilda Radner, The
(1989, C, 59m, NR)
Highlights from Gilda Radnnr's skits on "Saturday Night Live," featuring Roseanne Roseannadanna, Baba Wawa, Emily Litella, Lisa Loobner, and more. With Steve Martin. **CO13, ST150**

Best of John Belushi, The
(1985, C, 60m, NR)
The Killer Bees, Samurai Everything, Joe Cocker—they're all here on this collection of Belushi highlights from "Saturday Night Live." **CO13**

Best of Spike Jones, Volumes 1–3, The
(1954, B&W, 158m, NR)
Trio of tapes providing rare look at the man who murdered the classics, Tin Pan Alley, and all other musical forms. Drawn from his early 1950s TV show. **CO16**

Best of the Badmen (1951, C, 84m, NR)
Western drama about a former Union officer's vendetta against a detective and how famous outlaws help him get revenge. Robert Ryan and Robert Preston star, with Jack Beutel, Walter Brennan, and Lawrence Tierney as Jesse James. **HF16, ST193, WE3, WE5**

Best of the Best (1989, C, 95m, PG-13)
Drama set around a martial arts competition in Korea. Eric Roberts stars, with James Earl Jones, Sally Kirkland, and Phillip Rhee. **AC26, DR22, ST99**

Best of the Best II (1993, C, 100m, R)
Martial arts action with Eric Roberts and Phillip Rhee playing karate school instructors out for vengeance when their partner (Christopher Penn) is murdered in an illegal fighting match. **AC26**

Best of Times, The (1986, C, 105m, PG-13)
A pair of former high school football teammates get a chance to redeem themselves in a twenty-year anniversary rematch of the Big Game they lost. Robin Williams and Kurt Russell star in this comedy, with Pamela Reed and Holly Palance. Agreeable comedy, with all four stars shining. **CO3, CO19, ST191, ST228**

Best of W.C. Fields, The
(1930, B&W, 58m, NR)
Three of Fields's early short comedies, produced by Mack Sennett. **ST67**

Best Revenge (1984, C, 92m, NR)
Two Americans in Spain try to pull off a major hashish deal, with the usual double crosses. John Heard and Levon Helm star. **MU12**

Best Seller (1987, C, 110m, R)
A former hit man for a corporation turns to a bestselling novelist (and former cop) to write his life story. James Woods and Brian Dennehy star in this cat-and-mouse thriller. **MY9, ST233**

Best Years of Our Lives, The
(1946, B&W, 170m, NR)
Three World War II veterans (Dana Andrews, Oscar winners Fredric March and Harold Russell) adjust to life back home in this stirring drama. Oscar winner for Best Picture and Director (William Wyler). With Myrna Loy, Hoagy Carmichael, Teresa Wright, and Virginia Mayo. One of Wyler's best films. **CL8, DR26, DT142, ST142, ST148, XT1, XT2, XT4, XT6,** *Essential, Recommended*

Betrayal (1978, C, 100m, NR)
True drama of a psychiatrist who sexually harrassed his female patient. Lesley Ann Warren and Rip Torn star, with Ron Silver and Richard Masur. Originally made for TV. **DR6, ST216**

Betrayal (1983, C, 95m, R)
Harold Pinter adapted his play about a romantic triangle, beginning at the very end of the affair, flashing back in stages to the beginning. Jeremy Irons, Ben Kingsley and Patricia Hodge star. Superbly acted, with generous helpings of that unmistakable Pinter dialogue. **DR3, DR23, ST116, WR26,** *Recommended*

Betrayed (1954, C, 108m, NR)
Clark Gable and Lana Turner star in this World War II drama of the Resistance, set in Holland. **AC1, ST77, ST219**

Betrayed (1988, C, 123m, R)
An inexperienced FBI agent (Debra Winger) is assigned to go undercover to investigate a white supremacist group. What she doesn't count on is falling in love with one of the group's leaders (Tom Berenger). With John Heard and John Mahoney. Costa-Gavras directed. The story's topical urgency is undercut by unbelievable characters and situations. **DR3, MY5, ST231**

Betsy, The (1978, C, 125m, R)
Laurence Olivier stars as the head of a family-owned auto manufacturing plant. Trashy drama from Harold Robbins's bestseller. Supporting cast includes Robert Duvall, Katharine Ross, Tommy Lee Jones, Jane Alex-

ander, Kathleen Beller, Lesley-Anne Down, and Edward Herrmann. Olivier has a great time and you may, too, if you put your brain in neutral. **DR24, ST63, ST168**

Betsy's Wedding (1990, C, 97m, PG)
Comedy of family dealing with nuptials of prized daughter. Alan Alda and Madeline Kahn are the parents, Molly Ringwald is Betsy, Ally Sheedy her older sister. With Joe Pesci, Joey Bishop, and Catherine O'Hara. **CO5, CO14, ST172, XT20**

Bette Midler—Art or Bust
(1984, C, 82m, NR)
The Divine One in concert at the University of Minnesota, on her last (to date) national tour. **ST156**

Bette Midler's Mondo Beyondo
(1988, C, 60m, NR)
Bette stars in this comedy special (made for cable TV) as an Italian sexpot hosting a raunchy cable TV show. **CO16, ST156**

Betty Blue (1986, C, 117m, NR)
Erotic story of a writer's affair with a free-spirited young woman, whose mental instability begins to threaten their lives. Jean-Hughes Anglade and Beatrice Dalle star; Jean-Jacques Beineix directed. **CU6, FF1**

Between Friends (1983, C, 100m, NR)
Elizabeth Taylor and Carol Burnett play middle-aged women who offer each other moral support as they begin a new life in the singles world. Originally made for cable TV. **DR10, ST212**

Between Heaven and Hell
(1956, C, 94m, NR)
Robert Wagner plays a pampered Southern boy coming of age during World War II. With Terry Moore, Broderick Crawford, Buddy Ebsen, and L.Q. Jones. **AC1**

Between the Lines (1977, C, 101m, R)
An alternative newspaper in Boston is the setting for this charming comedy about a group of idealistic friends. Outstanding cast of young performers: Lindsay Crouse, John Heard, Jeff Goldblum, Jill Eikenberry, Gwen Welles, Bruno Kirby, and Stephen Collins. Directed by Joan Micklin Silver. **CO2, ST90,** *Recommended*

Beverly Hills Cop (1984, C, 105m, R)
Eddie Murphy plays Axel Foley, a Detroit cop who travels to California to investigate the murder of a friend. Action comedy costarring Lisa Eilbacher, Judge Reinhold, Ronny Cox, and John Ashton. **CO9, CO13, CO20, XT10**

Beverly Hills Cop II (1987, C, 105m, R)
The further adventures of Axel Foley; this

time, he's on the trail of a gang of murderous thieves. Eddie Murphy stars, with Ronny Cox, John Ashton, Judge Reinhold, Brigitte Nielsen, Dean Stockwell, and Jurgen Prochnow. **CO9, CO13, CO20, ST208, XT10**

Beverly Hills Madam
(1986, C, 100m, PG-13)
Faye Dunaway plays the title role in this drama of a woman with a very lucrative business. Among her associates: Robin Givens, Donna Dixon, and Melody Anderson. Originally made for TV. **ST61**

Beverly Hills, 90210 (1990, C, 92m, NR)
Opening episode of popular TV series about a pair of twins (Jason Priestly and Shannen Doherty) who move from Minnesota to Southern California and must adjust to life at a school where the students' cars far outclass their teachers'. Directed by Tim Hunter. **DR9, DR25, XT10**

Beware, My Lovely (1952, B&W, 77m, NR)
A lonely woman (Ida Lupino) hires a handyman (Robert Ryan), only to discover that he's a psychopath. Good performances. **MY3, ST193**

Beyond a Reasonable Doubt
(1956, C, 80m, NR)
Mystery, based on true story, of a usually peaceful New Zealand town that turns violent when an innocent farmer is charged with double murder. Dana Andrews and Joan Fontaine star. Fritz Lang directed. **DT70, MY8, ST73**

Beyond Obsession (1984, C, 116m, NR)
Marcello Mastroianni and Tom Berenger star in this thriller, set in Marrakesh, about an Italian ex-diplomat and an American and their mutual interest in the same woman. **ST154**

Beyond the Door (1974, C, 94m, R)
Horror film from Italy about the possession of a young girl, with *Exorcist* overtones. Juliet Mills and Richard Johnson star. **FF2, HO8**

Beyond the Door 2 (1979, C, 92m, R)
A little boy is possessed by the soul of his dead father seeking revenge on his wife. Horror drama from Italy, directed by Mario Bava. **FF2, HO8**

Beyond the Forest (1949, B&W, 96m, NR)
Bette Davis vehicle has her playing a scheming, small-town woman married to a doctor (Joseph Cotten). Directed by King Vidor. **DT126, ST44**

Beyond the Law (1968, C, 91m, NR)
Lee Van Cleef plays an outlaw who decides

to go straight when he learns that, as sheriff, he can claim a silver mine. **ST221, WE13**

Beyond the Limit (1983, C, 103m, R)
A British doctor in a South American country gets in over his head when he becomes involved with a diplomat's wife and with revolutionaries. Richard Gere, Michael Caine, and Bob Hoskins star in this adaptation of Graham Greene's *The Honorary Consul*. **DR27, ST25, ST84, ST111, WR11**

Beyond the Poseidon Adventure (1979, C, 122m, PG)
Sequel to *The Poseidon Adventure* about a race to recover treasure from the capsized ship before it sinks. Michael Caine and Sally Field star, with Telly Savalas, Slim Pickens, and Shirley Knight. **AC23, ST25, ST66**

Beyond the Stars (1989, C, 94m, NR)
Science fiction thriller has young boy genius investigating NASA coverup of botched moon landing. Christian Slater stars, with Martin Sheen, Olivia d'Abo, and F. Murray Abraham. **SF3, ST200**

Beyond the Valley of the Dolls (1970, C, 109m, R)
Spoofy "sequel" to famous trash story of three casualties of wicked Hollywood, with all-girl rock band clawing and sleeping their way to the top. Directed by Russ Meyer; written by Roger Ebert. **CU2, CU6**

Beyond Therapy (1987, C, 93m, R)
Comedy of two souls trying for romance but thwarted by their respective therapists. Julie Hagerty and Jeff Goldblum star, with Glenda Jackson, Tom Conti, and Christopher Guest. Robert Altman directed. **DT4, ST90, ST117**

Beyond Tomorrow (1940, B&W, 84m, NR)
Christmas fantasy of three millionaires reaching out to play matchmakers for a young couple. Richard Carlson, Jean Parker, Harry Carey, C. Aubrey Smith, and Charles Winninger star. **FA13**

Bhowani Junction (1956, C, 110m, NR)
Drama set in postwar India, with Ava Gardner as half-caste in love with a British officer (Stewart Granger). Directed by George Cukor. **DT32, ST79**

Bible, The (1966, C, 174m, NR)
Religious epic detailing many familiar stories from the first book of Genesis. John Huston directed and stars as Noah; also in the cast: Michael Parks (as Adam), George C. Scott (as Abraham), plus Peter O'Toole, Ava Gardner, and Richard Harris. **CL13, DT60, ST79, ST169, ST196**

Bicycle Thief, The (1949, B&W, 90m, NR)
Classic Italian drama of a poor man and his son searching the streets of Rome for their stolen bicycle. Vittorio De Sica directed; winner of a special Oscar. **DT37, XT7, *Essential***

Big (1988, C, 102m, PG)
Tom Hanks stars in this engaging comedy of a twelve-year-old boy who wakes up one morning in the body of a thirty-year-old man. With Elizabeth Perkins, Robert Loggia, and John Heard. Directed by Penny Marshall. **CO4, CO20, ST97, XT23, *Recommended***

Big Bad Mama (1974, C, 83m, R)
Depression-era action comedy with a shady lady, her male accomplices, and her two sexy daughters. Angie Dickinson stars, with Tom Skerritt, William Shatner, Susan Sennett, and Robbie Lee. Has a cult following for its numerous sex scenes. **CU6**

Big Bang, The (1990, C, 82m, R)
Utterly fascinating, one-of-a-kind documentary by James Toback, who interviewed a disparate group of people (from a young boy and girl to athletes to Holocaust survivors) about their theories on how life began, the afterlife, sin, and morality. Provocative, funny, and well worth a second viewing. **CU16, *Recommended***

Big Blue, The (1988, C, 118m, PG)
Adventure story of a pair of rival French free divers (men who use no equipment in their underwater diving), one of whom falls in love with an American woman. Rosanna Arquette stars, with Jean-Marc Barr and Jean Reno. **AC12**

Big Brawl, The (1980, C, 95m, R)
Martial arts star Jackie Chan is featured in this action drama set in 1930s gangster-era Chicago. Lots of action and not a few laughs. **AC26**

Big Bus, The (1976, C, 88m, PG)
Spoof of disaster movies set on a mammoth bus making an accident-prone cross-country trip. Stockard Channing, Joseph Bologna, John Beck, Lynn Redgrave, and Ned Beatty head the cast. **CO7**

Big Business (1988, C, 94m, PG)
Comedy starring Bette Midler and Lily Tomlin as two sets of twins mismatched at birth. One set grows up to run a New York corporation; the other grows up poor in rural West Virginia. Trouble starts when the country sisters travel to New York and run into you-know-who. Falls somewhat short of the classic it could have been. **CO3, CO5, ST156, ST215, XT27**

Big Carnival, The
(1951, B&W, 112m, NR)
Hard-bitten is a polite way to describe this
drama from writer-director Billy Wilder,
based loosely on the true story of a man
trapped in a cave and the media circus his
plight attracts. Kirk Douglas stars in a signature role as a cynical reporter looking for his
big exclusive. With Jan Sterling and Bob
Arthur. Also known as *Ace in the Hole*. Accurately forecasts current craze for eye-witness
reporting of personal tragedies. UNAVAIL-
ABLE ON VIDEO. **XT29**

Big Chill, The (1983, C, 108m, R)
A group of college friends from the 1960s are
reunited when one of their group commits
suicide. Slick portrait of a generation, starring
William Hurt, Glenn Close, Kevin Kline,
JoBeth Williams, Mary Kay Place, Tom
Berenger, and Jeff Goldblum, with Meg Tilly.
Glib and slick; see *The Return of the Secaucus
Seven* for a better take on the same subject.
DR7, ST33, ST90, ST114, ST127

Big Clock, The (1948, B&W, 95m, NR)
Exciting thriller of a magazine editor trying
to escape the clutches of a megalomaniacal
boss, getting ensnared as a suspect in murder
of the boss's mistress. Ray Milland and the
inimitable Charles Laughton star, with
Maureen O'Sullivan as Milland's wife and
George Macready as Laughton's henchman.
Directed by John Farrow. Storyline will sound
familiar to fans of the Kevin Costner-Gene
Hackman thriller, *No Way Out*. UNAVAIL-
ABLE ON VIDEO. **XT29**

Big Combo, The (1955, B&W, 89m, NR)
A cop (Cornel Wilde) takes on a mobster
with the help of the crook's mistress. With
Jean Wallace, Brian Donlevy, Richard Conte,
and Lee Van Cleef. One of the better *films
noirs*. **MY1, ST221,** *Recommended*

Big Country, The (1958, C, 166m, NR)
From director William Wyler comes an epic
tale of the Old West, with a land battle
erupting between settlers. Gregory Peck and
Charlton Heston head the cast, which also
includes Oscar winner Burl Ives, Jean Simmons, Carroll Baker, and Chuck Connors.
Widescreen will be lost on video. **CU20,
DT142, ST171, WE1, XT4**

Big Deal on Madonna Street
(1956, B&W, 91m, NR)
Classic Italian comedy about an inept band
of crooks and their bungling attempts to pull
off a heist. Vittorio Gassman and Marcello
Mastroianni star. **FF2, MY18, ST154,**
Recommended

Big Easy, The (1987, C, 106m, R)
A thriller set in New Orleans, with an easy-
going police detective (Dennis Quaid) trying
to solve a series of drug-related murders and
a nosy district attorney (Ellen Barkin) getting
in his way. First-rate soundtrack of contemporary New Orleans music. **MY2, MY5, ST7,
XT14**

Big Fix, The (1978, C, 108m, PG)
Richard Dreyfuss plays Moses Wine, a hippie
turned private eye. He's on the trail of a fellow former activist. **MY10, ST60**

Big Girls Don't Cry . . . They Get Even
(1992, C, 96m, PG)
Comedy of teen-ager tired of dealing with
her multiple step-parents and half-siblings
resulting from her parents' divorces; she
ducks out during a family vacation. Hillary
Wolf stars, with David Strathairn, Margaret
Whitton, Griffin Dunne, Patricia Kalembar,
and Adrienne Shelly. Directed by Joan Micklin Silver. **CO4, CO5, FA6**

Big Hand for the Little Lady, A
(1966, C, 95m, NR)
Comic Western about high-stakes poker
game and its lone female player (Joanne
Woodward). Henry Fonda costars, with Jason
Robards, Charles Bickford, and Burgess Meredith. **ST71, ST185, ST234, WE8, WE14**

Big Heat, The (1953, B&W, 90m, NR)
An ex-cop becomes obsessed with a case
when his wife is killed by a car bomb meant
for him. Glenn Ford, Gloria Grahame, and
Lee Marvin star. Directed by Fritz Lang at the
top of his American form. Virtually defines
the *film noir* genre. **AC22, DT70, MY1,
ST151,** *Essential, Recommended*

Big Hangover, The (1950, B&W, 82m, NR)
Melodrama of lawyer (Van Johnson) with
allergic reaction to booze, fighting his prob-
lem and trying to win heart of wealthy girl
(Elizabeth Taylor). With Leon Ames, Edgar
Buchanan, and Rosemary DeCamp. **ST212**

Big Jake (1971, C, 110m, PG)
John Wayne swings into action to save his
grandson's life. Richard Boone, Maureen
O'Hara, and Wayne's real-life son Patrick
costar in this Western drama. **ST167, ST224,
XT8**

Big Jim McLain (1952, B&W, 90m, NR)
John Wayne's on the trail of Commie spies
in Hawaii. A real artifact of the late, not-so-
great Cold War. With James Arness, Nancy
Olson, and Hans Conried. **ST224**

Big Knife, The (1955, B&W, 111m, NR)
One of the best portraits of the dark under-

belly of glamorous Hollywood, focusing on the tormented life of an actor. Jack Palance stars, with Rod Steiger, Ida Lupino, and Shelley Winters. Incisive script by Clifford Odets, sharp direction by Robert Aldrich. UNAVAILABLE ON VIDEO. **XT29**

Big Lift, The (1950, B&W, 120m, NR) Drama set against Berlin airlift, with American soldiers romancing German women. Montgomery Clift and Paul Douglas star. **ST32**

Big Mouth, The (1967, C, 107m, NR) Jerry Lewis comedy about a treasure hunt and its unscrupulous participants. **ST139**

Big Parade, The (1925, B&W, 126m, NR) Silent classic set in World War I Europe, starring John Gilbert and Renee Adoree. Box-office smash was also one of the first major films to deal with the war and its chilling effects. Directed by King Vidor. **AC2, CL12, DT126, XT25,** *Essential, Recommended*

Big Payoff, The see *Win, Place or Steal*

Big Picture, The (1989, C, 99m, PG-13) Satire of contemporary Hollywood, with Kevin Bacon as an up-and-coming director, Martin Short as an agent. The supporting cast includes Emily Longstreth, J.T. Walsh, Jennifer Jason Leigh, Michael McKean, and in a cameo, John Cleese. **CO8, CO14, CO15, ST136**

Big Red (1962, C, 89m, NR) Disney drama of a young boy's adventures with one very special Irish setter. **FA5**

Big Red One, The (1980, C, 113m, PG) World War II drama of tough sergeant (Lee Marvin) pushing his young recruits through several European campaigns. Samuel Fuller directed with customary verve; the story reflects many of his own experiences. **AC1, DT49, ST151,** *Recommended*

Big Shots (1987, C, 91m, PG-13) A pint-sized version of *The Sting*, with streetwise Darius McCrary and his new-found suburban pal Ricky Busker hustling their way through the streets of Chicago. With Paul Winfield. **CO4, FA7, ST230, XT11**

Big Show, The (1936, B&W, 70m, NR) Gene Autry plays two roles, a conceited movie cowboy and his look-alike stunt man, in this musical Western. The Sons of the Pioneers (with Roy Rogers, billed as Leonard Slye) do some harmonizing. **ST5, ST188**

Big Sky, The (1952, B&W, 122m, NR) Kirk Douglas and a rowdy band of 1830s fur trappers set out on a back-breaking expedi-

tion up the Missouri River. Howard Hawks directed. Based on the novel by A.B. Guthrie, Jr. **DT53, ST57, WE1**

Big Sleep, The (1946, B&W, 114m, NR) Private eye Philip Marlowe (Humphrey Bogart) falls for the lovely sister (Lauren Bacall) of a girl he's hired to protect in Raymond Chandler's classic thriller. Howard Hawks directed. Even when the story loses its way, the stars more than compensate. **CL15, DT53, MY1, ST15, WR2,** *Essential, Recommended*

Big Sleep, The (1978, C, 100m, R) Robert Mitchum plays Philip Marlowe in an updated version of Raymond Chandler's novel, closer to the actual story than the Bogart version, although the setting is London. With Sarah Miles, Candy Clark, Oliver Reed, Richard Boone, and James Stewart. **ST158, ST207, WR2**

Big Sombrero, The (1949, C, 77m, NR) Gene Autry comes to the aid of a lovely senorita whose fiancé is in cahoots with a swindler. **ST5**

Big Steal, The (1949, B&W, 71m, NR) Fast-moving chase thriller about a payroll heist and pursuit through the American Southwest and Mexico, starring Robert Mitchum (never more laconic) and Jane Greer, with William Bendix and Ramon Novarro. Directed by Don Siegel. **DT116, MY18, ST158, XT18,** *Recommended*

Big Store, The (1941, B&W, 80m, NR) The Marx Bros. go shopping at a department store. Margaret Dumont is not buying any of their nonsense. **ST152**

Big Street, The (1942, B&W, 88m, NR) A Damon Runyon story about a shy busboy (Henry Fonda) idolizing an embittered former show girl (Lucille Ball) who is wheelchair-bound. **ST71**

Big Top Pee-wee (1988, C, 86m, PG) Pee-wee Herman finds a circus in his farmyard and he decides to join the action, especially when he catches sight of a lovely trapeze artist. With Kris Kristofferson and Valeria Golino. **CO11, CO12, FA6, MU12**

Big Town, The (1987, C, 109m, R) Matt Dillon plays a small-town gambler looking to make it in the title locale—1950s Chicago. With Diane Lane, Tommy Lee Jones, Lee Grant, Bruce Dern, and Suzy Amis. **DR15, ST56**

Big Trail, The (1930, B&W, 110m, NR) Epic Western featuring John Wayne in one of his first starring roles, as a giant-sized, tender-hearted cowboy. Filmed in 70mm. Directed by Raoul Walsh. **DT131, ST224, WE1**

Big Trees, The (1952, C, 89m, NR)
Loggers battle homesteaders in this Western drama starring Kirk Douglas, with Eve Miller, Patrice Wymore, and Edgar Buchanan. **ST57**

Big Trouble (1985, C, 93m, R)
Comic retelling of familiar *film noir* tale of faithless wife (Beverly D'Angelo) and boyfriend (Peter Falk) trying to bump off her hubbie (Alan Arkin) for insurance money. With Charles Durning, Robert Stack, Paul Dooley, Valerie Curtin, and Richard Libertini. Directed by John Cassavetes. **CO10, XT23**

Big Trouble in Little China
(1986, C, 99m, PG-13)
A truck driver agrees to help his Chinese-American pal rescue the guy's fiancée from a cult operating beneath the streets of Chinatown. Kurt Russell stars in this action adventure from director John Carpenter. **AC21, AC26, DT23, ST191**

Big Wednesday (1978, C, 120m, PG)
Three surfing buddies from the 1960s find that the passing years aren't kind to them. Jan-Michael Vincent, Gary Busey, and William Katt star, with Barbara Hale (Katt's real-life mother). John Milius wrote and directed. **DR22, XT8**

Bigamist, The (1953, B&W, 80m, NR)
Title says it all: Edmond O'Brien tries to juggle marriage to two women, played by Joan Fontaine and Ida Lupino; the latter directed. **ST73, XT23**

Biggles: Adventures in Time
(1986, C, 100m, PG)
Time travel drama, with British man (Alex Hyde-White) moving between 1986 New York and World War I Europe, where he assists an aviator. With Neil Dickson and Peter Cushing. **SF4, SF19, ST43**

Bill (1981, C, 100m, NR)
True story of a retarded man released to the world after forty-six years in a mental hospital. Mickey Rooney won an Emmy for his starring performance. With Dennis Quaid; made for TV. **DR6, ST189**

Bill and Ted's Bogus Journey
(1991, C, 98m, PG)
Those masters of the air guitar we met in *B&T's Excellent Adventure* return for more time travel, as they battle that horrendous dude Death in a game of Twister. Keanu Reeves and Alex Winter star, with William Sadler as the Grim Reaper, Joss Ackland, Pam Grier, and George Carlin. **CO20, SF4**

Bill and Ted's Excellent Adventure
(1989, C, 90m, PG)
Time-travel comedy featuring a pair of lame-brained high school buddies (Keanu Reeves and Alex Winter) who get a crash course in history, thanks to a hip dude of a wizard (George Carlin). With Don Shor as Billy the Kid, Robert V. Barton as Lincoln, and Terry Camilleri as Napoleon. **CO20, HF1, HF18, HF19, SF4**

Bill Cosby: 49 (1987, C, 67m, NR)
The comedian holds forth on his impending middle age, his family, and a host of other topics, all grist for his comic mill. **CO16**

Bill Cosby: Himself (1981, C, 104m, NR)
An extended Cosby concert, filmed in Canada, featuring his observations on fatherhood and other modern dilemmas. **CO16**

Bill of Divorcement, A
(1932, B&W, 69m, NR)
Katharine Hepburn's first film, in which she's the daughter of a man (John Barrymore) just released from a mental hospital. Directed by George Cukor. **DT32, ST8, ST103**

Bill: On His Own (1983, C, 100m, NR)
Sequel to *Bill* has Mickey Rooney returning as the retarded man trying to make his way in the world after years of confinement in a mental hospital. With Teresa Wright and Dennis Quaid. Originally made for TV. **DR6, ST189**

Billie (1965, C, 87m, NR)
Comedy with Patty Duke playing a teen tomboy who proves to be a better athlete than many of the boys in her class. With Jim Backus, Jane Greer, and Warren Berlinger. **CO4, FA6**

Billion Dollar Hobo, The
(1978, C, 96m, G)
Disney comedy featuring Tim Conway as a man who becomes a bum to gain an inheritance. **FA1**

Billy Bathgate (1991, C, 106m, R)
Adaptation of E.L. Doctorow's novel about young man's initiation into the violent world of gangster Dutch Schultz. Dustin Hoffman stars as Schultz, with Nicole Kidman, Loren Dean as Billy, Bruce Willis, Steven Hill, and Steve Buscemi. Written by Tom Stoppard; directed by Robert Benton. **AC22, DR5, DR9, DR16, DR19, DT9, ST105, ST229**

Billy Budd (1962, B&W, 112m, NR)
Terence Stamp, Robert Ryan, Melvyn Douglas, and Peter Ustinov star in this intelligent, subtly played version of Herman Melville's classic novel about a naive sailor's

court-martial. Directed by Ustinov. **CL1, ST58, ST193, XT23,** *Recommended*

Billy Crystal: A Comic's Line
(1984, C, 59m, NR)
The "Saturday Night Live" alumnus leaves no comic stone unturned in this concert tape. **CO13, CO16**

Billy Crystal: Don't Get Me Started
(1986, C, 60m, NR)
Plenty of Billy's best bits, plus a "documentary" on his life and a spoof of a 1950s kiddie TV show. With Rob Reiner and Eugene Levy. **CO13, CO14, CO16, DT103**

Billy Crystal: Midnight Train to Moscow (1989, C, 72m, NR)
The comedian travels to the former Soviet Union to explore his family roots in this special made for cable TV. **CO13, CO16**

Billy Jack (1971, C, 112m, PG)
Pacifist schoolteacher is harassed by bullies at her school for Indians; karate expert shows up to help her out. Cult movie that has it both ways: preaches non-violence, presents a hero who kicks people's teeth out. Tom Laughlin and Delores Taylor star. **AC26, CU9**

Billy Liar (1963, B&W, 96m, NR)
British comedy-drama about a young man who prefers fantasies of heroic action to his drab everyday life. Tom Courtenay and Julie Christie star. John Schlesinger directed. **CO17, DR23, DT113, ST30**

Billy Rose's Jumbo see *Jumbo*

Billy the Kid Returns
(1938, B&W, 60m, NR)
Roy Rogers is mistaken for the legendary outlaw. **HF1, ST161**

Biloxi Blues (1988, C, 106m, PG-13)
Neil Simon comedy, a sequel to *Brighton Beach Memoirs,* with Eugene Jerome (Matthew Broderick) now in the U.S. Army. Christopher Walken costars. Mike Nichols directed. **CO6, CO21, DT91, ST222, WR23**

Bingo (1991, C, 87m, PG)
Young boy adopts unwanted dog, then his family has to move from Denver to Green Bay and leave the mutt behind. Guess who sets out to find his master? Cindy Williams, David Rasche, and Robert J. Steinmiller, Jr., star. **FA5**

Bingo Long Traveling All-Stars and Motor Kings, The (1976, C, 110m, PG)
The comic adventures of a black baseball team barnstorming the countryside in the 1930s. Billy Dee Williams, James Earl Jones, and Richard Pryor star. **CO19, ST118, ST180, ST227**

Birch Interval (1977, C, 104m, PG)
Drama of an eleven-year-old girl who is sent to live with relatives in Pennsylvanna's Amish community. Eddie Albert, Rip Torn, Ann Wedgeworth, and Susan McClung star. **FA7, ST216**

Birch Wood (1970, C, 99m, NR)
Polish director Andrzej Wajda's drama of the relationship between a tubercular musician and his brother, who is grieving the loss of his young wife. **DT130**

Bird (1988, C, 160m, R)
The life of pioneering jazz musician Charlie Parker, marked by artistic triumphs and personal setbacks, leading to his death at age thirty-four. Forest Whitaker stars, with Diane Venora as Parker's wife, Chan. Clint Eastwood directed. Purists scoffed but this is as good a mainstream movie about a major jazz figure as we're likely to get for some time. **DR12, MU5, ST64,** *Recommended*

Bird of Paradise (1932, B&W, 80m, NR)
A soldier of fortune falls in love with a native woman. Joel McCrea and Dolores Del Rio star, with Lon Chaney, Jr. Directed by King Vidor. **AC14, DT126, ST27, ST144**

Bird on a Wire (1990, C, 111m, PG-13)
Action comedy starring Mel Gibson as a man hiding out with the Federal Witness Protection Program, Goldie Hawn as his long-ago fiancée who runs into him just as the men he fingered are released from prison. With David Carradine and Bill Duke. **CO9, ST85, ST99, XT18**

Bird with the Crystal Plumage, The
(1969, C, 98m, PG)
An American writer in Rome witnesses a Jack the Ripper–style murder, tries to help the police, but finds himself involved with the case. Tony Musante and Suzy Kendall star. **FF2, HO9**

Birdman of Alcatraz
(1962, B&W, 143m, NR)
True story of Robert Stroud, a convicted murderer confined to the famed maximum security prison and how he became an expert on birds. Burt Lancaster stars, giving one of his best performances, with Karl Malden, Thelma Ritter, Neville Brand, and Edmond O'Brien. Directed by John Frankenheimer. **DR4, DR18, ST129,** *Recommended*

Birds, The (1963, C, 120m, NR)
Alfred Hitchcock's classic chiller finds a coastal California community terrorized by thousands of birds. Rod Taylor, Tippi Hedren, Jessica Tandy, and Suzanne Pleshette star. Based on a story by Daphne du Maurier.

More shock than substance, although that final image is a haunting one. **DT57, HO16, WR6**

Birdy (1985, C, 120m, R)
Two boyhood friends go to Vietnam and come back shattered, one with his face disfigured, the other retreating into his boyhood fantasies of being a bird. Matthew Modine and Nicolas Cage star. Based on William Wharton's novel; Alan Parker directed. Good adaptation of difficult book, but that ending leaves a bad taste. **DR7, DR19, ST23**

Birth of a Nation, The
(1915, B&W, 159m, NR)
D.W. Griffith's controversial account of the Civil War and Reconstruction from the South's perspective. Lillian Gish, Henry B. Walthall, Mae Marsh, and Miriam Cooper star, with Joseph Henabery as Abraham Lincoln and future director Raoul Walsh as John Wilkes Booth. A landmark in film history, making brilliant use of primitive techniques. **AC5, CL3, CL12, DT52, DT131, HF18, ST87,** *Essential, Highly Recommended*

Bishop's Wife, The
(1947, B&W, 108m, NR)
David Niven plays a bishop in need who's visited by a charming angel (Cary Grant). Loretta Young costars in this classic Christmastime fantasy. **FA13, SF2, ST92**

Bite the Bullet (1975, C, 131m, PG)
Western drama of an epic horse race, starring Gene Hackman, James Coburn, Ben Johnson, Jan-Michael Vincent, and Candice Bergen. Written for the screen and directed by Richard Brooks. **ST96, WE1**

Bitter Harvest (1981, C, 104m, NR)
Ron Howard and Art Carney star in this topical drama about dairy farmers whose herd is dying from chemical poisoning. Originally made for TV. **DT58**

Bitter Sweet (1940, C, 92m, NR)
Nelson Eddy and Jeanette MacDonald teamed up for the sixth time in this musical drama set in turn-of-the-century Vienna, with songs by Noel Coward. **CL15, WR4**

Bitter Tears of Petra van Kant, The
(1973, C, 119m, NR)
Director Rainer Werner Fassbinder's drama of a lesbian fashion designer and her unhappy love life. Margit Carstensen and Hanna Schygulla star. **DT42**

Bittersweet Love (1976, C, 92m, PG)
Soap opera story of a young couple about to have their first child, discovering that they are half-brother and -sister. Lana Turner stars,

with Robert Lansing, Celeste Holm, Robert Alda, Scott Hylands, and Meredith Baxter Birney. **ST219**

Black and White in Color
(1976, C, 90m, NR)
Frenchmen living in Africa at the outbreak of World War I decide to attack a nearby German fort. This droll comedy won an Oscar for Best Foreign Language Film. **FF1, XT7**

Black Arrow, The (1948, B&W, 76m, NR)
Robert Louis Stevenson swashbuckling adventure set in England follows the exploits of a young soldier (Louis Hayward) out to solve his father's murder. George Macready is the villain, Janet Blair the lady fair. **AC13, WR33**

Black Arrow (1984, C, 93m, NR)
Remake of the 1948 film of an exiled archer who returns to England and swears revenge on the villain (Oliver Reed) who drove him from his homeland. Disney swashbuckler made for cable TV. **FA1, WR33**

Black Beauty (1946, B&W, 74m, NR)
Mona Freeman stars as the young girl who develops a very special bond with a wild horse. Based on Anna Sewell's famed novel. **FA5**

Black Beauty (1971, C, 106m, G)
This version of Anna Sewell's classic tale takes a dramatic stand for animal rights. Mark Lester and Walter Slezak star. **FA5**

Black Caesar (1973, C, 96m, R)
Fred Williamson stars in this violent gangster melodrama directed by Larry Cohen. With Art Lund, Julius W. Harris, and Gloria Hendry. **AC22, DT28**

Black Castle, The (1952, B&W, 81m, NR)
A strange Austrian count plays host to two visitors who then disappear. Richard Greene stars in this low-budget horror film, with Boris Karloff, Stephen McNally, and Lon Chaney, Jr. **ST27, ST119**

Black Cat, The (1934, B&W, 65m, NR)
The bizarre home of an architect who is also a devil worshipper is the setting for this tale about a man who seeks vengeance for the death of his wife. Boris Karloff and Bela Lugosi star in this horror classic that is genuinely scary without resorting to on-screen gore. Not based on Edgar Allan Poe's story; directed by Edgar G. Ulmer. **HO1, ST119, ST143,** *Recommended*

Black Christmas (1975, C, 100m, R)
Sorority sisters prepare for their Christmas holiday while a madman stalks them. Margot

Kidder, Olivia Hussey, and Keir Dullea star, with Andrea Martin. **CO14, HO12**

Black Dragons (1949, B&W, 62m, NR)
Japanese agents sabotage the American war effort. Bela Lugosi and Clayton Moore star. **ST143**

Black Fury (1935, B&W, 92m, NR)
Paul Muni plays a coal miner who attempts to improve conditions for his fellow laborers in this classic social drama. **CL8**

Black Hand, The (1950, B&W, 93m, NR)
In a rare dramatic role, Gene Kelly plays a young man in turn-of-the-century New York who avenges his father's murder by a secret society. **ST123**

Black Hole, The (1979, C, 97m, PG)
Disney science fiction adventure of distant space travelers encountering title phenomenon. Maximilian Schell and Anthony Perkins star. **FA1, SF3, SF13, SF14**

Black Magic (1944) see *Meeting at Midnight*

Black Magic (1949, B&W, 105m, NR)
Orson Welles plays the eighteenth-century Italian charlatan Cagliostro in this biographical drama. With Akim Tamiroff, Nancy Guild, and Raymond Burr. The star co-directed but took no screen credit. **CL3, DT134**

Black Marble, The (1980, C, 110m, PG)
Romance blossoms between cops Paula Prentiss and Robert Foxworth when they're assigned to the case of a dognapper. Harry Dean Stanton and James Woods costar in this adaptation of Joseph Wambaugh's novel. **CO10, ST205, ST233**

Black Moon Rising (1986, C, 100m, R)
A high-tech car is the bone of contention between an organized car theft ring and a freelance thief. Tommy Lee Jones, Linda Hamilton, and Robert Vaughn star. **AC10**

Black Narcissus (1946, C, 99m, NR)
Drama set in the Himalayas finds three nuns (Deborah Kerr, Jean Simmons, and Flora Robson) faced with overwhelming obstacles when they try to set up a hospital. Breathtaking color photography by Jack Cardiff; directed by Michael Powell. **CL9, DT99, ST125**

Black Orchid, The (1959, B&W, 96m, NR)
A businessman and a widow fall in love, but she must persuade her children that the marriage will make them happy, too. Anthony Quinn and Sophia Loren star. Directed by Martin Ritt. **DT105, ST141**

Black Orpheus (1959, C, 98m, NR)
Oscar-winning drama from Brazil is based on Greek myth, transferred to Rio at Carnival time. Colorful imagery, with memorable music by Luis Bonfa and Antonio Carlos Jobim. **CL9, FF6, XT7,** *Recommended*

Black Pirate, The (1926, B&W, 132m, NR)
Douglas Fairbanks's silent swashbuckler classic. Billie Dove and Donald Crisp costar in this adventure for the entire family. **AC13, FA4**

Black Rain (1989, C, 125m, R)
A pair of American cops (Michael Douglas and Andy Garcia) invade Japan to bring an escaped gangster back to the States. With Ken Takakura, Kate Capshaw, and Yusaku Matsuda. Directed by Ridley Scott. **AC9, AC22, DT115, ST59**

Black Rain (1989, B&W, 123m, NR)
Japanese drama of the effects of Hiroshima's deadly radiation, directed by Shohei Imamura. Yoshiko Tanaka and Kazuo Kitamura star. **FF4**

Black Rainbow (1990, C, 113m, R)
Rosanna Arquette plays a psychic touring the South with her alcoholic father (Jason Robards). When she predicts the death of a murdered man in one of her public shows, she becomes a target for a hit man. With Tom Hulce. Written and directed by Mike Hodges. Fans of the offbeat may be interested. **HO7, MY3, ST185**

Black Robe (1991, C, 100m, R)
Drama of French missionaries in seventeenth-century Quebec, battling the wilderness and the Indians' resistance to their message. Lothaire Bluteau stars, with Adam Young, Sandrine Holt, and August Schellenberg. Directed by Bruce Beresford; adapted from Brian Moore's novel. Scenic locations enhance downbeat story. **DR5, DR27, DT10, XT26,** *Recommended*

Black Room, The (1935, B&W, 67m, NR)
Boris Karloff plays cursed twins, one of whom is literally a ladykiller. When he's suspected of the murders, he kills the good brother and impersonates him. **HO15, ST119**

Black Sabbath (1964, C, 99m, NR)
A compilation of three horror stories. *The Drop of Water* is about a nurse who steals a ring from a corpse, which comes back to haunt her through her tap. *The Telephone* is about a prostitute who receives mysterious phone calls. *The Wurdalak* features a Russian vampire who infects his whole family. Boris Karloff stars. Directed by Mario Bava. **HO23, ST119**

Black Sleep, The (1956, B&W, 81m, NR)
Standard horror tale of mad doctor and brain transplants, energized by excellent cast: Basil Rathbone, Akim Tamiroff, Lon Chaney, Jr., John Carradine, and Bela Lugosi. **ST25, ST122**

Black Stallion, The (1980, C, 120m, G)
Walter Farley's magical tale of the famed black horse and the boy who loved him. Mickey Rooney, Kelly Reno, Teri Garr, and Hoyt Axton star. Directed by Carroll Ballard, lovingly photographed by Caleb Deschanel. **FA5, MU12, ST189**, *Highly Recommended*

Black Stallion Returns, The
(1983, C, 93m, PG)
The young hero of *The Black Stallion* is off to Morocco when his best friend is horse-napped. Kelly Reno, Vincent Spano, and Teri Garr star. **FA5**

Black Sunday (1961, B&W, 83m, NR)
Barbara Steele stars in an Italian-made horror opus about an emissary from Satan wreaking havoc on the descendants of her executioners. **HO10**

Black Sunday (1977, C, 143m, R)
Arab terrorists plot to kill the President at the Super Bowl. Bruce Dern stars, with Marthe Keller and Robert Shaw. **MY6**

Black Widow (1986, C, 103m, R)
An offbeat tale about a woman who's been widowed by wealthy men so many times that she's aroused the suspicions of a government investigator. Theresa Russell and Debra Winger star in this cat-and-mouse thriller. With Sami Frey, Nicol Williamson, and Dennis Hopper. Directed by Bob Rafelson. The stars strike sparks, but the wrap-up takes too long. **MY9, ST110, ST231**

Black Windmill, The (1974, C, 106m, PG)
A secret agent (Michael Caine) investigates the kidnapping of his son. Directed by Don Siegel. Good suspense. **DT116, MY6, ST25**

Blackbeard, The Pirate
(1952, C, 99m, NR)
Robert Newton plays the infamous buccaneer, the terror of the Seven Seas. With Linda Darnell, William Bendix, and Richard Egan. Directed by Raoul Walsh. **AC15, DT131**

Blackbeard's Ghost (1968, C, 107m, G)
Dean Jones conjures up the spirit of the famed pirate (Peter Ustinov) to protect his descendants' home from racketeers. Suzanne Pleshette costars in this Disney comedy-adventure. **FA1**

Blackboard Jungle, The
(1955, B&W, 101m, NR)
Seminal wild youth movie of the nervous 1950s, with Glenn Ford as the schoolteacher besieged by a classful of trouble. Vic Morrow's the truly bad boy, Sidney Poitier the good bad boy; look for future director Paul Mazursky and Jameel Farah (Jamie Farr) in the class. Based on Evan Hunter's novel; directed by Richard Brooks. Bill Haley & the Comets sang "Rock Around the Clock" over the opening credits and movie music was never the same again. **CL8, DR25, DT87, ST174**, *Essential, Recommended*

Blackmail (1929, B&W, 86m, NR)
Alfred Hitchcock's first talking picture, about a woman who kills a man in self-defense and then has to prove her innocence when she's trapped between her detective boyfriend and a blackmailer. Originally shot as a silent film. **DT57**

Blacksmith, The/The Balloonatic
(1922/1923, B&W, 57m, NR)
Two Buster Keaton comedy shorts on one tape. In the first, he's the apprentice to the village smithy. In the second, he's trapped on a runaway hot-air balloon. **DT66**, *Recommended*

Blacula (1972, C, 92m, PG)
An African prince is transformed into a vampire, imprisoned in a coffin, then unleashed in modern Los Angeles. William Marshall and Vonetta McGee star. **HF7, HO5**

Blade Master, The (1984, C, 92m, PG)
Adventure saga featuring the title character, who leads the forces of good against the evil ones who would possess the Sword of Knowledge. Miles O'Keeffe and Lisa Foster star. **AC18**

Blade Runner (1982, C, 114m, R)
Harrison Ford plays a cop hunting down criminal androids in Los Angeles of the next century. With Rutger Hauer, Sean Young, Joanna Cassidy, and Daryl Hannah. Ridley Scott directed; spectacular sets almost steal the show. One video version contains some scenes of violence not shown in theaters. Also available in director's cut, which is letterboxed and does not contain Ford's narration—a big improvement; its running time is 112 minutes. A visual treat best seen on a big screen. **CU10, CU19, DT115, MY2, SF14, SF17, ST74**, *Recommended*

Blaise Pascal (1971, C, 131m, NR)
Roberto Rossellini's portrait, made for Italian TV, of the seventeenth-century philosopher

who wrestled with matters of science vs. religion. **DT109**

Blame It on Rio (1984, C, 110m, R)
Comedy about two married men on holiday in Rio with their teen-aged daughters and the trouble that develops when one man begins an affair with his pal's daughter. Michael Caine, Joseph Bologna, Demi Moore, and Michelle Johnson star. Directed by Stanley Donen. **DT38, ST25**

Blame It on the Bellboy
(1992, C, 77m, PG-13)
Farce set at a Venetian hotel employing a bellboy with a knack for mangling names. Dudley Moore, Bryan Brown, and Richard Griffiths star, with Andreas Katsoulis, Patsy Kensit, Alison Steadman, and Bronson Pinchot in the title role. **CO17, ST160**

Blaze (1989, C, 120m, R)
Raucous portrait of legendary Louisiana politician Earl K. Long and his well-publicized affair with exotic dancer Blaze Starr. Paul Newman gives a full-blooded performance much less restrained than most of his recent work; with Lolita Davidovich, Jerry Hardin, Gailard Sartain, and Jeffrey DeMunn. Written and directed by Ron Shelton. **DR4, DR21, ST162,** *Recommended*

Blazing Saddles (1974, C, 93m, R)
Mel Brooks's Western free-for-all, starring Gene Wilder and Cleavon Little, with Harvey Korman, Madeline Kahn, Slim Pickens, and David Huddleston. Brooks also plays two roles. Crude, vulgar, and often very, very funny. Kahn's Marlene Dietrich is a real treat; she should have the Oscar. **CO7, DT17, WE14, XT28,** *Recommended*

Bleak House (1985, C, 391m, NR)
Charles Dickens's story of nineteenth-century London's criminal class, starring Denholm Elliott and Diana Rigg. Originally made as a miniseries for British TV. **DR5, DR23, WR5**

Bless the Beasts and Children
(1972, C, 109m, PG)
At a summer camp, six city youths plan to save a herd of buffalo from their demise. Directed by Stanley Kramer. **DT67, FA7**

Blessed Event (1932, B&W, 83m, NR)
Fast-moving, spicy tale of show-biz gossip columnist whose shenanigans land him in hot water. Lee Tracy stars, with Mary Brian, Dick Powell (his debut), and Frank McHugh. Tracy's delightful. **CL7, ST175**

Blind Alley see *Perfect Strangers*

Blind Date (1984, C, 100m, R)
A blind man (Joseph Bottoms), obsessed that a psychopathic killer be brought to justice, implants a sight-giving computer chip in his head. Kirstie Alley costars. **MY11**

Blind Date (1987, C, 95m, PG-13)
A young executive is fixed up with an unpredictable woman for an important business dinner, with wildly comic events leading to apocalyptic wedding scene. Bruce Willis and Kim Basinger star, with John Larroquette and William Daniels. Directed by Blake Edwards. **CO1, DT40, ST229, XT20**

Blind Husbands (1919, B&W, 98m, NR)
Erich Von Stroheim stars in and directed this silent drama about a military man who falls for a doctor's wife. **CL12, DT129**

Blind Man's Bluff see *Cauldron of Blood*

Bliss (1985, C, 93m, R)
From Australia, a dark comedy about a successful businessman who suffers a nearly fatal heart attack and recovers with a new perspective on his greedy lifestyle and uncaring family. Barry Otto stars. **CO12, FF5**

Bliss of Mrs. Blossom, The
(1968, C, 93m, PG)
British comedy of frustrated wife of brassiere manufacturer; she keeps a secret lover in their attic. Shirley MacLaine and Richard Attenborough star; look for John Cleese in a small part. **CO15, CO17, ST145**

Blithe Spirit (1945, C, 96m, NR)
Rex Harrison stars in this comic fantasy by Noel Coward about a man haunted by the ghost of his first wife, who tries to ruin his second marriage. Margaret Rutherford costars. David Lean directed. **DR23, DT71, WR4, XT24**

Blob, The (1958, C, 86m, NR)
Jelly-like mass from outer space begins devouring everything—and everyone—in a small town, whose teens rush to the rescue. Classic 1950s science fiction, starring Steve McQueen. **SF1, SF9, ST146**

Block-Heads (1938, B&W, 55m, NR)
Laurel and Hardy comedy, with Stanley still thinking World War I is on, Ollie having to bring him out of the trenches. **ST133**

Blockhouse, The (1973, C, 90m, NR)
Drama of men trapped in an underground bunker during the D-Day invasion. Peter Sellers stars, with Per Oscarsson and Charles Aznavour. **ST198**

Blonde Crazy (1931, B&W, 79m, NR)
James Cagney vehicle has him playing a

small-time con man up against the big boss of the city (Louis Calhern). With Joan Blondell and Ray Milland. **ST24**

Blonde Venus (1932, B&W, 97m, NR)
Marlene Dietrich becomes the sole provider when her husband becomes ill; she returns to her career as a nightclub singer until a suave playboy (Cary Grant) makes her an irresistible offer. With Herbert Marshall and Dickie Moore. Directed by Josef von Sternberg. Perhaps the least stylized and most enjoyable of the Dietrich-von Sternberg collaborations. **DT128, ST55, ST92,** *Essential, Recommended*

Blood Alley (1955, C, 115m, NR)
Action drama starring John Wayne and Lauren Bacall as a couple fleeing the Chinese Communists for Hong Kong. Directed by William Wellman. **DT135, ST224**

Blood and Black Lace (1964, C, 88m, NR)
A man becomes a psychopathic killer when he can no longer hide his desire for beautiful women. Cameron Mitchell and Eva Bartok star. Directed by Mario Bava. **HO9**

Blood and Sand (1922, B&W, 80m, NR)
One of the early Rudolf Valentino vehicles, about a matador's daring brushes with death. With Lila Lee and Nita Naldi. **CL12**

Blood and Sand (1941, C, 123m, NR)
A bullfighter spurns his faithful love for an attractive temptress. Tyrone Power stars, with Linda Darnell and Rita Hayworth. Directed by Rouben Mamoulian. Oscar-winning color cinematography. **DT83, ST101, ST177**

Blood Beast Terror, The
(1969, C, 81m, NR)
An entomologist conducts experiments on his own daughter, turning her into a blood-thirsty insect. Peter Cushing stars. **ST43**

Blood Couple (1973, C, 83m, R)
Cult horror film involving a black vampire, African rituals, and a deadly romance. Duane Jones, Marlene Clark, and Bill Gunn star; Gunn directed. Also known as *Ganja and Hess*. **CU4, HO5**

Blood Feast (1963, C, 75m, PG)
An Egyptian preparing to bring a goddess to life needs body parts and organs from various women to complete the ritual. One of the first horror films to use explicit gore; directed by Herschell Gordon Lewis. **HO18**

Blood Feud (1979, C, 112m, NR)
Drama set in Sicily in the 1920s, with widow (Sophia Loren) romanced by two men (Marcello Mastroianni and Giancarlo Giannini).

Directed by Lina Wertmuller. **DT137, ST141, ST154**

Blood in the Face (1991, C, 77m, NR)
Documentary exploring the White Supremacist movement in America. Produced and directed by Anne Bohler, Kevin Rafferty, and James Ridgeway. **CU16**

Blood Link (1986, C, 98m, R)
A doctor begins to have a recurring dream that he is committing a murder. He discovers that he was once a Siamese twin and that his brother is still alive and deranged. Michael Moriarty stars. **HO15**

Blood Money (1988, C, 110m, NR)
Romance and mystery mix in this tale of a smuggler and prostitute running guns to the Contras in Nicaragua. Andy Garcia and Ellen Barkin star, with Morgan Freeman. Made for cable TV; also known as *Clinton and Nadine*. **ST7, ST76**

Blood Oath see *Prisoners of the Sun*

Blood of a Poet (1930, B&W, 55m, NR)
French director Jean Cocteau's meditation on an artist's inner world is a study in striking imagery, although not for every taste. **DT26, FF1, SF2**

Blood of Fu Manchu, The see *Against All Odds* (1968)

Blood of Heroes, The (1990, C, 102m, R)
Rutger Hauer stars in this action-adventure tale of a futuristic band of warriors known as "juggers." With Joan Chen. **AC24**

Blood of Others, The (1984, C, 176m, NR)
World War II drama of woman torn between her boyfriend in the French Resistance and a wealthy German. Jodie Foster stars, with Michael Ontkean, Sam Neill, and Stephane Audran. Directed by Claude Chabrol. Originally made for cable TV. **ST75**

Blood on Satan's Claw (1971, C, 93m, R)
A farmer unearths the corpse of a half man/half beast and evil takes hold of the community, eventually possessing a young girl. Linda Hayden and Patrick Wymark star. **HO10**

Blood on the Moon (1948, B&W, 88m, NR)
Western drama starring Robert Mitchum and Robert Preston as rivals in a land fraud scheme. Robert Wise directed. **DT140, ST158**

Blood on the Sun (1945, B&W, 98m, NR)
James Cagney stars in this drama about an American living in Japan during the 1930s and foreseeing that country's war plans. **ST24**

Blood Red (1989, C, 91m, R)
Western drama, set in Northern California, focuses on immigrant grape growers and their struggle against a tyrannical industrialist. Eric Roberts stars, with Giancarlo Giannini, Dennis Hopper, Burt Young, and Susan Anspach. **ST110**

Blood Simple (1985, C, 96m, R)
A jealous husband hires a seedy private detective to murder his wife and her lover. Contemporary cult thriller, written by Joel and Ethan Coen, directed by Joel. John Getz, Frances MacDormand, M. Emmet Walsh, and Dan Hedaya star. Creepy, clever, but not up to the Coens' later standards. **DR16, DT27, MY2**

Blood Tide (1982, C, 82m, R)
Greek locations star in this monster-from-the-deep saga. The human prey includes James Earl Jones, José Ferrer, Lila Kedrova, and Deborah Shelton. **ST118**

Bloodbath at the House of Death
(1984, C, 92m, NR)
British spoof of horror films, about paranormal researchers setting up shop in a house that was scene of many murders. Kenny Everett, Pamela Stephenson, Vincent Price star. **HO26, ST179**

Bloodbrothers (1978, C, 116m, R)
Young New Yorker is torn between following his father and uncle into construction work and following his own dream of becoming a teacher. Richard Gere stars, with Paul Sorvino and Tony LoBianco. Based on Richard Price's novel. Good early look at Gere's promise. **DR8, ST84**

Bloodfist (series)

Bloodfist (1989, C, 86m, R)

Bloodfist II (1991, C, 84m, R)

Bloodfist III: Forced to Fight
(1991, C, 90m, R)

Bloodfist IV: Die Trying (1992, C, 90m, R)
Martial arts series starring Don "The Dragon" Wilson, with the standard stories of revenge as an excuse to demolish entire rooms and dispatch faceless armies of baddies. **AC26**

Bloodhounds of Broadway
(1988, C, 101m, PG)
Four Damon Runyon stories set in 1928 New York are the basis for this nostalgic comedy of colorful horse players, show girls, and mobsters. Among the stars: Julie Hagerty, Randy Quaid, Madonna, Matt Dillon, Jennifer Grey, and Rutger Hauer. **CO6, DR19, MU12, ST56**

Bloodline see *Sidney Sheldon's Bloodline*

Bloodsport (1987, C, 92m, R)
Martial arts drama of American who enters the Kumite, a secret fighting contest. Jean Claude Van Damme stars; based on a true story. **AC26**

Bloodsuckers, The (1970, C, 87m, R)
An Oxford don visiting Greece takes up with a mysterious woman who leads him into black magic and vampirism. Patrick Mower stars, with Peter Cushing. **HO5, HO11, ST43**

Bloody Mama (1970, C, 90m, R)
Shelley Winters plays the notorious Ma Barker, the gangster who included her sons in her criminal affairs. Robert De Niro, Don Stroud, Pat Hingle, and Bruce Dern costar. Directed by Roger Corman. For fans of sleaze, a must. **AC22, DT30, ST51, ST232**

Blossoms in the Dust (1941, C, 100m, NR)
Greer Garson tearjerker about a woman who loses her child and decides to open an orphanage in Texas. With Walter Pidgeon. **CL6, ST83**

Blow Out (1981, C, 107m, R)
Director Brian De Palma's thriller about a sound effects engineer (John Travolta) unwittingly uncovering a political conspiracy. With Nancy Allen, John Lithgow, and Dennis Franz. **DR13, DT36, MY6, MY11**

Blowing Wild (1953, B&W, 90m, NR)
Barbara Stanwyck romances two men: oil tycoon husband (Anthony Quinn) and a wildcatter (Gary Cooper). **ST37, ST207**

Blow-Up (1966, C, 110m, NR)
An innocent London photographer takes snapshots of a couple that later, when enlarged, expose what appears to be a murder. Director Michelangelo Antonioni's most accessible film is a pinpoint portrait of Swingin' London, complete with a famous guitar-smashing appearance by the Yardbirds. David Hemmings stars, with Vanessa Redgrave and Sarah Miles. **DT5, MY11, ST182, XT15,** *Essential, Recommended*

Blue and the Gray, The
(1982, C, 295m, NR)
Epic drama of the Civil War, originally a TV miniseries. Stacy Keach stars as a Pinkerton's agent who manages to get involved with many of the war's major moments. With Gregory Peck as Lincoln, Lloyd Bridges, Colleen Dewhurst, John Hammond, Sterling Hayden, Warren Oates, Rip Torn, and Paul Winfield. **AC5, DR5, HF18, ST166, ST171, ST216, ST230**

Blue Angel, The (1930, B&W, 103m, NR)
German classic about an aging professor's

pathetic infatuation with a heartless nightclub singer. Marlene Dietrich and Emil Jannings star. Josef von Sternberg directed; his first of seven films with Dietrich and the one that launched her illustrious career. **DT128, FF3, ST55,** *Essential, Recommended*

Blue Bird, The (1940, C, 88m, NR)
Classic fantasy about the search for the special bird which will bring happiness. Shirley Temple stars. **SF13, ST213**

Blue Canadian Rockies
(1952, B&W, 58m, NR)
Gene Autry's boss sends him to Canada on a personal expedition to discourage his daughter's marriage to a fortune hunter. **ST5, WE10**

Blue City (1986, C, 83m, R)
Thriller of a young man (Judd Nelson) trying to solve the murder of his father in a corrupt small town. With Ally Sheedy and Paul Winfield. Based on a Ross MacDonald novel. **DR26, ST230, WR19**

Blue Collar (1978, C, 114m, R)
A trio of auto workers discover their union has been ripping off its workers, and they decide to get even. Hard-bitten drama from director Paul Schrader, still his best film. Richard Pryor, Yaphet Kotto, and Harvey Keitel star. First-rate bluesy soundtrack featuring Captain Beefheart and Ry Cooder. **DR7, DR14, ST180,** *Recommended*

Blue Fin (1977, C, 93m, NR)
Family adventure of a young boy on a fishing trip; he must take over the boat from his father in a storm. **FA7**

Blue Fire Lady (1983, C, 96m, NR)
Family drama of a girl's love for horses and her training of an obstinate mare, Blue Fire Lady, for racing. Catherine Harrison stars. **FA5**

Blue Hawaii (1961, C, 101m, NR)
Elvis Presley musical has The King as a cashiered soldier working in a tourist agency in Honolulu. Angela Lansbury costars. **ST131, ST178**

Blue Knight, The (1973, C, 103m, R)
Veteran cop, about to retire, wants to bring in one more criminal. William Holden stars in this adaptation of the Joseph Wambaugh novel. Originally made for TV. **AC9, ST106**

Blue Lamp, The (1950, B&W, 84m, NR)
British thriller about Scotland Yard manhunt for a cop killer. Jack Warner (not the Hollywood mogul) stars, with Jimmy Hanley, Dirk Bogarde, Robert Flemyng, and Bernard Lee. Directed by Basil Dearden. **MY15, ST14**

Blue Manhattan see *Confessions of a Peeping John*

Blue Max, The (1966, C, 156m, NR)
Drama of aerial combat during World War I, starring George Peppard, James Mason, and Ursula Andress. **AC2, AC11, ST153**

Blue Monkey (1987, C, 87m, R)
Monster movie set in a hospital, starring Steve Railsback, Gwynyth Walsh, Susan Anspach, John Vernon, and Joe Flaherty. **CO14**

Blue Steel (1990, C, 95m, R)
A female cop is stalked by a psycho in this urban thriller starring Jamie Lee Curtis and Ron Silver. **MY3, MY13, ST42**

Blue Thunder (1983, C, 108m, R)
Los Angeles police develop super-helicopter for crowd control, but political conspiracy has other ideas. Roy Scheider stars, with Daniel Stern, Malcolm McDowell, Warren Oates, and Candy Clark. **AC11, ST166, XT10**

Blue Velvet (1986, C, 120m, R)
Nightmarish, disturbing, and artfully told story from writer-director David Lynch about a naive young man's discovery of the dark side of a small American town. Kyle MacLachlan, Dennis Hopper, and Isabella Rossellini star, with Laura Dern, Dean Stockwell, and Brad Dourif. You'll never listen to Bobby Vinton's title tune or Roy Orbison's "In Dreams" the same way after you see this. **CU1, CU12, DR26, DT79, MY2, MY11, ST53, ST110, ST208,** *Recommended*

Blue Yonder, The (1985, C, 89m, NR)
Disney drama of a young boy (Huckleberry Fox) who travels back in time to share flying adventures with his grandfather (Peter Coyote), an ace aviator. Originally made for cable TV. **FA1**

Bluebeard (1972, C, 125m, R)
Richard Burton plays the legendary ladykiller whose victims include Raquel Welch, Virna Lisi, and Joey Heatherton. **ST22**

Bluebeard's Eighth Wife
(1938, B&W, 80m, NR)
Delightful film from the king of film comedy, director Ernst Lubitsch, about an oft-married millionaire (Gary Cooper) and the woman who means to snare him (Claudette Colbert). With David Niven and Edward Everett Horton. Written by Billy Wilder and Charles Brackett. UNAVAILABLE ON VIDEO. **XT29**

Blues Brothers, The (1980, C, 133m, R)
John Belushi and Dan Aykroyd extend their "Saturday Night Live" routine into a gargantuan musical comedy, featuring a great array

of black performers, including Aretha Franklin, James Brown, Ray Charles, Cab Calloway, and many more. Watch for bit parts by John Candy and others. The streets of Chicago take a pounding in the grand finale car chase. Directed by John Landis with his usual flair for overdoing everything. **CO3, CO13, CO14, MU9, XT11**

Blume in Love (1973, C, 116m, R)
A lawyer's brief indiscretion has his wife packing her bags and has him pleading to get her back. Sharp romantic comedy-drama from director Paul Mazursky, starring George Segal and Susan Anspach, with Kris Kristofferson, Marsha Mason, Shelley Winters, and the director. **CO1, DT87, MU12, ST232,** *Recommended*

Boat Is Full, The (1983, C, 100m, NR)
German refugees fleeing the Nazis are turned away by neutral Swiss officials in this drama produced in Switzerland. **FF7**

Boatniks, The (1970, C, 99m, G)
Disney comedy has an accident-prone Coast Guard ensign (Robert Morse) tangling with a band of jewel thieves. With Phil Silvers, Stephanie Powers, Norman Fell, Wally Cox, and Don Ameche. **FA1**

Bob & Carol & Ted & Alice
(1969, C, 104m, R)
A California couple are happily married until they meet a "modern" husband and wife, who believe in getting in touch with one's real inner feelings. Hilarious satire directed by Paul Mazursky, starring Robert Culp & Natalie Wood & Elliott Gould & Dyan Cannon. The latter should have won an Oscar. **CO2, DT87, XT28,** *Recommended*

Bob le Flambeur (1955, B&W, 102m, PG)
A middle-aged Parisian gambler decides to pull off a casino heist in this first-rate crime story directed by Jean-Pierre Melville. Roger Duchesne and Isabel Corey star. **FF1, MY18, XT16,** *Recommended*

Bob Roberts (1992, C, 105m, PG-13)
Satire of contemporary politics stars Tim Robbins (who also scripted and directed) as a right-wing, folk-singing candidate for a Pennsylvania senate seat. The large supporting cast includes Giancarlo Esposito, Ray Wise, Gore Vidal (as Roberts's opponent), Rebecca Jenkins, John Cusack, Peter Gallagher, Pamela Reed, Alan Rickman, James Spader, David Strathairn, Fred Ward, Bob Balaban, Helen Hunt, Fisher Stevens, and Susan Sarandon in a small role. The documentary-style approach has its limitations, and Robbins plays his hand too hard too often. Best potshots

reserved for bubble-brained newscasters. **CO2, DR7, DR21, ST194, ST203, XT23**

Bobby Deerfield (1977, C, 124m, PG)
Drama of a race car driver and his love for a German woman who is afflicted with a terminal disease. Al Pacino and Marthe Keller star. Sydney Pollack directed. **DR22, DT98, ST170**

Bobo, The (1967, C, 105m, NR)
Peter Sellers plays an aspiring singing matador who tries to seduce a lovely but remote senorita (Britt Ekland). **ST198**

Bocaccio '70 (1962, C, 165m, NR)
Three-part Italian sex comedy: a timid man wins a night with a lovely woman in a raffle, the bored wife of a businessman takes a job as his mistress, and a voluptuous poster girl comes to life. Directed by Federico Fellini, Vittorio De Sica, and Luchino Visconti, featuring Anita Ekberg, Sophia Loren, and Romy Schneider. **DT37, DT43, DT127, ST141**

Body and Soul (1947, B&W, 104m, NR)
John Garfield stars in the classic boxing drama of man who cuts every corner on his way to the championship. Robert Rossen directed. **DR22, ST80**

Body and Soul (1981, C, 100m, R)
Remake of the John Garfield classic, with Leon Isaac Kennedy as the hard-driving fighter. **CU18, DR22**

Body Double (1984, C, 110m, R)
From director Brian De Palma, the story of an unemployed actor whose spying on a voluptuous neighbor involves him in a twisted plot. Craig Wasson stars, with Gregg Henry, Melanie Griffith, Dennis Franz, and Deborah Shelton. **DT36, MY5, ST93**

Body Heat (1981, C, 113m, R)
A lawyer and a married woman plot to murder her wealthy husband. Steamy thriller stars William Hurt and Kathleen Turner (her film debut), with Richard Crenna, Ted Danson, and Mickey Rourke. Written and directed by Lawrence Kasdan. A notch below its classic *film noir* predecessors but still well worth seeing. **CU6, DR3, MY2, MY4, MY5, ST95, ST190, ST218, XT21,** *Recommended*

Body in the Library, The
(1984, C, 153m, NR)
Miss Marple, Agatha Christie's elderly sleuth, investigates the murder of a young woman whose corpse is found in a stately mansion. Joan Hickson stars. Originally made for British TV. **MY12, WR3**

Body of Evidence (1993, C, 99m, R)
Thriller about a gallery owner accused of

causing her lover, a wealthy older man who named her sole heir in his will, to have a fatal heart attack during lovemaking. She's soon involved with her attorney, too. Madonna and Willem Dafoe star, with Joe Mantegna, Anne Archer, Jurgen Prochnow, and Frank Langella. Available in an unrated version with about two mintues of extra footage—and it isn't of courtroom testimony. Laughable attempt at daring contemporary *film noir*. Note to Madonna: Keep the day job. **CU6, CU10, DR3, DR17, MU12, MY2, MY4**

Body Parts (1991, C, 88m, R)
A criminal psychologist loses an arm in an accident, has a "used" one sewn on—and it turns out to be from the body of a killer. Jeff Fahey stars, with Lindsay Duncan, Kim Delaney, Brad Dourif, and Zakes Mokae. **HO20**

Body Rock (1984, C, 93m, PG-13)
Breakdancing musical about a group of "downtown" kids showing the folks at an "uptown" club what good music and dancing is all about. Lorenzo Lamas stars. **MU9**

Body Snatcher, The
(1945, B&W, 77m, NR)
Val Lewton production about the macabre relationship between a doctor and the grave robber who steals bodies for the doctor's experiments. Boris Karloff stars, with Bela Lugosi. Directed by Robert Wise. Based on a story by Robert Louis Stevenson. **DT140, HO1, HO19, ST119, ST149, WR33**

Bodyguard, The (1992, C, 129m, R)
Pop singer menaced by a murderous fan and her hired protector fall in love. Kevin Costner and Whitney Houston star, with Gary Kemp, Bill Cobbs, and Ralph Waite. Screenplay by Lawrence Kasdan, directed by Mick Jackson. **DR1, DR12, ST38**

Boeing Boeing (1965, C, 102m, NR)
Pre-feminist comedy of bachelor buddies, one of them trying to juggle affairs with three stewardesses. Tony Curtis is the Don Juan, an unusually restrained Jerry Lewis is his pal. For the record, the women are played by Dany Saval, Christiane Schmidtmer, and Suzanna Leigh. **CO1, ST139**

Bohemian Girl, The
(1936, B&W, 70m, NR)
Laurel and Hardy adopt an abandoned girl who turns out to be the heir to a throne. **ST133**

Bombardier (1943, B&W, 99m, NR)
Randolph Scott plays a fighter cadet being trained for battle during air raids over World War II Japan. With Robert Ryan. **AC1, ST193, ST197**

Bombay Talkie (1970, C, 110m, PG)
Drama set in India of a visiting American writer who falls in love with a movie star. Jennifer Kendall and Shashi Kapoor star. Early collaboration from the filmmaking team of Ismail Merchant (producer), James Ivory (director), and Ruth Prawer Jhabvala (writer). **DR27, DT61**

Bombshell (1933, B&W, 95m, NR)
Jean Harlow plays the title role, a Hollywood star protected by her no-holds-barred publicist (Lee Tracy). Comedy about the picture business also features Frank Morgan, Franchot Tone, and Una Merkel. **CL7, ST98,** *Recommended*

Bon Voyage! (1962, C, 130m, NR)
Disney comedy of a family touring Europe, starring Fred MacMurray, Jane Wyman, Michael Callan, and Deborah Walley. **FA1**

Bon Voyage, Charlie Brown
(1980, C, 76m, G)
The "Peanuts" comic strip gang goes overseas as exchange students in this feature-length animated film. **FA10**

Bonfire of the Vanities, The
(1990, C, 126m, R)
Tom Wolfe's saga of 1980s New York drowning in a sea of greed, envy, and lust limps to the screen. Tom Hanks stars as financial wizard Sherman McCoy, with Melanie Griffith, Bruce Willis, Kim Cattrall, Saul Rubinek, Morgan Freeman (as a preaching judge), and F. Murray Abraham. Directed by Brian De Palma. Inept film finds no equivalent for Wolfe's super-heated prose, which carried the book along over many rough spots. **DR7, DR15, DR17, DR19, DR24, DT36, ST76, ST93, ST97, ST229, XT9**

Bonjour Tristesse (1958, C/B&W, 94m, NR)
Well-acted, coolly directed drama of relationship between a young woman (Jean Seberg) and her unattached father (David Niven), who's romancing an old friend (Deborah Kerr). Set in Paris and the South of France; based on Françoise Sagan's bestseller. Directed by Otto Preminger. Widescreen cinematography will lose something on video. **CU20, DR8, DT100, ST125,** *Recommended*

Bonnie and Clyde (1967, C, 111m, NR)
Brilliant, controversial portrait of Depression-era outlaws who became folk heroes. Warren Beatty and Faye Dunaway star, with Gene Hackman, Oscar winner Estelle Parsons, Michael J. Pollard, and Gene Wilder. Written by Robert Benton and David Newman; directed

by Arthur Penn. An entertaining and intelligent look at how myths often replace the facts of history. Should have won the Oscar for Best Picture. **DR5, DR16, DT96, ST10, ST61, ST96, XT5, XT18, XT26, XT28,** *Essential, Highly Recommended*

Bonnie Scotland (1935, B&W, 80m, NR) Laurel and Hardy are a pair of Scots assigned to a military outpost in the desert. **ST133**

Boogeyman, The (1980, C, 86m, R) A boy kills his mother's lover but is witnessed by his sister. Years later the girl returns to the scene of the crime to confront her fears. **HO8**

Boom Town (1940, B&W, 116m, NR) Oil drilling saga stars Clark Gable and Spencer Tracy as rival wildcatters, Claudette Colbert and Hedy Lamarr as their women. **ST34, ST77, ST217**

Boomerang (1992, C, 118m, R) Eddie Murphy vehicle has him playing a successful advertising executive with woman problems. The ladies in his life are played by Halle Berry, Robin Givens, Eartha Kitt, Grace Jones, and Tisha Campbell; also on hand are David Alan Grier, Martin Lawrence, Geoffrey Holder, and Chris Rock. Directed by Reginald Hudlin. Fitfully amusing but Murphy's smug performance too often spoils the fun. **CO1, CO2, CO13, MU12**

Boost, The (1988, C, 95m, R) A young couple find that sudden success in business has exacted a heavy price—they've become cocaine addicts. James Woods and Sean Young star. **DR7, ST233**

Boots and Saddles (1937, B&W, 59m, NR) A young Englishman becomes a real Western rancher after Gene Autry shows him the ropes. **ST5**

Border, The (1982, C, 107m, R) Jack Nicholson plays a Tex-Mex border cop who begins taking bribes to let illegals in and becomes involved with a desperate Mexican woman and her child. With Valerie Perrine, Warren Oates, and Harvey Keitel. Music by Ry Cooder. Story seems overly familiar, even if its heart is in the right place. **DR7, ST163, ST166**

Borderline (1980, C, 105m, PG) Charles Bronson is a Border Patrol officer tracking a dangerous killer. With Bruno Kirby, Bert Remsen, and Kenneth McMillan. **ST19**

Boris and Natasha (1992, C, 92m, PG) Dave Thomas and Sally Kellerman play the Soviet spy team from the old "Rocky & Bullwinkle" cartoons in this dated Cold War comedy. With Paxton Whitehead, Andrea Martin, and John Candy in a bit part. Made in 1988; debuted on cable TV. **CO10, CO14**

Born Free (1966, C, 96m, NR) Drama based on the true story of Joy Adamson, the wife of a British game warden living in Kenya, who raised a lioness as a pet in the wilds of Africa. **FA5**

Born in East L.A. (1987, C, 87m, R) Cheech Marin stars in a comedy about a legal resident of Los Angeles who's rounded up with a group of illegals and deported to Mexico. With Paul Rodriguez, Daniel Stern, and Jan-Michael Vincent. **ST28**

Born on the Fourth of July (1989, C, 144m, R) The true story of Ron Kovic, decorated and crippled Vietnam veteran who became an antiwar activist. Tom Cruise stars, with Raymond J. Barry, Carolina Kava, Kyra Sedgwick, Willem Dafoe, and Tom Berenger. Kovic and Oscar-winning director Oliver Stone adapted Kovic's memoir. Heartfelt and passionate but Cruise doesn't hold the film together. **AC4, DR4, DR7, DR8, DT120, ST41, XT6, XT25**

Born To Be Bad (1950, B&W, 94m, NR) Joan Fontaine plays a rare unsympathetic role, a manipulative woman, in this melodrama. With Robert Ryan, Joan Leslie, Mel Ferrer, and Zachary Scott. Directed by Nicholas Ray. **DT101, MY1, MY4, ST73, ST193**

Born To Dance (1936, B&W, 105m, NR) MGM musical featuring Eleanor Powell and James Stewart dancing and singing to a Cole Porter score that includes "I've Got You Under My Skin." **MU1, ST207**

Born To Kill (1947, B&W, 92m, NR) Classic *film noir* about a man who marries a woman for her money, but is really attracted to her divorced sister. Lawrence Tierney, Claire Trevor, Walter Slezak, and Audrey Long star. Directed by Robert Wise. **DT140, MY1, MY3,** *Recommended*

Born To Kill (1974) see *Cockfighter*

Born To Rock see *That Was Rock*

Born To Win see *Addict*

Born Yesterday (1950, B&W, 103m, NR) Garson Kanin's Broadway comedy about a wisecracking girl (Oscar winner Judy Holliday) in need of some polish. Her sugar daddy (Broderick Crawford) hires a tutor (William Holden) to smooth over her rough edges.

George Cukor directed. Holliday is perfection and her male costars play off her brilliantly. Some scenes shot on location in Washington, D.C. **CO1, CL10, DT32, ST106, ST107, XT3, XT12,** *Essential, Recommended*

Born Yesterday (1993, C, 101m, PG)
Remake and updating of 1950 comedy of loutish businessman visiting Washington, D.C., with his ditsy mistress, hiring her a tutor who turns suitor. John Goodman, Melanie Griffith, and Don Johnson star, with Edward Herrmann, Max Perlich, Fred Dalton Thompson, Nora Dunn, and several Washington celebs in small roles, including Benjamin C. Bradlee and Sally Quinn. **CO1, CO2, CU18, ST93, XT12**

Boston Strangler, The
(1968, C, 120m, NR)
Intense, gripping drama based on the exploits of the crazed killer who terrorized Boston for over a year. Henry Fonda and Tony Curtis star, with George Kennedy. **MY8, MY13, ST71**

Bostonians, The (1984, C, 120m, NR)
In nineteenth-century New England, feminists have a new young spokeswoman. She's also the center of a tug-of-war between a Southern reporter and one of her colleagues in the movement. Vanessa Redgrave, Christopher Reeve, and Madeleine Potter star in this version of Henry James's novel. Directed by James Ivory. Redgrave should have the Oscar for Best Actress. **DT61, ST182, WR14, XT28**

Botany Bay (1953, C, 94m, NR)
Alan Ladd's a prisoner and James Mason's the cruel captain aboard a convict ship bound for 1790 Australia. With Patricia Medina and Cedric Hardwicke. **AC16, ST128, ST153**

Boudu Saved From Drowning
(1932, B&W, 87m, NR)
French comedy from director Jean Renoir about a tramp rescued by a book dealer and the havoc he wreaks on the man's household. Michel Simon stars. American remake: *Down and Out in Beverly Hills.* **DT104, FF8**

Bound for Glory (1976, C, 147m, PG)
Superb portrait of folk music composer and singer Woody Guthrie, concentrating on his life during the Great Depression. David Carradine stars and sings Guthrie's music; with Ronny Cox, Melinda Dillon, and Randy Quaid. Directed by Hal Ashby; photographed by Haskell Wexler. **MU5,** *Recommended*

Bounty, The (1984, C, 130m, PG)
Latest version of the *Mutiny on the Bounty* story, with Mel Gibson as Fletcher Christian and Anthony Hopkins as Captain Bligh. Laurence Olivier has a small role. Look quickly for Daniel Day-Lewis. Hopkins makes Bligh somewhat sympathetic, but Gibson's not up to his role. **AC12, AC16, ST48, ST85, ST109, ST168**

Bounty Hunter, The (1989, C, 91m, R)
Robert Ginty stars as a one-man wrecking crew out to avenge a buddy's death. **AC19, AC25**

Bowery at Midnight
(1942, B&W, 63m, NR)
A killer is stalking the inhabitants of the Bowery. Bela Lugosi stars. **ST143**

Boxcar Bertha (1972, C, 97m, R)
Trashy tale of Depression-era train robbers, starring David Carradine and Barbara Hershey, directed by Martin Scorsese. Produced by Roger Corman. John Carradine has a small role. **CU14, DT114, ST104, XT8**

Boy and His Dog, A (1975, C, 87m, R)
A post-nuclear wasteland is the setting for this cult science fiction tale of a young hustler and his "dog" robot. Don Johnson and Jason Robards, Jr., star. **CU4, SF12, SF22, ST185**

Boy, Did I Get a Wrong Number!
(1966, C, 99m, NR)
Bob Hope comedy, costarring Phyllis Diller and Elke Sommer, with Ol' Ski Nose a fast-talking real estate man helping to conceal a fugitive movie star. **ST108**

Boy Friend, The (1971, C, 135m, G)
Lavish spoof of old-fashioned Hollywood musicals, starring Twiggy, with Christopher Gable (who choreographed), Moyra Fraser, Tommy Tune, and Glenda Jackson in a small role. Directed by Ken Russell. **DT111, MU3, MU4, ST117**

Boy in Blue, The (1986, C, 98m, R)
True story of nineteenth-century rowing champion Ned Hanlan, starring Nicolas Cage, with Christopher Plummer and David Naughton. **DR22, ST23**

Boy Named Charlie Brown, A
(1969, C, 85m, G)
Movie debut of the "Peanuts" gang, with Charlie Brown going for the grand prize in a national spelling bee. **FA10**

Boy Who Could Fly, The
(1986, C, 114m, PG)
Story of a fourteen-year-old boy whose fantasy is to soar away from his unhappy home life. Jay Underwood, Lucy Deakins, and Bonnie Bedelia star. **DR9, FA7**

Boy Who Left Home to Find Out About the Shivers, The (1981, C, 60m, NR)
Brothers Grimm tale about a boy (Peter Mac-Nichol) who's fearless until he's put to a test against the Evil Sorcerer. Christopher Lee and Dana Hill star, with Vincent Price in this Faerie Tale Theatre production. **FA12, ST135, ST179**

Boy With Green Hair, The (1948, C, 82m, NR)
Dean Stockwell stars in this social parable about a war orphan who's an outcast because of his unusually colored locks. With Pat O'Brien, Robert Ryan, and Barbara Hale. Directed by Joseph Losey. Stockwell's performance is worth a look. **CL8, ST193, ST208**

Boyfriends and Girlfriends (1988, C, 102m, PG)
The concluding chapter in French director Eric Rohmer's six-film "Comedies and Proverbs" series. It's about a quartet of young people in the throes of romantic angst in a Paris suburb. **DT107**

Boys From Brazil, The (1978, C, 123m, R)
Bizarre tale of an army of Hitler-cloned youth intended for use in a neo-Nazi take-over. Gregory Peck is the villain; Laurence Olivier costars as a Nazi hunter. With James Mason. Based on a novel by Ira Levin. Mildly entertaining. **MY6, ST153, ST168, ST171**

Boys From Brooklyn see *Bela Lugosi Meets a Brooklyn Gorilla*

Boys in Company C, The (1978, C, 127m, R)
Tough Army sergeant trains young recruits for Vietnam combat. Stan Shaw, Andrew Stevens, and Craig Wasson star. **AC4**

Boys in the Band, The (1970, C, 119m, R)
Mart Crowley's play about a group of homosexual friends at a birthday party, starring Kenneth Nelson, Peter White, Leonard Frey, Cliff Gorman, and Laurence Luckinbill. **DR3, DR20**

Boys Next Door, The (1985, C, 91m, R)
Disturbing drama of two seemingly normal teen-agers who go on a crime spree on the eve of their graduation. Charlie Sheen and Maxwell Caulfield star. Penelope Spheeris directed. **DR9**

Boys Town (1938, B&W, 96m, NR)
Oscar winner Spencer Tracy is kindly Father Flanagan and Mickey Rooney is Whitey, the kid he reforms, in this stirring drama of the real-life priest and his orphanage. **CL8, ST189, ST217, XT2**

Boyz N the Hood (1991, C, 107m, R)
Writer-director John Singleton's up-to-the-minute report on the crisis in urban life: the immense pressures on young black men to succumb to the temptations of the streets. Rap star Ice Cube, Cuba Gooding, Jr., and Morris Chestnutt play a trio of friends; Larry Fishburne is the father who tries to save one of them. Shot on the streets of south central Los Angeles. Moving, urgent filmmaking. **DR7, DR8, DR14, DR15, MU12, XT10,** *Recommended*

Braddock: Missing in Action III (1988, C, 101m, R)
Chuck Norris returns once again to Vietnam as former POW Colonel Braddock, this time to rescue his long-lost Vietnamese wife and their son. **AC4, ST165**

Brain, The (1969, C, 100m, G)
Comic heist story set aboard a speeding train, starring David Niven, Jean-Paul Belmondo, Bourvil, and Eli Wallach. **CO10, MY18, ST11**

Brain Damage (1988, C, 94m, R)
From Frank Henenlotter, the director of *Basket Case*, a horror story of a teen-ager plagued by a monstrous parasite which acts like a narcotic. **HO12**

Brain Donors (1992, C, 80m, PG)
Marx Brothers–style comedy of a trio of bumblers out to bamboozle a matron; she wants to start a ballet company. John Turturro, Bob Nelson, and Mel Smith star, with Nancy Marchand. **CO3**

Brain From Planet Arous, The (1958, B&W, 70m, NR)
Title creature inhabits scientist John Agar's head, while the brain of a cop occupies Agar's dog in this low-budget science fiction drama. **SF1, SF9**

Brain That Wouldn't Die, The (1963, B&W, 81m, NR)
A doctor keeps alive the head of his decapitated fiancée while he searches for a body. **HO20**

Brainstorm (1983, C, 106m, PG)
Research scientists discover a telepathic device; the military can't wait to use it for a weapon. Christopher Walken, Louise Fletcher, Cliff Robertson, and Natalie Wood (in her last film) star. **SF5, ST222**

Bram Stoker's Dracula (1973 version) see *Dracula* (1973 version)

Bram Stoker's Dracula (1992, C, 123m, R)
The familiar tale of this bloodsucking count, given a sexy spin by director Francis Ford

Coppola. Gary Oldman stars, with Winona Ryder as his love object, Anthony Hopkins as von Helsing, Keanu Reeves, Richard E. Grant, Cary Elwes, Bill Campbell, Sadie Frost, and Tom Waits as a Renfield to rival Dwight Frye. Photographed by Michael Ballhaus, production design by Thomas Sanders; Oscars for costume design by Eiko Ishioka, and makeup by Greg Cannom, Michele Burke, and Matthew W. Mungle. The stunning visuals carry the film over some rough narrative patches. **DT29, HF7, HO4, HO25, MU12, ST109,** *Recommended*

Branded (1950, C, 95m, NR)
Alan Ladd Western has him used by outlaws to impersonate a rancher's long-lost son. With Charles Bickford and Mona Freeman. **ST128, WE3**

Brannigan (1975, C, 111m, PG)
A tough Chicago detective (John Wayne) is off to London to bring home a fugitive. Richard Attenborough costars. **ST224, XT15**

Brasher Doubloon, The
(1947, B&W, 72m, NR)
Raymond Chandler's detective mystery stars George Montgomery as Philip Marlowe, who's after some rare coins linked to a series of murders. **WR2**

Brass Target (1978, C, 111m, PG)
World War II drama that imagines General Patton was murdered to cover up a gold theft by his men. John Cassavetes, Sophia Loren, and George Kennedy star. **ST141**

Bravados, The (1958, C, 98m, NR)
Gregory Peck stars in this Western tale of a man seeking revenge on the four outlaws who raped and then killed his wife. With Joan Collins, Stephen Boyd, Albert Salmi, and Lee Van Cleef. **ST171, ST221, WE5**

Brave Little Toaster, The
(1987, C, 89m, NR)
Disney animated feature about anthropomorphic household appliances. With the voices of Jon Lovitz, Tim Stack, and Timothy E. Day. **FA2**

Brazil (1985, C, 130m, R)
Futuristic tale of a bureaucrat mistakenly targeted as a terrorist, brilliantly directed by Terry Gilliam. Jonathan Pryce stars, with Robert De Niro, Kim Greist, Bob Hoskins, and Michael Palin. Eye-filling sets, special effects. **CO15, CU4, SF11, SF14, ST51, ST111, XT26,** *Highly Recommended*

Break of Hearts (1935, B&W, 80m, NR)
Katharine Hepburn plays a young composer married to a famous conductor (Charles Boyer) in this drama. **ST16, ST103**

Breaker! Breaker! (1977, C, 86m, PG)
Trucker uses his CB to rescue his son from a crooked judge. Chuck Norris stars. **ST165**

Breaker Morant (1979, C, 107m, PG)
Edward Woodward stars in this Australian drama set during the Boer War, about the court-martial of several soldiers on questionable charges. Directed by Bruce Beresford. **DT10, FF5**

Breakfast at Tiffany's
(1961, C, 115m, NR)
Audrey Hepburn is Holly Golightly, a nonworking girl living off a series of wealthy men in New York. With George Peppard, Patricia Neal, Buddy Ebsen, Mickey Rooney, and Martin Balsam. Based on Truman Capote's story; directed by Blake Edwards. **DR1, DR15, DT40, ST102, ST189, XT9,** *Recommended*

Breakfast Club, The (1985, C, 95m, R)
Five high-school students, confined to the school for a Saturday detention, become fast friends, despite their outward differences. Emilio Estevez, Molly Ringwald, Ally Sheedy, Anthony Michael Hall, and Judd Nelson star. Written and directed by John Hughes. Hughes's best film but, like his others, insufferably glib. **DR9, DR25, DT59**

Breakheart Pass (1976, C, 95m, PG)
Western drama about secret agent (Charles Bronson) on the trail of gunrunners. Action takes place mostly on a train; good supporting cast includes Ben Johnson, Richard Crenna, Charles Durning, Ed Lauter, Archie Moore, and Jill Ireland. **ST20, XT19**

Breakin' (1984, C, 90m, PG)
A waitress hopes to crash the show business world as a breakdancer. Lucinda Dickey stars in this musical drama. **MU9**

Breakin' 2: Electric Boogaloo
(1984, C, 94m, PG)
Lucinda Dickey and her breakdancing partners are back for more musical numbers in this sequel to *Breakin'*. **MU9**

Breaking Away (1979, C, 100m, PG)
A Midwestern teen-ager trains for a major bike race in this warm comedy-drama starring Dennis Christopher, Dennis Quaid, and Paul Dooley. Written by Steve Tesich. **CO4, DR22, DR26,** *Recommended*

Breaking Glass (1980, C, 104m, PG)
British musical drama of a singer (Hazel O'Connor) determined to make it with her own style of punkish music. Phil Daniels, Jon Finch, and Jonathan Pryce costar in this look behind the scenes of the music business. **MU4, MU9**

Breaking In (1989, C, 94m, R)
Wry, low-key comedy-drama from director
Bill Forsyth, starring Burt Reynolds as an
aging burglar who takes on a young appren-
tice (Casey Siemaszko). Written by John
Sayles. **CO10, DT46, DT112, ST183,**
Recommended

Breaking Up Is Hard to Do
(1979, C, 96m, NR)
Drama of the dissolution of a marriage, told
from the husband's point of view. Robert
Conrad stars, with Ted Bessell, Jeff Conaway,
and Billy Crystal. Originally made for TV
with a running time of 201 minutes. **CO13**

Breakout (1975, C, 96m, PG)
True-life action drama of an American held
in Mexican prison and a helicopter pilot's attempts to spring him. Charles Bronson,
Robert Duvall, Randy Quaid, and John Huston star. **DT60, ST20, ST63**

Breakthrough (1978, C, 115m, PG)
Sequel to World War II drama *Cross of Iron*,
starring Richard Burton, Robert Mitchum,
Rod Steiger, and Curt Jurgens. **AC1, ST22,
ST158**

Breath of Scandal, A (1960, C, 98m, NR)
Costume drama starring Sophia Loren as a
princess wooed by an American (John
Gavin). Maurice Chevalier and Angela Lansbury costar. **ST131, ST141**

Breathless (1959, B&W, 89m, NR)
A petty thief and an American girl find romance and death on the streets of Paris. Director Jean-Luc Godard's highly influential
feature debut. Jean-Paul Belmondo (his first
major role) and Jean Seberg star. U.S. remake
released in 1983. **DT50, FF8, ST11, XT16,
XT21,** *Essential, Recommended*

Breathless (1983, C, 100m, R)
American remake of the French classic; this
time the drifter is an American who's enthralled with rock music and comic books
and his lover is a French exchange student.
Richard Gere and Valerie Kaprisky star. **DR1,
FF8, ST84**

Breed Apart, A (1984, C, 95m, R)
Adventure drama of a couple living in the
mountains of North Carolina, protecting a
rare species of bird. Enter a mysterious
stranger, with orders to capture the bird.
Kathleen Turner, Rutger Hauer, and Powers
Boothe star. **AC12, ST218**

Brenda Starr (1992, C, 87m, PG)
Brooke Shields plays the red-headed reporter
from the comic pages in this romantic
adventure. With Tony Peck, Timothy Dalton

as Basil St. John, Diana Scarwid, Jeffrey Tambor, and Charles Durning. Made in 1986.
AC14

Brewster McCloud (1970, C, 101m, R)
Offbeat comedy about a young man who be-
lieves he's a bird and tries to fly in the
Houston Astrodome. Packed with absurd bits
and throwaway gags, this comedy has a cult
following. Directed by Robert Altman. Bud
Cort stars, with Sally Kellerman, Michael
Murphy, Shelley Duvall, Stacy Keach, and
Margaret Hamilton. Widescreen will be lost
on video. **CO12, CU5, CU20, DT4,**
Recommended

Brewster's Millions (1985, C, 97m, PG)
Frequently filmed comic story about a man
who must spend $30 million in thirty days
in order to inherit $300 million (the amounts
in this version have been adjusted for infla-
tion). Richard Pryor and John Candy star.
Walter Hill directed. **CO3, CO14, DT56,
ST180**

Brian's Song (1970, C, 73m, NR)
Tearjerker about the friendship between Chicago Bears running back Gayle Sayers (Billy
Dee Williams) and his terminally ill team-
mate, Brian Piccolo (James Caan). Originally
made for TV. **DR2, DR22, ST227**

Bride, The (1985, C, 118m, PG-13)
Remake of *The Bride of Frankenstein*, starring
Sting as the mad doctor and Jennifer Beals as
his creation. **CU18, HF10, HO20, MU12**

Bride Came C.O.D., The
(1941, B&W, 92m, NR)
James Cagney and Bette Davis team in a
comedy about a flier and a bride on the lam.
ST24, ST44

Bride Is Much Too Beautiful, The
(1958, B&W, 90m, NR)
Brigitte Bardot plays a simple farm girl whose
life is turned upside-down when she's recruited to become a fashion model. Louis
Jourdan costars. **ST6**

Bride of Frankenstein, The
(1935, B&W, 75m, NR)
Masterful follow-up to the first great *Franken-
stein* film, with Boris Karloff "wed" to Elsa
Lanchester. Colin Clive and Ernest Thesiger
play the matchmakers. James Whale directed.
CU4, DT138, HF10, HO1, HO20, ST119,
Essential, Highly Recommended

Bride of Re-Animator (1991, C, 99m, R)
Inevitable sequel to gory film about mad
young doctor reviving the dead. Jeffrey
Combs returns as the crazed revival artist.
CU7, HO18, HO20

Bride of the Gorilla
(1951, B&W, 76m, NR)
Camp classic about a newlywed who discovers that her husband is regularly transformed into a hairy beast. Raymond Burr,
Barbara Payton, and Lon Chaney, Jr., star.
CU2, ST27

Bride of the Monster
(1955, B&W, 69m, NR)
Inept horror film from the king of inept
movies, Ed Wood, Jr. Bela Lugosi stars as a
mad scientist; Tor Johnson is his immense
assistant Lobo. Must be seen to be believed.
DT141, ST143

Bride Walks Out, The
(1936, B&W, 81m, NR)
Romantic comedy starring Barbara Stanwyck
and Gene Raymond as a young couple trying
to make ends meet. **ST206**

Bride Wore Black, The
(1968, C, 107m, NR)
Jeanne Moreau plays a woman whose husband is murdered on their wedding day;
she spends the rest of her life tracking down
the men responsible. Directed by François
Truffaut; based on a story by William Irish
(Cornell Woolrich). **DT125, FF1, MY4,
ST161, WR39, XT20**

Bride Wore Red, The
(1937, B&W, 103m, NR)
Joan Crawford vehicle in which she's torn
between two men, Robert Young and Franchot Tone. Directed by Dorothy Arzner. **CL5,
ST39**

Brides of Dracula, The
(1960, C, 85m, NR)
British take on the count's domestic life, with
Peter Cushing baring his fangs, David Peel as
his disciple and scout for women, Martita
Hunt and Yvonne Monlaur as marital candidates. **HF7, HO5, HO26, ST43**

Brideshead Revisited (1981, C, 540m, NR)
Public TV miniseries based on Evelyn
Waugh's masterful study of a crumbling fam-
ily of British aristocrats. Jeremy Irons and
Anthony Andrews star, with Diana Quick,
Laurence Olivier, John Gielgud, Claire
Bloom, and Stéphane Audran. Directed by
Charles Sturridge. Richly satisfying adapta-
tion. **DR8, DR19, DR23, ST86, ST116,
ST168,** *Recommended*

Bridge at Remagen, The
(1969, C, 115m, PG)
World War II saga of Allies holding their
position at crucial river crossing near the
war's end. George Segal, Robert Vaughn, and
Ben Gazzara star. **AC1**

Bridge on the River Kwai, The
(1957, C, 161m, NR)
British prisoners of war are forced to construct a bridge vital to the Japanese; meanwhile, commandos are sent to destroy it.
Well-deserving winner of seven Oscars,
including Best Picture, Director (David Lean),
and Actor (Alec Guinness). William Holden,
Sessue Hayakawa, and Jack Hawkins costar.
Widescreen cinematography will be lost on
video. **AC7, CU20, DT71, ST95, ST106,
XT1, XT2, XT6,** *Essential, Highly
Recommended*

Bridge to Nowhere (1986, C, 82m, NR)
Five city kids head into trouble on a hike in
the country when they trespass on a madman's property. **AC24**

Bridge Too Far, A (1977, C, 175m, PG)
World War II epic about ill-fated Allied
attempt to surround German forces in Hol-
land. Among the many stars: Dirk Bogarde,
James Caan, Michael Caine, Sean Connery,
Edward Fox, Gene Hackman, Anthony Hop-
kins, Laurence Olivier, Robert Redford, and
Liv Ullmann. Richard Attenborough directed;
Joseph E. Levine produced. Reasonably enter-
taining, but the cast seems to be just passing
through. **AC1, ST14, ST25, ST36, ST96,
ST109, ST168, ST181, ST220, XT23**

Bridges at Toko-Ri, The
(1954, C, 103m, NR)
Korean war drama focusing on fighter pilot
and his qualms about the U.S. involvement.
William Holden, Grace Kelly, Fredric March,
and Mickey Rooney star. **AC3, AC11, ST106,
ST124, ST148, ST189**

Brief Encounter (1945, B&W, 85m, NR)
Classic romance by Noel Coward finds Celia
Johnson and Trevor Howard in World War II
England as ordinary, middle-aged people who
have a bittersweet affair. Directed by David
Lean. A small but still moving story. **CL4,
CL6, DT71, WR4,** *Essential, Recommended*

Brief Encounter (1974, C, 103m, NR)
Richard Burton and Sophia Loren star in this
made-for-TV remake of the classic Noel Coward romance. **CU18, ST22, ST141, WR4**

Brief History of Time, A
(1992, C, 84m, G)
Documentary examination of physicist Stephen Hawking's theories, adapted from his
bestselling book. Imaginative presentation
by director Errol Morris of abstract concepts.
Photographed by John Bailey, music by
Philip Glass. **CU16, DT89,** *Recommended*

Brigadoon (1954, C, 108m, NR)
Lerner and Loewe Broadway hit, with Gene

Kelly and Van Johnson as two Americans discovering a magical Scottish village. Directed by Vincente Minnelli. **DT88, MU1, MU2, MU8, ST123**

Bright Eyes (1934, B&W, 83m, NR)
Shirley Temple sings "On the Good Ship Lollipop" in this sentimental story of a custody battle. With Shirley's fellow child star Jane Withers. **ST213**

Bright Lights, Big City (1988, C, 107m, R)
Portrait of young New Yorker coming apart at the seams, as his partying and drug habit take their toll on his marriage and job at a prestigious magazine. Michael J. Fox stars, with Kiefer Sutherland, Phoebe Cates, Tracy Pollan, and Jason Robards. Based on Jay McInerney's novel. **DR15, DR19, ST185, XT9**

Brighton Beach Memoirs
(1986, C, 110m, PG-13)
Nostalgic comedy about growing up in Brooklyn in the 1940s, adapted by Neil Simon from his Broadway hit. Jonathan Silverman, Bob Dishy, Blythe Danner, and Judith Ivey star. **CO5, CO6, WR30**

Brighton Rock (1947, B&W, 86m, NR)
Early role for Richard Attenborough in this adaptation of Graham Greene's story of a young gangster. With Carol Marsh and Hermione Baddeley. Written by Greene and Terence Ratigan. Also known as *Young Scarface*. **AC22, DR23, WR11**

Brighty of the Grand Canyon
(1967, C, 89m, NR)
The adventures of a lovable pack mule, set in the splendor of northern Arizona, starring Joseph Cotten and Dick Foran. **FA4, FA5**

Brimstone and Treacle (1982, C, 85m, R)
Bizarre tale of strange young man who moves in uninvited with a couple; their teen-aged daughter is in a coma from an auto accident. Sting stars, with Denholm Elliott, Joan Plowright, and Suzanna Hamilton. Written by Dennis Potter. Generally unpleasant stuff. **DR23, MU12**

Bring Me the Head of Alfredo Garcia
(1974, C, 112m, R)
Director Sam Peckinpah's story of honor and revenge, with Warren Oates as a lowly piano player traveling on the title mission at the behest of a greedy Mexican. With Isela Vega, Gig Young, Robert Webber, Kris Kristofferson, and Emilio Fernandez. **DT95, MU12, MY2, ST166, XT18**

Bring on the Night (1985, C, 97m, PG-13)
Documentary about rock star Sting and his formation of a jazz-rock band. **MU11**

Bringing Up Baby (1938, B&W, 102m, NR)
Classic screwball comedy featuring a socially inept zoologist (Cary Grant), a ditsy heiress (Katharine Hepburn), and her Baby—a pet leopard. Howard Hawks directed. A bit frantic but still lots of fun. **CL10, DT53, ST92, ST103,** *Essential, Recommended*

Brink of Life (1958, B&W, 84m, NR)
Drama from director Ingmar Bergman about the lives of three women in a maternity ward. Eva Dahlbeck, Ingrid Thulin, and Bibi Andersson star. **DT11**

Brink's Job, The (1978, C, 103m, PG)
Seriocomic version of the famed 1950 robbery of armored car offices in Boston by a motley crew, played by Peter Falk, Peter Boyle, Allen Goorwitz, and Warren Oates. Directed by William Friedkin. **MY8, MY18, ST166**

Britannia Hospital (1982, C, 115m, R)
British comedy, set in an ineptly run hospital, takes swipes at socialized medicine, quack medical research, and corrupt unions. Malcolm McDowell stars. Watch for Alan Bates in a small role. Lindsay Anderson directed. A loose continuation of the McDowell/Anderson film, *O Lucky Man!* Occasionally on-target; humor probably makes more sense across the pond. **CO2, CO17, ST9**

British Intelligence
(1940, B&W, 62m, NR)
Boris Karloff plays a butler working during World War II as a possible spy. With Margaret Lindsay. **ST119**

Broadcast News (1987, C, 125m, R)
Romantic comedy set in a Washington, D.C., TV newsroom, involving a dynamo producer (Holly Hunter) and two reporters (William Hurt, Albert Brooks) who both love her. With Joan Cusack, Robert Prosky, and Peter Hackes; Jack Nicholson has a small role as a network anchorman. James L. Brooks wrote and directed. One of the few recent films that shows how a job can overwhelm a person's life and distort his (or her) judgment. **CO1, CO2, DT16, ST113, ST114, ST163, XT12,** *Recommended*

Broadway Bill (1934, B&W, 90m, NR)
Frank Capra directed this comedy of a man married to money but involved with horse-racing scene. Warner Baxter, Myrna Loy, and Walter Connolly star. **DT22, ST142**

Broadway Danny Rose
(1984, C, 86m, PG)
A luckless New York talent agent gets mixed up with a mobster's wife. Woody Allen and Mia Farrow star in this gentle comedy about

the less glamorous side of show business. **CO8, DT2, ST65, XT9, XT30,** *Recommended*

Broadway Melody (1929, B&W, 104m, NR) A pair of sisters try to break into show biz and fall for the same entertainer. The first musical to win the Best Picture Oscar. Bessie Love and Anita Page star. **MU4, MU7, XT1**

Broadway Melody of 1936 (1935, B&W, 110m, NR) MGM musical with Jack Benny as a sneaky columnist, Robert Taylor as a Broadway producer, and Eleanor Powell as his star dancer. Songs include "You Are My Lucky Star" and "Broadway Rhythm." **MU1, MU4**

Broadway Melody of 1938 (1937, B&W, 110m, NR) Eleanor Powell stars as a dancer torn between two men (Robert Taylor and George Murphy). Judy Garland and Sophie Tucker costar. **MU1, MU4, ST81**

Broadway Melody of 1940 (1940, B&W, 102m, NR) Fred Astaire and George Murphy are dance partners and rivals for dancing star Eleanor Powell. Songs by Cole Porter. **MU1, MU4, ST4**

Broadway Rhythm (1944, C, 114m, NR) MGM musical of ex-vaudeville star and his son, a producer, quarreling. George Murphy and Charles Winninger star, with Ginny Simms, Gloria De Haven, Nancy Walker, and Tommy Dorsey and His Orchestra. **MU1, MU4**

Broadway Serenade (1939, B&W, 114m, NR) Musical about a songwriter (Lew Ayres) and singer (Jeanette MacDonald) who have to choose between their careers and marriage. With Ian Hunter and Frank Morgan. **MU4**

Broken Arrow (1950, C, 93m, NR) Classic Western drama of the Apache Indian chief Cochise and his struggle to make peace with white settlers. James Stewart and Jeff Chandler star. **ST207, WE7**

Broken Blossoms (1919, B&W, 95m, NR) D.W. Griffith's silent tragedy, with Lillian Gish as an abused child who's befriended by a gentle Chinaman (Richard Barthelmess). Proves that Griffith was a master of intimacy as well as spectacle; Gish is sensational. **CL12, DT52, ST87,** *Essential, Recommended*

Broken Lance (1954, C, 96m, NR) Spencer Tracy plays a rancher in charge of a crumbling empire in this Western remake of *House of Strangers*. With Robert Wagner, Jean Peters, Richard Widmark, Katy Jurado, and

Hugh O'Brian. Directed by Edward Dmytryk. **ST217**

Bronco Billy (1980, C, 119m, PG) A Wild West Show entrepreneur (Clint Eastwood) leads his ragged troupe from one improbable adventure to the next. With Sondra Locke and Scatman Crothers. Eastwood directed. **ST64, WE12**

Bronze Venus see *The Duke Is Tops*

Brood, The (1979, C, 90m, R) David Cronenberg directed this gory story of a therapist experimenting with a treatment that allows patients to express their inner rage in physical ways. Art Hindle, Samantha Eggar, and Oliver Reed star. Like many Cronenberg films, this has a cult following, but the faint of heart should beware. **CU4, CU7, DT31, H013,** *Recommended*

Brother, Can You Spare a Dime? (1975, B&W, 103m, PG) Documentary of American life during the Great Depression combines newsreel footage and clips from popular films of the day. **CU16**

Brother from Another Planet, The (1984, C, 110m, NR) Dark-skinned alien fugitive lands in Harlem, where he's treated like just another strange dude. Science fiction with its tongue in its cheek; written and directed by John Sayles, who also plays a small role. Joe Morton stars. **DR14, DR15, DR27, DT112, SF9**

Brother John (1972, C, 94m, PG) Sidney Poitier stars in this story of the return of the Messiah in the form of a black man, who can't get anyone to believe him. With Will Geer, Beverly Todd, and Paul Winfield. **DR14, ST174, ST230**

Brother Orchid (1940, B&W, 91m, NR) Edward G. Robinson gangster film in which he tries to gather class about his person. With Ann Sothern, Humphrey Bogart, and Ralph Bellamy. **AC22, ST15, ST186**

Brother Sun, Sister Moon (1973, C, 121m, PG) Italian director Franco Zeffirelli's portrait of Francis of Assisi, starring Graham Faulkner and Judi Bowker, with Alec Guinness. Music by Donovan. **FF2, ST95**

Brotherhood, The (1968, C, 98m, NR) Kirk Douglas and Alex Cord play clashing brothers in this drama of organized crime. Directed by Martin Ritt. **DR16, DT105, ST57**

Brotherhood of Satan (1971, C, 92m, PG) A coven of witches takes over a small town and three outsiders fight for their lives. Strother Martin stars. **HO11**

Brotherhood of the Rose, The
(1989, C, 103m, PG-13)
A pair of young men, raised as brothers and trained in the art of espionage, are betrayed by a man they thought was their father. Robert Mitchum, Peter Strauss, and David Morse star, with Connie Sellecca, James B. Sikking, and M. Emmet Walsh. Originally made for TV with running time of 200 minutes. **MY6, MY14, ST158**

Brothers Karamazov, The
(1958, C, 146m, NR)
Dostoyevsky's classic tragedy, an exploration of good, evil, and faith involving a father and his three sons. Lee J. Cobb, Yul Brynner, Richard Basehart, and William Shatner star. Directed by Richard Brooks. **CL1**

Brothers Lionheart, The
(1977, C, 108m, G)
Family fantasy of siblings brought together in death in a medieval world, where they fight dragons. **FA8, SF13**

Brothers O'Toole, The (1973, C, 94m, NR)
This Western comedy follows the misadventures of two drifters who ride into a broken-down 1890s mining town. **WE14**

Brubaker (1980, C, 132m, R)
An idealistic warden at a Southern prison farm uncovers massive corruption. Robert Redford stars, with Yaphet Kotto, Jane Alexander, David Keith, Morgan Freeman, and Tim McIntire. **DR18, ST76, ST181**

Bruce Lee: The Legend
(1984, C, 88m, NR)
Documentary about the great martial arts star, with rare footage and out-takes, plus interviews with Steve McQueen and other friends of Lee. **ST134, ST146**

Bruce Lee: The Man/The Myth
(1984, C, 90m, PG)
Dramatized biography of the martial arts star, featuring real footage of Lee in action. **ST134**

Brute, The (1952, B&W, 81m, NR)
To break a tenants' strike, a slumlord hires an ignorant slaughterhouse worker, who falls into an affair with the slumlord's wife. Luis Buñuel directed this drama, filmed in Mexico. Katy Jurado and Pedro Armendariz star. **DT19**

Brute Man, The (1946, B&W, 60m, NR)
A college football hero is disfigured by a lab accident, which turns him into the Creeper, a psychopathic killer. Rondo Hatton stars. **HO9**

Buccaneer, The (1958, C, 121m, NR)
Drama set during the War of 1812, with Andrew Jackson (Charlton Heston) teaming up with pirate Lafitte (Yul Brynner) to fight the bloody British. With Charles Boyer. Produced by Cecil B. DeMille; directed by Anthony Quinn. **AC6, AC16, ST16, XT23**

Buck and the Preacher
(1972, C, 102m, PG)
Sidney Poitier stars in and directed this Western about a couple of con men. Harry Belafonte and Ruby Dee costar. **ST174**

Buck Privates (1941, B&W, 84m, NR)
Abbott and Costello's first starring roles, in a wacky service comedy. The Andrews Sisters sing "Boogie Woogie Bugle Boy." **CO21, ST1**

Buck Privates Come Home
(1947, B&W, 77m, NR)
Abbott and Costello sequel to their service comedy has the boys returning to civilian life, smuggling a European orphan into the U.S. **ST1**

Bucket of Blood, A
(1959, B&W, 66m, NR)
Legendary low-budget Roger Corman horror film about sculptor Walter Paisley (Dick Miller) who uses live models to create sculptures. With Barboura Morris and Antony Carbone. Written by Charles Griffith. Sequel of sorts: *The Little Shop of Horrors.* **DT30**

Buddy Buddy (1981, C, 96m, R)
A suicidal man and a hit man wind up in the same hotel room in this comedy starring Jack Lemmon and Walter Matthau. Billy Wilder directed. With Klaus Kinski. Remake of French comedy *A Pain in the A- -.* **CO3, DT139, FF8, ST126, ST138, ST155**

Buddy Holly Story, The
(1978, C, 113m, PG)
The short but brilliant life of rock music pioneer Buddy Holly, portrayed with gusto by Gary Busey, who also performs Holly's ground-breaking music. Don Stroud and Charles Martin Smith costar. **MU5, XT26,** *Recommended*

Buddy System, The (1984, C, 110m, PG)
Romantic comedy starring Richard Dreyfuss and Susan Sarandon as a couple trying to decide whether to get involved. **CO1, ST60, ST194**

Buffalo Bill (1944, C, 90m, NR)
Joel McCrea plays the legendary Westerner in this glossy Hollywood bio. With Maureen O'Hara, Linda Darnell, Thomas Mitchell, and Anthony Quinn. Directed by William Wellman. **DT135, HF3, ST144, ST167**

Buffalo Bill and the Indians
(1976, C, 120m, PG)
A moody portrait of the Hero of the Plains in his final days, when he ran a traveling Wild West Show. Paul Newman stars, with Burt Lancaster as Ned Buntline, Geraldine Chaplin as Annie Oakley, John Considine, Harvey Keitel, and Will Sampson. Directed by Robert Altman. One of Newman's better performances. **DT4, HF3, HF20, ST129, ST162, WE11,** *Recommended*

Buffalo Stampede (1933, B&W, 60m, NR)
Randolph Scott plays a buffalo hunter in one of his early Westerns. With Buster Crabbe, Harry Carey, and Noah Beery. **ST197**

Buffet Froid (1979, C, 95m, NR)
French comedy of a bumbling trio of killers (Gérard Depardieu, Bernard Blier, and Jean Carmet). Directed by Bertrand Blier, son of actor Bernard. **FF1, ST52**

Buffy the Vampire Slayer
(1992, C, 86m, PG-13)
Spoofy tale of contemporary high school cheerleader endowed with talent for knocking off vampires. Kristy Swanson stars, with Donald Sutherland, Luke Perry, and, as her opponents, Rutger Hauer and Paul Reubens. **HO5, HO12, HO24**

Bug (1975, C, 100m, PG)
An earthquake lets loose a swarm of insects capable of setting anything on fire. Bradford Dillman stars. **HO16**

Bugs and Daffy: The Wartime Cartoons
(1943–45, C, 120m, NR)
Time-capsule look at World War II through the eyes of the Warner Brothers cartoon gang. **FA11**

Bugs and Daffy's Carnival of the Animals (1976, C, 26m, NR)
Bugs Bunny and Daffy Duck combine their talents with a live orchestra conducted by Michael Tilson Thomas in this fantasy based on Camille St. Saëns's title composition. Directed by Chuck Jones; originally made for TV. **FA11,** *Recommended*

Bugs Bunny and Elmer Fudd Cartoon Festival (1940–46, C, 54m, NR)
Seven classic Bugs and Elmer shorts, including *Wabbit Twouble, Stage Door Cartoon,* and *The Big Snooze.* **FA11**

Bugs Bunny Cartoon Festival
(1942–46, C, 34m, NR)
Cartoon delights from directors Friz Freleng, Chuck Jones, and Bob Clampett. **FA11**

Bugs Bunny Classics (1941–48, C, 60m, NR)
Among the highlights of this collection are

Heckling Hare, directed by Tex Avery, and *Haredevil Hare,* directed by Chuck Jones. **FA11**

Bugs Bunny in King Arthur's Court
(1977, C, 25m, NR)
That wascally wabbit and his pals retell Mark Twain's *Connecticut Yankee in King Arthur's Court.* Directed by Chuck Jones; originally made for TV. **FA11, WR35**

Bugs Bunny/Road Runner Movie, The
(1979, C, 92m, G)
Warner Brothers classic cartoon compilation features Bugs, Daffy Duck, Elmer Fudd, The Road Runner, Wile E. Coyote, Porky Pig, and Pepe LePew. **FA11**

Bugs Bunny Superstar (1975, C, 90m, G)
A nine-cartoon collection from the 1930s and 1940s, most of them directed by Bob Clampett. **FA11**

Bugs Bunny's 3rd Movie: 1001 Rabbit Tales (1982, C, 76m, G)
A collection of old and new Warner Brothers favorites. Voices by Mel Blanc. **FA11**

Bugs Bunny's Wacky Adventures
(1957, C, 59m, NR)
Eight prized tales featuring that wascally wabbit. **FA11**

Bugsy (1991, C, 135m, R)
Gangster bio of Benjamin "Don't Call Me Bugsy" Siegel, credited with the founding of modern Las Vegas and its multibillion-dollar casino scene. With Annette Bening as Virginia Hill, his showgirl lover, Ben Kingsley as Meyer Lansky, Elliott Gould as Harry Greenberg, Joe Mantegna as George Raft, and Bill Graham as Lucky Luciano. Well-written by James Toback; directed by Barry Levinson. Great looking film that is consistently entertaining, only sags at the end. **AC22, DR4, DR16, DR24, DT75, ST10, ST12,** *Recommended*

Bugsy Malone (1976, C, 94m, G)
Jodie Foster heads the all-child cast in a musical which spoofs gangster films. Music by Paul Williams; directed by Alan Parker. It sounds like a bad idea and it plays like it, too. **FA9, MU16, ST75**

Bull Durham (1988, C, 108m, R)
A veteran catcher, wrapping up his career in the minor leagues, befriends a goofy young pitcher with great talent but no brains for the game, while the team's most devoted female fan makes a play for both men. Kevin Costner, Tim Robbins, and Susan Sarandon star in this sensational comedy from writer-director Ron Shelton. **CO1, CO19, ST38, ST194, XT26,** *Recommended*

Bulldog Drummond (series)

Bulldog Drummond
(1929, B&W, 89m, NR)

Bulldog Drummond at Bay
(1937, B&W, 62m, NR)

Bulldog Drummond Comes Back
(1937, B&W, 64m, NR)

Bulldog Drummond Escapes
(1937, B&W, 65m, NR)

Bulldog Drummond in Africa
(1938, B&W, 60m, NR)

Bulldog Drummond Striies Back
(1947, B&W, 65m, NR)

Bulldog Drummond's Bride
(1939, B&W, 55m, NR)

Bulldog Drummond's Peril
(1938, B&W, 66m, NR)

Bulldog Drummond's Revenge
(1937, B&W, 60m, NR)

Bulldog Drummond's Secret Police
(1939, B&W, 56m, NR)
The exploits of Hugh "Bulldog" Drummond, a high-flying ex-British officer with dashing good looks who always got his man with the help of his constant companion Algy. Ronald Colman stars in the first film; John Howard appears in all others in the series. John Barrymore costars as Drummond's pal, the master of disguises, in three entries (in *Comes Back*, *Peril*, and *Revenge*). **HF8, ST8, ST35**

Bulldog Jack (1934, B&W, 62m, NR)
British comedian Jack Hulbert stars in this mystery; he takes famed sleuth Bulldog Drummond's place on the case of a jewel thief. With Ralph Richardson as the villain and Fay Wray. Climax filmed in London's Underground. Original running time: 73 minutes. Also known as *Alias Bulldog Drummond*. **MY15, ST184, XT15**

Bullet for Sandoval, A (1970, C, 96m, PG)
A Civil War veteran swears revenge on those who caused the death of his son. Western action starring Ernest Borgnine. **WE9**

Bullet for the General, A
(1967, C, 115m, NR)
Italian-made Western with American gunfighter joining marauding Mexicans for mayhem. Gian Maria Volonté, Lou Castel, and Klaus Kinski star. **ST126**

Bulletproof (1988, C, 95m, R)
Gary Busey plays a seemingly unstoppable ex-CIA agent who takes on a gang of terrorists. With Darlanne Fluegel and Henry Silva. **AC25**

Bullets or Ballots (1936, B&W, 81m, NR)
Warner Brothers melodrama has cop (Edward G. Robinson) going after mobster by faking his resignation from the force. With Barton MacLane, Joan Blondell, Humphrey Bogart, and Frank McHugh. **AC22, ST15, ST186**

Bullfighter and the Lady, The
(1951, B&W, 124m, NR)
An American visiting Mexico finds a matador to teach him bullfighting. Robert Stack and Gilbert Roland star, with Joy Page and Katy Jurado. Budd Boetticher directed and was Stack's stand-in on many of the bullfighting scenes. No better film has ever been made on the subject. New video version adds footage to restore film to original running time. **CU10, DT14,** *Recommended*

Bullfighters, The (1945, B&W, 61m, NR)
Laurel and Hardy comedy, with Stanley mistaken for a famed matador and forced into the ring. **ST133**

Bullies (1986, C, 96m, R)
A clan of mountain rednecks terrorize a small community, with only a teen-aged boy to stand up to them. **AC25**

Bullitt (1968, C, 113m, PG)
Modern classic cop drama, with Steve McQueen the cool San Francisco detective caught up in political machinations, trying to protect a criminal witness. With Robert Vaughn, Jacqueline Bisset, and (in a small part) Robert Duvall. Memorable car chase sequence. **AC9, ST63, ST146, XT13,** *Recommended*

Bull'seye! (1989, C, 89m, PG-13)
Comic caper has Michael Caine and Roger Moore playing double roles: criminals who bear a striking resemblance to a couple of corrupt nuclear scientists. With Sally Kirkland, Lee Patterson, Deborah Barrymore (Moore's daughter in real life), and John Cleese in a bit part. **CO10, CO15, ST25, XT8, XT27**

Bullshot (1983, C, 85m, PG)
Send-up of *Bulldog Drummond* detective series, adapted from a play by Alan Shearman, Diz White, and Ron House, who all star as well. **CO7, CO17, MY17**

Bundle of Joy (1956, C, 98m, NR)
Debbie Reynolds takes custody of an abandoned baby, creating problems with fiancé Eddie Fisher, in this musical remake of *Bachelor Mother*. **MU14**

'Burbs, The (1989, C, 105m, PG)
Tom Hanks plays a suburbanite who's suspicious of his new neighbors in this comedy from director Joe Dante. **DT33, ST97**

Burden of Dreams (1982, C, 94m, NR)
Documentary about the filming of *Fitzcarraldo*, a movie plagued by physical hardships, a feuding star (Klaus Kinski) and director (Werner Herzog), and remote locations. Jason Robards and Mick Jagger appear briefly in clips from an earlier version of Herzog's film. Directed by Les Blank. One of the best behind-the-scenes documentaries ever made. **CU16, DT54, ST126, ST185, XT26,** *Highly Recommended*

Bureau of Missing Persons (1933, B&W, 75m, NR)
Drama set in big-city title agency, starring Lewis Stone, with Bette Davis, Pat O'Brien, and Allen Jenkins. **ST44**

Burglar (1987, C, 103m, R)
A bookshop owner who moonlights as a cat burglar witnesses a murder and can't go to the police with her story. Whoopi Goldberg stars in this comedy with Bobcat Goldthwait. **CO10, ST89**

Buried Alive (1990, C, 91m, R)
Horror film set in a mansion for wayward girls, based on tales by Edgar Allan Poe ("The Black Cat" and "The Cask of Amontillado"). Robert Vaughn stars, with Donald Pleasence, Karen Witter, John Carradine (his last film), and Ginger Lynn Allen. **WR27**

Buried Alive (1990, C, 100m, NR)
Thriller of man who wakes up in a grave, manages to escape to exact revenge on faithless wife and her lover. Jennifer Jason Leigh, Tim Matheson, William Atherton, and Hoyt Axton star. Originally made for cable TV. **MU12, MY4, ST136**

Burke and Wills (1986, C, 140m, PG-13)
Historical drama, set in 1860 Australia, of the first two men to cross that continent. Jack Thompson, Nigel Havers, and Greta Scacchi star. **DR5, FF5**

Burn! (1969, C, 112m, PG)
Marlon Brando stars in this story of British meddling on an eighteenth-century Caribbean island. Superb political drama from Italian director Gillo Pontecorvo; dialogue in English. **CU9, DR5, DR27, FF2, ST18,** *Recommended*

Burning Bed, The (1984, C, 100m, NR)
An abused wife reaches the breaking point and sets fire to the bed in which her husband is sleeping. Farrah Fawcett and Paul LeMat star in this harrowing true-life story. Originally made for TV. **DR6, DR10**

Burning Cross, The see *Klansman, The*

Burning Secret (1988, C, 107m, R)
Post–World War I Vienna is the setting for this romantic drama starring Faye Dunaway as an American woman seduced by a dashing nobleman (Klaus Maria Brandauer). **ST61**

Burnt Offerings (1976, C, 115m, PG)
There's something spooky about the summer house Karen Black and Oliver Reed have rented for their family. Bette Davis costars. **HO3, ST44**

Bus Stop (1956, C, 96m, NR)
Marilyn Monroe stars as a small-town singer bound for Hollywood; she has a boisterous rodeo cowboy (Don Murray) in love with her. Based on a play by William Inge. **DR20, DR26, ST159**

Bushido Blade, The (1979, C, 104m, R)
In nineteenth-century Japan, Commander William Perry attempts to recover a valuable stolen sword. Action adventure starring Richard Boone, James Earl Jones, and Toshiro Mifune. **ST118, ST157**

Bushwackers, The (1952, B&W, 70m, NR)
Western drama about Confederate army vet turned gunfighter. Dorothy Malone and John Ireland star, with Wayne Morris, Lawrence Tierney, and Lon Chaney, Jr. **ST27**

Business As Usual (1988, C, 89m, PG)
British drama of a sexual harassment suit, starring Glenda Jackson and Cathy Tyson. **DR10, DR23, ST117**

Buster (1988, C, 93m, R)
Pop star Phil Collins plays the mastermind behind Britain's 1963 Great Train Robbery. Julie Walters costars as Buster's wife. **DR6, DR16, MU12, MY18**

Buster Keaton: A Hard Act to Follow (1989, B&W/C, 106m, NR)
Documentary, made for British TV, about the great silent clown. Directed by Kevin Brownlow and David Gill. A must for fans of Keaton. **CU16, DT66,** *Recommended*

Buster Keaton Festival Vol. I (1921–22, B&W, 55m, NR)
Three classic comedy shorts: *Paleface, Blacksmith, Cops.* **DT66,** *Recommended*

Buster Keaton Festival Vol. II (1923, B&W, 55m, NR)
Three more classic comedy shorts: *The Boat, The Frozen North,* and *The Electric House.* **DT66,** *Recommended*

Buster Keaton Festival Vol. III (1919/1923, B&W, 54m, NR)
Three more great silent comedy shorts: *Daydreams, The Balloonatic,* and *The Garage.* **DT66,** *Recommended*

**Buster Keaton Rides Again/
The Railrodder** (1965, B&W, 81m, NR)
The Railrodder is one of Keaton's last films; shot in Canada, it tries to re-create his classic style, as Buster travels cross-country on a railroad handcar. *Rides Again* is a documentary on the making of *The Railrodder*, with revealing footage about Keaton's working methods. **DT66,** *Recommended*

Buster Keaton: The Golden Years
(1921–22, B&W, 60m, NR)
Three early films: *The Paleface* (1921), *Day Dreams* (1922), and *The Blacksmith* (1922). **DT66**

Buster Keaton: The Great Stone Face
(1917–27, B&W, 60m, NR)
A clip show of footage including *Coney Island* (1917), and *The Balloonatic* (1923). **DT66**

Bustin' Loose (1981, C, 94m, R)
Richard Pryor plays an ex-con who's hustled into driving a school bus full of ornery kids to a camp. Cicely Tyson costars in this comedy. **ST180, XT18**

But Not for Me (1959, B&W, 105m, NR)
Clark Gable plays an executive trying to fend off the interest of a young secretary (Carroll Baker). With Lilli Palmer, Barry Coe, and Lee J. Cobb. **ST77**

Butch and Sundance: The Early Days
(1979, C, 110m, PG)
Prequel to *Butch Cassidy and the Sundance Kid* shows the formative years of the famous outlaw duo. Tom Berenger and William Katt star. Directed by Richard Lester. Attractive leads, but script doesn't give them much to do. **DT74, WE3, WE14**

Butch Cassidy and the Sundance Kid
(1969, C, 112m, PG)
Paul Newman and Robert Redford play the legendary outlaws in this comic Western. With Katharine Ross, Strother Martin, and Ted Cassidy. Written by William Goldman; directed by George Roy Hill. Widescreen will be lost on video. Undeniably popular but slick and smug to some. **CU20, DT55, ST162, ST181, WE3, WE11, WE14,** *Essential*

Butcher's Wife, The
(1991, C, 104m, PG-13)
Romance set in New York, where the title character, a psychic, changes the lives of everyone she meets, including a young doctor. Demi Moore and Jeff Daniels star, with George Dzundza, Margaret Colin, Mary Steenburgen, and Frances McDormand. **CO1, XT9**

Butterfield 8 (1960, C, 109m, NR)
Elizabeth Taylor won an Oscar as the call girl of John O'Hara's novel. She's attracted to a married client (Laurence Harvey) and counseled by her best friend (Eddie Fisher). **ST212, WR24, XT3**

Butterflies Are Free (1972, C, 109m, PG)
Romance blossoms between a young blind man (Edward Albert) and his goofy neighbor (Goldie Hawn), despite the interference of his mother (Oscar winner Eileen Heckart). **ST99, XT5**

Butterfly (1981, C, 107m, R)
Sexy young woman seduces a man who may be her father in this trashy version of the James M. Cain story. Pia Zadora, Stacy Keach, and Orson Welles star. **CU6, DT134, WR1**

Buying Time (1989, C, 97m, R)
Dean Stockwell and Jeff Schultz star in this drama about a dishonest bookie, drug dealers, and an undercover cop. **ST208**

By Dawn's Early Light
(1990, C, 100m, NR)
Thriller centering on debate over whether to push the Big Button that will ignite nuclear war. Powers Boothe and Rebecca De Mornay star, with James Earl Jones, Martin Landau, Darren McGavin, Rip Torn, and Peter MacNichol. Originally made for cable TV. **MY6, ST118, ST216**

By Love Possessed (1961, C, 115m, NR)
Romantic drama of relationship between lovelorn woman (Lana Turner) and a prominent attorney (Efrem Zimbalist, Jr.). With Jason Robards and George Hamilton. **CL5, ST185, ST219**

By the Light of the Silvery Moon
(1953, C, 102m, NR)
Sequel to musical *On Moonlight Bay* follows courtship of couple in small Midwest town in years after World War I. Doris Day and Gordon MacRae star, with Leon Ames, Rosemary DeCamp, Mary Wickes, Billy Gray, and Merv Griffin in a bit role. **MU6, ST47**

Bye Bye Birdie (1963, C, 112m, NR)
Musical about rock star, loosely modeled on Elvis, coming to small town just before he's drafted. Janet Leigh, Dick Van Dyke, Ann-Margret, and Paul Lynde star. **MU2, MU6, MU9**

Bye Bye Brazil (1979, C, 100m, R)
A troupe of entertainers tour the Brazilian countryside in this comedy-drama. **FF6**

CB4 (1993, C, 86m, R)
Spoof of rap music scene, about title group (CB stands for cell block) and their rise to

fame. Chris Rock stars, with Allen Payne, Deezer D, Chris Elliott, Phil Hartman, and Charlie Murphy. Watch for real rap stars Ice-T and Ice Cube in cameos. Written by Rock and Nelson George, directed by Tamra Davis. **CO8**

C.H.O.M.P.S. (1979, C, 89m, G)
The title means: Canine HOMe Protection System. A young inventor perfects a mechanical guard dog in this family comedy starring Wesley Eure and Valerie Bertinelli. **FA6**

C.H.U.D. (1984, C, 90m, R)
Derelicts who live in the New York sewer system are turned into flesh-eating mutants, Cannabilistic Humanoid Underground Dwellers, by nuclear waste. John Heard, Daniel Stern, and Kim Greist star. **HO21**

Cabaret (1972, C, 128m, PG)
Broadway musical, set in the early days of the Third Reich, about a decadent Berlin nightclub featuring an American singing star (Liza Minnelli) and nasty emcee (Joel Grey). Minnelli, Grey, and director Bob Fosse won three of the film's eight Oscars. Musical remake of *I Am a Camera*. Stunning mix of musical theater and social commentary. **DR27, DT47, MU2, MU7, MU14, XT3, XT4, XT6,** *Essential, Recommended*

Cabin in the Cotton, The
(1932, B&W, 77m, NR)
Early Bette Davis melodrama has her playing a Southern belle who tells a lovestruck sharecropper, "I'd like to kiss you, but I just washed my hair." With Richard Barthelmess and Dorothy Jordan. Directed by Michael Curtiz. **ST44**

Cabin in the Sky (1943, B&W, 100m, NR)
Black musical fantasy about one man's struggle with the forces of good and evil. Eddie "Rochester" Anderson is the man, and the musical stars include Lena Horne, Ethel Waters, and Louis Armstrong. Directed by Vincente Minnelli. **DT88, MU8, MU13**

Cabinet of Dr. Caligari, The
(1919, B&W, 69m, NR)
Silent German classic about an evil doctor and his zombie-like creation. Sensational sets and imagery; the first great flowering of German film expressionism. Werner Krauss stars; Robert Wiene directed. **FF3, HO1,** *Essential, Recommended*

Caboblanco (1980, C, 87m, R)
Intrigue set in wartime South America, with bartender Charles Bronson keeping an eye on Nazi Jason Robards and other characters. Dominique Sanda and Fernando Rey costar. **ST20, ST185**

Cactus (1986, C, 95m, NR)
Love story involving a blind man (Robert Menzies) and a woman who is losing her sight (Isabelle Huppert). Australian Paul Cox directed. **FF5**

Cactus Flower (1969, C, 103m, PG)
Goldie Hawn won an Oscar for her role as the kookie girlfriend of a swinging middle-aged dentist (Walter Matthau). Ingrid Bergman plays Matthau's nurse, who breaks out of her shell when she realizes she's in love with him. **CO1, ST13, ST99, ST155, XT5**

Caddie (1976, C, 107m, NR)
Helen Morse stars in this true story of an Australian woman trying to raise two children and manage a career during the 1920s. **FF5**

Caddy, The (1953, B&W, 95m, NR)
Martin and Lewis comedy set on the golf links, with Donna Reed and guest appearances by several golf pros. **CL15, CO19, ST139, ST149**

Caddyshack (1980, C, 99m, R)
Comic shenanigans at a snooty country club, starring Rodney Dangerfield, Ted Knight, Bill Murray, and Chevy Chase. Directed by Harold Ramis. **CO13, CO14**

Caddyshack II (1988, C, 103m, PG)
More hijinks at Bushwood Country Club, featuring Jackie Mason, Dyan Cannon, Robert Stack, Paul Bartel, and "guest appearances" by Chevy Chase and Dan Aykroyd. Directed by Allan Arkush. **CO13, DT6, DT8**

Cadence (1991, C, 97m, PG-13)
Charlie and Martin Sheen star in a drama of a rebel soldier imprisoned in a West German brig with a group of black G.I.s. With F. Murray Abraham and Larry Fishburne. **DR7, DR18, XT8**

Cadillac Man (1990, C, 97m, R)
Robin Williams stars as a fast-talking car salesman whose talents are put to the test when a madman invades his dealership and holds everyone there hostage. With Tim Robbins, Pamela Reed, Fran Drescher, and Zack Norman. **CO10, ST228**

Caesar and Cleopatra (1946, C, 134m, NR)
Rendition of George Bernard Shaw's play with Claude Rains and Vivien Leigh as the mighty conqueror and his young Egyptian queen. **CL1, CL3, ST137, WR29**

Caged Heat (1974, C, 84m, R)
Women-in-prison drama, directed by Jonathan Demme, produced by Roger Corman, has Barbara Steele as warden confined to a

wheelchair, the usual shower scenes, etc.
CU14, DR18, DT35

Cahill—U.S. Marshal (1973, C, 103m, PG)
John Wayne plays a lawman whose son is
tempted by a life of crime. **ST224**

Caine Mutiny, The (1954, C, 125m, NR)
Humphrey Bogart stars in the Herman Wouk
story of Navy officers who join forces to
relieve their captain of his ship when they
find him mentally unfit. With José Ferrer,
Van Johnson, Fred MacMurray, E.G. Marshall, and Lee Marvin. Directed by Edward
Dmytryk. **DR19, ST15, ST151**

Cal (1984, C, 102m, R)
An Irish youth who was involved in the murder of a British policeman falls in love with
his widow. John Lynch and Helen Mirren
star. Produced by David Puttnam; music by
Mark Knopfler. **DR3, DR7, DR23**

Calamity Jane (1953, C, 101m, NR)
Doris Day plays the Wild West sharpshooter.
Howard Keel costars as Wild Bill Hickok. Fea-
tures the Oscar-winning song "Secret Love."
HF11, MU6, ST47, WE8

California Suite (1978, C, 103m, PG)
A series of comic sketches, all set in the Bev-
erly Hills Hotel. The cast features Jane Fonda,
Richard Pryor, Bill Cosby, Maggie Smith (an
Oscar winner), Michael Caine, Elaine May,
Walter Matthau, and Alan Alda. Written by
Neil Simon. The Caine-Smith segment is best;
the Pryor-Cosby is an embarrassment. **DT86,
ST25, ST72, ST155, ST180, WR23, XT5,
XT10**

Caligula (1980, C, 156m, NR)
Lavish, violent, sexually explicit portrait of
ancient Rome from *Penthouse* magazine pub-
lisher Bob Guccione, starring Malcolm Mc-
Dowell, Peter O'Toole, and John Gielgud.
Also available in an R-rated version with a
running time of 105 minutes. **CU6, CU7,
DR5, ST86, ST169**

Call Him Mr. Shatter (1976, C, 90m, R)
Stuart Whitman plays a hit man in Hong
Kong who's had enough. Peter Cushing
costars. **ST43**

Call It Murder (1934, B&W, 80m, NR)
Humphrey Bogart stars in a mystery about a
jury foreman's daughter who gets the death
penalty when she's romantically linked to a
gangster. Also known as *Midnight*. **ST15**

Call of the Canyon (1942, B&W, 71m, NR)
Gene Autry and his radio ranch are caught
under hoof when a crooked meat packer
starts a stampede. **ST5**

Call of the Wild, The (1972, C, 100m, PG)
The Jack London adventure tale of gold fever
in the turn-of-the-century Klondike, starring
Charlton Heston. **AC12, AC24**

Callie and Son (1981, C, 97m, NR)
Melodrama of Texas waitress who overcomes
adversity (including the birth of an illegitimate son) to work her way into Dallas society. Lindsay Wagner stars, with Dabney
Coleman, Jameson Parker, and Michelle
Pfeiffer. Originally made for TV. Also known
as *Rags to Riches*. **DR10, ST173**

Camelot (1967, C, 178m, NR)
Broadway musical of the Knights of the
Round Table, featuring Vanessa Redgrave,
Richard Harris, and Franco Nero as Guin-
evere, King Arthur, and Sir Lancelot, respec-
tively. **FA9, MU2, MU8, MU17, ST182**

Cameraman, The (1928, B&W, 70m, NR)
Buster Keaton comedy has him playing a
newsreel photographer recording a ticker
tape parade, and a Chinese tong war. Highlight: Keaton's one-man baseball game at
Yankee Stadium. **DT66, XT9,** *Recommended*

Cameron's Closet (1988, C, 86m, R)
Horror tale of a psychic child whose powers
cause the deaths of those who would control him. Cotter Smith, Mel Harris, and Tab
Hunter star. **HO7, HO13**

Camila (1984, C, 105m, NR)
Romantic drama, based on true events, of a
young socialite's love for a priest. This Argen-
tinean film was nominated for an Oscar for
Best Foreign Language Film. **FF6**

Camille (1936, B&W, 108m, NR)
Greta Garbo, Robert Taylor, and Lionel Barrymore star in Alexandre Dumas's story of the
tragic heroine who is thwarted in her desire
for the man she truly loves. Directed by
George Cukor. Garbo was never lovelier. **CL1,
CL4, CL5, DT32, ST78,** *Recommended*

Camille Claudel (1989, C, 149m, R)
Isabelle Adjani plays the student-mistress of
sculptor Auguste Rodin who eventually became an artist in her own right. Gérard
Depardieu costars as Rodin. Original French
running time: 173 minutes. **FF1, ST52**

Camorra (1986, C, 115m, R)
Italian thriller of an ex-prostitute taking on
the Mob in Naples. Angela Molina stars. Lina
Wertmuller directed. **DT137**

Can-Can (1960, C, 131m, NR)
Gay Nineties setting for this lavish musical
featuring Cole Porter music. Frank Sinatra,
Shirley MacLaine, Maurice Chevalier, Louis
Jourdan, and Juliet Prowse star. Musical num-

bers are presented in letterboxed format. **CU19, MU2, ST145, ST199**

Cancel My Reservation (1972, C, 99m, G)
Bob Hope comedy of a New York talk show host, on vacation in Arizona, becoming implicated in murder. Based on a novel by Louis L'Amour. **ST108, WR16**

Candidate, The (1972, C, 109m, PG)
A novice office seeker suddenly finds himself the front-runner in a senatorial race against a veteran incumbent. Sharp observations on the media-dominated political climate in contemporary America. Robert Redford stars, with Don Porter, Melvyn Douglas, and Peter Boyle. Oscar-winning screenplay by Jeremy Larner; directed by Michael Ritchie. **DR21, ST58, ST181, XT26,** *Recommended*

Candles at Nine (1944, B&W, 84m, NR)
In order to inherit her late uncle's estate, an innocent showgirl must first live a month in his home, which his other relatives have booby-trapped. Jessie Matthews stars in this British thriller. **MY3, MY15**

Candleshoe (1977, C, 101m, G)
Jodie Foster stars as an orphan pawn in a con man's swindle to steal heiress Helen Hayes's fortune. Disney comedy costars David Niven. **FA1, ST75**

Candy Mountain (1987, C, 91m, PG)
Unusual tale of musician's search for legendary guitar maker, with several prominent pop musical figures playing roles, including Dr. John, Tom Waits, Leon Redbone, Joe Strummer, and David Johansen (Buster Poindexter). Directed by photographer Robert Frank and writer Rudy Wurlitzer. **CU17**

Candyman (1992, C, 93m, R)
Genuinely spooky horror tale set in contemporary Chicago, centering on figure of urban legend, a nineteenth-century free black man who was mutilated by a white mob and now wears a hook for a hand. Virginia Madsen stars as a social scientist investigating the Candyman's appearances; with Tony Todd, Xander Berkeley, and DeJuan Guy. Written and directed by Bernard Rose, music by Philip Glass. **DR15, XT11, XT24,** *Recommended*

Cannery Row (1982, C, 120m, PG)
Adaptation of John Steinbeck's story about opposites who attract: a marine biologist (Nick Nolte) meets a goofy drifter (Debra Winger) in Monterey, California, in the 1930s. John Huston narrates this sweet tale of love. **DT60, ST164, ST231, WR32,** *Recommended*

Cannonball (1976, C, 93m, R)
Low-budget road race movie starring David Carradine, Veronica Hamel, and Robert Carradine. Directed by Paul Bartel. Watch for Roger Corman, Sylvester Stallone, Martin Scorsese, and others in bit parts. **AC10, DT8, DT30, DT114, ST204**

Cannonball Run, The (1981, C, 95m, PG)
Burt Reynolds and pals race across country in vehicles of all makes and descriptions. Roger Moore, Farrah Fawcett, Dom DeLuise, Dean Martin, Sammy Davis, Jr., and many more guest drivers and pedestrians show up. **AC10, CO9, ST149, ST183**

Cannonball Run II (1984, C, 108m, PG)
More road racing action with Burt Reynolds and friends, this time including Dom DeLuise, Shirley MacLaine, and Marilu Henner. Look quickly for Frank Sinatra. **AC10, CO9, ST145, ST149, ST183, ST199**

Can't Stop the Music (1980, C, 118m, PG)
Rock musical featuring The Village People, with Valerie Perrine, Bruce Jenner, and Steve Guttenberg on hand for dramatic flourishes. **MU9**

Canterbury Tale, A
(1944, B&W, 124m, NR)
Loose adaptation of Chaucer's classic poem, set in wartime British village, concerning the interactions of three people (Eric Portman, Sheila Sim, and John Sweet). Codirected by Michael Powell and Emeric Pressburger. **DT99**

Canterville Ghost, The
(1944, B&W, 96m, NR)
Charles Laughton plays a seventeenth-century spirit trying to break free of his spell in this lighthearted fantasy. With Margaret O'Brien, William Gargan, Rags Ragland, and Robert Young. **SF2, ST112, XT24**

Canterville Ghost, The
(1986, C, 96m, NR)
Updating of classic tale of spirit imprisoned by spell until he can perform a good deed. John Gielgud stars, with Ted Wass and Andrea Marcovicci. **FA8, ST86, XT24**

Cape Fear (1962, B&W, 105m, NR)
An ex-convict, out for revenge, terrorizes the family of the attorney who convicted him. Robert Mitchum and Gregory Peck star. With Polly Bergen, Lori Martin, and Martin Balsam. Music by Bernard Herrmann. Based on John D. MacDonald's novel *The Executioners*. **MY2, MY3, MY9, ST158, ST171,** *Recommended*

Cape Fear (1991, C, 128m, R)
Remake of the classic thriller thickens the plot by portraying the victimized family as one already in crisis. Nick Nolte and Robert De Niro star in the Peck and Mitchum roles; with Jessica Lange, Juliette Lewis (sensational), Joe Don Baker, Illeana Douglas, and, from the original film, Peck, Mitchum, and Martin Balsam. Directed by Martin Scorsese; Elmer Bernstein adapted Bernard Herrmann's original score. Widescreen will be lost on video. **CU18, CU20, DT114, MY2, MY3, MY9, ST51, ST130, ST158, ST164, ST171,** *Highly Recommended*

Captain America (1989, C, 97m, PG-13)
Adventure tale of comic book hero, created in 1944 but frozen in Alaska until present day. He's back to battle an army general who wants to control the President with a brain implant. Matt Salinger and Dabney Coleman star, with Ronny Cox, Ned Beatty, Michael Nouri, and Melinda Dillon. **AC17**

Captain Apache (1971, C, 94m, PG)
Western saga of a Union intelligence officer investigating the murder of an Indian commissioner. Lee Van Cleef stars, with Carroll Baker and Stuart Whitman. **ST221**

Captain Blood (1935, B&W, 118m, NR)
Doctor turns pirate but doesn't ignore a certain attractive damsel. Errol Flynn's first swashbuckler; Olivia de Havilland and Basil Rathbone costar. This is the newly restored, 118-minute version. **AC13, CU10, ST49, ST69**

Captain Horatio Hornblower
(1951, C, 117m, NR)
Gregory Peck plays the title character, the hero of C.S. Forester's saga of the Napoleonic Wars. With Virginia Mayo, Robert Beatty, and Christopher Lee. Directed by Raoul Walsh. **AC6, AC13, DT131, ST135, ST171**

Captain January (1936, B&W, 75m, NR)
Shirley Temple drama of a kindly lighthouse keeper (Guy Kibbee) and his charge. Buddy Ebsen and Shirley trip the light fantastic. **ST213**

Captain Kidd (1945, B&W, 89m, NR)
Adventures on the high seas with the notorious pirate (Charles Laughton) in search of treasure. Randolph Scott costars. **AC15, ST132, ST197**

Captain Kronos: Vampire Hunter
(1974, C, 91m, R)
From Britain's Hammer Studios, a spoof of horror and adventure serials, with a caped superhero and his two sidekicks who travel the world searching for vampires to kill. **HO5, HO26**

Captain Newman, M.D.
(1963, C, 126m, NR)
Army psychiatrist (Gregory Peck) counsels patients, does battle with military brass in this comedy-drama. With Angie Dickinson, Tony Curtis, Bobby Darin, and in a small role, Robert Duvall. **CO21, MU12, ST63, ST171**

Captain Ron (1992, C, 100m, PG-13)
Comedy of dweeb who decides to sail an inherited yacht with his family from a Caribbean island to Miami, hires a disreputable salt to pilot the voyage. Martin Short and Kurt Russell star, with Mary Kay Place, Benjamin Salisbury, and Meadow Sisto. **CO14, ST191**

Captain Sinbad (1963, C, 85m, NR)
Guy Williams plays the title role in this family adventure of the man who sailed the seven seas. **AC15, FA4**

Captains Courageous
(1937, B&W, 116m, NR)
Classic family adventure about a spoiled little rich kid (Freddie Bartholomew) whose attitude improves when he falls from a cruise ship and into the custody of a very wise Portuguese fisherman (Oscar winner Spencer Tracy). With Melvyn Douglas. Based on Rudyard Kipling's novel. **AC13, CL1, FA3, ST58, ST217, XT2**

Captain's Paradise, The
(1953, B&W, 77m, NR)
Alec Guinness stars in this British comedy about a sea captain with wives in two ports. Yvonne de Carlo and Celia Johnson are his mates. **CO17, ST95**

Car Wash (1976, C, 97m, PG)
Multi-character comedy set at an inner-city car wash. Richard Pryor and Franklin Ajaye head the cast; fine rock soundtrack. **ST180**

Caravans (1978, C, 123m, PG)
Adventure tale of the search in the Middle East for a U.S. senator's daughter. Anthony Quinn and Jennifer O'Neill star, with Michael Sarrazin, Christopher Lee, and Joseph Cotten. **ST135**

Carbine Williams (1952, B&W, 91m, NR)
Biographical drama of firearm inventor, starring James Stewart, with Jean Hagen, Wendell Corey, and James Arness. **CL2, ST207**

Carbon Copy (1981, C, 92m, PG)
Comedy of a successful executive confronted with a seventeen-year-old black youth who claims he's the man's son from a long-ago

affair. George Segal, Susan Saint James, Denzel Washington, and Paul Winfield star. **C02, ST230**

Cardinal, The (1963, C, 175m, NR)
From director Otto Preminger comes the epic story of a priest's rise to power in the Catholic Church. Tom Tryon stars, with Romy Schneider, Carol Lynley, Burgess Meredith, Raf Vallone, and John Huston. Plodding stuff. **DT60, DT100**

Care Bears Movie, The (1985, C, 75m, G)
Those roly-poly, lovable little bears are on a mission to help people share their feelings and to prevent evildoers like Professor Coldheart from taking over the world. Mickey Rooney supplies one of the character voices; songs by Carole King and John Sebastian. **FA10, ST189**

Career (1959, B&W, 105m, NR)
Backstage drama of young actor (Anthony Franciosa) climbing the ladder to fame on Broadway. With Dean Martin, Shirley MacLaine, and Carolyn Jones. **CL7, ST145, ST149**

Career Opportunities
(1991, C, 84m, PG-13)
John Hughes produced and wrote this comedy about a young night watchman, a lovely young shoplifter, and two bumbling crooks. Frank Whaley and Jennifer Connelly star. Look fast for John Candy. **C010, C014, DT59**

Carefree (1938, B&W, 80m, NR)
Fred Astaire plays a psychiatrist, with Ginger Rogers as his patient, in this Irving Berlin musical. **CL15, ST4, ST187**

Careful, He Might Hear You
(1983, C, 116m, PG)
Moving drama from Australia, based on Sumner Locke Elliott novel of a young boy caught in a bitter custody battle between two aunts. Wendy Hughes, Robyn Nevin, and Nicholas Gledhill star. **DR2, FF5,** *Recommended*

Cariboo Trail (1950, C, 81m, NR)
Randolph Scott Western featuring standard cattlemen vs. settlers tale. With George "Gabby" Hayes, Bill Williams, Victor Jory, and Jim Davis. **ST197**

Carlin at Carnegie (1983, C, 60m, NR)
Comedian George Carlin in concert at New York's venerable Carnegie Hall. **C016**

Carlton-Browne of the F.O.
(1959, B&W, 88m, NR)
The British Foreign Office discovers a forgotten island that's still part of the Commonwealth and dispatches a bumbling diplomat

to take charge. Terry-Thomas and Peter Sellers star. Also known as *Man in a Cocked Hat.* **ST198**

Carmen (1918) see *Gypsy Blood*

Carmen (1983, C, 102m, R)
Spanish troupe rehearses for dance interpretation of the famed opera, with the choreographer and his female star playing out the story backstage. Antonio Gades and Laura Del Sol star. Carlos Saura directed. Brilliant dance numbers. **FF7, MU3, MU4,** *Recommended*

Carnal Knowledge (1971, C, 96m, R)
Drama of two college friends who treat women as objects and don't understand why they can't find love. Jack Nicholson, Art Garfunkel, Ann-Margret, and Candice Bergen star. Banned in at least one state and subject of a famous trial. Directed by Mike Nichols; written by Jules Feiffer. Widescreen photography will be lost on video. Cold, almost clinical approach seems somehow appropriate. Nicholson and Ann-Margret are terrific. **CU8, CU20, DR7, DT91, MU12, ST163,** *Recommended*

Carnival of Souls (1962, B&W, 80m, NR)
After surviving a car crash into a river, a woman is pursued by a zombie-like man. Low-budget horror film with cult following. Candace Hilligoss stars. Written and directed by Herk Harvey, his only feature film; he also plays the zombie man. Genuinely unsettling. **CU4, CU15, HO6, XT24,** *Recommended*

Carnival Rock (1957, B&W, 75m, NR)
Early film from director Roger Corman, a romantic triangle drama set in the nightclub world, with appearances by The Platters and David Houston. Susan Cabot and Dick Miller star. **DT30**

Carny (1980, C, 107m, R)
Life behind the scenes at a traveling carnival, with young runaway (Jodie Foster) getting a liberal education from barker (Robbie Robertson) and his pal (Gary Busey). Underrated portrait of little-seen slice of American life. **DR12, MU12, ST75,** *Recommended*

Carousel (1956, C, 128m, NR)
Colorful Broadway musical of a ne'er-do-well carnival barker and his love. Gordon MacRae and Shirley Jones star, with Cameron Mitchell and Barbara Ruick. Rodgers and Hammerstein songs include "If I Loved You" and "Soliloquy." **FA9, MU2, MU6**

Carpetbaggers, The (1964, C, 150m, NR)
Florid saga of Howard Hughes–like figure (tycoon with his fingers in aircraft industry

and movie production, romancing movie stars), adapted from the Harold Robbins best-seller. George Peppard stars, with Carroll Baker (never sexier), Alan Ladd (as Nevada Smith, in his last film), Bob Cummings, Martha Hyer, Elizabeth Ashley, Lew Ayres, and Archie Moore. Directed by Edward Dmytryk. Trashy fun, although its virtues are largely with impressive physical production. Wide-screen cinematography will be lost without letterboxing. **CL7, DR19, DR24, ST128, XT22**

Carrie (1952, B&W, 118m, NR)
Theodore Dreiser story of a farm girl turned actress and her married lover. Laurence Olivier and Jennifer Jones star, with Miriam Hopkins and Eddie Albert. Directed by William Wyler with his usual sure hand for this kind of material. **CL1, CL6, DR19, DT142, ST168,** *Recommended*

Carrie (1976, C, 97m, R)
High school wallflower gets even with her tormentors and her strict mother by using her telekinetic powers. Horror shocker directed by Brian De Palma, based on a story by Stephen King. Sissy Spacek stars, with Piper Laurie, William Katt, Nancy Allen, Amy Irving, and John Travolta. De Palma's best film and one of the few watchable King adaptations. **DR25, DT36, HO7, HO12, ST202, WR12,** *Essential, Recommended*

Carry On Doctor (1968, C, 95m, NR)
British comedy in the long-running *Carry On . . .* series, with hospital setting and the usual bedpan humor. **CO17**

Cars That Ate Paris, The
(1974, C, 91m, PG)
Black comedy from Australia about a small town which creates traffic accidents to reap scrap metal and spare parts. Directed by Peter Weir. **CO12, DT133, FF5**

Carson City Kid (1940, B&W, 68m, NR)
Roy Rogers cleans up yet another Western town and gets in a few tunes as well. With Dale Evans and Gabby Hayes. **ST188**

Cartoon Moviestars: Bugs!
(1942–48, CC 60m, NR)
Among the highlights of this collection of Warner Brothers cartoons are *Bugs Bunny and the Three Bears* and *Bugs Bunny Gets the Boid.* **FA11**

Cartoon Moviestars: Daffy!
(1938–48, B&W/C, 60m, NR)
Eight cartoons featuring that crazy duck, including the debut of Elmer Fudd in *Daffy Duck and Egghead.* **FA11**

Cartoon Moviestars: Elmer!
(1940–48, B&W/C, 60m, NR)
First-wate cowection featuwing that bald butt of Bugs's and Daffy's jokes. **FA11**

Cartoon Moviestars: Porky!
(1935–47, B&W/C, 60m, NR)
The stuttering porker is featured in this collection which includes his debut in *I Haven't Got a Hat.* **FA11**

Casablanca (1942, B&W, 102m, NR)
The Oscar-winning romantic classic that just gets better and better. Humphrey Bogart and Ingrid Bergman make the perfect pair of war-torn lovers. Sydney Greenstreet, Dooley Wilson, Claude Rains, and Paul Henreid costar. Director Michael Curtiz also won an Academy Award; Bogart should have picked up one, too. **CL4, CL6, ST13, ST15, XT1, XT6, XT28,** *Essential, Highly Recommended*

Casanova's Big Night (1954, C, 86m, NR)
Joan Fontaine mistakes Bob Hope for the infamous Casanova (Vincent Price) and havoc ensues throughout Venice. With Lon Chaney, Jr. **ST27, ST73, ST108, ST179**

Casey at the Bat (1986, C, 52m, NR)
The famous poem of the blustering baseball slugger, starring Elliott Gould, with narration by Howard Cosell. Entry in Shelley Duvall's "Tall Tales and Legends" series. **FA3**

Casey's Shadow (1978, C, 117m, PG)
A free-wheeling horse trainer has to raise three sons when his wife leaves him. Walter Matthau stars in this family drama. Directed by Martin Ritt. **DT105, FA5, FA7, ST155**

Casino Royale (1967, C, 130m, NR)
Anything-for-a-laugh spoof of James Bond movies with amazing cast (Peter Sellers, Woody Allen, David Niven, Ursula Andress, Orson Welles, William Holden, Deborah Kerr, Charles Boyer, and in a bit role, Jean-Paul Belmondo) and plenty of sight gags, including explosive finale in Monte Carlo casino. Co-directed by John Huston. **CO7, CU17, DT2, DT60, DT134, HF2, ST11, ST16, ST106, ST125, ST198**

Cassandra Crossing, The
(1977, C, 127m, R)
Disaster drama centering on a train carrying plague and a shaky bridge. Richard Harris, Sophia Loren, Burt Lancaster, Ava Gardner, Martin Sheen, and O.J. Simpson star. **AC23, ST79, ST129, ST141**

Cast a Giant Shadow (1966, C, 142m, NR)
True-life drama about Mickey Marcus, Israeli freedom fighter. Kirk Douglas stars, with Angie Dickinson and many guest stars in bit

parts, including John Wayne and Frank Sinatra. **DR4, ST57, ST199, ST224**

Castaway (1987, C, 118m, R)
True story of middle-aged man and young woman who intentionally set themselves up on a desert island for a year. Oliver Reed and Amanda Donohoe star. Nicolas Roeg directed. **DR6, DT106**

Castaway Cowboy, The (1974, C, 91m, G)
Cowboy James Garner goes Hawaiian to help a farm widow (Vera Miles). Robert Culp co-stars as the bad guy in this tropical Disney Western. **FA1, ST82**

Castle in the Desert
(1942, B&W, 62m, NR)
It's the crafty detective Charlie Chan (Sidney Toler) up against a modern version of the Borgia clan in this mystery. **HF4**

Castle of Blood (1964, B&W, 85m, NR)
A poet decides to spend a night in a haunted castle in this adaptation of Edgar Allan Poe's poem, "Berenice." Barbara Steele stars. Also known as *Castle of Terror*. **HO3, WR27**

Castle of Fu Manchu
(1968, B&W, 92m, PG)
Fu Manchu and his minions are out to create havoc in the world one more time. Christopher Lee stars. **ST135**

Castle of Terror see *Castle of Blood*

Castle of the Living Dead
(1964, B&W, 90m, NR)
A mysterious nobleman turns his visitors into mummies. Christopher Lee stars, with Donald Sutherland. **ST135**

Casualties of War (1989, C, 113m, R)
True story of Vietnam War atrocity, starring Michael J. Fox and Sean Penn. Directed by Brian De Palma. Wildly overpraised by critics prone to adore De Palma's work. **AC4, DR6, DT36**

Cat and Mouse (1975, C, 107m, PG)
Comic mystery from France about a murdered husband whose less-than-faithful ways leave a long list of suspects. Michele Morgan and Serge Reggiani star. Claude Lelouch directed. **FF1**

Cat and the Canary, The
(1978, C, 90m, NR)
British remake of the classic tale finds a group of guests visiting a mansion on your basic dark and stormy night, becoming victims of a series of bizarre pranks. Michael Callan, Carol Lynley, and Olivia Hussey star. **MY15**

Cat and the Fiddle, The
(1934, B&W/C, 90m, NR)
Jeanette MacDonald's musical debut for MGM, in the Jerome Kern-Oscar Hammerstein operetta about a struggling composer (Ramon Novarro). Final sequence in color. **MU1**

Cat Ballou (1965, C, 96m, NR)
Comic Western featuring Jane Fonda as a cowgirl avenging her father's murder and Oscar winner Lee Marvin in two roles: a broken-down gunslinger and his evil twin brother. **CO7, ST72, ST151, WE8, WE14, XT2, XT27**

Cat Chaser (1989, C, 90m, R)
Thriller about a former Marine, who once fought in Santo Domingo, returning there, becoming involved with the wife of the former chief of secret police. Peter Weller and Kelly McGillis star, with Charles Durning, Frederic Forrest, and Tomas Milian. Based on a novel by Elmore Leonard. Also available in an unrated version with additional footage; running time: 98 minutes. **CU10, MY16, WR19**

Cat from Outer Space, The
(1978, C, 104m, G)
An extraterrestrial feline crashes on Earth, creating mayhem with the U.S. government. Disney comedy starring Ken Berry, Sandy Duncan, Harry Morgan, and McLean Stevenson. **FA1**

Cat on a Hot Tin Roof
(1958, C, 108m, NR)
Elizabeth Taylor and Paul Newman star in this drama of a deceptive Southern family who cozy up to their dying patriarch (Burl Ives), hoping to get a piece of his inheritance. Based on Tennessee Williams's play. **DR8, ST162, ST212, WR38**

Cat on a Hot Tin Roof
(1984, C, 148m, NR)
Jessica Lange, Tommy Lee Jones, and Rip Torn star in this version of the Tennessee Williams drama. **DR8, ST130, ST216, WR38**

Cat People (1942, B&W, 73m, NR)
Producer Val Lewton's first horror film is about a mysterious bride obsessed with a curse that will transform her into a deadly panther. Directed by Jacques Tourneur. One of the classic, non-gory horror films. **DT124, HO19, HO27, MY1, Essential, Recommended**

Cat People (1982, C, 118m, R)
An erotic remake of the 1942 Val Lewton classic, set in New Orleans. Nastassja Kinski, Malcolm McDowell, John Heard, and

Annette O'Toole star. Directed by Paul Schrader. A prime example of contemporary horror overkill. **CU18, HO25, XT14**

Catch Me a Spy (1971, C, 94m, NR)
Comic mystery of a man arrested as a Soviet spy. Kirk Douglas stars, with Marlene Jobert, Trevor Howard, and Tom Courtenay. Also known as *To Catch a Spy*. **MY17, ST57**

Catchfire see *Back Track*

Catch-22 (1970, C, 121m, R)
Joseph Heller's darkly comic view of World War II, with pilot Alan Arkin frustrated and near a breakdown. Incredible supporting cast includes Martin Balsam, Bob Newhart, Buck Henry, Jon Voight, Orson Welles, Art Garfunkel, Martin Sheen, Charles Grodin, Anthony Perkins, and Paula Prentiss. Directed by Mike Nichols. **CO12, CO21, CU17, DR19, DT91, DT134, MU12, ST94, XT25,** *Recommended*

Catered Affair, The (1956, B&W, 93m, NR)
Bette Davis plays the wife of a New York cabbie determined to give her daughter a first-class wedding. With Debbie Reynolds, Ernest Borgnine, Barry Fitzgerald, and Rod Taylor. Gore Vidal adapted Paddy Chayefsky's TV play. **ST44, XT20**

Cat's Eye (1985, C, 93m, PG-13)
A trio of Stephen King short stories are linked by a cat involved in all three. James Woods, Drew Barrymore, and Robert Hayes star. **HO23, ST233, WR15**

Cattle Queen of Montana
(1954, C, 88m, NR)
Barbara Stanwyck stars in the title role; Ronald Reagan's an undercover federal agent investigating cattle thievery. **ST206, WE5, WE8**

Caught (1949, B&W, 88m, NR)
A young woman (Barbara Bel Geddes) trapped in a miserable marriage to a millionaire (Robert Ryan) finds happiness with a struggling doctor (James Mason). Directed by Max Ophuls; his best Hollywood film, full of subtle touches. **DT93, MY1, MY3, ST153, ST193,** *Recommended*

Caught in the Draft
(1941, B&W, 82m, NR)
Service comedy has Bob Hope playing pampered movie star afraid of the draft, then accidentally enlisting. With Dorothy Lamour and Eddie Bracken. **CO21, ST108**

Cauldron of Blood (1967, C, 95m, PG)
A blind sculptor uses skeletons provided by his murderous wife. Boris Karloff, Viveca Lindfors, and Jean-Pierre Aumont star. **ST119**

Cavalcade (1933, B&W, 110m, NR)
Family chronicle, based on Noel Coward play, covering years from turn of the century to the Great Depression. Diana Wynyard, Clive Brook, Herbert Mundin, Ursula Jeans, and Margaret Lindsay star. Oscar winner for Best Picture and Director (Frank Lloyd). **DR8, WR4, XT1, XT6**

Caveman (1981, C, 92m, PG)
Comedy of life in prehistoric times, featuring Ringo Starr as a lovable Neanderthal. Barbara Bach, John Matuszak, Shelley Long, and Dennis Quaid costar. **MU12**

Celebrating Bird: The Triumph of Charlie Parker (1987, B&W/C, 58m, NR)
Documentary portrait of great jazz innovator, directed by Gary Giddins and Kendrick Simmons. **CU16**

Cemetery Club, The
(1993, C, 106m, PG-13)
Ellen Burstyn, Olympia Dukakis, and Diane Ladd play a trio of widows trying to get on with their lives in this drama. With Danny Aiello, Lainie Kazan, Bernie Casey, and Wallace Shawn. Screenplay by Ivan Menchell, adapted from his play. **DR10, DR20**

Certain Fury (1985, C, 87m, R)
Two girls, accused of a crime they didn't commit, are on the run from both police and hoods. Tatum O'Neal and Irene Cara star. **AC24, MU12**

César (1936, B&W, 117m, NR)
Third in classic trilogy of life in France's Provence region, with Fanny's son learning the true identity of his father. Preceded by *Marius* and *Fanny*. Raimu, Pierre Fresnay, and Orane Demazis star. Marcel Pagnol wrote and directed. **FF1**

César and Rosalie (1972, C, 104m, R)
Yves Montand, Romy Schneider, and Sami Frey star in this superbly directed and acted French drama of a woman's longtime love for two men. Directed by Claude Sautet. **FF1,** *Recommended*

Chain Lightning (1950, B&W, 94m, NR)
Humphrey Bogart plays a bomber pilot adjusting to life in the postwar world. With Eleanor Parker and Raymond Massey. **AC11, ST15**

Chain Reaction (1980, C, 87m, NR)
An accident at a nuclear power plant forces a worker to confront the dangers of nuclear power. Australian drama stars Steve Bisley. **FF5**

Chained (1934, B&W, 71m, NR)
Joan Crawford melodrama has her torn between two men (Otto Kruger and Clark

Gable). With Mickey Rooney. **CL5, ST39, ST77, ST189**

Chalk Garden, The (1964, C, 106m, NR)
British drama of relationship between governess (Deborah Kerr) and rebellious teen (Hayley Mills). Adapted from Enid Bagnold's play. With John Mills (Hayley's dad) and Edith Evans. **DR20, DR23, ST125, XT8**

Challenge, The (1982, C, 112m, R)
An American boxer visiting Japan becomes embroiled in a feud between two brothers. Scott Glenn and Toshiro Mifune star. John Frankenheimer directed. **DR27, ST157**

Challenge to Lassie (1949, C, 76m, NR)
Drama set in nineteenth-century Edinburgh, based on true story of a dog faithful to its master even after the man has died. Edmund Gwenn, Donald Crisp, and Geraldine Brooks star. **FA5**

Chamber of Fear (1968, C, 88m, NR)
A madman tortures all those who visit his castle. Boris Karloff and Isela Vega star. Also known as *The Fear Chamber*. **ST119**

Chamber of Horrors
(1940, B&W, 80m, NR)
A charming man (Leslie Banks) is secretly a killer of beautiful women; he has already selected his next victim (Lilli Palmer). **HO9**

Champ, The (1931, B&W, 87m, NR)
Wallace Beery won an Oscar for his portrayal of a broken-down boxer trying to keep custody of his son (Jackie Cooper). A classic three-hankie movie directed by King Vidor. Remake released in 1979. **CL6, DR22, DT126, XT2**

Champ, The (1979, C, 121m, PG)
An ex-fighter (Jon Voight) may lose custody of his son (Ricky Schroder) in this tearjerker remake of the 1931 film. Faye Dunaway costars. **CU18, DR22, FA7, ST61**

Champagne (1928, B&W, 93m, NR)
Alfred Hitchcock silent drama of a rich father who pretends he's penniless to teach his spoiled daughter a lesson. Betty Balfour, Jean Bradin, and Gordon Harker star. **DT57**

Champagne for Caesar
(1950, B&W, 99m, NR)
This comedy poking fun at television game shows features a contestant (Ronald Colman) winning big prizes and the show's worried sponsor (Vincent Price) trying to distract him. **CO8, ST35, ST179**

Champion (1949, B&W, 90m, NR)
Kirk Douglas plays the ultimate boxing machine in this gripping drama of an overly ambitious fighter. With Marilyn Maxwell and Arthur Kennedy. **DR22, ST57,** *Recommended*

Chan Is Missing (1982, B&W, 80m, NR)
Two San Francisco cabdrivers hunt for the title character, a Chinese who has their $4,000. Comedy-drama directed by Wayne Wang. More compelling as a cultural document than for its storytelling. **CO2, DR15, XT13**

Chances Are (1989, C 108m, PG-13)
A Washington widow (Cybill Shepherd) has a new man in her life—a young man to whom her daughter is attracted. The real complication: he's her late husband reincarnated. Robert Downey, Jr., Mary Stuart Masterson, and Ryan O'Neal costar. **CO1, CO20, XT12, XT24**

Chandu on the Magic Island
(1940, B&W, 67m, NR)
Chandu the magician travels to a lost island to battle an evil cult of devil worshippers. Bela Lugosi stars. **ST143**

Change of Habit (1969, C, 93m, G)
Elvis Presley puts down his guitar and picks up a stethoscope to play a doctor in this drama set in an inner-city neighborhood. Mary Tyler Moore plays a nun who admires Dr. P greatly. **ST178**

Change of Seasons, A (1980, C, 102m, R)
A professor takes one of his students for a lover, and his wife retaliates by taking up with a younger man. Anthony Hopkins, Shirley MacLaine, Bo Derek, and Michael Brandon star in this comedy. **ST109, ST145**

Changeling, The (1979, C, 109m, R)
A composer who has lost his wife and child in an accident rents an old house, discovers it is haunted by the ghost of a murdered child, then sets out to solve the murder. George C. Scott, Trish Van Devere, and Melvyn Douglas star. **HO2, HO19, ST58, ST196**

Chaplin (1992, C, 144m, PG-13)
Bio of film's greatest artist, starring Robert Downey, Jr., covers his life up to his 1972 appearance at the Academy Awards. With Dan Aykroyd as Mack Sennett, Geraldine Chaplin as both Charlie's mother (her grandmother), Kevin Dunn as Herbert Hoover, Moira Kelly as both Chaplin's first love and his last wife, Milla Jovovich, Kevin Kline as Douglas Fairbanks, Diane Lane as Paulette Goddard, Penelope Ann Miller, Paul Rhys, Marisa Tomei as Mabel Normand, Nancy Travis, James Woods in a small role as a lawyer, and Anthony Hopkins as a fictional editor working with Chaplin on his memoirs.

Directed by Richard Attenborough; based on Chaplin's autobiography and David Robinson's superb biography. No movie of modest length could do Chaplin justice, but Downey's performance makes this worth seeing for anyone with an interest in the subject. **CO13, DR4, DR13, DT24, ST109, ST127, ST233, XT23, XT27**

Chaplin Essanay Book I, The
(1915, B&W, 51m, NR)
Collection of Charlie Chaplin's early short films, including *The Tramp* and *The Champion*. **DT24,** *Recommended*

Chaplin Revue, The
(1958, B&W, 121m, NR)
Charlie Chaplin personally assembled this collection in 1958 of his early silent shorts, including *Shoulder Arms* (1918) and *The Pilgrim* (1923). **CO21, DT24,** *Essential, Recommended*

Chapter Two (1979, C, 124m, PG)
Neil Simon's autobiographical drama of a writer trying to get over the death of his wife and falling all too quickly in love with another woman. James Caan and Marsha Mason star. **DR1, WR30**

Charade (1963, C, 114m, NR)
A young widow finds that several men are interested in a secret that killed her husband. Audrey Hepburn and Cary Grant star in this classy romantic mystery set in Paris, with Walter Matthau, George Kennedy, and James Coburn. Directed by Stanley Donen. **DT38, MY3, ST92, ST102, ST155, XT16,** *Recommended*

Charge of the Light Brigade, The
(1936, B&W, 116m, NR)
Adventure tale of fateful British maneuver during the Crimean War, starring Errol Flynn and Olivia de Havilland. Directed by Michael Curtiz. **AC6, AC13, AC16, ST49, ST69**

Chariots of Fire (1981, C, 123m, PG)
Oscar-winning drama, based on a true story, of rival runners in the 1924 Olympics. Ben Cross, Ian Charleson, Ian Holm, and Alice Krige star, with guest appearances by John Gielgud and Lindsay Anderson. Directed by Hugh Hudson; produced by David Puttnam. Music by Vangelis. Not a bad movie, but hardly the best of its year. **DR22, DR23, ST68, XT1**

Charley and the Angel (1973, C, 93m, G)
Fred MacMurray learns a heavenly lesson from a wise angel (Harry Morgan): shape up his strict ways with his family or he'll be shipped off to the hereafter. Drama from the Disney studios. With Kurt Russell. **FA1, ST191, XT24**

Charley Varrick (1973, C, 111m, PG)
Robber of small-town bank gets more than he bargained for when he learns the loot is laundered Mob money. Walter Matthau stars, with Joe Don Baker, Felicia Farr, John Vernon, and Andy Robinson. First-rate action drama directed by Don Siegel. **DT116, MY9, MY18, ST155,** *Recommended*

Charlie Chan and the Curse of the Dragon Queen (1981, C, 97m, PG)
Peter Ustinov plays the Oriental detective in this comic mystery. With Lee Grant, Angie Dickinson, Richard Hatch, Brian Keith, Michelle Pfeiffer, and Roddy MacDowall. **HF4, ST173**

Charlie Chan at the Opera
(1936, B&W, 68m, NR)
An opera singer (Boris Karloff) seems the perfect suspect for the sleuthing of Chan (Warner Oland). William Demarest costars as a rival detective. **HF4, ST119**

Charlie Chan at the Wax Museum
(1940, B&W, 64m, NR)
An escaped killer vows vengeance against the wily detective (Sidney Toler) who put him behind bars. **HF4**

Charlie Chan in Paris
(1935, B&W, 72m, NR)
On the trail of forged bank bonds, Chan (Warner Oland) is soon caught up in a murder investigation in the City of Light. **HF4**

Charlie Chan in Rio
(1941, B&W, 60m, NR)
A suspected murderess is herself found dead, and Chan (Sidney Toler) sets out to find the real killer. **HF4**

Charlie Chan's Secret
(1936, B&W, 72m, NR)
A seance turns deadly, and Chan (Warner Oland) must divine the killer's identity. **HF4**

Charlie Chaplin Carnival
(1916, B&W, 80m, NR)
This collection of silent comedy classics includes *The Vagabond, The Fireman, The Count,* and *One A.M.* **DT24,** *Recommended*

Charlie Chaplin Cavalcade
(1916, B&W, 81m, NR)
Includes these silent shorts: *One A.M., The Pawnshop, The Floorwalker,* and *The Rink.* **DT24,** *Essential, Recommended*

Charlie Chaplin Festival
(1917, B&W, 80m, NR)
More Chaplin classics: *The Cure, The Adven-*

turer, *The Immigrant*, and *Easy Street*. **DT24,** *Recommended*

Charlie Chaplin—The Early Years, Volumes I–IV
(1916–17, B&W, approx. 60m each, NR)
Gems from Chaplin's first years in Hollywood. Volume I includes *The Immigrant* and *Easy Street*. Volume II features *The Pawnshop* and *One A.M.* Volume III has *The Cure* and *The Vagabond*. Volume IV: *The Rink* and *The Fireman*. **DT24,** *Recommended*

Charlie Chaplin's Keystone Comedies
(1914, B&W, 59m, NR)
Six one-reelers that helped to introduce Chaplin to the world: *Making a Living* (Chaplin as a villain), *Kid's Auto Races, A Busy Day, Mabel's Married Life, Laughing Gas,* and *The New Janitor*. **DT24,** *Recommended*

Charlie Chaplin's Keystone Comedies 2
(1914, B&W, 60m, NR)
Includes *Getting Acquainted* and *The Fatal Mallet*. **DT24,** *Recommended*

Charlie Chaplin's Keystone Comedies 3
(1914, B&W, 57m, NR)
Three shorts: *Caught in a Cabaret, The Masquerader,* and *Between Showers*. **DT24,** *Recommended*

Charlie Chaplin's Keystone Comedies 4
(1914, B&W, 54m, NR)
Four more films from the foremost clown of the silent screen: *His Million Dollar Job, Caught in the Rain, Mabel's Busy Day,* and *The Face of the Bar Room Floor*. **DT24,** *Recommended*

Charlie Chaplin's Keystone Comedies 5
(1914, B&W, 57m, NR)
This quartet of Chaplin shorts includes *Mabel's Strange Predicament, The Rounders, The Star Boarder,* and *Tango Tangles*. **DT24,** *Recommended*

Charlie, the Lonesome Cougar
(1968, C, 75m, G)
Disney's animal adventure-comedy stars a likable cougar who befriends a rugged logger. **FA5**

Charlotte's Web (1973, C, 85m, G)
E.B. White's famous story of Wilbur the pig and his friendship with Charlotte the spider is transformed into an animated musical. **FA10**

Charly (1968, C, 103m, NR)
Through a scientific experiment, a retarded man is given powers of superintelligence. Oscar winner Cliff Robertson and Claire Bloom star. Based on Daniel Keyes's story, *Flowers for Algernon*. **DR19, XT2**

Charro! (1969, C, 98m, G)
Elvis Presley Western has him playing a reformed bandit but not his guitar. **ST178, WE3**

Chase, The (1946, B&W, 86m, NR)
The chauffeur for a crooked Miami businessman decides to help his employer's unhappy wife escape to Cuba. Robert Cummings, Michele Morgan, and Steve Cochran star. Based on a story by Cornell Woolrich. **MY1, WR39**

Chase, The (1966, C, 135m, NR)
Delirious melodrama, with super cast, about a small Texas town awaiting the return of a notorious escaped convict. Marlon Brando, Robert Redford, Jane Fonda, Robert Duvall, Angie Dickinson, E.G. Marshall, James Fox, and Janice Rule star, with Jocelyn Brando, Paul Williams, and Martha Hyer. Written by Lillian Hellman; directed by Arthur Penn. Preposterous but irresistible. **CU17, DR26, DT96, ST18, ST63, ST72, ST181, XT8,** *Recommended*

Chasing Dreams (1982, C, 105m, PG)
Drama of a farm boy whose life turns around when he goes out for his college baseball team. David G. Brown stars, with Kevin Costner in a small role as his brother. **DR22, ST38**

Chato's Land (1972, C, 110m, R)
Charles Bronson plays an Indian accused of murdering a U.S. marshal. With Jack Palance, Richard Basehart, and Jill Ireland. **ST20, WE7**

Chattahoochee (1990, C, 103m, R)
True story of a Korean war veteran (Gary Oldman) confined, after a shooting spree, to a hellhole of a prison. With Dennis Hopper, Frances McDormand, Pamela Reed, M. Emmet Walsh, and Ned Beatty. **DR6, DR18, ST110**

Cheap Detective, The (1978, C, 92m, PG)
Peter Falk stars in this Neil Simon spoof of Humphrey Bogart's detective movies. With Ann-Margret, Eileen Brennan, Sid Caesar, Madeline Kahn, and Marsha Mason. **CO7, CO10, WR30**

Cheat, The (1915, B&W, 55m, NR)
Silent melodrama from director Cecil B. DeMille: socialite in debt to Japanese moneylender finds that his penalty for late payments exacts a terrible price. Fanny Ward and Sessue Hayakawa star. **DT34**

Cheech and Chong's Next Movie
(1980, 99m, R)
The second set of adventures featuring that stoned L.A. comedy team. **ST28**

Cheech and Chong's The Corsican Brothers (1984, C, 90m, R)
C&C play three roles each in this broad spoof of the swashbuckler adventures. Among the supporting cast: Rae Dawn and Robbi Chong (Tommy's kids) and Rikki Marin (Cheech's wife). **ST28, XT8, XT27**

Cheetah (1989, C, 84m, G)
American teens (Lucy Deakins and Keith Coogan) adopt an orphaned cheetah cub in Africa, then try to teach it to adapt to the wild. Disney drama shot on location. **FA1, FA5**

Chernobyl: The Final Warning see *Final Warning*

Cherry 2000 (1988, C, 93m, PG-13)
Futuristic adventure saga with Melanie Griffith as a kind of bounty hunter guiding a male companion (David Andrews) in search of a female robot. With Ben Johnson and Harry Carey, Jr. **SF8, ST93**

Cheyenne Autumn (1964, C, 154m, NR)
Director John Ford's last Western tells the epic story of the Cheyenne tribe's relocation by the U.S. government. Richard Widmark stars, with Carroll Baker, Edward G. Robinson, Karl Malden, and Dolores Del Rio. A Dodge City sequence featuring James Stewart as Wyatt Earp and Arthur Kennedy as Doc Holliday was restored to the home video edition. Widescreen will be lost on video. **CU10, CU20, DT44, HF9, HF13, ST186, ST207, WE1, WE7**

Cheyenne Social Club, The (1970, C, 103m, PG)
Comic Western has James Stewart inheriting a house of ill repute, running it with the help of Henry Fonda. Directed by Gene Kelly. **ST71, ST123, ST207, WE14**

Chicago Joe and the Showgirl (1990, C, 103m, R)
True-life crime case of 1944 murder spree by U.S. serviceman and his British girlfriend. Kiefer Sutherland and Emily Lloyd star, with Patsy Kensit and Keith Allen. **DR16, DR23**

Chicken Ranch (1983, C, 84m, NR)
Documentary on Nevada's notorious—and legal—house of prostitution. Directed by Nicholas Broomfield and Sandi Sissel. **CU16**

Chiefs (1983, C, 200m, NR)
A murder in a small Southern town goes unsolved from 1924 to 1962, until the town's first black chief takes a personal interest in the case. Charlton Heston, Billy Dee Williams, Brad Davis, and Keith Carradine star in this epic drama. Originally made for TV. **DR16, DR26, ST227**

Child Is Waiting, A (1963, B&W, 102m, NR)
Burt Lancaster and Judy Garland star in this drama of teachers trying to help retarded children. With Gena Rowlands; directed by John Cassavetes. **DR9, ST81, ST129, XT23**

Child of Glass (1978, C, 93m, NR)
Disney drama of a boy who discovers a ghost in his parents' New Orleans home; together they solve a mystery. Originally made for TV. **FA1**

Children Are Watching Us, The (1944, B&W, 92m, NR)
Early film by director Vittorio De Sica concerns a family falling apart, as seen through the eyes of a child. Isa Pola, Emilio Cigoli, and De Sica star. **DT37**

Children of a Lesser God (1986, C, 119m, R)
A teacher at a school for the deaf and one of his most difficult pupils embark on a tempestuous affair. William Hurt and Oscar winner Marlee Matlin star, with Piper Laurie. Directed by Randa Haines. Based on Mark Medoff's play. Leads' chemistry is very believable. **DR1, DR20, ST114, XT3,** *Recommended*

Children of Paradise (1944, B&W, 195m, NR)
French drama of a beautiful woman (Arletty) and the four men in her life: an actor, a mime, a thief, and a nobleman. With Jean-Louis Barrault, Pierre Brasseur, Albert Remay, and Maria Casares. Written by Jacques Prévert; directed by Marcel Carne. Richly conceived and played; one of the true monuments of film history. **FF1,** *Essential,* *Highly Recommended*

Children of the Corn (1984, C, 93m, R)
A Stephen King short story is the basis for this tale of a young couple passing through a small Midwestern town, discovering that the children are murderers. Linda Hamilton and Peter Horton star. **HO11, HO13, WR15**

Children of the Corn II: The Final Solution (1993, C, 92m, R)
Belated sequel to the 1984 Stephen King tale of small-town children drawn into a murderous cult. Terence Knox, Paul Scherrer, and Ryan Bollman star. **HO11, HO13, WR15**

Children of the Damned (1964, B&W, 90m, NR)
Sequel to sci-fi/horror classic *Village of the Damned*, with more shenanigans in a deceptively placid British village. Ian Hendry, Alan Badel, and Barbara Ferris star. **HO13, HO26**

Children of the Night (1992, C, 90m, R)
Horror story pits a vampire mom and
her daughter (Karen Black and Maya
McLaughlin) against a teacher and his
girlfriend (Peter Deluise and Ami Dolenz).
H05, H014

Children of Theatre Street, The
(1977, C, 92m, G)
Documentary about Leningrad's famed Kirov
Ballet School, whose alumni include Barysh-
nikov and Nureyev. Narrated by Princess
Grace of Monaco (Grace Kelly). **CU16, ST124**

**Children Shouldn't Play With Dead
Things** (1972, C, 85m, PG)
An acting company goes to a burial island to
shoot a movie. When the director tries to
raise the dead to use in his film, he succeeds
too well. **H06**

Children's Hour, The
(1962, B&W, 107m, NR)
Lillian Hellman's play about the gossip that
infects a town about the relationship
between a pair of female schoolteachers
(Audrey Hepburn and Shirley MacLaine).
With James Garner, Miriam Hopkins, Fay
Bainter, and Veronica Cartwright. Directed
by William Wyler, who filmed the play
before under the title *These Three*. **CU18,
DR20, DT142, ST82, ST102, ST145**

**Children's Songs and Stories With the
Muppets** (1985, C, 56m, NR)
The Muppets are joined by guest stars Julie
Andrews, Judy Collins, John Denver, Brooke
Shields, and Twiggy. **FA14, ST2**

Child's Play (1988, C, 87m, R)
An innocent-looking toy doll is possessed by
the soul of a mass killer, who continues his
crime spree. Chris Sarandon, Catherine
Hicks, and Alex Vincent star. **H08, H016**

Child's Play 2 (1990, C, 84m, R)
Chucky, the doll with a killer attitude, is
back for more mischief. Alex Vincent reprises
his role as the doll's human owner and Brad
Dourif returns as the voice of Chucky. With
Jenny Agutter and Gerrit Graham. **H08,
H016**

Child's Play 3 (1991, C, 98m, R)
Eight years after the events of the first two
Chucky adventures, the scene shifts to a military school, where the killer's soul infects
the body of a black cadet. **H08, H016**

Chilly Scenes of Winter
(1979, C, 96m, PG)
A determined young man tries to win back
his former sweetheart in this adaptation of
Ann Beattie's novel. John Heard and Mary

Beth Hurt star, with Peter Riegert, Kenneth
McMillan, and Gloria Grahame. Also known
as *Head Over Heels*. **DR1, DR19**

Chimes at Midnight
(1967, B&W, 115m, NR)
Orson Welles offers this pastiche of five
Shakespeare plays; he plays Falstaff. With
Jeanne Moreau, Margaret Rutherford, and
John Gielgud; narrated by Ralph Richardson.
Also known as *Falstaff*. **DT134, ST86,
ST161, ST184, WR28**

China Gate (1957, B&W, 95m, NR)
In one of the first films to deal with the Viet-
nam War, French soldiers attack a commu-
nist outpost. Gene Barry stars, with Angie
Dickinson, Lee Van Cleef, and Nat King Cole.
Samuel Fuller directed. **AC4, DT49, MU12,
ST221**

China Girl (1987, C, 90m, R)
Gang warfare breaks out between hot-headed
youths in the adjoining New York neighborhoods of Chinatown and Little Italy. An interracial couple is caught in the crossfire.
Directed by Abel Ferrara. **AC8, XT9**

China Is Near (1967, B&W, 110m, NR)
Italian drama from director Marco Bellocchio, who depicts a man in political and sexual turmoil. Glauco Mauri and Elda Tattoli
star. **FF2**

China Seas (1935, B&W, 90m, NR)
Clark Gable takes to the high seas as the captain of a shipping vessel bound for the Orient, with pirates and a deadly typhoon to
contend with. Jean Harlow and Rosalind
Russell costar. **AC12, ST77, ST98, ST192**

China Sky (1945, B&W, 78m, NR)
Randolph Scott plays a doctor who joins
the Chinese to fight the Japanese in World
War II. Based on a story by Pearl Buck. **AC1,
ST197**

China Syndrome, The
(1979, C, 123m, PG)
A TV news reporter and her cameraman
learn that officials at a nuclear power plant
are covering up certain details of an accident.
Jane Fonda, Michael Douglas, and Jack Lemmon star. Solid thriller was released coinci-
dentally with the Three Mile Island nuclear
accident, giving it even more urgency. Lemmon's performance should have won an
Oscar. **DR7, ST59, ST72, ST138, XT28,
*Essential, Recommended***

Chinatown (1974, C, 131m, R)
Director Roman Polanski's tale of love and
mystery in Depression-era Los Angeles. A
moody, hard-boiled detective, (Jack Nichol-

son) is hired to find the missing husband of a shady lady (Faye Dunaway). With John Huston, Perry Lopez, and the director as the little man with the knife. Written by Robert Towne. Widescreen photography will be hurt on video but still well worth seeing. **CU20, DT60, DT97, MY2, MY10, ST61, ST163, XT10,** *Essential, Highly Recommended*

Chinese Cat, The (1944, B&W, 65m, NR)
Charlie Chan mystery, with young woman enlisting detective's son to investigate her father's murder. Sidney Toler stars, with Benson Fong and Joan Woodbury. **HF4**

Chinese Connection, The
(1980, C, 107m, R)
Bruce Lee martial arts saga of young man avenging the death of his instructor. **ST134**

Chinese Roulette (1976, C, 96m, NR)
German director Rainer Werner Fassbinder's drama set in a country house where a group gathers for truth and sex games, orchestrated by one couple's paraplegic daughter. Anna Karina, Margit Carstensen, Ulli Lommel, and Brigitte Mira star. **DT42**

Chino (1973, C, 98m, PG)
Western drama starring Charles Bronson as a half-breed whose ranch is under attack from prejudiced locals. **ST20, WE7**

Chipmunk Adventure, The
(1987, C, 76m, G)
Alvin, Simon, and Theodore take to the skies in this full-length animated feature. **FA10**

Chisum (1970, C, 111m, G)
A cattle baron (John Wayne) wages war on local political corruption. With Forrest Tucker, Christopher George, Ben Johnson, Bruce Cabot, and Lynda Day. **ST224**

Chitty Chitty Bang Bang
(1968, C, 142m, G)
Dick Van Dyke portrays an eccentric inventor whose wild imagination takes him, his two children, and a beautiful woman named Truly Scrumptious (Sally Ann Howes) into a mystical world—all in a magical car. Family musical fun. **FA9**

Chloe in the Afternoon
(1972, C, 97m, NR)
Eric Rohmer directed this French comedy of a married man's obsession with a store clerk. Bernard Verley and Zouzou star. **DT107**

Chocolat (1989, C, 105m, PG-13)
A woman recalls her girlhood in French Cameroon in this drama set in the 1950s. Cecile Ducasse and Isaach De Bankole star; Claire Denis directed. **FF1**

Chocolate War, The (1989, C, 103m, R)
At a Catholic boys' school, a freshman defies both the stern principal and a secret student society known as The Vigils. Ilan Mitchell-Smith, John Glover, and Wally Ward star in this effective drama based on Robert Cormier's novel. Directed by Keith Gordon. **DR9, DR25, XT23,** *Recommended*

Choice of Arms (1983, C, 114m, NR)
Yves Montand and Gérard Depardieu are the antagonists in this French drama of a retired mobster and a young punk who threatens him and his wife (Catherine Deneuve). **FF1, ST50, ST52**

Choice of Weapons, A (1976, C, 88m, NR)
A man's investigation into the death of his father leads him to a society of modern-day knights. David Birney, Barbara Hershey, Donald Pleasence, and Peter Cushing star. Also known as *Dirty Knight's Work*. **ST43, ST104**

Choirboys, The (1977, C, 119m, R)
Joseph Wambaugh's comic novel of a profane and rowdy group of Los Angeles cops, adapted for the screen by director Robert Aldrich. Among the cast: Charles Durning, Louis Gossett, Jr., Perry King, Tim McIntire, Randy Quaid, and James Woods. **CO10, DT1, ST233**

Choke Canyon (1986, C, 94m, PG)
Scientist attempts to keep ruthless conglomerate out of protected wilderness area. Plenty of high-flying aerial action. Bo Svenson and Stephen Collins star. **AC11**

Choose Me (1984, C, 106m, R)
Romantic drama set largely in a big-city bar run by a loveless woman (Lesley Ann Warren). She's attracted to a smooth-talking newcomer (Keith Carradine); he's attracted to a radio talk-show host (Genevieve Bujold). Alan Rudolph directed. **DR1, DT110**

Chopping Mall (1986, C, 76m, R)
Horror story of shopping mall's automated security robots going haywire, with quartet of shoppers trapped inside after hours. Russell Todd and Barbara Crampton star, with Paul Bartel. **DT8, HO22**

Chorus Line, A (1985, C, 117m, PG-13)
Film version of Broadway's long-running musical, the backstage tale of a group of dancers auditioning for a show that may give them their first break. Michael Douglas stars, with Alyson Reed, Audrey Landers, Janet Jones, and Nicole Fosse. Directed by Richard Attenborough. **MU2, MU3, MU4, ST59, XT23**

Chorus of Disapproval, A
(1988, C, 100m, PG)
British comedy about a shy widower's
involvement in amateur theatrical group.
Jeremy Irons stars, with Anthony Hopkins,
Prunella Scales, Sylvia Sims, Lionel Jeffries,
and Patsy Kensit. Adapted from Alan
Ayckbourn's play. **CO8, CO17, DR20,
ST109, ST116**

Chosen, The (1978, C, 105m, PG)
Horror story of a nuclear power company
executive (Kirk Douglas) who discovers his
son is the Antichrist. With Agostina Bell,
Simon Ward, and Anthony Quayle. Also
known as *Holocaust 2000*. **HO10, ST57**

Chosen, The (1981, C, 108m, G)
In 1940s Brooklyn, two Jewish boys, one
Hassidic, the other Americanized, strike up
a wary friendship. Robby Benson and Barry
Miller star, with Rod Steiger and Maximilian
Schell. **DR15**

Christ Stopped at Eboli
(1979, C, 120m, NR)
Italian drama of an anti-Fascist writer living
in exile at a small village during the 1930s.
Gian Maria Volonte stars. Francesco Rosi
directed. **FF2**

Christian the Lion (1976, C, 89m, G)
Family drama of a lion raised in the London
Zoo, then returned to the wild. Bill Travers
and Virginia McKenna (the stars of *Born Free*)
star, with George Adamson (whom Travers
portrayed in *Born Free*). **FA5**

Christiane F. (1981, C, 124m, R)
A teen-ager enters Berlin's seamy underworld
of prostitution and drug addiction in this
disturbing German drama based on true
events. Nadja Brunkhorst stars; David Bowie
concert appearance is included. **FF3**

Christine (1983, C, 111m, R)
A 1958 Plymouth Fury turns into a killing
machine in this adaptation of the Stephen
King novel, directed by John Carpenter.
Keith Gordon stars, with Alexandra Paul and
Harry Dean Stanton. **DT23, HO22, ST205,
WR15**

Christmas Carol, A (1938, B&W, 70m, NR)
Reginald Owen stars in this British-produced
version of the Dickens tale. With Gene Lockhart as Bob Cratchit. **FA13, WR5**

Christmas Carol, A (1951, B&W, 86m, NR)
Charles Dickens's classic story of the nasty,
stingy Scrooge; he learns a few of life's lessons through the help of the ghost of his late
partner, Marley, and the ghosts of Christmas
Past, Present, and Future. Alistair Sim stars.
FA13, WR5

Christmas Coal Mine Miracle, The
(1977, C, 100m, NR)
Drama based on true story of three miners
trapped in a Christmas Eve cave-in. Kurt
Russell stars, with Melissa Gilbert, Andrew
Prine, and John Carradine. Also known as
Christmas Miracle in Caufield, U.S.A. **FA13,
ST191**

Christmas in Connecticut
(1945, B&W, 101m, NR)
Barbara Stanwyck stars in this comedy about
a recipe author who's really at a loss in the
kitchen, and her attempts to host a lonely
sailor with no place to go for the holidays.
Dennis Morgan and Sydney Greenstreet
costar. **FA13, ST206**

Christmas in July (1940, B&W, 67m, NR)
Preston Sturges wrote and directed this comedy of a man who mistakenly thinks he has
won the grand prize in a contest. Dick Powell stars, with Ellen Drew, William Demarest,
and Franklin Pangborn. **DT121, ST175**

Christmas Lilies of the Field
(1984, C, 98m, NR)
Billy Dee Williams takes on the Sidney Poitier role in this holiday-theme follow-up to
the story of a black handyman and a group
of German nuns in the Arizona desert. With
Maria Schell; originally made for TV. **FA13,
ST227**

Christmas Miracle in Caufield, U.S.A.
see *Christmas Coal Miracle, The*

Christmas Story, A (1983, C, 98m, PG)
Nostalgic holiday story, set in the Midwest of
the early 1940s, about a boy whose only wish
is to have a Red Ryder BB gun for Christmas.
Peter Billingsley stars, with Darren McGavin
and Melinda Dillon. Written and narrated by
Jean Shepherd. **CO6, FA6, FA13,**
Recommended

Christmas to Remember, A
(1978, C, 100m, NR)
During the Depression, an elderly farm couple is visited by their grandson for the holidays. Jason Robards, Eva Marie Saint, and
Joanne Woodward star. Originally made for
TV. **FA13, ST185, ST234**

Christmas Tree, The (1969, C, 110m, G)
Sentimental tale of a wealthy man's reconcil-
iation with his dying young son. William
Holden stars. Also known as *When Wolves
Cry*. **FA13, ST106**

Christmas Wife, The (1988, C, 73m, NR)
Lonely widower (Jason Robards) "hires" a
female companion (Julie Harris) for the holidays. Originally made for cable TV. **DR11,
ST185**

Christopher Columbus
(1949, C, 104m, NR)
Fredric March plays the famed explorer in this British-produced biography. With Florence Eldridge (March's real-life wife), Francis L. Sullivan, and Linden Travers. **CL2, ST148**

Christopher Columbus: The Discovery
(1992, C, 120m, PG-13)
George Corraface stars as history's first Italian-American. With Marlon Brando as Torquemada, Tom Selleck and Rachel Ward as Ferdinand and Isabella, Robert Davi, and Nigel Terry. Directed by John Glen. **DR5, ST18**

Christopher Strong
(1933, B&W, 77m, NR)
A female aviator (Katharine Hepburn) goes into a tailspin over a married man (Colin Clive). **CL5, ST103**

Chuck Berry: Hail! Hail! Rock 'n' Roll
(1987, C, 120m, PG)
Documentary about one of rock's Founding Fathers effortlessly blends amusing interview material with footage from a historic concert in Berry's hometown, St. Louis. Performers include Keith Richards, Eric Clapton, Linda Ronstadt, Etta James, and Robert Cray; interviewees include Bruce Springsteen, Little Richard, Bo Diddley, the Everly Brothers, and Jerry Lee Lewis. **MU11,** *Highly Recommended*

Chump at Oxford, A
(1940, B&W, 63m, NR)
Laurel and Hardy matriculate at England's most prestigious university. With Peter Cushing. **ST43, ST131**

Cimarron (1931, B&W, 124m, NR)
Oscar-winning Western epic of a family settling the frontier, based on Edna Ferber's novel. Richard Dix stars, with Irene Dunne and Estelle Taylor. **ST62, WE1, XT1**

Cincinnati Kid, The (1965, C, 113m, NR)
Steve McQueen stars as a poker-playing ace who challenges rich Edward G. Robinson to a high-stakes game. With Ann-Margret, Tuesday Weld, Rip Torn, Karl Malden, and Joan Blondell. Directed by Norman Jewison. **DT63, ST146, ST186, ST216**

Cinderella (1950, C, 75m, G)
Disney's full-length animated fairy tale finds a beautiful maiden dominated by an evil stepmother and ugly stepsisters until her fairy godmother and Prince Charming come to her rescue. **FA2,** *Recommended*

Cinderella (1964, C, 77m, NR)
Musical version of the famed fairy tale, with Lesley Ann Warren, Ginger Rogers, Celeste

Holm, and Walter Pidgeon, plus a Rodgers and Hammerstein score. Originally made for TV. **FA9, MU8, ST187**

Cinderella (1984, C, 60m, NR)
Jennifer Beals is the over-worked, under-loved maiden, Matthew Broderick is the charming prince, Jean Stapleton plays her fairy godmother, and Eve Arden is the wicked stepmother in this Faerie Tale Theatre presentation. **FA12**

Cinderfella (1960, C, 91m, NR)
Jerry Lewis spoofs the famed fairy tale as an orphaned boy who has to cook and clean for his evil stepbrothers. **FA6, ST139**

Cinema Paradiso (1989, C, 123m, NR)
Oscar-winning drama from Italy, set in a Sicilian village, where a young boy befriends the projectionist at the local theater. Filled with clips from classic Italian and American films of the 1930s and 1940s. Philippe Noiret stars, with Salvatore Cascio and Jacques Perrin. Written and directed by Giuseppe Tornatore. A must for any movie lover. **FF2, XT7, XT26, XT31,** *Recommended*

Circle of Iron (1979, C, 102m, R)
Martial arts combines with fantasy in this tale of an American searching for perfect peace and Zen awareness. David Carradine, Jeff Cooper, Roddy McDowall, and Christopher Lee star. Based on an idea by James Coburn and Bruce Lee. **AC26, ST135**

Circle of Love (1964, C, 105m, NR)
Remake of *La Ronde*, classic story of sexual roundelay, starring Jane Fonda, Jean-Claude Brialy, and Maurice Ronet. Directed by Roger Vadim; screenplay by Jean Anouilh. Original running time: 110 minutes. **CU18, ST72**

Circle of Two (1980, C, 105m, PG)
Richard Burton plays an artist who develops a special friendship with a young model (Tatum O'Neal). **ST22**

Circus, The (1928, B&W, 72m, NR)
Charlie Chaplin classic silent comedy finds him charmed by the circus owner's stepdaughter. Also available on a tape which includes Chaplin's 33-minute short, *A Day's Pleasure*, about a family's mishaps during a day set aside for fun and games. **CL11, DT24,** *Essential, Recommended*

Circus of Horrors (1960, C, 89m, NR)
A plastic surgeon and his nurse hide out in an unusual circus to escape a patient they once disfigured. Donald Pleasence stars. **HO20, HO26**

Circus World (1964, C, 135m, NR)
After a fifteen-year absence, a circus owner attempts to locate his ex-lover, who's also the mother of the child he's raised. John Wayne and Rita Hayworth star. **CL7, ST101, ST224**

Citadel, The (1938, B&W, 112m, NR)
Robert Donat plays a doctor who compromises his ideals for a life of luxury in this version of the A.J. Cronin novel. With Rosalind Russell, Ralph Richardson, and Rex Harrison. Directed by King Vidor. **DT126, ST184, ST192**

Citizen Cohn (1992, C, 112m, R)
James Woods plays Roy Cohn, the flashy and controversial lawyer who first gained the limelight as Senator Joseph McCarthy's aide, later became one of New York's most flamboyant characters. Originally made for cable TV. **DR4, ST233**

Citizen Kane (1941, B&W, 119m, NR)
The story of publishing tycoon Charles Foster Kane marks the stunning Hollywood debut of Orson Welles, who stars and also cowrote, directed, and produced. Joseph Cotten, Agnes Moorehead, Everett Sloane, Dorothy Comingore, and Ruth Warrick are among the supporting players. Watch for Alan Ladd as a reporter. On any shortlist of the greatest films of all time; easily deserving of the Best Picture and Director Oscars it didn't win. **CL2, DR24, DT134, ST128, XT21, XT28,** *Essential, Highly Recommended*

Citizens Band (1977, C, 98m, PG)
Comedy focusing on activities of CB enthusiasts in a small town, full of rich characters. Paul LeMat stars, with Candy Clark, Ann Wedgeworth, Marcia Rodd, Charles Napier, and Bruce McGill. Written by Paul Brickman; directed by Jonathan Demme. Also known as *Handle With Care*. Some good touches, but the director had yet to hit his stride. **CO2, DT35**

City for Conquest (1940, B&W, 101m, NR)
James Cagney melodrama about a boxer protecting his young brother (Arthur Kennedy) from the Wrong Elements. With Donald Crisp, Frank McHugh, George Tobias, and future director Elia Kazan. **DR22, DT65, ST24**

City Heat (1984, C, 94m, PG)
Spoof of 1930s gangster films starring Clint Eastwood as a cop and Burt Reynolds as his pal, a private eye. Rip Torn is the villain; Richard Roundtree, Madeline Kahn, Jane Alexander, and Irene Cara head the supporting cast. Directed by Richard Benjamin. Pretty strained stuff. **CO3, CO7, ST64, ST183, ST216**

City in Fear (1980, C, 150m, NR)
David Janssen plays a reporter on the trail of a psycho killer who's terrorizing a city. Robert Vaughn, Perry King, and Mickey Rourke costar. Originally made for TV. **AC9, MY13, ST190**

City Lights (1931, B&W, 86m, NR)
Charlie Chaplin is the poor tramp whose sudden fortune brings sight to a blind girl in this delightful and moving silent classic. **CL6, CL11, DT24,** *Essential, Highly Recommended*

City Limits (1985, C, 85m, PG-13)
The familiar post-apocalypse story, with a plague-decimated population and youth gangs ruling the cities. Darrell Larson, John Stockwell, and Kim Cattrall star, with Rae Dawn Chong, Robby Benson, and Danny De La Paz; narrated by James Earl Jones. **SF12, ST118**

City of Hope (1991, C, 129m, NR)
Writer-director John Sayles's ambitious drama about corruption in a big city. Vincent Spano and Joe Morton star, with Tony LoBianco, Anthony John Denison, Barbara Williams, David Strathairn, and the director. Widescreen will be lost on video. Interesting and ambitious, but never very compelling. Worth a look for fans of the director or genre. **DR7, DR15, DT112**

City of Joy (1992, C, 134, PG-13)
Drama of American surgeon who comes to Calcutta and awakens to severity of impoverished conditions there. Patrick Swayze stars, with Pauline Collins and Om Puri. Written by Mark Medoff, directed by Roland Joffe. **DR7, DR15, DR27**

City of the Walking Dead
(1983, C, 92m, R)
Zombies come to life in search of humans to feast on. Mel Ferrer stars. **HO21**

City of Women (1981, C, 139m, NR)
Federico Fellini fantasy of a man (Marcello Mastroianni) who dreams that he is a prisoner in a town run by females. **DT43, ST154**

City on Fire (1979, C, 101m, R)
Disaster story of a city endangered by a blaze set by an embittered refinery worker. Barry Newman, Henry Fonda, Ava Gardner, Shelley Winters, and Susan Clark star. **AC23, ST71, ST79, ST232**

City Slickers (1991, C, 108m, PG-13)
A trio of New York men, suffering through various personal crises, sign on with a dude ranch to drive a herd of cattle from New

Mexico to Colorado. Comedy-drama stars Billy Crystal, Daniel Stern, and Bruno Kirby, with Oscar winner Jack Palance (wonderful), Helen Slater, Patricia Wettig, and Tracey Walter. Best when it's funny, worst when it strains for significance. **CO2, CO13, CO20, WE12, XT4**

City That Never Sleeps
(1953, B&W, 90m, NR)
A Chicago cop (Gig Young) is involved in an affair with a nightclub singer, which leads to blackmail and murder. With Mala Powers, William Talman, and Edward Arnold. **MY1, XT11**

Civil War, The (1990, 680m, B&W/C, NR)
Landmark documentary on America's darkest hours, originally presented in nine installments on public TV. Deftly combines evocative still photographs, incisive commentary from contemporary historians, and moving narration of public and private documents. Directed by Ken Burns. **CU16,** *Highly Recommended*

Claire's Knee (1971, C, 103m, PG)
A groom-to-be develops an obsession with the daughter of a friend, or more specifically, the knee of a daughter of a friend. Comedy from French director Eric Rohmer. **DT107**

Clambake (1967, C, 97m, NR)
Elvis Presley musical, with El as a rich Miami boy who wants to be treated just like everyone else. Shelley Fabares costars. **ST178**

Clan of the Cave Bear (1986, C, 100m, R)
Prehistoric adventure saga, based on Jean M. Auel novel, starring Daryl Hannah, Pamela Reed, and James Remar. Directed by Michael Chapman. **AC12**

Clara's Heart (1988, C, 108m, PG-13)
A Jamaican housekeeper brings a young boy out of his emotional shell in this sentimental drama starring Whoopi Goldberg. Neil Patrick Harris, Kathleen Quinlan, and Michael Ontkean costar. **DR2, DR8, ST89**

Clarence (1991, C, 92m, G)
Robert Carradine plays Clarence Oddbody, the angel from *It's a Wonderful Life*; his mission this time is to help a young mother. **FA8**

Clarence Darrow (1978, C, 81m, NR)
Henry Fonda's one-man show, dramatizing the life of the famed lawyer, adapted from the play by Irvin Stone. Originally made for TV. **DR4, DR20, ST71**

Clarence, the Cross-Eyed Lion
(1965, C, 98m, NR)
Family adventure tale set in the wilds of Africa was the basis for the "Daktari" TV series. Marshall Thompson, Betsy Drake, and Cheryl Miller star. **FA4, FA5**

Clash by Night (1952, B&W, 105m, NR)
Barbara Stanwyck plays a restless woman who finally settles down with a fisherman (Paul Douglas), but she's hooked on her husband's best friend (Robert Ryan). Marilyn Monroe has a small part. Fritz Lang directed. **DT70, ST159, ST193, ST206**

Clash of the Titans (1981, C, 118m, PG)
Fantasy adventure retells ancient Greek mythology with the help of contemporary special effects by Ray Harryhausen. Laurence Olivier stars as Zeus, with Harry Hamlin, Maggie Smith, Claire Bloom, Ursula Andress, and Burgess Meredith. Terrific special effects, but "human" factor is missing. **SF13, ST168**

Class Act (1992, C, 98m, PG-13)
Sequel of sorts to comedy *House Party* reunites rappers Kid 'N Play (Christopher Reid, Christopher Martin). One's a nerd, the other's a tough guy; they decide to switch identities at their new school. With Karyn Parsons and Alysin Rogers. Directed by Randall Miller. **CO19, CO20**

Class Action (1991, C, 109m, R)
Gene Hackman and Mary Elizabeth Mastrantonio play opposing attorneys who are also father and daughter in this courtroom drama. He represents plaintiff in suit against car company she works for. With Colin Friels, Joanna Merlin, and Larry Fishburne. Directed by Michael Apted. **DR8, DR17, ST96**

Class of Miss MacMichael, The
(1978, C, 99m, R)
Glenda Jackson is the teacher of a class of disadvantaged rebels in this schoolroom drama. Oliver Reed costars. **DR25, ST117**

Class of 1984 (1982, C, 93m, R)
Violent melodrama of a lone teacher (Perry King) confronting a vicious gang of "students." Timothy Van Patten leads the truants; watch for Michael J. Fox. Over-the-top violence destroys any credibility. **DR25**

Class of 1999 (1990, C, 98m, R)
Futuristic look at high school life which Andy Hardy wouldn't recognize: gangs have taken over schools and a trio of androids are trying to (literally) whip the kids into shape. Bradley Gregg stars, with Traci Lin, Malcolm McDowell, and Stacy Keach. **DR25**

Class of Nuke 'Em High (1986, C, 81m, R)
A New Jersey high school becomes a nuclear waste dump and the students are transformed into obnoxious mutants. **CO18, HO21**

Clean and Sober (1988, C, 124m, R)
Absorbing drama of an investment counselor
(Michael Keaton) and his battle against alcohol abuse and drug addiction. With Morgan
Freeman, Kathy Baker, and M. Emmet Walsh.
DR7, ST76, ST122, *Recommended*

Clean Slate (1981, C, 128m, NR)
Hilarious black comedy set in French colonial
Africa about a police chief who gains revenge
on everyone who has mistreated him. Philippe Noiret, Stephane Audran, and Isabelle
Huppert star. Bertrand Tavernier directed;
based on Jim Thompson's novel, *Pop. 1280*.
French title: *Coup de Torchon*. Should have
won the Foreign Language Film Oscar.
DT123, MY16, WR34, XT28, *Recommended*

Cleopatra (1934, B&W, 95m, NR)
Claudette Colbert plays the Queen of the Nile
in this lavish historical drama directed by
Cecil B. DeMille. With Warren William and
Henry Wilcoxon. **CL2, CL3, DT34, ST34**

Cleopatra (1963, C, 243m, G)
The legendary film that made Elizabeth Taylor and Richard Burton the celebrity couple
of our time and nearly bankrupted one
movie studio. Rex Harrison costars, with
Roddy MacDowall and Martin Landau. Joseph L. Mankiewicz directed. Also available
in a 194-minute version. The director does
add some flourishes, but it's pretty heavy
going most of the time. **CL2, CL3, CL15,
DT84, ST22, ST212,** *Essential*

Cleopatra Jones (1973, C, 89m, PG)
Tamara Dobson stars as a secret agent skilled
in the martial arts in this adventure saga. Shelley Winters plays her nemesis. **AC26, ST200**

Cleopatra Jones and the Casino of Gold
(1975, C, 96m, R)
Second chapter in *Cleo* saga, with Tamara
Dobson squaring off against dragon lady
Stella Stevens. **AC26**

Clinton and Nadine see *Blood Money*

Cloak and Dagger (1946, B&W, 106m, NR)
Gary Cooper plays a professor caught up in
espionage on a trip to Germany. Fritz Lang
directed. **DT70, ST37**

Clock, The (1945, B&W, 90m, NR)
Classic romance between soldier on leave
in New York and an office worker. Robert
Walker and Judy Garland star, with James
Gleason and Keenan Wynn. Directed by Vincente Minnelli. **CL4, DT88, ST81, XT9**

Clockmaker, The (1973, C, 105m, NR)
French drama of simple man (Philippe
Noiret) whose life is turned upside down

when his son is charged with murder.
Bertrand Tavernier directed. **DT123**

Clockwise (1986, C, 96m, PG)
A British schoolmaster who prides himself on
his punctuality encounters a series of comic
disasters on the most important day of his
career. John Cleese stars. **CO15**

Clockwork Orange, A (1971, C, 137m, R)
In the ultra-violent future, Alex and his
droogs (gang members) lead merry lives of
crime until the authorities catch him and
subject him to a gruesome form of rehabilitation. Malcolm McDowell stars in director
Stanley Kubrick's chilling version of Anthony
Burgess's novel. With Patrick Magee. Originally rated X. Since 1973, banned from theatrical exhibition in Britain. Superb soundtrack, with imaginative use of Beethoven.
CU1, CU4, CU8, DR19, DT68, SF17, *Essential, Recommended*

Close Encounters of the Third Kind
(1977, C, 135m, PG)
Steven Spielberg's epic science fiction drama
of aliens landing in Wyoming, tipping off
their arrival ahead of time to certain Earthlings. Richard Dreyfuss and Melinda Dillon
star, with Bob Balaban and François Truffaut.
This is the *Special Edition*, which contains
footage added for the film's theatrical
rerelease. **DT118, DT125, FA8, SF9, SF16,
ST60,** *Essential, Recommended*

Close My Eyes (1991, C, 105m, R)
British drama of forbidden love, as a young
wife and her brother fall into a sexual relationship. Saskia Reeves, Clive Owen, and
Alan Rickman star. Directed by Stephen Poliakoff. Sensitive handling of explosive material, but it doesn't quite convincingly
dramatize the transition from affection to
lust. **DR1, DR3, DR8, DR23**

Closely Watched Trains
(1966, B&W, 89m, NR)
Oscar-winning comedy-drama from Czechoslovakia about a young railway worker's first
brush with sex. Set during the Nazi occupation. Directed by Jiri Menzel. **FF7, XT7,
XT19**

Closet Land (1991, C, 89m, R)
Two-character drama: a writer of children's
books is interrogated by the police official of
a totalitarian country. Madeleine Stowe and
Alan Rickman star. **DR21, ST209**

Clouds Over Europe
(1939, B&W, 78m, NR)
Laurence Olivier stars with Ralph Richardson
in a light-hearted mystery about a test pilot
and British inspector assigned to unravel a

case of missing bombers. Also known as *Q Planes*. **MY15, ST168, ST184**

Clown Murders, The (1975, C, 96m, NR)
Canadian drama about buddies at a Halloween party who fake a kidnapping to spoil a business deal. Stephen Young stars, with Susan Keller, Lawrence Dane, and John Candy. **CO14**

Clowns, The (1971, C, 90m, NR)
Documentary from Federico Fellini about the merry men and women of the circus, with some serious commentary on the human condition as well. **DT43**

Club, The (1980, C, 99m, NR)
Australian drama of off-field politics among a football team. Jack Thompson and Graham Kennedy star. Bruce Beresford directed. **DT10, FF5**

Club Extinction (1990, C, 112m, R)
Berlin is the setting for this futuristic mystery about a group of suicides linked to a mysterious media mogul. Alan Bates stars, with Jennifer Beals, Jan Niklas, and Andrew McCarthy. Directed by Claude Chabrol; dialogue in English. Based on same novel that inspired Fritz Lang's classic Dr. Mabuse films. **MY16, ST9**

Club Paradise (1986, C, 104m, PG-13)
A Chicago fireman moves to a Caribbean island with hopes of opening a swank resort for swingin' singles. Robin Williams stars, with Twiggy, Jimmy Cliff, Peter O'Toole, Andrea Martin, Rick Moranis, and Eugene Levy. Directed by Harold Ramis. **CO14, ST169, ST228**

Clue (1985, C, 87m, PG)
Comic mystery, based on the popular board game, starring Tim Curry, Eileen Brennan, Madeline Kahn, Martin Mull, Michael McKean, Christopher Lloyd, Lesley Ann Warren, and Lee Ving among the suspects. Released theatrically with three different endings; all are featured on the video version. **CO10, MU12, MY17**

Coal Miner's Daughter
(1980, C, 125m, PG)
Oscar winner Sissy Spacek stars as country music queen Loretta Lynn in this drama about her roller-coaster life and career. Tommy Lee Jones plays her husband, Beverly D'Angelo is Patsy Cline, Levon Helm is Lynn's father. Both actresses do their own singing, part of the charm of this entertaining look at the country music scene. **MU5, MU12, ST202, XT3**, *Recommended*

Cobra (1986, C, 87m, R)
Sylvester Stallone is a take-no-prisoners police

detective who's after a gang of vicious killers. Brigitte Nielsen costars. **AC9, ST204**

Coca-Cola Kid, The (1985, C, 94m, R)
Charming, offbeat comedy about a brash American marketing expert sent to the Australian outback to push the title product. Eric Roberts and Greta Scacchi star. Directed by Dusan Makavejev. **CO2, CO12, CO20, XT26**, *Recommended*

Cocaine Cowboys (1979, C, 87m, R)
Andy Warhol produced this comedy about a rock band that doubles as dope smugglers. Jack Palance, Tom Sullivan, and Warhol star. **CU3**

Cocaine Fiends (1936, B&W, 74m, NR)
Serious "message" film from the distant past warning audiences of the consequences of cocaine use (prostitution and suicide) is now regarded a camp "bad" movie. **CU11**

Cocaine: One Man's Seduction
(1983, C, 97m, NR)
Dennis Weaver plays a real estate salesman who gets hooked on drugs. With Karen Grassle, Pamela Belwood, and James Spader. Originally made for TV. **DR7, ST203**

Cockfighter (1974, C, 83m, R)
Warren Oates plays a man who drifts through the rural South training fighting birds in this cult film adapted from Charles Willeford's novel. With Harry Dean Stanton, Troy Donahue, and Millie Perkins. Also known as *Born To Kill*. **ST166, ST205**

Cocktail (1988, C, 104m, R)
Tom Cruise stars in this light romantic drama about a young man whose claim to fame in New York is his considerable bartending skills. Bryan Brown plays his mentor, Elisabeth Shue his girlfriend. **DR1, ST41**

Cocoanuts, The (1929, B&W, 96m, NR)
The Marx Brothers' debut film, about phony land sales in Florida, adapted from their Broadway hit. Some laughs, but the best was yet to come. **ST152**

Cocoon (1985, C, 118m, PG-13)
Senior citizens in Florida and aliens disguised as humans collide in this ingratiating comedy-drama starring Hume Cronyn, Wilford Brimley, Jessica Tandy, Maureen Stapleton, Gwen Verdon, Steve Guttenberg, Brian Dennehy, and Oscar winner Don Ameche. Directed by Ron Howard. **DR11, DT58, SF9, XT4**, *Recommended*

Cocoon: The Return (1988, C, 116m, PG)
This sequel to the story of alien visitors and oldsters in Florida reunites virtually the

entire cast of the first film for more adventures. **DR11, SF9**

Code Name: Wild Geese
(1986, C, 101m, R)
Action in the jungles of Southeast Asia, as a hand-picked mercenary force lays siege to a major opium smuggling operation. Lee Van Cleef, Klaus Kinski, and Ernest Borgnine star. **AC20, ST126, ST221**

Code of Silence (1985, C, 102m, R)
Chicago police detective is shunned by his colleagues when he turns in a crooked cop, and is also caught between warring gangs. Chuck Norris and Henry Silva star. **AC9, ST165, XT11**

Cold Feet (1989, C, 91m, R)
Loopy, offbeat comedy, set in the contemporary West, of jewel smugglers using a horse to carry their booty. Keith Carradine, Sally Kirkland, and Tom Waits star, with Bill Pullman, Rip Torn, and in a cameo role, Jeff Bridges. Written by Jim Harrison and Thomas McGuane. Pretty silly; if the principals interest you and you're in a mood for something light, you could do worse. **CO9, CO12, ST19, ST216, XT18**

Cold Heaven (1992, C, 105m, R)
Drama of unfaithful wife whose surgeon husband is killed in an accident just before she's to tell him of her affair. Or is his death only in her mind? Theresa Russell stars, with Mark Harmon, James Russo, Talia Shire, and Will Patton. Based on Brian Moore's novel. Directed by Nicolas Roeg. **DR10, DR19, DT106, XT30**

Cold River (1982, C, 94m, PG)
Family adventure of a brother and sister stranded in the wilderness when their father suffers a fatal heart attack. Filmed on location in the Adirondack Mountains; set in 1932. **FA4**

Cold Room, The (1984, C, 95m, NR)
A German vacation for a father (George Segal) and his college-age daughter (Amanda Pays) turns into a series of bizarre incidents when a mysterious man is found hiding out in her hotel room. Originally made for cable TV. **MY14**

Cold Sassy Tree (1989, C, 100m, NR)
Faye Dunaway stars in this drama set in a small Southern town at the turn of the century. She's from the North and shocks the residents by marrying an elderly store owner (Richard Widmark). With Neil Patrick Harris. Originally made for TV. **DR1, DR26, ST61**

Cold Sweat (1971, C, 94m, PG)
Charles Bronson plays an American expatriate in France who gets involved with drug dealing. James Mason, Liv Ullmann, and Jill Ireland costar. **AC8, ST20, ST153, ST220**

Cold Turkey (1971, C, 99m, PG)
Comedy of small-town minister who tries to get his entire community to give up smoking for a huge cash reward. Dick Van Dyke stars, with Pippa Scott, Tom Poston, Bob Newhart, and Bob Elliott & Ray Goulding (Bob & Ray). Directed by Norman Lear; music by Randy Newman. **CO2**

Collection, The (1975, C, 64m, NR)
Harold Pinter drama of a romantic triangle, starring Alan Bates, Malcolm McDowell, Helen Mirren, and Laurence Olivier. Directed by Michael Apted. Originally made for British TV. **DR3, DR20, DR23, ST9, ST168**

Collector, The (1965, C, 119m, NR)
A shy young man (Terence Stamp) wins a fortune in a football pool and buys an estate, where he keeps a beautiful girl (Samantha Eggar) captive in hopes that she'll fall in love with him. Chilling cult film directed by William Wyler. **CU13, DR3, DT142, MY3,** *Recommended*

College (1927, B&W, 65m, NR)
Buster Keaton goes out for the football team to impress a sweet coed. **CL11, CO18, DT66**

College Swing (1938, B&W, 86m, NR)
George Burns-Gracie Allen comedy with musical numbers set on campus; thin plot revolves around Gracie's inability to matriculate. With Bob Hope, Martha Raye, Edward Everett Horton, Florence George, Ben Blue, Betty Grable, and John Payne. **CO18, ST91, ST108**

Colonel Redl (1985, C, 144m, R)
Klaus Maria Brandauer stars in this Hungarian drama about an army officer's rise to power in the days before World War I. Istvan Szabo directed. **FF7**

Color of Money, The (1986, C, 119m, R)
Sequel to *The Hustler*, set twenty-five years later, with Paul Newman's "Fast Eddie" Felson training a hot new young prospect (Tom Cruise). With Mary Elizabeth Mastrantonio and Helen Shaver. Newman won an Oscar under Martin Scorsese's direction. Written by Richard Price; music supervised by Robbie Robertson. Not quite up to high standards of the original but still plenty to like. **DR22, DT114, ST41, ST162, XT2,** *Recommended*

Color Purple, The (1985, C, 155m, PG-13)
Drama of two black sisters and their painful separation and enduring love for one another.

Whoopi Goldberg stars, with Danny Glover, Oprah Winfrey, Margaret Avery, Rae Dawn Chong, and Adolph Caesar. Steven Spielberg directed; based on Alice Walker's novel. Available in letterboxed format. **CU19, DR8, DR10, DR14, DR19, DT118, ST88, ST89**

Colorado (1940, B&W, 54m, NR)
Roy Rogers and partner Gabby Hayes saddle up and head out for the wilds of Colorado. **ST188**

Colorado Sunset (1939, B&W, 61m, NR)
Gene Autry plays a sheriff who battles a phony protective association stirring up trouble among ranchers. **ST5**

Colors (1988, C, 120m, R)
On the streets of Los Angeles, two police officers (Robert Duvall and Sean Penn) try to keep the peace amid warring gangs. Directed by Dennis Hopper; some brief footage added for video release. Good performances, but the nightly TV news has more drama. **AC9, CU10, DR15, ST63, ST110, XT10**

Colossus: The Forbin Project
(1970, C, 100m, PG)
Science fiction tale of a super-computer that begins to develop a mind of its own, overriding all attempts to thwart it. Eric Braeden and Susan Clark star. Also known as *The Forbin Project*. **SF6**

Columbo: Prescription Murder
(1967, C, 99m, NR)
The disarming sleuth in the rumpled raincoat, Lt. Columbo (Peter Falk) is on the trail of a philandering psychiatrist. Originally made for TV; pilot for the successful series. **MY10**

Coma (1978, C, 113m, PG)
A doctor discovers a horrifying secret when her patients begin to suffer major brain damage after relatively minor surgery. Genevieve Bujold stars, with Michael Douglas and Rip Torn. Mildly entertaining; Torn is wonderful, as always. **HO19, MY3, MY11, SF5, ST59, ST216**

Comancheros, The (1961, C, 107m, NR)
A Texas ranger (John Wayne) goes undercover in an attempt to halt the sale of guns and liquor to the Comanches. Lee Marvin costars. **ST151, ST224, WE6**

Come Along With Me (1984, C, 60m, NR)
Newly widowed, a middle-aged woman embarks on a new career—as a seer. Based on an unfinished novel by Shirley Jackson. Estelle Parsons stars; Paul Newman provides the voice of her late husband. Directed by Joanne Woodward. Originally made for TV. **DR10, ST162, ST234, XT23**

Come and Get It (1936, B&W, 99m, NR)
Frances Farmer plays dual roles in this drama set in Wisconsin timber country. Edward Arnold and Joel McCrea star as the men in her life; Oscar winner Walter Brennan costars. A cult favorite, mainly for Farmer's amazing performance. Codirected by Howard Hawks and William Wyler. **CL14, DT53, DT142, ST144, XT4, XT27,** *Recommended*

Come Back, Little Sheba
(1952, B&W, 99m, NR)
Shirley Booth (in her film debut) won an Oscar for her portrayal of a put-upon housewife married to an alcoholic man (Burt Lancaster). Adaptation of William Inge play also features Terry Moore and Richard Jaeckel. **DR20, ST129, XT3, XT21**

Come Back to the Five & Dime, Jimmy Dean, Jimmy Dean (1992, C, 110m, NR)
A reunion of women who hung around the set of Dean's last film (*Giant*) in a small Texas town is shaken up by the arrival of a stranger. Cher, Sandy Dennis, and Karen Black star. Robert Altman directed this drama based on Ed Graczyk's play. Altman's fluid direction can't always disguise the thinness of the material. **DR20, DR26, DT4, ST29**

Come Blow Your Horn
(1963, C, 112m, NR)
Quintessential Frank Sinatra vehicle has him playing a swinger teaching his younger brother (Tony Bill) the ropes. With Lee J. Cobb, Jill St. John, Molly Picon, Barbara Rush, and Dean Martin in a bit role. From Neil Simon's first hit play. **CO5, ST199, WR30**

Come On, Rangers (1938, B&W, 54m, NR)
Roy Rogers and Gabby Hayes demonstrate the cowboy way in this musical Western. **ST188**

Come See the Paradise (1990, C, 132m, R)
World War II–era drama of West Coast labor organizer married to a Japanese-American woman; they're separated when she's forced into an internment camp. Dennis Quaid and Tamlyn Tomita star. Written and directed by Alan Parker. **DR5**

Comedians, The (1967, C, 148m, NR)
Political thriller, adapted from Graham Greene novel, of disparate lives colliding in Papa Doc Duvalier's Haiti. Elizabeth Taylor and Richard Burton star, with Alex Guinness, Peter Ustinov, Paul Ford, Lillian Gish, Raymond St. Jacques, Zakes Mokae, Cicely Tyson, and James Earl Jones. Fascinating subject matter is compromised only somewhat by glossy Liz 'n' Dick shenanigans; ter-

rific supporting cast. **CL15, DR27, MY6, ST22, ST87, ST95, ST118, ST212, WR11**

Comedy of Terrors (1964, C, 84m, NR)
Horror comedy about an undertaker (Vincent Price) and his inept assistant (Peter Lorre). With Boris Karloff, Basil Rathbone, and Joe E. Brown. Directed by Jacques Tourneur. **DT124, HO24, ST119, ST179**

Comes a Horseman (1978, C, 118m, PG)
A cattle baron plots to rustle up the land in his territory, but there's a feisty woman in his way. James Caan, Jane Fonda, and Jason Robards star in this quietly observed, well acted Western set in the late 1940s. Directed by Alan J. Pakula. **DT94, ST72, ST185, WE8, WE12,** *Recommended*

Comfort and Joy (1984, C, 105m, PG)
Disarmingly charming comedy about a Scottish disc jockey who looks for "meaning" in his life after his girlfriend leaves him; he gets involved in a feud between local ice cream truck companies. Bill Paterson stars. Bill Forsyth directed; music by Mark Knopfler. **CO17, DT46, FA13,** *Recommended*

Comfort of Strangers, The
(1991, C, 105m, R)
Strange drama, adapted from Ian McEwan's novel, about British couple visiting Venice, getting mixed up with kinky nobleman and his suffering wife. Rupert Everett and Natasha Richardson star, with Christopher Walken and Helen Mirren. Written by Harold Pinter; directed by Paul Shrader. Much ado about very little, although the views of Venice are magnificent. **DR19, DR27, ST222, WR26**

Comic, The (1969, C, 94m, PG)
Drama of a self-destructive silent film clown, played by Dick Van Dyke. With Mickey Rooney and Michele Lee. **DR13, ST189**

Comic Relief 2 (1987, C, 120m, NR)
The second comedians' benefit concert to aid the homeless, hosted by Robin Williams, Billy Crystal, and Whoopi Goldberg. Among the participants: Catherine O'Hara, Dudley Moore, Peter Cook, Harry Anderson, Arsenio Hall, Bobcat Goldthwait, Andrea Martin, Robert Klein, Penn and Teller. **CO13, CO14, CO16, ST89, ST160, ST228**

Comic Relief III (1989, C, 120m, NR)
More stand-up comedy from Billy Crystal, Whoopi Goldberg, Robin Williams, and friends in a benefit concert to aid the homeless. Among the guests: Bobcat Goldthwait, Arsenio Hall, Shelley Long, Garry Shandling, and Steven Wright. **CO13, CO16, ST89, ST228**

Coming Home (1978, C, 127m, R)
In the late 1960s, a crippled Vietnam vet, now opposed to the war, has an affair with the wife of a gung-ho Marine. Oscar winners Jon Voight and Jane Fonda star, with Bruce Dern, Penelope Milford, and Robert Carradine. Directed by Hal Ashby, who did deserve an Oscar in an admittedly weak year. Prime sixties peace 'n' love nostalgia overstuffed with "classic rock" that hasn't worn well with passage of time. **DR3, DR7, ST72, XT2, XT3, X28,** *Essential*

Coming to America (1988, C, 116m, R)
Eddie Murphy comedy about an African prince who decides to look for a bride in the land of the brave and the home of the free—namely, Queens, New York. Arsenio Hall heads the supporting cast; he and Murphy play several character parts in disguises. With James Earl Jones, Madge Sinclair, John Amos, and Shari Headley. Only mildly amusing; the Art Buchwald trial had more laughs. **CO13, CO20, ST118, XT9**

Command Decision (1948, C, 112m, NR)
Clark Gable plays a flight commander sending men off to almost certain death in World War II missions. With Walter Pidgeon, Van Johnson, Brian Donlevy, Charles Bickford, John Hodiak, and Edward Arnold. Adapted from a play by William Wister Haines. **AC1, DR20, ST77**

Commando (1985, C, 90m, R)
Former fighting man (Arnold Schwarzenegger) swings into action when nasties kidnap his daughter. A one-man army movie if ever there was one. Rae Dawn Chong costars. **AC25, ST195**

Commandos (1968, C, 89m, PG)
World War II drama of Americans working with Allies-siding Italians in North Africa. Lee Van Cleef and Jack Kelly star. **AC1, ST221**

Commandos Strike at Dawn
(1942, B&W, 96m, NR)
A Norwegian comes to the aid of British soldiers when Nazis invade his homeland. Paul Muni stars, with Anna Lee and Lillian Gish. **ST87**

Commissar, The (1967, B&W, 105m, NR)
Soviet drama, long banned in its native land, about the oppression of Jewish villagers by a female bureaucrat. **CU8, FF7**

Commitments, The (1991, C, 116m, R)
Engaging comedy of Dublin working-class youths forming a band that plays American soul music (including Otis Redding and Aretha Franklin). Robert Arkins heads the exuberant young cast; with Johnny Murphy

(as Joey the Lips Fagan), Andrew Strong (great voice), Michael Aherne, Angeline Ball, and Maria Doyle. Directed by Alan Parker. **CO8, CO17, MU9,** *Recommended*

Common Threads: Stories From the Quilt (1989, C/B&W, 80m, NR)
Oscar winner for Best Documentary Feature focuses on individuals represented in giant quilt memorializing victims of AIDS. Narrated by Dustin Hoffman. Simply done, very moving. **CU16, ST105,** *Recommended*

Communion (1989, C, 103m, R)
Novelist Whitley Strieber's nonfiction account of an encounter he had with alien visitors. Christopher Walken stars as the author; Lindsay Crouse plays his wife. **DR6, SF9, ST222**

Company of Wolves, The (1984, C, 95m, R)
Fantasy about a granny (Angela Lansbury) who tells various werewolf stories to her granddaughter (Sarah Patterson), which culminate in an erotic twist on the "Little Red Riding Hood" fairy tale. Directed by Neil Jordan. **HO4, HO17, ST131**

Competition, The (1980, C, 129m, PG)
Richard Dreyfuss and Amy Irving play rival pianists at a classical contest who fall in love. **DR12, ST60**

Compleat Beatles, The (1982, C, 120m, NR)
Superb, evocative documentary portrait of the four lads from Liverpool, packed with familiar and rare footage of their performances and fans. Narrated by Malcolm McDowell. **MU11,** *Recommended*

Compleat, "Weird Al" Yankovic, The (1985, C, 100m, NR)
Videos from rock 'n' roll's wacky parodist, including "Eat it," "I Love Rocky Road," I Lost on Jeopardy," and "Like a Surgeon." **CO16**

Compromising Positions (1985, C, 98m, R)
Long Island housewife turns sleuth when her lecherous dentist is murdered. A suspense comedy starring Susan Sarandon, with Raul Julia, Judith Ivey, and Mary Beth Hurt. Some funny moments, especially between Sarandon and Hurt. **CO10, MY11, ST194**

Computer Wore Tennis Shoes, The (1970, C, 91m, G)
Disney comedy with Kurt Russell as a college student who accidentally gets zapped by a computer and then has gangsters, gamblers, and college deans fighting for his knowledge. **CO18, FA1, ST191**

Conan the Barbarian (1982, C, 129m, R)
Arnold Schwarzenegger plays Robert Howard's pulp hero in this tale of his origins and battle against Thulsa Doom (James Earl Jones). With Max von Sydow and Sandahl Bergman. John Milius directed. Ponderously silly. **AC17, AC18, ST118, ST195**

Conan the Destroyer (1984, C, 103m, PG)
Arnold Schwarzenegger returns for more sword-wielding action. Grace Jones and Wilt Chamberlain costar. **AC17, AC18, MU12, ST195**

Concert for Bangladesh, The (1972, C, 90m, G)
Documentary of 1971 rock concert in Madison Square Garden to benefit victims of famine in Asia. George Harrison (who organized) performs with Bob Dylan, Leon Russell, and Ringo Starr. **MU10,** *Recommended*

Concorde, The—Airport '79 (1979, C, 123m, PG)
Fourth *Airport* adventure has more mid-air disasters with an entirely new lineup of stars, featuring Robert Wagner, Alain Delon, Susan Blakely, Sylvia Kristel, John Davidson, and Martha Raye. **AC23**

Condorman (1981, C, 90m, PG)
A cartoonist is transformed into a superhero to help a lovely Russian spy defect. Michael Crawford, Oliver Reed, and Barbara Carrera star. Produced by the Disney studios in Britain. **AC17, FA1**

Confessions of a Peeping John (1970, C/B&W, 87m, R)
Hip comedy about a Vietnam vet (Robert De Niro) who shoots blue movies and conducts bombing raids on New York apartment buildings. With Allen Garfield, Lara Parker, Jennifer Salt, and Gerrit Graham. Directed by Brian De Palma. Originally titled *Hi, Mom!* Also known as *Blue Manhattan.* **CO2, DT36, ST51**

Confidentally Yours (1983, B&W, 110m, PG)
French comedy-mysterr about a wrong man framed for murder, while his devoted secretary (Fanny Ardant) tries to prove his innocence. Director François Truffaut's last film. Based on Charles Williams's *The Long Saturday Night.* **DT125, MY16**

Conflict (1945, B&W, 86m, NR)
Rare later career bad-guy role for Humphrey Bogart, as he plays a man out to murder his wife (Rose Hobart) so he can marry her sister (Alexis Smith). **MY3, ST15**

Conformist, The (1971, C, 115m, R)
In the 1930s, an Italian fascist is ordered to murder his former professor. Chilling, atmo-

spheric, unforgettable drama from director Bernardo Bertolucci; his breakthrough film. Jean-Louis Trintignant, Dominique Sanda, and Stefania Sandrelli star. **DT13,** *Essential, Recommended*

Connecticut Yankee, A
(1931, B&W, 78m, NR)
Will Rogers stars in this version of the Mark Twain story of time travel back to Merrie Ole England. With Maureen O'Sullivan, Myrna Loy, and Frank Albertson. **CL10, SF4, ST167, WR35**

Connecticut Yankee in King Arthur's Court, A (1949, C, 107m, NR)
Bing Crosby plays Mark Twain's resourceful hero in this musical version of the time-travel tale. With Rhonda Fleming, William Bendix, and Cedric Hardwicke. **FA3, FA9, MU8, SF4, ST40, WR35**

Conqueror, The (1956, C, 111m, NR)
John Wayne portrays the mighty warlord Genghis Khan in this adventure drama which has acquired a cult following for its unintentionally hilarious moments. With Susan Hayward, Pedro Armendariz, Agnes Moorehead, and Lee Van Cleef. Directed by Dick Powell. **AC16, CU2, ST100, ST175, ST221, ST224**

Conqueror Worm, The
(1968, C, 98m, NR)
Horror tale set in Cromwell's England about a lustful witchfinder (Vincent Price). Cult horror film directed by Michael Reeves. Edgar Allan Poe's title poem is quoted, but the story is unrelated. Gloomy, but genre fans should take a look. **CU4, HO26, ST179**

Conquest (1937, B&W, 112m, NR)
Historical drama focusing on relationship between Napoleon (Charles Boyer) and a Polish countess (Greta Garbo). **CL3, HF19, ST16, ST78**

Conquest of the Planet of the Apes
(1972, C, 87m, PG)
Fourth in the *Apes* series is a flashback story to the origin of the famed planet, and how the apes took control. Roddy McDowall stars. **FA8, SF8, SF13, SF23**

Conrack (1974, C, 107m, PG)
True story of Pat Conroy, an idealistic young Southerner who tries to give a good education to poor black children living in rural Georgia. Jon Voight stars, with Paul Winfield, Hume Cronyn, and Madge Sinclair. Directed by Martin Ritt. **DR6, DR25, DR27, DT105, ST230**

Consenting Adults (1992, C, 100m, R)
Suburban husband, encouraged by his new neighbor, has a little fling with the man's wife, become prime suspect in her murder. Kevin Kline, Mary Elizabeth Mastrantonio, Kevin Spacey, and Rebecca Miller star in this thirller, with Forest Whitaker and E.G. Marshall. Directed by Alan J. Pakula. **DT94, MY7, MY9, MY19, ST127**

Consolation Marriage
(1931, B&W, 82m, NR)
Drama of a couple who marry when their respective lovers desert them. Years later, they face a tough decision when their ex-lovers return. Pat O'Brien and Irene Dunne star, with John Halliday and Myrna Loy. **ST62, ST142**

Conspirator (1949, B&W, 85m, NR)
British-produced drama starring Elizabeth Taylor and Robert Taylor as married couple; she suspects him of being a Communist agent. With Honor Blackman and Wilfrid Hyde-White. **ST212**

Consuming Passions (1988, C, 98m, R)
Dark British comedy of a candy firm that discovers success with its new flavor—created when several workers accidentally fall into a vat of chocolate. Based on a play by Monty Python's Michael Palin and Terry Jones. Vanessa Redgrave and Jonathan Pryce star. **CO12, CO17, ST182**

Contempt (1963, C, 103m, NR)
Director Jean-Luc Godard's wry comedy about modern filmmaking, with respectable writer selling out to write a potboiler version of *The Odyssey.* Jack Palance stars, with Brigitte Bardot, Michel Piccoli, and Fritz Lang as himself. **DT50, DT70, ST6, XT26,** *Essential, Recommended*

Continental Divide (1981, C, 103m, PG)
A Chicago reporter and a Colorado ornithologist manage to find love on a disastrous hiking expedition in the Rockies. John Belushi and Blair Brown star. **CO1, CO13, XT11**

Control (1987, C, 83m, NR)
Fifteen people volunteer to be confined to a fallout shelter in an experiment. They're trapped when a real nuclear emergency occurs. Burt Lancaster stars, with Kate Nelligan and Ben Gazzara. **ST129**

Conversation, The (1974, C, 113m, PG)
Gene Hackman plays a professional surveillance man who thinks he's heard a couple plotting a murder. With John Cazale, Robert Duvall, Harrison Ford, Cindy Williams, and Frederic Forrest. Brilliantly directed by

Francis Ford Coppola on location in San Francisco. One of the greatest psychological thrillers of all time. **DR7, DT29, MY11, ST63, ST74, ST96, XT13, XT26,** *Essential, Highly Recommended*

Conversation Piece (1976, C, 122m, R)
A middle-aged professor becomes involved with a woman, her wild children, and her young lover. Burt Lancaster, Silvana Mangano, and Helmut Berger star. Directed by Luchino Visconti. **DT127, ST129**

Convicts Four (1962, B&W, 105m, NR)
Prison drama of con turned artist stars Ben Gazzara, with Stuart Whitman, Ray Walston, Vincent Price, Rod Steiger, Broderick Crawford, and Sammy Davis, Jr. **DR18, ST179**

Convoy (1978, C, 110m, R)
A big rig driver (Kris Kristofferson), accompanied by his good buddies of the road, form the world's longest truck escort. With Ali MacGraw and Ernest Borgnine. Directed by Sam Peckinpah. **AC10, DT95, MU12, XT18**

Coogan's Bluff (1968, C, 100m, R)
A modern-day sheriff pursues his quarry from the West to the streets of New York. Clint Eastwood stars, with Don Stroud and Susan Clark. Directed by Don Siegel with his customary verve for action dramas. **AC9, DT116, ST64, WE12, XT9,** *Recommended*

Cook, The Thief, His Wife and Her Lover, The (1990, C, 120m, NR)
Controversial British drama from director Peter Greenaway, set in and around a swanky French restuarant. Violent, sexually explicit; perhaps the ultimate Love It or Hate It film. The title roles are played by Richard Bohringer, Michael Gambon, Helen Mirren, and Alan Howard. Widescreen photography by Sacha Vierney can only be appreciated in letterboxed version. Also available in an "R"-rated version; running time: 98 minutes. If you're going to check it out, see only the letterboxed original. **CU6, CU7, CU19, DR1, DR23, DT51,** *Recommended*

Cookie (1989, C, 93m, R)
Comedy of mobster released from prison, reuniting with his street-smart daughter. Peter Falk and Emily Lloyd star, with Dianne Wiest, Brenda Vacarro, Michael V. Gazzo, and Jerry Lewis. Directed by Susan Seidelman. **CO5, CO10, ST139**

Cool and the Crazy, The
(1958, B&W, 78m, NR)
1950s version of *Reefer Madness*, with high school kids "turned on" to marijuana, suffering dire consequences. **CU2**

Cool Hand Luke (1967, C, 126m, NR)
A rebellious prisoner on a Southern chain gang becomes a folk hero to his fellow cons. Paul Newman stars, with Oscar winner George Kennedy, Strother Martin, Harry Dean Stanton, Wayne Rogers, Clifton James, Joe Don Baker, Ralph Waite, Dennis Hopper, J.D. Cannon, and Jo Van Fleet. Widescreen will be lost on video. First-rate star vehicle for Newman in his Loner Rebel phase. **CU20, DR18, ST110, ST162, ST205,** *Highly Recommended*

Cool World (1992, C, 102m, PG-13)
Ex-con turns to cartooning, suddenly finds himself pulled into the crime-packed world he has created. Combination of live action and animation stars Gabriel Byrne, with Kim Basinger as cartoon figure Holli Would, who wants to "get real," and Brad Pitt as a flesh and blood detective trapped in the world since the 1940s. Directed by Ralph Bakshi. **DR27**

Cooley High (1975, C, 107m, PG)
Nostalgic comedy set in 1964 Chicago detailing life at an inner-city high school. Glynn Turman stars, with Garrett Morris, Lawrence Hilton-Jacobs, and Cynthia Davis. Lots of Motown music on soundtrack. Basis for TV sitcom, "What's Happening!!" **CO4, CO6, CO18, DR14, XT11**

Cop (1987, C, 110m, R)
James Woods plays a policeman at the breaking point in this intense drama, costarring Lesley Ann Warren, Charles Durning, and Charles Haid. **DR16, ST233**

Copacabana (1947, B&W, 92m, NR)
Comedy about the mix-ups that occur at a famous New York nightclub when a girl applies for two different jobs. Groucho Marx and Carmen Miranda costar (their only film together), with journalists Abel Green and Earl Wilson. **ST152**

Coquette (1929, B&W, 78m, NR)
Early sound melodrama starring Oscar winner Mary Pickford as a Southern belle who falls for a man her father won't accept. With John Mack Brown, Matt Moore, and John Sainpolis. **XT3**

Corn Is Green, The (1945, B&W, 114m, NR)
Bette Davis plays a middle-aged teacher who devotes much of her time and attention to one of her star pupils. **CU18, DR25, ST44**

Corn Is Green, The (1979, C, 100m, NR)
Remake of the 1945 film about an unmarried teacher in a Welsh mining town reunites Katharine Hepburn with one of her favorite directors, George Cukor. With Ian Saynor,

Bill Fraser, and Anna Massey. Originally made for TV. **CU18, DT32, ST103**

Cornbread, Earl and Me
(1975, C, 95m, R)
A black youth's idolization of a neighborhood basketball star is shattered when the older boy is accidentally shot by a policeman. Moses Gunn, Bernie Casey, Rosalind Cash, and Keith (Jamal) Wilkes star. **DR14, DR15**

Cornered (1945, B&W, 102m, NR)
Thriller staring Dick Powell, who's on a manhunt in Buenos Aires chasing his wife's killer. Directed by Edward Dmytryk. **MY1, MY6, ST175**

Coroner Creek (1948, C, 93m, NR)
Randolph Scott Western has him seeking revenge for the murder of his fiancée. **ST197, WE5**

Corpse Vanishes, The
(1942, B&W, 64m, NR)
A scientist kidnaps young women to use in his rejuvenation serum for his elderly wife. Bela Lugosi stars. **ST143**

Corridors of Blood (1958, B&W, 86m, NR)
A nineteenth-century doctor experiments with a way to anesthetize patients, becomes addicted to one of the drugs he tries, and resorts to robbing graves to maintain his experiments. Boris Karloff stars, with Christopher Lee. **ST119, ST135**

Corrupt (1983, C, 99m, PG)
A New York cop (Harvey Keitel) finds himself immersed in illegal activities in order to catch a killer. Rock singer John Lydon costars, with Nicole Garcia and Sylvia Sidney. **MU12**

Corsican Brothers, The
(1941, B&W, 112m, NR)
Classic swashbuckler, based on the Dumas tale of separated twins. Douglas Fairbanks, Jr., stars. **CL13**

Cotter (1973, C, 94m, NR)
An Indian rodeo clown returns to his small town to pick up the pieces of his life after a tragic accident. Don Murray stars, with Rip Torn, Carol Lynley, and Sherry Jackson. **ST216, WE12**

Cotton Club, The (1984, C, 127m, R)
Colorful tale set in and around Harlem's famed night spot, where gangsters and movie stars mingled to watch the likes of Duke Ellington and Cab Calloway perform. Richard Gere, Diane Lane, Gregory Hines, Bob Hoskins, Fred Gwynne, and James Remar head the cast. Directed by Francis Ford Coppola. Lots of fringe benefits, but the two

leads are stiff and unappealing. **AC22, DR5, DR14, DR15, DT29, ST23, ST84, ST111**

Couch Trip, The (1988, C, 97m, R)
Dan Aykroyd stars in this comedy about an escaped mental patient who takes over the radio call-in show of a vacationing therapist. Charles Grodin, Walter Matthau, and Donna Dixon costar. **CO13, CO20, ST94, ST155**

Count Dracula (1970, C, 98m, R)
Christopher Lee plays the vampire with an eye for ladies' necks. Klaus Kinski costars. **HF7, HO5, ST126, ST135**

Count Dracula and His Vampire Bride
(1973, C, 84m, R)
British horror drama about the greatest vampire of them all, set in modern times starring Christopher Lee and Peter Cushing. The finale in Hammer Studios' series of scary films. Original running time: 87 minutes. Also known as *Satanic Rites of Dracula*. **HF7, HO5, HO26, ST43, ST135**

Count of the Old Town, The
(1934, B&W, 90m, NR)
Swedish film with young Ingrid Bergman is set in small town trying to deal with gang of smugglers. **ST13**

Count Yorga, Vampire (1970, 91m, PG)
A vampire in modern Los Angeles holds seances as a way of attracting women into his lair. Robert Quarry stars. **HO5**

Countdown (1968, C, 101m, NR)
Drama centering on the approaching launch of a manned satellite, starring Robert Duvall and James Caan. Directed by Robert Altman. **DT4, ST63**

Counterfeit Traitor, The
(1962, C, 140m, NR)
William Holden stars in this true story of a World War II double agent. With Lilli Palmer and Hugh Griffith. **AC1, ST106**

Country (1984, C, 109m, PG)
An embattled farm couple struggles to hold on to their land against overwhelming economic pressures. Jessica Lange and Sam Shepard star. **DR7, DR8, ST130**

Country Girl, The (1954, B&W, 104m, NR)
Drama of aging alcoholic singer trying for a comeback. Bing Crosby and Oscar winner Grace Kelly star; William Holden plays a director with a professional interest in Crosby and a personal one in Grace. **CL7, ST40, ST106, ST124, XT3**

Country Girl, The (1982, C, 137m, NR)
Remake of the 1954 drama of an aging alcoholic actor (Dick Van Dyke), his younger wife

(Faye Dunaway), and their director friend (Ken Howard). Originally made for TV. **CU18, DR12, ST61**

Country Music with the Muppets
(1985, C, 55m, NR)
Compilation of favorite country music highlights from "The Muppet Show" features Johnny Cash, Roy Clark, Crystal Gayle, and Roger Miller. **FA14**

Coup de Grace (1976, C, 96m, NR)
German drama of a countess pining for the love of a no-good military officer. Margarethe von Trotta stars; her husband, Volker Schlondorff, directed. **FF3**

Coup de Torchon see *Clean Slate*

Coupe de Ville (1990, C, 99m, PG-13)
Road comedy set in the early 1960s, involving three brothers who drive a 1954 powder-blue Cadillac convertible from Detroit to their father's home in Florida. Patrick Dempsey, Arye Gross, and Daniel Stern star, with Annabeth Gish, Rita Taggert, and Alan Arkin. **CO5, CO6, XT18**

Courage (1986, C, 141m, NR)
In this true-life drama, Sophia Loren plays an American housewife who becomes a drug agent after she discovers that her own son is an addict. Billy Dee Williams costars. Originally made for TV. **DR6, DR10, ST141, ST227**

Courage Mountain (1989, C, 98m, PG)
Updating of classic children's tale *Heidi* has Swiss teen-ager sent off to boarding school at the outbreak of World War I. Juliette Caton stars, with Charlie Sheen, Leslie Caron, and Joanna Clarke. **FA4, FA15**

Courage of Lassie (1946, C, 92m, NR)
Change-of-pace role for the famed collie, who plays a World War II killer dog. Fortunately, there's a patient and loving girl (Elizabeth Taylor) around to retrain him. With Frank Morgan and Tom Drake. **FA5, ST212**

Courageous Mr. Penn
(1941, B&W, 79m, NR)
British-made biography of William Penn, focusing on his religious freedom trial and founding of the Pennsylvania colony. Clifford Evans and Deborah Kerr star. **CL2, DR23, ST125**

Court Jester, The (1956, C, 101m, NR)
Danny Kaye impersonates a clown; soon the joke's on him when a band of outlaws ask him to dethrone their nasty king. With Glynis Johns, Basil Rathbone, and Angela Lansbury. **CL10, ST120, ST131**

Court-Martial of Billy Mitchell, The
(1955, C, 100m, NR)
Gary Cooper stars as the Army officer whose obstreperous ways landed him in trouble with the brass in 1925. Charles Bickford, Ralph Bellamy, and Rod Steiger costar. Directed by Otto Preminger. **DR17, DT100, ST37**

Courtship of Eddie's Father, The
(1963, C, 117m, NR)
Glenn Ford plays a widower, the object of several young women's attentions. With Ronny Howard, Shirley Jones, Stella Stevens, and Dina Merrill. Directed by Vincente Minnelli. **DT58, DT88, FA6**

Cousin Bobby (1992, C, 70m, NR)
Director Jonathan Demme's documentary portrait of his relative, Robert Castle, a socially conscious Episcopal priest working some of New York's meanest streest. **CU16, DT35**

Cousin, Cousine (1975, C, 95m, R)
French comedy about an affair between two people who have become cousins by marriage. Marie-Christine Barrault and Victor Lanoux star. American remake: *Cousins*. **FF1, FF8, XT20**

Cousins (1989, C, 110m, R)
American remake of French romantic comedy *Cousin, Cousine*, with married man and woman falling in love at a wedding which is about to make them cousins. Ted Danson and Isabella Rossellini star, with William Petersen, Sean Young, Lloyd Bridges, Keith Coogan, and Norma Aleandro. Directed by Joel Schumacher. Refreshing take on well-worn material. **CO1, FF8, XT20,** *Recommended*

Cover Girl (1944, C, 107m, NR)
Colorful musical starring Rita Hayworth as the title character, an overnight success, romanced by Gene Kelly. With Phil Silvers and Eve Arden. **CL9, ST101, ST123**

Covered Wagon, The
(1923, B&W, 60m, NR)
Silent Western epic, directed by James Cruze, with pioneers making their way across the frontier. J. Warren Kerrigan stars, with Lois Wilson and Alan Hale. **CL12, WE1**

Cow Town (1950, B&W, 70m, NR)
Gene Autry's homesick on the range when ranchers take stake in their land with a fence war to protect it from cattle rustlers. **ST5**

Cowboy and the Ballerina, The
(1984, C, 96m, NR)
Aging cowhand and dancer defecting from a

touring Russian company fall in love. Lee Majors and Leslie Wing star, with Christopher Lloyd and Anjelica Huston. Originally made for TV. **ST115**

Cowboy and the Lady, The
(1938, B&W, 91m, NR)
Gary Cooper and Merle Oberon play the title roles, a rodeo rider and an aristocrat, in this romantic comedy. With Patsy Kelly, Walter Brennan, and Fuzzy Knight. **ST37, WE12**

Cowboy and the Senorita, The
(1944, B&W, 56m, NR)
Roy Rogers finds a missing girl and wins the love of her cousin (Dale Evans). **ST188**

Cowboys, The (1972, C, 128m, PG)
A veteran cattleman is forced to employ a group of young boys on his four-hundred-mile cattle drive. John Wayne stars, with Bruce Dern as a dastardly villain. **ST224, WE5**

Crack see *Strike Force*

Crackers (1984, C, 92m, PG)
Comic heist film with gang of misfits led by Donald Sutherland: Jack Warden, Sean Penn, Wallace Shawn, Trinidad Silva, Larry Riley. Directed by Louis Malle. Despite all that talent, it doesn't come off. **CO10, DT82, MY18**

Cracking Up (1983, C, 83m, PG)
Jerry Lewis comedy, a series of skits revolving around stories told by a suicidal patient to his shrink. With Herb Edelman, Dick Butkus, Sammy Davis, Jr., and Foster Brooks. Directed by Lewis; originally titled *Smorgasbord*. **ST139**

Cradle Will Fall, The (1983, C, 100m, NR)
Thriller about a desperate woman (Lauren Hutton) who can't convince her family and friends that she witnessed a murder. Ben Murphy and James Farentino costar. Originally made for TV. **MY3**

Craig's Wife (1936, B&W, 75m, NR)
Rosalind Russell plays a material girl who loves her possessions more than her man (John Boles). **CL5, ST192**

Crashout (1955, B&W, 90m, NR)
Prison drama of an escape attempt, starring William Bendix, Arthur Kennedy, Luther Adler, and William Talman. **DR18**

Crawling Eye, The (1958, B&W, 85m, NR)
A small town in the Swiss Alps is plagued by an immobile cloud and a series of gruesome murders. A psychic discovers that the cloud is an alien invader that resembles a large eye. **SF1, SF9**

Crawlspace (1986, C, 82m, R)
A landlord spies on his female tenants from an elaborate network in the ceilings of their apartments. Klaus Kinski stars in this horror drama. **ST126**

Crazies, The (1973, C, 103m, R)
A strange plague transforms and controls the inhabitants of a small town. Directed by George Romero. **DT108, HO21**

Crazy for Love (1952, B&W, 80m, NR)
French comedy about a village idiot who can inherit the town's inn if he earns a diploma within a year. Brigitte Bardot, Bourvil, and Janie Marken star. **ST6**

Crazy From the Heart (1991, C, 94m, NR)
Romantic drama about small Texas town principal (Christine Lahti) taking up with Mexican-American handyman (Rubén Blades). Originally made for cable TV. **DR1, DR26, MU12**

Crazy in Love (1992, C, 93m, NR)
Drama of three generations of women living on an island in Washington's Puget Sound, focusing on young married filmmaker (Holly Hunter) and her flirtation with a British photographer (Julian Sands). With Gena Rowlands, Frances McDormand, Bill Pullman, and Herta Ware. Directed by Martha Coolidge. Originally made for cable TV. Good observations about family interaction, but Hunter's character is irritatingly immature. **DR1, DR10, ST113**

Crazy Mama (1975, C, 82m, R)
Comic crime saga, set in the 1950s, about a grandmother, mother, and daughter as they wend their way from California to Arkansas. Ann Sothern, Cloris Leachman, and Linda Purl star. Directed by Jonathan Demme. **CO10, DT35, XT18**

Crazy People (1990, C, 90m, R)
Comedy of an ad man (Dudley Moore) who suggests telling the truth to customers and winds up in an asylum. With Daryl Hannah, Paul Reiser, and Mercedes Ruehl. Directed by Tony Bill. **CO2, ST160, XT23**

Crazy Ray, The (1923, B&W, 60m, NR)
Silent comedy from French director René Clair, about a scientist's experiment that paralyzes virtually all of Paris. Also available on this tape: *Entr'acte*, Clair's 1924 surrealistic short film. **DT25, FF1**

Creation of the Humanoids
(1962, C, 78m, NR)
In a post–World War III world, robots that thrive on human blood perform menial tasks, and a security officer discovers that his sister has fallen in love with one. **SF12**

Creator (1985, C, 108m, R)
Peter O'Toole stars in this comedy-drama
about a scientist who preserves some of his
late wife's tissue in the hopes that he can re-
create her in his laboratory. With Mariel
Hemingway, Vincent Spano, and Virginia
Madsen; Ivan Passer directed. Agreeably
charming; O'Toole's delightful. **CO2, ST169**

Creature (1985, C, 97m, R)
Science fiction horror drama about an expedition to one of Saturn's moons making a
gruesome and deadly discovery. Stan Ivar and
Klaus Kinski star. **SF20, ST126**

Creature from Black Lake
(1976, C, 97m, PG)
Two men come across Bigfoot in a Louisiana
swamp. Jack Elam stars. **HO16**

Creature From the Black Lagoon
(1954, B&W, 79m, NR)
Trip to Amazon results in find of Gill-Man
who lives underwater. Classic 1950s science
fiction starring Richard Carlson, Julia Adams,
Richard Denning, and Ricou Browning as the
Creature. The kids will love it; adults may
find it either amusing or stupid. **SF1, SF10,
SF13**

Creature from the Haunted Sea
(1961, B&W, 72m, NR)
A gangster aboard a boat fakes a story about
a sea monster killing off his companions—
only to discover that he's unwittingly telling
the truth. Anthony Carbone and Edward
Wain (writer Robert Towne) star; Roger Corman directed. **DT30**

Creepers (1985, C, 82m, R)
A psychopath stalks a young girl who can
communicate with insects via telepathy.
Donald Pleasence and Jennifer Connelly star.
Directed by Dario Argento. **HO7, HO16**

Creeping Flesh, The (1972, C, 91m, PG)
A scientist injects his daughter with an
experimental serum which turns out to be
the essence of evil. Peter Cushing and Christopher Lee star. **HO26, ST43, ST135**

Creeping Terror, The
(1964, B&W, 75m, NR)
Legendarily awful monster movie, with no
dialogue, about a creepy, carpet-like creature.
Directed by Art J. Nelson, who also stars
under the name Vic Savage. **CU11**

Creepshow (1982, C, 120m, R)
Five tales of revenge by Stephen King filmed
in the style of the old E.C. comic books. Hal
Holbrook, Adrienne Barbeau, Leslie Nielsen,
Ted Danson, and King star. Directed by
George Romero. **DT108, HO23, WR15**

Creepshow 2 (1987, C, 89m, R)
George Romero adapted three Stephen King
short stories for this sequel to *Creepshow*. Lois
Chiles and George Kennedy are among the
stars. **DT108, HO23, WR15**

Cries and Whispers (1972, C, 106m, R)
Stunning drama from Ingmar Bergman about
four women: three sisters (one of whom is
dying) and their servant. Harriet Andersson,
Liv Ullmann, Ingrid Thulin, and Kari Sylwan
star. Oscar-winning photography by Sven
Nykvist. Accessible, moving summation of
many Bergman concerns from late 1960s to
early 1970s. He should have won the Oscar.
DR10, DT11, ST220, XT28, XT30, *Essential, Recommended*

Crime of Monsieur Lange, The
(1936, B&W, 90m, NR)
Employees of publishing house take over
business after their wicked boss disappears.
French drama stars Rene Lefevre and Jules
Berry. Directed by Jean Renoir. Afflicted with
wobbling tone, but worth checking out for
fans of director. **DT104**

Crime Zone (1988, C, 92m, R)
Futuristic crime saga of a fugitive couple
from the wrong "caste" and their mentor,
starring David Carradine, Peter Nelson, and
Sherilyn Fenn. **SF17**

Crimes and Misdemeanors
(1989, C, 107m, PG-13)
Woody Allen's twofold story of a prominent
physician (Martin Landau) becoming
involved with murder-for-hire, and a documentary filmmaker (Allen) hired to record
the life of his obnoxiously successful brother-
in-law (Alan Alda). With Mia Farrow, Jerry
Orbach, Anjelica Huston, Sam Waterston,
and Claire Bloom. Because of its structure,
conclusive proof that Woody's comic gifts
(the Allen/Alda story) far outweigh his talent
for dramatic narrative (the Landau/Waterston
story). **CO8, DR8, DT2, ST65, ST115,
XT30**

Crimes of Passion (1984, C, 101m, R)
Successful businesswoman moonlights as a
prostitute, runs into trouble from a crazed
preacher. Kathleen Turner and Anthony
Perkins star. Ken Russell directed. An unrated
version of the film is also available, containing more explicit sexual material; running
time: 107 minutes. Russell's taste for bombast
overwhelms a good turn by the lead. **CU6,
CU10, DR3, DT111, ST218**

Crimes of the Heart
(1986, C, 105m, PG-13)
A trio of Southern sisters (Diane Keaton,

Sissy Spacek, and Jessica Lange) muddle through life in this adaptation of Beth Henley's play. With Sam Shepard and Tess Harper. Directed by Bruce Beresford. **CO5, DR10, DR20, DT10, ST121, ST130, ST202**

Criminal Code, The (1931, B&W, 98m, NR) Director Howard Hawks presents the story of a young man convicted of manslaughter and sent off to prison. Walter Huston, Phillips Holmes, Boris Karloff, and Constance Cummings star. Probably the first great prison drama; Huston is especially good as the warden with a heart. **DR18, DT53, ST119,** *Recommended*

Criminal Court (1946, B&W, 63m, NR) A lawyer involved in a murder trial knows the defendant is innocent—because he committed the crime. Robert Wise directed this thriller starring Tom Conway. NOTE: Packaged on videocassette with *The Saint Strikes Back.* **DT140, MY7**

Criminal Law (1989, C, 113m, R) After a young attorney successfully defends his client on a murder charge, he begins to suspect that the man really is a killer. Gary Oldman and Kevin Bacon star. **DR16, DR17, MY9, MY13**

Criminal Life of Archibaldo de la Cruz, The (1955, B&W, 91m, NR) Offbeat drama from director Luis Buñuel of a man fascinated by death as a result of a childhood trauma. Also known as *Ensayo de un Crimen (Rehearsal of a Murder).* **DT19**

Crimson Pirate, The (1952, C, 104m, NR) Exhilarating pirate classic, with Burt Lancaster and former fellow acrobat Nick Cravat swinging, climbing, and somersaulting their way across the Mediterranean. With Christopher Lee. **AC13, FA4, ST129, ST135,** *Essential, Highly Recommended*

Crimson Romance (1934, B&W, 72m, NR) World War I drama of American pilot involved with the German military because of loyalty to his best friend. Ben Lyon and Erich von Stroheim star. **AC2, DT129**

Crisis at Central High (1981, C, 125m, NR) Fact-based drama of 1957 integration of Little Rock high school, the focus of national attention for weeks. Joanne Woodward plays a real-life teacher whose journal was the inspiration for the screenplay written by Richard Levinson and William Link. With Charles Durning and Henderson Forsythe. Originally made for TV. **DR5, DR25, ST234**

Criss Cross (1949, B&W, 87m, NR) Moody thriller about an armored car heist, with Burt Lancaster as a loser whose fatal flaw is his devotion to his deceitful ex-wife (Yvonne de Carlo). **MY1, MY18, ST129,** *Recommended*

Criss Cross (1992, C, 100m, R) Goldie Hawn plays a single mom in this drama set in 1967 Key West about her struggles to raise a rebellious twelve-year-old son. With Arliss Howard, James Gammon, David Arnott, Steve Buscemi, and David Carradine as Goldie's ex. Directed by Chris Menges, best known as a cinematographer on *The Killing Fields* and other films. **DR8, DR9, ST99**

Critical Condition (1987, C, 99m, R) A convict in the hospital for treatment finds himself mistaken for a doctor during a power failure. Richard Pryor stars in this comedy, with Rachel Ticotin, Rubén Blades, and Garrett Morris. **CO13, CO20, MU12, ST180**

Critters (1986, C, 86m, PG-13) Hairy little aliens crash-land in Kansas and proceed to eat all the humans they can. A little boy and two intergalactic hunters try to save the day. Dee Wallace Stone and Scott Grimes star. **HO16, HO24**

Critters 2: The Main Course (1988, C, 87m, PG-13) More chompin' by those furry little demons from outer space. Scott Grimes and Liane Curtis try to stay out of the sauce. **HO16, HO24**

Crocodile Dundee (1986, C, 98m, PG-13) Romantic comedy with an international twist: an American journalist travels to Australia to interview a rough-and-tumble bush guide. He then comes to New York and learns how to "survive" in the urban jungle. Paul Hogan and Linda Kozlowski star. Hogan's signature role is all that distinguishes this. **CO1, CO9, CO20, FF5, XT9**

Crocodile Dundee II (1988, C, 110m, PG) Sequel to the romantic comedy about an Australian bush guide (Paul Hogan) and his American sweetheart (Linda Kozlowski). This time, the couple's adventures begin in New York and continue Down Under. **CO1, CO9, CO20, FF5, XT9**

Cromwell (1970, C, 145m, G) Richard Harris plays the British rebel soldier in this historical epic, with Alec Guinness, Robert Morley, Frank Finlay, and Timothy Dalton. **DR5, ST95**

Crooked Hearts (1991, C, 105m, NR) Drama of family troubled by father's infidelity, rebellious older son. Peter Coyote and

Vincent D'Onofrio star, with Jennifer Jason Leigh, Cindy Pickett, Noah Wyle, and Juliette Lewis. Adapted from Robert Boswell's novel. **DR8, DR19, ST136**

Crooks and Coronets (1969, C, 106m, PG)
Telly Savalas and Warren Oates are con artists at work on an elderly English lady (Edith Evans) in this comedy. Also known as *Sophie's Place.* **ST166**

Cross Creek (1983, C, 122m, PG)
True story of author Marjorie Kinan Rawlings, who abandoned Long Island society in the 1920s to homestead in a Florida swamp and become a writer. Mary Steenburgen stars, with fine support from Rip Torn, Alfre Woodard, Dana Hill, and as Maxwell Perkins, Malcolm McDowell. Directed by Martin Ritt. **DR4, DT105, ST216**

Cross My Heart (1987, C, 90m, R)
Comic chronicle of a modern couple's "crucial" third date, starring Martin Short and Annette O'Toole. **CO1, CO14**

Cross of Iron (1977, C, 119m, R)
Director Sam Peckinpah's drama follows the lives of German officers (James Coburn and Maximilian Schell) amidst World War II. With James Mason. Recommended only for fans of director or genre; others may find it numbingly downbeat. **AC1, DT95, ST153**

Crossed Swords see *Prince and the Pauper, The* (1978)

Crossfire (1947, B&W, 86m, NR)
One of the first postwar films to explore the issue of bigotry. A Jewish man is beaten to death, and three soldiers are held for questioning. Robert Young stars, with Robert Mitchum and Robert Ryan. Directed by Edward Dmytryk. Terrific blend of suspense and social comment. Ryan should have won a Supporting Actor Oscar. **CL8, MY1, ST158, ST193, XT28,** *Recommended*

Crossing Delancey (1988, C, 97m, PG)
A New York woman finds herself the object of an arranged courtship in this engaging romantic comedy-drama starring Amy Irving and Peter Riegert, with Reizl Bozyk, Jeroen Krabbe, and Sylvia Miles. **CO1, DR10, DR15, XT9,** *Recommended*

Crossover Dreams (1985, C, 86m, NR)
Musical drama about a salsa singing star (Rubén Blades) who gets a swelled head over his forthcoming album. **MU4**

Crossroads (1986, C, 100m, R)
Young guitar player journeys the Mississippi back roads in search of someone to teach him authentic blues licks. Ralph Macchio

and Joe Seneca star. Walter Hill directed; music by Ry Cooder. **DR12, DT56**

Crowd, The (1928, B&W, 104m, NR)
Classic silent drama from director King Vidor about the triumphs and tragedies of an "ordinary" couple living in New York. Eleanor Boardman and James Murray star. **CL8, CL12, DT126, XT9,** *Essential, Highly Recommended*

Crucible of Horror (1971, C, 91m, PG)
A man murdered by a member of his family comes back to haunt them. **HO14**

Cruel Sea, The (1953, B&W, 121m, NR)
British World War II drama set aboard a warship. Jack Hawkins stars, with Donald Sinden, Denholm Elliott, and Stanley Baker. **AC1, DR23**

Cruising (1980, C, 106m, R)
A New York cop goes undercover to solve a series of murders in the gay community. Al Pacino stars. Directed by William Friedkin. **DR16, ST170**

Crusoe (1989, C, 95m, PG-13)
The classic adventure tale of a marooned man, this time portrayed as an American slave trader (Aidan Quinn). Written by Walon Green; directed by Caleb Deschanel. A sleeper worth checking out. **AC12, AC24,** *Recommended*

Cry-Baby (1990, C, 85m, PG-13)
Early 1950s Baltimore is the setting for this affectionate send-up of teen movies, directed by John Waters. Johnny Depp and Amy Locane star, with Susan Tyrrell, Polly Bergen, Iggy Pop, Ricki Lake, Traci Lords, David Nelson, Joey Heatherton, and Mink Stole. **CO6, CO7, DT132, MU12**

Cry Blood, Apache (1970, C, 82m, R)
Western drama about a group of prospectors who kill a band of Indians; the lone survivor, a young girl, promises to lead them to a gold strike. Jody McCrea, Dan Kemp, and Jack Starrett star; Joel McCrea (Jody's real-life dad) appears in a small role. **ST144, XT8**

Cry Danger (1951, B&W, 79m, NR)
Wrong-man thriller stars Dick Powell as Rocky, framed for murder and robbery, sent to prison, now trying to prove his innocence. With Rhonda Fleming and William Conrad. **MY1, MY7, ST175**

Cry Freedom (1987, C, 157m, PG)
True drama of South African activist Steven Biko and his friendship with white reporter Donald Woods, who smuggled the story of Biko's torture and death to the outside world. Denzel Washington and Kevin Kline star.

Richard Attenborough directed. **DR6, DR14, ST127, ST223, XT23**

Cry in the Dark, A (1988, C, 120m, PG-13)
Fact-based drama about the sensational case of Australian Lindy Chamberlain, a mother accused of murdering her infant baby (whom she claimed was carried off by a wild dog). Meryl Streep and Sam Neill star. Directed by Fred Schepisi. Widesceen will be lost on video. Streep is terrific, and the film effectively dramatizes how public perception of an issue becomes reality. **CU20, DR6, DR17, FF5, ST210,** *Recommended*

Cry of the Banshee (1970, C, 87m, PG)
A witch and a satanist seek revenge against a nobleman who is on a witch hunt. Vincent Price stars. **ST179**

Cry, the Beloved Country
(1951, B&W, 100m, NR)
British-produced version of the Alan Paton novel of life under South Africa's apartheid policy. A black minister travels to the city to find his son, now a criminal. Canada Lee stars, with Charles Carson, Sidney Poitier, and Geoffrey Keen. Directed by Zoltan Korda. Original running time: 111 minutes. **DR7, DR14, DR19, DR23, ST174**

Crying Game, The (1992, C, 113m, R)
Original, absorbing British thriller about an IRA operative (Stephen Rea) who gets more than he bargained for when he makes a promise to a kidnapped British soldier. With Miranda Richardson, Forest Whitaker, and the bewitching Jaye Davidson. Written and directed by Neil Jordan, who won an Oscar for his screenplay. If you still don't know the plot twist in this one-of-a-kind film, count yourself lucky—and rent this as soon as you can. **DR1, DR3, DR16, DR23, XT26,** *Highly Recommended*

Cuba (1979, C, 121m, PG)
Love story set against the downfall of dictator Batista and rise of Castro, starring Sean Connery and Brooke Adams. Directed by Richard Lester. Underrated drama about little-examined time and place. **DT74, ST36,** *Recommended*

Cuban Rebel Girls see *Assault of the Rebel Girls*

Cujo (1983, C, 91m, R)
Stephen King story about a woman and her son who are terrorized by a rabid dog. Dee Wallace stars. **HO16, WR15**

Culpepper Cattle Company, The
(1972, C, 92m, PG)
A Western cult favorite about a sixteen-year-

old boy who quickly becomes a man when he joins a cattle drive through violent post–Civil War Texas. Gary Grimes stars, with Billy "Green" Bush, Luke Askew, and Bo Hopkins. **WE15**

Curly Sue (1991, C, 101m, PG)
James Belushi and Alisan Porter are a pair of con artists who work their way into the cushy apartment of a sympathetic lady lawyer (Kelly Lynch). Sentimental comedy was written, produced, and directed by John Hughes. **CO10, CO13, DR2, DT59**

Curly Top (1935, B&W, 75m, NR)
Shirley Temple classic finds the greatest child star of them all playing matchmaker and singing "Animal Crackers in My Soup." **ST213**

Curse, The (1987, C, 90m, PG-13)
A meteorite lands on a farm in Tennessee, and soon everyone in the family, except the young son, is acting strangely. Wil Wheaton and John Schneider star. **HO14, HO21**

Curse of Frankenstein, The
(1957, C, 83m, NR)
The first horror film from Britain's Hammer Studios, about Mary Shelley's doctor who becomes obsessed by his experiments and his creation. Peter Cushing, Christopher Lee, and Hazel Court star. **HF10, HO20, HO26, ST43, ST135**

Curse of the Cat People, The
(1944, B&W, 70m, NR)
A lonely little girl is befriended by the ghost of her father's first wife in this sequel to *Cat People*. Produced by Val Lewton; codirected by Robert Wise. **DT140, HO2, HO14, HO27**

Curse of the Demon (1958, B&W, 95m, NR)
An American professor (Dana Andrews) comes face to face with the dark side of the occult when he tries to solve the mysterious death of a colleague. Directed by Jacques Tourneur. **DT124, HO1, HO11, HO19**

Curse of the Living Dead see *Kill, Baby, Kill*

Curse of the Pink Panther
(1983, C, 109m, PG)
The final *Pink Panther* film, made after Peter Sellers's death, with Ted Wass playing Inspector Clouseau. Cameo appearances by Panther alumni David Niven, Herbert Lom, Bert Kwouk, and Capucine. Directed by Blake Edwards. **CO10, DT40**

Curse of the Werewolf, The
(1961, C, 91m, NR)
A servant girl is raped and eventually gives birth to a son who, when he reaches adult-

hood, discovers that strange things happen to him when the moon is full. Oliver Reed stars in this British horror film. **HO4, HO26**

Cut and Run (1985, C, 87m, R)
A pair of ambitious reporters stumble onto a big scoop when they travel to South America in search of an evil disciple of Jim Jones. Lisa Blount, Willie Aames, and Karen Black star. **AC24**

Cutter's Way (1981, C, 105m, R)
In Santa Barbara, California, a cynical, crippled Vietnam vet (John Heard), his alcoholic girlfriend (Lisa Eichorn), and their beach bum pal (Jeff Bridges) set out to prove that a local pillar of society is involved in a sordid murder case. Directed by Ivan Passer; written by Jeffrey Alan Fiskin. Superbly captures the ripe rot of a wealthy community and its darker side. **DR7, MY2, ST19,** *Recommended*

Cutting Edge, The (1992, C, 101m, PG)
Romantic comedy about an Olympic hopeful, a figure skater (Moira Kelly) forced to take on a new partner, a brash hockey player (D.B. Sweeney). With Roy Dotrice and Terry O'Quinn. Directed by Paul Michael Glaser. **CO1, CO19, XT23**

Cyborg (1989, C, 86m, R)
Martial arts star Jean Claude Van Damme plays the title role in this post-apocalyptic tale of revenge. **AC24, AC26, SF12**

Cyclops, The (1957, B&W, 75m, NR)
An expedition discovers the man they are searching for has been transformed into a monster by a radiation blast. Gloria Talbott, Lon Chaney, Jr., and Tom Drake star. Directed by Bert I. Gordon. **HO21, ST27**

Cyrano de Bergerac
(1950, B&W, 112m, NR)
José Ferrer won an Oscar for his portrayal of the long-nosed romantic of Edmond Rostand's play. **DR20, XT2**

Cyrano de Bergerac (1990, C, 138m, PG)
Gérard Depardieu plays the soldier-poet with a nose the size of Florida. With Anne Brochet. Dialogue in French; English subtitles by Anthony Burgess. **DR20, FF1, ST52**

D.A.R.Y.L. (1985, C, 99m, PG)
A young boy (Barret Oliver) baffles his parents because he is too "perfect." He soon becomes the most popular kid around—wanted even by the government. Michael McKean and Mary Beth Hurt costar. **DR9, FA7, FA15**

D.C. Cab (1983, C, 99m, R)
Amiable comedy about a wacked-out collection of cabbies cruising the streets of Our Nation's Capital. Adam Baldwin stars, with Max Gail, Gary Busey, Mr. T, and Irene Cara. **CO2, XT12**

D-Day the Sixth of June
(1956, C, 106m, NR)
Dramatic recreation of the Normandy invasion, starring Robert Taylor and Richard Todd as, respectively, American and British officers. **AC1**

D.O.A. (1949, B&W, 83m, NR)
A man is given poison—he has a few days to find his killer. Edmond O'Brien stars in this classic thriller. **MY1**

D.O.A. (1988, C, 100m, R)
Remake of the *film noir* classic, with Dennis Quaid as the poisoning victim trying to track down his killer. Meg Ryan costars. **CU18, MY2**

D.W. Griffith Triple Feature
(1913, B&W, 50m, NR)
A trio of short films from the movies' first great director: *The Battle of Elderbush Gulch, Iola's Promise,* and *The Goddess of Sagebrush Gulch.* Lillian Gish, Mary Pickford, and Mae Marsh are among the stars. **DT52, ST87**

Da (1988, C, 102m, G)
An Irish-American playwright returns to his homeland when his father dies. The old man's ghost confronts his son as they recall their good and bad times together. Martin Sheen and Barnard Hughes star; based on Hugh Leonard's play. **DR8, DR20**

Dad (1989, C, 117m, PG)
Heartfelt drama of the relationship between an ailing, elderly man (Jack Lemmon) and his grown son (Ted Danson). With Olympia Dukakis, Kathy Baker, Kevin Spacey, and Ethan Hawke. **DR8, DR11, ST138**

Daddy Long Legs (1955, C, 126m, NR)
Musical version of popular story about a playboy who anonymously gives an orphan her education—and when she grows up, she falls in love with him. Fred Astaire and Leslie Caron star, with Thelma Ritter, Fred Clark, and Terry Moore. Previously filmed as *Curly Top* with Shirley Temple. **MU14, ST4**

Daddy Nostalgia (1990, C, 105m, PG)
Drama of young woman (Jane Birkin) coming to the south of France to be reunited with her dying father (Dirk Bogarde). Directed by Bertrand Tavernier; dialogue in both French and English. **DT123, ST14**

Daddy's Dyin' ... Who's Got the Will?
(1990, C, 95m, PG-13)
Frantic comedy of scramble for inheritance among loopy family members. Beau Bridges,

Beverly D'Angelo, Tess Harper, Judge Reinhold, and Amy Wright star, with Bert Remsen and, in a bit role, Keith Carradine. **CO5**

Daffy Duck Cartoon Festival: Ain't that Ducky (1942–48, C, 35m, NR)
Donald Duck's Number One cartoon rival stars in these frenetic adventures, featuring Bob Clampett's *The Wise Quacking Duck*. **FA11**

Daffy Duck: The Nuttiness Continues (1956, C, 59m, NR)
Daffy's very own collection of cartoon classics, including *Beanstalk Bunny, Deduce You Say, Dripalong Daffy*, and *The Scarlet Pumpernickel*. **FA11**

Daffy Duck's Movie: Fantastic Island (1983, C, 78m, G)
Collection of ten classic Warner Brothers cartoons features Speedy Gonzales, Bugs Bunny, Porky Pig, Sylvester, Tweety, Pepe LePew, Pirate Sam, Foghorn Leghorn, and of course, Daffy Duck, who provides linking storyline that spoofs TV's "Fantasy Island." **FA11**

Daffy Duck's Quackbusters see *Quackbusters*

Dagora, the Space Monster (1964, C, 80m, NR)
Japanese science fiction drama of a flying jellyfish, gangsters, and stolen diamonds. **SF18**

Dain Curse, The (1978, C, 118m, NR)
James Coburn and Jean Simmons star in this Dashiell Hammett thriller. A private eye assigned to a relatively easy case of theft uncovers a series of complex murders in the process. Originally made for TV. **WR9**

Daisy Miller (1974, C, 91m, G)
Cybill Shepherd stars as the heroine of Henry James's comic novel about a headstrong American girl touring the Continent. With Barry Brown, Cloris Leachman, Mildred Natwick, and Eileen Brennan. Directed by Peter Bogdanovich. **CO20, WR14**

Dakota (1945, B&W, 82m, NR)
John Wayne battles land grabbers in this Western saga. Vera Ralston costars. **ST192**

Daleks: Invasion Earth 2150 A.D. (1966, C, 84m, NR)
Dr. Who travels to London 2150 A.D. and helps out a small band of resistance fighters in their battle against the Daleks, robots who want to kill all humans. Peter Cushing and Bernard Cribbins star. **SF4, SF19, ST43**

Damage (1992, C, 112m, R)
British drama of respectable middle-aged man who falls into mad affair with his son's fiancée, with catastrophic results. Jeremy Irons stars, with Juliette Binoche, Miranda Richardson, Rupert Graves, Ian Bannen, and Leslie Caron. David Hare adapted Josephine Hart's novel, Louis Malle directed. Available in an unrated version with about sixty seconds of extra footage, presumably material that nearly earned the film an NC-17 rating. **CU6, CU10, DR1, DR3, DR19, DR23, DT82, ST116**

Dames (1934, B&W, 90m, NR)
Busby Berkeley musical about a millionaire who tries to prevent the opening of a Broadway show. Dick Powell and Ruby Keeler star. **DT12, MU4, ST175**

Damien: Omen II (1978, C, 107m, R)
Sequel to *The Omen* opens seven years later, with Damien a student at a military academy where he discovers his true identity as the Antichrist. William Holden and Lee Grant star as Damien's uncle and aunt, who are now his legal guardians. **HO10, HO13, ST106**

Damn the Defiant! (1962, C, 101m, NR)
Adventure of sea battles during Napoleonic Wars, with Dirk Bogarde and Alec Guinness on opposing sides. **AC6, ST14, ST95**

Damn Yankees (1958, C, 110m, NR)
Musical fantasy of baseball fan who makes deal with the devil to be a young star who will help his beloved Washington Senators beat the hated New York Yankees. Tab Hunter, Ray Walston, and Gwen Verdon star. Directed by Stanley Donen and George Abbott; choreography by Bob Fosse, who appears in one dance number. **DT38, DT47, HO10, MU2, MU6,** *Recommended*

Damnation Alley (1977, C, 91m, PG)
Five survivors of a nuclear holocaust travel the wasteland in search of other human life. Jan-Michael Vincent, George Peppard, Dominique Sanda, Paul Winfield, and Jackie Earle Haley star. **SF12, ST230**

Damned, The (1969, C, 155m, R)
A dark portrait from Italian director Luchino Visconti of a decadent family of German arms merchants and their ties to the Third Reich. Dirk Bogarde, Ingrid Thulin, Helmut Griem, Helmut Berger, and Charlotte Rampling star in this controversial drama, originally rated "X." Impressively presented story but repellent; the characters have nowhere to go but down. **DR5, DT127, ST14**

Damsel in Distress, A
(1937, B&W, 101m, NR)
George Gershwin musical comedy stars Fred Astaire as a London dancer who pursues Joan Fontaine. With George Burns and Gracie Allen. George Stevens directed. **DT119, ST4, ST73**

Dance, Fools, Dance
(1931, B&W, 81m, NR)
Joan Crawford melodrama has her playing a journalist out to bring down a gangster (Clark Gable). **ST39, ST77**

Dance, Girl, Dance (1940, B&W, 89m, NR)
Classic woman's picture with cult following: Maureen O'Hara stars as a dancer with serious ambitions who gets sidetracked into a career in burlesque. With Louis Hayward, Lucille Ball, and Ralph Bellamy. Directed by Dorothy Arzner. **CL5, CL7, ST167**

Dance of the Damned (1989, C, 83m, R)
Horror drama with cult following about one-night stand between vampire (Cyril O'Reily) and suicidal stripper (Starr Andreef). Directed by Katt Shea Ruben. Remake: *To Sleep With a Vampire*. **CU4, HO5**

Dance With a Stranger (1985, C, 102m, R)
The true story of Ruth Ellis (Miranda Richardson), a divorced woman who killed her younger lover (Rupert Everett) and was hanged for her crime—the last woman in Britain to be executed. Ian Holm costars. Absorbing, with Richardson and Holm outstanding. **DR5, DR16, DR23, MY2, MY8, MY15,** *Recommended*

Dance with Me Henry
(1956, B&W, 79m, NR)
Last teaming of Abbott and Costello finds them running a shabby amusement park and trying to handle two orphan kids (Gigi Perreau and Rusty Hamer). **ST1**

Dancers (1987, C, 99m, PG)
Mikhail Baryshnikov stars in this drama set in the ballet world, where a pair of dancers imitate in real life the love story they're performing on stage. Directed by Herbert Ross. **DR12**

Dances With Wolves
(1990, C, 181m, PG-13)
Absorbing epic Western of a cavalry soldier's first-hand encounter with the Dakota Sioux. Director Kevin Costner stars, with Mary McDonnell, Graham Greene, Rodney A. Grant, and Floyd Red Crow Westerman. Six Oscars, including Best Picture, Director, and Screenplay Adaptation (Michael Blake, from his own novel). **ST38, WE1, WE4, WE7, XT1, XT6,** *Recommended*

Dancing Lady (1933, B&W, 94m, NR)
Joan Crawford plays a dancer in this backstage musical that finds her choosing between playboy Franchot Tone and no-nonsense producer Clark Gable. Fred Astaire is featured in his film debut and there's comic relief from the original Three Stooges. **CL7, CU17, ST4, ST39, ST77,** *Recommended*

Dancing Princesses, The
(1984, C, 60m, NR)
A princess (Lesley Ann Warren) teaches her overly strict father a lesson when his daughters break out of their locked rooms and into their dancing slippers with the help of a handsome prince (Peter Weller). From The Faerie Tale Theatre series. **FA12**

Dandy in Aspic, A (1968, C, 107m, NR)
A Russian double agent (Laurence Harvey) tires of his dangerous profession but can see no way out. With Tom Courtenay and Mia Farrow. Director Anthony Mann died during production; Harvey finished the film. **DT85, MY6, ST65**

Danger Lights (1930, B&W, 73m, NR)
Drama of young woman (Jean Arthur) engaged to an older man, a railroad supervisor (Louis Wolheim), but falling for a young engineer (Robert Armstrong). **ST3**

Dangerous (1935, B&W, 72m, NR)
Oscar winner Bette Davis plays a star on the downside of her career who finds redemption in the arms of a handsome suitor (Franchot Tone). **ST44, XT3**

Dangerous Liaisons (1988, C, 120m, R)
Deliciously played drama of intrigue in eighteenth-century France, with villainous schemers John Malkovich and Glenn Close plotting to divest innocent married woman Michelle Pfeiffer of her virtue. With Uma Thurman, Keanu Reeves, and Swoosie Kurtz. Christopher Hampton adapted his play; Stephen Frears directed. Material previously filmed as *Les Liaisons Dangereuses* and subsequently as *Valmont*. **DR1, DR5, DR20, DT48, ST33, ST147, ST173,** *Recommended*

Dangerous Mission (1954, C, 75m, NR)
A witness to a gangland killing flees cross-country with the killers in hot pursuit. Piper Laurie and Vincent Price star. **ST179**

Dangerous Moonlight
(1941, B&W, 83m, NR)
British drama of classical musician turned bomber pilot, set during World War II. Anton Walbrook stars. **AC1**

Dangerous Moves (1984, C, 95m, PG)
Oscar-winning drama from Switzerland about an international chess match and the

behind-the-scenes machinations that accompany it. Michel Piccoli, Leslie Caron, and Liv Ullmann star. **ST220, XT7**

Dangerous Summer, A
(1981, C, 100m, NR)
Australian drama of arsonist who's out to burn down a summer resort. Tom Skerritt stars, with Ian Gilmour, James Mason, and Wendy Hughes. **FF5, ST153**

Dangerous When Wet (1953, C, 95m, NR)
Esther Williams musical has her paddling her way across the English Channel. Fernando Lamas, Jack Carson, Charlotte Greenwood, and Tom and Jerry provide dry-land support. **MU1**

Dangerously Close (1986, C, 95m, R)
Melodrama of a society of high school vigilantes bullying kids who don't fit their clean-cut standards. John Stockwell stars. **DR25**

Daniel (1983, C, 130m, R)
Drama about a brother and sister whose parents were executed as spies in the 1950s and how that event still haunts them years later. Timothy Hutton and Amanda Plummer star, with Lindsay Crouse, Mandy Patinkin, Ed Asner, and Ellen Barkin. Based on E.L. Doctorow's novel, *The Book of Daniel*; directed by Sidney Lumet. Promising material but only Plummer really scores among the lead performers. **DR5, DR19, DT78, ST7**

Daniel Boone, Trail Blazer
(1956, C, 76m, NR)
Low-budget adventure saga of America's famed frontier explorer, starring Ismael Rodriguez, Bruce Bennett, and Lon Chaney, Jr. **ST27**

Dante's Inferno (1967, B&W, 90m, NR)
Oliver Reed plays Italian poet and painter Dante Gabriel Rossetti in this film from director Ken Russell. Originally made for British TV. **DR4, DR23, DT111**

Danton (1982, C, 136m, PG)
French-language drama from Polish director Andrzej Wajda, about the stormy days of the French Revolution. Gérard Depardieu stars in the title role. **DT130, ST52**

Darby O'Gill and the Little People
(1959, C, 93m, G)
Deep in the emerald forest of Ireland, a weaver of tall tales falls into the land of leprechauns in this Disney fantasy. An early role for Sean Connery. **FA1, ST36**

Dark Command (1940, B&W, 94m, NR)
In Civil War Kansas, John Wayne is the town marshal who clashes with local vigilante leader Walter Pidgeon. With Claire Trevor,

Gabby Hayes, and Roy Rogers. Directed by Raoul Walsh. The Duke and Roy's only screen pairing. That's about the only reason to see this. **DT131, ST188, ST224, WE6**

Dark Corner, The (1946, B&W, 99m, NR)
Lucille Ball plays an amateur sleuth in this mystery about a secretary who clears her boss from a murder charge. With Mark Stevens, Clifton Webb, and William Bendix. **MY15**

Dark Crystal, The (1983, C, 93m, PG)
Fantasy adventure from director Jim Henson and producer George Lucas, about the quest to replace the missing shard in the all-powerful Dark Crystal. Family entertainment, packed with unique creatures. **FA8, SF13**

Dark Eyes (1987, C, 118m, NR)
Marcello Mastroianni stars in this comedy-drama about a faded Italian aristocrat who takes one last, mad fling at love. **FF2, ST154**

Dark Forces (1980, C, 96m, PG)
An updating of the Rasputin story, about a faith healer who gains access into a senator's family by apparently curing the son, then developing a psychic power over the senator. Robert Powell stars. **HO7**

Dark Habits (1984, C, 116m, NR)
Irreverent comedy by Spanish director Pedro Almodóvar: a singer on the lam hides out in a convent. Christina Pascual, Julieta Serrano, and Carmen Maura star. **DT3**

Dark Journey (1937, B&W, 82m, NR)
Romantic suspense with Vivien Leigh as a World War I British spy who gets involved with a German intelligence officer (Conrad Veidt) while in Stockholm. **MY6, ST137**

Dark Mirror, The (1946, B&W, 85m, NR)
Twin sisters, one evil and the other good, are implicated in a murder case. Olivia de Havilland plays both sisters. **MY1, MY4, MY14, ST49, XT27**

Dark Obsession (1989, C, 97m, NC-17)
British drama of man whose life is coming unraveled: his marriage is floundering and he and his buddies are involved in the cover-up of a fatal accident. Gabriel Byrne and Amanda Donohoe star. Rating is for sexual content; also available in an R-rated version. Original British title: *Diamond Skulls*. Sodden stuff. **CU6, DR23**

Dark Passage (1947, B&W, 106m, NR)
An escaped convict (Humphrey Bogart) undergoes plastic surgery to cover up his identity while a beautiful girl (Lauren Bacall) tries to prove his innocence. **CL15, MY1, ST15**

Dark Past, The (1948, B&W, 75m, NR)
Hostage tale of a psycho killer and a psychologist. William Holden and Lee J. Cobb star. **ST106**

Dark Places (1973, C, 91m, PG)
Three people out to defraud a man of his inheritance are haunted by the ghost of a murderer. Christopher Lee and Joan Collins star. **HO2, ST135**

Dark Secret of Harvest Home, The (1978, C, 200m, NR)
A New York City family moves to a small town in New England. A mysterious old woman (Bette Davis) slowly draws the wife and daughter into her circle while the husband tries to solve some mysterious happenings. Originally made for TV. **HO11, ST44**

Dark Star (1974, C, 83m, PG)
Low-budget science fiction adventure from director John Carpenter that pokes fun at sci-fi epics such as *2001*. **CO7, CU4, DT23, SF21**

Dark Victory (1939, B&W, 106m, NR)
A young woman (Bette Davis) with a fatal disease decides to live her last few months to the fullest in this classic love story. With George Brent, Humphrey Bogart, Geraldine Fitzgerald, and Ronald Reagan. **CL4, CL6, ST15, ST44,** *Essential*

Darkman (1990, C, 95m, R)
Violent, delirious crime melodrama about a scientist maimed by vicious big city crooks, disguising himself with temporary makeup to achieve his revenge. Liam Neeson stars, with Frances McDormand, Colin Friels, and Larry Drake. Directed by Sam Raimi. Lots of echoes of other, better movies. **AC8, AC19, HO20**

Darling (1965, C, 122m, NR)
Drama of a successful London fashion model and her inability to find real love or meaning in her life. Oscar winner Julie Christie stars, with Dirk Bogarde and Laurence Harvey. Written by Frederic Raphael; directed by John Schlesinger. One of the first films to suggest the Swingin' Sixties scene in Europe masked a hollow shell. All three leads are terrific and Schesinger's direction should have won him an Oscar. **DR10, DR23, DT113, ST14, ST30, XT3, XT15, XT28,** *Essential, Recommended*

Das Boot (1981, C, 145m, R)
Stunning World War II drama set aboard a German submarine, starring Jurgen Prochnow, directed by Wolfgang Petersen. This is the dubbed version of the original German-language film. **AC1, FF3,** *Recommended*

Date With Death, A, see *McGuire, Go Home!*

Date With Judy, A (1948, C, 113m, NR)
Comedy with music revolving around two mischievous teen-agers and their families. Wallace Beery, Jane Powell, Elizabeth Taylor, and Carmen Miranda star. **ST212**

Daughter of Dr. Jekyll (1957, B&W, 71m, NR)
A young woman believes she is cursed by the experiments of a famous relative. Gloria Talbott and John Agar star. Directed by Edgar G. Ulmer. **HO14, HO20**

Daughter of Horror (1955, B&W, 60m, NR)
Offbeat horror film, with no dialogue, about a woman whose paranoia edges her into murder. Adrienne Barrett stars. Also known as *Dementia*. **HO9**

Daughters of Darkness (1971, C, 87m, R)
Horror film with a cult following about a pair of lesbian vampires who prey on honeymooning couples. Filmed in France; Delphine Seyrig stars. **CC4, CU6, HO5**

David and Bathsheba (1951, C, 116m, NR)
Gregory Peck and Susan Hayward play the title roles in this religious drama of the biblical king and his consort. **CL13, ST100, ST171**

David and Lisa (1963, B&W, 94m, NR)
Two mentally disturbed young people meet in a therapy session and develop a friendship that slowly blossoms into romance. Keir Dullea and Janet Margolin star, with Howard DaSilva. Written by Eleanor Perry; directed by Frank Perry. **DR9**

David Copperfield (1935, B&W, 130m, NR)
An all-star production of the life and times of Charles Dickens's character in Victorian England. Directed by George Cukor. Freddie Bartholomew stars, with Frank Lawton, W.C. Fields (as Micawber), Lionel Barrymore, Roland Young, Basil Rathbone, and Maureen O'Sullivan. **DT32, FA3, ST67, WR5,** *Recommended*

David Holtzman's Diary (1968, B&W, 74m, NR)
Amusing, provocative story about a filmmaker (L.M. Kit Carson) obsessed with his daily life, recording it with a camera. Directed by Jim McBride. Independently produced film speaks volumes about contemporary self-absorption and effect of electronic media on our lives. UNAVAILABLE ON VIDEO. **XT29**

Davy Crockett (1955, C, 88m, G)
Disney portrait of the King of the Wild Frontier (Fess Parker), as he takes on wild bears and nasty Indians before making his last stand at the Alamo. Buddy Ebsen costars. **FA1**

Davy Crockett and the River Pirates (1956, C, 81m, G)
Two episodes from the Disney TV series: Davy and riverboat king Mike Fink (Jeff York) square off in a boat race; Davy and his sidekick George Russell (Buddy Ebsen) take on some pesky Indians. **FA1**

Dawn! (1976, C, 114m, NR)
Australian film bio of Olympic swimming champ Dawn Fraser. Bronwyn Mackay-Payne stars. **DR22, FF5**

Dawn of the Dead (1979, C, 126m, NR)
Gruesome and darkly funny sequel to *Night of the Living Dead* finds a quartet of humans holed up in an abandoned shopping mall besieged by flesh-eating zombies. George Romero directed. **CU1, CU4, CU7, DT108, HO6, HO18**, *Recommended*

Dawn Patrol, The (1938, B&W, 103m, NR)
World War I drama of brave pilots on the edge of collapse from exhaustion, starring David Niven and Errol Flynn. **AC2, AC11, ST69**, *Recommended*

Dawning, The (1988, C, 97m, PG)
British drama, set in 1920 Ireland, about friendship between eighteen-year-old girl and middle-aged IRA operative. Anthony Hopkins and Rebecca Pidgeon star, with Jean Simmons, Trevor Howard (his last film), and Hugh Grant. **DR9, DR23, ST109**

Day After, The (1983, C, 120m, NR)
Controversial portrait of America undergoing nuclear attack and the attendant devastation. Jason Robards, JoBeth Williams, Steve Guttenberg, and John Lithgow star. Nicholas Meyer directed; originally made for TV. **DR7, SF12, ST185**

Day After Trinity, The (1980, C/B&W, 88m, NR)
Superb documentary about the building of the first nuclear weapons and the devastating effect the experience had on scientist J. Robert Oppenheimer. **CU16**, *Recommended*

Day at the Races, A (1937, B&W, 111m, NR)
The Marx Brothers invade a race track. Chico sells tutti-frutti ice cream and hot tips on the ponies. Margaret Dumont tries to ignore him. **ST152**

Day for Night (1973, C, 120m, PG)
Loving look at filmmaking from director François Truffaut, who also plays the director of a romantic comedy in production, with the usual behind-the-scenes crises, affairs, hopes, and dreams. Jean-Pierre Leaud, Jacqueline Bisset, Jean-Pierre Aumont, and Valentina Cortese costar. Oscar winner for Best Foreign Film. **DR13, DT125, XT7, XT31**, *Essential, Recommended*

Day in the Country, A (1936, B&W, 36m, NR)
French director Jean Renoir's evocative short film, about a family's outing, suggests some of the inspirations for Impressionist painters like his father. A mini-classic. **DT104**, *Recommended*

Day in the Death of Joe Egg, A (1972, C, 106m, R)
Darkly comic story of a British couple trying to deal with their severely handicapped daughter. Alan Bates and Janet Suzman star in this adaptation of Peter Nichols's play. **CO12, CO17, DR20, ST9**

Day of the Dead (1985, C, 91m, NR)
The third of the . . . *Dead* trilogy that began with *Night of the Living* and continued with *Dawn of the* has the zombies in control of everything and the last of the humans in a bunker waiting for the final battle. Directed by George Romero. **DT108, HO6, HO18**

Day of the Dolphin, The (1973, C, 104m, PG)
A marine biologist uses his trained dolphins to thwart an assassination plot. George C. Scott stars. Mike Nichols directed. Intriguing possibilities, but soggy results. **DT91, FA5, ST196**

Day of the Jackal, The (1973, C, 141m, PG)
Classy, intricately plotted thriller based on the Frederick Forsyth bestseller about a young British assassin's plot to kill de Gaulle in Paris and French officials' desperate race to catch him. Edward Fox stars, with Alan Badel, Cyril Cusack, Michel Lonsdale, and Delphine Seyrig. Directed by Fred Zinnemann. **DT144, MY6, WR10, XT16**, *Recommended*

Day of the Locust, The (1975, C, 144m, R)
Drama about the dark underside of Hollywood in the 1930s, with an impressionable painter meeting a gallery of grotesque show biz characters. Adapted from Nathanael West's classic novel. William Atherton stars, with Donald Sutherland, Karen Black, Burgess Meredith, and Geraldine Page. Directed

by John Schlesinger. Use of widescreen will be lost on video. Near-perfect adaptation (except for Black's casting) of the great novel about Hollywood. **CU20, DR13, DR19, DT113, XT10,** *Recommended*

Day of the Triffids, The
(1963, C, 95m, NR)
Science fiction drama about blinding meteor showers and invasion of mutant monsters. Howard Keel stars in this British production. **SF7, SF19**

Day of Wrath (1943, B&W, 110m, NR)
From Danish director Carl Dreyer, a tale of sixteenth-century superstition and revenge. An old woman, accused of witchcraft, places a curse on the clergyman who fingered her. **DT39**

Day the Earth Caught Fire, The
(1962, B&W, 99m, NR)
Earth comes dangerously close to the sun in this British science fiction drama starring Edward Judd and Leo McKern. **SF7, SF19**

Day the Earth Stood Still, The
(1951, B&W, 92m, NR)
Classic 1950s science fiction drama, with spaceship landing in Washington, D.C., alien trying to warn Earth of its disastrous nuclear arms race. Michael Rennie, Sam Jaffe, Patricia Neal, Billy Gray, and "Gort" star. Robert Wise directed. Has lost none of its punch or relevance after forty years. **CU4, DT140, FA8, SF1, SF9, SF13, XT12,** *Essential, Highly Recommended*

Day the Hot Line Got Hot, The see *Hot Line*

Day Time Ended, The (1980, C, 79m, PG)
Family living in the desert experiences a strange alien visitation. Jim Davis, Dorothy Malone, and Christopher Mitchum star. Also known as *Time Warp*. **SF9**

Day Will Dawn, The
(1942, B&W, 99m, NR)
British thriller set during World War II, with journalist helping to put a U-boat base out of commission. Hugh Williams stars, with Griffiths Jones, Deborah Kerr, and Ralph Richardson. Also known as *The Avengers*. **AC1, ST125, ST184**

Daydreamer, The (1966, C, 98m, NR)
Live action mixes with animation in this tale of a young Hans Christian Andersen thinking of the fairy tale characters he will later write about. Jack Gilford and Margaret Hamilton star, with the voices of Boris Karloff and Tallulah Bankhead. **ST119**

Days of Glory (1944, B&W, 86m, NR)
World War II action between the Nazis and the Russians, with Gregory Peck in his starring debut. Directed by Jacques Tourneur. **AC1, DT124, ST171**

Days of Heaven (1978, C, 95m, PG)
Romantic drama, set in Texas wheatfields at the turn of the century, about a farm owner who woos an itinerant worker, only to find that her "brother" is really her lover. Stunning photography by Nestor Alemendros and Haskell Wexler won an Oscar. Richard Gere, Brooke Adams, Sam Shepard, and Linda Manz star. Directed by Terrence Malick; music by Ennio Morricone. Visuals will lose something on video but Malick's ability to tell a story with imagery still impresses. **DR1, DT81, ST84,** *Essential, Highly Recommended*

Days of Jesse James (1939, B&W, 63m, NR)
Roy Rogers plays the notorious outlaw, in one of his early films. **HF16, ST188**

Days of Thunder (1990, C, 107m, PG-13)
Souped-up drama of hot-shot race car driver (Tom Cruise), from the same filmmaking team (producers Don Simpson and Gerry Bruckheimer, director Tony Scott) that fueled *Top Gun*. With Robert Duvall, Nicole Kidman, Randy Quaid, Michael Rooker, and Cary Elwes. Written by Robert Towne. Nothing you haven't seen before in this genre. **AC10, DR22, ST41, ST63**

Days of Wine and Roses, The
(1962, B&W, 117m, NR)
Intense, well-acted drama of an alcoholic couple and how they ruin their lives before one of them makes a recovery. Jack Lemmon and Lee Remick star. Blake Edwards directed. **DR7, DT40, ST138,** *Recommended*

Dead, The (1987, C, 83m, PG)
James Joyce's short story is the basis for this richly felt drama of family life in turn-of-the-century Dublin, centering around a holiday party and the memories it evokes. Anjelica Huston stars; her father, John, directed—his last film. **DR8, DR19, DT60, ST115,** *Recommended*

Dead Again (1991, C/B&W, 111m, R)
British thriller about a private eye trying to help a woman who thinks she has lived another life in the past. Kenneth Branagh and Emma Thompson star, with Derek Jacobi, Robin Williams, and Hanna Schygulla. Branagh directed. Stylish fun at times, but the leads seem curiously out of synch with the material. **MY3, MY5, MY10, ST228, XT23**

Dead and Buried (1981, C, 92m, R)
A sheriff investigating a series of bizarre murders discovers that some of his neighbors are actually zombies. James Farentino, Melody Anderson, and Jack Albertson star. **HO6**

Dead-Bang (1989, C, 109m, R)
Don Johnson stars in a crime saga of a relentless police detective whose pursuit of a cop killer uncovers a nest of verminous white supremacists. **AC9**

Dead Calm (1989, C, 97m, R)
Australian suspense drama has a couple on a yacht encountering a stranger on another boat who, they belatedly discover, has murdered all on board. Sam Neill, Nicole Kidman, and Billy Zane star. Phillip Noyce directed. **FF5**

Dead End (1937, B&W, 93m, NR)
Socially conscious drama paints a vivid portrait of life on New York's Lower East Side during the Depression. Sylvia Sidney, Joel McCrea, and Humphrey Bogart star, with the film debut of The Dead End Kids, later The Bowery Boys. Lillian Hellman adapted Sidney Kingsley's hit play; directed by William Wyler. **CL8, DR20, DT142, ST15, ST144,** *Essential, Recommended*

Dead Heat (1988, C, 86m, R)
Buddy-cop/horror story, with a pair of detectives (Joe Piscopo, Treat Williams) on the trail of a mad doctor (Vincent Price) who's reviving criminals from the dead. **AC9, HO6, ST179**

Dead Heat on a Merry-Go-Round
(1966, C, 104m, NR)
Heist drama centering on the robbery of an airport bank. Plenty of twists and double crosses. James Coburn stars, with Camilla Sparv, Aldo Ray, and Ross Martin. Harrison Ford makes a brief appearance, in his first film. **MY18, ST74**

Dead Man Out (1989, C, 87m, NR)
A state-appointed psychiatrist attempts to deal with a convict whose insanity has prevented the state from executing him. Danny Glover and Rubén Blades star. Originally made for cable TV. **DR18, MU12, ST88**

Dead Men Don't Wear Plaid
(1982, B&W, 89m, PG)
A comedy thriller starring Steve Martin as a private detective with a very bizarre assortment of suspects. Includes scenes from many *film noir* classics of the 1940s skillfully woven into the story. With Rachel Ward, Reni Santoni, and Carl Reiner, who also directed. **CO7, MY17, ST150**

Dead Men Walk (1943, B&W, 67m, NR)
An evil twin involved with the black arts resorts to vampirism to get back at his good brother. **HO15**

Dead of Night (1945, B&W, 102m, NR)
An architect discovers that the cottage he is to redesign and its occupants are exactly the same as those in his recurring nightmare. His story prompts the other guests to tell of their own brushes with the supernatural. Highlight: the tale of the nervous ventriloquist and his independent dummy, featuring Michael Redgrave. Would that the other tales were as memorable. **HO1, HO2, HO23, HO26**

Dead of Night (1973) see *Deathdream*

Dead of Winter (1987, C, 100m, R)
An aspiring actress (Mary Steenburgen) is lured to a remote farmhouse with the promise of a movie role. Once there, she finds herself trapped in a bizarre game of deception. Directed by Arthur Penn. **DT96, MY3**

Dead Poets Society (1989, C, 128m, PG)
Drama set in a private boys' school in 1959, with an unorthodox teacher (Robin Williams) inspiring devotion from his pupils, controversy among his colleagues and the boys' parents. Robert Sean Leonard and Ethan Hawke costar. Directed by Peter Weir. **DR9, DR25, DT133, ST228**

Dead Pool, The (1988, C, 91m, R)
Clint Eastwood's fifth outing as Dirty Harry has him trailing a killer with a hit list of San Francisco celebrities—a list which includes Harry. **AC9, ST64, XT13**

Dead Reckoning (1947, B&W, 100m, NR)
A World War II veteran (Humphrey Bogart) attempts to solve the murder of a fellow officer. **MY1, MY4, ST15**

Dead Ringer (1964, B&W, 115m, NR)
Bette Davis plays twin sisters; the evil one is plotting revenge over a failed romance. With Karl Malden, Peter Lawford, and Jean Hagen. Directed by Paul Henreid. **MY4, ST44, XT23, XT27**

Dead Ringers (1988, C, 115m, R)
Disturbing psychological study of twin doctors who share an apartment, a gynecological practice—and more. Jeremy Irons stars as both twins, with Genevieve Bujold. Brilliantly directed by David Cronenberg; based loosely on a true story. **DR8, DT31, HO15, ST116, XT27,** *Recommended*

Dead Zone, The (1983, C, 103m, R)
An accident victim comes out of a coma after five years and discovers he now has psychic

powers. Christopher Walken, Martin Sheen, Brooke Adams, and Tom Skerritt star. Directed by David Cronenberg; based on a novel by Stephen King. Walken is well cast and Cronenberg offers a more intelligent approach than King's material usually gets. **DT31, HO7, HO19, ST222, WR12,** *Recommended*

Deadbolt (1992, C, 95m, NR)
Thriller of woman taking in male roommate who turns out to be a possessive psycho. Justine Bateman and Adam Baldwin star. **MY3, MY19**

Deadline (1987, C, 100m, R)
Thriller about a journalist (Christopher Walken) covering the civil war in Lebanon. **MY6, ST222**

Deadline at Dawn (1946, B&W, 83m, NR)
Susan Hayward plays an aspiring actress who tries to clear the name of a sailor (Bill Williams) accused of murder. Written by Clifford Odets; directed by Harold Clurman, his only stint behind a film camera. Based on a novel by William Irish (Cornell Woolrich). **CU15, MY1, MY11, ST100, WR38**

Deadlock (1991, C, 100m, NR)
A pair of prison escapees (Rutger Hauer and Mimi Rogers), "wedded" by an electronic device that will kill them if they separate, seek revenge on the people who framed them. Thriller set in the near future also features James Remar and Joan Chen. Directed by Lewis Teague; original title: *Wedlock*. Promising premise weakened by indifferent performances, overextended plot. **AC24, DR18**

Deadly Blessing (1981, C, 102m, R)
A young couple moves to a farm that borders the compound of a community called The Hittites. A series of strange murders begins. Maren Jenson and Lisa Hartman star. Directed by Wes Craven. **HO11**

Deadly Companions, The
(1961, C, 90m, NR)
Brian Keith plays a tough gunfighter who accidentally kills the son of a dance-hall girl (Maureen O'Hara). Director Sam Peckinpah's first film, worth seeing for fans of him or Westerns in general. **DT95, ST167**

Deadly Friend (1986, C, 92m, R)
A teen-aged genius has two friends—the girl next door and his special robot. When the girl dies, he pushes his experiments into a deadly realm. Directed by Wes Craven. **HO20**

Deadly Hero (1975, C, 102m, PG)
Cop drama of a policeman who seems to be

a hero when he kills a woman's attacker. Don Murray stars, with Diahn Williams, James Earl Jones, and Lilia Skala. **ST118**

Deadly Illusion (1987, C, 87m, R)
A detective is framed for murder in this thriller starring Billy Dee Williams, with Vanity, Morgan Fairchild, and John Beck. Written and co-directed by Larry Cohen. **DT28, ST227**

Deadly Sanctuary (1970, C, 93m, R)
Horror drama focusing on the writings of the Marquis De Sade (Klaus Kinski), starring Jack Palance, Sylva Koscina, and Mercedes McCambridge. **ST126**

Deadly Tower, The (1975, C, 100m, NR)
True story of Charles Whitman, sniper who terrorized University of Texas campus in 1966. Kurt Russell stars, with Richard Yniquez, John Forsythe, Ned Beatty, Pernell Roberts, and Clifton James. **DR5, ST191**

Deadly Trackers, The (1973, C, 110m, PG)
Western revenge drama has sheriff (Richard Harris) riding to Mexico in search of the robbers who killed his wife and son. With Rod Taylor, Al Lettieri, Neville Brand, and Isela Vega. Story by Sam Fuller. **WE5, WE9**

Deadly Trap, The (1971, C, 96m, PG)
A former espionage agent is harrassed by his ex-employers, who use his unstable wife as a tool for revenge. Frank Langella and Faye Dunaway star. Directed by Rene Clement. Also known as *Death Scream*. **ST61**

Deal of the Century (1983, C, 99m, PG)
Chevy Chase stars in this satire on the arms race; he plays a fast-talking salesman of high-tech military hardware. Gregory Hines and Sigourney Weaver costar. Directed by William Friedkin. Chase has one good scene—his sales pitch. The satire never gets off the ground. **CO2, CO13, ST225**

Dear America: Letters Home From Vietnam (1987, C/B&W, 87m, NR)
Moving documentary composed of TV news footage and home movies of the war in Vietnam, with a soundtrack of actual letters written by servicemen and nurses (read by such stars as Robin Williams, Robert De Niro, and Kathleen Turner), plus well-chosen pop and rock music of the period. Originally made for cable TV. **AC4, CU16, ST51, ST218, ST228,** *Recommended*

Dear Brigitte (1965, C, 100m, NR)
James Stewart stars in a comedy about an eight-year-old boy's infatuation with French "sex kitten" Brigitte Bardot. Glynis Johns and Fabian costar; Bardot makes a guest appearance. **ST6, ST207**

Dear Detective (1977, C, 105m, NR)
French thriller starring Annie Girardot as a
detective who takes time out from several
murder investigations for a little romance
with a college professor. Also known as *Dear
Inspector*. **FF1, MY16**

Dear Inspector see *Dear Detective*

Dear Wife (1949, B&W, 88m, NR)
William Holden stars in this comedy about
an aspiring politician competing against a
much older man (Edward Arnold) for state
office. **ST106**

Death Becomes Her
(1992, C, 103m, PG-13)
Special effects comedy about a Hollywood
plastic surgeon, an aging actress, her jealous
rival, and a potion that promises immortality.
Bruce Willis, Meryl Streep, and Goldie Hawn
star, with Isabella Rossellini and Sydney Pollack. Directed by Robert Zemeckis. The effects
won an Oscar. **CO11, CO12, DT98, DT143,
SF15, ST99, ST210, ST229, XT24**

Death Before Dishonor
(1986, C, 95m, R)
A Marine sergeant (Fred Dryer) and his elite
unit track down a terrorist in the Middle
East. With Paul Winfield. **AC20, ST230**

Death Collector see *Enforcer, The* (1975)

Death Corps see *Shock Waves*

Death Hunt (1981, C, 97m, R)
A Mountie (Lee Marvin) pursues a trapper
(Charles Bronson) accused of murder across
the frozen Canadian landscape. **AC12, ST20,
ST151**

Death in Venice (1971, C, 130m, PG)
Italian drama, based on Thomas Mann novel,
of a composer's final days in Venice, as he
struggles to come to terms with his homosexuality and art. Dirk Bogarde stars; Luchino
Visconti directed. **DR19, DT127, ST14**

Death Kiss, The (1933, B&W, 75m, NR)
Thriller set during the filming of a movie,
when an actor is murdered. Bela Lugosi and
David Manners star. **ST143**

Death of a Centerfold
(1981, C, 100m, NR)
Jamie Lee Curtis plays Dorothy Stratten, the
Playboy model who was murdered by her
boyfriend-manager (Bruce Weitz). Same story
filmed as *STAR 80*. Originally made for TV.
DR6, DR13, ST42

Death of a Salesman
(1985, C, 150m, NR)
Dustin Hoffman plays Willy Loman in the
latest adaptation of the classic Arthur Miller

play. Kate Reid, John Malkovich, Stephen
Lang, and Charles Durning costar. Directed
by Volker Schlondorff. Originally made for
TV. **DR8, DR20, ST105, ST147**

Death on the Nile (1978, C, 140m, PG)
All-star production of the Agatha Christie
novel, in which Hercule Poirot (Peter
Ustinov) must determine who killed an
heiress aboard a ship. Bette Davis, Angela
Lansbury, Mia Farrow, and David Niven are
among the suspects. **MY12, ST44, ST65,
ST131, WR3**

Death Race 2000 (1975, C, 78m, R)
Low-budget science fiction adventure about
a road race that awards points for hitting
pedestrians. David Carradine, Sylvester Stallone, and Mary Woronov star; Paul Bartel
directed. Sequel: *Deathsport*. **AC10, CU4,
DT8, SF21, ST204**

Death Rides a Horse (1969, C, 114m, PG)
Western tale of revenge, starring John Phillip
Law as a man tracking a gang of killers, un-
aware that one of them is riding with him.
With Lee Van Cleef. **ST221, WE5**

Death Scream see *Deadly Trap, The*

Death Sentence (1974, C, 78m, NR)
A juror discovers that the wrong man is
on trial for murder when her husband is
revealed as a killer. Cloris Leachman stars,
with Nick Nolte. Originally made for TV.
MY3, ST164

Death Squad, The (1973, C, 74m, NR)
Urban drama focuses on a band of vigilante
cops involved with gangland executions.
Robert Forster stars, with Melvyn Douglas
and Michelle Phillips. **MU12, ST58**

Death Valley (1982, C, 87m, R)
A young boy visiting Arizona is witness to a
murder and flees for his life from a psychotic
killer. Paul LeMat, Catherine Hicks, Peter Billingsley, and Stephen McHattie star. **AC24**

Death Wish (series)

Death Wish (1974, C, 93m, R)

Death Wish II (1982, C, 89m, R)

Death Wish 3 (1985, C, 100m, R)

Death Wish 4: The Crackdown
(1987, C, 100m, R)
Charles Bronson plays Paul Kersey in these
violent, often-imitated action melodramas. In
the first film, his wife is killed and his daughter brutally assaulted by street thugs, and he
goes on a vigilante-style killing spree. Subsequent chapters have him in both New York
and Los Angeles, dealing out his brand of

justice to criminals. Jeff Goldblum made his film debut as a mugger in the first film. **AC19, ST20, ST90 (Death Wish), XT9 (Death Wish),** *Essential (Death Wish)*

Deathdream (1972, C, 90m, PG)
A veteran is discovered to be responsible for a series of murders because he is a zombie in need of human blood. Directed by Bob Clark. Also known as *Dead of Night.* **HO6**

Deathsport (1978, C, 82m, R)
Sequel to *Death Race 2000*, with deadly road race featuring killer cycles. David Carradine and Claudia Jennings star. Allan Arkush directed. **AC10, DT6**

Deathstalker (1984, C, 80m, R)
Sword and sorcery saga featuring a lovely princess (Barbi Benton), who's the prize for the bravest warrior of them all. **AC18**

Deathstalker II (1987, C, 85m, R)
Name-only sequel in this adventure tale of a brave fighting man. Monique Gabrielle and John Terlesky star. **AC18**

Deathtrap (1982, C, 116m, PG)
Complicated thriller about a burned-out playwright, his smothering wife, and an ambitious student who's written a very good play. Michael Caine, Dyan Cannon, and Christopher Reeve star. Based on Ira Levin's hit play; directed by Sidney Lumet. Undeniably clever, but not especially memorable. **DR20, DT78, MY9, ST25**

Deathwatch (1980, C, 128m, R)
A dying woman is followed by a TV reporter who has a camera imbedded in his head, transmitting her story on national TV. Romy Schneider, Harvey Keitel, and Harry Dean Stanton star in this science fiction drama from France, with English dialogue. Directed by Bertrand Tavernier. Fascinating premise gets wan treatment; worth a look if you want something different. **DT123, MY16, SF5, SF19, ST205**

Decameron Nights (1953, C, 87m, NR)
British adaptation of Boccaccio's medieval tales. Louis Jourdan and Joan Fontaine star. **CL1, DR23, ST73**

Deceived (1991, C, 103m, PG-13)
Goldie Hawn stars in a thriller about an art restoration expert who becomes increasingly suspicious of her husband (John Heard)—especially after his "death" in an accident. **MY3, MY11, ST99**

December 7th (1943, B&W, 85m, NR)
Full-length version of John Ford's Oscar-winning documentary about the attack on Pearl Harbor. Among the narrators: Walter Huston and Dana Andrews. Codirector was cinematographer Gregg Toland. Shorter version is available on tape titled *This Is Korea/December 7th.* **AC1, CU16, DT44**

Deception (1946, C, 112m, NR)
Bette Davis melodrama of a pianist whose benefactor (Claude Rains) keeps a tight rein on her. **ST44**

Decision at Sundown (1957, C, 77m, NR)
Randolph Scott Western has him on trail of a man he thinks caused his wife's suicide. With John Carroll, Karen Steele, and Noah Beery. Directed by Budd Boetticher. **DT14, ST197, WE5**

Decline of the American Empire, The (1986, C, 101m, R)
Canadian drama, with French dialogue, about a group of Quebec University professors and their wives. The men prepare a dinner while the women work out at a gym; the groups engage in conversation at the dinner. Directed by Denys Arcand. **FF7**

Decline of Western Civilization, The (1981, C, 100m, NR)
Documentary of the Los Angeles punk music scene, directed by Penelope Spheeris, featuring such household names as Black Flag, Fear, X, and Catholic Discipline. **MU11**

Decline of Western Civilization Part II: The Metal Years, The (1988, C, 90m, R)
Director Penelope Spheeris follows up her documentary on the punk music scene with a look at the heavy metal artists who've made it (Ozzy Osbourne, Joe Perry, Steven Tyler, and Gene Simmons) and the younger generation of musicians looking for the same kind of fame. **MU11**

Decoration Day (1990, C, 100m, NR)
Retired judge (James Garner) who has long refused Congressional Medal of Honor decides to accept it after childhood friend, a black pilot (Bill Cobbs), urges him to. With Judith Ivey, Ruby Dee, and Larry Fishburne. Originally made for TV. **ST82**

Deep, The (1977, C, 123m, PG)
Couple on an innocent skindiving expedition in Caribbean wind up finding treasure and drugs. Nick Nolte, Jacqueline Bisset, and Robert Shaw star. **AC12, ST164**

Deep Cover (1992, C, 112m, R)
Cop goes undercover on narcotics case, falls in with crooked lawyer, other shady types. Larry Fishburne and Jeff Goldblum star, with Victoria Dillard, Charles Martin Smith, Gregory Sierra, Clarence Williams III, and Glynn Turman. Directed by Bill Duke. Goldblum is

convincingly nasty; strictly for hardcore fans of genre. **AC9, MY2, ST90**

Deep in My Heart (1954, C, 132m, NR)
José Ferrer plays Sigmund Romberg in this biographical musical which features guest stars Gene Kelly, Ann Miller, and Tony Martin. Directed by Stanley Donen. **DT38, MU5, ST123**

Deep Red (1975, C, 98m, R)
A man who witnessed an ax murder and a journalist set out to investigate a series of similar killings. David Hemmings and Daria Nicolodi star. Directed by Dario Argento. **HO9**

Deep Six, The (1958, C, 105m, NR)
Alan Ladd plays a Quaker naval officer who gets into the thick of World War II action. With Dianne Foster, William Bendix, James Whitmore, and Joey Bishop. **AC1, ST128**

Deepstar Six (1988, C, 103m, R)
An underwater expedition encounters a sea monster in this high-tech horror story. Greg Evigan, Cindy Pickett, and Taurean Blacque star. **HO16**

Deer Hunter, The (1978, C, 183m, R)
Drama of small-town buddies whose experiences in Vietnam shatter their lives. Robert De Niro, Christopher Walken, John Savage, John Cazale, and Meryl Streep star. Directed by Michael Cimino. Oscar winner for Best Picture, Director, and Supporting Actor (Walken). A touchstone film about U.S. involvement with first-rate performances lost in overlong, incoherent story. **AC4, DR7, DR26, ST51, ST210, ST222, XT1, XT4, XT6, XT20, *Essential***

Def by Temptation (1990, C, 95m, R)
Horror tale of religious young black man (James Bond III) tempted by female vampire. With Kadeem Hardison, Bill Nunn, Samuel L. Jackson, Melba Moore, and Cynthia Bond as the Temptress. Written, produced, and directed by Bond; photographed by Ernest Dickerson. Provocative attempt to infuse genre with spiritual overtones will interest somē viewers. **DR14, HO10, HO25**

Defence of the Realm (1985, C, 96m, PG)
A journalist's story forces a British officer to resign. When the writer learns of the result, he attempts to uncover the entire story. Gabriel Byrne and Greta Scacchi star, with Denholm Elliott, Ian Bannen, and Bill Patterson. **MY6**

Defending Your Life (1991, C, 111m, PG)
Comic story of ad man (Albert Brooks) killed in car crash, discovering that the first stop after death is a trial that determines your future back on Earth or in another world. With Meryl Streep, Rip Torn, Lee Grant, Buck Henry, and in a bit role, Shirley MacLaine. Brooks wrote and directed; sweeter than his previous films but still likable. **CO1, DT16, ST145, ST210, ST216, XT24, *Recommended***

Defenseless (1991, C, 104m, R)
Barbara Hershey stars as an attorney whose affair with a married businessman explodes in her face when the man is found murdered. She winds up defending his wife (an old college friend of hers), knowing that some circumstantial evidence links herself to the crime. With Sam Shepard, Mary Beth Hurt, and J.T. Walsh. **DR17, MY3, ST104**

Defiance (1980, C, 102m, PG)
Urban loner (Jan-Michael Vincent) takes on New York street gangs. With Art Carney, Theresa Saldana, and Danny Aiello. **AC8**

Defiant Ones, The (1958, B&W, 97m, NR)
Tony Curtis and Sidney Poitier play two escaped cons who must look past the color of their skin to survive. With Lon Chaney, Jr., and Cara Williams. Directed by Stanley Kramer. **CL8, DT67, ST27, ST174**

Déjà Vu (1985, C, 95m, R)
Whodunit focusing on couple involved in torrid affair, with echoes of similar situation fifty years ago that resulted in murder. Jaclyn Smith and Nigel Terry play both couples. With Claire Bloom and Shelley Winters. Directed by Anthony Richmond, Ms. Smith's husband. **MY5, ST232, XT27**

Deliberate Stranger, The (1986, C, 188m, NR)
The twisted tale of notorious serial killer Ted Bundy. Mark Harmon stars, with Frederic Forrest, George Grizzard, Ben Masters, Glynnis O'Connor, M. Emmet Walsh, and Billy Green Bush. Originally made for TV. **DR6**

Delicate Delinquent, The (1957, B&W, 100m, NR)
Jerry Lewis stars in this film *sans* Dean Martin as a hoodlum reformed by a friendly cop. With Darren McGavin and Martha Hyer. **ST139**

Delicate Sound of Thunder (1989, C, 100m, NR)
Concert film of rock group Pink Floyd's "Momentary Lapse of Reason" tour, featuring four songs not on the album of the same name. **MU10**

Delicatessen (1992, C, 95m, NR)
Dark French comedy set in post-apocalypse future, when meat is scarce. A landlord who

doubles as a butcher supplies his old tenants—with the help of new roomers. Directed by Marc Caro and J.P. Jeunet. Consistently amusing, espcially for fans of Jacques Tati and Terry Gilliam. **CO12, FF1,** *Recommended*

Delirious (1991, C, 96m, PG)
John Candy comedy about a soap opera writer who finds himself a character in the fictional town he has created. With Mariel Hemingway, Emma Samms, Raymond Burr, Dylan Baker, Charles Rocket, and Robert Wagner playing himself. **CO8, CO14, CO20**

Deliverance (1972, C, 109m, R)
Four men on a canoe trip down an isolated stretch of river encounter disaster. Burt Reynolds, Jon Voight, Ned Beatty, and Ronny Cox star. John Boorman directed this adaptation of James Dickey's novel; Dickey makes a brief appearance as a sheriff. Boorman's artful direction lifts this from the run-of-the-mill adventure film it might have been. Widescreen will be lost on video. **AC24, DR19, DR27, DT15, ST183,** *Recommended*

Delta Force, The (1986, C, 129m, R)
When terrorists commandeer an airliner and its terrified passengers, a special squad of fighting men swing into action. Chuck Norris and Lee Marvin are the rescuers; Shelley Winters and Martin Balsam are among the hostages. **AC20, ST151, ST165, ST232**

Delta Force 2 (1990, C, 110m, R)
Chuck Norris and his combat-happy commandos are off to South America to wipe out a drug market. With Billy Drago and Richard Jaeckel. **AC20, ST165**

Dementia see *Daughter of Horror*

Dementia 13 (1963, B&W, 81m, NR)
Low-budget thriller about murders in and around an Irish castle. Directed by Francis Ford Coppola; produced by Roger Corman. **CU14, DT29, HO14**

Demetrius and the Gladiators
(1954, C, 101m, NR)
Saga of ancient Rome, with Victor Mature the stalwart hero, Susan Hayward his royal lover, and a flamboyant Jay Robinson as the emperor Caligula. **CL3, ST100**

Demi-Paradise, The (1943, B&W, 115m, NR)
British comedy starring Laurence Olivier as a Russian engineer visiting England, falling in love with local girl (Penelope Dudley Ward). With Leslie Henson and Margaret Rutherford. Also known as *Adventure for Two*. **CO17, ST168**

Demon see *God Told Me To*

Demon Seed (1977, C, 94m, R)
Computer goes mad, attacks scientist's wife (Julie Christie) for purposes of reproduction in this science fiction thriller. Donald Cammell directed. **HO22, HO25, SF6, SF22, ST30**

Demons (1986, C, 89m, R)
An audience watching a slasher film is terrorized by a demonic army and transformed into hideous creatures. Directed by Lamberto Bava. **HO17**

Dentist, The (1932, B&W, 22m, NR)
W.C. Fields stars in this comedy short about a man with a mission for removing molars. **ST67**

Derby (1971, C, 96m, PG)
Documentary about America's great trash sport, the roller derby, focusing on Dayton, Ohio, fan Mike Snell and his obsession with skating dynamo Charlie O'Connell. Directed by Robert Kaylor. Precisely observed piece of Americana. **CU16,** *Recommended*

Dersu Uzala (1975, C, 140m, G)
Oscar-winning drama from Japan's Akira Kurosawa about the friendship between a Japanese guide and a Russian explorer in turn-of-the-century Siberia. Slow-moving, but worthwhile. **DT69, XT7,** *Recommended*

Descending Angel (1990, C, 96m, R)
George C. Scott plays a Romanian refugee to the U.S. suspected by his daughter's fiancé of being a Nazi collaborator. With Diana Lane and Eric Roberts. Originally made for cable TV. **DR8, ST196**

Desert Bloom (1986, C, 106m, PG)
Sensitive portrait of a teen-ager with family problems in 1950s Las Vegas, at the time of A-bomb testing. Annabeth Gish stars, with Jon Voight (especially good), JoBeth Williams, and Ellen Barkin. **DR8, DR9, ST7,** *Recommended*

Desert Fox, The (1951, B&W, 88m, NR)
James Mason plays Field Marshal Rommel in this World War II drama. With Cedric Hardwicke, Jessica Tandy, and Luther Adler as Adolf Hitler. **AC1, HF12, ST153**

Desert Hearts (1986, C, 96m, R)
In the 1950s, a female professor in Reno to get a divorce falls in love with another woman. Helen Shaver and Patricia Charbonneau star. **DR3, DR10**

Desert Rats, The (1953, B&W, 88m, NR)
James Mason reprises his role from *The Desert Fox* as Field Marshal Rommel in this World War II drama costarring Richard Burton. Directed by Robert Wise. **AC1, DT140, ST22, ST153**

Design for Living (1933, B&W, 90m, NR)
One of the great director Ernst Lubitsch's
most delightful comedies, based on Noel
Coward's play about two painters sharing the
same woman. Gary Cooper, Fredric March,
and Miriam Hopkins star. Screenplay by Ben
Hecht. UNAVAILABLE ON VIDEO. **XT29**

Designing Woman (1957, C, 118m, NR)
Romantic comedy features Gregory Peck as a
sportswriter, Lauren Bacall as a fashion designer. With Dolores Gray, Sam Levene, and
Chuck Connors. Directed by Vincente Minnelli. **CO1, DT88, ST171**

Desire and Hell at the Sunset Motel
(1992, C, 90m, PG-13)
Offbeat comedy set in 1958 Anaheim, Cali-
fornia, about wife of a toy salesman involved
with blackmail and double-cross. Sherilyn
Fenn stars, with Whip Hubley, David
Hewlett, David Johansen, and Paul Bartel.
CO10, CO12, DT8, MU12

Desire Under the Elms
(1958, B&W, 114m, NR)
Drama based on Eugene O'Neill play set in
nineteenth-century New England. Mother
loves stepson, family bickers over land.
Sophia Loren, Anthony Perkins, and Burl
Ives star. **DR8, ST141, WR25**

Desiree (1954, C, 110m, NR)
Marlon Brando plays Napoleon; Jean Sim-
mons, his love object; Merle Oberon,
Empress Josephine in this historical drama.
CL3, HF19, ST18

Desk Set (1957, C, 103m, NR)
Spencer Tracy-Katharine Hepburn comedy
of a computer expert and a TV network
researcher matching wits. With Joan Blondell, Gig Young, and Dina Merrill. **CL15,
CO2, ST103, ST217**

Despair (1979, C, 119m, R)
A Russian emigre starts a successful business
in Germany, only to see the Nazis come to
power and ruin his life. Dirk Bogarde stars
in this version of Vladimir Nabokov's book.
Written by Tom Stoppard; directed by Rainer
Werner Fassbinder. **DR19, DT42, ST14**

Desperate (1947, B&W, 73m, NR)
Thriller of a truck driver who is victimized by
gangsters and flees for his life with his wife.
Steve Brodie and Audrey Long star, with Ray-
mond Burr. Directed by Anthony Mann.
DT85, MY1

Desperate Hours, The
(1955, B&W, 112m, NR)
Humphrey Bogart stars in this drama of an
escaped convict and his gang hiding out in

the house of a middle-class family. Fredric
March, Arthur Kennedy, and Martha Scott
costar. Loosely based on a true incident. William Wyler directed. Remake released in 1990
as *Desperate Hours.* **DT142, MY8, ST15,
ST148**

Desperate Hours (1990, C, 106m, R)
Remake of Bogart true-life thriller about con-
victs holding middle-class family hostage.
Mickey Rourke stars, with Anthony Hopkins,
Mimi Rogers, Lindsay Crouse, and Kelly
Lynch. Directed by Michael Cimino. **CU18,
MY8, ST109, ST190**

Desperate Journey (1942, B&W, 107m, NR)
Thrilling World War II adventure of downed
Allied fliers trying to make their way out of
occupied territory. Errol Flynn and Ronald
Reagan star, with Raymond Massey, Nancy
Coleman, and Arthur Kennedy. Directed by
Raoul Walsh. **AC1, DT131, ST69,**
Recommended

Desperate Living (1977, B&W, 87m, NR)
Baltimore's gift to movies, director John
Waters, strikes again with this story of a murderous housewife (Mink Stole), her accomplice maid (Jean Hill), and other not-of-this-
earth characters. Edith Massey and Liz Renay
costar. Don't say you weren't warned. **CU12,
DT132**

Desperate Siege see *Rawhide*

Desperately Seeking Susan
(1985, C, 104m, PG-13)
New Jersey housewife and New York con
artist get their identities switched in this
madcap, modern comedy. Rosanna Arquette
and Madonna star, with Aidan Quinn. **CO2,
CO20, MU12, XT9,** *Recommended*

Destination Moon (1950, C, 91m, NR)
Early example of postwar science fiction,
with rocketship making perilous trip to the
moon. Oscar-winning special effects; cowritten by Robert Heinlein. **SF1, SF3, SF15**

Destination Tokyo
(1943, B&W, 135m, NR)
World War II drama set aboard a submarine
in Japanese waters. Cary Grant stars, with
John Garfield, Alan Hale, and Dane Clark.
AC1, ST77, ST80

Destiny (1921, B&W, 122m, NR)
Early film from German director Fritz Lang,
a fantasy of a woman's desperate attempt to
rescue her lover from the hands of death.
DT70, FF3

Destroyer (1943, B&W, 99m, NR)
World War II sea saga about veteran (Edward
G. Robinson) clashing with young sailor

(Glenn Ford). With Marguerite Chapman, Edgar Buchanan, and Leo Gorcey. **AC1, ST186**

Destructors, The (1974, C, 89m, R)
Paris is the setting for this crime drama, starring Michael Caine as an assassin, Anthony Quinn as a federal drug agent, and James Mason as a narcotics kingpin. **ST25, ST153, XT16**

Destry Rides Again (1939, B&W, 94m, NR)
One of the great Western comedies, with sheriff James Stewart trying to clean up the town—without resorting to violence. Marlene Dietrich costars. **ST55, ST207, WE8, WE14,** *Essential, Recommended*

Detective, The (1954, B&W, 91m, NR)
Alec Guinness stars as Father Brown, the cleric-turned-detective created by G.K. Chesterton. **MY11, MY15, ST95**

Detective, The (1968, C, 114m, NR)
Frank Sinatra plays a police detective who's overzealous in his search for a killer and sends the wrong man to the electric chair. With Al Freeman, Jr., Lee Remick, and, in a small role, Robert Duvall. **AC9, ST63, ST199**

Detour (1945, B&W, 69m, NR)
A hitchhiker gets involved in a murder after he encounters a mysterious woman. A low-budget classic, starring Tom Neal and Ann Savage, directed by Edgar G. Ulmer. **MY1, MY4,** *Recommended*

Detroit 9000 (1973, C, 106m, R)
Jewel thieves and cops shoot it out on the streets of Motown. Alex Rocco, Hari Rhodes, and Vonetta McGee star. **AC8**

Devi (1960, B&W, 96m, NR)
India's preeminent director, Satyajit Ray, offers this drama of a farmer who persuades his daughter that she is divine. **DT102**

Devil and Daniel Webster, The
(1941, B&W, 85m, NR)
Fantasy about a young farmer who meets up with the devil. A flop in its original release, now a cult favorite. Edward Arnold and Walter Huston star. **CL14, HO10, SF2**

Devil and Max Devlin, The
(1981, C, 96m, PG)
Deceased Max Devlin (Elliott Gould) bargains with the devil (Bill Cosby) for another chance at life—in exchange, he'll provide three souls. Comedy from the Disney studios. **FA1, HO10**

Devil and Miss Jones, The
(1941, B&W, 92m, NR)
Classic comedy about a store owner (Charles Coburn) who goes undercover to spy on his employees. Jean Arthur stars, with Robert Cummings and Spring Byington. **CL10, ST3**

Devil at 4 O'Clock, The
(1961, C, 126m, NR)
Spencer Tracy plays a priest sent to rescue sickly children from the shadow of an erupting volcano. Frank Sinatra costars. **AC23, ST199, ST217**

Devil Bat, The see *Killer Bats*

Devil Doll, The (1936, B&W, 79m, NR)
A madman shrinks humans to the size of small dolls and gets them to carry out various crimes. Lionel Barrymore and Maureen O'Sullivan star. Directed by Tod Browning. Creepy stuff, best appreciated by fans of director. **DT18, HO1**

Devil in the Flesh (1986, C, 110m, R)
Sexually explicit drama of a young woman who's torn between her terrorist lover and a younger man. Maruschka Detmers, Federico Pitzalis, and Riccardo De Torrebruna star. Italian filmmaker Marco Bellocchio directed. Also available in an unrated version which contains footage that earned the film its original "X" rating. **CU6, FF2**

Devil Walks at Midnight, The see *Devil's Nightmare, The*

Devils, The (1971, C, 109m, R)
Religious hysteria grips a convent in seventeenth-century France, and a lecherous priest attempts to aid the delirious nuns. Ken Russell directed this controversial, highly charged drama starring Oliver Reed and Vanessa Redgrave. The usual Russell overkill. **DR5, DT111, HO11, ST182**

Devil's Brigade, The (1968, C, 130m, NR)
William Holden stars in a World War II drama focusing on a group of misfit soldiers whipped into a fighting unit. With Cliff Robertson, Vince Edwards, Michael Redgrave, Dana Andrews, and Carroll O'Connor. **AC1, ST106**

Devil's Brother, The
(1933, B&W, 88m, NR)
Laurel and Hardy operetta, in which Stan and Ollie play assistants to a dashing bandit (Dennis King). With Thelma Todd and James Finlayson. **ST133**

Devil's Disciple, The
(1959, B&W, 82m, NR)
George Bernard Shaw's satire, set during the American Revolution, stars Kirk Douglas, Burt Lancaster, and Laurence Olivier. **CL3, ST57, ST129, ST168, WR29**

Devil's Eye, The (1960, B&W, 90m, NR)
Director Ingmar Bergman's drama of the
Devil's emissary sent to take a young
woman's virginity. Jarl Kulle and Bibi
Andersson star. **DT11**

Devil's Nightmare, The (1971, C, 90m, R)
A sexy succubus seduces and slays seven travelers at a remote villa, with each killing paralleling the Seven Deadly Sins. Erika Blanc
stars. Also known as *The Devil Walks at Midnight* and *Succubus.* **HO10**

Devil's Partner, The
(1958, B&W, 75m, NR)
An old man possessed by the devil returns to
life as his mysterious "nephew" to torment a
small town in New Mexico. Ed Nelson stars.
HO10

Devil's Playground, The
(1976, C, 107m, NR)
Life at an Australian Catholic boys' school,
whose students and teachers are wrestling
with sexual problems. Fred Schepisi directed.
One of the more intelligent films on the subject. **DR25, FF5,** *Recommended*

Devil's Rain, The (1975, C, 85m, PG)
Ernest Borgnine is the reincarnation of a
seventeenth-century witch who is to deliver
souls to the Devil. He and his coven melt
everyone who gets in his way. William Shatner costars. **HO10, HO11**

Devil's Triangle, The (1978, C, 59m, NR)
Vincent Price narrates this documentary
about the strange occurrences in the Ber-
muda Triangle area. **ST179**

Devil's Undead, The (1972, C, 90m, PG)
Members of a satanic cult who yearn for
immortality try to project their souls into
children. Christopher Lee, Peter Cushing,
and Diana Dors star. Also known as *Nothing
but the Night.* **HO8, HO11, HO26, ST43,
ST135**

Devil's Wanton, The
(1949, B&W, 72m, NR)
Ingmar Bergman drama of an unhappy pros-
titute and her love affair with a writer. Doris
Svenlund stars. Released in the U.S. in 1962.
DT11

Diabolically Yours (1967, C, 94m, NR)
French suspense tale of a man who awakens
after an accident with a wife and huge house
he has no memory of. Alain Delon and Senta
Berger star. Directed by Julien Duvivier. **FF1**

Diabolique (1955, B&W, 107m, NR)
Classic French thriller about a wife and mistress who murder a heartless schoolteacher—
and the surprising aftermath. Simone Sig-

noret and Vera Clouzot star. Henri-Georges
Clouzot directed. **FF1, MY16,** *Essential,
Recommended*

Dial M for Murder (1954, C, 105m, NR)
A faithless husband (Ray Milland) plots the
murder of his wealthy, adulterous wife (Grace
Kelly). Robert Cummings costars. Directed by
Alfred Hitchcock, at about half-speed. **DT57,
MY3, ST124**

Diamond Skulls see *Dark Obsession*

Diamonds (1975, C, 101m, PG)
Heist drama, with Robert Shaw playing two
roles: the lead crook and his twin brother,
the designer of the target vault's security system. With Richard Roundtree, Shelley Winters, and Barbara Seagull (Hershey). Filmed in
Israel. **MY18, ST104, ST232**

Diamonds Are Forever
(1971, C, 119m, PG)
James Bond travels to Las Vegas, but it's not
to catch any of the shows or play the slots.
Sean Connery stars, with Jill St. John and
Charles Gray in support. Car chases galore,
not much more. **HF2, ST36**

Diary of a Chambermaid
(1946, C, 81m, NR)
Jean Renoir directed this English-language
drama about a disruptive servant (Paulette
Goddard). Written by and costarring Burgess
Meredith. Original running time: 98 minutes.
DT104

Diary of a Chambermaid
(1964, B&W, 79m, NR)
A French maid (Jeanne Moreau) discovers a
world of hypocrisy and corruption when she
takes a job with a country family during the
Nazi Occupation. Luis Buñuel directed this
remake of Jean Renoir's film. **CU18, DT19,
FF1, ST161**

Diary of a Country Priest
(1950, B&W, 120m, NR)
French director Robert Bresson paints a moving portrait of a young idealist assigned to a
rural parish. An important director's most
accessible work. **FF1,** *Essential*

Diary of a Hitman (1992, C, 91m, R)
Unusual thriller of title character, about to
retire, persuaded by his last victim to spare
her. Forest Whitaker and Sherilyn Fenn star,
with John Bedford-Lloyd, James Belushi, Lois
Chiles, Sharon Stone, and Seymour Cassel.
Written by Kenneth Pressman, directed by
Roy London. **CO13, DR16, MY3**

Diary of a Lost Girl
(1929, B&W, 104m, NR)
Silent classic from Germany starring the

extraordinary Louise Brooks as a woman whose life is a virtual catalogue of tragedy, from rape to residence in a bordello. Directed by G.W. Pabst. **CL12, FF3, ST21,** *Recommended*

Diary of a Mad Housewife
(1970, C, 95m, R)
A Manhattan woman, fed up with her status-seeking husband, tries to find solace in an affair with an actor. Carrie Snodgress stars, with Richard Benjamin and Frank Langella. **DR10**

Diary of a Madman (1963, C, 96m, NR)
Vincent Price horror film about a nineteenth-century man possessed by an evil spirit that leads him to murder. **HO8, ST179**

Diary of Anne Frank, The
(1959, C, 170m, NR)
The true account of a Jewish family's hiding out from the Nazis, as told by a teen-aged daughter in her diary. Millie Perkins stars, with Oscar winner Shelley Winters, Joseph Schildkraut, Richard Beymer, and Ed Wynn. George Stevens directed. **CL2, DT119, ST232, XT5**

Diary of Forbidden Dreams
(1973, C, 112m, R)
Roman Polanski directed this bizarre (even for him) comedy of a lovely young woman (Sydne Rome) whose stay at the home of a millionaire causes no end of commotion. With Marcello Mastroianni, Hugh Griffith, and the director in a small role. Original title: *What?* **DT97, ST154**

Dick Tracy (1990, C, 103m, PG)
The square-jawed police detective of the comic strips battles a rogue's gallery of villains. Warren Beatty stars, with Al Pacino, Dustin Hoffman, Madonna, Glenne Headly, Mandy Patinkin, and Charlie Korsmo. Beatty directed; production design by Richard Sylbert; cinematography by Vittorio Storraro. The visuals are the real star; on video they're much diminished. **AC9, AC22, ST10, ST105, ST170**

Dick Tracy Meets Gruesome
(1947, B&W, 65m, NR)
From the low-budget *Tracy* series made in the 1940s comes this case of master criminal Gruesome, who is using a gas to freeze people in the middle of his bank robberies. Ralph Byrd stars, with Boris Karloff. **ST119**

Die Hard (1988, C, 131m, R)
Riveting, breathlessly paced thriller set in a Los Angeles high-rise office building, with a terrorist gang holding hostages and battling a lone New York cop trapped inside. Bruce Willis stars, with Alan Rickman, Alexander Gudonov, and Bonnie Bedelia. **AC8, AC25, ST229,** *Recommended*

Die Hard 2: Die Harder
(1990, C, 124m, R)
More wisecracking, one-man army stuff with Bruce Willis taking on a gang of terrorists making life miserable for Christmas fliers at Washington, D.C.'s Dulles Airport. With Bonnie Bedelia, William Atherton, Franco Nero, and William Sadler. **AC25, ST229**

Die, Monster, Die! (1965, C, 80m, NR)
Boris Karloff stars in this British horror story of a hermit who's given strange powers by a fallen meteor. Based on an H.P. Lovecraft story. **ST119**

Diggstown (1992, C, 97m, R)
Con man just out of prison returns to his old ways by setting up boxing match to sting crime boss who controls title burg. James Woods, Louis Gossett, Jr., and Bruce Dern star, with Oliver Platt, Heather Graham, and Randall (Tex) Cobb. Directed by Michael Ritchie. **DR16, DR22, ST233**

Dillinger (1973, C, 96m, R)
Portrait of America's most notorious Depression-era gangster, played with roguish charm by Warren Oates. Costarring Ben Johnson (as Melvin Purvis), Cloris Leachman (as the Lady in Red), Richard Dreyfuss (as Baby Face Nelson), Michelle Phillips, and Harry Dean Stanton. Directed by John Milius. Rowdy fun. **AC22, MU12, ST60, ST166, ST205,** *Recommended*

Dim Sum: a little bit of heart
(1985, C, 88m, PG)
Drama set in San Francisco's Chinatown, focusing on the relationship between a mother with her Old World ways, and her more modern, Americanized daughter. Directed by Wayne Wang. **DR15, XT13**

Dimples (1936, B&W, 78m, NR)
Shirley Temple classic finds the child star taking on the burden of her father's financial difficulties to help ease his mind. Songs include: "Oh Mister Man Up In the Moon," "What Did the Bluebird Say?" **ST213**

Diner (1982, C, 110m, R)
Baltimore in the late 1950s is the setting for this nostalgic comedy about five young men reluctant to get on with their adult lives. Mickey Rourke, Daniel Stern, Kevin Bacon, Steve Guttenberg, Paul Reiser, and Timothy Daly star, with Ellen Barkin and Michael Tucker. Written and directed by Barry Levinson. One of the few films made in recent

years that improves with each viewing. **CO6, DT75, ST7, ST190,** *Highly Recommended*

Dingo (1991, C, 109m, NR)
Miles Davis plays an expatriate jazz musician whose trip to Australia inspires a young boy to take up music. Years later, the same young man travels to Paris to meet his idol. With Colin Friels and Bernadette Lafont. Music by Michel Legrand and Davis, making his last film appearance. **DR12, FF5, XT16**

Dinner at Eight (1933, B&W, 113m, NR)
Comedy classic from George Cukor stars Lionel Barrymore and Billie Burke as a high-falutin' couple who throw swell parties, where guests open up to reveal deep-dark secrets. All-star MGM cast also includes Wallace Beery, Jean Harlow, Lee Tracy, John Barrymore, Jean Hersholt, Marie Dressler, and many more. **CL10, CU17, DT32, ST8, ST98,** *Recommended*

Dinosaurus! (1960, C, 85m, NR)
Science fiction adventure about a pair of cavemen and a dinosaur discovered on a remote tropical island. **SF4**

Diplomatic Courier
(1952, B&W, 97m, NR)
Tale of international espionage, set in Trieste, Italy, has Tyrone Power avenging a friend's death. With Patricia Neal, Stephen McNally, Hildegarde Neff, and Karl Malden. Watch for unbilled bits by Lee Marvin and Charles Bronson. **MY6, ST20, ST151, ST177**

Dirt Bike Kid, The (1986, C, 90m, PG)
Peter Billingsley plays a precocious teen with an unusual bike that rides him right into mischief. **DR22, FA7**

Dirty Dancing (1987, C, 100m, PG-13)
Romantic drama, set in the summer of 1963 at a mountain resort hotel, where a sixteen-year-old girl blossoms under the eye of a handsome dance instructor. Jennifer Grey and Patrick Swayze star, with Jerry Orbach, Cynthia Rhodes, and Jack Weston. **DR1, MU3**

Dirty Dozen, The (1967, C, 150m, NR)
Allies recruit twelve convicts for nasty job behind Nazi lines. Lee Marvin trains the misfit gang, which includes Charles Bronson, Jim Brown, John Cassavetes, Telly Savalas, and Clint Walker; with Robert Ryan, Ernest Borgnine, Ralph Meeker, and Richard Jaeckel. Directed by Robert Aldrich. Often imitated, never duplicated. **AC1, AC20, DT1, ST20, ST151, ST193,** *Essential, Recommended*

Dirty Dozen: The Next Mission, The
(1985, C, 100m, NR)
Lee Marvin, Ernest Borgnine, and Richard Jaeckel return from the original film to train more recruits for another suicide mission. With Ken Wahl, Larry Wilcox, and Sonny Landham. Originally made for TV. **AC1, AC20, ST151**

Dirty Harry (1971, C, 102m, R)
The first film in the series about the San Francisco cop (Clint Eastwood) who makes his own rules—whatever it takes to keep the streets clean. A psychotic killer (Andy Robinson) is terrorizing the city, and Harry Callahan is ordered to bring him in. Directed by Don Siegel. If the politics are dubious, the results are undeniably powerful. **AC9, DT116, ST64, XT13,** *Essential, Recommended*

Dirty Knight's Work see *Choice of Weapons, A*

Dirty Rotten Scoundrels
(1988, C, 110m, PG)
A pair of hustlers who romance wealthy women wager on a common target—the one who succeeds first has the French Riviera to himself. Steve Martin and Michael Caine are the title characters. With Glenne Headly, Anton Rodgers, and Barbara Harris. Remake of *Bedtime Story*. **CO3, CU18, ST25, ST150**

Disappearance of Aimee, The
(1976, C, 110m, NR)
Faye Dunaway and Bette Davis star in this drama, set in the 1920s, about the much-publicized disappearance and reappearance of the evangelist Aimee Semple McPherson. With James Woods. Originally made for TV. **ST44, ST61, ST233**

Discreet Charm of the Bourgeoisie, The
(1972, C, 100m, R)
Straight-faced comedy about the inability of a group of well-to-do friends to conclude a dinner party. Director Luis Buñuel's film deservedly won the Oscar for Best Foreign Language Film. Dialogue in French. One of a great director's true masterworks. **DT19, XT7,** *Essential, Highly Recommended*

Disorderly Orderly, The
(1964, C, 90m, NR)
Jerry Lewis comedy set in a nursing home. Directed by Frank Tashlin. **ST139**

Disorganized Crime (1989, C, 101m, R)
A quartet of inept crooks, waiting for their leader to show up for a big heist, manage to create plenty of havoc in the meantime. Fred Gwynne, William Russ, Rubén Blades, and Lou Diamond Phillips are the crooks; Corbin Bernsen is their leader. **CO10, MU12, MY18**

Disraeli (1929, B&W, 89m, NR)
Oscar winner George Arliss plays the controversial British prime minister. With Joan Ben-

nett, Florence Arliss (the star's real-life wife), and Anthony Bushell. **CL2, XT2**

Distant Drums (1951, C, 101m, NR)
Gary Cooper is swamped by Seminole Indians in nineteenth-century Florida. Directed by Raoul Walsh. **DT131, ST37**

Distant Thunder (1973, C, 100m, NR)
Indian director Satyajit Ray presents a devastating drama of the great 1942 famine in Bengal. Soumitra Chatterji stars. **DT102**

Distant Thunder (1988, C, 114m, R)
A Vietnam veteran, living in isolation in a woodsy retreat since the war, confronts his teen-age son, whom he abandoned sixteen years before. John Lithgow and Ralph Macchio star. **DR7, DR8**

Distant Voices, Still Lives
(1989, C, 85m, PG-13)
Drama set in 1940s Liverpool, England, centering on one family and important events: the death of the father and weddings of two of the children. Terence Davies directed. **DR8, DR23**

Distinguished Gentleman, The
(1992, C, 113m, R)
Eddie Murphy comedy has him playing a con man with the same name as recently deceased congressman, taking the lawmaker's place in Washington. With Lane Smith, Sheryl Lee Ralph, Joe Don Baker, Victoria Rowell, Grant Shaud, Kevin McCarthy, and Charles S. Dutton. Watch for James Garner in a bit role. Directed by Jonathan Lynn. **CO2, CO13, CO20, ST82, XT12**

Diva (1982, C, 123m, R)
Contemporary French thriller, set in Paris, about a young courier's obsession with an opera singer and his accidental possession of a valuable tape recording. Stylish fun, directed by Jean-Jacques Beineix. **FF1, MY16, XT16,** *Recommended*

Dive Bomber (1941, C, 133m, NR)
Errol Flynn stars in this aviation drama about experiments to combat pilot blackout. With Fred MacMurray, Ralph Bellamy, Alexis Smith, and Craig Stevens. **AC11, ST69**

Divine (1990, C, 110m, NR)
Tribute to late transvestite star of many of cult director John Waters's films. Contains an early Waters/Divine short, *The Diane Linkletter Story,*and a performance by Divine in a stage show called *The Neon Woman*. **DT132**

Divine Madness (1980, C, 95m, R)
Concert film featuring Bette Midler, in all her campy glory. **MU10, ST156**

Divine Nymph, The (1979, C, 90m, R)
Costume drama starring Marcello Mastroianni, Laura Antonelli, and Terence Stamp as points of a love triangle. **ST154**

Divorce His—Divorce Hers
(1972, C, 144m, NR)
Richard Burton and Elizabeth Taylor play a husband and wife who offer two sides to the story behind a marriage breakup. Originally made for TV. **CL15, ST22, ST212**

Divorce—Italian Style
(1962, B&W, 104m, NR)
Supremely funny comedy starring Marcello Mastroianni as a man married to a shrew (Daniela Rocca), pining to shed her for a sweet young thing (Stefania Sandrelli). Directed by Pietro Germi. One of the landmark films of postwar Italian cinema. **FF2, ST154,** *Essential; Recommended*

Divorce of Lady X, The
(1938, C, 91m, NR)
A British debutante (Merle Oberon) pretends she's married to trick her lawyer (Laurence Olivier). With Ralph Richardson. **ST168, ST184**

Divorcee, The (1930, B&W, 83m, NR)
Oscar winner Norma Shearer plays one of her typical roles, the long suffering wife of an uncaring man (Chester Morris). With Conrad Nagel and Robert Montgomery. **CL5, XT3**

Dixie Dynamite (1976, C, 89m, PG)
After their father is killed by a deputy sheriff, two lovely sisters arm for revenge. Jane Anne Johnstone and Kathy McHaley star, with Warren Oates and Christopher George. **AC19, ST166**

Django (1968, C, 90m, PG)
Spaghetti Western finds a group of Americans feuding with Mexican bandits. **WE9, WE13**

Django Shoots First (1974, C, 96m, NR)
In this spaghetti Western, a cowboy is out to avenge the murder of his father. Glenn Saxon stars. **WE5, WE13**

Do the Right Thing (1989, C, 120m, R)
Writer-director-actor Spike Lee's uncompromising look at contemporary race relations in New York City, in a one-day portrait of Brooklyn's Bedford Stuyvesant neighborhood. The action centers around a pizza parlor run by Italians. Danny Aiello costars, with Ossie Davis, Ruby Dee, John Turturro, Richard Edson, Giancarlo Esposito, Joie Lee (the director's sister), and John Savage. Provocative, sometimes wrongheaded, but exceptionally well-made. Lee's best film to date. **DR7, DR14, DR15, DT72, XT8, XT9,** *Highly Recommended*

Doc Hollywood (1991, C, 103m, PG-13)
On his way to Southern California, an aspiring young plastic surgeon is waylaid by an accident and is stranded in a small Southern town. Michael J. Fox stars in this comedy, with Julie Warner, Barnard Hughes, Woody Harrelson, David Ogden Stiers, George Hamilton, and Bridget Fonda. **CO20, ST70**

Doc Savage: The Man of Bronze
(1975, C, 100m, G)
Pulp hero created by author Kenneth Robeson makes his movie debut in this adventure about a super scientist/muscle man and his five colleagues. Ron Ely stars. **AC17**

Docks of New York, The
(1928, B&W, 76m, NR)
Classic silent drama about a man who falls for the emotionally unstable woman he's just saved from drowning. Directed by Josef von Sternberg. **CL12, DT128**

Doctor, The (1991, C, 125m, PG-13)
William Hurt plays an arrogant physician who has the tables turned on him when he's diagnosed with a potentially serious affliction. Affecting, topical drama set in San Francisco features Christine Lahti, Elizabeth Perkins, Mandy Patinkin, Adam Arkin, and Charlie Korsmo. Directed by Randa Haines. One of Hurt's finest performances. **DR2, DR7, DR8, ST114,** *Recommended*

Doctor and the Devils, The
(1985, C, 93m, R)
Two grave robbers provide corpses to a dedicated surgeon who needs them for practice. Based on a screenplay written in the 1940s by Dylan Thomas. Timothy Dalton, Jonathan Pryce, and Twiggy star. **HO26**

Doctor at Large (1957, C, 98m, NR)
In this entry in the British comedy-drama series about a young physician, Dirk Bogarde takes a job in a wealthy hospital. With Muriel Pavlow, Donald Sinde, James Robertson Justice, and Shirley Eaton. Directed by Ralph Thomas. **CO17, ST14**

Doctor at Sea (1955, C, 93m, NR)
British comedy-drama of young doctor (Dirk Bogarde) signing on to work a freighter. With Brigitte Bardot. **CO17, ST6, ST14**

Doctor Detroit (1983, C, 89m, R)
A college professor finds himself involved with pimps, prostitutes, and other low-lifes in this comedy starring Dan Aykroyd and Howard Hesseman. **CO13**

Doctor Dolittle (1967, C, 144m, NR)
Rex Harrison is the magical doctor who can talk to the animals, in a musical based on

Hugh Lofting's children's stories. Samantha Eggar and Anthony Newley costar. **FA9, MU8, MU17**

Doctor Faustus (1968, C, 93m, NR)
Richard Burton stars in this drama based on Christopher Marlowe's play of an embittered scholar in need of some soul searching. Elizabeth Taylor appears briefly as Helen of Troy. **CL15, ST22, ST212**

Doctor in Distress (1963, C, 102m, NR)
Last appearance for Dirk Bogarde in series of British comedy-dramas about a young physician's adventures concerns the love lives of a young assistant and chief of surgery. With Samantha Eggar and James Robertson Justice. **CO17, ST14**

Doctor in the House (1954, C, 92m, NR)
Classic British comedy about medical students majoring in female anatomy. Dirk Bogarde stars in this first of a long-running series. **CO17, ST14**

Doctor Terror's House of Horrors
(1965, C, 98m, NR)
Five tales are linked together by the mysterious Dr. Schreck, foretelling the futures of five people on a train. Peter Cushing, Christopher Lee, and Donald Sutherland star. **HO23, HO26, ST43, ST135**

Doctor X (1932, C, 80m, NR)
The path of a murderer is traced back to a mysterious doctor. Lionel Atwill and Fay Wray star. **HO1**

Doctors' Wives (1971, C, 100m, R)
Trashy drama about the murder of a wife who had been cheating on her physician husband. Gene Hackman stars, with Richard Crenna and Rachel Roberts. **ST96**

Dodes'ka-den (1970, C, 140m, NR)
Japanese drama centering on the lives of shanty dwellers in a Tokyo slum is both funny and terribly moving. Directed by Akira Kurosawa; one of his most underrated films. **DT69,** *Recommended*

Dodge City (1939, C, 105m, NR)
Western saga starring Errol Flynn as a two-fisted marshal. With Olivia de Havilland, Ann Sheridan, Bruce Cabot, Alan Hale, and Ward Bond. **ST49, ST69**

Dodsworth (1936, B&W, 101m, NR)
A middle-aged American couple discover on a European holiday that their marriage is no longer solid. Walter Huston, Ruth Chatterton, and Mary Astor star in this excellent version of Sinclair Lewis's novel, directed by William Wyler. **DT142, WR20,** *Essential, Recommended*

Dog Day (1983, C, 101m, NR)
French drama starring Lee Marvin as a U.S. traitor on the run who bargains with some farmers for refuge. **ST151**

Dog Day Afternoon (1975, C, 130m, R)
True-life drama of a bank robbery in summertime New York that goes awry, with the desperate thieves holding hostages. Taut suspense mixed with humor. Al Pacino and John Cazale star, with John Forsythe and Chris Sarandon. Directed by Sidney Lumet, who's usually at his best at dealing with chaos of contemporary New York. **DR6, DT78, ST170, XT9,** *Recommended*

Dog of Flanders, A (1959, C, 96m, NR)
A badly abused dog is cared for and loved back to good health by a Dutch boy and his grandpa in this animal story. **FA5**

Dogfight (1991, C, 92m, R)
Affecting drama set on night before JFK assassination; title event involves a group of young Marines, about to ship out to Vietnam, challenged to bring the ugliest woman each can find to the same San Francisco club. River Phoenix plays one of the Marines; Lili Taylor is his "date," an idealistic young waitress. Directed by Nancy Savoca. **DR1, DR7, XT13,** *Recommended*

Dogs in Space (1986, C, 105m, NR)
Australian musical drama set in the late 1970s, centering on that country's punk music scene. Michael Hutchence stars. **FF5, MU9**

Dogs of Hell (1983, C, 90m, R)
The U.S. Army trains a pack of Rottweilers to be the perfect killing machines. The dogs escape and terrorize a nearby town. Earl Owensby stars. **HO16**

Dogs of War, The (1980, C, 102m, R)
Frederick Forsyth's story of a band of ruthless mercenaries that tries to overthrow a sadistic African dictator. Christopher Walken and Tom Berenger star, with JoBeth Williams. **AC20, ST222, WR10**

Dollar (1938, B&W, 74m, NR)
Swedish-language drama starring a pre-Hollywood Ingrid Bergman as the wife of an industrialist who suspects her husband is having an affair. **ST13**

$ (Dollars) (1972, C, 119m, R)
Comic tale of elaborate heist, with wild chase sequence. Warren Beatty and Goldie Hawn star in this caper film shot in Germany. Valiant attempt at sophisticated entertainment falls flat. **CO10, MY18, ST10, ST99**

Dollmaker, The (1984, C, 140m, NR)
Moving drama of one woman's struggle to keep her family together when they move from the rural South to Detroit in search of work. Jane Fonda won an Emmy for her performance; Levon Helm costars as her husband. Based on Harriette Arnow's novel. Originally made for TV. **DR10, MU12, ST72** *Recommended*

Dolls (1987, C, 77m, R)
A family and a couple of hitchhikers are forced by a storm to take refuge in a mysterious house owned by an old couple who make dolls that can kill. Directed by Stuart Gordon. **HO16**

Doll's House, A (1973, C, 95m, G)
Claire Bloom and Anthony Hopkins star in Henrik Ibsen's drama of one woman's struggle for respect and independence. With Ralph Richardson, Denholm Elliott, Anna Massey, and Edith Evans. **DR20, ST109, ST184**

Doll's House, A (1973, C, 103m, G)
Jane Fonda stars in this adaptation of the Ibsen play about a nineteenth-century housewife's fight for independence. With David Warner, Trevor Howard, Delphine Seyrig, and Edward Fox. **DR20, ST72**

Dolly Dearest (1992, C, 94m, R)
Horror story of an American family who takes over a Mexican doll factory, only to discover that it's built over an ancient burial ground—with predictable effects on the inventory. Rip Torn, Sam Bottoms, and Denis Crosby star. **HO16, ST216**

Dominick and Eugene
(1988, C, 111m, PG-13)
Sentimental tale of two Pittsburgh brothers (Tom Hulce, Ray Liotta), one slow-witted, well-meaning child-man, the other an aspiring doctor. Trouble arises when the intern must continue his studies in another city. With Jamie Lee Curtis. **DR2, DR8, ST42**

Domino Principle, The (1977, C, 97m, R)
Thriller about a man recruited by a political conspiracy to be an assassin. Gene Hackman stars, with Candice Bergen, Richard Widmark, and Mickey Rooney. Directed by Stanley Kramer. **DT67, MY6, ST96, ST189**

Don Juan (1926, B&W, 156m, NR)
Drama from late silent era, with music and sound effects, stars John Barrymore as the legendary lover. With Mary Astor, Myrna Loy, and Warner Oland. **AC13, CL12, ST8, ST142**

Don Q: Son of Zorro
(1925, B&W, 148m, NR)
Douglas Fairbanks stars in this silent classic

about the Mexican swordsman and his off-spring, who is determined to follow in his father's famous footsteps. **AC13**

Doña Flor and Her Two Husbands
(1978, C, 106m, R)
Brazilian comedy about a lovely young widow who remarries, then has to satisfy her sex-starved husband's ghost. Sonia Braga stars. U.S. remake: *Kiss Me Goodbye*. **FF6, FF8, ST17, XT24**

Donkey Skin (1971, C, 90m, NR)
Comic fairy tale starring Catherine Deneuve as a princess whose mother's dying request leads to a rather delicate situation with her father. **FF1, ST50**

Donovan's Reef (1963, C, 109m, NR)
Classic action comedy stars John Wayne as an ex-Navy man living the island high-life in the South Pacific until a prudish New England girl arrives in search of her dad. With Elizabeth Allen, Lee Marvin, Jack Warden, Cesar Romero, and Mike Mazurki. John Ford directed. Unabashedly old-fashioned, but pretty irresistible, too. **CO9, DT44, ST151, ST224,** *Recommended*

Don's Party (1976, C, 91m, NR)
Australian comedy about an election-night bash featuring heated political debates and some sexual escapades as well. Bruce Beresford directed. John Hargreaves heads the splendid cast. **DT10, FF5,** *Recommended*

Don't Answer the Phone
(1980, C, 94m, R)
A psychopath stalks and attacks the patients of a beautiful talk show psychologist. James Westmoreland and Flo Gerrish star. **HO9**

Don't Bother To Knock
(1952, B&W, 76m, NR)
Early Marilyn Monroe starring role: she plays a mentally disturbed babysitter working in a hotel. With Richard Widmark, Anne Bancroft, Jeanne Cagney, and Elisha Cook, Jr. **ST159**

Don't Fence Me In (1945, B&W, 71m, NR)
Roy Rogers plays a singin' cowpoke who can't be tied down. **ST188**

Don't Look Back (1967, B&W, 96m, NR)
Unsparing, often very funny documentary about singer Bob Dylan's 1965 tour of England. Incisive portrait of a brilliant, difficult subject. Directed by D.A. Pennebaker. **MU11, XT26,** *Essential, Highly Recommended*

Don't Look Now (1973, C, 110m, R)
Julie Christie and Donald Sutherland star in a gripping thriller about a couple who try to make contact with their dead child. Directed

by Nicolas Roeg; adapted from a Daphne du Maurier story. Venice setting is especially well used by the director. **DT106, HO14, HO19, MY14, ST30, WR6,** *Recommended*

Don't Raise the Bridge, Lower the River (1968, C, 99m, NR)
Jerry Lewis plays an American living in England whose free-spending ways are financed by his get-rich-quick schemes. **ST139**

Don't Tell Mom the Babysitter's Dead
(1991, C, 105m, PG-13)
Title says all: group of kids, headed by savvy teen-ager (Christina Applegate) decide to make it on their own with single parent off on long vacation and elderly sitter dead of heart attack. With Joanna Cassidy, John Getz, John Charles, and Keith Coogan. **CO4, CO5**

Doolins of Oklahoma, The
(1949, B&W, 90m, NR)
Randolph Scott Western has the famed outlaws going straight. With George Macready, Louise Albritton, and John Ireland. **ST197, WE3**

Doomed To Die (1940, B&W, 68m, NR)
Boris Karloff plays Mr. Wong, the wily Chinese detective, in this mystery of a fire aboard a luxury liner. **ST119**

Doors, The (1991, C, 135m, R)
The rise and fall of the rock group led by the high-living Jim Morrison (Val Kilmer). With Meg Ryan as Morrison's wife, Kevin Dillon, Kyle MacLachlan, and Frank Whaley as the rest of the band, and Kathleen Quinlan, Mimi Rogers, Crispin Glover, Will Jordan, and Bill Graham. Cowritten and directed by Oliver Stone. Best at capturing the details of the era, less successful at finding significance in Morrison's life and work. Lack of widescreen on video will hurt film's powerful concert scenes. **CU20, DT120, MU5**

Dorothy in the Land of Oz
(1981, C, 60m, NR)
Animated musical based on the popular Wizard of Oz tales, with old friends and some new members added to the Oz family. **FA10**

Dorrit's Story see *Little Dorrit*

Double-Crossed (1991, C, 111m, NR)
Thriller based on true story of drug dealer turned government informant, snitching on Colombia's ties to the Sandinistas. Dennis Hopper stars, with Robert Carradine, G.W. Bailey, and Adrienne Barbeau. **ST110**

Double Dynamite (1951, B&W, 80m, NR)
Frank Sinatra stars in this comedy about a bank clerk mistakenly accused of embezzle-

ment. With Jane Russell and Groucho Marx. Not a shining moment for any of the stars. **ST152, ST199**

Double Edge (1992, C, 86m, PG-13)
Faye Dunaway stars in this topical drama about a New York reporter involved with a story on Israel's West Bank. With Amos Kollek (who directed), his uncle Teddy Kollek (the mayor of Jerusalem), and interview footage with Meier Kahane, Hanan Ashrawi, and Abba Eban. **DR7, DR27, ST62, XT8**

Double Hit see *Next Man, The*

Double Impact (1991, C, 108m, R)
Jean-Claude Van Damme kickfest has the martial arts star playing twin brothers out to avenge their parents' murders. With Geoffrey Lewis and Alonna Shaw. **AC26, XT27**

Double Indemnity
(1944, B&W, 106m, NR)
Classic *film noir* with Barbara Stanwyck the ultimate femme fatale, Fred MacMurray the ultimate sap in this murder for love story. Edward G. Robinson costars. Billy Wilder directed and wrote the screenplay with Raymond Chandler, based on the James M. Cain novel. Perhaps the best film of its kind. Both film and Wilder deserved Oscars. **DT139, MY1, MY4, MY5, ST186, ST206, WR1, XT28,** *Essential, Highly Recommended*

Double Life, A (1947, B&W, 104m, NR)
A serious actor (Oscar winner Ronald Colman) finds he can't separate his work from his personal life when he takes on the role of Othello. With Signe Hasso, Edmond O'Brien, and Shelley Winters. Directed by George Cukor. **CL7, DT32, ST35, ST232, XT2**

Double Life of Veronique, The
(1991, C, 100m, NR)
French-Polish drama stars Irene Jacob as look-alike women living in different countries, having unseen effect on each other's lives. Directed by Krzysztof Kieslowski. Intriguing but not always coherent. Jacob is splendid. **FF1, FF7, XT27**

Double McGuffin, The
(1979, C, 101m, PG)
A trio of inquisitive kids get mixed up in a plot to assassinate a Middle Eastern leader. The adult stars of this family adventure include Ernest Borgnine, George Kennedy, Elke Sommer, and Lyle Alzado. **FA7**

Double Suicide (1969, B&W, 105m, NR)
Japanese drama of ill-fated affair between a merchant and a prostitute. Directed by Masahiro Shinoda. **FF4**

Double Trouble (1967, C, 90m, NR)
Elvis Presley musical about a pop star and one of his teen fans in Britain. With Annette Day and John Williams. **ST178**

Double Vision (1992, C, 92m, PG-13)
When a young woman's twin is murdered, she assumes her sister's identity to catch the killer. Kim Cattrall stars as both sisters, with Gale Hansen and Christopher Lee. Based on a Mary Higgins Clark story. **MY3, MY11, ST135, XT27**

Doubting Thomas (1935, B&W, 78m, NR)
Will Rogers comedy set in small town where everyone is a bit strange or a stuffed shirt. With Billie Burke, Alison Skipworth, Sterling Holloway, and Gail Patrick. **CL10**

Doughboys (1930, B&W, 79m, NR)
World War I service comedy starring Buster Keaton, with Sally Eilers, Cliff Edwards, and Edward Brophy. **CO21, DT66**

Dove, The (1975, C, 105m, PG)
True adventure tale of sixteen-year-old boy's quest to sail solo around the world. Joseph Bottoms stars, with Deborah Raffin and Dabney Coleman. **AC12, FA4**

Down Among the Z-Men
(1952, B&W, 70m, NR)
Britain's Goon Show radio team stars in this comedy about an inept gang of crooks trying to steal a secret formula. Harry Secombe, Spike Milligan, and Peter Sellers head the cast. Also known as *Stand Easy.*
ST194

Down and Dirty (1976, C, 115m, NR)
Italian comedy, directed by Ettore Scola, about a poverty-stricken family and their ribald adventures in a Rome slum. Nino Manfredi stars. **FF2**

Down and Out in America
(1985, C, 60m, NR)
Oscar-winning documentary on America's working-class poor. Directed by Lee Grant. **CU16, XT23**

Down and Out in Beverly Hills
(1986, C, 103m, R)
Homeless man tries to commit suicide in Beverly Hills swimming pool, is rescued and moves in with nutsy family. Comic look at modern lifestyles starring Nick Nolte, Richard Dreyfuss, and Bette Midler, with Elizabeth Pena, Tracy Nelson, and Little Richard. Directed by Paul Mazursky, who plays a small role. Remake of French classic, *Boudu Saved From Drowning.* **CO2, CO20, DT87, FF8, ST60, ST156, ST164, XT10,** *Recommended*

Down Argentine Way (1940, C, 94m, NR)
Betty Grable musical has her romanced by
horse breeder Don Ameche. With Carmen
Miranda and the Nicholas Brothers. **ST91**

Down by Law (1986, B&W, 90m, R)
A trio of jailbirds escape from a Louisiana
pokey for a series of comic adventures. John
Lurie, Tom Waits, and Roberto Benigni star,
with Ellen Barkin. Jim Jarmusch directed this
offbeat comedy. **CO12, DT62, MU12, ST7**

Down Dakota Way (1949, B&W, 67m, NR)
Roy Rogers is on the trail of the bad guys
when he learns of his friend's death. Dale
Evans costars. **ST188**

Down Mexico Way (1941, B&W, 78m, NR)
Gene Autry and sidekick Smiley Burnette
wind up among a ring of thieves. **ST5**

Downhill Racer (1969, C, 102m, PG)
Cocky ski champ and his coach clash all the
way to the Olympics. Robert Redford and
Gene Hackman star. Michael Ritchie directed.
DR22, ST96, ST181, *Recommended*

Downtown (1990, C, 96m, R)
A white Philadelphia cop is transferred from
a suburban beat to one of the city's worst
neighborhoods, where he's teamed up with a
young black cop. Anthony Edwards and Forest Whitaker star in this action film with
moments of comedy. **AC9**

Dr. Butcher, M.D. (1980, C, 88m, NR)
An investigation of mutilated corpses leads a
doctor and scientist to an island where can-
nibalism is practiced. They find a mad doctor
experimenting with strange transplants and
creating a race of monstrous zombies. **HO18**

Dr. Cyclops (1940, C, 75m, NR)
A mad scientist in the Peruvian jungle transforms a quartet of colleagues into miniaturized humans. Oscar-winning special
effects highlight this classic fantasy. **SF2,
SF5, SF15**

Dr. Giggles (1992, C, 95m, R)
Horror comedy stars Larry Drake as a mad
doctor avenging his father's death (he was
lynched after attempting a heart transplant
for his ailing wife). **HO20, HO24**

Dr. Goldfoot and the Bikini Machine
(1966, C, 90m, NR)
Comic nonsense about a mad scientist (Vincent Price) creating an army of lovely gold
diggers. With Frankie Avalon and Dwayne
Hickman. **ST179**

Dr. Jekyll and Mr. Hyde
(1920, B&W, 63m, NR)
A silent version of Robert Louis Stevenson's
story about a doctor (John Barrymore) who
is experimenting with a way to separate the
good half and the evil half in humans. **HO1,
HO20, ST8, WR33**

Dr. Jekyll and Mr. Hyde
(1932, B&W, 98m, NR)
Superb version of the Robert Louis Stevenson
tale, with an Oscar-winning performance by
Fredric March, solid support from Miriam
Hopkins, excellent direction by Rouben
Mamoulian. The transformation scenes are
especially effective. Video version restores
footage trimmed by censors after the film's
initial release. **CU10, DT83, HO1, HO17,
HO20, ST148, WR33, XT2,** *Essential,
Recommended*

Dr. Jekyll and Mr. Hyde
(1941, B&W, 114m, NR)
Spencer Tracy and Ingrid Bergman star in
this version of Robert Louis Stevenson's classic tale. With Lana Turner and Donald Crisp.
HO1, HO20, ST13, ST217, ST219, WR33

Dr. Jekyll and Mr. Hyde
(1973, C, 73m, NR)
Kirk Douglas plays the good doctor/bad guy.
With Michael Redgrave, Susan George, and
Donald Pleasence. **HO20, ST57, WR33**

Dr. Mabuse, the Gambler
(1922–23, B&W, 242m, NR)
Fritz Lang's landmark silent epic about a
master criminal (Rudolf Klein-Rogge) and his
operations. Originally released in two parts.
DT70, *Essential*

Dr. No (1962, C, 111m, PG)
The first film appearance of James Bond
(Sean Connery), as he battles a sinister mas-
termind (Joseph Wiseman) in the Carib-
bean. Ursula Andress costars. **HF2, ST36,**
Recommended

Dr. Phibes Rises Again (1972, C, 89m, PG)
Sequel to *The Abominable Dr. Phibes* has the
bad doctor in Egypt to perform a ritual that
will bring his late wife back to life. Vincent
Price, Robert Quarry, and Peter Cushing star.
HO20, HO26, ST43, ST179

**Dr. Strangelove or; How I Learned to
Stop Worrying and Love the Bomb**
(1964, B&W, 93m, NR)
Landmark black comedy about a crazy Air
Force general who orders U.S. planes to
bomb the Soviet Union, triggering frantic
actions by the President to save the world.
Peter Sellers stars in three roles, with Sterling
Hayden, George C. Scott, Keenan Wynn,
Slim Pickens, Peter Bull, and James Earl Jones
in support. Cowritten by Terry Southern;
directed by Stanley Kubrick. Should have

picked up both Best Picture and Director Oscars. **CO2, CO12, DT68, ST118, ST196, ST198, XT25, XT27, XT28,** *Essential, Highly Recommended*

Dr. Terror's Gallery of Horrors
(1967, C, 90m, NR)
Five-part horror anthology featuring John Carradine as a warlock, Lon Chaney, Jr., as a mad doctor, Mitch Evans as Dracula, and more. Alternate titles: *Alien Massacre, Return From the Past, Gallery of Horrors.* **HF7, ST27**

Dr. Who and the Daleks
(1965, C, 85m, NR)
Science fiction adventure, inspired by popular British TV character, with Dr. Who and his friends on another planet with robot-like creatures. Peter Cushing and Jennie Linden star. **SF19, ST43**

Dr. Zhivago (1965, C, 197m, NR)
An epic of the Russian Revolution and the people whose lives it changed. Omar Sharif and Julie Christie star, with Geraldine Chaplin, Rod Steiger, Alec Guinness, Ralph Richardson and Tom Courtenay. Robert Bolt's screenplay was based on Boris Pasternak's novel; directed by David Lean. Lacks the urgency of Lean's two previous epics (*The Bridge on the River Kwai* and *Lawrence of Arabia*), due in part to weak central character. **CL3, CL4, DT71, ST30, ST95, ST184**

Dracula (1931, B&W, 75m, NR)
Bela Lugosi re-creates his famous stage role as the mysterious nobleman who only comes out at night and lives to drink human blood. With Dwight Frye. Directed by Tod Browning. **DT18, HF7, HO1, HO5, ST143,** *Essential, Recommended*

Dracula (1931, B&W, 104m, NR)
Spanish-language version of neck-biter's story, shot on same sets as the Tod Browning-Bela Lugosi version, but with a sexier approach to the material. Lupita Tovar and Carlos Villarias star. Directed by George Melford. **HF7, HO5**

Dracula (1973, C, 99m, NR)
Jack Palance bares his fangs in the title role. With Simon Ward, Nigel Davenport, Pamela Brown, and Fiona Lewis. Written by Richard Matheson. Originally made for TV. Also known as *Bram Stoker's Dracula.* **HF7, HO5**

Dracula (1979, C, 109m, R)
Frank Langella plays the famous vampire in this version of Bram Stoker's novel, which gives the old count sexier appeal. Laurence Olivier costars. **HF7, HO5, HO19, ST168**

Dracula and Son (1979, C, 90m, PG)
Dracula's boy just wants to play football and date girls; he won't bite anyone, even when his father punishes him. Christopher Lee stars. **HF7, HO5, ST135**

Dracula vs. Frankenstein
(1971, C, 90m, PG)
Dracula (Lon Chaney, Jr.) goes to see Dr. Frankenstein (J. Carrol Naish) to arrange for a continuous blood supply. **HF7, HF10, ST27**

Dracula's Daughter
(1936, B&W, 70m, NR)
Bela Lugosi's second outing in the cape; his offspring (Gloria Holden) is interested in female victims. With Otto Kruger, Marguerite Churchill, Irving Pichel, and Hedda Hopper. **HF7, HO5**

Dragnet (1987, C, 106m, PG-13)
Dan Aykroyd stars as the nephew of TV's Sgt. Joe Friday in this continuation of that show's tight-lipped traditions, with a few contemporary comic touches. Tom Hanks costars, with Dabney Coleman, Alexandra Paul, Christopher Plummer, and Harry Morgan. The leads are good, but the plot's just too silly. **CO10, CO13, ST97**

Dragon Seed (1944, B&W, 145m, NR)
A Chinese town bands together to ward off a Japanese invasion in this classic drama based on Pearl Buck's novel. Katharine Hepburn and Walter Huston star. **ST103**

Dragon That Wasn't (Or Was He?), The
(1983, C, 96m, NR)
An animated feature about Ollie B. Bear, a jolly bruin who raises a baby dragon he finds on his doorstep. **FA10**

Dragonslayer (1981, C, 108m, PG)
Sorcerer's apprentice (Peter MacNicol, not Mickey Mouse) learns his craft well when he takes on an enormous dragon. Caitlin Clarke and Ralph Richardson costar in this adventure tale with dazzling special effects. **AC18, ST184**

Draughtsman's Contract, The
(1983, C, 103m, R)
Unusual drama of seventeenth-century artist hired on commission by wealthy nobleman, asked by the man's wife to provide sexual favors. Anthony Higgins, Janet Suzman, Anne Louise Lambert, and Hugh Fraser star. Directed by Peter Greenaway. **DR5, DR23, DT51**

Draw! (1984, C, 98m, NR)
Kirk Douglas and James Coburn play a couple of has-been outlaws in this old-fashioned

Western comedy. Originally made for cable TV. **ST57, WE14**

Dream a Little Dream
(1989, C, 114m, PG-13)
A smitten teen-ager exchanges personalities with an old man in this comedy-drama starring Corey Feldman and Jason Robards. With Meredith Salenger, Piper Laurie, and Harry Dean Stanton. **CO20, ST185, ST205**

Dream for Christmas, A
(1973, C, 100m, NR)
Family drama of a black pastor moving his brood to California to start a new congregation. George Spell, Hari Rhodes, and Beah Richards star. **DR14, FA13**

Dream Lover (1986, C, 104m, R)
Thriller about a woman undergoing "dream therapy" to uncover the source of her ongoing nightmares. Kristy McNichol stars, with Ben Masters and Paul Shenar. Directed by Alan J. Pakula. **DT94, MY3**

Dream Street (1921, B&W, 138m, NR)
D.W. Griffith's silent drama looks at London's seamy lower depths, where two brothers are both in love with the same girl. **DT52**

Dream Team, The (1989, C, 113m, PG-13)
A quartet of psychiatric patients are set adrift in New York City when their doctor is injured during a field trip. Comedy starring Michael Keaton, Christopher Lloyd, Peter Boyle, and Stephen Furst. **CO3, CO20, ST122, XT9**

Dreamchild (1985, C, 94m, PG)
Imaginative drama of elderly English woman who, as a little girl, was the inspiration for Lewis Carroll's *Alice in Wonderland*, now coming to New York to attend a program honoring the late author. Coral Browne stars, with Ian Holm (as Carroll in flashbacks), Peter Gallagher, and Nicola Cowper. Written by Dennis Potter. **DR5, DR11,** *Recommended*

Dreams (1955, B&W, 86m, NR)
Drama from Ingmar Bergman about a model and the head of her photo agency, their problems with men and their careers. Eva Dahlbeck and Harriet Andersson star. **DT11**

Dreamscape (1984, C, 99m, PG-13)
A research project into dreams is secretly used for sinister political purposes in this science fiction thriller. Dennis Quaid, Kate Capshaw, and Max von Sydow star. **SF5**

Dressed To Kill (1946, B&W, 72m, NR)
Super sleuth Sherlock Holmes uncovers a music box with some valuable hints concerning a theft at the Bank of England. Basil Rathbone and Nigel Bruce star. **HF14**

Dressed To Kill (1980, C, 105m, R)
An adulterous wife (Angie Dickinson) is brutally murdered and her son launches his own investigation by seeking out a prime witness. Michael Caine, Keith Gordon, and Nancy Allen costar. Directed by Brian De Palma. Genuinely shocking but finally just too preposterous. **DT36, MY5, MY11, MY13, MY19, ST25**

Dresser, The (1983, C, 118m, PG)
In postwar Britain, the temperamental star of a traveling troupe is tended to by his loyal valet. Albert Finney and Tom Courtenay star, with Edward Fox. Directed by Peter Yates. The stars are fine but the story overstays its welcome. **DR12, DR23, ST68**

Dressmaker, The (1988, C, 92m, NR)
In 1944 Liverpool, England, a seventeen-year-old girl under the care of two aunts falls in love. Joan Plowright, Billie Whitelaw, and Jane Horrocks star. **DR8, DR23**

Drive, He Said (1972, C, 90m, R)
Jack Nicholson directed this intense drama of life on a college campus during the height of the Vietnam War. A basketball star drifts into an affair with a professor's wife and his roommate cracks under the threat of being drafted. William Tepper stars, with Karen Black, Michael Margotta, Bruce Dern, Robert Towne, and Michael Warren. Adapted from Jeremy Larner's novel. A great time-capsule movie with first-rate performances, especially by Dern, and good basketball action. UNAVAILABLE ON VIDEO. **XT29**

Driver, The (1978, C, 90m, R)
Stripped-down, stylized thriller (characters have no names) about a getaway man (Ryan O'Neal), a detective (Bruce Dern), and a lovely lady (Isabelle Adjani). Directed by Walter Hill. **AC8, DT56, MY2**

Driver's Seat, The (1973, C, 101m, R)
Thriller, made in Italy, stars Elizabeth Taylor as a psychotic on a rendezvous with death. **ST212**

Driving Me Crazy (1991, C, 88m, PG-13)
Comedy about an inventor whose car runs on turnips. Thomas Gottschalk stars, with Billy Dee Williams and Dom Deluise. **ST227**

Driving Miss Daisy (1989, C, 99m, PG)
The ongoing relationship between a Southern Jewish widow and her black chauffeur form the basis for this touching drama. Jessica Tandy and Morgan Freeman star, with Dan Aykroyd. Based on the play by Alfred

Uhry; directed by Bruce Beresford. Six Oscars, including Best Picture and Actress. **CO13, DR8, DR11, DR20, DT10, ST76, XT1, XT3,** *Recommended*

Drop Dead Fred (1991, C, 98m, PG-13)
Wacky comedy of a young repressed woman (Phoebe Cates) who turns to her imaginary childhood pal (Rik Mayall) to solve her family problems. With Marsha Mason, Tim Matheson, and Carrie Fisher. **CO5**

Drowning by Numbers
(1987, C, 118m, NR)
British director Peter Greenaway presents another unusual drama, this one about a coroner involved with three generations of women linked by mysterious deaths by water. Joan Plowright, Bernard Hill, Juliet Stephenson, and Joely Richardson star. **DT51**

Drowning Pool, The (1976, C, 108m PG)
Paul Newman plays private eye Lew Harper in Ross MacDonald's mystery about the murder of a businessman. With Joanne Woodward, Anthony Franciosa, and Melanie Griffith. Set in New Orleans. Decent adaptation, but change of scene is puzzling to fans of MacDonald's peculiarly Southern California stories. **MY10, ST76, ST162, ST234, WR22, XT14**

Drugstore Cowboy (1989, C, 100m, R)
Matt Dillon stars in a comedy-drama set in the early 1970s about a junkie who steals drugs or cash in a one-day-at-a-time lifestyle. With Kelly Lynch, James Le Gros, Heather Graham, and William Burroughs. Directed and cowritten by Gus Van Sant, Jr. Amusing, sometimes horrifying, but overpraised. **DR7, DR16, ST56**

Drum (1976, C, 110m, R)
Sequel to *Mandingo*, with further adventures of fighting slaves, lusting massas, and their women. Warren Oates, Ken Norton, and Pam Grier star. **ST166**

Drum Beat (1954, C, 111m, NR)
Alan Ladd Western about Indian wars. Audrey Dalton costars; watch for Charles Bronson in a small role. **ST20, ST128**

Drums (1938, C, 99m, NR)
British troops in India are aided by a native lad in this classic adventure tale. Sabu, Raymond Massey, and Valerie Hobson star. **AC13**

Drums Along the Mohawk
(1939, C, 103m, NR)
Henry Fonda and Claudette Colbert star in this drama of settlers living in upstate New York during the colonists' fight against the British. Directed by John Ford. **AC6, DT44, ST34, ST71**

Drunken Angel (1948, B&W, 102m, NR)
A young gangster (Toshiro Mifune) is treated by a kindly doctor (Takashi Shimura) for a bullet wound and learns that he has tuberculosis. Japanese drama from director Akira Kurosawa. **DT69, ST157**

Dry White Season, A (1989, C, 106m, R)
Intensely felt drama of racial divisions in contemporary South Africa, focusing on one white man's growing realization of the injustices of apartheid. Donald Sutherland stars, with Winston Ntshona, Zakes Mokae, Jurgen Prochnow, Susan Sarandon, Janet Suzman, and Marlon Brando. Directed by Euzhan Palcy. **DR7, DR14, ST18, ST194,** *Recommended*

DuBarry Was a Lady (1943, C, 101m, NR)
Red Skelton plays a patsy who dreams he's in the court of Louis XIV. With Lucille Ball and Gene Kelly. Outstanding color photography and sets. **CL9, ST123**

Duchess and the Dirtwater Fox, The
(1976, C, 98m, PG)
Western comedy teams George Segal and Goldie Hawn; he's a bumbling cardsharp and she's a kooky dance-hall girl. **ST99, WE14**

Duchess of Idaho (1950, C, 98m, NR)
Esther Williams musical has her taking to the slopes of Sun Valley to rescue a roommate's romance. With Van Johnson, John Lund, Paula Raymond, Amanda Blake, Eleanor Powell, and Lena Horne. **MU1**

Duck Soup (1933, B&W, 70m, NR)
The Marx Brothers take over a country called Freedonia. Zeppo's last appearance with Groucho, Chico, and Harpo. Margaret Dumont acts offended. A classic satire on politics, perhaps the best Marxist movie. Directed by Leo McCarey. **CL10, DT80, ST152,** *Essential, Highly Recommended*

Duck Tales: The Movie—Treasure of the Lost Lamp (1990, C, 73m, G)
Donald Duck, his Uncle Scrooge, and his nephews go off in search of a genie's lamp that can make ice cream fall from the sky in this Disney feature cartoon. **FA2**

Duck, You Sucker see *Fistful of Dynamite, A*

Dudes (1988, C, 90m, R)
On a cross-country trip, a trio of punk rockers from New York are harassed by a gang of rednecks. Jon Cryer, Daniel Roebuck, Catherine Mary Stewart, and Lee Ving star. Penelope Spheeris directed. **DR7, MU12**

Duel (1971, C, 90m, NR)
Steven Spielberg directed this terrifying tale of a businessman (Dennis Weaver) being

stalked on the highway by an unseen truck driver. Originally made for TV. **DT118, MY9, XT18,** *Recommended*

Duel at Diablo (1966, C, 103m, NR)
James Garner and Sidney Poitier star in an Indians vs. the cavalry Western. **ST82, ST174, WE4**

Duel in the Sun (1946, C, 130m, NR)
Producer David O. Selznick's colorful Western saga, with Jennifer Jones, a hot-blooded half-breed caught between brothers Gregory Peck and Joseph Cotten. The supporting cast includes Lionel Barrymore, Walter Huston, Lillian Gish, and Butterfly McQueen. Directed by King Vidor. Gloriously over-the-top entertainment. **CL9, DT126, ST87, ST170, WE1, WE8, WE15,** *Essential, Recommended*

Duel of Champions (1961, C, 105m, NR)
Alan Ladd plays a general in ancient Rome who takes on the forces of Alba in this sword-and-sandal epic. **ST128**

Duellists, The (1977, C, 101m, PG)
A pair of feuding soldiers carry their grudge through many years and campaigns in this drama set in the Napoleonic era. Harvey Keitel and Keith Carradine star, with Cristina Raines and Albert Finney. Ridley Scott directed. Sumptuous visuals overcome weak lead performances. **DT115, ST68,** *Recommended*

Duet for One (1987, C, 110m, R)
A concert violinist is struck with a debilitating disease, throwing her shaky marriage onto the rocks, forcing her into therapy. Julie Andrews stars, with Alan Bates, Max von Sydow, and Rupert Everett. **DR2, DR10, ST2**

Duke Is Tops, The (1938, B&W, 80m, NR)
All-black musical about a girl trying for her first break in show business. Lena Horne stars, in one of her first screen appearances. Also known as *Bronze Venus*. **MU13**

Dumb Waiter, The (1987, C, 60m, NR)
Harold Pinter comedy about two hit men waiting for instructions, getting mixed up. John Travolta and Tom Conti star. Directed by Robert Altman. **CO10, DT4, WR26**

Dumbo (1941, C, 64m, G)
Disney animation brings this poignant tale of the tiny elephant with oversized ears to life. **FA2,** *Highly Recommended*

Dune (1984, C, 140m, PG-13)
Science fiction epic, based on Frank Herbert's classic novel, about intergalactic war and intrigue in the distant future. David Lynch directed. Kyle MacLachlan stars, with Jurgen Prochnow, Sting, Francesca Annis, Sean

Young, Kenneth McMillan, Brad Dourif, Dean Stockwell, and Linda Hunt. Widescreen visuals will be lost on video, and they're the best thing about the film. Even Lynch fans might question their devotion based on this one. **CU20, DT79, MU12, SF11, ST208**

Dunera Boys, The (1985, C, 150m, R)
Epic drama set during World War II, when a POW camp was set up in Australia to house Jewish outcasts from Britain, who incredibly were suspected of being Nazi spies. Joseph Spano and Bob Hoskins star. **AC7, ST111**

Dunwich Horror, The (1970, C, 90m, PG)
An evil warlock (Dean Stockwell) menaces a lovely young woman (Sandra Dee). Based on a story by H.P. Lovecraft. **ST208**

Dutch (1991, C, 105m, PG-13)
Road comedy of working-class stiff (Ed O'Neill) and prep-school kid (Ethan Randall) trying to get home for the holidays. With JoBeth Williams. Written by John Hughes. **CO4, DT59, XT18**

Dying Young (1991, C, 105m, R)
Tearjerker about young man with fatal disease and his lovely hired companion falling in love. Julia Roberts and Campbell Scott star, with Colleen Dewhurst (Scott's real-life mom), Vincent D'Onofrio, David Selby, and Ellen Burstyn. Directed by Joel Schumacher. **DR1, DR2, XT8**

Dynasty of Fear see *Fear in the Night*

E.T.—The Extra-Terrestrial
(1982, C, 115m, PG)
Box-office champion about friendly visitor and the kids who protect him from uncaring adults. Directed by Steven Spielberg, with Oscar-winning special effects. Henry Thomas, Drew Barrymore, Robert McNaughton, Peter Coyote, and Dee Wallace star. **DT118, FA8, FA15, SF9, SF13, SF15**

Each Dawn I Die (1939, B&W, 92m, NR)
James Cagney prison drama, with our hero a framed man trying to prove his innocence. George Raft and George Bancroft costar. **DR18, ST24**

Eagle Has Landed, The (1977, C, 123m, PG)
World War II espionage drama about an attempt to kidnap Winston Churchill. Michael Caine, Donald Sutherland, Robert Duvall, Jenny Agutter, and Donald Pleasence star. Based on the Jack Higgins novel. **AC1, MY6, ST25, ST64**

Eagle's Wing (1979, C, 100m, PG)
An Indian renegade and a white trapper come to blows over a white stallion in this

British-made Western. Martin Sheen, Sam Waterston, and Harvey Keitel star. **WE7**

Early Summer (1951, B&W, 135m, NR)
Japanese drama from director Yasujiro Ozu, with a young woman resisting an arranged marriage. **FF4**

Earrings of Madame de . . . , The
(1954, B&W, 105m, NR)
Elegant costume drama of wealthy woman's gift passing from hand to hand and eventually ruining her marriage. Danielle Darrieux, Charles Boyer, and Vittorio De Sica star; Max Ophuls directed. **DT37, DT93, ST16**

Earth (1930, B&W, 63m, NR)
Russian silent classic dealing with the formation of a peasant farm in the Ukraine. **CL12, FF7**

Earth Girls Are Easy (1989, C, 100m, PG)
Comedy with musical numbers about a manicurist (Geena Davis) living in the San Fernando Valley and her close encounter with three handsome aliens (Jeff Goldblum, Jim Carrey, Damon Wayans). With Julie Brown and Michael McKean. Julien Temple directed. Davis shines; the movie is hit and miss. **CO2, SF9, SF21, ST45, ST90**

Earth vs. the Flying Saucers
(1956, B&W, 82m, NR)
Unfriendly aliens come out of the skies in this 1950s science fiction classic starring Hugh Marlowe and Joan Taylor. Finale featuring the destruction of Washington, D.C., is not to be missed. **SF1, SF9, XT12, Recommended**

Earthling, The (1980, C, 102m, PG)
Family drama of an orphaned boy (Ricky Schroder) and a terminally ill man (William Holden) learning the ways of the bush country. **FA7, FA15, ST106**

Earthquake (1974, C, 129m, PG)
Los Angeles is hit by a catastrophic quake in this all-star disaster drama. Charlton Heston, Ava Gardner, Lorne Greene, Genevieve Bujold, Marjoe Gortner, Richard Roundtree, George Kennedy, and (in a bit part) Walter Matthau try to keep their balance. For confirmed fans of the genre only. **AC23, ST79, ST155**

East of Eden (1955, C, 115m, NR)
Two brothers become rivals for the love of their father in John Steinbeck's transplanting of the Cain and Abel story to early 1900s California. James Dean's starring debut won him an Oscar nomination. Raymond Massey, Julie Harris, and Oscar winner Jo Van Fleet costar. Elia Kazan directed, and he should

have won an Oscar. Widescreen photography is unfortunately lost on video, but otherwise, a stirring film. **CU20, DR8, DR26, DT65, WR32, XT5, XT21, Essential, Recommended**

East of Eden (1982, C, 240m, NR)
TV miniseries based on the Steinbeck classic, starring Timothy Bottoms and Bruce Boxleitner as the rival brothers, with Jane Seymour and Warren Oates. **DR8, ST166, WR32**

East Side Kids Meet Bela Lugosi see
Ghosts on the Loose

East Side, West Side
(1949, B&W, 108m, NR)
Drama of Manhattan couple (Barbara Stanwyck and James Mason) and their shaky marriage. With Ava Gardner and Van Heflin. **ST79, ST153, ST206**

Easter Parade (1948, C, 103m, NR)
MGM musical, with tunes by Irving Berlin, about a dancer (Fred Astaire) caught between his current partner (Judy Garland) and his old one (Ann Miller). **MU1, MU6, ST4, ST81**

Easy Living (1949, B&W, 77m, NR)
An aging football star (Victor Mature) can't face his impending retirement or his nagging wife (Lizabeth Scott) until the team secretary (Lucille Ball) comes up with her own strategy. Directed by Jacques Tourneur. **DR22, DT124**

Easy Money (1983, C, 95m, R)
Comedy starring Rodney Dangerfield as a slob who has to give up all his vices for a year to gain an inheritance. With Joe Pesci, Geraldine Fitzgerald, and Jennifer Jason Leigh. **CO20, ST136, ST172**

Easy Rider (1969, C, 94m, R)
Two California bikers hit the road for New Orleans with money from a drug deal. Legendary "head" movie starring Dennis Hopper (who directed), Peter Fonda, and Jack Nicholson (who deserved an Oscar). Photographed by Laszlo Kovacs; superb rock soundtrack. Box-office success spurred pursuit of young audiences for the next twenty years. A prime artifact of sixties counterculture paranoia. **CU3, DR7, ST110, ST163, XT14, XT18, XT26, XT28, Essential, Recommended**

Easy To Love (1953, C, 96m, NR)
Esther Williams musical set in Florida's Cypress Gardens, with numbers choreographed by Busby Berkeley. Van Johnson and Tony Martin play rivals for Esther's fin, er, hand. **DT12, MU1**

Easy Virtue (1927, B&W, 79m, NR)
Early film from Alfred Hitchcock, a silent melodrama about a married woman whose

husband is an alcoholic and whose lover commits suicide. Based on a play by Noel Coward. **DT57, WR4**

Eat My Dust! (1976, C, 90m, PG)
Ron Howard stars in this car-chase comedy, produced by Roger Corman. **AC10, DT58**

Eat the Peach (1987, C, 95m, NR)
Genial Irish comedy about two friends who come up with a plan to put their village on the map with a daring motorcycle act borrowed from the Elvis Presley movie *Roustabout*. Stephen Brenna and Eammon Morrissey star, with Catherine Byrne. **CO17, Recommended**

Eaten Alive (1976, C, 96m, NR)
A demented hotel owner keeps a live crocodile in his front yard and feeds it any troublesome guests. Neville Brand, Carolyn Jones, and Mel Ferrer star in this horror film from director Tobe Hooper. **HO16**

Eating Raoul (1982, C, 87m, R)
Strange comedy with cult following about a couple who murder swingers for their money to pay for a new restaurant. Paul Bartel and Mary Woronov star; Bartel directed. **CU5, DT8**

Ebony Tower, The (1983, C, 80m, NR)
An aging artist living in a country house with two young women hosts an art critic, who begins a romance with one of the women. Laurence Olivier, Roger Rees, and Greta Scacchi star. Based on a novel by John Fowles. Originally made for cable TV. **DR19, ST168**

Echo Park (1986, C, 93m, R)
Title refers to shabby Los Angeles neighborhood, scene of drama about trio of people sharing a house: a single mother/aspiring actress, a pizza delivery man/would-be poet, and an Austrian weightlifter/Hollywood hopeful. Susan Dey, Tom Hulce, and Michael Bowen star, with Richard (Cheech) Marin. **DR15, ST28, XT10**

Eclipse, The (1962, B&W, 123m, NR)
From Italian director Michelangelo Antonioni, a drama of doomed love between a young Roman translator and a handsome broker, starring Monica Vitti and Alain Delon. **DT5, XT17**

Ecstasy (1933, B&W, 88m, NR)
Notorious film, banned for many years in some states, mainly for brief nude swimming and suggestive love-making scenes. The story is of a bored young wife (Hedy Lamarr) and her affair with a workman. It's still fairly sexy, though that's about all there is. **CU6, CU8, FF7**

Eddie and the Cruisers
(1983, C, 92m, PG)
A rock group's debut album is a smash hit, but their leader disappears with the tapes for their follow-up record. Years later, a journalist opens an investigation of the mystery. Tom Berenger, Michael Paré, and Ellen Barkin star. **DR12, MU4, ST7**

Eddie and the Cruisers II: Eddie Lives!
(1989, C, 103m, PG-13)
Second chapter in the *Eddie* saga, with Michael Paré returning as the mysterious rock 'n' roll singer. **DR12, MU4**

Eddie Macon's Run (1983, C, 95m, PG)
An escaped con (John Schneider) leads a determined lawman (Kirk Douglas) on a wild chase across the Southwest toward Mexico. **ST57, XT18**

Eddie Murphy: Delirious
(1983, C, 60m, NR)
This live concert, taped at Washington, D.C.'s Constitution Hall, features some of Murphy's most outrageous routines, with no-holds-barred language and wit. **CO13, CO16**

Eddie Murphy Raw (1987, C, 91m, R)
More concert comedy featuring the outrageous humor of Eddie Murphy, filmed at New York's Madison Square Garden. Directed by Robert Townsend. **CO13, CO16**

Eddy Duchin Story, The
(1956, C, 123m, NR)
Bio of pianist-bandleader famed in the 1930s and 1940s, starring Tyrone Power, with Kim Novak and Victoria Shaw. **MU5, ST177**

Edge of Darkness (1943, B&W, 120m, NR)
Errol Flynn stars in this wartime drama about Norwegian resistance to the Nazi takeover. With Ann Sheridan, Walter Huston, Helmut Dantine, and Judith Anderson. Screenplay by Robert Rossen, directed by Lewis Milestone. **ST69**

Edison, the Man (1940, B&W, 107m, NR)
Spencer Tracy plays the famed American inventor in this glossy MGM biography. **CL2, ST217**

Educating Rita (1983, C, 110m, PG)
A young wife (Julie Walters) who works as a hairdresser wants to improve her life, and she selects an alcoholic professor (Michael Caine) to do the job. **CO17, ST25**

Edward Scissorhands
(1990, C, 100m, PG-13)
Fantasy of scientist's creation, a young man with very sharp hands, and his encounters with suburban neighbors. Johnny Depp stars, with Winona Ryder, Dianne Wiest,

Alan Arkin, Anthony Michael Hall, and Vincent Price. Directed by Tim Burton. The director's visual flair goes only so far with this underdeveloped idea. **DT20, SF5, SF13, ST179**

Edward II (1991, C, 91m, R)
British-produced version of the Christopher Marlowe play about the fourteenth-century monarch who took a male lover. Steven Waddington, Kevin Collins, Andrew Tiernan, and Tilda Swinton star. Directed by Derek Jarman, who adds stylized touches (some actors wear contemporary costumes) and emphasizes the gay aspects of the story. **DR3, DR4, DR20, DR23**

Efficiency Expert, The see *Spotswood*

Egg and I, The (1947, B&W, 108m, NLR)
Comedy of city girl (Claudette Colbert) and her new marriage to a down-home egg farmer (Fred MacMurray). With Marjorie Main and Percy Kilbride, making their debut as the Ma and Pa Kettle characters. **CO20, ST34**

Egyptian, The (1954, C, 140m, NR)
Elaborate historical drama set in ancient Egypt, centering on a physician to the Pharaoh and his love affairs. Edmund Purdom stars, with Victor Mature, Gene Tierney, Michael Wilding, Jean Simmons, and Peter Ustinov. **CL3, ST214**

Eiger Sanction, The (1975, C, 128m, R)
Clint Eastwood directed and stars in this drama of a professor who moonlights as a CIA agent. He leads a mountain-climbing expedition designed to expose a traitorous agent. **AC12, MY6, ST64**

8½ (1963, B&W, 135m, NR)
Oscar-winning film from Federico Fellini about a film director unsure what his next project is to be. This autobiographical film has had an enormous influence on many other movies. Marcello Mastroianni stars, with Claudia Cardinale and Anouk Aimee. **DR13, DT43, ST154, XT7, XT31,** *Essential, Highly Recommended*

Eight Men Out (1988, C, 120m, PG-13)
Superbly detailed re-creation of the major league scandal that forever changed the sport, when players on the 1919 Chicago White Sox conspired to "fix" the World Series. John Cusack, David Strathairn, D.B. Sweeney, and Charlie Sheen star, with Christopher Lloyd, Clifton James, Michael Rooker, and Studs Terkel. Written and directed by John Sayles, who plays sportswriter Ring Lardner. **DR5, DR22, DT112,** *Highly Recommended*

8 Million Ways to Die (1986, C, 115m, R)
Urban action drama of an alcoholic ex-cop (Jeff Bridges) involved with a prostitute (Rosanna Arquette) and her vicious pimp (Andy Garcia). With Alexandra Paul. **AC8, ST18**

18 Again! (1988, C, 100m, PG)
A teenager (Charlie Schlatter) recovers from an accident to find that the mind of his lively grandfather (George Burns) has taken over his body. **CO5, CO20, XT24**

84 Charing Cross Road (1987, C, 99m, PG)
True-life drama of New York writer Helene Hanff and her twenty-year correspondence with a London bookseller. A small gem of a film starring Anne Bancroft and Anthony Hopkins. Based in part on a play adapted from Hanff's memoirs. **DR4, DR6, DR20, ST109,** *Recommended*

84 Charlie Mopic (1989, C, 95m, R)
Vietnam War drama, presenting events as seen through the eyes (and lens) of a documentary filmmaker. Written and directed by Patrick Duncan. A unique and unforgettable view of the war. **AC4,** *Recommended*

El Amor Brujo (1986, C, 100m, PG)
Romantic drama with dance from Spain, about two young lovers separated by a twist of fate. Choreographed by Antonio Gades. **FF7**

El Cid (1961, C, 184m, R)
The story of the legendary eleventh-century Christian hero (Charlton Heston) who freed Spain from Moorish invaders. Directed by Anthony Mann. Sophia Loren costars. Widescreen will be lost on video. **AC16, CU20, DT85, ST141**

El Condor (1970, C, 102m, R)
Western tale set in Mexico, with two cowpokes searching for a cache of gold. Jim Brown and Lee Van Cleef star. **ST221, WE9**

El Dorado (1967, C, 126m, NR)
From director Howard Hawks comes this tale of an aging gunslinger (John Wayne) who stands up to a land-grabbing cattle baron. Robert Mitchum costars. **DT53, ST158, ST224**

El Norte (1983, C, 141m, R)
Heartrending story of a brother and sister (Zaide Silvia Gutierrez and David Villalpando) fleeing their Latin American country because of political persecution and heading for the United States, where they encounter a different set of problems. Directed by Gregory Nava; produced by Anna Thomas. Beau-

tifully observed story on urgent subject.
DR7, DR27, *Recommended*

El: This Strange Passion
(1952, B&W, 82m, NR)
Director Luis Buñuel's haunting, amusing
portrait of the typical Spanish male's sexual
paranoia. Arturo De Cordova and Delia
Garces star. **DT19,** *Recommended*

Eleanor Roosevelt Story, The
(1965, B&W, 91m, NR)
Oscar-winning documentary portrait of the
First Lady who charmed millions and an-
gered not a few with her forthright views.
Narrated by Archibald MacLeish, Eric
Sevareid, and Francis Cole. **CU16**

Electra Glide in Blue (1973, C, 106m, R)
Robert Blake stars as an Arizona highway
patrolman in this hot wheels action drama.
AC9, AC10

Electric Horseman, The
(1979, C, 120m, PG)
A reporter (Jane Fonda) rounds up a rodeo
star (Robert Redford) for a scoop, but she
winds up with more than she bargained for.
With Valerie Perrine, Willie Nelson, John
Saxon, and Wilford Brimley. Sydney Pollack
directed this romantic comedy that leans too
hard on its stars for charm. **CO1, DT98,
MU12, ST72, ST181, WE12**

Elena and Her Men (1956, C, 98m, NR)
Ingrid Bergman plays a Polish princess who's
juggling affairs with the likes of Jean Marais
and Mel Ferrer. Jean Renoir directed. Also
known as *Paris Does Strange Things.* **DT104,
ST13**

Eleni (1985, C, 116m, PG)
Drama based on New York reporter Nicholas
Gage's search for the man who executed
Gage's mother in war-torn Greece in the late
1940s. John Malkovich and Kate Nelligan
star. **DR6, ST147**

Elephant Man, The
(1980, B&W, 125m, PG)
The life of John Merrick, a Victorian-age
Briton who suffered from a terrible, deform-
ing disease. John Hurt and Anthony Hopkins
star, with Anne Bancroft, John Gielgud, and
Freddie Jones. Directed with enormous inge-
nuity by David Lynch. **DR4, DT79, ST86,
ST109,** *Essential, Recommended*

Elephant Walk (1954, C, 103m, NR)
Elizabeth Taylor stars in a drama set in
Ceylon; she's the new bride of plantation
owner Peter Finch. With Dana Andrews. Taylor replaced the ailing Vivien Leigh, who can
be seen in some long shots. **ST212**

Elevator to the Gallows see *Frantic* (1958)

11 Harrowhouse (1974, C, 98m, PG)
Spoof of heist movies, written by and starring Charles Grodin as a diamond merchant
who decides to pull off the ultimate jewel
theft. With Candice Bergen, James Mason,
and John Gielgud. **CO7, CO10, MY18,
ST86, ST94, ST153**

Ellis Island (1984, C, 310m, NR)
TV miniseries focusing on trio of immigrants
passing through New York at the turn of the
century. Richard Burton, Faye Dunaway, and
Ben Vereen star, with Melba Moore, Ann Jillian, Peter Riegert, and Kate Burton (Richard's
real-life daughter). **DR5, ST22, ST61, XT8**

Elmer Fudd Cartoon Festival
(1940–48, C, 33m, NR)
A quartet of cartoons starring that balding,
wovable, wittle man. **FA11**

Elmer Fudd's Comedy Capers
(1950–57, C, 57m, NR)
Cartoon comedy at its finest, including *The
Rabbit of Seville, Hare Brush,* and *What's
Opera, Doc?* **FA11,** *Recommended*

Elmer Gantry (1960, C, 145m, NR)
Burt Lancaster won an Oscar as the smooth-
talking tent preacher of Sinclair Lewis's
novel. Jean Simmons and Oscar winner Shirley Jones costar as the women in Elmer's
life—and his downfall. Richard Brooks
directed. **ST129, WR20, XT2, XT5**

Elmore Leonard's Criminal Records
(1991, C, 61m, NR)
Documentary portrait of America's top crime
fiction novelist, featuring an extended interview with its subject and a description of his
working methods. A must for anyone interested in this great writer. **CU16, WR19,**
Recommended

Elusive Corporal, The
(1962, B&W, 108m, NR)
From French director Jean Renoir, the story
of a World War II POW and his attempts to
escape. **DT104**

Elusive Pimpernel, The
(1950, C, 109m, NR)
Remake of *The Scarlet Pimpernel,* starring
David Niven as the nobleman turned swords-
man. With Margaret Leighton, Cyril Cusack,
Jack Hawkins, and Patrick MacNee. Written
and directed by Michael Powell and Emeric
Pressburger. Originally filmed as a musical,
but numbers were deleted before release.
AC15, DT99

Elvira Madigan (1967, C, 89m, NR)
Lushly filmed romance from Sweden, about

two young people who run away to be together, only to meet tragedy. Pia Degermark and Thommy Berggren star. Directed by Bo Widerberg. **DR1, FF7**

Elvis '56 (1987, C, 61m, NR)
Documentary, narrated by Levon Helm, focuses on the year when Elvis rocked the nation with stunning performances in concert and on national television. Directed by Alan and Susan Raymond; originally made for cable TV. **MU11, ST178,** *Highly Recommended*

Elvis—1968 Comeback Special
(1968, C, 76m, NR)
This live television broadcast marked The King's long-awaited return to the concert stage. **MU10, ST178,** *Highly Recommended*

Elvis on Tour (1972, C, 93m, NR)
Elvis Presley, on-stage and off, on one of his cross-country tours. **MU11, ST178**

Elvis: That's the Way It Is
(1970, C, 97m, NR)
Behind the scenes with Elvis, as he prepares for his debut on the Las Vegas stage. **MU11, ST178**

Elvis: The Movie (1979, C, 117m, NR)
Kurt Russell plays the King in this TV movie, with Shelley Winters as Gladys, Pat Hingle as Vernon, Season Hubley as Priscilla, Ed Begley, Jr., and Joe Mantegna. Directed by John Carpenter. Original running time: 150 minutes. **DT23, MU5, ST178, ST191, ST232**

Embryo (1976, C, 104m, PG)
Rock Hudson plays a scientist who develops a fetus into a full-grown woman right in his laboratory. **SF5, ST112**

Emerald Forest, The (1985, C, 113m, R)
Stirring adventure tale, based on fact, of an American father looking in the Amazon jungles for his long-lost son, who was actually kidnapped and raised by natives. Powers Boothe and Charley Boorman star; John Boorman (Charley's father) directed. **AC12, DR27, DT15,** *Recommended*

Emil and the Detectives
(1964, C, 99m, NR)
Disney adventure about a young boy who is robbed and enlists the help of his detective friends to catch the thief. **FA1**

Emperor Jones, The
(1933, B&W, 72m, NR)
Paul Robeson stars in this adaptation of the Eugene O'Neill play about a black fugitive who escapes a chain gang and becomes the king of a Caribbean island. **DR14, WR25**

Emperor's New Clothes, The
(1984, C, 60m, NR)
This story from the Faerie Tale Theatre collection features Art Carney and Alan Arkin as two con men who pull the invisible wool over the eyes of a vain king (Dick Shawn). **FA12**

Empire of the Ants (1977, C, 90m, PG)
Vacationers on an island are attacked by monster ants in this loose adaptation of an H.G. Wells story. Joan Collins and Robert Lansing star. **SF10, WR37**

Empire of the Sun (1987, C, 152m, PG)
A British boy living in Shanghai when Japanese invade in the 1930s finds himself separated from his parents and on his own during the war. Based on J.G. Ballard's autobiographical novel; Steven Spielberg directed. Christian Bale and John Malkovich star. Impressive production, small emotional payoff. **DR5, DR9, DT118, FA15, ST147**

Empire Strikes Back, The
(1980, C, 124m, PG)
The first sequel to *Star Wars* features a developing romance between Han Solo (Harrison Ford) and Princess Leia (Carrie Fisher), while Luke Skywalker (Mark Hamill) meets the kindly sage Yoda. With Billy Dee Williams, Alec Guinness, and James Earl Jones as the voice of Darth Vader. Special effects won an Oscar. **FA8, SF11, SF13, SF15, SF23, ST74, ST95, ST118, ST227,** *Essential, Recommended*

Employees Entrance
(1933, B&W, 75m, NR)
Fast-moving, snappy melodrama of life in a department store, with Warren William as the manager who virtually defines the word "ruthless" in his professional and personal lives. With Loretta Young, Wallace Ford, Alice White, and Allen Jenkins. Entertaining stuff, with William a magnetic antihero. **DR24,** *Recommended*

Empty Canvas, The (1964, B&W, 118m, NR)
Bette Davis plays the mother of a model who is the obsession of a young French artist. Horst Buchholz and Catherine Spaak costar. **ST44**

Enchanted Cottage, The
(1945, B&W, 91m, NR)
Dorothy McGuire and Robert Young portray two misfits who fall in love in a magical New England cottage. **CL4**

Enchanted Forest, The
(1945, C, 78m, NR)
Fantasy of a young boy who learns about life from his visits to an old man who lives in the forest. Edmund Lowe stars. **FA8**

Encino Man (1992, C, 89m, PG)
A pair of teens uncover a Cro-Magnon man in an L.A. backyard, take him to school as a transfer student. Sean Astin and Pauly Shore star in this comedy, with Brendan Fraser as the title dude, and Megan Ward, Mariette Hartley, and Richard Masur. **CO18, CO20**

Encore (1952, B&W, 89m, NR)
Sequel to *Quartet* and *Trio* presents three more tales by W. Somerset Maugham, with Anthony Pelissier, Nigel Patrick, and Glynis Johns heading the cast. **DR23, WR23**

End, The (1978, C, 100m, R)
Burt Reynolds stars in this black comedy about a terminally ill man whose friends and relatives can't seem to deal with his imminent demise. With Sally Field, Dom DeLuise, Joanne Woodward, Myrna Loy, Pat O'Brien, and Kristy McNichol. **CO12, ST66, ST142, ST183, ST234**

End of Innocence, The (1991, C, 102m, R)
Dyan Cannon stars in a drama about a woman who grows up the only child of quarreling parents and lives with the effects the rest of her life. With Rebecca Schaeffer, John Heard, and George Coe. The star wrote and directed. **DR10, XT23**

End of St. Petersburg, The
(1927, B&W, 75m, NR)
Silent Soviet drama from director V.I. Pudovkin, about a worker becoming aware of the need to participate in the Revolution. **FF7**

End of the Line (1987, C, 105m, PG)
Drama of a railroad man and his buddy (Wilford Brimley, Levon Helm) from Arkansas who protest the closing of a depot. With Mary Steenburgen, Holly Hunter, and Kevin Bacon. **DR7, MU12, ST113**

End of the Road (1969, C, 110m, R)
Drama of romantic triangle in college community is a springboard for commentary on variety of late-1960s social issues. Bizarre film stars Stacy Keach, Harris Yulin, Dorothy Tristan, and James Earl Jones; based on John Barth's novel. **DR7, DR19, ST118**

End of the World (1977, C, 87m, PG)
Christopher Lee plays two roles: a priest and his grotesque, murderous double in this science fiction drama about alien invaders. **ST135, XT27**

End of the World in Our Usual Bed in a Night Full of Rain see *Night Full of Rain, A*

Endangered Species (1982, C, 97m, R)
New York cop on vacation stumbles onto mystery in small Wyoming town involving cattle mutilations. Robert Urich, JoBeth Williams, Paul Dooley, and Hoyt Axton star. Alan Rudolph directed. **DR26, DT110**

Endgame (1985, C, 98m, PG-13)
Science fiction adventure set in a vaguely post-apocalyptic world, with survival the real name of the game. Al Cliver and Moira Chen star. **SF8**

Endless Love (1981, C, 115m, R)
Adaptation of Scott Spencer's splendid novel of a young man's obsession with a girl and her wealthy family. Martin Hewitt and Brooke Shields star as the lovers. With Shirley Knight, Don Murray, Richard Kiley, and Beatrice Straight; James Spader and Tom Cruise (his debut) appear in small roles. Directed by Franco Zeffirelli. An unmitigated disaster, thanks in part to unappealing and ineffective leads. Read the book, skip the movie. **DR1, DR19, ST41, ST203**

Endless Night (1971, C, 99m, NR)
A chauffeur marries an heiress (Hayley Mills), and they move into a mysterious old house. Based on an Agatha Christie novel. **MY15, WR3**

Enemies, A Love Story (1989, C, 119m, R)
Seriocomic story of a man living in 1949 New York who is married, has a mistress—and then is stunned when his first wife, whom he thought had died in a World War II concentration camp, shows up. Ron Silver stars, with Margaret Sophie Stein, Lena Olin, and Anjelica Huston as his women. With Alan King and Paul Mazursky, who also directed. Based on an Isaac Bashevis Singer story. Mazursky's best film in many years, a rich blend of tragedy and poignant comedy. **DR1, DR5, DR19, DT87, ST115,** *Recommended*

Enemy Below, The (1957, C, 98m, NR)
World War II submarine action, with Robert Mitchum, Curt Jurgens, and Theodore Bikel. Directed by Dick Powell. **AC1, ST158, ST175**

Enemy Mine (1985, C, 108m, PG-13)
When an astronaut crashes on a remote planet, he is forced to join with an alien to survive various hardships. Dennis Quaid and Louis Gossett, Jr., star. **SF8**

Enemy of the People, An
(1977, C, 103m, G)
Steve McQueen stars in this version of Henrik Ibsen's nineteenth-century drama about a doctor warning a small town of the dangers of water pollution. With Bibi Andersson and Charles Durning. **DR20, ST146**

Enemy Territory (1987, C, 89m, R)
A white insurance salesman is trapped inside a ghetto tenement by a vicious street gang.

Only a local resident can help him escape. Gary Frank and Ray Parker, Jr., star. **AC8, MU12**

Enforcer, The (1951, B&W, 87m, NR)
Humphrey Bogart stars as a crusading district attorney determined to put a syndicate boss (Everett Sloane) behind bars. **ST15**

Enforcer, The (1975, C, 85m, R)
Low-budget drama of small-time hood trying to make a rep for himself. Joseph Cortese, Lou Criscuolo, and Joe Pesci star. Also known as *Family Enforcer* or *Death Collector*. **ST172**

Enforcer, The (1976, C, 96m, R)
Third in the *Dirty Harry* series, with Clint Eastwood taking on a female partner (Tyne Daly), as they hunt down terrorists who have kidnapped the mayor of San Francisco. By the numbers. **AC9, ST64, XT13**

Enola Gay: The Men, the Mission, the Atomic Bomb (1980, C, 150m, NR)
Behind-the-scenes drama of the plane that dropped the atomic bomb on Hiroshima, starring Billy Crystal, Kim Darby, Patrick Duffy, Gary Frank, and Gregory Harrison. Originally made for TV. **CO13, DR5**

Enormous Changes (1983, C, 115m, NR)
Trio of dramas based on stories from Grace Paley's *Enormous Changes at the Last Minute*, centering on women's problems in contemporary New York. Maria Tucci, Lynn Milgrim, Ellen Barkin, Ron McLarty, and Kevin Bacon star. Cowritten by John Sayles. Also known as *Trumps*. **DR10, DR15, DR19, DT112, ST7, XT9**

Ensayo de un Crimen (Rehearsal of a Murder) see *Criminal Life of Archibaldo de la Cruz, The*

Ensign Pulver (1964, C, 104m, NR)
This sequel to *Mister Roberts* follows the shenanigans of Ensign Pulver (Robert Walker, Jr.) as he tries to save the captain (Burl Ives), who has been washed overboard. With Walter Matthau, Jack Nicholson, and Larry Hagman. **CO21, ST155, ST163**

Enter Laughing (1967, C, 112m, NR)
Carl Reiner wrote and directed this semi-autobiographical comedy about a struggling young actor. Reni Santoni stars, with José Ferrer, Shelley Winters, Elaine May, and Rob Reiner in a small role. **CO8, DT86, DT103, ST232**

Enter the Dragon (1973, C, 97m, R)
Martial arts classic, with cult following, starring Bruce Lee in his last finished film. He's invited to a fighting tournament on an island stronghold run by a criminal kingpin.

Exciting action sequences; the one Lee film to see to understand his enormous appeal. **CU7, ST134, XT22,** *Essential, Highly Recommended*

Entertainer, The (1960, B&W, 97m, NR)
John Osborne's drama of a third-rate British vaudevillian causing his family no end of pain. Laurence Olivier stars, with Brenda de Banzie, Roger Livesey, Joan Plowright, Daniel Massey, Shirley Anne Field, and (in their debuts) Alan Bates and Albert Finney. Osborne adapted his play; Tony Richardson directed. **DR12, DR20, DR23, ST9, ST68, ST168**

Entertaining Mr. Sloane (1970, C, 94m, NR)
In this offbeat comedy based on the Joe Orton play, a handsome young criminal becomes sexually involved with both a widow and her brother. Beryl Reid, Harry Andrews, and Peter McEnery star. **CO12, CO17**

Entity, The (1983, R, 115m, R)
Barbara Hershey stars in a drama, based on real events, in which a woman is sexually assaulted by a giant unseen mass. With Ron Silver and Jacqueline Brooks. **DR6, MY3, ST104**

Entr'acte see *Crazy Ray, The*

Entre Nous (1983, C, 110m, PG)
Touching drama of two women whose friendship for each other over a twenty-year span proves stronger than what they feel for their husbands. Isabelle Huppert and Miou Miou star. Diane Kurys directed. **DR10, FF1,** *Recommended*

Epic That Never Was, The (1965, C/B&W, 74m, NR)
Documentary detailing the troubled 1937 film version of *I, Claudius*, directed by Josef von Sternberg, which was shelved after its star, Merle Oberon, was injured in an auto accident. Charles Laughton was to play Claudius; also appearing are Flora Robson, Emlyn Williams, Robert Newton, author Robert Graves, and Dirk Bogarde. **CU16, DT128, ST14, ST132,** *Recommended*

Equalizer 2000 (1986, C, 85m, R)
In a post-apocalypse world, only Slade, the one-man army, will take on the brutal dictatorship of The Ownership. Richard Norton and Corinne Wahl star. **AC25**

Equinox Flower (1958, C, 118m, NR)
Japanese director Yasujiro Ozu's first color film, about a business executive (Chishu Ryu) who rejects his daughter's suitor. **FF4**

Equus (1977, C, 138m, R)
A psychiatrist (Richard Burton) tries to unravel the problems of a stable boy (Peter Firth) who intentionally blinds horses. Based on the Peter Shaffer play; directed by Sidney Lumet. **DR20, DT78, ST22**

Eraserhead (1978, B&W, 90m, NR)
Director David Lynch's legendary cult film about a reclusive young man (John Nance), the deformed baby he fathers, and his bizarre imaginary life. A midnight-screening favorite. **CU1, CU12, DT79, HO14**

Erendira (1983, C, 103m, NR)
Offbeat drama, based on a story by Gabriel Garcia Marquez, about a woman who travels the countryside with a carnival starring her young granddaughter as a sexual slave. Irene Papas stars; filmed in Mexico. **FF6**

Eric Bogosian—Funhouse
(1987, C, 60m, NR)
Record of the comic's one-man show in which he plays a variety of characters. Originally made for public TV. Also known as *Funhouse*. **CU16**

Erik the Viking (1989, C, 103m, PG-13)
Spoof of Viking films stars Tim Robbins, with Gary Cady, Mickey Rooney, John Cleese, and Terry Jones, who also wrote and directed. **CO7, CO15, ST189**

Ernest Film Festival, The
(1986, C, 55m, NR)
Collection of TV ads starring Jim Varney as his hick character, Ernest P. Worrell. **CO16**

Ernest Goes to Camp (1987, C, 93m, PG)
Ernest P. Worrell, world's most inept human, gets his wish when he envisions himself as a camp counselor. Jim Varney stars in this silly family comedy. **FA6**

Ernest Goes to Jail (1990, C, 81m, PG)
A bank janitor is wrongly fingered for a robbery and winds up in stir with hardened cons. Jim Varney plays the title character in this family comedy. **CO10, FA6**

Ernest Saves Christmas
(1988, C, 89m, PG)
Jim Varney stars as Ernest P. Worrell, the good-natured hayseed who's out to fill in when Santa can't make his annual trip. **FA6, FA13**

Ernest Scared Stupid (1991, C, 91m, PG)
Jim Varney's fourth outing as the bubble-brained Ernest P. Worrell takes place at Halloween, when an evil witch (Eartha Kitt) releases a wicked troll. **FA6, MU12**

Ernie Kovacs: Between the Laughter
(1984, C, 100m, NR)
Jeff Goldblum stars as TV's pioneering comic genius; this drama focuses on his bitter battle for custody of his two daughters from his first marriage. With Melody Anderson as Edie Adams. **DR4, ST90**

Errand Boy, The (1961, B&W, 92m, NR)
Star Jerry Lewis directed this tale of a nutty young nerd set loose in a movie studio. **CO20, ST139**

Escape Artist, The (1982, C, 96m, PG)
Young magician tries to follow in his late father's footsteps in this offbeat drama starring Griffin O'Neal, with Teri Garr, Raul Julia, Joan Hackett, and Desi Arnaz. Directed by Caleb Deschanel; written by Stephen Zito and Melissa Mathison. **DR9, FA7, FA15,** *Recommended*

Escape From Alcatraz (1979, C, 112m, PG)
Clint Eastwood stars as bank robber Frank Morris, who led the only escape from the famed maximum security prison in which no one was caught. Directed by Don Siegel; his last collaboration with Clint and one of their very best. **DR18, DT116, ST64,** *Recommended*

Escape From New York (1981, C, 99m, R)
In the near future, Manhattan has become a maximum-security prison for the worst criminal elements. When the president's plane crashes there, the government hires a soldier of fortune to rescue him. John Carpenter directed; Kurt Russell stars, with Lee Van Cleef, Harry Dean Stanton, Isaac Hayes, and Adrienne Barbeau. Great idea, wonderful cast—so why isn't it better? **AC21, DT23, MU12, SF8, ST191, ST205, ST221**

Escape From the Planet of the Apes
(1971, C, 98m, PG)
Third in *Apes* series of sci-fi adventures, with the ape characters in contemporary Los Angeles. Roddy McDowall, Kim Hunter, and Bradford Dillman star. **FA8, SF8, SF13, SF23**

Escape Me Never (1947, B&W, 104m, NR)
Offbeat role for Errol Flynn, as he plays a composer who marries a young waif (Ida Lupino) and then cheats on her. With Eleanor Parker and Gig Young. **ST69**

Escape to Athena (1979, C, 101m, PG)
World War II POWs plan an escape and art heist. Roger Moore, Telly Savalas, and David Niven star, with Claudia Cardinale, Richard Roundtree, Sonny Bono, and in a bit role, William Holden. **AC7, MU12, MY18, ST106**

Escape to Burma (1955, C, 87m, NR)
Barbara Stanwyck's the tough mistress of
a tea plantation who's confronted by a desperate fugitive (Robert Ryan). **ST193,
ST206**

Escape to Witch Mountain
(1975, C, 97m, G)
Two children with mysterious powers are
the object of a villain's plans in this Disney
adventure. Ray Milland, Eddie Albert, and
Donald Pleasence costar. **FA1, FA15**

Escape 2000 (1981, C, 92m, R)
Futuristic action drama about a society where
criminals are hunted down like animals.
Filmed in Australia. Steve Railsback and
Olivia Hussey star. **FF5, SF11**

Escapes (1985, C, 71m, NR)
Five-part horror-science fiction anthology,
done *Twilight Zone*-style, dealing with time
travel, alien visitors, and telepathy. Introduced by Vincent Price. **HO23, SF4, ST179**

Eternal Return, The
(1943, B&W, 100m, NR)
French drama, based on the Tristan and
Isolde legend, starring Jean Marais. Jean
Cocteau contributed to the screenplay.
FF1

Ethan Frome (1993, C, 99m, PG)
Edith Wharton's novel of a man trapped in
marriage to invalid, falling in love with his
cousin. Liam Neeson, Patricia Arquette, and
Joan Allen star. Directed by John Madden.
DR1, DR19

Eureka (1981, C, 130m, R)
Offbeat drama, set on a Caribbean island,
about a wealthy ex-prospector, his daughter
and her shady lover, and a pair of hit men.
Gene Hackman and Theresa Russell star, with
Rutger Hauer, Joe Pesci, and Mickey Rourke.
Nicolas Roeg directed; his fractured way with
narrative doesn't serve him well here.
DT106, ST96, ST172, ST190, XT30

Europa see *Zentropa*

Europa, Europa (1991, C, 115m, R)
French-German production (dialogue in Ger-
man) based on true story of a young Polish
Jew (Salomon Perel) who posed as a Nazi to
avoid persecution. Written and directed by
Agnieszka Holland. **FF3,** *Recommended*

Europa '51 (1951, B&W, 110m, NR)
Ingrid Bergman stars in a drama of a wealthy
woman's search for peace after the death of
her son. Roberto Rossellini, then Bergman's
husband, directed. Also known as *The Greatest Love.* **DT109, ST13, XT30**

Europeans, The (1979, C, 90m, NR)
A staid American family living in 19th-
century New England tries to cope with the
arrival of two foreign cousins. Ismail Merchant produced and James Ivory directed this
drama, adapted from the Henry James novel
by Ruth Prawer Jhabvala. Lee Remick stars,
with Robin Ellis, Wesley Addy, Lisa Eichorn,
and Tim Woodward. **DR27, DT61, WR14**

Eve of Destruction (1991, C, 98m, R)
Female scientist invents robot in her likeness;
it goes berserk and she has to find a way to
stop it. Gregory Hines and Renee Soutendijk
star. **SF5, SF6**

Even More Ripping Yarns see *Ripping
Yarns* (series)

**Evening With Bobcat Goldthwait:
Share the Warmth, An**
(1987, C, 83m, NR)
The comedian whom one critic called "a
cross between Joe Cocker and a serial killer"
performs in concert. **CO16**

Evening With Robin Williams, An
(1982, C, 92m, NR)
The fastest funny man in America goes wild
in this energetic comedy special. **CO16,
ST228**

Eversmile, New Jersey (1989, C, 88m, PG)
Daniel Day-Lewis stars in this strange comedy about a traveling missionary who doubles as a dentist, working his way through
Argentina. **CO12, ST48**

Every Girl Should Be Married
(1948, B&W, 85m, NR)
Comedy about a determined girl (Betsy
Drake) who sets out to capture the affections
of a bachelor (Cary Grant). **ST92**

**Every Man for Himself and God
Against All** (1975, C, 110m, NR)
German drama, based on fact, about a
strange, child-like man who appeared one
day in nineteenth-century Nuremberg. Directed by Werner Herzog; one of the films
that deservedly won him acclaim. Also
known as *The Mystery of Kasper Hauser.*
DT54, *Recommended*

Every Time We Say Goodbye
(1987, C, 97m, PG-13)
An American soldier recuperating in a Jerusalem hospital falls in love with a Jewish girl,
whose family opposes the romance. Tom
Hanks and Cristina Marsillach star in this
drama set during World War II. **DR3, ST97**

Every Which Way But Loose
(1978, C, 114m, PG)
Clint Eastwood plays a two-fisted truck driver

who travels the country with his pet orangutan Clyde in pursuit of a country and western singer (Sondra Locke). Beverly D'Angelo and Ruth Gordon costar in this action comedy. Ham-handed stuff. **CO9, ST64**

Everybody Sing (1938, B&W, 80m, NR)
Musical about a family determined to put on a really big show stars Fanny Brice, Reginald Owen, Billie Burke, and a young Judy Garland. **ST81**

Everybody Wins (1990, C, 97m, R)
Nick Nolte is an insurance investigator, Debra Winger a small-town prostitute who hires him in this mystery written by Arthur Miller. With Will Patton and Judith Ivey. Directed by Karel Reisz. **MY10, ST164, ST231**

Everybody's All-American
(1988, C, 122m, R)
Dennis Quaid and Jessica Lange star in a romantic drama of a college football star and homecoming queen who marry and then have to deal with his post-sports career problems. With Timothy Hutton and John Goodman. **DR1, DR22, ST130**

Everything You Always Wanted to Know About Sex (But Were Afraid to Ask) (1972, C, 87m, R)
Writer-director Woody Allen serves up seven comic sketches, each answering a valid question about sexuality. With Gene Wilder, John Carradine, Louise Lasser, Lou Jacobi, Lynn Redgrave, Burt Reynolds, and Tony Randall. The last bit, "What Happens During Orgasm?," is particularly funny. **DT2, ST183,** *Recommended*

Evil Dead, The (1982, C, 85m, NR)
Gruesome horror film about five college pals on a woodsy vacation in a remote cabin and how they're possessed by spirits of the dead. Directed by Sam Raimi. Followed by two sequels. **CU7, HO8**

Evil Dead 2: Dead by Dawn
(1987, C, 85m, X)
The remaining survivior from *The Evil Dead* returns to the site of the murders, where supernatural demons once again take over. Directed by Sam Raimi. Sequel: *Army of Darkness: Evil Dead 3.* **HO8**

Evil Mind, The (1934, B&W, 80m, NR)
A phony clairvoyant begins to predict events that do happen. Claude Rains and Fay Wray star. **HO7, MY15**

Evil of Frankenstein, The
(1964, C, 98m, NR)
The baron tries to manipulate his monster

with the help of a hypnotist, but the monster runs amok. Peter Cushing stars in this British-made film. **HF10, HO26, ST43**

Evil That Men Do, The (1984, C, 89m, R)
Charles Bronson action thriller, with the hero tracking down a doctor who advises dictators on torture techniques. Joseph Maher plays the villain. **ST20**

Evil Under the Sun (1982, C, 102m, PG)
Hercule Poirot (Peter Ustinov) investigates a murder at a resort hotel. Based on the Agatha Christie novel. Jane Birkin, James Mason, Sylvia Miles, Diana Rigg, and Maggie Smith costar. **MY12, ST153, WR3**

Evilspeak (1982, C, 89m, R)
An orphan at a military academy uses black magic on the cadets who have tormented him. **HO13**

Excalibur (1981, C, 140m, R)
The King Arthur legend, starring Nigel Terry, Helen Mirren, Nicol Williamson, and Cherie Lunghi. Directed by John Boorman. Dazzling visuals but muddled dramatics. Worth a look for devotees of the genre. **AC18, DT15**

Execution, The (1985, C, 100m, NR)
Five female friends, survivors of a Nazi death camp, plot revenge on the doctor hiding in America who tortured them years ago. Loretta Swit, Valerie Harper, Sandy Dennis, Jessica Walter, and Rip Torn star. Originally made for TV. **DR10, ST216**

Execution of Private Slovik, The
(1974, C, 122m, NR)
Drama of the only soldier court-martialed and executed (for desertion) in World War II. Martin Sheen stars, with Ned Beatty and Gary Busey. Written by Richard Levinson and William Link. Originally made for TV. **DR5,** *Recommended*

Execution of Raymond Graham, The
(1989, C, 96m, NR)
True story of lawyers and family of death row convict trying to hold off his execution. Morgan Freeman stars, with Jeff Fahey, Kate Reid, and Laurie Metcalf. Originally made for TV. **DR6, ST88**

Executioner's Song, The
(1982, C, 200m, NR)
Dramatic account of murderer Gary Gilmore and his fight to be executed by the state of Utah. Emmy winner Tommy Lee Jones costars with Rosanna Arquette; Norman Mailer adapted his own book. Originally made for TV; video version contains footage not shown in original broadcast. **CU10, DR6, DR16**

Executive Action (1973, C, 91m, PG)
Burt Lancaster stars in this thriller claiming a conspiracy was behind President Kennedy's assassination. Robert Ryan costars in one of his last screen appearances. Pretty turgid. Recommended only for viewers who can't get enough of JFK assassination lore. **MY6, ST129, ST193**

Executive Suite (1954, B&W, 104m, NR)
High-powered corporate soap opera, with all-star cast: William Holden, June Allyson, Barbara Stanwyck, Fredric March, Walter Pidgeon, and Shelley Winters. Directed by Robert Wise. **DR7, DR24, DT140, ST106, ST148, ST206, ST232**

Ex-Lady (1933, B&W, 65m, NR)
Early Bette Davis film has her playing an independent woman who's in love but not ready for marriage. With Gene Raymond and Frank McHugh. **ST44**

Ex-Mrs. Bradford, The
(1936, B&W, 80m, NR)
Comic mystery starring William Powell as a detective who teams up with his ex (Jean Arthur) to solve a case. With James Gleason, Eric Blore, and Robert Armstrong. **MY17, ST3, ST176**

Exodus (1960, C, 213m, NR)
Paul Newman and Eva Marie Saint star in this epic drama of the birth of the modern state of Israel and the Palestinian war that resulted. With Ralph Richardson, Lee J. Cobb, Sal Mineo, John Derek, Peter Lawford, and Jill Haworth. Directed by Otto Preminger; screenplay by Dalton Trumbo based on Leon Uris's novel. Some good scenes (the prison breakout) but script retains some of the book's weaker characters and film needs a less detached approach. **DR5, DR19, DT100, ST162, ST184**

Exorcist, The (1973, C, 121m, R)
A young girl is possessed by the devil and a special priest is called in to perform a horrifying ritual of exorcism. Linda Blair, Ellen Burstyn, Max von Sydow, and Jason Miller star in this modern horror classic. Based on the bestseller by William Peter Blatty, set in Washington, D.C. **HO8, HO13, XT12**, *Essential, Recommended*

Exorcist II: The Heretic
(1977, C, 110m, R)
Delirious sequel to *The Exorcist*, with Linda Blair the subject of experiments by priest Richard Burton and researcher Louise Fletcher. With James Earl Jones. Directed by John Boorman; some scenes shot in Washington, D.C. A prime example of stretching a thin concept well beyond the bounds of credibility or entertainment value. **DT15, HO8, HO13, ST22, ST118, XT12**

Exorcist III: Legion (1990, C, 110m, R)
Third go-round for Washington, D.C., tale of possession, directed by *Exorcist* author William Peter Blatty. George C. Scott is a police detective investigating serial killings that connect with events of original story. With Ed Flanders, Brad Dourif, Jason Miller, Nicol Williamson, and Scott Wilson. **HO8, HO9, ST196, XT12**

Experiment in Terror
(1962, B&W, 123m, NR)
An FBI agent (Glenn Ford) tracks a killer who has terrorized a bank teller (Lee Remick) into embezzlement by kidnapping her sister. Directed by Blake Edwards on location in San Francisco. **DT40, MY2, XT13**

Experiment Perilous
(1944, B&W, 91m, NR)
An unsuspecting wife (Hedy Lamarr) is tormented by her overbearing husband (Paul Lukas), who is set on driving her mad. Directed by Jacques Tourneur. **DT124, MY3**

Experts, The (1989, C, 94m, PG-13)
Comedy adventures of a pair of hip (but not too bright) dudes who travel from New York to what they think is a Nebraska town to open a night club. In reality, they're in a mock American town inside the Soviet Union, unwittingly teaching pop culture to Russian agents masquerading as Americans. John Travolta and Arye Gross star, with Charlie Martin Smith and Kelly Preston. Directed by Dave Thomas. Limp and lame. **CO2, CO14, CO20**

Explorers (1985, C, 109m, PG)
A young science fiction buff gets his wish for space travel in a scheme concocted by his friend. Joe Dante directed this special effects comedy. **CO11, DT33, FA8, FA15, SF3, SF13**

Exterminating Angel, The
(1962, B&W, 95m, NR)
Surrealistic masterwork from director Luis Buñuel: a party of well-to-do friends suddenly find they cannot leave a room. Silvia Pinal stars. **DT19**, *Essential, Highly Recommended*

Exterminator, The (1980, C, 101m, R)
Robert Ginty plays a Vietnam veteran with vengeance on his mind when his buddy is blown away by the Mob. This extremely violent action thriller was directed by James Glickenhaus. **AC19**

Exterminator 2, The (1984, C, 88m, R)
Star Robert Ginty returns for more adventures of the man with the blowtorch. Directed by Mark Buntzman. **AC19**

Exterminators of the Year 3000 (1983, C, 101m, R)
Science fiction adventure with the world gone dry from years without rain and warring factions fighting for every precious drop of water. **SF8**

Extreme Prejudice (1987, C, 104m, R)
Violent action drama about boyhood friends who grow up on opposite sides of the law and on opposite sides of the Tex-Mex border. Nick Nolte is the Texas Ranger, Powers Boothe the drug kingpin. With Maria Conchita Alonso and Rip Torn. Walter Hill directed. For fans of the genre only. **DT56, ST164, ST216**

Extremities (1986, C, 89m, R)
A woman is nearly raped in her home but turns the tables on her attacker and holds him prisoner, trying to decide how to dispense justice. Farrah Fawcett stars, with James Russo, Alfre Woodard, and Diana Scarwid. Based on a play by William Mastrosimone. **DR10, DR20**

Eye for an Eye, An (1981, C, 106m, R)
Chuck Norris is a cop whose partner is killed by drug dealers. He swears vengeance and singlehandedly takes on the gang leader (Christopher Lee) and his men. **AC19, AC25, ST135, ST165**

Eye of the Needle (1981, C, 112m, R)
Donald Sutherland is a German spy stranded on a British island during World War II. He seduces a lonely woman (Kate Nelligan) in hopes of using her to effect his plans. **MY5, MY6**

Eye of the Storm (1992, C, 93m, R)
Strange drama about two brothers who witness their parents' murder as youngsters, with one of them blinded in the attack. Ten years later they're running a gas station/motel when a couple shows up, triggering memories of their tragedy. Craig Sheffer, Bradley Gregg, Lara Flynn Boyle, and Dennis Hopper star. Directed by Yuri Zeltser. **MY14, ST110**

Eye of the Tiger (1986, C, 90m, R)
A newcomer to a small town battles local corruption, goes on a rampage when his wife and child are murdered. Gary Busey and Yaphet Kotto star. **AC19, AC25**

Eyeball (1977, C, 87m, R)
Horror story of a psychopathic murderer and his particularly gruesome calling card. **HO9**

Eyes of a Stranger
(1981, C, 85m, R)
A newswoman is on the trail of a psychopathic killer after she finds that her sister, a blind and deaf young girl, could be his next victim. Lauren Tewes and Jennifer Jason Leigh star. **HO9, MY3, ST136**

Eyes of Laura Mars
(1978, C, 103m, R)
A fashion photographer (Faye Dunaway) has premonitions of brutal murders, but she can't persuade anyone to believe her. Tommy Lee Jones costars in this stylish thriller directed by Irvin Kershner. Dazzling surface barely conceals overly familiar story. **HO7, MY2, MY3, ST61**

Eyes of Texas (1948, B&W, 54m, NR)
Roy Rogers turns his ranch into a camp for boys orphaned by World War II. With Andy Devine. **ST188**

Eyes, the Mouth, The (1982, C, 100m, R)
A young man tries to come to grips with his twin brother's suicide in this drama from Italian director Marco Bellocchio. Lou Castel stars. **FF2**

Eyes Without a Face
(1960, B&W, 84m, NR)
Classic French horror film about a scientist's experiments on his disfigured daughter. Georges Franju directed; cinematography by Eugen Shuftan. Pierre Brasseur stars. Also known as *The Horror Chamber of Dr. Faustus.* **FF1, HO1, HO20**

Eyewitness (1981, C, 102m, R)
A New York janitor (William Hurt) pretends he has access to evidence in a baffling murder case, just to get acquainted with a TV news reporter (Sigourney Weaver) he admires. With Christopher Plummer, James Woods, Morgan Freeman, and Pamela Reed. Colorful characters, good chemistry between leads. **MY5, ST76, ST114, ST225, ST233, XT9,** *Recommended*

FBI Story, The (1959, C, 149m, NR)
James Stewart plays a longtime agent assigned to many of the Bureau's most famous cases. With Vera Miles, Murray Hamilton, Larry Pennell, and Nick Adams. **AC9, CL3, ST207**

F.I.S.T. (1978, C, 145m, PG)
Sylvester Stallone plays a union boss who unsuccessfuly attempts to resist corruption in this drama based loosely on the life of Jimmy Hoffa. With Rod Steiger, Peter Boyle, and Melinda Dillon. Directed by Norman Jewison. **DR7, DT63, ST204**

FM (1978, C, 104m, PG)
Comedy revolving around wigged-out radio personalities at rock 'n' roll station. Michael Brandon stars, with Eileen Brennan, Alex Karras, Cleavon Little, Martin Mull, and Cassie Yates, with concert appearances by Linda Ronstadt and Jimmy Buffet. Soundtrack features variety of late 1970s FM rock stars, including Steely Dan (doing the title tune), Bob Seger, Joe Walsh, Tom Petty & the Heartbreakers, Boz Scaggs, the Eagles, and Boston. The inspiration for TV series "WKRP in Cincinnati." Slick to a fault. **CO8**

F/X (1986, C, 106m, R)
A movie special effects expert is hired to stage the phony killing of a government witness against the Mob. When the man actually dies, the effects man realizes he has been set up. Bryan Brown stars, with Brian Dennehy, Jerry Orbach, and Mason Adams. Directed by Robert Mandel. Clever but not particularly memorable. Genre fans will want to see it. **AC19, DR13, MY9**

F/X 2: The Deadly Art of Illusion (1991, C, 109m, PG-13)
Bryan Brown and Brian Dennehy reunite as the movie effects wizard and his detective pal, out to solve a murder. With Rachel Ticotin, Joanna Gleason, Philip Bosco, and Kevin J. O'Connor. **DR13, MY9**

Fabulous Baker Boys, The (1989, C, 113m, R)
Real-life brothers Jeff and Beau Bridges star as a piano-playing act whose career is on the skids—until they hire a lovely singer (Michelle Pfeiffer). Written and directed by Steve Kloves. Well-played by all three leads; a polished but totally engaging view of the fringes of show biz. **DR1, DR8, DR12, ST19, ST173, XT8,** *Recommended*

Fabulous Dorseys, The (1947, B&W, 88m, NR)
Biography of those great bandleaders and musicians, Tommy and Jimmy Dorsey, with the brothers playing themselves. Musicians Art Tatum and Charlie Barnet appear in one memorable jam session. **MU5**

Face in the Crowd, A (1957, B&W, 125m, NR)
Andy Griffith portrays a country bumpkin who rises to sudden fame as a television star and develops dangerous political ambitions. Patricia Neal and Walter Matthau costar, with Lee Remick making her film debut. Written by Budd Schulberg; directed by Elia Kazan. Scores points about the manipulation of the media that still hold true. **CL7, DT65, ST155,** *Recommended*

Face of Fu Manchu, The (1965, C, 96m, NR)
First in contemporary British series about the evil doctor bent on world domination. Christopher Lee stars, with Nigel Green and James Robertson Justice. **ST135**

Faces (1968, B&W, 130m, NR)
Intense drama from director John Cassavetes, his breakthrough film, taking place during one night and the following morning. The focus is on the failed marriage of a couple (John Marley, Lynn Carlin) who respectively visit a prostitute (Gena Rowlands) and take a young lover (Seymour Cassel). Very talky, with dialogue probably improvised, but remarkably moving for the patient viewer. UNAVAILABLE ON VIDEO. **XT29**

Fade-In (1968, C, 93m, NR)
Love story set against filmmaking backdrop, utilizing scenes from real Western film *Blue* (not available on video). Burt Reynolds and Barbara Loden star. **DR13, ST183**

Fade to Black (1980, C, 100m, R)
A lonely young man who fantasizes about movies begins dressing up like famous film villains and eliminating his tormentors. Dennis Christopher stars. **HO9**

Fahrenheit 451 (1967, C, 111m, NR)
In a future society, firemen start fires, urged by a dictatorship to burn books and keep the population ignorant. Oskar Werner and Julie Christie (playing two roles) star. Cult film was directed by François Truffaut and based on Ray Bradbury's novel. Stiff and cold, unlike most of Truffaut's other work. **CU4, CU13, DR19, DT125, SF11, ST30**

Fail-Safe (1964, B&W, 111m, NR)
A U.S. Air Force plane is accidentally ordered to bomb the Soviet Union, which could start a nuclear war. Henry Fonda stars, with Walter Matthau and Fritz Weaver. Sidney Lumet directed. **DT78, ST71, ST155**

Falcon and the Snowman, The (1985, C, 131m, R)
True story of two boyhood friends (Timothy Hutton and Sean Penn) who grow up to become spies and sell American secrets to the Russians. Directed by John Schlesinger. Penn's good, Hutton not, and the story seems shapeless. **DR6, DR16, DR26, DT113, MY6**

Falcon Takes Over, The (1942, B&W, 63m, NR)
George Sanders stars as the suave crimesolver in this entry of the popular mystery series. Based on Raymond Chandler's *Farewell, My Lovely.* **WR2**

Fall of the House of Usher, The
(1949, B&W, 74m, NR)
British version of the Edgar Allan Poe story
of a mad nobleman and his late sister. Gwen
Watford, Kaye Tendeter, and Irving Steen
star. **WR27**

Fall of the House of Usher, The
(1960, C, 79m, NR)
A beautiful young girl is brought to her
fiancé's mysterious house, where the skeletons come out of the closets with hair-raising
results. Vincent Price stars; Roger Corman
directed this first of his eight films based on
the works of Edgar Allan Poe. Also known as
House of Usher. **DT30, ST179, WR27**

Fall of the House of Usher, The
(1982, C, 101m, PG)
Poe's tale of family decadence, starring Martin Landau, Robert Hays, and Charlene
Tilton. Originally made for TV. **WR27**

Fall of the Roman Empire, The
(1964, C, 153m, NR)
An epic drama of Livius, the renegade general (Stephen Boyd) who's torn between
his country and his lover (Sophia Loren).
Anthony Mann directed; the cast also includes Alec Guinness, James Mason, Christopher Plummer, and Omar Sharif. **CL3,
DT85, ST95, ST141, ST153**

Fallen Idol, The (1948, B&W, 94m, NR)
Absorbing British drama of relationship
between young boy and household servant,
who is under suspicion of murdering his
wife. Ralph Richardson and Bobby Henrey
star, with Michele Morgan, Jack Hawkins,
and Bernard Lee. Directed by Carol Reed;
based on a Graham Greene novel, *The Basement Room.* Superbly drawn character study.
DR23, ST184, WR11, *Recommended*

Fallen Sparrow, The
(1943, B&W, 94m, NR)
World War II–era thriller, with John Garfield
as a Spanish Civil War veteran hunted by
Nazis in New York City. With Maureen
O'Hara and Walter Slezak. **ST80, ST167**

Falling Down (1993, C, 115m, R)
Melodrama of contemporary man gone haywire. He's walking across Los Angeles to be
reunited with his estranged wife and daughter, creating havoc in his wake and attracting
the attention of a police detective about to
retire from the force. Michael Douglas and
Robert Duvall star, with Barbara Hershey,
Rachel Ticotin, Tuesday Weld, Frederic Forrest, and Lois Smith. Written by Ebbe Roe
Smith, directed by Joel Schumacher. Scores
some points about urban alienation, but

loses its delicate balance about halfway into
the story when the Douglas character takes a
violent turn. **DR7, DR15, ST59, ST63,
ST104, XT10**

Falling From Grace
(1992, C, 100m, PG-13)
John Cougar Mellencamp stars in this drama
of a country singer who returns to his small
hometown in Indiana to deal with family
problems. With Kay Lenz, Mariel Hemingway, Claude Akins, and Dub Taylor. Written
by Larry McMurtry, directed by Mellencamp.
DR8, DR26, XT23

Falling in Love (1984, C, 107m, PG-13)
Robert De Niro and Meryl Streep star as two
married Manhattan-bound commuters who
strike up a friendship that develops into
something more serious. With Harvey Keitel,
Jane Kaczmarek, and Dianne Wiest. The stars
never develop any real passion. **DR3, ST51,
ST210, XT9**

Falling in Love Again (1980, C, 103m, R)
Middle-aged man is nostalgic for his youth-
ful, romantic days. Elliott Gould stars, with
Susannah York and Michelle Pfeiffer. **ST173**

Falstaff see *Chimes at Midnight*

Fame (1980, C, 134m, R)
New York City's High School for the Performing Arts is the backdrop for this story of
aspiring students who struggle to make it in
show business. Directed by Alan Parker. Irene
Cara, Lee Curreri, Eddie Barth, Laura Dean,
Paul McCrane, and Gene Anthony Ray star.
Michael Gore's music and several stirring
production numbers are offset by dippy dramatics. **DR25, MU9, XT9**

Family, The (1970, C, 100m, R)
An ex-con seeks retribution against the man
who framed him and stole his girlfriend
while he was in prison. Charles Bronson
stars, with Jill Ireland and Telly Savalas.
AC19, ST20

Family, The (1987, C, 127m, PG)
Drama of eighty years in the life of one fam-
ily in Rome, directed by Ettore Scola. Vittorio
Gassman stars, with Fanny Ardant, Philippe
Noiret, and Stefania Sandrelli. **FF2**

Family Business (1989, C, 115m, R)
Crime comedy of three generations of a Mob
clan: irrepressible grandfather (Sean Connery), reluctant son (Dustin Hoffman), and
eager grandson (Matthew Broderick). Directed by Sidney Lumet. **CO5, CO10, DT78,
ST36, ST105**

Family Enforcer, The see *Enforcer, The*
(1975)

Family Game, The (1984, C, 107m, NR)
Comedy centering on Japanese family who hires a tutor for one of its sons and winds up being totally dominated by the teacher. Directed by Yoshimitsu Morita. **FF4**

Family Jewels, The (1965, C, 100m, NR)
Jerry Lewis plays seven outrageously different roles, as potential guardians to a little heiress. **ST139, XT27**

Family Plot (1976, C, 120m, PG)
Alfred Hitchcock's final film is about a phony psychic who, along with her private-eye boyfriend, tries to find a missing heir. Barbara Harris, Bruce Dern, William Devane, and Karen Black star. Hitch goes out on a relatively high note, thanks to a quartet of well-drawn characters. **DT57,** *Recommended*

Family Secrets (1984, C, 96m, NR)
Drama of three women from different generations of the same family spending a weekend together. Maureen Stapleton, Stefanie Powers, and Melissa Gilbert star, with James Spader. Originally made for TV. **DR8, DR10, ST203**

Family Upside Down, A
(1978, C, 100m, NR)
Emmy-winning performance by Fred Astaire highlights this drama of an elderly couple who become dependent on their grown-up offspring. With Helen Hayes, Efrem Zimbalist, Jr., Pat Crowley, and Patty Duke Astin. Originally made for TV. **DR11, ST4**

Fan, The (1981, C, 95m, R)
Stalker thriller about glamorous actress (Lauren Bacall) hounded by unbalanced fan (Michael Biehn). With James Garner and Maureen Stapleton. **MY3, MY19, ST82**

Fancy Pants (1950, C, 92m, NR)
Remake of comic Western *Ruggles of Red Gap*, with Bob Hope (billed as "Mr. Robert Hope") as an English valet, Lucille Ball a nouveauriche lady. **CU18, ST108, WE8, WE14**

Fandango (1985, C, 91m, PG)
A group of college friends decide to go off for one last "fandango" by driving across Texas to Mexico before they're drafted to fight in the Vietnam War. Judd Nelson and Kevin Costner star in this comedy-drama, with Sam Robards, Chuck Bush, Glenne Headly, and Suzy Amis. Expansion of student film by director Kevin Reynolds and self-conscious as only a student film can be. Reynolds and Costner later collaborated on *Robin Hood*. **CO4, ST38, XT18**

Fanny (1932, B&W, 120m, NR)
Second part of famed trilogy by French writer-director Marcel Pagnol (*Marius* is first,

César is last). Fanny (Orane Demazis) is abandoned by her true love Marius (Pierre Fresnay). **DR1, FF1**

Fanny (1961, C, 133m, NR)
Condensation of Marcel Pagnol's trilogy about a wandering sailor and the girl he leaves behind. Leslie Caron and Horst Buchholz star, with Charles Boyer and Maurice Chevalier. Directed by Joshua Logan. **DR1, ST16**

Fanny and Alexander (1983, C, 197m, R)
Oscar-winning family epic from director Ingmar Bergman, a mixture of comedy and drama set in turn-of-the-century Sweden. The point of view is that of a young boy and his sister, as they witness their beloved father's death and their mother's remarriage to a stern minister. Less forbidding than many of Bergman's films but no less powerful. **DT11, XT7,** *Recommended*

Fantasia (1940, C, 120m, G)
Walt Disney's landmark marriage of animation and classical music, underappreciated in its time, gaining prestige and fans over the years through numerous reissues, at one point adopted as a "head" movie by certain cultists. NOTE: Dealers had a limited time (November 1991–January 1992) to buy the film for sale and rent; copies may be difficult to find. **CL14, CU3, FA2,** *Essential, Recommended*

Fantastic Planet, The (1973, C, 72m, NR)
From France, an animated science fiction adventure about a planet where men are slaves to gigantic mechanical creatures. **FF1, SF19**

Fantastic Voyage (1966, C, 100m, NR)
Team of scientists is miniaturized and injected into the body of a patient in need of advanced micro-surgery. Oscar-winning special effects highlight this science fiction adventure. Donald Pleasence, Stephen Boyd, Raquel Welch, and Edmond O'Brien star. **SF3, SF15**

Far and Away (1992, C, 140m, PG-13)
Epic story of pair of Irish immigrants coming to late nineteenth-century Boston, moving west to participate in Oklahoma Land Rush. Tom Cruise and Nicole Kidman star, with Thomas Gibson, Robert Prosky, Barbara Babcock, Rance Howard, and Clint Howard. Directed by Ron Howard (Rance's son, Clint's brother). Mildly entertaining star vehicle that carries no urgency or extra sparkle. **DR1, DR5, DT58, ST41, XT8**

Far Country, The (1955, C, 97m, NR)
Western tale about a cattleman (James Stewart) in search of a boomtown on the Alaskan tundra. Directed by Anthony Mann; out-

standing color photography. **CL9, DT85, ST207, WE10**

Far From the Madding Crowd
(1967, C, 169m, NR)
Thomas Hardy's story of one passionate woman's effect on three very different men, starring Julie Christie, Alan Bates, Peter Finch, and Terence Stamp. Cinematography by Nicolas Roeg; adapted by Frederic Raphael and directed by John Schlesinger. Perhaps the best big-screen treatment of Hardy. **CL1, DR1, DR19, DT113, ST9, ST30,**
Recommended

Far Frontier, The (1948, B&W, 67m, NR)
Roy Rogers rides to the rescue of a kidnapped Border Patrol agent. With Andy Devine.
ST188

Far North (1988, C, 88m, PG-13)
Sam Shepard wrote and directed this drama of a woman's struggle to reconcile herself with her father. Jessica Lange and Charles Durning star, with Anne Wedgeworth. **DR8, DR10, ST130**

Far Off Place, A (1993, C, 105m, PG)
Disney adventure story of two American teens stranded in African wilderness when their parents are murdered by poachers. They're guided to safety by a young bushman. Reese Witherspoon, Ethan Randall, and Sarel Bok star, with Jack Thompson and Maximilian Schell. **DR27, FA1, FA15**

Far Out Man (1990, C, 91m, R)
Tommy Chong stars in this comic tale of a '60s burnout in search of his ex-lover and love child (played by his real-life wife and daughter, Shelley and Paris Chong). With C. Thomas Howell, Martin Mull, and Chong's old partner, Richard "Cheech" Marin in a cameo. Chong wrote and directed. **ST28, XT8**

Far Pavilions, The (1984, C, 108m, NR)
Romance between British officer and Indian princess, starring Ben Cross and Amy Irving. With Christopher Lee and Omar Sharif. Originally made for cable TV as a miniseries.
DR1, DR3, ST135

Farewell, Friend see *Honor Among Thieves*

Farewell, My Lovely (1975, C, 97m, R)
Robert Mitchum plays Philip Marlowe, Raymond Chandler's famous detective, who is hired to find an ex-con's sweetheart. With Charlotte Rampling, John Ireland, Harry Dean Stanton, and in a small role, Sylvester Stallone. Filmed in 1944 as *Murder My Sweet.*
CU18, ST158, ST204, ST205, WR2

Farewell to Arms, A
(1932, B&W, 78m, NR)
Tragic love story, based on the Ernest Hemingway novel, about an affair between an army nurse (Helen Hayes) and a young soldier (Gary Cooper) during World War I. **AC2, CL4, ST37, WR13**

Farewell to Arms, A (1957, C, 152m, NR)
Rock Hudson and Jennifer Jones star in this lavish version of the Hemingway classic. Producer David O. Selznick's last film. With Vittorio De Sica. **AC2, CL4, DT37, ST112, WR13**

Farewell to the King
(1989, C, 114m, PG-13)
During World War II, a renegade American soldier successfully leads natives on a South Pacific island against the Japanese. Nick Nolte stars in this action drama from writer-director John Milius. **AC1, ST164**

Farmer Takes a Wife, The
(1935, B&W, 91m, NR)
Henry Fonda's film debut, in a story of nineteenth-century romance along the Erie Canal. With Janet Gaynor and Charles Bickford. **ST71**

Farmer Takes a Wife, The
(1953, C, 81m, NR)
Remake of 1935 romance, filmed as a musical with Betty Grable, Dale Robertson, and Thelma Ritter. **MU14, ST91**

Farmer's Daughter, The
(1947, B&W, 97m, NR)
Loretta Young gave an Academy Award–winning performance in this comedy of a Swedish housemaid and her boss, a Washington politician. With Joseph Cotten, Ethel Barrymore, and Charles Bickford. **XT3**

Fashions of 1934 (1934, B&W, 78m, NR)
Bette Davis plays a fashion designer who, along with a con man (William Powell), conquers the Paris fashion world. **ST44, ST176**

Fast Break (1979, C, 107m, PG)
A New York City basketball coach accepts a position in the Midwest and brings his streetwise players with him. Gabriel Kaplan stars in this comedy. **CO19**

Fast Company (1978, C, 90m, NR)
True story of race car driver Lonnie Johnson, starring William Smith, with John Saxon and Claudia Jennings. Directed by David Cronenberg. **DR22, DT31**

Fast Forward (1985, C, 110m, PG)
Eight teen-agers from a small town in Ohio venture to New York City to enter a national

dance contest. Directed by Sidney Poitier. **DR12, ST174**

Fast Talking (1986, C, 93m, NR)
A bright fifteen-year-old from a broken home uses his wits to wriggle out of sticky situations. Family comedy-drama stars Steve Bisley. **FA7**

Fast Times at Ridgemont High
(1982, C, 92m, R)
Witty, knowing comedy about high school life with energetic young cast. Jennifer Jason Leigh stars as the "nice" girl, Phoebe Cates as her more knowing friend. With Judge Reinhold, Robert Romanus, and Sean Penn as the spaced-out Spicoli. Directed by Amy Heckerling. **CO4, CO18, ST136**, *Recommended*

Fastest Guitar Alive, The
(1968, C, 87m, NR)
Civil War Western starring rock star Roy Orbison. He's the leader of a band of Confederate soldiers trying to return money they stole just before the end of the conflict. Title refers to Orbison's instrument, which converts to a gun; he does sing several songs. **MU16, WE6**

Fast-Walking (1982, C, 116m, R)
James Woods is Fast-Walking Miniver, a cynical prison guard who is ordered to assassinate a new black con (Robert Hooks) but can't resist an offer of $50,000 to help the same man escape. With Tim McIntire and Kay Lenz. Mean, even for a film of this genre, but exceptionally well done. McIntire is riveting. **DR18, ST233**, *Recommended*

Fat City (1972, C, 100m, PG)
John Huston directed this story of a small-time boxer trying to pass on some of his ring savvy to a young fighter. Stacy Keach and Jeff Bridges star, with Susan Tyrrell and Candy Clark. Written by Leonard Gardner; based on his novel. Huston and his collaborators score a knockout. **DR19, DR22, DT60, ST19**, *Recommended*

Fat Man and Little Boy
(1989, C, 126m, PG-13)
True-life drama of the development of the atomic bomb at Los Alamos, New Mexico. Paul Newman stars as General Leslie Groves, Dwight Schultz as J. Robert Oppenheimer. With Bonnie Bedelia, John Cusack, and Laura Dern. Directed by Roland Joffe. **DR5, ST53, ST162**

Fatal Attraction (1987, C, 119m, R)
A family man (Michael Douglas) has a weekend fling with a young woman (Glenn Close), who turns murderously possessive, threatening to ruin his entire life. With Anne

Archer. Directed by Adrian Lyne. A jolting experience that falls apart in retrospect. Available in special Director's Edition with film's originally shot ending, plus a 35-minute behind-the-scenes documentary. **CU10, DR3, MY13, MY14, ST33, ST59**

Fatal Beauty (1987, C, 104m, R)
Whoopi Goldberg goes undercover to track the dealers of a dangerous drug, Fatal Beauty. She gets help from a bodyguard (Sam Elliott) whom she suspects of knowing more about distribution of the drug than he admits. With Rubén Blades. **AC9, MU12, ST89**

Fatal Glass of Beer, A/Pool Sharks
(1933/1915, B&W, 29m, NR)
Two classic shorts starring W.C. Fields. In the first, Fields is in the frozen North battling the elements. In the second, one of his early silent films, Fields gets involved in a duel over a beautiful girl; no pistols or swords are brandished, only pool cues. **ST67**

Fatal Hour, The (1940, B&W, 67m, NR)
Fourth in series of Mr. Wong mysteries, starring Boris Karloff as Oriental sleuth, here investigating murder of a policeman. With Marjorie Reynolds, Grant Withers, and Jason Robards, Sr. **ST119**

Fatal Vision (1984, C, 200m, NR)
True story about an army doctor (Gary Cole) accused of killing his wife and two daughters. His father-in-law is sure of his guilt, and pursues the case in a bitter trial. With Karl Malden and Andy Griffith. Excellent adaptation of the book by Joe McGinniss. Originally made for TV. **DR6, DR16, MY8,** *Recommended*

Father (1966, B&W, 96m, NR)
Hungarian drama of a young boy (Andras Balint) who imagines a new father for himself after his real one dies in World War II. Written and directed by Istvan Szabo. **FF7**

Father Brown see *The Detective* (1954)

Father Goose (1964, C, 115m, NR)
Cary Grant plays a beach bum on a South Pacific island during World War II. He winds up protecting a teacher (Leslie Caron) and her girl students, who are fleeing the Japanese. **ST92**

Father of the Bride (1950, B&W, 93m, NR)
Spencer Tracy is the father, Elizabeth Taylor is the bride in this warm comedy about preparations for a wedding. Vincente Minnelli directed. **DT88, ST212, ST217, XT20,** *Essential, Recommended*

Father of the Bride (1991, C, 105m, PG)
Remake of the Tracy-Taylor classic, with
Steve Martin in the title role. Kimberly Wil-
liams is the loving daughter, with Diane Kea-
ton, Martin Short, George Newbern, B.D.
Wong, and Eugene Levy in a bit role. Bland
as a piece of wedding cake. **C05, C014,
CU18, ST121, ST150, XT20**

Father, Son and the Mistress see *For
Richer, For Poorer*

Father's Little Dividend
(1951, B&W, 82m, NR)
Sequel to original *Father of the Bride* has
Spencer Tracy adjusting to the idea of becom-
ing a grandfather. Elizabeth Taylor costars.
Vincente Minnelli directed. **DT88, ST212,
ST217**

Faust (1926, B&W, 100m, NR)
Silent German drama based on the famed
legend, with Gosta Ekman in the title role,
Emil Jannings as The Devil. Directed by F.W.
Murnau. **FF3, HO10**

**Favor, The Watch, and the Very Big
Fish, The** (1991, C, 89m, R)
British comedy about a man asked to pose
for a painting of Christ, beginning to take
his role seriously. Jeff Goldblum stars, with
Bob Hoskins and Natasha Richardson. **C017,
HF17, ST90, ST111**

Fawlty Towers, Volumes 1–4
(1975, C, approx. 75m. each, NR)
Each of these four volumes contains three
episodes of the hilarious British TV series
starring John Cleese as the frantic owner of
a slightly rundown seaside hotel. Prunella
Scales and Connie Booth costar; Cleese and
Booth wrote the scripts. **C015,** *Highly
Recommended*

Fear (1955, B&W, 84m, NR)
Ingrid Bergman stars as a woman who begins
to collapse from the everyday pressures of
life. Directed by Roberto Rossellini, then her
husband. **DT109, ST13, XT30**

Fear Chamber, The see *Chamber of Fear*

Fear City (1984, C, 96m, R)
Tom Berenger and Jack Scalia play the
owners of a New York talent agency that spe-
cializes in "exotic dancers." They're looking
for a killer who has been eliminating their
clients. With Billy Dee Williams, Melanie
Griffith, and Rae Dawn Chong. Worth checking out for fans of cast members but nothing
really special. **AC8, DR15, ST93, ST227**

Fear in the Night (1947, B&W, 72m, NR)
Thriller about a man hypnotized and forced
to commit murder, later recalling the deeds

in a nightmare. Paul Kelly stars, with
DeForest Kelley and Ann Doran. Based on
a story by Cornell Woolrich. **MY1,
WR39**

Fear in the Night (1972, C, 94m, NR)
Peter Cushing and Joan Collins star in this
tale of a tormented wife whose fear drives
her to the brink of insanity. **ST43**

Fear Strikes Out (1957, B&W, 100m, NR)
Tony Perkins stars as Red Sox outfielder
Jimmy Piersall, whose battle with mental ill-
ness nearly cost him his ballplaying career.
With Karl Malden. **DR4, DR22**

Fearless Vampire Killers, The
(1967, C, 98m, NR)
Roman Polanski's comic vampire story show-
cases his penchant for dark humor. Jack Mac-
Gowran, Sharon Tate, and the director star.
Footage added for home video release. Has
lost a lot of its bite with passage of time.
CU10, DT97, HO5, HO24

Fedora (1978, C, 114m, PG)
Movie producer tries to lure reclusive star
from retirement, discovers well-kept secret
about her life. William Holden stars in this
drama based on the Thomas Tryon novel.
With Marthe Keller, Hildegarde Knef, José
Ferrer, and Henry Fonda and Michael York in
small roles. Cowritten and directed by Billy
Wilder. Echoes of Wilder's classic *Sunset Boulevard* abound, but the spark isn't there this
time. **DR13, DT139, ST71, ST106**

Feds (1988, C, 83m, PG-13)
A pair of female recruits (Rebecca DeMornay
and Mary Gross) bungle their way through
training at the FBI Academy. **C03**

Feed (1992, C, 75m, NR)
Documentary of 1992 New Hampshire presidential primary, capturing candidates in un-
guarded moments by compiling footage
not used by networks. Directed by Kevin
Rafferty and James Ridgeway. Fascinating
behind-the-scenes stuff that's occasionally
petty and cruel. A must for close followers
of the political process. **CU16,** *Recommended*

Feel My Pulse (1928, B&W, 65m, NR)
Silent comedy about a girl who discovers
that a sanitarium she has inherited is a
haven for rumrunners. Bebe Daniels stars,
with Richard Arlen and William Powell.
ST176

Fellini Satyricon see *Satyricon*

Fellini's Roma (1972, C, 128m, R)
Documentary about the famed director's
favorite location. **DT43, XT17**

Female (1933, B&W, 60m, NR)
Drama of female auto company executive, ruthless in her business and personal affairs, given extra spice because it was produced before restrictive Production Code was enforced. Ruth Chatterton stars, with George Brent, Ferdinand Gottschalk, and Philip Faversham. Directed by Michael Curtiz. **CL5, DR24**

Female on the Beach
(1955, B&W, 97m, NR)
Late Joan Crawford melodrama has her romanced by muscle boy Jeff Chandler in what is now regarded as a camp classic. **CU2, ST39**

Female Trouble (1975, B&W, 95m, NR)
Director John Waters's follow-up to *Pink Flamingos* stars Divine as a girl gone wrong who finally suffers for her sins in the electric chair. Camp or crude? It's up to the viewer. **CU12, DT132**

Ferngully ... The Last Rainforest
(1992, C, 76m, G)
Animated feature about creatures in title forest fighting developers. Character voices by Tim Curry, Samantha Mathis, Christian Slater, Robin Williams, Grace Zabriskie, Cheech Marin, and Tommy Chong. **FA10, ST28, ST200, ST228**

Ferris Bueller's Day Off
(1986, C, 103m, PG-13)
A suburban high school senior (Matthew Broderick) with a knack for ducking trouble takes a day off from school with two pals and heads for downtown Chicago. Written and directed by John Hughes. Mia Sara and Alan Ruck costar, with Jeffrey Jones, Jennifer Grey, and in a small role, Charlie Sheen. Virtually defines the word "smarmy." **CO4, DT59, XT11**

Feud, The (1989, C, 96m, R)
Amusing comic tale set in small-town 1950s America, with two clans from adjoining burgs waging war over a petty misunderstanding. Director Bill D'Elia cowrote the screenplay, adapted from Thomas Berger's novel. Featured in the large cast are Rene Auberjonois, Ron McLarty, Joe Grifasi, Gale Mayron, and David Strathairn. Deftly captures Berger's dark sense of humor. **CO6, DR19, DR26**

Fever Mounts in El Pao
(1959, B&W, 97m, NR)
Comedy-drama, made in Mexico by Luis Buñuel, about a dictator and an imaginary South American country. Also known as *Los Ambicosos*. **DT19**

Few Good Men, A (1992, C, 138m, R)
Military courtroom drama has callow but clever young defense attorney unraveling possible coverup surrounding death of Marine at Cuba's Guantanamo base. Tom Cruise stars, with Demi Moore, Kevin Pollak, Kevin Bacon, James Marshall, Wolfgang Bodison, J.T. Walsh, Kiefer Sutherland, and Jack Nicholson as Cruise's main adversary, the colonel in charge of the base. Aaron Sorkin adapted his play, Rob Reiner directed. Genuinely entertaining; a better vehicle for Cruise than, say, *Far and Away*, thanks in large part to Nicholson's presence. **DR17, DR20, DT103, ST41, ST163,** *Recommended*

ffolkes (1980, C, 99m, PG)
Tongue-in-cheek action film, with Roger Moore as an unorthodox agent (loves cats, hates women) hired to battle terrorists on two North Sea oil rigs. With James Mason and Anthony Perkins. **ST153**

Fiddler on the Roof (1971, C, 181m, G)
Popular Broadway musical about a humble Ukrainian farmer at the turn of the century who has no dowries for his five unwed daughters. Great family viewing. Directed by Norman Jewison. **DT63, FA9, MU2,** *Recommended*

Field, The (1990, C, 107m, PG-13)
Drama set in 1930s Ireland involving struggle over title piece of land between a stubborn tenant farmer (Richard Harris) and an American businessman (Tom Berenger). With John Hurt, Sean Bean, and Brenda Fricker. Written and directed by Jim Sheridan. **DR23**

Field of Dreams (1989, C, 106m, PG)
An Iowa farmer (Kevin Costner) builds a baseball diamond in his cornfield, where the spirits of long-gone baseball stars like Shoeless Joe Jackson (Ray Liotta) come to play. Sentimental drama also features Amy Madigan, James Earl Jones, and Burt Lancaster. The sentiment finally overwhelms the film's best intentions. **DR2, DR8, DR22, ST38, ST118, ST129**

Field of Honor (1986, C, 93m, R)
Drama of a Dutch soldier's horrifying experiences in the Korean War. Based on a true story; Everett McGill stars. **AC3**

Fiend Without a Face
(1958, B&W, 74m, NR)
Superb special effects enhance this gruesome tale of a scientist whose thoughts materialize in the form of invisible creatures. These creatures then seek out victims to feed on their brains. **HO20, SF1**

Fiendish Plot of Dr. Fu Manchu, The
(1980, C, 108m, PG)
Peter Sellers's last film casts him in two roles:
Fu Manchu and his nemesis, Inspector Nayland Smith. As Fu Manchu tries to conquer the world, his bumbling foe tries to stop him. **ST194**

Fifth Avenue Girl (1939, B&W, 83m, NR)
Ginger Rogers comedy has her playing a homeless lass taken in by a friendly millionaire (Walter Connolly). **ST187**

Fifth Musketeer, The (1979, C, 103m, PG)
Remake of Dumas's swashbuckler *The Man in the Iron Mask*. Beau Bridges stars, with Sylvia Kristel, Ursula Andress, Cornel Wilde, Ian McShane, Lloyd Bridges, Alan Hale, Jr., Rex Harrison, and Olivia de Havilland. **AC15, ST49, XT8**

55 Days at Peking (1963, C, 150m, NR)
Epic account of events in China surrounding the 1900 Boxer Rebellion, starring Charlton Heston, Ava Gardner, and David Niven. Directed by Nicholas Ray. **CL3, DT101, ST79**

52 Pick-Up (1986, C, 114m, R)
A self-made businessman (Roy Scheider) is blackmailed by three creeps who know he has been cheating on his wife (Ann-Margret). With John Glover and Clarence Williams III. Based on Elmore Leonard's novel; directed by John Frankenheimer. The best screen version of a Leonard novel to date. **AC19, MY2, WR19,** *Recommended*

Fighting Back (1982, C, 98m, R)
A deli owner in South Philadelphia organizes his neighbors into a vigilante group to fight local thugs, with unexpected results. Tom Skerritt stars, with Patty LuPone, Michael Sarrazin, and Yaphet Kotto. **AC19**

Fighting Caravans (1932, B&W, 80m, NR)
Gary Cooper takes to the great outdoors in this Western based on a Zane Grey story.
ST37

Fighting Kentuckian, The
(1949, B&W, 100m, NR)
John Wayne comes to rescue of homesteaders in colonial Kentucky. Oliver Hardy costars in a rare dramatic role. **ST133, ST224**

Fighting Mad (1976, C, 90m, R)
Melodrama of farmer who seeks revenge on wealthy landowner trying to squeeze him off his spread. Peter Fonda stars, with Lynn Lowry, John Doucette, and Scott Glenn. Directed by Jonathan Demme. **AC19, DT35**

Fighting Mad (1977, C, 96m, R)
A soldier in Vietnam is left to die by his company, only to be captured by Japanese troops

who think that World War II is still on. James Iglehart, Jayne Kennedy, and Leon Isaac Kennedy star. **AC4**

Fighting Prince of Donegal, The
(1966, C, 112, NR)
Disney swashbuckler has the new head of an Irish family in the sixteenth century fighting for his people against British troops. **FA1**

Fighting Seabees, The
(1944, B&W, 100m, NR)
John Wayne and Dennis O'Keefe are soldiers stationed in the South Pacific, both fighting for the same woman (Susan Hayward). **AC1, ST100, ST224**

Fighting Sullivans, The
(1944, B&W, 111m, NR)
True story of five brothers who served—and died—together in World War II. Anne Baxter and Thomas Mitchell star. Also known as *The Sullivans*. **AC1**

Final Analysis (1992, C, 124m, R)
San Francisco shrink takes on lovely patient, falls into affair with her equally attractive sister, who's caught in an abusive marriage with a gangster—who winds up murdered. Richard Gere, Uma Thurman, Kim Basinger, and Eric Roberts star. Cowritten by Wesley Strick, directed by Phil Joanou. Trashy fun, helped by attractive stars, delirious plotting, and dramatic locations. But: next time you're in San Francisco, don't try to find that lighthouse by the Golden Gate Bridge! **MY2, MY4, MY5, MY14, ST84, XT13,** *Recommended*

Final Comedown, The (1972, C, 84m, R)
Drama of black radical activist trying to enlist white revolutionaries in his cause. Billy Dee Williams stars, with D'Urville Martin and Raymond St. Jacques. **DR14, ST227**

Final Conflict, The (1981, C, 108m, R)
This third and final chapter of *The Omen* saga follows Antichrist Damien Thorn to adulthood, as he moves toward the presidency. **HO10**

Final Countdown, The
(1980, C, 104m, PG)
Modern aircraft carrier passes through a time warp to Pearl Harbor on the eve of the Japanese attack. Kirk Douglas and Martin Sheen star in this science fiction adventure. **SF4, ST57**

Final Mission, The (1984, C, 101m, NR)
A Vietnam veteran, now a policeman, gets a chance for revenge against a man who betrayed him in Southeast Asia. **AC19**

Final Option, The (1982, C, 125m, R)
Terrorists try to take over American embassy in London; a Special Air Services team is dispatched to stop them. Lewis Collins stars, with Judy Davis, Richard Widmark, Robert Webber, and Edward Woodward. **AC20, ST46**

Final Terror, The (1981, C, 82m, R)
A psychopathic killer stalks teen-agers in a forest. Daryl Hannah and Rachel Ward star. **HO12**

Final Warning (1991, C, 100m, NR)
Jon Voight plays a California surgeon trying to help the victims of the Chernobyl nuclear disaster. With Jason Robards as Armand Hammer. Originally made for TV. Also known as *Chernobyl: The Final Warning.* **DR6, ST185**

Find the Lady (1976, C, 79m, NR)
John Candy and Lawrence Dane play a pair of inept cops looking for a kidnapped socialite. With Mickey Rooney and Peter Cook. **CO14, ST189**

Finders Keepers (1984, C, 96m, PG)
Frantic comedy, set mostly on a train, involving con men, coffins, hired killers, and a fortune in stolen money. Michael O'Keefe, Beverly D'Angelo, and Louis Gossett, Jr., star. Richard Lester directed. Some Lester fans find it funny; this one doesn't. **CO10, DT74, XT19**

Fine Madness, A (1966, C, 104m, NR)
Sean Connery plays an iconoclastic poet in this comedy-drama about society's attempts to tame a misfit. With Joanne Woodward, Jean Seberg, and Patrick O'Neal. Has some funny moments; worth a look for fans of Connery or offbeat. **CO20, ST33, ST234**

Fine Mess, A (1986, C, 88m, PG)
Comedy about a pair of bumblers (Ted Danson, Howie Mandel) who overhear plans to fix a horse race, and wind up with the Mob and the police on their trail. Directed by Blake Edwards. **CO3, DT40**

Finishing School (1934, B&W, 73m, NR)
Drama set in girls' school, with usual competition, backbiting, love with boy from wrong side of town. Frances Dee stars, with Ginger Rogers, Beulah Bondi, Billie Burke, and Bruce Cabot. **ST187**

Fingers (1978, C, 91m, R)
Cult movie with exceptionally nasty violence about a young man torn between career as a concert pianist and loyalty to his father, a numbers runner. Harvey Keitel stars, with Michael V. Gazzo, Tisa Farrow, Jim Brown,

Tanya Roberts, Marian Seldes, and Danny Aiello. James Toback wrote and directed. The director's talent for creating vivid characters is undercut by wallowing in repellent situations. **CU7, DR16**

Finian's Rainbow (1968, C, 145m, NR)
Musical fantasy, adapted from the Broadway hit, starring Fred Astaire as an Irishman who moves to the American South in search of his pot of gold. With Petula Clark, Tommy Steele, Keenan Wynn, Al Freeman, Jr., and Don Francks. Francis Ford Coppola directed, breathing enormous life into this dated material. Songs include "That Old Devil Moon" and "Look to the Rainbow." Widescreen will be lost on video. **CU20, DT29, MU2, MU8, ST4,** *Recommended*

Fire and Ice (1983, C, 81m, PG)
Animated adventure saga based on Frank Frazetta's "Dungeons and Dragons" characters, directed by Ralph Bakshi. **AC18**

Fire Birds (1990, C, 85m, PG-13)
Action drama featuring U.S. Army's Apache assault helicopters, used here against a South American drug cartel. Nicolas Cage stars, with Tommy Lee Jones and Sean Young. **AC11, ST23**

Fire Down Below (1957, C, 116m, NR)
Shipboard romantic triangle, with Robert Mitchum and Jack Lemmon in conflict over Rita Hayworth on a tramp steamer. **ST101, ST138, ST158**

Fire in the Sky (1993, C, 107m, PG-13)
Allegedly true story of Arizona lumberjack who mysteriously disappeared for five days, turned up claiming he was abducted by aliens. D.B. Sweeney stars, with Robert Patrick, Craig Sheffer, Peter Berg, and James Garner. **DR6, SF9, ST82**

Fire Over England (1937, B&W, 89m, NR)
Vivien Leigh and Laurence Olivier portray young lovers in the court of Queen Elizabeth during the British-Spanish conflict. With James Mason. **CL3, ST137, ST153, ST168**

Firebird 2015 A.D. (1981, C, 97m, PG)
In this science fiction adventure, cars have been banned because of an oil shortage. Darren McGavin and Doug McClure star. **SF8**

Firefly, The (1937, B&W, 131m, NR)
Jeanette MacDonald operetta has her playing a Spanish spy during the Napoleonic Wars. With Allan Jones singing "The Donkey Serenade." **MU1**

Firefox (1982, C, 124m, PG)
An American undercover agent (Clint Eastwood) steals a super-secret plane from the

Russians and heads for the border with Soviet aircraft in pursuit. Eastwood also directed. **AC11, ST64**

Firemen's Ball, The (1968, C, 73m, NR)
Comedy from Czechoslovakia about a volunteer firemen's dance that turns into a full-scale disaster. Directed by Milos Forman. **DT45, FF7**

Firepower (1979, C, 104m, R)
Action drama, set in the Caribbean, starring Sophia Loren as a woman seeking revenge for the murder of her husband. With James Coburn, O.J. Simpson, and Eli Wallach. **AC19, ST141**

Fires on the Plain (1959, B&W, 105m, NR)
Japanese war drama focuses on the suffering of several soldiers during the final days of World War II. Directed by Kon Ichikawa. **AC1, FF4, XT25**

Fires Within (1991, C, 86m, R)
Romantic triangle drama involving recently released prisoner from Cuban jail, his Miami-based wife, and her rescuer from a boating accident. Jimmy Smits, Greta Scacchi, and Vincent D'Onofrio star. Directed by Gillian Armstrong. **DT7**

Firestarter (1984, C, 115m, R)
Drew Barrymore plays a child who inherits the ability to start fires at a glance. Based on the Stephen King bestseller. With George C. Scott, Art Carney, and Martin Sheen. **HO13, ST196, WR15**

Firewalker (1986, C, 104m, R)
Tongue-in-cheek adventure story, with Chuck Norris and Louis Gossett, Jr., as two bumbling soldiers of fortune. **AC21, ST165**

First Blood (1982, C, 97m, R)
Sylvester Stallone's first appearance as John Rambo, the Vietnam vet with a chip on his shoulder. Here, he's harassed by a small-town sheriff and he leads law enforcement officials and a National Guard company on a wild backwoods chase. With Richard Crenna and Brian Dennehy. For Stallone and genre fans only. **AC25, ST204**

First Deadly Sin, The (1980, C, 112m, R)
Frank Sinatra stars as a New York City cop who tracks a psycho. With Faye Dunaway, Brenda Vaccaro, and James Whitmore. **AC9, ST61, ST199**

First Family (1980, C, 104m, R)
This political satire casts Bob Newhart as a president trying to deal with his scatter-brained wife (Madeline Kahn) and sex-crazed daughter (Gilda Radner). With Rip Torn, Richard Benjamin, and Harvey Korman.

Written and directed by Buck Henry. **CO5, CO13, ST216, XT12**

First Howie Mandel Special, The (1983, C, 53m, NR)
The former star of TV's "St. Elsewhere" gives an energetic standup comedy performance. **CO16**

First Legion, The (1951, B&W, 86m, NR)
A priest is skeptical of events surrounding a miracle in his town. Charles Boyer stars in this drama directed by Douglas Sirk. **DT117**

First Men in the Moon
(1964, C, 103m, NR)
H.G. Wells tale of space explorers, with outstanding special effects by Ray Harryhausen. Edward Judd, Martha Hyer, and Lionel Jeffries star. **SF3, WR37**

First Monday in October
(1981, C, 98m, R)
This light comedy concerns the first female member of the Supreme Court locking horns with a fellow justice. Jill Clayburgh and Walter Matthau star. **CO2, DR10, ST31, ST155, XT12**

First Name: Carmen (1983, C, 85m, NR)
French director Jean-Luc Godard's meditation on the Carmen story, with updating to make the heroine a terrorist/filmmaker. Maruschka Detmers stars; Godard plays her "Uncle Jean," a has-been director. **DT50**

First Power, The (1990, C, 98m, R)
The Devil grants a mad killer immortality, and he immediately seeks vengeance against a young cop. Lou Diamond Phillips stars as the cop, with Jeff Kober and Tracy Griffith. **HO9, HO10**

Firstborn (1984, C, 100m, PG-13)
A teen-ager is suspicious of his divorced mother's new boyfriend, especially when he finds evidence that the man is dealing drugs. Christopher Collet, Teri Garr, and Peter Weller star in this underrated drama. **DR8,** *Recommended*

Fish Called Wanda, A (1988, C, 108m, R)
Knockabout British caper comedy featuring a gang composed of one thick-headed macho American (Oscar winner Kevin Kline), his sexy girlfriend (Jamie Lee Curtis), and a stuttering accomplice (Michael Palin)—all mixed up with a confused barrister (John Cleese). Cowritten by Cleese. Small dog or tropical fish lovers, beware. **CO10, CO15, CO17, MY18, ST42, ST127, XT4,** *Recommended*

Fisher King, The (1991, C, 137m, R)
Topical urban comedy-drama of New York radio disc jockey, on the skids after being

linked to a murderous rampage, and a homeless man whose wife was killed in the same incident. Jeff Bridges and Robin Williams star, with Oscar winner Mercedes Ruehl, Amanda Plummer, and Michael Jeter. Screenplay by Richard LaGravenese; directed by Terry Gilliam. Ambitious and often touching, anchored by two strong leads and the fantastic Ruehl. **CO15, DR7, DR15, ST19, ST228, XT5, XT9, XT26,** *Recommended*

Fist of Fear, Touch of Death
(1980, C, 90m, R)
Drama set at a karate championship at Madison Square Garden, starring Fred Williamson and Ron Van Clief. Bruce Lee appears in a short segment. **ST134**

Fistful of Dollars, A (1964, C, 96m, NR)
A mysterious gunfighter (Clint Eastwood) is caught between two feuding families in this classic spaghetti Western directed by Sergio Leone. Remake of Japanese samurai drama, *Yojimbo.* **DT73, FF8, ST64, WE2, WE13,** *Recommended*

Fistful of Dynamite, A (1972, C, 138m, R)
A peasant thief (Rod Steiger) and an explosives mastermind (James Coburn) join forces during the Mexican Revolution. Directed by Sergio Leone. Also known as *Duck, You Sucker.* **DT73, WE9, WE13**

Fists of Fury (1972, C, 103m, R)
Bruce Lee's first feature film has him playing a martial arts student out to avenge his teacher's death. **ST134**

Fitzcarraldo (1982, C, 157m, NR)
Epic drama from German director Werner Herzog about an obsessed man's attempt to build an opera house in the midst of the Amazon jungles. Klaus Kinski stars in this bold, memorable drama. Be sure to check out behind-the-scenes documentary, *Burden of Dreams.* **DT54, ST126,** *Recommended*

Five Card Stud (1968, C, 103m, NR)
Western action with Dean Martin as a gambler, Robert Mitchum as a psychotic preacher. With Inger Stevens and Roddy McDowall. **ST149, ST158**

Five Corners (1988, C, 92m, R)
In 1964, a Bronx neighborhood is shaken by the return of an ex-con looking for revenge. A young idealist (Tim Robbins) agrees to protect a girl (Jodie Foster) from the criminal. Written by John Patrick Shanley; directed by Tony Bill. **DR15, ST75, XT23**

Five Days One Summer
(1983, C, 93m, PG)
A middle-aged man and his young female companion travel in 1930s Switzerland posing as man and wife—although their relationship is secretly quite different. Sean Connery and Betsy Brantley star. Fred Zinnemann directed. Original running time: 108 minutes. **DR3, DT144, ST36**

Five Easy Pieces (1970, C, 96m, R)
Breakthrough role for Jack Nicholson in this tale of a drifter who chooses a blue-collar job rather than follow his family of classical musicians. Written by Carol Eastman (under the name Adrien Joyce) and directed by Bob Rafelson. Karen Black and Susan Anspach costar, with Billy "Green" Bush, Lois Smith, Toni Basil, and Helena Kallianiotes. Wonderful soundtrack of Tammy Wynette and Mozart. Still powerful; Black should have won an Oscar for her touching performance. **DR8, ST163, XT18, XT28,** *Essential, Highly Recommended*

5 Fingers (1952, B&W, 108m, NR)
Spy thriller stars James Mason as a Nazi agent working in Britain. With Danielle Darrieux and Michael Rennie. Written and directed by Joseph Mankiewicz. **DT84, MY6, ST153**

Five Golden Dragons (1967, C, 93m, NR)
International intrigue in Hong Kong setting, with Robert Cummings as a naive American. With Margaret Lee, Maria Perschy, Brian Donlevy, and Christopher Lee. **MY16, ST135**

Five Heartbeats, The (1991, C, 120m, R)
Show-biz saga of black pop group, loosely based on exploits of the Dells, starring Robert Townsend (who cowrote and directed), with Michael Wright, Leon, and Harry J. Lennix. **DR12, DR14**

Five Pennies, The (1959, C, 117m, NR)
Danny Kaye plays trumpeter Red Nichols in this musical film bio. With Barbara Bel Geddes, Tuesday Weld, and musical performances by Louis Armstrong and Bob Crosby. **MU5, ST120**

5,000 Fingers of Dr. T, The
(1953, C, 88m, NR)
Classic children's fantasy of a little boy who suffers nightmares dominated by his strict piano teacher. Tommy Rettig and Hans Conried star; written by Dr. Seuss. **FA8, FA15**

Five Weeks in a Balloon
(1962, C, 101m, NR)
Jules Verne adventure about a hot-air balloon expedition to Africa. Red Buttons, Barbara Eden, and Fabian star. **FA4, WR36**

Flame and the Arrow, The
(1950, C, 88m, NR)
Burt Lancaster stars as a swashbuckler in medieval Italy who leads his people to victory against the Hessians. Virginia Mayo and Nick Cravat costar. Jacques Tourneur directed. **AC13, DT124, ST129**

Flame of the Barbary Coast
(1945, B&W, 91m, NR)
John Wayne Western with the Duke competing for the hand of a saloon singer (Ann Dvorak). **ST224**

Flaming Star (1960, C, 92m, NR)
Elvis Presley plays a half-breed who must choose sides when an Indian uprising threatens his family. Directed by Don Siegel. Widescreen will be lost on video. **CU20, DT116, ST178, WE7**

Flamingo Kid, The
(1984, C, 100m, PG-13)
Engaging comic story of inner-city kid working a Long Island swim club in the summer of 1963, getting involved with club cardshark and a rich girl. Matt Dillon stars, with Richard Crenna, Hector Elizondo, Jessica Walter, Fisher Stevens, Janet Jones, Bronson Pinchot, and in small roles, Marisa Tomei and John Turturro. Directed by Garry Marshall. Dillon and Crenna are terrific. **CO4, CO6, CO20, ST56**, *Recommended*

Flamingo Road (1949, B&W, 94m, NR)
Joan Crawford is a carnival dancer stranded in a small Southern town, romancing (as usual) two men. With Zachary Scott and David Brian; Sydney Greenstreet plays the quintessential corrupt Dixie politician. **DR26, ST39**

Flash Gordon (1980, C, 110m, PG)
The hero of the old movie serials gets a big-budget, tongue-in-cheek treatment in this spoofy adventure. Sam J. Jones, Max von Sydow, Ornella Muti, Melody Anderson, Topol, and Timothy Dalton star. Music by Queen. **SF21**

Flashback (1990, C, 108m, R)
A legendary 1960s activist, now a fugitive from the law, is captured and transported by a young FBI agent from San Francisco to Washington State to stand trial. Comedy stars Dennis Hopper and Kiefer Sutherland, with Carol Kane, Paul Dooley, Cliff De Young, Richard Masur, and Michael McKean. Hopper's wonderful, but the rest of the film limps along. **CO10, CO20, ST110, XT18, XT19**

Flashdance (1983, C, 96m, R)
A young female welder moonlights as an exotic dancer, although she aspires to audition for a ballet company. Jennifer Beals and Michael Nouri star; music by Giorgio Moroder, which is the best thing about this silly film. **DR12, DR15, MU3**

Flashpoint (1984, C, 94m, R)
A pair of border cops stumble onto some evidence that will help solve a political assassination. Kris Kristofferson and Treat Williams star, with Rip Torn. **MU12, MY6, ST216**

Flask of Fields, A (1930, B&W, 61m, NR)
A trio of shorts starring the inimitable W.C. Fields: *The Golf Specialist, A Fatal Glass of Beer,* and *The Dentist.* **ST67**

Flatbed Annie (1979, C, 100m, NR)
Original title, *Flatbed Annie & Sweetiepie: Lady Truckers,* says it all, good buddy. Annie Potts and Kim Darby star, with (get this) Harry Dean Stanton, Arthur Godfrey, Rory Calhoun, and Billy Carter (yes, *that* Billy Carter). Originally made for TV. **AC10, ST205**

Flatliners (1990, C, 111m, R)
Group of hot-shot med students experiment with dying and reviving one another. Kiefer Sutherland, Julia Roberts, Kevin Bacon, William Baldwin, and Oliver Platt star in this drama. **DR7, HO20, XT24**

Flesh (1968, B&W, 90m, NR)
Paul Morrissey directed and Andy Warhol produced this cult comedy about a male hustler (Joe Dallesandro) and his many conquests. **CU12, DT90**

Flesh & Blood (1922, B&W, 74m, NR)
A lawyer goes to jail for fifteen years for a crime he didn't commit. Lon Chaney, Sr., stars in this silent melodrama. **ST26**

Flesh and Blood (1985, C, 126m, R)
Adventure tale of lovely young princess captured by a band of roving thieves, with her intended in hot pursuit. Rutger Hauer, Jennifer Jason Leigh, and Tom Burlinson star. Paul Verhoeven directed. Genre devotees will love the violence (and nudity). **AC18, ST136**

Flesh and the Devil
(1927, B&W, 103m, NR)
Greta Garbo silent drama in which she plays the ultimate temptress, breaking up the friendship of John Gilbert and Lars Hanson. **CL4, CL12, ST78**

Flesh and the Fiends, The see *Mania*

Fleshburn (1984, C, 91m, R)
Confined to an asylum for five years, a Vietnam veteran escapes and seeks revenge

against the doctors who had him committed. **AC19**

Fletch (1985, C, 96m, PG)
Chevy Chase plays a wise-guy reporter who relies on disguises to get the scoop on a drug ring. With Richard Libertini, Dana Wheeler-Nicholson, Tim Matheson, Geena Davis, M. Emmet Walsh, and George Wendt. **CO10, CO13, ST45**

Fletch Lives (1989, C, 95m, PG-13)
Chevy Chase returns as the investigative reporter and master of disguises. Here, he inherits a Southern mansion and a mystery that goes with the house. **CO10, CO13**

Flight of Dragons, The
(1982, C, 98m, NR)
Enter a world of dragons, dungeons, and castles, and mysterious happenings in this full-length animated feature. **FA10**

Flight of the Eagle, The
(1982, C, 139m, NR)
Swedish adventure story, based on historical events, about a daring hot-air balloon trip to the North Pole in 1897. Max von Sydow stars. **AC12, AC16, FF7**

Flight of the Intruder
(1991, C, 113m, PG-13)
Vietnam War flyboys drama, set in 1972, starring Danny Glover and Willem Dafoe. With Brad Johnson and Rosanna Arquette. Directed by John Milius. **AC4, AC11, ST88**

Flight of the Navigator
(1986, C, 90m, PG)
Fantasy about a twelve-year-old boy who leaves earth on an alien spacecraft, but returns as a twelve-year-old eight years later. Veronica Cartwright and Joey Cramer star. **FA8, FA15**

Flight of the Phoenix (1966, C, 147m, NR)
Tense tale of survival, starring James Stewart as the leader of a squadron whose plane crashes in the Arabian desert. With Richard Attenborough, Peter Finch, and Ernest Borgnine. Directed by Robert Aldrich. Widescreen will be lost on video. **AC12, CU20, DT1, ST207**, *Recommended*

Flight to Fury (1966, B&W, 80m, NR)
Adventure saga set in the Philippines, about a search for missing diamonds. Dewey Martin, Fay Spain, and Jack Nicholson star. Directed by Monte Hellman. **ST163**

Flight to Mars (1951, C, 72m, NR)
Low-budget science fiction adventure about trip to the Red Planet and discovery of a lost civilization. **SF3**

Flim Flam Man, The (1967, C, 115m, NR)
Likable comedy of con man (George C. Scott) stealing his way through the South with a new young apprentice (Michael Sarrazin). With Sue Lyon, Harry Morgan, Jack Albertson, and Slim Pickens. Directed by Irvin Kershner. **CO10, ST196**

Flipper (1963, C, 90m, NR)
Family adventure of a boy and his friendly dolphin, the basis for the TV series. Chuck Connors, Luke Halpin, and Kathleen McGuire star. **FA5**

Flipper's New Adventure
(1964, C, 103m, G)
The smart dolphin returns to help thwart a band of escaped convicts. Luke Halpin and Pamela Franklin star. **FA5**

Flirting (1991, C, 96m, R)
Australian coming-of-age drama, set in 1965, of a loner at a boys' school, in love with a Ugandan student at a neighboring girls' school. Noah Taylor and Thandie Newton star, with Nicole Kidman. Sequel to writer-director John Duigan's *The Year My Voice Broke*. **DR9, DR25, FF5**

Floating Weeds (1959, C, 119m, NR)
From Japan, a drama about an actor visiting his illegitimate son and ex-lover after many years' absence. Directed by Yasujiro Ozu. **FF4**

Flood! (1976, C, 100m, NR)
Disaster drama set in motion when weak dam breaks loose, inundating small town. Robert Culp stars, with Martin Milner, Barbara Hershey, Richard Basehart, and Carol Lynley. Originally made for TV. **AC23, ST104**

Flower Drum Song (1961, C, 133m, NR)
Rodgers and Hammerstein musical about life in San Francisco's Chinatown. Nancy Kwan, James Shigeta, and Miyoshi Umeki star. **MU2, MU6**

Flowers in the Attic (1987, C, 95m, PG-13)
A widowed mother of four is desperate to be reinstated in her father's good graces—and in his will. She and her kids move into his house, where she keeps the children confined to one room. Based on the novel by V.C. Andrews. **HO14**

Flowers of St. Francis, The
(1950, B&W, 75m, NR)
Roberto Rossellini's austere drama about the controversial saint and his followers. Federico Fellini can be seen among the supporting cast. **DT43, DT109**

Fly, The (1958, B&W, 94m, NR)
An experiment turns into a disaster as a scientist's machine mixes some of his molecules with those of a fly. Vincent Price, Herbert Marshall, and David Hedison star. Final scene is a chiller. **HO20, SF1, SF5, ST179**

Fly, The (1986, C, 96m, R)
Intelligent, well-acted remake of the horror science fiction film about an experiment gone terribly wrong, with much more explicit and gruesome detail. Jeff Goldblum and Geena Davis star. David Cronenberg directed. **CU7, CU18, DT31, HO17, HO20, SF5, SF20, ST45, ST90,** *Recommended*

Fly II, The (1989, C, 104m, R)
Follow-up to 1986 remake of the sci-fi horror classic has the son of the scientist/insect following in his father's fateful footsteps. Eric Stoltz and Daphne Zuniga star. **HO20, SF5, SF20**

Flying Deuces, The (1939, B&W, 65m, NR)
Laurel and Hardy join the foreign legion to forget Ollie's recent lost love. **ST133**

Flying Down to Rio
(1933, B&W, 89m, NR)
Fred Astaire and Ginger Rogers dance "The Carioca" in their first screen teaming. Dolores Del Rio costars. **CL15, ST4, ST187**

Flying Leathernecks (1951, C, 102m, NR)
John Wayne and Robert Ryan play two Marine officers who argue over Wayne's treatment of his troops during World War II. Nicholas Ray directed. **AC1, DT101, ST193, ST224**

Flying Tigers (1942, B&W, 102m, NR)
World War II action over China, starring John Wayne. **AC1, AC11, ST224**

Fog, The (1980, C, 91m, R)
An old fisherman in a California coastal town creates havoc when he tells a ghost story to a group of young children. John Carpenter directed. Jamie Lee Curtis and John Houseman star, with Janet Leigh (Jamie's real-life mom). **DT23, HO2, ST42, XT8**

Foghorn Leghorn's Fractured Funnies
(1948–55, C, 58m, NR)
Collection of classic Warner Brothers cartoons featuring the best of Foghorn Leghorn's adventures. Included are *Lovelorn Leghorn, The Leghorn Blows at Midnight,* and *Leghorn Swaggled.* **FA11**

Folks! (1992, C, 107m, PG-13)
Tom Selleck stars in a comedy of accommodation, about a man whose elderly parents (Anne Jackson and Don Ameche), one recovering from surgery, the other exhibiting

signs of senility, move in with him. With Christine Ebersole and Michael Murphy. Directed by Ted Kotcheff. **CO5**

Follow Me, Boys! (1966, C, 131m, NR)
Disney drama set in 1930s Midwest, with Fred MacMurray starting a Boy Scout troop in a small town. With Vera Miles, Lillian Gish, and Kurt Russell. **FA1, ST87, ST191**

Follow Me Quietly (1949, B&W, 59m, NR)
Thriller about a vigilante killer who calls himself The Judge. William Lundigan, Dorothy Patrick, and Jeff Corey star. **MY1, MY13**

Follow That Bird (1985, C, 88m, G)
Big Bird, Sesame Street's favorite giant, is placed in a foster home, and slowly makes his way back to his friends. Many guest stars include Dave Thomas, John Candy, Joe Flaherty, and Chevy Chase. Also known as *Sesame Street Presents Follow That Bird.* **CO13, CO14, FA9**

Follow That Dream (1962, C, 110m, NR)
Elvis Presley musical about a young man whose family moves to Florida and is not accepted by the local townspeople. **ST178**

Follow the Fleet (1936, B&W, 110m, NR)
Fred Astaire dances his way through the Navy to Irving Berlin tunes. Ginger Rogers and Randolph Scott costar; Betty Grable has a bit part. **CL15, ST4, ST91, ST187, ST197**

Food of the Gods (1976, C, 88m, PG)
H.G. Wells tale of animals growing to gigantic proportions after eating an unusual substance. Marjoe Gortner, Pamela Franklin, and Ida Lupino star. **SF10, WR37**

Fool for Love (1985, C, 107m, R)
Two lovers meet at a desert motel and try to sort out their past in this drama written by and starring Sam Shepard, with Kim Basinger, Harry Dean Stanton, and Randy Quaid. Robert Altman directed. Loses steam before a so-what ending. **DR3, DT4, ST205**

Foolish Wives (1922, B&W, 107m, NR)
Erich Von Stroheim's classic silent about a corrupt man who poses as a Russian count in Monte Carlo. With Mae Busch and Cesare Gravina. **CL12, DT129**

Fools (1970, C, 97m, PG)
San Francisco is the setting for this May-December romance between a middle-aged actor (Jason Robards) and the bored wife (Katharine Ross) of an attorney. **DR1, ST185, XT13**

Fools of Fortune (1990, C, 109m, PG-13)
Saga of family involved with both the British and the Irish Republican Army stars Iain

Glen, Julie Christie, and Mary Elizabeth Mastrantonio. **DR23, ST30**

Footlight Parade (1933, B&W, 104m, NR)
Classic backstage musical about the difficulty of putting on a show. James Cagney, Ruby Keeler, and Dick Powell star, with choreography by Busby Berkeley. **DT12, MU4, ST24, ST175**, *Essential, Recommended*

Footloose (1984, C, 107m, PG)
A young high-school student (Kevin Bacon) shakes up a town where dancing has been outlawed by a powerful minister. With Lori Singer, John Lithgow, Dianne Wiest, Christopher Penn, and Sarah Jessica Parker. **CO4, DR9, DR26, DR27, MU3**

For a Few Dollars More
(1965, C, 130m, PG)
In this sequel to *A Fistful of Dollars*, Clint Eastwood is a cigar-smoking bounty hunter out to track down a vicious bandit. Lee Van Cleef costars, with Klaus Kinski. Directed by Sergio Leone. **DT73, ST64, ST126, ST221, WE2, WE13**, *Recommended*

For All Mankind (1989, C, 90m, NR)
NASA footage of the nine manned space flights to the moon between 1968 and 1972, compiled and edited by Al Reinert. **CU16**

For Keeps (1988, C, 98m, PG-13)
In this comedy, Molly Ringwald plays a high school senior whose unplanned pregnancy forces her to postpone college. **CO4**

For Love of Ivy (1968, C, 102m, NR)
A brother and sister fix up their family's black maid with a trucking company owner. Romantic comedy stars Sidney Poitier and Abbey Lincoln as the lovers; Beau Bridges and Lauri Peters are the matchmakers. **DR14, ST174**

For Love or Money (1963, C, 108m, NR)
Comedy of widow (Thelma Ritter) hiring lawyer (Kirk Douglas) to find matches for her three daughters. With Mitzi Gaynor, Julie Newmar, Leslie Parrish, and Gig Young. **ST57**

For Me and My Gal
(1942, B&W, 104m, NR)
Gene Kelly made his film debut opposite Judy Garland in this musical about a vaudeville couple's attempts to hit the big time. Busby Berkeley directed. **DR12, MU4, ST81, ST123**

For Pete's Sake (1974, C, 90m, PG)
Barbra Streisand stars as the well-intentioned wife of a cab driver (Michael Sarrazin); her schemes to help him make money immerse them in comic misadventures. **ST211**

For Queen and Country
(1989, C, 105m, R)
Denzel Washington stars in a British drama of a veteran who finds his home country hostile to his aspirations. **DR7, DR14, DR23, ST223**

For Richer, For Poorer (1992, C, 90m, NR)
Jack Lemmon stars in a comedy about a millionaire who intentionally goes broke to teach his selfish family a lesson in starting over. With Talia Shire, Joanne Gleason, Jonathan Silverman, and Madeline Kahn. Originally made for cable TV. Also known as *Father, Son and the Mistress*. **CO2, CO5, ST138**

For the Boys (1991, C, 145m, R)
Sentimental musical drama of show-biz team (Bette Midler and James Caan) entertaining the troops through three wars (WWII, Korea, and Vietnam). With George Segal and Patrick O'Neal. **DR2, DR12, ST156**

For the Love of Benji (1977, C, 84m, G)
The lovable canine stars in his second adventure; this time, he's running through the streets of Athens, dodging criminals who want a formula tattooed on his paw. **FA5**

For Us, the Living (1983, C, 90m, NR)
The life and death of civil rights leader Medgar Evers (Howard Rollins, Jr.). With Irene Cara, Margaret Avery, Roscoe Lee Browne, Larry Fishburne, and in a small role, Paul Winfield. Originally made for public TV. **DR4, DR7, DR14, ST230**

For Your Eyes Only (1981, C, 127m, PG)
James Bond adventure, with the usual exotic locales and sinister villains, but less emphasis on gadgetry and gimmicks. Roger Moore stars, with Carole Bouquet, Chaim Topol, and Lynn-Holly Johnson. **HF2**

Forbidden Alliance see *Barretts of Wimpole Street, The*

Forbidden Games (1951, B&W, 87m, NR)
Oscar-winning French film about an orphan girl (Brigitte Fossey) and her stepbrother retreating into their own world. René Clement directed. **FF1, XT7**, *Essential, Recommended*

Forbidden Planet (1956, C, 98m, NR)
Classic 1950s science fiction drama about astronauts discovering planet occupied by wicked scientist and his lovely daughter. A loose adaptation of Shakespeare's *The Tempest*, starring Walter Pidgeon, Anne Francis, and Leslie Nielsen. **CU4, SF1, WR28**, *Essential, Recommended*

Forbidden Zone (1980, C, 76m, R)
This unusual, campy musical deals with an underground kingdom set in the Sixth Dimension. Herve Villechaize stars. **CU2, MU16**

Forbin Project, The see *Colossus: The Forbin Project*

Force of Evil (1948, B&W, 78m, NR)
A small-time attorney (John Garfield) gives up his ideals to find success working for a racketeer. Classic *film noir*, written and directed by Abraham Polonsky. **MY1, ST80,** *Essential, Recommended*

Force of One, A (1979, C, 90m, PG)
Chuck Norris stars in this karate-kicking sequel to *Good Guys Wear Black*, about a small California town overrun by drug dealers and the man who would stop them. **ST165**

Force 10 From Navarone
(1978, C, 118m, PG)
This sequel to *The Guns of Navarone* features Harrison Ford and Robert Shaw as members of a force out to blow up a bridge that is vital to the Nazis. **AC1, ST74**

Forced Vengeance (1982, C, 90m, R)
In Hong Kong, a Vietnam War veteran, now the head of security at a casino, tangles with some gangsters. Chuck Norris stars. **ST165**

Foreign Correspondent
(1940, B&W, 119m, NR)
Joel McCrea is a journalist who falls for a British girl and uncovers a spy ring headed by her father. With Laraine Day, Herbert Marshall, and George Sanders. Directed by Alfred Hitchcock. **DT57, MY6, ST144**

Forever and a Day (1943, B&W, 104m, NR)
Epic story of one house and its eighty years of inhabitants, featuring a parade of British and American performers, including Charles Laughton, Buster Keaton, Robert Cummings, Ida Lupino, Herbert Marshall, Ray Milland, Merle Oberon, Claude Rains, Elsa Lanchester, Edward Everett Horton, and Edmund Gwenn. Co-directed by René Clair. **CU17, DR8, DR23, DT25, DT66, ST132**

Forever Darling (1956, C, 96m, NR)
Lucille Ball and Desi Arnaz play a bickering couple reunited by a guardian angel (James Mason). **ST153**

Forever Young (1992, C, 102m, PG)
Mel Gibson plays a World War II–era pilot who, after his romance takes a tragic turn, persuades an inventor buddy to freeze his body, to be reawakened in the near future. Instead, he doesn't thaw out for another forty years. Romantic drama also features Jamie Lee Curtis, Elijah Wood, Isabel Glasser, George Wendt, and Joe Morton. **DR1, DR2, DR27, SF4, ST42, ST85**

Formula, The (1980, C, 117m, R)
A Los Angeles cop investigates the murder of his friend and discovers a conspiracy involving a formula for synthetic fuel. Marlon Brando and George C. Scott star, with John Gielgud, Marthe Keller, G.D. Spradlin, and Beatrice Straight. Directed by John Avildsen. **DR24, MY6, MY9, ST18, ST86, ST196**

Forsaking All Others
(1934, B&W, 84m, NR)
Clark Gable-Joan Crawford melodrama has him carrying a torch for her for twenty years. With Robert Montgomery, Charles Butterworth, Billie Burke, and Rosalind Russell. **CL5, ST39, ST77, ST192**

Fort Apache (1948, B&W, 127m, NR)
John Ford directed this classic Western about cavalrymen (John Wayne and Henry Fonda) who protect the frontier from the Indians. With Shirley Temple, Victor McLaglen, and Ward Bond. **DT44, ST71, ST213, ST224, WE4,** *Essential, Recommended*

Fort Apache, The Bronx
(1981, C, 125m, R)
Paul Newman plays a weary, streetwise cop trying to do his job against often impossible odds in a dangerous neighborhood. With Ed Asner, Ken Wahl, Pam Grier, and Danny Aiello. Newman and Grier are both very good, but the story's too contrived. **DR15, ST162, XT9**

Fortress (1985, C, 89m, NR)
Australian action drama of kidnapping of a teacher and her students in the Australian outback. Rachel Ward stars. **FF5**

Fortune and Men's Eyes
(1971, C, 102m, R)
Drama set in men's prison focuses on homosexual relations between prisoners. Wendell Burton stars, with Michael Greer and Zooey (David) Hall. Based on John Herbert's play. **DR3, DR18, DR20**

Fortune Cookie, The
(1966, B&W, 125m, NR)
Barbarous comedy of TV reporter injured during Cleveland Browns game, encouraged by his shady brother-in-law to sue everyone in sight. Jack Lemmon and Oscar winner Walter Matthau star, with Ron Rich, Cliff Osmond, and Judi West. Directed and co-written by Billy Wilder. **CO2, CO3, DT139, ST138, ST155, XT4**

Fortunes of War (1989, C, 350m, NR)
Kenneth Branagh and Emma Thompson star
in this British TV miniseries about a couple's
adventures in the Baltics on the brink of
World War II. Based on Olivia Manning's trilogy of novels. Originally shown in the U.S.
on public TV. **DR5, DR19, DR23**

Forty Carats (1973, C, 110m, PG)
Liv Ullmann is a middle-aged divorced
woman who falls in love with a man half her
age. Gene Kelly and Edward Albert costar in
this comedy. **CO1, ST123, ST220**

48 HRS (1982, C, 96m, R)
Eddie Murphy made his screen debut in this
action/thriller about a weary San Francisco
cop (Nick Nolte) who gets a con (Murphy)
out of jail for two days to help track a deranged killer. With Annette O'Toole, James
Remar, and Frank McRae. Directed by Walter
Hill. Less than the sum of its entertaining
parts. **AC9, CO13, DT56, ST164, XT13,
XT21**

49th Parallel, The (1941, B&W, 105m, NR)
When a Nazi U-boat is sunk in Canadian
waters, its survivors struggle to reach neutral
territory. Suspense from director Michael
Powell, starring Anton Walbrook, Eric Portman, Leslie Howard, and Laurence Olivier.
AC1, DT99, ST168

42nd Street (1933, B&W, 89m, NR)
The star of a Broadway show gets sick, and
a naive girl (Ruby Keeler) is picked to go on
in her place. Great songs, including "Shuffle
Off to Buffalo," and superb choreography by
Busby Berkeley. Look quickly for Ginger
Rogers. **DT12, MU4, ST175, ST187,** *Essen-
tial, Recommended*

**Forty-Seven Ronin, The
Part One** (1941, B&W, 113m, NR)

Part Two (1942, B&W, 112m, NR)
Epic Japanese historical drama about a group
of royal retainers out to avenge the honor of
their lord. Directed by Kenji Mizoguchi. **FF4**

Forty Thousand Horsemen
(1941, B&W, 84m, NR)
World War I adventure of the Australian
Light Brigade's adventures in Palestine. Grant
Taylor and Chips Rafferty star. **AC2, FF5**

Foul Play (1978, C, 116m, PG)
Suspense comedy, set in San Francisco, about
a woman caught in a murder plot. No one
will believe her, except a detective who happens to be falling in love with her. Goldie
Hawn and Chevy Chase star, with Dudley
Moore. **CO10, CO13, ST99, ST160, XT13**

Fountainhead, The
(1949, B&W, 114m, NR)
Gary Cooper plays an idealistic architect who
won't compromise his designs for the com-
pany he works for or for the woman he loves
(Patricia Neal). Cult camp based on the Ayn
Rand novel. Directed by King Vidor. **CU2,
DT126, ST37**

4D Man (1959, C, 85m, NR)
Science fiction drama of a scientist whose
experiments give him the power to pass
through solid matter. Robert Lansing and
Lee Meriwether star. **SF1, SF5**

**Four Adventures of Reinette and
Mirabelle** (1986, C, 99m, NR)
French director Eric Rohmer's drama of the
friendship between a country girl and a city
girl rooming together in Paris. Joelle Miquel
and Jessica Forde star. **DT107**

Four Daughters (1938, B&W, 90m, NR)
Drama of small-town life, about quartet of
sisters with different men in their lives.
Claude Rains stars, with Rosemary Lane, Lola
Lane, Priscilla Lane, Gale Page, John Garfield
(his debut), Jeffrey Lynn, Frank McHugh,
May Robson, and Dick Foran. Directed by
Michael Curtiz. Lanes were real-life sisters.
CL5, DR26, ST80, XT8

Four Faces West (1948, B&W, 90m, NR)
Western drama of sheriff tracking down a
fugitive, starring Joel McCrea, with Frances
Dee, Charles Bickford, and Joseph Calleia.
ST144

Four Feathers, The (1939, C, 115m, NR)
A cowardly British officer decides to prove
his prowess when he helps fellow soldiers in
the Sudan uprising. Ralph Richardson and
C. Aubrey Smith star in this early Technicolor saga. **AC6, AC13, CL9, ST184**

Four for Texas (1963, C, 124m, NR)
Comic Western, set in 1870 Galveston, star-
ring Frank Sinatra and Dean Martin, with
Victor Buono, Anita Ekberg, Ursula Andress,
Charles Bronson, Richard Jaeckel, and Mike
Mazurki. Directed by Robert Aldrich. **DT1,
ST20, ST199, WE14**

Four Friends (1981, C, 115m, R)
A young Yugoslavian immigrant to the U.S.
grows up during the turbulent 1960s. Craig
Wasson stars, with Jodi Thelen and Jim
Metzler. Written by Steve Tesich; directed
by Arthur Penn. **DR7, DT96**

Four Horsemen of the Apocalypse, The
(1961, C, 153m, NR)
Vincente Minnelli directed this remake and
updating of the silent classic about the break-

up of a family whose members fight on opposite sides during World War II (World War I in the original). Glenn Ford and Charles Boyer star. **CL3, DT88, ST16**

400 Blows, The (1959, B&W, 99m, NR) Stunning account of a young Parisian boy's desperate search for affection in a loveless household. Jean-Pierre Leaud stars in this first of several films about the same character, Antoine Doinel. Director François Truffaut's groundbreaking debut. **DT125, XT16,** *Essential, Highly Recommended*

Four Musketeers, The (1975, C, 108m, PG) Sequel to 1974 version of *The Three Musketeers* (filmed at the same time), with grand cast indulging in more swordplay and double-dealing. Oliver Reed, Faye Dunaway, Frank Finlay, Michael York, and Richard Chamberlain star, with Christopher Lee, Charlton Heston, Raquel Welch, and Roy Kinnear. Brilliantly directed by Richard Lester. **AC15, DT74, ST61, ST135,** *Highly Recommended*

Four Seasons, The (1981, C, 107m, PG) Three middle-aged couples vacation together during each of the seasons of the year. Alan Alda stars, with Carol Burnett, Rita Moreno, Jack Weston, Len Cariou, and Bess Armstrong. Alda wrote and directed. Slick and occasionally funny, but more than a little smug. **CO1**

1492: Conquest of Paradise (1992, C, 150m, PG-13) Gérard Depardieu is Columbus, Sigourney Weaver is Queen Isabella in this lavish epic from director Ridley Scott. With Armand Assante, Loren Dean, Angela Molina, Fernando Rey, and Frank Langella. Widescreen visuals will be lost on video without letterboxing. Most interesting for its portrayal of the tragic events surrounding the first settlements in the New World. Not an embarrassment, though not up to Scott's best work, either. **DR5, DT115, ST52, ST225**

Fourth Man, The (1979, C, 104m, NR) A bisexual writer begins an affair with a seductive young woman, but is more attracted to her current boyfriend. Then he learns that the woman's three husbands all died mysteriously. Dutch film with cult reputation for its sexy explicitness, directed by Paul Verhoeven. **CU6, FF7, MY5, MY16,** *Recommended*

Fourth Protocol, The (1987, C, 119m, R) A British spy (Michael Caine) tries to stop a Russian plot to sever ties between England and America. Pierce Brosnan and Joanna Cassidy costar as the Russian agents. Based on a Frederick Forsyth novel. **MY6, ST25, WR10**

Fourth War, The (1990, C, 95m, R) Roy Scheider and Jurgen Prochnow play rival American and Soviet military officers poised on opposite sides of the Eastern Europe border in this pre-*glasnost* thriller. With Harry Dean Stanton and Tim Reid. **MY6, ST205**

Fox and His Friends (1975, C, 123m, NR) German drama of a gay carnival worker who is exploited by his wealthy lover. Rainer Werner Fassbinder directed himself in the title role. **DT42**

Foxes (1980, C, 106m, R) The trials and tribulations of four teen-age girls growing up fast in the San Fernando Valley, starring Jodie Foster, Cherie Curie, Marilyn Kagan, and Kandice Stroh, with Scott Baio, Sally Kellerman, and Randy Quaid. Not bad, considering how many truly dumb movies have been made on the subject. **DR9, MU12, ST75**

Foxtrot (1976, C, 91m, R) Peter O'Toole stars in this drama about a wealthy couple who flee Europe in the late 1930s to escape the approaching madness of World War II. They settle on an island off the coast of Mexico. With Charlotte Rampling and Max von Sydow. **ST169**

Fozzie's Muppet Scrapbook (1985, C, 58m, NR) Milton Berle, Raquel Welch, and Beverly Sills join "The Muppet Show's" lovable Fozzie Bear in some of his greatest adventures. **FA14**

Framed (1990, C, 87m, NR) Thriller about an artist (Jeff Goldblum) mixed up with a con woman (Kristin Scott). **ST90**

Frances (1982, C, 140m, R) Jessica Lange is riveting to watch as Frances Farmer, the Hollywood actress of the 1930s, whose brushes with the law and conflicts with her domineering mother cut short her career. With Kim Stanley as Frances's monster mother and Sam Shepard. Watch for Kevin Costner in a small role. **DR4, DR13, ST38, ST130,** *Recommended*

Frankenhooker (1990, C, 90m, NR) Violent horror story of scientist whose girlfriend is sliced up by a power mower; he seeks to reconstruct her by murdering prostitutes for the body parts. James Lorinz and Patty Mullen star. Cowritten and directed by Frank Henelotter. **CU1, CU4, CU7, HO18, HO20**

Frankenstein (1931, B&W, 71m, NR)
The definitive Man-Made Monster movie, with Boris Karloff the creation of mad scientist Colin Clive. Video version restores footage not seen since the original release. Directed by James Whale. **CU10, DT138, HF10, HO1, HO20, SF2, ST119,** *Essential, Recommended*

Frankenstein (1973, C, 130m, NR)
Made-for-television version of the Mary Shelley story features Bo Svenson as the creation, more a dashing rogue than a monster. Robert Foxworth and James Mason costar. **HF10, HO20**

Frankenstein (1982, C, 81m, NR)
In this version of the familiar tale, the monster actually speaks with his creator, and both die in the Arctic. Robert Powell stars, with David Warner as the monster, Carrie Fisher, and John Gielgud. **HF10, HO20, ST86**

Frankenstein and the Monster From Hell (1974, C, 93m, R)
British entry in the seemingly endless series has young doctor conducting experiments with human bodies; Dr. F is running an asylum, and the two join forces. Peter Cushing and Shane Briant star, with David Prowse as the monster. **HF10, HO26, ST43**

Frankenstein Island (1978, C, 88m, NR)
Four balloonists crash on an uncharted island and encounter zombies, mad doctors, scantily clad women, and . . . well, more we dare not tell. Deservedly obscure "bad" film. **CU11**

Frankenstein Meets the Wolf Man (1943, B&W, 72m, NR)
Summit meeting of film monsters, starring Bela Lugosi and Lon Chaney, Jr. **HF10, HO1, ST27, ST143**

Frankenstein—1970 (1958, B&W, 83m, NR)
This version of the classic horror story stars Boris Karloff as a mad scientist and takes more of a science fiction approach to the familiar material. **HF10, ST119**

Frankenstein Unbound (1990, C, 85m, R)
A new twist on the familiar story finds a twenty-first-century scientist (John Hurt) transported in time to meet Dr. F (Raul Julia) and his creation (Nick Brimble). With Jason Patric as Lord Byron, rock star Michael Hutchence as Percy Shelley, and Bridget Fonda as Mary Shelley. Directed by Roger Corman. **DT30, HF10, HO20, MU12, SF4, ST70**

Frankenweenie (1984, C, 28m, NR)
Cartoon short from director Tim Burton (his debut) about a boy named Victor Franken-

stein bringing his pet dog back to life. **DT20, HF10**

Frankie and Johnny (1966, C, 87m, NR)
Elvis Presley plays a riverboat gambler caught in a love triangle. **ST178**

Frankie and Johnny (1991, C, 118m, R)
New York love story of ex-con turned cook (Al Pacino) and defensive waitress (Michelle Pfeiffer). With Hector Elizondo, Nathan Lane, Kate Nelligan, and Jane Morris. Screenplay by Terrence McNally, from his play. Directed by Garry Marshall. Touching story of lost souls in a big, cold city. **DR1, DR15, DR20, ST170, ST173, XT9,** *Recommended*

Frantic (1958, B&W, 90m, NR)
A man and woman plan to murder her husband, but the plan backfires, and the man gets accused of murders he didn't commit. Jeanne Moreau stars. Louis Malle directed; great musical score by Miles Davis. Also known as *Elevator to the Gallows*. **DT82, MY16, ST161**

Frantic (1988, C, 120m, R)
Thriller starring Harrison Ford as an American whose wife is kidnapped while they're vacationing in Paris. With Emmanuelle Seigner and Betty Buckley. Directed by Roman Polanski, playing it unusually straight but still delivering a solid thriller. **DT97, MY16, ST74, XT16,** *Recommended*

Freaks (1932, B&W, 64m, NR)
Classic horror film, banned for many years in Britain, about circus troupe, starring real "human oddities." Directed by Tod Browning. **CU4, CU8, DT18, HO1, HO19,** *Recommended*

Freaky Friday (1977, C, 95m, G)
This Disney comedy features Barbara Harris and Jodie Foster as a mother and daughter who switch personalities for a day. Pretty lame, despite two expert leads. **CO20, FA1, ST75**

Freddie as F.R.O.7 (1992, C, 90m, PG)
Animated tale of secret agent frog, featuring voices of Ben Kingsley, Jenny Agutter, Brian Blessed, Nigel Hawthrone, Michael Hordern, and Edmund Kingsley. **FA4, FA10**

Freddy's Dead: The Final Nightmare see *Nightmare on Elm Street* (series)

Free and Easy (1930, B&W, 92m, NR)
Buster Keaton stars in this comedy with musical numbers about an aspiring movie star. With Anita Page, Robert Montgomery, Lionel Barrymore, and lots of Hollywood personalities playing themselves, including Cecil B. DeMille. **CL7, DT34, DT66**

Free Soul, A (1931, B&W, 91m, NR)
Lionel Barrymore won an Oscar for his performance as an attorney whose daughter
(Norma Shearer) falls in love with a gangster
(Clark Gable) he is defending. **ST77, XT2**

Freejack (1992, C, 108m, R)
Science fiction tale of race car driver who
"dies" in 1991, only to be reincarnated in
2009 as host body for a dying rich man living in dystopian New York. Emilio Estevez
stars, with Anthony Hopkins, Mick Jagger,
Rene Russo, David Johansen, and Amanda
Plummer. **MU12, SF4, ST109**

French Cancan (1955, C, 93m, NR)
Jean Renoir directed this colorful story of the
early days of the Moulin Rouge. Jean Gabin
plays a showman who invents the title
dance. Also known as *Only the French Can.*
DT104

French Connection, The
(1971, C, 104m, R)
Oscar winner Gene Hackman plays Popeye
Doyle, a hard-driving New York City detective on the trail of a heroin smuggling ring.
Oscars for Best Picture and Director (William
Friedkin). With Roy Scheider and Fernando
Rey. Hackman's performance carries the day
in the first of the urban anything-to-stop-
drug-lords dramas. **AC9, ST96, XT1, XT2,
XT6, XT9,** *Essential, Recommended*

French Connection II, The
(1975, C, 119m, R)
Popeye Doyle travels to France in an attempt
to locate the drug kingpin who eluded him
in New York. Gene Hackman and Fernando
Rey star. John Frankenheimer directed. **AC9,
ST96**

French Lieutenant's Woman, The
(1981, C, 123m, R)
Intelligent, daring screen version of John
Fowles's story of ill-fated Victorian love affair
adds a parallel modern story about actor and
actress shooting a film and becoming lovers.
Meryl Streep and Jeremy Irons star. Written
by Harold Pinter and directed by Karel Reisz.
Streep's performance should have won her
an Oscar. **DR1, DR13, ST116, ST210,
WR26, XT28,** *Recommended*

French Postcards (1979, C, 92m, PG)
A group of American teen-agers studying in
Paris get involved in many misadventures.
Early screen appearances for Debra Winger,
Mandy Patinkin, and Blanche Baker. **CO4,
ST231, XT16**

Frenzy (1972, C, 116m, R)
Alfred Hitchcock's gripping story of a London strangler known as The Necktie Mur-
derer, and the innocent man who is suspected of the killer's crimes. Jon Finch and
Barry Foster star, with Barbara Leigh-Hunt,
Anna Massey, Alec McCowen, and Vivien
Merchant. **DT57, MY3, MY7, MY13, XT15,**
Recommended

Fresh Horses (1988, C, 104m, PG-13)
A soon-to-be-married young man has second
thoughts when he meets a sensual young
woman, although they're from very different
backgrounds. Andrew McCarthy and Molly
Ringwald star in this romantic drama. **DR1**

Freshman, The (1925, B&W, 70m, NR)
In this silent comedy classic, Harold Lloyd
plays a college freshman who will do anything to be accepted by his fellow students.
CL11, CO18, *Essential*

Freshman, The (1990, C, 102m, PG)
Sweet, loopy comedy about a naive young
man (Matthew Broderick) enrolling in New
York University Film School, getting mixed
up with a crime boss (Marlon Brando, in a
parody of his *Godfather* role). With Penelope
Ann Miller, Bruno Kirby, Paul Benedict, Maximilian Schell, and Bert Parks (who sings Bob
Dylan's "Maggie's Farm"). Written and
directed by Andrew Bergman. **CO10, CO12,
CO18, ST18, XT9,** *Recommended*

Friday the 13th (series)
Part I (1980, C, 95m, R)
Part II (1981, C, 87m, R)
Part III (1982, C, 96m, R)
The Final Chapter (1984, C, 91m, R)
Part V: A New Beginning
(1985, C, 102m, R)
Part VI: Jason Lives (1986, C, 87m, R)
Part VII: The New Blood
(1988, C, 90m, R)
Part VIII: Jason Takes Manhattan
(1989, C, 100m, R)
This horror series portrays a mad, seemingly
indestructible killer named Jason, who masquerades behind a hockey mask, murdering
innumerable teen-agers at a summer camp.
HO12, HO18, *Essential (Part I)*

Fried Green Tomatoes
(1991, C, 130m, PG-13)
Drama of parallel stories about women in
the South. A vibrant nursing home resident
(Jessica Tandy) tells an unhappy, middle-aged
housewife (Kathy Bates) a tale of two young
women (Mary Stuart Masterson and Mary-
Louise Parker) in the 1930s and their friendship in the face of bigotry and cruelty. Based
on Fannie Flagg's novel. Tough to dislike, but
Masterson seems more at her ease than Parker, and the wrap-up is drawn out. **DR10,
DR11, DR26**

Friendly Persuasion (1956, C, 140m, NR)
A family of Quakers hold fast to their faith during the Civil War. Gary Cooper and Dorothy McGuire star. William Wyler directed. **AC5, DT142, ST37**

Fright Night (1985, C, 106m, R)
A teen-ager hires a TV horror movie host to kill a new neighbor, whom he suspects of being a vampire. William Ragsdale, Chris Sarandon, and Roddy McDowall star, with Amanda Bearse. **HO5, HO19**

Fright Night II (1989, C, 108m, R)
Sequel to *Fright Night* has same teen and TV horror show host teaming to trap a seductive vampire (Julie Carmen). **HO5**

Fringe Dwellers, The (1986, C, 98m, PG)
Australian drama about an aborigine family moving into a white, middle-class neighborhood, with expected problems. Directed by Bruce Beresford. **DT10, FF5**

Frisco Kid, The (1979, C, 122m, PG)
A wild Western about a Polish rabbi (Gene Wilder) who sets out on the 1850s frontier to meet his San Francisco congregation. Harrison Ford costars. Directed by Robert Aldrich. **DT1, ST74, WE14**

Frogs (1972, C, 91m, PG)
Ray Milland stars as a man who destroys the natural wildlife near his home, only to have his family threatened by an onslaught of avenging amphibians. **HO16**

From Beyond (1986, C, 85m, R)
A scientist's insatiable search for a sixth sense eventually drives his staff to insanity. Based on an H.P. Lovecraft tale; exceptionally gory. **CU7, HO20, HO25**

From Beyond the Grave
(1973, C, 97m, PG)
Four horror stories centering on a British antique shop, where the mysterious owner (Peter Cushing) helps his customers meet terrible fates. Margaret Leighton, Diana Dors, and David Warner costar. **HO23, HO26, ST43**

From Here to Eternity
(1953, B&W, 118m, NR)
The James Jones story of army life in Pearl Harbor just before the Japanese attack, starring Burt Lancaster, Deborah Kerr, Montgomery Clift, and Oscar winners Frank Sinatra and Donna Reed. Winner of six other Academy Awards, including Best Picture, Director (Fred Zinnemann), and Screenplay Adaptation (Daniel Taradash). Filled with classic moments and sensational performances. **AC1, DR19, DT144, ST32, ST125, ST129,** **ST199, XT1, XT4, XT5, XT6,** *Essential, Highly Recommended*

From Hollywood to Deadwood
(1989, C, 102m, R)
A pair of private eyes (Scott Paulin and Jim Haynie) go looking for a missing movie star. Written and directed by Rex Pickett. **MY10**

From Russia With Love
(1963, C, 118m, NR)
The second James Bond adventure, and one of the very best, with Sean Connery sparring with lovely Soviet spy Daniela Bianchi. Robert Shaw and Lotte Lenya make an especially colorful pair of villains. Outstanding fight sequence aboard the Orient Express. **HF2, ST36, XT19,** *Highly Recommended*

From the Earth to the Moon
(1958, C, 100m, NR)
Jules Verne's fantasy adventure about man's first voyage to the moon, starring George Sanders, Debra Paget, and Cedric Hardwicke. **FA8, SF13, WR36**

From the Life of the Marionettes
(1980, C/B&W, 104m, R)
Drama from director Ingmar Bergman about a respectable businessman involved in the murder of a prostitute. Robert Atzorn stars. **DT11**

From the Mixed-Up Files of Mrs. Basil E. Frankweiler (1973, C, 105m, NR)
Two children hide out in New York City's Metropolitan Museum and befriend a reclusive woman (Ingrid Bergman). **FA7, ST13**

From the Terrace (1960, C, 144m, NR)
John O'Hara story of a war veteran rising to social prominence on the backs of everyone who gets in his way. Paul Newman stars, with Joanne Woodward and Myrna Loy. **ST142, ST162, ST234, WR24**

Front, The (1976, C, 94m, PG)
Woody Allen stars in a drama of a restaurant cashier who fronts for a group of blacklisted television writers in 1950s New York. He slowly becomes a celebrity as he accepts the praise and recognition for their work. Written by Walter Bernstein (himself a blacklisted writer); directed by Martin Ritt. **DR5, DR12, DT2, DT105**

Front Page, The (1931, B&W, 101m, NR)
First screen version of the Ben Hecht-Charles MacArthur stage comedy about the ruthless world of journalism. Pat O'Brien plays the star reporter, and Adolphe Menjou is his hard-driving editor. Remade in 1940 (as *His Girl Friday*), in 1974, and in 1988 (as *Switching Channels*). **CL10, DR20**

Front Page, The (1974, C, 105m, PG)
Director Billy Wilder's take on the often-filmed newspaper comedy. Walter Matthau (as Walter) and Jack Lemmon (as Hildy) star, with Susan Sarandon, Carol Burnett, and Vincent Gardenia. Not up to its predecessors. **CO3, CU18, DT139, ST138, ST155, ST194**

Frontier Pony Express
(1939, B&W, 54m, NR)
Roy Rogers and Trigger ride into action to round up Pony Express bandits. **ST188**

Frozen Assets (1992, C, 93m, PG-13)
Romantic comedy set in a sperm bank (yes, you read right), starring Corbin Bernsen and Shelley Long, with Larry Miller, Dody Goodman, Matt Clark, Gerrit Graham, and Paul Sand. **CO1**

Fugitive, The (1947, B&W, 104m, NR)
Drama of a priest (Henry Fonda) in Mexico involved with revolutionaries. Directed by John Ford. Based on Graham Greene's novel *The Power and the Glory.* **DT44, ST71, WR11**

Fugitive Kind, The
(1959, B&W, 135m, NR)
A drifter (Marlon Brando) arrives in a Southern town and begins romancing two women (Joanne Woodward and Anna Magnani). Tennessee Williams drama directed by Sidney Lumet. **DT78, ST18, ST234, WR38**

Full Metal Jacket (1987, C, 120m, R)
After a grueling basic training period, a cynical young army journalist (Matthew Modine) is plunged into combat in Vietnam. A gritty, violent tale from director Stanley Kubrick. With Vincent D'Onofrio, Lee Ermey, and Adam Baldwin. **AC4, DT68,** *Recommended*

Full Moon in Blue Water
(1988, C, 96m, R)
Gene Hackman plays the owner of a run-down seaside bar whose bad fortune is reversed by the arrival of a young woman (Teri Garr). **ST96**

Full Moon in Paris (1984, C, 102m, R)
French comedy about an independent young woman juggling three lovers. Pascale Ogier stars. Eric Rohmer directed. **DT107**

Fun in Acapulco (1963, C, 97m, NR)
Elvis Presley plays a lifeguard by day and nightclub entertainer at night in this musical set in Mexico. **ST178**

Fun With Dick and Jane
(1977, C, 95m, PG)
Comedy about modern lifestyles stars Jane Fonda and George Segal as an upwardly mobile couple who turn to robbery when he loses his job. **CO2, CO10, ST72**

Funeral in Berlin (1966, C, 102m, NR)
Michael Caine's second film as British spy Harry Palmer; here he arranges for the defection of a Russian officer. **MY6, ST25**

Funhouse, The (1981, C, 96m, R)
Four teen-agers decide to spend the night in a carnival funhouse, where they are terrorized by an unknown assailant. Directed by Tobe Hooper. **HO12**

Funhouse (1987) see *Eric Bogosian—Funhouse*

Funny About Love (1990, C, 101m, PG-13)
Gene Wilder stars in a comedy about a couple who can't conceive a child, so he takes up with a younger woman. With Christine Lahti, Mary Stuart Masterson, Robert Prosky, Anne Jackson, Susan Ruttan, and basketball star Patrick Ewing in a bit part. Directed by Leonard Nimoy. **CO1, XT23**

Funny Face (1957, C, 103m, NR)
Fred Astaire is a fashion photographer who takes a plain Audrey Hepburn and turns her into a beautiful Paris model. Stanley Donen directed; songs by George Gershwin. **CL9, DT38, ST4, ST102, XT16**

Funny Farm (1988, C, 101m, PG)
Chevy Chase is a sportswriter looking for a rural retreat—and finding nothing but trouble. Madolyn Smith costars. Directed by George Roy Hill. **CO13, DT55**

Funny Girl (1968, C, 155m, G)
Barbra Streisand, in her debut film, won an Academy Award for re-creating her Broadway success as Fanny Brice, the comedy legend who rose to stardom in the Ziegfeld Follies. With Omar Sharif and Kay Medford. Directed by William Wyler. **DT142, MU2, MU5, MU7, ST211, XT3, XT9, XT21,** *Essential*

Funny Lady (1975, C, 137m, PG)
This sequel to *Funny Girl* portrays Fanny Brice (Barbra Streisand) at the peak of her career, married to showman Billy Rose (James Caan). **MU5, ST211**

Funny Thing Happened on the Way to the Forum, A (1966, C, 99m, NR)
Zero Mostel portrays a sly slave in ancient Rome with a yearning to be free. Based on the Broadway musical, with costars Buster Keaton, Jack Gilford, and Michael Crawford. Directed by Richard Lester, who stretches the material even further than one would think possible. Widescreen will be lost on home video, severely affecting film's impact. **CU20, DT66, DT74, MU2**

Fury (1936, B&W, 94m, NR)
Trenchant social drama, with Spencer Tracy the innocent object of a small-town lynch

mob, escaping aad turning vengeful. With Sylvia Sidney, Walter Abel, Bruce Cabot, and Walter Brennan. Fritz Lang's first American film remains among his very best. **CL8, DR26, DT70, ST217,** *Essential, Recommended*

Fury, The (1978, C, 118m, R)
Young girl and boy with telekinetic powers are united against evil American agents. Kirk Douglas, Amy Irving, John Cassavetes, and Andrew Stevens star. Brian De Palma directed, as nearly always, deliriously and to no great effect. **DT36, HO7, ST57**

Future-Kill (1984, C, 83m, R)
Science fiction action with a band of rowdy fraternity boys taking on antinuclear activists in a city wasteland. Edwin Neal and Marilyn Burns star. **SF8**

Futureworld (1976, C, 104m, PG)
Sequel to *Westworld*, with that film's robots hatching a Take Over the World scheme. Science fiction drama starring Peter Fonda, Blythe Danner, and Yul Brynner. **SF6**

Fuzz (1972, C, 92m, PG)
Cop drama, with moments of dark humor, about Boston policemen and their attempts to stay sane amid the chaos of big city life. Burt Reynolds stars, with Raquel Welch, Yul Brynner, Jack Weston, Tom Skerritt, and Peter Bonerz. **CO9, ST183**

G.I. Blues (1960, C, 104m, NR)
Elvis Presley stars as a guitar-playing soldier in Germany who romances a leggy dancer (Juliet Prowse). **ST178**

"G" Men (1935, B&W, 85m, NR)
James Cagney stars as a young man turned FBI agent when his friend, a crook who raised him, is gunned down by rivals. With Ann Dvorak, Margaret Lindsay, Robert Armstrong, and Barton MacLane. **AC22, ST24**

Gabriel Over the White House
(1933, B&W, 86m, NR)
Fantasy of crooked politician (Walter Huston) ascending to the White House, suddenly having a change of heart, deciding to clean up the country using dictatorial powers. With Karen Morley and Franchot Tone. Directed by Gregory La Cava. Fascinating time-capsule look at how some Americans fantasized a way out of the Depression. **DR21, SF2,** *Recommended*

Gabriela (1983, C, 102m, R)
Barkeeper takes on lovely young woman as a cook, and romance follows. Marcello Mastroianni and Sonia Braga costar in this Brazilian film. **FF6, ST16, ST154**

Gaby—A True Story (1987, C, 110m, R)
True-life drama of a young woman afflicted with cerebral palsy, struggling to overcome her handicap and her parents' overprotectiveness to become a bestselling writer. Rachel Levin stars, with Liv Ullmann, Robert Loggia, and Norma Aleandro. Levin is very good. **DR2, DR6, ST220**

Galaxina (1980, C, 95m, R)
Science fiction spoof of both *Star Wars* and *Star Trek* movies, starring Avery Schreiber and sexy Dorothy Stratten. **SF21, SF22**

Galaxy of Terror (1981, C, 80m, R)
Astronauts confront monsters while on a rescue mission in this science fiction/horror tale. Edward Albert, Erin Moran, and Ray Walston star. **SF20**

Gallagher (series)
(1984–85, C, approx. 60m ea., NR)
Stand-up comic Gallagher appears in this series of five separate performances: *The Bookkeeper, The Maddest, Melon Crazy, Over Your Head,* and *Stuck in the '60s.* **CO16**

Gallant Hours, The
(1960, B&W, 111m, NR)
James Cagney plays Admiral William F. Halsey in this World War II drama focusing on the 1944 Battle of Leyte Gulf. **AC1, CL2, ST24**

Gallery of Horrors see *Dr. Terror's Gallery of Horrors*

Gallipoli (1981, C, 110m, PG)
World War I drama, starring Mel Gibson and Mark Lee as two naive young Australian recruits thrown into fierce battle. Directed by Peter Weir, his best film. **AC2, DT133, ST85, XT25,** *Recommended*

Gambit (1966, C, 109m, NR)
A crook (Michael Caine) wants to steal a valuable statue, and he hires a kooky young woman (Shirley MacLaine) to help him do the job. Fairly entertaining, with good ending. **MY18, ST25, ST145**

Gamble, The (1988, C, 108m, R)
Costume drama of young nobleman (Matthew Modine) out to recoup his father's gambling losses to an evil, lusty countess (Faye Dunaway). **ST61**

Gambling Samurai, The
(1960, C, 93m, NR)
Toshiro Mifune stars in this tale of a wandering warrior. **FF5, ST157**

Game Is Over, The (1966, C, 96m, NR)
French drama of a woman's marriage to a wealthy man and her affair with his son.

Jane Fonda stars. Roger Vadim directed. **FF1, ST72**

Game of Death (1979, C, 102m, R)
Bruce Lee finished twenty minutes of fighting scenes for this film before he died; a story was composed around those sequences to take advantage of his phenomenal popularity. With Chuck Norris, Kareem Abdul-Jabbar, Gig Young, and Hugh O'Brian. **ST134, ST165**

Gandhi (1982, C, 188m, PG)
Ben Kingsley won an Oscar for his portrayal of India's modern spiritual leader, whose courage inspired his countrymen to reject British colonial rule. With John Gielgud, Edward Fox, Martin Sheen, and in a small role, Daniel Day-Lewis. The film and director Richard Attenborough also won Academy Awards. **DR4, DR23, ST48, ST86, XT1, XT2, XT6, XT23,** *Recommended*

Gangs, Inc. (1941, B&W, 72m, NR)
Innocent woman takes the rap on trumped-up charges to shield her boyfriend, then decides on revenge. Joan Woodbury stars, with Jack LaRue, Linda Ware, and Allan (Alan) Ladd in a small, early role. **ST128**

Gangster, The (1947, B&W, 84m, NR)
Barry Sullivan plays the title role, the product of a disadvantaged youth. With Belita, Joan Lorring, Akim Tamiroff, Harry Morgan, and Shelley Winters. **AC22, MY1, ST232**

Ganja and Hess see *Blood Couple*

Garbo Talks (1984, C, 103m, PG-13)
A son works to grant his mother's dying wish—she wants to meet Greta Garbo, who is living in seclusion in New York City. Anne Bancroft and Ron Silver star, with Carrie Fisher, Catherine Hicks, Steven Hill, Howard da Silva, Dorothy Loudon, and Harvey Fierstein. Directed by Sidney Lumet. The author of this book can be glimpsed as an extra in a party scene. **CO5, DT78, XT9**

Garden of Allah, The (1936, C, 80m, NR)
Charles Boyer and Marlene Dietrich star in this romance set in the Algerian desert. Lovely color photography. A must for fans of old-fashioned romance. **CL9, ST16, ST55**

Garden of the Finzi-Continis, The (1971, C, 95m, R)
Oscar-winning drama from Italy about an aristocratic Jewish family in wartime Italy oblivious to the Holocaust until it is too late to escape. Vittorio De Sica directed. Dominique Sanda stars. **DT37, XT7**

Gardens of Stone (1987, C, 111m, R)
Title refers to Arlington National Cemetery, scene of this drama set during the early days of the Vietnam War. An army company that buries the dead welcomes a young recruit yearning for combat experience. James Caan, James Earl Jones, and D.B. Sweeney star, with Mary Stuart Masterson, Anjelica Huston, Dean Stockwell, and Bill Graham. Francis Ford Coppola directed. **DR7, DT29, ST115, ST118, ST208**

Garlic Is as Good as Ten Mothers (1977, C, 51m, NR)
Ode to the odoriferous plant whose bulbs have enriched the palates of millions. Directed by Les Blank, who enhanced his personal appearances with the film by cooking garlic in the rear of the theater, giving a new twist to the term Smell-o-Vision. **CU16**

Garry Shandling: Alone in Vegas (1984, C, 52m, NR)
The popular comedian is shown in a live performance in Las Vegas. **CO16**

Garry Shandling Show, 25th Special (1985, C, 57m, NR)
The comic who's best at lampooning talk show hosts offers this mock special. **CO16**

Gas, Food, Lodging (1992, C, 100m, R)
Small town in New Mexico is the setting for this drama of a waitress mom (Brooke Adams) deserted by her husband, trying to raise two teen-age daughters (Ione Skye and Fairuza Balk). Told from the point of view of the younger daughter. With James Brolin, Robert Knepper, David Lansbury, Jacob Vargas, and Donovan Leitch (Skye's real-life brother). Directed by Allison Anders. Familiar story contains some nicely observed moments. **DR8, DR9, DR10, DR26, XT8**

Gaslight (1944, B&W, 114m, NR)
Ingrid Bergman won an Academy Award for playing a tormented woman whose husband (Charles Boyer) is slowly driving her insane. With Angela Lansbury. Directed by George Cukor. **DT32, MY3, ST13, ST16, ST131, XT3**

Gas-s-s-s (1970, C, 79m, PG)
Roger Corman directed this free-spirited comedy about a lethal gas destroying everyone in the United States over thirty. Robert Corff and Elaine Giftos star, with Bud Cort, Cindy Williams, Ben Vereen, and Talia Coppola (Shire). Full title: *Gas-s-s-s . . . Or, It May Become Necessary to Destroy the World in Order to Save It!* **CO2, DT30**

Gate, The (1987, C, 92m, PG-13)
A young boy is grounded, and he and a friend discover the gate to hell in his backyard. **HO10**

Gate of Hell (1954, C, 89m, NR)
Japanese drama of a twelfth-century samurai who falls in love with a married woman, then discards her. Oscar winner for Best Foreign Language Film. **FF4, XT7**

Gate II (1992, C, 95m, R)
Somewhat belated sequel to 1987 horror tale of boy finding entrance to hell in his backyard. Louis Tripp returns, now as a teen, to unleash some nasty demons that will grant his desires. **HO12**

Gates of Heaven (1978, C, 85m, NR)
Funny and surprisingly touching documentary about pet cemeteries, the people who use them, the people who run them. Directed by Errol Morris. **CU16, DT89, *Recommended***

Gathering of Eagles, A
(1963, C, 115m, NR)
Strategic Air Command drama set in peacetime, starring Rock Hudson as a tough colonel. With Rod Taylor, Mary Peach, Barry Sullivan, and Kevin McCarthy. **AC11, ST112**

Gathering of Old Men, A see *Murder on the Bayou*

Gathering Storm (1974, C, 72m, NR)
Richard Burton plays Winston Churchill in this biogrpahical drama concentrating on the years before World War II. With Virginia McKenna and Ian Bannen. Original title: *Walk With Destiny*. **DR4, ST22**

Gator (1976, C, 116m, PG)
Good ol' boy Burt Reynolds teams up with the feds to get the goods on a crooked politician in this sequel to *White Lightning*. **ST183**

Gauntlet, The (1977, C, 109m, R)
A cop is assigned to escort a prostitute, set to testify against the Mob, from Las Vegas to Phoenix; both are unaware they've been set up for assassination. Clint Eastwood and Sondra Locke star. Over-the-top gunplay turns this into a comic-strip movie. **AC9, ST64, XT18**

Gay Divorcee, The (1934, B&W, 107m, NR)
Fred Astaire and Ginger Rogers dance to Cole Porter music. Also includes the first Oscar-winning song, "The Continental." Watch for Betty Grable in a bit part. **CL15, ST4, ST91, ST187**

Gay Ranchero, The (1947, B&W, 53m, NR)
Roy Rogers and sidekick Andy Devine go searching for a downed airplane in this contemporary Western. **ST188**

Geisha Boy, The (1958, C, 98m, NR)
Jerry Lewis comedy about a bumbling magician touring the Orient. With Marie McDonald, Sessue Hayakawa, and Suzanne Pleshette in her film debut. Directed by Frank Tashlin. **ST139**

General, The (1927, B&W, 74m, NR)
Buster Keaton plays a man trying to steal a train during the Civil War, with riotous results. One of the truly great comedies, silent or sound. **CL11, DT66, XT19, *Essential, Highly Recommended***

General Della Rovere
(1960, B&W, 129m, NR)
Vittorio De Sica stars in a drama of an Italian impersonating a general during World War II and beginning to believe his ruse. Roberto Rossellini directed. **DT37, DT109, FF2**

General Died at Dawn, The
(1936, B&W, 97m, NR)
Gary Cooper stars in this tale of romance and intrigue in the mysterious East, with Madeleine Carroll as the agent he falls for, Akim Tamiroff his wily adversary. **MY6, ST37**

General Idi Amin Dada
(1974, C, 90m, NR)
Documentary profile of Uganda's monstrous dictator, directed by Barbet Schroeder. **CU16**

General Line, The (1929, B&W, 90m, NR)
Soviet director Sergei Eisenstein's silent drama of a rural woman's struggle to start a collective. **DT41**

General Spanky (1936, B&W, 71m, NR)
Civil War setting for this adult romance whose real stars are three of the Our Gang kids: George "Spanky" McFarland, Carl "Alfalfa" Switzer, and Billie "Buckwheat" Thomas. **FA6**

Gentleman Jim (1942, B&W, 104m, NR)
Errol Flynn plays Jim Corbett, the famed heavyweight boxing champion of the early twentieth century, in this colorful drama. With Alexis Smith, Jack Carson, and Alan Hale. Directed by Raoul Walsh. **CL2, DR22, DT131, ST69**

Gentleman's Agreement
(1947, B&W, 118m, NR)
Laura Z. Hobson's story about a lawyer who goes undercover as a Jew to better understand discrimination. Gregory Peck stars, with Dorothy McGuire, John Garfield, Celeste Holm, Anne Revere, June Havoc, Albert Dekker, Jane Wyatt, and Dean Stockwell. Screen adaptation by Moss Hart, directed by Elia Kazan. Oscar Winner for Best

Picture, Director, and Supporting Actress (Holm). **CL8, DT65, ST80, ST171, ST208, XT1, XT5, XT6**

Gentlemen Prefer Blondes
(1953, C, 91m, NR)
Marilyn Monroe and Jane Russell are two showgirls who set out to find themselves husbands in this vibrant adaptation of the Broadway musical. Monroe proves that "Diamonds Are a Girl's Best Friend." Directed by Howard Hawks. **CO8, DT53, ST157**

George Carlin on Campus
(1984, C, 59m, NR)
The stand-up comedian in concert on the UCLA campus, doing his great "A Place for My Stuff" routine. **CO16**

George Stevens: A Filmmaker's Journey
(1984, C, 110m, NR)
Katharine Hepburn, Ginger Rogers, Joel McCrea, and Warren Beatty are among the performers who add insight to this insightful documentary about director Stevens's films. Includes scenes from *Alice Adams, Swing Time, Giant*, and *A Place In the Sun*. Directed by George Stevens, Jr. **CU16, DT119, ST4, ST10, ST103, ST144, ST187,** *Recommended*

George Washington Slept Here
(1942, B&W, 93m, NR)
New York couple move to house in the country, with predictably comic results. Jack Benny and Ann Sheridan star, with Charles Coburn, Hattie McDaniel, Percy Kilbride, and Franklin Pangborn. Adapted from the George S. Kaufman-Moss Hart play. **CO20, DR20**

Georgy Girl (1966, B&W, 100m, NR)
Lynn Redgrave is an ugly duckling London girl who's romanced by a wealthy older gentleman (James Mason). Alan Bates and Charlotte Rampling costar. Redgrave and Mason are wonderful. **CO17, DR3, ST9, ST153, XT15**

Germany Year Zero
(1947, B&W, 75m, NR)
Roberto Rossellini's neorealist drama of a young boy's experiences in postwar Germany. **DT109**

Geronimo (1962, C, 101m, NR)
Chuck Connors plays the famed Apache chief in this sympathetic portrait. With Kamala Devi, Ross Martin, and Adam West. **WE7**

Gertrud (1964, B&W, 116m, NR)
Director Carl Dreyer's intense drama of a middle-aged Danish woman's desertion of her husband for solitary life in Paris. Nina Pens Rode and Baard Owe star. **DT39**

Get Back (1991, C/B&W, 90m, NR)
Documentary of Paul McCartney's 1990 world tour, directed by Richard Lester, who filmed Paul in *A Hard Day's Night* and *Help!* **DT74, MU10**

Get Crazy (1983, C, 92m, NR)
A theater owner plans to stage the biggest rock concert ever on New Year's Eve, but everything goes wrong. Cult comedy with many characters resembling real-life rock stars, lots of in-jokes about the music business. Daniel Stern stars, with Malcolm McDowell, Ed Begley, Jr., Lou Reed, Bobby Sherman, and Fabian Forte. Directed by Allan Arkush. **CU5, DT6, MU9,** *Recommended*

Get Out of My Room (1985, C, 53m, NR)
Cheech and Chong perform in this compilation of four crazy comedy and music videos, including *Love Is Strange* and *Born in East L.A.* **ST28**

Get Out Your Handkerchiefs
(1978, C, 109m, R)
Dark comedy from France about a man so desperate to keep his wife happy that he urges her to take a lover. Gerard Depardieu, Patrick Dewaere, and Carole Laure star. Directed by Bertrand Blier. Oscar winner for Best Foreign Langauge Film. **FF1, ST52, XT7**

Getaway, The (1972, C, 122m, PG)
Sam Peckinpah's violent tale about a bank robber and his wife (Steve McQueen and Ali MacGraw) who lead a corrupt politician and the police on a wild chase across Texas. With Ben Johnson, Al Lettieri, Sally Struthers, Dub Taylor, John Bryson, and Slim Pickens. Based on a novel by Jim Thompson. Nasty but never less than entertaining in Peckinpah's hands. **AC9, DT95, MY18, ST146, WR26, XT18,** *Recommended*

Getting Even (1986, C, 90m, R)
A crazed businessman threatens to unleash poison gas on Dallas if he's not paid $50 million. Joe Don Baker stars, with Edward Albert and Audrey Landers. **AC8**

Getting It Right (1989, C, 102m, R)
British comedy of a thirty-one-year-old virgin and his one-night initiation into the world of sex. Jesse Birdsall stars, with Helena Bonham Carter, Peter Cook, John Gielgud, Jane Horrocks, and Lynn Redgrave. **CO17, ST86**

Getting of Wisdom, The
(1977, C, 100m, NR)
Australian drama of a girl from the outback holding her own at a stuffy boarding school. Directed by Bruce Beresford. **DT10, FF5**

Getting Straight (1970, C, 124m, R)
A graduate student (Elliott Gould) is caught between his loyalty to his studies and the student activist movement taking place on campus. Candice Bergen costars; watch for Harrison Ford in a small role. Perhaps the worst of the bad crop of sixties student protest films. **CO18, ST74**

Ghidrah, the Three-Headed Monster (1965, C, 85m, NR)
Monster movie from Japan, with Godzilla, Mothra, and Rodan battling the title character. **FF4, SF18**

Ghost (1990, C, 127m, PG-13)
Unabashedly sentimental story of young woman whose ghost of a husband tries to warn her of danger. Demi Moore and Patrick Swayze star, with Oscar winner Whoopi Goldberg and Tony Goldwyn. Goldberg is wonderful, but the film's about twenty minutes too long. **DR1, DR2, MY3, ST89, XT5, XT24**

Ghost and Mrs. Muir, The (1947, B&W, 104m, NR)
Fantasy of lonely woman (Gene Tierney) romanced by a suave spirit (Rex Harrison). Written by Philip Dunne and directed by Joseph L. Mankiewicz. Music by Bernard Herrmann. **DT84, SF2, ST214**

Ghost Breakers, The (1940, B&W, 85m, NR)
Bob Hope comedy has him and Paulette Goddard stuck in a haunted Cuban mansion. With Richard Carlson, Paul Lukas, Anthony Quinn, and Willie Best. Remade as the Martin and Lewis vehicle, *Scared Stiff.* **HO2, HO3, HO19, HO24, ST108**

Ghost Dad (1990, C, 84m, PG)
Bill Cosby comedy; he's the title character who returns from the dead to wreak havoc on his family. Directed by Sidney Poitier. **CO5, CO11, ST174, XT24**

Ghost Goes West, The (1936, B&W, 82m, NR)
The new owner of a castle finds it's haunted by the ghost of a playboy. Eugene Pallette and Robert Donat star. René Clair directed. **DT25, SF2**

Ghost in the Noonday Sun (1973, C, 89m, NR)
Pirate comedy starring Peter Sellers, Anthony Franciosa, Spike Milligan, and Peter Boyle. **ST198**

Ghost of Yotsuya, The (1950, C, 100m, NR)
Japanese horror film about a man tortured by an evil spirit. **FF4**

Ghost Story (1981, C, 110m, R)
Four elderly men are tormented by an event which took place fifty years before. Fred Astaire, Melvyn Douglas, Douglas Fairbanks, Jr., and John Houseman star, with Craig Wasson, Patricia Neal, and Alice Krige. Based on the novel by Peter Straub. **HO2, HO19, ST4, ST58**

Ghost Warrior (1984, C, 86m, R)
A samurai warrior found frozen in modern-day Japan is brought to Los Angeles. When he thaws out and someone tries to steal his sword, all hell breaks loose on the streets. **AC25**

Ghostbusters (1984, C, 107m, PG)
A trio of nutty paranormal researchers (Bill Murray, Dan Aykroyd, Harold Ramis) decide to start their own business, flushing out ghosts in New York. Dazzling special effects and a brilliant comic performance by Murray. With Sigourney Weaver, Ernie Hudson, Rick Moranis, William Atherton, and Annie Potts. **CO9, CO11, CO13, CO14, ST225, XT9,** *Highly Recommended*

Ghostbusters II (1989, C, 102m, PG)
Return of the spook-chasing trio and their associates, with stars from first installment reprising their roles. Watch for Cheech Marin in a cameo. **CO9, CO11, CO13, CO14, ST28, ST225, XT9**

Ghosts on the Loose (1943, B&W, 65m, NR)
A honeymooning couple has to spend the night in a haunted house, and the East Side Kids go there pretending to haunt the place. Bela Lugosi and Ava Gardner, in one of her first roles, star. Also known as *The East Side Kids Meet Bela Lugosi.* **HO24, ST79, ST143**

Ghoul, The (1933, B&W, 73m, NR)
British horror tale, with Boris Karloff as a man buried with jewels from an Egyptian tomb, resurrected when they're stolen. With Cedric Hardwicke, Ernest Thesiger, and (in his film debut) Ralph Richardson. **HO26, ST119, ST184**

Ghoul, The (1975, C, 88m, NR)
Innocent people are accosted by the monster of a wealthy man (Peter Cushing). John Hurt costars. **HO26, ST43**

Ghoulies (1985, C, 84m, PG-13)
On his eighteenth birthday, a young man inherits a rambling mansion and an ability to conjure up evil spirits. **HO16**

Giant (1956, C, 201m, G)
Elizabeth Taylor, Rock Hudson, and James Dean (in his last film) star in Edna Ferber's

sprawling story of Texas cattlemen who strike it rich with oil. With Mercedes McCambridge, Dennis Hopper, Carroll Baker, Chill Wills, Jane Withers, and Sal Mineo. Directed by Oscar winner George Stevens. Dean's terrific, but his costars have more to do and less to do it with. **DR24, DT119, ST110, ST112, ST212, WE12, XT6, XT22,** *Essential*

Gideon's Trumpet (1980, C, 104m, NR)
Henry Fonda plays a convict whose battle for his basic rights became a landmark Supreme Court decision. With José Ferrer as Abe Fortas. Originally made for TV. **DR6, ST71**

Gig, The (1985, C, 92m, NR)
An amateur group of jazz musicians get their first big break—but aren't sure if they can handle the pressures. Wayne Rogers and Cleavon Little star. **DR12**

Gigi (1958, C, 116m, NR)
Winner of nine Academy Awards, including Best Picture, this is the story of a young Parisian girl (Leslie Caron) who chooses marriage over becoming a courtesan. Louis Jourdan, Maurice Chevalier, and Hermione Gingold costar. Directed by Oscar winner Vincente Minnelli. **DT88, MU1, MU7, XT1, XT6**

Gilda (1946, B&W, 110m, NR)
Rita Hayworth's most famous role, a woman married to a wealthy South American casino owner, whose right-hand man (Glenn Ford) is a love from her past. **CL4, MY1, MY4, ST101**

Gilda Live (1980, C, 90m, NR)
Former "Saturday Night Live" regular Gilda Radner re-creates many of her characters in this filmed version of her Broadway show. Directed by Mike Nichols. **CO13, CO16, DT91**

Gimme Shelter (1970, C, 91m, NR)
Stunning documentary of The Rolling Stones' 1969 concert tour of America includes footage from their tragic appearance at Altamont, where an audience member was murdered. Directed by Albert and David Maysles, with Charlotte Zwerin. Raises all kinds of issues about the responsibilities of performing artists to their audience, about the power of film to accurately record history, etc. **MU10, XT26,** *Essential, Recommended*

Gin Game, The (1984, C, 82m, NR)
Filmed performance of Broadway play about an aging couple (Jessica Tandy and Hume Cronyn) living in a nursing home. Directed by Mike Nichols. Originally made for cable TV. **DR11, DR20, DT91**

Ginger and Fred (1986, C, 126m, PG-13)
A couple of small-time Italian entertainers who once imitated Astaire and Rogers are reunited thirty years later for a television show. Giulietta Masina and Marcello Mastroianni star. Directed by Federico Fellini. **CO8, DT43, ST154**

Ginger in the Morning
(1973, C, 89m, PG)
Love story between an unlikely pair: a lonely traveling salesman (Monte Markham) and a free-spirited hitchhiker (Sissy Spacek). **ST202**

Girl, The (1986, C, 104m, R)
A wealthy attorney's affair with a teen-ager soon leads to murder in this thriller starring Franco Nero and Christopher Lee. **ST135**

Girl Can't Help It, The
(1956, C, 99m, NR)
A gangster hires an agent to promote his girlfriend, who wants to be a singer. Edmond O'Brien, Tom Ewell, and Jayne Mansfield are the leads, but the real stars are the rock performers (Little Richard, Eddie Cochran, and Gene Vincent) who appear in concert segments. Directed by Frank Tashlin. Widescreen will be lost on video. **CU20, MU9,** *Recommended*

Girl Crazy (1943, B&W, 99m, NR)
Mickey Rooney plays a hypochondriac who moves from New York to Arizona, where he falls for a local girl (Judy Garland). Directed by Norman Taurog, with songs by George and Ira Gershwin. **DT12, MU1, ST81, ST189**

Girl From Missouri, The
(1934, B&W, 75m, NR)
Jean Harlow stars as a country girl wooed by an older millionaire. With Lionel Barrymore, Franchot Tone, and Lewis Stone. **ST98**

Girl From Petrovka, The
(1974, C, 104m, PG)
A Russian ballerina (Goldie Hawn) falls in love with an American correspondent (Hal Holbrook). With Anthony Hopkins. **DR1, ST99, ST109**

Girl Happy (1965, C, 96m, NR)
Elvis Presley chaperones a gangster's daughter (Shelley Fabares) to Fort Lauderdale. **ST178**

Girl Hunters, The (1963, B&W, 103m, NR)
Author Mickey Spillane wrote and starred in this tale of detective Mike Hammer, who travels to Europe to find his missing secretary. **WR31**

Girl in a Swing, The (1989, C, 112m, NR)
Erotic drama starring Meg Tilly as a mysterious woman who marries a lonely ceramics

dealer (Rupert Fraser). Based on a Richard Adams novel. **CU6**

Girl in Every Port, A
(1952, B&W, 86m, NR)
Groucho Marx and William Bendix star in a comedy about two sailors who hide a racehorse aboard ship. **ST152**

Girl of the Golden West, The
(1938, B&W, 120m, NR)
Jeanette MacDonald and Nelson Eddy star in a musical Western about a desperado and the woman who loves him. Walter Pidgeon, Leo Carillo, and Buddy Ebsen head the supporting cast. **CL15, WE8**

Girl Who Had Everything, The
(1953, B&W, 69m, NR)
Elizabeth Taylor drama has her playing an impressionable young woman who falls for the criminal her attorney father is representing. With Fernando Lamas, William Powell, Gig Young, and James Whitmore. **ST176, ST212**

Girl Who Spelled Freedom, The
(1986, C, 90m, NR)
Disney drama, based on a true story of a Cambodian girl who comes to the United States and becomes a spelling bee champion. Wayne Rogers, Mary Kay Place, and Jade Chinn star; originally made for TV. **FA1, FA7**

Girls! Girls! Girls! (1962, C, 106m, NR)
Elvis Presley musical about a man with women on his mind. El sings "Return to Sender." Stella Stevens costars. **ST178**

Girls of Huntington House, The
(1973, C, 73m, NR),
Drama set at school for unwed mothers, as one teacher gets personally involved with her students' problems. Shirley Jones stars, with Mercedes McCambridge, Sissy Spacek, and William Windom. Originally made for TV. **DR10, DR25, ST202**

Girls of the White Orchid
(1983, C, 100m, NR)
American girl in Japan with ambitions to become a singer is abducted by Yakuza gangsters and forced to become a prostitute. Jennifer Jason Leigh stars, with Ann Jillian, Thomas Byrd, and Mako. Directed by Jonathan Kaplan. Video version contains sexy footage not contained in original, made-for-TV version. **CU10, ST136**

Git Along, Little Dogies
(1937, B&W, 60m, NR)
Gene Autry sings his heart out for a banker's daughter. **ST5**

Give a Girl a Break (1953, C, 82m, NR)
After temperamental star quits a show, a trio of hopefuls auditions for her part. Musical drama stars Marge and Gower Champion, Debbie Reynolds, Helen Wood, and Bob Fosse. Directed by Stanley Donen. **DT38, DT47, MU4**

Give My Regards to Broad Street
(1984, C, 108m, PG)
A rock star (Paul McCartney) searches for his stolen master recordings. Paul plays some new tunes, as well as a few ditties he wrote when he was with a band called The Beatles. With Bryan Brown, Ringo Starr, Linda McCartney, Barbara Bach, Tracey Ullman, Ralph Richardson, and Dave Edmunds. **MU4, MU9, ST184**

Gizmo! (1977, C/B&W, 77m, G)
Documentary tribute to inventors and their wacky creations, directed by Howard Smith. **CU16**

Gladiator (1992, C, 98m, R)
Two up-and-coming boxers, also buddies, are forced to fight each other by crooked promoter. Cuba Gooding, Jr., James Marshall, and Brian Dennehy star, with Robert Loggia, Ossie Davis, and John Heard. Directed by Rowdy Herrington. **DR22**

Glass House, The (1972, C, 73m, NR)
Truman Capote story of life behind bars, starring Vic Morrow, Clu Gulager, and Billy Dee Williams. Originally made for TV. **DR18, ST228**

Glass Bottom Boat, The
(1966, C, 110m, NR)
Doris Day comedy has her playing a writer hired by a scientist (Rod Taylor) to pen his biography. With Arthur Godfrey, Paul Lynde, Ellen Corby, John McGiver, and Dom De Luise. Directed by Frank Tashlin. **ST47**

Glass Key, The (1942, B&W, 85m, NR)
An unscrupulous politician calls on his right-hand man to clear him of a murder frameup in this version of the Dashiell Hammett novel. Brian Donlevy, Alan Ladd, and Veronica Lake star. **MY1, ST128, WR12**

Glass Menagerie, The (1987, C, 134m, PG)
Paul Newman directed this adaptation of the Tennessee Williams play about a timid cripple (Karen Allen), her faded Southern belle mother (Joanne Woodward), her shiftless brother (John Malkovich), and the dream worlds they live in. **DR20, ST147, ST162, ST234, WR38, XT30**

Glass Slipper, The (1955, C, 94m, NR)
Cinderella story set to music stars Leslie Caron, with Michael Wilding, Keenan Wynn,

Estelle Winwood, Elsa Lanchester, and Amanda Blake. **FA9, MU8**

Gleaming the Cube
(1989, C, 104m, PG-13)
Skateboarding high school student decides to investigate the murder of his adopted Vietnamese brother. Christian Slater stars, with Steven Bauer and Ed Lauter. Pretty strained; skateboarders will find it rad enough. **MY11, ST200**

Glen and Randa (1971, C, 94m, R)
Science fiction drama with cult following about the end of the world and a surviving couple (Steven Curry, and Shelley Plimpton). Directed by Jim McBride. **CU4, SF12**

Glen or Glenda? (1953, B&W, 61m, NR)
Contender for title of Worst Movie Ever, with (naturally) a cult following. Serious attempt to document one man's struggle with sexuality winds up a hilarious comedy. Bela Lugosi "hosts." Directed by Ed Wood, Jr., who also stars. **CU11, DT141, ST143**

Glengarry Glen Ross (1992, C, 100m, R)
David Mamet's drama of real estate salesmen hustling to sell worthless property or face a jobless future. Jack Lemmon stars, with Al Pacino, Ed Harris, Alan Arkin, Kevin Spacey, Jonathan Pryce, and Alec Baldwin. Mamet adapted his play, James Foley directed. Exhilarating use of language, superb performances. **DR20, DR24, ST138, ST170,** *Recommended*

Glenn Miller Story, The
(1954, C, 116m, G)
A sentimental musical biography that follows the life of the legendary big band leader. James Stewart stars, with June Allyson. Anthony Mann directed. **DT85, MU5, ST207**

Glitter Dome, The (1984, C, 95m, NR)
Drama of Los Angeles cops investigating film producer's death, adapted from the Joseph Wambaugh novel. James Garner stars, with Margot Kidder, John Lithgow, Colleen Dewhurst, John Marley, and Stuart Margolin (who directed). Originally made for cable TV. **AC9, ST82**

Glitz (1988, C, 100m, NR)
Elmore Leonard story, set in Atlantic City, of a cop, a psycho killer devoted to his mother, and a lounge singer. Jimmy Smits, Markie Post, and John Diehl star. Originally made for TV. Lacks the edge and meanness of the author's work. **MY3, MY13, WR19**

Gloria (1980, C, 121m, R)
A feisty New York woman takes a young Puerto Rican boy under her protection after

his parents are rubbed out by mobsters. Gena Rowlands stars, with John Adames, Buck Henry, and Julie Carmen. John Cassavetes directed. **AC8, DR10, XT23, XT30**

Glorifying the American Girl
(1929, B&W, 87m, NR)
Flo Ziegfeld produced this musical revue featuring the top talent of the day, including Helen Morgan, Rudy Vallee, and Eddie Cantor. **MU15**

Glory (1989, C, 122m, R)
Stirring, true story of the first black regiment to fight in the Civil War, commanded by a white New Englander. Matthew Broderick stars, with Morgan Freeman and Oscar winner Denzel Washington. Available in a letterboxed format. **AC5, CU19, DR5, DR14, ST76, ST223, XT4,** *Recommended*

Glory Stompers, The (1967, C, 85m, NR)
Motorcycle saga stars Dennis Hopper (still two years away from *Easy Rider* glory), with Jody McCrea, Chris Noel, Jock Mahoney, and Lindsay Crosby. **ST110**

Gnome-Mobile, The (1967, C, 90m, NR)
Disney adventure starring Walter Brennan as an elderly businessman who, along with his grandchildren, discovers gnomes in a forest. The three try to protect them from being captured by freak show owners. **FA1**

Gnomes, Vol. 1 (1980, C, 52m, NR)
This animated feature introduces the Gnomes, tiny creatures who battle the Trolls, who are trying to ruin a Gnome wedding. **FA10**

Go Masters, The (1982, C, 123m, NR)
Japanese-Chinese production traces relationship of two families, one from each country, from the 1920s to the 1950s. Title refers to chess-like game played by various members of each clan. **FF4**

Go Tell the Spartans (1978, C, 114m, R)
Vietnam War drama starring Burt Lancaster as a commander during the early days of that conflict. With Craig Wasson and Marc Singer. **AC4, ST129**

Go West (1940, B&W, 81m, NR)
The Marx Brothers take a train ride through the Old West. A few funny moments, but their best films were already behind them. **ST152, WE14, XT19**

Goalie's Anxiety at the Penalty Kick, The (1971, C, 110m, NR)
German drama about a soccer player's depression over a crucial misplay and his subsequent breakdown. Directed by Wim

Wenders; adapted from a Peter Handke story. **DT136**

Goat, The see *La Chevre*

Go-Between, The (1971, C, 116m, PG)
Subtle, rewarding drama, from L.P. Hartley story of young boy used as messenger between illicit lovers. Julie Christie and Alan Bates star, with Dominic Guard, Margaret Leighton, Michael Redgrave, and Edward Fox. Script by Harold Pinter; directed by Joseph Losey. **DR1, ST9, ST30, WR26,** *Recommended*

God Told Me To (1977, C, 95m, R)
Horror film about normal New Yorkers driven to unexplained acts of madness. Larry Cohen directed. Also known as *Demon.* **DT28**

Goddess, The (1958, B&W, 105m, NR)
Drama, loosely based on Marilyn Monroe story, of Hollywood star at the breaking point. Kim Stanley and Lloyd Bridges star. Screenplay by Paddy Chayefsky. **DR13**

Godfather, The (1972, C, 175m, R)
Sensational adaptation of Mario Puzo's look into the world of a Mafia chieftain (Marlon Brando) in 1930s New York City. The supporting cast includes James Caan, Diane Keaton, Robert Duvall, and Al Pacino. Winner of three Oscars, including Best Picture and Actor (Brando). Masterfully directed by Francis Ford Coppola. **AC22, DR5, DR24, DT29, ST18, ST63, ST121, ST170, XT1, XT2, XT20,** *Essential, Highly Recommended*

Godfather, Part II, The
(1974, C, 200m, R)
Sequel to *The Godfather* combines two stories: the rise to power of the Corleones' youngest son, Michael (Al Pacino), and the struggles of his young immigrant father (Robert De Niro) in early twentieth-century New York City. Winner of six Oscars, including Best Picture, Best Director (Francis Ford Coppola), and Best Supporting Actor (De Niro). Pacino deserved one, too. With Diane Keaton, John Cazale, Robert Duvall, Talia Shire, Lee Strasberg, Michael V. Gazzo, Harry Dean Stanton, Roger Corman (as a Congressman), and in one flashback scene, James Caan. **AC22, DR5, DR24, DT29, DT30, ST51, ST63, ST121, ST170, ST205, XT1, XT4, XT6, XT28,** *Essential, Highly Recommended*

Godfather, Part III, The
(1990, C, 170m, R)
Third chapter in Corleone saga focuses on relationship between Michael (Al Pacino) and his headstrong daughter (Sofia Coppola), plus his attempts to pull out of the rackets.

With Diane Keaton, Talia Shire, Andy Garcia, Eli Wallach, Joe Mantegna, George Hamilton, Bridget Fonda, and Raf Vallone. Directed by Francis Ford Coppola; photographed by Gordon Willis. Nine minutes of footage were added for video. Great looking but can't match standards of first two. Still worth seeing for followers of series and its principals. **AC22, CU10, DR24, DT29, ST70, ST121, ST170**

Godfather: The Complete Epic, 1902–1958, The (1981, C, 386m, NR)
Combination of the first two *Godfather* films sets story in chronological order, with some footage added. Originally produced for TV. **AC22, DR5, DR24, DT29, DT30, ST18, ST51, ST63, ST121, ST170, ST205,** *Highly Recommended*

Godfather Trilogy, 1901–1980, The
(1992, C, 593m, R)
Francis Ford Coppola's epic tale of organized crime, edited into one chronological story, with new footage added. See the individual films' entries for details on cast members. **AC22, CU10, DR5, DR24, DT29, DT30, ST18, ST51, ST63, ST70, ST121, ST170, ST205**

God's Little Acre (1958, B&W, 110m, NR)
A Georgia farmer (Robert Ryan) destroys his land in search of sunken treasures. With Tina Louise, Aldo Ray, Buddy Hackett, and Jack Lord. This version of the Erskine Caldwell novel was directed by Anthony Mann. **DR19, DT85, ST193**

Gods Must Be Crazy, The
(1981, C, 108m, PG)
Comedy, set in South Africa, with two intertwining tales: a community of Bushmen encounter civilization in the form of a soft drink bottle, and a clumsy scientist romances a pretty schoolteacher. **CO2**

Gods of the Plague (1969, C, 92m, NR)
German director Rainer Werner Fassbinder's story of a robbery gone bad. Hanna Schygulla, Harry Baer, and the director star. **DT42**

Godsend, The (1979, C, 93m, R)
Horror story of a couple who take in a little girl left with them by a strange woman, and the death and destruction she brings to their lives. **HO13**

Godzilla, King of the Monsters
(1956, B&W, 80m, NR)
The film that started the cycle of Japanese monster movies, featuring that Tokyo-stomping behemoth. Raymond Burr costars. **FF4, SF10, SF18**

Godzilla 1985 (1985, C, 91m, PG)
The big guy returns and is reunited—more or less—with Raymond Burr. **FF4, SF10, SF18**

Godzilla on Monster Island
(1971, C, 90m, NR)
A children's amusement park is the site for this version of Monster Wrestlemania, starring Godzilla, Ghidrah, Gaigan, and Angorus. **FF4, SF10, SF18**

Godzilla vs. Megalon (1976, C, 80m, G)
Godzilla, now a good guy, joins forces with a robot monster to square off against Megalon and his buddy in a monster tag-team match. **FF4, SF10, SF18**

Godzilla vs. Monster Zero
(1966, C, 90m, G)
Nick Adams and Rodan costar with the Big Guy, as he takes on yet another foe of Japanese civilization. **FF4, SF10, SF18**

Godzilla vs. Mothra (1964, C, 90m, G)
The Protector of Japan meets a flying monster that no moth ball could hope to stop. Also known as *Godzilla vs. The Thing*. **FF4, SF10, SF18**

Godzilla vs. The Thing see *Godzilla vs. Mothra*

Goin' South (1978, C, 109m, PG)
Jack Nicholson stars in this romantic Western comedy about an outlaw who ties the knot to save his neck. With Mary Steenburgen, John Belushi, and Danny DeVito. Nicholson directed. Fairly funny, but there are long dry stretches, too. **CO13, ST54, ST163, WE9, WE14**

Going Ape! (1981, C, 87m, PG)
Tony Danza plays a man who must care for three primates to qualify for an inheritance. Comedy costars Danny DeVito and Jessica Walter. **ST54**

Going Berserk (1983, C, 85m, R)
John Candy plays a scatter-brained chauffeur who saves his future father-in-law from a religious cult. With Joe Flaherty and Eugene Levy. **CO14**

Going Hollywood (1933, B&W, 80m, NR)
MGM musical starring Marion Davies as a determined young woman pursuing a crooner (Bing Crosby) to the West Coast. With Fifi D'Orsay and Stuart Erwin. Directed by Raoul Walsh. **DT131, MU1, MU4, ST40**

Going in Style (1979, C, 96m, PG)
Touching comedy-drama about a trio of elderly men (George Burns, Art Carney, and Lee Strasberg) who decide to rob a bank for the hell of it. Directed by Martin Brest. **DR11, MY18,** *Recommended*

Going My Way (1944, B&W, 126m, NR)
Bing Crosby and Barry Fitzgerald play parish priests with different approaches to their flock in this heartwarming classic. Oscars went to both actors, writer-director Leo McCarey, and the film. **CL6, DT80, ST40, XT1, XT2, XT4, XT6,** *Essential*

Going Places (1974, C, 117m, R)
French drama, with darkly comic overtones, of two drifters (Gérard Depardieu and Patrick Dewaere) and their determinedly carefree lifestyle. With Brigitte Fossey and Jeanne Moreau. Directed by Bertrand Blier. Well regarded by some critics, but pretty distasteful stuff for most. **FF1, ST52, ST161, XT18**

Gold Diggers of 1933
(1933, B&W, 96m, NR)
Busby Berkeley choreographed this musical about a songwriter (Dick Powell) who can't finance his extravaganza until some spunky show girls (Ginger Rogers and Ruby Keeler) save the day. **DT12, MU4, ST175, ST187**

Gold Diggers of 1935
(1935, B&W, 95m, NR)
More singing and dancing from Busby Berkeley and his talented collection of performers, headed by Dick Powell. With Adolphe Menjou and Gloria Stuart. Musical highlight: "Lullaby of Broadway." **DT12, MU4, ST175**

Gold of Naples, The
(1954, B&W, 107m, NR)
Vittorio De Sica directed this quartet of vignettes of Italian life, starring Sophia Loren, Silvana Mangano, Toto, and the director. **DT37, ST141**

Gold Raiders (1983, C, 106m, NR)
A plane carrying $200 million in gold is shot down over Laos and a commando squad tries to retrieve the precious cargo. Robert Ginty stars. **AC20**

Gold Rush, The (1925, B&W, 72m, NR)
Charlie Chaplin classic set in the Yukon Gold Rush days. With Georgia Hale and Mack Swain. **CL11, DT24,** *Essential, Highly Recommended*

Golden Age of Looney Tunes, The
(1930s–50s, 60m each, C/B&W, NR)
Ten-volume set of some of the greatest cartoons ever made, from the geniuses at Warner Bros. Volume 1: 1930s Musicals; 2: Firsts (Debuts of Famed Characters); 3: Tex Avery; 4: Bob Clampett; 5: Chuck Jones; 6: Friz Freleng; 7: Bugs Bunny by Each Director, or "Six Men in Search of a Wabbit;" 8: 1940s Zanies; 9: Hooray for Hollywood; 10: The Art of Bugs. **FA11,** *Highly Recommended*

Golden Boy (1939, B&W, 99m, NR)
A would-be musician turns to boxing to make a living. Clifford Odets drama has William Holden making his screen debut opposite Barbara Stanwyck. With Lee J. Cobb and Adolphe Menjou. Directed by Rouben Mamoulian. **DR22, DT83, ST106, ST206, XT21**

Golden Child, The (1986, C, 96m, PG-13)
A youth with magical powers is kidnapped by a cult, and it's up to Eddie Murphy to rescue him in this adventure comedy packed with special effects. **CO9, CO11, CO13**

Golden Coach, The (1952, C, 105m, NR)
French director Jean Renoir's classic drama of a theatrical troupe in eighteenth-century Peru, starring Anna Magnani as a lady of many affairs. Superb color photography. **CL9, CL14, DT104**

Golden Demon, The (1953, C, 95m, NR)
From Japan, a drama about a young man in love with the daughter of his adopted parents. His frustration grows when she is given in an arranged marriage to a wealthy businessman. **FF4**

Golden Seal, The (1983, C, 93m, PG)
Family drama about a young boy who befriends a seal. Steve Railsback, Penelope Milford, and Michael Beck star. **FA5**

Golden Stallion, The
(1949, B&W, 67m, NR)
Trigger gets the spotlight in this Roy Rogers Western, as he tries to set a small mare free from her nasty owners. **ST188**

Golden Voyage of Sinbad, The
(1974, C, 104m, G)
John Phillip Law stars as the swashbuckling pirate in this adventure/fantasy which features great special effects. **FA8**

Goldenrod (1977, C, 100m, NR)
A rodeo champion (Tony LoBianco) reevaluates his life after a debilitating accident. Originally made for TV. **WE12**

Goldfinger (1964, C, 111m, NR)
Third James Bond adventure has 007 foiling plan to rob Fort Knox. Sean Connery stars, but Gert Frobe, Harold Sakata, and Honor Blackman steal the show as Goldfinger, Odd Job, and Pussy Galore. **HF2, ST36,** *Essential, Highly Recommended*

Goldilocks and the Three Bears
(1985, C, 60m, NR)
Tatum O'Neal stars as the little girl who invades the lives of three bears in this Faerie Tale Theatre adventure. John Lithgow, Alex Karras, and Carole King costar. **FA12, MU12**

Goldy: The Last of the Golden Bears
(1984, C, 91m, NR)
An orphaned child adopted by a prospector goes on an incredible adventure to rescue a golden bear from the circus. **FA5**

Golem, The (1920, B&W, 118m, NR)
Classic silent horror film about a legendary robot-like creature created to save German Jewish peasants from persecution. **FF3, HO1**

Goliath Awaits (1981, C, 200m, NR)
Adventure tale of an oceanographer who comes upon the survivors of a maritime disaster, living in a boat that capsized forty years ago. Mark Harmon stars, with Christopher Lee, Eddie Albert, John Carradine, Alex Cord, Robert Forster, and Frank Gorshin. Originally made for TV. **AC24, ST134**

Gone in 60 Seconds (1974, C, 103m, PG)
A professional car thief eludes police with his incredible driving skills. This action drama features a forty-minute car chase. Written and directed by H.B. Halicki. **AC10**

Gone With the Wind (1939, C, 222m, G)
Civil War epic of Scarlett O'Hara (Vivien Leigh) and her tempestuous romance with Rhett Butler (Clark Gable). Winner of ten Oscars, including Best Picture, Best Actress, Best Supporting Actress (Hattie McDaniel), and Best Director (Victor Fleming). With Olivia de Havilland, Leslie Howard, Thomas Mitchell, and Butterfly McQueen. **AC5, CL3, ST49, ST77, ST137, XT1, XT3, XT5, XT6,** *Essential, Highly Recommended*

Good Earth, The (1937, B&W, 138m, NR)
Oscar winner Luise Rainer costars with Paul Muni in Pearl Buck's story of Chinese peasants coming to ruin over greed. **DR19, XT3**

Good Father, The (1987, C, 90m, R)
An embittered man whose marriage has just broken up takes out his frustrations by interfering in the domestic problems of a friend. Anthony Hopkins stars in this British drama. **DR8, DR23, ST109**

Good Guys Wear Black
(1979, C, 96m, PG)
Karate action drama with Chuck Norris, featuring his incredible stunt of leaping through the windshield of a moving car. Anne Archer costars. **ST165**

Good Morning, Babylon
(1987, C, 115m, NR)
Two Italian stonemasons emigrate to America in search of work, wind up laboring on the sets of D.W. Griffith's silent film epic, *Intolerance*. Vincent Spano and Joaquim de Almeida star, with Greta Scacchi, Desiree

Becker, and Charles Dance as Griffith. Dialogue in Italian and English. **DR5, DR13**

Good Morning, Vietnam
(1987, C, 120m, R)
Robin Williams stars as a zany disc jockey who shakes up Armed Forces Radio during the Vietnam War. With Forest Whitaker, Bruno Kirby, and J.T. Walsh. Loosely based on the real-life exploits of Adrian Cronauer. Barry Levinson directed. Williams at the peak of his powers. **AC4, CO6, CO21, DT75, ST228,** *Recommended*

Good Mother, The (1988, C, 104m, R)
Diane Keaton plays a divorced woman locked in a bitter battle for custody of her young daughter. With Liam Neeson, Jason Robards, Ralph Bellamy, and Teresa Wright. Based on Sue Miller's novel; directed by Leonard Nimoy. Worth seeing if only for subject matter, but falls short of being fairly good. **DR8, DR10, ST121, ST185, XT23**

Good Neighbor Sam (1964, C, 130m, NR)
An advertising executive out to impress a new client gets caught up in a complicated masquerade involving a lovely neighbor who's mistaken for his wife. Jack Lemmon stars, with Edward G. Robinson, Romy Schneider, and Dorothy Provine. Frantic, with diminishing returns. **CO20, ST138, ST186**

Good News (1947, C, 95m, NR)
A college football star (Peter Lawford) won't graduate unless he passes his French exam in this MGM musical set in the Roaring Twenties. June Allyson costars. **MU1, MU3, MU6**

Good Sam (1948, B&W, 128m, NR)
A good samaritan (Gary Cooper) creates tension in his home life when he overdoes his generosity. Ann Sheridan costars. Directed by Leo McCarey. **DT80, ST37**

Good, the Bad, and the Ugly, The
(1967, C, 161m, NR)
Three unscrupulous men (Clint Eastwood, Lee Van Cleef, and Eli Wallach) hunt for a treasure while the Civil War rages around them. The third in director Sergio Leone's *Dollars* trilogy and also the best. Unfortunately, widescreen compositions will be lost on video. **CU20, DT73, ST64, ST221, WE1, WE3, WE6, WE13,** *Essential, Highly Recommended*

Good To Go see *Short Fuse*

Good Woman of Bangkok, The
(1991, C, 82m, NR)
Offbeat Australian film blends fiction and fact in tale of Thai prostitute and her daily life. **DR10, FF5**

Goodbye Again (1961, B&W, 120m, R)
Ingrid Bergman stars in the melodrama of a lonely woman's affair with a younger man (Anthony Perkins). Yves Montand costars. **ST13**

Goodbye, Columbus (1969, C, 105m, R)
Romantic comedy-drama of a naive young Jewish man falling for snobbish girl, getting involved with her family. Richard Benjamin and Ali MacGraw star, with Jack Klugman, Nan Martin, and Michael Meyers. Engaging adaptation of Philip Roth's short novel. **DR1, DR19, XT20,** *Recommended*

Goodbye Girl, The (1977, C, 110m, PG)
An aspiring actor (Oscar winner Richard Dreyfuss) shares an apartment with a divorced woman (Marsha Mason) and her precocious daughter (Quinn Cummings) in this consistently funny Neil Simon comedy. **CO1, ST60, WR23, XT2,** *Recommended*

Goodbye, Mr. Chips (1939, B&W, 114m, NR)
Robert Donat won an Oscar for his portrayal of a devoted schoolmaster in this classic drama. Greer Garson costars in her film debut. **DR25, ST83, XT2, XT21**

Goodbye, Mr. Chips (1969, C, 151m, G)
Musical remake of the classic drama of a beloved schoolteacher, starring Peter O'Toole and Petula Clark. With Michael Redgrave and George Baker. **DR25, MU14, MU17, ST169**

Goodbye, My Lady (1956, B&W, 95m, NR)
Family drama, set in rural Mississippi, of a boy and his dog. Brandon de Wilde stars, with Walter Brennan, Phil Harris, and Sidney Poitier. Directed by William Wellman. **DT135, FA5, ST174**

GoodFellas (1990, C, 146m, R)
Stunning look at life of Henry Hill, onetime gangster involved with major New York airport heist that landed him in the government's witness protection program. Ray Liotta stars, with Robert De Niro, Oscar winner Joe Pesci, Lorraine Bracco, and Paul Sorvino, plus brief appearances by Henny Youngman, Jerry Vale, and Bobby Vinton as themselves. Martin Scorsese directed; he and Nicholas Pileggi adapted the latter's book, *WiseGuy.* Watch for the director's mother (as Pesci's mom) and father (as a cellmate of Liotta). Sensational use of period pop, soul, and rock music. Should have won Oscars for Best Picture and Director. **AC22, DR6, DR16, DT114, ST51, ST172, XT4, XT28,** *Highly Recommended*

Goon Show Movie, The
(1953, B&W, 75m, NR)
The zany antics of Britain's "Goon Show" are

presented in this collection of their sketches. Spike Milligan, Harry Secombe, and Peter Sellers star. Also known as *Stand Easy.* **CO17, ST198**

Goonies, The (1985, C, 111m, PG)
Group of misfit kids take on ugly band of thieves in search of buried treasure in this comedy-adventure. Sean Astin, Josh Brolin, Jeff Cohen, Corey Feldman, Kerri Green, Martha Plimpton, and Ke Huy Quan star. **FA15**

Gorath (1964, C, 77m, NR)
Japanese science fiction drama about a meteor forcing scientists to change Earth's orbit. **FF4, SF18**

Gordon's War (1973, C, 90m, R)
Paul Winfield plays a Vietnam veteran who returns to the States to find his wife hooked on drugs. He forms a fighting force to rid his neighborhood of drug pushers. **AC8, AC20, ST230**

Gore Vidal's Billy the Kid
(1989, C, 96m, NR)
Val Kilmer plays the legendary Western outlaw in this new version of the Vidal TV play, previously filmed as *The LeftHanded Gun.* Originally made for cable TV. **HF1, WE3**

Gorgeous Hussy, The
(1936, B&W, 102m, NR)
Joan Crawford drama of the scandalous events surrounding the wife of Andrew Jackson. With Lionel Barrymore, Robert Taylor, Franchot Tone, Melvyn Douglas, and James Stewart in a small role. **CL3, ST39, ST58, ST207**

Gorgo (1961, C, 78m, NR)
A baby sea monster is captured and placed in a London zoo, and its giant parent comes to the rescue. Bill Travers stars. **SF10, XT15**

Gorgon, The (1964, C, 83m, NR)
After she is possessed by an evil spirit, a beautiful girl's gaze turns people to stone. Peter Cushing, Christopher Lee, and Barbara Shelley star. **HO26, ST43, ST135**

Gorilla, The (1939, B&W, 66m, NR)
The Ritz Brothers play detectives who investigate a series of murders that take place at the stroke of midnight. With Bela Lugosi. **MY17, ST143**

Gorillas in the Mist
(1988, C, 129m, PG-13)
Sigourney Weaver plays Dian Fossey, the anthropologist whose defense of mountain gorillas from hunters led to her murder. Bryan Brown costars. **DR6, DR10, DR27, ST225**

Gorky Park (1983, C, 128m, R)
Three corpses found in Moscow's Gorky Park set a Russian police captain (William Hurt) off on a twisted case. Based on the bestseller by Martin Cruz Smith. With Lee Marvin, Brian Dennehy, and Joanna Pacula. **MY6, MY16, ST114, ST151**

Gospel According to St. Matthew, The
(1966, B&W, 135m, NR)
Low-key dramatization of the life of Christ, from Italian director Pier Paolo Pasolini. Enrique Irazoqui stars. **FF2, HF17**

Gospel According to Vic, The
(1985, C, 92m, PG)
A teacher at a Catholic school embarks on a skeptical inquiry into miracles that have been occurring at his school. Tom Conti and Helen Mirren star in this offbeat British comedy. **CO17, CO18**

Gosta Berling's Saga
(1924, B&W, 123m, NR)
Silent Swedish drama of a defrocked priest (Lars Hanson) and a married woman (Greta Garbo). Directed by Mauritz Stiller. Also known as *The Atonement of Gosta Berling.* **ST78**

Gotham (1988, C, 93m, NR)
A private eye (Tommy Lee Jones) is hired by a man who's certain that his dead wife (Virginia Madsen) is following him. Originally made for cable TV. **MY10**

Gothic (1987, C, 87m, R)
One dark and stormy night in the lives of writers Lord Byron, Percy Shelley, and Mary Shelley, as imagined by flamboyant director Ken Russell. Julian Sands, Gabriel Byrne, and Natasha Richardson star. **DT111, HO25**

Grace Quigley
(1985, C, 87m, PG)
Katharine Hepburn plays an elderly woman who hires hit man Nick Nolte to kill her and other friends who would rather be dead. Another version is known as *The Ultimate Solution of Grace Quigley.* **CO12, DR11, ST103, ST164**

Graduate, The (1967, C, 105m, PG)
A naive college graduate (Dustin Hoffman) is seduced by a middle-aged woman (Anne Bancroft) but falls in love with her daughter (Katharine Ross). Director Mike Nichols won an Oscar for this brilliant, groundbreaking youth comedy which should have won the Best Actor Oscar, too. Now available in a letterboxed edition. **CO2, CO4, CU19, DT91, ST105, XT6, XT20, XT28**, *Essential, Highly Recommended*

Graduation Day (1981, C, 96m, R)
Horror story about members of a high school track team who are brutally murdered a few days before graduation. **HO12**

Graffiti Bridge (1990, C, 95m, PG-13)
Rock star Prince's followup to *Purple Rain*: more anguished dramatics behind the scenes with a pop star, more of Prince's unique brand of music. With Ingrid Chavez, Morris Day, Jerome Benton, Mavis Staples, and George Clinton. The star directed. **DR12, MU9, XT23**

Grand Canyon (1991, C, 134m, R)
Dramatic story of six intertwining lives and how they reflect problems of contemporary urban America. Kevin Kline, Danny Glover, Steve Martin, Mary McDonnell, Mary-Louise Parker, and Alfre Woodard star. Filmed in Los Angeles; directed and cowritten by Lawrence Kasdan. **DR7, DR15, ST88, ST127, ST150, XT10**

Grand Canyon Trail
(1948, B&W, 68m, NR)
Roy Rogers's mine may have him sitting pretty on pay dirt, or it could just be useless gravel. Only the town swindler knows for sure. **ST188**

Grand Highway, The (1988, C, 104m, NR)
French drama of a nine-year-old boy sent to live in a village in Brittany while his mother has a baby. Directed by Jean-Loup Hubert, based on his own experiences. U.S. remake: *Paradise* (1991). **FF1**

Grand Hotel (1932, B&W, 113m, NR)
Drama set in luxury hotel featuring a mind-boggling cast of MGM stars: Wallace Beery, Greta Garbo, John Barrymore, Joan Crawford, Lionel Barrymore, and Jean Hersholt, for starters. Grand, old-fashioned entertainment; winner of Best Picture Oscar. **CU17, ST8, ST39, ST78, XT1,** *Essential, Highly Recommended*

Grand Illusion (1937, B&W, 111m, NR)
Director Jean Renoir's masterful antiwar drama, set in a World War I prisoner of war camp. Jean Gabin, Erich Von Stroheim, and Pierre Fresnay star. Deserved to win the Oscar. **AC7, DT104, DT129, XT25, XT28,** *Essential, Highly Recommended*

Grand Isle (1991, C, 94m, NR)
A late-nineteenth-century Louisiana resort is the setting for this drama of a married woman tempted into adultery, adapted from Kate Chopin's novel, *The Awakening*. Kelly McGillis stars, with Adrian Pasdar, Julian Sands, Glenne Headley, and Ellen Burstyn. Originally made for cable TV. **DR10, DR19**

Grand Prix (1966, C, 176m, NR)
Big-budget, all-star drama about racing on the European circuit. James Garner, Eva Marie Saint, Yves Montand, and Toshiro Mifune head the cast. John Frankenheimer directed. Stunning visuals are compromised without letterboxing. **AC10, CU20, DR22, ST82, ST157**

Grand Theft Auto (1977, C, 89m, PG)
Ron Howard is the star, cowriter, and debuting director of this car-chase comedy. Produced by Roger Corman. **AC10, CU14, DT59**

Grandview, U.S.A. (1984, C, 97m, R)
Smalltown drama of kids trying to stay out of trouble, with C. Thomas Howell, Patrick Swayze, Jamie Lee Curtis, and Jennifer Jason Leigh. **DR9, DR26, ST42, ST136**

Grapes of Wrath, The
(1940, B&W, 129m, NR)
John Steinbeck story of a poor family in the midst of the Depression and their hopes for a better life in Caliiornia. Henry Fonda stars; Oscars went to actress Jane Darwell and director John Ford. As good an adaptation of a classic American novel as you'll see. **CL8, DT44, ST71, WR32, XT5, XT6,** *Essential, Recommended*

Grass Is Always Greener Over the Septic Tank, The (1978, C, 100m, NR)
Carol Burnett and Charles Grodin play a New York couple whose move to suburbia precipitates a number of adjustments. Adapted from Erma Bombeck's bestselling humor book. Originally made for TV. **CO2, ST94**

Grass Is Greener, The (1960, C, 105m, NR)
Cary Grant and Deborah Kerr play a British couple whose marriage is threatened by a handsome tourist (Robert Mitchum) in this comedy. Directed by Stanley Donen. **DT38, ST92, ST125, ST158**

Grateful Dead Movie, The
(1977, C, 131m, NR)
Rock concert film starring those tie-dyed wonders of laid-back rock 'n' roll. Outstanding animated sequence opens the film. A must for Dead Heads. **MU10**

Graveyard Shift (1987, C, 89m, R)
Horror story about a New York cabbie with a deadly secret—he's a vampire who prefers a nip on the neck to a tip. **HO5**

Graveyard Shift (1990, C, 87m, R)
Stephen King story of small town mill infected with rats—and worse. David Andrews, Kelly Wolf, Stephen Macht, and Brad Dourif are the human stars. **HO16, WR15**

Gray Lady Down (1978, C, 111m, PG)
A downed submarine is the object of a daring rescue mission in this adventure saga. Charlton Heston and David Carradine star, with Stacy Keach, Ned Beatty, and Ronny Cox. **AC24**

Grease (1978, C, 110m, PG)
Olivia Newton-John and John Travolta star in this screen version of the long-running Broadway musical about high school life in the 1950s. In the supporting cast: Stockard Channing, Eve Arden, Edd Byrnes, and Frankie Avalon. Loud and seemingly endless; made me long for *Blackboard Jungle*. **MU2, MU9**

Grease 2 (1982, C, 114m, PG)
More musical adventures of the students at Rydell High in the 1950s. Maxwell Caulfield and Michelle Pfeiffer star. **MU9, ST173**

Greased Lightning (1977, C, 94m, PG)
In a dramatic change of pace, Richard Pryor portrays Wendell Scott, the first black race car driver. **DR22, ST180**

Greaser's Palace (1972, C, 91m, R)
Midnight movie favorite sets the story of Christ in a town of the Old West. Allan Arbus stars, with Albert Henderson, Luana Anders, and George Morgan. Directed by Robert Downey. **CU1, HF16, WE15**

Great American Cowboy, The
(1974, C, 90m, NR)
An Oscar-winning documentary about modern-day rodeo cowboys. Narrated by Joel McCrea. **ST144, WE12**

Great Balls of Fire
(1989, C, 108m, PG-13)
Dennis Quaid plays rock legend Jerry Lee Lewis in this flamboyantly told account of his early career, including his controversial marriage to a cousin (Winona Ryder). With Alec Baldwin as Jimmy Swaggart and Michael St. Gerard as Elvis Presley. Intentionally cartoonish but that approach wears thin. **DR12, MU5**

Great Battle, The see *Battle Force*

Great Caruso, The (1951, C, 109m, NR)
Ann Blyth and Mario Lanza star in this biographical film about the opera star's life. **MU1, MU5**

Great Day in the Morning
(1956, C, 92m, NR)
In pre–Civil War Colorado, a separationist wants to finance the impending war with gold. Robert Stack and Ruth Roman star. Directed by Jacques Tourneur. **DT124**

Great Dictator, The
(1940, B&W, 128m, NR)
Charlie Chaplin's classic spoof of Hitler, as he plays "Adenoid Hynkel," dictator of Tomania. Jack Oakie costars as "Benzino Napaloni." **CL10, DT24, HF12, XT27,** *Essential, Recommended*

Great Escape, The (1963, C, 168m, NR)
Superb drama of World War II POWs and a massive breakout from a Nazi prison, based on a true story. James Garner, Steve McQueen, Charles Bronson, Richard Attenborough, James Coburn, and Donald Pleasence head the cast. Still the most exciting POW movie of them all. **AC7, ST20, ST82, ST146,** *Highly Recommended*

Great Expectations
(1946, B&W, 118m, NR)
David Lean directed this splendid adaptation of Charles Dickens's story of a poor orphan who becomes a wealthy young gentleman, thanks to an unknown benefactor. John Mills, Alec Guinness (in his film debut), and Jean Simmons star. **DT71, FA3, ST95, WR5, XT21,** *Essential, Recommended*

Great Flamarion, The
(1945, B&W, 78m, NR)
Drama of faithless circus star and her jilted lover. Erich Von Stroheim and Mary Beth Hughes star, with Dan Duryea. Directed by Anthony Mann. **DT85, DT129**

Great Gabbo, The (1929, B&W, 95m, NR)
Erich Von Stroheim plays a boastful ventriloquist in this backstage drama with musical numbers. **CL7, DT129**

Great Gatsby, The (1974, C, 144m, PG)
Robert Redford portrays the mysterious Jay Gatsby in this lavish adaptation of F. Scott Fitzgerald's novel of the Jazz Age. With Mia Farrow, Sam Waterston, Bruce Dern, and Karen Black. Strong on the edges (Dern and Black), weak in the center (Redford and Farrow). **ST65, ST181, WR8**

Great Guns (1941, B&W, 74m, NR)
After their boss joins the army, a gardener and a chauffeur (Stan Laurel and Oliver Hardy) enlist, too. **CO21, ST133**

Great Guy (1936, B&W, 75m, NR)
James Cagney plays an inspector out to crack down on illegal dealings in the meat business. **DR24, ST24**

Great Lie, The (1941, B&W, 107m, NR)
Bette Davis soap opera of a woman who marries a man with a scheming ex-wife. With George Brent and Oscar winner Mary Astor. **ST44, XT5**

Great Locomotive Chase, The
(1956, C, 85m, NR)
Disney adventure based on the true story of
a Union spy who led a band of renegades in
the theft of a train during the Civil War.
Story previously filmed as *The General*. **FA1,
XT19**

Great Lover, The (1949, B&W, 80m, NR)
Bob Hope plays a Boy Scout leader aboard a
cruise ship with a lovely redhead (Rhonda
Fleming) and a fugitive killer (Roland Young).
ST108

Great McGinty, The (1940, B&W, 81m, NR)
Classic comedy of a bum maneuvered into
the governor's mansion by a political machine, which finds to its dismay that their
man is actually honest. Brian Donlevy and
Akim Tamiroff star. Written and directed by
Preston Sturges. **CO20, DT121, XT26,** *Essential, Recommended*

Great McGonagall, The (1975, C, 95m, NR)
British comedy of a Scot trying to become
poet laureate of England. Spike Milligan
stars, with Peter Sellers as Queen Victoria.
ST198

Great Man Votes, The
(1939, B&W, 72m, NR)
John Barrymore plays a former professor
turned to the bottle, struggling to gain custody of his children. Title refers to setting,
during a political campaign. With Virginia
Weidler and William Demarest. Directed by
Garson Kanin. **ST8**

Great Moment, The (1944, B&W, 83m, NR)
Joel McCrea plays the inventor of anesthesia
in this unusual comedy-drama from director
Preston Sturges. **CL2, DT121, ST144**

Great Mouse Detective, The
(1986, C, 80m, G)
Disney animated version of *Basil of Baker
Street*, story of a mouse who solves crimes à la
Sherlock Holmes. Vincent Price supplies the
voice of the villainous Professor Ratigan. Discontinued from manufacture in April 1993;
copies may be hard to find. **FA2, ST179**

Great Muppet Caper, The
(1981, C, 95m, G)
Kermit, Fozzie, and Gonzo travel to London
as newspaper reporters in search of jewel
thieves. Miss Piggy is close on their heels to
keep an eye on "Kermie." Featuring Diana
Rigg, John Cleese, and Charles Grodin.
CO15, FA14, ST94

Great Northfield, Minnesota, Raid, The
(1972, C, 91m, PG)
Western with cult following about Cole

Younger (Cliff Robertson) and Jesse James
(Robert Duvall) and their ill-fated attempt
to rob a bank in the title town. Written and
directed by Philip Kaufman. Stylized approach works well; Duvall a standout as
the mad Jesse. **HF16, ST63, WE15,**
Recommended

Great Outdoors, The (1988, C, 90m, PG)
Comic tale of a family's vacation ruined
by the arrival of obnoxious relatives. John
Candy and Dan Aykroyd star, with Annette
Bening and Stephanie Faracy. Written and
produced by John Hughes. **CO5, CO13,
CO14, DT59, ST12**

Great Race, The (1965, C, 150m, NR)
Blake Edwards directed this old-fashioned,
big-budget comedy about an intercontinental
road race. Jack Lemmon, Tony Curtis, and
Natalie Wood star. Fun for a while, but runs
out of gas. **AC14, CO6, DT40, FA6, ST138,
XT18**

Great Santini, The (1979, C, 116m, PG)
Portrait of a career Marine whose peacetime
battles are mainly with his teen-age son.
Robert Duvall, Michael O'Keefe, and Blythe
Danner star. Duvall's good but not enough to
lift the movie above the ordinary. **DR8,
ST63**

Great Scout and Cathouse Thursday
(1976, C, 102m, PG)
Lee Marvin, Oliver Reed, and Robert Culp
star as a crazy trio of gold prospectors who
strike it rich in 1908 Colorado. **ST151, WE14**

Great Smokey Roadblock, The
(1976, C, 84m, PG)
An aging truckdriver's rig is repossessed while
he is in the hospital. He escapes, steals the
truck, and decides to go across the country
one last time. Henry Fonda stars, with Eileen
Brennan and Susan Sarandon. **ST71, ST194,
XT18**

Great Spy Mission, The see *Operation
Crossbow*

Great Train Robbery, The
(1979, C, 111m, PG)
Victorian England is the setting for this heist
thriller, starring Sean Connery, Donald Sutherland, and Lesley-Anne Down. **MY18,
ST36, XT19**

Great Waldo Pepper, The
(1975, C, 107m, PG)
Robert Redford stars as a barnstorming pilot
of the 1920s in this affectionate comedy-
drama about aerial daredevils. With Susan
Sarandon. Directed by George Roy Hill. The
flying sequences carry the film. **AC11, DT55,
ST181, ST194**

Great Waltz, The (1938, B&W, 102m, NR)
The story of Austria's great composer, Johann Strauss, starring Luise Rainer and Fernand Gravet. Oscar-winning cinematography by Joseph Ruttenberg. **MU5**

Great White Hope, The
(1970, C, 101m, PG)
Howard Sackler's play, based on the life of Jack Johnson, the first black heavyweight boxing champion. James Earl Jones re-creates his stage role, with Jane Alexander as his mistress. Directed by Martin Ritt. Jones is wonderful re-creating his stage role but the rest of the film doesn't measure up to him. **DR4, DR14, DR20, DR22, DT105, ST118**

Great Ziegfeld, The (1936, B&W, 176m, NR)
Musical bio of the legendary showman, played by William Powell. Oscar winner for Best Picture and Actress (Luise Rainer). Also in the cast: Myrna Loy, Fanny Brice, and Ray Bolger. **CL15, MU5, MU7, ST142, ST176, XT1, XT3**

Greatest, The (1977, C, 101m, PG)
This screen biography of Muhammad Ali traces his life from boyhood in Louisville to his incredible achievements as heavyweight champ. Ali stars as himself, with support from Ernest Borgnine, James Earl Jones, and Robert Duvall. Even this Ali fan had trouble making it to the last round. **DR4, DR14, ST63, ST118**

Greatest Love, The see *Europa '51*

Greatest Show on Earth, The
(1952, C, 141m, NR)
Oscar-winning drama about life in the circus, directed by Cecil B. DeMille, starring Charlton Heston, Betty Hutton, and James Stewart. Spectacular train wreck is the highlight. **CL7, DT34, ST207, XT1**

Greatest Story Ever Told, The
(1965, C, 196m, NR)
George Stevens directed this lavish epic detailing the life of Christ. Max von Sydow plays the lead, with guest appearances by many Hollywood stars, including Charlton Heston, Sidney Poitier, Angela Lansbury, John Wayne, and Shelley Winters. **CL13, DT119, HF17, ST131, ST174, ST224, ST232**

Greed (1924, B&W, 133m, NR)
Director Erich Von Stroheim's masterpiece, a searing version of the Frank Norris novel *McTeague*. A simple dentist (Gibson Gowland) and his wife (ZaSu Pitts) become bitter enemies over money and her former suitor (Jean Hersholt). Video version contains new musical score by Carl Davis. **CL1, CL12, DT129, XT20**, *Essential, Highly Recommended*

Greeks Had a Word for Them, The see *Three Broadway Girls*

Green Berets, The (1968, C, 141m, NR)
John Wayne stars in this Vietnam War drama that makes no apologies for American involvement in that conflict. Wayne and Ray Kellogg directed. Whatever your politics, it's still not one to remember Wayne by. **AC4, ST224**

Green Card (1991, C, 108m, PG-13)
Romantic comedy of modern arranged marriage in New York, starring Gérard Depardieu and Andie MacDowell. With Bebe Neuwirth, Gregg Edelman, and Robert Prosky. Written and directed by Peter Weir. Amiable entertainment. **CO1, DT133, ST52, XT9**

Green Dolphin Street
(1947, B&W, 141m, NR)
Romantic drama set in seventeenth-century New Zealand, starring Lana Turner, Donna Reed, and Van Heflin. **ST219**

Green Eyes (1976, C, 100m, NR)
Paul Winfield plays a Vietnam veteran returning to Southeast Asia to find the son he left behind. Originally made for TV. **ST230**

Green for Danger (1946, B&W, 93m, NR)
British whodunit starring Alastair Sim as Scotland Yard detective looking into double murder at hospital. With Sally Gray and Trevor Howard. Clever script, with Sim outstanding as rumpled sleuth. **MY12, MY15,** *Recommended*

Green Grow the Rushes
(1951, B&W, 80m, NR)
British comedy of village involved with brandy smuggling. Richard Burton stars (his last film before departing for Hollywood), with Honor Blackman and Roger Livesey. **CO17, ST21**

Green Pastures, The
(1936, B&W, 90m, NR)
Adaptation of Marc Connelly play features all-black cast enacting stories from the Bible. Rex Ingram stars as "de Lawd," with Oscar Polk, Eddie Anderson, and Frank Wilson. Directed by Connelly and William Keighley. **CL13, DR20**

Green Room, The (1978, C, 95m, PG)
A writer obsessed with World War I casualties builds a memorial in their honor. Adaptation of Henry James story directed by François Truffaut, who also stars. **DT125, WR14**

Greetings (1968, C, 88m, R)
Comedy of a trio of New Yorkers (Jonathan Warden, Robert De Niro, and Gerrit Graham) and their obsessions: women, ducking the draft, and the Kennedy assassination. Di-

rected by Brian De Palma. Originally rated "X." Still funny but dated in less interesting ways than many films of the time. **CU5, DT36, ST51, XT9**

Gregory's Girl (1981, C, 91m, PG)
A young Scottish goalie develops a crush on the new girl on the soccer team. Charming comedy from director Bill Forsyth. **CO4, CO17, CO18, DT46, FA7**

Gremlins (1984, C, 111m, PG)
A teen-ager's unusual pet produces offspring that turn violent when not properly cared for. Zach Galligan, Phoebe Cates, and Hoyt Axton star in this horror comedy directed by Joe Dante. Frantic and just plain irritating. **CO11, DT33, HO16, HO24, MU12**

Gremlins 2: The New Batch
(1990, C, 106m, PG-13)
More madcap nonsense from those fuzzy, furry creatures, as they invade a Manhattan skyscraper. The humor is often at the expense of modern media and business institutions. Zach Galligan and Phoebe Cates return, with John Glover, Christopher Lee, Dick Miller, and cameos from Hulk Hogan, Paul Bartel, and Leonard Maltin. **CO2, CO11, DT8, DT33, HO16, HO24, ST135**

Grey Fox, The (1982, C, 92m, PG)
After thirty-three years in prison, a gentleman bandit (Richard Farnsworth) just can't go straight, so he stages a train robbery. Western drama filmed in Canada. **DR11, WE3, WE10, WE11, XT19**

Grey Gardens (1976, C, 95m, PG)
Lifestyles of the formerly rich and truly eccentric: a documentary portrait of seventy-nine-year-old Edith Bouvier Beale and her fifty-seven-year-old daughter, Edie. This aunt and cousin of Jacqueline Kennedy Onassis are shown living in squalor in a barren mansion in East Hampton, New York. Filmed by the redoubtable team of Albert and David Maysles. Fascinating, not a little creepy. **CU16,** *Recommended*

Greyfriars Bobby (1961, C, 91m, NR)
Disney drama about a terrier who became a "community pet" in Edinburgh in the nineteenth century. **FA1**

Greystoke: The Legend of Tarzan, Lord of the Apes (1984, C, 129m, PG)
This version of the Tarzan story starts at the very beginning when, as a baby, Greystoke's parents are shipwrecked in Africa and die, leaving the jungle apes to raise him. Christopher Lambert stars, with Ralph Richardson, Ian Holm, and Andie MacDowell (whose voice was allegedly dubbed by Glenn Close). Best in

its opening third, but Lambert and MacDowell can't carry the film. **DR27, HF22, ST184**

Griffin and Phoenix: A Love Story
(1976, C, 100m, NR)
Peter Falk and Jill Clayburgh star in this tearjerker of a couple with incurable diseases who meet and fall in love. Originally made for TV. **DR1, DR2, ST31**

Grifters, The (1990, C, 119m, R)
A trio of con artists converge in this lurid tale from pulp master Jim Thompson. Anjelica Huston, Annette Bening, and John Cusack star, with Pat Hingle, J.T. Walsh, and Charles Napier. Screenplay by Donald Westlake; directed by Stephen Frears and produced by Martin Scorsese. The women are sensational. **DR16, DT48, MY2, MY4, MY14, ST12, ST115, WR34,** *Recommended*

Grim Prairie Tales (1990, C, 94m, R)
Two cowpokes (James Earl Jones, Brad Dourif) hunker down in front of a camp fire and swap a quartet of ghost stories dealing with life on the frontier. With Will Hare, Marc McClure, Lisa Eichorn, and William Atherton. **HO23, ST118**

Grissom Gang, The (1971, C, 127m, R)
Violent action comedy about a 1920s heiress kidnapped by a strange family. Kim Darby stars, with Scott Wilson, Irene Dailey, and Tony Musante. Directed by Robert Aldrich. **CO9, DT1**

Groove Tube, The (1974, C, 75m, R)
Chevy Chase is among the stars in this wild collection of satirical skits about television. **CO8, CO13**

Gross Anatomy (1989, C, 107m, PG-13)
Comedy-drama of life in medical school, with Matthew Modine and Daphne Zuniga the students, Christine Lahti their hard-nosed teacher. **CO18**

Ground Zero (1988, C, 100m, PG-13)
Australian drama, based on actual events, about a 1950s atomic test that turned disastrous, leading to a government coverup, which a cameraman discovers thirty years later. Colin Friels stars. **FF5**

Groundhog Day (1993, C, 103m, PG)
Bill Murray plays an arrogant Pittsburgh TV weatherman who journeys to a small town in Pennsylvania for title holiday, wakes up next morning to find himself repeating the day, wakes up the next morning . . . With Andie MacDowell, Chris Elliott, Stephen Tobolowsky, and Brian Doyle-Murray (Bill's real-life brother). Directed and cowritten by Harold Ramis, who has a bit part. Sur-

prisingly sweet romantic comedy about redemption is Murray's best starring vehicle yet, with MacDowell terrific in support. **CO1, CO13, CO14, CO20, XT8,** *Recommended*

Group, The (1966, C, 150m, NR)
Film version of Mary McCarthy novel about a clique of Vassar students and their lives after college. Candice Bergen, Joanna Pettet, Joan Hackett, Elizabeth Hartman, Shirley Knight, Jessica Walter, Kathleen Widdoes, and Mary-Robin Redd star. Directed by Sidney Lumet. **DR10, DR19, DT78**

Grown-Ups (1986, C, 106m, NR)
Adaptation of Jules Feiffer's stage drama about the disintegration of a family, starring Charles Grodin, with Martin Balsam, Jean Stapleton, and Marilu Henner. Originally made for cable TV. **DR8, DR20, ST94**

Guadalcanal Diary (1943, B&W, 93m, NR)
World War II action in the South Pacific, with Preston Foster, Lloyd Nolan, William Bendix, Richard Conte, and Anthony Quinn. **AC1**

Guardian, The (1990, C, 93m, R)
A couple entrust their young daughter to a nanny (Jenny Seagrove) who is secretly a child-stealer who sacrifices infants to a monstrous tree. Directed by William Friedkin. **HO14, MY19**

Guardsman, The (1931, B&W, 89m, NR)
Only screen-starring roles for stage legends Alfred Lunt and Lynn Fontanne, in this adaptation of the Fredric Molnar comedy of jealousy. **CL1, DR20**

Guess Who's Coming to Dinner (1967, C, 108m, NR)
Spencer Tracy (in his last film) and Katharine Hepburn (an Oscar winner) team in this drama about a couple whose daughter tells them she's marrying a black doctor (Sidney Poitier). Directed by Stanley Kramer. **CL15, DR7, DT67, ST103, ST174, ST217, XT3, XT22**

Guest Wife (1945, B&W, 90m, NR)
Comedy of impetuous woman (Claudette Colbert) posing as another man's wife, much to her own spouse's dismay. With Don Ameche and Dick Foran. **ST34**

Guide for the Married Man, A (1967, C, 89m, NR)
Walter Matthau stars as a befuddled husband who is guided in the fine art of adultery by a lecherous pal (Robert Morse). Gene Kelly directed this comedy, essentially a series of skits with guest stars including Lucille Ball, Jack Benny, Sid Caesar, and Jayne Mansfield.

With Inger Stevens as Matthau's wife. Leering stuff. **ST123, ST155**

Guilty by Suspicion (1991, C, 105m, PG-13)
Robert De Niro is a Hollywood director whose career is sidelined by the McCarthyera witch hunts. With Annette Bening, George Wendt, Patricia Wettig, Sam Wanamaker, and Martin Scorsese as a filmmaker loosely based on Joseph Losey (who fled America at the time and never returned). Written and directed by Irwin Winkler. Heartfelt and necessary but just shy of a solid film. **DR5, DR13, DR21, DT114, ST12, ST51**

Gulliver's Travels (1939, C, 74m, NR)
Jonathan Swift's adventure comes to the screen in this full-length animated feature. **FA10**

Gumball Rally, The (1976, C, 107m, PG)
A variety of characters gather for a crosscountry road race in this action-filled comedy. Michael Sarrazin, Tim McIntire, Raul Julia, and Gary Busey star. **AC10, CO9**

Gumshoe (1972, C, 88m, NR)
Albert Finney stars in this comic thriller about a man obsessed with Bogart who decides to solve a murder. Directed by Stephen Frears. **CO17, DT48, MY11, MY15, ST68,** *Recommended*

Gun Crazy (1949, B&W, 86m, NR)
Film noir with strong cult following, about a couple on the lam; she's the deadlier of the two, a former carnival sharpshooter. Peggy Cummins stars, with John Dall; Rusty Tamblyn plays Dall as a child. Directed by Joseph H. Lewis. Appropriate alternate title: *Deadly Is the Female.* **MY1, MY4, MY5,** *Recommended*

Gun Fury (1953, C, 83m, NR)
Rock Hudson plays a cowboy who tracks down the men who kidnapped his fiancée. Lee Marvin and Donna Reed costar. Directed by Raoul Walsh. **DT131, ST112, ST151**

Gun in Betty Lou's Handbag, The (1992, C, 89m, PG-13)
Comedy of milquetoast librarian finding a gun, concocting a story around it that soon ensnares her in real crimes. Penelope Ann Miller stars, with Eric Thal, Alfre Woodard, Julianne Moore, Cathy Moriarty, and William Forsythe. Directed and cowritten by Allan Moyle. **CO10**

Guncrazy (1992, C, 93m, R)
Loose remake of *film noir* classic of pistolpackin' babe (Drew Barrymore) leading her

boyfriend (James LeGros) into life of crime. With Billy Drago, Rodney Harvey, Joe Dallesandro, Michael Ironside, and Ione Skye. Directed by Tamra Davis. **CU18, DR16, MY4**

Gunfight, A (1971, C, 90m, PG)
Two aging gunslingers decide to sell tickets to a final shootout with themselves as the star attractions. Kirk Douglas, Raf Vallone, and Johnny Cash star. **MU12, ST57**

Gunfight at the O.K. Corral
(1957, C, 122m, NR)
Burt Lancaster and Kirk Douglas join forces as Wyatt Earp and Doc Holliday in this Western about the fabled Dodge City shootout. With Rhonda Fleming, Jo Van Fleet, John Ireland, Lee Van Cleef, and Dennis Hopper. **HF9, HF13, ST57, ST110, ST129, ST221,** *Recommended*

Gunfighter, The (1950, B&W, 84m, NR)
Gregory Peck plays Johnny Ringo, a disillusioned gunslinger who feels it's time to hang up the holster. **ST171, WE2**

Gung Ho! (1943, B&W, 88m, NR)
Randolph Scott prepares Marine recruits for World War II action. With Robert Mitchum. **AC1, ST158, ST197**

Gung Ho (1986, C, 111m, PG-13)
The foreman of an auto plant about to go under persuades a Japanese car company to take over management of the factory. Michael Keaton stars in this underrated topical comedy, with Gedde Watanabe, George Wendt, and Mimi Rogers. Directed by Ron Howard. **CO2, DT58, ST122,** *Recommended*

Gunga Din (1939, B&W, 117m, NR)
Rousing adventure classic, from Kipling's poem, about three British soldiers fighting the natives—and each other—in nineteenth-century India. Cary Grant, Douglas Fairbanks, Jr., and Victor McLaglen star, with Sam Jaffe in the title role and Joan Fontaine. George Stevens directed. **AC13, DT119, FA4, ST73, ST92,** *Essential, Highly Recommended*

Gunrunner, The (1984, C, 92m, R)
Early Kevin Costner film about a 1920s Canadian gangster trying to help Chinese rebels obtain arms. **AC22, ST37**

Guns at Batasi (1964, C, 103m, NR)
Drama of life in African country wracked by political strife, with British military trying to stay out of harm's way. Richard Attenborough, Jack Hawkins, and Mia Farrow star. **DR27, ST65**

Guns of Navarone, The
(1961, C, 157m, NR)
Adventure yarn about a group of World War II commandoes out to destroy massive Nazi guns. Gregory Peck, David Niven, Anthony Quinn, and Stanley Baker star. Widescreen will be lost on video. Great finale but takes too long getting there. **AC1, CU20, ST171**

Gunslinger, The (1956, C, 83m, NR)
Female marshal tries to keep the peace in this low-budget western directed by Roger Corman. Beverly Garland and John Ireland star. **DT30, WE8**

Gus (1976, C, 96m, G)
This Disney comedy features a mule named Gus with a talent for kicking footballs. A group of evildoers plots to kidnap the talented animal for their own purposes. Edward Asner, Don Knotts, and Tim Conway star. **FA1**

Guy Named Joe, A (1943, B&W, 120m, NR)
Spencer Tracy plays an angel who comes to Earth to help a World War II soldier in trouble. With Irene Dunne, Van Johnson, Ward Bond, Barry Nelson, and Lionel Barrymore. Remade as *Always*. As solid as Tracy usually is, he seems slightly miscast here, and Johnson is impossibly young for Garson. **SF2, ST62, ST217, XT24**

Guyana Tragedy: The Story of Jim Jones (1980, C, 192m, NR)
Powers Boothe plays the messianic cult leader whose followers committed mass suicide. With Ned Beatty, Irene Cara, Veronica Cartwright, Rosalind Cash, Brad Dourif, Meg Foster, Diane Ladd, and James Earl Jones. Originally made for TV. **DR6, ST118**

Guys And Dolls (1955, C, 150m, NR)
Frank Sinatra, Marlon Brando, and Jean Simmons star in this classic Damon Runyon story about a gambler and a missionary, set to a Frank Loesser score. Joseph L. Mankiewicz directed. Final number is presented in letterboxed format. **CU19, DT84, MU2, MU6, MU17, ST18, ST199**

Gypsy (1962, C, 149m, NR)
Natalie Wood plays Gypsy Rose Lee in this musical account of the stripper's life, with Rosalind Russell as Mama Rose. **MU5, ST192**

Gypsy Blood (1918, B&W, 104m, NR)
Silent film drama based on the classic story that inspired Bizet's opera *Carmen*, with Pola Negri as the temptress. Directed by Ernst Lubitsch. Original title: *Carmen*. **DT76**

HBO Comedy Club
(1987, C, 60m each, NR)
This series of three tapes highlight the best of today's comedy. The first is *Howie From Maui*, featuring Howie Mandel in concert. The sec-

ond, *Tenth Anniversary Young Comedians Special*, is a reunion of comics featuring Robin Williams. The third, *Roseanne Barr*, stars the sharp-tongued comedienne. **CO16, ST228**

H-Man, The (1958, C, 79m, NR)
Japanese science fiction story set in Tokyo with twin plots: radioactive substance causes havoc, while police and dope dealers battle it out. **FF4, SF18**

Hail! Hail! Rock 'n' Roll see *Chuck Berry: Hail! Hail! Rock 'n' Roll*

Hail, Hero! (1969, C, 100m, PG)
Michael Douglas's film debut, as he plays a son rebelling against his parents over the Vietnam War. With Arthur Kennedy and Teresa Wright. **DR7, DR8, ST59**

Hail Mary (1985, C, 107m, NR)
Director Jean-Luc Godard's controversial drama about a contemporary young woman's unexplained pregnancy. Any resemblances to the well-known biblical story are purely intentional. **CU8, DT50**

Hail the Conquering Hero
(1944, B&W, 101m, NR)
An Army reject is mistakenly taken for a war hero by his hometown. Preston Sturges wrote and directed this satire starring Eddie Bracken. **CL10, CO20, DT121**

Hair (1979, C, 121m, R)
The Broadway musical about a group of New York hippies opposed to the Vietnam War. Treat Williams, John Savage, and Beverly D'Angelo star. Milos Forman directed; choreography by Twyla Tharp. Only intermittently effective, usually during the musical numbers. **DT45, MU2, MU9, XT9**

Hairspray (1988, C, 90m, PG)
Baltimore in the early 1960s: a TV teen dance show is disrupted when one of the "regulars" tries to bring her black friends to the show. A marvelously nostalgic comedy from director John Waters, starring Ricki Lake, Divine (in two roles), Jerry Stiller, Sonny Bono, Debby Harry, Ruth Brown, and the director in a bit part. Waters's most "accessible" film. **CO6, DT132, MU12,** *Recommended*

Hairy Ape, The (1944, B&W, 90m, NR)
Eugene O'Neill's play of a ship's stoker in love with a haughty passenger. William Bendix and Susan Hayward star. **ST100, WR25**

Half a Sixpence (1967, C, 148m, NR)
Family musical, based on an H.G. Wells story, about a young man who tried to break into society with his newly inherited fortune.

Tommy Steele stars, with Julia Foster, Penelope Horner, and Cyril Ritchard. **FA9, WR37**

Half Moon Street (1986, C, 90m, R)
Sigourney Weaver plays an American researcher in London who turns to prostitution to make ends meet, becomes involved in political intrigue. Michael Caine costars in this limp adaptation of Paul Theroux's novella. **MY6, ST25, ST225**

Half of Heaven (1987, C, 127m, NR)
Spanish drama, with elements of comedy and fantasy, starring Angela Molina as a woman who molds herself into a successful restaurant owner. Directed by Manuel Guttierez Aragon. **FF7**

Hallelujah (1929, B&W, 90m, NR)
Early sound musical featuring all-black cast in tale of cotton picker turned preacher, tempted by a young vixen. Daniel L. Haynes and Nina Mae McKinney star. Directed by King Vidor. Original running time: 106 minutes. May seem dated to most viewers but does offer rare mainstream look at performers and subject matter for many years confined to films made for segregated audiences. **DT126, MU13**

Halloween (1978, C, 93m, R)
A young boy murders his teen-age sister, is locked up, and escapes years later, looking for more victims. Cult horror film was also a hit movie spawning dozens of imitators and several sequels. Jamie Lee Curtis and Donald Pleasence star. John Carpenter directed; his most influential and best film to date. **CU4, DT23, HO9, ST42,** *Essential, Recommended*

Halloween II (1981, C, 92m, R)
Terror continues as the killer stalks his victims on Halloween night, taking up where *Halloween* left off. Jamie Lee Curtis and Donald Pleasence return, too. **HO9, ST42**

Halloween III: Season of the Witch
(1983, C, 96m, R)
A mad scientist hatches a plot to slaughter millions of children on Halloween. Not a sequel to earlier *Halloween* films. **HO20**

Halloween 4: The Return of Michael Myers (1988, C, 88m, R)
As the title suggests, the monstrous killer from the first two *Halloween* horrorfests is back, with the same good doctor (Donald Pleasence) in pursuit. **HO9**

Halloween 5: The Revenge of Michael Myers (1989, C, 96m, NN)
Dr. Loomis (Donald Pleasence) continues to explore the psychic connection between madman Michael Myers and his young niece (Danielle Harris). **HO9**

Halls of Montezuma (1950, C, 113m, NR)
Marines hit the beach in this World War II
saga, starring Richard Widmark, Walter (Jack)
Palance, Robert Wagner, and Jack Webb. Directed by Lewis Milestone. **AC1**

Hambone and Hillie (1984, C, 89m, G)
Lillian Gish plays a woman who's separated
from her beloved dog at an airport in this
family drama. **FA5, ST87**

Hamburger Hill (1987, C, 104m, R)
War drama of American company caught up
in bloody battle for a strategic position in
Vietnam. Michael Dolan, Daniel O'Shea, and
Dylan McDermott star. **AC4**

Hamlet (1948, B&W, 135m, NR)
Laurence Olivier directed and stars in this
peerless adaptation of the Shakespeare play
about the tormented Danish prince. With
Jean Simmons and Peter Cushing. Winner of
four Academy Awards, including Best Picture
and Actor. **ST43, ST168, WR28, XT1, XT2,**
Essential, Recommended

Hamlet (1969, C, 114m, G)
Nicol Williamson is the star of this version of
Shakespeare's tragedy, with Gordon Jackson,
Anthony Hopkins, and Marianne Faithfull
as Ophelia. Directed by Tony Richardson.
MU12, ST109, WR28

Hamlet (1990, C,,TH135m, PG)
Mel Gibson is the moody prince of Denmark,
with Glenn Close as Gertrude, Alan Bates as
Claudius, and Paul Scofield, Ian Holm, and
Helena Bonham Carter. Co-adapted and di-
rected by Franco Zeffirelli. **ST9, ST33, ST85,**
WR28

Hammersmith Is Out (1972, C, 108m, R)
Elizabeth Taylor and Richard Burton team
up in this strange story of a violent mental
patient who is determined to escape from the
hospital. With Peter Ustinov, Beau Bridges,
and George Raft. **CL15, ST22, ST212**

Hammett (1983, C, 97m, PG)
Real-life author Dashiell Hammett gets in-
volved in a real-life mystery. Based on Joe
Gores's novel about Hammett's career as a
Pinkerton detective. Frederic Forrest stars,
with Peter Boyle, Marilu Henner, Elisha
Cook, Samuel Fuller, and R.G. Armstrong.
Wim Wenders directed; outstanding produc-
tion design by Dean Tavoularis. Despite
production problems, a finely observed mys-
tery. **DT49, DT136, MY2, MY8, WR12,**
Recommended

Hand, The (1981, C, 104m, R)
Michael Caine plays a cartoonist whose
severed hand comes back to haunt him.

Written and directed by Oliver Stone.
DT120, ST25

Hand That Rocks the Cradle, The
(1992, C, 110m, R)
Young mother hires nanny, not knowing the
woman is out for revenge; the mom sued the
nanny's husband for malpractice, causing
him to commit suicide and her to miscarry
her own baby. Annabella Sciorra and Rebecca
De Mornay star in this thriller, with Matt
McCoy and Ernie Hudson. **MY3, MY4,**
MY9, MY14, MY19

Handful of Dust, A (1988, C, 118m, PG)
Evelyn Waugh story of a failed marriage
between a sensitive aristocrat (James Wilby)
and his self-centered wife (Kristin Scott-
Thomas). With Rupert Graves, Judi Dench,
Anjelica Huston, and Alec Guinness. Well-
handled, especially in the difficult final
scenes in the jungle. **DR1, DR19, DR23,**
ST95, ST115, *Recommended*

Handle With Care see *Citizens Band*

Handmaid's Tale, The (1990, C, 109m, R)
Futuristic tale of society where a class of
women is subservient to men for procrea-
tion. Natasha Richardson stars, with Robert
Duvall, Faye Dunaway, Aidan Quinn, Eliz-
abeth McGovern, and Victoria Tennant.
Adapted by Harold Pinter from Margaret
Atwood's novel; directed by Volker Schlön-
dorff. **DR7, DR10, DR19, ST61, ST63,**
WR26

Hands Across the Border
(1944, B&W, 54m, NR)
Roy Rogers does his bit to promote good relations between the U.S. and Mexico in this
Western adventure. **ST188**

Hands of Orlac, The (1960, C, 95m, NR)
Horror story of a pianist who gets a hand
transplant and feels an urge to kill. Mel Ferrer stars, with Lucille Saint-Simon and Christopher Lee. **ST135**

Hang 'em High (1968, C, 114m, NR)
Cowboy (Clint Eastwood) vows revenge
on the men who tried to kill him. This
American-made spaghetti Western features
Inger Stevens, Ed Begley, Pat Hingle, Ben
Johnson, and Dennis Hopper. **ST64, ST110,**
WE13

Hangin' With the Homeboys
(1991, C, 88m, R)
Twenty-four hours in the lives of four South
Bronx buddies trying not to succumb to the
temptations of crime in the big city. Doug E.
Doy, Mario Joyner, John Leguizano, and Nestor Serrano star. Written and directed by Joseph P. Vasquez. **DR15, XT9**

Hanging Tree, The (1959, C, 106m, NR)
Gary Cooper Western has him playing a
frontier doctor who helps a blind girl (Maria
Schell). With Karl Malden and George C.
Scott in his film debut. **ST37, ST196, WE8**

Hangman's Knot (1952, C, 81m, NR)
Civil War Western of Rebel officer (Randolph
Scott) trying to persuade his men to return
a cache of stolen gold. With Donna Reed,
Claude Jarman, Jr., and Lee Marvin. **ST151,
ST197, WE6**

Hanky Panky (1982, C, 110m, PG)
Comic thriller about a woman looking for
the men who murdered her brother and
involving an innocent bystander in her
investigation. Gilda Radner and Gene Wilder
star; directed by Sidney Poitier. **CO13, MY17,
ST174**

Hanna K. (1983, C, 108m, R)
Jill Clayburgh plays a lawyer in Israel who is
juggling a persistent ex-husband, an amorous district attorney, and a mysterious Arab
defendant she is representing. Topical drama
from director Costa-Gavras. **DR3, DR7,
DR10, ST31**

Hannah and Her Sisters
(1986, C, 106m, PG)
Woody Allen comedy-drama of a family of
neurotic New Yorkers whose lives mingle
over three Thanksgivings. Dianne Wiest and
Michael Caine won Oscars, as did Allen's
screenplay. With Mia Farrow, Barbara Hershey, Carrie Fisher, Lloyd Nolan, Maureen
O'Sullivan (Mia's mom), Daniel Stern, Max
von Sydow, and John Turturro. One of the
director's best films of the last ten years.
**CO5, DT2, ST25, ST65, ST104, XT4, XT5,
XT8, XT9, XT30,** *Recommended*

Hanna's War (1988, C, 148m, PG-13)
True-life drama of a Hungarian woman who
worked for the Allies in World War II on rescue missions. She was captured and tortured
by the Nazis. Maruschka Detmers stars, with
Ellen Burstyn, Anthony Andrews, and
Donald Pleasence. **DR5**

Hannie Caulder (1972, C, 85m, R)
Raquel Welch stars in a Western drama of a
woman who seeks revenge on the men who
attacked her. With Robert Culp as a friendly
bounty hunter, Ernest Borgnine, Jack Elam,
Strother Martin, and, in a bit role, Christopher Lee. **ST135, WE5, WE8**

Hanoi Hilton, The (1987, C, 130m, R)
Drama of Vietnam War POWs; the title refers
to their sarcastic name for their quarters.
Michael Moriarty, Jeffrey Jones, and Paul
LeMat star. **AC7**

Hanover Street (1979, C, 109m, PG)
World War II romance between British wife
and American serviceman, starring Harrison
Ford and Lesley-Anne Down. **DR1, ST60**

Hans Christian Andersen
(1952, C, 120m, NR)
Danny Kaye stars in this family musical
about the famous storyteller. **FA9, ST120**

Hansel and Gretel (1984, C, 58m, NR)
Two hungry children (Ricky Schroder and
Bridgette Anderson) stop to snack on a gin-
gerbread house and almost become dinner
for the witch (Joan Collins) who lives there.
A Faerie Tale Theatre presentation. **FA12**

Happiest Millionaire, The
(1967, C, 118m, NR)
This Disney musical features Fred MacMurray and Greer Garson as an eccentric Philadelphia couple dealing with life in the early
1900s. With Geraldine Page and Lesley Ann
Warren. **FA1, ST83**

Happiness Cage, The (1972, C, 94m, PG)
Thriller has German doctor using controversial experiments on soldiers to curb aggressive behavior. Christopher Walken stars, with
Joss Ackland and Ralph Meeker. Also known
as *The Mind Snatcher.* **ST222**

**Happy Anniversary 007: 25 Years of
James Bond** (1987, C, 59m, NR)
Documentary of clips from the long-running
series featuring all four actors who've played
Mr. Bond: Sean Connery, Roger Moore,
George Lazenby, and Timothy Dalton. **HF2,
ST36**

Happy Birthday, Gemini
(1980, C, 107m, R)
Comedy of young man coming of age, sort-
ing out his true sexual preferences. Madeline
Kahn, Rita Moreno, and Robert Viharo star.
Based on Albert Innaurato's play, *Gemini.*
CO4, DR20

Happy Birthday to Me (1981, C, 108m, R)
Horror story of a high school student who
may be killing off her classmates in retribution
for the accidental death of her mother. **HO9**

Happy Ending, The (1969, C, 112m, PG)
Contemporary drama of a middle-aged
woman walking out on her marriage, starring
Jean Simmons, with John Forsythe, Lloyd
Bridges, Shirley Jones, and Robert (Bobby)
Darin. **DR10, MU12**

Happy New Year (1973, C, 112m, PG)
A pair of jewel thieves plot a heist, only to
have one fall in love with the proprietor of
the store next to their target. French comedy
stars Lino Ventura, Francoise Fabian, and

Charles Gerard. U.S. remake released in 1987. **FF1, FF8, MY18**

Happy New Year (1987, C, 85m, PG)
Remake of French comedy about two jewel thieves and romantic complications, starring Peter Falk, Wendy Hughes, Charles Durning, and Tom Courtenay. **FF8, MY18**

Hard Choices (1986, C, 90m, NR)
Drama of social worker and her teen-aged client, a juvenile offender, falling in love, with her helping him to escape custody. Gary McCleery and Margaret Klenck star, with John Sayles. **DR1, DR3, DT112**

Hard Day's Night, A
(1964, B&W, 85m, NR)
Richard Lester directed this brilliant rock musical about a day in the life of The Beatles, shot on location in London. **DT74, FA9, MU9, XT15**, *Essential, Highly Recommended*

Hard Frame (1970, C, 100m, NR)
Drama of ex-con returning to his hometown to mend fences with stern father and former lover. Burt Reynolds stars, with Melvyn Douglas, Suzanne Pleshette, and Martin Balsam. Originally made for TV, where it was titled "Hunters Are for Killing." **DR8, ST58, ST183**

Hard Promises (1991, C, 95m, PG)
Romantic comedy set in small Texas town of woman about to embark on second marriage, with her ex showing up to disrupt the wedding. Sissy Spacek, William Petersen, and Brian Kerwin star, with Mare Winningham and Ann Wedgeworth. **CO1, ST202, XT20**

Hard Rock Zombies (1985, C, 94m, R)
Four heavy metal musicians are murdered but return from the grave for their scheduled concert as zombies. **HO6**

Hard Times (1975, C, 97m, R)
Drama about street fighter in Depression-era New Orleans, starring Charles Bronson, James Coburn, and Strother Martin. Directed by Walter Hill. Strictly for genre devotees. **AC8, DT56, ST20, XT14**

Hard To Kill (1990, C, 95m, R)
Steven Seagal stars as Mason Storm, an agent left for dead by his enemies, back after seven years in a coma, looking for revenge. With Kelly LeBrock. **AC19, AC25, AC26**

Hard Way, The (1979, C, 88m, NR)
Familiar action tale of hired killer hired for one last job. Patrick McGoohan and Lee Van Cleef star. **ST221**

Hard Way, The (1991, C, 111m, R)
A soft-headed movie star researches his latest role by teaming up with a hard-bitten cop—

and they wind up cracking the case of a serial killer. Action comedy with plenty of movie jokes. Michael J. Fox and James Woods star, with Stephen Lang, Annabella Sciorra, and rap star LL Cool J. **AC9, CO8, CO9, CO20, MU12, ST233**

Hardcore (1979, C, 108m, R)
Religious father from the Midwest tries to find runaway daughter in the midst of the porno film and prostitution worlds. George C. Scott stars, with Season Hubley. Paul Schrader wrote and directed. One of Scott's many good performances and Schrader's few good films. **DR7, ST196**, *Recommended*

Harder They Come, The (1973, C, 98m, R)
A poor youth in Jamaica gains fame as both a singer and an outlaw in this midnight movie classic starring Jimmy Cliff. Great reggae music soundtrack. **CU1, CU9, MU9**, *Recommended*

Harder They Fall, The
(1956, B&W, 109m, NR)
Humphrey Bogart's last screen appearance has him playing a press agent who befriends an exploited prizefighter. Rod Steiger costars. **DR22, ST15, XT22**

Hardly Working (1981, C, 91m, PG)
An unemployed circus clown (Jerry Lewis) stumbles through a series of odd jobs, all with disastrous results. With Susan Oliver, Steve Franken, and Harold J. Stone. Lewis directed. **ST139**

Hardware (1990, C, 92m, R)
Sci-fi horror story set in post-apocalypse wasteland: a scavenger brings his alchemist girlfriend a hunk of rubble which turns into a killing machine. Very violent, almost earned an "X" rating. Dylan McDermott and Stacey Travis star, with John Lynch, and the voice of Iggy Pop as a manic deejay. **CU1, CU7, MU12, SF6, SF12, SF20**

Harlan County, U.S.A.
(1977, C, 103m, PG)
Oscar-winning documentary about a bitter and violent coal miner's strike in Kentucky. Directed by Barbara Kopple. **CU16**

Harlem Nights (1989, C, 118m, R)
Comedy set in 1930s New York, with Eddie Murphy and Richard Pryor as club owners fighting off a crime boss who wants a piece of their action—a big piece. With Redd Foxx, Della Reese, Danny Aiello, Michael Lerner, and in a small role, Arsenio Hall. **CO6, CO13, ST180**

Harley Davidson & the Marlboro Man
(1991, C, 93m, R)
Mickey Rourke and Don Johnson play the

title dudes in this urban action drama, about a pair of 1996 drifters who help out their buddy by robbing a bank. **AC8, ST190**

Harlow (1965, C, 125m, NR)
The short and, according to this film, less than happy life of 1930s movie queen Jean Harlow. Carroll Baker stars, with Peter Lawford, Red Buttons, Michael Connors, and Raf Vallone and Angela Lansbury as Jean's parents. **DR4, DR13, ST131**

Harold and Maude
(1972, C, 90m, PG)
Offbeat romantic comedy about a suicidal rich boy (Bud Cort) and a life-loving eighty-year-old (Ruth Gordon) finding romance. A cult favorite at midnight screenings. **CO12, CU1, CU5, CU17**

Harold Lloyd: The Third Genius
(1990, B&W/C, 110m, NR)
First-rate British-made documentary exalts bespectacled silent clown, including interviews with producer Hal Roach and Jack Lemmon. Directed by Kevin Brownlow and David Gill. **CU16, ST138**, *Recommended*

Harold Lloyd's World of Comedy
(1962, B&W, 80m, NR)
Compilation of the classic silent comedian's short films from the early 1920s, including his masterpiece, *Safety Last.* **CL11,**
Recommended

Harper (1966, C, 121m, NR)
Paul Newman plays detective Lew Harper, hired by a frustrated wife (Lauren Bacall) to find her missing husband. With Janet Leigh, Arthur Hill, Robert Wagner, Shelley Winters, Julie Harris, Strother Martin, and Robert Webber. Based on the Ross MacDonald novel, *The Moving Target.* Directed by Jack Smight. Pretty entertaining, just not up to MacDonald's high standards. **ST162, ST232, WR22**

Harry and Son (1984, C, 117m, PG)
Star Paul Newman also cowrote, coproduced, and directed this drama of a strained relationship between a widowed construction worker and his idealistic son. Robby Benson costars, with Joanne Woodward, Morgan Freeman, and Ellen Barkin. **DR8, ST7, ST76, ST162, ST234, XT30**

Harry and Tonto (1974, C, 115m, R)
Touching odyssey of a senior citizen and his pet cat on the road from New York to California, with Oscar winner Art Carney magnificent. With Ellen Burstyn and Larry Hagman. Directed by Paul Mazursky. **DR11, DT87, XT2, XT18**, *Recommended*

Harry and Walter Go to New York
(1976, C, 123m, PG)
Two unsuccessful vaudevillians (Elliott Gould and James Caan) resort to theft and land in jail in 1890s New York. Diane Keaton and Michael Caine costar in this comedy. **CO6, ST25, ST121**

Harry Tracy, Desperado
(1982, C, 100m, PG)
A wanted criminal's exploits made him the envy of all and a folk hero to most. Bruce Dern and singer Gordon Lightfoot star in this Canadian-produced Western. **MU12, WE3, WE10**

Harum Scarum (1965, C, 86m, NR)
Elvis Presley musical about a movie star who gets involved in an attempted assassination in the Middle East. **ST178**

Harvey (1950, B&W, 104m, NR)
James Stewart stars in the screen version of Mary Chase's play about Elwood P. Dowd, a man who has a large, invisible rabbit for a companion. With Oscar winner Josephine Hull. **CL10, DR20, ST207, XT5**

Harvey Girls, The (1946, C, 101m, NR)
Judy Garland stars in this musical about a girl who travels west to work for Fred Harvey and his railroad-stop restaurants. Ray Bolger, Angela Lansbury, and Preston Foster costar. **MU1, MU6, ST81, ST131**

Hatari! (1962, C, 159m, NR)
John Wayne is the leader of a group of big-game stalkers who capture wild animals for zoos. With Elsa Martinelli, Red Buttons, and Hardy Kruger. Directed by Howard Hawks; music by Henry Mancini. Good family entertainment. Not one of director Hawks's best, though. **AC12, DT53, FA4, ST224**

Haunted Honeymoon
(1986, C, 82m, PG-13)
A recently married couple (Gene Wilder and Gilda Radner) spend their honeymoon in a haunted house. Dom DeLuise costars in this horror comedy directed by Wilder. **CO13, XT23**

Haunted Palace, The (1963, C, 85m, NR)
A New England castle is haunted by an evil spirit, which possesses the new owner. Vincent Price stars, with Debra Paget, Lon Chaney, Jr., and Frank Maxwell. Directed by Roger Corman, based on a story by H.P. Lovecraft. **DT30, HO3, HO8, ST27, ST179**

Haunted Strangler, The
(1958, B&W, 81m, NR)
A mystery writer (Boris Karloff) investigates a series of murders that took place in London

twenty years before, believing that an innocent man was hanged for the crimes. **ST119**

Haunted Summer (1988, C, 106m, R)
Drama based on actual meeting of nineteenth-century English poets Lord Byron (Philip Anglim) and Percy Bysshe Shelley (Eric Stoltz). Laura Dern and Alice Krige costar. **DR5, ST53**

Haunting, The (1963, B&W, 112m, NR)
Two women who have had clairvoyant experiences are invited to a mysterious house where strange and terrifying events have occurred. Claire Bloom and Julie Harris star. Directed by Robert Wise. Widescreen will be lost on video. **CU20, DT140, HO1, HO2, HO3, HO19**

Haunting of Julia, The (1976, C, 96m, R)
Mia Farrow stars as a tormented woman who, after the death of her young daughter, moves to a house inhabited by a spirit. Keir Dullea and Tom Conti costar in this British horror film. **HO2, HO3, HO19, HO26, ST65**

Haunting of Morella, The
(1990, C, 87m, R)
Sexy rendering of Edgar Allan Poe story of a witch who is executed, then comes back to life to possess her nubile niece. Produced by Roger Corman. **HO8, HO25, WR27**

Havana (1990, C, 145m, R)
Robert Redford plays a gambler adrift in Cuba in this romantic drama set during the dying days of the Bautista dictatorship. With Lena Olin, Alan Arkin, Tomas Milian, and Raul Julia. Directed by Sydney Pollack. **DR1, DR5, DT98, ST181**

Having Wonderful Time
(1938, B&W, 71m, NR)
Ginger Rogers comedy set in the Catskills, where she finds romance on her vacation. With Douglas Fairbanks, Jr., Lucille Ball, Red Skelton, and Eve Arden. **ST187**

Hawaii (1966, C, 171m, NR)
Missionaries try to bring Christianity to Hawaiian Islands in the nineteenth century. Julie Andrews and Max von Sydow star, with Richard Harris, Gene Hackman, Carroll O'Connor, and as an extra, Bette Midler. Directed by George Roy Hill; adapted from the James Michener novel. Also available in a 192-minute "director's cut" version. **CU10, DR5, DT55, ST2, ST96, ST156**

Hawmps! (1976, C, 113m, G)
Camels are trained as army mounts for desert maneuvers in this family comedy based on a true story. **FA6**

Haxan see *Witchcraft through the Ages*

He Knows You're Alone (1981, C, 94m, R)
A mad killer is after women who are about to be married. Don Scardino and Caitlin O'Heaney star; watch for Tom Hanks in a small part. **MY3, ST97**

He Said, She Said (1991, C, 115m, PG-13)
Romantic comedy set in Baltimore TV station, with pair of commentators fighting loving. Story is told twice, from both parties' points of view. Kevin Bacon and Elizabeth Perkins star. Codirected by Ken Kwapis and Marisa Silver. **CO1**

He Walked by Night
(1948, B&W, 79m, NR)
Los Angeles homicide investigators are looking for a cop killer in this classic thriller. Anthony Mann codirected with Alfred Werker. **DT85, MY1**

Head (1968, C, 86m, G)
The Monkees made their film debut in this wild collection of skits, written by Jack Nicholson and directed by Bob Rafelson. With Terry (Teri) Garr, Frank Zappa, and guest stars Annette Funicello, Sonny Liston, and Victor Mature. **CU3, MU9**

Head Office (1986, C, 86m, PG-13)
A naive college graduate (Judge Reinhold) gets a job with a powerful conglomerate after his father pulls some strings. Comedy about big business also features Rick Moranis, Danny De Vito, Eddie Albert, and Jane Seymour. **CO14, ST54**

Head Over Heels (1967) see *A Coeur Joie*

Head Over Heels (1979) see *Chilly Scenes of Winter*

Hear My Song (1991, C, 104m, R)
Drama loosely based on life of expatriate Irish tenor Josef Locke, whom a London nightclub owner is trying to lure in for an engagement. Ned Beatty and Adrian Dunbar star, with Shirley Anne Field, Tara Fitzgerald, and David McCallum. Directed by Peter Chelsom. **DR12, DR23, MU5**

Hear No Evil (1993, C, 97m, R)
Thriller about a deaf physical trainer menaced after one of her clients conceals a valuable coin in her beeper. Marlee Matlin stars, with D.B. Sweeney, Martin Sheen, and John C. McGinley. **MY3**

Heart Beat (1980, C, 109m, R)
The life and times of Beat writer Jack Kerouac (John Heard) and his pal Neal Cassady (Nick Nolte). Sissy Spacek plays Carolyn Cassady and Ray Sharkey is very funny as Allen Gins-

berg. Only Sharkey shines in this disappointment. **DR4, ST164, ST202**

Heart Condition (1990, C, 95m, R)
A racist cop suffers a heart attack, winds up with the transplanted heart of a murdered black lawyer. The lawyer's spirit appears to the cop, and they solve the mystery of the killing. Bob Hoskins and Denzel Washington star in this comedy, with Chloe Webb and Roger E. Mosley. **CO10, CO20, ST111, ST223**

Heart Is a Lonely Hunter, The
(1968, C, 125m, G)
Touching version of Carson McCullers novel about a young girl's coming of age in a small Southern town. Sondra Locke and Alan Arkin star, with Stacy Keach, Chuck McCann, and Cicely Tyson. Arkin's moving performance deserved an Oscar. A bonafide tearjerker that is just a shade too long. **DR2, DR9, DR19, DR26, XT28,** *Recommended*

Heart Like a Wheel (1983, C, 113m, PG)
The true story of Shirley Muldowney, the first woman to dent the all-male barrier in modern drag racing. Bonnie Bedelia, Beau Bridges, and Hoyt Axton star. Directed by Jonathan Kaplan. **DR4, DR10, DR22, MU12,** *Recommended*

Heart of a Nation (1943, B&W, 111m, NR)
French drama, a family saga covering years from Franco-Prussian War through both world wars. Louis Jouvet, Raimu, and Suzy Prim star, with narration by Charles Boyer. Prints were nearly destroyed during Nazi Occupation. **FF1, ST16**

Heart of Dixie, The (1989, C, 95m, PG)
At a girls' college in 1957 Alabama, a young white student learns of the civil rights struggle firsthand. Ally Sheedy stars, with Virginia Madsen, Phoebe Cates, and Treat Williams. **DR7, DR25**

Heart of Glass (1976, C, 93m, NR)
Werner Herzog directed this drama of how a glassblower's death affects his small town, as he takes his secret formula to the grave. **DT54**

Heart of Midnight (1988, C, 93m, R)
Thriller starring Jennifer Jason Leigh as a young woman whose fragile mental state is further weakened when she inherits a sex club. With Peter Coyote, Gale Mayron, and Brenda Vaccaro. **MY3, ST136**

Heart of the Golden West
(1942, B&W, 54m, NR)
Roy Rogers comes to the rescue of Cherokee City ranchers. **ST188**

Heart of the Rio Grande
(1942, B&W, 70m, NR)
Gene Autry sings his way out of the middle of a family feud. **ST5**

Heart of the Rockies
(1951, B&W, 54m, NR)
Roy Rogers plays a highway engineer battling a crooked rancher in this contemporary Western. **ST188**

Heartbeeps (1981, C, 79m, PG)
The ultimate futuristic romance: two robots fall in love. Andy Kaufman and Bernadette Peters star. Allan Arkush directed. **DT6, FA8, SF21**

Heartbreak Hotel (1988, C, 101m, PG-13)
To cheer up his widowed mother who's an avid Elvis Presley fan, her teen son and his buddies kidnap The King from his hotel and take him to their small Ohio town. Comedy, set in the early 1970s, stars Charlie Schlatter and Tuesday Weld, with David Keith as Elvis. **CO6, ST178**

Heartbreak Kid, The (1972, C, 104m, PG)
A Jewish man (Charles Grodin) marries, but has a change of heart when he meets a beautiful WASP (Cybill Shepherd) on his honeymoon in Miami. Elaine May directed this dark and supremely funny comedy, adapted by Neil Simon from a Bruce J. Friedman story. With Jeannie Berlin and Eddie Albert. **CO1, CU5, DT86, ST94, WR30, XT20,** *Highly Recommended*

Heartbreak Ridge (1986, C, 130m, R)
A tough Marine sergeant (Clint Eastwood) shapes up his young recruits for action in the Grenada invasion. With Marsha Mason, Everett McGill, and Mario Van Peebles. Eastwood directed. **AC6, ST64**

Heartburn (1986, C, 108m, R)
Jack Nicholson and Meryl Streep are a seemingly happily married couple, until she learns during her pregnancy that he's having an affair. Directed by Mike Nichols; Nora Ephron adapted her novel. Filmed partly on location in Washington, D.C. With Jeff Daniels, Maureen Stapleton, Stockard Channing, Richard Masur, Catherine O'Hara, Milos Forman, and Karen Akers. It's good for the most part, but falls short of fulfilling its promise. Worth a look if you're a fan of the principals. **CO1, CO2, CO14, DT45, DT91, ST163, ST210, XT12, XT20**

Heartland (1979, C, 96m, PG)
A western woman's saga of life on the 1910 Wyoming frontier, based on a true story. Conchata Ferrell and Rip Torn star. **ST216, WE8,** *Recommended*

Heartland Reggae (1980, C, 87m, NR)
Concert film shot in Jamaica in April 1978, featuring some of reggae's superstars, including Bob Marley and Peter Tosh. **MU10**

Hearts and Minds (1974, C, 110m, R)
Oscar-winning documentary explores America's involvement in the Vietnam War. Directed by Peter Davis. Does not aspire to objectivity but makes a very convincing case against U.S. participation. **CU16,** *Recommended*

Hearts of Darkness: A Filmmaker's Apocalypse (1991, C, 96m, NR)
Sensational documentary of the incredible set of events that marked the making of *Apocalypse Now*. Directed and written by Fax Bahr and George Hickenlooper, with footage and commentary by Eleanor Coppola, wife of the original film's director, Francis Ford Coppola. Includes interviews with Dennis Hopper, Martin Sheen, Frederic Forrest, George Lucas, and John Milius, plus footage of Marlon Brando struggling with his role. An absolute must for anyone interested in how movies get made. **CU16, DT29, DT72, ST18, ST63, ST110, XT26, XT31,** *Highly Recommended*

Hearts of Fire (1987, C, 95m, R)
Drama of a romantic triangle among pop singers, starring Bob Dylan, Fiona, and Rupert Everett. **DR12**

Hearts of the West (1975, C, 102m, PG)
Jeff Bridges plays an aspiring novelist in the 1930s who goes to Hollywood to work as a screenwriter, but winds up acting in low-budget Westerns. Charming comedy also stars Blythe Danner, Alan Arkin, and Andy Griffith. Directed by Howard Zieff. **CO6, CO8, ST19,** *Recommended*

Hearts of the World
(1918, B&W, 122m, NR)
Sentimental silent drama from director D.W. Griffith, made to persuade America to enter World War I. Robert Harron is the young man who goes off to fight; Lillian and Dorothy Gish costar. Erich Von Stroheim has a small role as a German soldier. **AC2, DT52, DT129, ST87, XT8**

Heat (1972, C, 100m, NR)
Andy Warhol–produced takeoff on *Sunset Boulevard*, with Joe Dallesandro and Sylvia Miles as the writer and faded star. Directed by Paul Morrissey. **CU2, CU12, DT90**

Heat (1987, C, 101m, R)
Burt Reynolds is a mystery man based in Vegas, protecting the innocent, teaching a neophyte gambler the ropes. Adapted by William Goldman from his novel. **ST157**

Heat and Dust (1983, C, 130m, NR)
Two-pronged story of a pair of English-women (Greta Scacchi and Julie Christie) who a century apart journey to India and fall in love with the country and one of its natives. From the filmmaking team of producer Ismail Merchant, director James Ivory, and writer Ruth Prawer Jhabvala who adapted her own novel. The Scacchi story works much better. **DR10, DR23, DR27, DT61, ST30**

Heat of Desire (1980, C, 90m, R)
A respectable professor is seduced by a free-spirited woman, and both his marriage and career are ruined. Patrick Dewaere, Clio Goldsmith, and Jeanne Moreau star. **FF1, ST161**

Heat Wave (1990, C, 100m. NR)
Drama centering on 1965 urban riots in the Watts neighborhood of Los Angeles. Cicely Tyson, Blair Underwood, and James Earl Jones star, with Sally Kirkland, David Strathairn, Robert Hooks, Adam Arkin, Charlie Korsmo, and Margaret Avery. Directed by Kevin Hooks. Originally made for cable TV. **DR6, DR14, DR15, ST118**

Heathers (1989, C, 102m, R)
Dark comedy starring Winona Ryder as a high school girl vying to be accepted into a clique of snotty princesses, until she meets a rebel student (Christian Slater). Murders trumped up to look like suicides are his specialty. Written by Daniel Waters; directed by Michael Lehmann. Sharp satire blunted only in the last scenes. **CO4, CO12, CO18, CU5, ST200,** *Recommended*

Heatwave (1983, C, 99m, R)
A radical activist leads a fight against a multi-million-dollar development which will destroy a neighborhood. Matters get complicated when she and the project architect fall in love. Australian drama starring Judy Davis. **FF5, MY16, ST46**

Heaven (1987, C, 80m, NR)
Diane Keaton directed this documentary about people's perceptions of heaven. Film alternates between clips of Hollywood movies on the subject and interviews. **CU16, ST121**

Heaven Can Wait (1943, C, 112m, NR)
Ernst Lubitsch directed this comedy classic of a man (Don Ameche) who recalls his wicked past as he awaits admission through the Pearly Gates. With Gene Tierney, Charles Coburn, Marjorie Main, and Laird Cregar as the Devil. **CL10, DT76, HO10, ST214, XT24,** *Recommended*

Heaven Can Wait (1978, C, 100m, PG)
Remake (and updating) of *Here Comes Mr. Jordan*, with Warren Beatty as a football player taken to heaven before his time and allowed to return to Earth. With Julie Christie, James Mason, Dyan Cannon, and Charles Grodin. Codirected by Beatty and screenwriter Buck Henry. Grodin and Cannon provide the real spark to this damp comedy. **CO20, CU18, ST10, ST30, ST94, ST153, XT24**

Heaven Help Us (1985, C, 104m, R)
A New York Catholic boys' school in the early 1960s is the setting for this wonderful coming of age comedy. Andrew McCarthy and Kevin Dillon are the students; Donald Sutherland, John Heard, and Wallace Shawn are in charge. **CO4, CO18**, *Recommended*

Heaven Is a Playground
(1991, C, 111m, R)
Drama set on the Chicago outdoor basketball courts, starring D.B. Sweeney as the only white boy in the games. With former roundball stars Michael Warren and Bo Kimble, Richard Jordan, Victor Love, and Janet Julian. **DR22, XT11**

Heavens Above (1963, B&W, 105m, NR)
A deeply devoted reverend wreaks havoc when he becomes a bishop on a nuclear missile base in outer space. Peter Sellers stars. **ST198**

Heaven's Gate (1980, C, 219m, R)
Western epic of a war between immigrant settlers and cattle barons in Johnson County, Wyoming. Kris Kristofferson, Christopher Walken, Isabelle Huppert, and Jeff Bridges star, with John Hurt, Sam Waterston, Brad Dourif, Joseph Cotten, Geoffrey Lewis, and in a small role, Mickey Rourke. Michael Cimino directed; photographed by Vilmos Zsigmond, with music by David Mansfield. Lovely to look at, impossible to follow. Should be seen once, to understand how a filmmaker can run away with a major production. (Also available in a 149 minute version, which makes even less sense.) **MU12, ST19, ST190, ST222, WE1**, *Essential*

Heavy Petting (1988, C, 80m, R)
Documentary look at sexual mores of the uptight 1950s uses period clips interspersed with interviews of celebrities (David Byrne, Ann Magnuson, Allen Ginsberg, Abbie Hoffman) about their sexual experiences. **CU16**

Hedda (1975, C, 104m, PG)
Glenda Jackson stars in a Royal Shakespeare Company production of Ibsen's *Hedda Gabler*. With Peter Eyre, Timothy West, and Jennie Linden. **DR20, DR23, ST117**

Heidi (1937, B&W, 88m, NR)
Shirley Temple stars as the little girl living in the Swiss Alps with her grandfather whose life turns upside down when she moves to the city to live with a wealthy invalid girl. **FA2, ST213**

Heir to Genghis Kahn, The see *Storm Over Asia*

Heiress, The (1949, B&W, 115m, NR)
The plain daughter of a wealthy doctor is threatened with disinheritance when she falls in love with a young social climber. Oscar winner Olivia de Havilland stars, with Ralph Richardson and Montgomery Clift. Superbly directed by William Wyler; based on the Henry James novel, *Washington Square*. Richardson should have won the Best Supporting Actor Oscar. **CL1, CL4, CL6, DT142, ST32, ST49, ST184, WR14, XT3**, *Recommended*

Hellfighters, The (1969, C, 121m, NR)
John Wayne leads a team of brave men who put out oil well fires. Jim Hutton and Katharine Ross costar. **ST224**

Hell in the Pacific (1968, C, 103m, G)
A Pacific island during World War II is the setting for this unusual and riveting survival drama, as a U.S. Marine (Lee Marvin) and Japanese officer (Toshiro Mifune) match wits. Directed by John Boorman. **AC1, AC24, DR27, DT15, ST151, ST157**, *Recommended*

Hell Is for Heroes
(1962, B&W, 90m, NR)
World War II action, with Steve McQueen excellent as a cynical loner whose outfit includes Bobby Darin, Fess Parker, Harry Guardino, Nick Adams, and Bob Newhart. Directed by Don Siegel. **AC1, DT116, MU12, ST146**, *Recommended*

Hell Night (1981, C, 101m, R)
Four girls pledging a sorority must spend the night in a haunted mansion supposedly occupied by the ghost of a killer. But as the night wears on, they're not sure he's really dead. **HO12**

Hell on Frisco Bay (1955, C, 98m, NR)
Gangster saga, set in contemporary San Francisco, with good guy Alan Ladd against baddie Edward G. Robinson. With Joanne Dru, William Demarest, Fay Wray, and Jayne Mansfield. **AC22, ST128, ST186**

Hell Up in Harlem (1973, C, 96m, R)
Sequel to *Black Caesar* stars Fred Williamson as a vengeance-seeking gangster. Directed by Larry Cohen. With Julius W. Harris, Gloria Hendry, and Margaret Avery. **AC22, DT28**

Hellbound: Hellraiser II
(1988, C, 93m, R)
The demons who haunted the couple in *Hellraiser* are back for more sport, this time with the couple's daughter (Ashley Laurence). Available in an unrated version with a 98 minute running time. **CU10, HO14, XT24**

Helldorado (1946, B&W, 54m, NR)
Roy Rogers and Dale Evans travel to Las Vegas for Nevada's Frontier Days. **ST188**

Heller in Pink Tights (1960, C, 100m, NR)
Sophia Loren travels the 1880s West with a theatrical troupe, entertaining in the face of Indian uprisings, bill collectors, and thieves. With Anthony Quinn, Steve Forrest, Eileen Heckart, Margaret O'Brien, and Ramon Novarro. Directed by George Cukor; based on a Louis L'Amour story. Underrated film features outstanding use of color. **CL9, DT32, ST141, WE8, WR13,** *Recommended*

Hello Again (1987, C, 96m, PG)
Comedy of housewife choking to death, raised from her grave by a witch-like sister after one year. Shelley Long stars, with Judith Ivey, Corbin Bernsen, Gabriel Byrne, and Sela Ward. **XT24**

Hello, Dolly! (1969, C, 146m, G)
In this screen version of the Broadway smash, Barbra Streisand plays Dolly Levi, a widowed matchmaker in old New York who finds herself attracted to a bachelor merchant (Walter Matthau). Directed by Gene Kelly. Musical remake of Thornton Wilder's *The Matchmaker*. **MU2, MU14, ST123, ST155, ST211**

Hellraiser (1987, C, 94m, R)
Clive Barker wrote and directed this harrowing tale about a man whose dead brother comes back to haunt him and his family. Two sequels: *Hellbound: Hellraiser II* and *Hellraiser III: Hell on Earth*. **HO14, XT24**

Hellraiser III: Hell on Earth
(1992, C, 92m, R)
Third chapter of horror series created by Clive Barker has new human characters but same villains, led by Pinhead. A TV newsman contacts PH through the ghost of a World War I soldier. Terry Farrell stars, with Doug Bradley as both Pinhead and the solider. **XT24, XT27**

Hell's Angels (1930, B&W/C, 127m, NR)
Saga of World War I fliers, two English brothers, one a straight arrow with a faithless girlfriend, the other a dissolute playboy. Ben Lyon, James Hall, and Jean Harlow star. Directed by Howard Hughes over several years (when filming began, it was to be a silent); James Whale, credited as dialogue director, reportedly wrote and directed much of the story. Spectacular aerial footage, including a nighttime attack on a German zeppelin, offset a pedestrian, awkwardly staged ground story—though Harlow's plunging necklines are a real attraction. One party sequence in early technicolor; some other sequences tinted. **AC2, AC11, DT138,** *Essential; Recommended*

Hell's Angels on Wheels
(1967, C, 95m, NR)
Low-budget nonsense about the infamous motorcycle gang. Jack Nicholson stars as a gas station attendant named Poet. **ST163**

Hell's House (1932, B&W, 72m, NR)
A young boy is sent to a reformatory after he takes the blame for a crime to protect someone else. Bette Davis appears in one of her first film roles. **ST44**

Hellstrom Chronicle, The
(1971, C, 90m, G)
Oscar-winning documentary which proposes that insects may take over the world from man by weight of sheer numbers. **CU16**

Help! (1965, C, 90m, NR)
In their second film, The Beatles dodge a crazy cult that's after a sacrificial ring that Ringo possesses. With Leo McKern, Eleanor Bron, Victor Spinetti, and Roy Kinnear. Richard Lester directed. Irresistible. **DT74, FA9, MU9,** *Highly Recommended*

Helter Skelter (1976, C, 194m, NR)
Chilling dramatization of the Charles Manson murders and the subsequent trials, based on prosecutor Vincent Bugliosi's book. Steve Railsback is a very creepy Manson. Originally made for TV. **DR6, DR16,** *Recommended*

Henry & June (1990, C, 134m, NC-17)
Drama of Henry Miller, his wife June, and writer Anaïs Nin forming an erotic triangle in Paris. Fred Ward, Uma Thurman, and Maria de Medeiros star, with Richard E. Grant and Kevin Spacey. Directed by Philip Kaufman, who cowrote with Rose Kaufman. **CU6, DR3, DR4, DT64**

Henry V (1945, C, 137m, NR)
Laurence Olivier produced, directed, and stars in this colorful adaptation of Shakespeare's classic. Olivier won a special Oscar for his achievement. One of the great Shakespeare films. **CL9, DR5, DR23, ST168, WR28,** *Essential, Recommended*

Henry V (1989, C, 138m, NR)
Kenneth Branagh stars as Shakespeare's dashing warrior monarch. He also directed a cast

that includes Derek Jacobi, Brian Blessed, Ian Holm, Emma Thompson, and Paul Scofield. Available in letterboxed format. Magnificently cinematic; Branagh should have won the Oscar for his direction. **CU19, DR5, DR23, WR28, XT23, XT28,** *Recommended*

Henry IV (1984, C, 95m, PG-13)
Marcello Mastroianni stars as a mad nobleman who believes he's Emperor Henry IV in this version of the Pirandello play, directed by Marco Bellocchio. Claudia Cardinale co-stars. **FF2, ST154**

Henry: Portrait of a Serial Killer
(1990, C, 83m, NR)
Violent, affecting crime drama stars Michael Rooker as a character whose exploits are loosely based on a real-life murderer. Directed by John McNaughton on locations in and around Chicago. Recommended only for those not easily disturbed by screen violence. **CU7, MY13, XT11,** *Recommended*

Her Alibi (1989, C, 110m, PG)
Comic mystery of a novelist (Tom Selleck) who's not sure if the lovely new woman in his life (Paulina Porizkova) is really guilty of murder. With William Daniels. Directed by Bruce Beresford. **DT10, MY11, MY17**

Herbie Goes Bananas (1980, C, 93m, G)
Herbie, the magical Volkswagen from *The Love Bug*, travels to South America to enter a car race. Fourth in the series from the Disney studios. **FA1**

Herbie Goes to Monte Carlo
(1977, C, 104m, G)
Herbie gets involved in a Monte Carlo race and his driver (Dean Jones) is unaware that a spy ring has a diamond hidden in the gas tank. Third in the Disney series. **FA1**

Herbie Rides Again (1974, C, 88m, G)
This sequel to *The Love Bug* casts Helen Hayes as a woman trying to thwart a villain who wants to get his hands on Herbie. **FA1**

Hercules (1959, C, 107m, NR)
Strongman Steve Reeves plays the mighty warrior in this adventure that set off a wave of sequels and imitators. **FF2**

Hercules Goes Bananas (1970, C, 75m, G)
Silly takeoff on muscleman movies features Arnold Schwarzenegger (billed as Arnold Strong, with his voice dubbed) hanging out in the Big Apple. With Arnold Stang, Tania Elg, and James Karen. Original running time: 91 minutes. Also known as *Hercules in New York*. Arnie's film debut; we'd guess it doesn't appear on his resume. **CO20, ST195**

Hercules in New York see *Hercules Goes Bananas*

Hercules in the Haunted World
(1961, C, 83m, NR)
The legendary strongman finds himself imprisoned in the devil's kingdom. Reg Park and Christopher Lee star. **ST135**

Herdsmen of the Sun (1990, C, 52m, NR)
Documentary from German filmmaker Werner Herzog, detailing the nomadic lives of the Woodabe tribe in the Sahara Desert. **CU16, DT54**

Here Come the Girls (1953, C, 78m, NR)
Bob Hope comedy has him playing an entertainer involved with an escaped killer. With Arlene Dahl, Rosemary Clooney, Tony Martin, Robert Strauss, and the Four Step Brothers. **ST108**

Here Come the Littles (1985, C, 72m, G)
Based on the children's books, this animated feature follows the adventures of the Littles, tiny people who live in the walls of people's houses. In this story, they get involved with a twelve-year-old boy. **FA10**

Here Comes Mr. Jordan
(1941, B&W, 93m, NR)
Classic comic fantasy of boxer taken to heaven before his time and returned to Earth in another man's body. Robert Montgomery, Claude Rains, Evelyn Keyes, and Edward Everett Horton star. Remade in 1978 as *Heaven Can Wait*. **CO20, SF2, XT24**

Here Comes the Groom
(1951, B&W, 113m, NR)
Bing Crosby musical has him playing odd man out at his old flame's wedding, trying to disrupt the proceedings. With Jane Wyman and Franchot Tone; musical appearances by Louis Armstrong and Phil Harris. Directed by Frank Capra. Oscar-winning Johnny Mercer song: "In the Cool, Cool, Cool of the Evening." **DT22, ST40, XT20**

Hero (1992, C, 116m, PG-13)
Satire of distorting effects of media spotlight stars Dustin Hoffman as a nebbish who anonymously helps rescue folks from a downed airplane. One, a TV news reporter (Geena Davis), launches a search for her savior and an imposter (Andy Garcia) steps forward. With Joan Cusack, Kevin J. O'Connor, Tom Arnold, and Chevy Chase. Written by David Webb Peoples, directed by Stephen Frears. **CO2, CO13, DT48, ST45, ST105**

Hero Ain't Nothin' but a Sandwich, A
(1978, C, 105m, PG)
Drama of young black boy lured into world

of drugs. Cicely Tyson, Paul Winfield, Larry B. Scott, and Glynn Turman star. **DR7, DR9, DR14, DR15, FA7, ST230**

Hero and the Terror (1988, C, 97m, R)
Chuck Norris plays a cop who puts away a superhuman killer, only to have the man escape, precipitating another manhunt led by you-know-who. **ST165**

Heroes (1977, C, 113m, PG)
A disturbed Vietnam vet (Henry Winkler) embarks on a cross-country trip and meets a confused young girl (Sally Field) along the way. With Harrison Ford. **ST66, ST74, XT18**

Heroes for Sale (1933, B&W, 73m, NR)
Melodrama of World War I veteran going through improbable series of hardships—drug addiction, failed business, homelessness—and remaining optimistic. Richard Barthelmess stars in this social problem drama, with Loretta Young, Aline MacMahon, and Robert Barrat. Screenplay by Wilson Mizner and Robert Lord; directed by William Wellman. Real time-capsule stuff that still has relevance, too. **CL8, DT135,** *Recommended*

Hester Street (1975, B&W, 92m, PG)
In turn-of-the-century New York, a young immigrant wife struggles to adapt to the ways of her new life. Carol Kane stars. Joan Micklin Silver directed. **DR5, DR15,** *Recommended*

Hexed (1993, C, 90m, R)
Comedy about nerd finding out his lovely one-night stand is really a crazed killer. Arye Gross and Claudia Christian star, with Adrienne Shelly and R. Lee Ermey. **CO10, MY19**

Hey Babu Riba (1986, C, 109m, NR)
Yugoslavian comedy centering on four men and their memories of youthful 1950s fascination with the same girl. Gala Videnovic plays the object of their desire. **FF7**

Hey There, It's Yogi Bear
(1964, C, 89m, G)
Yogi Bear and Boo Boo star in this animated musical feature about life in Jellystone Park. As spring and picnic basket season approach, the bears try to outsmart Ranger Smith. **FA10**

Hi, Mom! see *Confessions of a Peeping John*

Hidden, The (1987, C, 96m, R)
A police detective joins forces with an alien cop (in human form) to track a sinister force that possesses people and causes them to go berserk. Michael Nouri and Kyle MacLachlan

star in this science fiction/action thriller. **AC8, SF17**

Hidden Agenda (1990, C, 108m, R)
Drama, set in 1982 Belfast, of coverup of police involvement in murder of IRA sympathizer and an American lawyer. Brian Cox and Frances McDormand star, with Brad Dourif and Mai Zetterling. Directed by Ken Loach. **DR23, MY6**

Hidden Fortress, The
(1958, B&W, 139m, NR)
Japanese adventure starring Toshiro Mifune as the loyal companion to a spoiled princess making a dangerous journey with precious royal cargo. Directed by Akira Kurosawa. Video version is completely restored print. **CU10, DT69, ST157**

Hide in Plain Sight (1980, C, 98m, PG)
True story of man (James Caan, who directed) who frantically searches for his children after they disappear with his ex-wife. With Jill Eikenberry. Solid, without a memorable moment. **MY8, XT23**

Hideous Sun Demon, The
(1959, B&W, 74m, NR)
Low-budget science fiction yarn about scientist (Robert Clarke) exposed to radiation who turns into the title character in sunlight. Clarke also directed. **SF10**

Hide-Out (1934, B&W, 83m, NR)
Robert Montgomery plays a gangster on the lam at a farm, falling in love with you-know-who's daughter (Maureen O'Sullivan). With Edward Arnold, Elizabeth Patterson, and Mickey Rooney. **ST189**

High and Low (1962, B&W/C, 142m, NR)
Akira Kurosawa directed this suspenseful study of a businessman (Toshiro Mifune) whose chauffeur's son is mistakenly kidnapped; he agrees to pay the ransom anyway. Deliberately paced, but exceptionally exciting. Based on a story by Ed McBain. One key segment in color. Available in letterboxed format. **CU19, DT69, MY16, ST157,** *Recommended*

High Anxiety (1977, C, 94m, PG)
Mel Brooks spoof of Hitchcock films, about a psychiatrist (Brooks) who finds trouble behind every door when he becomes the head of a sanitarium. With Madeline Kahn, Harvey Korman, and Cloris Leachman. Watch for future director Barry Levinson as a bellhop. Labored, with some occasional laughs courtesy Kahn and Leachman. **CO7, DT17, DT75**

High Bright Sun, The see *McGuire, Go Home!*

High Command, The
(1937, B&W, 90m, NR)
British crime drama set at an African outpost, with an army officer involved in blackmail and murder. Lionel Atwill stars, with Lucie Mannheim, Steven Geray, and a young James Mason. **ST153**

High Heels (1972, C, 100m, NR)
Jean-Paul Belmondo stars in this French comedy-mystery about a doctor who marries an unattractive woman and falls in love with her sister. Directed by Claude Chabrol. With Mia Farrow and Laura Antonelli. **FF1, ST11, ST65**

High Hopes (1988, C, 110m, NR)
British comedy-drama of life in Thatcher's world, with Ruth Sheen and Philip Davis as a working-class couple trying to make ends meet and sense of their zany family. Written and directed by Mike Leigh. **CO2, CO17,** *Recommended*

High Noon (1952, B&W, 85m, NR)
Gary Cooper's performance as the honorable sheriff who faces a showdown with outlaws on his wedding day won him an Oscar. With Grace Kelly, Lon Chaney, Jr., Thomas Mitchell, Katy Jurado, Lloyd Bridges, and Lee Van Cleef. Directed by Fred Zinnemann. Still important to see, but hasn't worn its classic mantle well. **DR26, DT144, ST27, ST37, ST124, ST221, WE2, XT2,** *Essential*

High Noon, Part II: The Return of Will Kane (1980, C, 100m, NR)
Lee Majors plays a retired marshal who takes the law into his hands when he returns to find a corrupt sheriff in his town. **WE2**

High Plains Drifter (1973, C, 105m, R)
Clint Eastwood directed this spooky, violent Western tale about a mysterious character (Eastwood) in a strange frontier town. A must for Clint fans and lovers of the offbeat. **ST64, WE5,** *Recommended*

High Road to China (1983, C, 120m, PG)
A soldier of fortune agrees to fly a spoiled young woman on a rescue mission to help her father out of China. Tom Selleck and Bess Armstrong star. **AC11, AC14, AC21**

High Rolling (1977, C, 88m, PG)
Australian drama of two unemployed carnival workers and their encounter with a drug runner. Joseph Bottoms, Grigor Taylor and Judy Davis star. **FF5, ST46**

High School Confidential!
(1958, B&W, 85m, NR)
Camp cult classic which opens with Jerry Lee Lewis singing the title tune (on the back of a flatbed truck) and goes downhill from there. Story has Russ Tamblyn as an undercover agent investigating widespread marijuana use by teens. Also in the cast: Mamie Van Doren, Jackie Coogan, Charlie Chaplin, Jr., and Michael Landon. **CU2, DR25**

High Sierra (1941, B&W, 100m, NR)
Humphrey Bogart plays a gangster running from the police, with the help of his girlfriend (Ida Lupino). Cowritten by John Huston; Raoul Walsh directed. One of the roles that helped define Bogart's screen persona. **AC22, DT131, MY1, ST15,** *Essential, Recommended*

High Society (1956, C, 107m, NR)
In this musical remake of *The Philadelphia Story*, Grace Kelly is a wealthy socialite trying to avoid nosy reporters (Frank Sinatra and Celeste Holm) and her ex-husband (Bing Crosby) on the eve of her wedding. Louis Armstrong appears as himself. Perfect casting, terrific music. **MU1, MU14, ST40, ST124, ST199, XT20,** *Recommended*

High Spirits (1988, C, 99m, PG-13)
Peter O'Toole plays an impoverished nobleman who claims his castle is haunted, to attract American tourists Steven Guttenberg and Beverly D'Angelo for a paying visit. Daryl Hannah costars as a real live ghost in this comedy. **CO11, ST169, XT24**

High Tide (1987, C, 120m, PG-13)
Australian drama of a woman (Judy Davis) whose aimless life on the road with musical groups is changed when she's reunited with the daughter she abandoned many years ago. Superbly subtle direction by Gillian Armstrong. **DR9, DR10, DT7, FF5, ST46,** *Recommended*

High Velocity (1977, C, 105m, PG)
A band of Vietnam vets rescue a kidnapped executive. Ben Gazzara stars, with Paul Winfield, Britt Ekland, and Keenan Wynn. **AC20, ST230**

High Voltage (1929, B&W, 57m, NR)
A bus is stranded in a mountain snowstorm and its passengers seek help from a lineman, who is in reality a fugitive from justice. William Boyd, Owen Moore, and Carole (billed as "Carol") Lombard star. **ST140**

Higher and Higher (1943, B&W, 90m, NR)
Frank Sinatra made his starring debut in this musical about a down-on-his-luck gentleman who conspires with his servants to raise money. **ST199**

Highlander (1986, C, 111m, R)
Adventure tale of an ancient Scottish warrior who pursues his arch-rival to contemporary

Manhattan. Christopher Lambert stars, with Sean Connery. Music by Queen. **SF4, ST36, XT9**

Highlander II: The Quickening
(1991, C, 96m, R)
Christopher Lambert and Sean Connery return for more time-traveling adventures, as a villain tries to thin the ozone layer. With Michael Ironside and Virginia Madsen. **SF4, ST36**

Highpoint (1980, C, 88m, PG)
An innocent man gets involved in a murder after he begins working for a wealthy family in this comedy/thriller. Richard Harris, Christopher Plummer, and Beverly D'Angelo star. **MY9**

Highway to Hell (1992, C, 93m, R)
Horror comedy about an eloping young couple who take the wrong road and wind up confronting a highway cop who's really from hell. He kidnaps the girl, and the guy has twenty-four hours to free her. Chad Lowe and Kristy Swanson star, with Patrick Bergin as Beezle (aka the Devil), Adam Storke, Pamela Gidley, Richard Farnsworth, and Gilbert Gottfried as Adolf Hitler. **HF12, HO10, HO24, XT18**

Hillbillys in a Haunted House
(1967, C, 88m, NR)
A group of country singers get stranded at a haunted house during a storm in this comic horror story. Lon Chaney, Jr., and Basil Rathbone star. **HO24, ST27**

Hills Have Eyes, The (1977, C, 89m, R)
Horror film about family whose car breaks down in the desert; they are attacked by crazed "family" of mutants. Wes Craven directed this cult film. **CU4, HO14**

Hills of Utah, The (1951, B&W, 70m, NR)
Gene Autry uncovers the truth about his father's death when he visits his hometown. **ST5**

Himatsuri (1984, C, 120m, NR)
Japanese drama of a man who renounces modern ways for Shinto way of life, winds up killing his family and himself. **FF4**

Hindenburg, The (1975, C, 125m, PG)
Drama centering on the disastrous crash in 1937 of the famed German dirigible, starring George C. Scott, Anne Bancroft, William Atherton, Charles Durning, and Burgess Meredith. Directed by Robert Wise. **AC16, AC23, DT140, ST196**

Hired Hand, The (1971, C, 93m, PG)
Peter Fonda directed this Western drama set in 1880s New Mexico. He plays a cowhand

who returns to work for the woman he abandoned years earlier. Warren Oates costars. **ST166, WE15, XT23**

Hiroshima, Mon Amour
(1960, B&W, 88m, NR)
Groundbreaking drama about an affair between French woman and Japanese man, with echoes of atomic bomb catastrophe lurking in the background. French-language film directed by Alain Resnais has influenced many others for its artful editing. **FF1,** *Essential*

His Double Life (1933, B&W, 67m, NR)
When a famous but retiring artist is thought dead, he happily accepts oblivion to marry a spinster. Roland Young and Lillian Gish star. **ST71**

His Girl Friday (1940, B&W, 92m, NR)
Cary Grant is a newspaper editor whose star reporter, also his ex-wife (Rosalind Russell), is planning to remarry. Ralph Bellamy costars in this breakneck comedy based on the play *The Front Page*. Written by Ben Hecht and Charles Lederer; Howard Hawks directed. My nominee for the funniest movie ever made. **CL10, DT53, ST92, ST192,** *Essential, Highly Recommended*

His Kind of Woman
(1951, B&W, 120m, NR)
Robert Mitchum plays a fall guy for a criminal (Raymond Burr) who wants to reenter the country from Mexico. With Jane Russell and Vincent Price. **MY1, ST158, ST179**

His Majesty O'Keefe (1953, C, 92m, NR)
Swashbuckler set in the South Seas, featuring Burt Lancaster as a daring buccaneer. With Joan Rice, Benson Fong, and Philip Ahn. **AC15, ST129**

History Is Made at Night
(1937, B&W, 97m, NR)
Jean Arthur stars in a drama of a woman fleeing her jealous husband, falling in love with a Parisian waiter (Charles Boyer). **CL4, ST3, ST16**

History of the World—Part I
(1981, C, 92m, R)
Mel Brooks's revisionist view of human history, starting with prehistoric times. Brooks stars, with Gregory Hines, Dom DeLuise, Madeline Kahn, Harvey Korman, Sid Caesar, Paul Mazursky, and John Hurt as Jesus Christ. Caesar's good in the opening sketch, but it's mostly downhill from there. **CO6, DT17, DT87, HF16**

Hit, The (1984, C, 98m, R)
Comedy-drama of crime informer (Terence Stamp) being transported by a pair of hit

men to his doom. With John Hurt, Tim Roth, and Laura Del Sol. Directed by Stephen Frears. Music by Roger Waters and Eric Clapton. Has cult following; I'm not a member. **DT48, XT18**

Hit and Run (1982, C, 93m, NR)
A cabdriver's involvement with a mysterious woman leads to murder. **MY7**

Hit List (1989, C, 87m, R)
Jan-Michael Vincent and Rip Torn star in this action drama of an innocent man whose best friend and son are victimized by a Mob hit man. **ST216**

Hit the Deck (1955, C, 112m, NR)
MGM musical of fun-loving sailors on shore leave, starring Jane Powell, Tony Martin, Debbie Reynolds, Ann Miller, and Vic Damone. Final musical number is presented in letterboxed format. **CU19, MU1**

Hit the Ice (1943, B&W, 82m, NR)
Abbott and Costello are newspaper photographers who get involved with a gangster and his minions at the winter resort of Sun Valley. **ST1**

Hitcher, The (1986, C, 97m, R)
Horror tale of lone driver picking up man who turns out to be homicidal maniac; he keeps reappearing, even after it appears he's been killed. C. Thomas Howell is the victim, Rutger Hauer the madman. With Jennifer Jason Leigh. **HO9, ST136**

Hitch-Hiker, The (1953, B&W, 71m, NR)
Film noir tale of hitcher who abducts a pair of fishermen on his way to Mexico. William Talman, Edmond O'Brien, and Frank Lovejoy star. Directed by Ida Lupino. **MY1, XT23**

Hitler (1962, B&W, 107m, NR)
Film portrait of the Nazi dictator, starring Richard Basehart. **DR4, HF12**

Hitler—Dead or Alive
(1943, B&W, 70m, NR)
Low-budget wartime thriller about con men trying to assassinate Hitler. Ward Bond stars, with Bobby Watson as Der Führer. **HF12**

Hitler: The Last Ten Days
(1973, C, 108m, PG)
Alec Guinness stars in this re-creation of the dying days of the Third Reich. **HF12, ST95**

Hitman, The (1991, C, 95m, R)
Cop stuff with Chuck Norris as an undercover man working to united Italian and French mobs in Seattle for big job. With Michael Parks, Al Waxman, and Albert Watson. **AC9, ST165**

Hobbit, The (1978, C, 78m, NR)
Based on the J.R.R. Tolkien fantasy novel, this animated feature deals with a magical hobbit named Bilbo Baggins. **FA8, FA10, SF13**

Hobson's Choice (1954, B&W, 107m, NR)
A bootshop owner (Charles Laughton) in 1890s Britain decides whom his daughters shall marry, despite their objections. Directed by David Lean. **CO17, DT71, ST132**

Hobson's Choice (1983, C, 100m, NR)
TV movie remake of the classic comedy about a shopowner's attempts to control his daughters' lives. Richard Thomas, Sharon Gless, Jack Warden, and Lillian Gish star. **CU18, ST87**

Hoffa (1992, C, 140m, R)
Jack Nicholson plays the controversial Teamsters president in this portrait that follows him from his early organizing days to his disappearance (the filmmakers suggest a solution). With Danny DeVito, Armand Assante, J.T. Walsh as Frank Fitzsimmons, John C. Reilly, Frank Whaley, Kevin Anderson as Robert Kennedy, and Natalija Nogulich. Written by David Mamet, directed by DeVito. Widescreen will be lost without letterboxing. Maddeningly unspecific about dates, key details; pluses are Nicholson's persuasive performance and clever story-framing device that leads to terrific ending. Certainly worth seeing for anyone with an interest in the subject. **DR4, DR24, ST54, ST163**

Holcroft Covenant, The
(1985, C, 112m, R)
A former henchman for Hitler leaves his son (Michael Caine) a fortune intended to make amends for Nazi atrocities. Thriller based on the bestseller by Robert Ludlum. **MY6, ST25, WR21**

Hold That Ghost (1941, B&W, 86m, NR)
Abbott and Costello are bumbling gas station attendants who inherit a gangster's mysterious mansion. **ST1**

Hold the Dream (1986, C, 200m, NR)
Sequel to *A Woman of Substance* continues story of wealthy businesswoman (Deborah Kerr), now turning over her empire to granddaughter (Jenny Seagrove). With Stephen Collins, John Mills, Claire Bloom, and James Brolin. Originally made for TV. **DR10, ST125**

Hold Your Man (1933, B&W, 86m, NR)
Comedy-drama starring Jean Harlow as a young woman who falls for a jailbird (Clark Gable). With Stuart Erwin and Elizabeth Patterson. **ST77, ST98**

Hole in the Head, A (1959, C, 120m, NR)
Drama of relationship between a Miami
ne'er-do-well (Frank Sinatra) and his ador-
ing son (Eddie Hodges). With Edward G.
Robinson, Eleanor Parker, and Thelma Ritter.
Directed by Frank Capra; features the Oscar-
winning song, "High Hopes." **DT22, ST186,
ST199**

Holiday (1938, B&W, 93m, NR)
Bright, amusing comedy about a nonconformist (Cary Grant) who becomes engaged
to the daughter of a high society family, then
falls for her sister (Katharine Hepburn). Directed by George Cukor. **CL10, DT32, ST92,
ST103,** *Essential, Recommended*

Holiday Affair (1949, B&W, 87m, NR)
Christmas story of young widow (Janet
Leigh), her sons, and two suitors (Robert Mit-
chum and Wendell Corey). **FA13, ST158**

Holiday in Mexico (1946, C, 127m, NLR)
MGM musical comedy about diplomat's
daughter smitten by famous musician. Walter
Pidgeon and Ilona Massey star, with Roddy
McDowall, José Iturbi, Xavier Cugat, and
Jane Powell. **MU1**

Holiday Inn (1942, B&W, 101m, NR)
Bing Crosby breaks with show-biz partner
and rival Fred Astaire to run a Connecticut
inn which only opens on holidays. This film
introduced the Irving Berlin songs "White
Christmas" and "Easter Parade." **MU4, MU6,
ST4, ST40**

Hollywood Boulevard (1976, C, 83m, R)
Determinedly low-budget, intentionally
sleazy comedy about a young girl trying to
"make it" in movies, with dozens of inside
gags, especially about filmmaking for producer Roger Corman. Candice Rialson stars,
with Mary Woronov, Rita George, Dick Miller, and Paul Bartel. Joe Dante and Allan
Arkush directed. **CO8, CU5, CU14, DT6,
DT8, DT33**

Hollywood Canteen
(1944, B&W, 124m, NR)
Story of World War II home front romance is
just an excuse to visit Los Angeles, favorite
hangout for G.I.s, founded by Bette Davis
and John Garfield. Guest spots by, among
others, Joan Crawford, Barbara Stanwyck,
Olivia de Havilland, Peter Lorre and Sydney
Greenstreet, Jack Benny, Roy Rogers, and
Jane Wyman. **CL7, ST39, ST44, ST49,
ST80, ST188, ST206**

Hollywood or Bust (1956, C, 95m, NR)
Jerry Lewis plays a zealous movie fan who
wins a car in a raffle and travels to Hollywood with a gambler (Dean Martin) to meet

his idol, Anita Ekberg. Martin and Lewis's last
film. **CL15, CO8, FA6, ST139, ST149, XT18**

Hollywood Shuffle (1987, C, 82m, R)
Comic saga of a young black actor (Robert
Townsend) and his attempts to make an impression in Hollywood. Spoofs various genres
of black exploitation filmmaking and racial
stereotypes on the screen. Townsend directed
and cowrote. **CO8**

Hollywood Vice Squad (1986, C, 100m, R)
Episodic action thriller set on the mean
streets of Hollywood, starring Ronny Cox,
Carrie Fisher, Frank Gorshin, and Leon Isaac
Kennedy. **AC9**

Holocaust (1978, C, 450m, NR)
Meryl Streep, Fritz Weaver, and Michael Mor-
iarty star in this gripping account of the
Nazis' efforts to exterminate all European
Jews, and the effects on one family. With
James Woods. Originally made for TV. Grip-
ping drama with outstanding performances.
DR5, ST210, ST233, *Recommended*

**Holocaust Survivors . . . Remembrance
of Love** (1982, C, 100m, NR)
Widower meets woman he had affair with in
the Warsaw Ghetto forty years before. Kirk
Douglas stars, with Pam Dawber and Chana
Eden. Also known as *Remembrance of Love.*
ST57

Holocaust 2000 see *Chosen, The* (1978)

Holy Innocents (1984, C, 108m, NR)
Spanish drama of rural peasants in revolt
against wealthy landowners. Alfredo Landa
and Francisco Rabal star. **FF7**

Hombre (1967, C, 111m, NR)
A white man (Paul Newman) raised by
Indians is the victim of prejudice in frontier
Arizona. With Fredric March, Richard Boone,
Martin Balsam, and Diane Cilento. Based on
a story by Elmore Leonard; directed by Mar-
tin Ritt. Good cast but only middling results;
Newman gives an opaque performance.
DT105, ST149, ST162, WE7, WR19

Home Alone (1990, C, 102m, PG-13)
Hit comedy of resourceful little boy acciden-
tally left home when his family takes off for
Paris at Christmas. Macaulay Culkin stars,
with Joe Pesci and Daniel Stern as bungling
would-be burglars. With Catherine O'Hara,
John Heard, Roberts Blossom, and John
Candy in a small role. Produced by John
Hughes. It wouldn't be Scrooge-ish to suggest
that a little of the slapstick humor goes over-
board. **CO4, CO14, DT59, FA6, FA13,
FA15, ST172**

Home Alone 2: Lost in New York
(1992, C, 120m, PG)
Inevitable sequel to popular comedy repeats formula of kid stranded by family on holiday trip. The twist here is he's not really home but in the Big Apple—and pursued by those zany crooks from the first story. Macaulay Culkin stars, with Joe Pesci and Daniel Stern, plus John Heard, Catherine O'Hara, Tim Curry, Brenda Fricker, and Eddie Bracken. Produced and written by John Hughes, directed by Chris Columbus. **CO4, CO14, DT59, FA6, FA15, ST172, XT9**

Home and the World, The
(1984, C, 130m, NR)
From Indian director Satyajit Ray, a drama about a woman caught up in the political turmoil that swept her country in the first decade of the twentieth century. **DT102**

Home for the Holidays
(1972, C, 74m, NR)
An elderly man, threatened by a killer, is protected by his four daughters. Eleanor Parker, Sally Field, Jessica Walter, Julie Harris, Jill Haworth, and Walter Brennan star. Originally made for TV. **DR8, ST66**

Home from the Hill (1960, C, 150m, NR)
Melodrama of Texas patriarch (Robert Mitchum) and his two competing sons (George Peppard and George Hamilton). With Eleanor Parker. Directed by Vincente Minnelli. **DR8, DT88, ST158**

Home in Oklahoma
(1947, B&W, 54m, NR)
Roy Rogers plays a newspaper editor, Dale Evans a reporter; they're investigating a shifty rancher. **ST188**

Home Is Where the Heart Is see *Square Dance*

Home Movies (1979, C, 90m, PG)
An egotistical film director (Kirk Douglas) gives the star treatment to a nerd, who then decides to pursue his brother's girlfriend. Comedy about show-biz life directed by Brian De Palma. **CO8, DT36, ST57, XT31**

Home of the Brave (1949, B&W, 85m, NR)
A black G.I. is abused by his fellow soldiers during World War II in this classic drama about the effects of racism. James Edwards stars, with Jeff Corey and Lloyd Bridges. **AC1, CL8,** *Essential*

Home Sweet Home (1914, B&W, 62m, NR)
D.W. Griffith directed this silent drama inspired by the work of poet and composer John Howard Payne. Dorothy and Lillian Gish star. **DT52, ST87, XT8**

Home To Stay (1978, C, 74m, NR)
A young girl runs away from home with her elderly grandfather (Henry Fonda) to avoid her family sending him to a nursing home. Originally made for TV. **DR11, ST71**

Homeboy (1989, C, 112m, R)
Boxing saga set in Miami, starring Mickey Rourke as the determined young fighter. With Christopher Walken and Rubén Blades. **DR22, MU12, ST190, ST222**

Homer and Eddie (1990, C, 99m, R)
Jim Belushi and Whoopi Goldberg are an unlikely road couple: he's a mentally retarded dishwasher, and she's a homicidal cancer patient. **CO13, ST89, XT18**

Hometown Story (1951, B&W, 61m, NR)
Low-budget drama of political feud in small town, notable for early screen appearance by Marilyn Monroe. Jeffrey Lynn and Donald Crisp star. **DR21, ST159**

Homeward Bound: The Incredible Journey (1993, C, 84m, G)
Remake of 1963 Disney tale of two dogs and cat setting off across wilderness to be reunited with their family owners. This one provides voiceovers for the animals by Don Ameche, Michael J. Fox, and Sally Field. **FA1, FA5, ST66**

Homicide (1991, C, 100m, R)
Writer-director David Mamet's hard-bitten drama of a Jewish cop (Joe Mantegna) under tremendous pressure to solve murder of Jewish shopkeeper, dealing with racial tensions in city. With William H. Macy, Natalija Nogulich, and Ving Rhames. Shot in Baltimore. Muffled dramatics, with Mantegna's character unclear on motivation. Fans of Mamet should see it. **AC9, DR7, DR15**

Honey, I Blew Up the Kid
(1992, C, 89m, PG)
Second comic adventure of fumblebrained inventor (Rick Moranis) who previously miniaturized his offspring has him accidentally enlarging his two-year-old. The toddler proceeds to go on a rampage in, among other places, Las Vegas. With Marcia Strassman, Robert Oliveri, Lloyd Bridges, and John Shea. **CO5, CO11, CO14, FA6**

Honey, I Shrunk the Kids
(1989, C, 86m, PG)
A nerdy scientist accidentally trains his miniaturization invention on his own children. Special effects comedy stars Rick Moranis and Matt Frewer. The video version includes a Roger Rabbit cartoon, *Tummy Trouble.* **CO5, CO11, CO14, FA6, FA15**

Honey Pot, The (1967, C, 131m, NR)
Writer-director Joseph L. Mankiewicz updates
Ben Jonson's *Volpone*, the story of a wealthy
rogue who pretends to be dying to see which
of his women will try hardest to curry favor
with him. Rex Harrison stars, with Susan
Hayward, Cliff Robertson, Capucine, Edie
Adams, and Maggie Smith. **DT84, ST100**

Honeymoon (1985, C, 98m, R)
A French woman visiting New York marries a
man in order to stay in America, only to find
that he's a psychotic killer. Nathalie Baye and
John Shea star. **HO9, MY3**

Honeymoon in Vegas
(1992, C, 95m, PG13)
Comedy, set during title event, of young
hubby who goes into debt to ruthless gambler, who in turn promises to erase losses if
he can spend a weekend with the new wife.
Nicolas Cage, James Caan, and Sarah Jessica
Parker star, with Anne Bancroft, Pat Morita,
Peter Boyle, and Burton Gillian. Set amid a
convention of Elvis impersonators. Written
and directed by Andrew Bergman. Fitfully
amusing. **CO1, ST23**

Honeymoon Killers, The
(1970, B&W, 108m, R)
Cult melodrama, based on fact, about a
nurse and her lover posing as brother and
sister to lure lonely, rich women to their
deaths. Shirley Stoler and Tony LoBianco
star. Leonard Kastle directed, his only credit
behind the camera and a pretty impressive
one at that. **CU15, DR16, MY8,**
Recommended

Honeymoon Machine, The
(1961, C, 87m, NR)
Steve McQueen plays a sailor who devises a
system to beat the roulette tables in Venice.
Comedy also stars Jim Hutton and Paula
Prentiss, with Dean Jagger and Jack Weston.
ST146

Honeysuckle Rose (1980, C, 119m, PG)
Willie Nelson plays a country singer who
romances one of his back-up singers, much
to his wife's dismay. With Amy Irving, Dyan
Cannon, and Slim Pickens. Willie sings "On
the Road Again" and many of his hits. **DR12**

Honky Tonk (1941, B&W, 105m, NR)
Western starring Clark Gable as a gambler,
Lana Turner as the lady in his life. With
Frank Morgan and Chill Wills. **ST77, ST219,
WE8**

Honky Tonk Freeway (1981, C, 107m, R)
Comic free-for-all of the effect on a small
Florida town split by a highway overpass.
The ensemble cast includes William Devane,

Beverly D'Angelo, Hume Cronyn, Jessica
Tandy, Beau Bridges, and Geraldine Page.
Directed by John Schlesinger. Painfully
unfunny, given the talent involved. **CO2,
DT113**

Honkytonk Man (1982, C, 122m, PG)
Clint Eastwood stars in this drama set in the
Depression about a broken-down country
singer who won't get off the road. Eastwood's
son Kyle plays his son on screen. **DR12,
MU17, ST64, XT8**

Honolulu (1939, B&W, 83m, NR)
MGM musical stars Eleanor Powell in familiar identity-switch tale, this time between
film star and plantation owner. With Robert
Young, George Burns, and Gracie Allen. **MU1**

Honor Among Thieves (1968, C, 115m, R)
Charles Bronson and Alain Delon star in this
action drama of French mercenaries in Marseilles with a big heist in their plans. Also
known as *Farewell, Friend*. **MY18, ST20**

Hook (1991, C, 144m, PG)
Director Steven Spielberg's new version of the
Peter Pan story, with Peter (Robin Williams) a
corporate attorney whose children are kidnapped by his archenemy (Dustin Hoffman).
With Julia Roberts as Tinkerbell, Bob Hoskins
as Smee, Maggie Smith as Granny Wendy,
and Caroline Goodall and Charlie Korsmo as
Peter's kids. Phil Collins and David Crosby
have small roles; watch for Glenn Close in
disguise as a pirate. Overlong, overproduced.
Obviously a personal film for the director but
he's incapable of subtly or gently presenting
the message. **DT118, FA4, FA15, MU12,
ST33, ST105, ST228**

Hooper (1978, C, 100m, PG)
Burt Reynolds portrays an aging Hollywood
stuntman who is challenged by a young
maverick to perform a dangerous stunt. Sally
Field and Jan-Michael Vincent costar. Some
thrilling moments, a few laughs. **CO8, ST66,
ST183**

Hoosiers (1986, C, 114m, PG)
Moving drama about a middle-aged man
(Gene Hackman) who accepts a job coaching
basketball in smalltown Indiana in the 1950s.
He meets opposition from the townspeople
for his methods, until the school begins win-
ning. With Barbara Hershey and Dennis
Hopper. Based on a true story. All three leads
are sensational. **DR22, DR26, ST96, ST104,
ST110,** *Recommended*

Hope and Glory (1987, C, 113m, PG-13)
A young boy suddenly becomes the man of
the house when his father goes off to war.
John Boorman wrote, produced, and directed

this nostalgic, comic view of Britain during World War II. Sebastian Rice-Edwards and Sarah Miles star, with David Hayman, Sammi Davis, Ian Bannen, and Charley Boorman. **CO4, CO5, CO6, CO17, DT15,** *Highly Recommended*

Hopscotch (1980, C, 104m, R)
A CIA man who's been phased out of The Company decides to get revenge on his boss by publishing his memoirs. Walter Matthau stars in this comedy, with Glenda Jackson, Sam Waterston, and Ned Beatty. **CO10, ST117, ST155**

Horizons West (1952, C, 81m, NR)
Western drama of brothers on opposing side of the law. Robert Ryan and Rock Hudson star, with Julia (Julie) Adams, Raymond Burr, James Arness, and Dennis Weaver. Directed by Budd Boetticher. **DT14, ST112, ST193**

Horn Blows at Midnight, The
(1945, B&W, 78m, NR)
Comic fantasy starring Jack Benny as an angel assigned to destroy Earth with a blast from his horn. With Alexis Smith, Dolores Moran, Allyn Joslyn, Margaret Dumont, Franklin Pangborn, and Bobby (Robert) Blake. Directed by Raoul Walsh. Not the stinker that Benny claimed for years afterward. **CL10, CU5, DT131, XT24**

Horror Castle (1963, C, 83m, NR)
Victim of World War II runs castle of horrors in Germany. Christopher Lee stars, with Rossana Podesta and George Riviere. Made in Italy. Also known as *Terror Castle*. **ST135**

Horror Express (1972, C, 88m, NR)
A frozen monster thaws out and comes to life on train traveling through Asia, while two anthropologists (Peter Cushing, Christopher Lee) lock horns. **HO8, ST43, ST135, XT19**

Horror Hotel (1960, B&W, 76m, NR)
The spirit of a witch burned at the stake in the seventeenth century lives at a Massachusetts inn. Several young people who stay there become human sacrifices to the Devil. Christopher Lee stars. **HO10, ST135**

Horror of Dracula (1958, C, 82m, NR)
This British film from the famed Hammer studios features Christopher Lee as the cursed count. Peter Cushing costars as Professor Van Helsing. **HF7, HO1, HO5, HO26, ST43, ST135**

Horror of Frankenstein, The
(1970, C, 95m, R)
A self-destructive doctor does away with his father, best friend, and wife while creating a

monster. This British version of the classic horror tale is strictly tongue-in-cheek. **HF10, HO26**

Horse Feathers (1932, B&W, 67m, NR)
The Marx Brothers matriculate at Huxley College, and campus life will never be the same again. Thelma Todd costars. Highlights: the speakeasy "password" scene and the football game. **CO18, ST152,** *Recommended*

Horse in the Gray Flannel Suit, The
(1968, C, 113m, G)
An advertising executive (Dean Jones) designs a campaign to take advantage of his daughter's love for horses. Disney comedy with Diane Baker and Kurt Russell. **FA1, ST191**

Horse Soldiers, The (1959, C, 119m, NR)
Set during the Civil War, this Western drama stars John Wayne as a soldier who leads his cavalry troops into Confederate territory. Directed by John Ford. William Holden costars. **DT44, ST106, ST224, WE4, WE6**

Horse's Mouth, The (1958, C, 93m, NR)
Alec Guinness plays an iconoclastic British painter who doesn't need a canvas to work on. Guinness also adapted the Joyce Cary novel. **CO17, DR19, ST95**

Hospital, The (1971, C, 103m, PG)
This offbeat comedy casts George C. Scott as a disillusioned doctor who gets involved with a nutty woman (Diana Rigg) and her father amid the sloppy workings of an inner-city hospital. Written by Paddy Chayevsky, directed by Arthur Hiller. Scott's terrific but the film overplays its hand. **CO12, ST196**

Hostage Tower, The (1980, C, 105m, NR)
Thriller about a psycho who takes over the Eiffel Tower, holding the U.S. President's mother hostage. Written by Alistair MacLean. Peter Fonda and Billy Dee Williams star, with Keir Dullea, Douglas Fairbanks, Jr., and Rachel Roberts. **MY16, ST227**

Hot Lead and Cold Feet (1978, C, 90m, G)
Disney Western features a ranching patriarch and his two sons, a gunfighter and his timid twin, all played by Jim Dale. **FA1**

Hot Line (1969, C, 92m, PG)
Political thriller of what happens when secret agents foul up communications between Washington and Moscow. Robert Taylor stars (his last film), with Charles Boyer and George Chakiris. Also known as *The Day the Hot Line Got Hot*. **MY6, ST16**

Hot Pepper (1980, C, 54m, NR)
Documentary portrait of Louisiana's great zydeco accordion player, Clifton Chenier.

Directed by Les Blank and Maureen Gosling. **CU16**

Hot Rock, The
(1972, C, 105m, PG)
A group of thieves blunder their way through a jewel heist. Robert Redford and George Segal star. Based on Donald Westlake's novel. Modest rewards. **AC9, CO10, MY18, ST181**

Hot Shot (1986, C, 94m, PG)
Rich American boy runs off to Brazil to meet his idol, soccer superstar Pelé (playing himself). Jim Youngs stars in this family drama. **DR22, FA7**

Hot Shots! (1991, C, 85m, PG-13)
Spoof of glamorous flyboy movies stars Charlie Sheen, Cary Elwes, and Valeria Golino, with Lloyd Bridges, Kevin Dunn, Jon Cryer, and Efrem Zimbalist, Jr. **AC11, CO7, CO21**

Hot Spell (1958, B&W, 86m, NR)
Anthony Quinn stars as an unfaithful husband whose breakup with his nagging wife (Shirley Booth) has a strong impact on their recently jilted daughter (Shirley MacLaine). **DR8, ST145**

Hot Spot, The (1990, C, 130m, R)
Small-town shenanigans, with car salesman (Don Johnson) hooking up with voracious, murderous wife (Virginia Madsen) of his boss, while eying the young company secretary (Jennifer Connelly). With Charles Martin Smith, William Sadler, Jack Nance, and Jerry Hardin. Directed by Dennis Hopper. Good score of blues music. Sexy but just too long and drawn-out to have maximum impact. Still, fans of the genre will want a look. **DR3, MY2, MY4, MY5, ST110**

Hot Tomorrows (1977, B&W, 73m, NR)
One-of-a-kind film takes place in one night in Los Angeles. The main character is obsessed with death, and he embarks on an odyssey in which he meets a number of characters for whom the word "weird" seems inadequate. Ken Lerner stars, with Ray Sharkey, Herve Villechaize, Victor Argo, George Memmoli, and the voice of Orson Welles. Director Martin Brest made this, his feature debut, for the American Film Institute, and exhibition rights are tied up. UNAVAILABLE ON VIDEO. **XT29**

Hotel (1967, C, 124m, NLR)
Multi-character saga taking place at ritzy establishment, adapted from Arthur Hailey bestseller. Rod Taylor stars, with Catherine Spaak, Karl Malden, Melvyn Douglas, Richard Conte, Michael Rennie, Merle Oberon, and Kevin McCarthy. **ST58**

Hotel Colonial (1987, C, 104m, R)
International intrigue, involving an Italian man's journey to Colombia to investigate the death of his brother. John Savage stars, with Rachel Ward and Robert Duvall. **MY16, ST63**

Hotel New Hampshire, The
(1984, C, 110m, R)
This film version of John Irving's bestselling novel deals with an unusual family's sexual and social adventures. Rob Lowe, Nastassja Kinski, Jodie Foster, and Beau Bridges head the cast. Directed by Tony Richardson. A misfire in every scene. **CO5, DR19, ST75**

Hotel Reserve (1944, B&W, 79m, NR)
Eric Ambler thriller set in a French resort during World War II, revolving around the identity of a mysterious stranger. James Mason stars, with Lucille Mannheim, Herbert Lom, and Patricia Medina. **MY6, MY15, ST153**

Hotel Terminus (1988, C/B&W, 267m, NR)
Oscar-winnning documentary from director Marcel Ophuls that explores the trial in Lyons, France, of Nazi torture specialist Klaus Barbie. **CU16, DT92**

Houdini (1953, C, 106m, NR)
Tony Curtis stars as the master of escape in this glossy film bio. With Janet Leigh and Torin Thatcher. **CL2**

Hound of the Baskervilles, The
(1939, B&W, 80m, NR)
A wealthy British family is cursed by a violent hound until Sherlock Holmes (Basil Rathbone) solves the mystery. The first of the series starring Rathbone and Nigel Bruce. **HF14**

Hound of the Baskervilles, The
(1959, C, 84m, NR)
Peter Cushing portrays Sherlock Holmes in this remake of the Conan Doyle novel. Produced by Hammer Films; costarring Christopher Lee. **HF14, ST43, ST135**

Hound of the Baskervilles, The
(1977, C, 84m, PG)
Sherlock Holmes spoof starring Peter Cook as the great detective, Dudley Moore as Watson (and Holmes's mother), plus Denholm Elliott, Joan Greenwood, Spike Milligan, and Roy Kinnear. Directed by Paul Morrissey. **DT90, HF14, ST160**

Hour of the Gun (1967, C, 100m, NR)
Western drama of Wyatt Earp (James Garner), Doc Holliday (Jason Robards), and the O.K. Corral. With Robert Ryan, Albert Salmi, and, making his debut in a small part, Jon Voight. **HF9, HF13, ST82, ST185, ST193**

Hour of the Star (1985, C, 96m, NR)
A nineteen-year-old girl from the impoverished northern region of Brazil holds fast to her dream of some day breaking out of her dreary surroundings. **FF6**

Hour of the Wolf (1968, B&W, 88m, NR)
Ingmar Bergman drama, set on a deserted island, of a painter and his wife—he's having strange visions. Max von Sydow, Liv Ullmann, and Erland Josephson star. **DT11, ST220, XT30**

House (1986, C, 93m, R)
A novelist (William Katt), plagued by the break-up of his marriage and the disappearance of his son, moves to a house where his late aunt hung herself. **HO3, HO19**

House by the River, The
(1950, B&W, 88m, NR)
Melodrama of a dishonest man who commits a crime and gets his wife and brother involved. Louis Hayward, Jane Wyatt, and Lee Bowman star. Directed by Fritz Lang. **DT70**

House Calls (1978, C, 98m, PG)
A widowed doctor (Walter Matthau), who enjoys the single life, meets an opinionated divorcée (Glenda Jackson) who wants a commitment. Art Carney costars in this adult romantic adult comedy. Good script by Max Shulman and Julius J. Epstein. Adroit direction by Howard Zieff. **CO1, ST117, ST155,** *Recommended*

House of Fear (1945, B&W, 69m, NR)
Sherlock Holmes (Basil Rathbone) and Dr. Watson (Nigel Bruce) investigate a murder at Drearcliff, a club whose members are being killed off one at a time. **HF14**

House of Frankenstein
(1944, B&W, 71m, NR)
Boris Karloff gets to wield the scalpel in this installment of the Mad Doc Tampers With Life story. With J. Carroll Naish as his hunchback assistant, Lon Chaney, Jr., John Carradine as Dracula, and Glenn Strange as the Monster. **HF7, HF10, HO20, ST27, ST119**

House of Games (1987, C, 102m, R)
A psychologist (Lindsay Crouse) whose patient is a compulsive gambler seeks out the con men who have set him up. Fascinated by their techniques, she allows herself to be used by one (Joe Mantegna), then seeks revenge. Written and directed by David Mamet. Not flashy, just solid and satisfying. **DR15, MY9,** *Recommended*

House of 1,000 Dolls (1967, C, 83m, NR)
Vincent Price plays an illusionist involved with a white slave racket in Tangiers. With

Martha Hyer, George Nader, Anne Smyrner, and Wolfgang Kieling. **ST179**

House of Strangers (1949, B&W, 101m, NR)
Edward G. Robinson plays a hard-driving financier using his sons to no good end. With Susan Hayward, Richard Conte, Luther Adler, Efrem Zimbalist, Jr., and Debra Paget. Directed by Joseph L. Mankiewicz. **DR24, DT84, ST100, ST186**

House of the Long Shadows
(1983, C, 96m, PG)
Four notable horror film stars—Vincent Price, Peter Cushing, John Carradine, and Christopher Lee—have small roles in this tale of a mystery writer (Desi Arnaz, Jr.) spending the night with his girlfriend at mysterious mansion. **HO19, ST43, ST135, ST179**

House of Usher see *The Fall of the House of Usher*

House of Wax (1953, C, 88m, PG)
A vengeful sculptor (Vincent Price), disfigured by a fire, rebuilds his gallery by using human corpses as wax statues. With Frank Lovejoy and Charles Buchinsky (Charles Bronson). Remake of *Mystery of the Wax Museum.* **CU18, HO1, HO19, ST20, ST179**

House on Carroll Street, The
(1988, C, 111m, PG-13)
Thriller set in 1950s New York, with a photo researcher uncovering a plot to smuggle Nazis into the country. Kelly McGillis, Jeff Daniels, and Mandy Patinkin star. **MY3, MY6**

House on Haunted Hill
(1958, B&W, 75m, NR)
Vincent Price plays a wealthy eccentric who offers a group of people $50,000 each if they'll spend the night in a mansion with a history of murder. **HO3, HO19, ST179**

House Party (1990, C, 105m, R)
Comedy centering around a black youth's attempts to make it to the hippest party of the week. Christopher Reid and Christopher Martin (the rap group Kid 'n Play) star, with Robin Harris. **CO4,** *Recommended*

House Party 2 (1991, C, 94m, R)
Kid (Christopher Reid) 'n Play (Christopher Martin) are off to college for more comic adventures. With Tisha Campbell, Iman, Martin Lawrence, Georg Stanford Brown, and Queen Latifah. **CO18**

House That Dripped Blood, The
(1971, C, 101m, NR)
Christopher Lee, Peter Cushing, and Denholm Elliott star in this four-part horror story about a new owner of a mysterious-

looking mansion who has doubts about living there. **HO23, ST43, ST135**

House II: The Second Story
(1987, C, 88m, PG-13)
Sequel in name only to *House*, with another young man discovering evil that lurks behind the walls of a creepy piece of real estate. **HO3**

House Where Evil Dwells, The
(1982, C, 88m, R)
An American family moves into a house in Japan, ignoring warnings that the house is dominated by the ghosts of a nineteenth-century love affair that ended in tragedy. **HO3**

Houseboat (1958, C, 110m, NR)
A Washington, D.C., widower (Cary Grant) with three children hires a housekeeper (Sophia Loren), and romance blossoms. Pretty creaky; nice use of locations. **ST92, ST141, XT12**

Householder, The (1963, B&W, 100m, NR)
In India a young schoolteacher relates experiences of his early married life, when his wife and mother didn't get along. English-language comedy from the filmmaking team of producer Ismail Merchant, director James Ivory, and writer Ruth Prawer Jhabvala, who adapted her own novel. **DT61**

Housekeeper, The (1986, C, 96m, R)
An illiterate woman with severely repressed anxieties takes a job as a maid to a well-to-do family—with murderous results. Rita Tushingham stars. Also known as *A Judgment in Stone*. **MY13, MY19**

Housekeeping (1987, C, 117m, PG)
Two orphaned sisters are taken in by their loony aunt in this drama set in Montana in the 1940s. Christine Lahti stars in this deliberate but rewarding drama, with Sara Walker and Andrea Burchill. Bill Forsyth directed; based on a novel by Marilynne Robinson. **DR9, DR10, DR19, DT46**, *Recommended*

HouseSitter (1992, C, 102m, PG)
Steve Martin and Goldie Hawn star in a comedy of misunderstanding, as a one-night stand leads to a wacky woman disrupting the life of a man about to be married. With Dana Delany, Julie Harris, Donald Moffat, Christopher Durang, and Heywood Hale Broun. Written by Mark Stein, directed by Frank Oz. **CO1, ST99, ST150**

Housewife (1972, C, 96m, R)
A couple is held hostage in their Beverly Hills home by vengeance-seeking man. Yaphet Kotto, Andrew Duggan, Joyce Van Patten,

and Jeannie Berlin star. Directed by Larry Cohen. **DT28**

How Green Was My Valley
(1941, B&W, 118m, NR)
Beautifully realized story of Welsh coal miners from director John Ford. Walter Pidgeon and Maureen O'Hara star, with Donald Crisp, Anna Lee, Roddy McDowall, John Loder, Sara Allgood, and Barry Fitzgerald. Adapted by Philip Dunne from Richard Llewellyn's novel. Oscar winner for Best Picture, Director, and Supporting Actor (Crisp). **CL6, CL8, DT44, ST167, XT1, XT4, XT6**, *Highly Recommended*

How I Got Into College
(1989, C, 89m, PG-13)
A high school senior (Corey Parker) determines his choice of colleges by where a certain young lady (Lara Flynn Boyle) is going. **CO18**

How I Won the War (1967, C, 109m, PG)
A man recalls his career in World War II with hilariously exaggerated details. Michael Crawford stars, with John Lennon, Michael Hordern, and Roy Kinnear in this dark comedy from director Richard Lester. British accents and humor may not come through on first viewing, but patience will reap rewards. **CO6, CO12, CO17, CO21, DT74, MU12, XT25**, *Recommended*

How Many Miles to Babylon?
(1980, C, 106m, NR)
World War II drama of two young men from different economic backgrounds becoming friends. When one deserts, the other is ordered to oversee his execution. Daniel Day-Lewis and Christopher Fairbank star. Originally made for British TV. **ST48**

How Sweet It Is! (1968, C, 99m, NR)
Comedy of couple on second honeymoon in France, with lusty Frenchman making eyes at the wife. James Garner and Debbie Reynolds star, with Maurice Ronet and Paul Lynde. **ST82**

How the West Was Won
(1963, C, 155m, G)
Spencer Tracy narrates this monumental drama about the men and the women who explored and settled the great American West. John Wayne, Henry Fonda, and James Stewart star, with Gregory Peck as Abraham Lincoln. John Ford directed one of the four segments. Despite the talent, it's nothing special, except for a wild train scene. **DT44, HF17, ST71, ST171, ST207, ST217, ST224, WE1, WE6, XT19**

How To Beat the High Co$t of Living
(1980, C, 110m, PG)
Susan Saint James, Jane Curtin, and Jessica

Lange play three fed-up housewives who plan a robbery at a local shopping mall. **CO13, MY18, ST110**

How To Get Ahead in Advertising
(1989, C, 95m, R)
British satire of the ad game, with Richard E. Grant a rising executive who's troubled by a strange growth on his neck that takes on a life of its own. With Rachel Ward. Written and directed by Bruce Robinson. **CO2, CO17**

How To Marry a Millionaire
(1953, C, 95m, NR)
Marilyn Monroe, Betty Grable, and Lauren Bacall are the man-hungry young women in pursuit of rich husbands in this comedy. With William Powell, Rory Calhoun, and David Wayne. Widescreen will be lost on video. **CU20, ST91, ST159, ST176**

How To Murder Your Wife
(1965, C, 118m, NR)
Jack Lemmon stars in a comedy about a cartoonist who marries a lovely woman in a weak moment and learns she's a shrew. His solution to his problems is described in the title. With Virna Lisi and Terry-Thomas. **CO10, ST138**

How To Steal a Million
(1966, C, 127m, NR)
Irresistible pairing of Audrey Hepburn and Peter O'Toole in this caper comedy from director William Wyler. They're out to execute a heist at a Paris art museum. With Charles Boyer, Eli Wallach, and Hugh Griffith. UNAVAILABLE ON VIDEO. **XT29**

How To Succeed in Business Without Really Trying
(1967, C, 121m, NR)
Title says it all, in this Broadway musical starring Robert Morse as the aspiring window washer making good in Rudy Vallee's conglomerate. Michele Lee costars. **MU2**

Howard the Duck (1986, C, 111m, PG)
A duck from another planet comes to Earth and saves the planet from alien invaders. Spoofy special effects comedy stars Lea Thompson. **CO9, CO20**

Howards End (1992, C, 140m, PG)
Rich and moving adaptation of the E.M. Forster novel of two families' interlocking fortunes, mainly over a property left in a will. Anthony Hopkins and Emma Thompson star, with Vanessa Redgrave, Helena Bonham-Carter, James Wilby, and Jemma Redgrave (Vanessa's real-life daughter). Produced by Ismail Merchant, directed by James Ivory, adapted by Ruth Prawer Jhabvala; this long-running team's most splendid achievement. Well-deserved Oscars to Thompson and Jhab-

vala. **DR8, DR23, DT61, ST109, ST182, XT3, XT8,** *Highly Recommended*

Howards of Virginia, The
(1940, B&W, 122m, NR)
Cary Grant plays a colonel during the Revolutionary War, caught between his father-in-law's loyalist views and his own principles. With Martha Scott, Cedric Hardwicke, and Alan Marshal. Look for Alan Ladd in a small role. **AC6, ST92, ST128**

Howie From Maui see *HBO Comedy Club*

Howling, The (1981, C, 91m, R)
Gory tale of a news reporter sent to a California retreat after she experiences a sexual trauma, only to realize that everyone there is a werewolf. Joe Dante directed; memorable transformation scenes, plenty of in-jokes about other horror movies. Dee Wallace stars, with Patrick Macnee, Dennis Dugan, Kevin McCarthy, John Carradine, Slim Pickens, and (very briefly) Roger Corman. Cowritten by John Sayles. **DT30, DT33, DT112, HO4, HO17, XT26,** *Recommended*

Howling II (1984, C, 91m, R)
After the death of his sister, a law officer discovers that she may have been the victim of a werewolf. Christopher Lee stars in this name-only sequel. Full title: *Howling II: Your Sister Is a Werewolf.* **HO4, ST135**

Howling III: The Marsupials
(1987, C, 94m, R)
Australia is the setting for this horror tale about a scientist's investigation into a new breed of werewolf. Barry Otto stars. **HO4**

Howling IV, The (1988, C, 94m, R)
Fourth installment in werewolf series has lovely writer on a woodsy retreat, with predictable results. **HO4**

Huckleberry Finn (1975, C, 78m, NR)
TV movie version of Mark Twain's classic, starring Ron Howard, with Antonio Fargas, Jack Elam, and Merle Haggard. **DT59, FA3, MU12, WR35**

Hucksters, The (1947, B&W, 115m, NR)
Drama set in competitive world of big business and advertising. Clark Gable, Deborah Kerr, Sydney Greenstreet, Adolphe Menjou, and Ava Gardner star. **DR24, ST77, ST79, ST125**

Hud (1963, B&W, 112m, NR)
In contemporary Texas, an arrogant cattleman plays by his own set of rules—and gets away with it. Paul Newman and Oscar winners Patricia Neal and Melvyn Douglas star. Based on Larry McMurtry's novel, *Horseman, Pass By*; directed by Martin Ritt. Newman

and Neal are splendid, and the view of the contemporary West is still refreshingly unromantic. Widescreen cinematography by James Wong Howe will be lost on video. **CU20, DR19, DT105, ST58, ST162, WE12, XT3, XT4,** *Recommended*

Hudson Hawk (1991, C, 95m, R)
Bruce Willis stars in this caper film about a cat burglar and his pal (Danny Aiello) set up by criminal masterminds to steal a precious artifact from the Vatican. With Andie MacDowell, James Coburn, Richard E. Grant, and Sandra Bernhard. Written by Steven de Souza and Daniel Waters (with an assist from an ad-libbing Willis); directed by Michael Lehmann. Not nearly as bad as you've heard, although non-Willis fans aren't likely to be converted. **CO9, CO10, MY18, ST229**

Hullabaloo Over Georgie and Bonnie's Pictures (1979, C, 85m, NR)
Comedy set in India of American and Indian art dealers competing for the art collection of a prince and his sister. Victor Bannerjee stars, with Aparna Sen, Larry Pine, Saeed Jeffrey, and Peggy Ashcroft. Produced by Ismail Merchant, directed by James Ivory, written by Ruth Prawer Jhabvala. **DT61**

Human Comedy, The
(1943, B&W, 118m, NR)
William Saroyan's affectionate portrait of small-town life in World War II America. Mickey Rooney stars, with Frank Morgan, Jackie "Butch" Jenkins, James Craig, Marsha Hunt, and in a small role, Robert Mitchum. **DR19, DR26, ST158, ST189**

Human Condition, The
Part I (1958, B&W, 200m, NR)

Part II (1959, B&W, 180m, NR)

Part III (1961, B&W, 190m, NR)
Epic Japanese tale of a pacifist's wartime experiences. In Part I, Kaji (Tatsuya Nakadai) is sent to Manchuria to supervise mine workers; he is betrayed by his enemies and is eventually served with a draft notice. Part II (originally titled *Road to Eternity*) finds Kaji at the Front, where he distinguishes himself in battle. In Part III (original title: *A Soldier's Prayer*), Kaji is thrown into despair during the final days of the war, as he comes to understand the true madness of the conflict. Directed and cowritten by Masaki Kobayashi. **FF4, XT25**

Human Desire (1954, B&W, 90m, NR)
Drama of weak-willed man involved with a married woman, who'd like to be rid of her husband. Glenn Ford, Gloria Grahame, and Broderick Crawffrd star. Fritz Lang directed this remake of Jean Renoir's *La Bête Humaine*. **CU18, DT70, FF8**

Human Gorilla, The (1948, B&W, 62m, NR)
Low-budget thriller of a reporter who tracks a judge under suspicion of illegal activity to an asylum. Richard Carlson and Lucille Bremer star. Directed by Oscar (Budd) Boetticher. Original title: *Behind Locked Doors*. **DT14, MY1**

Human Monster, The
(1939, B&W, 73m, NR)
Bela Lugosi plays the evil owner of a home for blind men. He persuades them to buy more life insurance, then plots to kill them off. **HO9, ST143**

Human Vapor, The (1964, B&W, 79m, NR)
Japanese science fiction drama of an experiment which transforms a man into a gaseous, deadly monster. **FF5, SF18**

Humanoids from the Deep
(1980, C, 80m, R)
A seaside village is menaced by mutated sea monsters who rape women to produce their offspring. Doug McClure, Vic Morrow, and Ann Turkel star. Trashy fun. **HO16, HO25,** *Recommended*

Humoresque (1946, B&W, 125m, NR)
Melodrama of violinist (John Garfield) and his patroness (Joan Crawford). With Oscar Levant, J. Carrol Naish, and Craig Stevens. **CL5, CL7, ST39, ST80**

Hunchback (1982, C, 102m, PG)
This version of *The Hunchback of Notre Dame* stars Anthony Hopkins as the deformed bellringer, with Derek Jacobi, Lesley-Anne Down, and John Gielgud. Originally made for TV under the familiar title with a 150-minute running time. **CL1, ST86, ST109**

Hunchback of Notre Dame, The
(1923, B&W, 93m, NR)
Lon Chaney, Sr., portrays the Parisian hunchback in this first film version of the Victor Hugo novel. **ST26**

Hunchback of Notre Dame, The
(1939, B&W, 115m, NR)
Charles Laughton is sensationally moving as the handicapped bell-ringer attracted to a beautiful Gypsy girl (Maureen O'Hara) in this version of Victor Hugo's classic. With Cedric Hardwicke. **CL1, ST132, ST167,** *Recommended*

Hunchback of Notre Dame (1982 version) see *Hunchback*

Hunger, The (1983, C, 97m, R)
A two-thousand-year-old vampire (Catherine Deneuve) searches for fresh blood in a new

lover to replace her old one (David Bowie), who is aging rapidly. Susan Sarandon costars. Directed by Tony Scott. Visually stylish but empty otherwise. **HO5, MU12, ST50, ST194**

Hunt for Red October, The
(1990, C, 137m, PG)
A Soviet super-submarine sails toward the United States—is it defecting or about to attack America? This first-rate adaptation of Tom Clancy's thriller stars Sean Connery and Alec Baldwin, with Scott Glenn, Sam Neill, James Earl Jones, Joss Ackland, and Courtney B. Vance. Directed by John McTiernan. **MY6, ST36, ST118,** *Recommended*

Hunter, The (1980, C, 97m, PG)
Steve McQueen stars as contemporary bounty hunter Pappy Thorson in this action thriller set in Chicago. With Eli Wallach, Kathryn Harrold, and LeVar Burton. One of McQueen's last films and far from his best. **AC8, ST146, XT11**

Hunters, The (1958, C, 108m, NR)
Veteran pilot (Robert Mitchum) falls in love with wife of a young colleague (Robert Wagner). With Richard Egan and Mai Britt. Directed by Dick Powell. **ST158, ST175**

Hunters Are for Killing see *Hard Frame*

Hunter's Blood (1987, C, 102m, R)
Five city boys hunting in the country run afoul of some nasty poachers. Sam Bottoms, Kim Delaney, and Clu Gulager star in this survival adventure. **AC24**

Hurricane, The (1937, B&W, 102m, NR)
John Ford directed this tale of a South Seas island and its inhabitants being tormented by a vindictive governor. Climactic storm scenes will blow you away. Dorothy Lamour, Jon Hall, and Mary Astor star. **AC13, AC23, CU18, DT44**

Hurricane (1979, C, 119m, PG)
Remake of disaster story set on an otherwise idyllic South Pacific isle. Jason Robards and Mia Farrow star, with Max von Sydow and Trevor Howard. **AC23, CU18, ST65, ST185**

Hurry Up, or I'll Be 30 (1973, C, 88m, NR)
Comedy of New Yorker trying to get his act together. John Lefkowitz stars, with Linda De Coff, Ronald Anton, and a young Danny DeVito. **ST54**

Husbands and Wives (1992, C, 107m, R)
In this drama from writer-director Woody Allen, two Manhattan couples who are close friends undergo separate crises in their marriages. Allen, Mia Farrow, Sydney Pollack, and Judy Davis star, with Juliette Lewis, Liam Neeson, and Lysette Anthony. Allen's best work in years; whether his well-publicized personal problems gave this work the edge most of his recent films lacked, only time will tell. **DR7, DR15, DT2, DT98, ST46, ST65, XT9, XT30,** *Recommended*

Hush . . . Hush, Sweet Charlotte
(1965, B&W, 133m, NR)
Bette Davis plays a victimized Southern woman who cannot live down a scandal from her past. Olivia de Havilland and Joseph Cotten costar in this camp cult favorite. Directed by Robert Aldrich. **CU2, DT1, ST44, ST49**

Hustle (1975, C, 120m, R)
Burt Reynolds stars as a detective who gets involved with a call girl (Catherine Deneuve) while investigating a suicide. With Paul Winfield. Directed by Robert Aldrich. One of a good director's most underrated films. **AC9, DT1, MY2, ST50, ST183,** *Recommended*

Hustler, The (1961, B&W, 135m, NR)
Paul Newman plays Fast Eddie Felson, a jaded drifter with a talent for shooting pool who challenges the champ, Minnesota Fats (Jackie Gleason). George C. Scott and Piper Laurie costar in this superb drama from writer-director Robert Rossen. Based on a novel by Walter Tevis. Widescreen photography by Eugen Shuftan will be lost on video, but performances of four leads remain intact and outstanding. Should have won the Oscar for Best Picture, Director, and Scott's performance. **CU20, DR22, ST162, ST196,** *Essential, Highly Recommended*

Hustling (1975, C, 100m, NR)
Woman reporter (Lee Remick) goes undercover as Manhattan prostitute to write story on second-oldest profession. With Jill Clayburgh as the hooker who befriends her, Monte Markham, Alex Rocco, Dick O'Neill, Burt Young, and Melanie Mayron. Fay Kanin adapted Gail Sheehy's nonfiction book. Originally made for TV. **DR10, DR15, ST31, XT9**

I Am a Camera (1955, B&W, 98m, NR)
The John van Druten play of Sally Bowles, a young American living in pre–World War II Berlin, performing in a decadent nightclub. Julie Harris stars, with Laurence Harvey and Shelley Winters. Musical remake: *Cabaret.* **DR20, DR27, ST232**

I Am a Fugitive From a Chain Gang
(1932, B&W, 93m, NR)
Dramatic story of an innocent man (Paul Muni) who is sentenced to prison, victimized

by the system. Classic social problem of the desperate 1930s. **CL8,** *Essential*

I Am the Cheese (1983, C, 95m, PG)
Drama of a young boy who witnesses his parent's deaths, and the fantasies he imagines while under a doctor's care. **FA7**

I Am the Law (1938, B&W, 83m, NR)
Edward G. Robinson plays a law professor hired to clean up a corrupt city government. With Otto Kruger and Wendy Barrie. **ST186**

I Come in Peace (1990, C, 93m, R)
Dolph Lundgren stars in a science fiction thriller of an alien cop pursuing his quarry in Houston. With Brian Benben, Betsy Brantley, and Matthias Hues. **SF17**

I Confess (1953, B&W, 95m, NR)
Montgomery Clift portrays a priest who hears a confession of murder and becomes the prime suspect because of his vows of silence. Directed by Alfred Hitchcock. **DT57, MY7, ST32**

I Could Go On Singing
(1963, C, 99m, NR)
In her final film, Judy Garland plays an American singer on tour in London battling personal problems. Dirk Bogarde costars. **DR12, ST14, ST81**

I Cover the Waterfront
(1933, B&W, 70m, NR)
Drama of inquiring reporter mixed up with free spirit whose father is involved with smuggling illegal Chinese workers. Ben Lyon and Claudette Colbert star. Unusually frank about sex for its day. **ST34**

I Died a Thousand Times
(1955, C, 109m, NR)
Remake of the gangster saga *High Sierra* features Jack Palance in the Bogart role, with Shelley Winters, Lori Nelson, Lee Marvin, Earl Holliman, and Lon Chaney, Jr. Writer W.R. Burnett adapted his own novel. **AC22, CU18, MY1, ST27, ST151, ST232**

I Dood It (1943, B&W, 102m, NR)
MGM musical starring Red Skelton as a tailor, Eleanor Powell as his girlfriend, an actress. With Lena Horne, Hazel Scott, and Jimmy Dorsey and His Orchestra. Directed by Vincente Minnelli. **DT88, MU1**

I Dream Too Much
(1935, B&W, 95m, NR)
Henry Fonda plays an American composer having marital problems with his lovely opera star wife (Lily Pons). **CL7, ST71**

I Hate Your Guts see *Shame* (1961)

I Know Where I'm Going
(1945, B&W, 91m, NR)
British romance of an independent young woman (Wendy Hiller) forced to stay in a Scottish village, falling in love with local man (Roger Livesey). Codirected by Michael Powell and Emeric Pressburger. **DR1, DT99,** *Recommended*

I Live My Life (1935, B&W, 92m, NR)
Joan Crawford vehicle has her falling in love with a dashing archeologist (Brian Aherne). With Frank Morgan, Eric Blore, Arthur Treacher, and Stanley Holloway. Written by Joseph L. Mankiewicz. **CL5, ST39**

I Love All of You
(1983, C, 103m, NR)
French drama of career woman undecided on the men in her life. Catherine Deneuve stars, with Jean-Louis Trintignant and Gérard Depardieu. Directed by Claude Berri. **FF1, ST50, ST52**

I Love You (1981, C, 104m, R)
Brazilian drama of a man with nothing left to lose, who finds love. Sonia Braga stars. **FF6, ST17**

I Love You, Alice B. Toklas
(1968, C, 93m, R)
Peter Sellers plays a successful Los Angeles lawyer who becomes involved with a lovely flower child (Leigh Taylor-Young) in this comedy cowritten by Paul Mazursky, who also has a small role. **CO2, DT87, ST198**

I Love You to Death (1990, C, 96m, R)
Dark comedy, based on true story, of woman trying unsuccessfully to have her unfaithful husband murdered. Kevin Kline and Tracey Ullman star, with Joan Plowright, River Phoenix, William Hurt, and Keanu Reeves. Directed by Lawrence Kasdan. **CO10, CO12, ST114, ST127**

I Married a Monster from Outer Space
(1958, B&W, 78m, NR)
Newlywed can't figure out her husband's strange behavior. Tom Tryon and Gloria Talbott star in this classic of 1950s science fiction. **SF1, SF9,** *Recommended*

I Married a Witch
(1942, B&W, 76m, NR)
Fantasy comedy about a pesky sorceress (Veronica Lake) determined to make mischief on the descendants of the Puritan (Fredric March) who had her burned at the stake three hundred years ago. With Robert Benchley, Susan Hayward, and Cecil Kellaway. Directed by René Clair. **DT25, SF2, ST100, ST148, XT24**

I Married an Angel (1942, B&W, 84m, NR)
Nelson Eddy and Jeanette MacDonald's swan
song as a screen team, the lighthearted tale
of a playboy and the heavenly lady who
tames him. **CL15**

I, Mobster (1958, B&W, 80m, NR)
Standard, low-budget crime saga, starring
Steve Cochran, with Lita Milan and Robert
Strauss. Directed by Roger Corman. **AC22,
DT30**

I Never Sang for My Father
(1970, C, 93m, PG)
A middle-aged man (Gene Hackman) takes
the responsibility of caring for his elderly,
stubborn father (Melvyn Douglas) after his
mother dies. With Estelle Parsons. Based on
a play by Robert Anderson. Painfully raw at
times, but too often cliched. Worth seeing
for good performances; Hackman should
have won the Supporting Actor Oscar. **DR8,
DR11, DR20, ST96,** *Recommended*

I Ought to Be in Pictures
(1982, C, 107m, PG)
A young New Yorker (Dinah Manoff) travels
to Los Angeles to make it in the movies, but
her real ambition is to find her father (Walter
Matthau). Based on the Neil Simon play.
CO5, ST155, WR30

I Remember Mama
(1948, B&W, 134m, NR)
George Stevens directed this heartwarming
film of an immigrant family from Norway
adjusting to life in San Francisco. Irene
Dunne and Barbara Bel Geddes star. **DR8,
DT119, ST62**

I See a Dark Stranger
(1946, B&W, 98m, NR)
British drama of young Irish woman (Deborah Kerr) throwing in with the Germans
during World War II, to fight her hated enemy, the British. With Trevor Howard. Also
known as *The Adventuress*. **DR23, ST125**

I Sent a Letter to My Love
(1981, C, 96m, PG)
A woman and her invalid brother unknowingly begin a romance in a newspaper per-
sonals column. Simone Signoret and Jean
Rochefort star in this French drama. **FF1**

I Shot Jesse James (1949, B&W, 81m, NR)
The true tale of Bob Ford, the man who
killed the West's most famous desperado
(Reed Hadley). Director Sam Fuller's first film.
DT49, HF16

I Stand Condemned (1935, B&W, 75m, NR)
An officer gets framed by his superior as a
spy in a fit of jealousy over a woman. Lau-

rence Olivier stars in one of his early films.
ST168

I, the Jury (1982, C, 111m, R)
Hard-boiled detective Mike Hammer is played
by Armand Assante in this Mickey Spillane
thriller. **WR31**

I Vitelloni (1953, B&W, 104m, NR)
Comedy-drama from director Federico Fellini
about five boys on the verge of adulthood.
DT43

I Wake Up Screaming
(1941, B&W, 82m, NR)
An actress's agent (Victor Mature) is the
prime suspect in her murder, and he turns to
her sister (Betty Grable) for help in clearing
his name. With Laird Cregar and Carole
Landis. **MY1, MY7, ST91**

I Walked with a Zombie
(1943, B&W, 69m, NR)
Classic horror tale of nurse coming to Haiti
to treat victim of coma-like state, discovering
voodoo rituals. Directed by Jacques Tourneur;
produced by Val Lewton. **CU4, DT124, HO1,
HO6, HO27,** *Recommended*

I Wanna Hold Your Hand
(1978, C, 104m, PG)
Engaging comedy about a group of teen-
agers who use every trick they can think of
to get tickets to the Beatles' debut on "The
Ed Sullivan Show" in 1964. Robert Zemeckis
directed a lively cast, including Nancy Allen,
Bobby DiCicco, Marc McClure, Wendie Jo
Sperber, Eddie Deezen, and, as Sullivan, Will
Jordan. **CO6, DT143,** *Recommended*

I Want To Live! (1958, B&W, 120m, NR)
This classic prison drama deals with the story
of Barbara Graham, who was framed for
murder and sent to the gas chamber. Susan
Hayward won an Academy Award for her
performance, directed by Robert Wise. **DR18,
DT140, ST100, XT3**

I Was a Male War Bride
(1949, B&W, 105m, NR)
Hilarious Cary Grant comedy about a Frenchman who marries a WAC (Ann Sheridan)
during World War II but can't, because of
stupid restrictions, return with her to the
U.S. Their solution: dress him up as a G.I.
"bride." Directed by Howard Hawks.
UNAVAILABLE ON VIDEO. **XT29**

I Will Fight No More Forever
(1975, C, 100m, NR)
Historical account of Chief Joseph, who led
his tribe on a sixteen-hundred-mile trek to
Canada to avoid a U.S. Cavalry battle. James
Whitmore stars. Originally made for TV.
WE7

I Will, I Will . . . For Now
(1976, C, 110m, R)
Diane Keaton and Elliott Gould play a couple
who are bored with their ten-year marriage.
They try every means, including therapy and
a sex clinic, to rekindle the spark in this
comedy. **CO1, ST121**

Ice Palace (1960, C, 143m, NR)
Edna Ferber saga set in Alaska, about two
friends (Richard Burton and Robert Ryan)
turned rivals. With Carolyn Jones, Martha
Hyer, Jim Backus, and Shirley Knight. **ST22,
ST193**

Ice Pirates, The (1984, C, 91m, PG)
Science fiction comedy about band of lovable
cutthroats out to hijack a drought-stricken
galaxy's water supply. Robert Urich, Mary
Crosby, and Anjelica Huston star. **SF21,
ST115**

Ice Station Zebra (1968, C, 148m, G)
Cold War drama under the icecap of the
North Pole, starring Rock Hudson as a sub-
marine commander. With Ernest Borgnine,
Patrick McGoohan, Jim Brown, and Tony
Bill. **MY6, ST112**

Iceman Cometh, The (1973, C, 239m, PG)
Eugene O'Neill's marathon drama set in a
1912 saloon, as its defeated patrons await the
annual visit of their savior, the glib salesman
Hickey. Lee Marvin stars, with Fredric March
(his last film), Robert Ryan, Jeff Bridges,
and Moses Gunn. Directed by John Frankenheimer. Stunning stuff, even if Marvin is
something of a weak link. Occasionally
shown on TV in a 101-minute version.
UNAVAILABLE ON VIDEO. **XT29**

Icicle Thief, The (1989, C, 84m, NR)
Italian comedy satirizing the overabundance
of commercials during televised films. Director Maurizio Nichetti stars as a director
whose title film (a pun on the classic neorealist drama, *The Bicycle Thief*) is interrupted
so often by commericals that viewers can't
tell where one stops and the other starts.
FF2

Idaho (1943, B&W, 70m, NR)
Roy Rogers and Smiley Burnette clear a judge
who's been framed for murder. **ST188**

Identity Crisis (1990, C, 98m, R)
The sudden death of a French fashion designer results in his reincarnation in the
body of a hip black street dude. Mario van
Peebles wrote and stars in this comedy
directed by his father, Melvin, who plays a
small role as a police inspector. **CO20, XT8,
XT24**

Idiot, The (1951, B&W, 166m, NR)
Japanese director Akira Kurosawa adapts Dostoevsky's tale of two brothers in love with
the same woman. Toshiro Mifune, Masayuki
Mori, and Setsuko Hara star. **DT69, ST157**

Idiot's Delight (1939, B&W, 105m, NR)
Clark Gable, as a song and dance man and
Norma Shearer, as his former love, are
stranded in a hotel in the Italian Alps at the
outset of World War II. Comedy-drama features Gable performing "Puttin' on the Ritz."
Strange blend of social commentary and
musical numbers rates a look for those with
interest in offbeat. **MU17, ST77**

Idolmaker, The (1980, C, 119m, PG)
This fictionalized biography of music producer Bob Marcucci shows how he pushed
rock singers Frankie Avalon and Fabian to
the top of the charts in the early days of rock
'n' roll. Ray Sharkey stars. Taylor Hackford
directed. **DR12, MU4, MU9**

if . . . (1969, C/B&W, 111m, R)
Rebellious boys at a British boarding school
finally resort to violence in this drama with
darkly comic overtones. Malcolm McDowell
stars. Lindsay Anderson directed. One of the
few youth movies of the late sixties that
holds up today. **DR9, DR23, DR25,** *Essential, Recommended*

If It's Tuesday, This Must Be Belgium
(1969, C, 99m, G)
Family comedy about American tourists on
whirlwind tour of Europe. Suzanne Pleshette,
Ian McShane, Mildred Natwick, Murray Hamilton, and Peggy Cass star; cameo appearances include Ben Gazzara, John Cassavetes,
Vittorio De Sica, Donovan, Anita Ekberg, and
Joan Collins. **DT37, FA6, XT18**

If Looks Could Kill (1991, C, 88m, PG-13)
A high school student on a trip to Paris is
mistaken for a secret agent. This comedy
stars Richard Grieco, with Linda Hunt, Roger
Rees, and in a small role, Roger Daltrey. **CO9,
CO20, XT16**

If You Can't Say it, Just See It see *Whore*

Ike: The War Years (1978, C, 196m, NR)
TV miniseries, originally shown in six-hour
timeslot, stars Robert Duvall as Dwight Eisenhower and Lee Remick as his wartime mistress, Kay Summersby. With Dana Andrews,
J.D. Cannon, and Darren McGavin. **DR4,
ST63**

Ikiru (1952, B&W, 143m, NR)
Japanese drama of a bureaucrat who finds
that he has terminal cancer and searches for
a sense of purpose in his life. Akira Kurosawa

directed. Takashi Shimura stars. **DT69,** *Essential, Recommended*

Il Bidone (1955, B&W, 92m, NR)
Federico Fellini's comedy-drama of three crooks setting up an operation in Rome. Broderick Crawford, Giulietta Masina, and Richard Basehart star. Also known as *The Swindle.* **DT43**

Il Grido (1957, B&W, 115m, NR)
Italian director Michelangelo Antonioni's study of one man's breakdown, starring Steve Cochran, with Alida Valli, Dorian Gray, and Betsy Blair. Also known as *The Outcry.* **DT5**

I'll Cry Tomorrow (1955, B&W, 117m, NR)
Susan Hayward plays singer-actress Lillian Roth, whose battles with the bottle were the stuff of show-biz legend. **CL2, CL5, ST100**

Ill Met by Moonlight
(1957, B&W, 93m, NR)
World War II drama, set in Nazi-occupied Crete, about British commandos kidnapping a German general. Dirk Bogarde, Marius Goring, and Christopher Lee star. Michael Powell directed. Also known as *Night Ambush.*
DT99, ST14, ST135

I'll See You in My Dreams
(1951, B&W, 110m, NR)
Musical bio of composer Gus Kahn, starring Danny Thomas and Doris Day. Songs include "Makin' Whoopee," "Toot Toot Tootsie," "It Had To Be You," and "Pretty Baby." **MU5, ST47**

Illegal (1955, B&W, 88m, NR)
A former district attorney, turned to working as attorney for a gangster, tries to save his reputation by defending a former colleague on a murder charge. Edward G. Robinson stars, with Nina Foch, Hugh Marlowe, Jayne Mansfield, and Albert Dekker. Remake of *The Mouthpiece.* **DR17, ST186**

Illusion Travels by Streetcar
(1954, B&W, 90m, NR)
Luis Buñuel directed this comedy of a pair of drunken workers taking one last ride on a city's streetcars just before they're consigned to the scrap heap. Filmed in Mexico. **DT19**

I'm All Right, Jack
(1960, B&W, 104m, NR)
British comedy of a factory owner's elaborately crooked schemes being upset by the arrival of his strait-laced nephew. Ian Carmichael and Peter Sellers star. **CO17, ST198**

I'm Almost Not Crazy: John Cassavetes—The Man and His Work
(1989, C, 60m, NR)
Documentary study of actor/director focuses on his unique working methods outside the Hollywood system. **CU16**

I'm Dancing as Fast as I Can
(1982, C, 106m, PG)
TV producer gets hooked on pills and tries to quit cold turkey, with nearly disastrous results. Jill Clayburgh stars in this true story. With Nicol Williamson, Dianne Wiest, Daniel Stern, Joe Pesci, and Geraldine Page. **DR6, DR10, ST31, ST172**

I'm Dangerous Tonight
(1990, C, 100m, NR)
Horror story of demonic Aztec cloak which passes on curse to whoever wears it. Madchen Amick, Anthony Perkins, R. Lee Ermey, and Dee Wallace Stone star. Based on a Cornell Woolrich story. Directed by Tobe Hooper. Originally made for cable TV. **HO8, WR39**

I'm Gonna Git You Sucka!
(1989, C, 89m, R)
Loving spoof of blaxploitation films, starring Keenen Ivory Wayans (who wrote and directed), with Bernie Casey, Antonio Fargas, Jim Brown, and Isaac Hayes. **CO7, MU12,** *Recommended*

Image, The (1990, C, 110m, R)
Drama of ambitious TV anchorman, starring Albert Finney, with John Mahoney, Kathy Baker, Swoosie Kurtz, Marsha Mason, and Spalding Gray. Originally made for cable TV. **DR7, DR12, ST68**

Images (1972, C, 101m, R)
Director Robert Altman's stunning psychological portrait of a woman slowly losing her grip, with murderous results. Susannah York gives a great performance, with Rene Auberjonois, Marcel Bozzuffi, and Hugh Millais fine in support. Photographed on location in Ireland by Vilmos Zsigmond. UNAVAILABLE ON VIDEO. **XT29**

Imagine: John Lennon (1988, C, 103m, R)
Documentary tribute to the late musician, singer, and activist, with rare footage from his Beatle days and subsequent years of marriage to Yoko Ono. **MU11**

Imitation of Life (1959, C, 124m, NR)
Glossy tear-jerker deals with a white actress, her black housekeeper, and the conflicts they share with their teen-age daughters. Lana Turner and Sandra Dee star. Douglas Sirk directed. **CL6, DR2, DT117, ST219**

Immediate Family (1989, C, 100m, PG-13)
Childless, middle-class couple decides to adopt a baby conceived by a young woman and her boyfriend. Glenn Close, James

Woods, Mary Stuart Masterson, and Kevin Dillon star. **DR8, ST33, ST233**

Immortal Bachelor, The
(1979, C, 95m, NR)
In this Italian comedy, a woman juror (Claudia Cardinale) is skeptical of a female defendant's story—she killed her unfaithful husband—because the man sounds so attractive. With Monica Vitti and Giancarlo Giannini. **FF2**

Immortal Battalion, The
(1944, B&W, 91m, NR)
Drama of British civilians brought together in World War II as fighting unit. David Niven stars, with Stanley Holloway, James Donald, Peter Ustinov, and Trevor Howard (in his debut). Screenplay by Ustinov and Eric Ambler, directed by Carol Reed. Original British title: *The Way Ahead*; released at 116 minutes. **AC1, DR23**

Immortal Sergeant, The
(1943, B&W, 91m, NR)
Henry Fonda plays an inexperienced corporal who has to take command of the troops after their sergeant dies. With Maureen O'Hara and Thomas Mitchell. **AC1, ST71, ST176**

Importance of Being Earnest, The
(1952, C, 95m, NR)
Oscar Wilde's comedy of manners set in Victorian England stars Michael Redgrave and Margaret Rutherford. **CL1**

Imposter, The (1984, C, 100m, NR)
Con man goes undercover as high school principal to do his bit in the war on drugs. Anthony Geary stars, with Lorna Patterson, Jordan Charney, and Billy Dee Williams. **DR25, ST227**

Impromptu (1991, C, 109m, PG-13)
Farcical comedy of talented and famous spending weekend at a country house, starring Judy Davis as novelist George Sand, Hugh Grant as the man she adores, Frederic Chopin, Mandy Patinkin as Alfred de Musset (Sand's one-time lover), and Julian Sands as Franz Liszt. With Bernadette Peters, Ralph Brown, and Emma Thompson. Performances vary wildly, with Davis and Thompson coming off best. **CO6, ST46**

Impulse (1990, C, 108m, R)
Theresa Russell plays an undercover cop who unwittingly becomes involved with a killer. With Jeff Fahey and George Dzundza. Directed by Sondra Locke. **MY3, XT23**

In a Lonely Place (1950, B&W, 91m, NR)
Humphrey Bogart is a frustrated screenwriter in this moody drama from director Nicholas

Ray. Gloria Grahame costars. **DT101, MY1, ST15**

In a Shallow Grave (1988, C, 92m, R)
Low-key drama of a scarred war veteran's passion for the girl he left behind but couldn't forget. Michael Biehn and Patrick Dempsey star in this adaptation of the James Purdy novel. **DR1**

In Celebration (1975, C, 110m, PG)
David Storey's play of three brothers returning to coal-mining hometown for their parents' fortieth wedding anniversary. Alan Bates, James Bolam, and Brian Cox star. Directed by Lindsay Anderson. **DR8, DR20, DR23, ST9**

In Cold Blood (1967, B&W, 134m, NR)
Meticulously crafted drama based on Truman Capote's famed "non-fiction novel" about the senseless murder of a Kansas family by two drifters. Scott Wilson and Robert Blake star. Richard Brooks wrote and directed. Widescreen will be lost on video, but worth seeing for great lead performances and heart-wrenching finale. **CU20, DR16, MY8,** *Recommended*

In Country (1989, C, 120m, NR)
Drama of teen-ager trying to come to grips with the father she never knew—killed almost twenty years before in Vietnam. Emily Lloyd stars, with Bruce Willis, Joan Allen, and Kevin Anderson. Based on the novel by Bobbie Ann Mason; final scene shot at Washington, D.C.'s Vietnam Veterans Memorial. Directed by Norman Jewison. Lloyd and Willis are fine, but film seems unnecessarily padded. **DR7, DR8, DR19, DT63, ST229, XT12**

In Harm's Way (1965, B&W, 165m, NR)
All-star cast in World War II yarn of Navy heroics in the South Pacific, with John Wayne, Kirk Douglas, Patricia Neal, Brandon de Wilde, Jill Haworth, Burgess Meredith, Tom Tryon, Franchot Tone, Patrick Neal, George Kennedy, Slim Pickens, and Henry Fonda. Directed by Otto Preminger. Wayne's last really good performance, although he's too old for the role; other actors less convincing. Widescreen will lose much on video, especially in famous opening shot. **AC1, CU20, DT100, ST57, ST71, ST224**

In Like Flint (1967, C, 114m, NR)
James Coburn stars in this spoof of James Bond films as a secret agent who never loses his cool, even when a society of women threaten to take over the world. With Lee J. Cobb and Jean Hale. Second in series that began with *Our Man Flint*. **CO7**

In Name Only (1939, B&W, 94m, NR)
Cary Grant plays a married man trying to escape a loveless marriage for his beautiful mistress (Carole Lombard). With Kay Francis. Terrific chemistry between Grant and Lombard puts this one over the top. **CL6, ST92, ST140,** *Recommended*

In Old Amarillo (1951, B&W, 68m, NR)
During a drought, a courageous cowboy (Roy Rogers) organizes local ranchers. **ST188**

In Old Caliente (1939, B&W, 54m, NR)
A cowpoke (Roy Rogers) is framed for theft by an evil half-breed. With Gabby Hayes. **ST188**

In Old California (1942, B&W, 88m, NR)
A young Boston pharmacist (John Wayne) goes West during the California Gold Rush. **ST224**

In Old Cheyenne (1941, B&W, 60m, NR)
Roy Rogers Western, set in contemporary times, has the singin' cowpoke dealing a bank holdup and rustling. **ST188, WE12**

In Old Santa Fe (1934, B&W, 60m, NR)
Gene Autry helps veteran plainsman Ken Maynard recover his horse from bandits. **ST5**

In Person (1935, B&W, 85m, NR)
Comedy of movie star recovering from breakdown with the help of a new love. Ginger Rogers and George Brent star. **CL7, ST187**

In Search of the Castaways
(1962, C, 100m, NR)
An expedition looks for a missing sea captain, and along the way encounters many hardships. Hayley Mills, Maurice Chevalier, and George Sanders star in this Disney adventure based on a Jules Verne story. **FA1, WR36**

In the Good Old Summertime
(1949, C, 102m, NR)
Judy Garland and Van Johnson star in this musical remake of *The Shop Around The Corner*, about two coworkers who unknowingly become pen pals. **MU1, MU14, ST81**

In the Heat of the Night
(1967, C, 109m, NR)
Oscar winner Rod Steiger plays a small-town Southern sheriff who unwillingly receives help from a black police detective (Sidney Poitier) in a murder case. With Warren Oates and Lee Grant. Directed by Norman Jewison. Winner of four other Oscars, including Best Picture. Unintentionally spun off series of black-white cop movies that continues to this day. Enjoyable, but how does it look now next to *Bonnie and Clyde* and *The Gradu-*

ate, two other Best Picture nominees from 1967? **DR27, DT51, MY10, ST166, ST174, XT1, XT2,** *Essential, Recommended*

In the Mood (1987, C, 100m, PG-13)
Comedy based on the true story of Sonny Wisecarver, a 1940s teen-ager who ran away to marry an older woman and became known as "The Woo-Woo Kid." **CO6**

In the Navy (1941, B&W, 85m, NR)
Abbott and Costello service comedy, with Dick Powell and the Andrews Sisters. **CO21, ST1, ST175**

In the Realm of the Senses
(1976, C, 105m, NC-17)
Japanese drama, based on true story, of intense affair between ex-prostitute and master of house where she's a servant. Tatsuya Fuji and Eiko Matsuda star. Directed by Nagisa Oshima. Banned in some states for its explicit sexuality and disturbingly violent finale. **CU6, CU8, FF4**

In the Shadow of Kilimanjaro
(1986, C, 97m, R)
During a severe drought in the African bush country, herds of baboons begin attacking humans. **HO16**

In the Spirit (1990, C, 93m, R)
Comedy of a Californian (Elaine May) who moves to New York with her husband (Peter Falk) and is befriended by a ditsy mystic (Marlo Thomas). With Jeannie Berlin (May's daughter, who also cowrote the screenplay) and Melanie Griffith. **CO2, CO12, DT86, ST93, XT8**

In This Our Life (1942, B&W, 97m, NR)
Bette Davis plays the meddling sister to Olivia de Havilland in this melodrama directed by John Huston. With George Brent, Dennis Morgan, and Charles Coburn. **CL5, DT60, ST44, ST49**

In Which We Serve
(1942, B&W, 115m, NR)
World War II drama of men on board a British battleship recalling the events that shaped their lives. Written by Noel Coward, who also stars and codirected with David Lean. With John Mills, Celia Johnson, and Richard Attenborough. **AC1, DT71, WR4,** *Recommended*

Incident, The (1967, B&W, 107m, NR)
Two punks terrorize a New York subway car in this urban drama. Tony Musante and Martin Sheen star, with Beau Bridges, Thelma Ritter, Ed McMahon, Jack Gilford, and Gary Merrill. **DR15, XT19**

Incident, The (1990, C, 100m, NR)
Homefront drama, set in small town during
World War II, of lawyer defending German
POW on murder charge. Walter Matthau
stars, with Susan Blakely, Robert Carradine,
Peter Firth, and Barnard Hughes. Originally
made for TV. **DR17, DR26, ST155**

Incident at Oglala (1992, C, 89m, PG)
Documentary examining violent episode in
1975 on South Dakota's Pine Ridge reservation in which two FBI agents were killed in
shootout with Indian activists. Presents evidence that Leonard Peltier, the man charged
in the crime, has been wrongly imprisoned.
Narrated by Robert Redford, directed by Michael Apted. Companion piece to Apted's
mystery-drama *Thunderheart*. **CU16, ST181**

Incredible Invasion see *Sinister Invasion*

Incredible Journey, The
(1963, C, 80m, NR)
Two dogs and a cat make a two-hundred-
and-fifty-mile journey across Canada to be
reunited with their human owners in this
Disney adventure. **FA1, FA5**

Incredible Mr. Limpet, The
(1964, C, 102m, NR)
Family fantasy of a mild-mannered man
(Don Knotts) who imagines himself a dol-
phin who helps the U.S. Navy during World
War II. **FA8**

Incredible Sarah, The
(1976, C, 106m, PG)
Glenda Jackson plays famed stage and silent
screen actress Sarah Bernhardt. Daniel Massey costars. **DR4, DR12, ST117**

Incredible Shrinking Man, The
(1957, B&W, 81m, NR)
A radioactive mist has a terrifying effect on
an ordinary man, who's soon battling a spider five times his size. Classic 1950s science
fiction with cult following, directed by
Jack Arnold. **CU4, FA8, SF1,** *Essential,
Recommended*

Incredible Shrinking Woman, The
(1981, C, 88m, PG)
This take-off on *The Incredible Shrinking Man*
stars Lily Tomlin as a housewife who begins
to shrink after exposure to household products. With Charles Grodin and Ned Beatty.
Directed by Joel Schumacher. Tomlin's good,
the sets are wonderful, but it's just too silly
after awhile. **CO11, SF21, ST94, ST215**

**Incredibly Strange Creatures Who
Stopped Living and Became Mixed-up
Zombies, The** (1963, C, 82m, NR)
Cult horror story of sideshow proprietor who

disfigures patrons and puts them on display
in his show. Moody cinematography, atro-
cious acting and dialogue. **CU4**

Independence Day (1983, C, 110m, R)
Small-town woman with big ambitions
yearns to break free, but is held back in part
by a romance with a local mechanic. Kathleen Quinlan and David Keith star. **DR1,
DR10, DR26**

Indestructible Man, The
(1956, B&W, 70m, NR)
A thief returns from the dead to get revenge
on his cohorts who betrayed him during a
robbery. Lon Chaney, Jr., stars. **ST27, XT24**

Indian Fighter, The (1955, C, 88m, NR)
Kirk Douglas leads a wagon train through
hostile territory. With Walter Matthau, Elsa
Martinelli, Walter Abel, and Lon Chaney, Jr.
Directed by André de Toth. **ST27, ST57,
ST155**

Indian Runner, The (1991, C, 125m, R)
Drama of family in turmoil, focusing on
relationship between two brothers, one of
whom has just returned from duty in Vietnam. David Morse and Viggo Mortensen
star, with Valeria Golino, Patricia Arquette,
Charles Bronson, Sandy Dennis, and Dennis
Hopper. Written and directed by Sean Penn.
DR8, ST20, ST110, XT23

Indiana Jones and the Last Crusade
(1989, C, 127m, PG)
Third *Indy* adventure unites him with his
father for derring-do against the Nazis. Harrison Ford and Sean Connery star, with John
Rhys-Davies, Denholm Elliott, Alison Doody,
and River Phoenix as the young Indiana.
Steven Spielberg directed. Available in a
letterboxed edition. Fun mainly comes from
Connery. Protracted and confusing finale
really disappoints. **AC21, CU19, DT118,
ST36, ST74**

Indiana Jones and the Temple of Doom
(1984, C, 118m, PG)
This prequel to *Raiders of the Lost Ark* follows
the 1930s archaeologist as he tries to save a
group of children from a murderous cult.
Harrison Ford and Kate Capshaw star. Directed by Steven Spielberg. Available in a letterboxed edition. Series already seems old in
only its second installment. **AC21, CU19,
DT118, ST74**

Indiscreet (1931, B&W, 81m, NR)
Comedy-drama stars Gloria Swanson as
woman with shady past, trying to protect
current lover (Ben Lyon) from truth. Gloria
even sings two songs. Directed by Leo
McCarey. **DT80**

Indiscreet (1958, C, 100m, NR)
Cary Grant is a playboy who romances a famous actress (Ingrid Bergman) and realizes he may be falling seriously in love. Directed by Stanley Donen. **DT38, ST13, ST92**

Indiscretion of an American Wife
(1953, B&W, 63m, NR)
Jennifer Jones and Montgomery Clift play adulterous lovers in this drama from director Vittorio De Sica. Also known as *Terminal Station*. **DT37, ST32**

Indochine (1992, C, 158m, PG-13)
French drama set in 1930s Indochina, during early communist upheavals, starring Catherine Deneuve as manager of a rubber plantation. A naval officer is attracted to her, but her teen-age daughter falls in love with him. Oscar winner as Best Foreign Language Film. **FF1, ST50, XT7**

Industrial Symphony No. 1—The Dream of the Broken Hearted
(1989, C, 50m, NR)
David Lynch directed and wrote the lyrics for this opera about a love affair set in an industrial wasteland. Laura Dern, Nicolas Cage, and Julee Cruise star. Music by Angelo Badalamenti, who has contributed to most of Lynch's film and TV projects. **DT79, MU16, ST23, ST53**

Informer, The (1935, B&W, 91m, NR)
Victor McLaglen won an Oscar for his portrayal of a drunk who turns on a friend to collect reward money during the Irish Rebellion. Oscar-winning direction by John Ford. One of the few Ford films that hasn't aged well. **DT44, XT2, XT6**

Inherit the Wind (1960, B&W, 127m, NR)
Spencer Tracy, Fredric March, and Gene Kelly star in this effective drama of the Scopes Monkey Trial of 1925, in which a schoolteacher was indicted for teaching Darwin's theory of evolution. Based on the play by Jerome Lawrence and Robert E. Lee; directed by Stanley Kramer. The stars put over the material. **DR17, DR20, DT67, ST123, ST148, ST217,** *Recommended*

Inheritance, The (1976, C, 105m, R)
A dying patriarch plans to disinherit his entire family, save his lovely daughter-in-law, with whom he's having an affair. Italian drama starring Anthony Quinn and Dominique Sanda. **FF2**

Inheritors, The (1984, C, 89m, NR)
German drama of an impressionable youth caught up in a neo-Nazi movement. Directed by Walter Bannert. **FF3**

Initiation of Sarah, The
(1978, C, 100m, NR)
When she pledges a sorority, a young girl with telepathic powers falls under the spell of a witch. Kay Lenz stars, with Kathryn Crosby, Tony Bill, Morgan Brittany, and Shelley Winters as the witch. **HO7, HO12, ST232**

In-Laws, The (1979, C, 103m, PG)
A quiet, unassuming dentist (Alan Arkin) gets involved in the bizarre schemes of his daughter's father-in-law (Peter Falk), a man claiming to be a CIA agent. Zany comedy written by Andrew Bergman. With Richard Libertini as the demented dictator. **CO3, CO10,** *Recommended*

Inn of the Sixth Happiness, The
(1958, C, 158m, NR)
A missionary (Ingrid Bergman) leads children through enemy territory in pre–World War II China. Robert Donat costars. **ST13**

Inner Circle, The (1991, C, 134m, PG-13)
True story of Ivan Sanshin, movie projectionist for the KGB who was tapped to work for Stalin. Tom Hulce stars, with Lolita Davidovitch, Bob Hoskins, and Alexandre Zbruev as Stalin. Directed by Andrei Konchalovsky, a Russian émigré returning to his homeland to make this film. **DR5, ST111**

Innerspace (1987, C, 120m, PG)
Dennis Quaid plays a cocky Navy test pilot who is miniaturized for an experiment but is accidentally injected into the body of a timid grocery store clerk (Martin Short). Joe Dante directed. Available in a letterboxed edition. **CO9, CO11, CO14, CU19, DT33, SF3, SF21**

Innocent Blood (1992, C, 112m, R)
When a sexy female vampire infects a big city mobster it gives new meaning to the term "gang bloodbath." Anne Parillaud and Robert Loggia star, with Anthony LaPaglia and David Proval; cameos by directors Frank Oz, Sam Raimi, Michael Ritchie, and comedian Don Rickles. Directed by John Landis. **HO5, HO25**

Innocent Man, An (1989, C, 113m, R)
Tom Selleck stars in this thriller as a man set up by two crooked cops, sent off to prison, plotting his revenge. With F. Murray Abraham. **DR18, MY7**

Innocents, The (1961, B&W, 100m, NR)
Subtle, satisfying version of Henry James's *The Turn of the Screw*, starring Deborah Kerr as the governess whose own insecurities affect her relationship with her charges. Marvelous photography by Freddie Francis.

Directed by Jack Clayton. UNAVAILABLE ON VIDEO. **XT29**

Inserts (1976, C, 99m, R)
Richard Dreyfuss plays a 1930s Hollywood director who has turned to making pornographic movies. With Jessica Harper, Veronica Cartwright, and Bob Hoskins. **DR13, ST60, ST111**

Inside Daisy Clover (1965, C, 128m, NR)
The tale of an ambitious young actress, set in 1930s Hollywood. Natalie Wood stars, with Robert Redford, Christopher Plummer, Roddy McDowall, and Ruth Gordon. **CL7, ST181**

Inside Man, The (1984, C, 90m, NR)
Spy drama, made in Sweden, with agents vying for submarine-detecting device. Dennis Hopper stars. **ST110**

Inside Moves (1980, C, 113m, PG)
A suicide survivor (John Savage) who was left crippled gets involved with a group of handicapped men at a local bar. Through these friends and his love for basketball, he regains his self-esteem. With David Morse, Diana Scarwid, Amy Wright, and Harold Russell. **DR22**

Inside Out (1975, C, 97m, PG)
Action drama of attempt to free World War II criminal from East German prison—he knows where a cache of gold is hidden. Telly Savalas, James Mason, Robert Culp, and Aldo Ray star. **ST153**

Inside the Third Reich
(1982, C, 250m, NR)
Rutger Hauer stars in this adaptation of Albert Speer's memoir of Germany's darkest days. With John Gielgud, Maria Schell, Blythe Danner, Trevor Howard, Viveca Lindfors, Randy Quaid, Mort Sahl, and Derek Jacobi as Adolf Hitler. Originally made for TV. **DR5, HF12, ST86**

Insignificance (1985, C, 105m, R)
"Historical" drama about chance encounters between a scientist, a senator, a lovely movie star, and her baseball player husband—resembling Albert Einstein, Joseph McCarthy, Marilyn Monroe, and Joe DiMaggio. Michael Emil, Tony Curtis, Theresa Russell, and Gary Busey star. Nicolas Roeg directed. Russell's good, but everyone else seems uncomfortable in their roles, especially Busey. **DT106, XT30**

Inspector General, The
(1949, C, 102m, NR)
Musical comedy featuring Danny Kaye as a man who impersonates a bureaucrat in an Eastern European village. **ST120**

Inspiration (1931, B&W, 74m, NR)
Greta Garbo vehicle has her playing a Parisian whose past catches up to her. With Robert Montgomery and Lewis Stone. Directed by Clarence Brown. **ST78**

Instant Justice (1986, C, 101m, R)
A Marine swears vengeance on the drug smugglers who killed his sister. Michael Paré and Tawny Kitaen star. **AC19, AC25**

Interiors (1978, C, 93m, PG)
Woody Allen wrote and directed this drama of a guilt-ridden family trying to come to terms with each other. Geraldine Page, Diane Keaton, E.G. Marshall, Maureen Stapleton, Mary Beth Hurt, Kristin Griffith, Richard Jordan, and Sam Waterston star. Still Woody's most successful drama, but still feels like warmed-over Bergman. **DR8, DT2, ST121, XT30**

Intermezzo (1936, B&W, 88m, NR)
Swedish-language drama of a a young pianist (Ingrid Bergman) and her affair with a married violinist (Gosta Ekman). Remade two years later in the U.S. **FF7, FF8, ST13**

Intermezzo (1939, B&W, 70m, NR)
Remake of Ingrid Bergman's breakthrough Swedish film about a married violinist (Leslie Howard) who falls in love with his musical protégé (Bergman). **CL4, FF8, ST13**

Internal Affairs (1990, C, 115m, R)
Tense drama of two L.A. cops, one a corrupt womanizer (Richard Gere, very good), the other a newly married internal investigator (Andy Garcia) on his trail. With Nancy Travis and Laurie Metcalf. Directed by Mike Figgis. **DR16, ST84, MY9, MY19, XT10,** *Recommended*

International House
(1933, B&W, 70m, NR)
W.C. Fields stars with George Burns and Gracie Allen in this comedy set in a hotel in China, where a scientist has invented television and assorted people come from all over the world to buy the rights. With Stuart Erwin, Bela Lugosi, Franklin Pangborn, and Rudy Vallee. **ST67, ST143**

International Velvet (1978, C, 127m, PG)
This sequel to *National Velvet* follows a grown Velvet Brown as she primes her niece to take her place as a champion rider. Tatum O'Neal stars, with Nanette Newman, Anthony Hopkins, and Christopher Plummer. **FA5, ST109**

Intimate Strangers (1977, C, 100m, NR)
Drama of marriage falling apart at hands of abusive husband. Dennis Weaver and Sally Struthers star, with Tyne Daly, Larry

Hagman, Melvyn Douglas, and Rhea Perlman. Originally made for TV. **DR10, ST58**

Into the Fire (1987, C, 83m, R)
A weird couple at a remote estate involve a young musician and his girlfriend in a complex murder plot. Susan Anspach and Art Hindle star, with Lee Montgomery and Olivia D'Abo. Also known as *Legend of Wolf Lodge*. **MY9**

Into the Night (1985, C, 115m, R)
An insomniac finds himself involved with a beautiful girl, who is being chased by killers. Michelle Pfeiffer and Jeff Goldblum star in this comic thriller, with cameos by many film directors and pop music stars, including Paul Mazursky, Jonathan Demme, David Cronenberg, Don Siegel, David Bowie, and Carl Perkins. Dan Aykroyd can also be glimpsed briefly. The good leads get tangled in plot convolutions and distracting cameos. **AC14, CO13, CU17, DT31, DT35, DT87, DT116, MU12, ST90, ST173**

Into the Sun (1992, C, 100m, R)
Ego-ridden movie star hitches ride with military pilot to "do research" for upcoming film, gets involved in real action in the Middle East. Action comedy stars Anthony Hall and Michael Pare. **AC11, CO9**

Intolerance (1916, B&W, 175m, NR)
Four stories about man's inhumanity to man, stretching from ancient times to modern day, are interwoven in this silent classic directed by D.W. Griffith. Robert Harron, Mae Marsh, Constance Talmadge, and Bessie Love star, with Howard Gaye as Jesus Christ, Erich Von Stroheim in a small role, and Lillian Gish as the Hand That Rocks the Cradle. Now available in newly restored and tinted print with above running time; accept no substitutes. Amazingly successful at integrating the separate stories; Griffith's total mastery of the medium sweeps aside all quibbles. **CL12, CL14, DT52, DT129, HF16, ST87,** *Essential, Highly Recommended*

Intruder, The see *Shame* (1961)

Intruder in the Dust
(1949, B&W, 87m, NR)
Adaptation of William Faulkner novel of black man wrongly accused of murder in small town, aided by two whites, a lawyer, and a teen-age boy. David Brian, Claude Jarman, Jr., and Juano Hernandez star. Directed by Clarence Brown. One of the few Faulkner films that works, thanks in large part to Hernandez. **CL8, WR7,** *Recommended*

Invaders From Mars (1953, C, 78m, NR)
Small-town boy sees invasion of aliens who brainwash adults, but he can't get anyone to believe him. Classic 1950s science fiction drama, starring Helena Carter, Arthur Franz, and Jimmy Hunt. **SF1, SF9**

Invaders From Mars
(1986, C, 100m, PG)
Karen Black, Hunter Carson, and Laraine Newman star in this remake of the 1953 science fiction thriller. Tobe Hooper directed. **CO13, CU18, SF9**

Invasion of the Bee Girls
(1973, C, 85m, R)
Cult science fiction film about sinister alien force that turns women in a small town into sexually ravenous creatures. **CU4**

Invasion of the Body Snatchers
(1956, B&W, 80m, NR)
Pods from outer space begin duplicating humans in zombie-like form. Classic science fiction with political overtones for the 1950s, starring Kevin McCarthy, Dana Wynter, King Donovan, and Carolyn Jones, with Sam Peckinpah in a small role. Directed by Don Siegel. Still great as both a straight science fiction thriller and a subtle comment on '50s McCarthyism. **CU4, DT95, DT116, SF1, SF9,** *Essential, Highly Recommended*

Invasion of the Body Snatchers
(1978, C, 115m, PG)
Remake of the sci-fi classic, updated to 1970s San Francisco, with pointed commentary on self-help trends. Donald Sutherland and Brooke Adams star, with Jeff Goldblum, Veronica Cartwright, and Leonard Nimoy. With cameo appearances by Kevin McCarthy and Don Siegel, star and director of original film, and Robert Duvall. Brilliantly directed by Philip Kaufman; still his best film. **CU4, CU18, DT64, DT116, SF9, ST63, ST90, XT13,** *Highly Recommended*

Invasion U.S.A. (1985, C, 107m, R)
Chuck Norris does his very best to thwart a Russian-backed invasion of America. **AC20, ST165**

Investigation (1979, C, 116m, R)
French thriller set in a village where a businessman murders his wife to marry his pregnant mistress. Victor Lanoux, Jean Carmet, and Valerie Mairesse star. **FF1**

Invisible Ghost, The
(1941, B&W, 64m, NR)
A man commits murder after his domineering wife hypnotizes him. Bela Lugosi stars. **ST143**

Invisible Man, The (1933, B&W, 71m, NR)
Claude Rains's debut, as he stars in the H.G.
Wells story of the mad scientist who makes
himself invisible and causes great problems
in a small British town. Directed by James
Whale. **DT138, HO1, HO20, WR37, XT21,**
Recommended

Invisible Man Returns, The
(1940, B&W, 81m, NR)
Sequel to story of hard-to-find guy stars Vincent Price in title role, as the I.M. clears himself of a murder rap. With Cedric Hardwicke,
John Sutton, and Nan Grey. **ST179**

Invisible Ray, The (1936, B&W, 81m, NR)
Boris Karloff plays a man whose exposure to
radiation during an experiment slowly destroys his mind. Bela Lugosi costars. **HO21,
ST119, ST143**

Invitation to the Dance
(1957, C, 93m, NR)
Gene Kelly directed and stars in this trio of
stories told in dance. **MU1, MU3, ST123**

Invitation to the Wedding
(1973, C, 89m, PG)
Comedy of young American man invited to
wedding in England and falling in love with
the bride. Paul Nicholas and Elizabeth Shepherd star, with John Gielgud and Ralph Richardson. **ST86, ST184, XT20**

Ipcress File, The
(1965, C, 108m, NR)
Michael Caine stars in the first of his three
films as Harry Palmer, a British crook who
becomes a spy. Based on the character created by Len Deighton. **MY6, ST25**

Iphigenia (1978, C, 127m, NR)
Irene Papas stars in this screen version of the
classic Greek tragedy *Iphigenia in Aulis*. **FF7**

Irezumi (1983, C, 88m, R)
Japanese drama of sensual obsession, featur-
ing a woman who has her back elaborately
tattooed by her lover. Directed by Yoichi
Takabayashi. Also known as *Spirit of Tattoo.*
FF4

Irma La Douce (1963, C, 142m, NR)
Comedy of a Paris policeman (Jack Lemmon)
who falls for a prostitute (Shirley MacLaine).
Billy Wilder directed. Risque in its day; aw-
fully tame and not terrifically funny now.
DT139, ST138, ST145

Iron and Silk (1991, C, 90m, PG)
True-life drama of Mark Salzman, who stars
as an English teacher in contemporary
China. Salzman and director Shirley Sun
adapted his book. **DR6, DR27**

Iron Eagle (1986, C, 117m, PG-13)
When an Air Force officer is taken hostage by
terrorists in Northern Africa, his teen-age son
and another officer commandeer two jets
and attempt a daring rescue mission. Jason
Gedrick and Louis Gossett, Jr., star. **AC11**

Iron Eagle II (1988, C, 105m, PG)
More aerial action with Louis Gossett, Jr.,
teaming up with the Soviets to wipe out a
Middle East nuclear missile installation. Rock
soundtrack features Alice Cooper's version of
"I Got a Line on You." **AC11**

Iron Major, The (1943, B&W, 85m, NR)
True story of Frank Cavanaugh, football
coach turned World War I hero. Pat O'Brien
stars, with Ruth Warrick and Robert Ryan.
AC2, CL2, ST193

Iron Mask, The (1929, B&W, 87m, NR)
Silent swashbuckler starring Douglas Fairbanks (in his last such role) in Dumas's tale
of intrigue in the court of Louis XIV. **AC13,
CL12**

Iron Maze (1991, C, 102m, R)
Japanese businessman, planning to build an
amusement park on the site of an abandoned
steel mill in a small Pennsylvania town, is
severely assaulted. A laid-off worker charged
with the crime and the victim's American
wife, who was present, differ on details of the
incident. Bridget Fonda and Jeff Fahey star,
with Hiroaki Murakami and J.T. Walsh. Produced by Oliver Stone. Never as compelling
as it might have been; leads are bland. **DR7,
DR26, DR27, ST70**

Iron Triangle, The (1988, C, 94m, R)
Vietnam war drama, told from Vietcong
point of view, of American officer's capture
and treatment by the enemy. Beau Bridges
stars, with Haing S. Ngor. **AC4**

Ironweed (1987, C, 143m, R)
Jack Nicholson and Meryl Streep star as alcoholic outcasts weathering the storm of the
Great Depression. With Carroll Baker, Michael O'Keefe, Diane Venora, Fred Gwynne,
and Tom Waits. Based on the novel by William Kennedy; directed by Hector Babenco.
The stars are very strong but the film feels
hollow at the core. **DR19, MU12, ST163,
ST210**

Irreconcilable Differences
(1984, C, 117m, PG)
A young girl sues her selfish, materialistic
parents for divorce in this modern comedy-
drama. Ryan O'Neal and Shelley Long play
the parents, whose overnight Hollywood successes turn them into monsters, and Drew
Barrymore is the daughter. Lots of pointed

(and some in-) jokes about Hollywood, but tone wavers and some of the comedy is downright embarrassing. **CO5, CO8, DR8, DR17**

Is Paris Burning? (1966, B&W, 173m, NR) Drama of the liberation of Paris, with Nazis fleeing the city. Jean-Paul Belmondo heads a large cast of international stars, including Charles Boyer, Leslie Caron, Jean-Pierre Cassel, Claude Dauphin, Alain Delon, Kirk Douglas, Glenn Ford, Yves Montand, Simone Signoret, and Orson Welles. Screenplay by Gore Vidal and Francis Ford Coppola. Video version restores footage to original running time, from cut of 136 minutes. **AC1, CU10, DT134, ST11, ST16, ST57, XT16**

Isadora (1969, C, 131m, PG) Vanessa Redgrave is sensational as Isadora Duncan, who was as famous for her free-spirited lifestyle as she was for her influence on modern dance. With Jason Robards and James Fox. Directed by Karel Reisz. Video version restores some footage cut after original theatrical release. **CU10, DR4, ST182, ST185,** *Recommended*

Ishtar (1987, C, 107m, PG) Warren Beatty and Dustin Hoffman play two untalented singer-songwriters who can only get a gig in a war-torn North African kingdom. With Charles Grodin and Isabelle Adjani. Written and directed by Elaine May. Reviewed more for its runaway budget than its content; there are some funny moments and intentionally stupid songs by Paul Williams. **CO3, CO8, CO20, DT86, ST10, ST94, ST105**

Island, The (1962, B&W, 96m, NR) Japanese drama, with no dialogue, about family's struggle to survive on a rocky island. Directed by Kaneto Shindo. **FF4**

Island, The (1980, C, 114m, R) Drama of modern-day pirates kidnapping an unsuspecting tourist and his son in the Caribbean. Michael Caine and David Warner star. Directed by Michael Ritchie. An embarrassment. **AC24, ST25**

Island at the Top of the World, The (1974, C, 93m, G) An Arctic expedition uncovers a Viking civilization thought to be extinct. Adventure from the Disney studios. **FA1**

Island in the Sun (1957, C, 119m, NR) Racial strife and interracial love on a West Indies island, starring James Mason, Joan Fontaine, Dorothy Dandridge, Joan Collins, Michael Rennie, and Harry Belafonte. **DR3, ST73, ST153**

Island Monster (1953, B&W, 87m, NR) A group of cut-throat drug smugglers elude the law. Boris Karloff stars. **ST119**

Island of Dr. Moreau, The (1977, C, 104m, PG) Burt Lancaster plays a mad doctor who creates "humanimals" in his island laboratory. Based on an H.G. Wells story. Michael York and Barbara Carrera costar. **HO20, ST129, WR37**

Island of Terror (1966, C, 90m, NR) British science fiction drama of cancer research that gets out of hand, causing horrible mutations. Peter Cushing stars, with Edward Judd and Carole Gray. Directed by Terence Fisher. **SF5, SF19, ST43**

Island of the Blue Dolphins (1964, C, 93m, NR) Family adventure set in the nineteenth century, about a young Indian girl abandoned on a desert island and befriended by a pack of wild dogs. Celia Kaye stars. **FA4**

Island of the Burning Damned see *Island of the Burning Doomed*

Island of the Burning Doomed (1967, C, 94m, NR) British science fiction drama of aliens heating up things during winter, starring Christopher Lee and Peter Cushing. Also known as *Island of the Burning Damned* and *Night of the Big Heat.* **SF7, SF19, ST43, ST135**

Islands in the Stream (1977, C, 105m, PG) Drama based on Ernest Hemingway novel about an artist living in the Caribbean and his relationships with his three sons. George C. Scott stars, with David Hemmings, Claire Bloom, Susan Tyrrell, and Gilbert Roland. **DR8, ST196, WR13**

Isle of the Dead (1945, B&W, 72m, NR) Boris Karloff stars in this tale about a group of mysterious people stranded on a quarantined Greek island. Produced by Val Lewton. **HO06, HO27, ST119**

Isn't Life Wonderful? (1924, B&W, 90m, NR) Silent drama, from director D.W. Griffith, of life in post–World War I Germany. Carol Dempster and Neil Hamilton star. **DT52**

It (1927, B&W, 72m, NR) Clara Bow plays the "it" girl, a gold-digger who has designs on her boss, in this silent comedy. Gary Cooper has a small role. **CL11, ST37,** *Essential*

It Came from Beneath the Sea (1955, B&W, 80m, NR) Science fiction monster story of massive octopus wreaking havoc in San Francisco.

Kenneth Tobey and Faith Domergue star. Special effects by Ray Harryhausen. **SF10**

It Came From Hollywood
(1982, C, 80m, PG)
Comedy stars, including Gilda Radner, Dan Aykroyd, and Cheech and Chong, introduce scenes from some of Hollywood's worst science fiction and horror films. **CO13, ST28**

It Came From Outer Space
(1953, B&W, 81m, NR)
Classic 1950s science fiction from director Jack Arnold, about an alien spaceship crashing in the desert and its passengers assuming human identities. Richard Carlson and Barbara Rush star. **SF1, SF9,** *Recommended*

It Came Upon a Midnight Clear
(1984, C, 100m, NR)
Christmas story of an ex-New York cop, now an angel, trying to help his grandson celebrate an old-fashioned holiday. Mickey Rooney stars. Originally made for TV. **FA13, ST189**

It Conquered the World
(1956, B&W, 68m, NR)
Early low-budget science fiction opus from director Roger Corman, about monsters from Venus shaped like carrots. Peter Graves, Beverly Garland, and Lee Van Cleef star. **DT30, SF9, ST221**

It Happened at the World's Fair
(1963, C, 105m, NR)
Elvis Presley plays a pilot who finds romance during the Seattle World's Fair. With Joan O'Brien, Gary Lockwood, and in a small role, Kurt Russell. **ST178, ST191**

It Happened in Brooklyn
(1947, B&W, 105m, NR)
Musical of group of Brooklynites trying to make it in show biz. Frank Sinatra stars, with Kathryn Grayson, Jimmy Durante, Peter Lawford, and Gloria Grahame. **MU4, ST199**

It Happened One Night
(1934, B&W, 105m, NR)
Clark Gable is a newspaper reporter who meets an heiress (Claudette Colbert); she's running away from her father, who is against her marriage. This classic comedy was an Academy Award winner for Best Actor, Best Actress, Best Picture, and Best Director (Frank Capra). Sublime. **CL10, DT22, ST34, ST77, XT1, XT2, XT3, XT6, XT18,** *Essential, Highly Recommended*

It Happened One Summer see *State Fair* (1945)

It Lives Again (1978, C, 91m, R)
Sequel to *It's Alive*, featuring more mayhem, this time by three demonic infants. Frederic Forrest and Kathleen Lloyd star. Directed by Larry Cohen. **DT28, HO13**

It Should Happen to You
(1954, B&W, 81m, NR)
Judy Holliday plays an unemployed actress who uses her savings to buy New York City billboards to publicize her name. This comedy marked Jack Lemmon's film debut. Directed by George Cukor. **DT32, ST107, ST138, XT9**

It Started in Naples (1960, C, 100m, NR)
Clark Gable is an American lawyer, Sophia Loren an aunt reluctant to let her nephew go to America in this comedy. With Vittorio De Sica. **DT37, ST77, ST141**

It Takes Two (1988, C, 79m, PG-13)
Comedy about a young couple about to be married, only he's getting cold feet. His solution—buy the sportscar of his dreams and ride off for a fling. George Newbern and Leslie Hope star. **CO1**

Italian Job, The (1969, C, 101m, NR)
Michael Caine and Noel Coward head a gang that's competing with the Mafia to pull off a $4 million heist in Turin. With Maggie Blye, Benny Hill, Rossano Brazzi, and Raf Vallone. **MY16, MY18, ST25, WR4**

Italian Straw Hat (1927, B&W, 72m, NR)
René Clair directed this silent French comedy of a misunderstanding in which newlyweds must find a replacement for a hat eaten by a horse. **FF1, DT25**

It's a Date (1940, B&W, 103m, NR)
Deanna Durbin musical has her playing a young singer competing with her mother (Kay Francis) for the same role. With Walter Pidgeon and Eugene Pallette. **MU4**

It's a Dog's Life (1955, C, 98m, NR)
Family film dramatizing a canine's rise from poverty to the lap of luxury, told from the pooch's point of view. Jeff Richards, Edmund Gwenn, and Dean Jagger star. Also known as *Bar Sinister*. **FA5**

It's a Gift (1934, B&W, 73m, NR)
W.C. Fields plays a grocer bedeviled by insomnia, clumsy blind men, and an indifferent family. A classic comedy, perhaps Fields's funniest. **CL10, CU5, ST67,** *Essential, Highly Recommended*

It's a Great Feeling (1949, C, 85m, NR)
Doris Day comedy about filmmakers in Hollywood. With Dennis Morgan and Jack Carson, plus bit appearances by Joan Crawford, Gary Cooper, Edward G. Robinson, King

Vidor, Raoul Walsh, and Ronald Reagan as themselves. **CL10, DT126, DT131, ST37, ST39, ST47, ST186**

It's a Mad Mad Mad Mad World
(1963, C, 175m, NR)
Comedy featuring a truly all-star cast of comic performers, with police detective Spencer Tracy watching a frantic group of people search for stolen bank money. Jonathan Winters, Sid Caesar, Dick Shawn, Phil Silvers, Ethel Merman, and Mickey Rooney are among the treasure hunters; watch for guest appearances by dozens of comic personalities, including Buster Keaton, the Three Stooges, Jack Benny, Jerry Lewis, Stan Freberg, and Jimmy Durante. Directed by Stan-. ley Kramer. This is the restored version, with over twenty minutes of footage added and a modified letterbox format. Tries awfully hard but winds up carrying a pretty weak batting average. **C09, CU10, CU17, CU19, DT66, DT67, FA6, ST139, ST189, ST217, XT18**

It's a Wonderful Life
(1946, B&W, 129m, NR)
George Bailey (Jimmy Stewart) wishes he had never been born, and an angel shows him what life in his hometown would have been like without him. With Donna Reed and Lionel Barrymore. Frank Capra directed. Not highly regarded on first release, it has grown into an American institution. Not to my taste. **CL6, CL14, DT22, FA13, ST207, *Essential***

It's Alive! (1974, C, 91m, PG)
Newborn baby turns into rampaging demon in this cult horror film. Directed by Larry Cohen. Sequels: *It Lives Again* and *It's Alive III.* **DT28, HO13**

It's Alive III: Island of the Alive
(1987, C, 91m, R)
Third in series about monstrous baby throws in social commentary in story of infants on desert island, with oblique references to intolerance of AIDS victims. Michael Moriarty stars, with Karen Black, Laurene Landon, and Gerrit Graham. **DT28, HO13**

It's Always Fair Weather
(1955, C, 102m, NR)
Gene Kelly, Dan Dailey, and Michael Kidd are three wartime buddies who meet ten years later, only to find that they have nothing in common. Musical written by Betty Comden and Adolph Green, directed by Kelly and Stanley Donen. Widescreen will be lost on video. **CU20, MU1, DT38, ST123**

It's an Adventure, Charlie Brown
(1983, C, 50m, NR)
The "Peanuts" gang joins in for these six vi-gnettes about a boy named Charlie Brown. **FA10**

It's Good To Be Alive (1974, C, 100m, NR)
Paul Winfield plays all-star Dodger catcher Roy Campanella, who suffered a paralyzing injury that cut short his career. With Louis Gossett, Jr., and Ruby Dee. Originally made for TV. **DR22, ST230**

It's in the Bag (1945, B&W, 87m, NR)
Rare film outing for comic Fred Allen, as the proprietor of a flea circus in search of a hidden inheritance. His encounter with archrival Jack Benny is a classic bit. **CL10**

It's My Turn (1980, C, 91m, R)
A young New York woman (Jill Clayburgh) tries to have it all as a career woman and a lover. With Michael Douglas and Charles Grodin. Small rewards; devotees of leads should check it out. **CO1, CO2, ST31, ST59, ST94, XT9**

It's the Old Army Game
(1926, B&W, 75m, NR)
W.C. Fields silent has him playing Elmer Prettywillie, village druggist put upon by nocturnal customers and errant firemen. With Louise Brooks. **CL11, ST21, ST67**

Ivan the Terrible
Part One (1943, B&W, 96m, NR)
Part Two (1946, C, 84m, NR)
Russian director Sergei Eisenstein's historical epic about Czar Ivan IV is packed with mesmerizing imagery and features music by Sergei Prokofiev. Tapes available separately or in one package. **DT41, *Essential, Highly Recommended (both parts)***

Ivanhoe (1952, C, 106m, NR)
Elizabeth Taylor and Robert Taylor star in this family adventure of knights and their ladies fair, based on the Sir Walter Scott novel. With James Mason and Harold Warrender as Robin Hood. **AC13, FA4, HF15, ST73, ST153, ST212**

I've Heard the Mermaids Singing
(1987, C, 81m, PG)
Comedy-drama, with cult following, about an aimless young woman who finally finds happiness working at a trendy art gallery. Sheila McCarthy stars. **CO12**

Ivory Hunters (1990, C, 94m, NR)
A writer and scientist team to block elephant poachers in Africa. John Lithgow and Isabella Rossellini star, with James Earl Jones. Coproduced by the National Audubon Society. Originally made for cable TV under the title *The Last Elephant.* **AC12, ST118**

JFK (1991, C/B&W, 189m, R)
Stunning historical polemic by director
Oliver Stone on how and why President
John F. Kennedy was assassinated. Discredits
Warren Commission findings and uses New
Orleans District Attorney Jim Garrison as
clearinghouse for theories about Lee Harvey
Oswald, the Mafia, the CIA, the Pentagon,
Cuban exiles, and gays in New Orleans.
Kevin Costner stars as Garrison, with Sissy
Spacek as his wife, Joe Pesci, Tommy Lee
Jones, Gary Oldman (as Oswald), John
Candy, Jack Lemmon, Walter Matthau (as
Earl Long, in one scene), Ed Asner, Donald
Sutherland, Kevin Bacon, Brian Doyle-Murray
(as Jack Ruby), and Jim Garrison (as Earl
Warren!). Available in a "Director's Cut" with
17 minutes of additional footage. Not always
convincing but always powerful, disturbing,
and provocative. **CO14, CU9, CU10, DR5,
DR21, DT120, MY6, MY8, ST38, ST138,
ST155, ST172, ST202, XT12, XT14,**
Recommended

Jabberwocky (1977, C, 100m, PG)
Black comedy set in the Middle Ages, directed by Terry Gilliam, stars Michael Palin,
both from the Monty Python troupe. **CO15**

J'Accuse (1937, B&W, 95m, NR)
French director Abel Gance's classic anti-war
statement, banned in France as treasonous. A
scientist (Victor Francen) finds his work is
being exploited by the government and military to bring about destruction of human
lives. **CU8, FF1, XT25**

Jack and the Beanstalk (1952, B&W/
C, 87m, NR)
Abbott and Costello star in a version of the
children's fairy tale. **ST1**

Jack and the Beanstalk
(1983, C, 60m, NR)
Dennis Christopher stars as the young boy
who trades a cow for magic beans, climbs a
beanstalk, and encounters a husband/wife
giant team (Jean Stapleton and Elliott Gould)
in this classic story from the Faerie Tale Theatre collection. **FA12**

Jack London (1943, B&W, 94m, NR)
Bio of famed writer and adventurer, starring
Michael O'Shea and Susan Hayward. **CL2,
ST100**

Jack the Bear (1993, C, 98m, PG-13)
Danny Devito stars as a widowed father trying to raise two young sons in this heartfelt
drama set in 1972 Oakland. With Robert Steinmiller, Jr., Miko Hughes, Gary Sinise, Julia
Louis-Dreyfus, and Reese Witherspoon. Based

on a novel by Dan McCall, directed by Marshall Herskovitz. **DR2, DR8, DR9, ST54**

Jack the Giant Killer (1962, C, 94m, G)
The children's fairy tale, expanded to a fea-
ture film starring Kerwin Mathews, with Judi
Meredith and Torin Thatcher. **FA4**

Jack the Ripper (1980, C, 82m, R)
Klaus Kinski plays the notorious ladykiller of
Victorian London. **HO9, ST126**

Jack the Ripper (1988, C, 200m, NR)
Michael Caine plays a Scotland Yard inspec-
tor after the notorious killer; this thriller
offers a solution to the unsolved crime.
With Armand Assante, Ray McAnally, Susan
George, and Jane Seymour. **MY3, MY8,
MY13, ST25**

Jackie Chan's Police Force
(1987, C, 90m, PG-13)
Martial arts thriller about a cop framed for
murder. Jackie Chan stars. **AC9, AC26**

Jackie Mason on Broadway
(1988, C, 60m, NR)
Highlights from the veteran comic's hilarious
one-man Broadway show, *The World According to Me.* **CO16,** *Recommended*

Jackie Robinson Story, The
(1950, B&W, 76m, NR)
Bio of pioneering black baseball player, with
Robinson portraying himself. **DR4, DR22**

Jacknife (1989, C, 102m, R)
A Vietnam veteran (Robert De Niro) tries to
pull his one-time war buddy (Ed Harris) out
of postwar trauma. Kathy Baker costars in
this topical drama. **DR7, ST51**

Jack's Back (1988, C, 97m, R)
Mystery set in contemporary Los Angeles,
where a killer is imitating Jack the Ripper's
crimes on their one-hundredth anniversary.
James Spader plays a young intern who discovers the killer's identity. Cynthia Gibb is
one of the potential victims. Absorbing, with
one of Spader's better performances. **MY3,
MY7, MY13, ST203,** *Recommended*

Jacob's Ladder (1990, C, 115m, R)
A Vietnam War veteran living in New York
begins suffering from hallucinations which
may be a result of his tour of duty. Tim
Robbins stars, with Elizabeth Pena, Danny
Aiello, and as Robbins's son, Macaulay
Culkin. **DR7, DR15, XT9, XT24**

**Jacqueline Susann's Once Is Not
Enough** see *Once Is Not Enough*

Jade Mask, The (1944, B&W, 66m, NR)
Charlie Chan (Sidney Toler) is on the trail of
a clever couple who murder people and then

disguise their victims to make it appear they're still alive. With Mantan Moreland and Edwin Luke. **HF4**

Jagged Edge (1985, C, 108m, R)
Glenn Close plays an attorney who gets romantically involved with her client (Jeff Bridges), a newspaper publisher accused of murdering his heiress wife. With Peter Coyote and Robert Loggia. Strains credulity, with a so-what ending. **DR3, DR17, MY3, MY5, ST19, ST33**

Jaguar Lives! (1979, C, 91m, PG)
A karate expert is hired to travel all over the world to track down narcotics kingpins. Joe Lewis, Christopher Lee, and Barbara Bach star. **ST135**

Jail Bait (1954, B&W, 70m, NR)
From cult director Ed Wood, Jr., comes the tragic tale of a youth led into a crime and then forced to alter his face through plastic surgery to avoid capture. Timothy Farrell, Lyle Talbot, and Steve Reeves star. **DT141**

Jailhouse Rock (1957, B&W, 96m, NR)
Early Elvis Presley musical, perhaps his best, about a young man who learns to play the guitar while in jail and becomes a successful rock star after his release. **ST178**, *Recommended*

Jake Speed (1986, C, 104m, PG)
A fictional adventure hero and his trusty companion come to life to rescue a lady in distress. Wayne Crawford and Dennis Christopher star as the heroes; John Hurt is the villain. **AC21**

Jamaica Inn (1939, B&W, 98m, NR)
Alfred Hitchcock directed this version of Daphne du Maurier's novel about an orphan girl (Maureen O'Hara) who gets involved with a band of smugglers. Charles Laughton costars. **DT57, MY3, ST132, ST167, WR6**

Jamaica Inn (1985, C, 200m, NR)
New version of the du Maurier classic of a lovely lass in distress at the hands of her evil uncle. Jane Seymour stars, with Patrick McGoohan, John McEnery, and Billie Whitelaw. Made for TV. **CU18, MY3, WR6**

James Dean Story, The
(1957, B&W, 82m, NR)
Documentary about the legendary movie star, codirected by Robert Altman. **CU16, DT4**

James Joyce: A Portrait of the Artist as a Young Man see *Portrait of the Artist as a Young Man*

Jane Austen in Manhattan
(1980, C, 108m, NR)
Backstage drama of rival theatrical companies competing to produce a recently discovered play by Jane Austen. Robert Powell and Anne Baxter star, with Michael Wager, Tim Choate, Katrina Hodiak, and Sean Young. Produced by Ismail Merchant, directed by James Ivory, written by Ruth Prawer Jhabvala. **DR12, DT61**

Jane Doe (1983, C, 103m, NR)
Karen Valentine plays an amnesiac stalked by a killer who wants her dead before she can incriminate him. Originally made for TV. **MY3**

Jane Eyre (1944, B&W, 96m, NR)
Charlotte Brontë's tale of the orphan girl who becomes a governess and falls under the spell of her employer. Joan Fontaine and Orson Welles star, with Margaret O'Brien, Agnes Moorehead, Elizabeth Taylor, and Peggy Ann Garner. **CL1, DT134, ST73, ST212**

Janis (1975, C, 96m, NR)
Documentary about the short life and career of blues/rock singer Janis Joplin; includes extensive concert footage. **MU11**

January Man, The (1989, C, 122m, R)
Kevin Kline is a suspended New York cop on the trail of a serial killer in this crime drama with comic overtones. With Susan Sarandon, Harvey Keitel, and Rod Steiger. **AC9, MY17, ST127, ST194**

Jason and the Argonauts
(1963, C, 104m, NR)
Jason sets out to find the Golden Fleece in order to regain his rightful place on the throne, and encounters many obstacles along the way. Great special effects highlight this fantasy. **AC18, FA8**

Java Head (1934, B&W, 70m, NR)
British drama of sea captain marrying a Mandarin princess. Anna May Wong and John Loder star, with Elizabeth Allan, Edmund Gwenn, and Ralph Richardson. **DR23, ST184**

Jaws (1975, C, 124m, PG)
Blockbuster horror film about a great white shark's attacks on swimmers at a New England beach. Richard Dreyfuss, Roy Scheider, and Robert Shaw star. Now available in a letterboxed edition. Steven Spielberg directed; still his best film. **CU19, DT118, HO16, ST60,** *Essential, Highly Recommended*

Jaws 2 (1978, C, 117m, PG)
The saga of the great white shark continues, with Roy Scheider and his wife in Florida, where they're bedeviled by further attacks. **HO16**

Jaws 3 (1983, C, 97m, PG)
In the third chapter, personnel at a sea world park in Florida are under siege from a shark enraged that its offspring has been captured. Dennis Quaid, Bess Armstrong, and Louis Gossett, Jr., star. **HO16**

Jaws the Revenge (1987, C, 87m, PG-13)
Lorraine Gary, who played Roy Scheider's wife in the first and second installments, is back to battle another mammoth shark, this time in the Caribbean. Michael Caine co-stars. **HO16, ST25**

Jayhawkers, The (1959, C, 100m, NR)
Western set in pre–Civil War Kansas, about a government agent infiltrating a vigilante gang. Jeff Chandler and Fess Parker star. **WE6**

Jayne Mansfield Story, The
(1980, C, 100m, NR)
The life and times of the buxom blonde bombshell, starring Loni Anderson and Arnold Schwarzenegger as Jayne's hubbie, Mickey Hargitay. Originally made for TV. **DR4, ST195**

Jazz on a Summer's Day
(1959, C, 85m, NR)
Highlights from the 1955 Newport Jazz Festival, featuring performances by Louis Armstrong, Dinah Washington, Gerry Mulligan, Thelonius Monk, and Mahalia Jackson. Perfectly captures ambience of era. **CU16,** *Recommended*

Jazz Singer, The (1927, B&W, 89m, NR)
Al Jolson stars as the son of a cantor who'd rather be singing on the stage instead of in a synagogue. With Mary McAvoy, Warner Oland, William Demarest, and Myrna Loy as a chorus girl. A milestone for its use of sound in musical numbers and some dialogue scenes. **MU4, ST142,** *Essential*

Jazz Singer, The (1980, C, 115m, PG)
Remake of the classic melodrama stars Neil Diamond as the son of a Jewish cantor (Laurence Olivier); Neil breaks with family tradition to become a rock star. **CU18, MU4, ST168**

Jean de Florette (1986, C, 122m, PG)
French drama, based on Marcel Pagnol's tale, about a scheming landowner who conspires with his dim-witted nephew to deprive their new neighbor of water for his crops. Yves Montand, Daniel Auteuil, and Gérard Depardieu are the principals. Directed by Claude Berri. Story concludes in *Manon of the Spring*. Lovingly made. **FF1, ST52,** *Recommended*

Jekyll & Hyde . . . Together Again
(1982, C, 87m, R)
Mark Blankfield stars in this update of the

Robert Louis Stevenson tale, given a comic spin. With Bess Armstrong, Krista Errickson, Tim Thomerson, and George Chakiris. Directed by Jerry Belson. **CO11, WR33**

Jennifer (1978, C, 90m, PG)
A shy girl is ostracized when she moves to a new school, and her telekinetic powers allow her to unleash deadly snakes on those who snubbed her. **HO7**

Jennifer Eight (1992, C, 124m, R)
Thriller set in small Northern California community, where a visiting L.A. cop finds himself involved in local case of serial killer preying on blind women. Moreover, he falls in love with a potential victim. Andy Garcia and Uma Thurman star, with Lance Henricksen, Kathy Baker, and John Malkovich in a small role. Written and directed by Bruce Robinson. Quirky story is helped immensely by Conrad Hall's outstanding cinematography. **MY2, MY3, MY7, ST147,** *Recommended*

Jenny's War (1985, C, 192m, PG)
True story of American teacher working her way into a World War II concentration camp in search of her son. Dyan Cannon stars, with Elke Sommer and Robert Hardy. Originally made for TV. **DR5**

Jeremiah Johnson (1972, C, 107m, PG)
A mountain man (Robert Redford) who has turned his back on civilization goes to war with the Crow Indians, who killed his family. Cult Western directed by Sydney Pollack, one of his best films. **DT98, ST181, WE15,** *Recommended*

Jerk, The (1979, C, 94m, R)
Steve Martin stars as the title character, a stupid young man who attempts to adjust to life in the "normal" world. Directed by Carl Reiner. Lame. **ST150**

Jerry Lewis Live (1985, C, 77m, NR)
This live concert, filmed in Las Vegas, includes many of Jerry Lewis's zaniest routines. **ST139**

Jesse James (1939, C, 105m, NR)
A biography of the famed outlaw starring Henry Fonda in the title role, with Tyrone Power and Randolph Scott. **HF16, ST71, ST177, ST197, WE3**

Jesse James at Bay (1941, B&W, 54m, NR)
Roy Rogers and Gabby Hayes team up in a saga of the notorious outlaw's battles with the railroads. **HF16, ST188**

Jesus Christ, Superstar (1973, C, 103m, G)
Screen version of the successful Broadway rock opera portrays the last seven days in the

life of Christ. Ted Neeley (in the title role), Carl Anderson, and Yvonne Elliman star. Directed by Norman Jewison. **DT63, FA9, HF16, MU2, MU9**

Jesus of Montreal (1989, C, 119m, R) French-Canadian drama about an acting troupe putting on Passion Play. Lothaire Bluteau stars. Written and directed by Denys Arcand. **FF7**

Jesus of Nazareth (1977, C, 371m, NR) The life of Christ, portrayed by Robert Powell, features an all-star supporting cast, including Laurence Olivier, James Mason, and Anne Bancroft. Directed by Franco Zeffirelli; originally made for TV. **CL13, HF16, ST153, ST168**

Jet Benny Show, The (1986, C, 77m, NR) Science fiction spoof featuring a character who resembles Jack Benny. Steve Norman and Kevin Dees star. **CO7, SF21**

Jet Pilot (1957, C, 112m, NR) Legendary aviation/Cold War drama from producer Howard Hughes has All-American pilot John Wayne falling in love with Soviet spy Janet Leigh. With Jay C. Flippen, Paul Fix, and Hans Conried. Directed by Josef von Sternberg, obviously working for hire this time out. Made in 1950 and shelved for seven years. Hard to imagine anyone even at the height of the Cold War taking this seriously; now it's regarded as a camp cult classic. **AC11, CU2, DT128, ST224**

Jetsons: The Movie (1990, C, 82m, G) The cartoon characters from the popular animated sci-fi TV show. Voice characterizations by George O'Hanlon, Mel Blanc, and Penny Singleton. **FA10**

Jewel of the Nile (1985, C, 104m, PG) Kathleen Turner, Michael Douglas, and Danny DeVito return in this sequel to *Romancing the Stone*, set in a North African kingdom. Author Joan Wilder is kidnapped by a mad prince, and soldier of fortune Jack Colter is off to the rescue. Pretty limp next to sprightly original. **AC14, AC21, ST54, ST59, ST218**

Jezebel (1938, B&W, 103m, NR) Bette Davis plays a willful Southern belle who defies social customs to make her fiancé (Henry Fonda) jealous. Davis and supporting actress Fay Bainter both won Oscars under William Wyler's direction. **CL3, DT142, ST44, ST71, XT3, XT5**

Jigsaw Man, The (1984, C, 91m, PG) A British agent (Michael Caine) who defected to Russia comes back to Britain for a final mission. Laurence Olivier costars. **MY6, ST25, ST168**

Jim Thorpe—All American (1951, B&W, 107m, NR) Burt Lancaster plays the famous athlete who starred in the Olympics, professional football, and major league baseball—seventy years before Bo Jackson. With Charles Bickford, Steve Cochran, and Phyllis Thaxter. **CL2, ST129**

Jimi Hendrix (1973, C, 102m, NR) This documentary on rock's greatest guitarist features interviews with his friends and musical associates, plus rare concert footage. **MU11,** *Recommended*

Jimi Plays Berkeley (1973, C, 55m, NR) Master musician Jimi Hendrix in concert. **MU10**

Jimmy the Kid (1983, C, 85m, PG) A stuffy young boy, the child of wealthy parents, is kidnapped by a group of bumblers who teach him how to be a kid. Gary Coleman and Paul LeMat star. **FA7**

Jinxed! (1982, C, 103m, R) Dark comedy of shady doings in Las Vegas involving a lounge singer (Bette Midler), her obnoxious lover (Rip Torn), and a handsome young blackjack dealer (Ken Wahl). Directed by Don Siegel. **DT116, ST156, ST216**

Jo Jo Dancer, Your Life Is Calling (1986, C, 97m, R) Richard Pryor stars in this semi-autobiographical story of a comedian who nearly dies from drug abuse. He reflects on his past, starting with his youth in his grandmother's brothel. With Debbie Allen, Art Evans, Barbara Williams, Carmen McRae, and Billy Eckstine. Pryor cowrote and directed. **DR12, DR14, MU12, ST180**

Joan of Arc (1948, C, 100m, NR) Ingrid Bergman portrays the tragic heroine in this adaptation of the Maxwell Anderson play. **CL2, ST13**

Joan of Paris (1942, B&W, 91m, NR) During World War II, a brave Frenchwoman (Michele Morgan) helps to smuggle downed Allied fliers back to safety. With Paul Henreid, Thomas Mitchell, Laird Cregar, and Alan Ladd. **AC1, ST128**

Jocks (1987, C, 91m, R) Teen comedy about a traveling tennis team whose hijinks in Las Vegas overshadow their tennis tournament. With Christopher Lee and Richard Roundtree in small roles. **CO19, ST135**

Joe (1970, C, 107m, R)
Working-class bigot (Peter Boyle) blackmails business executive after the latter murders his daughter's hippie boyfriend. With Dennis Patrick, K. Callan, and Susan Sarandon in her debut. Directed by John Avildsen. Hateful, although Boyle does give a full-blooded performance. **DR7, ST194**

Joe Bob Briggs Dead in Concert
(1985, C, 60m, NR)
America's favorite connoisseur of drive-in movies (in real life, movie critic John Bloom) offers commentary on the state of our culture. Includes a performance of his controversial anthem "We Are the Weird." **CO16**

Joe Cocker: Mad Dogs and Englishmen
(1971, C, 119m, NR)
This documentary features highlights of Joe Cocker's 1970 American tour, with outstanding performances by Cocker and Leon Russell. **MU10**

Joe Kidd (1972, C, 88m, PG)
Clint Eastwood is hired on the wrong side of a land war between Mexican-Americans and a greedy landowner. Robert Duvall costars. Written by Elmore Leonard, directed by John Sturges. **ST63, ST64, WR19**

Joe Piscopo New Jersey Special
(1986, C, 60m, NR)
TV special stars funny man Piscopo kidding his home state, with guest star Danny DeVito. **CO16, ST54**

Joe Piscopo Video, The
(1984, C, 60m, NR)
"Saturday Night Live" alumnus does it all in this one-man show, highlighting many of his famous impressions. **CO16**

Joe Vs. the Volcano (1990, C, 94m, PG)
Thinking he has only a few months to live, a mild-mannered young man agrees to become a human sacrifice on a small South Pacific island. Tom Hanks stars in this comedy, with Meg Ryan (in three roles), Lloyd Bridges, Robert Stack, and Dan Hedaya. Written and directed by John Patrick Shanley. **CO1, ST97, XT27**

Johnny Apollo (1940, B&W, 93m, NR)
Tyrone Power is a young man who turns to crime to spite his father (Edward Arnold), a criminal with a spotless public reputation. With Dorothy Lamour and Lloyd Nolan. **AC22, ST177**

Johnny Be Good (1988, C, 84m, R)
A high school quarterback is the object of a mad scramble among unscrupulous recruiters. Anthony Michael Hall and Robert

Downey, Jr., star in this comedy. Rated PG-13 in its theatrical release; video version contains additional footage to earn the "R" rating. **CO4, CO19, CU10**

Johnny Belinda (1948, B&W, 103m, NR)
Jane Wyman's Oscar-winning performance highlights this tale of a deaf-mute and the doctor (Lew Ayres) who comes to her aid. **CL6, XT3**

Johnny Come Lately
(1943, B&W, 97m, NR)
James Cagney stars as an itinerant journalist who comes to the aid of a small-town editor (Grace George). With Marjorie Main, Marjorie Lord, and Hattie McDaniel. **DR26, ST24**

Johnny Dangerously
(1984, C, 90m, PG-13)
Spoof of Prohibition-era gangster movies, starring Michael Keaton, Joe Piscopo, and Danny DeVito. **CO7, CO10, ST54, ST122**

Johnny Got His Gun (1971, C, 111m, PG)
A war veteran whose body has been virtually obliterated recalls his past from his hospital bed. Antiwar parable stars Timothy Bottoms, with Jason Robards and Donald Sutherland. Dalton Trumbo adapted and directed his novel. **DR7, DR19, ST185, XT25**

Johnny Guitar (1954, C, 110m, NR)
Offbeat Western with women in the two leads: Joan Crawford as a tough saloon owner who learns her wealth can't buy everything, and Mercedes McCambridge as her rival. With Sterling Hayden. Nicholas Ray directed. Effective melodramatics. **CU17, DT101, ST39, WE8, WE15,** *Recommended*

Johnny Handsome (1989, C, 95m, R)
Betrayed in a robbery, a disfigured criminal gets a shot at a new life in prison when a surgeon rebuilds his face. Out on parole, he goes looking for the couple that left him behind. Mickey Rourke stars, with Ellen Barkin, Elizabeth McGovern, Lance Henriksen, Morgan Freeman, and Forest Whitaker. Walter Hill directed on locations in New Orleans. Nasty, unpleasant; a real disappointment considering the talent involved. **DR16, DT56, ST7, ST76, ST190, XT14**

Johnny Tremain (1957, C, 80m, NR)
Based on the Esther Forbes novel, this Disney film deals with a young boy's involvement in the Revolutionary War. **FA1**

Joke of Destiny, A (1983, C, 105m, PG)
Italian comedy of a government official locked inside his high-tech limo by a computer. Lina Wertmuller directed. **DT137**

Jolson Sings Again (1949, C, 96m, NR)
This sequel to *The Jolson Story* continues the success story of American entertainer Al Jolson. Larry Parks stars; Jolie supplied the vocals. **MU5**

Jolson Story, The (1946, C, 128m, NR)
Larry Parks plays Al Jolson in this biographical film tracing his rise to stardom. **MU5**

Jonathan Winters: On the Ledge
(1987, C, 60m, NR)
One of America's premier funnymen stars in this series of sketches, also featuring Robin Williams and Milton Berle. **CO16, ST228**

Josephine Baker Story, The
(1991, C, 130m, R)
Bio of black American dancer who wowed 1920s Paris audiences with her sexy stage routines. Lynn Whitfield gives an Emmy-winning performance in the lead role; with Rubén Blades, David Dukes, Louis Gossett, Jr., and Craig T. Nelson. Originally made for cable TV. **DR4, DR14**

Joshua Then and Now (1985, C, 127m, R)
James Woods plays a Jewish writer trying to live down his father's reputation as a gangster. Comedy-drama, adapted from Mordecai Richler's novel, costars Alan Arkin and Gabrielle Lazure. Originally a TV miniseries in Canada, which accounts for its choppy exposition. Arkin is wonderful as Woods's reprobate of a father. **DR8, DR19, ST233**

Jour de Fête (1949, B&W, 70m, NR)
Comedy from French director Jacques Tati about a postman's bizarre attempts to mechanize mail delivery. **DT122**

Journey Back to Oz (1974, C, 90m, G)
This animated sequel to *The Wizard of Oz* features the voices of Liza Minnelli, Mickey Rooney, Margaret Hamilton (the witch from the original), and Milton Berle. **FA10, ST189**

Journey for Margaret
(1942, B&W, 81m, NR)
World War II tearjerker of British children left homeless by German bombing raids. Margaret O'Brien stars in a stunning debut; with Robert Young, Laraine Day, and Fay Bainter. **CL6, FA15, XT21**

Journey Into Fear (1942, B&W, 69m, NR)
An American armaments smuggler (Orson Welles) flees from Turkey in this World War II thriller, adapted from an Eric Ambler novel. Joseph Cotten costars; he and Welles wrote the screenplay. **DT134, MY1, MY6**

Journey Into Fear (1975, C, 103m, R)
Remake of the 1942 Orson Welles classic, starring Sam Waterston as a geologist involved with World War II intrigue. With Zero Mostel, Yvette Mimieux, Vincent Price, and Shelley Winters. **CU18, ST179, ST232**

Journey of Honor (1992, C, 106m, PG-13)
Swashbuckling adventure follows a seventeenth-century voyage from Japan to Spain. Sho and Kane Kosugi (real-life father and son) star, with David Essex, Christopher Lee, Norman Lloyd, John Rhys-Davies, Polly Walker, and Toshiro Mifune in a small role. **AC15, ST135, ST157, XT8**

Journey of Hope (1990, C, 110m, NR)
Swiss drama of Turkish couple emigrating to Switzerland to build a new life. Winner of Academy Award for Best Foreign Language Film. Directed by Xavier Koller. **FF7, XT7**

Journey of Natty Gann, The
(1985, C, 101m, PG)
During the Depression, a young girl travels cross-country to see her father and is protected along the way by a pet wolf. John Cusack and Meredith Salenger star in this Disney family adventure. **FA1, FA4, XT18, XT19**

Journey Through Fairyland
(1989, C, 95m, NR)
Animated adventure for children about a brave hero's exciting travels, featuring many classical music pieces on the soundtrack. **FA10**

Journey to the Center of the Earth
(1959, C, 132m, NR)
Jules Verne fantasy tale of nineteenth-century expedition, packed with perils and wonders. James Mason, Arlene Dahl, Pat Boone, and Diane Baker star. **FA4, SF1, SF3, SF13, ST153, WR36**

Journey to the Center of the Earth
(1989, C, 79m, PG)
Remake of the Jules Verne classic of "inner space" travel, starring Nicola Cowper, Ilan Mitchell-Smith, and Paul Carafotes. **FA4, SF3, SF13, WR36**

Journey to the Far Side of the Sun
(1969, C, 99m, G)
British science fiction adventure, with space voyagers finding a hidden planet. Roy Thinnes, Lynn Loring, and Herbert Lom star. **SF3, SF19**

Journey to the Lost City
(1958–59, C, 95m, NR)
Romantic adventure of exotic dancer and architect battling an evil maharajah. Debra Paget and Paul Hubschmid star. Directed by Fritz Lang. This is a melding of two Lang films, *The Tiger of Eschnapur* (1958, 101m) and *The Indian Tomb* (1959, 97m). **DT70**

Joy House (1964, B&W, 98m, NR)
A playboy (Alain Delon) with a secret past stumbles into a mansion in France run by two American women. Jane Fonda costars. **ST72**

Joy of Knowledge see *Le Gai Savior*

Joy of Living (1938, B&W, 90m, NR)
Comedy with musical numbers stars Douglas Fairbanks as a playboy who romances a singer (Irene Dunne). With Alice Brady, Guy Kibbee, Eric Blore, and Lucille Ball. Music by Jerome Kern, directed by Tay Garnett. **ST62**

Joy of Sex, The (1984, C, 93m, R)
A high school girl, thinking she has only weeks to live, decides to experience it all before it's too late. Michelle Meyrink and Christopher Lloyd star in this comedy. **C04**

Joyless Street (1925, B&W, 96m, NR)
Silent German drama set in post–World War I Viennese neighborhood, starring Greta Garbo as professor's daughter trying to hold her family together. With Asta Nielsen and Werner Krauss. Directed by G.W. Pabst. **FF3, ST78**

Joyride (1977, C, 92m, R)
Two couples on the road to Alaska fall into a life of crime. Desi Arnaz, Jr., Robert Carradine, Melanie Griffith, and Anne Lockhart star. **DR16, ST93, XT18**

Ju Dou (1989, C, 98m, PG-13)
Chinese drama, set in the 1920s, about cruel old dye-maker and his young wife, who's attracted to her husband's young nephew. Gong Li, Li Bao-Tian, and Li Wei star. Directed by Zhang Yimou. Banned in China for its implicit political criticism of older leaders. **CU8, FF7**

Juarez (1939, B&W, 132m, NR)
This biographical drama stars Paul Muni as Mexican leader Juarez, with Bette Davis as Carlotta. With Brian Aherne, Claude Rains, and John Garfield. **CL2, ST44, ST80**

Jubal (1956, C, 101m, NR)
A rancher becomes jealous of his best friend, who he thinks is having an affair with his lovely wife. Ernest Borgnine and Glenn Ford star, with Valerie French, Rod Steiger, and Charles Bronson. Western take on Shakespeare's *Othello*. **ST20, WR28**

Jubilee Trail (1954, C, 103m, NR)
Vera Ralston plays a saloon singer turned rancher in this Western drama. With Joan Leslie, Forrest Tucker, John Russell, and Pat O'Brien. **WE8**

Judge and the Assassin, The (1975, C, 130m, NR)
French drama of a jurist (Philippe Noiret) who must decide the sanity of a man (Michael Galabru) on trial. With Isabelle Huppert. Directed by Bertrand Tavernier. **DT123**

Judge Priest (1934, B&W, 80m, NR)
John Ford directed this humorous tale of a controversial judge (Will Rogers) in a small town. **DR26, DT44**

Judgment at Nuremberg (1961, B&W, 178m, NR)
Spencer Tracy plays an American judge who presides over the Nuremberg war crimes trials. Outstanding performances by Burt Lancaster, Judy Garland, Montgomery Clift, Marlene Dietrich, and Maximilian Schell, who won an Academy Award as the German defense attorney. Directed by Stanley Kramer, written by Abby Mann. Undeniably powerful, although mostly on the weight of its acting. **CL8, DR17, DT67, ST32, ST55, ST81, ST129, ST217, XT2,** *Recommended*

Judgment in Stone see *The Housekeeper*

Judith of Bethulia (1914, B&W, 65m, NR)
Director D.W. Griffith's first foray into feature-length filmmaking, the biblical tale of the siege of a Judean city and its effect on a pair of lovers. Blanche Sweet and Henry B. Walthall star, with Mae Marsh, Robert Harron, and Lillian and Dorothy Gish. **CL12, CL13, DT52, ST87, XT8**

Juggernaut (1937, B&W, 64m, NR)
A doctor (Boris Karloff) is hired by a woman to murder her husband. But he doesn't stop with one corpse, as he continues to poison people. **ST119**

Juggernaut (1974, C, 109m, PG)
A madman plants four bombs aboard an ocean liner and demands blackmail money from the shipping company. First-rate adventure, with touches of sly wit, starring Richard Harris, Anthony Hopkins, and Shirley Knight, with Omar Sharif, Roy Kinnear, Ian Holm, David Hemmings, and Freddie Jones. Directed by Richard Lester. **AC23, DT74, ST109,** *Highly Recommended*

Juice (1992, C, 96m, R)
Life on the mean streets of New York, with quartet of black teen-agers involved in simple store robbery that goes awry. Omar Epps, Tupac Shakur, Jermaine Hopkins, and Khalil Kain star, with Cindy Herron. Directed and cowritten by Ernest Dickerson, best known for his outstanding cinematography on Spike Lee's films. **DR9, DR14, DR15, MU12, XT9**

Jules and Jim (1961, B&W, 104m, NR)
Director François Truffaut's modern classic:
two men try to share the same free-spirited
woman. Jeanne Moreau, Oskar Werner, and
Henri Serre star. U.S. remake: *Willie and Phil.*
Stick with the original. **DT125, FF8, ST161,
XT26,** *Essential, Highly Recommended*

Julia (1977, C, 118m, PG)
True story of how writer Lillian Hellman got
involved with World War II resistance move-
ment in Europe, thanks to a courageous
friend. Jane Fonda and Oscar winner Vanessa
Redgrave star; Jason Robards also won an
Oscar for playing Dashiell Hammett. Meryl
Streep's screen debut, in a small role. Di-
rected by Fred Zinnemann. **DR4, DT144,
ST72, ST182, ST185, ST210, WR12, XT4,
XT5,** *Recommended*

Julia and Julia (1988, C, 98m, R)
Kathleen Turner stars as a woman whose
husband is killed on their wedding day; years
later, he returns with their six-year-old son.
She's unable to sort reality from fantasy,
which creates tension with her new lover
(Sting). **MU12, ST218, XT24**

Julia Misbehaves (1948, B&W, 99m, NR)
Comedy of show girl (Greer Garson) return-
ing to her ex (Walter Pidgeon) in time for the
wedding of their daughter (Elizabeth Taylor).
With Peter Lawford, Cesar Romero, and Mary
Boland. **ST83, ST212**

Juliet of the Spirits (1965, C, 148m, NR)
Director Federico Fellini's dream-movie about
the fantasies of an ordinary housewife (Giulietta Masina) who's afraid that her husband
is cheating on her. **DT43, XT30**

Julius Caesar (1953, B&W, 120m, NR)
The Shakespeare drama of power politics in
ancient Rome, with Marlon Brando as Mark
Anthony, and James Mason, John Gielgud,
Louis Calhern, Greer Garson, and Deborah
Kerr. Joseph L. Mankiewicz directed. **CL3,
DT84, ST18, ST83, ST86, ST125, ST153,
WR28,** *Recommended*

Julius Caesar (1970, C, 117m, G)
Charlton Heston, Jason Robards, Diana Rigg,
John Gielgud, and Christopher Lee are fea-
tured in this adaptation of Shakespeare's play
about political intrigue in Rome. **DR5,
ST86, ST135, ST185, WR28**

Jumbo (1962, C, 125m, NR)
Rodgers and Hart songs and Busby Berkeley
choreography highlight this circus musical
starring Doris Day, Stephen Boyd, Jimmy
Durante, and Martha Raye. Also known as
Billy Rose's Jumbo. **DT12, MU4, ST47**

Jumpin' Jack Flash (1986, C, 100m, R)
Whoopi Goldberg plays a computer programmer who gets involved in international intrigue when a spy contacts her on her computer screen. With Stephen Collins, John
Wood, Carol Kane, Annie Potts, and Jim
Belushi. Directed by Penny Marshall. Not
enough sense in story, which seems to be
making it up as it goes along. **CO10, CO13,
ST89, XT23**

Jumping Jacks (1952, B&W, 96m, NR)
Martin and Lewis comedy has them joining
paratroopers. Don DeFore and Robert Strauss
offer support. **CL15, CO21, ST139, ST149**

June Bride (1948, B&W, 97m, NR)
Comedy pairs Bette Davis and Robert Mont-
gomery as reporters doing story on title sub-
ject. With Fay Bainter, Tom Tully, and Debbie
Reynolds, making her debut in a small role.
ST44

June Night (1940, B&W, 90m, NR)
Ingrid Bergman stars in this melodrama,
made in Sweden before her Hollywood career
began, about a woman trying to escape her
scandalous past. Also known as *A Night in
June.* **FF7, ST13**

Jungle Book, The (1942, C, 109m, NR)
Colorful live action fantasy about a boy
raised by wolves in the jungle. Great family
entertainment, based on the Kipling book.
FA4

Jungle Book, The (1967, C, 78m, G)
Animated version from the Disney studios
of the Kipling classic, featuring the voices
of Phil Harris, Sebastian Cabot, Louis Prima,
George Sanders, and Sterling Holloway. **FA2**

Jungle Fever (1991, C, 132m, R)
Spike Lee directed this story of the effect an
interracial love affair between a successful,
married black architect (Wesley Snipes) and
his temporary secretary (Annabella Sciorra),
an Italian-American from the Bensonhurst
neighborhood of New York, has on their
families and friends. With Ossie Davis, Ruby
Dee, Samuel L. Jackson, Lonette McKee, John
Turturro, Anthony Quinn, and the director.
Songs by Stevie Wonder. A bit too diffuse to
score any real points, but still strong and
provocative filmmaking. Turturro and Jackson make the strongest impressions. **DR3,
DR7, DR8, DR14, DR15, DT72, ST201,
XT9,** *Recommended*

Jungle Raiders (1985, C, 102m, PG-13)
Adventure story featuring Captain Yankee, a
fearless soldier of fortune who's off in search
of the Ruby of Gloom. Christopher Connelly
and Lee Van Cleef star. **AC21, ST221**

Junior Bonner (1972, C, 103m, PG)
Steve McQueen plays a fading rodeo star who
returns to his hometown show, determined
to be in the spotlight again. With Robert
Preston, Ida Lupino, Joe Don Baker, and Ben
Johnson. Sam Peckinpah directed. Wide-
screen will be lost on video. Entire cast is
superb; Peckinpah in a rare relaxed mood.
CU20, DR8, DT95, ST146, WE12,
Recommended

Juno and the Paycock
(1930, B&W, 85m, NR)
Early Alfred Hitchcock drama of troubles in
Dublin, based on Sean O'Casey play. Sara
Allgood, Edward Chapman, and Sidney Mor-
gan star. **DT57**

Jupiter's Darling (1955, C, 96m, NR)
Esther Williams gets historical in this musical
of a temptress who seduced Hannibal (How-
ard Keel) to stall his attack on Rome. With
George Sanders and Marge and Gower
Champion. **MU1**

Jupiter's Thigh (1983, C, 90m, NR)
Sequel to French comic thriller *Dear Detective*
teams up same stars (Annie Girardot and Philippe Noiret) for a mystery that takes place
on their honeymoon. **FF1**

Just a Gigolo (1979, C, 96m, R)
Atmospheric drama of Prussian war veteran
(David Bowie) adrift in Berlin. Sydne Rome,
Kim Novak, and David Hemmings costar;
Marlene Dietrich makes a brief appearance.
MU12, ST55

Just Another Girl on the I.R.T.
(1993, C, 92m, R)
Drama of cocky black high school student
who's certain she is going to break out of her
Brooklyn neighborhood for better things.
Ariyan Johnson stars, with Kevin Thigpen,
Ebony Jerido, and Chequito Jackson. Written
and directed by Leslie Harris. **DR9, DR14,
DR15**

Just Around the Corner
(1938, B&W, 70m, NR)
Shirley Temple teams with Bill "Bojangles"
Robinson for some of their best musical
numbers, as Shirley puts an end to the Depression by persuading an elderly tycoon to
create more jobs. Bert Lahr and Joan Davis
costar. **ST213**

Just Between Friends
(1986, C, 110m, PG-13)
When a woman's husband is killed in an
accident, she learns a terrible secret about
her new best friend. Mary Tyler Moore and
Christine Lahti star, with Ted Danson and
Sam Waterston. **DR10**

Just Me and You (1978, C, 100m, NR)
A New York eccentric (Louise Lasser) and a
salesman (Charles Grodin) take to the road
in this comedy-drama written by Lasser.
Originally made for TV. **ST94, XT18**

Just Tell Me What You Want
(1980, C, 112m, R)
A business executive (Alan King)
unknowingly pushes his mistress (Ali Mac-
Graw) into the arms of a younger man (Peter
Weller), then does everything in his power to
get her back. Slam-bang New York comedy
directed by Sidney Lumet. With Myrna Loy
and Dina Merrill. King is wonderful, Mac-
Graw much less so. **DT78, ST142, XT9**

Justine (1969, C, 116m, NR)
A banker's wife (Anouk Aimée) gets involved
with politicians from the Middle East. Adaptation of the Lawrence Durrell novel also
stars Dirk Bogarde, Robert Forster, and Michael York. Directed by George Cukor. **DR19,
DT32, ST14**

K2 (1992, C, 111m, R)
Adventure tale of an attorney and physics
professor who attempt to climb the Himalayas' steepest and most remote peak. Michael Biehn, Matt Craven, and Raymond J.
Barry star, with Patricia Charbonneau. Based
on a play by Patrick Myers, directed by Franc
Roddam. **AC12, DR20**

K-9 (1989, C, 102m, PG-13)
James Belushi plays a cop whose new partner
is a German shepherd in this action comedy.
CO10, CO13

Kafka (1991, B&W/C, 98m, PG-13)
Jeremy Irons plays the famed writer in this
dramatic exploration of the influences on his
work, set in 1919 Prague. With Theresa Russell,
Joel Grey, Ian Holm, Jeroen Krabbe, Armin
Mueller-Stahl, and Alec Guinness. Written by
Lem Dobbs, directed by Steven Soderbergh.
One fourteen-minute sequence in color. Inter-
mittent rewards. **DR4, ST95, ST116**

Kagemusha (1980, C, 159m, PG)
Epic adventure tale of thief who assumes
identity of dead warlord, directed by Japan's
premier filmmaker, Akira Kurosawa. Tatsuya
Nakadai stars. **DT69,** *Recommended*

Kameradschaft (1931, B&W, 89m, NR)
Classic German drama of post–World War I
enmity between Germans and French forgotten during mining disaster rescue. Directed
by G.W. Pabst. **FF3**

Kamikaze '89 (1982, C, 106m, NR)
Thriller set in futuristic Germany about a
detective (Rainer Werner Fassbinder) foiling
a bomb plot. **FF3, DT42**

Kanal (1956, B&W, 90m, NR)
From Polish director Andrzej Wajda, an un-bearably tense drama of the Polish resistance fighters taking their last stand against the Nazis during the Warsaw uprising. **DT130,**
Recommended

Kangaroo (1986, C, 105m, R)
Australian drama, based on D.H. Lawrence's autobiographical novel, of a writer scorned in his native England. He and his German-born wife emigrate to Australia, where they become involved with a band of Fascists. Colin Friels and Judy Davis star. **FF5, ST46, WR17**

Kansas (1988, C, 111m, R)
Two aimless young men (Matt Dillon and Andrew McCarthy) pull off an impromptu bank robbery. One hides the money, and his partner comes looking for him. **DR16, ST56**

Kansas City Confidential
(1952, B&W, 98m, NR)
Film noir of ex-con framed for robbery, look-ing for revenge on a crime boss. John Payne stars, with Coleen Gray, Preston Foster, Nev-ille Brand, Lee Van Cleef, and Jack Elam. Directed by Phil Karlson. **MY1, ST221**

Kaos (1984, C, 188m, R)
Italian drama adapted from Luigi Pirandello stories of childhood memories, set in turn-of-the-century Sicily. Directed by Paolo and Vit-torio Taviani. Originally made for Italian TV. **FF2**

Karate Kid, The (1984, C, 126m, PG)
The new kid in town is the punching bag for neighborhood bullies until a kindly handy-man teaches him self-defense. Ralph Macchio and Noriyuki "Pat" Morita star. Overlong, overdone. **DR9, DR22, FA7**

Karate Kid, Part II, The
(1986, C, 113m, PG)
Further adventures of the young karate stu-dent, now in Japan for martial arts tourna-ment, and his kindly teacher. **DR9, DR22, FA7**

Karate Kid, Part III, The
(1989, C, 111m, PG)
Daniel (Ralph Macchio) won't participate in a karate tournament until a bully gets his goat. Noriyuki "Pat" Morita costars. **DR9, DR22, FA7**

Katherine (1975, C, 100m, NR)
Sissy Spacek plays a young woman who turns from political activist to terrorist. With Art Carney and Henry Winkler. Originally made for TV. **DR7, ST202**

Keep 'em Flying (1941, B&W, 86m, NR)
Abbott and Costello join the Air Force. With Dick Foran and Martha Raye as twins. **CO21, ST1**

Keep the Change (1992, C, 95m, NR)
Drama of contemporary West, set in small Montana town, where an expatriate returns to claim his family land from the clutches of a greedy rancher. William Petersen stars, with Lolita Davidovich, Rachel Ticotin, Jack Palance, Fred Thompson, and Buck Henry. Adapted from a novel by Tom McGuane. Originally made for cable TV. Misses the edginess of McGuane but does capture some feel for his milieu. **DR19, WE12**

Keeper, The (1984, C, 96m, NR)
The patients at an insane asylum are tortured by their sadistic keeper. Christopher Lee stars in this horror drama. **ST135**

Keeper of the Flame
(1942, B&W, 100m, NR)
Spencer Tracy is a reporter out to break a story on late American hero; Katharine Hep-burn is the man's widow. Directed by George Cukor. **CL15, DT32, ST103, ST217**

Keeping On (1981, C, 75m, NR)
Drama of union organizer who doubles as a preacher. Dick Anthony Williams stars, with Carol Kane, James Broderick, Marcia Rodd, Rosalind Cash, and Danny Glover. Directed by Barbara Kopple. Originally made for TV. **DR7, ST88**

Keeping Track (1985, C, 102m, R)
A newsman and a bank teller become pawns in a game of international intrigue after $5 million falls into their laps. Michael Sarrazin and Margot Kidder star. **MY6**

Kelly's Heroes (1970, C, 145m, PG)
A gang of GIs plans a daring robbery behind enemy lines during World War II. Clint East-wood stars in this comedy-adventure, with Telly Savalas, Donald Sutherland, Carroll O'Connor, and Harry Dean Stanton. **CO21, MY18, ST64, ST205**

Kennel Murder Case, The
(1933, B&W, 73m, NR)
William Powell plays Philo Vance, the sophisticated detective, as he investigates a murder in New York City. **MY10, ST176**

Kent State (1981, C, 150m, NR)
Dramatic recreation of events of May 4, 1970, when four students were murdered by National Guardsman at an Ohio campus dur-ing a Vietnam War protest. Jane Fleiss, Char-ley Lang, Talia Balsam, Keith Gordon, John Getz, and Ellen Barkin star. Emmy-winning

direction by James Goldstone. Originally made for TV. **DR6, ST7**

Kentuckian, The (1955, C, 104m, NR)
Burt Lancaster stars in this Western about a man starting life over with his son in 1820s Texas. With Diana Lynn and Walter Matthau. Lancaster directed. **ST129, ST155**

Kentucky Kernels (1934, B&W, 75m, NR)
Comic team of Bert Wheeler and Robert Woolsey star in this story of the Old South. They aid a youngster (Spanky McFarland) trying to collect his inheritance and find themselves embroiled in a family feud. Directed by George Stevens. **DT119**

Kermit and Piggy Story, The (1985, C, 57m, NR)
The rags-to-riches show biz saga of The Muppets' Miss Piggy, as told by Cheryl Ladd, Raquel Welch, and Tony Randall. **FA14**

Key, The (1958, B&W, 125m, NR)
In World War II London, a woman whose apartment key has passed from one sea captain to another, in a series of affairs, finally finds true love with a Canadian officer. Sophia Loren and William Holden star. Directed by Carol Reed. **ST106, ST141**

Key Largo (1948, B&W, 101m, NR)
A gangster (Edward G. Robinson) holds people captive in a Florida hotel during a hurricane. Humphrey Bogart and Lauren Bacall star, with Claire Trevor, who won an Oscar for Best Supporting Actress. Directed by John Huston. Impeccable star power smooths over rough edges. **CL15, DT60, MY1, ST15, ST186, XT5,** *Recommended*

Keys of the Kingdom (1944, B&W, 137m, NR)
Drama of a missionary sent to China, adapted from the novel by A.J. Cronin. Gregory Peck stars, with Thomas Mitchell and Vincent Price. **DR27, ST171, ST179**

Khartoum (1966, C, 134m, NR)
True story of British Major "Chinese" Gordon (Charlton Heston) and his confrontation in 1833 Africa with a wily Arab spiritual leader (Laurence Olivier). With Richard Johnson, Ralph Richardson, Alexander Knox, and Michael Hordern. **DR5, ST168, ST184**

Kickboxer (1989, C, 97m, R)
Jean-Claude Van Damme plays this title role in this martial arts saga. **AC26**

Kid, The/The Idle Class (1921, B&W, 85m, NR)
In his first feature-length film, Charlie Chaplin plays The Little Tramp, who adopts an orphan (Jackie Coogan). Also included on this tape is the Chaplin short, *The Idle Class.* **DT24,** *Essential, Highly Recommended*

Kid for Two Farthings, A (1955, C, 91m, NR)
British drama of boy fascinated by legend of unicorn who finds a goat with horns he dubs one. Celia Johnson, Diana Dors, David Kossoff, and Jonathan Ashmore star. Directed by Carol Reed. **DR23, FA7**

Kid From Brooklyn, The (1946, C, 113m, NR)
Danny Kaye comedy about a milkman turned pugilist, with Virginia Mayo, Vera-Ellen, and Eve Arden. **CO19, ST120**

Kid Galahad (1937, B&W, 101m, NR)
Edward G. Robinson plays a boxing promoter who loses his girl (Bette Davis) to his new fighter (Wayne Morris). With Humphrey Bogart and Harry Carey. Remade in 1962 as Elvis Presley musical. **DR22, ST15, ST44, ST186**

Kid Galahad (1962, C, 95m, NR)
Elvis Presley plays a successful boxer who would rather be a mechanic. Charles Bronson has a small role. **DR22, MU14, ST20, ST178**

Kid Vengeance (1977, C, 94m, NR)
Western drama of revenge, with young man (Leif Garrett) tracking down the men who murdered his parents and kidnapped his sister. With Lee Van Cleef, Jim Brown, John Marley, and Glynnis O'Connor. **ST221, WE5**

Kid Who Loved Christmas, The (1990, C, 100m, NR)
Tale of black orphan attempting to cut red tape to be with his adopted dad for the holidays. Trent Cameron stars, with Cicely Tyson, Michael Warren, Sammy Davis, Jr. (his last movie), Della Reese, and Esther Rolle. Produced by Eddie Murphy. Originally made for TV. **DR14, FA13**

Kidnap Syndicate (1975, C, 83m, R)
Italian-made crime saga of two gangsters who snatch the sons of a millionaire and auto mechanic, with violent retribution in the offing. James Mason stars, with Valentina Cortese and Luc Merenda. **ST153**

Kidnapped (1960, C, 97m, NR)
Disney adaptation of Robert Louis Stevenson's book, about a young heir who looks for his uncle, only to be abducted along the way and sold into slavery. Peter Finch and James MacArthur star, with Peter O'Toole. **FA1, ST169, WR33**

Kidnapping of the President, The (1980, C, 113m, R)
Thriller of terrorists who abduct the Chief

Executive. William Shatner stars as a Secret Service agent, with Hal Holbrook, Van Johnson, and Ava Gardner. **MY6, ST79**

Kids Are Alright, The (1979, C, 108m, NR)
Documentary on the British rock group The Who, concentrating on the group's memorable concert performances. With brief appearances by Ringo Starr, Tom Smothers, and Steve Martin. **MU11, ST150**

Kid's Auto Race/Mabel's Married Life (1914/1915, B&W, 21m, NR)
Charlie Chaplin stars in two of his most famous short films. The first deals with a kiddie-car contest. The second focuses on two married people who flirt in the park. **DT24**

Kill and Kill Again (1981, C, 100m, R)
Sequel to *Kill or Be Killed*, with karate star James Ryan foiling the plans of an evil scientist. **AC26**

Kill, Baby, Kill (1966, C, 90m, NR)
The ghost of a murdered girl returns to her European village to avenge her death. Directed by Mario Bava. Also known as *Curse of the Living Dead*. **HO13**

Kill Me Again (1989, C, 94m, R)
A down-and-out private eye decides to help a woman fake her murder—unaware that she's trying to shake a psychotic boyfriend. Joanne Whalley-Kilmer, Val Kilmer, and Michael Madsen star. Wan, with married leads especially disappointing. **MY2, MY4, MY10**

Kill or Be Killed (1980, C, 90m, PG)
Karate champ James Ryan stars in a drama about an ex-Nazi and his Japanese counterpart from World War II meeting years later in a martial arts tournament. **AC26**

Killer, The (1989, C, 110m, NR)
Bullet-riddled tale, made in Hong Kong, of hired killer out to go straight after he accidentally blinds a lovely singer during a nightclub rubout. Written and directed with tremendous flair by John Woo. The final shootout in a church is a real jaw-dropper. **AC25, CU7, FF7,** *Recommended*

Killer Bait (1949, B&W, 98m, NR)
Film noir of a couple who stumble into ill-gotten money; he wants to return it, but she'll do anything to keep it. Lizabeth Scott, Don DeFore, Dan Duryea, and Arthur Kennedy star. Also known as *Too Late for Tears*. Good use of Los Angeles locations. Genre fans only. **MY1, MY4, XT10**

Killer Bats (1941, B&W, 67m, NR)
A cosmetics manufacturer deprives his partner (Bela Lugosi) of his share of the profits, and the partner plots revenge. Also known as *The Devil Bat*. **ST143**

Killer Elite, The (1975, C, 122m, R)
A tale of two professional assassins (James Caan and Robert Duvall) who end up stalking each other. Sam Peckinpah directed on locations in San Francisco. Some sequences show flashes of the director's talent, but there's a lot of dead air, too. **AC8, AC19, DT95, MY6, ST63, XT13**

Killer Force (1975, C, 100m, PG)
A diamond mine in South Africa is the scene for skullduggery in this action-adventure story, starring Peter Fonda and Telly Savalas, with Hugh O'Brian, Christopher Lee, and O.J. Simpson. **ST135**

Killer Inside Me, The (1976, C, 99m, R)
Stacy Keach plays a deputy sheriff who is near the breaking point. Based on a novel by Jim Thompson. **MY13, WR34**

Killer Party (1986, C, 92m, R)
A trio of sorority pledges are special guests at an April Fool's party held in an abandoned fraternity house. Horror drama starring Elaine Wilkes, with Paul Bartel. **DT8, HO12**

Killers, The (1964, C, 95m, NR)
Thriller, loosely based on Hemingway short story, about hit men learning about their victim's past. Lee Marvin, Angie Dickinson, John Cassavetes, and Ronald Reagan (in his last film) star. Directed by Don Siegel. Originally made for TV but deemed too violent, so it was released to theaters. Cult reputation for Reagan's role as sadistic hoodlum. Relentlessly downbeat; worth a look for fans of stars or genre. **CU2, DT116, ST151, WR13, XT22**

Killer's Kiss (1955, B&W, 67m, NR)
Early film from director Stanley Kubrick about a boxer looking for revenge after his manager is murdered. Frank Silvera, Jamie Smith, and Irene Kane star. Story behind its filming was inspiration for *Stranger's Kiss*. **DT68, MY1, XT26**

Killing, The (1956, B&W, 83m, NR)
Breakthrough film for director Stanley Kubrick, a taut tale of a gang pulling off a complex robbery at a racetrack. Sterling Hayden stars, with Coleen Gray, Vince Edwards, Elisha Cook, Jr., and Timothy Carey. Screenplay by Kubrick and Jim Thompson. **DT56, MY1, MY18, WR34,** *Recommended*

Killing Fields, The (1984, C, 142m, R)
Fact-based, unbearably tense drama about *New York Times* reporter escaping Cambodia during Vietnam War and his subsequent re-

union with his translator. Sam Waterston and Oscar winner Haing S. Ngor star. Directed by Roland Joffe. **DR6, XT4,** *Recommended*

Killing of Angel Street, The
(1981, C, 101m, PG)
A political activist and a geologist team up to halt greedy real estate developers who are forcing residents to sell their homes. Australian drama stars Liz Alexander and John Hargreaves. **FF5**

Killing of Randy Webster, The
(1981, C, 100m, NR)
True-life drama of teen killed by Houston police, with his father investigating the circumstances. Hal Holbrook stars, with Dixie Carter, James Whitmore, Jr., and Jennifer Jason Leigh. Originally made for TV. **DR6, ST136**

Killing of Sister George, The
(1968, C, 138m, R)
A middle-aged British actress loses her job on a popular TV series and is also in danger of losing her young female lover to another woman. Beryl Reid, Susannah York, and Coral Browne star. Robert Aldrich directed this drama. **DR3, DT1**

Killings at Outpost Zeta, The
(1980, C, 92m, NR)
Science fiction mystery about team of scientists and soldiers investigating murders at a remote planet. **SF17**

Killjoy (1981, C, 100m, NR)
Whodunit about a murdered woman and the many possible suspects. Robert Culp and Kim Basinger star. **MY12**

Kim (1950, C, 113m, NR)
Rudyard Kipling's tale of British soldiers fighting against fierce tribesmen in India, starring Errol Flynn and Dean Stockwell. **AC13, FA4, ST69, ST208**

Kind Hearts and Coronets
(1949, B&W, 104m, NR)
The black sheep of a wealthy family decides to kill them off. Alec Guinness plays all eight victims in this delightful comic British mystery. **CL10, CL17, MY15, MY17, ST95, XT27,** *Essential, Recommended*

Kind of Loving, A (1962, B&W, 112m, NR)
British drama of a young couple wed because of her pregnancy. Alan Bates and June Ritchie star. Directed by John Schlesinger. **DR23, DT113, ST9**

Kindergarten Cop (1990, C, 110m, PG-13)
Arnold Schwarzenegger plays a hard-bitten cop forced to go undercover as a kinder-garten teacher. With Penelope Ann Miller, Pamela Reed, Linda Hunt, Carroll Baker, and Richard Tyson. Uneasy blend of comedy and violence, especially because it involves young children. **CO18, CO20, ST195**

Kindred, The (1987, C, 92m, R)
A young man discovers that he has been the guinea pig for an experiment combining his tissue with that of a sea monster. Rod Steiger and Kim Hunter star. **HO13**

King (1978, C, 272m, NR)
TV miniseries on the life of Dr. Martin Luther King, Jr. and his leadership in the civil rights struggle. Paul Winfield stars, with Cicely Tyson, Ossie Davis, Roscoe Lee Browne, and Howard Rollins, Jr. Written and directed by Abby Mann. **DR4, DR7, DR14, ST230**

King and Four Queens, The
(1956, C, 86m, NR)
Clark Gable Western has him looking for money hidden by the husbands of four women. With Eleanor Parker, Jo Van Fleet, Jean Willes, and Barbara Nichols. Directed by Raoul Walsh. **DT131, ST77, WE8**

King and I, The (1956, C, 133m, NR)
Yul Brynner won an Oscar for his performance as the King of Siam in this version of the Rodgers and Hammerstein Broadway musical. Deborah Kerr stars as Anna, the governess hired to teach his many children. **FA9, MU2, MU7, ST125, XT2**

King Creole (1958, B&W, 116m, NR)
A nightclub singer (Elvis Presley) with a troubled past gets involved with criminals in New Orleans. With Walter Matthau. **ST155, ST178**

King David (1985, C, 114m, PG-13)
Richard Gere stars as the biblical monarch in this drama costarring Edward Woodward as Saul and Alice Krige as Bathsheba. Directed by Bruce Beresford. **CL13, DT10, ST84**

King in New York, A
(1957, B&W, 105m, NR)
Charlie Chaplin comedy about a European monarch who visits America during the McCarthy witch hunts and gets a strong taste of American morality. **CO20, DT24**

King Kong (1933, B&W, 100m, NR)
The granddaddy of all oversized animal movies, with the big hairy ape terrorizing Skull Island and then demolishing Manhattan. Robert Armstrong, Bruce Cabot, and Fay Wray star. Makes you feel like a nine-year-old all over again. **CU4, FA8, HO1, HO16, SF2, SF10, SF13, SF16, XT9,** *Essential, Highly Recommended*

King Kong (1976, C, 134m, PG)
Jeff Bridges and Jessica Lange star in this remake of the classic story about a gigantic ape who captures a young woman and terrorizes Manhattan. With Charles Grodin. One of the great unnecessary remakes of all time. **CU18, HO16, ST19, ST94, ST130, XT9**

King Lear (1971, B&W, 137m, PG)
Shakespeare's tragedy of a lonely monarch, starring Paul Scofield, Irene Worth, and Jack MacGowran. Directed by Peter Brook. **DR23, WR28**

King Lear (1987, C, 91m, PG)
The title is Shakespeare, but the director is French iconoclast Jean-Luc Godard, who "updates" the tale in his own way. Peter Sellars, Burgess Meredith, and Molly Ringwald head the cast, with appearances by Woody Allen and Norman Mailer. **DT2, DT50, WR28**

King of Comedy, The (1983, C, 109m, PG)
A stand-up comic kidnaps a popular talk-show host in hopes of getting a shot at the big time. Dark comedy about success and fame, starring Robert De Niro and Jerry Lewis, with Sandra Bernhard. Directed by Martin Scorsese. Not one of a great director's best films but still provocative and mordantly funny. **CO2, CO12, CU5, DT114, MY19, ST51, ST139, XT9**, *Recommended*

King of Hearts (1966, C, 102m, NR)
Midnight movie classic, a fantasy about a World War I soldier separated from his division and coming upon a town occupied only by inmates escaped from an asylum. Alan Bates and Geneviève Bujold star. Available in a letterboxed edition. **CU1, CU5, CU19, ST9**

King of Jazz, The (1930, C, 93m, NR)
This revue features a cartoon sequence by Walter Lantz, plus Bing Crosby and the Rhythm Boys, and a performance of Gershwin's "Rhapsody in Blue." **MU15, ST40**

King of Kings, The
(1927, B&W/C, 115m, NR)
Cecil B. DeMille's silent spectacular on the life of Christ (H.B. Warner). The Resurrection is presented in two-color Technicolor. **CL12, CL13, DT34, HF17**

King of Kings (1961, C, 168m, NR)
Nicholas Ray directed this epic drama centering on the life of Christ. Jeffrey Hunter stars, with Robert Ryan, Rip Torn, and Hurd Hatfield. **CL13, DT101, HF17, ST193, ST216**

King of New York (1990, C, 103m, R)
Violent melodrama with cult following, focuses on ex-con (Christopher Walken) resuming his drug-dealing ways, wiping out rivals, battling police. Set in New York, with David Caruso, Larry Fishburne, Victor Argo, Wesley Snipes, and Janet Julian. Directed by Abel Ferrara. Overkill would be a polite way to describe the proceedings. **AC8, AC9, AC22, CU7, ST201, ST222, XT9**

King of the Cowboys
(1943, B&W, 67m, NR)
Roy Rogers fights contemporary saboteurs who are plotting to destroy a defense installation. With Smiley Burnette. **ST188**

King of the Grizzlies (1970, C, 93m, G)
In this Disney film, an Indian youth befriends a bear cub, only to grow up to face the same animal as a full-grown grizzly. **FA1**

King of the Gypsies (1978, C, 112m, R)
Eric Roberts stars in the title role as a young man destined to rule his wandering modern clan. With Judd Hirsch, Susan Sarandon, Sterling Hayden, Shelley Winters, Annette O'Toole, and Brooke Shields. **DR8, ST194, ST232**

King of the Kongo, The
(1929, B&W, 213m, NR)
Silent serial starring Boris Karloff in a tale of ivory thieves in Africa. **ST119**

King of the Mountain (1981, C, 90m, PG)
A mechanic and his pals spend their spare time racing on Los Angeles's winding Mulholland Drive. Harry Hamlin stars, with Joseph Bottoms, Deborah Van Valkenburgh, and Dennis Hopper as the one-time King of the Mountain. **AC10, ST110**

King of the Roaring '20s—The Story of Arnold Rothstein (1961, B&W, 106m, NR)
David Janssen stars in this story of the legendary gangster which doesn't let facts get in the way. With Dianne Foster, Jack Carson, Diana Dors, and Mickey Rooney. **AC22, ST189**

King Ralph (1991, C, 97m, PG)
Comedy of lovable American slob (John Goodman) who, through no fault of his own, ascends to the throne of England. With Peter O'Toole, John Hurt, and Richard Griffiths. **CO20, ST169**

King Rat (1965, B&W, 133m, NR)
In a Japanese POW camp during World War II, an American hustler inspires envy and grudging admiration from his fellow captives. George Segal stars, with Tom Courtenay and James Fox. Directed by Bryan Forbes; probably his best film. **AC7**, *Recommended*

King Solomon's Mines
(1937, B&W, 80m, NR)
First screen version of classic tale of African exploration, starring Paul Robeson, Cedric Hardwicke, and Roland Young. **AC12, AC13, AC21**

King Solomon's Mines
(1950, C, 102m, NR)
Second and most popular version of the H. Rider Haggard tale of African adventure, starring Stewart Granger and Deborah Kerr. **AC12, AC13, AC21, FA4, ST125**

King Solomon's Mines
(1985, C, 100m, PG-13)
Richard Chamberlain stars as the classic British adventurer, Allan Quatermain, as he plunges into deepest, darkest Africa in search of a fabled treasure. **AC12, AC21**

Kings Go Forth (1958, B&W, 109m, NR)
Drama of American G.I.s in World War II France, starring Frank Sinatra, Tony Curtis, and Natalie Wood. **AC1, ST199**

Kings of the Road (1976, B&W, 176m, NR)
Rambling drama from director Wim Wenders about two drifters making their way through the contemporary German landscape. **DT136, XT18**

King's Row (1942, B&W, 127m, NR)
Classic drama of small-town life in the years prior to World War I. Ronald Reagan and Robert Cummings star. **CL6, DR26, Essential**

Kinjite: Forbidden Subjects
(1989, C, 97m, R)
A Los Angeles cop (Charles Bronson) with a grudge against Orientals must change his tune when he must track down the kidnapped daughter of a visiting Japanese businessman. **AC9, ST20**

Kismet (1955, C, 113m, NR)
Howard Keel and Ann Blyth star in this colorful musical based on the Broadway show about the Arabian Nights. Directed by Vincente Minnelli. **DT88, MU1, MU2, MU8**

Kiss, The (1929, B&W, 89m, NR)
Greta Garbo's last silent, a drama of a married woman's harmless flirtation with a young man leading to tragedy. With Lew Ayres and Conrad Nagel. **CL12, ST78**

Kiss, The (1988, C, 101m, R)
Horror tale of a young girl (Meredith Salenger) and her spooky aunt (Joanna Pacula), who is determined to infect her niece with the family curse. **HO14**

Kiss and Kill see *Against All Odds* (1969)

Kiss Before Dying, A (1991, C, 95m, R)
Remake of 1956 thriller (not available on video) about an ambitious young man not above murder in his rise to social prominence. Matt Dillon stars, with Sean Young (as sisters), Max von Sydow, James Russo, and Diane Ladd. **MY3, ST56, XT27**

Kiss Me Deadly (1955, B&W, 105m, NR)
Ralph Meeker plays Mickey Spillane's famous private eye, Mike Hammer, as he uncovers the secret behind a lead-lined box that's causing a lot of mayhem. With Albert Dekker, Paul Stewart, Cloris Leachman (in her debut, in a raincoat), Maxine Cooper, Gaby Rodgers, Jack Elam, and Strother Martin. Directed by Robert Aldrich. Watch for those opening credits—they roll backwards! Hardboiled and true to Spillane in every way; quintessential *film noir*. **DT1, MY1, MY4, WR31**, *Essential, Highly Recommended*

Kiss Me Goodbye (1982, C, 101m, PG)
Sally Field plays a young New York socialite visited by the ghost of her dead husband (James Caan) just as she's about to marry another man (Jeff Bridges). Loosely based on *Doña Flor and Her Two Husbands*. **FF8, ST19, ST66, XT24**

Kiss Me Kate (1953, C, 109m, NR)
Cole Porter's musical version of *The Taming of the Shrew* stars Howard Keel, Kathryn Grayson, and Ann Miller. Watch for Bob Fosse. **DT47, MU1, MU2, MU14, WR28**

Kiss Me, Stupid (1964, B&W, 126m, NR)
Farce about preening show-biz demi-legend (Dean Martin) stalled in small town of Climax, Nevada, being pitched to by a pair of aspiring songwriters (Ray Walston, Cliff Osmond), who aren't above using a local prostitute (Kim Novak) to help the cause. With Felicia Farr as Walston's put-upon wife. Directed by Billy Wilder, who scripted with I.A.L. Diamond. Target of heavy Catholic condemnation which now seems ludicrous. Cult following claims this as underrated Wilder work. **CO8, CU5, CU6, CU8, DT139, ST149**

Kiss of Death (1947, B&W, 98m, NR)
Film noir about thief (Victor Mature) who throws in with cops to catch a gang. With Brian Donlevy, Coleen Gray, Richard Widmark (as a giggling psycho), and Mildred Dunnock. **AC22, MY1**, *Recommended*

Kiss of the Spider Woman
(1985, C/B&W, 119m, R)
Oscar winner William Hurt stars with Raul Julia and Sonia Braga in this drama of cellmates, one a political prisoner, the other a

homosexual with his film fantasies. Directed by Hector Babenco. A one-hour idea stretched to two. **DR18, FF6, ST17, ST114, XT2**

Kiss Tomorrow Goodbye
(1950, B&W, 102m, NR)
James Cagney plays the most ruthless of all criminals in one of his last tough-guy roles. **ST24**

Kissin' Cousins (1964, C, 96m, NR)
Elvis Presley in a dual role: a military officer and his down-home relative. The army man is trying to persuade the hick to sell his farm as a site for a missile base. **ST178, XT27**

Kitchen Toto, The (1987, C, 96m, PG-13)
Drama set in Kenya in the 1950s, as that country was breaking away from British rule. A young black boy working in the house of the British chief of police watches the violent events of revolution unfold. Edwin Mahinda, Bob Peck, and Phyllis Logan star. Directed by Harry Hook. **DR5, DR9, DR14**

Kitty and the Bagman (1982, C, 95m, R)
Australian comedy-drama about true-life couple in Roaring Twenties, a crooked cop (John Stanton) and his lover (Liddy Clark), the Underworld Queen of Sydney. **FF5**

Kitty Foyle (1940, B&W, 107m, NR)
Ginger Rogers won an Academy Award for her performance as a working-class girl who falls in love with her boss. **CL5, CL6, ST187, XT3**

Klansman, The (1974, C, 112m, R)
Lee Marvin is a small-town Southern sheriff, Richard Burton the wealthy landowner in this melodrama of boiling racial tensions. With Cameron Mitchell, Lola Falana, Linda Evans, and O.J. Simpson. Cowritten by Sam Fuller. Also known as *The Burning Cross*. **DR14, DR26, ST22, ST151**

Klute (1971, C, 114m, R)
Oscar winner Jane Fonda stars as a New York call girl who is being threatened by sadistic phone calls. She attracts the attention of Klute (Donald Sutherland), a small-town detective searching for a missing friend. With Charles Cioffi, Roy Scheider, Dorothy Tristan, and Jean Stapleton. Directed by Alan J. Pakula. Use of widescreen will be lost on video; still an absorbing film, with Fonda outstanding. **CU20, DT94, MY3, MY5, MY10, ST72, XT3,** *Recommended*

Knife in the Water (1962, B&W, 94m, NR)
Director Roman Polanski's groundbreaking drama of a couple who pick up a hitchhiker and invite him on a boating holiday. In Polish. Superbly orchestrated suspense. **DT97, FF7,** *Essential, Recommended*

Knight Without Armor
(1937, B&W, 101m, NR)
Robert Donat is the secret agent who helps Russian noblewoman Marlene Dietrich escape vengeful revolutionaries. **MY6, ST55**

Knightriders (1981, C, 145m, R)
George Romero wrote and directed this unusual drama about a traveling motorcycle gang who stage medieval fairs in which knights joust on cycles. Ed Harris stars. **DT108**

Knights and Emeralds (1986, C, 94m, PG)
Racial tension develops when a young white musician (Christopher Wild) befriends black musicians in this British drama-musical. **DR23**

Knights of the City (1985, C, 87m, R)
Action drama set on the mean streets of Miami, where a street gang tries to go straight and start a career in the music industry. Leon Isaac Kennedy, Nicholas Campbell, and singer Smokey Robinson star. **AC8**

Knights of the Round Table
(1953, C, 115m, NR)
Robert Taylor, Ava Gardner, and Mel Ferrer star in this lavish drama of the King Arthur legend. **AC13, ST79**

Knock on Any Door
(1949, B&W, 100m, NR)
Humphrey Bogart plays a prominent attorney who defends a young hoodlum accused of killing a cop. With John Derek and George Macready. Directed by Nicholas Ray. **CL8, DT101, MY1, ST15**

Knockout, The/Dough and Dynamite
(1914, B&W, 54m, NR)
Charlie Chaplin stars in both of these comedy shorts, featuring some of his most famous routines. *The Knockout* features Chaplin as the referee of a big fight. *Dough and Dynamite* is about a strike at a bakery where Chaplin works. **DT24**

Knute Rockne, All American
(1940, B&W, 84m, NR)
Pat O'Brien plays the legendary Notre Dame football coach and Ronald Reagan is his star player, George Gipp. **CL2, DR22**

Kojiro (1967, C, 152m, NR)
In a followup to Japanese director Hiroshi Inagaki's *Samurai Trilogy*, Tatsuya Nakadai plays a famed swordsman whose exploits young Kojiro (Kikunosuke Onoe) emulates. **FF4**

Kotch (1971, C, 113m, G)
Walter Matthau plays an elderly man who resists his family's attempts to write him off. Jack Lemmon directed this comedy-drama. **DR11, ST138, ST155**

Koyaanisqatsi (1983, C, 87m, NR)
Impressions of nature and man-made structures blend together in this one-of-a-kind documentary meditation on contemporary life. Directed by Godfrey Reggio; music by Philip Glass. **CU16**

Kramer vs. Kramer (1979, C, 104m, PG)
Drama of a marriage breakup and the father's learning to care for his young son, starring Dustin Hoffman, Meryl Streep, and Justin Henry, with JoBeth Williams and Howard Duff. Written and directed by Robert Benton. Oscar winner for Best Picture, Actor, Supporting Actress, and Director. **DR8, DR17, DT9, ST105, ST210, XT1, XT2, XT5, XT6,** *Essential, Recommended*

Krays, The (1990, C, 119m, R)
True saga of twin brother British gangsters who terrorized London during the Swinging '60s. Musicians Gary and Martin Kemp (brothers, not twins) star, with Billie Whitelaw as their manipulative mum. Directed by Peter Medak. Brutal, moody, with Whitelaw especially good. **AC22, DR4, DR16, DR23, MU12, XT8, XT15**

Kriemhilde's Revenge
(1924, B&W, 95m, NR)
This silent film, directed by Fritz Lang, is the sequel to *Siegfried*, based on a popular legend of German mythology. **DT70, FF3**

Kronos (1957, B&W, 78m, NR)
A metallic monster from outer space crashlands off the coast of Mexico and begins absorbing all the Earth's energy. Science fiction drama stars Jeff Morrow, Barbara Lawrence, and John Emery. **SF1**

Krull (1983, C, 117m, PG)
Sword and sorcery adventure of young man in search of a lost jewel, starring Ken Marshall and Lysette Anthony. Lavish production values. Directed by Peter Yates. **AC18**

Kuffs (1992, C, 101m, PG-13)
Action comedy starring Christian Slater as a young smart-aleck who inherits his murdered brother's private cop business. With Tony Goldwyn, Bruce Boxleitner, George de la Pena, and Milla Jovovich. Filmed in San Francisco. **AC9, CO9, ST200, XT13**

Kwaidan (1964, C, 164m, NR)
A quartet of horror stories from Japan, based on works by Lafcadio Hearn. Imaginative use of color; directed by Masaki Kobayashi. Now available in letterboxed edition. **CU19, FF4**

L.A. Story (1991, C, 95m, PG-13)
Steve Martin stars in this gentle comedy as a TV weatherman in love with his town and a visiting Britisher (Victoria Tennant). With Richard E. Grant, Marilu Henner, and Sarah Jessica Parker. Martin wrote the screenplay. Lightly likable. **CO1, CO2, ST150, XT10**

La Balance (1982, C, 102m, R)
Gritty, no-apologies cop drama from France about a Parisian prostitute and her boyfriend forced to inform on crime boss by a ruthless cop. Nathalie Baye, Philippe Léotard, and Richard Berry star. An American, Bob Swaim, directed. **FF1, XT16,** *Recommended*

La Bamba (1987, C, 108m, PG-13)
Biography of rock 'n' roll's first Hispanic star, Ritchie Valens, starring Lou Diamond Phillips. With Esai Morales, Elizabeth Pena, Marshall Crenshaw as Buddy Holly, and Howard Huntsberry as Jackie Wilson. Los Lobos performs Valens's music on the soundtrack. **MU5, XT26,** *Recommended*

La Bête Humaine (1938, B&W, 102m, NR)
French drama of a railway worker's obsession with a married woman, who tries to persuade him to kill her husband. Jean Renoir directed; Jean Gabin, Simone Simon, and the director star. U.S. remake: *Human Desire*. **DT104, FF8,** *Recommended*

La Boum (1981, C, 100m, PG)
A teen-age girl tries to stay out of the way of her quarreling parents in this comedy-drama from France. Claude Brasseur, Brigitte Fossey, and Sophie Marceau star. **FF1**

La Cage aux Folles (1979, C, 110m, R)
French comedy about a gay couple (Ugo Tognazzi and Michel Serrault), one with a son about to be married, both trying to keep their private lives secret from the future in-laws. **CU5, FF1**

La Cage aux Folles II (1981, C, 101m, R)
More misadventures with the popular gay couple (Ugo Tognazzi and Michel Serrault), this time involving espionage and multiple mistaken identities. **FF1**

La Cage aux Folles III: The Wedding
(1986, C, 88m, PG-13)
In the third chapter, the oddest couple are about to land an inheritance, but only if one of them is married. **FF1, XT20**

La Chèvre (1981, C, 91m, NR)
French comedy starring Pierre Richard and Gérard Depardieu as a pair of inept detectives on the trail of a kidnapped businessman's

daughter. Also known as *The Goat*. U.S. remake: *Pure Luck*. **FF1, FF8, ST52**

La Chienne (1931, B&W, 95m, NR)
Director Jean Renoir's first sound film, about a timid bank clerk led astray by a prostitute and her scheming pimp. Michel Simon, Janie Mareze, and Georges Flamant star. U.S. remake: *Scarlet Street*. **DT104, FF8**

La Dolce Vita (1960, B&W, 175m, NR)
Exuberant, sobering, one-of-a-kind look at contemporary Rome from director Federico Fellini. Marcello Mastroianni stars as a jaded journalist who thinks he's seen it all, but really hasn't. Anita Ekberg heads the supporting cast of this drama filmed on many well-known locations in Rome. **DT43, ST154, XT17,** *Essential, Recommended*

La Favorita (1952, B&W, 82m, NR)
Film version of the opera, with Sophia Loren in an early supporting role. **ST141**

La Femme Nikita (1990, C, 117m, R)
French action thriller about female punk turned government agent. Anne Paillard stars, with Jean-Hughes Anglade, Tcheky Karyo, and Jeanne Moreau. Stylishly empty. U.S. remake: *Point of No Return*. **FF1, FF8, ST161**

La Grande Bourgeoise
(1974, C, 115m, NR)
Italian drama, based on true story, of a man who murders his sister's no-good husband. Giancarlo Giannini and Catherine Deneuve star. **FF2, ST50**

La Marseillaise (1938, B&W, 130m, NR)
From director Jean Renoir, a drama about the turbulent times of the French Revolution. **DT104**

La Nuit de Varennes (1982, C, 133m, R)
This historical drama has Casanova and Thomas Paine sharing a coach during the violent days of the French Revolution. Marcello Mastroianni, Harvey Keitel, and Hanna Schygulla star. Directed by Ettore Scola. **FF2, ST154**

La Passante (1983, C, 106m, NR)
Romy Schneider plays a dual role in this French drama; she's a German refugee and the wife of a world leader. Story of political intrigue also features Michel Piccoli and Maria Schell. **FF1**

La Ronde (1950, B&W, 97m, NR)
Director Max Ophuls spins a romantic web about the interlocking lives and loves of a group of people in Vienna. Anton Walbrook, Serge Reggiani, Simone Simon, Simone Signoret, Daniel Gelin, Danielle Darrieux, and

Fernand Gravet star. Peerlessly sophisticated sex drama. **DT93, FF1,** *Recommended*

La Signora di Tutti (1934, B&W, 90m, NR)
Early drama from director Max Ophuls, starring Isa Miranda as an actress at the end of her rope. Dialogue in Italian. **DT93**

La Strada (1954, B&W, 115m, NR)
Oscar-winning drama from Federico Fellini about a traveling circus and three diverse characters: a lonely waif (Guilietta Masina), a strongman (Anthony Quinn), and an acrobat (Richard Basehart). **DT43, XT7, XT30,** *Essential*

La Tartuffe (1984, C, 100m, NR)
Star Gérard Depardieu adapted and directed Molière's attack on religious and sexual hypocrisy. With Elizabeth Depardieu (star's wife) and François Perier. **DR20, ST52**

La Terra Trema (1947, B&W, 160m, NR)
Documentary-style look at the lives of Sicilian fisherman from director Luchino Visconti. One of the key films of the Italian neorealist movement. **DT127,** *Essential*

La Truite (1982, C, 105m, R)
French country girl (Isabelle Huppert) becomes enmeshed in the shady world of high finance in this contemporary French-language drama from director Joseph Losey. With Jacques Spiesser, Jeanne Moreau, and Jean-Pierre Cassel. Also known as *The Trout*. **FF1, ST161**

La Vie Continue (1982, C, 93m, NR)
French drama of a woman (Annie Girardot) who must pick up the pieces of her life when her husband suddenly dies. American remake: *Men Don't Leave*. **FF1, FF8**

Labyrinth (1986, C, 101m, PG)
A young girl wishes her brother would be captured by goblins—and when her wish comes true, she sets out to rescue him. Family adventure starring Jennifer Connelly and David Bowie, with Terry Jones. **CO15, FA8, FA15, MU12, SF13**

Labyrinth of Passion (1982, C, 100m, NR)
Sex farce from Spanish director Pedro Almodóvar, mixing odd assortment of characters: transvestites, punk rockers, and the sex-starved of both genders. Celia Roth, Imanol Arias, and Helga Line star. **DT3**

Lacemaker, The (1977, C, 107m, NR)
Low-key drama of shy young girl (Isabelle Huppert) adrift, taking up with young man (Yves Beneyton) she thinks she loves. Directed by Claude Goretta. Huppert is superb but film doesn't dramatize her true problems well. **FF1**

Lacombe, Lucien (1974, C, 137m, R)
French drama from director Louis Malle of
a simple young peasant who becomes a
Gestapo agent during the Nazi Occupation.
Pierre Blaise and Aurore Clement star in this
masterful portrait of personal corruption.
UNAVAILABLE ON VIDEO. **XT29**

L'Addition (1985, C, 85m, R)
French prison drama, starring Richard Berry
and Richard Bohringer. **FF1**

Ladies Club, The (1986, C, 86m, R)
Frustrated with the criminal justice system,
a policewoman, a rape victim, and several
other angry women set out to get justice
their own way. **AC19**

Ladies' Man, The (1961, C, 106m, NR)
Jerry Lewis comedy has him playing a
handyman at a girls' school. With Helen
Traubel, Kathleen Freeman, and Harry James
and His Band. **CO18, ST139**

Ladies of the Chorus
(1949, B&W, 61m, NR)
Early Marilyn Monroe film has her and Adele
Jergens playing a mother and daughter dancing in burlesque shows. **ST159**

Ladies They Talk About
(1933, B&W, 68m, NR)
Barbara Stanwyck stars in this women's
prison melodrama, spicier than you might
expect, because it was made prior to enforcement of Production Code restrictions. With
Preston S. Foster, Lyle Talbot, Dorothy Burgess, and Lillian Roth. **DR18, ST206**

Lady and the Tramp (1955, C, 75m, G)
Classic Disney animated feature about a
pampered cocker spaniel and her romance
with a street mutt. Widescreen will be lost
on video. **CU20, FA2,** *Highly Recommended*

Lady by Choice (1934, B&W, 78m, NR)
Sequel to *Lady for a Day* stars May Robson in
her street person role; this time, she's taken
in by a dancer (Carole Lombard). **ST140**

Lady Caroline Lamb
(1972, C, 118m, PG)
True story of wife of British politician and
her open affair with poet Lord Byron. Sarah
Miles, Jon Finch, and Richard Chamberlain
form the romantic triangle; with Laurence
Olivier and Ralph Richardson. **DR5, ST168,
ST184**

Lady Chatterley's Lover
(1955, B&W, 102m, NR)
French-language version of D.H. Lawrence's
story of forbidden love, starring Danielle Darrieux. **DR3, WR17**

Lady Chatterley's Lover
(1981, C, 105m, R)
Second, and more explicit, version of the
D.H. Lawrence tale of passion, starring Sylvia
Kristel and Nicholas Clay. **DR3, WR17**

Lady Eve, The (1941, B&W, 94m, NR)
A preoccupied scientist (Henry Fonda) is
thoroughly confused and fleeced by a
smooth con woman (Barbara Stanwyck) in
this classic comedy from writer-director Preston Sturges. With Charles Coburn, William
Demarest, and Eugene Pallette. Great fun,
with Sturges and his cast in top form. **CL10,
DT121, ST71, ST206,** *Essential, Highly
Recommended*

Lady for a Day (1933, B&W, 88m, NR)
Damon Runyon's tale of New York gangster
befriending old street woman, Apple Annie.
Warren William and May Robson star.
Directed by Frank Capra, who remade it
years later as *A Pocketful of Miracles*. **DT22**

Lady for a Night (1941, B&W, 87m, NR)
A gambling boat owner tries marriage to a
wealthy man but is framed for murder. Joan
Blondell and John Wayne star in this drama.
ST224

Lady From Louisiana
(1941, B&W, 82m, NR)
John Wayne plays a crusading lawyer in
old New Orleans who falls in love with the
daughter of a gambling boss he wants to put
behind bars. **ST224**

Lady From Shanghai, The
(1948, B&W, 87m, NR)
Orson Welles directed this bizarre thriller
about a sailor's infatuation with the lovely
wife (Rita Hayworth) of a sleazy lawyer.
Welles plays the sap, with Everett Sloane as
the crippled lawyer. Famous climax in house
of mirrors. **DT134, MY1, ST101,**
Recommended

Lady Ice (1973, C, 93m, PG)
An insurance investigator tracks a gang of
jewel thieves in this caper mystery. Donald
Sutherland, Jennifer O'Neill, and Robert
Duvall star. **MY18, ST63**

Lady in a Cage (1964, B&W, 93m, NR)
Olivia de Havilland stars in a thriller about a
woman trapped in her home and terrorized
by hoodlums. With Ann Sothern, Jeff Corey,
James Caan, and Rafael Campos. **MY3, ST49**

Lady in Cement (1968, C, 93m, NR)
Frank Sinatra plays a seedy private eye who's
investigating the murder of a woman who
was given special, hard-to-remove footwear.
With Raquel Welch, Dan Blocker, Richard

Conte, and Joe E. Lewis. Sequel to *Tony Rome*. **MY10, ST199**

Lady in Question, The
(1940, B&W, 81m, NR)
Unusual love story of juror and the woman defendant he saves, starring Brian Aherne and Rita Hayworth. With Glenn Ford, Irene Rich, and George Coulouris. **DR17, ST101**

Lady in the Lake, The
(1946, B&W, 103m, NR)
Robert Montgomery plays Raymond Chandler's famed detective Philip Marlowe in this mystery seen totally from Marlowe's point of view. With Audrey Totter, Lloyd Nolan, Tom Tully, and Jayne Meadows. Directed by Montgomery. **MY1, WR2, XT23**

Lady in White (1988, C, 112m, PG-13)
In 1962, a ten-year-old boy, locked in a school coatroom, witnesses a murder which took place ten years before. A ghost story with plenty of scares but very little violence. Lukas Haas stars. **HO2, HO19**

Lady Jane (1985, C, 140m, PG-13)
The true story of the sixteenth-century teenaged Queen of England, her dramatic rise to the throne, and her sudden downfall. Helena Bonham Carter and Cary Elwes star in this lavish historical drama. **DR5, DR23**

Lady Killer (1933, B&W, 74m, NR)
James Cagney plays a gangster who turns to movie acting. With Mae Clark (his grapefruit friend in *Public Enemy*), Leslie Fenton, and Margaret Lindsay. **AC22, CL7, ST24**

Lady of Burlesque (1943, B&W, 91m, NR)
Barbara Stanwyck plays detective when a murderer begins eliminating strippers in this comic mystery. Directed by William Wellman. With Michael O'Shea, Iris Adrian, and Pinky Lee. **DT135, MY17, ST206**

Lady of the Evening (1979, C, 110m, PG)
Italian comedy features Sophia Loren and Marcello Mastroianni as a prostitute and a crook who become partners. **FF2, ST141, ST154**

Lady on the Bus (1978, C, 102m, R)
A new bride finds her husband unattractive in bed but learns that she is attracted to nearly every other man in sight. Sexy comedy from Brazil starring Sonia Braga. **FF6, ST17**

Lady Sings the Blues (1972, C, 144m, R)
Diana Ross plays famed singer Billie Holiday, who fought a losing battle with drug addiction. With Billy Dee Williams and Richard Pryor. Ross does her best, even on the sing-

ing, but the film has no shape or feel for the characters. **DR14, MU5, ST180, ST227**

Lady Takes a Chance, A
(1943, B&W, 86m, NR)
John Wayne is a rodeo star and Jean Arthur is the city girl he tames in this light-hearted Western. **ST3, ST224, WE12, WE14**

Lady Vanishes, The (1938, B&W, 97m, NR)
Hitchcock mystery set aboard a speeding train with a disappearing lady, lots of suspects, sly comedy. Margaret Lockwood, Michael Redgrave, and Dame May Whitty star. Seamless entertainment. **DT57, MY15, XT19,** *Highly Recommended*

Lady Vanishes, The (1979, C, 99m, PG)
Remake of Hitchcock's classic thriller, starring Cybill Shepherd, Elliott Gould, and Angela Lansbury. **CU18, ST131, XT19**

Lady Windermere's Fan
(1925, B&W, 80m, NR)
Silent screen version of the Oscar Wilde play of blackmail, deception, and infidelity among British nobility. Ronald Colman, Irene Rich, and May McAvoy star. Ernst Lubitsch directed. **DT76, ST35**

Lady Without Camellias, The
(1953, B&W, 106m, NR)
Early drama from Italian director Michelangelo Antonioni of relationship between an actress and producer who has discovered her. Lucia Bose, Andrea Cecchi, and Alain Cuny star. **DT5**

Ladybugs (1992, C, 89m, PG-13)
Rodney Dangerfield stars as a reluctant coach of a little girls' soccer team (he's angling for a promotion at work). Complications arise when he recruits his fiancée's son to dress in drag as a ringer. With Jackee, Jonathan Brandis, Nancy Parsons, and Tommy Lasorda. Directed by Sidney J. Furie. **CO19**

Ladyhawke (1985, C, 124m, PG-13)
A curse has doomed a knight (Rutger Hauer) and his maiden fair (Michelle Pfeiffer) always to be apart—until they meet a young pickpocket (Matthew Broderick). The stars are fine, but the direction's leaden and the music intrusively inappropriate. **AC14, AC18, ST173**

Ladykillers, The (1955, C, 90m, NR)
Classic British comedy about a bungling band of crooks and a little old (but quite resourceful) lady. Alec Guinness and Peter Sellers head the cast. **CL10, CO10, CO17, CU5, MY15, MY17, ST95, ST198,** *Recommended*

L'Age d'Or (1930, B&W, 63m, NR)
Legendary surrealistic film directed by Luis
Buñuel, cowritten with Salvador Dali. A scan-
dal in its time for its startling imagery. **DT19,**
Essential, Recommended

Laguna Heat (1987, C, 115m, NR)
Private eye mystery has Harry Hamlin trying to solve the murder of his partner. With
Jason Robards, Rip Torn, Catherine Hicks,
and Ann Francis. Written by Pete Hamill,
from T. Jefferson Parker's novel. Originally
made for TV. **MY10, ST185, ST216**

Lair of the White Worm
(1988, C, 93m, R)
Director Ken Russell takes on a story by Bram
Stoker, about a sexy female vampire. Amanda
Donohoe, Catherine Oxenberg, and Sammi
Davis star. **DT111, HO5, HO25**

Land Before Time, The (1988, C, 66m, G)
Animated feature set in prehistoric times,
with cute dinosaur and his friends undergoing many adventures. **FA10**

Land of Faraway, The (1988, C, 95m, PG)
Family fantasy of an eleven-year-old boy who
becomes a knight when he releases a spirit
from a bottle. Christian Bale stars, with Timothy Bottoms, Susannah York, and Christopher Lee. **FA8, SF13, ST135**

Land of the Minotaur (1976, C, 88m, PG)
A devil-worshipping cult in Greece kidnaps
tourists for their bizarre rituals. Donald Pleasence and Peter Cushing star. **HO11, ST43**

Land of the Pharaohs
(1955, C, 106m, NR)
Epic historical drama centering on the construction of the Great Pyramid, starring Jack
Hawkins, Joan Collins, James Robertson Justice, and Dewey Martin. William Faulkner
contributed to the script, Howard Hawks directed. Despite pedigree, now regarded as a
camp classic, especially for finale, when evil
Collins is entombed with a bevy of eunuchs.
CL3, CU2, DT53, WR7

Land That Time Forgot, The
(1975, C, 90m, PG)
Science fiction fantasy about Germans and
Americans discovering a prehistoric land in
Latin America. Doug McClure stars. **SF4**

Land Without Bread
(1932, B&W, 28m, NR)
Director Luis Buñuel's searing documentary
about Las Hurdes, one of the poorest regions
of rural Spain. **CU16, DT19,** *Recommended*

Landlord, The (1970, C, 113m, PG)
Stinging comedy of naive young dilettante
who inherits ghetto apartment building,
becomes involved with lives of his black ten-
ants. Beau Bridges stars, with Pearl Bailey,
Diana Sands, Louis Gossett (with hair!), Lee
Grant, Susan Anspach, and Bob (Robert)
Klein. Screenplay by Bill Gunn, directed by
Hal Ashby, photographed by Gordon Willis.
Ashby's stunning debut deftly satirizes racial
phobias. UNAVAILABLE ON VIDEO. **XT29**

L'Année des Meduses (1986, C, 110m, NR)
Sexy French drama of a battle between a
nymphet (Valerie Kaprisky) and a gigolo (Bernard Giraudeau). Also known as *The Year of
the Jellyfish.* **CU6, FF1**

Laserblast (1978, C, 90m, PG)
A young boy finds a laser gun left behind by
aliens and uses it to get even with his tormentors. Family science fiction drama. **SF13**

Lassie Come Home (1943, C, 88m, NR)
Family classic of a collie who is separated
from the family who loves him and embarks
on a dramatic journey to return to them.
Roddy McDowall, Donald Crisp, Dame Mae
Whitty, and Edmund Gwenn star, with a
young Elizabeth Taylor in a small role. **FA5,
ST212**

Lassiter (1984, C, 110m, R)
A cat burglar is forced to go undercover for
Scotland Yard against the Nazis. Tom Selleck
stars, with Lauren Hutton, Jane Seymour,
and Bob Hoskins. **AC14, ST111**

Last American Hero, The
(1973, C, 100m, PG)
Jeff Bridges plays a moonshine runner whose
driving skills catapult him to fame on the
stock-car racing circuit. With Valerie Perrine,
Geraldine Fitzgerald, and Gary Busey. Loosely
based on the life of Junior Johnson. Engaging
performances, nice feel for the stock-car circuit life. **DR22, ST19,** *Recommended*

Last Angry Man, The
(1959, B&W, 100m, NR)
An elderly doctor who has devoted his life to
patients in a Brooklyn slum finds himself the
unwilling subject of a TV documentary. Paul
Muni stars, with Luther Adler, Betsy Palmer,
Godfrey Cambridge, Billy Dee Williams, and
Cicely Tyson. **CL8, DR15, ST227**

Last Boy Scout, The (1991, C, 105m, R)
Buddy action movie, with Bruce Willis as a
private eye, Damon Wayans as ex-football
star banned from the NFL for gambling,
looking to find the killer of his girlfriend.
With Chelsea Field, Noble Willingham, Danielle Lewis, Halle Berry, and Taylor Negron. If
you like Willis's wisecracking and plenty of
car crashes, this one's for you. **AC8, AC19,
ST229**

Last Chase, The (1981, C, 101m, R)
In the future, an oil shortage has virtually doomed auto travel—until one man reassembles his Porsche and leads police on a cross-country chase. Lee Majors stars. **AC10, SF11**

Last Command, The
(1928, B&W, 88m, NR)
An expatriate Russian general is reduced to playing out his life as a Hollywood extra. Oscar winner Emil Jannings stars, with Evelyn Brent and William Powell. Josef von Sternberg directed this silent classic. **CL7, CL12, DT128, ST176, XT2,** *Recommended*

Last Days of Chez Nous, The
(1992, C, 96m, R)
Absorbing drama from Australian director Gillian Armstrong about two sisters in conflict over one's involvement with the other's husband. Lisa Harrow, Kerry Fox, and Bruno Ganz star. **DR8, DR10, DT7, FF5,** *Recommended*

Last Days of Dolwyn, The
(1949, B&W, 95m, NR)
British drama about Welsh village in turmoil over construction project. Edith Evans and Emlyn Williams star; notable as Richard Burton's film debut. Written and directed by Williams. **DR23, ST22**

Last Days of Man on Earth, The
(1973, C, 79m, R)
British science fiction, with comic overtones, about an impudent scientist who creates a "new messiah" as the world comes to an end. Jon Finch stars. **SF19, SF21**

Last Days of Patton, The
(1986, C, 150m, NR)
George C. Scott returns to the role which won him an Oscar in this drama of the general's life immediately after the end of World War II. With Eva Marie Saint, Richard Dysart, Murray Hamilton, and Kathryn Leigh Scott. Originally made for TV. **DR4, ST196**

Last Detail, The (1973, C, 105m, R)
Rollicking, ultimately sad comedy-drama about a pair of Navy "lifers" (Jack Nicholson and Otis Young) transporting a young seaman (Randy Quaid) from Norfolk, Virginia, to a naval prison in New Hampshire. With Clifton James, Carol Kane, Michael Moriarty, Nancy Allen, and in a small role, Gilda Radner. Written by Robert Towne; directed by Hal Ashby. **CO13, CO21, ST163, XT12, XT18,** *Recommended*

Last Dragon, The (1985, C, 109m, PG-13)
Kung Fu meets Motown in this martial arts adventure with musical numbers. Taimak provides the kicks and Vanity the music. **AC26, MU16**

Last Elephant, The see *Ivory Hunters*

Last Embrace (1979, C, 102m, R)
A CIA agent's wife is murdered and he believes the killers are after him, too. Roy Scheider and Janet Margolin star in this fine thriller from director Jonathan Demme. With Charles Napier, Christopher Walken, John Glover, and Sam Levene. One of the better Hitchcock homages. **DT35, MY4, MY6, ST222,** *Recommended*

Last Emperor, The (1987, C, 160m, R)
Winner of nine Oscars (including Best Picture and Director), this lavish drama tells the incredible story of Pu Yi, the Chinese emperor set adrift in the currents of twentieth-century history. John Lone stars, with Peter O'Toole and Joan Chen. Bernardo Bertolucci directed. A visual treat. **DR4, DT9, ST169, XT1, XT6,** *Recommended*

Last Exit to Brooklyn (1990, C, 102m, R)
Hubert Selby, Jr.'s cult novel of life in 1952 Brooklyn's lower depths, starring Stephen Lang and Jennifer Jason Leigh with Burt Young, Jerry Orbach, and Ricki Lake. Music by Mark Knopfler. Give it points for not compromising on its source grimness. **DR3, DR15, DR19, ST136**

Last Flight of Noah's Ark, The
(1980, C, 97m, G)
Disney adventure about a pilot, a female missionary, two young stowaways, and a pair of Japanese soldiers converting a crippled plane into a boat. Elliott Gould and Genevieve Bujold star. **FA1**

Last Four Days, The (1977, C, 91m, PG)
Drama recounting the final days of Italian dictator Benito Mussolini. Rod Steiger and Henry Fonda star. **DR4, ST71**

Last Holiday (1950, B&W, 89m, NR)
British comedy of young man (Alec Guinness) who thinks he's dying, living it up at resort where customers thinks he's a V.I.P. With Kay Walsh. **CO17, ST95**

Last House on the Left (1972, C, 91m, R)
Two teen-age girls are tortured and murdered by a sadistic gang, and one girl's father exacts his own revenge. Cult horror film directed by Wes Craven. A loose remake of *The Virgin Spring*. **FF8, HO12**

Last Hurrah, The (1958, B&W, 121m, NR)
Spencer Tracy stars as a Boston Irish politician in the twilight of his career. Directed by John Ford. **DR21, DT44, ST217**

Last Laugh, The (1924, B&W, 77m, NR)
Classic silent drama from Germany about a
doorman at a hotel and his meager existence,
starring Emil Jannings. Directed by F.W. Murnau. **FF3, CL12,** *Essential, Recommended*

Last Man on Earth, The
(1964, B&W, 86m, NR)
Vincent Price plays the sole survivor of a
world-wide plague who must fight nightly
battles against blood-seeking victims. **SF12,
ST179**

Last Metro, The (1980, C, 133m, PG)
Director François Truffaut's drama of a theater troupe in occupied Paris. Gérard Depardieu and Catherine Deneuve star. **DT125,
ST50, ST52**

Last Movie, The (1971, C, 108m, R)
Offbeat drama about an American film company shooting on location in a poor village
in Peru. Director Dennis Hopper stars, with
Peter Fonda, Kris Kristofferson, Dean Stockwell, Julie Adams, Sylvia Miles, Rod Cameron, and Sam Fuller. The film that put
Hopper's directing career on hold for many
years; it's a noble failure. **DR13, DT49,
MU12, ST110, ST208**

Last Night at the Alamo
(1983, B&W, 80m, NR)
The denizens of a Houston bar that's about
to be demolished gather for one last stand in
this comedy about urban cowboys. **WE12**

Last of Mrs. Cheyney, The
(1937, B&W, 98m, NR)
Joan Crawford's a jewel thief, William Powell
a British lord in this romantic drama. With
Robert Montgomery and Frank Morgan.
ST39, ST176

Last of Sheila, The (1973, C, 120m, PG)
A yacht party featuring a mystery game turns
into something more serious when the hostess is found murdered. James Coburn, Dyan
Cannon, James Mason, and Joan Hackett
star. Anthony Perkins and Stephen Sondheim
wrote the script. **MY9, MY12, ST153**

Last of the Finest, The (1990, C, 106m, R)
Brian Dennehy plays an overzealous cop suspended for his activities against drug dealers;
he and his buddies uncover a political conspiracy involving city officials. **AC8**

Last of the Mohicans, The
(1936, B&W, 91m, NR)
Randolph Scott stars in this adaptation of
James Fenimore Cooper's adventure of the
French and Indian War. **AC6, AC13, CL1,
ST197**

Last of the Mohicans, The
(1992, C, 114m, R)
The hardy James Fenimore Cooper tale of
the French and Indian War is given a lushly
romantic treatment by director and cowriter
Michael Mann. Daniel Day-Lewis (as Hawkeye) and Madeleine Stowe (Cora) are the
stars; with Russell Means, Eric Schweig, Jodhi
May, Steven Waddington, Maurice Roëves,
and Wes Studi as a memorable Magua. One
difference from book: shift of Cora's romance
from Uncas to Hawkeye. North Carolina
locations do admirable job standing in for
upstate New York. Available only in letterboxed edition. Thrilling in ways its original
author may have never anticipated. **AC6,
AC12, AC14, CL1, CU19, ST48, ST209,**
Recommended

Last of the Pony Riders
(1953, B&W, 80m, NR)
Gene Autry saddles up for his last feature
film, with sidekick Smiley Burnette. **ST5**

Last of the Red Hot Lovers
(1972, C, 98m, PG)
Neil Simon comedy about a married man's
inept attempts at various romantic affairs.
Alan Arkin, Sally Kellerman, and Paula Prentiss star. **WR30**

Last Picture Show, The
(1971, B&W, 118m, NR)
Drama adapted from Larry McMurtry's novel,
set in 1950s, of a dying small Texas town and
its frustrated inhabitants. Timothy Bottoms
and Jeff Bridges star, with Cybill Shepherd,
Ellen Burstyn, Cloris Leachman, Ben Johnson, Clu Gulager, Randy Quaid, and Sam
Bottoms. Leachman and Johnson won Oscars. Directed by Peter Bogdanovich. A career
launcher for its director and several stars
and a renewal for veteran Johnson. Finely
observed, terrifically acted. **DR19, DR26,
ST11, XT4, XT5,** *Essential, Recommended*

Last Polka, The (1984, C, 54m, NR)
John Candy and Eugene Levy play their
hilarious "SCTV" characters, polka kings
Yosh and Stan Schmenge, in this spoof of
music documentaries and *The Last Waltz* in
particular. With Rick Moranis and Catherine
O'Hara. Originally made for cable TV. Further
proof that "SCTV" was the funniest TV program ever. **CO7, CO14,** *Recommended*

Last Prostitute, The (1991, C, 100m, NR)
A pair of 1960s teens decide to seek out a leg-
endary prostitute, only to find that she has
retired. Wil Wheaton, Woody Watson, and
Sonia Braga star. Originally made for cable
TV. **ST17**

Last Remake of Beau Geste, The
(1977, C, 83m, PG)
Spoof of French Foreign Legion movies, directed by and starring Marty Feldman, with Ann-Margret, Michael York, Peter Ustinov, James Earl Jones, and Trevor Howard. **CO7, ST118**

Last Resort (1986, C, 80m, R)
Nightmare vacation comedy with family man (Charles Grodin) stuck at Club Med-style spot. With Robin Pearson Rose, John Ashton, Ellen Blake, and Jon Lovitz. **ST94**

Last Ride of the Dalton Gang, The
(1979, C, 150m, NR)
The story of the Old West's notorious gang of outlaws. Cliff Potts and Randy Quaid star, with Jack Palance and Dale Robertson. Originally made for TV. **WE14**

Last Rites (1988, C, 103m, R)
A mysterious woman, seeking sanctuary in a New York church, draws a young priest into a story of murder and revenge. Tom Berenger and Daphne Zuniga star. **DR16**

Last Starfighter, The (1984, C, 100m, PG)
A video game whiz is recruited into an interplanetary war. Science fiction adventure starring Lance Guest, Robert Preston, and Dan O'Herlihy. **SF8, SF13**

Last Summer (1969, C, 97m, R)
Quartet of teens come together at resort for games that turn violent. Richard Thomas, Bruce Davison, Barbara Hershey, and Cathy Burns star. Character motivation is murky, a crucial fault for a film with this ending. **DR9, ST104**

Last Tango in Paris (1973, C, 129m, X)
Controversial drama about a casual affair involving an American whose wife has just committed suicide and a free-spirited young Frenchwoman. Marlon Brando and Maria Schneider star, with Jean-Pierre Leaud. Bernardo Bertolucci directed. Brando's last grand performance should have won him an Oscar; Bertolucci supplies supple direction. **CU6, CU13, DR1, DR3, DT13, ST18, XT16, XT28,** *Essential, Recommended*

Last Temptation of Christ, The
(1988, C, 160m, R)
Director Martin Scorsese's controversial adaptation of the Nikos Kazantzakis novel about Christ's human side. Willem Dafoe stars, with Barbara Hershey, Harvey Keitel, Harry Dean Stanton, John Lurie, and David Bowie. Music by Peter Gabriel. Brilliant if flawed by overlength, occasional scenes that go nowhere. **DR19, DT114, HF16, MU12, ST104, ST205,** *Recommended*

Last Time I Saw Paris, The
(1954, C, 116m, NR)
Elizabeth Taylor and Van Johnson star in this drama, loosely based on an F. Scott Fitzgerald story, about Americans adrift in late 1940s Paris. **ST212, WR8**

Last Train From Gun Hill
(1959, C, 94m, NR)
Western drama of sheriff trying to get out of town with murder suspect. Kirk Douglas and Anthony Quinn star, with Carolyn Jones and Earl Holliman. **ST57**

Last Tycoon, The (1976, C, 125m, PG)
F. Scott Fitzgerald's final novel, the story of a driven movie executive and the people who support and oppose his power. Robert De Niro stars, with Jack Nicholson, Jeanne Moreau, and Robert Mitchum, Theresa Russell, Ingrid Boulting, Tony Curtis, John Carradine, Ray Milland, Dana Andrews, and in a small role, Anjelica Huston. Written by Harold Pinter; directed by Elia Kazan and produced by Sam Spiegel. **CU17, DR13, DT65, ST51, ST115, ST158, ST161, ST163, WR8, WR26,** *Recommended*

Last Unicorn, The (1982, C, 95m, PG)
Animated story about a mythical beast trying to survive in an unfriendly world. Voices supplied by Alan Arkin, Jeff Bridges, and Mia Farrow. **FA10, ST19, ST65**

Last Valley, The (1971, C, 128m, PG)
Adventure saga of a troop of seventeenth-century soldiers who stumble into a valley unchanged by the Thirty Years' War. Michael Caine and Omar Sharif star. Directed by James Clavell. **ST25**

Last Voyage, The (1960, C, 91m, NR)
Disaster drama of luxury ship slowly sinking, with usual mix of heroism and cowardice in the offing. Robert Stack stars, with Dorothy Malone, George Sanders, Edmond O'Brien, and Woody Strode. **AC23**

Last Waltz, The (1978, C, 117m, PG)
Concert film of rock group The Band's farewell performance on Thanksgiving Day, 1976, featuring many of their hits, plus performances by Bob Dylan, Neil Young, Eric Clapton, Muddy Waters, Van Morrison, Joni Mitchell, Dr. John, Ronnie Hawkins, Paul Butterfield, The Staples, and Emmylou Harris. Directed by Martin Scorsese. As good as a rock concert film can get; hook up your VCR to your speakers and turn up the volume. **DT114, MU10,** *Highly Recommended*

Last War, The (1962, C, 79m, G)
From Japan, a science fiction drama about a future conflict that escalates into nuclear annihilation. **FF4, SF18**

Last Wave, The (1977, C, 106m, PG)
Richard Chamberlain stars in this Australian drama about a lawyer who gets more than he bargained for in defending an aborigine on a murder charge. Directed by Peter Weir. **DT133**

Last Woman on Earth, The
(1961, C, 71m, NR)
Low-budget sci-fi drama from director Roger Corman, about a trio of survivors of an atomic holocaust. Antony Carbone, Edward Wain (Robert Towne), and Betsy Jones-Moreland star. Written by Wain. **DT30, SF12**

Last Year at Marienbad
(1962, B&W, 93m, NR)
Cryptic, hypnotic film about a young man's attempts to seduce an attractive but enigmatic woman. Directed by Alain Resnais. Artful or pretentious—take your pick. **FF1,** *Essential*

L'Atalante (1934, B&W, 89m, NR)
Classic romance/fantasy about a French couple living on a barge on the Seine, directed by Jean Vigo. Running time reflects restored, 89-minute version. **FF1,** *Essential*

Late Chrysanthemums
(1954, B&W, 101m, NR)
Japanese drama of geisha in her declining years, directed by Mikio Naruse. **FF4**

Late for Dinner (1991, C, 92m, PG)
Comic shaggy dog story of two men cryogenically frozen in 1962, waking up twenty-nine years later. Brian Wimmer and Peter Berg star, with Marcia Gay Harden and Colleen Flynn. **CO20, SF4**

Late Show, The (1977, C, 94m, R)
Art Carney plays a private eye who gets help from a kooky woman (Lily Tomlin) in solving the murder of his ex-partner. An offbeat, likable mystery from writer-director Robert Benton. **DT9, MY10, ST215, XT26,** *Recommended*

Laughing Policeman, The
(1974, C, 111m, R)
San Francisco police track down a crazed killer who has shot up a busload of people. Walter Matthau, Bruce Dern, and Louis Gossett, Jr., star. **AC9, ST132, XT13**

Laura (1944, B&W, 88m, NR)
Classic mystery starring Gene Tierney as supposed victim, Dana Andrews as police detective smitten by her portrait, and Clifton Webb as columnist Waldo Lydecker, the key to the crime. With Vincent Price and Judith Anderson. Otto Preminger directed. Webb deserved a Best Supporting Actor Oscar for his witty performance. **DT100, MY1, MY3,** **MY5, ST179, ST214, XT28,** *Essential, Recommended*

Laurel and Hardy: At Work
(1932–33, B&W, 70m, NR)
Three L&H shorts: *Towed in a Hole* (1932), *Busy Bodies* (1933), and the Oscar-winning *The Music Box* (1932). **ST133**

Laurel and Hardy Comedy Classics
(9 volumes: each B&W, 70–90m, NR)
Each volume of this series contains several short films by the great comedy duo. **ST133,** *Recommended*

Laurel and Hardy's Laughing 20's
(1965, B&W, 90m, NR)
Compilation of silent Laurel and Hardy classic moments also includes some Charlie Chase footage. **ST133**

Laurel and Hardy: On the Lam
(1930–34, B&W, 90m, NR)
A quartet of shorts from Stan and Ollie: *Scram!* (1932), *Another Fine Mess* (1930), *One Good Turn* (1931), *Going Bye Bye* (1934). **ST133**

Laurel and Hardy: Stan "Helps" Ollie
(1930–33, B&W, 85m, NR)
Four shorts from Laurel & Hardy's great years: *County Hospital* (1932), *Me and My Pal* (1933), *Hog Wild* (1930), and *Helpmates* (1931). **ST133**

Laurence Olivier—A Life
(1982, C/B&W, 159m, NR)
Documentary portrait of Britain's titan of the stage and screen, featuring interviews with and film clips of Olivier's wives (Joan Plowright, Vivien Leigh) and his acting colleagues (John Gielgud, Ralph Richardson, Douglas Fairbanks, Jr., and Peggy Ashcroft). Originally made for TV. **CU16, ST86, ST137, ST168, ST184**

Lavender Hill Mob, The
(1951, B&W, 82m, NR)
Caper comedy, one of the first of its kind, from Britain starring Alec Guinness as a bank clerk who masterminds a safe-cracking scheme. Watch for Audrey Hepburn in a brief appearance. **CO10, CO17, MY15, MY17,** **MY18, ST95, ST102,** *Essential, Recommended*

L'Avventura (1960, B&W, 145m, NR)
On a weekend boating trip to a remote island, a woman disappears, prompting the others in her party to examine their lives. Deliberately paced drama from Italian director Michelangelo Antonioni. Available in a letterboxed edition. **CU19, DT5,** *Essential*

Law and Jake Wade, The
(1958, C, 86m, NR)
Western drama of outlaws, once buddies,

now adversaries over cache of loot. Robert Taylor and Richard Widmark star, with Patricia Owens and Robert Middleton. **WE3**

Law of Desire (1986, C, 100m, NR)
Comedy from Spanish director Pedro Almodovar about a homosexual director of adult movies, his transsexual sister, and their various liaisons. Carmen Maura and Eusebio Poncala star. **DT3**

Lawless Street, A (1955, C, 78m, NR)
Randolph Scott Western: he's a marshal cleaning up a wicked town, confronting long-lost love (Angela Lansbury). **ST131, ST197**

Lawnmower Man, The
(1992, C, 137m, NR)
Stephen King story of mentally defective handyman given shot of super-intelligence by experimenting scientist, whose government connections suddenly become *very* interested in his work. Pierce Brosnan and Jeff Fahey star, with Jenny Wright and Geoffrey Lewis. Directed by Brett Leonard. This video version restores over thirty minutes of footage cut from film before its original release. Original version, which runs 105 minutes and is rated R, is also available. Impressive computer-animated special effects but thin story doesn't merit length; shorter version, however, reportedly makes much less sense. **CU10, HO20, WR15**

Lawrence of Arabia (1962, C, 222m, G)
Peter O'Toole's stunning star debut as T.E. Lawrence, the Englishman who led Arab tribesmen against the Turks in the 1920s. With Omar Sharif, Alec Guinness, Anthony Quinn, Arthur Kennedy, Stanley Baker, and Jack Hawkins. Directed by David Lean; screenplay by Robert Bolt, masterful cinematography by Freddie Young. Available in a letterboxed edition which includes footage restored from original cut of the film. O'Toole should have won the Oscar. Magnificent, although should be seen on big screen for full impact. **CL2, CU10, CU19, DR27, DT71, ST95, ST169, XT1, XT6, XT21, XT28,** *Essential, Highly Recommended*

Le Bal (1982, C, 112m, NR)
One-of-a-kind musical, set in Parisian dance hall, spanning fifty years, told with only music, no dialogue. French lyrics, with English subtitles. Ettore Scola directed. **FF1, MU16**

Le Beau Mariage (1982, C, 97m, R)
From French director Eric Rohmer, a comedy about a determined young woman who decides it's time she got married—even

though her intended has no idea of her plans. **DT107**

Le Bourgeois Gentilhomme
(1958, C, 97m, NR)
Performance of Molière's classic stage comedy about a social climber, featuring Jean Meyer, Louis Seigner, Jacques Charon, and other members of the Comédie-Française. **FF1**

Le Dernier Combat (1984, B&W, 90m, R)
After the apocalypse, a survivor wanders a bizarre landscape and encounters equally strange characters. French film with no dialogue, only music and sound effects. Directed by Luc Besson. **FF1, SF19**

Le Doulos (1961, B&W, 108m, NR)
French thriller of ex-con and pal he suspects of being an informant. Jean-Paul Belmondo stars, with Serge Reggiani and Michel Piccoli. Directed by Jean-Pierre Melville. **FF1, ST11**

Le Gai Savior (1967, B&W, 96m, NR)
From French director Jean-Luc Godard, a debate between two Maoists: Patricia, daughter of Patrice Lumumba, and Emil Rousseau, descendant of Jean-Jacques. The subject is the philosophical basis of contemporary communication. Jean-Pierre Leaud and Juliette Berto star. Originally made for French TV; released in the U.S. in 1970. Also known as *The Joy of Knowledge*. **DT50**

Le Jour Se Lève (1939, B&W, 85m, NR)
Classic French drama of a factory worker (Jean Gabin) driven to murder, trying to sort out his life before he's captured. Marcel Carne directed. **FF1,** *Recommended*

Le Magnifique (1976, C, 84m, NR)
A novelist falls in love with a young student, who admires one of his superhero creations. Jean-Paul Belmondo and Jacqueline Bisset star in this French comedy. **ST11**

Le Mans (1971, C, 106m, G)
Grand Prix racing drama starring Steve McQueen. **AC10, DR22, ST146**

Le Million (1931, B&W, 85m, NR)
René Clair directed this French comedy of a lucky lottery ticket that sets off a frantic search. **DT25, FF1**

Le Plaisir (1951, B&W, 97m, NR)
Trio of stories by Guy de Maupassant about romance, starring Jean Gabin, Danielle Darrieux, Simone Simon, and Claude Dauphin. Directed by Max Ophuls. **DT93**

Le Repos du Guerrier (1962, C, 100m, NR)
Brigitte Bardot starts in this French drama about a woman involved with a suicidal

lover. Directed by Roger Vadim. Also known as *Warrior's Rest*. **ST6**

Le Sex Shop (1973, C, 92m, R)
The owner of a book shop finds his business multiplying when he begins selling pornographic material. A light, naughty comedy from France, directed by Claude Berri. **FF1**

League of Gentlemen, The
(1960, B&W, 114m, NR)
Comic heist featuring British colonel and former officers as gang. Jack Hawkins stars, with Nigel Patrick, Roger Livesey, Richard Attenborough, and Bryan Forbes, who also scripted. **MY15, MY17, MY18**

League of Their Own, A
(1992, C, 128m, PG)
Comedy centering on World War II–era women's baseball leagues, starring Tom Hanks as a dissolute manager finding some self-respect, Geena Davis and Lori Petty as sisters and fellow players. With Madonna, Jon Lovitz, David Strathairn, Rosie O'Donnell, Megan Cavanagh, Garry Marshall, and David L. Lander. Directed by Penny Marshall. Available in a letterboxed edition. A crowd-pleaser all the way, marred by protracted wrap-up. **CO6, CO19, CU19, MU12, ST45, ST97, XT23,** *Recommended*

Lean on Me (1989, C, 104m, PG-13)
Real-life story of New Jersey high school principal Joe Clark, who brought order to an inner-city school plagued by crime and dropouts. Morgan Freeman stars. **DR6, DR25, ST76**

Leap of Faith (1992, C, 108m, PG-13)
Steve Martin plays a traveling evangelist who's stranded in a small Kansas town with a full troupe of singers and musicians and a testy business manager (Debra Winger). With Lolita Davidovich, Liam Neeson, Lukas Haas, and Meat Loaf. Comedy-drama directed by Richard Pearce. **DR26, MU12, ST150, ST231**

Learning Tree, The (1969, C, 107m, PG)
Gordon Parks directed this version of his autobiographical novel about a young black boy growing up in 1920s Kansas. **DR14**

Leather Jackets (1992, C, 90m, R)
Drama of gang leader tangling with Vietnamese thugs, fleeing for his life with his girlfriend and buddy. Cary Elwes, D.B. Sweeney, and Bridget Fonda star, with Christopher Penn, James LeGros, and Jon Polito. **ST70**

Leave 'em Laughing (1981, C, 100m, NR)
Mickey Rooney plays a clown who takes in homeless kids in this true story set in Chicago. Originally made for TV. **DR6, ST189**

Leaves From Satan's Book
(1919, B&W, 165m, NR)
Silent drama from Danish master Carl Dreyer examines Satan's impact on man from the days of Christ to the Russian Revolution. **DT39**

Leaving Normal (1992, C, 110m, R)
Jaded waitress (Christine Lahti) and thrice-wed twentysomething (Meg Tilly) hit the highway for a better life in Alaska. With Lenny Van Dohlen, Maury Chaykin, and James Gannon. Directed by Edward Zwick, photographed by Ralf Bode. **DR10, XT18**

Left Hand of God, The
(1955, C, 87m, NR)
A priest is caught in the political turbulence of post–World War II China. Humphrey Bogart, Gene Tierney, and Lee J. Cobb star. **DR27, ST15, ST214**

Left-Handed Gun, The
(1958, B&W, 102m, NR)
Paul Newman plays Billy the Kid in this psychological study of the Kid's outlaw ways. Based on Gore Vidal's TV play. Directed by Arthur Penn. Newman and the film are mannered in the excess, which works in small doses. **DT96, HF1, ST162, WE3**

Legacy, The (1979, C, 100m, R)
Two Americans are kidnapped and taken to a British mansion where a secret cult prepares to deal with them. Katharine Ross and Sam Elliott star. **HO11**

Legal Eagles (1986, C, 114m, PG)
When a New York attorney is caught in a compromising situation with his female client who's suspected of murder, he calls on a female lawyer for help. Robert Redford, Debra Winger, and Daryl Hannah star in this comedy-mystery. Directed by Ivan Reitman. Overproduced, packaged star vehicle evinces no chemistry among leads. **MY17, ST181, ST231, XT9**

Legend (1986, C, 89m, PG)
A young hermit living in a magical forest sets off to rescue a lovely maiden from the forces of evil. Tom Cruise stars in this lavishly produced adventure fantasy. Ridley Scott directed. **AC18, DT115, SF13, SF14, ST41**

Legend of Billie Jean, The
(1985, C, 96m, PG-13)
Drama of teen-ager and her brother on the run after misunderstanding and shooting. Media attention on her plight winds up saddling her with crimes she doesn't commit. Helen Slater stars, with Keith Gordon, Christian Slater, Richard Bradford, Peter Coyote, and Dean Stockwell. **DR9, ST200, ST208**

Legend of Frenchie King, The
(1971, C, 97m, NR)
Brigitte Bardot stars in a Western comedy
about female outlaws in New Mexico. With
Claudia Cardinale. Dubbed in English. **ST6**

Legend of Hell House, The
(1973, C, 95m, PG)
Horror tale of researchers spending a week in
a haunted house. Roddy McDowall and Pamela Franklin star. Richard Matheson wrote the
screenplay. **HO2, HO3**

Legend of Lobo, The (1962, C, 67m, NR)
Family drama about a wild wolf from his
days as a pup. Disney production features
songs by Sons of the Pioneers. **FA5**

Legend of Sleepy Hollow, The
(1949, C, 49m, G)
Washington Irving's fantasy about Ichabod
Crane and the Headless Horseman comes to
life in this Disney animated feature. Narrated
and sung by Bing Crosby. **FA2, ST40**

Legend of Sleepy Hollow, The
(1980, C, 98m, NR)
Jeff Goldblum stars in this version of Washington Irving's classic. With Dick Butkus,
Paul Sand, and Meg Foster. Originally made
for TV. **FA3, ST90**

Legend of the Lone Ranger, The
(1981, C, 98m, PG)
The Masked Man rides again in this
big-screen account of his origins. Klinton
Spilsbury stars, with Michael Horse, Jason
Robards, and Christopher Lloyd. Stick with
Clayton Moore and Jay Silverheels, although
Twin Peaks fans may want to check out Dep-
uty Hawk in his younger, slimmer days.
ST185, WE2

Legend of the Lost (1957, C, 109m, NR)
Action in the Sahara, with John Wayne and
Rossano Brazzi battling the elements—and
each other, over Sophia Loren. **AC12, ST141,
ST224**

Legend of the Seven Golden Vampires
(1972, C, 72m, NR)
Dracula tale is enlivened with martial arts
fighting in this British horror film. Peter
Cushing stars. **AC26, HF7, HO5, HO26,
ST43**

Legend of the Werewolf
(1975, C, 87m, R)
A Parisian zoo worker has a hairy problem
when the moon is full. Peter Cushing stars
as the investigator on his trail. **HO4, ST43**

Legend of Wolf Mountain, The
(1992, C, 91m, PG)
Family adventure of three kids on an outing

in a national park, encountering a pair of
prison escapees. Nicole Land, Matthew Lewis,
and Jonathan Best star, with Bo Hopkins,
Mickey Rooney, Robert Z'Dar, and Don
Shanks. **AC12, FA4, FA15, ST189**

Lemon Drop Kid, The
(1951, B&W, 91m, NR)
Bob Hope is in hock to a gangster and tries
to use his prowess at the racetrack to make
the payment. **ST108**

Lemon Sisters, The (1990, C, 89m, PG-13)
Diane Keaton stars in this wistful comedy
about a family show-biz act. With Kathryn
Grody, Elliott Gould, Aidan Quinn, Rubén
Blades, and Richard Libertini. **CO8, ST121**

Lenny (1974, B&W, 112m, R)
Dustin Hoffman plays controversial comic
Lenny Bruce, whose life was plagued by trou-
bles with the law and drugs. With Valerie
Perrine. Bob Fosse directed. Imaginative
directing can't overcome central miscasting.
DR4, DT47, ST105

Lenny Bruce Performance Film, The
(1967, B&W, 60m, NR)
The only filmed performance of the controversial stand-up comic. **CU16,** *Recommended*

Leonor (1975, C, 90m, NR)
Liv Ullmann stars in this strange drama
about a woman who makes herself mistress
to the Devil. **HO10, ST220**

Leopard Man, The (1943, B&W, 59m, NR)
Horror film about a small desert town terror-
ized by what it thinks is an escaped animal.
Directed by Jacques Tourneur; produced by
Val Lewton. Based on a story by William
Irish (Cornell Woolrich). **DT124, HO16,
HO27, WR39**

Lepke (1975, C, 110m, R)
Tony Curtis plays real-life gangster Louis
Lepke Buchalter, the head of Murder Inc.,
in this violent crime saga. **AC22**

Leprechaun (1993, C, 92m, R)
Horror tale of title creature (Warwick Davis)
transported to the U.S. by a thieving Irishman, set free after ten years, on a rampage
to recover his pot o' gold. With Jennifer
Aniston and Ken Olandt. **HO16**

Les Biches see *Bad Girls*

Les Carabiniers (1962, B&W, 80m, NR)
Jean-Luc Godard's antiwar drama of two
young layabouts shanghaied into military
service. Anna Karina stars. **DT50, XT25**

Les Comperes (1985, C, 109m, PG)
A French comedy about two bachelors with
an ex-lover in common whose missing child

may be one of theirs. Gérard Depardieu and Pierre Richard star. **FF1, ST52**

Les Girls (1957, C, 114m, NR)
A star of a variety show (Gene Kelly) romances three dancing girls (Taina Elg, Kay Kendall, and Mitzi Gaynor). Cole Porter wrote the score; Orry-Kelly won an Oscar for his costumes. George Cukor directed. **DT32, MU1, MU4, ST123**

Les Liaisons Dangereuses
(1959, B&W, 111m, NR)
Updating of the eighteenth-century tale of sexual intrigue among the French aristocracy, starring Gérard Phillipe as Valmont and Jeanne Moreau as Mme. Merteuil. With Jeanne Valerie and Annette Vadim; directed by Roger Vadim. Music by Thelonius Monk and Art Blakey. *Dangerous Liaisons* and *Valmont* used the same material in its original setting. **FF1, ST161**

Les Misérables (1935, B&W, 108m, NR)
Victor Hugo's epic novel of the thief Jean Valjean (Fredric March) and Inspector Javert (Charles Laughton). With Cedric Hardwicke, Rochelle Hudson, Frances Drake, and in a small role, John Carradine. **CL1, ST132, ST148**

Les Miserables (1978, C, 150m, NR)
Richard Jordan is the escaped con Jean Valjean, Anthony Perkins the relentless Inspector Javert in this version of the Victor Hugo classic. With Cyril Cusack, Claude Dauphin, and John Gielgud. Originally made for TV. **CL1, ST86**

Less Than Zero (1987, C, 100m, R)
A wealthy young crowd in Los Angeles hops from party to party and drug to drug. Adapted from the bestselling novel by Bret Easton Ellis. Andrew McCarthy, Jami Gertz, and Robert Downey, Jr., star. **DR9, DR19, ST203**

Lesson in Love, A (1954, B&W, 95m, NR)
From director Ingmar Bergman, the story of a married couple's separate affairs. Gunnar Bjornstrand and Eva Dahlbeck star. **DT11**

Let Him Have It (1991, C, 100m, R)
British drama of sensational 1950s cop murder trial in which trigger man, legally a juvenile, could not be executed, so his older accomplice, a slightly retarded young man, was sentenced to hang. Paul Reynolds and Chris Eccleston star, with Tom Courtenay. Directed by Peter Medak. **DR5, DR17, DR23**

Let It Be (1970, C, 80m, G)
Documentary chronicles The Beatles recording one of their last albums. Some memora-

ble musical moments and insights into why the band broke up. **MU11**

Let It Ride (1989, C, 86m, PG-13)
Racetrack comedy, with Richard Dreyfuss as a compulsive gambler on a roll. With Teri Garr and David Johansen. **CO19, MU12, ST60**

Let There Be Light (1945, B&W, 60m, NR)
Director John Huston's documentary about the psychological effects of World War II combat. **CU16, DT60**

L'Eté Meurtrier see *One Deadly Summer*

Lethal Weapon (1987, C, 110m, R)
Mel Gibson and Danny Glover are cop partners on the trail of vicious drug smugglers. With Gary Busey, Mitchell Ryan, Tom Atkins, and Darlene Love. Gibson's wild man routine wears thin, as does the movie's overstated violence. Preposterous finale. **AC9, ST85, ST88**

Lethal Weapon 2 (1989, C, 113m, R)
More buddy-cop action on the streets of L.A., with Mel Gibson and Danny Glover, with the latter marked for murder by South African government agents. With Joe Pesci and Patsy Kensit. If you loved the first one . . . **AC9, ST85, ST88, ST172, XT10**

Lethal Weapon 3 (1992, C, 118m, R)
More mayhem with Mel Gibson and Danny Glover, reunited with their favorite motormouth accountant (Joe Pesci). The plot this time revolves around an ex-cop supplying guns to gangs. With Rene Russo, Stuart Wilson, and Darlene Love. Cowritten by Jeffrey Boam, directed by Richard Donner. **AC9, MU12, ST85, ST88, ST172**

Let's Dance (1950, C, 112m, NR)
Fred Astaire and Betty Hutton star in this musical tale of former dance partners fighting for custody of her young son. **ST4**

Let's Do It Again (1975, C, 112m, PG)
Sequel to *Uptown Saturday Night* has Sidney Poitier and pal Bill Cosby as wacky lodge brothers hoping to cash in on a "hypnotized" boxer (Jimmie Walker). **CO10, ST174**

Let's Get Harry (1986, C, 98m, R)
An American businessman (Mark Harmon) is kidnapped by terrorists in South America, and a soldier of fortune leads his buddies on a rescue mission. Robert Duvall heads the expedition; Gary Busey and Glen Frey follow his orders. **AC20, ST63, MU12**

Let's Get Lost (1989, B&W, 120m, NR)
Documentary portrait of jazz trumpeter and singer Chet Baker, whose turbulent life was marked by drug addiction. Baker died from a

hotel window fall shortly after filming was completed. Directed by Bruce Weber. Sometimes too caught up in mythmaking but generally absorbing and fascinating. **CU16,** *Recommended*

Let's Make It Legal (1951, B&W, 77m, NR)
Comedy of couple divorcing but staying friends. Claudette Colbert and Macdonald Carey star, with Zachary Scott, Robert Wagner, and Marilyn Monroe. **ST34, ST159**

Let's Make Love (1960, C, 118m, NR)
Yves Montand plays a millionaire who falls for Marilyn Monroe in this show-biz saga. Bing Crosby, Milton Berle, and Gene Kelly have bit parts. George Cukor directed. **DT32, ST40, ST123, ST159**

Let's Spend the Night Together
(1982, C, 94m, PG)
Concert film of the Rolling Stones' 1981 tour. Directed by Hal Ashby. **MU10**

Letter, The (1940, B&W, 95m, NR)
Bette Davis stars in the Somerset Maugham drama of a woman who claims self-defense in a twisted murder case. With Herbert Marshall. Directed by William Wyler. **CL5, DT142, ST44, WR23**

Letter From an Unknown Woman
(1948, B&W, 90m, NR)
Joan Fontaine stars as a woman hopelessly in love with a dashing musician (Louis Jourdan). Directed with great style by Max Ophuls; written by Howard Koch. **CL4, CL6, DT93, ST73,** *Recommended*

Letter to Brezhnev (1985, C, 95m, NR)
Comedy about two Liverpool working-class girls who meet a pair of lonely Russian sailors, with love unexpectedly blossoming between one couple. Alexandra Pigg and Peter Firth star. **CO17**

Letter to Three Wives, A
(1949, B&W, 103m, NR)
Wicked social comedy about trio of women receiving the same letter from small-town flirt, claiming she has run off with one of their husbands. Jeanne Crain, Linda Darnell, and Ann Sothern star, with Kirk Douglas, Paul Douglas, and Jeffrey Lynn; Celeste Holm is the voice of the letter writer. Joseph L. Mankiewicz won an Oscar for his screenplay and direction. Witty stuff, played with great relish by entire cast. **DR26, DT84, XT6,** *Recommended*

Leviathan (1989, C, 98m, R)
Undersea adventure, with something very strange and very large lurking in the depths. Peter Weller stars, with Richard Crenna, Amanda Pays, and Daniel Stern. **AC12**

Lianna (1983, C, 110m, R)
A married woman finds herself attracted to another woman in this drama from writer-director John Sayles. Linda Griffiths and Jane Hallaren star, with Sayles in a small role. **DR3, DR10, DT112**

Liar's Moon (1981, C, 105m, PG)
Love story of poor boy (Matt Dillon) and rich girl (Cindy Fisher) trying to overcome the usual odds. With Christopher Connelly and Hoyt Axton. **DR1, MU12, ST56**

Libeled Lady (1936, B&W, 98m, NR)
Classic comedy of a ruthless newspaper editor (Spencer Tracy) who uses his fiancée (Jean Harlow) and a reporter (William Powell) to get the lowdown on an heiress (Myrna Loy). Starts fast, never lets up. Four stars at their best. **CL10, ST98, ST142, ST176, ST217,** *Recommended*

Liberation of L.B. Jones, The
(1970, C, 102m, R)
A hotly contested divorce case threatens to blow the lid off simmering race relations in a small Southern town. Lee J. Cobb stars in this drama from director William Wyler. With Anthony Zerbe, Lola Falana, Roscoe Lee Browne, Lee Majors, and Barbara Hershey. **DR14, DR26, DT142, ST85**

Licence To Kill (1989, C, 133m, PG-13)
James Bond tracks a drug kingpin in the second series installment to star Timothy Dalton. With Carey Lowell, Talisa Soto, Anthony Zerbe, Robert Davi, and Frank McRae. **HF2**

License To Kill (1984, C, 96m, NR)
Drama of young girl killed by drunk driver, her parents trying to bring public awareness of problem. James Farentino stars, with Don Murray, Penny Fuller, Millie Perkins, and Denzel Washington. Originally made for TV. **DR7, ST223**

Liebelei (1933, B&W, 88m, NR)
Max Ophuls directed this German-language drama of a young officer challenged to a duel by an aristocrat who mistakes the man's intentions toward his wife. Magda Schneider and Wolfgang Liebeneiner star. **DT93**

Liebestraum (1991, C, 116m, NR)
Offbeat story of romantic triangle echoing forty-year-old affair, starring Kevin Anderson, Pamela Gidley, and Bill Pullman. Directed by Mike Figgis. Also available in original 109 minutes, R-rated version. **CU10, DR3**

Lt. Robin Crusoe, USN (1966, C, 110m, G)
Navy pilot Dick Van Dyke makes the most of his being stranded on a desert island in a family comedy from the Disney studios. **FA1**

Life and Death of Colonel Blimp, The
(1943, C, 115m, NR)
Epic drama of British soldier through many
campaigns and personal crises, starring Roger
Livesey and Deborah Kerr (in four roles). Co-
directed by Michael Powell and Emeric Pressburger. Original running time: 163 minutes.
One of Powell's best films but should be seen
at full length. **DT99, ST125, XT27**

Life and Nothing But (1990, C, 135m, PG)
French drama starring Philippe Noiret as
army officer still trying, two years after the
end of World War I, to sort out records of
war dead, being approached by woman looking for her husband. Directed by Bertrand
Tavernier. **DT123**

Life and Times of Grizzly Adams, The
(1976, C, 93m, G)
Family adventure about a fur trapper and his
unlikely friendship with a bear. Dan Haggerty
stars. **FA4**

Life and Times of Judge Roy Bean, The
(1972, C, 120m, PG)
Offbeat Western drama from director John
Huston, about the famous hanging judge of
Texas. Paul Newman heads the cast, which
includes Jacqueline Bisset, Stacy Keach,
Victoria Principal, Anthony Perkins, Ava
Gardner, and the director himself. One of
Huston's experiments that didn't work.
Worth a look if you're interested in the prin-
cipals. **DT60, ST79, ST162, WE15**

Life Begins for Andy Hardy
(1941, B&W, 100m, NR)
Eleventh in popular series finds Andrew
in New York looking for a real job. Mickey
Rooney stars; Judy Garland makes her third
and final appearance in the series, with her
songs cut from final version of film. **CL15,
ST81, ST189**

Life of Emile Zola, The
(1937, B&W, 116m, NR)
Classic biography of French writer, high-
lighted by his role in the Dreyfus scandal.
Paul Muni stars, with Oscar winner Joseph
Schildkraut as Dreyfus. Film won Best Picture
Oscar as well. **CL2, XT1, XT4**

Life of Oharu, The
(1952, B&W, 146m, NR)
From Japan, the story of a woman banished
because of her forbidden love for a samurai
warrior (Toshiro Mifune). Kenji Mizoguchi
directed. **FF4, ST157**

Life of Python (1990, C, 56m, NR)
Documentary on Monty Python's Flying
Circus, featuring clips and interviews. **CO15**

Life Stinks (1991, C, 95m, PG-13)
Mel Brooks comedy about zillionaire developer who bets a rival he can survive for
thirty days in a slum with no money or,
worse, no credit cards. With Lesley Ann
Warren, Jeffrey Tambor, Stuart Pankin, and
Howard Morris. **CO2, CO20, DT17**

Life With Father (1947, C, 118m, NR)
Long-running Broadway comedy by Howard
Lindsay and Russell Crouse about colorful
family headed by a strong patriarch, in turn-
of-the-century New York City. William Powell, Irene Dunne, and Elizabeth Taylor star.
CO5, DR20, ST62, ST176, ST212

Lifeboat (1944, B&W, 96m, NR)
The survivors of a German submarine attack
struggle to survive in a small boat. Alfred
Hitchcock thriller starring Tallulah Bankhead,
Walter Slezak, and William Bendix. **AC24,
DT57**

Lifeforce (1985, C, 100m, R)
Astronauts return to Earth as blood-sucking
vampires in this horror-science fiction film
from director Tobe Hooper. **HO5, SF20**

Lift, The (1985, C, 95m, R)
From Holland, a horror film about an ele-
vator that begins attacking its passengers.
HO22

Light at the Edge of the World, The
(1971, C, 126m, PG)
Jules Verne saga of lighthouse keeper (Kirk
Douglas) and pirate (Yul Brynner) battling for
possession of an island and a lovely woman
(Samantha Eggar). **AC12, ST57, WR36**

Light in the Forest, The
(1958, C, 93m, NR)
Disney adventure of a white boy raised by
Indians and returned to his original family.
James MacArthur, Carol Lynley, and Fess
Parker star. **FA1**

Light of Day (1987, C, 107m, PG-13)
A factory worker and his single-parent sister
spend their evenings performing in a bar
band in Cleveland. Michael J. Fox, Joan Jett,
and Gena Rowlands star in this drama about
a family in crisis. Directed by Paul Shrader.
Jett's surprisingly good, Fox is not. **DR8,
DR12**

Light Sleeper (1992, C, 113m, R)
Low-key drama of New York drug runner
who's starting to look for a better line of
work. Willem Dafoe stars, with Susan Sarandon, Dana Delaney, David Clennon, and
Mary Beth Hurt. Written and directed
by Paul Schrader, his best work in years.
DR7, DR15, DR16, ST194, XT9, XT26,
Recommended

Light Years (1988, C, 79m, PG)
Animated science fiction fantasy about a prince traveling into the future. Sensibility is aimed more at adult than youth audience. Featuring the voices of Glenn Close, Christopher Plummer, Jennifer Grey, Bridget Fonda, and John Shea. **SF4, ST33, ST70**

Lighthorsemen, The (1987, C, 111m, PG)
Australian adventure tale of a company of horse soldiers and their disastrous World War I campaign against the Turks. Directed by Simon Wincer. **AC2, FF5**

Lightning Over Water (1980, C, 91m, NR)
Heartfelt documentary portrait of American film director Nicholas Ray, by his German colleague Wim Wenders. Shot during the final days of Ray's life. **CU16, DT101, DT136,** *Recommended*

Lightning: The White Stallion
(1986, C, 93m, PG)
A horse trainer has his prize stallion stolen and recovers it with the help of two youngsters. Mickey Rooney stars in this family adventure. **FA1, FA4, ST189**

Lights of Old Santa Fe
(1944, B&W, 79m, NR)
A rodeo trick rider leaves the big time to help a struggling friend's show. Roy Rogers stars, with Dale Evans and Gabby Hayes. **ST188**

Lightship, The (1985, C, 89m, R)
A trio of crooks lay siege to a lightship in this offbeat thriller starring Robert Duvall and Klaus Maria Brandauer. Directed by Jerzy Skolimowski. **ST63**

Like Father, Like Son
(1987, C, 98m, PG-13)
Identity-switching comedy of teen-ager (Kirk Cameron) and his doctor dad (Dudley Moore). With Margaret Colin and Catherine Hicks. **CO5, CO20, ST160**

Li'l Abner (1959, C, 113m, NR)
Film version of Broadway musical of Al Capp's comic strip about denizens of Dogpatch, U.S.A. Peter Palmer stars in the title role, with Leslie Parrish as Daisy Mae, Stubby Kaye as Marryin' Sam, and Howard St. John, Julie Newmar, and Stella Stevens. Garish, stagy, with some good songs but little of Capp's satirical wit. **FA9, MU2, MU6**

Lili (1953, C, 81m, G)
Leslie Caron plays a teen-age orphan who joins a circus and helps a bitter puppeteer (Mel Ferrer) see the good things in life. The theme song, "Hi Lili, Hi Lo," helped the film score to win an Oscar. **MU1**

Lilies of the Field (1963, B&W, 93m, NR)
Sidney Poitier won an Oscar for his performance as a handyman who comes to the aid of a group of German nuns trying to build a chapel in the Arizona desert. With Lilia Skala, who should have won an Oscar. Pretty thin but not hard to sit through once. **ST174, XT2, XT28**

Liliom (1934, B&W, 85m, NR)
Charles Boyer plays a man who goes to heaven, stands trial for his life's deeds. Made in France by director Fritz Lang, his first film after leaving Nazi Germany. **DT70, ST16, XT24**

Lilith (1964, B&W, 114m, NR)
Warren Beatty plays a naive young therapist who falls under the spell of one of his patients. With Jean Seberg, Peter Fonda, and Gene Hackman. Directed by Robert Rossen. Deliberate but very rewarding; Beatty's first strong performance. **DR3, ST10, ST96,** *Recommended*

Limelight (1952, B&W, 120m, NR)
Charlie Chaplin's sentimental drama of a washed-up comedian who's given inspiration by a young ballerina (Claire Bloom). Buster Keaton appears as a colleague of Chaplin's in one unforgettable scene. Original running time: 145 minutes. Chaplin lets the maudlin aspects of the story get the upper hand early. **CL6, CL7, DT24, DT66,** *Essential*

Limit Up (1989, C, 88m, PG-13)
Offbeat drama of Chicago grain trader (Nancy Allen) making a deal with the Devil's messenger. With Dean Stockwell, Brad Hall, Danitra Vance, and Ray Charles. **DR24, HO10, ST208**

Lindbergh Kidnapping Case, The
(1976, C, 150m, NR)
Cliff DeYoung plays the famed aviator, Anthony Hopkins is accused child stealer Bruno Hauptmann in this dramatization of the controversial 1930s case. With Joseph Cotten and Denise Alexander. Origianlly made for TV. **DR5, DR17, ST109**

Linguini Incident, The (1992, C, 98m, R)
Romantic comedy, set in New York restaurant, of waitress impulsively robbing her employer to buy an antique ring. At same time, a waiter is trying to rob the till to cover a gambling loss. Rosanna Arquette and David Bowie star, with Eszter Balint, Andre Gregory, Buck Henry, Viveca Lindfors, and Marlee Matlin; cameo appearances by Julian Lennon and Iman. Directed by Richard Shepard. **CO1, MU12**

Link (1986, C, 103m, R)
A crazed scientist and his lovely assistant are endangered species when his experimental chimps launch a revolt. Terence Stamp and Elisabeth Shue star. **HO16, HO19, HO20**

L'Innocente (1979, C, 115m, R)
A faithless Sicilian husband finds that his lovely wife has her own lovers, too. Giancarlo Giannini and Laura Antonelli star. Director Luchino Visconti's last film. Now available in a letterboxed edition. **CU19, DT127**

Lion Has Wings, The
(1939, B&W, 76m, NR)
Drama of the early days of the British Air Defense, starring Merle Oberon, Ralph Richardson, and Flora Robson. Codirected by Michael Powell, Brian Desmond Hurst, and Adrian Brunel. **AC1, DT99, ST184**

Lion in Winter, The (1968, C, 135m, PG)
Katharine Hepburn is Eleanor of Aquitaine, Peter O'Toole is Henry II in this drama of familial and political intrigue in medieval England. Hepburn won her third Oscar for her performance. With Jane Merrow, Nigel Terry, Anthony Hopkins, and Timothy Dalton. **DR5, ST103, ST109, ST169, XT3**

Lion Is in the Streets, A
(1953, C, 88m, NR)
James Cagney plays a fast-talking salesman turned politician in this drama. With Barbara Hale, Anne Francis, Lon Chaney, Jr., and Jeanne Cagney (the star's real-life sister). Directed by Raoul Walsh. **DR21, DT131, ST24, ST27, XT8**

Lion of the Desert (1981, C, 162m, PG)
Epic drama of Omar Mukdtar, Libyan guerrilla leader who waged war against Italians between 1911 and 1931. Anthony Quinn stars, with Oliver Reed, John Gielgud, and Rod Steiger as Benito Mussolini. **DR5, ST86**

Lion, the Witch, and the Wardrobe, The (1983, C, 95m, NR)
When four children walk through a magic wardrobe closet, they're transported into a magical land and meet an evil witch and a kindly lion. An animated adventure based on C.S. Lewis's *Narnia* tales. **FA10**

Lionheart (1987, C, 104m, PG)
Family adventure tale of a young knight (Eric Stoltz) off to join King Richard for the Crusades. With Gabriel Byrne. **AC16, FA4**

Lionheart (1990, C, 105m, R)
Jean-Claude Van Damme applies his kickboxing skills to this story of a foreign legion deserter turned street fighter. **AC26**

Liquid Sky (1983, C, 112m, R)
Cult science fiction film about aliens who land in New York in the middle of the punk-downtown scene. Anne Carlisle plays a male and female role in this highly original film. **CU4, CU6, SF22, XT9,** *Recommended*

Lisbon (1956, C, 90m, NR)
A suave thief (Claude Rains) hires a soldier of fortune (Ray Milland) to rescue the husband of a lovely woman (Maureen O'Hara) from a Communist prison. Directed by Milland. **ST167, XT23**

List of Adrian Messenger, The
(1963, B&W, 98m, NR)
Whodunit set on an Irish estate during hunting season, with guest stars in disguise as the suspects. George C. Scott plays detective; Kirk Douglas, Frank Sinatra, Tony Curtis, Robert Mitchum, and Burt Lancaster are the guest stars. Directed by John Huston, who also appears in a small role. **DT60, MY12, ST57, ST129, ST158, ST196, ST199**

Listen, Darling (1938, B&W, 70m, NR)
Judy Garland and Freddie Bartholomew star in a comedy of a brother and sister searching for a husband for their mom (Mary Astor). Judy sings "Zing Went The Strings Of My Heart." **ST81**

Listen to Me (1989, C, 90m, PG-13)
Drama of college students competing on debate squad, with abortion as the Big Topic. Jami Gertz and Kirk Cameron star, with Roy Scheider. **DR7, DR25**

Listen Up: The Lives of Quincy Jones
(1990, C, 114m, PG-13)
Documentary portrait of musician-arranger-composer-producer features appearances by long list of friends and colleagues: George Benson, Ray Charles, Miles Davis, Billy Eckstine, Ahmet Ertegun, Ella Fitzgerald, Dizzy Gillespie, Lionel Hampton, Ice-T, Jesse Jackson, Sidney Lumet, Frank Sinatra, Steven Spielberg, Barbra Streisand, Sarah Vaughan, and the voice of Michael Jackson. **CU16, DT78, DT118, ST199, ST211**

Lisztomania (1975, C, 105m, R)
A stylized, anything-goes biography of composer Franz Liszt, starring rock singer Roger Daltrey, directed by Ken Russell. As with most Russell films, not for viewers with tender sensibilities. **DT111, MU5**

Little Big Man (1970, C, 150m, PG)
The tall tale of Jack Crabbe, a one-hundred-twenty-one-year-old man who claims he was the only white to survive Custer's Last Stand. Dustin Hoffman stars, with Faye Dunaway, Chief Dan George, Richard Mulligan as

George Armstrong Custer, and Jeff Corey as Wild Bill Hickok. Arthur Penn directed; based on the novel by Thomas Berger. Determinedly revisionist Western that loses much of the poetry and irony of its source but still worth seeing. **DR19, DT96, HF6, HF11, ST61, ST105, WE1, WE7,** *Recommended*

Little Boy Lost (1953, B&W, 95m, NR)
A journalist travels to post–World War II France to find his son. Bing Crosby stars. **ST40**

Little Caesar (1930, B&W, 80m, NR)
Edward G. Robinson is sensational as Rico, the mob boss modeled on Al Capone, in this early gangster classic. **AC22, ST186,** *Essential, Highly Recommended*

Little Colonel, The (1935, B&W, 80m, NR)
In the Reconstruction South, a little girl reunites her feuding mother and grandpa. Shirley Temple, Lionel Barrymore, and Bill Robinson star. **ST213**

Little Darlings (1980, C, 95m, R)
Smirky comedy of two teen girls at summer camp vying to see who can lose her virginity first. Tatum O'Neal and Kristy McNichol star, with Armand Assante and Matt Dillon. Only fans of the stars need check this one out. **CO4, ST56**

Little Dorrit (1988, C, 360m, G)
Epic version of the Charles Dickens novel about the trials and tribulations of a young girl and her father. Divided into two films: *Nobody's Fault* (177m) and *Dorrit's Story* (183m). Derek Jacobi and Sarah Pickering star, with Alec Guinness. **DR23, ST95, WR5**

Little Drummer Girl, The
(1984, C, 130m, R)
From John Le Carré's novel, the story of a British actress recruited by Israeli intelligence to trap a terrorist. Diane Keaton and Klaus Kinski star. Directed by George Roy Hill. Keaton may not sound British but she's right in every other way. **DT55, MY6, ST121, ST126, WR18,** *Recommended*

Little Foxes, The (1941, B&W, 116m, NR)
Lillian Hellman drama about the collapse of a Southern family, starring Bette Davis in one of her showcase performances. Herbert Marshall and Teresa Wright costar. Directed by William Wyler. **DR20, DT142, ST44**

Little Girl Who Lives Down the Lane, The (1976, C, 94m, PG)
Subtle horror mystery about a strange girl whose father has been missing for a long time and a menacing man with a special interest in her. Jodie Foster and Martin Sheen star. **HO13, ST75**

Little Gloria . . . Happy at Last
(1982, C, 200m, NR)
True story of bitter custody fight over young Gloria Vanderbilt, with Bette Davis, Angela Lansbury, and Christopher Plummer. Originally made for TV. **DR5, ST44, ST131**

Little Lord Fauntleroy
(1936, B&W, 98m, NR)
Freddie Bartholomew plays the young American who suddenly finds himself a British lord in this adaptation of the classic children's story. C. Aubrey Smith and Mickey Rooney costar. **FA3, ST189**

Little Lord Fauntleroy
(1980, C, 100m, NR)
TV movie remake of the children's classic about an American lad in Britain. Ricky Schroder and Alec Guinness star. **FA3, ST95**

Little Man Tate (1991, C, 99m, PG)
Drama of child prodigy (Adam Hann-Byrd) and his single, working-class mother (Jodie Foster), who reluctantly agrees to let him attend college. With Dianne Wiest and Harry Connick, Jr. Foster directed. Strong performances, especially from Hann-Byrd and Wiest. **DR9, DR10, DR25, FA7, MU12, ST75,** *Recommended*

Little Mermaid, The (1984, C, 55m, NR)
A Faerie Tale Theatre presentation of the Hans Christian Andersen tale. A lovely sea creature (Pam Dawber) has to choose between her home in the ocean and life on land with a sailor (Treat Williams). **FA12**

Little Mermaid, The (1989, C, 82m, G)
Disney animated feature, based on the Hans Christian Andersen tale, with an Oscar-winning musical score. **FA2,** *Recommended*

Little Minister, The
(1934, B&W, 110m, NR)
Katharine Hepburn plays a gypsy girl who falls in love with a Scottish minister. **ST103**

Little Miss Broadway
(1938, B&W, 70m, NR)
Shirley Temple stars in a musical about a theatrical boarding house. George Murphy and Jimmy Durante are on hand, too. **ST213**

Little Miss Marker (1980, C, 103m, PG)
Comedy set in the 1930s about a little girl left with a bookie as an IOU. Walter Matthau, Julie Andrews, Bob Newhart, and Sara Stimson star. **FA6, ST2, ST155**

Little Monsters (1989, C, 103m, PG)
Fantasy-comedy of a young boy discovering a gang of monsters under his bed. Fred Savage stars, with Howie Mandel and Daniel Stern. **CO11, FA8**

Little Murders (1971, C, 110m, PG)
Dark comedy, written by cartoonist Jules
Feiffer, about life in a New York City where
random killings are the order of the day.
Elliott Gould and Marcia Rodd star, with
Vincent Gardenia, Elizabeth Wilson, Donald
Sutherland, and Alan Arkin, who directed.
CO2, CO12, CU5, XT23

Little Nellie Kelly (1940, B&W, 100m, NR)
Judy Garland stars in this George M. Cohan
musical of a girl mending fences between her
father and grandfather. With George Murphy
and Charles Winninger. **ST81**

**Little Nemo: Adventures in Slumber-
land** (1992, C, 85m, G)
Animated feature based on the landmark
early twentieth-century comic strip by
Winsor McCay. Voices by Gabriel Damon,
Mickey Rooney, and Rene Auberjonois. **FA8,
FA10, ST189**

Little Night Music, A (1978, C, 124m, PG)
Stephen Sondheim musical, based on Ingmar
Bergman's comedy *Smiles of a Summer Night*,
about summertime romance among the rich
and beautiful people. Elizabeth Taylor and
Diana Rigg star. Musical highlight: "Send in
the Clowns." **MU2, MU14, MU17, ST212**

Little Nikita (1988, C, 98m, PG)
FBI agent has the tough task of telling an
American teen that his parents are Soviet
agents. Sidney Poitier and River Phoenix star.
MY6, MY14, ST174

Little Prince, The (1974, C, 88m, G)
Unusual musical based on children's book
about a young boy and his friendship with
an aviator. Richard Kiley, Bob Fosse, Gene
Wilder, and Steven Warner star. Stanley
Donen directed. **DT38, DT47, MU16**

Little Princess, The
(1939, B&W/C, 93m, NR)
Shirley Temple stars as a Victorian waif
searching for her soldier father. With Cesar
Romero and Arthur Treacher. **ST213**

Little Red Riding Hood
(1985, C, 60m, NR)
This Faerie Tale Theatre presentation features
Mary Steenburgen as the unsuspecting girl
and Malcolm McDowell as the evil wolf.
FA12

Little Romance, A (1979, C, 108m, PG)
Laurence Olivier plays matchmaker in Paris
to a young American girl (Diane Lane) and
her new French boyfriend (Thelonius Bernard). Directed by George Roy Hill. **CO4,
DT55, ST168, XT16**

Little Shop of Horrors, The
(1960, B&W, 70m, NR)
Low-budget horror comedy (supposedly
filmed in three days) about a man-eating
plant and its nerdy keeper. Jonathan Haze
stars; Jack Nicholson has a small part as a
pain-loving dental patient. Directed by Roger
Corman. Occasionally funny; a must for
devotees of the offbeat. **CU4, DT30, HO24,
ST163**

Little Shop of Horrors
(1986, C, 88m, PG-13)
Musical version of the horror comedy about
a man-eating plant named Audrey II. Rick
Moranis and Steve Martin star. Bill Murray,
John Candy, and Jim Belushi make brief appearances. Amusing, but layers of production
values can't conceal the cheap, shallow origins. **CO13, CO14, MU8, MU14, MU16,
ST150**

Little Theatre of Jean Renoir, The
(1971, C, 100m, NR)
Three short films from the French master,
his last effort: *The Last Christmas Dinner, The
Electric Floor Waxer*, and *A Tribute to Tolerance*.
Jeanne Moreau heads the cast. **DT104, ST161**

Little Thief, The (1989, C, 104m, R)
French drama of a rebellious adolescent girl
growing up in the stifling 1950s, starring
Charlotte Gainsbourg. **FF1**

Little Treasure (1985, C, 95m, R)
An American stripper journeys to Mexico to
visit her father but winds up searching for
treasure with an amiable adventurer. Margot
Kidder, Burt Lancaster, and Ted Danson are
the stars. **ST129**

Little Vegas (1990, C, 91m, R)
Offbeat comedy set in isolated desert town:
the mob wants to transform it with casinos,
but residents of a trailer park have other
ideas. Anthony John Denison, Catherine
O'Hara, and Michael Nouri star, with Jerry
Stiller, Perry Lang, John Sayles, Jay Thomas,
and Bobcat Goldthwait. **CO10, CO14, DT112**

Little Vera (1989, C, 110m, NR)
Comedy from the Soviet Union, centering on
a rebellious, sexy teen-ager (Natalya Negoda)
and her family problems. **FF7**

Little Women (1933, B&W, 115m, NR)
Louisa May Alcott's classic novel of a family
full of varied sisters, starring Katharine Hepburn and Joan Bennett. Directed by George
Cukor. **CL1, DT32, ST103**

Little Women (1949, C, 121m, NR)
All-star MGM cast is featured in this version of Louisa May Alcott's book, with June

Allyson, Margaret O'Brien, Elizabeth Taylor, and Peter Lawford leading the way. **CL1, ST212**

Littlest Horse Thieves, The
(1977, C, 104m, G)
Three children attempt to save a herd of abused ponies who work in the mines. Disney drama set in turn-of-the-century England. **FA1**

Littlest Outlaw, The (1955, C, 75m, NR)
A Mexican boy, fearful that a horse will be destroyed, runs away with it. Disney family drama. **FA1**

Littlest Rebel, The (1935, B&W, 70m, NR)
A little girl saves her father from prison during the Civil War by pleading directly to President Lincoln. Shirley Temple stars, with Bill Robinson and Frank McGlynn as Lincoln. **HF17, ST213**

Live a Little, Love a Little
(1968, C, 90m, NR)
Elvis Presley plays a photographer who moonlights at a second job—and manages to fit in a little singin' as well. With Michele Carey and Rudy Vallee. **ST178**

Live and Let Die (1973, C, 121m, PG)
Roger Moore's debut as James Bond has 007 chasing down a madman who's distributing drugs as part of his scheme to take over the world. Yaphet Kotto costars. **HF2**

Lives of a Bengal Lancer, The
(1935, B&W, 109m, NR)
Gary Cooper heads the cast of this classic adventure tale about a British regiment on patrol in India. With Franchot Tone, Richard Cromwell, Sir Guy Standing, C. Aubrey Smith, and Monte Blue. Directed by Henry Hathaway. **AC13, FA4, ST37**

Livin' Large (1991, C, 96m, R)
Comedy of young black man, a dry-cleaning truck driver, suddenly turned TV news reporter. Terrence (T.C.) Carson stars, with Lisa Arrindell, Blanche Baker, Nathaniel (Afrika) Hall, and Julia Campbell. **CO2, CO20**

Living Daylights, The
(1987, C, 130m, PG)
Timothy Dalton takes over the James Bond role in this story of a rogue Soviet general (Jeroen Krabbe) and a crooked international arms dealer (Joe Don Baker). Maryam D'Abo and John Rhys-Davies costar. **HF2**

Living Desert, The (1953, C, 73m, G)
Oscar-winning documentary about flora and fauna in the American desert, from the Disney studios. **FA1**

Living Free (1972, C, 91m, G)
Sequel to *Born Free* features more action with Elsa and her cubs in the African wilderness. Susan Hampshire and Nigel Davenport star. **FA5**

Living on Tokyo Time (1987, C, 83m, NR)
Comedy centering on a marriage of convenience between a Japanese woman visiting San Francisco who barely speaks English, and a Japanese-American who speaks no Japanese. Minako Ohashi and Ken Nakagawa star. **CO1, CO2**

Loaded Pistols (1948, B&W, 80m, NR)
Gene Autry shoots and sings his way through another Western adventure. **ST5**

Local Hero (1983, C, 111m, PG)
Charming, original comedy about an American oil company trying to buy a Scottish fishing village as a site for a refinery. Peter Riegert and Burt Lancaster star, with Fulton MacKay, Denis Lawson, Jenny Seagrove, and Peter Capaldi. Written and directed by Bill Forsyth; memorable music by Mark Knopfler. **CO2, CO17, CO20, DT46, ST129, XT26,** *Highly Recommended*

Lock Up (1989, C, 105m, R)
Prison drama of rebel convict (Sylvester Stallone) and sadistic warden (Donald Sutherland). **DR18, ST204**

Lodger, The (1926, B&W, 75m, NR)
Silent thriller from Alfred Hitchcock, his first foray into suspense, about a mysterious man suspected of committing a series of murders in London. Ivor Novello stars. **DT57, MY13**

Logan's Run (1976, C, 120m, PG)
Science fiction adventure about a society of unlimited pleasures but extermination at the age of thirty, and one man's attempt to escape that fate. Michael York and Jenny Agutter star. The special effects won an Oscar. **SF8, SF15**

Lola (1961, B&W, 90m, NR)
Comedy-drama from France, about a cabaret entertainer (Anouk Aimée) trying to remain faithful to her lover, who left her seven years ago. Written and directed by Jacques Demy. **FF1**

Lola (1969, C, 88m, PG)
A teen-ager (Susan George) and a middle-aged writer (Charles Bronson) fall in love. Also known as *Twinky*. **DR3, ST20**

Lola Montes (1955, C, 110m, PG-13)
The story of a famed circus performer and her many affairs with European nobility. A classic unappreciated on its initial release. Directed by Max Ophuls. Available in letter-

boxed format. Highly regarded among Ophuls afficionados, but Martine Carol's stiff performance as Lola is a real drawback. **CL14, CU19, DT93**

Lolita (1962, B&W, 152m, NR)
Dark comedy about a middle-aged man's obsession with a sexy teen-ager. James Mason stars, with Sue Lyon, Peter Sellers, and Shelley Winters. Stanley Kubrick directed; Vladimir Nabokov adapted his own novel. Perfectly cast, adroitly directed. **CO12, DR19, DT68, ST153, ST198, ST232,** *Recommended*

London Kills Me (1992, C, 107m, R)
Urban drama of the drug trade in contemporary London, with Justin Chadwick, Steven Mackintosh, Fiona Shaw, and Brad Dourif. Written and directed by Hanif Kureishi. **DR15, DR23, XT15**

Lone Wolf McQuade (1983, C, 107m, PG)
Chuck Norris, as a Texas Ranger, and David Carradine, as a drug lord, square off in this modern-day Western with plenty of martial arts thrown in. **ST165**

Loneliness of the Long Distance Runner, The (1962, B&W, 103m, NR)
Influential British drama of reform school student with knack for track, defying authorities during big race. Tom Courtenay stars, with Michael Redgrave, Alec McCowen, and James Fox. Alan Sillitoe adapted his own story, Tony Richardson directed. Flashback structure, impressionistic camerawork make this a key entry in postwar British films. **DR22, DR23, DR25,** *Essential, Recommended*

Lonely Are the Brave (1962, B&W, 107m, NR)
In the contemporary West, a rebellious cowboy leads a posse on a wild chase. Kirk Douglas, Gena Rowlands, and Walter Matthau star. Dalton Trumbo adapted Edward Abbey's novel, *Brave Cowboy*. Heavy-handed at times, but undeniably stirring. **ST57, ST155, WE12,** *Recommended*

Lonely Guy, The (1984, C, 91m, R)
When Steve Martin's girlfriend walks out on him, he joins the official ranks of America's lonely guys in this contemporary comedy. Charles Grodin costars. Based on Bruce Jay Friedman's book of humorous essays. **CO2, ST94, ST150**

Lonely Hearts (1981, C, 95m, R)
A romantic drama from Australia about the unlikely pairing of a piano tuner and an awkwardly shy office worker. Wendy Hughes and Norman Kaye star. **FF5**

Lonely Lady, The (1983, C, 92m, R)
A screenwriter claws (and sleeps) her way to the top of the Hollywood heap. This adaptation of the Harold Robbins novel stars Pia Zadora and virtually defines the word "trash." **CU2**

Lonely Man, The (1957, B&W, 87m, NR)
Western drama of a gunfighter trying to put his killing days behind him and find peace with his son. Jack Palance and Anthony Perkins star, with Neville Brand, Claude Akins, and Lee Van Cleef. **ST221, WE2**

Lonely Passion of Judith Hearne, The (1987, C, 110m, R)
Maggie Smith stars in this drama of an Irish spinster's troubles. With Bob Hoskins and Wendy Hiller. Based on Brian Moore's novel. Good performances but too much of the novel's delicacy is gone. **DR19, DR23, ST111**

Lonelyhearts (1958, B&W, 101m, NR)
A reporter takes on his newspaper's advice to the lovelorn column and begins to take his readers' problems to heart. Montgomery Clift stars in this version of Nathanael West's novel, with Robert Ryan, Myrna Loy, and Maureen Stapleton. **DR19, ST32, ST142, ST193**

Loners, The (1972, C, 79m, R)
Biker saga set on the highways and byways of the American Southwest. Dean Stockwell stars, with Todd Susman, Scott Brady, and Gloria Grahame. **ST208, XT18**

Lonesome Dove (1989, C, 375m, NR)
Larry McMurtry's sprawling Western story of two ex-Texas Rangers who agree to drive a herd of cattle from Texas north to Montana. Robert Duvall and Tommy Lee Jones star, with Danny Glover, Rick Schroder, Robert Urich, Anjelica Huston, Diane Lane, and Frederic Forrest. Adapted by William Wittliff; directed by Simon Wincer. Originally a TV miniseries. The best Western of the past twenty years; it will also appeal to non-fans of the genre. Outstanding performances including one of Duvall's strongest ever. **DR19, ST63, ST88, ST115, WE1, WE8,** *Highly Recommended*

Long, Dark Hall, The (1951, B&W, 86m, NR)
Rex Harrison plays a man accused of murder, but his wife (Lilli Palmer) stands by his claims of innocence. **MY15**

Long Day's Journey Into Night (1962, B&W, 136m, NR)
Eugene O'Neill's famous autobiographical play about a family in turmoil, starring

Katharine Hepburn, Ralph Richardson, Jason Robards, and Dean Stockwell. Directed by Sidney Lumet. As good a rendition of this classic play as you're likely to see with Hepburn giving a performance that deserved an Oscar. **DR8, DT78, ST103, ST184, ST185, ST208, WR25, XT28,** *Highly Recommended*

Long Day's Journey Into Night
(1987, C, 169m, NR)
Jack Lemmon stars in this made-for-TV version of the O'Neill classic, with Bethel Leslie, Peter Gallagher, and Kevin Spacey. **DR8, ST138, WR25**

Long Gone (1987, C, 110m, NR)
Comedy-drama of life in baseball's minor leagues, starring William Petersen and Virginia Madsen. Originally made for cable TV. **DR22**

Long Good Friday, The (1980, C, 114m, R)
British gangster saga, with Bob Hoskins superb as a London crime boss whose empire suddenly begins to crumble. Helen Mirren costars. **AC22, DR23, ST111, XT15,** *Highly Recommended*

Long Goodbye, The (1973, C, 112m, R)
Hip, non-traditional version of Raymond Chandler's private eye novel features Elliott Gould as a laconic Philip Marlowe. With Nina Van Pallandt, Sterling Hayden, Henry Gibson, Mark Rydell, Jim Bouton, and in a small role, Arnold Schwarzenegger. Written by Leigh Brackett; directed by Robert Altman and photographed by Vilmos Zsigmond. Funny without sacrificing genuine suspense; purists need not apply. **DT4, MY2, ST195, WR2,** *Recommended*

Long Gray Line, The (1955, C, 138m, NR)
Saga of West Point cadet who rises to become beloved athletic trainer there. Tyrone Power stars, with Maureen O'Hara, Robert Francis, Ward Bond, and Donald Crisp. Directed by John Ford. Widescreen photography is lost on video. **CL3, CU20, DT44, ST167, ST177**

Long, Hot Summer, The
(1958, C, 117m, NR)
William Faulkner's stories are the basis for this starpowered melodrama of Mississippi life, with Paul Newman, Joanne Woodward, Orson Welles, Lee Remick, Anthony Franciosa, and Angela Lansbury. Directed by Martin Ritt. The cast obviously has a great time with their Southern accents, but the film misses much of the source's nuance. **DT105, DT134, ST131, ST162, ST234, WR7**

Long Hot Summer, The
(1985, C, 208m, NR)
TV miniseries remake of the 1958 film, based on Faulkner stories, stars Don Johnson, Cybill Shepherd, Jason Robards, Judith Ivey, Ava Gardner, and Wings Hauser. **ST79, ST185, WR7**

Long, Long Trailer, The
(1954, C, 103m, NR)
Lucille Ball and Desi Arnaz comedy of couple on their event-filled honeymoon. With Marjorie Main and Keenan Wynn. Directed by Vincente Minnelli. **DT88, FA6, XT18**

Long Riders, The (1980, C, 100m, R)
The story of the James Brothers and their friends and enemies, with four real-life sets of brothers starring. Stacy and James Keach play Frank and Jesse James; David, Keith, and Robert Carradine are the Younger brothers; Randy and Dennis Quaid are the Miller brothers; Nicholas and Christopher Guest are the Ford boys. With Pamela Reed as Belle Starr, Savannah Smith, and Harry Carey, Jr. Directed by Walter Hill; music by Ry Cooder. Major disappointment; it's not really bad but given the story, the stars, the director, it coulda been a contender. **DT56, HF16, WE3, XT8**

Long Voyage Home, The
(1940, B&W, 105m, NR)
Drama of Swedish seamen, starring John Wayne, Thomas Mitchell, and Barry Fitzgerald. Adapted from Eugene O'Neill's plays; directed by John Ford. **DT44, ST224, WR25**

Long Walk Home, The (1990, C, 97m, PG)
Drama of 1955 Montgomery, Alabama, bus boycott, with housewife (Sissy Spacek) coming to terms with racial discrimination through the eyes of her maid (Whoopi Goldberg). With Dwight Schultz, Ving Rhames, and Dylan Baker; narrated by Mary Steenburgen. Directed by Richard Pearce. Modestly rewarding. **DR5, DR14, ST89, ST202**

Longest Day, The (1962, B&W, 180m, NR)
Mammoth re-creation of the Normandy Invasion, featuring an all-star, nearly all-male cast, including John Wayne, Henry Fonda, Richard Burton, Robert Mitchum, Sean Connery, Robert Ryan, and many more. Produced by Darryl F. Zanuck; a real labor of love for him that actually worked out well. **AC1, ST22, ST36, ST71, ST158, ST193, ST224,** *Recommended*

Longest Drive, The (1976, C, 92m, NR)
Kurt Russell and Tim Matheson star in a Western drama of two brothers searching for

their long-lost sister. With Brian Keith, Keenan Wynn, Neville Brand, Cameron Mitchell, and Iron Eyes Cody. Originally made for TV under the title "The Quest." **ST190**

Longest Yard, The (1974, C, 123m, R)
Prison comedy-drama, with an ex-pro football star (Burt Reynolds) leading the cons in a rousing game against the vicious guards and their tyrannical warden. Eddie Albert is the warden; among the players are Michael Conrad, Ed Lauter, and Richard Kiel. Directed by Robert Aldrich. Crowd pleaser for its big-game finale; unbearably slow in spots before it gets there. **CO19, DR18, DT1, ST183**

Longshot, The (1986, C, 89m, PG)
Tim Conway-Harvey Korman comedy set at a racetrack, directed by Paul Bartel. **DT8**

Longtime Companion (1990, C, 96m, R)
Drama of the effect of AIDS in the 1980s on a group of gay friends. Stephen Caffrey stars, with Patrick Cassidy, Brian Cousins, and Bruce Davison. Originally made for public TV. Intensely moving. **DR3, DR7,** *Recommended*

Look Back in Anger
(1958, B&W, 99m, NR)
Classic contemporary British drama of angry young man (Richard Burton) lashing out at society for all its injustices. With Mary Ure and Claire Bloom. Tony Richardson directed on location in London. Based on the play by John Osborne. One of Burton's very best performances, when he still had fire in his belly. **DR20, DR23, ST22, XT15,** *Essential, Recommended*

Look Who's Talking
(1989, C, 90m, PG-13)
Gimmick comedy has single mother giving birth to baby whose wisecracking thoughts are voiced by Bruce Willis. Kirstie Alley and John Travolta costar. **CO5, ST229**

Look Who's Talking Too
(1990, C, 81m, PG-13)
More out-of-the-minds-of-babies comedy with original cast (Travolta, Alley, and voice of Willis), Olympia Dukakis, and the voices of Roseanne Barr, Damon Wayans, and Mel Brooks. **CO5, DT17, ST229**

Looker (1981, C, 94m, PG)
A plastic surgeon uncovers a corporate plot to reproduce female models by computer image and eliminate the real people. Albert Finney, James Coburn, and Susan Dey star in this science fiction mystery. **SF5, ST68**

Looking for Mr. Goodbar
(1977, C, 135m, R)
Schoolteacher Diane Keaton prowls singles

bars at night, with disastrous consequences. Drama based on a true story. With Tuesday Weld, Richard Kiley, William Atherton, Richard Gere, and Tom Berenger. Written and directed by Richard Brooks. Good performance by Keaton smothered by purple writing and crude direction. **DR3, DR7, ST84, ST121**

Looking Glass War, The
(1970, C, 108m, PG)
John Le Carré thriller about a photographer out to get picture of a secret rocket in East Berlin. Christopher Jones, Ralph Richardson, and Anthony Hopkins star. **MY6, ST109, ST184, WR18**

Looney, Looney, Looney Bugs Bunny Movie, The (1981, C, 79m, G)
Bugs and all his pals, from Yosemite Sam to Daffy Duck and Porky Pig, are on hand for this collection of Warner Brothers cartoons. **FA11**

Loophole (1980, C, 105m, NR)
Albert Finney stars in a thriller about an unemployed architect who takes part in a bank heist. With Martin Sheen and Susannah York. **MY18, ST68**

Loose Cannons (1990, C, 94m, R)
Buddy cop comedy matches weary veteran (Gene Hackman) and nutty younger partner (Dan Aykroyd). With Dom DeLuise, Ronny Cox, Nancy Travis, and Robert Prosky. **CO10, CO13, ST96**

Loose Shoes (1980, C, 74m, PG)
Comic collection of coming attractions for movies you'll never see: "Skateboarders From Hell," "Welcome to Bacon County," "The Yid and the Kid," etc. The cast of this spoof includes Bill Murray, Howard Hesseman, Ed Lauter, Susan Tyrrell, and Buddy Hackett. **CO7, CO13**

Loot (1972, C, 101m, PG)
Dark comedy, based on Joe Orton play, about a pair of bank robbers who hide their stash in a coffin. Lee Remick, Richard Attenborough, Roy Holder, and Hywel Bennett star. **CO12, CO17**

Lord Jim (1965, C, 154m, NR)
Peter O'Toole stars in Joseph Conrad's tale of a British sailor living with guilt over a single act of cowardice. With James Mason, Curt Jurgens, and Eli Wallach. Adapted and directed by Richard Brooks. **DR19, ST153, ST169**

Lord Love a Duck (1966, B&W, 104m, NR)
Scathing social satire of high school mores, starring Tuesday Weld as status-seeking teen

fixated on acceptance. With Roddy McDowall, Lola Albright, Martin West, Ruth Gordon, and Harvey Korman. Directed and cowritten by Geroge Axelrod. Cult reputation well deserved for this forerunner of *Heathers*. UNAVAILABLE ON VIDEO. **XT29**

Lord of the Flies (1963, B&W, 90m, NR)
After an atomic holocaust, a planeload of young boys escaping the devastation crashes on a jungle island. Adapted from William Golding's bestselling novel. Directed by Peter Brook. **AC12, AC24, DR9, DR19, DR23, SF12**

Lord of the Flies (1990, C, 90m, R)
Second version of the Golding classic changes boys to American military school students, removes references to atomic holocaust. **AC12, AC24, CU18, DR9, DR19**

Lord of the Rings (1978, C, 133m, PG)
Animated feature of the famous J.R.R. Tolkien books about the fantastic characters of Middle Earth. **FA8, FA10, SF13**

Lords of Flatbush, The
(1974, C, 88m, PG)
Comedy about a gang of fun-loving guys living in Brooklyn in the 1950s. Sylvester Stallone, Henry Winkler, and Perry King star, with Susan Blakely. Minor rewards; *The Wanderers* covers the same turf with more style. **CO6, ST204**

Lorenzo's Oil (1992, C, 135m, PG-13)
True story of couple whose young son was diagnosed with rare, fatal genetic disorder, and their personal struggle to find a cure. Susan Sarandon and Nick Nolte star, with Peter Ustinov, Kathleen Wilhoite, and Zack O'Malley Greenburg as the young Lorenzo. Directed and cowritten by George Miller. His direction and Sarandon's performance are first-rate; to its credit, the film avoids ennobling the characters or stooping to cheap sentiment. **DR2, DR6, DR8, ST164, ST194,** *Recommended*

Los Ambicosos see *Fever Mounts in El Pao*

Los Olvidados (1950, B&W, 88m, NR)
Drama about the street boys of Mexico City is one of the most powerful films on the subject of rebellious youth. Luis Buñuel directed. **DT19, XT26,** *Essential, Highly Recommended*

Losin' It (1983, C, 104m, R)
A trio of teens make their way to Tijuana for a wild weekend. Tom Cruise, Jackie Earle Haley, and John Stockwell star, with Shelley Long. **ST41**

Lost and Found (1979, C, 112m, PG)
Glenda Jackson and George Segal star in a

romantic comedy about a widower and divorcée whose passion dies when they marry. With Maureen Stapleton, Hollis McLaren, Paul Sorvino, and, in small roles, John Candy and Martin Short. Directed by Melvin Frank. **CO1, CO14, ST117**

Lost Angels (1989, C, 116m, R)
An institution for the children of wealth with emotional problems is the setting for this drama of life in Los Angeles, starring Adam Horovitz and Donald Sutherland. Directed by Hugh Hudson. Well-intentioned but dramatically impoverished. **DR9, MU12, XT10**

Lost Boys, The (1987, C, 97m, R)
Horror story of two teen-age brothers up against a gang of teen vampires in a small town. Jason Patric, Corey Haim, and Kiefer Sutherland star, with Dianne Wiest, Barnard Hughes, Edward Herrmann, Corey Feldman, and Jami Gertz. **DR26, HO5, HO13**

Lost Command (1966, C, 130m, NR)
Combat action between French and Algerian forces, starring Anthony Quinn, Alain Delon, George Segal, and Claudia Cardinale. **AC6**

Lost Honor of Katharina Blum, The
(1975, C, 97m, R)
Political thriller from Germany about a woman (Margarethe von Trotta) who's persecuted by officials after she spends the night with a suspected terrorist. Directed by Volker Schlondorff. **FF3**

Lost Horizon (1937, B&W, 132m, G)
Director Frank Capra's classic fable about a group of stranded travelers who stumble onto the kingdom of Shangri-La. Ronald Colman stars, with Jane Wyatt, Thomas Mitchell, Margo, and Sam Jaffe. The video version restores about 15 minutes of footage from the film's original release. Adapted from the novel by James Hilton. Reputation precedes it; stunning cinematography and production design are now its main virtues. **CU10, DT22, SF2, ST35,** *Essential*

Lost in a Harem (1944, B&W, 89m, NR)
Abbott and Costello comedy, fully explained by title. With Marilyn Maxwell, John Conte, and Douglas Dumbrille. **ST1**

Lost in America (1985, C, 91m, R)
Writer-director Albert Brooks stars in this brilliant satire about a middle-class couple who decide to quit their jobs and take to the great American road. With Julie Hagerty and Garry Marshall. Brooks's funniest film and one of the few comedies to perfectly sum up the '80s. **CO2, DT16, XT18, XT26,** *Highly Recommended*

Lost in the Stars (1974, C, 114m, NR)
The Kurt Weill-Maxwell Anderson musical
based on Alan Paton's novel *Cry, the Beloved
Country*, about a South African minister's tri-
als and tribulations under apartheid. Brock
Peters heads the all-black cast. **DR14, MU13**

Lost Moment, The (1947, B&W, 88m, NR)
Drama, based on Henry James's *Aspern Papers*, of publisher looking in Italy for famed
writer's long-lost love letters, coming upon
woman who claims to have them. Robert
Cummings and Susan Hayward star. **ST100,
WR14**

Lost Patrol, The (1934, B&W, 65m, NR)
A British army patrol is stranded in the African desert, and Arab tribesmen pick them
off one by one. Classic adventure directed
by John Ford, starring Victor McLaglen
and Boris Karloff. **AC13, DT44, ST119,**
Recommended

Lost Squadron, The
(1932, B&W, 79m, NR)
Drama of former World War I aces working
as movie stunt pilots. Richard Dix stars, with
Mary Astor, Joel McCrea, and Erich Von
Stroheim as an egomaniacal director. **CL7,
DT129, ST144**

Lost Weekend, The
(1945, B&W, 101m, NR)
Ray Milland plays an alcoholic who lives
only for his next drink in this drama. Oscar
winner for Best Picture, Actor, and Director
(Billy Wilder). Still harrowing after all these
years. **CL8, DT139, XT1, XT2, XT6,** *Essential, Recommended*

Lost World, The (1925, B&W, 60m, NR)
Classic silent adventure about a modern
expedition stumbling onto a prehistoric
region. One of the first films to make extensive use of special effects techniques. **AC13,
SF4, SF16**

Lots of Luck (1985, C, 88m, NR)
An unlucky family find their fortunes
reversed when they win a lottery. Unfortunately, they also lose all claims to privacy.
Disney comedy stars Martin Mull, Annette
Funicello, and Fred Willard. Originally made
for cable TV. **FA1**

Louisiana Purchase (1941, B&W, 98m, NR)
Irving Berlin songs enliven this Bob Hope
comedy about a congressman caught in a
position of compromise. With Vera Zorina,
Victor Moore, and Irene Bordoni. **MU6,
ST108**

Louisiana Story (1948, B&W, 79m, NR)
Classic documentary, directed by Robert
Flaherty, centering on the arrival of an oil-
drilling operation in the Louisiana bayou.
Made on commission from Standard Oil
Company. Music by Virgil Thomson. **CU16,**
Essential, Recommended

Loulou (1980, C, 110m, NR)
French drama of a lout (Gérard Depardieu)
who persuades a married woman (Isabelle
Huppert) to leave her husband. Directed by
Maurice Pialat. **FF1, ST52**

Love Affair (1939, B&W, 87m, NR)
Comedy-drama of shipboard romance stars
Irene Dunne and Charles Boyer. Directed by
Leo McCarey, who remade same story as *An
Affair to Remember*, also on tape. One tape
version substitutes entirely new musical score
for original. **CL4, DT80, ST16, ST62**

Love Among the Ruins
(1975, C, 100m, NR)
An aging actress hires a barrister to defend
her in a breach of promise suit. She's unaware, but he still recalls that the two were
long-ago lovers. Katharine Hepburn and Laurence Olivier star. George Cukor directed.
Originally made for TV. Star power supreme,
with astute direction by veteran Cukor.
DR1, DR11, DR17, DT32, ST103, ST168,
Recommended

Love and Anarchy (1973, C, 108m, R)
From Italian director Lina Wertmuller, a
drama of an Italian peasant's plan to assassinate Mussolini. Giancarlo Giannini stars.
DT137

Love and Bullets (1979, C, 103m, PG)
Charles Bronson plays an FBI agent assigned
to retrieve a mobster's girlfriend from Switzerland; instead, he falls in love with her.
ST20

Love and Death (1975, C, 82m, PG)
Woody Allen spoofs foreign movies, Russian
literature, Napoleon (James Tolkan), and
more. With Diane Keaton and Alfred Lutter.
Hit and miss. **DT2, HF18, ST121, XT30**

Love and Money (1982, C, 90m, R)
Bizarre drama of rich businessman (Klaus
Kinski) and the wayward man (Ray Sharkey)
he tries to hire. With Ornella Muti and King
Vidor. Written and directed by James Toback.
Like all this director's films, it has a certain
verve, but diminishing returns. Vidor is won-
derful. **DT126, ST126**

Love and the Frenchwoman
(1961, B&W, 143m, NR)
French drama from several directors (including René Clair) on the seven ages of love in a
woman's life. With Martine Lambert, Claude

Rich, and Jean-Paul Belmondo. **DT25, FF1, ST11**

Love at First Bite (1979, C, 96m, PG)
Comic twist on the Dracula story has George Hamilton as a lovesick vampire, traveling to New York to meet (and nip on) the girl of his dreams. **CO7, HF7, HO5, HO24**

Love at First Sight (1974, C, 85m, NR)
Comedy starring a pre-"Saturday Night Live" Dan Aykroyd as a blind man who falls in love. With Mary Ann McDonald. Made in Canada. **CO13**

Love at Large (1990, C, 97m, R)
A private eye, hired by a mysterious woman to tail her lover, winds up following the wrong man, who turns out to be a bigamist. Tom Berenger stars in this mystery with its share of comic moments. With Elizabeth Perkins, Anne Archer, Ted Levine, Annette O'Toole, Kate Capshaw, Ann Magnuson, and Neil Young. Directed by Alan Rudolph. Berenger and Perkins are a quirky team but too many supporting characters don't make sense. **CO1, DR1, DT110, MU12, MY10**

Love at Stake (1988, C, 88m, R)
Unlikely comedy about Salem witch trials, starring Patrick Cassidy and Kelly Preston (as a baker named Sara Lee), with Dave Thomas, Bud Cort, and Barbara Carrera. **CO6, CO14**

Love Bug, The (1968, C, 108m, G)
Herbie is a Volkswagen with a mind of his own in this popular Disney comedy that spun off many sequels. Dean Jones and Michele Lee costar. **FA1**

Love Butcher, The (1975, C, 84m, R)
A nerdy gardener, spurned by women, turns up as an alter ego seducer, his "twin" brother, to murder them. Horror film stars Erik Stern. **HO9**

Love Crazy (1941, B&W, 99m, NR)
William Powell and Myrna Loy team in a romantic comedy of marital misunderstandings. With Gail Patrick and Jack Carson. **CL15, ST142, ST176**

Love Crimes (1992, C, 85m, R)
An assistant district attorney (Sean Young) goes undercover to expose a photographer (Patrick Bergin) who's taking compromising pictures of women and then blackmailing them. Directed by Lizzie Borden. Also available in an unrated version with several additional minutes of compromising, er, sexy, scenes added. **CU10, MY3**

Love 'Em and Leave 'Em
(1926, B&W, 70m, NR)
Silent comedy-drama of sisters involved with gambling, also rivals in love. Evelyn Brent and Louise Brooks star. **ST21**

Love Field (1992, C, 104m, PG-13)
Drama set in 1963 of Dallas waitress so unnerved by the John F. Kennedy assassination that she decides to take a bus to Washington, D.C., for the funeral. Along the way, she befriends a young black man traveling with his daughter for reasons he doesn't immediately disclose. Michelle Pfeiffer stars, with Dennis Haysbert, Stephanie McFadden, and Brian Kerwin. Directed by Jonathan Kaplan. **DR5, ST173, XT18**

Love Finds Andy Hardy
(1938, B&W, 90m, NR)
Mickey Rooney has true romance problems, trying to decide among Judy Garland, Lana Turner, and Ann Rutherford. Judy sings three songs. **CL15, ST81, ST189, ST219**

Love Flower, The (1920, B&W, 70m, NR)
Silent drama from director D.W. Griffith, about a man who murders his wife's lover, then flees with his daughter to a desert island. Carol Dempster and Richard Barthelmess star. **DT52**

Love From a Stranger
(1947, B&W, 81m, NR)
Agatha Christie story of a woman (Sylvia Sidney) who learns that her husband is a killer. With John Hodiak and John Howard. **MY3, WR3**

Love Happy (1949, B&W, 91m, NR)
Late Marx Brothers film about putting on a show. Marilyn Monroe has a small part. For hard-core Marxists only. **ST152, ST159**

Love in Germany, A (1984, C, 110m, R)
German-produced story of soldier's wife (Hanna Schygulla) and her affair with a Polish POW. With Marie-Christine Barrault and Armin Mueller-Stahl. Directed by Andrzej Wajda. **DT130**

Love in the Afternoon
(1957, B&W, 130m, NR)
Romance blossoms between Gary Cooper and Audrey Hepburn in this comedy set in Paris. Billy Wilder directed. **CL4, DT139, ST37, ST102**

Love in the City (1953, B&W, 90m, NR)
Six Italian directors demonstrate different aspects of love in Rome. Contributors include Federico Fellini and Michelangelo Antonioni. **DT5, DT43, XT17**

Love Is a Many Splendored Thing
(1955, C, 102m, NR)
Glossy romantic drama, with a Eurasian woman (Jennifer Jones) and American

reporter (William Holden) learning the meaning of the title. Drama set in Hong Kong during the Korean War. **CL4, ST106**

Love Is Better Than Ever
(1952, B&W, 81m, NR)
Elizabeth Taylor and Larry Parks star in this MGM musical of relationship between dancer and agent. With Josephine Hutchinson, Tom Tully, Elinor Donahue, and Gene Kelly in a bit part. Directed by Stanley Donen. **DT38, MU1, MU4, ST123, ST212**

Love Laughs at Andy Hardy
(1946, B&W, 93m, NR)
Andy is home from World War II and back in the romantic soup. Mickey Rooney and Bonita Granville star. **ST189**

Love Letters (1983, C, 98m, R)
A young woman discovers after her mother's death of a secret affair with a married man; she takes up with one herself. Jamie Lee Curtis and James Keach star, with Amy Madigan, Bud Cort, and Sally Kirkland. **DR1, DR3, ST42**

Love Machine, The (1971, C, 108m, R)
Melodrama of a TV executive who stops at nothing to quench his unslakable thirst for power, power, power. John Phillip Law stars, with Dyan Cannon, Robert Ryan, and David Hemmings. Adapted from the novel by Jacqueline Susann. Originally made for TV. **DR12, ST193**

Love Me or Leave Me (1955, C, 122m, NR)
Musical drama about real life singer Ruth Etting and her affair with a domineering gangster. Doris Day and James Cagney star. **MU5, ST24, ST47**

Love Me Tender (1956, B&W, 89m, NR)
Elvis Presley made his film debut in this Civil War Western about family conflicts. **ST178, WE6**

Love Nest (1951, B&W, 84m, NR)
Comedy about an army veteran and his wife making do in a rundown apartment house. June Haver and William Lundigan star, with Frank Fay, Marilyn Monroe, and Jack Paar. **ST159**

Love on the Dole (1941, B&W, 100m, NR)
Drama of London family trying to survive the Great Depression. Deborah Kerr, Clifford Evans, and Mary Merrall star. **DR23, ST125**

Love on the Run (1979, C, 93m, PG)
The fifth installment in French director François Truffaut's series of films about Antoine Doinel, starring Jean-Pierre Leaud. **DT125**

Love Potion No. 9 (1992, C, 97m, PG-13)
Romantic comedy of two wonks (Tate Donovan, Sandra Bullock) who become irresistible after ingesting title fluid. With Anne Bancroft as the gypsy. Written and directed by Dale Launer. **CO1**

Love Songs (1986, C, 107m, NR)
A woman is deserted by her husband and is uncertain of her new-found freedom. Drama from France, starring Catherine Deneuve. **FF1, ST50**

Love Story (1970, C, 99m, PG)
The contemporary classic about a Harvard student (Ryan O'Neal) and his short-lived marriage to a working-class girl (Ali MacGraw). With John Marley and Ray Milland. Erich Segal adapted his bestselling novel. **DR1, DR2,** *Essential*

Love Streams (1984, C, 141m, PG-13)
Drama from director John Cassavetes, who stars with his real-life wife Gena Rowlands in a tangled tale of a brother-sister relationship. With Diahnne Abbott and Seymour Cassel. Adapted from a play by Ted Allan. **DR8, DR20, XT23, XT30**

Love With the Proper Stranger
(1963, B&W, 100m, NR)
New York is the setting for this romance between a jazz musician (Steve McQueen) and working girl (Natalie Wood). With Herschel Bernardi, Edie Adams, and Tom Bosley. **DR1, ST146, XT9**

Loved One, The (1965, B&W, 116m, NR)
Very dark comedy, based on Evelyn Waugh's novel about a Britisher (Robert Morse) visiting Los Angeles and getting mixed up in the funeral racket when his uncle (John Gielgud) is fired from his job at a movie studio and commits suicide. Incredible supporting cast includes Jonathan Winters (in two roles), Anjanette Comer, Robert Morley, Liberace, Dana Andrews, Milton Berle, James Coburn, Paul Williams, Tab Hunter, Roddy McDowall, Lionel Stander, and Rod Steiger as Mr. Joyboy. Written by Terry Southern and Christopher Isherwood; directed by Tony Richardson. Advertised as "The movie with something to offend everyone." It's true, it's true. **CO8, CO12, CO20, CU12, CU17, DR19, ST86, XT10, XT27**

Lover, The (1992, C, 110m, R)
Love story set in 1920s Vietnam focuses on intensely sexual affair between a fifteen-year-old and a Chinese businessman. French drama adapted from Marguerite Duras's autobiographical novel, directed by Jean-Jacques Annaud. Available in an unrated version with about twelve minutes of extra footage. **CU6, CU10, DR1, DR19, FF1**

Lover Come Back (1961, C, 107m, NR)
Rock Hudson-Doris Day comedy about rival
advertising executives finding romance. With
Tony Randall and Edie Adams. **ST47, ST112**

Loverboy (1989, C, 98m, PG-13)
A pizza delivery boy finds that many of his
customers—bored women—are interested in
more than just his pies. Patrick Dempsey
stars in this comedy, with Kate Jackson,
Nancy Valen, Barbara Carrera, Kirstie Alley,
and Carrie Fisher. Directed by Joan Micklin
Silver. **CO1**

Lovers, The (1959, B&W, 90m, NR)
Jeanne Moreau plays a bored wife who finds
true love with an overnight guest and runs
away with him. Louis Malle directed. Subject
to censorship in famous Ohio case that went
to the Supreme Court. **CU8, DT82, ST161**

Lovers (1991, C, 103m, NR)
Sexy crime drama based on 1955 Madrid case
of young man taking up with his older land-
lady and deserting his fiancee, who seeks
revenge. Victoria Abril, Jorge Senz, and Mari-
bel Verda star in this Spanish-language film.
Also available in slightly shorter, R-rated version. **CU6, FF7, MY8**

Lovers and Liars (1979, C, 96m, R)
Giancarlo Giannini and Goldie Hawn are the
frantic lovers in this dark comedy made in
Italy. **FF2, ST99**

Lovers and Other Strangers
(1970, C, 106m, PG)
Comedy centering around the wedding of a
young couple, with the impending ceremony
bringing out the best—and worst—in both
families. Michael Brandon, Bonnie Bedelia,
Bea Arthur, Richard Castellano, and Gig
Young star. Diane Keaton's film debut. A surprise hit on its release that has dated badly.
CO5, ST121, XT20

Lovers Like Us (1975, C, 103m, PG)
French comedy starring Catherine Deneuve
and Yves Montand as runaway spouses falling in love. **FF1, ST50**

Loves of a Blonde (1965, B&W, 88m, NR)
Boy meets girl, Czech style, in this poignant
drama from director Milos Forman. **DT45,
FF7**

Loves of Carmen, The (1948, C, 99m, NR)
The famous opera story of passion and be-
trayal, told in dramatic terms, starring Rita
Hayworth and Glenn Ford. **ST101**

Lovesick (1983, C, 95m, PG)
Psychiatrist falls in love with his own patient
and calls on Sigmund Freud for advice. Dudley Moore and Elizabeth McGovern star in

this romantic comedy, with John Huston,
Alec Guinness as Freud, Wallace Shawn, Alan
King, Renee Taylor, and Ron Silver. Written
and directed by Marshall Brickman. Moore
overacts; long stretches without laughs. **CO1,
DT60, ST95, ST160**

Lovespell (1979, C, 91m, NR)
Retelling of Tristan and Isolde legend, filmed
in Ireland. Kate Mulgrew and Nicholas Clay
star, with Richard Burton. Also known as
Tristan and Isolde. **DR1, DR3, ST22**

Loving (1970, C, 90m, R)
Richly textured story of architect whose
career and personal life are floundering.
George Segal stars, with Eva Marie Saint, Sterling Hayden, Keenan Wynn, Nancie Phillips,
Roy Scheider, and Sherry Lansing. Directed
by Irvin Kershner. Skillfully drawn portrait of
contemporary man yielding to temptations.
UNAVAILABLE ON VIDEO. **XT29**

Loving Couples (1980, C, 97m, PG)
Mate-switching comedy starring Shirley Mac-
Laine, James Coburn, Susan Sarandon, and
Stephen Collins. **ST145, ST194**

Loving You (1957, C, 101m, NR)
Elvis Presley's second film finds him playing a gas jockey whose singing doesn't go
unnoticed by a talent scout (Lizabeth Scott).
One of the King's better efforts. **ST178**

Lower Depths, The (1936, B&W, 92m, NR)
Loose adaptation of Maxim Gorky's play
about life in home for derelicts, filmed by
Jean Renoir. Jean Gabin, Louis Jouvet, Suzy
Prim, and Vladimir Sokoloff star. **DT104**

Lower Depths, The
(1957, B&W, 125m, NR)
Japanese version of the famed Maxim Gorky
play, directed by Akira Kurosawa. Toshiro
Mifune plays a thief whose life is changed by
an itinerant priest. Kurosawa brings an amazing amount of dynamism to stagy story.
DT69, ST157, *Recommended*

Lucas (1986, C, 100m, PG-13)
A sixteen-year-old boy tries out for the
school football team, despite his lack of size,
to impress his first love. Corey Haim, Charlie
Sheen, and Kerri Green star in this family
drama. **DR9, FA7**

Lucky Luciano (1974, C, 110m, R)
Drama depicting the final years of the
deported crime kingpin, starring Gian-Maria
Volonte, Rod Steiger, and Edmond O'Brien.
AC22

Lucky Me (1954, C, 100m, NR)
Doris Day musical, with D.D. playing a
Miami gig in a theatrical troupe, hoping for

her big break. With Robert Cummings, Phil Silvers, Eddie Foy, and Nancy Walker. **MU4, ST47**

Lucky Partners (1940, B&W, 99m, NR) Comedy starring Ronald Colman and Ginger Rogers as a pair of sweepstakes winners trying to decide what they'll do with their fortune. **ST35, ST187**

Lullaby of Broadway (1951, C, 92m, NR) In this Doris Day musical, she plays a New York star reunited with her singer mother. With Gene Nelson, Gladys George, S.Z. Sakall, and Billy de Wolfe. **MU4, ST47**

Lulu in Berlin (1985, C/B&W, 50m, NR) Documentary portrait of actress Louise Brooks, featuring a rare interview plus generous clips from *Pandora's Box*, *Diary of a Lost Girl*, and her other films. Directed by Richard Leacock and Susan Woll. **CU16, ST21, XT26,** *Recommended*

Lumière (1976, C, 95m, R) Star Jeanne Moreau also directed this drama about four women and their friendships. **DR10, FF1, ST161**

Lunatics and Lovers (1975, C, 93m, PG) Italian comedy about a man with an imaginary wife. Marcello Mastroianni stars, with Claudia Mori. **FF2, ST154**

Lust for a Vampire (1970, C, 95m, R) An all-girls' boarding school is really a haven for vampires in this sexy horror tale. **HO5, HO25, HO26**

Lust for Life (1956, C, 122m, NR) Biography of tormented painter Vincent Van Gogh (Kirk Douglas), directed by Vincente Minnelli, with an Oscar-winning performance by Anthony Quinn as Paul Gauguin. Outstanding color photography. **CL2, CL9, DT88, ST57, XT4**

Lust in the Dust (1985, C, 85m, R) Spoof of Westerns has Divine and Lainie Kazan playing saloon singers with different parts of a treasure map tattooed on their posteriors. With Tab Hunter, Geoffrey Lewis, and Woody Strode. Directed by Paul Bartel. **CO7, DT8, WE14**

Lusty Men, The (1952, B&W, 113m, NR) Susan Hayward, Robert Mitchum, and Arthur Kennedy star in this contemporary Western drama about the men who tour the rodeo circuit. Directed by Nicholas Ray. His fans love it; others beware. **DT101, ST100, ST158, WE12**

Luv (1967, C, 95m, NR) In this comedy, Jack Lemmon plays a would-be suicide who is "saved" by a pal (Peter Falk) who persuades him to take his wife (Elaine May) off his hands. With Eddie Mayehoff, Severn Darden, and in a small role, Harrison Ford. Based on a play by Murray Shisgal. **DR20, DT86, ST74, ST138**

M (1931, B&W, 99m, NR) Classic German thriller about a child molester (Peter Lorre) who's hunted down by criminal gangs. Directed by Fritz Lang. Repellent subject matter artfully presented. **DT70, FF3, HO1, MY13,** *Essential, Highly Recommended*

M*A*S*H (1970, C, 116m, R) Uproarious military comedy about a trio of fun-loving surgeons and their operating procedures during the Korean War. Donald Sutherland, Elliott Gould, and Tom Skerritt star, with Robert Duvall, Sally Kellerman, René Auberjonois, Gary Burghoff, Michael Murphy, and Fred Williamson. Robert Altman directed; Ring Lardner, Jr., won an Oscar for his screenplay adaptation of the Richard Hooker novel. **AC3, CO6, CO12, CO21, DT2, ST63, XT25,** *Essential, Highly Recommended*

MUSE Concert: No Nukes, The (1980, C, 103m, NR) Concert film, shot at benefit rally opposing nuclear power, includes performances by Bruce Springsteen, James Taylor, Carly Simon, Jackson Browne, and Crosby, Stills & Nash. Also known as *No Nukes.* **MU10**

MacArthur (1977, C, 130m, PG) Gregory Peck plays the fabled general who led the U.S. to victories in World War II but clashed with President Truman over how to wage the Korean War. **DR4, ST171**

MacArthur's Children (1984, C, 120m, PG) Japanese drama of the effects of the American postwar occupation on a village, especially its youngsters. Directed by Masahiro Shinoda. **FF4**

McBain (1991, C, 102m, R) Action drama of soldier of fortune (Christopher Walken) making good on promise to Vietnam vet buddy to overthrow Colombian drug cartel. With Maria Conchita Alonso, Michael Ironside, Steve James, and Jay Patterson. **AC21, ST222**

Macbeth (1948, B&W, 112m, NR) Orson Welles's legendary adaptation of the Shakespeare play, done with authentic Scottish accents. This is the restored version, which contains twenty-one minutes of additional footage. With Jeanette Nolan, Dan

O'Herlihy, Edgar Barrier, and Roddy Mc-Dowall. **CU10, DT134, WR28**

Macbeth (1971, C, 140m, R)
Director Roman Polanski's version of the Shakespeare play of political intrigue in Scotland. Jon Finch and Francesca Annis star. **DT97, WR28**

McCabe and Mrs. Miller
(1971, C, 121m, R)
Warren Beatty is a gambler, Julie Christie a frontier madam in this richly textured Western set in the Pacific Northwest. With René Auberjonois, Keith Carradine, Bert Remsen, Shelley Duvall, Michael Murphy, and Hugh Millais. Directed by Robert Altman; songs by Leonard Cohen. Glorious use of widescreen will be lost on video but essential story, with finely shaded performances, remains strong. **CU20, DT4, ST10, ST30, WE8, WE10, WE11, WE15,** *Highly Recommended*

McConnell Story, The (1955, C, 107m, NR)
Bio of famed test pilot of jets, starring Alan Ladd, with June Allyson, James Whitmore, and Frank Faylen. **CL2, ST128**

McGuire, Go Home! (1966, C, 101m, NR)
Drama set in 1954 Cyprus, as British soldiers battle terrorists. Dirk Bogarde stars, with Susan Strasberg and George Chakiris. Also known as *A Date With Death* and *The High Bright Season.* **ST14**

Mackenna's Gold (1969, C, 128m, PG)
Western saga of the search for a lost canyon filled with gold, starring Gregory Peck, Omar Sharif, Telly Savalas, and Edward G. Robinson. **ST171, ST186, WE1**

McLintock! (1963, C, 122m, NR)
Broad comic Western with cult following stars John Wayne as fun-loving cowpoke trying to loosen up his strait-laced wife, played by Maureen O'Hara. With Patrick Wayne (the Duke's real-life son), Stefanie Powers, Yvonne De Carlo, and Chill Wills. Directed by Andrew McLaglen. Widescreen will be lost on home video. Beware budget-label edition with compromised video quality. **CU20, ST167, ST224, WE14, XT8**

McQ (1974, C, 116m, PG)
John Wayne takes to the streets of Seattle as a veteran cop out to avenge the murder of his partner. Best thing about film was promotional line: "Wayne on Wheels!" **AC9, ST224**

McVicar (1980, C, 111m, R)
True-life story of England's most dangerous criminal and his escape from prison. Roger Daltrey stars. **MU12**

Macabre Serenade (1968, C, 95m, NR)
Boris Karloff stars in this horror film, one of his last, about a wicked toymaker whose creations are deadly weapons. **ST119**

Macao (1952, B&W, 80m, NR)
Robert Mitchum and Jane Russell star in an adventure yarn set in the exotic title port. Josef von Sternberg directed. **DT128, ST158**

Macaroni (1985, C, 104m, PG)
Marcello Mastroianni and Jack Lemmon are the stars of this comedy about an American returning to the Italian village where he served in World War II. **CO3, FF2, ST138, ST154**

Machine Gun Kelly (1958, B&W, 80m, NR)
Charles Bronson plays the notorious gangster who made his rep when he turned from bank robbery to kidnapping. With Susan Cabot, Barboura Morris, and Morey Amsterdam. Directed by Roger Corman. **AC22, DT30, ST20**

Macho Callahan (1970, C, 99m, R)
David Janssen plays a prison escapee in a Civil War Western about revenge. **WE5, WE6**

Mack, The (1973, C, 110m, R)
An Oakland pimp just released from prison finds that his old territory has been taken over. Urban action starring Max Julien, Richard Pryor, and Roger E. Mosley. **AC8, ST180**

Mackintosh Man, The
(1973, C, 105m, PG)
Espionage thriller about the elimination of a double agent, starring Paul Newman and James Mason, directed by John Huston. Written by Walter Hill. Ordinary. **DT60, MY6, ST153, ST162**

Mad at the Moon (1992, C, 98m, R)
Supernatural tale set on the 1892 Western frontier, with young virgin wife discovering something hairy about her new hubby when the moon comes out. Mary Stuart Masterson and Hart Bochner star, with Fionnula Flanagan, Stephen Blaka, and Daphne Zuniga. Directed by Martin Donovan. **HO4, WE8, XT23**

Mad Dog and Glory (1993, C, 96m, R)
When a Chicago police photographer saves a loan shark's life, the crook offers him the use for a week of a lovely young bartender who's indebted to him. Offbeat romantic drama stars Robert De Niro and Bill Murray, with Uma Thurman, David Caruso, Mike Starr, Tom Towles, and Kathy Baker. Written by Richard Price (who appears as a cop in one scene), directed by John McNaughton. Ter-

rific screenplay, with Murray especially effective as the swaggering but insecure gangster. **CO13, DR1, DR15, ST51, XT11,** *Recommended*

Mad Dog Morgan (1976, C, 102m, R)
Fact-based story of a nineteenth-century outlaw who terrorized the Australian countryside and outwitted the law, starring Dennis Hopper. **FF5, ST110, WE3**

Mad Love (1935, B&W, 70m, NR)
Subtle horror tale stars Peter Lorre as a crazed doctor in love with a married woman; he's about to perform a critical operation on her pianist husband. With Frances Drake and Colin Clive. Directed by Karl Freund. **HO1, HO19, HO20,** *Recommended*

Mad Max (1979, C, 93m, R)
In the near future, a gang of cyclists rule the outback roads of Australia, and only a fearless cop (Mel Gibson) can stop them. George Miller directed this non-stop action adventure. Followed by two sequels, *The Road Warrior* and *Mad Max Beyond Thunderdome*. This one is the quirkiest and meanest. **AC10, AC25, CU7, FF5, ST85, XT18,** *Highly Recommended*

Mad Max Beyond Thunderdome
(1985, C, 106m, PG-13)
In the third *Mad Max* adventure, Mel Gibson squares off against Tina Turner and her mangy minions in a desert battle to the death. One *Max* too many. **AC10, AC24, AC25, FF5, MU12, ST85**

Mad Max 2 see *Road Warrior, The*

Mad Miss Manton, The
(1938, B&W, 80m, NR)
A mystery comedy, with socialite Barbara Stanwyck and her society pals involved. Henry Fonda costars. **MY17, ST71, ST206**

Mad Monster Party? (1967, C, 94m, NR)
Animated children's feature, with Frankenstein announcing his retirement at a gathering of famous monsters. Features the voice of Boris Karloff. **FA10, ST119**

Madam Satan (1930, B&W, 105m, NR)
Hokum from director Cecil B. DeMille about drab housewife who takes on new identity as notorious socialite to win her wandering spouse back. Kay Johnson stars, with Reginald Denny, Roland Young, and Lillian Roth. Some amusing scenes, including a party aboard a zeppelin. **DT34**

Madame Bovary (1934, B&W, 102m, NR)
French-language adaptation of Flaubert's classic, directed by Jean Renoir. Valentine Tessier and Pierre Renoir (the director's brother) star. **CL1, CL5, DT104**

Madame Bovary (1949, B&W, 115m, NR)
The Flaubert story of a woman's sacrifice for her husband, lushly told by director Vincente Minnelli. Jennifer Jones and James Mason star. **CL1, CL5, DT88, ST153**

Madame Bovary (1991, C, 130m, NR)
French-language version of the Flaubert classic, starring Isabelle Huppert, directed by Claude Chabrol. **CL1, FF1**

Madame Curie (1943, B&W, 124m, NR)
Greer Garson plays the Nobel Prize-winning scientist. Walter Pidgeon costars, Henry Travers, Robert Walker, and C. Aubrey Smith. **CL2, ST83**

Madame Rosa (1977, C, 105m, NR)
Oscar-winning French drama of a madam (Simone Signoret) who shelters the children of prostitutes. **FF1, XT7**

Madame Sin (1971, C, 73m, NR)
Bette Davis stars as an evil foreign agent out to make trouble for the U.S. Navy. With Robert Wagner. Originally made for TV. **MY4, MY6, ST44**

Madame Sousatzka (1988, C, 121m, PG-13)
Shirley MacLaine plays an eccentric Russian piano teacher in this drama, with Navin Chowdhry, Twiggy, and Peggy Ashcroft. Directed by John Schlesinger. **DT113, ST145**

Madame X (1966, C, 100m, NR)
The classic soap story about a woman accused of murder, defended by a man who has no idea she is really his mother. Lana Turner stars. **CL5, CL6, DR2, ST219**

Made for Each Other
(1939, B&W, 93m, NR)
Young marrieds James Stewart and Carole Lombard have their ups and downs, mainly the latter, in this classic melodrama. **CL6, ST140, ST207**

Made for Each Other (1971, C, 107m, PG)
Hilarious comedy of two lost New York souls, the son of an Italian-American clan and a dizzy Jewish show-biz aspirant, trying to find romance. Renee Taylor and Joseph Bologna star, with Paul Sorvino and Olympia Dukakis. The stars also wrote the script. Many highlights, including one of the funniest family dinners ever filmed. UNAVAILABLE ON VIDEO. **XT29**

Made in Heaven (1987, C, 103m, PG)
Two souls meet in heaven and begin a romance that is interrupted when one of them is sent down to Earth. Timothy Hutton and Kelly McGillis star in this romantic drama from director Alan Rudolph. With Maureen Stapleton, Don Murray, Amanda

Plummer, Mare Winningham, Timothy Daly, and small roles for Ellen Barkin, Debra Winger, Neil Young, Tom Petty, and Gary Larson. **DR1, DT110, ST7, ST231**

Madeleine (1949, B&W, 101m, NR)
British drama of woman accused of murdering her lover. Ann Todd stars, with Leslie Banks and Elizabeth Sellars. Directed by David Lean. Also known as *The Strange Case of Madeleine.* **DT71, MY15**

Mademoiselle Fifi (1944, B&W, 69m, NR)
Allegorical tale, set during Franco-Prussian War, with parallels to World War II, of laundress on coach ride who displays more patriotism than her jaded fellow passengers. Simone Simon stars, with John Emery, Kurt Krueger, Alan Napier, and Jason Robards, Sr. Produced by Val Lewton, directed by Robert Wise. **DT140, HO27**

Mademoiselle Striptease
(1957, B&W, 99m, NR)
Brigitte Bardot stars in this caper comedy about the theft of a rare art book. Also known as *Please! Mr. Balzac.* **ST6**

Madhouse (1974, C, 89m, PG)
British mystery stars Vincent Price as a horror film actor attempting a comeback, implicated in a string of murders. With Peter Cushing. **MY7, MY15, ST43, ST179**

Madigan (1968, C, 101m, NR)
A police detective (Richard Widmark) and his commissioner boss (Henry Fonda) disagree on how to keep the peace in New York. Directed by Don Siegel. Superb portrait of police department politics. Use of widescreen will be lost on video. **AC9, CU20, DT116, ST71, XT9,** *Recommended*

Madigan's Millions (1967, C, 86m, NR)
Comedy about an incompetent U.S. Treasury agent sent to Italy to recover stolen funds belonging to a late gangster. Dustin Hoffman stars. Made before *The Graduate* but released only after its success; Hoffman's voice is dubbed. **FF2, ST105**

Madman (1979, C, 92m, PG)
A Russian Jew survives years of forced confinement in an asylum and swears revenge. Sigourney Weaver, Michael Beck, and F. Murray Abraham star. **ST225**

Madwoman of Chaillot, The
(1969, C, 132m, G)
Katharine Hepburn stars in the Jean Giraudoux play about an elderly woman who clings to her ideals in a modern, cynical world. With Charles Boyer, Claude Dauphin, Edith Evans, John Gavin, Paul Henreid, Yul

Brynner, and Danny Kaye. **DR20, ST16, ST103, ST120**

Maedchen in Uniform
(1931, B&W, 90m, NR)
German drama, once considered daring, takes place in an oppressive girls' school, where one student and her teacher form a lesbian relationship. Dorothea Wieck and Hertha Thiele star. Leontine Sagan directed. **FF3**

Magic (1978, C, 106m, R)
A high-strung ventriloquist lets his dummy take over his life. Anthony Hopkins and Ann-Margret star. Directed by Richard Attenborough. William Goldman adapted his novel, which was far scarier, although Hopkins gives it his all. **HO8, HO19, ST109, XT23**

Magic Christian, The (1970, C, 93m, PG)
Far-out Terry Southern comedy about the world's wealthiest man testing to see just what people will do for money. Peter Sellers and Ringo Starr head the cast, which also includes Graham Chapman, John Cleese, Richard Attenborough, Roman Polanski, Yul Brynner (in drag), and Christopher Lee as Dracula. Not to be confused with or compared to *Indecent Proposal.* **CO12, CO15, CO17, DT97, HF7, MU12, ST135, ST198**

Magic Flute, The (1974, C, 134m, G)
Change of pace from director Ingmar Bergman: a screen version of Mozart's classic opera. **DT11**

Magic of Lassie, The (1978, C, 100m, G)
Remake of *Lassie Come Home*, with the popular collie the object of a custody battle. James Stewart stars—and even sings, too. With Mickey Rooney. **FA5, ST189, ST207**

Magic Sword, The (1962, C, 80m, NR)
Adventure film about a young knight's quest to rescue a princess from an evil sorcerer. Basil Rathbone stars. **AC18**

Magic Town (1947, C, 103m, NR)
James Stewart plays a pollster who finds the perfectly average American small town in this comedy. With Jane Wyman, Kent Smith, Regis Toomey, and Donald Meek. Directed by William Wellman. **DR26, DT135, ST207**

Magical Mystery Tour (1967, C, 60m, NR)
The Beatles' legendary "home movie," originally made for TV, is a loosely connected series of skits incorporating songs from their album of the same name. A midnight movie favorite. **CU1, MU9**

Magician, The (1959, B&W, 102m, NR)
A magician (Max von Sydow) has more than

simple tricks up his sleeve in this somber drama from director Ingmar Bergman. **DT11**

Magician of Lublin, The
(1979, C, 105m, R)
Drama set in turn-of-the-century Poland about a wizard, adapted from a story by Isaac Bashevis Singer. Alan Arkin stars, with Louise Fletcher, Valerie Perrine, and Shelley Winters. **DR19, ST232**

Magnificent Ambersons, The
(1942, B&W, 88m, NR)
Orson Welles's second film as a director (he narrates but does not appear on screen) is a rich portrait of a turn-of-the-century Midwest family resisting the modern era. Tim Holt, Joseph Cotten, and Agnes Moorehead star. Despite cutting from its original two-hour length, a worthy follow-up to *Citizen Kane*; deserved the Best Picture Oscar. **CL14, DR26, DT134, XT28,** *Essential, Recommended*

Magnificent Dope, The
(1942, B&W, 83m, NR)
Comedy of a rube (Henry Fonda) and city slicker (Don Ameche) and the woman in between them (Lynn Bari). **ST71**

Magnificent Matador, The
(1955, C, 94m, NR)
An aging bullfighter grooms his young protégé for a future in the bullring. Anthony Quinn stars, with Maureen O'Hara, Thomas Gomez, Richard Denning, and Lola Albright. Directed by Budd Boetticher. **DT14, ST167**

Magnificent Obsession
(1954, C, 108m, NR)
A playboy carelessly blinds a woman in an auto accident and decides to become a surgeon to restore her sight. Rock Hudson and Jane Wyman star in this tearjerker from director Douglas Sirk. **CL6, DT117, ST112**

Magnificent Seven, The
(1960, C, 126m, NR)
Seven cowboys assemble to help a Mexican village besieged by bandits. Yul Brynner heads the cast of future stars, including Steve McQueen, Charles Bronson, Robert Vaughn, and James Coburn. A remake of the Japanese classic, *The Seven Samurai*. **CU17, FF8, ST20, ST146, WE1,** *Recommended*

Magnum Force (1973, C, 124m, R)
The second Dirty Harry adventure, with Clint Eastwood hunting down a band of rogue San Francisco cops trying to dispense justice their own way. **AC9, ST64, XT13**

Mahler (1974, C, 115m, PG)
Director Ken Russell's dramatic portrait of the great composer: his torments, his relationship with his lovely wife, and his triumphs. Robert Powell stars. **DT111, MU5**

Mahogany (1975, C, 109m, PG)
Diana Ross plays a fashion designer with love life problems in this soap opera costarring Billy Dee Williams and Anthony Perkins. **DR1, DR10, DR14, ST227**

Maid's Night Out (1938, B&W, 64m, NR)
Comedy of mistaken identity stars Joan Fontaine as an heiress taken for a servant. With Allan Lane, Hedda Hopper, and Billy Gilbert. **ST73**

Main Event, The (1979, C, 112m, PG)
Barbra Streisand comedy has her playing a business executive who decides to manage a luckless prizefighter (Ryan O'Neal). With Patti D'Arbanville. **CO19, ST211**

Main Street to Broadway
(1953, B&W, 102m, NR)
Romantic story is jumping-off point for parade of guest star appearances from the Broadway theater, including Ethel and Lionel Barrymore, Shirley Booth, Rex Harrison, Lilli Palmer, Helen Hayes, Henry Fonda, Tallulah Bankhead, and Mary Martin. **CL7, ST71, XT8**

Maîtresse (1975, C, 112m, R)
French drama of cat burglar breaking into house of woman who caters to sexual masochists; he becomes her assistant. Gérard Depardieu and Bulle Ogier star. Directed by Barbet Schroeder. **CU6, FF1, ST52**

Major Barbara (1941, B&W, 135m, NR)
George Bernard Shaw's play of a wealthy girl who enlists in the Salvation Army. Wendy Hiller and Rex Harrison star, with Robert Morley, Robert Newton, and in her film debut, Deborah Kerr. **DR23, ST125, WR29**

Major Dundee (1965, C, 124m, NR)
Civil War Western about a ragged band of Confederate soldiers at war with the Apaches and French troops. Charlton Heston and Richard Harris star, with Jim Hutton, James Coburn, Warren Oates, Ben Johnson, and Slim Pickens. Sam Peckinpah directed. Heavy editing by producer hurt whatever chances this had; still worth seeing for Peckinpah fans. **DT95, ST166, WE6**

Major League (1989, C, 107m, R)
The new owner of the Cleveland Indians baseball team wants to move the franchise to Miami, so she assembles a ragtag collection to ensure that attendance figures will justify the move. The plan backfires when the misfits are inspired by a flaky pitcher (Charlie

Sheen) and veteran catcher (Tom Berenger). With Corbin Bernsen, Wesley Snipes, and Margaret Whitton. David S. Ward wrote and directed this comedy. This Indians fan found it amusing but never truly wonderful. Ball games were filmed in Milwaukee. **CO19, ST201**

Make Mine Mink (1960, B&W, 80m, NR) Terry-Thomas heads a gang of fur thieves in this British comedy. Original running time: 100 minutes. **CO17**

Making Contact (1985, C, 80m, PG) After his father's death, a nine-year-old boy finds he has new powers which he uses to thwart demons from another dimension. **SF13**

Making Love (1982, C, 113m, R) A married doctor discovers his true sexual identity when he is attracted to one of his male patients. Michael Ontkean, Harry Hamlin, and Kate Jackson star. **DR3**

Making Mr. Right (1987, C, 100m, PG-13) Clever, offcenter comedy about a hip public relations expert (Ann Magnuson) hired to "sell" a mandroid astronaut to the public. John Malkovich plays the mandroid and his scientist creator. With Glenne Headly, Ben Masters, Laurie Metcalf, and Polly Bergen. Directed by Susan Seidelman. **CO2, ST147, XT26,** *Recommended*

Making of a Legend—Gone With the Wind (1989, C/B&W, 120m, NR) Behind the scenes with the most popular film of all time, including rare outtakes and screen tests. Footage of Clark Gable, Vivien Leigh, Olivia de Havilland, Jean Arthur, Carole Lombard, Melvyn Douglas, and Lana Turner, among many others. Written by David Thomson. Originally made for cable TV. **CU16, ST3, ST49, ST58, ST77, ST137, ST140, ST219,** *Recommended*

Makioka Sisters, The (1983, C, 140m, NR) Japanese drama set in 1938 Osaka, where heiresses to a shipping business watch their family fortune slowly dissolve. Directed by Kon Ichikawa. **FF4**

Malcolm (1986, C, 90m, PG-13) A kooky inventor teams up with a larcenous couple to pull off a heist in this Australian comedy. Colin Frields, John Hargreaves, and Lindy Davies star. Directed by Nadia Tass; written by her husband, David Parker. **CO12, FF5, MY18**

Malcolm X (1992, C, 201m, PG-13) Spike Lee's epic bio of the famed black activist, starring Denzel Washington, with Angela Bassett, Albert Hall, Al Freeman, Jr., as Elijah Muhammad, and Delray Lindo. Look for Bobby Seale, Karen Allen, Christopher Plummer, Al Sharpton, Peter Boyle, and William Kunstler in small roles; that's Ossie Davis's voice over final montage reciting the same eulogy he read at Malcolm's funeral. Packed with moving moments, highlighted by Washington's magnetic performance, outstanding cinematography and costumes, although it comes up short on crucial details of Malcolm's later years. **DR4, DR14, DT72, ST223,** *Recommended*

Male and Female (1919, B&W, 100m, NR) Silent comedy starring Gloria Swanson as a British aristocrat stranded on an island, falling in love with her butler. With Thomas Meighan. Based on James M. Barrie's play *The Admirable Crichton*. Directed by Cecil B. DeMille. **DR20, DT34**

Malice in Wonderland (1985, C, 100m, NR) Elizabeth Taylor and Jane Alexander play Louella Parsons and Hedda Hopper, the feuding gossip columnists of 1930s and 1940s Hollywood. Originally made for TV. Also known as *The Rumor Mill*. **DR13, ST212**

Malicious (1973, C, 97m, R) Laura Antonelli plays a lusty housekeeper who's the love object of both a father and his teen-age son in this Italian comedy. **FF2**

Malone (1987, C, 92m, R) An ex-CIA agent blows into a small Western town, discovers it's dominated by a rich racist and his hate organization. Burt Reynolds and Cliff Robertson star. **AC25, ST183**

Malta Story, The (1953, B&W, 98m, NR) World War II action with British air forces, starring Alec Guinness and Jack Hawkins. **AC1, ST95**

Maltese Falcon, The (1941, B&W, 100m, NR) Classic Dashiell Hammett detective story of Sam Spade (Humphrey Bogart) and "the stuff that dreams are made of"—the statue of a black bird. With Sydney Greenstreet, Mary Astor, Peter Lorre, and Elisha Cook, Jr. Written and directed by John Huston. Virtually flawless, no matter how many times you see it. **DT60, MY1, ST15, WR12,** *Essential, Highly Recommended*

Mambo (1954, B&W, 94m, NR) Venice is the setting for this story of a saleswoman aspiring to be a dancer, dragged down by her involvements with a gambler and a nobleman. Silvana Mangano stars, with Michael Rennie, Shelley Winters, and

Vittorio Gassman. Original running time: 107 minutes. **ST232**

Mambo Kings, The (1992, C, 104m, R)
Show-biz saga of two Cuban brothers who emigrate to postwar New York with dream of heading their own successful orchestra. Armand Assante and Antonio Banderas star, with Cathy Moriarty, Maruschka Detmers, Desi Arnaz, Jr. (as his father), Talisa Soto, Celia Cruz, and Tito Puente. Adapted from the marvelously sensual Oscar Hijuelos novel. Wonderful music and a nice feel for the period (on what was probably a limited budget), but fans of the book will feel something essential is missing. **DR8, DR12, DR19**

Mame (1974, C, 131m, PG)
Broadway musical version of the Auntie Mame tale of a grande dame taking in her impressionable nephew. Lucille Ball and Robert Preston star. **MU2, MU14**

Man, a Woman and a Bank, A
(1979, C, 100m, PG)
Canadian-produced heist thriller, starring Donald Sutherland, Brooke Adams, and Paul Mazursky. **DT87, MY18**

Man Alone, A (1955, C, 96m, NR)
Ray Milland plays a fugitive from a lynch mob hiding under the protection of a sheriff's daughter. Milland also directed this Western. With Raymond Burr and Lee Van Cleef. **ST221, WE3**

Man and a Woman, A
(1966, C, 102m, NR)
Romantic drama about a widow and widower finding that love is even better the second time around. Anouk Aimee and Jean-Louis Trintignant star. Oscar winner for Best Foreign Language Film. **FF1, XT7**

Man and a Woman: 20 Years Later, A
(1986, C, 112m, PG)
Sequel to the popular romantic drama, with the same stars (Anouk Aimee and Jean-Louis Trintignant) continuing their love affair. **FF1**

Man Betrayed, A see *Wheel of Fortune*

Man Called Flintstone, A
(1966, C, 87m, NR)
Feature-length adventures of Fred, Barney, and all the Stone Age cartoon gang, in a spoof of spy movies. **FA10**

Man Called Horse, A (1970, C, 114m, PG)
Richard Harris stars as an English aristocrat captured by Indians and initiated into their tribal ways. Followed by two sequels: *Return of . . .* and *Triumphs of . . .* **WE7**

Man Called Peter, A (1955, C, 119m, NR)
The true story of Peter Marshall, a Scotsman who became a Presbyterian minister and eventually chaplain of the U.S. Senate. Richard Todd and Jean Peters star. **DR4**

Man Called Sledge, A (1970, C, 93m, R)
Italian-made Western with James Garner in a typical bad guy role; he heads a gang that breaks into a prison for a cache of gold. With Dennis Weaver, Claude Akins, and Laura Antonelli. Directed by Vic Morrow. **ST82, XT23**

Man Facing Southeast (1986, C, 105m, R)
From Argentina, a science fiction drama about a man who mysteriously appears in a mental hospital, claiming to be an alien. **FF6, SF19**

Man for All Seasons, A
(1966, C, 120m, NR)
Paul Scofield plays Thomas More, the cleric who defied Henry VIII (Robert Shaw) at the risk of execution. With Wendy Hiller, Susannah York, John Hurt, Orson Welles, and in a small role, Vanessa Redgrave. Oscar winner for Best Picture, Actor, and Director (Fred Zinnemann); Wendy Hiller should have won, too. **DR5, DT134, DT144, ST182, XT1, XT2, XT6, XT28,** *Recommended*

Man for All Seasons, A
(1988, C, 168m, NR)
Charlton Heston heads the cast of this adaptation of Robert Bolt's life of Thomas More. With Vanessa Redgrave and John Gielgud. Originally made for cable TV. **DR5, ST86, ST182**

Man Friday (1976, C, 115m, R)
The Robinson Crusoe story, with a contemporary race relations angle emphasized. Peter O'Toole and Richard Roundtree star. **AC24, ST169**

Man From Cheyenne
(1942, B&W, 54m, NR)
A government agent (Roy Rogers) investigates a rustling ring run by a lovely lady. Gabby Hayes costars. **ST188**

Man From Colorado, The
(1948, C, 99m, NR)
William Holden stars in a Western drama of a cowboy forced to deal with an old Civil War comrade (Glenn Ford) who has become a judge dispensing a brutal form of frontier justice. **ST106**

Man From Laramie, The
(1955, C, 104m, NR)
Western revenge drama, with James Stewart out to bring in the men who murdered his

brother. Anthony Mann directed. Widescreen will be lost on video. **CU20, DT85, ST207, WE5**

Man From Music Mountain, The
(1938, B&W, 54m, NR)
Gene Autry and partner Smiley Burnette foil the plans of a swindler. **ST5**

Man From Snowy River, The
(1982, C, 115m, PG)
Australian adventure about a pack of wild horses and the young cowboy who would capture them. Tom Burlinson and Sigrid Thornton star, with Kirk Douglas as twin brothers in this family film. Sequel: *Return to Snowy River, Part II.* **AC12, FF5, ST57, XT27**

Man From the Alamo, The
(1953, C, 79m, NR)
Glenn Ford plays a Texan who escapes from the carnage at the Alamo to warn others but is accused of desertion. Directed by Budd Boetticher. **DT14**

Man in a Cocked Hat see *Carlton-Browne of the F.O.*

Man in Grey, The (1943, B&W, 116m, NR)
British costume drama of rivals in romance (Phyllis Calvert, Margaret Lockwood). With Stewart Granger and, in a breakthrough early role, James Mason. **DR23, ST153**

Man in Love, A (1987, C, 117m, R)
American actor on location in Rome falls in love with leading lady. Peter Coyote, Greta Scacchi, Peter Riegert, and Jamie Lee Curtis star. Directed by Diane Kurys. **DR1, DR13, ST42**

Man in the Gray Flannel Suit, The
(1956, C, 153m, NR)
Gregory Peck stars as the quintessential 1950s Madison Avenue executive. With Jennifer Jones, Fredric March, Marisa Pavan, Lee J. Cobb, and Keenan Wynn. **DR24, ST148, ST171**

Man in the Iron Mask, The
(1939, B&W, 110m, NR)
Adventure tale of twin brothers, one ascending to royalty, the other becoming a musketeer. Louis Hayward, Joan Bennett, and Warren William star. James Whale directed. **AC15, FA4, DT138**

Man in the Iron Mask, The
(1977, C, 100m, NR)
Richard Chamberlain stars in this version of the Dumas adventure tale. With Patrick McGoohan, Louis Jourdan, Jenny Agutter, Vivien Merchant, Ian Holm, and Ralph Richardson. Originally made for TV. **AC15, FA4, ST184**

Man in the Moon, The
(1991, C, 99m, PG-13)
Coming-of-age drama set in small-town 1957 Louisiana, focusing on fourteen-year-old girl (Reese Witherspoon) who's attracted to the guy next door—and he's smitten by her older sister. With Sam Waterston, Tess Harper, and Gail Strickland. **DR9, DR26**

Man in the Saddle (1951, C, 87m, NR)
Randolph Scott Western has him involved in deadly romantic triangle. With Joan Leslie and Ellen Drew. Directed by Andre de Toth. **ST197**

Man in the Santa Claus Suit, The
(1979, C, 100m, NR)
Fred Astaire plays seven characters in this holiday story. With Gary Burghoff, John Byner, Bert Convy, and Nanette Fabray. Originally made for TV. **FA13, ST4**

Man in the White Suit, The
(1952, B&W, 84m, NR)
Classic British comedy about an inventor (Alec Guinness) who comes up with a miracle fabric and is hounded by the clothing establishment. **CO17, ST95**

Man in the Wilderness
(1971, C, 105m, PG)
Richard Harris plays a frontier trapper left for dead, fighting his way across wintry wasteland to wreak revenge. With John Huston, John Bindon, and Ben Caruthers. Pretty soggy going, though Huston does get to chew up the scenery in one of his Demented Man roles. **AC24, DT60, WE5**

Man Like Eva, A (1983, C, 92m, NR)
A young woman impersonates film director Rainer Werner Fassbinder in this drama from Germany. **DT42, FF3**

Man of a Thousand Faces
(1957, B&W, 122m, NR)
Bio of Lon Chaney, film's first great horror star, played with gusto by James Cagney. With Dorothy Malone, Jane Greer, Marjorie Rambeau, Robert Evans, and Roger Smith as the adult Lon Chaney, Jr. **CL2, CL7, ST24, ST26, ST27**

Man of Aran (1934, B&W, 75m, NR)
Classic documentary look at isolated village on the western coast of Ireland, directed by Robert Flaherty. **CU16,** *Essential*

Man of Flowers (1984, C, 91m, R)
Australian drama about a wealthy bachelor who pays an artist's model to take off her clothes for him. Norman Kaye stars; Werner Herzog plays Kaye's father in flashback scenes. Directed by Paul Cox. **FF5, DT54**

Man of Iron (1980, C, 140m, PG)
Sequel to *Man of Marble*, this Polish drama
follows a documentary filmmaker and her
romance with the son of a worker-hero
whose story she filmed. Andrzej Wajda directed. Unique view of changing political
scene in contemporary Poland. **DT130,**
Essential

Man of La Mancha (1972, C, 130m, G)
Musical version of the classic novel *Don
Quixote*, about a knight in search of his
dream. Peter O'Toole and Sophia Loren head
the cast. **MU2, MU17, ST141, ST169**

Man of Marble (1977, C, 160m, NR)
Epic Polish drama of a woman filmmaker
shooting a documentary about the leader
of a workers' uprising. Directed by Andrzej
Wajda. Sequel: *Man of Iron*. **DT130,** *Essential*

Man of the Forest (1933, B&W, 62m, NR)
Randolph Scott Western has him framed for
murder by Noah Beery, Sr. Based on a Zane
Grey novel. **ST197**

Man of the Frontier
(1936, B&W, 60m, NR)
Early Gene Autry Western, featuring the
debut of his mighty horse, Champion. Also
titled *Red River Valley*. **ST5**

Man of the West (1958, C, 100m, NR)
Cult Western starring Gary Cooper as former
outlaw forced to ride with old boss and ruth-
less gang. With Julie London, Lee J. Cobb,
Arthur O'Connell, Jack Lord, and Neville
Brand. Directed by Anthony Mann. Wide-
screen will be lost on video. **CU20, DT85,
ST37, WE3, WE15**

Man on Fire (1987, C, 93m, R)
Action drama of ex-CIA pacifist who turns
into a one-man army when the young
woman he's protecting is kidnapped. Scott
Glenn stars, with Jade Malle, Paul Shenar,
Brooke Adams, Jonathan Pryce, Joe Pesci,
and Danny Aiello. **AC25, ST172**

Man on the Eiffel Tower, The
(1949, C, 97m, NR)
Georges Simenon's creation Inspector Mai-
gret is after a murderer in this mystery
directed by Burgess Meredith. Charles
Laughton and Franchot Tone star. **MY16,
ST132, XT16, XT23**

Man They Could Not Hang, The
(1939, B&W, 72m, NR)
A mad scientist is executed for his crimes but
brought back to life for revenge on the judge
and jury that convicted him. Boris Karloff
stars. **HO20, ST119**

Man Trouble (1992, C, 100m, PG-13)
Offbeat romantic comedy stars Jack
Nicholson as a dog trainer hired by opera
singer Ellen Barkin to provide her with protection. With Harry Dean Stanton, Beverly
D'Angelo, Michael McKean, Veronica Cartwright, David Clennon, and Paul Mazursky
in a small role. Written by Carole Eastman,
directed by Bob Rafelson. The writer, director,
and star who hit gold with *Five Easy Pieces*
come up with something closer to dross
here, though it's not the bomb some critics
claimed. Certainly worth a look for fans of
the participants. **CO1, DT87, ST7, ST163,
ST205**

Man Who Broke 1,000 Chains, The
(1987, C, 115m, NR)
Story of Robert Elliot Burns, Depression-era
convict whose story was told in classic *I Am
a Fugitive From a Chain Gang*. Val Kilmer
stars, with Charles Durning, Sonia Braga,
William Sanderson, and Kyra Sedgwick. **DR4,
ST17**

Man Who Came to Dinner, The
(1941, C, 112m, NR)
The classic play, by George S. Kaufman and
Moss Hart, of an obnoxious guest taking up
permanent residence in an ordinary house-
hold. Monty Woolley stars, with Bette Davis,
Ann Sheridan, Billie Burke, and Jimmy
Durante. **DR20, ST44**

Man Who Could Work Miracles, The
(1937, B&W, 82m, NR)
A shy bank clerk suddenly discovers he has
the power to do anything he wants. Family
fantasy film, based on an H.G. Wells story,
stars Roland Young and Ralph Richardson.
SF13, ST184, WR37

Man Who Fell to Earth, The
(1976, C, 140m, R)
Science fiction drama about an alien (David
Bowie) who comes to Earth in search of wa-
ter for his parched planet but is unable to
return home. Brilliantly directed by Nicolas
Roeg. With Candy Clark, Rip Torn, and Buck
Henry. **CU4, DR27, DT106, MU12, SF9,
ST216,** *Highly Recommended*

Man Who Haunted Himself, The
(1970, C, 94m, PG)
Low-key horror film set in London about a
man who begins seeing a double of himself
after he's injured in a car crash. Roger Moore
stars. **HO15**

Man Who Knew Too Much, The
(1934, B&W, 75m, NR)
Hitchcock thriller about a couple who accidentally learn intelligence information, and

their daughter is kidnapped by spies. Leslie Banks, Edna Best, and Peter Lorre star. **DT57, MY6, MY7**

Man Who Knew Too Much, The
(1956, C, 120m, PG)
Hitchcock remake of his own film, with the setting now North Africa. James Stewart plays the title character; Doris Day is his wife. Widescreen will be lost on video. **CU18, CU20, DT57, MY6, MY7, ST47, ST207**

Man Who Lived Again, The
(1936, B&W, 61m, NR)
British horror drama of mad doctor (Boris Karloff) experimenting with personality transfer. **HO20, HO26, ST119**

Man Who Loved Cat Dancing, The
(1973, C, 114m, PG)
Burt Reynolds and Sarah Miles are trail companions in this Western about two people on separate quests. **ST183, WE8**

Man Who Loved Women, The
(1977, C, 119m, R)
A man who simply loves all kinds of women tries to come to grips with his obsession by writing his life story. Charles Denner stars, with Brigitte Fossey, Nelly Borgeaud, Leslie Caron, and Genevieve Fontanel. French comedy-drama directed by François Truffaut. American remake released in 1983. **DT125, FF8**

Man Who Loved Women, The
(1983, C, 110m, R)
Burt Reynolds stars in a remake of the French comedy about a man with insatiable romantic tendencies. Julie Andrews plays his analyst; Kim Basinger, Marilu Henner, and Cynthia Sikes are the objects of his affections. Directed by Blake Edwards. **DT40, FF8, ST2, ST183, XT30**

Man Who Never Was, The
(1956, C, 103m, NR)
World War II espionage story, with Allies planting false man to divert attack on Sicily. Produced in Britain. Clifton Webb stars, with Gloria Grahame and Robert Flemyng. **AC1, MY15**

Man Who Saw Tomorrow, The
(1981, C, 88m, PG)
Documentary on Nostradamus, sixteenth-century astrologer, physician, and prophet, who allegedly foresaw many historical trends and events. Narrated by Orson Welles. **DT134**

Man Who Shot Liberty Valance, The
(1962, C, 122m, NR)
A peace-loving lawyer confronts a violent outlaw. James Stewart, John Wayne, and Lee Marvin star in this Western classic, directed by John Ford. With Vera Miles, Woody Strode, and Lee Van Cleef. **DT44, ST151, ST207, ST221, ST224, WE11, Essential, Recommended**

Man Who Would Be King, The
(1975, C, 129m, PG)
Sean Connery and Michael Caine star in the Rudyard Kipling story of two adventurers held captive by a mountain tribe who think one of them is a god. With Christopher Plummer as Kipling. John Huston directed. Immensely entertaining; one of Huston's best late-career films. **AC12, DT60, ST25, ST36, Recommended**

Man With Bogart's Face, The
(1980, C, 106m, PG)
Would-be detective has plastic surgery to resemble Bogart, goes on to solve comic caper. Robert Sacchi stars, with Michelle Phillips, Olivia Hussey, George Raft (in his last film), and Mike Mazurki. **MY17, ST15**

Man With One Red Shoe, The
(1985, C, 92m, PG)
An innocent man is mistaken for a spy and is caught in a comic crossfire of international agents. Tom Hanks and Jim Belushi star. Remake of French film, *The Tall Blonde Man With One Black Shoe*. **CO10, CO13, FF8, ST97**

Man With the Golden Arm, The
(1955, B&W, 119m, NR)
Classic drama of a drug addict (Frank Sinatra) and his desperate attempts to control his problem. With Kim Novak, Darren McGavin, Arnold Stang, Robert Strauss, and Eleanor Parker. Directed by Otto Preminger; based on Nelson Algren's novel. Subject of controversial attempt by motion picture rating board to deny it seal of approval; still powerful, with Sinatra especially good; he deserved an Oscar. **CL8, DR19, DT100, ST199, XT28, Essential, Recommended**

Man With the Golden Gun, The
(1974, C, 125m, PG)
James Bond (Roger Moore) takes on a vicious international assassin (Christopher Lee). Britt Ekland and Maud Adams costar. **HF2, ST135**

Man With Two Brains, The
(1983, C, 93m, R)
Comic tale of a mad scientist (Steve Martin) who marries a lovely but cold woman (Kathleen Turner); his real love is another woman's brain, which he keeps in his laboratory. Sissy Spacek supplies the voice of the brain. Directed by Carl Reiner. **CO7, SF21, ST150, ST202, ST218**

Man Without a Star (1955, C, 89m, NR)
Kirk Douglas is the gunslinger who helps
a farm woman (Jeanne Crain) in distress.
Directed by King Vidor. **DT126, ST57, WE2**

Manchurian Candidate, The
(1962, B&W, 126m, PG)
Intelligent, stylish political thriller about a
war hero (Laurence Harvey) programmed by
communists to be an assassin. Frank Sinatra,
Angela Lansbury, and Janet Leigh costar.
Adapted by George Axelrod from Richard
Condon's novel. Directed by John Frankenheimer. Special video version includes
interview with Sinatra, Axelrod, and Frankenheimer. **CU9, DR19, DR21, MY2, MY6,
ST131, ST199,** *Essential, Highly Recommended*

Mandela (1987, C, 135m, NR)
Danny Glover plays South Africa's Nelson
Mandela, the heroic leader who has struggled
against apartheid. With Alfre Woodard as his
wife, Winnie. Originally made for cable TV.
DR4, DR7, DR14, ST88

Mandingo (1975, C, 127m, R)
Melodrama of antebellum plantation life,
with James Mason, Susan George, Perry
King, and Ken Norton. Dreadful. **DR5,
ST153**

Manfish (1956, C, 76m, NR)
Adaptation of Edgar Allan Poe's classic
story, *The Gold Bug*, about a search for buried
treasure. Joan Bromfield, Lon Chaney, Jr.,
Victor Jory, and Barbara Nichols star. **ST27,
WR27**

Mango Tree, The (1977, C, 93m, NR)
Drama set in Australia around the time of
World War I about a young man's coming
of age in a small town. Christopher Pate
and Geraldine Fitzgerald star. **FF5**

Manhattan (1979, B&W, 96m, R)
Woody Allen's comedy about the endless
possibilities of love—and heartbreak—in the
Big Apple. Diane Keaton, Mariel Hemingway,
and Meryl Streep costar as the women in
Woody's life. With Michael Murphy and
Anne Byrne. Available in letterboxed format.
**CO1, CO2, CU19, DT2, ST121, ST210,
XT9, XT30,** *Essential, Recommended*

Manhattan Melodrama
(1934, B&W, 93m, NR)
Crime drama starring Clark Gable and William Powell as opponents on opposite sides
of the law. With Myrna Loy and Mickey
Rooney. The last movie outlaw John Dillinger
ever saw; he was shot down by federal agents
coming out of a screening. **CL15, ST77,
ST142, ST176, ST189**

Manhattan Merry-Go-Round
(1938, B&W, 80m, NR)
A gangster takes control of a record company—but the story is just an excuse
to present musical numbers by the likes of
Gene Autry, Cab Calloway, Louis Prima, and
(believe it or not) Joe DiMaggio. **ST5**

Manhattan Project, The
(1986, C, 117m, PG-13)
A teen-ager creates a unique science project
with stolen plutonium. Drama starring Christopher Collet, John Lithgow, and Jill Eikenberry. **DR9**

Manhunt for Claude Dallas
(1986, C, 100m, NR)
True story of mountain man (Matt Salinger)
who's arrested for murder and escapes, to be
pursued by relentless sheriff (Rip Torn). With
Claude Akins and Pat Hingle. Originally
made for TV. **DR6, ST216**

Manhunter (1986, C, 119m, R)
An FBI agent comes out of retirement to
catch a vicious serial killer by imagining how
the psycho must plan his crimes. Superb sus-
pense drama, based on Thomas Harris's novel
Red Dragon (which was its title when shown
on TV). William Petersen stars, with Kim
Greist, Brian Cox (as Hannibal Lecter), Joan
Allen, and Dennis Farina. Directed by Mi-
chael Mann. Sequel of sorts: *Silence of the
Lambs*. **DR19, MY2, MY9, MY13,**
Recommended

Mania (1959, B&W, 87m, NR)
British horror tale stars Peter Cushing as an
Edinburgh scientist who robs graves to supply his experiments. With Donald Pleasence,
George Rose, and Billie Whitelaw. Originally
released as *The Flesh and the Fiends* at 97
minutes. **HO20, HO26, ST43**

Maniac (1980, C, 87m, R)
Extremely graphic horror film about a homi-
cidal killer with a talent for mutilation. Joe
Spinell stars. **CU7, HO18**

Manipulator, The (1971, C, 91m, R)
Horror story of crazed movie makeup man
who kidnaps young actresses. Mickey Rooney
stars, with Luana Anders and Keenan Wynn.
ST189

Mannequin (1937, B&W, 95m, NR)
Working girl (Joan Crawford) and wealthy
man (Spencer Tracy) try to find love. With
Alan Curtis, Ralph Morgan, and Leo Gorcey.
CL5, ST39, ST217

Mannequin (1987, C, 89m, PG)
Comedy of timid guy who's the only person
to know that a store dummy has come to life

(she's been possessed by the spirit of an ancient Egyptian). Andrew McCarthy and Kim Cattrall star, with Estelle Getty, James Spader, and Meshach Taylor. **ST203, XT24**

Manon of the Spring (1987, C, 113m, PG) Concluding chapter of Marcel Pagnol story, begun with *Jean de Florette*: daughter of wronged French landowner seeks revenge on the neighbors responsible. Emmanuelle Beart, Yves Montand, and Daniel Auteil star. Directed by Claude Berri. A shade below its predecessor but still absorbing and moving. **FF1,** *Recommended*

Manos, The Hands of Fate (1966, C, 90m, NR) A couple on an idyllic vacation falls captive to cultists. Ultra low-budget, ultra-bad horror film shot in Texas. **CU11, HO11**

Man's Favorite Sport? (1964, C, 120m, NR) Phony fishing expert (Rock Hudson) is forced to enter an angling competition in this comedy from director Howard Hawks. Paula Prentiss costars. **CO19, DT53, ST112**

Manxman, The (1929, B&W, 90m, NR) Hitchcock's last silent film, a drama about two best friends, a lawyer and fisherman, who love the same woman. **DT57**

Marat/Sade (1967, C, 115m, NR) Harrowing version of the stage hit about the Marquis de Sade directing his fellow lunatic asylum inmates in a play about the French Revolution and the murder of Jean-Paul Marat. Patrick Magee is a magnetic de Sade, Glenda Jackson is Charlotte Corday. Full title: *The Persecution and Assassination of Jean-Paul Marat as Performed by the Inmates of the Asylum of Charenton Under the Direction of the Marquis de Sade*. **DR5, DR20, DR23, ST117,** *Recommended*

Marathon Man (1976, C, 125m, R) Thriller about an innocent New Yorker caught up in international intrigue set in motion by the murder of his secret agent brother. Dustin Hoffman, Laurence Olivier, and Roy Scheider star, with Marthe Keller, William Devane, and Fritz Weaver. William Goldman adapted his novel; directed by John Schlesinger. Efficient but heartless, with some important changes from the book weakening film. **DT113, MY7, ST105, ST168, XT9**

March of the Wooden Soldiers (1934, C, 73m, NR) Laurel and Hardy star in the Victor Herbert operetta, *Babes in Toyland* (the film's original title). Colorized for home video. **FA9, ST133**

March or Die (1977, C, 104m, PG) Old-fashioned adventure tale of the French Foreign Legion, starring Gene Hackman, Terence Stamp, Max von Sydow, and Catherine Deneuve. Handsome looking, empty dramatics. **AC12, ST50, ST96**

Maria's Lovers (1984, C, 100m, R) Drama set in small Pennsylvania town, to which a World War II veteran returns, with problems for his new bride. John Savage, Nastassja Kinski, Robert Mitchum, and Keith Carradine star. **DR26, ST158**

Marie (1985, C, 113m, PG-13) The true story of a woman who blew the whistle on corruption in the highest levels of Tennessee state government. Sissy Spacek and Jeff Daniels star, with Morgan Freeman. **DR6, DR10, DR21, ST76, ST202**

Marie Antoinette (1938, B&W, 149m, NR) Norma Shearer plays the haughty French monarch in this lavish costume epic. With Tyrone Power, John Barrymore, and Robert Morley. **CL2, ST8, ST177**

Marine Raiders (1944, B&W, 91m, NR) Saga of marines in training for combat action in World War II. Pat O'Brien stars, with Robert Ryan, Ruth Hussey, and Frank McHugh. **AC1, ST193**

Marius (1931, B&W, 125m, NR) French comedy-drama of life in the Provence region, written by Marcel Pagnol. Pierre Fresnay plays the title character, a man torn between his love for Fanny (Orane Demazis) and life at sea. The first of a trilogy, followed by *Fanny* and *César*. **FF1**

Marjoe (1972, C, 88m, PG) Documentary portrait of pseudo-evangelist Marjoe Gortner. **CU16**

Marjorie Morningstar (1958, C, 123m, NR) Natalie Wood plays a naive young girl with great ambitions; Gene Kelly is her summer lover. With Claire Trevor, Ed Wynn, Everett Sloane, Martin Milner, and Martin Balsam. Based on Herman Wouk's novel. **DR19, ST123**

Mark of the Hawk, The (1957, C, 83m, NR) Sidney Poitier drama set in contemporary Africa, centering on the debate over the means of achieving racial equality. With Eartha Kitt, Juano Hernandez, and John McIntire. **DR14, ST174**

Mark of the Vampire (1935, B&W, 61m, NR) Bela Lugosi and his Dracula director, Tod

Browning, are reunited for more bloodsucking thrills. Lionel Barrymore costars. **DT18, HO5, ST143**

Mark of Zorro, The
(1920, B&W/C, 90m, NR)
Quintessential Douglas Fairbanks role, as he carves Z's across Old Mexico. With Marguerite De La Motte and Noah Beery. Video version is color-tinted. **AC13, AC15, CL12, FA4,** *Essential, Recommended*

Mark of Zorro, The (1940, B&W, 93m, NR)
Tyrone Power plays the dashing swordsman in this adventure classic. With Linda Darnell, Basil Rathbone, Gale Sondergaard, and Eugene Pallette. Directed by Rouben Mamoulian. **AC13, AC15, DT83, FA4, ST177**

Marked for Death (1990, C, 94m, R)
Steven Seagal stars in this bone-crushing action tale of a former DEA agent tangling with Jamaican drug dealers. With Basil Wallace, Keith David, and Joanna Pacula. **AC8, AC25**

Marked Woman (1937, B&W, 99m, NR)
Crusading district attorney (Humphrey Bogart) persuades four women to testify against their gangster boss. Bette Davis costars. **ST15, ST44**

Marlene (1984, C/B&W, 96m, NR)
Actor Maximilian Schell's documentary about fabled performer Marlene Dietrich, filmed with her very reluctant cooperation. Fascinating portrait of a fascinating subject. **CU16, ST55, XT26,** *Recommended*

Marlon Brando (1985, C/B&W, 120m, NR)
Documentary portrait of the controversial and charismatic actor, made for Italian TV. **CU16, ST18**

Marlowe (1969, C, 95m, PG)
Raymond Chandler's detective novel, *The Little Sister*, starring James Garner as Philip M, with Gayle Hunnicutt, Carroll O'Connor, Rita Moreno, William Daniels, Jackie Coogan, and Bruce Lee. Watchable without ever being wonderful, except for Lee's two big scenes of mayhem. **MY2, ST82, ST134, WR2**

Marnie (1964, C, 129m, NR)
A compulsive thief is caught by her boss, who has fallen in love with her. She agrees to marry him to avoid prosecution. Hitchcock thriller starring Tippi Hedren and Sean Connery. With Diane Baker, Martin Gabel, and in small roles, Bruce Dern and Mariette Hartley. Hitch at low ebb; one of Connery's few stiff performances. **DT57, MY5, ST36**

Marooned (1969, C, 134m, PG)
A group of astronauts is trapped in space, unable to return to Earth, in this science fiction thriller. Gregory Peck, Richard Crenna, and Gene Hackman costar. Special effects won an Oscar. **SF3, SF15, ST96, ST171**

Marriage Circle, The
(1924, B&W, 90m, NR)
Silent comedy, directed by Ernst Lubitsch, of unfaithful couples in Vienna. Florence Vidor, Monte Blue, Marie Prevost, and Adolphe Menjou star. **DT76**

Marriage of Maria Braun, The
(1978, C, 120m, R)
In postwar Germany, a war widow builds a financial empire. Acclaimed drama from director Rainer Werner Fassbinder. Hanna Schygulla stars. Key film in New German cinema is also one of Fassbinder's more accessible works. **DT42,** *Essential, Recommended*

Married Man, A (1984, C, 200m, NR)
British drama of content barrister, his bored wife, and her lover. Anthony Hopkins, Ciaran Madden, and Lise Hilboldt star. Originally made for TV. **DR23, ST109**

Married to the Mob (1988, C, 103m, PG)
Wacky crime comedy set in New York and Miami Beach, with a Mafia hit man's widow pursued by her late husband's boss (and killer), his jealous wife, and a bumbling FBI agent. Michelle Pfeiffer stars, with Dean Stockwell, Mercedes Ruehl, Matthew Modine, Alec Baldwin, and Sister Carol. Witty direction by Jonathan Demme. **CO10, DT35, ST173, ST208, XT9,** *Recommended*

Married Woman, A (1965, B&W, 94m, NR)
Director Jean-Luc Godard's study of a marriage in crisis, with a bored wife taking on a lover. **DT50**

Marrying Man, The (1991, C, 115m, R)
Neil Simon comedy of title character beginning long-running relationship with Bugsy Siegel's girlfriend during his bachelor party in Las Vegas. Kim Basinger and Alex Baldwin star, with Robert Loggia, Elisabeth Shue, and Armand Assante as Siegel. **CO1, WR30**

Martin (1978, C, 95m, R)
A teen-age vampire struggles with his terrible secret in this cult horror film from director George Romero. **CU4, DT108, HO5,** *Recommended*

Marty (1955, B&W, 91m, NR)
Oscar-winning story of an ordinary guy, a Bronx butcher, who unexpectedly finds love. Star Ernest Borgnine, director Delbert Mann, and writer Paddy Chayefsky all won Oscars.

With Betsy Blair, Joe Mantell, and Joe De Santis. **CL4, XT1, XT2, XT6,** *Essential*

Marvin and Tige (1983, C, 104m, PG)
Drama of unusual friendship between young runaway black boy (Gibran Brown) and middle-aged loner (John Cassavetes). With Billy Dee Williams. **DR14, DR15, ST195**

Mary of Scotland (1936, B&W, 123m, NR)
Katharine Hepburn plays the doomed sixteenth-century queen. With Fredric March and Florence Eldredge. John Ford directed. **CL3, DT44, ST103, ST148**

Mary Poppins (1964, C, 140m, G)
Classic Disney musical about a nanny with magical powers. Oscar winner Julie Andrews (in her movie debut) and Dick Van Dyke star in this combination of live action and animation. **FA1, FA9, MU7, MU8, ST2, XT3, XT21**

Masada (1981, C, 131m, NR)
Drama of Roman siege of Jewish town during first century. Peter O'Toole and Peter Strauss star, with Barbara Carrera, Anthony Quayle, and David Warner. Originally made for TV, where it ran as an eight-hour miniseries. **DR5, ST169**

Masculine-Feminine
(1966, B&W, 103m, NR)
A love affair between a journalist and a would-be rock star is the springboard for director Jean-Luc Godard's exploration of mid-1960s Paris. Jean-Pierre Leaud stars. **DT50, XT16**

Mask (1985, C, 120m, PG-13)
True story about a mother's patient love for her teen-age son, whose face is disfigured by an incurable disease. Cher and Eric Stoltz star in this heart-wrenching drama. With Sam Elliott, Estelle Getty, Harry Carey, Jr., and Laura Dern. Directed by Peter Bogdanovich. **DR2, DR6, DR8, DR9, ST29, ST53,** *Recommended*

Mask of Fu Manchu, The
(1932, B&W, 72m, NR)
Boris Karloff plays the Oriental master criminal in this horror/adventure classic. With Lewis Stone, Karen Morley, and Myrna Loy as Fu's daughter. Corny stuff that hasn't aged too well. **HO1, HO9, ST119, ST142**

Masks of Death, The (1980, C, 80m, NR)
Peter Cushing plays Sherlock Holmes in this mystery about three unidentified corpses found in London's North End. **HF14, ST43**

Masque of the Red Death, The
(1964, C, 86m, NR)
Vincent Price stars as evil Prince Prospero,

the madman who throws a massive ball in his castle while a plague sweeps the land. Roger Corman directed this adaptation of two Edgar Allan Poe stories: the title tale and *Hop-Frog*. **DT30, HO1, ST179, WR27**

Masque of the Red Death
(1989, C, 83m, R)
Second telling of the Poe tale, produced by Roger Corman, starring Patrick Macnee, Claire Hoak, Jeff Osterhage, and Tracy Reiner. **WR27**

Masquerade (1988, C, 91m, R)
A shy young heiress meets a handsome stranger shortly after her mother's mysterious death. Is her stepfather using the man to romance her out of her money? Meg Tilly, Rob Lowe, and John Glover star in this thriller. **MY3, MY5**

Mass Appeal (1984, C, 100m, PG)
Conflict between an eager young priest and a veteran pastor forms the basis of this comedy starring Jack Lemmon and Zeljko Ivanek. **ST138**

Massacre at Fort Holman
(1974, C, 92m, NR)
A Civil War Western involving the bloody battle for a heavily fortified position. James Coburn and Telly Savalas lead the opposing armies. **WE6**

Massacre in Rome (1973, C, 103m, PG)
During World War II, a Vatican priest pleas for the lives of 330 villagers condemned by Hitler's orders. Richard Burton and Marcello Mastroianni star. **FF2, ST22, ST154**

Master of Ballantrae, The
(1953, C, 89m, NR)
Errol Flynn stars in this version of the Robert Louis Stevenson novel of Scottish efforts to put Bonnie Prince Charlie on the throne. **AC15, ST69**

Master of the House
(1925, B&W, 81m, NR)
Silent comedy from Danish director Carl Dreyer, with a woman deserting her abusive husband, returning when he has learned his lesson at the hands of an old nurse. **DT39**

Master of the World
(1961, C, 104m, NR)
Vincent Price wants to rule the world from his zeppelin in this science fiction adventure. With Charles Bronson. Based on several Jules Verne stories. **ST20, ST179, WR36**

Master Touch, The (1973, C, 96m, PG)
Kirk Douglas plays a safecracking pro who takes on a new challenge for a million-dollar payday. Filmed on European locations with

an international supporting cast, including Florinda Bolkan and Giuliano Gemma. **MY16, ST57**

Masters of the Universe
(1987, C, 106m, PG)
A science fiction adventure tale based on the popular children's toys. Dolph Lundgren stars. **AC17, FA8, SF13**

Mata Hari (1932, B&W, 90m, NR)
Greta Garbo plays the famed World War I spy who used sex to gain information. With Ramon Novarro, Lionel Barrymore, Lewis Stone, and Karen Morley. **CL2, ST78**

Matador (1986, C, 102m, NR)
Dark, sexy comedy with cult following from Spanish director Pedro Almodóvar, about a retired matador who makes snuff films. Assumpta Serna, Antonio Banderas, and Nacho Martinez star. **CU5, DT3**

Matchmaker, The (1958, B&W, 101m, NR)
Thornton Wilder's comic play about a middle-aged widower who hires a woman to find him a wife. Shirley Booth stars, with Anthony Perkins, Shirley MacLaine, Paul Ford, and Robert Morse. Musical remake: *Hello, Dolly!* **CL10, DR20, ST145**

Matewan (1987, C, 130m, PG-13)
Drama based on events surrounding a bitter and bloody coal miner's strike in 1920 West Virginia. Chris Cooper and James Earl Jones star. Written and directed by John Sayles, who also plays a small role. Deliberately paced drama which rewards with stunning final impact. **DR5, DT112, ST118,** *Recommended*

Matilda (1978, C, 103m, G)
Family comedy about a boxing kangaroo, starring Elliott Gould, Robert Mitchum, and Lionel Stander. **CO19, FA6, ST158**

Matinee (1993, C, 99m, PG)
Sweet comedy set in Key West, Florida, at time of Cuban Missile Crisis, about teen-age film fan (Simon Fenton) eagerly awaiting arrival of schlock horror film producer (John Goodman), in town to promote his new film, *Mant* ("Half man! Half insect!!"). With Cathy Moriarty, Omri Katz, Lisa Jakub, Kellie Martin, the inimitable team of Dick Miller and John Sayles (as con men), Jesse White, Kevin McCarthy, and William Schallert. Co-written by Charlie Haas, directed by Joe Dante. Numerous affectionate send-ups of Cold War sci-fi films and Goodman's charm offset disappointingly dippy teen romance story. **CO4, CO6, CO7, CO8, DT33, DT112, FA6, XT31,** *Recommended*

Matter of Time, A (1976, C, 99m, PG)
Liza Minnelli and Ingrid Bergman star in this drama about a chambermaid taught lessons in life by a daft noblewoman. With Charles Boyer. Director Vincente Minnelli's last film. **DT88, ST13, ST16**

Maurice (1987, C, 140m, NR)
Drama based on E.M. Forster's novel about a young Englishman's gradual awakening to his homosexual nature. Produced by Ismail Merchant; directed by James Ivory. **DR3, DT61, WR9**

Mausoleum (1983, C, 96m, R)
A housewife is possessed by a demon from the 17th century in this horror film starring Marjoe Gortner. **HO8**

Maverick Queen, The (1956, C, 92m, NR)
Barbara Stanwyck plays a lady outlaw who falls for a lawman in this Western drama. **ST206, WE8**

Max Dugan Returns (1983, C, 98m, PG)
From Neil Simon, a comedy about a school-teacher whose ex-con father turns up one day with gifts to charm her and her teen-age son. Marsha Mason, Jason Robards, and Matthew Broderick star. **CO5, ST185, WR30**

Max Headroom (1986, C, 60m, NR)
Comic adventure about a computer-created character and his alter ego, a TV news reporter. Matt Frewer and Amanda Pays star. The original episode of the TV series which had a deserved cult following for its witty view of the future of television. **CO2, CO11,** *Recommended*

Maxie (1985, C, 90m, PG)
Glenn Close stars in this fantasy-comedy about a contemporary San Francisco woman possessed by the spirit of a Roaring Twenties flapper. Mandy Patinkin costars, with Ruth Gordon. **CO20, ST33, XT24**

Maximum Force (1990, C, 90m, R)
Trio of renegade cops infiltrate L.A. crime gang. Sam Jones, Sherrie Rose, and Jason Lively star, with John Saxon, Richard Lynch, and Mickey Rooney. **AC9, ST189**

Maximum Overdrive (1986, C, 97m, R)
Horror tale directed by Stephen King, based on one of his stories, about the passing of a comet and its effects on all the machinery at a truck stop in the South. Emilio Estevez stars. **HO22, WR15**

May Fools (1990, C, 108m, R)
A French family gathers in the countryside for the funeral of the clan's grandmother. Comedy-drama from director Louis Malle set against backdrop of turbulent 1968 strikes in

Paris. Michel Piccoli and Miou-Miou star. Music by Stephane Grapelli. **FF1, DT82**

Mayerling (1936, B&W, 89m, NR)
Classic story of doomed love, with Charles Boyer as Crown Prince Rudolph of Austria, Danielle Darrieux as the commoner who wins his heart. **CL3, CL4, DR3, ST16**

Maytime (1937, B&W, 132m, NR)
Nelson Eddy and Jeanette MacDonald team for this love story about a married opera star and poor singer; John Barrymore plays the jealous husband. **CL15, ST8**

Mazes and Monsters (1982, C, 100m, NR)
Four college students get a bit too involved in a game similar to the Dungeons and Dragons craze that has periodically infected contemporary campuses. Tom Hanks, Wendy Crewson, David Wallace, and Chris Makepeace star. Based on Rona Jaffe's novel. Originally made for TV. **DR25, ST97**

Me and Him (1989, C, 93m, R)
Offbeat comedy of a man and his talking penis. Griffin Dunne and the voice of Mark Linn-Baker star. Directed by Doris Dörrie. **CO12**

Mean Frank and Crazy Tony
(1975, C, 85m, R)
Lee Van Cleef and Tony LoBianco play a mob boss and a street punk who break out of prison together in this crime thriller from Italy. **AC22, FF2, ST221**

Mean Machine, The (1973, C, 89m, R)
Chris Mitchum plays a man with a mission— he's out to get even with the Mob. **AC19**

Mean Season, The (1985, C, 103m, R)
Miami journalist strikes up "relationship" with serial killer in this drama about the way the media handles such sensational crimes. Kurt Russell stars, with Mariel Hemingway, Richard Jordan, Richard Masur, and Andy Garcia. **MY11, MY13, ST191**

Mean Streets (1973, C, 110m, R)
In New York's Little Italy, a young hood tries to rise within the organization while keeping his crazy cousin out of trouble. Brilliant portrait of modern urban life, directed by Martin Scorsese, starring Harvey Keitel and Robert De Niro, with Richard Romanus, David Proval, and Amy Robinson. Wonderful soundtrack mixes rock 'n' roll and opera. **DR15, DR16, DT114, ST51, XT9,** *Essential,* *Highly Recommended*

Meatballs (1979, C, 92m, PG)
Bill Murray stars as an amiable camp counselor in this comedy. **CO1**

Mechanic, The (1972, C, 100m, R)
Hit man Charles Bronson passes on his knowledge to understudy Jan-Michael Vincent. **DR16, ST20**

Medicine Man
(1992, C, 106m, PG-13)
Sean Connery plays a maverick scientist working on a cancer cure in the Amazon rainforest; he's confronted by an obnoxious young researcher (Lorraine Bracco) sent to check on his progress. Directed by John McTiernan. **DR7, ST36**

Mediterraneo (1991, C, 92m, NR)
Charming comic tale of Italian soldiers who occupy idyllic, isolated Greek isle during World War II and never get the message the war is over—not that they care. Directed by Gabriele Salvatores. Oscar winner for Best Foreign Language Film. Consistently entertaining. **FF2, XT7,** *Recommended*

Medium Cool (1969, C, 110m, R)
Intense, original drama set in Chicago, during the 1968 Democratic National Convention. An apolitical TV reporter (Robert Forster) is galvanized by the turmoil in the city. With Verna Bloom and Peter Bonerz. Haskell Wexler directed. Terrific collection of rock music on soundtrack. A true time capsule movie. **DR7, DR15, XT11,** *Essential,* *Highly Recommended*

Medusa Touch, The
(1978, C, 110m, R)
Richard Burton stars in a psychological thriller about a man who can will people to their deaths. Lee Remick plays his psychiatrist. **HO7, ST22**

Meet John Doe (1941, B&W, 132m, NR)
A sleazy politician hires a naive ex-baseball player to persuade the public that they never had it so good. Gary Cooper and Barbara Stanwyck star in this comedy-drama, with Edward Arnold, Walter Brennan, and James Gleason. Directed by Frank Capra. Fascinating document for its time, but its cardboard characters and confused ending haven't aged well. **DT22, ST37, ST206,** *Essential*

Meet Me in St. Louis
(1944, C, 113m, NR)
Musical glimpse into the life of a family visiting the 1903 World's Fair. Judy Garland and Margaret O'Brien, who won a special Academy Award, star. Vincente Minnelli directed. Available in special edition with improved color, plus one song not used in the film and previews of coming attractions. **DT88, FA9, MU1, MU6, ST81, XT30,** *Essential,* *Recommended*

Meet the Applegates see *Applegates, The*

Meeting at Midnight
(1944, B&W, 67m, NR)
Charlie Chan mystery, set in London, starring Sidney Toler. Also known as *Black Magic.* **HF4**

Meeting Venus (1991, C, 117m, PG-13)
Glenn Close stars as a temperamental opera diva in this comedy-drama about an international production of Wagner's *Tannhäuser,* set in a Paris opera house. With Neils Arestrup as her conductor; Kiri Te Kanawa supplied Close's singing voice. Directed by István Szabo; dialogue in English. Immensely entertaining look at contemporary world of international art and its politics. **CO1, CO8, ST33,** *Recommended*

Mélo (1986, C, 110m, NR)
French drama, adapted from stage play, of a romantic triangle set in the world of classical music. Alain Resnais directed a cast headed by Sabine Azéma, Pierre Arditi, and Fanny Ardant. **FF1**

Melodie en Sous-Sol
(1963, B&W, 118m, NR)
Caper film, French style, as veteran crook (Jean Gabin) and young hothead (Alain Delon) set to take on a Riviera casino. Also known as *Any Number Can Win.* **FF1**

Melody Ranch (1940, B&W, 80m, NR)
Unusual Gene Autry Western, mainly because of his costars: Jimmy Durante and Ann Miller. Otherwise, it's business as usual for the singing cowboy. **ST5**

Melody Trail (1935, B&W, 60m, NR)
Gene Autry wins $1000 in a rodeo, only to lose it to a gypsy. With Smiley Burnette. **ST5**

Melvin and Howard (1980, C, 95m, R)
Comedy based on the true story of Melvin Dummar, the gas station owner who claimed to be an heir to billionaire Howard Hughes. Paul LeMat stars, with Jason Robards as Hughes, Oscar winner Mary Steenburgen, Jack Kehoe, Pamela Reed, Dabney Coleman, Michael J. Pollard, Gloria Grahame, Charles Napier, and the real Dummar in a small role. Gently satirical look at fame and fortune directed by Jonathan Demme; Oscar-winning screenplay by Bo Goldman. **CO2, DT35, ST185, XT5,** *Highly Recommended*

Member of the Wedding, The
(1952, B&W, 91m, NR)
Poignant story of twelve-year-old Frankie, a young girl confused by her brother's upcoming marriage. Julie Harris stars, with Ethel Waters and Brandon de Wilde. Fred Zin-

nemann directed this adaption of Carson McCullers' play. **DR9, DR20, DT144**

Memoirs of an Invisible Man
(1992, C, 99m, PG-13)
Political thriller starring Chevy Chase in rare straight role as a securities analyst turned invisible after an accident, pursued by CIA for their own use. With Daryl Hannah, Sam Neill, and Michael McKean. Directed by John Carpenter on locations in San Francisco. **CO13, DT23, MY6, XT13**

Memorial Day (1983, C, 100m, NR)
Drama of successful lawyer organizing reunion with buddies he served with in Vietnam. Mike Farrell stars, with Shelley Fabares, Keith Mitchell, Bonnie Bedelia, Robert Walden, Edward Herrmann, and Danny Glover. Originally made for TV. **ST88**

Memories of Me (1988, C, 103m, PG-13)
A surgeon suffers a heart attack and while recovering decides to seek a reconciliation with his estranged father, who works as a professional extra in Hollywood. Billy Crystal and Alan King star in this drama, with Jo-Beth Williams. **CO13, DR8**

Memories of Underdevelopment
(1968, B&W, 104m, NR)
Cuban-produced drama of an alienated intellectual who harbors doubts about his country's post-revolutionary society. Directed by Tomas Gutierrez Alea. **FF6**

Memphis Belle (1990, C, 101m, PG-13)
World War II saga based on exploits of young crew of title B-17 aircraft that was memorialized in famous wartime documentary by William Wyler. Matthew Modine, Eric Stoltz, Tate Donovan, D.B. Sweeney, Billy Zane, Sean Astin, and Harry Connick, Jr., star. Made in Britain. Directed by Michael Caton-Jones. **AC1, AC11, DR23, MU12**

Men . . . (1985, C, 99m, R)
From Germany, a comedy about a business executive who becomes buddies with his wife's lover, an artist. Directed by Doris Dörrie. **FF3**

Men, The (1950, B&W, 85m, NR)
Marlon Brando made his film debut in this drama about handicapped World War II veterans trying to adjust to their disabilities. Teresa Wright and Jack Webb costar. Directed by Fred Zinnemann. **CL8, DT144, ST18, XT21,** *Recommended*

Men at Work (1990, C, 99m, PG-13)
Emilio Estevez and real-life brother Charlie Sheen star in a comedy about two garbagemen who find the body of a political candi-

date and uncover a political conspiracy. Written and directed by Estevez. **CO10, XT8, XT23**

Men Don't Leave (1990, C, 113m, PG-13)
A mother with two sons is suddenly widowed and must adjust to life without a mate. Jessica Lange stars in this comedy-drama, with Chris O'Donnell, Charlie Korsmo, Arliss Howard, Joan Cusack, and Kathy Bates. Directed by Paul Brickman. Remake of French film, *La Vie Continue*. Refreshingly unpolished and heartfelt. **DR8, DR10, FF8, ST130,** *Recommended*

Men in War (1957, B&W, 104m, NR)
Korean War drama starring Robert Ryan, Aldo Ray, and Vic Morrow. Directed by Anthony Mann. **AC3, DT85, ST193**

Men of Boys Town (1941, B&W, 106m, NR)
Sequel to successful *Boys Town* reunites Spencer Tracy as Father Flanagan and Mickey Rooney as Whitey, the bad boy gone good. **CL8, ST189, ST217**

Men of Bronze (1977, B&W/C, 59m, NR)
Documentary of courageous black regiments who fought in World War I. Directed by William Miles. **AC2, CU16, DR14,** *Recommended*

Men of Respect (1991, C, 113m, R)
Oddball version of *Macbeth* in gangster trappings, with John Turturro as an ambitious mobster. With Rod Steiger, Dennis Farina, and Peter Boyle. **AC22, WR28**

Men Who Tread on the Tiger's Tail, The (1945, B&W, 58m, NR)
Early film from Japanese director Akira Kurosawa, based on a historical incident: a medieval general flees with his retinue, disguised as priests, from his rival brother. Also known as *They Who Step on the Tiger's Tail*. **DT69**

Men's Club, The (1986, C, 100m, R)
Drama adapted by Leonard Michaels from his novel about a men's support group whose members decide one evening to adjourn to a brothel. The ensemble cast features Richard Jordan, Harvey Keitel, Frank Langella, Roy Scheider, Treat Williams, and Craig Wasson, with Stockard Channing and Jennifer Jason Leigh. **DR7, DR19, ST136**

Mephisto (1981, C, 135m, NR)
Oscar-winning Hungarian drama of a vain actor throwing in with the Nazis during the Occupation, paying a terrible price. Klaus Maria Brandauer stars. **FF7, XT7**

Mephisto Waltz, The (1971, C, 108m, R)
A journalist falls in with a satanic cult after meeting a renowned concert pianist. Alan Alda stars in this horror film, with Jacqueline Bisset, Curt Jurgens, and Barbara Parkins. **HO10, HO11**

Merchant of Four Seasons, The (1971, C, 88m, NR)
German drama of simple man whose frustrations with his marriage and life in general lead to tragedy. Han Hirschmuller, Irm Hermann, and Hanna Schygulla star. Directed by Rainer Werner Fassbinder. **DT42**

Mermaids (1990, C, 110m, PG-13)
Set in the early 1960s, this comedy-drama focuses on a fifteen-year-old girl (Winona Ryder) and her relationship with her single, eccentric mother (Cher). With Bob Hoskins, Michael Schoeffling, and Christina Ricci. **CO4, CO5, CO6, ST29, ST111**

Merry Christmas, Mr. Lawrence (1983, C, 122m, R)
Prisoner-of-war drama, with British captives Tom Conti and David Bowie locked in struggle against two Japanese officers (Ryuichi Sakamoto and Takeshi). In English and Japanese; directed by Nagisa Oshima. **AC7, FF4, MU12**

Merry Widow, The (1934, B&W, 88m, NR)
Operetta, starring Jeanette MacDonald and Maurice Chevalier, of a rich widow's courtship in Paris. Directed by Ernst Lubitsch. Original running time: 99 minutes. **DT76**

Merry Widow, The (1952, C, 105m, NR)
MGM remake of the operetta about a wealthy widow's romance in Paris, starring Lana Turner and Fernando Lamas. **MU1**

Messenger of Death (1988, C, 92m, R)
Charles Bronson plays an investigative reporter looking into a mass murder which may be linked to a splinter sect of Mormons. **ST20**

Messiah, The (1978, C, 145m, NR)
Director Roberto Rossellini's final film, a portrayal of Christ as a morally perfect man. **HF17, DT109**

Metalstorm: The Destruction of Jared-Syn (1983, C, 84m, PG)
A peacekeeping ranger is assigned to destroy the evil Jared-Syn, who holds the planet of Lemuria under his tyrranical reign. Adventure fantasy with plenty of swordplay and special effects. **AC18**

Meteor (1979, C, 103m, PG)
A runaway meteor threatens destruction of the Earth in this all-star disaster adventure. Sean Connery, Natalie Wood, and Henry Fonda head the cast. **AC23, SF7, ST36, ST71**

Metropolis (1926, B&W, 120m, NR)
Director Fritz Lang's legendary science fiction drama takes place in an underground city, whose workers are enslaved by a cruel dictatorship. Rereleased in 1984 in an 87-minute version with some color tinting and a rock music score composed by Giorgio Moroder. Both editions available on home video; purists may prefer the original but Moroder's experiment actually works. **CL12, DT58, FF3, SF2, SF5, SF14, SF16,** *Essential (first edition), Highly Recommended (both editions)*

Metropolitan (1990, C, 98m, PG-13)
Social comedy, set in Manhattan during Christmas holidays, of set of upper-crust young people flitting from party to party. Edward Clements stars as an outsider to the clique, with Carolyn Farina, Christopher Eigeman, Taylor Nichols, and Allison Rutledge-Parisi. Written and directed by Whit Stillman. A bit repetitious but worth seeing for view of segment of society neglected by contemporary films. **CO2, CO4, XT9,** *Recommended*

Mexicali Rose (1939, B&W, 60m, NR)
Gene Autry finds out his radio show is sponsored by a crooked oil company. **ST5**

Mexican Bus Ride (1951, B&W, 85m, NR)
Luis Buñuel directed this drama of a newly-wed adrift in the big city. Lilia Prado and Esteban Marquez star. **DT19**

Mexican Hayride (1948, B&W, 77m, NR)
Abbott and Costello go south of the border to recover a mine deed. Though based on the Cole Porter musical, there are no songs. With Virginia Grey, Luba Malina, and John Hubbard. **ST1**

MGM's Big Parade of Comedy
(1964, B&W, 100m, NR)
Clip show includes appearances (many of them brief) by Joan Crawford, Buster Keaton, Jean Harlow, Clark Gable, Cary Grant, Spencer Tracy, Carole Lombard, W.C. Fields, Laurel and Hardy, Katharine Hepburn, William Powell, Myrna Loy, Abbott and Costello, Greta Garbo, Melvyn Douglas, and the Marx Brothers. **DT66, ST1, ST39, ST58, ST67, ST78, ST92, ST98, ST103, ST133, ST140, ST142, ST152, ST176**

Miami Blues (1990, C, 97m, R)
Middle-aged police detective and blithe psychopath play a cat-and-mouse game on the streets of Miami. Fred Ward and Alec Baldwin star, with Jennifer Jason Leigh, Charles Napier, and Nora Dunn. Adapted from the Charles Willeford novel by director George

Armitage; coproduced by Jonathan Demme. **AC9, MY9, ST136, XT26,** *Recommended*

Micki & Maude (1984, C, 115m, PG-13)
Dudley Moore stars as a man whose wife and mistress both announce they're pregnant—and they have the same doctor. Frantic comedy from director Blake Edwards costars Ann Reinking and Amy Irving. **CO1, DT40, ST160**

Microwave Massacre (1983, C, 75m, NR)
Comedian Jackie Vernon stars in this horror comedy about man and his mysterious oven. **HO24**

Midnight (1934) see *Call It Murder*

Midnight (1939, B&W, 94m, NR)
Delightful romantic comedy of penniless but plucky American (Claudette Colbert) impersonating a Hungarian countess in Paris society, pursued by dashing cab driver (Don Ameche). With John Barrymore, Mary Astor, Francis Lederer, Hedda Hopper, and Monty Woolley. Written by Billy Wilder and Charles Brackett, directed by Mitchell Leisen. Irresistible fluff. UNAVAILABLE ON VIDEO. **XT29**

Midnight Clear, A (1992, C, 107m, R)
Antiwar drama set in 1944 Ardennes Forest, where a small unit of young American GIs encounter Germans who want to surrender—but not without a mock battle. Ethan Hawke, Peter Berg, Kevin Dillon, Arye Gross, Gary Sinise, and Frank Whaley star. Director Keith Gordon adapted from William Wharton's autobiographical novel. Solid for the first two-thirds, but loses its way toward the end. **AC1, DR19, XT23, XT25**

Midnight Cowboy (1969, C, 113m, R)
Naive young man comes to New York and falls in with a hustling vagrant. Jon Voight stars as Joe Buck and Dustin Hoffman is Ratso Rizzo, with Sylvia Miles, John McGiver, Brenda Vaccaro, Barnard Hughes, Jennifer Salt, and Bob Balaban. Won Oscars for Best Picture, Director (John Schlesinger), and Screenplay Adaptation (Waldo Salt). Based on James Leo Herlihy's novel. Originally rated X; eventually rerated although no changes were made. Voight should have won the Oscar, though Hoffman would have been a good choice. **DR15, DT113, ST105, XT1, XT6, XT9, XT26, XT28,** *Essential, Recommended*

Midnight Crossing
(1988, C, 104m, R)
Intrigue, double cross, and murder aboard a charter boat on a voyage from the Florida Keys to recover a stolen fortune. Daniel J. Travanti and Faye Dunaway star. **ST61**

Midnight Express (1978, C, 121m, R)
Billy Hayes, an American visiting Turkey, is caught at the airport trying to smuggle drugs out of the country and is thrown into a barbaric prison. Brad Davis, Randy Quaid, and John Hurt star in this true story. Written by Oliver Stone; directed by Alan Parker. Music by Giorgio Moroder. Effectively overheated for a while, then becomes ludicrous and repellent. **DR6, DR18, DR27**

Midnight Girl, The (1925, B&W, 84m, NR)
Silent drama starring Lila Lee as a Russian immigrant in New York and Bela Lugosi as a sophisticated suitor. **ST143**

Midnight Lace (1960, C, 108m, NR)
Thriller set in London with a wife (Doris Day) the victim of anonymous threats that may be coming from her husband (Rex Harrison). With John Gavin, Myrna Loy, and Roddy McDowall. **MY3, ST47, ST142, XT15**

Midnight Run (1988, C, 125m, R)
A bounty hunter (Robert De Niro) accompanies a former Mob accountant (Charles Grodin) on a cross-country journey, with the FBI, Mafia hit men, and a rival bounty hunter all in pursuit. Directed by Martin Brest. Action comedy also features Yaphet Kotto, Dennis Farina, and John Ashton. The leads put over the material. **CO9, ST51, ST94, XT18,** *Recommended*

Midsummer Night's Dream, A
(1935, B&W, 117m, NR)
Shakespeare's classic comedy, with an all-star cast, including Mickey Rooney, James Cagney, Dick Powell, and Olivia de Havilland.
ST24, ST49, ST175, ST189, WR28

Midsummer Night's Sex Comedy, A
(1982, C, 88m, PG)
Sex and romance at a country estate in this Woody Allen comedy set at the turn of the century. The lovers include Mia Farrow, José Ferrer, Julie Hagerty, Mary Steenburgen, and Tony Roberts. Fluffy stuff. **CO1, DT2, ST65, XT30**

Midway (1976, C, 132m, G)
Drama centering on the key naval battle of World War II, using many clips from previous war films and documentary footage. Charlton Heston heads the cast, which also includes Henry Fonda, Robert Mitchum, and Toshiro Mifune. **AC1, ST71, ST157, ST158**

Mighty Ducks, The (1992, C, 101m, PG)
Young lawyer, convicted on drunk driving charge, has to serve community by coaching pee-wee hockey team. Emilio Estevez stars in this comedy-drama, with Joss Ackland, Lane

Smith, Heidi Kling, Joseph Sommer, and Joshua Jackson. **DR22, FA7**

Mighty Quinn, The (1989, C, 98m, R)
Mystery on a Caribbean island, with murdered white businessman, black police chief, and his boyhood friend (and prime suspect) the main ingredients. Denzel Washington and Robert Townsend star, with James Fox, Mimi Rogers, and M. Emmet Walsh. **MY16, ST223**

Mikado, The (1987, C, 131m, NR)
Performance of the Gilbert and Sullivan operetta by the English National Opera Company, filmed at the London Coliseum. Eric Idle stars as the Lord High Executioner. Produced by Jonathan Miller. **CO15**

Mike's Murder (1984, C, 97m, R)
After her boyfriend is murdered, a young woman decides to investigate and finds that he has been involved with drug dealers. Debra Winger and Paul Winfield star. **MY11, ST230, ST231**

Mikey and Nicky (1976, C, 119m, R)
Drama about the friendship of two hoods, one of whom may be setting up his buddy for a rubout. Peter Falk and John Cassavetes star. Elaine May wrote and directed. **DR16, DT86**

Milagro Beanfield War, The
(1988, C, 118m, R)
Comedy-drama set in a small New Mexico town, whose citizens are up in arms over water rights and a new recreation development. Robert Redford directed. The cast is headed by Chick Vennera, with Sonia Braga, John Heard, Rubén Blades, Melanie Griffith, Daniel Stern, Freddy Fender, and Christopher Walken. Based on John Nichols's novel. It captures some of the book's best episodes but misses its exuberant spirit. **CO2, DR19, DR26, MU12, ST17, ST93, ST181, ST222**

Mildred Pierce (1945, B&W, 109m, NR)
Joan Crawford's classic role (an Oscar winner, too), as a woman whose success in business can't disguise her problems with headstrong daughter Ann Blyth. Based on the James M. Cain novel. **CL5, CL6, MY1, ST39, WR1, XT3,** *Essential*

Miles From Home (1988, C, 108m, R)
When a bank forecloses on their family farm, a pair of brothers burn the house and flee the law. Soon, they're regarded as folk heroes. Richard Gere and Kevin Anderson star, with John Malkovich. **DR7, DR16, ST84, ST147**

Miles To Go (1986, C, 100m, NR)
Tearjerker of a wife and mother dying of cancer looking for a woman to take her place after she dies. Jill Clayburgh stars, with Tom Skerritt and Mimi Kuzyk. Originally made for TV. **DR2, DR8, ST31**

Milky Way, The (1936, B&W, 89m, NR)
Harold Lloyd comedy of a timid milkman accidentally turned prizefighter. With Adolphe Menjou and Verree Teasdale. Directed by Leo McCarey. **XL11, DT80**

Milky Way, The (1970, C, 105m, NR)
Director Luis Buñuel's meditations on the history of Christianity. A funny, irreverent film from the master of surrealistic movie art. Paul Frankeur and Laurent Terzieff star, with Bernard Verley as Jesus Christ. **DT15, HF16**

Mill on the Floss, The
(1937, B&W, 94m, NR)
George Eliot's novel of a millowner's quarrel with a solicitor, starring Frank Lawton, with Victoria Hopper, Fay Compton, Geraldine Fitzgerald, and in a small role, James Mason. **CL1, ST153**

Millennium (1989, C, 108m, PG-13)
Time-travel science fiction drama, with Kris Kristofferson as an airplane crash investigator, Cheryl Ladd as a commando from a thousand years in the future. **MU12, SF4**

Miller's Crossing (1990, C, 115m, R)
Urban gangster story of betrayal and shifting loyalties, starring Gabriel Byrne and Albert Finney, with Marcia Gay Harden, Jon Polito, John Turturro, and J.E. Freeman. Written by Joel and Ethan Coen; directed by Joel. Photographed by Barry Sonnenfield. The Coens' stylistic flourishes work more in service of the story than in their other films. **AC19, AC22, DR16, DT27, ST68,** *Highly Recommended*

Millhouse: A White Comedy
(1971, B&W, 93m, NR)
A scathing documentary about Richard Nixon, using extensive and by now famous clips from his checkered career. Directed by Emile De Antonio. **CU16,** *Recommended*

Million Dollar Duck, The
(1971, C, 92m, G)
Disney comedy about a duck that, after exposure to radiation, lays eggs with gold yolks. Dean Jones and Sandy Duncan play the lucky owners. **FA1**

Million Dollar Mermaid
(1952, C, 115m, NR)
Esther Williams plays Annette Kellerman, Olympic swimming champion and silent movie star, in this MGM musical. Production numbers staged by Busby Berkeley. With Victor Mature. **DT12, MU1**

Million to One, A (1937, B&W, 60m, NR)
Drama of athlete training for Olympic glory, starring Herman Brix (Bruce Bennett), himself a real Olympian. With Joan Fontaine and Monte Blue. **ST73**

Millionairess, The (1960, C, 90m, NR)
British comedy of snooty heiress (Sophia Loren) and Indian doctor (Peter Sellers), based on a play by George Bernard Shaw. With Vittorio De Sica. **CO17, DR20, DT37, ST141, ST198, WR29**

Mind Snatchers, The see *Happiness Cage, The*

Mindwalk (1991, C, 110m, PG)
Offbeat drama, really a talkfest among poet (Liv Ullmann), physicist (Sam Waterston), and politician (John Heard), covering range of topical subjects. **DR7, ST220**

Mines of Kilimanjaro, The
(1987, C, 88m, PG-13)
A soldier of fortune swears revenge on the Nazis who murdered his professor. Their trail leads to Africa, where he encounters many unexpected adventures. Christopher Connelly stars. **AC21**

Mingus (1968, B&W, 58m, NR)
Documentary on the influential jazz bassist and composer, much of it filmed while he awaited eviction from his New York loft. **CU16**

Minute to Pray, A Second to Die, A
(1967, C, 97m, R)
Italian Western about an outlaw, subject to seizures of paralysis, on the run. Alex Cord stars, with Arthur Kennedy and Robert Ryan. **ST193, WE3, WE13**

Miracle, The (1948, B&W, 43m, NR)
Director Roberto Rossellini's drama of a deluded peasant woman (Anna Magnani) who thinks her seduction by a stranger (Federico Fellini) will result in the birth of Christ. Subject of exceptional controversy when released in U.S., with temporary banning in New York. **CU8, DT43, DT109**

Miracle, The (1991, C, 96m, R)
A young Irish musician is fascinated by a visiting American film actress whom he thinks might be his mother. Niall Byrne and Beverly D'Angelo star, with Donal McCann and Lorraine Pikington. **DR1, DR23**

Miracle Down Under (1986, C, 107m, NR)
Loose adaptation of Dickens's *A Christmas Carol*, set in frontier Australia, as a small boy

warms a miser's heart. Dee Wallace, John Waters, and Charles Tingwell star. **FA13, FF5, WR5**

Miracle in Milan (1951, B&W, 95m, NR) Italian comedy from director Vittorio De Sica focuses on village of poor people and the plight of displaced persons in postwar Europe. **DT37**

Miracle Mile (1989, C, 87m, R) Thriller about a musician who learns from a ringing pay phone that nuclear war is about to start—and he can't convince anyone of the truth. Anthony Edwards stars, with Mare Winningham and John Agar. Music by Tangerine Dream. Fairly exciting, but stretches credibility a bit too far. **MY6**

Miracle of Morgan's Creek, The (1944, B&W, 99m, NR) Wacky comedy about a girl who attends an all-night party with wartime soldiers on leave, gets pregnant, but isn't sure who's the father. Betty Hutton, Eddie Bracken, and William Demarest star, with Bobby Watson as Adolf Hitler and brief appearances by Brian Donlevy and Akim Tamiroff in the roles they played in *The Great McGinty*. Preston Sturges wrote and directed. The fun starts to wear thin after a while. **DT121, HF12**

Miracle of the Bells, The (1948, B&W, 120m, NR) When a famous movie star is buried in her hometown, it sets off an unexplained chain of miracles. Frank Sinatra stars as a priest in this drama. **ST199**

Miracle of the White Stallions, The (1963, C, 117m, NR) True adventure of the evacuation of prized horses from Vienna during World War II. Family fare from the Disney studios. **FA1, FA5**

Miracle on 34th Street (1947, C, 96m, NR) Classic holiday story of a department store Santa proving to a little girl (and the world) that Mr. Claus (and the spirit he embodies) lives. Oscar winner Edmund Gwenn and Natalie Wood star, with Maureen O'Hara. **FA13, ST167, XT4**

Miracle Worker, The (1962, B&W, 107m, NR) Oscar winners Patty Duke and Anne Bancroft play Helen Keller and her teacher Anne Sullivan in this vivid re-creation of their relationship. Directed by Arthur Penn, from the play by William Gibson. **DR4, DR20, DT96, XT3, XT5**

Mirage (1965, B&W, 109m, NR) Gregory Peck plays an amnesia victim in this New York-based thriller, with Diane Baker, Walter Matthau, and Kevin McCarthy. **MY7, ST155, ST171, XT9**

Mirror Crack'd, The (1980, C, 105m, PG) Agatha Christie whodunit, with Angela Lansbury as Miss Marple. Elizabeth Taylor, Rock Hudson, Kim Novak, and Tony Curtis are among the suspects. Strained; the stars look ill at ease. **ST112, ST131, ST212, WR3**

Misadventures of Merlin Jones, The (1964, C, 88m, NR) A college whiz kid shows off his powers of mind-reading and hypnotism in this Disney comedy starring Tommy Kirk. **FA1**

Misery (1990, C, 107m, R) Stephen King tale of writer stranded by accident in isolated cabin of his biggest fan—a crackpot nurse with her own ideas on how he should complete his latest work. James Caan and Oscar winner Kathy Bates star, with Frances Sternhagen, Richard Farnsworth, and Lauren Bacall. Screenplay by William Goldman; directed by Rob Reiner. **DT103, MY9, MY19, WR15, XT3**

Misfits, The (1961, B&W, 124m, NR) Clark Gable and Marilyn Monroe star in a drama (the last film for both) about horse trappers in modern Nevada. With Montgomery Clift, Eli Wallach, and Thelma Ritter. Written by Arthur Miller; John Huston directed. **DT60, ST32, ST77, ST159, WE8, WE12, XT22,** *Recommended*

Mishima (1985, C/B&W, 120m, R) The turbulent life of Japan's controversial novelist and self-styled samurai, Yukio Mishima, is told in this stylized film from American director Paul Schrader. Ken Ogata plays Mishima, but the cinematography by Donald Bailey, production design by Eiko Ishioka, and musical score by Philip Glass are the real stars. An underrated film about a difficult subject. **FF4,** *Recommended*

Miss Annie Rooney (1942, B&W, 84m, NR) Shirley Temple gets her first screen kiss (from Dickie Moore) in this tale of a poor girl in love with a boy from a wealthy family. **ST213**

Miss Firecracker (1989, C, 102m, PG) Loopy comedy set in Yazoo City, Mississippi, about a local beauty contest and its eccentric entrants. Holly Hunter stars, with Mary Steenburgen, Alfre Woodard, Tim Robbins, and Scott Glenn. Beth Henley adapted her play, *The Miss Firecracker Contest.* **CO12, DR20, ST113**

Miss Grant Takes Richmond
(1947, B&W, 87m, NR)
Lucille Ball plays a secretary who does a little amateur sleuthing in this comic mystery with William Holden. **ST106**

Miss Mary (1986, C, 100m, R)
A drama set in Argentina about a British governess (Julie Christie) and her strange relationship to her family of employers. **FF6, ST30**

Miss Sadie Thompson (1953, C, 91m, NR)
Musical remake of Somerset Maugham's *Rain*, with Rita Hayworth as the South Seas lady of the night who seduces a respectable minister. With José Ferrer, Aldo Ray, and Charles Bronson. **MU14, ST20, ST101, WR23**

Missing (1982, C, 122m, R)
Fact-based drama about an American in a Latin American country who's abducted by state police, with his wife and father desperate to find his whereabouts. Jack Lemmon and Sissy Spacek star, with John Shea and Melanie Mayron. Costa-Gavras directed. Effective drama about ineffective U.S. diplomatic corps in the face of brutal dictatorship. Lemmon is terrific. **DR6, ST138, ST202,** *Recommended*

Missing in Action (1984, C, 101m, R)
Chuck Norris stars as a former POW who returns to Vietnam to free more Americans being held captive. **AC4, ST165**

Missing in Action 2: The Beginning
(1985, C, 96m, R)
In this sequel to *Missing in Action*, the story of Chuck Norris's captivity in Vietnam and his escape are told. **AC4, AC7, ST165**

Mission, The (1986, C, 126m, PG)
The true story of missionaries in seventeenth-century South America clashing with slave traders. Robert De Niro and Jeremy Irons star, with Aidan Quinn and Roy McAnally. Oscar-winning cinematography by Chris Menges; directed by Roland Joffe. Stunning visuals but the story works only intermittently. **DR5, DR27, ST51, ST116, XT26,** *Recommended*

Mission of Justice (1992, C, 95m, R)
Martial arts action, with Jeff Wincott as an undercover cop battling a corrupt politician. With Brigitte Nielsen. **AC26**

Missionary, The (1982, C, 90m, R)
Comedy about a cleric just back from Africa who is assigned to run a home for women of weak virtue. Michael Palin and Maggie Smith star. **CO15**

Mississippi Blues (1983, C, 96m, NR)
Filmmakers Bertrand Tavernier and Robert Parrish traveled the American South to make this documentary on its music. **CU16, DT123**

Mississippi Burning (1988, C, 125m, R)
The 1964 murder of three civil rights workers is the jumping-off point for this melodrama about the subsequent FBI investigation. Gene Hackman and Willem Dafoe star, with Frances McDormand and Brad Dourif. Directed by Alan Parker, whose heavy hand is all too evident. Hackman is excellent, as always (he deserved an Oscar), but the other Southerners are virtually all caricatures. **DR5, DR7, ST96**

Mississippi Masala (1992, C, 118m, R)
Denzel Washington stars in this romantic drama as a black carpet cleaner who falls in love with an Indian immigrant from Uganda. Their affair sparks strong reactions from both communities in a small Mississippi town. With Sarita Choudhury, Roshan Seth, Charles S. Dutton, and Joe Seneca. Directed by Mira Nair. Intercultural romance given interesting spin with detailed portrait of little-known immigrant enclave. **DR1, DR3, DR27, ST223,** *Recommended*

Mississippi Mermaid (1969, C, 110m, PG)
Jean-Paul Belmondo is a plantation owner, Catherine Deneuve is his mail-order bride (or so he thinks) in this romantic drama from director François Truffaut. Based on a story by William Irish (Cornell Woolrich). One of Truffaut's great little-seen works. **DT125, ST11, ST50, WR39,** *Recommended*

Missouri Breaks, The (1976, C, 126m, PG)
Bounty hunter Marlon Brando squares off against reformed outlaw Jack Nicholson in a leisurely Western drama. With Harry Dean Stanton, Randy Quaid, and Kathleen Lloyd. Written by Tom McGuane; directed by Arthur Penn. It should be Nicholson's film but Brando's histrionics steal the show. Unfairly reviled, although no classsic, either. **DT96, ST18, ST163, ST205, WE3, WE15**

Missouri Traveler, The
(1958, C, 104m, NR)
An orphan tries to find a home in a small Southern town in the 1910s. Brandon de Wilde stars, with Lee Marvin and Gary Merrill. **ST151**

Mistress (1992, C, 109m, R)
Seriocomic tale of Hollywood screenwriter finally getting someone interested in his dream script; unfortunately it's a down-and-out producer who also wants to "make a few

changes." Robert Wuhl stars, with Martin Landau, Robert De Niro (who also produced), Danny Aiello, Eli Wallach, Jane Alexander, Sheryl Lee Ralph, Christopher Walken in a small role, and Ernest Borgnine as himself. Directed by Barry Primus. Worth a look for fans of participants. **CO8, ST51, ST222**

Misty (1961, C, 92m, NR)
Family drama based on book by Marguerite Henry about wild ponies on islands off Virginia's Atlantic shore. David Ladd and Pam Smith star, with Arthur O'Connell. Filmed on location on Chincoteague and Assateague islands. **FA5**

Misunderstood (1984, C, 91m, PG)
Gene Hackman stars in this drama about a family torn apart when the wife dies and the son (Henry Thomas) retreats into a world of his own. With Rip Torn and Susan Anspach. **DR8, ST96, ST216**

Mixed Blood (1985, C, 98m, R)
A comedy-drama about a gang of Brazilian toughs trying to muscle in on New York's drug trade, thwarted by romance between their leader and the daughter of a rival boss. Directed by Paul Morrissey. **DT90**

Mo' Better Blues (1990, C, 129m, R)
A jazz musician's troubles, both with his band and his women, are dramatized by writer-director Spike Lee. Denzel Washington stars, with Wesley Snipes, Joie Lee (the director's sister), Cynda Williams, Giancarlo Esposito, Robin Harris, Bill Nunn, Dick Anthony Williams, Rubén Blades, John and Nicholas Turturro, and Spike himself. Ambitious, perhaps overly so, with a lead character whose travails grow increasingly tiring. Very unfortunate ending. **DR12, DR14, DT72, MU12, ST201, ST223, XT8**

Mo' Money (1992, C, 89m, R)
Real-life brothers Damon and Marlon Wayans star in this comedy about a punk who's trying to set a good example for his sibling, only to wind up involved in a credit card scam and blackmail. **CO10, XT8**

Mobsters (1991, C, 104m, R)
How four of history's biggest gangsters got their starts in the business of crime. Christian Slater (Lucky Luciano), Patrick Dempsey (Meyer Lansky), Richard Grieco (Bugsy Siegel), and Costas Mandylor (Frank Costello) star, with F. Murray Abraham as Arnold Rothstein, Lara Flynn Boyle, Michael Gambon, Christopher Penn, and Anthony Quinn. **AC22, DR4, ST200**

Moby Dick (1956, C, 116m, NR)
Herman Melville's classic tale of Captain Ahab (Gregory Peck) and his obsession with the white whale. With Richard Basehart as Ishmael, Friedrich Ledebur, Leo Genn, James Robertson Justice, and Harry Andrews. Orson Welles has one memorable scene as a priest. Directed by John Huston. A valiant attempt to land a towering book, undercut heavily by Peck's flat performance. **CL1, DT60, DT134, ST171**

Modern Love (1990, C, 109m, R)
Romantic comedy from Robby Benson who stars as regular guy pulled into marriage, fatherhood—the whole domestic trip. Benson also wrote, produced, and directed. With his real-life wife, Karla DeVito, Rue McClanahan, Burt Reynolds, Frankie Valli, and Louise Lasser. **CO1, MU12, ST183, XT20**

Modern Problems (1981, C, 91m, PG)
Chevy Chase stars in this comedy about an air traffic controller who discovers he has telekinetic powers. **CO11, CO13**

Modern Romance (1981, C, 93m, R)
A film editor (Albert Brooks) drives his girlfriend (Kathryn Harrold) crazy with his obsessive behavior about their relationship. With Bruno Kirby, Jane Hallaren, James L. Brooks, George Kennedy as himself, and Brooks's brother Bob Einstein in a small role. Brooks cowrote and directed. Lead character may drive *you* nuts but there's real truth and humor in there. **CO1, CO8, DT16, XT8,** *Recommended*

Modern Times (1936, B&W, 89m, G)
Charlie Chaplin's sublime comedy of contemporary man bedeviled by machines. Paulette Goddard costars in this silent, which features music composed by Chaplin. **CL11, DT24,** *Essential, Highly Recommended*

Moderns, The (1988, C, 126m, R)
Drama set in 1926 Paris, amid the art and literary world of expatriate Americans, including Ernest Hemingway (Kevin O'Connor) and Gertrude Stein. Keith Carradine plays an art forger, Wallace Shawn a columnist, John Lone a wealthy art collector, Linda Fiorentino his wife and Carradine's former lover. With Geraldine Chaplin and Genevieve Bujold. Alan Rudolph directed. About half the scenes work but most of the acting seems mannered or bloodless. **DR5, DT110, WR13**

Mogambo (1953, C, 115m, NR)
Remake of classic adventure story *Red Dust,* with Clark Gable once again the plantation foreman caught between advances of Ava Gardner and Grace Kelly. John Ford directed on location in Africa. **AC12, AC14, CU18, DT44, ST77, ST79, ST124**

Mohawk (1956, C, 79m, NR)
An Indian war is prevented by a white man (Scott Brady) and a lovely Indian (Rita Gam). **WE7**

Molly Maguires, The (1970, C, 123m, PG)
In nineteenth-century Pennsylvania, striking coal miners are betrayed by a union-busting spy. Sean Connery, Richard Harris, and Samantha Eggar star in this historical drama. Directed by Martin Ritt. First-rate production values, strong performances. Widescreen cinematography of James Wong Howe will be lost on video. **CU20, DR5, DT105, ST36,** *Recommended*

Mom and Dad Save the World
(1992, C, 99m, PG)
Family comedy of typical suburban couple transported to another planet to do battle with an evil dictator. Teri Garr and Jeffrey Jones star, with Jon Lovitz, Thalmus Rasulala, Wallace Shawn, and Eric Idle. **CO11, CO15, CO20, FA6, SF21**

Mommie Dearest (1981, C, 129m, PG)
Movie star and (according to her daughter) monster mom Joan Crawford is portrayed by Faye Dunaway. With Diana Scarwid, Steve Forrest, Howard da Silva (as Louis B. Mayer), and Mara Hobel. Directed by Frank Perry. Has cult following for its campy portrayal of Crawford's obsessions. **CU2, DR12, ST61**

Mon Oncle see *My Uncle*

Mon Oncle Antoine (1971, C, 104m, NR)
French-Canadian drama of fifteen-year-old boy's coming of age in small town. Jacques Gagnon and Jean Ducappe star. Directed by Claude Jutra. **FF7**

Mon Oncle d'Amerique
(1980, C, 123m, PG)
From French director Alain Resnais, a comedy about modern life, focusing on the work habits of three individuals. Gérard Depardieu stars. **FF1, ST52**

Mona Lisa (1986, C, 104m, R)
In London, a hood just out of jail agrees to return to work for his old boss, chauffeuring (and spying on) a black prostitute who's suspected of pocketing her earnings. Bob Hoskins and Cathy Tyson star, with Michael Caine and Robbie Coltrane. Directed by Neil Jordan. Excellent performances.
DR16, DR23, ST25, ST111, XT15, XT26, *Recommended*

Mondo Cane (1963, C, 105m, NR)
First of the infamous "Mondo" series of documentaries about strange and repellent behavior by peoples all over the world—

the stuff you now can see any night of the week on those home-video shows on TV. Made in Italy. **CU16**

Mondo Trasho (1969, B&W, 95m, NR)
Director John Waters presents a self-described "gutter film" about one day in the life of a hit-and-run driver, played by the inimitable Divine. A cult favorite. **CU12, DT132**

Money Pit, The (1986, C, 91m, PG)
A young married couple (Tom Hanks and Shelley Long) discover that the house of their dreams needs more than a "little" fixing up. With Maureen Stapleton and Alexander Godunov. **CO2, ST97**

Monika see *Summer With Monika*

Monkey Business (1931, B&W, 77m, NR)
The Marx Brothers wreak havoc on a luxury liner. With Thelma Todd; cowritten by S.J. Perelman. **CL10, ST152**

Monkey Business (1952, C, 97m, NR)
Cary Grant plays a scientist looking for a youth serum in this zany comedy from director Howard Hawks. Ginger Rogers and Marilyn Monroe costar. **CL10, DT53, ST92, ST159, ST187**

Monkey Shines: An Experiment in Fear
(1988, C, 115m, R)
A quadraplegic is helped by a trained monkey, who performs daily tasks for him. Trouble develops when the animal, injected with human brain cells, begins acting strangely. Directed by George Romero. **HO16, DT108**

Monkeys, Go Home! (1967, C, 101m, G)
American inherits an olive farm in France and trains a group of monkeys to pick his harvest. Disney comedy starring Dean Jones and Maurice Chevalier (in his last film). **FA1**

Monkey's Uncle, The (1965, C, 87m, NR)
Sequel to Disney comedy *The Misadventures of Merlin Jones* has college brain Tommy Kirk inventing a flying machine. **FA1**

Monsieur Beaucaire
(1946, B&W, 93m, NR)
Costume comedy starring Bob Hope as a barber enlisted to become a spy. With Joan Caulfield, Patric Knowles, and Marjorie Reynolds. **CO6, ST108**

Monsieur Hire (1989, C, 88m, PG-13)
French thriller of middle-aged voyeur falling in love with object of his peeping, who in turn is involved with murder. Michel Blanc and Sandrine Bonnaire star. Based on a novel by Georges Simenon. **FF1**

Monsieur Verdoux (1947, B&W, 123m, NR)
Charlie Chaplin's dark comedy about a man
who marries, then murders, a string of
women for their money. With Martha Raye,
Isobel Elsom, and William Frawley. **DT24,**
Recommended

Monster Club, The (1980, C, 97m, PG)
Vincent Price plays a vampire who narrates
three tales of terror, all revolving around a
Transylvanian disco. **HO23, ST179**

Monster in a Box (1992, C, 96m, NR)
Spalding Gray offers another of his comic
monologues, this one about a novel he's
trying to write (the title reference) and
the adventures that interrupt his progress.
Directed by Nicholas Broomfield. **CO12,
CO16**

Monster in the Closet (1986, C, 87m, PG)
Comic tribute to 1950s sci-fi/horror films,
about a gang of monsters that hide in closets
and kill people. Donald Grant stars, with
Claude Akins, Henry Gibson, Howard Duff,
Paul Dooley, and John Carradine. **SF21**

Monster Squad, The (1987, C, 82m, PG-13)
A gang of plucky kids meet up with every
monster imaginable, from Frankenstein and
Dracula to the Wolf Man and the Mummy in
this horror comedy. **HF7, HF10, HO24**

Monte Walsh (1970, C, 106m, PG)
Old-time cowboys Lee Marvin and Jack Palance won't face the fact that the frontier is
closing down. With Jeanne Moreau. **ST151,
ST161, WE11**

Montenegro (1981, C, 98m, R)
A bored housewife discovers a new way to
approach life when she begins an affair with
a Yugoslavian worker. Susan Anspach stars.
Dusan Makavejev directed. **FF7**

Monterey Pop (1969, C, 72m, NR)
Concert film of ground-breaking 1967 Cali-
fornia pop festival, featuring Jimi Hendrix,
Janis Joplin, Otis Redding, The Who, Ravi
Shankar, Simon and Garfunkel, Eric Burdon
and the Animals, The Jefferson Airplane,
Country Joe and the Fish, Canned Heat,
Hugh Masakela, and The Mamas and the
Papas. Directed by D.A. Pennebaker. A must
for any fan of rock 'n' roll. **MU10,** *Highly
Recommended*

Montgomery Clift
(1985, C/ B&W, 120m, NR)
Documentary on the gifted and tormented
actor, made for Italian TV. **CU16, ST32**

Monty Python and the Holy Grail
(1974, C, 90m, PG)
The boys from TV's most wickedly funny

program take on the King Arthur legends.
CO7, CO15

**Monty Python Live at the Hollywood
Bowl** (1982, C, 77m, NR)
A record of Python's live stage show. **CO15**

Monty Python's Flying Circus
(1970–73, 22 volumes: all C, 60m, NR)
Each tape in this series contains two half-
hour programs (Vol. 22 is 90m. and contains
three) from the deliriously silly TV program
starring John Cleese, Eric Idle, Graham Chapman, Michael Palin, and Terry Jones, with
animated sequences by Terry Gilliam. **CO15,**
Highly Recommended

Monty Python's Life of Brian
(1979, C, 90m, R)
Britain's bad boys of humor tell their own
version of the Messiah story in this irreverent
spoof of religious epics. **CO7, CO15**

Monty Python's Meaning of Life
(1983, C, 103m, R)
More madness from the Python troupe,
as they attempt to answer some of life's
great questions in this series of bawdy
and naughty sketches. **CO15**

Moon and Sixpence, The
(1942, B&W/C, 89m, NR)
The W. Somerset Maugham tale of man who
moves to Tahiti to realize his ambition of
becoming a painter. George Sanders stars,
with Herbert Marshall (as Maugham), Doris
Dudley, and Eric Blore. Paintings shown in
color. **WR23**

Moon in the Gutter, The
(1983, C, 126m, R)
Gérard Depardieu and Nastassja Kinski star in
this stylized thriller about a man in search of
the thug who brutalized his sister. Directed
by Jean-Jacques Beneix. **FF1, ST52**

Moon Is Blue, The (1953, B&W, 95m, NR)
A young woman's virginity is at stake in this
comedy, considered daring in its day. William Holden, David Niven, and Maggie
McNamara star. Based on a play by F. Hugh
Herbert. Otto Preminger directed. Amusing
but hardly earth-shattering stuff—which is
what its defenders always claimed. **CO1,
DR20, DT100, ST106**

Moon Over Miami (1941, C, 91m, NR)
Quintessential Betty Grable musical has her
manhunting with pals Carole Landis and
Charlotte Greenwood in title town. With
Don Ameche and Robert Cummings. **ST91**

Moon Over Parador
(1988, C, 105m, PG-13)
An American movie actor, on location in a

Latin American country, is forced to impersonate the land's dictator after the despot suffers a fatal heart attack. Comedy, directed by Paul Mazursky, stars Richard Dreyfuss, with Sonia Braga, Raul Julia, Jonathan Winters, and the director (as the dictator's mother). Watch for appearances by Sammy Davis, Jr., Charo, and Dick Cavett. Dreyfuss is very good but the movie feels much longer than 105 minutes. **CO2, CO8, CO20, DT87, ST17, ST60, XT27**

Moon Pilot (1962, C, 98m, G)
Just before he blasts off, an astronaut meets a lovely alien. Disney comedy starring Tom Tryon, Brian Keith, and Dany Saval. **FA1**

Moonfleet (1955, C, 89m, NR)
Swashbuckling tale starring Stewart Granger, with Jon Whiteley, George Sanders, and Viveca Lindfors. Directed by Fritz Lang. **AC15, DT70**

Moonlighting (1982, C, 97m, PG)
Jeremy Irons plays the foreman of a gang of Polish workmen in London on a temporary construction job. He tries to keep news of political turmoil back home from his co-workers. Directed by Jerzy Skolimowski. Dialogue in English and Polish. **DR27, FF7, ST116**

Moonlighting (1985, C, 97m, NR)
A classy fashion model and a hip investigator team up to run a detective agency. Cybill Shepherd and Bruce Willis star in this mystery-comedy, originally the pilot for a TV series. **CO10, MY10, ST229,** *Recommended*

Moonraker (1979, C, 126m, PG)
James Bond blasts into outer space to take on a madman and his steel-toothed henchman. Roger Moore, Michael Lonsdale, and Richard Kiel star. **HF2**

Moonrise (1948, B&W, 90m, NR)
Melodrama of son of executed killer who's tormented by the memory. In self-defense, he commits a murder and hides out in the swamps. Dane Clark stars. **MY1**

Moon's Our Home, The
(1936, B&W, 76m, NR)
Margaret Sullavan and Henry Fonda star in this romantic comedy about the up-and-down relationship between a movie star and a New York writer. **CL7, ST71**

Moon-Spinners, The (1964, C, 118m, NR)
Hayley Mills stars in a Disney mystery about an innocent tourist in Crete becoming involved with a smuggling operation. **FA1**

Moonstruck (1987, C, 102m, PG)
A young Italian-American widow, set to marry a second time, falls in love with her fiancé's younger brother in this delightful romantic comedy set in Brooklyn. Cher and Olympia Dukakis won Oscars for their performances as the widow and her mother. With Nicolas Cage, Vincent Gardenia, and Danny Aiello. Directed by Norman Jewison; written by John Patrick Shanley. **CO1, DT63, ST23, ST29, XT3, XT5,** *Recommended*

More (1969, C, 110m, NR)
Love affair between German student and American woman degenerates into drug addiction odyssey that takes them from Paris to Ibiza. Mimsy Farmer and Klaus Grunberg star. Cowritten by Barbet Schroeder. Music by Pink Floyd. **CU3, DR1**

More American Graffiti
(1979, C, 111m, PG)
Sequel to tale of high school kids in small-town, early 1960s California pursues four stories: Ron Howard and Cindy Williams set up house and find something less than domestic bliss, Paul LeMat pursues a career as a race-car driver, Candy Clark trips out in Haight-Ashbury, and Charlie Martin Smith winds up in Vietnam. With Scott Glenn, Mary Kay Place, and in small roles, Rosanna Arquette and Harrison Ford. Directed by B.W.L. Norton. Ambitious, but rarely successful attempt to elaborate on original. **CO6, DT58, ST74**

More Ripping Yarns see *Ripping Yarns* (series)

More the Merrier, The
(1943, B&W, 104m, NR)
The housing shortage in Washington during World War II is the basis for this clever romantic comedy starring Joel McCrea and Jean Arthur, with Oscar-winning support from Charles Coburn (Arthur should have won, too). Directed by George Stevens. **CL10, DT119, ST3, ST144, XT4, XT28,** *Recommended*

Morgan: A Suitable Case for Treatment
(1966, B&W, 97m, NR)
Madcap British comedy about a loony artist (David Warner) who's obsessed with apes and his ex-wife (Vanessa Redgrave). Directed by Karel Reisz. Touching performance by Warner as misfit in proper society. **CO17, CO20, CU5, ST182,** *Recommended*

Morgan Stewart's Coming Home
(1987, C, 92m, PG-13)
Hip prep school student (Jon Cryer) shows his uptight parents (Lynn Redgrave and

Nicholas Pryor) how to loosen up in this comedy. **CO5**

Morituri (1965, B&W, 123m, NR)
Marlon Brando plays a German who helps British forces capture a cargo ship in World War II. Yul Brynner costars, with Trevor Howard, Janet Margolin, and Wally Cox. Also known as *Saboteur: Code Name Morituri.* **AC1, ST18**

Morning After, The (1986, C, 103m, R)
Jane Fonda stars in this mystery about an alcoholic actress who wakes up one morning next to a corpse—and can't remember what happened the night before. Jeff Bridges costars, with Raul Julia. Sidney Lumet directed. **DT78, MY3, MY5, ST19, ST72**

Morning Glory (1933, B&W, 74m, NR)
Katharine Hepburn won the first of her four Oscars for her role as an aspiring young actress in this drama. Adolphe Menjou and Douglas Fairbanks, Jr., costar. **CL5, ST103, XT3**

Morocco (1930, B&W, 92m, NR)
Marlene Dietrich's first American film has her succumbing to the charms of legionnaire Gary Cooper. Directed by Josef von Sternberg. **DT128, ST37, ST55**

Mortal Thoughts (1991, C, 104m, R)
Loutish husband is found murdered—did his wife or her best friend do it? Demi Moore and Glenne Headly star, with Bruce Willis and Harvey Keitel. Directed by Alan Rudolph. Flashback structure seems clever at first, then bogs story down in needless repetition. Willis believable in unsympathetic role. **DR10, DT110, MY3, ST229**

Mosby's Marauders (1966, C, 79m, NR)
Civil War action, with Kurt Russell as recruit to company of Confederate raiders. With James MacArthur, Jack Ging, Peggy Lipton, and Nick Adams. **AC5, ST191**

Moscow Does Not Believe in Tears
(1980, C, 152m, R)
Oscar-winning drama from the Soviet Union about a trio of women who emigrate to the capital city in the 1950s to seek their fortunes. **FF7, XT7**

Moscow on the Hudson
(1984, C, 115m, R)
A Soviet saxophonist defects—in the middle of Bloomingdale's—in this comedy-drama starring Robin Williams. With Maria Conchita Alonso, Cleavant Derricks, and Alejandro Rey. Paul Mazursky directed. Flagwaving finale leaves unnecessarily sour taste. **CO20, DR15, DR27, DT87, ST228, XT9**

Moses (1975, C, 141m, PG)
Burt Lancaster stars as the biblical prophet in this condensed version of a six-hour TV miniseries. **CL13, ST129**

Mosquito Coast, The (1986, C, 117m, PG)
Eccentric inventor (Harrison Ford) moves his family from New England to the jungles of Central America to escape the evil influences of "civilization." With River Phoenix, Helen Mirren, Martha Plimpton, and Andre Gregory. Peter Weir directed; based on Paul Theroux's novel. Source's point of view—it's told through son's eyes—is sorely missed. Ford is game, but he's miscast. **DR8, DR19, DT133, ST74**

Most Dangerous Game, The
(1932, B&W, 63m, NR)
Classic adventure saga, based on famous short story about a man and woman pursued for sport by a mad big game hunter. Joel McCrea and Fay Wray star, with Leslie Banks as Count Zaroff. Primitive but exciting. **AC13, AC24, ST144,** *Recommended*

Motel Hell (1980, C, 102m, R)
Horror film, played for laughs, about a brother and sister whose motel swallows up tourists and recycles them into a popular brand of sausage. Rory Calhoun stars. **HO24**

Mother (1952, B&W, 98m, NR)
Japanese drama of fatherless working-class family living in postwar Tokyo. Directed by Mikio Naruse. **FF4**

Mother, Jugs & Speed (1976, C, 95m, R)
Darkly comic adventures of city ambulance drivers, starring Bill Cosby, Raquel Welch, and Harvey Keitel, with Larry Hagman. **CO2**

Mother Kusters Goes to Heaven
(1975, C, 108m, NR)
Director Rainer Werner Fassbinder's drama of a woman dealing with her husband's mental breakdown. Brigitte Meara, Ingrid Craven, and Armin Meier star. **DT42**

Mother's Day (1980, C, 98m, NR)
A trio of women out for a hike are brutalized by two backwoods brothers, but the women have the final say in this gruesome horror story. **CU7, HO18**

Mothra (1962, C, 100m, NR)
Japanese monster movie about gigantic flying creature whose destructive ways can be checked only by two tiny twin sisters. **FF4, SF18**

Motown 25: Yesterday, Today, and Forever (1983, C, 130m, NR)
Celebration of the black pop music label that recorded such great performers as Stevie

Wonder, Marvin Gaye, The Supremes, The Four Tops, The Temptations, and The Jackson 5. Originally shown on TV. **MU10,** *Recommended*

Moulin Rouge (1952, C, 123m, NR)
The life of deformed French artist Toulouse-Lautrec, filmed in dazzling color by director John Huston. José Ferrer stars, with Zsa Zsa Gabor, Christopher Lee, and Peter Cushing. **CL2, CL9, DT60, ST43, ST135**

Mountain, The (1956, C, 105m, NR)
Adventure story of two brothers (Spencer Tracy and Robert Wagner) on climbing expedition to check out wreckage. With Claire Trevor, William Demarest, and Richard Arlen. **AC12, ST217**

Mountain Family Robinson
(1979, C, 100m, G)
Family drama of clan learning to survive in rugged mountain terrain, starring Robert F. Logan, Susan Damante-Shaw, and Heather Rattray. **FA4**

Mountain Road, The
(1960, B&W, 102m, NR)
World War II drama set in China during final days of conflict. James Stewart stars, with Lisa Lu, Glenn Corbett, and Henry (Harry) Morgan. **AC1, ST207**

Mountains of the Moon
(1990, C, 135m, R)
The true story of nineteenth-century British explorers Richard Burton and John Hanning Speke and their search for the source of the Nile River. Patrick Bergin plays Burton, Iain Glen is Speke, with Fiona Shaw (as Isabel Burton) and Richard E. Grant. Directed by Bob Rafelson, his best film in years. **AC12, AC16, AC24, DR4,** *Recommended*

Mouse That Roared, The
(1959, C, 83m, NR)
Peter Sellers plays three roles in this British comedy about a tiny, mythical kingdom declaring war on America so they can be eligible for generous foreign aid. **CO17, ST198, XT27**

Movers and Shakers (1985, C, 79m, PG)
Hollywood screenwriter tries to sell script called *Love in Sex* in this satire of the contemporary movie scene. Walter Matthau and Charles Grodin star; guest appearances by Steve Martin and Gilda Radner. **CO8, CO13, ST94, ST150, ST155**

Movie Movie (1978, C/B&W, 107m, PG)
Spoof of 1930s movies contains two films, one a boxing drama called *Dynamite Hands*, the other a big-budget musical called *Bathing*

Beauties of 1933. George C. Scott stars, with Trish Van Devere, Eli Wallach, Red Buttons, Barbara Harris, Harry Hamlin, Art Carney, and Ann Reinking. Stanley Donen directed. **CO7, DT38, ST196**

Movie Struck (1937, B&W, 70m, NR)
Typical tale of small-town girl looking for fame and fortune in Hollywood. Jack Haley, Rosina Lawrence, and Patsy Kelly star; Laurel and Hardy appear as "guest stars" in two scenes. Also known as *Pick a Star.* **ST133**

Moving (1988, C, 89m, R)
Richard Pryor stars in this comedy about a man whose job transfer from New Jersey to Idaho is one disaster after another. With Dave Thomas. **CO14, ST180, XT18**

Mr. and Mrs. Bridge
(1990, C, 124m, PG-13)
Drama set in the 1930s and 1940s of middle-class Kansas City couple (Paul Newman and Joanne Woodward), based on acclaimed pair of novels by Evan Connell. With Blythe Danner, Simon Callow, Kyra Sedgwick, and Robert Sean Leonard. Produced by Ismail Merchant, directed by James Ivory, and adapted by Ruth Prawer Jhabvala. The artful irony of the books is replaced with a dogged literalness and an infuriating ending. **DR8, DR19, DT61, ST162, ST234**

Mr. and Mrs. North (1941, B&W, 67m, NR)
Screen version of popular radio show, with fun-loving couple solving murder mystery. Gracie Allen stars. **MY17**

Mr. and Mrs. Smith (1941, B&W, 95m, NR)
Alfred Hitchcock takes a break from thrillers to make a comedy about a couple who finds that their marriage was never legal. Robert Montgomery and Carole Lombard star. **DT57, ST140**

Mr. Arkadin (1955, B&W, 99m, NR)
Twisted tale of mystery millionaire, directed by and starring Orson Welles. With Michael Redgrave, Patricia Medina, Akim Tamiroff, and Mischa Auer. Falls well short of Welles's *Kane* glory. **DR24, DT134**

Mr. Baseball (1992, C, 109m, PG-13)
Tom Selleck plays an American slugger whose fading career is revived when he signs on with a Japanese team. Comedy of culture clash features Ken Takakura and Aya Takanashi. Directed by Fred Schepisi. Widescreen cinematography will be lost without letterboxing. **CO19, CO20**

Mr. Blandings Builds His Dream House
(1948, B&W, 94m, NR)
New York couple decide to buy their dream

home in the Connecticut countryside; the fun begins when they decide to fix it up "a little." Cary Grant, Myrna Loy, and Melvyn Douglas star in this delightful comedy. **CL10, ST58, ST92, ST142,** *Recommended*

Mr. Deeds Goes to Town
(1936, B&W, 115m, NR)
Director Frank Capra won an Oscar for this comedy about an ordinary guy who inherits a fortune and decides to give it all away. Gary Cooper and Jean Arthur star, with George Bancroft and Lionel Stander. **CL8, DT22, ST3, ST37, XT6,** *Essential*

Mr. Destiny (1990, C, 110m, PG-13)
Comedy of second chance, with Jim Belushi as a guy who gets to start his life over again, beginning with crucial moment in a high school baseball game. With Linda Hamilton, Michael Caine, Jon Lovitz, and Hart Bochner. **CO13, ST25**

Mister Frost (1990, C, 92m, R)
Jeff Goldblum plays an imprisoned serial killer who believes he's the devil. With Kathy Baker, Alan Bates, Jean-Pierre Cassel, Daniel Gelin, and Vincent Schiavelli. **HO10, MY13, ST9, ST90**

Mr. Halpern and Mr. Johnson
(1983, C, 57m, NR)
Drama of two elderly men meeting after the funeral of one's wife, the second revealing a longtime secret friendship with the woman. Originally made for cable TV. Laurence Olivier and Jackie Gleason star. **DR11, ST168**

Mr. Hobbs Takes a Vacation
(1962, C, 116m, NR)
Family comedy about a father who's put through the wringer on a summer vacation. James Stewart and Maureen O'Hara star. **CO5, ST167, ST207**

Mr. Hulot's Holiday
(1953, B&W, 86m, NR)
The first film about M. Hulot, the comic Frenchman with a knack for getting into the strangest situations. Director Jacques Tati also plays the lead role. **DT122,** *Essential, Recommended*

Mister Johnson (1990, C, 101m, PG-13)
Drama set in 1920s Africa, based on Joyce Cary novel of relationship between British diplomat (Pierce Brosnan) and his black clerk (Maynard Eziashi). With Edward Woodward. Directed by Bruce Beresford. **DR5, DR19, DR27, DT10,** *Recommended*

Mr. Klein (1977, C, 122m, PG)
In Nazi-occupied France, an art dealer exploiting Jews finds himself confused with another man who's a Jew and under scrutiny from the Germans. Alain Delon and Jeanne Moreau star. Joseph Losey directed. **FF1, ST161**

Mr. Lucky (1943, B&W, 100m, NR)
Cary Grant stars as the dashing owner of a gambling ship who is out to bilk Laraine Day, but she charms him into respectability. **CL10, ST92,** *Recommended*

Mr. Majestyk (1974, C, 103m, PG)
A Colorado melon grower (Charles Bronson) won't knuckle under to the Mob, which decides to have him eliminated. Adapted by Elmore Leonard from his own novel. **ST20, WR19**

Mr. Mom (1983, C, 91m, PG)
When an executive loses his job and his wife goes to work, their roles are reversed and their lives turned upside-down. Comedy starring Michael Keaton, Teri Garr, and Martin Mull. Written by John Hughes. **CO2, CO5, CO20, DT59, ST122**

Mr. Music (1950, B&W, 113m, NR)
Bing Crosby musical has him playing a Broadway composer whose main priority is living the good life. With Nancy Olson, Charles Coburn, Ruth Hussey, Marge and Gower Champion, Peggy Lee, and Groucho Marx. **MU4, ST40, ST152**

Mr. North (1988, C, 92m, PG)
Gentle comic fable, set in 1920s Newport, Rhode Island, about an extraordinary young man who charms society with his very "electric" personality. Anthony Edwards stars, with Robert Mitchum, Harry Dean Stanton, Anjelica Huston, and Lauren Bacall. Based on a novel by Thornton Wilder. **CO6, DR19, ST115, ST158, ST205**

Mr. Peabody and the Mermaid
(1948, B&W, 89m, NR)
Comedy of a mild-mannered man (William Powell) and his encounter with a finned lady (Ann Blyth). **ST176**

Mr. Quilp see *Old Curiosity Shop, The (1975 version)*

Mister Roberts (1955, C, 123m, NR)
Classic comedy-drama about World War II shipboard battle between high-strung captain (James Cagney) and determined first mate (Henry Fonda). With Oscar winner Jack Lemmon (as Ensign Pulver) and William Powell (in his last film). Codirected by John Ford. Widescreen will be lost on video. **CL10, CU20, DT44, ST24, ST71, ST138, ST176, XT4, XT22,** *Recommended*

Mr. Saturday Night (1992, C, 119m, R)
Sentimental show-biz tale of comic Buddy
Young, Jr., character created on "Saturday
Night Live" by Billy Crystal. With David Pay-
mer, Julie Warner, Helen Hunt, Mary Maya,
Jerry Orbach, Ron Silver, Jackie Gayle, Carl
Ballantine, and Jerry Lewis as himself. Directed
by Crystal, who cowrote with Lowell Ganz
and Babaloo Mandel. **CO8, CO13, ST139**

Mr. Skeffington (1944, B&W, 140m, NR)
Bette Davis and Claude Rains star as a New
York society couple whose loveless marriage
warms with the passing years. The video version restores thirteen minutes of footage
from the film's original release. **CL4, CL5,
CU10, ST44**

Mr. Smith Goes to Washington
(1939, B&W, 129m, NR)
James Stewart plays an idealistic young Con-
gressman in conflict with the Old Guard
in the Nation's Capital. With Jean Arthur,
Thomas Mitchell, and Claude Rains. Frank
Capra directed. One of the quintessential
Capras, but not to my taste. **DT22, ST3,
ST207, XT12,** *Essential*

Mr. Sycamore (1974, C, 88m, NR)
Offbeat comedy of repressed mailman who
decides to turn into a tree to escape his
shrewish wife. Jason Robards stars, with
Sandy Dennis and Jean Simmons. **CO12,
ST185**

Mr. Winkle Goes to War
(1944, B&W, 80m, NR)
Comedy-drama of a mild-mannered man
(Edward G. Robinson) who's accidentally
drafted and winds up becoming a war hero.
CO20, CO21, ST186

Mr. Wong, Detective (1938, B&W, 69m, NR)
Boris Karloff plays an Oriental detective in
this low-budget mystery. **ST119**

Mr. Wong in Chinatown
(1939, B&W, 70m, NR)
Boris Karloff's third appearance as the wily
Oriental detective has him on the trail of the
murderer of a Chinese princess. **ST119**

Mrs. Miniver (1942, B&W, 134m, NR)
Classic story of the effects of World War II on
a middle-class British family. Winner of seven
Oscars, including Best Picture, Director (Wil-
liam Wyler), Actress (Greer Garson), and
Supporting Actress (Teresa Wright). Walter
Pidgeon costars. **CL8, DT142, ST83, XT1,
XT3, XT5, XT6,** *Essential*

Mrs. Soffel (1984, C, 110m, PG-13)
Prison warden's wife falls in love with a convict and helps him and his brother escape.

True-life romantic drama set in turn-of-the-
century Pittsburgh, starring Diane Keaton,
Mel Gibson, and Matthew Modine. Skillfully
directed by Gillian Armstrong. One of Gibson's better performances; a real sleeper.
DR1, DR16, DT7, ST85, ST121,
Recommended

Mrs. Wiggs of the Cabbage Patch
(1934, B&W, 80m, NR)
A poor woman raising five children on her
own finds time to play matchmaker to a
spinster. Pauline Lord stars, with ZaSu Pitts
and W.C. Fields as the matched couple. **ST67**

Ms. Don Juan (1973, C, 87m, R)
Brigitte Bardot plays a temptress whose con-
quests include her cousin, a priest. With
Maurice Ronet, Robert Hossein, and Jane
Birkin. Directed by Roger Vadim. **ST6**

Ms. 45 (1981, C, 84m, R)
In New York City, a mute seamstress is raped
twice and goes on a killing spree in revenge.
Zoe Tamerlis stars in this action film with a
cult following. Directed by Abel Ferrara. The
bizarre finale at a costume party is the one
good scene. **AC19, CU7, MY3, MY4**

Multiple Maniacs (1971, B&W, 90m, NR)
Cult favorite, described by its creator, director John Waters, as a "celluloid atrocity."
Divine stars as the proprietor of a "Cavalcade
of Perversions," a carnival at which customers are robbed and beaten. **CU12, DT132**

Mummy, The (1932, B&W, 72m, NR)
Boris Karloff plays the Egyptian wrapped in
bandages in the classic horror film. Directed
by Karl Freund. Atmospheric, intelligent.
HO1, ST119, *Recommended*

Mummy, The (1959, C, 88m, NR)
British remake of the horror fable of the
Egyptian's cursed tomb, starring Christopher
Lee and Peter Cushing. **HO26, ST43, ST135**

Mummy's Hand, The
(1940, B&W, 67m, NR)
First in the Kharis series of classic horror tales
centers on expedition to lost tomb of Egyptian princess. Dick Foran stars, with Wallace
Ford, Peggy Moran, and George Zucco. **HO1,
HO19**

Muppet Christmas Carol, The
(1992, C, 85m, G)
Retelling of the Dickens holiday story, with
Michael Caine playing Scrooge, Muppets fill-
ing all the supporting roles. **FA13, FA14,
ST25, WR5**

Muppet Moments (1985, C, 56m, NR)
A collection of musical numbers and comedy
skits from the popular TV series. Guest stars

include Lena Horne, Liza Minnelli, Pearl Bailey, and Zero Mostel. **FA14**

Muppet Movie, The (1979, C, 94m, G)
The Muppets' feature film debut, in a comedy loaded with human stars as well: Orson Welles, Mel Brooks, Steve Martin, Bob Hope, and Richard Pryor head the list. **DT17, DT134, FA14, ST108, ST150, ST180**

Muppet Revue, The (1985, C, 56m, NR)
More sketches and songs from the hit TV series, with guest stars Harry Belafonte, Linda Ronstadt, and Rita Moreno. **FA14**

Muppet Treasures (1985, C, 56m, NR)
Kermit, Miss Piggy, and friends welcome human stars Loretta Lynn, Ethel Merman, Peter Sellers, and Paul Simon in this collection of funny moments from the TV series. **FA14, ST198**

Muppets Take Manhattan, The
(1984, C, 94m, G)
Broadway-bound frog, pig, and friends take the Great White Way by storm. Liza Minnelli, Joan Rivers, Brooke Shields, Elliott Gould, Art Carney, and Dabney Coleman lend support. **FA14, XT9**

Murder! (1930, B&W, 108m, NR)
Herbert Marshall stars in this Hitchcock thriller about a jury member who has second thoughts about a condemned woman. **DT57**

Murder Ahoy (1964, B&W, 93m, NR)
Agatha Christie's amateur sleuth Miss Marple investigates a murder aboard a naval cadet training ship. Margaret Rutherford stars, with Lionel Jeffries and Charles Tingwell. **MY11, MY12, MY15, WR3**

Murder at the Baskervilles see *Silver Blaze, The*

Murder at the Gallop
(1963, B&W, 81m, NR)
Miss Marple (Margaret Rutherford) looks into the death of a wealthy recluse. With Robert Morley and Flora Robson. Based on a story by Agatha Christie. **MY11, MY12, MY15, WR3**

Murder at the Vanities
(1934, B&W, 89m, NR)
Combination mystery and musical, with detective Victor McLaglen investigating backstage killing. Duke Ellington and his band are among the performers. **MU16, MY12**

Murder by Death (1976, C, 94m, PG)
Mystery comedy featuring an all-star collection of detectives (Charlie Chan, Sam Spade, Miss Marple) attempting to solve a whodunit in the mansion of Truman Capote. Peter

Sellers, Peter Falk, and Alec Guinness star, with David Niven, Maggie Smith, James Coco, Elsa Lanchester, Eileen Brennan, Nancy Walker, and Truman Capote. Written by Neil Simon. **CO7, CO10, HF4, MY17, ST95, ST198, WR30**

Murder by Decree (1979, C, 121m, PG)
Sherlock and Dr. Watson track Jack the Ripper. Christopher Plummer and James Mason star. With Genevieve Bujold, Susan Clark, David Hemmings, and John Gielgud. **HF14, MY13, ST86, ST153**

Murder by Natural Causes
(1979, C, 100m, NR)
The unfaithful wife of a mentalist tries to scare her husband to death, with unexpected results. Katharine Ross and Hal Holbrook star. Written by Richard Levinson and William Link. Originally made for TV. **MY14**

Murder by Television
(1935, B&W, 60m, NR)
Low-budget mystery about the murder of a professor working on early TV technology. Bela Lugosi plays his assistant, the prime suspect. **ST143**

Murder Is Announced, A
(1984, C, 153m, NR)
Joan Hickson stars as Miss Marple, Agatha Christie's intrepid sleuth, in this whodunit involving a murder that is advertised ahead of schedule in the classified ads of a newspaper. Originally made for British TV. **MY11, MY12, MY15, WR3**

Murder Most Foul (1965, B&W, 90m, NR)
Agatha Christie's Miss Marple serves on a jury and holds out for the suspect's innocence. Margaret Rutherford stars, with Ron Moody and Charles Tingwell. **MY11, MY12, MY15, WR3**

Murder, My Sweet (1944, B&W, 95m, NR)
Dick Powell plays Raymond Chandler's famous detective Philip Marlowe in this version of *Farewell, My Lovely*. Filmed under the original title in 1975. **MY1, ST175, WR2**

Murder of Mary Phagan, The
(1988, C, 251m, PG)
True story of notorious case in 1913 Georgia, when Leo Frank, a Jewish factory superintendent, was convicted of murdering a fourteen-year-old worker, had his sentence commuted, but was eventually lynched. Peter Gallagher stars as Frank, Jack Lemmon plays the sympathetic governor; with Richard Jordan, Robert Prosky, Rebecca Miller, and Kathryn Walker. Originally a TV miniseries. **DR5, ST138**

Murder on the Bayou (1987, C, 100m, NR)
When a white racist is killed by an elderly
black man in rural Louisiana, all the accused
man's friends take responsibility for the
crime. Louis Gossett, Jr., and Richard Widmark star, with Holly Hunter, Joe Seneca,
Woody Strode, Papa John Creach, and Julius
Harris. Directed by Volker Schlöndorff. Originally made for TV under the title "A Gathering of Old Men." **DR14, MU12, ST113**

Murder on the Orient Express
(1974, C, 127m, PG)
Agatha Christie's master sleuth Hercule Poirot solves the killing of a rich American
aboard the famous luxury train. Albert Finney plays Poirot; among the suspects are
Oscar winner Ingrid Bergman, Lauren Bacall,
Sean Connery, Martin Balsam, Jacqueline
Bisset, John Gielgud, Rachel Roberts, Michael
York, and Vanessa Redgrave. Sidney Lumet
directed. The stars are fun but the film's
needlessly long. **DT78, MY12, ST13, ST36,
ST68, ST86, ST182, WR3, XT5, XT19**

Murder or Mercy (1974, C, 78m, NR)
True-life drama of physician implicated
in mercy killing of his terminally ill wife.
Melvyn Douglas stars, with Bradford Dill-
man, David Birney, and Mildred Dunnock.
Originally made for TV. **DR6, DR7, ST58**

Murder Over New York
(1940, B&W, 64m, NR)
Ace detective Charlie Chan (Sidney Toler)
attends a police convention and comes up
against saboteurs who are crippling the Allied
air effort. **HF4**

Murder, She Said (1962, B&W, 87m, NR)
Margaret Rutherford plays Miss Marple, the
Agatha Christie sleuth, as she goes undercover as a maid to solve a crime she witnessed. With Arthur Kennedy, Muriel Pavlow,
and James Robertson Justice. **MY11, MY12,
MY15, WR3**

Murder Story (1989, C, 90m, NR)
An aspiring young novelist copies the technique of his idol by piecing random newspaper clippings to form a mystery story.
Christopher Lee stars in this thriller, made
in Holland. **ST135**

Murderers' Row (1966, C, 108m, NR)
Second in the Matt Helm spy spoof series
pits Dean Martin against arch-villain Karl
Malden, who wants to melt Washington,
D.C. With Ann-Margret, Camilla Sparv, and
James Gregory. **CO9, ST149**

Murders in the Rue Morgue
(1932, B&W, 75m, NR)
The Edgar Allan Poe tale of a mad doctor and
his ape trained to bring him female victims.
Bela Lugosi and Sidney Fox star. Cowritten
by John Huston. **HO20, ST143, WR27**

Murders in the Rue Morgue
(1971, C, 87m, PG)
Horror story, based on Edgar Allan Poe tale,
of Parisian murders by a most mysterious
assailant. Jason Robards and Herbert Lom
star. **ST185, WR27**

Murders in the Rue Morgue, The
(1986, C, 100m, NR)
George C. Scott stars in this latest version
of the Poe detective tale. With Rebecca De
Mornay, Ian McShane, Neil Dickson, and
Val Kilmer. Originally made for TV. **ST196,
WR27**

Murmur of the Heart (1971, C, 118m, NR)
French comedy-drama from director Louis
Malle about an unlikely subject: the inti-
mate relationship that develops between a
fourteen-year-old boy and his mother. **DR3,
DT82, FF1,** *Recommended*

Murphy's Law (1986, C, 100m, R)
Charles Bronson plays a police detective
framed for murder by an ex-con (Carrie
Snodgrass). **ST20**

Murphy's Romance
(1985, C, 107m, PG-13)
A newly divorced mother moves to a small
Arizona town hoping for a new life, and she
falls in love with the town druggist. Sally
Field and James Garner star. Directed by Martin Ritt. The stars are worth seeing it for, if
you're in the mood for something very light.
CO1, DR26, DT105, ST66, ST82

Murphy's War (1971, C, 108m, PG)
Peter O'Toole stars in this drama of a British
seaman who survives a Nazi attack and
swears revenge. **AC1, ST169**

Murri Affair, The (1974, C, 120m, NR)
Catherine Deneuve plays a society woman
investigating her husband's murder. With
Giancarlo Giannini and Fernando Rey.
MY11, ST50

Music Box (1989, C, 123m, R)
In contemporary Chicago, an elderly man
is accused of participating in World War II
atrocities, and his attorney daughter agrees
to defend him. Jessica Lange and Armin
Mueller-Stahl star, with Frederic Forrest,
Donald Moffat, and Lukas Haas. Directed by
Costa-Gavras. Lange and Mueller-Stahl are
good; story suffers from so many red herrings
its conclusion seems obvious. **DR7, DR8,
DR17, ST130, XT11**

Music Box, The/Helpmates
(1932, B&W, 50m, NR)
Two classic Laurel and Hardy shorts; the first, about an inept piano-moving team, won them their only Oscar. **ST133**

Music Lovers, The (1971, C, 122m, R)
The life and flamboyant times of Tchaikovsky, as interpreted by director Ken Russell, who concentrates on allegations about the composer's homosexuality and the insatiable sexual appetite of his wife. Richard Chamberlain and Glenda Jackson star. Don't say you weren't warned. **DT111, MU5, ST117**

Music Man, The (1962, C, 151m, G)
A con man charms the people of River City, Iowa, in this all-American musical starring Robert Preston and Shirley Jones, with Buddy Hackett and Ronny Howard. Songs includes "Till There Was You" and "76 Trombones." **DT58, FA9, MU2, MU6,** *Recommended*

Mussolini and I (1985, C, 126m, PG-13)
Focus in this historical drama is on the dictator's son-in-law, Count Galeazzo (Anthony Hopkins). Bob Hoskins plays Il Duce, with Susan Sarandon as his daughter. Originally made for cable TV, where it was shown at 192 minutes. Also known as *Mussolini: The Decline and Fall of Il Duce.* **DR4, ST109, ST111, ST194**

Mutant (1984, C, 100m, R)
A chemical plant's deadly toxic waste finds its way into the town's water supply, turning everyone into a horrible monster. Wings Hauser, Bo Hopkins, and Jennifer Warren star. **HO21**

Mutilator, The (1985, C, 86m, R)
Five teens at a remote beach house are stalked by a mad killer out for revenge in this horror film. **HO12**

Mutiny (1952, C, 77m, NR)
The War of 1812 is the backdrop for this tale of romantic rivals. Mark Stevens, Patric Knowles, and Angela Lansbury star. **AC6, ST131**

Mutiny on the Bounty, The
(1935, B&W, 132m, NR)
The great sea adventure of Captain Bligh (Charles Laughton) and his rebellious first mate Fletcher Christian (Clark Gable). Oscar winner for Best Picture; Laughton should have won, too. **AC12, AC13, AC16, CL3, ST77, ST132, XT1, XT28,** *Essential, Recommended*

Mutiny on the Bounty
(1962, C, 179m, NR)
Remake of the true-life sea story, with Mar-

lon Brando as Christian and Trevor Howard as Captain Bligh. Although Brando's foppish interpretation is amusing, the film feels overproduced at every turn. **AC12, AC16, ST18**

My Beautiful Laundrette
(1985, C, 93m, R)
A young Pakistani émigré living in London borrows money from a wealthy uncle to open his own business. He also begins a secret affair with a white British youth. Perceptive comedy-drama, originally made for British TV, stars Saeed Jaffrey, Roshan Seth, Daniel Day-Lewis, and Gordon Warnecke. Directed by Stephen Frears; written by Hanif Kureishi. **DR3, DR7, DR23, DT48, ST48, XT15,** *Recommended*

My Best Girl (1927, B&W, 78m, NR)
Mary Pickford's last silent film, a comedy of a girl from a poor family working in a department store, in love with the store's owner (Charles "Buddy" Rogers). **CL11**

My Blue Heaven (1990, C, 95m, R)
Hip mobster (Steve Martin) hides out in suburbia under the watchful eye of a nerdy FBI agent (Rick Moranis) in this comedy. With Joan Cusack, Melanie Mayron, and Carol Kane. **CO2, CO3, CO10, CO14, ST150**

My Bodyguard (1980, C, 96m, PG)
When bullies harass a small high school student, he hires a very large friend to protect him. Comedy-drama starring Chris Makepeace, Adam Baldwin, and Matt Dillon, with Martin Mull and Ruth Gordon. Directed by Tony Bill. Quickly got overrated as sleeper; it's good but not that good. **CO4, CO18, ST56, XT23**

My Brilliant Career
(1979, C, 101m, G)
In turn-of-the-century Australia, a young woman finds her headstrong ways are getting her into loads of trouble. Judy Davis stars in this superb drama from director Gillian Armstrong. **DT7, FF5, ST46,** *Recommended*

My Cousin Vinny (1992, C, 119m, R)
Joe Pesci plays a New York lawyer who travels to a small town in the South to plead a case for his relative jailed on a bum murder rap. With Ralph Macchio, Oscar winner Marisa Tomei (marvelous as Vinny's girlfriend), Mitchell Winfield, Fred Gwynne, and Lane Smith. Courtroom scenes are very funny, but movie dawdles too much getting there. **CO20, ST172, XT5**

My Darling Clementine
(1946, B&W, 97m, NR)
Henry Fonda is Wyatt Earp, Victor Mature is Doc Holliday in this classic telling of the

gunfight at the O.K. Corral, directed by John Ford. With Linda Darnell and Walter Brennan. Western mythmaking at its best. **DT44, HF9, HF13, ST71, WE5, WE8,** *Essential, Highly Recommended*

My Dear Secretary (1948, B&W, 94m, NR) Romantic comedy set in the literary world: Laraine Day plays a bestselling author and Kirk Douglas is a struggling writer. With Keenan Wynn. **ST57**

My Demon Lover (1987, C, 86m, PG-13) Romantic comedy about a guy who has a problem around girls: whenever he gets turned on, he's transformed into a hideous beast. Scott Valentine and Michelle Little star. **CO11**

My Dinner With André (1981, C, 110m, NR) A New York playwright (Wallace Shawn) and director (André Gregory) share a meal and talk about their separate life experiences. A cult comedy, with the performers more or less playing themselves and improvising their dialogue. Directed by Louis Malle. Yes, it's different but it's not all that funny. At 70 minutes it coulda been a minor classic. **CO12, CU5, DT82**

My Dream Is Yours (1949, C, 101m, NR) Doris Day musical has her becoming a radio star with the help of Jack Carson. With Lee Bowman, Adolphe Menjou, and in an animated sequence, Bugs Bunny. **MU1, MU4, ST47**

My Fair Lady (1964, C, 170m, G) Hit Broadway musical about a Cockney flower girl learning her manners from stuffy professor. Audrey Hepburn, Rex Harrison, and a great Lerner and Loewe score share the spotlight. Musical version of George Bernard Shaw's play *Pygmalion*. Oscar winner for Best Picture, Actor, and Director (George Cukor). Hard to resist—but as much as we love Hepburn, we can't help but wonder what Julie Andrews would have been like. **DT32, FA9, MU2, MU7, MU17, ST102, WR29, XT1, XT2, XT6,** *Recommended*

My Father's Glory (1991, C, 110m, G) French comedy-drama based on Marcel Pagnol's autobiographical novel of life in Provence in early twentieth century. Philippe Canbere and Nathalie Roussel star. Directed by Yves Robert. Story continues in *My Mother's Castle*. **FF1**

My Favorite Blonde (1942, B&W, 78m, NR) Bob Hope and his trained penguin are enlisted as spies against the Nazis. (Did we really *win* that war?) With Madeleine Carroll, Gale Sondergaard, and George Zucco. **MY17, ST108**

My Favorite Brunette (1947, B&W, 87m, NR) Bob Hope comedy about a photographer involved with mobsters, costarring Dorothy Lamour, Peter Lorre, and Lon Chaney, Jr. Look for Bob's buddy, Bing Crosby. **MY17, ST27, ST40, ST108**

My Favorite Wife (1940, B&W, 88m, NR) A woman thought dead returns from a desert island to find her husband has remarried. Irene Dunne, Cary Grant, and Randolph Scott star in this comedy. **CL10, ST62, ST92, ST197**

My Favorite Year (1982, C, 92m, PG) Young writer for a popular 1950s TV program is assigned to keep watch over a tipsy Hollywood star who's to appear live on the show. Nostalgic comedy starring Peter O'Toole and Mark Linn-Baker, with Jessica Harper, Joseph Bologna, Bill Macy, Selma Diamond, Lainie Kazan, and Adolph Green. O'Toole's wonderful as the Errol Flynn type, but Bologna's hilarious as a knockoff of Sid Caesar. **CO6, CO8, ST169,** *Recommended*

My First Wife (1984, C, 95m, NR) Intense drama from Australian director Paul Cox of a man trying to cope when his wife leaves him after ten years of marriage. **FF5**

My Forbidden Past (1951, B&W, 81m, NR) Ava Gardner plays a Southern belle in this drama of antebellum New Orleans; she's out to avenge herself on a jilting man (Robert Mitchum). With Melvyn Douglas. **ST58, ST79, ST158**

My Friend Irma (1949, B&W, 103m, NR) Comedy of less-than-bright blonde who hooks up with singing soda jerk. Marie Wilson and Diana Lynn star, with Dean Martin and Jerry Lewis in their film debut. **CL15, ST139, ST149**

My Geisha (1962, C, 120m, NR) Actress tries to persuade director husband that she can play the lead in his new film. Shirley MacLaine stars in this comedy, with Yves Montand, Edward G. Robinson, and Robert Cummings. **CO8, ST145, ST186**

My Girl (1991, C, 102m, PG) Coming-of-age story set in 1972, about eleven-year-old girl (Anna Chlumsky) and her widowed dad (Dan Aykroyd). With Jamie Lee Curtis, Macaulay Culkin, and Richard Masur. **CO13, DR9, FA7, ST42**

My Heroes Have Always Been Cowboys
(1991, C, 106m, PG)
Aging rodeo rider returns to home town in Oklahoma to confront family problems. Scott Glenn stars, with Ben Johnson, Kate Capshaw, Balthazar Getty, Tess Harper, Gary Busey, and Mickey Rooney. **DR8, ST189, WE12**

My Left Foot (1989, C, 100m, R)
The life of Irish painter and writer Christy Brown, whose affliction afforded only his foot as a means of painting or typing. Oscar winners Daniel Day-Lewis and Brenda Fricker (as Christy's mother) star, with Ray McAnally and Fiona Shaw. Entire cast is sensational. **DR4, DR23, ST48, XT2, XT5,** *Recommended*

My Life as a Dog (1987, C, 101m, NR)
Swedish boy becomes too much for his ill mother to handle, so he's sent to live with relatives in a village. Gentle comedy about pains and pleasures of growing up in the late 1950s, written and directed by Lasse Hallström. (Available in both subtitled and dubbed versions.) **CO4, FF7**

My Life to Live (1962, B&W, 85m, NR)
Director Jean-Luc Godard's portrait of a Parisian prostitute (Anna Karina) is the subject of this groundbreaking experimental film. **DT50**

My Little Chickadee
(1940, B&W, 83m, NR)
Mae West and W.C. Fields team up to tame the Old West in this classic spoof. It has its moments, just not enough of them. **CL10, ST67, ST226, WE14**

My Little Girl (1986, C, 113m, R)
Drama of a naive girl from a wealthy family who takes a job in an inner city children's detention center. Mary Stuart Masterson stars, with James Earl Jones and Geraldine Page. **DR7, DR9, ST118**

My Little Pony: The Movie
(1986, C, 90m, G)
Animated feature film starring the beautiful Little Ponies, who befriend humans and fight against evil in the world. Among the voices: Danny DeVito, Madeline Kahn, Tony Randall, and Rhea Pearlman. **FA10, ST54**

My Man Adam (1985, C, 84m, R)
Pizza delivery boy lands girl of his dreams, only to wind up involved with a murder mystery. Raphael Sbarge and Page Hannah star, with Veronica Cartwright, Larry B. Scott, and Dave Thomas. **CO14**

My Man Godfrey (1936, B&W, 95m, NR)
Classic comedy of Depression era, with wealthy man turning hobo and becoming butler to a Park Avenue family of eccentrics. William Powell and Carole Lombard star, with Gail Patrick, Eugene Pallette, and Alice Brady. **CL10, CO20, ST140, ST176,** *Essential, Recommended*

My Mother's Castle (1991, C, 98m, PG)
Sequel to *My Father's Glory* continues Marcel Pagnol autobiographical story, with young protagonist in adolescence, his family still making trips to Provence. Philippe Canbere and Nathalie Roussel star. Directed by Yves Robert. **FF1**

My Name Is Nobody (1974, C, 115m, PG)
In this spaghetti Western, Henry Fonda plays an aging gunfighter who's idolized by a young cowpoke (Terence Hill). **ST71, WE2, WE13**

My New Gun (1992, C, 99m, R)
Dark comedy of New Jersey housewife embarking on series of adventures after well-meaning husband gives her a gun for protection. Diane Lane stars, with Stephen Collins, James LeGros, and Tess Harper. Written and directed by Stacy Cochran. **CO12**

My New Partner (1985, C, 104m, R)
A French comedy about a veteran cop (Philippe Noiret) training his young partner in the fine art of selective law enforcement. **FF1**

My Night at Maud's
(1970, B&W, 105m, PG)
An upright, uptight Catholic intellectual is fascinated by an attractive woman. Jean-Louis Trintignant stars in this breakthrough French comedy from director Eric Rohmer. **DT107,** *Essential*

My Old Man (1979, C, 104m, NR)
Ernest Hemingway's story of a racetrack trainer and his loving daughter stars Warren Oates and Kristy McNichol. Originally made for TV. **DR8, ST166, WR13**

My Outlaw Brother
(1951, B&W, 82m, NR)
South-of-the-border Western drama of Texas Ranger (Robert Preston) up against bad guy (Robert Stack). With Mickey Rooney. **ST189, WE9**

My Own Private Idaho (1991, C, 102m, R)
Offbeat tale of two male hustlers (River Phoenix and Keanu Reeves) hooking up in Portland, Oregon. With James Russo and William Richert. Incorporates material from Shakespeare's *Henry IV, Part 1*. Written and directed by Gus Van Sant. Impressive cinematography; dramatic pace lags too often. A must for devotees of the offbeat. **DR3, DR15, WR28**

My Pal Trigger (1946, B&W, 79m, NR)
Roy Rogers and his faithful horse ride the range in search of adventure. **ST188**

My Pet Monster (1986, C, 60m, NR)
A boy under a mysterious spell turns into a monster every time he gets hungry in this family adventure. **FA4**

My Science Project (1985, C, 94m, PG)
A group of high school students cook up something in their lab that could destroy the whole school. A comedy with plenty of special effects action. John Stockwell stars, with Danielle Von Zerneck and Dennis Hopper. **CO11, CO18, ST110**

My Side of the Mountain
(1969, C, 100m, G)
Family drama of a thirteen-year-old Toronto lad who runs away from home to live in a forest for a year. Teddy Eccles stars, with Theodore Bikel. **FA4, FA7**

My Sister Eileen (1955, C, 108m, NR)
Musical remake of 1942 comedy about two Ohio girls moving to Greenwich Village. Betty Garrett, Janet Leigh, and Jack Lemmon star, with Kurt Kaszner, Dick York, and Bob Fosse (who also did the choreography). **DT47, MU14, ST138**

My Stepmother Is an Alien
(1988, C, 108m, PG-13)
A widowed scientist is romanced by a sexy blonde—who is in reality an alien assigned to enlist his help in saving her imperiled planet. Dan Aykroyd and Kim Basinger star. **CO11, CO13**

My Twentieth Century
(1989, B&W, 104m, NR)
Hungarian story of two sisters, born in 1880 with birth of Edison's electric lights, separated shortly thereafter, one becoming a courtesan, the other a bomb-toting revolutionary. Dorothea Segda plays both roles. Disjointed narrative is a problem, but Segda is very impressive. Worth a look if you like movies with some intellectual heft. **FF7, XT27**

My Uncle (1958, C, 116m, NR)
Jacques Tati's Oscar-winning film about the misadventures of M. Hulot (Tati), whose simple life is in contrast to his sister and brother-in-law's gadget-filled home. Also known as *Mon Oncle*. **DT122, XT7**

My Wicked, Wicked Ways
(1985, C, 100m, NR)
The life of film star Errol Flynn through 1943, is dramatized in this TV movie starring Duncan Regehr, with Barbara Hershey, Dar-

ren McGavin, and Lee Purcell. **DR4, DR13, ST69, ST104**

Myra Breckenridge (1970, C, 94m, R)
Cult movie about decadent Hollywood scene, based on Gore Vidal's novel. Raquel Welch stars, with Mae West, Rex Reed, and John Huston. **CU1, CU2, DR19, DT60, ST226**

Mysterians, The (1959, C, 85m, NR)
Japanese science fiction drama about highly evolved aliens trying to take over our planet. **FF4, SF18**

Mysteries (1984, C, 93m, NR)
French drama starring Rutger Hauer as a rich man obsessed with a young woman he meets in a seaside town. With Sylvia Kristel, David Rappaport, and Rita Tushingham. **FF1**

Mysterious Island (1961, C, 101m, NR)
Jules Verne's tale of prison escapees landing on an island inhabited by gigantic animals. Michael Craig, Joan Greenwood, and Michael Callan star. Special effects by Ray Harryhausen. **FA3, FA4, SF10, WR36**

Mysterious Lady (1928, B&W, 96m, NR)
Greta Garbo silent has her playing a Russian spy romancing an Austrian officer (Conrad Nagel). **CL12, ST78**

Mysterious Mr. Wong
(1935, B&W, 56m, NR)
Oriental sleuth (Bela Lugosi) uncovers a deadly mystery in Chinatown involving the Twelve Coins of Confucious. **ST143**

Mystery Date (1991, C, 99m, PG-13)
Shy teen gets help from cool older brother setting up date with lovely girl—only to get into a world of trouble, thanks to two corpses in brother's car. Ethan Hawke stars in this comedy, with Teri Polo, B.D. Wong, and Fisher Stevens. **CO4, CO10**

Mystery of Kasper Hauser, The see *Every Man for Himself and God Against All*

Mystery of Mr. Wong
(1939, B&W, 67m, NR)
Second *Wong* mystery with Boris Karloff as Oriental sleuth on the case of a rare gem and an altered will. **ST119**

Mystery of the Mary Celeste: The Phantom Ship, The (1937, B&W, 63m, NR)
Story, based on fact, of a ship found in midocean with no one aboard. Bela Lugosi stars. **ST143**

Mystery of the Wax Museum
(1933, C, 77m, NR)
Classic horror film about a mad doctor (Lionel Atwill) dipping his victims in wax and putting them on display. One of the

early films shot in Technicolor. Fay Wray co-stars. **HO1**

Mystery Train (1989, C, 110m, R)
Trio of comic stories set in Memphis, in and around same fleabag hotel, relating in some way to Elvis Presley. In *Far From Yokohama,* two Japanese tourists (Masatoshi Nagase, Youki Kudoh) ruminate about their fondness for the King. *A Ghost* pairs a young widow (Nicholette Braschi) on her way back to Italy to bury her husband and a female drifter (Elizabeth Bracco); they share a room for the night and one sees a vision of Elvis. *Lost in Space* follows the trail of three bumbling fugitives (Joe Strummer, Joe Avies, Steve Buscemi) from a liquor store robbery and shooting. With Screamin' Jay Hawkins as the desk clerk, Sy Richardson, Rufus Thomas, and the voice of Tom Waits as a deejay. Directed by Jim Jarmusch. Available in letterboxed edition. A quirky director's most accessible and funniest work to date. **CO2, CO12, CU19, DT62, MU12,** *Recommended*

Mystic Pizza (1988, C, 101m, R)
In a seaside Connecticut town, three young women who work at a pizza restaurant try to figure what to do with the rest of their lives. Julia Roberts, Annabeth Gish, and Lili Taylor star, with Vincent Philip D'Onofrio, Conchata Ferrell, Adam Storke, and William R. Moses. Worth seeing for its up-and-coming stars, but nothing special otherwise. **DR10, DR26**

Nadine (1987, C, 83m, PG)
Austin, Texas, 1954: Vernon and Nadine are about to get divorced, but first there's this matter of some risqué photos, a dead photographer, and a sleazy gangster. Comedy from writer-director Robert Benton, starring Jeff Bridges, Kim Basinger, and Rip Torn. Basinger's delightful and Torn is, as always, pure pleasure. **CO6, DT9, ST19, ST216,** *Recommended*

Naked and the Dead, The
(1958, C, 131m, NR)
From Norman Mailer's first novel, a drama of men at war—often with each other—in the South Pacific. Aldo Ray and Cliff Robertson star. Directed by Raoul Walsh. **AC1, DR19, DT131**

Naked City, The (1948, B&W, 96m, NR)
Classic *film noir* tale of New York City police manhunt for killer of young woman. Barry Fitzgerald and Howard Duff star, with Dorothy Hart, Don Taylor, and Ted De Corsia. Excellent use of real locations, with Oscar-winning cinematography by William Daniels. **AC9, MY1, XT9,** *Essential*

Naked Civil Servant, The
(1980, C, 80m, NR)
John Hurt portrays Quentin Crisp, a British advocate of rights for homosexuals in the 1930s and 1940s, in this drama. **DR4**

Naked Edge, The (1961, B&W, 99m, NR)
Thriller set in London of American man suspected by his wife of murder, even though his testimony puts a suspect behind bars. Gary Cooper (his last film) and Deborah Kerr star. **MY3, MY11, ST37, ST125**

Naked Face, The (1985, C, 103m, R)
A psychiatrist, accused of murdering his own patient, turns detective to find the real killer. Roger Moore, Rod Steiger, and Elliott Gould star. **MY11**

Naked Gun, The (1988, C, 85m, R)
Spoof of cop movies, with Leslie Nielsen a poker-faced detective investigating a plot to assassinate Queen Elizabeth at an L.A. Dodgers baseball game. With O.J. Simpson, Priscilla Presley, George Kennedy, Ricardo Montalban, and Reggie Jackson. Very silly, very funny. **CO7, CO10, XT26,** *Recommended*

Naked Gun 2½: The Smell of Fear, The
(1991, C, 85m, PG-13)
Leslie Nielsen is back as Frank Drebin, the American Inspector Clouseau. Here he's uncovering a plot by energy-producing conglomerates to cover up a scientist's revolutionary discovery. With Priscilla Presley, George Kennedy, O.J. Simpson, Robert Goulet, and Richard Griffiths. **CO7, CO10**

Naked in the Sun (1957, C, 79m, NR)
Seminole Indians battle slave traders in this Western tale, based on a true story. James Craig and Lita Milan star. **WE7**

Naked Jungle, The (1954, C, 95m, NR)
Charlton Heston is a South American plantation owner whose property and life are threatened by a mammoth army of ravenous red ants. **AC12, AC24**

Naked Kiss, The
(1964, B&W, 93m, NR)
Writer-director Sam Fuller's devastating look at small-town hypocrisy, with an ex-prostitute starting a new life, only to be caught up in a first-class scandal when she murders her fiancé. Constance Towers stars, with Anthony Eisley, Virginia Grey, and Michael Dante. Available in letterboxed edition. **CU19, DR26, DT49,** *Recommended*

Naked Lunch (1991, C, 115m, R)
Writer-director David Cronenberg's loose adaptation of the William Burroughs novel of drug-induced hallucinations and free-form

associations. Peter Weller stars as William Lee, Burroughs' literary alter ego; Judy Davis plays two roles. With Ian Holm, Julian Sands, and Roy Scheider. **CU3, DR19, DT31, ST46, XT27**

Naked Night, The see *Sawdust and Tinsel*

Naked Prey, The (1966, C, 94m, NR) Cornel Wilde directed and stars in this adventure story of a Britisher pursued by murderous African tribesmen. **AC12, AC24, DR27,** *Recommended*

Naked Spur, The (1953, C, 91m, NR) Bounty hunter James Stewart and fugitive Robert Ryan play a cat-and-mouse game in this classic Western. Directed by Anthony Mann. **DT85, ST193, ST207**

Naked Truth, The (1957, B&W, 92m, NR) British comedy about an assortment of people united in their desire to do away with the sleazy editor of a pornographic magazine. Terry-Thomas and Peter Sellers star. Also known as *Your Past Is Showing*. **CO17, ST198**

Name of the Rose, The (1986, C, 130m, R) Sean Connery stars as a monk in fourteenth-century Italy who solves a bizarre series of murders in a monastery. Based on Umberto Eco's bestselling novel. With F. Murray Abraham and Christian Slater. Fairly entertaining while you watch it but doesn't linger much afterwards. **DR19, MY11, MY16, ST36, ST200**

Nana (1955, C, 118m, NR) French-language adaptation of Emile Zola's novel of an actress turned prostitute in 1880s Paris. Charles Boyer and Martine Carol star. **FF1, ST16**

Nancy Goes to Rio (1950, C, 99m, NR) MGM musical of mother and daughter competing for the same part—and man. Ann Sothern and Jane Powell star, with Barry Sullivan, Carmen Miranda, and Hans Conried. **MU1, MU4**

Nanook of the North (1922, B&W, 55m, NR) Pioneering documentary, directed by Robert Flaherty, about the daily lives of an Eskimo family. **CU16,** *Essential, Recommended*

Napoleon (1927, B&W/C, 235m, G) Grand, epic telling of the life of France's great emperor, played as an adult by Albert Dieudonné. This silent film, directed by Abel Gance, features tinted scenes and a three-screen Polyvision sequence that was far ahead of its time. **CL1, CL12, FF1, HF18,** *Essential, Highly Recommended*

Napoleon (1955, C, 115m, NR) Orson Welles and Erich Von Stroheim head the cast of this French-made drama about the famed emperor's life. Raymond Pellegrin stars in the title role. **DT129, DT134, HF18**

Napoleon and Samantha (1972, C, 92m, G) A pair of young children run off with a pet lion in this Disney drama. Johnny Whitaker, Jodie Foster, and Michael Douglas star. **FA1, ST59, ST75**

Narrow Margin (1990, C, 97m, R) Remake of *film noir* classic (minus "The" in title), with cop and gangster's widow on train speeding through Canadian Rockies. Gene Hackman and Anne Archer star. **CU18, MY2, MY3, ST96, XT19**

Narrow Margin, The (1952, B&W, 70m, NR) *Film noir* featuring a cop and gangster's widow on a train dodging hit men. Charles McGraw and Marie Windsor star. Directed by Richard Fleischer. Hard-boiled, expertly played. **MY1, MY3, XT19,** *Recommended*

Nashville (1975, C, 159m, R) Multi-character study of the music scene in Nashville and its connections to a political candidate. Henry Gibson, Karen Black, Ronee Blakley, Keith Carradine, Lily Tomlin, Michael Murphy, and Ned Beatty star, with Gwen Welles, Christina Raines, Jeff Goldblum, and Elliott Gould and Julie Christie as themselves. Robert Altman directed. Widescreen will be lost on video. To some, Altman's masterpiece; to me, the first sign that the director's career was in trouble: an indulgent, condescending mess. **CU20, DR12, DT2, MU6, ST30, ST90, ST215,** *Essential*

Nasty Girl, The (1990, C/B&W, 95m, PG-13) German story of adolescent girl (Lena Stolze) scandalizing her small town by writing an essay on what happened there during World War II. Directed by Michael Verhoeven. **FF3**

Nasty Habits (1977, C, 96m, PG) Dark comedy about political machinations inside a convent that mirror the Watergate affair. Glenda Jackson, Geraldine Page, Melina Mercouri, and Sandy Dennis star, with Rip Torn, Edith Evans, Jerry Stiller, and Eli Wallach. Despite that cast, pretty strained going. **CO12, ST117, ST216**

Nate and Hayes (1983, C, 100m, PG) Swashbuckling story of a pirate pair who roam the Caribbean in search of treasure and lovely women. Tommy Lee Jones and Michael O'Keefe star, with Jenny Seagrove. Written by John Hughes. **AC15, DT59**

National Lampoon's Animal House
(1978, C, 109m, R)
The groundbreaking comedy about life in the Delta House, the fraternity where disorder always reigns. John Belushi stars, with Tim Matheson, Peter Riegert, Thomas Hulce, Karen Allen, Donald Sutherland, John Vernon, Stephen Furst, Kevin Bacon, and Bruce McGill. Directed by John Landis. Its success is still being felt, mostly in negative ways, but . . . anyone who went to a college with fraternities during the '60s will recognize a lot of truth in this film. **CO4, CO13, CO18,** *Recommended*

National Lampoon's Christmas Vacation (1989, C, 97m, PG-13)
Third outing (following the two *Vacation* films) of the comic misadventures of the Griswold clan, headed by Chevy Chase and Beverly D'Angelo, as they entertain for the holidays. With Randy Quaid and Diane Ladd. Produced and written by John Hughes. **CO5, CO13, DT59, FA13**

National Lampoon's Class Reunion
(1982, C, 84m, R)
A psycho killer stalks a high school reunion party in this comedy written by John Hughes. Gerrit Graham stars. **CO18, DT59**

National Lampoon's European Vacation (1985, C, 94m, PG-13)
The wacky family from *National Lampoon's Vacation* invades the continent for more misadventures in tourism. Chevy Chase, Beverly D'Angelo, and Eric Idle star. Cowritten by John Hughes. **CO5, CO13, CO15, DT59, XT18**

National Lampoon's Loaded Weapon 1
(1993, C, 83m, PG-13)
Spoof of cops 'n' robbers films stars Emilio Estevez and Samuel L. Jackson as salt 'n' pepper team. With Jon Lovitz, Tim Curry, Kathy Ireland, Frank McRae, William Shatner, Whoopi Goldberg, F. Murray Abraham, and bit roles by Bruce Willis, Charlie Sheen, many others. **CO7, CO10, ST89, ST229, XT8**

National Lampoon's Vacation
(1983, C, 98m, R)
Chevy Chase and family take off for the summer and travel every back road in America on their way to mythical Wally World. Beverly D'Angelo costars, with Christie Brinkley, John Candy, Eddie Bracken, Imogene Coca, Randy Quaid, and Eugene Levy. Written by John Hughes; directed by Harold Ramis. It has its moments (Quaid and

Bracken are very funny), but a little Chevy goes a long way. **CO5, CO13, CO14, DT59, XT18**

National Velvet (1944, C, 125m, G)
Classic story of a girl and the horse she must ride in the Grand National—even if it means disguising herself as a boy. Elizabeth Taylor and Mickey Rooney star, with Oscar winner Anne Revere and Angela Lansbury. **FA5, ST131, ST189, ST212, XT5**

Native Son (1986, C, 112m, PG)
In 1940, a young black chauffeur accidentally murders the daughter of his employer and becomes the center of a highly publicized trial. Victor Love stars, with Elizabeth McGovern, Oprah Winfrey, and Matt Dillon. Adapted from Richard Wright's novel. **DR14, DR19, ST56**

Nativity, The (1978, C, 100m, NR)
Story of the birth of Christ, starring Madeleine Stowe and John Shea. Originally made for TV. **CL13, HF17, ST209**

Natural, The (1984, C, 134m, PG)
Robert Redford is baseball star Roy Hobbs, the man with a mysterious past. With Glenn Close, Robert Duvall, Barbara Hershey, Kim Basinger, Richard Farnsworth, Wilford Brimley, Darren McGavin, and Joe Don Baker. Adapted from the novel by Bernard Malamud. Directed by Barry Levinson; cinematography by Caleb Deschanel and music by Randy Newman. Redford would have been right ten years earlier. Overproduced and, for fans of the book, a distressingly different ending. **DR2, DR19, DR22, DT75, ST33, ST63, ST104, ST181**

Naughty Marietta (1935, B&W, 106m, NR)
Nelson Eddy and Jeanette MacDonald debuted together in this operetta about a runaway princess and dashing Indian scout. Songs include "Ah, Sweet Mystery of Life." **CL15**

Naughty Nineties, The
(1945, B&W, 76m, NR)
Abbott and Costello play a couple of riverboat gamblers in this comedy which includes their unforgettable "Who's on First?" routine. **ST1**

Navajo Joe (1966, C, 89m, NR)
Burt Reynolds plays an Indian who survives a massacre and swears revenge. **ST183, WE5, WE7**

Navigator, The (1924, B&W, 63m, NR)
Sublime Buster Keaton comedy about a millionaire and his ditsy girlfriend (Kathryn McGuire) stranded on an abandoned ocean liner. UNAVAILABLE ON VIDEO. **XT29**

Navy SEALS (1990, C, 113m, R)
Elite team of naval commandos are out to rescue hostages from Beirut. Charlie Sheen, Michael Biehn, and Joanne Whalley-Kilmer star. **AC20**

Nazarin (1961, B&W, 92m, NR)
From director Luis Buñuel, the story of a Mexican priest and his unsuccessful attempts to bring the word of God to the peasants. **DT21**

Near Dark (1987, C, 95m, R)
Teen-age boy in Oklahoma (Adrian Pasdar) is kidnapped by a family of vampires who roam the roads of the Midwest by night. With Jenny Wright, Lance Henriksen, Bill Paxton, and Jenette Goldstein. Atmospheric, stylishly made horror story with modern twists, directed by Kathryn Bigelow. Music by Tangerine Dream. **HO5, HO14, XT18,** *Recommended*

Necessary Roughness (1991, C, 108m, PG-13)
Football comedy set at fictitious Texas State University, rebuilding after being put on NCAA probation. Scott Bakula stars as their thirty-four-year-old quarterback, with Hector Elizondo, Robert Loggia, Harley Jane Kozak, Larry Miller, Sinbad, Fred Dalton Thompson, and Kathy Ireland. **CO18, CO19**

Necromancy (1972, C, 83m, PG)
Orson Welles play a cult leader who tries to lure a lovely young woman (Pamela Franklin) into his power. With Michael Ontkean and Lee Purcell. Also known as *The Witching.* **DT134, HO11**

Ned Kelly (1970, C, 100m, PG)
Cult Western stars Mick Jagger as real-life Irish outlaw who terrorized Australian outback and British army in particular. With Clarissa Kaye and Mark McManus. Directed by Tony Richardson. Songs written by Shel Silverstein, sung by Waylon Jennings; Jagger does warble traditional ballad "The Wild Colonial Boy." **MU12, WE3, WE15**

Negatives (1968, C, 90m, R)
Odd British drama of couple who enjoy masquerading as historical characters, particularly famed murderer Dr. Crippen and his wife. Peter McEnery, Diane Cilento, Glenda Jackson, and Maurice Denham star. Directed by Peter Medak. **DR23, ST117**

Neighbors (1981, C, 94m, R)
Placid suburban man is bedeviled by rude and lewd new next-door neighbors—but is he imagining it all? John Belushi and Dan Aykroyd star in this offbeat comedy, with Cathy Moriarty and Kathryn Walker. Based on Thomas Berger's novel. Belushi's last film only occasionally captures some of the book's tricky point of view, will seem ridiculous to those who haven't read it. **CO12, CO13, DR19, MY19**

Nelson Mandela, 70th Birthday Tribute (1988, C, 120m, NR)
Highlights from a benefit concert held at London's Wembley Stadium to honor the then-jailed South African activist. Among the performers: George Michael, The Eurythmics, Al Green, Tracy Chapman, Peter Gabriel, Whitney Houston, Stevie Wonder, Dire Straits, and Eric Clapton. With Whoopi Goldberg. **MU10, ST89**

Neptune's Daughter (1949, C, 93m, NR)
Esther Williams plays a bathing suit designer in this aquatic MGM musical costaring Red Skelton, Betty Garrett, and Mel Blanc. **MU1**

Nest, The (1988, C, 88m, R)
A scientific experiment gone wrong results in a breed of giant cockroaches. Robert Lansing, Lisa Langlois, and a lot of bugs star. **HO16**

Network (1976, C, 121m, R)
Aggressive programmer (Faye Dunaway) at a major TV network clashes with veteran producer (William Holden) and unstable anchorman (Peter Finch, in his last film). With Beatrice Straight, Robert Duvall, and Ned Beatty. Directed by Sidney Lumet; Paddy Chayefsky's script brilliantly anticipates many ills of current TV journalism. Finch, Dunaway, and Straight won Oscars; the film should have won, too. **DR7, DR12, DR61, DR63, DT78, ST106, XT2, XT3, XT5, XT22, XT28,** *Essential, Highly Recommended*

Nevada City (1941, B&W, 54m, NR)
Roy Rogers Western has him up against a crooked financier. **ST188**

Nevada Smith (1966, C, 135m, NR)
Steve McQueen is an obsessed cowboy out to avenge the murders of his parents. With Karl Malden, Brian Keith, Arthur Kennedy, Raf Vallone, Suzanne Pleshette, and Pat Hingle. **ST146, WE3, WE5**

Nevadan, The (1950, C, 81m, NR)
Randolph Scott Western about lawman on the trail of outlaws. With Dorothy Malone, Forrest Tucker, George Macready, and Jock Mahoney. **ST197**

Never a Dull Moment (1950, B&W, 89m, NR)
Irene Dunne's a New York songwriter who gives up the bright lights of Broadway for the moonlit prairies when she marries a Wyoming rancher (Fred MacMurray). With Wil-

liam Demarest, Andy Devine, Gigi Perreau, and Natalie Wood. **CO20, ST62**

Never a Dull Moment
(1968, C, 100m, G)
A TV star accidentally becomes involved with gangsters. Disney comedy starring Dick Van Dyke and Edward G. Robinson. **FA1, ST186**

Never Cry Wolf (1983, C, 105m, PG)
Based on a true story, this family adventure drama follows naturalist Farley Mowat as he braves Arctic conditions to study wolves up close. Charles Martin Smith stars. Directed by Carroll Ballard. Exciting story that will thrill kids and adults, too. **AC12, AC24, FA4,** *Recommended*

Never Give a Sucker an Even Break
(1941, B&W, 71m, NR)
W.C. Fields's last feature film appearance is a zany free-for-all of vintage Fields bits. Margaret Dumont costars. **ST67**

Never Let Go (1963, B&W, 90m, NR)
Rare dramatic outing for Peter Sellers, as he plays a gangster involved with car thefts. **ST198**

Never Love a Stranger
(1958, B&W, 91m, NR)
A young hood finds himself caught between his boyhood friends on the right side of the law and his colleagues in the Mob. John Drew Barrymore stars; Steve McQueen has a small supporting role. **ST146**

Never on Sunday (1960, B&W, 91m, NR)
An American visiting Greece tries to "educate" a carefree prostitute, who turns the tables on him. Melina Mercouri and husband Jules Dassin star; Dassin directed. **CO1**

Never Say Never Again
(1983, C, 134m, PG)
Sean Connery's return as an older but no less crafty James Bond is a remake of *Thunderball*. Klaus Maria Brandauer is the villain, Kim Basinger and Barbara Carrera are the ladies. Sean's not showing his age, but the series is. **CU18, HF2, ST36**

Never So Few (1959, C, 124m, NR)
Frank Sinatra leads a guerrilla band against the Japanese in World War II Burma. Steve McQueen and Charles Bronson head the supporting cast. **AC1, ST20, ST146, ST199**

Never Steal Anything Small
(1959, C, 94m, NR)
James Cagney plays a union boss in this offbeat musical comedy-drama. With Shirley Jones, Roger Smith, Cara Williams, and Nehemiah Persoff. **MU16, ST24**

Never Wave at a WAC
(1952, B&W, 87m, NR)
Service comedy starring Rosalind Russell as a socialite who joins the WACs. With Marie Wilson and Paul Douglas. **CO21, ST192**

NeverEnding Story, The
(1984, C, 92m, PG)
A young boy imagines that the fantasy story he is reading comes true—and he becomes part of a fabulous adventure. Noah Hathaway and Barrett Oliver star. Produced in Germany; dialogue in English. Directed by Wolfgang Peterson. **FA8, FF3, SF13**

NeverEnding Story II: The Next Chapter, The (1990, C, 92m, PG)
Continuation of tale of boy with large imagination, starring Jonathan Brandis. This time, his fantasy counterpart is off to Fantasia in search of a princess. Directed by Wolfgang Peterson. **FA8**

New Adventures of Pippi Longstocking, The (1988, C, 100m, G)
The children's book heroine embarks on more adventures with her friends Tommy and Annika. Tami Erin stars, with Eileen Brennan, Dennis Dugan, and Dick Van Patten. See also: *Pippi Longstocking* series. **FA4**

New Centurions, The (1972, C, 103m, R)
Joseph Wambaugh story of rookie cops in Los Angeles, starring George C. Scott as the impatient veteran, with Stacy Keach, Jane Alexander, Rosalind Cash, Scott Wilson, Erik Estrada, and James B. Sikking. **AC9, ST196**

New Jack City (1991, C, 97m, R)
Highly charged melodrama of crack epidemic ruining entire neighborhoods in New York, thanks to drug lord whose operations are housed in a huge tenement building. Wesley Snipes stars, with Ice-T, Judd Nelson, and Mario Van Peebles as the cops who try to bring him down. With Chris Rock. Van Peebles directed. Stirring but in some of the wrong ways—Snipes's character is bad but magnetic, too. Still, a fascinating document of the 1990s. **AC9, DR14, DR15, MU12, ST201, XT9,** *Recommended*

New Kids, The (1985, C, 90m, R)
A brother and sister off to live with their uncle suddenly find themselves confronted by a neighborhood gang. Shannon Presby, Lori Loughlin, and Eric Stoltz star in this drama. **DR9, ST203**

New Kind of Love, A (1963, C, 110m, NR)
Romantic comedy, set in Paris, starring Paul Newman and Joanne Woodward as a journalist and a fashion buyer. With Thelma Ritter,

Eva Gabor, and Maurice Chevalier. **ST162, ST234**

New Leaf, A (1971, C, 102m, PG)
Elaine May directed and stars in this comedy about a frumpy scientist who's wooed strictly for her money by an unscrupulous playboy (Walter Matthau). Matthau's cast against type but he's still good, as is May. It's just a bit thin but not to be missed by her fans. **CO12, DT86, ST155,** *Recommended*

New Life, A (1988, C, 104m, PG-13)
The comic mishaps of a New York couple who divorce and encounter the world of singles and "dating." Alan Alda and Ann-Margret star, with Hal Linden, Veronica Hamel, and John Shea. Alda wrote and directed. **CO1, CO2**

New Moon (1940, B&W, 105m, NR)
Jeanette MacDonald-Nelson Eddy musical set in Louisiana. Songs include "Softly as in a Morning Sunrise" and "Stout-Hearted Men." **CL15**

New York, New York (1977, C, 163m, R)
Drama set at the end of the Big Band era, centering on the stormy romance between a hot-tempered musician (Robert De Niro) and a rising singer (Liza Minnelli). With Lionel Stander, Mary Kay Place, Georgie Auld, Diahnne Abbott, George Memmoli, Barry Primus, and Dick Miller. Martin Scorsese directed. The video version contains the "Happy Endings" production number, which did not appear in the original release of the film. Also available in a letterboxed edition. Lavishly produced but so determinedly downbeat it's hard to tell what Scorsese was up to. **CU10, CU19, DR12, DT114, MU4, MU6, ST51**

New York Stories (1989, C, 130m, PG)
A trio of tales set in contemporary Manhattan. In *Life Lessons*, directed by Martin Scorsese, a temperamental artist (Nick Nolte) tries to prevent his protégé-lover (Rosanna Arquette) from leaving him. Francis Ford Coppola's *Life Without Zoe* focuses on the adventures of a girl who lives in a luxurious hotel while her parents are away tending to their separate careers. *Oedipus Wrecks* features director-star Woody Allen as a Jewish attorney whose dominating mother (Mae Questel) ruins his relationship with a Gentile woman (Mia Farrow). Watch for Peter Gabriel, Deborah Harry and Ed Koch in small roles. Scorsese's story is a trifle but brilliantly assembled; Coppola's is an empty soufflé; Allen's is a gem, harkening back to the best of his comic work. **CO2, DR1, DR9, DR15,**

DT2, DT29, DT114, ST65, ST164, XT9, XT30, *Recommended*

Newsfront (1978, C, 110m, PG)
Behind-the-scenes drama of the people who made newsreels in Australia during the 1940s and 1950s. **FF5,** *Recommended*

Newsies (1992, C, 125m, PG)
Musical centering on 1899 strike by New York newspaper boys against Joseph Pulitzer and William Randolph Hearst's papers. Christian Bale stars, with Bill Pullman, Robert Duvall (as Pulitzer), Ann-Margret, Michael Lerner, and Kevin Tighe. **FA9, MU6, ST63**

Next of Kin (1989, C, 108m, R)
Patrick Swayze plays a Chicago cop whose hometown clan from Kentucky helps him get revenge on the gangsters who killed his brother. **AC19**

Next Man, The (1976, C, 108m, R)
Sean Connery stars in a political thriller about a Saudi Arabian diplomat romantically involved with a hit woman (Cornelia Sharpe). Also known as *Double Hit* and *The Arab Conspiracy*. **MY5, MY6, ST36**

Next Voice You Hear, The
(1950, B&W, 83m, NR)
Unusual social comment drama has group of people hearing the voice of God through their radios. James Whitmore, Nancy Davis (Reagan), and Jeff Corey star. Directed by William Wellman. **CL8, DT135**

Next Year, If All Goes Well
(1981, C, 95m, R)
French comedy of a couple (Isabelle Adjani and Thierry Lhermitte) who can't decide if they're really in love, even after conceiving a child. **FF1**

Niagara (1953, C, 89m, NR)
Marilyn Monroe stars in this thriller about a woman planning to murder her new husband on their honeymoon. With Joseph Cotten and Jean Peters. Directed by Henry Hathaway. **MY1, MY4, ST159**

Nice Dreams (1981, C, 89m, R)
Cheech and Chong, those spaced-out L.A. hipsters, use their ice cream truck as a front for selling marijuana. With Stacy Keach and Timothy Leary. **ST28**

Nicholas and Alexandra
(1971, C, 183m, PG)
Epic tale of the final days of Czar Nicholas of Russia and his wife, with court intrigue aplenty. Michael Jayston and Janet Suzman star, with Tom Baker, Harry Andrews, Jack Hawkins, Laurence Olivier, and Michael Red-

grave. Directed by Franklin Schaffner. **DR5, ST168**

Nicholas Nickleby (1947, B&W, 108m, NR) The Charles Dickens tale of an impoverished family's relationship with their evil uncle. Derek Bond and Cedric Harwicke star, with Alfred Drayton, Bernard Miles, and Sally Ann Howes. **DR23, WR5**

Night Ambush see *Ill Met by Moonlight*

Night and Day (1946, C, 128m, NR) Cary Grant plays composer Cole Porter in this dramatic biography, with Eve Arden and Alexis Smith. Many Porter tunes on the soundtrack. **MU5, ST92**

Night and Fog (1955, B&W, 34m, NR) Classic documentary about the horrors of the Nazi death camps, directed by Alain Resnais. **CU16,** *Essential, Recommended*

Night and the City (1950, B&W, 101m, NR) *Film noir* classic of hustling American (Richard Widmark) out to promote boxing matches in London underworld. With Gene Tierney, Googie Withers, Hugh Marlow, Francis L. Sullivan, Herbert Lom, and Mike Mazurki. Directed by Jules Dassin. **DR15, DR27, MY1, ST214, XT15**

Night and the City (1992, C, 98m, R) Remake of the 1950 drama stars Robert De Niro as a nervy New York lawyer who gets in over his head when he turns sports promoter. With Jessica Lange, Cliff Gorman, Alan King, Jack Warden, Eli Wallach, and Barry Primus. Screenplay by Richard Price, directed by Irwin Winkler. **DR15, MY2, ST51, ST130**

Night at the Opera, A (1935, B&W, 92m, NR) The Marx Brothers journey to America, demolish a production of *Il Travatore*. Margaret Dumont takes a dim view of it all. Stateroom scene an all-time crowd pleaser. Kitty Carlisle and Allan Jones offer a few songs. **ST152,** *Essential, Recommended*

Night Before, The (1988, C, 85m, PG-13) Comedy of errors, set during a teen-age boy's prom night, starring Keanu Reeves, and Lori Loughlin, with Trinidad Silva. Songs by George Clinton, who appears in a nightclub scene. Okay for films of this type. **CO4**

Night Call Nurses (1972, C, 85m, R) Sexy comedy about wild goings-on at a hospital. Produced by Roger Corman; directed by Jonathan Kaplan. **CU14**

Night Crossing (1981, C, 106m, PG) True-life drama about two families escaping from East Berlin in a hot-air balloon. John Hurt, Jane Alexander, and Glynnis O'Connor star in this Disney production. **FA1**

Night Flight From Moscow (1973, C, 113m, PG) A Russian diplomat attempts to defect to the West. Spy thriller starring Yul Brynner, Henry Fonda, and Dirk Bogarde. **MY6, ST14, ST71**

Night Full of Rain, A (1978, C, 104m, R) Italian director Lina Wertmuller's first English-language film focuses on a turbulent affair between a journalist (Giancarlo Gianini) and feminist (Candice Bergen). Full title: *The End of the World in Our Usual Bed in a Night Full of Rain.* **DR1, DT137**

Night Gallery (1969, C, 98m, NR) Trio of creepy stories, narrated by Rod Serling, each originating with a separate painting. Roddy McDowall, Ossie Davis, and Joan Crawford are among the stars. Steven Spielberg directed the segment with Crawford. Originally made for TV. **DT118, HO23, ST39**

Night Has Eyes, The (1942, B&W, 79m, NR) British mystery involving a schoolteacher (Joyce Howard) and a friend who turn up missing on the moors. James Mason costars. Also known as *Terror House.* **MY5, ST153**

Night in Casablanca, A (1946, B&W, 85m, NR) The Marx Brothers turn a Moroccan hotel upside-down in search of Nazi spies. **ST152**

Night in June, A see *June Night*

Night in the Life of Jimmy Reardon, A (1988, C, 90m, R) The comic misadventures of a sexually precocious young man, set in 1962 suburban Chicago. River Phoenix stars, with Ann Magnuson, Meredith Salenger, and Ione Skye. **CO4**

Night Is My Future (1947, B&W, 87m, NR) Early film from director Ingmar Bergman about a blind veteran who is taken in by a caring housekeeper. Mai Zetterling stars. **DT11**

'night, Mother (1986, C, 97m, PG-13) A drama about a woman's determination to end her life and her mother's attempts to talk her out of suicide. Sissy Spacek and Anne Bancroft star in this screen version of Marsha Norman's play. **DR8, DR20, ST202**

Night Moves (1975, C, 95m, R) Detective, hired to find runaway rich girl, uncovers bizarre mystery plot in the Florida Keys. Cleverly plotted thriller, starring Gene

Hackman, with Jennifer Warren, Susan Clark, Melanie Griffith, Edward Binns, and James Woods. Directed by Arthur Penn; written by Alan Sharp. One of Hackman's best performances. **DT96, MY2, MY10, ST93, ST96, ST233,** *Highly Recommended*

Night My Number Came Up, The
(1955, B&W, 94m, NR)
Intriguing tale of group of people on flight in the Orient through dangerous weather; a crash would fulfill a vivid dream one of the passengers has had. Michael Redgrave stars, with Alexander Knox, Sheila Sim, Denholm Elliott, and Michael Hordern. Nifty British drama with the feel of a good "Twilight Zone" episode. **DR23,** *Recommended*

Night Nurse (1931, B&W, 72m, NR)
Barbara Stanwyck plays a nurse who's growing suspicious of the intrigue building in the private home where she works. With Ben Lyon, Joan Blondell, and Clark Gable. Directed by William Wellman. Spicy stuff for its time, with plenty of underwear showing. Worth watching for Stanwyck devotees. **DT135, ST77, ST206**

Night of the Big Heat see *Island of the Burning Doomed*

Night of the Bloody Apes
(1968, C, 82m, NR)
Mexican mishmash of horror and wrestling movie. A mad doctor transplants the heart of an ape into his son, who promptly goes bananas. Cult favorite of "bad" movie connoisseurs. **CU11**

Night of the Comet (1984, C, 94m, PG-13)
The passing of a strange comet over the skies of Los Angeles leaves two air-head sisters as survivors to battle zombie victims. Tongue-in-cheek science fiction, starring Catherine Mary Stewart and Kelli Maroney. **SF12, SF21, XT10,** *Recommended*

Night of the Creeps (1986, C, 89m, NR)
An alien organism is released through a human carrier, creating monsters and havoc. **HO21**

Night of the Generals, The
(1967, C, 148m, NR)
Someone is murdering the generals of the Third Reich in this mystery/war drama. Peter O'Toole, Omar Sharif, and Tom Courtenay star. **MY16, ST169**

Night of the Ghouls see *Revenge of the Dead*

Night of the Hunter, The
(1955, B&W, 93m, NR)
Moody thriller about two children fleeing

from murderous preacher (Robert Mitchum). With Shelley Winters, Lillian Gish, Peter Graves, Billy Chapin, and Sally Jane Bruce. The only film directed by actor Charles Laughton; adapted by James Agee from the novel by Davis Grubb. Cinematography by Stanley Cortez. A cult favorite. Mitchum is chilling. **CU15, MY1, ST87, ST132, ST158, ST232,** *Recommended*

Night of the Iguana, The
(1964, B&W, 118m, NR)
Tennessee Williams drama about a minister in Mexico and his worldly temptations. Richard Burton stars, with Ava Gardner, Deborah Kerr, and Sue Lyon as his temptations. John Huston directed. Heavy going, but Burton sees it through the rough spots. **DT60, ST22, ST79, ST125, WR38**

Night of the Living Dead
(1968, B&W, 96m, NR)
Low-budget horror classic about ghouls returning from the grave to feed on the living. George Romero directed this midnight movie staple. It is *very* effective in its own unpolished way. **CU1, CU4, CU7, HO6, HO18, DT108,** *Essential, Highly Recommended*

Night of the Living Dead
(1990, C, 89m, R)
Tom Savini, George Romero's makeup man on many of his horror films, directed this remake of the zombie classic, written by Romero. Tony Todd, Patricia Tallman, and Tom Towles star. **CU7, CU18, HO6, HO18**

Night of the Shooting Stars, The
(1982, C, 106m, R)
During the final days of World War II, the residents of an Italian village try to survive the Nazi retreat. Directed by Paolo and Vittorio Taviani. Intense, moving, deeply felt. **FF2,** *Recommended*

Night on Earth (1991, C, 130m, R)
Comedy-drama from cult director Jim Jarmusch hopscotches the world for five stories in five cities (New York, Helsinki, Los Angeles, Rome, and Paris) about variety of night life as seen through the eyes of cab drivers. Among the stars: Winona Ryer, Gena Rowlands, Giancarlo Esposito, Roberto Benigni, Armin Mueller-Stahl, and Beatrice Dalle. Songs by Tom Waits. Available in letterboxed edition. Hit and miss; impressive cinematography. **CO2, CU19, DR15, DT62, XT9, XT10, XT16, XT17**

Night Porter, The (1974, C, 115m, R)
A former concentration camp official and the prisoner he once abused meet years after the war and resume a bizarre sexual relationship.

Dirk Bogarde and Charlotte Rampling star in this drama. **CU6, ST14**

Night Shift (1982, C, 105m, R)
A nerd and a fast-talking hustler who work nights together at the New York City morgue decide to go into the call girl business. Sweet comedy starring Henry Winkler, Michael Keaton (a star-making performance), and Shelley Long. Directed by Ron Howard. **CO1, CO2, DT58, ST122, XT26,** *Recommended*

Night Stage to Galveston
(1952, B&W, 61m, NR)
Gene Autry and pal Pat Buttram are working to uncover corruption in the ranks of the Texas Rangers. With Clayton Moore (TV's Lone Ranger). **ST5**

Night They Raided Minsky's, The
(1968, C, 99m, PG)
Comedy set in burlesque era in New York, with Quaker girl (Britt Ekland) meeting baggy-pants comic (Jason Robards). Narrated by Rudy Vallee. **CO6, ST185**

Night Tide (1961, B&W, 84m, NR)
Atmospheric thriller about a lonely sailor (Dennis Hopper) obsessed with a sideshow mermaid (Linda Lawson) who may be the real thing. Shot in Venice, California; directed by Curtis Harrington. **CU4, ST110**

Night Time in Nevada (1948, C, 67m, NR)
A western town is caught in the grip of a pair of cattle thievin', embezzlin' varmints, and it's Roy Rogers to the rescue. With Andy Devine and Bob Nolan. **ST188**

Night to Remember, A
(1943, B&W, 91m, NR)
Comic mystery about a suspense novelist (Brian Aherne) and his wife (Loretta Young) solving a real murder case. **MY11, MY17**

Night to Remember, A
(1958, B&W, 123m, NR)
Dramatic recreation of the infamous sinking of the *Titanic*. Kenneth More and David McCallum head the cast of this disaster adventure. **AC23, CL3, DR5**

Night Visitor, The (1970, C, 106m, PG)
Liv Ullmann and Max von Sydow star in this suspense drama about a man who escapes from a mental institution, intent on revenge. English-language film, shot in Denmark and Sweden. **HO9, ST220**

Night Watch (1973, C, 105m, R)
A wealthy widow claims she witnessed a murder, but police can find no evidence a crime has been committed. Elizabeth Taylor and Laurence Harvey star in this thriller. **MY3, ST212**

Nightbreaker (1989, C, 99m, NR)
During the 1950s, the U.S. government deliberately exposes thousands of soldiers to an atomic bomb test to determine the effects of radiation. Emilio Estevez and Martin Sheen (son and father in real life) star, with Lea Thompson. Originally made for cable TV. **DR7, XT8**

Nightbreed (1990, C, 99m, R)
Clive Barker wrote and directed this grisly horror tale of a man determined to join a gang of monsters hiding beneath a small-town cemetery. Craig Sheffer stars, with David Cronenberg, Anne Bobby, and Charles Haid. **DT31, HO8, HO18**

Nightcomers, The (1972, C, 96m, R)
Prequel of sorts to Henry James's ghost tale *Turn of the Screw* tries to imagine how the children of that story came to be haunted. Marlon Brando and Stephanie Beacham star. Suggests a kinkier side to James but to little effect other than titillation. **ST18, WR14**

Nightforce (1986, C, 82m, R)
A strike force composed of young recruits engages terrorist during a rescue mission in the jungles of Southeast Asia. Linda Blair is in command. **AC20**

Nighthawks (1981, C, 99m, R)
Two New York police detectives (Sylvester Stallone and Billy Dee Williams) comb Manhattan for a cold-blooded terrorist (Rutger Hauer). **AC9, ST204, ST227, XT9**

Nightingale, The (1985, C, 60m, NR)
Mick Jagger stars in this Faerie Tale Theatre presentation of the story of a powerful emperor and a magical bird. With Barbara Hershey and Edward James Olmos. **FA12, MU12, ST104**

Nightmare Circus (1973, C, 86m, R)
Horror story of young man, victim of child abuse, who captures women for a traveling circus. Early film from director Alan Rudolph, working under the name Gerald Cormier. Also known as *Barn of the Living Dead* and *Terror Circus*. **DT110**

Nightmare on Elm Street (series)

Nightmare on Elm Street, A
(1984, C, 92m, R)

Nightmare 2: Freddy's Revenge
(1985, C, 87m, R)

Nightmare 3: Dream Warriors
(1987, C, 97m, R)

Nightmare 4: The Dream Master
(1988, C, 93m, R)

Nightmare 5: The Dream Child
(1989, C, 89m, R)

Freddy's Dead: The Final Nightmare
(1991, C, 90m, R)
Sextet of horror tales about teen-agers
with horrible dreams featuring the same demented, scarred killer. Robert Englund stars
as the evil Freddy Krueger in all six films.
HO12, HO18

Nightmare Weekend (1985, C, 88m, R)
Three college coeds answer an ad for an
experimental weekend in the country, only
to find themselves captives of a professor's
crazed assistant. **HO20**

Nightmares (1983, C, 99m, R)
Four-story horror film, starring Emilio Este-
vez, Cristina Raines, and William Sanderson.
HO23

Nights of Cabiria (1957, B&W, 110m, NR)
A prostitute in Rome dreams of a better life
for herself in this Oscar-winning drama from
director Federico Fellini. Giulietta Masina (his
real-life wife) stars. **DT43, XT7, XT30**

Nightwing (1979, C, 105m, PG)
Horror drama, set in Arizona, about killer
vampire bats. David Warner, Kathryn Harrold, and Strother Martin star. **HO16**

Nijinsky (1980, C, 125m, R)
True-life drama of relationship between
famed Russian dancer Nijinsky and impres-
sario Sergei Diaghilev. George de la Pena and
Alan Bates star, with Leslie Browne, Alan
Badel, and Jeremy Irons. Directed by Herbert
Ross. **DR3, DR4, DR12, ST9, ST116**

Nikki, Wild Dog of the North
(1961, C, 74m, NR)
Disney adventure about a Canadian wolfdog
and his master. **FA1, FA5**

9½ Weeks (1986, C, 113m, R)
Drama of an intense love affair between two
modern New Yorkers, with overtones of sa-
dism and masochism. Mickey Rourke and
Kim Basinger star. Directed by Adrian Lyne.
CU6, DR3, ST190

Nine to Five (1980, C, 110m, PG)
Comedy about three long-suffering secre-
taries (Jane Fonda, Lily Tomlin, and Dolly
Parton) who take out their frustrations on
their loutish boss (Dabney Coleman). Silly
and ultimately offensive, even if it does strike
a chord with plenty of women. **CO3, MU12,
ST72, ST215**

1918 (1984, C, 94m, NR)
Matthew Broderick stars in this drama about
a small Texas town devastated by the famous
influenza epidemic. Written by Horton Foote.
Prequel: *On Valentine's Day.* **DR5, DR26**

1984 (1984, C, 117m, R)
Screen version of the George Orwell novel
about life under a future dictatorship. John
Hurt and Richard Burton (in his last film)
star. **DR19, DR21, SF11, ST22**

1941 (1979, C, 118m, PG)
Panic erupts in Southern California when
residents believe a Japanese attack is imminent. Steven Spielberg directed this comedy
with a huge cast that includes John Belushi,
Ned Beatty, Treat Williams, Nancy Allen, Dan
Aykroyd, Toshiro Mifune, Robert Stack, Warren Oates, Christopher Lee, John Candy, and
Slim Pickens. Widescreen will be lost on
video. About every ten minutes, there's a real
laugh. **CO6, CO13, CO14, CU20, DT118,
ST135, ST157, ST166**

1900 (1977, C, 243m, R)
From Italian director Bernardo Bertolucci, the
epic story of two friends, one a landowner,
the other a peasant, and how they're affected
by the rise of fascism. Robert De Niro and
Gérard Depardieu star, with Dominique
Sanda, Burt Lancaster, Sterling Hayden,
Donald Sutherland, and Stefania Sandrelli.
Originally released in Europe at six-hour running time; 1991 theatrical rerelease restored
footage to 311 minutes. Even edited to this
length, it's very powerful and potent stuff
from a major director. **DT13, FF2, ST51,
ST52, ST129,** *Recommended*

92 in the Shade (1975, C, 93m, R)
Bizarre goings-on in the Florida Keys in this
comedy about rival fishing guides and their
wacky women. Peter Fonda, Warren Oates,
Margot Kidder, and Elizabeth Ashley star,
with William Hickey, Burgess Meredith,
Harry Dean Stanton, Sylvia Miles, and Joe
Spinell. Director Tom McGuane adapted his
own novel. A true original that richly deserves its cult status. **CO12, DR19, ST166,
ST205,** *Recommended*

Ninotchka (1939, B&W, 110m, NR)
Greta Garbo is a Russian agent who falls for
suave Parisian Melvyn Douglas. With Bela
Lugosi, Sig Ruman, and Ina Claire. Directed
by Ernst Lubitsch; written by Billy Wilder.
A rare comic outing for the star; it's almost
indescribably wonderful. **CL10, DT76,
ST58, ST78, ST143,** *Essential, Highly
Recommended*

No Deposit, No Return (1976, C, 112m, G)
Two clever kids stage their kidnapping, just
to get some attention. David Niven and Dar-

ren McGavin star as villains in this Disney comedy. **FA1**

No Holds Barred (1989, C, 92m, PG-13)
Wrestling star Hulk Hogan makes his motion picture debut in this light-hearted look at the world of professional rassling. **CO19**

No Man of Her Own
(1932, B&W, 85m, NR)
Clark Gable and Carole Lombard costar in this drama of a no-good guy and the woman who sets him straight. **ST77, ST140**

No Mercy (1986, C, 107m, R)
A Chicago cop (Richard Gere) travels to New Orleans to nab the gangster who killed his partner. Kim Basinger and Jeroen Krabbe costar. Okay for genre fans; others need not apply. **AC19, MY5, ST84, XT14**

No Nukes see *MUSE Concert: No Nukes, The*

No Regrets for Our Youth
(1946, B&W, 110m, NR)
Early film from Japanese director Akira Kurosawa, a drama of a housewife whose lover, a political activist, is executed for espionage. Setsuko Hara and Takashi Shimura star. **DT69**

No Retreat, No Surrender
(1985, C, 85m, PG)
A karate student squares off against a Russian bully. **AC26**

No Surrender (1985, C, 100m, R)
Comedy-drama set in a Liverpool nightclub, where a prankster has booked two senior citizen lodges—one Catholic, the other Protestant—plus a group of retarded patients from a hospital. Michael Angelis, Ray McAnally, and Joanne Whalley star, with Elvis Costello as an inept magician. Written by Alan Bleasdale. Sounds contrived but it works in strange and mysterious ways. **CO17, DR11, DR23, MU12,** *Recommended*

No Way Out (1950, B&W, 106m, NR)
Tense drama of white racist crook who's wounded, refuses treatment from black hospital doctor, eventually incites a race riot. Richard Widmark and Sidney Poitier (his debut) star, with Linda Darnell, Stephen McNally, Ruby Dee, and Ossie Davis. Written and directed by Joseph L. Mankiewicz. Although some details have dated, still a powerful social issues drama. UNAVAILABLE ON VIDEO. **XT29**

No Way Out (1987, C, 116m, R)
A naval aide to the Secretary of Defense finds himself incriminated in the death of the Secretary's mistress. Kevin Costner, Gene Hackman, and Sean Young star in this political

thriller filmed on location in Washington, D.C. With Will Patton, Howard Duff, George Dzundza, and Fred Dalton Thompson. Riveting stuff, with a terrific twist ending. **DR21, MY2, MY5, MY6, ST38, ST96, XT12,** *Recommended*

No Way To Treat a Lady
(1968, C, 108m, NR)
An actor with a mother fixation dons disguises to commit his crimes against women. Rod Steiger, George Segal, and Lee Remick star. As the villain, Steiger chews the scenery until there's nothing left for his costars. **MY3, MY13, XT27**

Nobody's Fault see *Little Dorrit*

Noises Off (1992, C, 104m, PG-13)
Farce adapted from the Michael Frayn play about a theatrical company trying to work out the kinks in a production headed for a New York opening. Film shows both backstage misadventures and onstage disasters. The ensemble cast is headed by Carol Burnett, Michael Caine (as the show's director), Denholm Elliott, Julie Hagerty, Marilu Henner, Mark Linn-Baker, Christopher Reeve, John Ritter, and Nicolette Sheridan. Directed by Peter Bogdanovich. **CO8, DR20, ST25**

Nomads (1986, C, 95m, R)
A scientist discovers a secret cult of ghosts living in modern-day Los Angeles. Horror thriller stars Pierce Brosnan, Lesley-Anne Down, and Adam Ant. **HO11, MU12**

Nomads of the North
(1920, B&W, 109m, NR)
In the wilderness of northern Canada, a lovely young woman is forced into marriage with a villain to absolve her father's debts. Silent melodrama starring Lon Chaney, Sr. **ST26**

None But the Brave (1965, C, 105m, NR)
Frank Sinatra stars in a World War II drama of fliers downed on a Japanese-occupied island. With Clint Walker, Tommy Sands, and Tony Bill. Sinatra directed. **AC1, MU12, ST199**

None But the Lonely Heart
(1944, B&W, 113m, NR)
Rare drama for Cary Grant as a Cockney trying to do right by his dying mother (Oscar winner Ethel Barrymore). With Barry Fitzgerald, Jane Wyatt, Dan Duryea, George Coulouris. Grant's only Oscar nomination; worth seeing for his performance. **ST92, XT5,** *Recommended*

Noose Hangs High, The
(1948, B&W, 77m, NR)
Abbott and Costello comedy, with the boys robbed of large sum of money, involved in

mistaken identity caper. With Joseph Calleia, Leon Errol, and Mike Mazurki. **ST1**

Norma Rae (1979, C, 113m, PG)
Sally Field won an Oscar for her portrayal of a Southern working woman who helps organize a union against enormous pressures. With Beau Bridges and Ron Liebman. Directed by Martin Ritt. Needs a lighter touch, but Field is very good. Try to imagine a big-screen movie on this subject getting made today. **DR10, DT105, ST66, XT3, XT26,** *Recommended*

Norman Loves Rose (1982, C, 98m, R)
Australian comedy of a teen-ager (Tony Owen) in love with his sister-in-law (Carol Kane), who becomes pregnant. **FF5**

North Avenue Irregulars, The
(1979, C, 99m, G)
A young priest and some of his female parishioners take on local criminals in this Disney comedy. Edward Herrmann, Barbara Harris, and Susan Clark star. **FA1**

North by Northwest (1959, C, 136m, NR)
Hitchcock chase drama, with innocent businessman Cary Grant mistaken for government agent. Many memorable scenes: the stabbing at the United Nations, the crop-duster chase in Indiana, the exciting climax on Mount Rushmore. With Eva Marie Saint, James Mason, Martin Landau, and Jesse Royce Landis. Written by Ernest Lehman. **DT57, MY7, ST92, ST153, XT9, XT18,** *Essential, Highly Recommended*

North Dallas Forty (1979, C, 119m, R)
A pro football player finds his love of the game soured by the win-at-all-costs attitudes of his team's coaches and management. A devastatingly funny portrait of modern professional sports, starring Nick Nolte and Mac Davis, with Dayle Haddon, Charles Durning, G.D. Spradlin, Bo Svenson, John Matuszak, and Dabney Coleman. My candidate for the best sports movie ever. It combines great entertainment with sharp critique of the business ends of sports. **CO2, CO19, MU12, ST164, XT26,** *Highly Recommended*

North of the Great Divide
(1950, C, 67m, NR)
Roy Rogers stars in this Western about a Canadian Mountie and an Indian agent joining forces against a corrupt cannery owner. **ST188, WE10**

North Shore (1987, C, 96m, PG)
Matt Adler and Gregory Harrison star in this drama about surfers living for the big wave on the California coast. **DR22**

North Star, The (1943, B&W, 105m, NR)
World War II drama set in a Russian village, with noble townspeople resisting the German army. Anne Baxter, Dana Andrews, Walter Huston, and Erich Von Stroheim star. Written by Lillian Hellman; directed by Lewis Milestone. A few years after its release, Cold War politics forced scenes especially sympathetic to the Soviets to be cut; film was retitled *Armored Attack*. **AC1, CU8, DT129**

North to Alaska (1960, C, 122m, NR)
Gold diggers on the northern frontier battle the elements and each other. John Wayne, Stewart Granger, and Fabian star. **MU12, ST224, WE10**

Northern Pursuit (1943, B&W, 94m, NR)
Errol Flynn plays a Canadian Mountie tracking a downed Nazi spy pilot. Directed by Raoul Walsh. **DT131, ST69**

Northwest Passage (1940, C, 125m, NR)
Spencer Tracy stars in this colorful historical drama about Rogers' Rangers, a group of scouts in Colonial America. With Robert Young, Walter Brennan, and Ruth Hussey. Directed by King Vidor. **CL3, DT126, ST217**

Nosferatu (1922, B&W, 63m, NR)
Silent film version of the Dracula story, directed by F.W. Murnau, is a classic of mood and atmosphere rather than blood and gore. **HF7, HO1, HO5,** *Essential*

Not as a Stranger (1955, B&W, 135m, NR)
Lengthy drama of nurse supporting her husband through medical school. Olivia de Havilland and Robert Mitchum star, with Frank Sinatra, Charles Bickford, Gloria Grahame, Broderick Crawford, Lee Marvin, and Lon Chaney, Jr. Produced by Stanley Kramer; also his directorial debut. **DT67, ST27, ST49, ST151, ST158, ST199**

Not for Publication (1984, C, 88m, PG)
Comedy about a reporter (Nancy Allen) who moonlights as a campaign worker for a zany mayor and her romance with a photographer (David Naughton). Paul Bartel directed. **DT8**

Not Without My Daughter
(1991, C, 114m, PG-13)
True-life story of Betty Mahmoody, American woman whose Iranian husband took her daughter back to his homeland for a visit and wouldn't return with her. She goes undercover to Iran to bring her home. Sally Field stars, with Alfred Molina. **DR6, DR10, DR27, ST66**

Notebook on Cities and Clothes
(1990, C, 80m, NR)
From German director Wim Wenders, a doc-

umentary on fashion designer Yohji Yamamoto. **CU16, DT136**

Nothing But the Night see *Devil's Undead, The*

Nothing But Trouble
(1944, B&W, 69m, NR)
Laurel and Hardy play servants whose master, a king, is in danger and needs their help. (Now he's *really* in danger.) With Mary Boland, Philip Merivale, and David Leland. **ST133**

Nothing But Trouble
(1991, C, 93m, PG-13)
A Manhattan couple driving through a small New York town are caught in a speed trap and subjected to a nightmare of horrors by the locals. Comedy stars Chevy Chase and Demi Moore, with Dan Aykroyd (in two roles) and John Candy. Aykroyd also wrote and directed. **CO13, CO14, XT27**

Nothing in Common (1986, C, 118m, PG)
After a hip advertising executive sees his parents' long-standing marriage fall apart, he finds that his ailing father is now dependent on him. Tom Hanks and Jackie Gleason star in this comedy-drama, with Eva Marie Saint, Hector Elizondo, Barry Corbin, Sela Ward, and Bess Armstrong. Directed by Garry Marshall; set in Chicago. Hanks and Gleason are superb; deftly mixes comic view of the ad business with on-target drama about family relationships. **DR8, DR24, ST97, XT11,** *Recommended*

Nothing Sacred (1937, C, 75m, NR)
Smooth-talking reporter gets fictional scoop on a Vermont girl supposedly dying of radium poisoning and turns her into a national celebrity. Fredric March and Carole Lombard star in this comedy. Written by Ben Hecht; directed by William Wellman. Hasn't worn too well, although stars are certainly worth watching. **CL10, DT135, ST140, ST148**

Notorious (1946, B&W, 101m, NR)
Alfred Hitchcock's classic mix of suspense and passion, with American agent Cary Grant forcing Ingrid Bergman to spy on Nazi Claude Rains. The ultimate blend of romance and intrigue; Grant and Bergman are as sexy a screen team as you'll ever see. Rains should have won the Best Supporting Actor Oscar. **CL4, DT57, MY3, MY5, MY6, ST13, ST92, XT28,** *Essential, Highly Recommended*

Now and Forever (1983, C, 93m, R)
An Australian couple's happiness is shattered when he's falsely accused of rape and sent to prison. Cheryl Ladd stars. **FF5**

Now, Voyager (1942, B&W, 117m, NR)
Classic Bette Davis tearjerker about a spinster's romance. Paul Henreid and Claude Rains costar. **CL4, CL5, ST44**

Now You See Him, Now You Don't
(1972, C, 88m, G)
College student Kurt Russell invents a spray that makes him invisible and is pursued by crooks who want the formula. Disney comedy also stars Cesar Romero and Jim Backus. **FA1, ST191**

Nowhere To Hide (1987, C, 90m, R)
Amy Madigan is a Marine whose husband, also a member of the Corps, is murdered by assassins. She uses her training to protect herself and her small son. **AC24, AC25**

Nowhere To Run (1993, C, 94m, R)
Jean Claude Van Damme action drama has him playing an escaped con who helps out a lonely farm widow (Rosanna Arquette) being pressured off her land. With Kieran Culkin, Ted Levine, Tiffany Taubman, and Joss Ackland. **AC25**

Number One With a Bullet
(1987, C, 101m, R)
Billy Dee Williams and Robert Carradine star as police detectives tracking a drug lord. With Valerie Bertinelli and Peter Graves. **ST227**

Number 17 (1932, B&W, 83m, NR)
Light-hearted Hitchcock thriller about a hobo who gets mixed up with gang of jewel thieves. **DT57, MY15**

Nuns on the Run (1990, C, 90m, PG-13)
British comedy of two small-time hoods on the lam, disguising themselves and hiding out in a convent. Eric Idle and Robbie Coltrane star. **CO15, CO17, CO20**

Nun's Story, The (1959, C, 149m, NR)
Audrey Hepburn stars as a young sister who serves as a missionary in Africa and later decides to leave her order. With Peter Finch, Edith Evans, and Peggy Ashcroft. Fred Zinnemann directed. One of Hepburn's finest performances but story has a few too many lulls. **DR10, DT144, ST102**

Nutcracker Prince, The (1990, C, 75m, G)
Animated version of Christmas classic about young girl helping toy soldiers to fight an evil Mouse King. Uses Tchaikovsky's music; voices by Kiefer Sutherland, Megan Follows, Peter O'Toole, and Phyllis Diller. **FA10, FA13, ST169**

Nutcracker, The Motion Picture
(1986, C, 89m, G)
Performance by Pacific Northwest Ballet of

Tchaikovsky's classic, directed by Carroll Ballard. Sets and costumes designed by Maurice Sendak. **FA13**

Nuts (1987, C, 116m, R)
Prostitute on trial for murdering a customer must battle her own lawyer and the legal system which wants to declare her insane. Barbra Streisand and Richard Dreyfuss star in this adaptation of Tom Topor's play. With Maureen Stapleton, Karl Malden, Eli Wallach, Robert Webber, James Whitmore, and Leslie Nielsen. Directed by Martin Ritt. **DR10, DR17, DR20, DT105, ST60, ST211**

Nutty Professor, The (1963, C, 107m, NR)
Comic variation on the Dr. Jekyll and Mr. Hyde story, with Jerry Lewis as the supremely nerdy scientist and his alter ego, suave crooner Buddy Love. Stella Stevens costars. **CL14, CO18, ST139**

O.C. & Stiggs (1987, C, 109m, R)
Comedy about two teen-agers determined one summer to wreak havoc on their neighborhood. Dan Jenkins and Neill Barry star, with Paul Dooley, Dennis Hopper, Jane Curtin, and Jon Cryer. Robert Altman directed. **CO13, DT2, ST110**

O Lucky Man! (1973, C, 173m, R)
Epic adventures of a plucky young Britisher (Malcolm McDowell) who becomes top coffee salesman, suffers humiliating failure, only to land on his feet again. Unique musical interludes featuring composer Alan Price. With Ralph Richardson, Rachel Roberts, Arthur Lowe, and Helen Mirren. Directed by Lindsay Anderson, who also has a small role. Ambitious and largely successful attempt at modern picaresque. **DR23, ST184,** *Recommended*

Object of Beauty, The (1991, C, 97m, R)
Offbeat comedy of unmarried couple living it up in posh London hotel, deciding whether to hock a valuable piece of art to finance their wicked, wicked ways. John Malkovich and Andie MacDowell star, with Lolita Davidovich, Joss Ackland, Bill Paterson, and Peter Riegert. **CO12, ST147**

Objective, Burma! (1945, B&W, 142m, NR)
World War II classic of American G.I.s slogging through jungle, battling Japanese. Errol Flynn stars, with William Prince and James Brown. Directed by Raoul Walsh. **AC1, DT131, ST69,** *Recommended*

Oblong Box, The (1969, C, 91m, PG)
Vincent Price and Christopher Lee star in this horror story of two brothers, one a respectable British aristocrat, the other his disfigured, reclusive brother. Based on an Edgar Allan Poe tale. **HO14, ST135, ST179, WR27**

Obsession (1976, C, 98m, PG)
Years after his wife and daughter are kidnapped and disappear, a New Orleans businessman meets a young woman with an uncanny resemblance to his wife. Cliff Robertson, Genevieve Bujold, and John Lithgow star in this thriller from director Brian De Palma. Music by Bernard Herrmann. One of the director's more effective Hitchcock-style thrillers suffers from weak lead performances. **DT36, MY5, XT14**

Ocean's Eleven (1960, C, 127m, NR)
Frank Sinatra heads a gang of thieves with plans to rob five Las Vegas casinos at one time. Dean Martin, Sammy Davis, Jr., Peter Lawford, and Angie Dickinson costar in this comic caper. **MY18, ST149, ST199**

Octagon, The (1980, C, 103m, R)
Chuck Norris plays a bodyguard whose client is in danger from an army of Ninja assassins. With Lee Van Cleef. **ST165, ST221**

Octopussy (1983, C, 130m, PG)
James Bond (Roger Moore) travels to India to tangle with a deadly female assassin (Maud Adams) and her cult. **HF2**

Odd Angry Shot, The (1979, C, 90m, R)
A group of Australian soldiers try to cope with combat life during the Vietnam War. John Hargreaves and Bryan Brown star. **FF5**

Odd Couple, The (1968, C, 105m, G)
Classic Neil Simon comedy about two newly divorced men (Walter Matthau and Jack Lemmon) sharing a New York apartment despite their totally incompatible lifestyles. Maybe it's the ubiquity of the TV show, but this does seem overly familiar stuff now; Lemmon and Matthau are wonderful. **CO3, ST138, ST155, WR30, XT9**

Odd Job, The (1978, C, 86m, NR)
British comedy starring Graham Chapman as a man who hires a killer to rub out his wife, only to regret the move and try to undo his orders. With David Jason and Diana Quick. Written by Chapman and Bernard McKenna; directed by Peter Medak. **CO15, CO17**

Odd Man Out (1947, B&W, 113m, NR)
James Mason plays a wounded Irish gunman on the lam, with no one to shelter him, in this classic thriller. With Robert Newton (quite good), Kathleen Ryan, and Cyril Cusack. Directed by Carol Reed. Consistently suspenseful, with Mason in top form. **MY15, ST153,** *Recommended*

Odd Obsession (1959, C, 96m, NR)
In this Japanese drama, an elderly man persuades his wife to take up with a younger man, with disastrous consequences. **FF4**

Odessa File, The (1974, C, 128m, PG)
Frederick Forsyth thriller about a German reporter tracking ex-Nazis in 1963 Berlin. Jon Voight and Maximilian Schell star. **MY6, WR10**

Of Human Bondage
(1934, B&W, 83m, NR)
Somerset Maugham story of a crippled man's infatuation with a scornful waitress, starring Bette Davis and Leslie Howard. Davis's performance now seems overwrought; Howard wimpy as always. **ST44, WR23**

Of Mice and Men (1939, B&W, 107m, NR)
Drama, based on John Steinbeck novel, about two itinerant workers, clever George (Burgess Meredith) and dim-witted Lenny (Lon Chaney, Jr.), and the tragic event that leads to their separation. **ST27, WR32**

Of Mice and Men (1992, C, 110m, PG)
John Malkovich (as Lenny) and Gary Sinise (as George) star in this version of the heartbreaking John Steinbeck tale of friendship between two farm workers. With Ray Walston, Casey Siemaszko, and Sherilyn Fenn. Adapted by Horton Foote, directed by Sinise. **DR2, WR32, XT23**

Of Unknown Origin (1983, C, 88m, R)
Horror story of a New York businessman doing battle in his home with a gigantic rodent. Peter Weller stars. **HO16**

Off Limits (1953, B&W, 89m, NR)
Service comedy, with Bob Hope and Mickey Rooney trying to put one (or two) over on the brass. **CO21, ST108, ST189**

Off Limits (1988, C, 102m, R)
A pair of American police detectives track down a killer in 1968 Saigon. Willem Dafoe and Gregory Hines star, with Amanda Pays, Fred Ward, and Scott Glenn. **AC9, MY16**

Officer and a Gentleman, An
(1982, C, 125m, R)
Romance blossoms between a headstrong naval pilot-in-training and a girl who works at a local factory. Richard Gere and Debra Winger star, with Oscar winner Louis Gossett, Jr., David Keith, Robert Loggia, Lisa Blount, and Lisa Eilbacher. Directed by Taylor Hackford. Crowd pleaser with good performances is slave to clichés. **DR1, ST84, ST231, XT4**

Official Story, The (1985, C, 110, R)
Oscar-winning film from Argentina about a woman who discovers that the parents of her adopted daughter may be among the "missing" persons executed by the secret police. Norma Aleandro stars. **FF6, XT7**

Offspring, The (1986, C, 99m, R)
A quartet of horror tales, narrated by an old man (Vincent Price) who lives in a mysterious small town. **HO23, ST179**

Oh! Calcutta! (1972, C, 108m, NR)
Long-running Broadway musical, actually a series of sketches about sexuality, in which the actors wear no clothes. **MU2**

Oh Dad, Poor Dad, Mama's Hung You in the Closet and I'm Feeling So Sad
(1967, C, 86m, NR)
Dark farce of mother-fixated young man (Robert Morse) and his mom (Rosalind Russell), who keeps her husband's corpse handy. With Barbara Harris, Hugh Griffith, and Jonathan Winters. Adapted from the Arthur Kopit play. Strained attempt at daring humor falls flat on its face. **CO12, DR20, ST192**

Oh, God! (1977, C, 104m, PG)
A supermarket manager strikes up a friendship with the earthly presence of the Supreme Being. John Denver and George Burns star in this family comedy. **FA6, MU12**

Oh, God! Book II (1980, C, 94m, PG)
George Burns returns as the Man Upstairs. This time, he's using a little girl to get out the word that reports of his demise have been greatly exaggerated. **FA6**

Oh, God! You Devil (1984, C, 96m, PG)
The third in the series finds George Burns playing both title roles in the story of a singer who sells his soul to you-know-who for fame and fortune. Ted Wass costars. **FA6**

Oh, Heavenly Dog! (1980, C, 103m, PG)
A private eye (Chevy Chase) is reincarnated in the body of a lovable dog (Benji) in this family comedy. **CO13, FA5, XT24**

Oh Susannah (1938, B&W, 59m, NR)
Gene Autry joins two drifters to find the men who robbed him. **ST5**

O'Hara's Wife (1982, C, 87m, PG)
Comedy of man trying to deal with his ghostly wife. Edward Asner and Mariette Hartley star, with Jodie Foster, Perry Lang, Tom Bosley, and Ray Walston. **ST75, XT24**

Oklahoma! (1955, C, 145m, G)
Classic Rodgers and Hammerstein musical about settlers in the Sooner State, starring Gordon MacRae and Shirley Jones, with

Charlotte Greenwood, Rod Steiger, Gloria Grahame, Eddie Albert, and James Whitmore. Songs include "Oh, What a Beautiful Mornin" and "People Will Say We're in Love." Directed by Fred Zinnemann. **DT144, FA9, MU2, MU6**

Oklahoma Kid, The
(1939, B&W, 85m, NR)
Unusual casting in this Western featuring Humphrey Bogart and James Cagney as the villain and lawman in a revenge struggle. **ST15, ST24, WE15**

Oklahoman, The (1957, C, 80m, NR)
Joel McCrea Western in which he tries to help Indians who were swindled out of their land. With Barbara Hale, Brad Dexter, and Gloria Talbott. **ST144**

Old Barn Dance, The
(1938, B&W, 58m, NR)
Singing cowboy Gene Autry exposes some evil businessmen in this modern-day Western. Roy Rogers is in the supporting cast under the name Dick Weston. **ST5, ST188**

Old Boyfriends (1979, C, 103m, R)
Drama about a woman who looks up her former lovers to try to understand herself better. Talia Shire stars; John Belushi, Richard Jordan, and Keith Carradine play the title roles. Directed by Joan Tewkesbury. **CO13, DR10**

Old Corral, The (1936, B&W, 56m, NR)
Contemporary cowboy Gene Autry battles gangsters on the range. The Sons of the Pioneers (featuring Roy Rogers) harmonize. With Lon Chaney, Jr. **ST5, ST27, ST188**

Old Curiosity Shop, The
(1935, B&W, 90m, NR)
The Charles Dickens story of an old gambler and his understanding young daughter. Ben Webster and Elaine Benson star. **WR5**

Old Curiosity Shop, The
(1975, C, 118m, G)
British musical version of the Dickens tale of a gambler and his daughter, starring Anthony Newley, who also wrote the songs. With David Hemmings, David Warner, Michael Hordern, and Jill Bennett. Also known as *Mr. Quilp.* **MU14, WR5**

Old Gringo (1989, C, 119m, R)
Historical drama, set during the Mexican Revolution, about an American schoolteacher's fascination with two men: an aging American journalist and a handsome Mexican soldier. Jane Fonda, Gregory Peck, and Jimmy Smits star in this adaptation of Carlos Fuentes's novel. **DR1, DR5, DR19, DR27, ST72, ST171**

Old Ironsides (1926, B&W, 111m, NR)
A trio of sailors ship out in search of adventure in this silent adventure classic, starring Wallace Beery, Boris Karloff, and Charles Farrell. **CL12, ST119**

Old Maid, The (1939, B&W, 95m, NR)
Bette Davis and Miriam Hopkins play cousins at war over Davis's illegitimate daughter in this melodrama set in the 1860s. With George Brent, Jane Bryan, and Donald Crisp. Directed by Edmund Golding. **CL5, ST44**

Old Yeller (1957, C, 83m, G)
A Texas pioneer family in the 1860s adopts a lovable stray dog in this Disney Western drama. Fess Parker, Dorothy McGuire, and Tommy Kirk star. **FA1, FA5**

Oldest Living Graduate, The
(1982, C, 75m, NR)
Henry Fonda plays an alumnus of a Texas school who is in conflict with his son. With George Grizzard, Harry Dean Stanton, Penelope Milford, and Cloris Leachman. Videotape of a stage performance, originally shown on public TV. **DR8, DR20, ST71, ST205**

Oldest Profession, The (1967, C, 97m, NR)
A comic look at prostitution through the ages, from the viewpoint of six directors, including Jean-Luc Godard. Among the stars: Jeanne Moreau, Elsa Martinelli, Raquel Welch, Anna Karina, and Jean-Pierre Leaud. **DT50, ST161**

Oliver! (1968, C, 153m, G)
Musical version of the Dickens story about an orphan's adventures in London won six Oscars, including Best Picture and Director (Carol Reed). Ron Moody, Oliver Reed, and Mark Lester star, with Shani Wallis, Jack Wild, Harry Secombe, and Hugh Griffith. Songs include "As Long as He Needs Me." **FA9, MU2, MU7, WR5, XT1, XT6**

Oliver Twist (1922, B&W, 77m, NR)
Silent version of the Charles Dickens tale of orphans and thieves, starring Jackie Coogan and Lon Chaney, Sr. **FA3, ST26, WR5**

Oliver Twist (1933, B&W, 77m, NR)
The Dickens classic of an orphan caught up in a world of thieves, starring Dickie Moore. **FA3, WR5**

Oliver Twist (1948, B&W, 118m, NR)
Director David Lean's version of the Dickens classic, starring John Howard Davies, Alec Guinness, Robert Newton, Kay Walsh, and Anthony Newley. Video restores footage once censored for U.S. release (Guinness's portrayal of Fagan was deemed anti-Semitic). Atmospheric sets and cinematography. **CU8,**

CU10, DT71, FA3, ST95, WR5,
Recommended

Olly, Olly, Oxen Free (1978, C, 83m, G)
Katharine Hepburn plays a junk dealer who
befriends two boys and takes them on a hot-
air balloon ride. With Kevin McKenzie and
Dennis Dimster. **FA4, ST103**

Olympia (1936, B&W, 215m, NR)
Legendary documentary of the 1936 Olympic
Games, directed by Leni Riefenstahl. Available on two tapes: Part I, *The Festival of the
People*, runs 119 minutes; Part II, *The Festival
of Beauty*, runs 96 minutes. Magnificently
directed record of what has turned out to be
the most historically significant Olympiad.
CU16, *Essential, Highly Recommended*

Omen, The (1976, C, 111m, R)
The American ambassador to England finds
out that his stepchild is actually the "Anti-
christ" incarnate. Horror drama starring
Gregory Peck, Lee Remick, and David War-
ner. First in a trilogy that continues with
Damien—Omen II and *The Final Conflict*.
HO10, HO13, ST171

On a Clear Day You Can See Forever
(1970, C, 129m, PG)
Musical fairy tale about a woman whose psychiatrist discovers she has lived a previous
life. Barbra Streisand and Yves Montand star;
Jack Nicholson has a small role. Directed by
Vincente Minnelli. Widescreen will be lost on
video. Glossy production values can't hide
creakiness of the vehicle. **CU20, DT88,
MU8, ST163, ST211**

On an Island With You
(1948, C, 107m, NR)
Esther Williams musical about a movie star
on location in Hawaii. With Peter Lawford,
Ricardo Montalban, Jimmy Durante, Xavier
Cugat, and Cyd Charisse. **MU1**

On Any Sunday (1971, C, 91m, G)
Documentary on the thrills and spills of
motorcycle racing, featuring Steve McQueen.
CU16, ST146

On Borrowed Time (1939, B&W, 99m, NR)
Classic fantasy of elderly man who traps
Death, called Mr. Brink, in a tree. Lionel Bar-
rymore and Cedric Hardwicke star. Based on
a play by Lawrence Edward Watkin. **DR20,
SF2**

On Dangerous Ground
(1951, B&W, 82m, NR)
A burned-out New York cop is assigned to
a small-town case that involves a teen-age
killer. Robert Ryan and Ida Lupino star in
this *film noir* directed by Nicholas Ray. Music
by Bernard Herrmann. **DT101, MY1, ST193**

On Golden Pond (1981, C, 109m, PG)
Katharine Hepburn won her fourth Oscar,
Henry Fonda his first (and in his last film),
for this sentimental drama about an elderly
couple and their clashes with their head-
strong daughter (Jane Fonda). With Doug
McKeon and Dabney Coleman. Ernest
Thompson adapted his play; directed by
Mark Rydell. **DR2, DR8, DR11, DR20,
ST71, ST72, ST103, XT2, XT3, XT8,
XT22**

On Her Majesty's Secret Service
(1969, C, 140m, PG)
James Bond not only takes on archenemy
Ernst Stavro Blofeld, but he also decides to
marry a contessa. George Lazenby (in his
only 007 film) stars, with Telly Savalas and
Diana Rigg. **HF2**

On Moonlight Bay (1951, C, 95m, NR)
Doris Day musical, adapted from Booth Tar-
kington's *Penrod* books, about a small-town
Midwestern tomboy and her coming of age
over a handsome neighbor (Gordon MacRae).
With Billy Gray, Mary Wickes, and Leon
Ames. Sequel: *By the Light of the Silvery Moon*.
MU6, ST47

On the Beach (1959, B&W, 133m, NR)
After the superpowers destroy one another
with atomic weapons, a group of survivors in
Australia await the deadly radiation clouds.
Classic 1950s science fiction, starring Gregory Peck, Ava Gardner, and Fred Astaire. Directed by Stanley Kramer. Adapted from
the novel by Nevil Shute. Urgency of subject undercut by stiff execution. **DT67,
SF1, SF12, ST4, ST79, ST171**

On the Edge (1985, C, 92m, PG)
Bruce Dern plays a middle-aged runner training for a grueling race that could turn his life
around. **DR22**

On the Nickel (1980, C, 96m, R)
Drama about street persons in Los Angeles,
starring Ralph Waite and Donald Moffat,
directed by Waite. **DR15, XT23**

On the Old Spanish Trail
(1947, B&W, 56m, NR)
Roy Rogers joins a traveling show to pay off
a debt. With Jane Frazee and Andy Devine.
ST188

On the Right Track (1981, C, 98m, PG)
Gary Coleman stars in this family comedy
about a shoeshine boy who lives in a train
station locker. **FA6, FA15**

On the Town (1949, C, 98m, NR)
Exuberant musical about three sailors (Gene
Kelly, Frank Sinatra, and Jules Munshin) on

shore leave in New York City trying to see all they can in twenty-four hours. Directed by Gene Kelly and Stanley Donen. Music by Leonard Bernstein; lyrics by Adolph Green and Betty Comden. **DT38, MU1, MU6, ST123, ST199, XT9,** *Essential, Recommended*

On the Waterfront
(1954, B&W, 108m, NR)
Drama of life on the New Jersey docks, with Marlon Brando the former prizefighter caught between his fellow workers and his brother, who works for a crooked union boss. With Eva Marie Saint (her debut), Rod Steiger, Karl Malden, and Lee J. Cobb. Written by Budd Schulberg, directed by Elia Kazan, produced by Sam Spiegel. Oscar winner for Best Picture, Actor, Supporting Actress, and Director. Seamless blend of social commentary and story of personal relationships; first-rate ensemble acting. **CL8, DT65, ST18, XT1, XT2, XT5, XT6, XT21,** *Essential, Highly Recommended*

On the Yard (1979, C, 102m, R)
Prison drama about young convict making the big mistake of taking on the top con in the joint. John Heard and Thomas Waites star. **DR16**

On Top of Old Smoky
(1953, B&W, 59m, NR)
Gene Autry is in hot water when he's mistaken for an outlaw. Smiley Burnette adds comic relief. **ST5**

On Valentine's Day (1986, C, 106m, PG)
A young woman from a small southern town shocks her family by marrying a man with few prospects. Matthew Broderick and Hallie Foote star. Horton Foote wrote this drama about his parents' marriage; prequel to *1918*. **DR5**

On Wings of Eagles (1986, C, 221m, NR)
Dramatization of businessman Ross Perot's attempt to rescue two of his employees from an Iranian prison. Burt Lancaster stars as the retired general who leads the mission, with Richard Crenna as Perot, Paul LeMat, and Jim Metzler. Originally made for TV. **DR6, ST129**

Once Around (1991, C, 115m, R)
Comedy-drama of ugly duckling daughter of Boston family meeting the man of her dreams, an aggressive salesman that no one in her clan can stand. Holly Hunter and Richard Dreyfuss star, with Danny Aiello, Gena Rowlands, and Laura San Giacomo. Written by Malia Scotch Marmo; directed by Lasse Hallström. Scores telling points about family dynamics with both humor and moving dramatics. **CO1, DR1, DR8, ST60, ST113,** *Recommended*

Once Is Not Enough (1975, C, 121m, R)
Soap opera deluxe from writer Jacqueline Susann, about young woman's affairs and her ongoing fascination with her father. Deborah Raffin and Kirk Douglas star, with Brenda Vacarro, Alexis Smith, Melina Mercouri, and George Hamilton. Also known as *Jacqueline Susann's Once Is Not Enough*. Sudsy to the max; Vacarro provides real laughs, Raffin unintentional ones. **ST57**

Once Upon a Crime (1992, C, 94m, PG)
Crime comedy set in Europe, revolving around a missing dachshund and his murdered owner. The ensemble cast includes John Candy, James Belushi, Cybill Shepherd, Sean Young, Richard Lewis, Ornela Muti, Giancarlo Giannini, and George Hamilton. Directed by Eugene Levy. **CO10, CO13, CO14**

Once Upon a Honeymoon
(1942, B&W, 117m, NR)
Ginger Rogers marries a man she does not know is a Nazi officer; Cary Grant comes to the rescue. Walter Slezak costars in this comedy directed by Leo McCarey. **DT80, ST92, ST187**

Once Upon a Midnight Scary
(1990, C, 50m, NR)
Trio of horror stories aimed at kids, including Washington Irving's *The Legend of Sleepy Hollow*. Hosted by Vincent Price. **FA8, HO23, ST179**

Once Upon a Time in America
(1984, C, 225m, R)
Rich, powerfully presented gangster epic about two Jewish buddies who grow up in New York and turn rivals as adults. Robert De Niro and James Woods star, with Elizabeth McGovern, Joe Pesci, Burt Young, Tuesday Weld, Treat Williams, Larry Rapp, William Forsythe, James Hayden, and Jennifer Connelly. Sergio Leone directed. Also available in a 143-minute version which was the one first released to U.S. theaters; don't bother with that one. A great, if flawed, portrait of America. **AC22, DR24, DT73, ST51, ST172, ST233,** *Highly Recommended (long version)*

Once Upon a Time in the West
(1969, C, 165m, PG)
The ultimate spaghetti Western—maybe the ultimate Western, with Henry Fonda (as a villain) pitted against Jason Robards and a vengeful Charles Bronson. Claudia Cardinale costars, with Jack Elam, Woody Strode, and Lionel Stander. Photographed on location in scenic Monument Valley, familiar to fans of

John Ford's classic Westerns. Directed by Sergio Leone. Lovely musical score by Ennio Morricone. Widescreen compositions will be lost on video. **CL14, CU20, DT73, ST20, ST71, ST185, WE1, WE5, WE8,** *Essential, Highly Recommended*

One Against the Wind (1992, C, 96m, PG)
Judy Davis stars in this true World War II story of an Englishwoman living in Nazi-occupied Paris who sheltered Allied fliers. With Sam Neill. Originally made for TV. **DR5, ST46**

One and Only, Genuine, Original Family Band, The (1968, C, 117m, G)
Disney comedy about a musical family from the Dakota Territories who lend their talents to the 1888 Presidential campaign. Walter Brennan stars, with Buddy Ebsen, Lesley Ann Warren, John Davidson, Janet Blair, and Kurt Russell; Goldie Hawn made her debut in a small role. **FA1, ST99, ST191**

One Arabian Night (1921, B&W, 85m, NR)
Silent drama of carnival dancer kidnapped by a sheik, starring Pola Negri, Ernst Lubitsch, and Paul Wegener. Lubitsch directed. **DT76**

One Body Too Many (1944, B&W, 75m, NR)
Jack Haley plays a salesman forced to solve a crime when he's mistaken for a detective. Comedy-mystery costars Bela Lugosi. **MY17, ST143**

One Crazy Summer (1986, C, 94m, PG)
Life on Nantucket Island during the tourist season is the basis for this freewheeling comedy, starring John Cusack, Demi Moore, and Joe Flaherty. **CO14**

One Deadly Summer (1983, C, 133m, R)
Isabele Adjani stars in this French thriller about a young girl whose eccentric manner disguises an intricate revenge plan. Also known as *L'Été Meurtrier*. **MY16**

One-Eyed Jacks (1961, C, 141m, NR)
Marlon Brando stars in this Western tale (which he directed) about an outlaw left for dead by his partner. Karl Malden costars as the object of Brando's vengeance. With Katy Jurado, Pina Pellicer, Ben Johnson, Slim Pickens, Timothy Carey, and Elisha Cook, Jr. Widescreen will be lost on video. Film was begun by Stanley Kubrick, who left early in production, but Brando's direction is exceptionally strong. Has well-deserved cult reputation. **CU15, CU20, ST18, WE5, WE15,** *Highly Recommended*

One-Eyed Swordsman, The (1963, C, 95m, NR)
Japanese samurai action drama starring Tetsuro Tanba. **FF4**

One False Move (1992, C, 105m, R)
Thriller in the *film noir* tradition, about a trio of drug dealers fleeing murder scene in Los Angeles for a small town in Arkansas, where one of them has family—and other—ties. Bill Paxton, Cynda Williams, Billy Bob Thornton, Michael Beach, and Jim Metzler star. Written by Thornton, directed by Carl Franklin. Standard plot given some new twists; Paxton and Williams very good. **DR26, MY2,** *Recommended*

One Flew Over the Cuckoo's Nest (1975, C, 133m, R)
A misfit decides to get himself committed to a mental hospital for "a little rest." But he doesn't anticipate clashing with a strong head nurse. Adaptation of the Ken Kesey novel won Oscars for Best Picture, Actor (Jack Nicholson), Actress (Louise Fletcher), and Director (Milos Forman). With Brad Dourif, Christopher Lloyd, Danny DeVito, Scatman Crothers, Will Sampson, and Vincent Schiavelli. Quintessential Nicholson role, with strong support from all. **DR19, DT45, ST54, ST163, XT1, XT2, XT3, XT6,** *Essential, Highly Recommended*

One from the Heart (1982, C, 100m, R)
From director Francis Ford Coppola, a stylized musical drama about a couple in Las Vegas who split up and find other momentary partners. Teri Garr, Frederic Forrest, Raul Julia, and Nastassja Kinski star, with Harry Dean Stanton, Lainie Kazan, Allen Goorwitz (Garfield), and in a small role, Rebecca De Mornay. Songs by Tom Waits, sung by Waits and Crystal Gayle. Stunning production design and fluid camera work almost camouflage thinness of story. **DT29, MU16, ST205**

One Good Cop (1991, C, 114m, R)
New York cop (Michael Keaton) and wife (Renée Russo) inherit three daughters of his slain partner. Mixes domestic comedy-drama and usual street action. With Anthony LaPaglia, Kevin Conway, and Rachel Ticotin. **AC9, DR8, DR15, ST122**

101 Dalmatians (1961, C, 79m, G)
Disney animated feature about dogs of London banding together to save kidnapped litter. Discontinued from manufacture as of March 1993. Copies may be hard to find. **FA2,** *Recommended*

100 Rifles (1969, C, 110m, PG)
A deputy sheriff pursues a gun thief into Mexico, where the lawman falls in love with a lovely revolutionary. Burt Reynolds, Jim Brown, and Raquel Welch star. **ST183, WE7, WE9**

One Little Indian (1973, C, 90m, G)
Disney comedy-drama set in Western desert,
with cavalry man (James Garner) befriending
Indian boy. With Vera Miles, Clay O'Brien,
Pat Hingle, and Jodie Foster. **FA1, ST75,
ST82**

One Magic Christmas (1985, C, 88m, G)
A modern Christmas fable about a harried
mother (Mary Steenburgen) who learns the
true meaning of the season from a special
angel (Harry Dean Stanton). **FA13, ST205**

One-Man Force (1989, C, 89m, R)
Title says it all, with this cop action drama
starring John Matuszak, with Ronny Cox and
Charles Napier. **AC25**

One Man's War (1991, C, 100m, NR)
True story of Joel Filartiga, physician in Para-
guay who was also a human rights activist.
Anthony Hopkins stars, with Norma
Aleandro and Rubén Blades. Originally made
for cable TV. **DR4, MU12, ST109**

One Million B.C. (1940, B&W, 80m, NR)
Life in prehistoric times, with cavemen bat-
tling dinosaurs. Victor Mature and Lon
Chaney, Jr., star. **AC16, ST27**

One Minute to Zero
(1952, B&W, 105m, NR)
Korean War drama starring Robert Mitchum,
with Ann Blyth, William Talman, and Richard Egan. **AC3, ST158**

One Night of Love (1934, B&W, 80m, NR)
Grace Moore musical has her playing opera
star involved with her teacher (Tullio Car-
minati). **MU4**

One of Our Aircraft Is Missing
(1941, B&W, 106m, NR)
Drama about British pilots who crash during
war mission over Holland and try to make
their way home. Godfrey Tearle, Eric Portman, and Hugh Williams star. Michael Powell and Emeric Pressburger directed. **AC1,
DT99**

One on One (1977, C, 98m, R)
A heavily recruited high school basketball
player finds he's just another player on the
team at a big university. Robby Benson is the
struggling jock; Annette O'Toole is his academic tutor. With G.D. Spradlin, Gail Strickland, and in a small role, Melanie Griffith.
DR22, DR25, ST93

One Shoe Makes it Murder
(1982, C, 100m, NR)
Robert Mitchum's a private eye looking for
the missing wife of a gambling king. With
Angie Dickinson and Mel Ferrer. Originally
made for TV. **MY10, ST135**

One Touch of Venus
(1948, B&W, 81m, NR)
Broadway musical with Kurt Weill-Ogden
Nash score about store window statue of
Venus coming to life. Ava Gardner and
Robert Walker star, with Dick Haymes and
Eve Arden. **MU2, ST79**

One-Trick Pony (1980, C, 98m, R)
Rock star tries to juggle the demands of his
marriage and his changing audience. Paul
Simon stars, with Blair Brown, Joan Hackett,
Mare Winningham, Rip Torn, Allen Goorwitz
(Garfield), Lou Reed as a slick record producer, and in a small role, Daniel Stern.
Musical performances by The Lovin' Spoonful and Sam and Dave. Written by Simon;
directed by Robert M. Young. Fatally flawed
by weak lead; still worth a look for those
with interest in subject. **DR12, DR25, MU9,
ST216**

One, Two, Three (1961, B&W, 108m, NR)
James Cagney plays a fast-talking American
Coca-Cola executive caught up in some hilar-
ious Cold War complications in Berlin. With
Arlene Francis, Horst Buchholz, and Pamela
Tiffin. Billy Wilder directed. Cagney's last
great performance. **CL10, CO2, DT139,
ST24,** *Highly Recommended*

One Woman or Two (1985, C, 97m, PG-13)
A comedy about a French scientist (Gérard
Depardieu) and his relationship with the
American woman (Sigourney Weaver) who
finances his work. **CO2, ST52, ST225**

Onion Field, The (1979, C, 122m, R)
True story, based on Joseph Wambaugh book,
about a Los Angeles policeman whose partner is murdered by two punks and how he
deals with the consequences. John Savage
stars, with James Woods, Franklyn Seales,
and Ted Danson. Woods steals the show as
the more clever of the two cons. **DR6,
DR16, ST233,** *Recommended*

Only Angels Have Wings
(1939, B&W, 121m, NR)
Superbly realized buddy adventure of mail
pilots working the dangerous routes through
the Andes. Cary Grant stars, with Jean
Arthur and Rita Hayworth as the women in
his life, Richard Barthelmess, Thomas Mitchell, and Noah Beery, Jr., as his fellow fliers.
Howard Hawks directed; arguably the greatest of his many great films. **AC11, AC13,
DT53, ST3, ST92, ST101, XT26,** *Essential,
Highly Recommended*

Only Game in Town, The
(1970, C, 113m, PG)
Low-key drama of affair between gambler

(Warren Beatty) and Vegas showgirl (Elizabeth Taylor). Directed by George Stevens. Beatty's good, but the film's pretty turgid. **DT119, ST10, ST212**

Only One Night (1938, B&W, 87m, NR) Swedish film with young Ingrid Bergman as society woman in love with the illegitimate son of an aristocrat. **ST13**

Only the French Can see *French Cancan*

Only the Lonely (1991, C, 102m, PG-13) John Candy's a Chicago cop, Maureen O'Hara his smothering mom in this dramatic change of pace for Candy. With Ally Sheedy, Kevin Dunn, Anthony Quinn, and Jim Belushi. Produced by John Hughes; written and directed by Chris Columbus. Yes, they do use the Roy Orbison tune on the soundtrack. **CO1, CO5, CO13, CO14, DT59, ST167**

Only the Valiant (1951, B&W, 105m, NR) Western drama of courageous army man (Gregory Peck) battling Indians. Lon Chaney, Jr., costars. **ST27, ST171**

Only Two Can Play (1962, B&W, 106m, NR) Peter Sellers comedy: he's a librarian making passes at a society lady (Mai Zetterling). With Virginia Maskell and Richard Attenborough. Based on a Kingsley Amis novel. **CO17, ST198**

Only When I Laugh (1981, C, 120m, R) Change of pace for Neil Simon in this drama about an actress who's a recovering alcoholic and her relationship with her teen-age daughter. Marsha Mason and Kristy McNichol star, with Joan Hackett and James Coco. Hackett's Oscar-worthy performance is the best thing about it. **DR8, WR30, XT28**

Open City (1946, B&W, 105m, NR) Influential Italian drama about the tense days of Rome's occupation during World War II. Directed by Roberto Rossellini. **DT109, FF2, XT17,** *Essential*

Open Doors (1990, C, 109m, R) Italian story of jurist in Fascist Sicily deciding fate of bureaucrat accused of triple homicide. Gian Maria Volonte stars. Directed by Gianni Amelio. Provocative drama effectively raises basic issues of justice. **FF2,** *Recommended*

Operation C.I.A. (1965, B&W, 90m, NR) Saigon-based thriller with Burt Reynolds as an American agent trying to prevent an assassination. **ST183**

Operation Crossbow (1965, C, 116m, NR) Adventure saga of World War II commandos out to destroy Nazi missile base. George Peppard stars, with Sophia Loren, Trevor Howard, Tom Courtenay, Anthony Quayle, and John Mills. Also known as *The Great Spy Mission.* **AC1, ST141**

Operation Pacific (1951, B&W, 111m, NR) John Wayne World War II drama of dedicated Navy man assigned to duty in the Pacific. With Patricia Neal and Ward Bond. **AC1, ST224**

Operation Petticoat (1959, C, 124m, NR) Cary Grant and Tony Curtis star in this service comedy set aboard a submarine. Directed by Blake Edwards. **CO21, DT40, ST92**

Operation Thunderbolt (1977, C, 125m, PG) Drama about the Entebbe hijack rescue by Israeli commandos on July 4, 1976. Klaus Kinski stars. This film version of those events was officially approved by the Israeli government. **DR6, ST126**

Opportunity Knocks (1990, C, 105m, PG-13) Dana Carvey plays a con artist in this comedy, with Robert Loggia, Todd Graff, and Julia Campbell. **CO10**

Opposing Force (1986, C, 97m, R) During a war games maneuver on a remote Pacific island, two officers discover that a third is waging war for real. Tom Skerritt and Lisa Eichhorn star, with Anthony Zerbe. **AC20, AC24**

Opposite Sex, The (1956, C, 117m, NR) Musical remake of *The Women,* starring June Allyson, Joan Collins, Dolores Gray, Ann Sheridan, Ann Miller, and Leslie Nielsen. **MU1, MU14**

Opposite Sex . . . And How To Live With Them, The (1993, C, 86m, R) Familiar comic story of blueblooded girl (Courtney Cox) and regular guy (Arye Gross) coming together, falling apart, advised by respective best friends (Kevin Pollak, Julie Brown). **CO1**

Orca (1977, C, 92m, PG) A giant whale goes on a rampage when bounty hunters murder his mate. Horror/disaster story starring Richard Harris and Charlotte Rampling. **HO16**

Orchestra Wives (1942, B&W, 98m, NR) Lighthearted musical centering on the Glenn Miller band and the problems their wives have while the boys are on the road. George Montgomery stars, with Lynn Bari, Carole Landis, Cesar Romero, Jackie Gleason, and the Nicholas Brothers. Songs: "I've Got a Gal in Kalamazoo," "At Last." **MU4**

Ordeal by Innocence
(1984, C, 87m, PG-13)
Agatha Christie tale of injustice in a small English town and the amateur sleuth who rights the wrong. Donald Sutherland, Faye Dunaway, and Christopher Plummer star. **ST61, MY11, WR3**

Ordet (1955, B&W, 125m, NR)
Danish director Carl Dreyer's classic story of feuding families who must resolve their religious differences when a love affair between one son and daughter of each clan is revealed. **DT39**

Ordinary People (1980, C, 123m, R)
A family is torn apart over the death of its oldest son in this drama. Donald Sutherland, Mary Tyler Moore, and Timothy Hutton (in his debut) star, with Judd Hirsch, Elizabeth McGovern, M. Emmet Walsh, Dinah Manoff, and James B. Sikking. Robert Redford directed. Adapted from the novel by Judith Guest by Alvin Sargent. The film, Redford, Hutton, and Sargent each won Oscars. Moore should have won. **DR2, DR8, DR9, DR19, ST181, XT1, XT4, XT6,** *Essential, Recommended*

Organization, The (1971, C, 107m, PG)
Sidney Poitier returns for his third stint as Detective Virgil Tibbs in this drama about a dope-smuggling operation. **AC9, ST174**

Ornette Coleman—Made in America
(1987, C, 80m, NR)
Documentary look at cutting-edge jazz musician, shown in performance with the Ft. Worth Symphony. Also includes interviews with Coleman colleagues Don Cherry and Charlie Haden. Directed by Shirley Clarke. **CU16**

Orphan Train (1979, C, 150m, NR)
Drama set in nineteenth century of abandoned children journeying by train from New York to the Western frontier, accompanied by a social worker and a newspaper photographer. Jill Eikenberry and Kevin Dobson star, with Linda Manz and Glenn Close. Originally made for TV. **DR5, FA4, FA15, ST33, XT19**

Orphans (1987, C, 120m, R)
Three-character drama about a gangster kidnapped by two loony brothers living in a ramshackle house in New Jersey. Albert Finney, Matthew Modine, and Kevin Anderson star. Lyle Kessler adapted his own stage play; directed by Alan Pakula. Strong performances, but what might have seemed claus-

trophobic on stage has been opened up and weakened. **DR20, DT94, ST68**

Orphans of the Storm
(1922, B&W, 125m, NR)
Silent drama from director D.W. Griffith set amid the turbulence of French Revolution, involving sisters unfairly separated. Lillian and Dorothy Gish star. **DT52, ST87, XT8**

Orpheus (1949, B&W, 95m, NR)
Jean Cocteau's retelling of the Orpheus legend, set in contemporary Paris. Jean Marais, François Perier, and Maria Casares star. Original French running time: 112 minutes. **DT26**

Orpheus Descending (1990, C, 150m, NR)
Tennessee Williams play about an Italian immigrant's romancing a wanderer while her husband lies dying. Vanessa Redgrave and Kevin Anderson star. Originally made for cable TV. **DR3, ST182, WR38**

Oscar (1991, C, 109m, PG)
Sylvester Stallone plays Snaps Provolone, a gangster whose daughter wants to get married to someone he hates, whose accountants may be stealing from him, and so on and so on. This farce features Ornella Muti, Don Ameche, Peter Riegert, Tim Curry, Vincent Spano, and in a small role, Kirk Douglas. Directed by John Landis. **CO10, ST57, ST204**

Oscar, The (1966, C, 119m, NR)
Behind-the-scenes soap opera centering on the annual Hollywood Academy Awards show. Eleanor Parker, Stephen Boyd, Elke Sommer, and Ernest Borgnine star. **DR12**

Ossessione (1942, B&W, 135m, NR)
Italian director Luchino Visconti's version of James M. Cain's story of infidelity and murder, *The Postman Always Rings Twice,* set in Fascist Italy. Massimo Girotti and Clara Calamai star. Early example of neorealism movement could not be legally shown in U.S. until 1975 because it was unauthorized adaptation. **CU8, DT127, WR1,** *Essential*

Osterman Weekend, The
(1983, C, 102m, R)
Talk show host is persuaded that several of his best friends are Soviet agents. Convoluted thriller, based on the Robert Ludlum novel, stars John Hurt, Rutger Hauer, and Burt Lancaster, with Craig T. Nelson, Dennis Hopper, and Helen Shaver. Director Sam Peckinpah's final film; not one to remember him by. **DT95, MY6, ST110, ST129, WR21**

Othello (1952, B&W, 92m, NR)
Orson Welles's take on the Shakespeare tragedy, with the director as the troubled Moor, and Michael MacLiammoir, Suzanne Cloutier,

and Robert Coote. Look for Joseph Cotten and Joan Fontaine in bit roles. Filmed between 1949 and 1952, whenever Welles wasn't working on other films and had enough money to continue production. This is the restored version of the film with its original music score recovered. **DT134, WR28**

Othello (1982, C, 120m, NR)
Shakespeare's play of the jealous Moor, starring Anthony Hopkins, Bob Hoskins, and Penelope Wilton. Originally produced for TV. **ST109, ST111, WR28**

Other, The (1972, C, 100m, PG)
Thriller, based on Thomas Tryon's novel, about young twin boys, one good, one evil. Uta Hagen, Diana Muldaur, and Chris and Martin Udvarnoky star. **HO15**

Other People's Money (1991, C, 101m, R)
Comedy of ruthless financial wizard (Danny DeVito) trying to swoop in on company run by old-fashioned businessman (Gregory Peck), who hires lovely lawyer (Penelope Ann Miller) to stop him. With Piper Laurie and Dean Jones. Alvin Sargent adapted Jerry Sterner's play; directed by Norman Jewison. **CO2, DR20, DR24, DT63, ST54, ST171**

Other Side of Midnight, The
(1977, C, 165m, R)
Epic soap opera, from the Sidney Sheldon bestseller, about a woman's ruthless climb to the top of the show business world. Marie-France Pisier, Susan Sarandon, and John Beck star. **DR2, ST194**

Our Daily Bread (1934, B&W, 74m, NR)
During the Depression, a couple living on a dilapidated farm invite homeless people to work their land and form a commune of sorts. Classic drama of hard-times 1930s, directed by King Vidor. **CL8, DT126**

Our Dancing Daughters
(1928, B&W, 97m, NR)
Silent melodrama of Roaring '20s flaming youth, starring Joan Crawford, caught in a romantic triangle with Johnny Mack Brown and Anita Page. **CL12, ST39**

Our Hospitality (1923, B&W, 74m, NR)
Buster Keaton's first feature-length comedy is about feuding Southern families. Highlight is incredible stunt rescue at a waterfall. With Natalie Talmadge (Buster's wife), Joseph Keaton (his father), and Buster Keaton, Jr. **CL11, DT66, XT8**

Our Little Girl (1935, C, 63m, NR)
Shirley Temple plays a girl who tries to bring her feuding parents (Rosemary Ames and Joel McCrea) together. **ST144, ST213**

Our Man Flint (1966, C, 107m, NR)
First in mercifully short-lived series of spoofs of James Bond films, starring James Coburn as unflappable secret agent. With Lee J. Cobb, Gila Golan, and Edward Mulhare. **CO7**

Our Modern Maidens
(1929, B&W, 70m, NR)
Silent drama of Jazz Age couple who fall in and out of love, starring Joan Crawford and Douglas Fairbanks, Jr. Sequel to *Our Dancing Daughters*. **ST39**

Our Relations (1936, B&W, 74m, NR)
Laurel and Hardy comedy in which the boys play two sets of twins, one set happy-go-lucky sailors, the others peaceable married men. **ST133**

Our Town (1940, B&W, 90m, NR)
Thornton Wilder's classic play about life in a small New England town stars William Holden, Martha Scott, and Thomas Mitchell. **DR20, DR26, ST106**

Our Vines Have Tender Grapes
(1945, B&W, 105m, NR)
Saga of family farm life in Wisconsin, seen through the eyes of a young girl (Margaret O'Brien). Edward G. Robinson and Agnes Moorehead star in this version of the George Victor Martin book; adaptation by Dalton Trumbo. **ST186**

Out (1982, C, 83m, NR)
Drama of counter-culture-kinda guy follows his road odyssey from the 1960s to the 1980s. Peter Coyote stars, with O-Lan Shepard (Sam's ex-wife), Jim Haynie, and Danny Glover. **DR7, ST88, XT18**

Out for Justice (1991, C, 91m, R)
Steven Seagal's an Italian cop who doesn't let old neighborhood ties bind him when his partner is murdered. With William Forsythe. **AC19, AC25**

Out of Africa (1985, C, 161m, PG)
Meryl Streep plays writer Isak Dinesen, who journeyed from her native Denmark to live on a plantation in Africa and write about her experiences there. Robert Redford and Klaus Maria Brandauer costar. Sydney Pollack directed this drama, which won seven Academy Awards, including Best Picture and Director. Intelligent and involving, although it does lean a bit heavily on the romantic angle. **DR1, DR4, DT98, ST181, ST210, XT1, XT6,** *Recommended*

Out of Bounds (1986, C, 93m, R)
A young man visiting Los Angeles from Iowa is mistaken for a drug courier in this thriller starring Anthony Michael Hall. **MY7**

Out of Control (1985, C, 78m, R)
A group of high school students are trapped on a desert island and forced to battle a ruthless gang of smugglers for survival. Martin Hewitt stars. **AC24**

Out of It (1969, B&W, 95m, PG)
Clever comedy of high school life, with Barry Gordon as quintessential nerd, Jon Voight as bullying jock, Lada Edmund, Jr., as class queen. Directed by Paul Williams. A sleeper that's superior to most recent films on the same subject. UNAVAILABLE ON VIDEO. **XT29**

Out of Season (1975, C, 90m, R)
Vanessa Redgrave stars in a moody drama about a woman, a stranger with whom she had an affair twenty years ago, and her grown daughter who's attracted to him. With Cliff Robertson and Susan George. Directed by Alan Bridges. Also known as *Winter Rates*. **DR3, ST182**

Out of the Blue (1980, C, 94m, R)
A teen-ager tries to deal with the problems of her parents, an ex-con and a drug addict, but finally loses control of her life, too. Linda Manz stars, with Dennis Hopper (who directed) and Sharon Farrell. Intense but also melodramatic to a fault. Manz is very believable. **DR8, ST110**

Out of the Past (1947, B&W, 97m, NR)
Classic *film noir* about an ex-con up to his neck in trouble from his former boss and a no-good woman. Robert Mitchum, Kirk Douglas, and Jane Greer are the points in the deadly triangle. Jacques Tourneur directed. Remade as *Against All Odds* (1984). One of the very best of a genre filled with good films. **DT124, MY1, MY5, ST57, ST158,** *Essential, Highly Recommended*

Out of the Rain (1990, C, 91m, R)
Drama of small town in the grip of drug problems, starring Bridget Fonda and Michael O'Keefe. **DR7, DR26, ST70**

Out on a Limb (1992, C, 82m, PG)
Comedy of young businessman on his way to complete deal, drawn to a small town to rescue his sister from villainous twins. Matthew Broderick stars, with Jeffrey Jones as the twins, Heidi Kling, and Courtney Peldon. **CO20, XT27**

Outcry, The see *Il Grido*

Outland (1981, C, 109m, R)
Sean Connery is an outer-space lawman in this futuristic thriller about drug smuggling at a space station. Peter Boyle costars. Tepid, even with Connery in good form. **SF17, ST36**

Outlaw, The (1943, B&W, 103m, NR)
Cult Western, initially banned in some cities, about Billy the Kid (Jack Buetel) and Doc Holliday (Walter Huston), was controversial for its allegedly steamy scenes with Jane Russell (in her film debut). Directed by Howard Hawks and Howard Hughes. **CU8, DT53, HF1, HF13, WE3, WE15, XT21**

Outlaw Josey Wales, The
(1976, C, 135m, PG)
Clint Eastwood Western saga of a man consumed with hatred for the Union soldiers who killed his family. With Chief Dan George, Sondra Locke, and John Vernon. Eastwood directed. Widescreen will be lost on video. One of Clint's strongest roles, with script (by Philip Kaufman) that has some refreshingly offbeat touches. **CU20, ST64, WE3, WE5, WE6,** *Recommended*

Out-of-Towners, The (1970, C, 97m, PG)
Jack Lemmon and Sandy Dennis play a couple of Ohio tourists who encounter every nightmare situation possible on a trip to New York City. With Sandy Baron, Anne Meara, Ann Prentiss, Graham Jarvis, Billy Dee Williams, Paul Dooley, Dolph Sweet, Robert Walden, and Richard Libertini. Written by Neil Simon. **CO2, CO20, ST138, ST227, XT9**

Outrageous! (1977, C, 100m, R)
A lonely young woman and a female impersonator strike up a friendship in this cult comedy starring Craig Russell and Hollis McLaren. **CO12, CU1**

Outrageous Fortune (1987, C, 100m, R)
Bette Midler and Shelley Long play two women who track down the man that two-timed them. Wild chase comedy with Peter Coyote and George Carlin. Some slam-bang comedy, mostly courtesy of Midler. **CO3, ST156, XT18**

Outside the Law (1921, B&W, 77m, NR)
Lon Chaney, Sr., and director Tod Browning's first collaboration is this silent melodrama with Chaney playing two roles: Black Mike, the slimy hoodlum, and Ah Wing, the faithful Chinese retainer to the story's heroine. **DT18, ST26**

Outsiders, The (1983, C, 91m, PG)
Three teen-age brothers try to get through life without parents in this drama adapted from S.E. Hinton's novel. C. Thomas Howell, Ralph Macchio, Patrick Swayze, and Matt Dillon star, with Rob Lowe, Emilio Estevez, Diane Lane, and Tom Cruise. Francis Ford Coppola directed. Certainly worth seeing for its cast of future stars and wannabes, but

Coppola's heavy hand crushes simple story elements. **CU17, DR9, DR19, DT29, ST41, ST56**

Over the Brooklyn Bridge
(1984, C, 106m, R)
Romantic comedy of Jewish man (Elliott Gould) who runs into family troubles when he romances a Catholic girl (Margaux Hemingway). With Sid Caesar, Burt Young, and Shelley Winters. **CO5, ST232**

Over the Edge (1979, C, 95m, R)
In a suburban community, a group of bored, restless teens clash with parents and law enforcement officials. Provocative, disturbing drama starring Michael Kramer and Matt Dillon. Written by Tim Hunter and Charlie Haas; directed by Jonathan Kaplan. Offhand drama perfectly captures restlessness of entire generation. **DR7, DR9, ST56, XT26,** *Recommended*

Over the Top (1987, C, 94m, PG)
Sylvester Stallone is a trucker involved in a custody battle and the national arm-wrestling championships. **DR22, ST204**

Overboard (1987, C, 112m, PG)
Goldie Hawn plays a snob who suffers amnesia when she falls off her yacht, and Kurt Russell is the carpenter who claims her for his wife (and mother to his frenetic kids) in this comedy. With Edward Herrmann, Katherine Helmond, and Roddy McDowall. Directed by Garry Marshall, who has a small role. **CO5, CO20, ST99, ST191**

Overcoat, The (1960, B&W, 78m, NR)
Soviet drama based on Nikolai Gogol's classic story of a common clerk who buys a new coat and finds his life transformed. **FF7**

Overland Stage Raiders
(1938, B&W, 55m, NR)
John Wayne B-Western in the Three Mesquiteers series has them guarding an airport that's scene to gold shipments. Notable for late career appearance by Louise Brooks. **ST21, ST224**

Owl and the Pussycat, The
(1970, C, 95m, R)
Barbra Streisand and George Segal star in this romantic comedy about a sassy New York prostitute and a fussy, would-be writer. With Robert Klein, Allen Garfield, and Roz Kelly. Written by Buck Henry; directed by Herbert Ross. Stars make the most of this familiar material. **CO1, ST211, XT26,** *Recommended*

Ox-Bow Incident, The
(1943, B&W, 75m, NR)
Western tale of injustice, about the lynching of a trio of cowboys who turn out to be innocent. Henry Fonda stars, with Dana Andrews, Mary Beth Hughes, Anthony Quinn, William Eythe, Henry (Harry) Morgan, and Jane Darwell. Directed by William Wellman. Excellent adaptation of Walter Van Tilburg Clark's novel raised sights of Westerns a notch. **DT135, ST71, WE5,** *Essential, Recommended*

Oxford Blues (1984, C, 93m, PG-13)
An American rower enrolls at Oxford to compete with the best that Britain has to offer. Rob Lowe, Ally Sheedy, and Amanda Pays star. **DR22**

P.O.W.: The Escape (1986, C, 90m, R)
David Carradine plays a hard-bitten officer determined to lead a group of American prisoners out of Vietnam. **AC7**

Pacific Heights (1990, C, 102m, PG-13)
Thriller of young San Francisco couple renting apartment to stranger who begins to terrorize them. Melanie Griffith, Matthew Modine, and Michael Keaton star, with Mako, Nobu McCarthy, Laurie Metcalf, and Tippi Hedren (Griffith's real-life mom). Directed by John Schlesinger. **DT113, MY9, MY19, ST93, ST122, XT8, XT13**

Pack, The (1977, C, 99m, R)
Wild dogs attack two families in this horror tale starring Joe Don Baker and R.G. Armstrong. **HO16**

Pack Up Your Troubles
(1932, B&W, 68m, NR)
Laurel and Hardy enlist in the army to fight in World War I. The Germans almost die laughing. **CO21, ST133**

Package, The (1989, C, 108m, R)
Thriller starring Gene Hackman as an army officer transporting a criminal (Tommy Lee Jones), whose escape begins to unravel a complex political conspiracy. With Joanna Cassidy, John Heard, and Dennis Franz. **MY6, ST96**

Padre Padrone (1977, C, 114m, NR)
Based on a true story, this Italian drama portrays the bitter childhood of a peasant boy who grows up to be a renowned scholar. Directed by Paolo and Vittorio Taviani. **FF2**

Pagan Love Song (1950, C, 76m, NR)
Esther Williams musical, with her playing a half-Tahitian in love with a visiting plantation owner (Howard Keel). With Minna Gombell and Rita Moreno. **MU1**

Pain in the A——, A (1974, C, 90m, PG)
A hit man and a would-be suicide wind up sharing the same hotel room in this dark

comedy from France. American remake: *Buddy, Buddy.* **FF1, FF8**

Paint Your Wagon (1969, C, 166m, G)
Lavish Lerner-Loewe Broadway musical about the gold rush in California, starring Clint Eastwood, Lee Marvin, and Jean Seberg, with Harve Presnell and Ray Walston. Yes, Clint and Lee do attempt to sing. **MU2, MU6, MU17, ST64, ST151**

Painted Desert, The
(1931, B&W, 75m, NR)
Western drama about two feuding families. Clark Gable's talking picture debut; he plays a baddie. **ST77**

Painted Veil, The (1934, B&W, 83m, NR)
Greta Garbo plays a faithless wife who's trying to change her ways. With Herbert Marshall, George Brent, Warner Oland, and Jean Hersholt. Adapted from a story by W. Somerset Maugham. **ST78, WR23**

Paisan (1946, B&W, 90m, NR)
Classic drama of Italian life during World War II, directed by Roberto Rossellini and cowritten by Federico Fellini. **DT109, FF2**

Pajama Game, The (1957, C, 101m, NR)
Doris Day and John Raitt square off in this Broadway musical about labor troubles. With Carol Haney, Eddie Foy, Jr., and Barbara Nichols. Directed by Stanley Donen and George Abbott; superb choreography by Bob Fosse. Songs include "Hey There" and "Hernando's Hideaway." Energetic, with Day at top of her appeal. **DT38, DT47, MU2, ST47,** *Recommended*

Pal Joey (1957, C, 111m, NR)
Broadway musical about a colorful hustler (Frank Sinatra) who builds a nightclub in San Francisco, then tries to decide between two lovely women (Rita Hayworth and Kim Novak). Based on a story by John O'Hara. Rodgers and Hart Songs include "The Lady Is a Tramp," "Bewitched," and "My Funny Valentine." Outstanding use of color. **CL9, MU2, ST101, ST199, WR24**

Pale Rider (1985, C, 113m, R)
Clint Eastwood stars in this Western story of a mysterious lone gunfighter who comes to the aid of persecuted prospectors. With Carrie Snodgress, John Russell, Michael Moriarty, and Christopher Penn. Eastwood directed. **ST64, WE2**

Paleface, The (1948, C, 91m, NR)
Bob Hope is the world's biggest dude, Jane Russell is his straight-shooting sidekick in this Western comedy. **ST108, WE14**

Palermo Connection, The
(1991, C, 100m, R)
Thriller of Italian-American New York mayoral candidate running on anti-crime platform, honeymooning in Sicily, where he's set up as fall guy in a murder. James Belushi stars, with Mimi Rogers, Joss Ackland, Philippe Noiret, and Vittorio Gassman. Cowritten by Gore Vidal, directed by Francesco Rosi. Comes close to pulling off rare feat of genre movie with something to say, but drab leads, incredible plot twists pull it down. **CO13, MY6, XT9**

Palm Beach Story, The
(1942, B&W, 90m, NR)
Classic comedy about a wife deciding to divorce her inventor husband because her tastes are too rich for them. Claudette Colbert and Joel McCrea star, with Rudy Vallee and Mary Astor. Preston Sturges wrote and directed. Among the highlights: Colbert's encounter with Quail & Ale Club on her train ride to Florida. Sturges at the peak of his powers. **CL10, DT121, ST34, ST144, XT19,** *Highly Recommended*

Panama Hattie (1942, B&W, 79m, NR)
Broadway musical from Cole Porter pen about a nightclub owner in Central America. Ann Sothern stars, with Red Skelton, and Lena Horne singing "Just One of Those Things." **MU1, MU2**

Pancho Villa (1972, C, 92m, PG)
Telly Savalas plays the legendary Mexican bandit/revolutionary in this Western adventure. **WE9**

Pandora's Box (1928, B&W, 110m, NR)
Classic silent drama of Lulu, the bewitching woman who casts an irresistible spell on all men. Louise Brooks gives a dynamic, sexy performance—the source of her considerable reputation. Directed by G.W. Pabst. **CL12, CU6, FF3, ST21,** *Essential, Highly Recommended*

Panic in Needle Park, The
(1971, C, 110m, PG)
Harrowing drama of two young New Yorkers (Al Pacino and Kitty Winn) and their descent into drug addiction. With Alan Vint, Richard Bright, Kiel Martin, and Raul Julia. Written by Joan Didion and John Gregory Dunne. **DR7, DR15, ST170**

Panic in the Streets
(1950, B&W, 93m, NR)
Tense story of New Orleans manhunt for two gangsters, one unwittingly carrying rare and deadly strain of plague. Richard Widmark stars, with Paul Douglas, Barbara Bel Geddes,

Jack Palance, and Zero Mostel. Directed by Elia Kazan. **DT65, MY1, XT14,** *Recommended*

Papa's Delicate Condition
(1963, C, 98m, NR)
Comedy set at turn of the century, about young girl's love for her father, a hard-drinking but kindly railroad man. Jackie Gleason stars, with Glynis Johns and Charlie Ruggles. **CO5, CO6**

Paper Chase, The (1973, C, 111m, PG)
Portrait of a first-year Harvard Law School student (Timothy Bottoms) and his affair with the daughter (Lindsay Wagner) of his most feared professor (John Houseman, in an Oscar-winning performance). Photographed by Gordon Willis, directed by James Bridges. Houseman is practically the whole show, but Willis's cimematography is a real plus, too. **DR25, XT4,** *Recommended*

Paper Lion (1968, C, 107m, G)
Writer George Plimpton (Alan Alda) goes on assignment with pro football's Detroit Lions, training with the team and quarterbacking in one exhibition game. Alex Karras, then a star lineman, steals the film; also in the cast: Lauren Hutton, Sugar Ray Robinson, and (in a small part) Roy Scheider. **CO19, CO20**

Paper Moon (1973, B&W, 102m, PG)
Depression-era comedy about a con man (Ryan O'Neal) and his daughter (Oscar winner Tatum O'Neal) traveling through Middle America with a Bible-selling routine. With Madeline Kahn. Directed by Peter Bogdanovich. **CO6, XT5, XT8, XT18**

Paper Tiger (1976, C, 99m, PG)
David Niven plays the cowardly tutor to a Japanese diplomat's son who musters all his courage when he and the boy are kidnapped. Toshiro Mifune costars in this family drama. **FA15, ST157**

Paperhouse (1989, C, 94m, PG-13)
British drama of a young girl (Charlotte Burke) whose bout with a fever allows her imagination to run riot. Directed by Bernard Rose. **DR9, DR23**

Papillon (1973, C, 150m, PG)
True story of Henri Charrière, played by Steve McQueen, and his dramatic escape from Devil's Island prison. Dustin Hoffman costars. **AC24, DR18, ST105, ST146**

Paradine Case, The
(1948, B&W, 116m, NR)
Alfred Hitchcock courtroom drama, starring Gregory Peck and Valli, with Ann Todd, Charles Laughton, and Ethel Barrymore. **DR17, DT57, ST132, ST171**

Paradise (1991, C, 110m, PG-13)
Nine-year-old boy is sent off to live with friends of his pregnant mother; couple has their own problems. Don Johnson and Melanie Griffith star in this sentimental drama, with Elijah Wood and Thora Birch. Remake of 1988 French film, *The Grand Highway*. **DR2, DR8, FA7, FF8, ST93**

Paradise Alley (1978, C, 109m, PG)
Sylvester Stallone stars in this comedy of three New York brothers and their dreams for fame and fortune, with one going for a career as a pro wrestler. With Armand Assante. Stallone directed. **CO5, CO19, ST204**

Paradise, Hawaiian Style
(1966, C, 91m, NR)
Elvis Presley returns to the islands after his success with *Blue Hawaii* for some more ukulele strumming and romancing with the local ladies. **ST178**

Parallax View, The (1974, C, 102m, R)
Reporter Warren Beatty uncovers a complex political conspiracy in this very contemporary thriller. With Paula Prentiss, Hume Cronyn, and Jim Davis. Directed by Alan J. Pakula; photographed by Gordon Willis in widescreen format, which will be lost on video. Superbly directed, if sometimes far-fetched, thriller. **CU9, CU20, DR21, DT94, MY6, MY11, ST10,** *Recommended*

Pardon Mon Affaire (1977, C, 105m, PG)
A happily married man is nevertheless fascinated by a gorgeous model he spots in a parking garage. French comedy was remade in the U.S. as *The Woman in Red.* **FF1, FF8**

Pardon My Sarong (1942, B&W, 84m, NR)
Abbott and Costello are shipwrecked, involved with jewel thieves. With Lionel Atwill, Virginia Bruce, William Demarest, and the Four Ink Spots. **ST1**

Pardon Us (1931, B&W, 55m, NR)
Laurel and Hardy are shipped off to prison for making homemade brew during the height of Prohibition. **ST133**

Parent Trap, The (1961, C, 124m, NR)
Hayley Mills plays twin sisters who are separated when their parents divorce and meet years later at a summer camp. Disney comedy costars Brian Keith and Maureen O'Hara. **FA1, ST167, XT27**

Parenthood (1989, C, 124m, PG-13)
Interlocking stories of a large family, with several generations of problems. Comedy-drama, directed by Ron Howard, stars Steve Martin, with Mary Steenburgen, Dianne

Wiest, Jason Robards, Rick Moranis, Thomas Hulce, Martha Plimpton, and Keanu Reeves. Very uneven, depending on whose story is being told. Martin, Robards and Wiest come off best. **CO5, CO14, DT58, ST150, ST185**

Parents (1989, C, 90m, R)
Dark comedy set in the 1950s, featuring a seemingly normal couple whose young son begins to suspect that their dinners are composed of human meat. Randy Quaid and Mary Beth Hurt star. **CO5, CO6, CO12**

Paris Blues (1961, B&W, 98m, NR)
Quartet of Americans in Paris—two jazz musicians, two female tourists—are the focus of this drama. Paul Newman, Sidney Poitier, Joanne Woodward, and Diahann Carroll star; Louis Armstrong makes an appearance. Directed by Martin Ritt. **DT105, ST162, ST174, ST234, XT16**

Paris Does Strange Things see *Elena and Her Men*

Paris Express, The (1953, C, 80m, NR)
A shy bookkeeper uncovers embezzling by his boss and follows him to Paris, where he's accused of the thief's murder. Claude Rains stars. **MY7**

Paris Holiday (1958, C, 100m, NR)
Bob Hope plays an American in Paris looking to purchase a screenplay, involved in misunderstandings and mix-ups. With Fernandel, Anita Ekberg, and writer-direetor Preston Sturges in a rare acting role. **DT121, ST108**

Paris Is Burning (1991, C, 71m, NR)
One-of-a-kind documentary on New York underground gay scene, with drag costume balls and competition held weekly in Bronx gymnasium. Directed by Jennie Livingston. Could have been a freak show but is touching portrait of desperate lives. **CU16, Recommended**

Paris, Texas (1984, C, 150m, R)
Drama of two brothers reunited years after one deserted his son and wife. Harry Dean Stanton, Nastassja Kinski, and Dean Stockwell star, with Hunter Carson. Written by Sam Shepard; directed by Wim Wenders. Music by Ry Cooder. Extreme length dissipates emotional impact, but worth seeing for fans of participants; Stanton's best role ever. **DR8, DT136, ST205, ST208, XT18**

Paris Trout (1991, C, 100m, NR)
Harrowing adaptation of Pete Dexter's novel of racism and betrayal in small-town South. Dennis Hopper is title character, a store-owner who's on trial for casual murder of black girl, Barbara Hershey is his long-suffering wife, Ed Harris his attorney who's attracted to her. Adapted by Dexter; directed by Stephen Gyllenhaal. Originally made for cable TV. Very powerful, with Hopper sensational. **DR17, DR19, DR26, MY3, ST104, ST110, Recommended**

Paris When It Sizzles (1964, C, 110m, NR)
An American screenwriter and his secretary are in Paris trying to work on a script in this comedy starring William Holden and Audrey Hepburn. Marlene Dietrich, Fred Astaire, Noel Coward, and Frank Sinatra are among the stars who appear in cameos. **ST4, ST55, ST102, ST106, ST199, WR4**

Parrot Sketch Not Included
(1990, C, 75m, NR)
Twentieth anniversary collection of Monty Python Flying Circus's greatest bits. **CO15**

Partner (1968, C, 112m, NR)
Complex drama from Italian director Bernardo Bertolucci, starring Pierre Clementi as a man bedeviled by his flesh-and-blood alter ego. With Tina Aumont and Stefania Sandrelli. **DT13, XT27**

Party, The (1968, C, 99m, NR)
Slapstick comedy set at a large Hollywood party, starring Peter Sellers and Claudine Longet. Directed by Blake Edwards. Sellers has some moments but this is one party you can skip. **DT40, ST198**

Party Girl (1958, C, 99m, NR)
A corrupt lawyer (Robert Taylor) and dancer (Cyd Charisse) attempt to break free of the clutches of the Chicago mob. With Lee J. Cobb and John Ireland. Directed by Nicholas Ray. **AC22, DT101**

Party Line (1988, C, 91m, R)
A brother and sister, unhinged by their mother's suicide and father's abuse, turn killers, using special telephone party lines to lure their victims. Leif Garrett and Greta Blackburn star. **MY14**

Pascali's Island (1988, C, 101m, PG-13)
British period drama set on a Mediterranean outpost, where a Turkish intelligence officer is frustrated in both his professional and love life. Ben Kingsley stars, with Helen Mirren and Charles Dance. **DR23**

Passage to India, A (1984, C, 163m, PG)
From director David Lean comes this screen version of the E.M. Forster novel about an impressionable Englishwoman's tragic experiences in India. Judy Davis, Victor Banerjee, Alec Guinness, and Oscar winner Peggy Ashcroft star. Doesn't quite capture novel's mysteries. **DR27, DT71, ST46, ST95, WR9, XT5**

Passage to Marseilles
(1944, B&W, 110m, NR)
Escape drama set on infamous Devil's Island, starring Humphrey Bogart, Claude Rains, Sydney Greenstreet, and Peter Lorre. **DR18, ST15**

Passed Away (1992, C, 96m, PG-13)
Black comedy about how death of family patriarch affects his heirs. The ensemble cast features Bob Hoskins, William Petersen, Helen Lloyd Breed, Maureen Stapleton, Pamela Reed, Tim Curry, Peter Riegert, Blair Brown, Nancy Travis, and Jack Warden as the deceased. Written and directed by Charlie Peters. **CO5, CO12, ST111**

Passenger, The (1975, C, 119m, PG)
A journalist in North Africa assumes the identity of a man he finds dead in a hotel room. Jack Nicholson and Maria Schneider star in this drama from director Michelangelo Antonioni. Falls just short of the mark, but followers of star and director won't want to miss it. **DR27, DT5, ST163**

Passenger 57 (1992, C, 83m, R)
Action drama of airline security expert who happens to be aboard a plane when it's hijacked by terrorists. Wesley Snipes stars, with Bruce Payne, Ernie Lively, and Robert Hooks. Directed by Kevin Hooks. **AC11, AC25, ST201**

Passion (1919, B&W, 135m, NR)
Silent version of *Madame du Barry*, starring Pola Negri and Emil Jannings and directed by Ernst Lubitsch. **CL12, DT76, FF3**

Passion (1954, C, 84m, NR)
Western drama of revenge set in California, starring Cornel Wilde, Yvonne de Carlo, and Lon Chaney, Jr. **ST27**

Passion Fish (1992, C, 134m, R)
Drama of TV soap actress whose career is on hold after a crippling accident and her relationship with young black nurse. Mary McDonnell and Alfre Woodard star, with David Strathairn and Vondie Curtis-Hall. Written, directed, and edited by John Sayles. Rewarding character study, with Woodard and Strathairn especially good. **DR10, DT112,** *Recommended*

Passion Flower (1986, C, 100m, NR)
Romantic drama set in Singapore involving banker and the daughter of a smuggler. Bruce Boxleitner and Barbara Hershey star, with Nicol Williamson. Originally made for TV. **ST104**

Passion of Anna, The (1969, C, 101m, R)
Superbly detailed drama from writer-director Ingmar Bergman about tangled relationship between lonely man (Max von Sydow) and a widow (Liv Ullmann). With Bibi Andersson and Erland Josephson. Photographed by Sven Nykvist. One of Bergman's strongest and most accessible films. **DR1, DT11, ST220, XT30,** *Highly Recommended.*

Passion of Beatrice, The see *Beatrice*

Passion of Joan of Arc, The
(1928, B&W, 114m, NR)
Director Carl Dreyer's austere, gripping recreation of the young martyr's trial and execution. A silent film classic. Maria Falconetti gives a mesmerizing performance. **CL12, DT39, FF1,** *Essential, Recommended*

Passion of Love (1982, C, 117m, NR)
Italian drama set in 1862, concerning the cousin of a military commander falling in love with a dashing captain. Valeria D'Obici and Bernard Giraudeau star, with Laura Antonelli and Jean-Louis Trintignant. Directed by Ettore Scola. **FF2**

Pat and Mike (1952, B&W, 95m, NR)
Very funny Spencer Tracy-Katharine Hepburn comedy of a hustling sports promoter and his latest find, a superb female athlete. With Aldo Ray, Willam Ching, Jim Backus, Carl ("Alfalfa") Switzer, and Charles Bronson (billed as Charles Buchinski). Directed by George Cukor; written by Garson Kanin and Ruth Gordon. **CL10, CL15, CO19, DT24, ST20, ST103, ST207,** *Recommended*

Pat Garrett and Billy the Kid
(1973, C, 122m, R)
The tragic tale of the famous outlaw and his sheriff friend who gunned him down. James Coburn and Kris Kristofferson star, with Richard Bright, Harry Dean Stanton, Slim Pickens, Katy Jurado, Jason Robards, Richard Jaeckel, R.G. Armstrong, Rita Coolidge, and L.Q. Jones. Directed by Sam Peckinpah, with music by Bob Dylan; both have small roles. This is the version that restores the director's original footage; also available at 106 minutes. Generally flawed at shorter length but restored footage (which details Garrett's character and background) pushes this into front rank of director's work. **CU10, DT95, HF1, MU12, ST185, ST205, WE3, WE15,** *Recommended (long version)*

Patch of Blue, A (1965, B&W, 105m, NR)
Heartfelt tale of a young blind woman who falls in love with a black man. Elizabeth Hartman and Sidney Poitier star, with Oscar winner Shelley Winters. Well-intentioned but hardly memorable. **DR3, ST174, ST232, XT5**

Paternity (1981, C, 94m, PG)
The manager of New York's Madison Square Garden decides to look for the perfect woman to father his first child. Burt Reynolds stars in this comedy, with Beverly D'Angelo, Elizabeth Ashley, and Lauren Hutton. **CO1, ST183**

Pather Panchali (1956, B&W, 112m, NR)
Indian director Satyajit Ray's first film in his *Apu* trilogy, about the day-to-day life of a poor family in Bengal. **DT102,** *Essential*

Paths of Glory (1957, B&W, 86m, NR)
World War I drama about a French general who orders his men on a suicide mission, then has three survivors court-martialed and executed. Powerful antiwar statement from director Stanley Kubrick. Kirk Douglas stars. Cowritten by Jim Thompson. **AC2, DT68, ST57, XT25,** *Essential, Highly Recommended*

Patrick (1978, C, 96m, PG)
A young murderer in a coma uses his telekinetic powers to further destroy those around him. Horror drama from Australia, directed by Richard Franklin. **FF5, HO7**

Patriot Games (1992, C, 116m, R)
Thriller, adapted from Tom Clancy's novel, about retired CIA man protecting his family from a vengeful Irish terrorist and his gang. Harrison Ford stars, with Anne Archer, Patrick Bergin, Sean Bean, Thora Birch, James Fox, Samuel L. Jackson, Polly Walker, James Earl Jones, and Richard Harris. Directed by Phillip Noyce. Gives new meaning to the phrase "strains credibility," even if you take it as a piece of escapist fluff. **MY6, MY14, ST74, ST118**

Patsy, The (1964, C, 101m, NR)
Nerdy bellhop agrees to impersonate a dead comedian so that the star's hangers-on can keep the money rolling in. Jerry Lewis stars. **ST139**

Patterns (1956, B&W, 83m, NR)
Absorbing drama of boardroom politics in New York corporation. Van Heflin, Ed Begley, and Everett Sloane star. Directed by Fielder Cook; adapted by Rod Serling from his TV play. **DR24, XT8,** *Recommended*

Patti Rocks (1988, C, 86m, R)
Foul-mouthed guy takes his buddy for a car ride to visit his pregnant girlfriend to talk her into an abortion. Comedy-drama stars Chris Mulkey, John Jenkins, and Karen Landry. Mulkey (as the obnoxious guy) is terrific, but it's a thin idea for 86 minutes. **CO2**

Patton (1970, C, 169m, PG)
George C. Scott won an Oscar (which he refused to accept) for his performance as the legendary U.S. Army general with a controversial record in Europe during World War II. The film and its director, Franklin Schaffner, also won Academy Awards. With Karl Malden as Omar Bradley. Widescreen will be lost on home video. **AC1, DR4, ST196, XT1, XT2, XT6,** *Essential, Recommended*

Patty Hearst (1988, C, 108m, R)
True story of publishing heiress kidnapped by political radicals and brainwashed into joining them in a crime spree. Natasha Richardson ann William Forsythe star. Paul Schrader directed. **DR6, DR16**

Pauline at the Beach (1983, C, 94m, R)
From French director Eric Rohmer, a comedy about a teen-age girl's experiences during a summer of growing up at a resort. **DT107**

Pawnbroker, The (1965, B&W, 116m, NR)
Rod Steiger stars as a Jewish survivor of the Nazi death camps who runs a pawn shop in Harlem, fighting against his horrible memories. With Jaime Sanchez, Geraldine Fitzgerald, and Brock Peters. Sidney Lumet directed. Steiger's best performance, but the film lays it on too hard for too long. **DR15, DT78, XT9**

Payday (1973, C, 103m, R)
A country singer pushes himself—and everyone around him—to the brink with his rowdy, uninhibited ways. Rip Torn is the magnetic star of this cult favorite. **DR12, ST216, XT18, XT26,** *Recommended*

Payoff (1991, C, 111m, R)
Standard revenge drama of ex-cop out for personal justice after mobsters murder his parents. Keith Carradine stars, with Kim Greist, Harry Dean Stanton, and John Saxon. **AC19, ST205**

Peanut Butter Solution, The (1985, C, 96m, PG)
Family comedy of an eleven-year-old boy with a very vivid imagination who finds himself in a strange house with more adventures than he ever dreamed of. **FA6, FA7**

Pearl, The (1948, B&W, 77m, NR)
Adaptation of the John Steinbeck parable of how a Mexican peasant's discovery of a large pearl changes his life. Pedro Armendariz and Maria Elena Marques star. **CL8, WR32**

Pearl of Death (1944, B&W, 69m, NR)
Sherlock Holmes adventure starring Basil Rathbone and Nigel Bruce. They're out to find a killer who calls himself The Creeper. **HF14**

Peeping Tom (1960, C, 109m, R)
Legendary cult film, censored and banned in

its original release, about a murderous cinematographer (Carl Boehm) who films his crimes. With Anna Massey and Moira Shearer. Michael Powell directed; he also plays the father of the killer in flashback scenes. Not for the squeamish but a provocative statement on the nature of filmmaking. **CU8, DT99, XT31,** *Recommended*

Pee-wee's Big Adventure
(1985, C, 90m, PG)
Pee-wee Herman discovers that his favorite bicycle has been stolen, and he embarks on a cross-country mission to recover it. Silly fun for kids of all ages. Directed by Tim Burton. **CO11, CO12, CU5, DT20, FA6, XT18,** *Recommended*

Peggy Sue Got Married
(1986, C, 103m, PG-13)
At her 20th anniversary high school reunion, a woman passes out and wakes up to find herself in high school again. Will she marry the same no-good guy? Kathleen Turner and Nicolas Cage star in this comedy from director Francis Ford Coppola. With Barry Miller, Catherine Hicks, Joan Allen, Barbara Harris, Maureen O'Sullivan, and John Carradine. Gets off to a bad start and never gains its footing. Turner's too old for the role, Cage is totally unsympathetic. **CO6, CO20, DT29, SF4, ST23, ST218**

Pelle the Conqueror (1988, C, 138m, PG-13)
Oscar-winning drama from Denmark, starring Max von Sydow as an impoverished Swedish widower who moves to Denmark to begin a new life with his son. **FF7, XT7**

Pendulum (1969, C, 106m, PG)
Police detective is framed for murder and must clear himself. George Peppard and Jean Seberg star. **MY7**

Penn & Teller Get Killed
(1989, C, 89m, R)
Magicians Penn and Teller star in this offbeat mystery as themselves, the targets of a mad killer. Directed by Arthur Penn. **DT96, MY17**

Pennies From Heaven (1981, C, 107m, R)
One-of-a-kind musical about a Depression-era sheet music salesman who sings his way through his various troubles. Steve Martin stars, with Bernadette Peters, Jessica Harper, and Christopher Walken. Based on a British TV miniseries created by Dennis Potter. Filled with lavish production numbers on sets designed by Ken Adam, brilliantly photographed by Gordon Willis. **MU3, MU16, ST150, ST222,** *Recommended*

Penny Serenade (1941, B&W, 125m, NR)
Cary Grant and Irene Dunne star in this tear-jerker about a couple who decide to adopt a baby. Directed by George Stevens. Has its fans, but I'm not one of them. **CL6, DT119, ST62, ST92**

People That Time Forgot, The
(1977, C, 90m, PG)
Sequel to *The Land That Time Forgot,* with more adventures in ancient world populated by fierce dinosaurs. Doug McClure stars. **SF4**

People Under the Stairs, The
(1991, C, 102m, R)
Contemporary haunted house tale, featuring a thirteen-year-old black kid and a lot of creepy folks living you-know-where. Brandon Adams stars, with Everett McGill and Wendy Robie. Directed by Wes Craven. **HO3**

Pepe LePew's Skunk Tales
(1948–60, C, 56m, NR)
A collection of Warner Brothers cartoons featuring that misunderstood and amorous skunk. Includes the Oscar-winning cartoon, *For Scent-imental Reasons.* **FA11**

Pepi, Luci, Bom (1980, C, 86m, NR)
Spanish director Pedro Almodóvar's debut film, a wacky comedy about three friends in Madrid. **DT3**

Perfect! (1985, C, 120m, R)
Reporter John Travolta is supposed to do an exposé on fitness clubs as a place to pick up dates; he finds himself falling for aerobics instructor Jamie Lee Curtis. With Laraine Newman and Marilu Henner. **CO2, ST42**

Perfect Furlough, The
(1958, B&W, 93m, NR)
Romantic comedy of young soldier (Tony Curtis) wooing military psychiatrist (Janet Leigh). Directed by Blake Edwards. **CO21, DT40**

Perfect Strangers (1984, C, 91m, R)
A three-year-old witnesses a murder, then watches as the killer romances his mom. Anne Carlisle, Brad Rijn, and Matthew Stockley star. Also known as *Blind Alley.* **DT28, MY14**

Perfect Weapon, The (1991, C, 112m, R)
Jeff Speakman stars in this martial arts saga of an expert in kenpo—a combination of judo, jujitsu, karate, and kung fu. **AC26**

Performance (1970, C, 105m, R)
A London gangster on the lam hides out in the home of a reclusive rock star, and their lives begin to intertwine. James Fox and Mick Jagger star in this cult drama, directed by Nicolas Roeg and Donald Cammell. Outstanding soundtrack features Ry Cooder, Randy Newman, The Last Poets, and Jagger's

rendition of "Memo from Turner." Originally rated X. **CU1, CU3, DR16, DT106, MY2,** *Recommended*

Period of Adjustment (1962, C, 112m, NR) Romantic comedy by Tennessee Williams of trails and tribulations of a pair of newlyweds. Jane Fonda and Jim Hutton star, with Tony Franciosa and Lois Nettleton. Directed by George Roy Hill. **CO1, DT55, ST72, WR38**

Permanent Record (1988, C, 91m, PG-13) A teen-ager who seems to have it all—good grades, popularity, girlfriends—commits suicide, leaving his friends to wonder why. Alan Boyce stars, with Keanu Reeves and Richard Bradford. **DR9, DR25**

Permission To Kill (1975, C, 96m, PG) British-made spy drama starring Dirk Bogarde as the head of a Western alliance, involved with attempt by opposition leader to return to his dictator-ruled country. With Bekim Fehmiu, Ava Gardner, Timothy Dalton, and Frederic Forrest. **MY6, ST14, ST79**

Persecution (1974, C, 92m, PG) Lana Turner stars in a British thriller about an overbearing mom's effect on her offspring. With Trevor Howard and Ralph Bates. **MY14, MY15, ST219**

Persecution and Assassination of Jean-Paul Marat as Performed by the Inmates of the Asylum of Charenton Under the Direction of the Marquis de Sade, The see *Marat/Sade*

Persona (1966, B&W, 81m, NR) Hypnotic drama from director Ingmar Bergman about the relationship between an actress and a nurse. Liv Ullmann and Bibi Andersson star. **DT11, ST220, XT30,** *Essential, Recommended*

Personal Best (1982, C, 124m, R) A pair of women runners, competing for a place on the Olympic team, become lovers. Mariel Hemingway, Patrice Donnelly, and Scott Glenn star. Written and directed by Robert Towne. Sorely needed look at neglected subject seems never to get going dramatically. Weak lead performances. **DR3, DR10, DR22**

Personal Property (1937, B&W, 84m, NR) Robert Taylor woos widow Jean Harlow in this romantic comedy set in England. **ST98**

Personal Services (1987, C, 105m, R) Julie Walters stars as a London working-class girl who stumbles into running a brothel and soon becomes very successful at it. Saucy comedy was directed by Terry Jones of the Monty Python troupe. **CO15, CO17**

Pet Sematary (1989, C, 102m, R) Stephen King horror tale of an ancient burial ground with powers that can bring dead animals back to life. Dale Midkiff and Fred Gwynne star. King adapted his novel and has a small role as a minister. **HO16, WR15**

Pet Sematary Two (1992, C, 100m, R) Name-only sequel to Stephen King tale of haunted burial ground. In this one, a young boy envisions his dead mother at title locale. Edward Furlong and Darlanne Fluegel star, with Anthony Edwards. **HO6**

Pete Kelly's Blues (1955, C, 95m, NR) Drama revolving around the jazz scene of the 1920s, starring Jack Webb as a trumpet player and featuring real-life music stars Peggy Lee and Ella Fitzgerald. With Janet Leigh and Lee Marvin. Webb directed. Widescreen will be lost on home video. Terrific cast can't quite strike necessary spark. **DR12, ST151**

Pete 'n' Tillie (1972, C, 100m, PG) Walter Matthau and Carol Burnett star in this romantic comedy-drama about a couple who meet and marry late in life. With Geraldine Page, Barry Nelson, and René Auberjonois. Adapted from Peter de Vries's novella, *Witch's Milk*, by Julius J. Epstein. Directed by Martin Ritt. Burnett is very good; story is best when it concentrates on leads. **CO1, DR1, DT105, ST155**

Peter and Paul (1981, C, 200m, NR) Biblical story of Apostles Peter (Robert Foxworth) and Paul (Anthony Hopkins) follows them from Christ's crucifixion to their deaths. With Eddie Albert, Raymond Burr, and José Ferrer. Originally made for TV. **CL13, ST109**

Peter Pan (1953, C, 76m, G) Disney feature-length cartoon about the young boy who never grows up, and the trio of children he takes to his magical kingdom. **FA2,** *Recommended*

Peter's Friends (1992, C, 100m, NR) British comedy of New Year's reunion of group of old friends at country house, with old lusts and animosities surfacing. Featured in the cast are Kenneth Branagh, Stephen Fry, Hugh Laurie, Rita Rudner, Alphonsia Emmanuel, Emma Thompson, Imelda Stanton, and Tony Slattery. Branagh produced and directed, Rudner and her husband Martin Bergman wrote the screenplay. Fitfully entertaining. Rudner's very funny. **CO17**

Pete's Dragon (1977, C, 134m, G) An orphan is befriended by a large and very friendly dragon in this Disney musical. Helen

Reddy, Jim Dale, Mickey Rooney, and Shelley Winters star. **FA1, ST189, ST232**

Petrified Forest, The
(1936, B&W, 83m, NR)
Escaped convict Humphrey Bogart holds waitress Bette Davis and drifter Leslie Howard hostage in this melodrama. Based on the play by Robert Sherwood. Pretty creaky, although Bogie makes indelible impression. **DR20, ST15, ST44**

Petulia (1968, C, 105m, PG)
Drama set in 1967 San Francisco about a divorced surgeon (George C. Scott) and his affair with a restless newlywed (Julie Christie). Powerful portrait of late-1960s America is brilliantly told through multiple flashbacks. With Richard Chamberlain, Arthur Hill, Shirley Knight, Joseph Cotten, Pippa Scott, Kathleen Widdoes, and musical appearances by the Grateful Dead and Big Brother and the Holding Company. Written by Lawrence B. Marcus and directed by Richard Lester; photographed by Nicolas Roeg. If I had one film to take to a desert island . . . **CL14, DR1, DR7, DR15, DT74, ST30, ST196, XT13,** *Essential, Highly Recommended*

Peyton Place (1957, B&W, 157m, NR)
Grace Metalious's notorious novel of small-town lust, turned into a respectable Hollywood production starring Lana Turner, with Hope Lange, Arthur Kennedy, Lloyd Nolan, Terry Moore, Russ Tamblyn, David Nelson, and Diane Varsi. Directed by Mark Robson. **DR26, ST219**

Phantom Creeps, The
(1939, B&W, 75m, NR)
Condensed version of serial adventure about the evil Dr. Zorka (Bela Lugosi) and his robot and mechanical spider. **ST143**

Phantom Empire (1935, B&W, 245m, NR)
A twelve-chapter Western serial starring Gene Autry, as he battles the "Thunder Riders" from an underworld kingdom beneath his ranch. Also available in an eighty-minute version titled *Radio Ranch*. **ST5**

Phantom of Liberty, The
(1974, C, 104m, R)
Director Luis Buñuel presents a series of surrealistic sketches, loosely connected, all designed to satirize contemporary society's claims to freedom. Jean-Claude Brialy, Monica Vitti, and Michel Piccoli star. **DT19**

Phantom of the Opera, The
(1925, B&W, 79m, NR)
Lon Chaney, Sr., silent version of the horror classic can't be beat for chills; unmasking

scene still an all-time movie highlight. **HO1, HO9, ST26,** *Highly Recommended*

Phantom of the Opera
(1943, C, 92m, NR)
Second version of horror classic adds brilliant color photography and set design (both Oscar winners). Claude Rains, Susanna Foster, and Nelson Eddy star. **CL9, CU18, HO9**

Phantom of the Opera, The
(1989, C, 90m, R)
Robert Englund stars as the masked man of the opera house in this version set in nineteenth-century London. With Jill Schoelen. **HO9**

Phantom of the Paradise
(1974, C, 92m, PG)
Rock 'n' roll version of *Phantom of the Opera*, with a little Faust thrown in. Paul Williams, William Finley, Jessica Harper, and Gerrit Graham star. Brian De Palma directed. Some sharp satire and some soggy musical numbers; one of the director's least pretentious films. **DT36, MU4, MU9, MU14**

Phantom Ship see *The Mystery of the Mary Celeste*

Phantom Tollbooth, The
(1969, C, 90m, G)
Live action and animation blend in this version of the classic children's book about a boy's adventures in a land of numbers and letters. Animation directed by Chuck Jones. Also known as *The Adventures of Milo in the Phantom Tollbooth*. **FA8**

Phar Lap (1984, C, 106m, PG)
In 1932, Phar Lap became a national hero, a pug ugly horse from New Zealand that won thirty-seven races in Australia. Tom Burlinson stars in this horse lover's drama. **DR22, FA5**

Phase IV (1974, C, 86m, PG)
Science fiction/horror story of three scientists at remote outpost beset by mutant ants. Clever photography and special effects. Directed by Saul Bass. **SF20,** *Recommended*

Philadelphia Experiment, The
(1984, C, 102m, PG)
Two American sailors fall through a time warp in 1943 and wind up in 1984. After one disappears, the other discovers he's part of a secret government experiment. Michael Paré, Nancy Allen, and Bobby Di Cicco star. **MY6, SF4**

Philadelphia Story, The
(1940, B&W, 112m, NR)
Witty story of spoiled society girl (Katharine Hepburn) who dumps one husband (Cary Grant), tries to marry another man, and falls

in love with a third (Oscar winner James Stewart). With Ruth Hussey, John Howard, Roland Young, and Virginia Wiedler. Donald Ogden Stewart adapted Philip Barry's play, which also starred Hepburn. Flawlessly directed by George Cukor. As good as Hollywood comedy gets. **CL4, CL10, DR20, DT32, ST92, ST103, ST207, XT2, XT20,** *Essential, Highly Recommended*

Philby, Burgess and MacLean: Spy Scandal of the Century
(1986, C, 83m, NR)
Dramatization of Britain's major spy scandal, involving three college chums recruited by the Russians and working undetected for thirty years. Anthony Bates, Derek Jacobi, and Michael Culver star. **MY6, MY8, MY15**

Phobia (1980, C, 90m, R)
John Huston directed this mystery about a doctor whose patients, all victims of various phobias, are being murdered one by one. Paul Michael Glaser stars. **DT60**

Phone Call From a Stranger
(1952, B&W, 96m, NR)
The survivor of a plane crash decides to visit the families of some of the victims. Gary Merrill and Bette Davis star, with Shelley Winters and Michael Rennie. **ST44, ST232**

Physical Evidence (1989, C, 99m, R)
Burt Reynolds is a suspended cop framed for murder whose only hope for acquittal is a snotty public defender (Theresa Russell). **MY7, ST183**

Piano for Mrs. Cimino, A
(1982, C, 100m, NR)
Bette Davis plays a widow who is declared senile but fights on for her dignity. With Penny Fuller and Keenan Wynn. Originally made for TV. **DR11, ST44**

Pick a Star see *Movie Struck*

Pick-up Artist, The (1987, C, 81m, R)
A young New York schoolteacher spends his spare time roaming the streets of the city, hitting on women. He meets his match when an attractive young woman accepts his offer for casual sex, then spurns him. Robert Downey, Jr., and Molly Ringwald star, with Dennis Hopper and Harvey Keitel. Written and directed by James Toback. Downey does his best with a tiresome character; Hopper's terrific in a small role. **DR1, ST110, XT9**

Pickup on South Street
(1953, B&W, 80m, NR)
Compact, razor-sharp thriller from director Sam Fuller about low-life pickpocket who accidentally gets hold of some microfilm that the Commies and the FBI are after. Richard Widmark stars, with Jean Peters, Thelma Ritter, and Richard Kiley. **DT49, MY1,** *Recommended*

Pickwick Papers (1954, B&W, 109m, NR)
British-produced version of the Charles Dickens tale about a clever actor and con artist, starring James Donald, with Hermione Baddeley, James Hayter, and Hermione Gingold. **DR23, WR5**

Picnic (1955, C, 115m, NR)
The William Inge play of a drifter who shakes things up in a small Kansas town. William Holden stars, with Rosalind Russell, Kim Novak, Betty Field, Cliff Robertson, and Arthur O'Connell. Directed by Joshua Logan. Available in letterboxed format. **CU19, DR20, DR26, ST106, ST192**

Picnic at Hanging Rock
(1975, C, 110m, PG)
Atmospheric drama set in turn-of-the-century Australia: a girls' school outing to the Outback turns tragic when three students and their teacher disappear. Rachel Roberts stars. Peter Weir directed; based on a true story. **DR5, FF5, DT133**

Picnic on the Grass (1959, C, 92m, NR)
French fantasy of politician falling in love with a peasant girl, directed by Jean Renoir. Paul Meurisse and Catherine Rouvel star. **DT104**

Picture of Dorian Gray, The
(1945, B&W, 110m, NR)
Oscar Wilde story of a man who never ages, despite a wild and carefree life. Hurd Hatfield, Angela Lansbury, and George Sanders star. Several short sequences in color. **CL1, HO1, HO26, ST131**

Piece of the Action, A
(1977, C, 135m, PG)
Con men Sidney Poitier and Bill Cosby are roped into helping a social worker and her young charges in this comedy. With James Earl Jones. **CO10, ST118, ST174**

Pied Piper of Hamelin, The
(1985, C, 60m, NR)
Eric Idle plays both the title role and poet Robert Browning in this Faerie Tale Theatre version of Browning's classic. **CO15, FA12**

Pierrot le Fou (1965, C, 110m, NR)
Episodic adventures of a couple on the lam, from French director Jean-Luc Godard. Screenplay was allegedly improvised as the film was shot. Jean-Paul Belmondo and Anna Karina star, with director Sam Fuller appearing as himself. Godard in top, mid-'60s form

with heady mixture of politics and B-movie homages. **DT49, DT50, ST11, XT18,** *Recommended*

Pillow Talk (1959, C, 105m, NR)
Doris Day and Rock Hudson share a party line, can't stand each other on the phone, but fall in love when they meet. Fluffy romantic comedy with Tony Randall and Thelma Ritter. Virtually defines Day's box office appeal. **CO1, ST47, ST112,** *Essential*

Pin (1988, C, 103m, R)
Horror tale of a young boy's fascination with his physician father's anatomical dummy, which comes to life for him. **HO16**

Pink Cadillac (1989, C, 122m, PG-13)
Clint Eastwood action comedy of a bounty hunter and the fugitive wife of a white supremacist. With Bernadette Peters. Buddy Van Horn directed. **CO10, ST64**

Pink Flamingos (1972, C, 95m, NR)
Director John Waters's look at the cheap and disgusting lives of certain denizens of Baltimore, Maryland. Divine stars in this midnight movie classic. **CU1, CU12, DT132**

Pink Floyd: The Wall (1982, C, 99m, R)
Gloomy rock musical, based on album by British rock group, about the decay of modern society. Bob Geldof and Bob Hoskins star. Directed by Alan Parker. **MU9, MU16, ST111**

Pink Panther, The (1964, C, 113m, NR)
The comedy that gave the madcap Inspector Clouseau (Peter Sellers) to the world. The theft of a rare jewel (the title reference) is the object of his investigation. With David Niven, Capucine, and Robert Wagner. Blake Edwards directed. **DT40, ST198**

Pink Panther Strikes Again, The (1976, C, 103m, PG)
The fifth in the series about the inept Inspector Clouseau (Peter Sellers) has his ex-boss gone loony and attempting to (dare we say it?) rule the world. Herbert Lom costars. Directed by Blake Edwards. **DT40, ST198**

Pinky (1949, B&W, 102m, NR)
Drama of light-skinned black girl (Jeanne Crain) passing for white up North, returning to her mother's home in the South. With Ethel Barrymore and Ethel Waters. Directed by Elia Kazan. Interesting attempt by Hollywood to deal with touchy subject. **CL8, DR14, DT65**

Pinocchio (1940, C, 87m, G)
Disney animated feature about a marionette who wants to become a boy and must learn some hard lessons about telling the truth.

One of the great cartoon features of all time. **FA2,** *Essential, Highly Recommended*

Pinocchio (1984, C, 60m, NR)
Paul Reubens (better known as Pee-wee Herman) stars as the marionette who wants to be a boy in this Faerie Tale Theatre presentation. With James Belushi. **CO13, FA12**

Pinocchio and the Emperor of the Night (1987, C, 87m, G)
Animated adventures of the famous marionette, who has now become a real boy. Voices supplied by Ed Asner, Tom Bosley, Lana Beeson, James Earl Jones, Ricky Lee Jones, and Don Knotts. **FA10, ST118**

Pin-up Girl (1944, C, 83m, NR)
Betty Grable musical; she plays the title role. With Martha Raye, John Harvey, Joe E. Brown, and Eugene Pallette. **ST91**

Pippi Longstocking (series)
Pippi Longstocking (1974, C, 99m, G)
Pippi in the South Seas (1974, C, 99m, G)
Pippi Goes on Board (1975, C, 84m, G)
Pippi on the Run (1978, C, 99m, G)
The adventures of a daring little Swedish girl who inherits her spunk from her sea captain father. See also: *The New Adventures of Pippi Longstocking.* **FA4**

Pippin (1982, C, 120m, NR)
Filmed performance of the Broadway musical about the adolescent son of Charlemagne. Tony winner Ben Vereen stars, with William Katt, Martha Raye, and Chita Rivera. Choreography by Bob Fosse. **DT47, MU2**

Piranha (1978, C, 92m, R)
Horror-movie spoof about a resort lake invaded by tiny but deadly fish. Joe Dante directed; written by John Sayles. Cult reputation hard to figure. **CU4, DT33, DT112, HO16, HO24**

Piranha II: The Spawning (1981, C, 95m, R)
A Club Med-style resort is the scene for an attack of mutated flying fish. Tricia O'Neil, Steve Marachuk, and Lance Henriksen star. Early effort from director James Cameron. Also known as *The Spawning.* **DT21, HO16**

Pirate, The (1948, C, 102m, NR)
Judy Garland believes that Gene Kelly is a famous pirate in this colorful MGM musical directed by Vincente Minnelli. **CL9, DT88, MU1, ST81, ST123, XT30**

Pirate Warrior (1964, C, 86m, NR)
Low-budget movie about fierce buccaneers, starring Ricardo Montalban and Vincent Price. **AC15, ST179**

Pirates (1986, C, 117m, PG-13)
Walter Matthau plays a one-legged rascal
seeking revenge on the crew that set him
adrift. With Damien Thomas, Richard Pearson, Cris Campion, Charlotte Lewis, and Roy
Kinnear. Directed by Roman Polanski. Amiable fun but certainly not top-rate Polanski by
any means. **AC15, DT97, ST155**

Pirates of Penzance, The
(1983, C, 112m, G)
Film version of the classic Gilbert and Sul-
livan operetta, starring Kevin Kline, Linda
Ronstadt, Angela Lansbury, Rex Smith, and
George Ross. **FA9, ST127, ST131**

Pistol: The Birth of a Legend, The
(1991, C, 100m, G)
Story of basketball superstar Pete Maravich
concentrates on his career beginnings, when
he was thirteen and was being coached by
his dad. Adam Grier stars, with Millie Perkins
and Nick Benedict. **DR4, DR22, FA7**

Pit and the Pendulum, The
(1961, C, 80m, NR)
Vincent Price stars in this adaptation of the
Edgar Allan Poe story of an evil torturer. Di-
rected by Roger Corman. **DT30, ST179,
WR27**

Pitfall, The (1948, B&W, 84m, NR)
Film noir drama of married man falling into
affair with woman he's supposed to be investigating. Dick Powell and Lizabeth Scott star,
with Jane Wyatt and Raymond Burr. Directed
by Andre de Toth. **MY1, MY4**

Pixote (1981, C, 127m, NR)
Powerful drama set on the streets of Rio de
Janeiro about a homeless boy's daily struggle
for survival. Directed by Hector Babenco.
FF6, XT26, *Highly Recommended*

Place in the Sun, A
(1951, B&W, 122m, NR)
Montgomery Clift is an ambitious man
trapped in a dead-end affair with a factory
worker (Shelley Winters) and really in love
with a society girl (Elizabeth Taylor). Adapted
from Theodore Dreiser's *An American Tragedy.*
Directed by Oscar winner George Stevens.
Meticulous production aided greatly by sensational, career-defining performance from
Clift. **CL4, CL6, CL8, DR19, DT119, ST32,
ST212, ST232, XT6,** *Essential, Recommended*

Places in the Heart (1984, C, 110m, PG)
Drama of a farm woman in Texas during the
1930s and her valiant attempts to bring in
the harvest after her husband dies. Oscar
winner Sally Field stars, with Danny Glover,
Lindsay Crouse, Ed Harris, Amy Madigan,
and John Malkovich. Written and directed by

Robert Benton. Heartfelt, but it didn't touch
me. **DR2, DR5, DR8, DT9, ST66, ST88,
ST147, XT3**

Plainsman, The (1936, B&W, 113m, NR)
With this lavish Western, director Cecil B.
DeMille manages to pack Annie Oakley (Jean
Arthur), Wild Bill Hickok (Gary Cooper), Buf-
falo Bill (James Ellison), and George Arm-
strong Custer (John Miljan) into one story.
**DT34, HF3, HF6, HF11, HF20, ST3, ST37,
WE1, WE8**

Plan 9 From Outer Space
(1959, B&W, 79m, NR)
Notoriously awful film (and, therefore, a cult
classic) from director Ed Wood, Jr., about
aliens raising the dead. Bela Lugosi's last film.
CU11, DT141, ST143

Planes, Trains and Automobiles
(1987, C, 93m, R)
Comedy about the agonies of holiday travel,
starring Steve Martin and John Candy as unwilling companions trying to get from New
York to Chicago for Thanksgiving. Directed
by John Hughes. Fairly enjoyable until a
soppy and all too predictable finale. **CO2,
CO3, CO14, DT59, ST150, XT18, XT19**

Planet of Blood (1966, C, 81m, NR)
Horror story of alien vampire landing on
Earth. John Saxon stars, with Basil Rathbone,
Judi Meredith, and Dennis Hopper. **SF20,
ST110**

Planet of the Apes (1968, C, 112m, PG)
Science fiction adventure about astronauts
landing on a planet inhabited by a race of
intelligent apes—that hold humans captive
as beasts. Charlton Heston stars. First film in
long-running series; see SF23 for a complete
list of titles. **FA8, SF8, SF12, SF13, SF23**

Platinum Blonde (1931, B&W, 90m, NR)
Society girl Jean Harlow marries down-to-
earth reporter Robert Williams, but her
friends put him off. With Loretta Young.
Directed by Frank Capra. **CL10, DT22, ST98**

Platoon (1986, C, 120m, R)
A young recruit is pitched into the horrors of
combat in Vietnam. Charlie Sheen, Willem
Dafoe, and Tom Berenger star. Oscar winner
for Best Picture and Director (Oliver Stone,
who also scripted). Along with *Apocalypse
Now,* the two great Vietnam movies. **AC4,
DT102, XT1, XT6, XT25, XT26,**
Recommended

Play It Again, Sam (1972, C, 87m, PG)
Woody Allen stars in this adaptation of his
play about a lovelorn New Yorker with a
Humphrey Bogart hang-up. With Diane Kea-

ton and Tony Roberts. Directed by Herbert Ross. **CO1, DT2, ST15, ST121, XT31**

Play It As It Lays (1972, C, 99m, R)
Astute psychological study of the wife of an ego-ridden film director. Tuesday Weld and Anthony Perkins star, with Adam Roarke, Tammy Grimes, and Tyne Daly in a small role. Adapted from the Joan Didion novel, directed by Frank Perry. Weld and Perkins have never been better. UNAVAILABLE ON VIDEO. **XT29**

Play Misty for Me (1971, C, 102m, R)
Clint Eastwood plays a disc jockey whose one-night stand with a fan (Jessica Walter) turns into a nightmare when the woman relentlessly pursues him. With Donna Mills and Don Siegel. Eastwood's first film as a director, and it's a good one. **DT116, MY13, MY19, ST64,** *Recommended*

Playboys, The (1992, C, 110m, PG-13)
Drama, set in small Irish town, of middle-aged constable smitten with single young woman who's pregnant but won't reveal the father's identity. The arrival of a traveling theatrical troupe with a handsome leading man soon complicates matters. Albert Finney, Robin Wright, and Aidan Quinn star, with Milo O'Shea. Screenplay by Shane Connaughton and Karry Crabbe, directed by Gillies MacKinnon. Well played, though the wrap-up's a bit protracted. **DR1, DR12, DR23, DR26, ST68,** *Recommended*

Player, The (1992, C, 123m, R)
Director Robert Altman's satire of contemporary Hollywood mores, wrapped around the story of a hotshot studio executive who thinks he can get away with murder—literally. Tim Robbins and Greta Scacchi star, with Vincent D'Onofrio, Fred Ward, Whoopi Goldberg, Peter Gallagher, Brion James, Cynthia Stevenson, Dean Stockwell, Richard E. Grant, Sydney Pollack, and Lyle Lovett. Cameo appearances by dozens of Hollywood denizens playing themselves; a shortlist includes Cher, Jeff Goldblum, Buck Henry, Anjelica Huston, Jack Lemmon, Nick Nolte, Burt Reynolds, Julia Roberts, Alan Rudolph, Susan Sarandon, Lily Tomlin, and Bruce Willis. Adapted by Michael Tolkin from his novel; he and real-life brother Stephen appear in several scenes as a screenwriting team. Must viewing for anyone with the slightest interest in the anthropology of Hollywood. **CU17, DR13, DT4, DT98, DT110, MU12, ST29, ST89, ST90, ST115, ST138, ST164, ST183, ST194, ST215, ST229, XT8,** *Highly Recommended*

Playgirls and the Bellboy, The see *Bellboy and the Playgirls, The*

Playing for Time (1980, C, 150m, NR)
Drama set in a Nazi concentration camp, where certain prisoners played in an orchestra while others met their deaths. Originally made for TV; Emmys to stars Vanessa Redgrave and Jane Alexander, plus writer Arthur Miller. **DR5, ST182**

Playmates (1941, B&W, 94m, NR)
John Barrymore's last film is a musical about a Shakespearean actor collaborating with a band leader (Kay Kyser) to settle up with the IRS. With Lupe Velez and May Robson. **ST8**

Playtime (1967, C, 108m, NR)
Jacques Tati directed and stars in this comedy about M. Hulot, the perpetually befuddled Parisian who is trying to keep an important appointment. **DT122**

Plaza Suite (1971, C, 115m, PG)
Trio of Neil Simon playlets about goings-on at famous hotel in New York. Walter Matthau stars in all three episodes; Maureen Stapleton, Lee Grant, and Barbara Harris costar. **ST155, WR30**

Please Don't Eat the Daisies
(1960, C, 111m, NR)
Jean Kerr's comic play about a New York drama critic, his patient wife, and their mischievous kids. David Niven and Doris Day star, with Janis Paige, Spring Byington, and Patsy Kelly. **DR20, FA6, ST47**

Please! Mr. Balzac see *Mademoiselle Striptease*

Plenty (1985, C, 119m, R)
Meryl Streep plays a British woman whose teen-age act of heroism during World War II makes the rest of her life seem dull and unrewarding. With Charles Dance, Tracey Ullman, John Gielgud, and Sting. Adaptation of David Hare's play. Use of widescreen will be lost on video. Directed by Fred Schepisi. Streep tries but the film fails to make sense of the character. **CU20, DR10, DR20, MU12, ST86, ST210**

Plot Against Harry, The
(1969, B&W, 81m, NR)
Comedy of Jewish gangster (Martin Priest) just released from prison, trying to adjust to life with his zany family. Directed by Michael Roemer. **CO5, CO10**

Ploughman's Lunch, The
(1983, C, 100m, R)
Dark view of British society and journalism in particular, focusing on the conduct of a

reporter (Jonathan Pryce) and colleagues during the Falklands war. **DR7, DR23**

Plumber, The (1980, C, 76m, NR)
An overbearing plumber destroys a young couple's bathroom in this comic thriller from Australian director Peter Weir. **DT133, HO24, MY3, MY16**

Pocket Money (1972, C, 102m, PG)
Contemporary Western comedy about two cowpokes (Paul Newman and Lee Marvin) looking to lift some money from a crooked cattleman. With Strother Martin, Christine Belford, Kelly Jean Peters. Written by Terrence Malick. **CO10, ST151, ST162, WE12, WE14**

Pocketful of Miracles (1961, C, 136m, NR)
Bette Davis is Apple Annie, a street-corner vendor of the Depression who's turned into a real lady by a producer (Glenn Ford). With Hope Lange, Arthur O'Connell, Thomas Mitchell, Peter Falk, Ann-Margret, and Sheldon Leonard. Directed by Frank Capra. Remake of his 1933 film, *Lady for a Day*. **CU18, DT22, ST44**

Pocketful of Rye, A (1984, C, 102m, NR)
Miss Marple, the indefatigable sleuth created by Agatha Christie, comes to the help of a protégé in this whodunit. Joan Hickson stars. Originally made for British TV. **MY12, WR3**

Point Blank (1967, C, 92m, NR)
Stylized, violent thriller about a man with a mission: to recover money his partner stole during a heist at abandoned Alcatraz Prison. Lee Marvin stars, with John Vernon, Keenan Wynn, Lloyd Bochner, Angie Dickinson, Carroll O'Connor, and James B. Sikking. Directed with great flair by John Boorman on locations in San Francisco and Los Angeles. Widescreen will be lost on video. **AC8, AC19, AC25, CU7, CU20, DR16, DT15, ST151, XT10, XT13,** *Highly Recommended*

Point Break (1991, C, 122m, R)
Young FBI agent goes undercover with group of surfers suspected of doubling as bank robbers (wearing masks of past Presidents). Keanu Reeves and Patrick Swayze star, with Gary Busey and Lori Petty. Directed by Kathryn Bigelow. Plenty of surfing and two memorable sky-diving scenes. Good escapist fun. **AC9, AC12,** *Recommended*

Point of No Return (1993, C, 109m, R)
Remake of French thriller *La Femme Nikita*, transposed to Washington, D.C., and California: the story of a psychotic criminal transformed by government agents into a lovely assassin. Bridget Fonda stars, with Gabriel Byrne, Dermot Mulroney, Miguel Ferrer,

Anne Bancroft, and Harvey Keitel. **AC25, FF8, ST70, XT12**

Point of Order (1964, B&W, 97m, NR)
Sensational documentary from director Emile de Antonio, a record of the famed Army-McCarthy hearings, in which Senator Joseph McCarthy's unethical tactics were exposed to a national TV audience. Riveting stuff. UNAVAILABLE ON VIDEO. **XT29**

Poison (1990, C/B&W, 85m, NR)
Trio of intertwined stories inspired by writings of Jean Genet: "Hero," about a young boy who murders his abusive father; "Horror," (in B&W) in which a scientist isolates the human sex drive in a serum which he accidentally ingests; "Homo," about a convict's sexual obsession for a fellow prisoner. Edith Meek, Larry Maxwell, and Scott Renderer star. Written and directed by Todd Haynes. At turns, fascinating and repellent; definitely not for casual moviegoers. Also available in an R-rated version with slightly shorter running time. **CU1, DR3, DR18**

Poison Ivy (1992, C, 89m, R)
Melodrama starring Drew Barrymore as a seductress who insinuates her way into a dysfunctional family: an alcoholic father (Tom Skerritt), a critically ill mother (Cheryl Ladd), and an impressionable teen (Sarah Gilbert). Directed by Katt Shea Ruben. **DR8, MY4**

Poker Alice (1987, C, 109m, NR)
Elizabeth Taylor plays a New Orleans gambler who makes her mark in a frontier saloon. George Hamilton and Tom Skerritt costar in this Western originally made for cable TV. **ST212, WE8**

Police (1984, C, 113m, NR)
French drama of brutal cop involved with a lovely drug dealer. Gérard Depardieu stars, with Sophie Marceau. Directed by Maurice Pialat. **FF1, ST52**

Pollyanna (1960, C, 134m, NR)
An orphan comes to live with her aunt in a small town in New England and her good spirits soon affect everyone around her. Disney classic, starring Hayley Mills, Jane Wyman, and Karl Malden. **DR26, FA1**

Poltergeist (1982, C, 115m, PG)
Suburban family is haunted by ghosts through their TV set, with youngest daughter kidnapped into another dimension. Craig T. Nelson and JoBeth Williams star, with Beatrice Straight, Dominique Dunne, Oliver Robins, Heather O'Rourke, and Zelda Rubinstein. Tobe Hooper directed; Steven Spielberg produced. **HO2, HO3, HO19**

Poltergeist II (1986, C, 91m, PG-13)
Same family, different house, same problems, as Craig T. Nelson, JoBeth Williams and children undergo more hauntings. **HO2, HO3**

Poltergeist III (1988, C, 97m, PG-13)
Heather O'Rourke, the young star of the first two chapters, is still in contact with otherworldly demons, while living with her aunt and uncle (Nancy Allen and Tom Skerritt) in a high-rise apartment. **HO2**

Polyester (1981, C, 86m, R)
Suburban Baltimore housewife Francine Fishpaw is romanced by drive-in movie theater owner Todd Tomorrow in this comedy from cult director John Waters. Divine and Tab Hunter star. **CU12, DT132**

Pony Express (1953, C, 101m, NR)
Drama about the founding of the famous mail route that helped to open the West. Buffalo Bill (Charlton Heston) and Wild Bill Hickok (Forrest Tucker) are among the historical figures portrayed. **HF3, HF11**

Poor Little Rich Girl
(1936, B&W, 72m, NR)
Shirley Temple is a runaway who teams up with a vaudeville couple in this show-business musical. Alice Faye and Jack Haley costar. **ST213**

Popcorn (1991, C, 93m, R)
Horror story of film students staging a marathon screening of scary films, with a mad killer stalking them. Jill Schoelen and Tom Villard star, with Dee Wallace Stone, Ray Walston, and Tony Roberts. **HO9, HO12**

Pope John Paul II (1984, C, 150m, NR)
Biography of the first Polish pontiff, portrayed by Albert Finney. Made for TV. **DR4, ST68**

Pope Must Diet, The
(1991, C, 97m, PG-13)
Comedy of mistaken identity in which a humble priest at an Italian orphanage is elected Supreme Pontiff, despite efforts of organized crime to fix the election. Robbie Coltrane stars, with Beverly D'Angelo, Herbert Lom, Paul Bartel, Balthazar Getty, and Alex Rocco. Original title: *The Pope Must Die.* **CO2, CO10, CO17, DT8**

Pope of Greenwich Village, The
(1984, C, 120m, R)
A pair of smalltime New York hoods (Mickey Rourke and Eric Roberts) decide to challenge the neighborhood crime boss. With Daryl Hannah. Lame stuff; for the real thing, check out *Mean Streets.* **DR15, ST190**

Popeye (1980, C, 114m, PG)
Live action musical of the famous cartoon and comic strip sailor with a taste for spinach. Robin Williams stars, with Shelley Duvall as Olive Oyl, Paul Dooley as Wimpy. Directed by Robert Altman; songs by Harry Nilsson. Williams is good, but Altman can't seem to find the handle on the material. **DT4, FA9, ST228**

Poppy Is Also a Flower, The
(1966, C, 100m, NR)
Drama with antidrug message demonstrates how illegal drugs are manufactured abroad and are smuggled into the United States. E.G. Marshall and Stephen Boyd star, with Senta Berger, Trevor Howard, Eli Wallach, Angie Dickinson, Marcello Mastroianni, Rita Hayworth, and Yul Brynner. Originally produced by the United Nations for TV showings. Also known as *The Opium Connection.* **DR7, ST101, ST154**

Pork Chop Hill (1959, B&W, 97m, NR)
Korean War action centering on battle for a strategic position. Gregory Peck, Harry Guardino, and Rip Torn star. **AC3, ST171, ST216**

Porky Pig and Daffy Duck Cartoon Festival (1943–47, C, 57m, NR)
A collection of Warner Brothers cartoons from the 1940s starring that st-st-stuttering pig and his foolish fowl of a friend. **FA11**

Porky's (series)
Porky's (1981, C, 94m, R)
Porky's II: The Next Day
(1983, C, 100m, R)
Porky's Revenge (1985, C, 95m, R)
These comedies depict the zany and raunchy misadventures of a gang of teen-agers at a Florida high school in the 1950s. **CO4, CO18**

Port of Call (1948, B&W, 99m, NR)
In a Swedish port town, a young outcast and a seaman strike up a friendship. Directed by Ingmar Bergman. **DT11**

Portnoy's Complaint (1972, C, 101m, R)
Adaptation of Philip Roth's controversial comic novel about a Jewish man's sexual odyssey. Richard Benjamin stars, with Karen Black, Lee Grant, Jack Somack, Jeannie Berlin, and Jill Clayburgh. Written and directed by Ernest Lehman. What was hilarious on the printed page just looks smutty on the screen. **CO5, DR19, ST31**

Portrait of Jennie
(1948, B&W/C, 86m, NR)
Classic love story of starving artist (Joseph Cotten) and the ethereal object of his desire (Jennifer Jones). With Ethel Barrymore and

Lillian Gish. Produced by David O. Selznick. Final scene in color. **CL4, ST87**

Portrait of the Artist as a Young Man
(1978, C, 93m, NR)
Irish-produced adaptation of James Joyce's autobiographical novel abut his struggles with the Catholic Church and its teachings. Bosco Hogan, T.P. McKenna, and John Gielgud star. Also known as *James Joyce: A Portrait of the Artist as a Young Man.* **DR19, FF7, ST86**

Poseidon Adventure, The
(1972, C, 117m, PG)
When a cruise ship is capsized by a tidal wave, a group of passengers engage in desperate battle for escape and survival. Gene Hackman stars, with Ernest Borgnine, Red Buttons, Stella Stevens, and Shelley Winters. Boatful of clichés. **AC23, ST96, ST232**

Positive I.D. (1987, C, 96m, R)
A housewife victimized by a rapist learns that he's being released from jail. Written and directed by Andy Anderson. **MY3**

Posse (1975, C, 94m, PG)
Kirk Douglas stars in this Western as a politically ambitious marshal who has his hands full when he captures a wily and popular outlaw (Bruce Dern). With Bo Hopkins and James Stacy. Douglas directed. **ST57, WE3**

Possessed (1931, B&W, 72m, NR)
Joan Crawford stars in a melodrama of a woman's sacrifice for the man she loves. With Clark Gable. **CL5, ST39, ST77**

Possessed (1947, B&W, 108m, NR)
Same title, same star (Joan Crawford) as 1931 film, but different story. This time, Joan loves one man (Van Heflin) but works for another (Raymond Massey) who marries her after his wife dies. **CL5, ST39**

Possession of Joel Delaney, The
(1972, C, 105m, R)
Shirley MacLaine plays a well-to-do New Yorker whose brother (Perry King) is possessed by an evil spirit. **HO8, HO14, ST145**

Postcards From the Edge
(1990, C, 101m, R)
Comedy-drama of relationship between film actress (Meryl Streep) and her domineering mother (Shirley MacLaine), a onetime star. With Dennis Quaid, Gene Hackman, Richard Dreyfuss, Rob Reiner, and Annette Bening. Screenplay by Carrie Fisher was based on her novel. Directed by Mike Nichols. Enjoyable but forgettable stuff. **CO5, CO8, DR8, DR13, DT91, DT103, ST12, ST60, ST96, ST145, ST210**

Postman Always Rings Twice, The
(1946, B&W, 113m, NR)
First screen version of the James M. Cain story of adultery and murder, with Lana Turner (in all-white outfits) and John Garfield the amorous killers. With Cecil Kellaway. Directed by Tay Garnett. **DR3, MY1, MY5, ST80, ST219, WR1, Essential, Recommended**

Postman Always Rings Twice, The
(1981, C, 123m, R)
Jack Nicholson and Jessica Lange are the lovers in this version of James M. Cain's classic tale of adultery and murder. With John Colicos, Michael Lerner, Christopher Lloyd, and in a small role, Anjelica Huston. David Mamet adapted Cain's novel; Bob Rafelson directed. With that much talent, how come it's not better than the 1946 version? **CU18, DR3, MY5, ST115, ST130, ST163, WR1**

Pot o' Gold (1941, B&W, 86m, NR)
James Stewart and Paulette Goddard star in this musical about a boy who wrangles a spot on his uncle's radio show. **ST207**

Potemkin (1925, B&W, 65m, NR)
Classic film based on real-life sailors' mutiny and subsequent massacre of citizens in 1905 Russia. Brilliant editing and imagery give this silent film, directed by Sergei Eisenstein, real emotional power. Also known as *Battleship Potemkin.* **CL12, CU9, DT41, Essential, Highly Recommended**

Power (1928, B&W, 60m, NR)
Early talkie about a pair of rival dam workers and their love affairs. William Boyd, Alan Hale, Carole Lombard, and Joan Bennett star. **ST140**

Power (1986, C, 111m, R)
A Washington political consultant finds himself representing a mysterious client with some nasty secrets. Richard Gere, Gene Hackman, and Julie Christie star, with Denzel Washington, Kate Capshaw, E.G. Marshall, and Beatrice Straight. Sidney Lumet directed. Gere's good, Hackman even better, but story feels preachy. **DR7, DR21, DT78, ST30, ST84, ST96, ST223, XT12**

Power of One, The (1992, C, 111m, PG-13)
Drama set in South Africa of British youth educated in 1930s to be a boxer, growing up to work against apartheid. Stephen Dorff stars, with Armin Mueller-Stahl, Morgan Freeman, John Gielgud, and Guy Witcher. Directed by John Avildsen. **DR7, DR14, DR22, ST86**

Power Play (1978, C, 102m, PG)
A group of military officers plot a coup in a country ruled by a dictatorship and secret

police. Peter O'Toole and David Hemmings star. **DR21, ST169**

Powwow Highway (1989, C, 91m, R)
Road comedy-drama focusing on two Native Americans driving a beat-up Buick from Montana to Santa Fe, one on a spiritual quest, the other to get his sister out of jail. Gary Farmer and A Martinez star. Good use of rock music on soundtrack. Amusing; of interest to fans of this kind of film. **DR7, XT18**

Prairie Moon (1938, B&W, 58m, NR)
Gene Autry is saddled with three young children after their father dies in this light-hearted Western. **ST5**

Prancer (1989, C, 103m, G)
A little girl nurses a sick reindeer back to health, believing that it's one of Santa's helpers. Sam Elliott, Rebecca Harrell, and Cloris Leachman star. **FA13**

Pray for Death (1985, C, 93m, R)
Sho Kosugi stars in this action drama about a former Ninja who reverts to his training when he and his family are threatened by mobsters. **AC26**

Prayer for the Dying, A
(1987, C, 107m, R)
A gunman for the Irish Republican Army decides to escape the country. But before he can, he has to carry out a hit for a ruthless mobster. Mickey Rourke, Alan Bates, and Bob Hoskins star. Rourke's off-putting performance is only tip of the iceberg of problems. **DR16, DR23, ST9, ST111, ST190**

Predator (1987, C, 107m, R)
Arnold Schwarzenegger and his jungle combat buddies are being picked off one by one by an alien creature. With Carl Weathers, Jesse Ventura, Elpidia Carrillo, Bill Duke, Sonny Landham, and Kevin Peter Hall as the monster. Directed by John McTiernan. **AC24, AC25, ST195**

Predator 2 (1990, C, 108m, R)
More monster alien action, this time set in 1997 Los Angeles. Danny Glover stars, with Gary Busey, Rubén Blades, Maria Conchita Alonso, Bill Paxton, and Kevin Peter Hall as the monster. **AC8, MU12, ST88**

Prelude to a Kiss (1992, C, 106m, PG-13)
Offbeat romantic drama of young woman at her wedding who exchanges souls with an elderly stranger by virtue of a kiss. Meg Ryan and Alec Baldwin star, with Kathy Bates, Ned Beatty, Patty Duke, and Sydney Walker as the old man. Craig Lucas adapted his own play. **DR1, DR20, XT20**

Premature Burial, The
(1962, C, 81m, NR)
Ray Milland plays a medical student with an obsession that he'll be buried alive. Roger Corman directed this loose adaptation of Edgar Allan Poe's story. **DT30, WR27**

Premonition (1971, C, 83m, PG)
Drama about three drug-using college students who all experience the same forebodings of death. Directed by Alan Rudolph. **DT110**

Presenting Lily Mars
(1143, B&W, 104m, NR)
Early Judy Garland musical about a young singer trying to make it big on Broadway. With Van Heflin, Fay Bainter, Richard Carlson, and Spring Byington. **MU4, ST81**

President's Analyst, The
(1967, C, 104m, NR)
James Coburn stars as the title character, a man who knows so many intimate details about the Chief Executive that every spy in the world is after him. Satirical comedy, with Godfrey Cambridge and William Daniels. Aims high and does score, although its view of '60s counterculture scene seemed dated even then. **CO2, XT12**

President's Plane Is Missing, The
(1971, C, 100m, NR)
Thriller, adapted from Robert Serling bestseller, about an attempted overthrow of the U.S. government. Buddy Ebsen, Arthur Kennedy, and Peter Graves star, with Rip Torn, Raymond Massey, and Mercedes McCambridge. Originally made for TV. **MY6, ST216**

Presidio, The (1988, C, 97m, R)
A San Francisco police detective (Mark Harmon) and an army officer (Sean Connery) clash over the investigation of a murder on the latter's base. With Meg Ryan. Ordinary stuff, with a romantic subplot that seems extraneous. **AC9, ST36, XT13**

Pressure Point (1962, B&W, 91m, NR)
Test-of-wills drama, starring Sidney Poitier as a prison psychiatrist, Bobby Darin as his patient, a neo-Nazi. Based on a true story. **DR18, MU12, ST174**

Presumed Innocent (1990, C, 127m, R)
Prosecutor finds himself target of murder investigation when his mistress is killed and circumstantial evidence points to him. Harrison Ford stars, with Raul Julia, Brian Dennehy, Paul Winfield, John Spencer, Bonnie Bedelia, and Greta Scacchi. Based on Scott Turow's bestselling novel; directed by Alan J. Pakula. Handsomely mounted with a few zingy performances (Winfield, Julia, and

Spencer), but Ford's less than impressive.
DR17, DR19, DT94, MY7, ST74

Pretty Baby (1978, C, 109m, R)
In New Orleans around the time of World
War I, a strange photographer asks permission of a madam to take pictures of her
prostitutes. Based on the true story of E.J.
Bellocq. Keith Carradine, Brooke Shields, and
Susan Sarandon star. Louis Malle directed;
photographed by Sven Nykvist. Great to look
at but Carradine's stiff and the film meanders
to no effect. **DR3, DR5, DT82, ST194,
XT14**

Pretty in Pink (1986, C, 96m, PG-13)
A girl from the wrong side of the tracks and
a guy from a wealthy family fall in love and
defy their respective crowds at the high
school prom. Molly Ringwald and Andrew
McCarthy star, with Harry Dean Stanton and
James Spader. John Hughes produced and
wrote the script. **DR9, DT59, ST203,
ST205**

Pretty Poison (1968, C, 89m, R)
Quirky thriller about an unstable arsonist
(Anthony Perkins) who meets his match
when he hooks up with a murderous teen-
ager (Tuesday Weld). With Beverly Garland,
John Randolph, and Dick O'Neill. Screenplay
by Lorenzo Semple, Jr. Cult following well
earned for this disturbing tale. **MY2, MY4,**
Recommended

Pretty Woman (1990, C, 119m, R)
A Los Angeles prostitute agrees to pose as an
escort to a high-powered takeover specialist,
and they fall in love. This Cinderella story
stars Julia Roberts and Richard Gere, with
Laura San Giacomo, Hector Elizondo, and
Ralph Bellamy. Directed by Garry Marshall.
The best Prostitute With Hopes for Some-
thing Better movie in recent memory. **CO1,
CO20, ST84, XT10**

Prick up Your Ears (1987, C, 111m, R)
The life of British playwright Joe Orton, who
authored several hit comedies before he was
murdered by his homosexual lover. Gary
Oldman and Alfred Molina star, with Vanessa
Redgrave, Wallace Shawn, and Julie Walters.
Directed by Stephen Frears. Sensational per-
formances from the leads but story just
seems to skim the surface. **DR3, DR4,
DR23, DT48, ST182**

Pride and Prejudice
(1940, B&W, 118m, NR)
Jane Austen's classic comedy of manners features Greer Garson and Laurence Olivier as
romantic sparring partners in nineteenth-
century England. **CL1, ST83, ST168**

Pride and the Passion, The
(1957, C, 132m, NR)
War drama set in nineteenth-century Spain,
focusing on the capture of a mammoth cannon. Cary Grant, Frank Sinatra, and Sophia
Loren star. Directed by Stanley Kramer.
DT67, ST92, ST141, ST199

Pride of St. Louis, The
(1952, B&W, 93m, NR)
The life and wacky times of St. Louis Cardi-
nals pitching great Dizzy Dean, played by
Dan Dailey. **CL2, DR22**

Pride of the Yankees, The
(1942, B&W, 127m, NR)
Gary Cooper plays New York Yankees star
Lou Gehrig, whose brilliant career was cut
short by a mysterious disease. With Teresa
Wright. Has its followers, but I'm not among
them. **CL2, DR22, ST37**

Priest of Love (1981, C, 125m, R)
Ian McKellan plays writer D.H. Lawrence in
this British-made drama of his last years.
With Janet Suzman, Ava Gardner, John Giel-
gud, and Sarah Miles. **DR4, DR23, ST79,
ST86, WR17**

Primary Motive (1992, C, 93m, R)
Political drama focusing on young press secretary to gubernatorial candidate who learns
that their opponent is corrupt. Judd Nelson
stars, with Justine Bateman, Richard Jordan,
John Savage, Malachi Throne, and Frank
Converse. **DR21**

Prime Cut (1972, C, 86m, R)
Rival mobsters Gene Hackman and Lee Mar-
vin duke it out over the Kansas City meat
packing business. Sissy Spacek's film debut.
Directed by Michael Ritchie. Trashy fun.
AC22, ST96, ST151, ST202, *Recommended*

Prime of Miss Jean Brodie, The
(1969, C, 116m, PG)
Maggie Smith's Oscar-winning performance
highlights this drama of an unconventional
teacher in a girls' school. With Robert Stephens and Pamela Franklin. **DR25, XT3**

Primrose Path, The
(1940, B&W, 93m, NR)
Ginger Rogers stars in this drama about a girl
from the wrong side of town in love with a
young man (Joel McCrea) with ambitions.
ST144, ST187

Prince and the Pauper, The
(1937, B&W, 120m, NR)
Screen version of Mark Twain's story of royal
son and commoner who trade places. Errol
Flynn stars, with real-life twins Billy and
Bobby Mauch. **FA3, ST69, WR35**

Prince and the Pauper, The
(1978, C, 113m, PG)
Remake of the Twain tale of prince and his subject. Mark Lester, Oliver Reed, Raquel Welch, George C. Scott, and Charlton Heston star. Also known as *Crossed Swords*. **FA3, ST196, WR35**

Prince and the Showgirl, The
(1957, C, 117m, NR)
Unique pairing of Laurence Olivier and Marilyn Monroe in this comedy: title says it all. Olivier directed. **ST159, ST168**

Prince of Darkness
(1987, C, 110m, R)
A group of students and scientists discover an ancient cannister in a church, and the contents reap terrifying results. Horror drama from director John Carpenter. **DT23**

Prince of Pennsylvania (1988, C, 93m, R)
Family troubles in a working-class suburb of Pittsburgh, with teen genius son (Keanu Reeves) hatching a plot to kidnap his father (Fred Ward). With Bonnie Bedelia and Amy Madigan. **DR8**

Prince of the City (1981, C, 167m, R)
True-life drama of New York City cop persuaded by special investigators to go undercover and expose corruption in the force. Treat Williams stars, with Jerry Orbach, Lindsay Crouse, and Richard Foronjy. Sidney Lumet directed. Despite length and somewhat weak lead performance, consistently absorbing drama, one of Lumet's best. **DR6, DR16, DT78, XT9, XT26,** *Recommended*

Prince of Tides, The
(1991, C, 132m, R)
Nick Nolte's a Southern man with family secrets who's in New York to tend to his ill sister; he falls in love with her psychiatrist (Barbra Streisand). With Kate Nelligan, Jeroen Krabbe, Melinda Dillon, George Carlin, and Jason Gould (Streisand's son). Based on Pat Conroy's novel. Directed by Streisand, whose performance weakens film's impact. **DR8, DR19, ST164, ST211, XT8**

Prince Valiant (1954, C, 100m, NR)
Hal Foster's comic strip hero of the Middle Ages comes to life in the screen person of Robert Wagner. With Janet Leigh, James Mason, Sterling Hayden, Debra Paget, and Victor McLaglen. **AC15, FA4, ST153**

Princess and the Pea, The
(1985, C, 60m, NR)
Liza Minnelli, Tom Conti, and Pat McCormick star in this Faerie Tale Theatre presentation of the children's classic. **FA12**

Princess and the Pirate, The
(1944, C, 94m, NR)
Pirate comedy with Bob Hope ducking buccaneers Victor McLaglen and Walter Brennan. Virginia Mayo costars. Look quickly for Bing Crosby. **ST40, ST108**

Princess Bride, The (1987, C, 98m, PG)
A fairy tale story for both grownups and kids, with a lovely princess (Robin Wright) tricked by an evil prince (Chris Sarandon) into believing that her lover (Cary Elwes) is dead. The supporting cast includes Mandy Patinkin, Wallace Shawn, Andre the Giant, Christopher Guest, and Billy Crystal. Directed by Rob Reiner; adapted by William Goldman from his novel. Intermittently engaging; Patinkin steals the show as vengeful swordsman. **AC14, AC15, CO13, DT103**

Princess Tam-Tam (1935, B&W, 77m, NR)
Josephine Baker stars in this French comedy of an African girl educated by a Frenchman and passed off as Indian royalty. **FF1**

Princess Who Had Never Laughed, The
(1984, C, 60m, NR)
A Faerie Tale Theatre presentation of the Brothers Grimm classic, starring Howie Mandel, Ellen Barkin, and Howard Hesseman. **FA12, ST7**

Principal, The (1987, C, 109m, R)
At an inner-city school, a new principal finds that discipline is his most important subject. Jim Belushi and Louis Gossett, Jr., star in the action drama. **CO13, DR25**

Prisoner, The (1955, B&W, 91m, NR)
Alec Guinness stars in this British drama, set in an Eastern Bloc country, about a cardinal interrogated by a brutal official (Jack Hawkins). **CL8, DR23, ST95**

Prisoner of Honor (1991, C, 115m, NR)
Historical drama starring Richard Dreyfuss as a French colonel who's court-martialed for supporting Alfred Dreyfus. With Oliver Reed, Peter Firth, Jeremy Kemp, and Lindsay Anderson. Directed by Ken Russell. Originally made for cable TV. **DR5, DT111, ST60**

Prisoner of Second Avenue, The
(1975, C, 105m, PG)
Neil Simon comedy-drama about an unemployed executive in Manhattan who can't cope with his troubles. Jack Lemmon and Anne Bancroft star. **CO2, ST138, WR30**

Prisoner of Zenda, The
(1937, B&W, 101m, NR)
First-rate version of the classic adventure tale of commoner filling in for regal relative, gaining revenge. Ronald Colman, Douglas

Fairbanks, Jr., and Madeleine Carroll star. **AC13, FA4, ST35,** *Recommended*

Prisoner of Zenda, The
(1952, C, 101m, NR)
The classic swashbuckler about a commoner mistaken for a king. Stewart Granger crosses swords with everyone in sight. With Deborah Kerr and James Mason. **AC13, ST125, ST153**

Prisoner of Zenda, The
(1979, C, 108m, PG)
Comic version of the classic swashbuckler, with Peter Sellers in the lead. **CO7, ST198**

Prisoners of the Sun (1990, C, 105m, R)
Wartime courtroom drama, based on true story, of Australians prosecuting Japanese POW camp commander for atrocities. Bryan Brown and George Takei star. Original title: *Blood Oath.* **AC7, DR5, DR17, FF5**

Private Affairs of Bel Ami, The
(1947, B&W, 112m, NR)
George Sanders stars as a rogue in 1880s Paris society, in this adaptation of the Guy de Maupassant novel. With Angela Lansbury, Ann Dvorak, Frances Dee, and John Carradine. **CL1, ST131**

Private Benjamin (1980, C, 100m, R)
A pampered young Jewish woman, widowed on her wedding night, enlists in the army and learns a few lessons in life. Goldie Hawn and Eileen Brennan star in this comedy, with Armand Assante, Harry Dean Stanton, and Albert Brooks. Film's early comic scenes are best, but turn toward drama doesn't help. **CO2, CO21, DT16, ST99, ST205**

Private Files of J. Edgar Hoover, The
(1977, C, 112m, PG)
Melodramatic recreation of the life of famed FBI chief, starring Broderick Crawford as the man with the goods on everyone in Washington. With Dan Dailey, José Ferrer, Rip Torn, Raymond St. Jacques as Martin Luther King, and Michael Parks as Bobby Kennedy. Directed by Larry Cohen. Seemed pretty outrageous at the time, less so in light of more recent revelations. **CU2, DR4, DT28, ST216**

Private Function, A (1985, C, 93m, R)
During the late 1940s, when meat rationing was still in force in Britain, an illegal pig becomes the focus of deception and double-dealing. This comedy stars Michael Palin and Maggie Smith. Funny, but won't convert non-fans of British humor. **CO6, CO15, CO17**

Private Hell 36 (1954, B&W, 81m, NR)
A pair of cops decide to keep some stolen money, then have second thoughts. Ida Lupino stars (she also cowrote and produced), with Steve Cochran and Howard Duff. Directed by Don Siegel. **DT116, MY1**

Private Life of Henry VIII, The
(1933, B&W, 97m, NR)
Oscar winner Charles Laughton stars as the much-married King of England, with Elsa Lanchester as one of his unfortunate brides. **CL2, ST132, XT2**

Private Life of Sherlock Holmes, The
(1970, C, 125m, PG)
As the title implies, not your everyday Holmes mystery. Robert Stephens, Colin Blakely, and Christopher Lee star in this film from writer-director Billy Wilder with a strong cult following. **DT139, HF14, ST135**

Private Lives (1931, B&W, 84m, NR)
Noel Coward's comic play of romantic entanglements, starring Norma Shearer and Robert Montgomery. **CL10, WR4**

Private Lives of Elizabeth and Essex, The (1939, C, 106m, NR)
Historical drama of the political—and personal—relationship of Queen Elizabeth I (Bette Davis) and the dashing Earl of Essex (Errol Flynn). With Vincent Price and Olivia de Havilland. **CL2, CL3, CL21, ST44, ST49, ST69, ST179**

Privates on Parade (1982, C, 100m, PG-13)
Comedy about a special theatrical unit performing for British troops in the Pacific during World War II, starring John Cleese. **CO6, CO15, CO21**

Private Parts (1972, C, 86m, R)
Dark comedy of teen-age girl living at her aunt's hotel, which is populated with all manner of weirdos, including a voyeuristic photographer who takes pictures of corpses. Ann Ruymen and Lucille Benson star, with Laurie Main and John Ventantonio. Directed by Paul Bartel. **CO12, DT8**

Prix de Beauté (1930, B&W, 78m, NR)
Louise Brooks in her first sound film plays a typist turned beauty queen in this drama. Cowritten by René Clair. **CL5, ST21**

Prize, The (1963, C, 136m, NR)
Paul Newman stars in this thriller of political intrigue set around the annual Nobel Prize ceremony in Stockholm. With Edward G. Robinson (playing twins) and Elke Sommer. Ernest Lehman adapted Irving Wallace's novel. **MY6, ST162, ST186, XT27**

Prize Fighter, The (1979, C, 99m, PG)
Family comedy about a lame-brained boxer and his mouthy manager, starring Don Knotts and Tim Conway. **FA6**

Prizzi's Honor (1985, C, 129m, R)
A pair of professional killers meet at a wedding and fall in love, even though one has been assigned to "hit" the other. Jack Nicholson and Kathleen Turner star in this darkly comic tale, based on Richard Condon's novel. With Oscar winner Anjelica Huston, John Randolph, Robert Loggia, William Hickey, and Lawrence Tierney. John Huston directed. Delightfully played by all. **DR16, DT60, ST115, ST163, ST218, XT5, XT20,** *Recommended*

Probe (1972, C, 97m, NR)
Investigator working on jewelry theft has a transmitter implanted in him to link him to control center. Hugh O'Brian stars, with Elke Sommer, John Gielgud, and Burgess Meredith. Also known as *Search.* Originally made for TV. **ST86**

Problem Child (1990, C, 81m, PG)
Slapstick comedy of title character (Michael Oliver) making life miserable for his adoptive dad (John Ritter). With Jack Warden and Gilbert Gottfried. **CO5**

Producers, The (1968, C, 88m, PG)
Mel Brooks's debut as a writer-director is a daring comedy about an unscrupulous Broadway producer's attempts to intentionally make a flop and walk away with his investors' money. Zero Mostel and Gene Wilder star, with Dick Shawn, Kenneth Mars, and Lee Meredith. Rowdy, rude, and very funny. Wilder deserved an Oscar. **CO8, DT17, XT28,** *Essential, Recommended*

Professionals, The (1966, C, 117m, NR)
In this Western drama, a wealthy man hires four soldiers of fortune to recapture his wife, who has been kidnapped by a Mexican bandit. Burt Lancaster, Lee Marvin, Robert Ryan, and Woody Strode star, with Jack Palance, Claudia Cardinale, and Ralph Bellamy. Cast carries the film. **ST129, ST151, ST193, WE9,** *Recommended*

Project X (1987, C, 108m, PG)
An Air Force enlisted man is assigned to a project involving chimpanzees and soon discovers the deadly secret behind the experiments. Matthew Broderick stars, with Helen Hunt. **DR2, DR7**

Prom Night (1980, C, 91m, R)
Horror story of teens stalked by killer looking for revenge for little girl's death. Leslie Nielsen, Jamie Lee Curtis, and Casey Stevens star. **HO12, ST42**

Promise Her Anything (1966, C, 98m, NR)
Romantic comedy starring Warren Beatty as an aspiring filmmaker stuck with caring for the baby of his widowed neighbor (Leslie Caron). With Bob Cummings, Hermione Gingold, Lionel Stander, and Keenan Wynn. **ST10**

Promised a Miracle (1988, C, 100m, NR)
True story of religious couple trusting their diabetic son to faith healing, only to have him die and find themselves accused of manslaughter. Rosanna Arquette and Judge Reinhold star. Directed by Stephen Gyllenhaal. Originally made for TV. **DR7, DR8, DR17**

Promised Land (1988, C, 101m, R)
Story of three small-town high school friends whose lives after graduation diverge and then converge, disastrously. Kiefer Sutherland, Jason Gedrick, and Tracy Pollan star, with Meg Ryan. Characters don't make much sense. **DR7, DR26**

Promoter, The (1952, B&W, 88m, NR)
Alec Guinness plays a brash young opportunist in this British comedy, costarring Glynis Johns. Written by Eric Ambler. **CO17, ST95**

Proof (1992, C, 91m, NR)
Australian drama of cynical blind man who takes photographs, his manipulative young housekeeper, and his friendship with a dishwasher. Hugo Weaving, Genevieve Picot, and Russell Crowe star. Written and directed by Jocelyn Moorhouse. Genuinely unsettling stuff, not easily forgotten. **FF5, MY4,** *Recommended*

Proof of the Man (1984, C, 100m, NR)
An American found murdered in Tokyo is the key to a mystery with international implications. Toshiro Mifune, George Kennedy, and Broderick Crawford star. **MY16, ST157**

Prophecy (1979, C, 95m, PG)
A doctor and his pregnant wife investigate mercury poisoning in Maine streams and come face to face with a mutant monster. Talia Shire, Robert Foxworth, and Armand Assante star in this science fiction/horror tale. Directed by John Frankenheimer. Dreadful. **SF10**

Prospero's Books (1991, C, 124m, R)
Cult director Peter Greenaway offers this unusual version of Shakespeare's *The Tempest,* with John Gielgud as Prospero, Michael Clark as Caliban, and Isabelle Pasco as Miranda. Most of the performers spend the film without clothing (not Gielgud). Visually stunning but determinedly obscure. **DR23, DT51, WR28**

Protector, The (1985, C, 94m, R)
Martial arts star Jackie Chan plays a New York City cop who's after a drug kingpin. **AC26**

Protocol (1984, C, 96m, PG)
Goldie Hawn stars in this comedy about a know-nothing who's given a do-nothing job in the State Department—and winds up involved in serious foreign relations matters. With Chris Sarandon, Richard Romanus, and Andre Gregory. **ST99, XT12**

Proud Rebel, The (1958, C, 103m, NR)
Alan Ladd plays a proud man seeking help for his mute son (David Ladd, the star's real-life son). Olivia de Havilland costars, with Dean Jagger, John Carradine, and (Harry) Dean Stanton. **ST49, ST128, ST205, XT8**

Providence (1977, C, 104m, R)
From French director Alain Resnais, an English-language film about an aging writer (John Gielgud), his attempts to finish his last novel, and his relationships with his family. With Dirk Bogarde, Ellen Burstyn, and David Warner. Subtle, suggestive; not to everyone's taste. **DR8, FF1, ST14, ST86,** *Recommended*

Psycho (1960, B&W, 109m, R)
Alfred Hitchcock's most memorable shocker, about a woman thief, a shabby motel, a shy clerk, and a murderous mother. Anthony Perkins and Janet Leigh star, with John Gavin, Vera Miles, and Martin Balsam. Amazingly effective even on repeated viewings. **DT57, HO1, HO9,** *Essential, Highly Recommended*

Psycho II (1983, C, 113m, R)
Norman Bates is out of prison for his fiendish crimes, but he just can't stay away from the Bates Motel. Anthony Perkins and Meg Tilly star, with Vera Miles. Richard Franklin directed. Some very macabre humor, including a jaw-dropping ending. **HO9**

Psycho III (1986, C, 93m, R)
The third entry in the saga of Norman Bates has director-star Anthony Perkins playing the horror for laughs. **HO9, XT23**

Psycho-Circus (1967, C, 65m, NR)
British mystery of killer stalking his victims under the big top, based on a story by Edgar Wallace. Christopher Lee and Suzy Kendall star. **MY15, ST135**

Psychomania (1971, C, 95m, R)
A British motorcycle gang returns from the dead after making a special deal in this adult horror film. George Sanders stars. **HO6**

Psychos in Love (1985, C, 88m, NR)
Horror comedy about a romance between a pair of demented killers. **HO24**

Psych-Out (1968, C, 82m, NR)
In late-1960s San Francisco, a young deaf runaway tries to locate her brother and falls in with a local rock band. Susan Strasberg,

Bruce Dern, Jack Nicholson, and Dean Stockwell star in this relic from the psychedelic era. Directed by Richard Rush. Good for a few laughs. **ST163, ST208, XT13**

Psycho Sisters (1972, C, 76m, PG)
A woman whose husband has just died goes to live with her sister, recently released from an insane asylum. Horror drama starring Susan Strasberg and Faith Domergue. **HO14**

Puberty Blues (1981, C, 86m, R)
Two young girls experience the joys and pains of adolescence while they hang out with the surfing crowd in Sydney, Australia. Directed by Bruce Beresford. **DT10, FF5**

Public Cowboy No. 1 (1937, B&W, 54m, NR)
Gene Autry Western set in modern dress with rustlers employing contemporary methods. **ST5**

Public Enemy (1931, B&W, 84m, NR)
James Cagney star-making turn as a tough-talking gangster who packs a mean wallop, especially with a grapefruit in his hand. With Jean Harlow, Eddie Woods, Joan Blondell, and Mae Clark. Directed by William Wellman. **AC22, DT135, ST24, ST98,** *Essential, Highly Recommended*

Public Eye, The (1992, C, 98m, R)
Joe Pesci stars in this drama set in 1940s New York about a tabloid photographer involved with helping a lovely nightclub owner (Barbara Hershey). The pictures of corpses and scenes of urban life on the edge are based loosely on the career of real-life photographer Weegee. Directed by Howard Franklin. Terrific period re-creation (Chicago and Cincinnati stand in for New York), good performance by Pesci. **MY2, MY4, MY11, ST104, ST112,** *Recommended*

Pudd'nhead Wilson (1984, C, 90m, NR)
Mark Twain's detective tale of mismatched twins and a murder, starring Ken Howard. Originally made for public TV. **WR35**

Puff the Magic Dragon (1985, C, 45m, NR)
Based on the children's song, this animated feature is about a lonely boy and his gigantic fire-breathing friend. **FA10**

Pulp (1972, C, 95m, PG)
Darkly comic tale of a retired Hollywood actor (Mickey Rooney) hiring a hack writer (Michael Caine) to pen his memoirs. With Lizabeth Scott and Lionel Stander. Directed by Michael Hodges. Offbeat and engaging; Rooney's hilarious. **CO12, ST25, ST189,** *Recommended*

Pump up the Volume (1990, C, 100m, R)
Christian Slater plays a shy high school student who lets loose when he's broadcasting over his homemade pirate radio station. Drama also features Samantha Mathis, Ellen Greene, Scott Paulin, and Annie Ross. Written and directed by Alan Moyle. Often funny and on-target look at disaffected young people. **DR9, DR25, MU12, ST200,** *Recommended*

Pumping Iron (1976, C, 85m, PG)
Documentary about the world of weightlifters and professional bodybuilders, featuring Arnold Schwarzenegger and Lou Ferrigno. **CU16, ST195**

Pumping Iron II: The Women (1985, C, 107m, NR)
Sequel to *Pumping Iron* concentrates on the female bodybuilders. Bev Francis is the star. **CU16**

Pumpkinhead (1988, C, 87m, R)
Horror story of a vengeance-seeking father who summons a legendary demon to deal with his son's murderers but cannot control it once the killing begins. **HO14**

Punchline (1988, C, 123m, R)
Tom Hanks and Sally Field play stand-up comics; he's the cynical veteran of the club scene, she's a housewife trying to break into the biz. With John Goodman, Mark Rydell, and in a small role, Paul Mazursky. David Seltzer directed this drama. Neither Hanks nor Field are convincing as comics—would-be or otherwise. **DR12, ST66, ST97**

Puppet Master (1989, C, 90m, R)
Horror tale of a group of psychics gathered at a remote hotel, terrorized by the fiendish creations of a mad inventor. Paul LeMat stars, with Irene Miracle, Matt Roe, and William Hickey. **HO16**

Pure Country (1992, C, 112m, PG)
George Strait plays a country singer looking to get back to the basics in this drama. With Lesley Ann Warren, Isobel Glasser, Kyle Chandler, Rory Calhoun, and John Doe. Screenplay by Rex McGee. **DR12**

Pure Luck (1991, C, 96m, PG)
Comic pairing of Martin Short as a disaster-plagued accountant and Danny Glover as a straight-arrow private eye, teaming in Mexico to find the missing daughter of a businessman. Remake of French comedy *La Chevre*. **CO3, CO10, CO14, FF8, ST88**

Purlie Victorious (1963, C, 97m, NR)
Musical fable about a black preacher standing up to a wicked plantation owner. Written by and starring Ossie Davis, with Ruby Dee, Sorrell Booke, and Godfrey Cambridge. **DR14, MU2**

Purple Heart, The (1944, B&W, 99m, NR)
World War II drama of U.S. fliers shot down during bombing raids on Tokyo, starring Dana Andrews, Farley Granger, Sam Levene, and Richard Conte. **AC1**

Purple Hearts (1984, C, 115m, R)
A Navy medic and a nurse fall in love against the backdrop of the war in Vietnam. Cheryl Ladd and Ken Wahl star. **AC4**

Purple People Eater (1988, C, 87m, PG)
Family comedy about character from 1959 hit song forming a rock band with a bunch of teen-agers. Ned Beatty stars, with Shelley Winters, Neil (Patrick) Harris, Peggy Lipton, Chubby Checker, Little Richard, and Sheb Woolley. **FA6, ST232**

Purple Rain (1984, C, 113m, R)
The movie debut of rock star Prince, as he plays a character named The Kid, a rocker battling rival musicians, his own band members, and family problems. With Apollonia Kotero, Morris Day, Jerome Benton, and Clarence Williams III. The music's terrific, the dramatics standard. Day and Benton have future as comic team; they steal the show from the lead. **DR12, MU9**

Purple Rose of Cairo, The (1985, C, 84m, PG)
During the Depression, a waitress trapped in a loveless marriage imagines her favorite movie star has come off the screen to romance her. Mia Farrow and Jeff Daniels star in this comedy written and directed by Woody Allen. With Danny Aiello, Dianne Wiest, Van Johnson, Edward Herrmann, Michael Tucker, and Glenne Headly. Too clever by half, with Farrow vacantly unappealing. **CO8, DT2, ST65, XT30**

Purple Taxi, The (1977, C, 107m, R)
Drama of various expatriates living in Ireland, starring Charlotte Rampling, Philippe Noiret, Peter Ustinov, and Fred Astaire. Original running time: 120 minutes. **ST4**

Pursued (1947, B&W, 101m, NR)
Robert Mitchum is a cowboy out to find his father's killers. Directed by Raoul Walsh. **DT131, ST158, WE5**

Pursuit of D.B. Cooper, The (1981, C, 100m, PG)
The tale of the legendary airline bandit who parachuted from the sky with thousands in ransom. Treat Williams and Robert Duvall star. Shaggy dog stuff. **DR6, ST63**

Pursuit of Happiness, The
(1971, C, 98m, PG)
Drama of moody young man bringing injustice on himself at a trial. Michael Sarrazin stars, with Barbara Hershey, Robert Klein, Sada Thompson, Arthur Hill, and E.G. Marshall. **DR17, ST104**

Pursuit of the *Graf Spee*
(1957, C, 106m, NR)
Michael Powell codirected this World War II drama about the British attempts to sink a German battleship. John Gregson, Anthony Quayle, and Christopher Lee star. **AC1, DT99, ST135**

Pursuit to Algiers (1945, B&W, 65m, NR)
Sherlock Holmes mystery, starring Basil Rathbone and Nigel Bruce, has the famous detective and his companion accompanying an heir to a foreign throne on a voyage. Not based on any Arthur Conan Doyle story. **HF14**

Puss in Boots (1984, C, 60m, NR)
Ben Vereen and Gregory Hines star in this Faerie Tale Theatre presentation of the beloved children's story. **FA12**

Putney Swope (1969, C/B&W, 88m, R)
Satirical comedy about a black man taking over a prestigious New York advertising agency and renaming it Truth and Soul, Inc. Arnold Johnson stars; Mel Brooks has a small part. Directed by Robert Downey. **CO2, CO12, DT17**

Pygmalion (1938, B&W, 95m, NR)
The George Bernard Shaw play about a professor's gamble that he can turn a Cockney flower girl into a lady of culture. Leslie Howard and Wendy Hiller star in this comedy that was the basis for *My Fair Lady*. **CL1, DR23, WR29**

Q (1982, C, 93m, R)
Horror comedy about a monster from Mexican legend terrorizing Manhattan, nesting on top of the Chrysler Building. Michael Moriarty, Richard Roundtree, and David Carradine star. Larry Cohen directed. Moriarty chews the scenery, the special effects are cheesy . . . fans of trash will love it. **DT28, HO16, XT9**

Q & A (1990, C, 134m, R)
Nick Nolte plays a racist New York cop, Timothy Hutton the assistant district attorney investigating him. With Armand Assante and Jenny Lumet. Written and directed by Sidney Lumet. Nolte and Assante's performances compensate for Hutton. **DR15, DR16, DT78, ST164, XT9**, *Recommended*

Q Planes see *Clouds Over Europe*

QB VII (1974, C, 313m, R)
Courtroom drama of noted British doctor suing novelist for libel for implicating him in war crimes. Anthony Hopkins and Ben Gazzara star, with Lee Remick, Leslie Caron, Juliet Mills, and John Gielgud. Based on Leon Uris's novel. Originally a TV miniseries. **DR17, DR19, ST109**

Quackbusters (1989, C, 76m, G)
Feature-length cartoon, spoofing *Ghostbusters*, starring Daffy Duck as a spook-hunting detective. **FA10**

Quackser Fortune Has a Cousin in the Bronx (1970, C, 90m, R)
Gene Wilder plays an amiable Irishman who collects horse manure from the streets of Dublin and sells it to gardeners. Margot Kidder is an American student who falls in love with him. **CO1**

Quadrophenia (1979, C, 115m, R)
Musical drama about a young Briton in the early 1960s with four separate personalities, based on the rock album by The Who. Superb marriage of music and imagery directed by Franc Roddam. Phil Daniels stars, with Sting in a small role. **MU9,** *Recommended*

Quality Street (1937, B&W, 84m, NR)
A woman pretends to be her own niece in order to woo a flame she hasn't seen in ten years. Katharine Hepburn and Franchot Tone star in this comedy directed by George Stevens. With Fay Bainter, Eric Blore, and Joan Fontaine. **DT119, ST73, ST103**

Quartet (1949, B&W, 120m, NR)
W. Somerset Maugham introduces four of his short stories, each with its own cast. Among the players: Mai Zetterling, Ian Fleming, and Dirk Bogarde. Sequels: *Trio* and *Encore*. **DR23, ST14, WR23**

Quartet (1981, C, 101m, R)
Suffocating drama of couple (Alan Bates and Maggie Smith) who take in young girl (Isabelle Adjani) for what seem to be altruistic motives; he then seduces her. Based on a novel by Jean Rhys. Directed by James Ivory; produced by Ismail Merchant. **DR19, DT61, ST9**

Quatermass Conclusion, The
(1980, C, 107m, NR)
British science fiction adventure about a professor who is the key to stopping a deadly ray from destroying the planet. John Mills stars. Originally made for TV. **SF19**

Que Viva Mexico! (1932, B&W, 85m, NR)
Russian director Sergei Eisenstein's legendary, unfinished documentary about life in Mexico. **DT41,** *Recommended*

Queen Christina (1933, B&W, 97m, NR)
One of Greta Garbo's signature roles: the seventeenth-century Swedish monarch who gave up her throne for love. With John Gilbert, Ian Keith, Lewis Stone, and C. Aubrey Smith. Directed by Rouben Mamoulian. Unbeatable romantic teaming and sympathetic direction lift this into first rank of Garbo films. **CL3, CL4, DT83, ST78,** *Essential, Recommended*

Queen Kelly (1929, B&W, 95m, NR)
Director Erich Von Stroheim's bizarre tale of a young girl's odyssey from a convent school to a brothel. Gloria Swanson stars in this reconstruction of a long-lost and never-finished classic silent drama. **CL12, DT129**

Queen of Hearts (1989, C, 112m, PG)
Charming comedy-drama of an Italian immigrant family living in postwar London, as seen through the eyes of its young son (Ian Hawkes). Joseph Long and Anita Zagaria star. Directed by Jon Amiel. A real sleeper that deserves discovery. **CO4, CO5, CO17,** *Recommended*

Queen of Outer Space (1958, C, 80m, NR)
Zsa Zsa Gabor in the title role; her home base is Venus. Favorite of bad movie connoisseurs everywhere. **CU11**

Queenie (1987, C, 200m, NR)
Drama of rise of film star from Calcutta poverty, based on Michael Korda's novel, in turn based loosely on life of Merle Oberon. Mia Sara stars, with Kirk Douglas (as character based on Korda's Uncle Alexander), Martin Balsam, Claire Bloom, Topol, and Joel Grey. **DR13, ST57**

Queens Logic (1991, C, 112m, R)
Group of New York neighborhood twenty-somethings gather for wedding of two friends. Ken Olin and Chloe Webb star as the intendeds, with Kevin Bacon, Linda Fiorentino, John Malkovich, Joe Mantegna, Tony Spiridakis (who wrote the screenplay), Tom Waits, and Jamie Lee Curtis. Amiably aimless at first, then irritatingly so. **DR7, DR15, MU12, ST42, ST147, XT9**

Querelle (1982, C, 120m, R)
Director Rainer Werner Fassbinder's last film, about a sailor's discovery of his homosexual nature. Brad Davis and Jeanne Moreau star. **DT42, ST161**

Quest, The (1976) see *Longest Drive, The*

Quest, The (1986, C, 93m, PG)
A young boy learns of an ancient myth in the Australian outback and confronts the source in this adventure. Henry Thomas stars. **FA4, FF5**

Quest for Fire (1981, C, 97m, R)
A drama of life in prehistoric times, filmed on several continents, with special languages and body movements designed for the film. Everett McGill, Ron Perlman, and Rae Dawn Chong star. Directed by French filmmaker Jean-Jacques Annaud. **AC12, AC24, FF1**

Question of Silence, A (1983, C, 92m, R)
Dutch film about three women on trial for murdering the same man, venting their hostility over a male-dominated society. **FF7**

Quick and the Dead, The
(1987, C, 93m, NR)
Louis L'Amour Western of a homesteading family falling under the protection of a mysterious stranger. Sam Elliott, Kate Capshaw, and Tom Conti star. Originally made for cable TV. **WR16**

Quick Change (1990, C, 89m, R)
Crime comedy of three bank robbers thwarted in attempt to escape Manhattan for airport getaway. Bill Murray, Geena Davis, and Randy Quaid star, with Jason Robards and Bob Elliott. Murray and Howard Franklin directed. **CO10, CO13, ST45, ST185, XT9**

Quick, Let's Get Married
(1971, C, 96m, NR)
Strange comedy of bordello madam (Ginger Rogers) and her relationship with one of her pregnant employees (Barbara Eden). With Ray Milland, Michael Ansara, and Elliott Gould (his debut). Made in 1964, but unreleased for seven years. **ST187**

Quiet Cool (1986, C, 80m, R)
A New York cop brings his special brand of street smarts to a small California town being overrun by a gang of pot growers. James Remar and Nick Cassavettes star. **AC9**

Quiet Earth, The (1985, C, 91m, R)
Only three people are left on Earth after a top-secret project goes haywire. Science fiction drama from New Zealand. **SF12**

Quiet Man, The (1952, C, 129m, NR)
American prizefighter returns to his native Ireland and courts local lass in this rollicking comedy from Oscar-winning director John Ford. John Wayne and Maureen O'Hara star, with Victor McLaglen and Barry Fitzgerald. Gorgeous, Oscar-winning color cinematography. Deserved, among that year's nominees, to win Best Picture Oscar. **CL9, DT44, ST167, ST224, XT6, XT28,** *Essential, Recommended*

Quiet One, The (1948, B&W, 67m, NR)
Low-budget drama, set in New York, of a black youth trying to stay out of trouble. Donald Thompson stars. **DR9, DR14**

Quigley Down Under
(1990, C, 120m, PG-13)
Tom Selleck plays an Amercian cowboy hired for a job in Australia. When he arrives and learns that it's exterminating aborigines, he refuses and is left to die in the desert by a villainous rancher. With Alan Rickman and Laura San Giacomo. Tepid, although Rickman is in full throttle as baddie. **AC24, DR27, WE5**

Quiller Memorandum, The
(1966, C, 105m, NR)
An American agent in Britain hunts down ex-Nazis in this spy thriller starring George Segal, Alec Guinness, and Max von Sydow. Written by Harold Pinter. **MY6, ST95, WR26**

Quintet (1979, C, 110m, R)
Science fiction drama about a frozen city of the future and its few inhabitants who play a bizarre game for survival. Paul Newman stars, with Bibi Andersson, Fernando Rey, and Nina Van Pallandt. Robert Altman directed. Opaque; setting is just too offputting for any real drama. **DT4, SF8, ST162**

Quo Vadis? (1951, C, 171m, NR)
Big-budget spectacle of ancient Rome in days of Nero (Peter Ustinov), starring Robert Taylor and Deborah Kerr, with Leo Genn, Finlay Currie, and Buddy Baer. **CL3, ST125**

R.P.M. (1970, C, 97m, R)
Drama of campus insurrection, starring Anthony Quinn as a lusty professor, with Ann-Margret, Gary Lockwood, and Paul Winfield as students. Directed by Stanley Kramer. **DR25, DT67, ST230**

Rabbit Test (1978, C, 86m, R)
Billy Crystal stars in a comedy about the world's first pregnant man. Joan Rivers directed. **CO13**

Rabid (1977, C, 90m, R)
From horror director David Cronenberg, the story of a woman who develops a thirst for human blood after she's had plastic surgery. Not for the squeamish. Marilyn Chambers stars. **DT31, HO18**

Race With the Devil (1975, C, 88m, PG)
Two couples on vacation tangle with some devil worshippers in this action thriller that features lots of motorcycle and car chases. Peter Fonda and Warren Oates star, with Loretta Swit, Lara Parker, and R.G. Armstrong. For genre fans only. **AC10, HO11, ST166**

Racers, The (1955, C, 112m, NR)
Kirk Douglas stars in a drama of high-speed auto racing on the European circuit. With

Bella Darvi, Gilbert Roland, Lee J. Cobb, and Cesar Romero. **AC10, DR22, ST57**

Rachel and the Stranger
(1948, B&W, 93m, NR)
A romantic triangle, Western-style, featuring Loretta Young, William Holden, and Robert Mitchum. **ST106, ST158, WE8**

Rachel Papers, The (1989, C, 92m, R)
Comedy-drama about young man who keeps files on prospective romances in his computer. Dexter Fletcher, Ione Skye, and James Spader star. Based on a novel by Martin Amis. **DR1, ST203**

Rachel, Rachel (1968, C, 101m, R)
Joanne Woodward stars in this drama about a lonely schoolteacher looking for love in her mid-thirties. With Estelle Parsons and James Olson. Paul Newman directed. Quietly observed. **DR10, ST162, ST234, XT30**

Rachel River (1987, C, 90m, PG-13)
Low-key drama of a Minnesota woman who lives in the title small town, eking out a living as a radio journalist. Pamela Reed stars, with Craig T. Nelson, James Olson, and Zeljko Ivanek. Reed is wonderful as always; story takes too long to develop. **DR10, DR26**

Racing With the Moon
(1984, C, 108m, PG)
Nostalgic drama set in small California coastal town in the early 1940s about the romance between a poor boy and a servant's daughter he mistakenly thinks is wealthy. Sean Penn, Elizabeth McGovern, and Nicolas Cage star. **DR1, DR26, ST23**

Racket, The (1951, B&W, 88m, NR)
Film noir of a cop (Robert Mitchum) and gangster (Robert Ryan) squaring off. With Lizabeth Scott, Ray Collins, William Talman, and William Conrad. Directed by John Cromwell. Good of kind. **MY1, ST158, ST193**

Racketeer (1929, B&W, 68m, NR)
A gangster tries to go straight for the love of a young woman. Robert Armstrong and Carole Lombard star. **ST140**

Rad (1986, C, 95m, PG)
Family drama centering on the world of BMX bike racing. Bill Allen is the kid with the hot wheels; Talia Shire, Ray Walston, and Jack Weston are the adults on the sidelines. **AC10, DR22, FA7**

Radio Days (1987, C, 85m, PG)
Woody Allen directed this affectionate portrait of New York in the early 1940s, when everyone listened to the nightly radio pro-

grams of adventure, romance, and mystery. Mia Farrow stars, with Seth Green, Julie Kavner, Josh Mostel, Michael Tucker, Dianne Wiest, Wallace Shawn (as the Masked Avenger), Danny Aiello, Jeff Daniels, Tony Roberts, and Diane Keaton in a small role as a band singer. Allen's best film of the last ten years. **CO5, CO6, CO8, DT1, ST65, ST121, XT9, XT26, XT30,** *Highly Recommended*

Radio Flyer (1992, C, 120m, PG-13)
Drama of two boys escaping into a fantasy world to avoid an abusive stepfather. Lorraine Bracco, Elijah Wood, and Joseph Mazzello star, with John Heard, Adam Baldwin, and Ben Johnson. Tom Hanks is the uncredited narrator. Directed by Richard Donner. **DR8, DR9, ST97**

Radio Ranch see *Phantom Empire*

Rafferty and the Gold Dust Twins
(1975, C, 92m, PG)
A nerdy driving instructor is forced by a pair of kooky women to drive them from Los Angeles to New Orleans. Alan Arkin, Sally Kellerman, and Mackenzie Phillips star, with Harry Dean Stanton. **ST205, XT18**

Rage (1972, C, 104m, PG)
Revenge drama of rancher (George C. Scott) whose son has been killed by careless government chemical testing. With Richard Basehart, Martin Sheen, and Barnard Hughes. Scott also directed. **DR7, ST196**

Rage at Dawn (1955, C, 87m, NR)
Randolph Scott and his saddle buddies hunt down an outlaw gang. **ST197**

Rage in Harlem, A (1991, C, 115m, R)
In 1950s New York, a seductress arrives from Mississippi to sell a stash of gold, putting a whole neighborhood in an uproar. Forest Whitaker, Gregory Hines, and Robin Givens star, with Zakes Mokae and Danny Glover. Based on a novel by Chester Himes. Directed by Bill Duke. **DR14, DR15, DR16, ST88**

Rage of Angels (1983, C, 200m, NR)
Sidney Sheldon soaper about a lovely lawyer (Jaclyn Smith) torn between two lovers: a married politician (Ken Howard) and a mob lawyer (Armand Assante). Originally made for TV. **DR2**

Raggedy Man (1981, C, 94m, PG)
Sissy Spacek stars as a widow in a small Texas town during the 1940s who has a romance with a sailor (Eric Roberts) on leave. Sam Shepard costars. Directed by Jack Fisk. Spacek and Roberts are good, but story seems contrived. **DR10, DR26, ST202**

Raggedy Rawney, The
(1988, C, 102m, NR)
Drama of an AWOL British soldier (Bob Hoskins) hiding out with Gypsies. Hoskins also directed. **ST111**

Raging Bull (1980, B&W/C, 128m, R)
Robert De Niro won an Oscar for his portrayal of New York boxer Jake LaMotta, as brutal outside the ring as in it. With Cathy Moriarty, Joe Pesci, Nicholas Colasanto, and Theresa Saldana. Martin Scorsese directed; photographed by Michael Chapman and edited by Oscar winner Thelma Schoonmaker. Scorsese's greatest achievement to date proves that film about unsympathetic character can be work of art. The film and Scorsese should have won Oscars. **DR4, DR22, DT114, ST51, ST172, XT2, XT9, XT28,** *Essential, Highly Recommended*

Rags to Riches see *Callie and Son*

Ragtime (1981, C, 156m, PG)
Epic panorama of turn-of-the-century America, adapted from E.L. Doctorow bestseller. Mary Steenburgen, Howard E. Rollins, Jr., Elizabeth McGovern, and Mandy Patinkin head the large cast, with James Olson, Brad Dourif, Kenneth McMillan, Donald O'Connor, Pat O'Brien, Moses Gunn, Debbie Allen, Norman Mailer, Jeff Daniels, and in modest but key role, James Cagney. Music by Randy Newman. Milos Forman directed. Packs a lot into two and a half hours but Doctorow's canvas is far too big to be captured effectively; might have been better as a TV miniseries. **DR5, DT45, ST24**

Raid on Entebbe
(1977, C, 150m, NR)
Drama about the July 4, 1976, rescue by Israeli commandos of hostages held in Uganda by terrorists. Charles Bronson and Peter Finch star. Originally made for TV. **DR6, ST20**

Raid on Rommel (1971, C, 99m, PG)
Richard Burton stars as the wily German commander in this World War II drama. **AC1, ST22**

Raiders of the Lost Ark
(1981, C, 115m, PG)
Steven Spielberg's modern tribute to the old-fashioned movie serials, with Harrison Ford as the bullwhip-toting professor, Karen Allen as his companion, and plenty of hair-raising escapes and breath-taking chases. With John Rhys-Davies and Denholm Elliott. Available in a letterboxed format. **AC14, AC21, CU19, DT118, ST74,** *Recommended*

Railroaded (1947, B&W, 71m, NR)
Gangster John Ireland makes life miserable for Sheila Ryan in this thriller. Directed by Anthony Mann. **DT85**

Railrodder, The see *Buster Keaton Rides Again/The Railrodder*

Railway Children, The (1972, C, 102m, G)
From Britain, a family adventure about a trio of plucky children determined to clear their father of false charges of espionage. Dinah Sheridan and Bernard Cribbins star. **FA4**

Rain (1932, B&W, 93m, NR)
Joan Crawford and Walter Huston square off in this version of W. Somerset Maugham's tale of a lady of ill repute and a reform-minded preacher. **ST39, WR23**

Rain Man (1988, C, 140m, R)
Cross-country odyssey of two brothers (Dustin Hoffman and Tom Cruise), one a hustler, the other a long-institutionalized autistic savant. With Valeria Golino. Oscar winner for Best Picture, Actor (Hoffman), Director (Barry Levinson, who has a small role as a doctor), and Original Screenplay (Ron Bass and Barry Morrow). Terrific soundtrack with artists from Aaron Neville and Etta James to Johnny Clegg and Lou Christie. **DR8, DT75, ST41, ST105, XT1, XT2, XT6, XT18,** *Recommended*

Rain People, The (1969, C, 102m, R)
A housewife deserts her family and takes to the road for an odyssey of self-discovery. Francis Ford Coppola directed this drama starring Shirley Knight, James Caan, and Robert Duvall. **DR10, DT29, ST63, XT18,** *Recommended*

Rainbow, The (1989, C, 112m, R)
D.H. Lawrence's story of young love awakening, focusing on a female character who later appeared in *Women in Love*. Sammi Davis stars, with Paul McGann, Amanda Donohoe, Glenda Jackson, and David Hemmings. Co-written and directed by Ken Russell. Rare restrained outing for Russell is solid but unexciting. **DR1, DR23, DT111, ST117, WR17**

Rainmaker, The (1956, C, 121m, NR)
Katharine Hepburn stars as a spinster living in a parched Southwest town who's wooed by a smooth-talking con man (Burt Lancaster). **CL4, ST103, ST129**

Raintree County (1957, C, 168m, NR)
Elizabeth Taylor is the selfish Southern belle, Montgomery Clift the schoolteacher she ruins in this historical drama of the Confederacy. With Eva Marie Saint and Lee Marvin. Directed by Edward Dmytryk. Widescreen

will be lost on video. The beginning of the end for Clift, who suffered disfiguring accident in the middle of filming schedule, although the film has plenty of other problems. **CL3, CU20, ST32, ST151, ST212**

Raise the Red Lantern
(1992, C, 126m, PG)
Drama from China, set in the 1920s, about intrigue among the four concubines of a wealthy man. Gong Li stars. Directed by Zhang Yimou. Absorbing story; artful use of color. **FF7,** *Recommended*

Raise the Titanic! (1980, C, 112m, PG)
Big-budget version of bestselling novel about the salvage job of a lifetime, starring Jason Robards, with Richard Jordan, David Selby, and Alec Guinness. **AC12, ST95, ST185**

Raisin in the Sun, A (1961, B&W, 128m, NR)
Drama of black family life in Chicago, adapted from Lorraine Hansberry's play. Sidney Poitier, Claudia McNeil, Ruby Dee, and Louis Gossett, Jr., star. **CL8, DR8, DR14, DR20, ST174**

Raisin in the Sun, A (1989, C, 171m, NR)
New version of Lorraine Hansberry's play stars Danny Glover and Esther Rolle, with Starlett Dupois. Directed by Bill Duke. **DR8, DR14, DR20, ST88**

Raising Arizona (1987, C, 94m, PG-13)
A childless couple decide to kidnap one of a set of quintuplets in this frantic action comedy starring Nicolas Cage and Holly Hunter. With John Goodman, William Forsythe, Trey Wilson (as Nathan Arizona), Randall (Tex) Cobb, and M. Emmet Walsh. Written by Joel and Ethan Coen; directed by Joel and produced by Ethan. Sensational camerawork by Barry Sonnenfeld and music by Carter Burwell steal the show from unappealing characters. **CO5, CO9, CO10, DT27, ST23, ST113**

Raising Cain (1992, C, 95m, R)
Complicated thriller from director Brian De Palma about a child psychologist with an evil twin brother. John Lithgow plays both twins, plus three other roles. With Lolita Davidovich, Steven Bauer, Frances Sternhagen, Gregg Henry, Tom Bower, and Mel Harris. **DT36, HO15, MY13, MY14, XT27**

Rambling Rose (1991, C, 113m, R)
Small Georgia town in 1935 is setting for drama recalled by grown man, then the teenage son of family welcoming wayward, sexy girl into its fold. Laura Dern stars, with Robert Duvall, Diane Ladd (Dern's real-life mom), and Lukas Haas. Calder Willingham adapted his own novel; directed by Martha Coolidge. Duvall's wonderful and Ladd has

one terrific scene; the wraparound story makes for one too many endings. **DR8, DR26, ST53, ST63, XT8**

Rambo: First Blood Part II
(1985, C, 95m, R)
Sylvester Stallone is the Special Forces maverick with a mission: to free Americans still held captive in Vietnam. **AC4, AC25, ST204**

Rambo III (1988, C, 101m, R)
In this installment, John Rambo travels to Afghanistan to rescue his old commander from the Soviet invaders. Sylvester Stallone and Richard Crenna star. **AC25, ST204**

Ramparts of Clay (1971, C, 87m, PG)
French-produced drama, set in Tunisia, concerning a woman's involvement in a strike by villagers. Directed by Jean-Louis Bertucelli. **FF1**

Ramrod (1947, B&W, 94m, NR)
Western tale of a ranch owner (Veronica Lake) involved in a land dispute with her father (Charlie Ruggles). With Joel McCrea, Arleen Whelan, Don DeFore, and Preston Foster. **ST144, WE8**

Ran (1985, C, 161m, R)
A Japanese version of Shakespeare's *King Lear*, with samurai warriors, Oscar-winning costumes, and some of the greatest battle scenes ever filmed. Tatsuya Nakadai stars. Directed by Akira Kurosawa. Widescreen will be lost on video; still, a stunning spectacle. **CU20, DT69, WR28,** *Highly Recommended*

Rancho Deluxe (1975, C, 93m, R)
Contemporary Western comedy with cult following stars Jeff Bridges and Sam Waterston as a laid-back pair of rustlers. With Elizabeth Ashley and Clifton James as their intended victims, Harry Dean Stanton and Richard Bright as their accomplices, Slim Pickens and Charlene Dallas as their adversaries, Patti D'Arbanville and Maggie Wellman as their girlfriends, and Joe Spinell as Waterston's Indian father. Written by Tom McGuane, directed by Frank Perry. Music by Jimmy Buffett, who appears in one scene. Shot in and around Livingston, Montana. Falling-down funny, even if you've never been west of Ohio. **CO2, CO10, CU5, ST19, ST205, WE12, WE14,** *Highly Recommended*

Rancho Notorious (1952, C, 89m, NR)
Cowboy Arthur Kennedy, seeking revenge for a murder, winds up at a strange hideout for outlaws run by Marlene Dietrich. Directed by Fritz Lang. **DT70, ST55, WE5, WE8, WE15**

Random Harvest (1942, B&W, 124m, NR)
Sentimental romantic drama of a wartime amnesia victim (Ronald Colman) and the woman (Greer Garson) whose love leads him to recovery. **CL4, ST35, ST83**

Ranger and the Lady, The
(1938, B&W, 54m, NR)
Roy Rogers finds romance in the Old West. Gabby Hayes costars—not as the love interest! **ST188**

Rape and Marriage: The Rideout Case
(1980, C, 96m, NR)
True story of the landmark court case in which a woman charged her estranged husband with rape. Mickey Rourke and Linda Hamilton star, with Rip Torn. Originally made for TV. **DR6, DR17, ST190, ST216**

Rape of Love (1977, C, 117m, NR)
French drama of a nurse who's sexually assaulted and then undergoes a worse ordeal in the criminal justice system. Nathalie Nell stars. **DR10, FF1**

Rapid Fire (1992, C, 95m, R)
Martial arts saga starring Brandon Lee (son of Bruce) as a pacifist student recruited by a renegade Chicago cop (Powers Boothe) as bait in a war between Mafia and Oriental drug dealers. With Nick Mancuso, Raymond J. Barry, Kate Hodge, and Tzi Ma. **AC26**

Rapture, The (1991, C, 102m, R)
Unusual story of woman leading hedonistic life suddenly having religious conversion to evangelical fundamentalist sect. Mimi Rogers stars, with Patrick Bachau, David Duchovny, and Kimberly Cullum. Written and directed by Michael Tolkin. Rogers is terrific in a difficult role. **DR7, DR10,** *Recommended*

Rapunzel (1983, C, 60m, NR)
The fairy tale of the girl with long flowing locks, presented by Faerie Tale Theatre. Shelley Duvall, Jeff Bridges, and Gena Rowlands star. **FA12, ST19**

Rare Breed, The (1966, C, 108m, NR)
James Stewart stars in this Western drama; Maureen O'Hara can't decide between him and Brian Keith. **ST167, ST207, WE8**

Rashomon (1951, B&W, 88m, NR)
Japanese drama of a criminal act in a forest and the various versions the story takes in the retelling. Breakthrough film for both star (Toshiro Mifune) and his director (Akira Kurosawa). Winner of an Oscar for Best Foreign Language Film. **DT69, ST157, XT7,** *Essential, Recommended*

Rasputin and the Empress
(1932, B&W, 123m, NR)
Historical saga of the last days of the Russian monarchy, starring John, Ethel, and Lionel

Barrymore in their only film together. **CL3, ST8, XT8**

Ratings Game, The (1984, C, 102m, NR)
TV producer (Danny DeVito) has terrible idea—and it leads him to overnight success in this comedy. With Rhea Perlman, Gerrit Graham, Kevin McCarthy, Jayne Meadows, Steve Allen, George Wendt, and Huntz Hall. DeVito directed. Originally made for TV. **CO8, ST54**

Raven, The (1935, B&W, 62m, NR)
Bela Lugosi stars in the bizarre tale of a mad doctor who's obsessed with Edgar Allan Poe and one of his female patients (Irene Ware). With Boris Karloff as a "victim" of the doctor's plastic surgery. Not based on the Poe poem, but does borrow elements from his tales. **HO1, ST119, ST143, WR27**

Raven, The (1963, C, 86m, NR)
A trio of magicians square off in this horror comedy, starring Vincent Price, Peter Lorre, and Boris Karloff. With Jack Nicholson. Roger Corman directed. Very loosely based on Poe's famous poem. Goofy fun. **DT30, ST119, ST163, ST179, WR27**

Ravishing Idiot (1965, B&W, 110m, NR)
Comedy about an inept crook who's out to steal some important NATO documents. Anthony Perkins and Brigitte Bardot star. **ST6**

Raw Deal (1986, C, 97m, R)
Arnold Schwarzenegger plays a special FBI agent assigned to clean up Mob activity in Chicago as only he can. **AC25, ST195**

Rawhide (1951, B&W, 86m, NR)
Western remake of gangster film *Show Them No Mercy*, with outlaws taking hostages at a stagecoach station. Tyrone Power stars, with Susan Hayward, Dean Jagger, Edgar Buchanan, and Jack Elam. Also known as *Desperate Siege*. **XT100, ST177**

Razorback (1984, C, 95m, R)
A wild hog terrorizes the Australian outback. Gregory Harrison stars. **FF5, HO16**

Razor's Edge, The (1946, B&W, 146m, NR)
Tyrone Power stars in this version of the W. Somerset Maugham story of a man's disillusionment after his experiences in World War I. With Oscar winner Anne Baxter, Gene Tierney, and Clifton Webb. **ST177, ST214, WR23, XT5**

Razor's Edge, The (1984, C, 128m, PG-13)
Bill Murray plays it straight in this second screen version of the Maugham story of a man looking for inner peace. With Theresa Russell, Catherine Hicks, James Keach, and Denholm Elliott. Directed by John Byrum. Murray struggles to overcome well-established comic persona but can't; film feels uncomfortably old-fashioned. **CO13, WR23**

Reaching for the Moon
(1931, B&W, 62m, NR)
Depression-era comedy stars Douglas Fairbanks as a financier fighting a booze problem. With Bebe Daniels and Edward Everett Horton; Bing Crosby sings one song. **ST40**

Real Bruce Lee, The (1980, C, 108m, R)
Highlights of martial arts star Bruce Lee in action from four of his early films. **ST134**

Real Genius (1985, C, 104m, PG)
Comedy about a group of college whiz kids getting revenge on their professor for using their research for a death-dealing government project. Val Kilmer stars, with Gabe Jarret, Michelle Meyrink, and William Atherton. Directed by Martha Coolidge. Genuine wit in a genre sorely lacking in it. **CO2, CO4, CO18,** *Recommended*

Real Glory, The (1939, B&W, 95m, NR)
Gary Cooper plays a medic assigned to the Philippines in the aftermath of the Spanish-American War. **AC6, ST37**

Real Life (1979, C, 99m, PG)
Pushy documentary filmmaker (Albert Brooks) invades home of typical family to make a movie about them. Brooks also directed and cowrote this comedy, costarring Charles Grodin. Always amusing commentary on our media-saturated lives. **CO8, DT16, ST94, XT31,** *Recommended*

Real Men (1987, C, 86m, R)
Jim Belushi and John Ritter star in this action comedy about a CIA agent and a civilian caught up in a dangerous game of international intrigue. **CO13**

Really Weird Tales (1986, C, 85m, NR)
Spoof of "Twilight Zone"-style TV shows, with three episodes starring John Candy, Martin Short, Joe Flaherty, and Catherine O'Hara. **CO14, SF21**

Re-Animator (1985, C, 86m, NR)
Extremely gory horror film with cult following about a young doctor's experiments reviving the dead. Jeffrey Combs and Barbara Crampton star. (Also available in an R-rated version with some of the violence trimmed.) **CU4, CU7, HO18, HO20**

Reap the Wild Wind (1942, C, 124m, NR)
Adventure tale of nineteenth-century salvagers working off the Georgia coast, starring

John Wayne, Ray Milland, and Paulette Goddard. With Raymond Massey, Robert Preston, Susan Hayward, Charles Bickford, and Hedda Hopper. Directed by Cecil B. DeMille. Oscar-winning special effects. **AC12, AC13, DT34, SF15, ST100, ST224**

Rear Window (1954, C, 112m, PG)
Classic Hitchcock thriller about a photographer spying on his neighbor, who may have murdered his wife. James Stewart and Grace Kelly star, with Thelma Ritter, Wendell Corey, and Raymond Burr. Based on a story by Cornell Woolrich. Supreme casting, ingenious direction make this one of Hitchcock's great films. **DT57, MY11, ST124, ST207, WR39, XT26,** *Essential, Highly Recommended*

Rebecca (1940, B&W, 130m, NR)
Daphne du Maurier story, directed by Alfred Hitchcock, about a young woman's marriage to a widower whose former wife dominates everything around them. Laurence Olivier and Joan Fontaine star, with Judith Anderson and George Sanders. Winner of the Best Picture Oscar. **DT57, ST73, ST168, WR6, XT1,** *Essential*

Rebecca of Sunnybrook Farm
(1938, B&W, 80m, NR)
Shirley Temple stars in this musical about a young radio star. Randolph Scott and Gloria Stuart add some romance. **ST197, ST213**

Rebel (1973, C, 80m, PG)
Sylvester Stallone plays a student radical in this drama made several years before his success with Rocky. **ST204**

Rebel (1986, C, 93m, R)
Matt Dillon is an American G.I. deserter adrift in World War II Australia. Bryan Brown costars in this drama. **DR27, FF5, ST56**

Rebel Rousers (1967, C, 78m, NR)
Low-budget melodrama about motorcycle gangs, famous mainly for pre-stardom pairing of Jack Nicholson and Bruce Dern. With (Harry) Dean Stanton. **ST163, ST205**

Rebel Without a Cause
(1955, C, 111m, NR)
Vintage 1950s drama of misunderstood teens. James Dean, Natalie Wood, and Sal Mineo form a memorable trio of outcasts. With Jim Backus, Corey Allen, Nick Adams, and Dennis Hopper. Directed by Nicholas Ray. Widescreen will be lost on video. **CL8, CU20, DR9, DT101, ST110,** *Essential, Highly Recommended*

Reckless (1935, B&W, 96m, NR)
Drama of chorus girl's effect on the lives of many people. Jean Harlow stars, with William Powell, Franchot Tone, May Robson, Rosalind Russell, and Mickey Rooney. **CL7, ST98, ST176, ST189, ST192**

Reckless (1984, C, 93m, R)
Straight-arrow student Daryl Hannah falls for moody rebel Aidan Quinn. Stylish high school romance, directed by James Foley. **DR9**

Reckless Moment, The
(1949, B&W, 82m, NR)
Max Ophuls directed this *film noir* of a blackmailer (James Mason) and his victim, a murderer (Joan Bennett). **DT93, MY1, MY3, ST153**

Red Badge of Courage, The
(1951, B&W, 69m, NR)
The classic Civil War story, adapted from Stephen Crane's novel, about a young soldier's initiation into the horrors of combat. Audie Murphy stars, with Bill Mauldin, John Dierkes, and Royal Dano. John Huston directed. Film suffered greatly from tampering by producer after it flopped on first release. **AC5, CL1, DT60, XT25**

Red Beard (1965, B&W, 185m, NR)
Toshiro Mifune stars as a crusty doctor who tries to impart his knowledge to a young, more kindly intern. Epic drama from director Akira Kurosawa. Available in letterboxed format. Ultimately too long but has some powerful individual scenes. Recommended for followers of director and star. **CU19, DT69, ST157**

Red Dawn (1984, C, 114m, PG-13)
When Soviet-backed troops invade a small town in the American Southwest, a band of teen-agers take to the hills and wages a guerrilla war. Patrick Swayze and C. Thomas Howell star, with Powers Boothe, Ben Johnson, and Harry Dean Stanton. Preposterous; prime time-capsule example of Red paranoia. **AC20, ST205**

Red Desert (1964, C, 116m, NR)
Director Michelangelo Antonioni's drama of a woman alienated from modern urban life, on the brink of a breakdown. Monica Vitti and Richard Harris star. Outstanding photography by Carlo DiPalma. **DT5**

Red Dragon see *Manhunter*

Red Dust (1932, B&W, 83m, NR)
Romantic triangle on a rubber plantation: Clark Gable has to pick between lusty Jean Harlow and demure Mary Astor. Classic romantic adventure, remade as *Mogambo*. Three stars in top form. **AC13, AC14, ST77, ST98, XT26,** *Highly Recommended*

Red-Headed Stranger, The
(1986, C, 105m, NR)
Willie Nelson stars in Western story, based
on his classic album, about a preacher who
swears revenge on an unfaithful wife. With
Katharine Ross and Morgan Fairchild. **MU12,
WE2, WE5**

Red-Headed Woman
(1932, B&W, 79m, NR)
Jean Harlow plays a gold digger out to land
her married boss (Chester Morris) in this
comedy. With Una Merkel, Lewis Stone, May
Robson, and Charles Boyer as an amorous
chauffeur. Written by Anita Loos, directed by
Jack Conway. Harlow is unscrupulously sexy
in this prime example of early 1930s raciness.
ST16, ST98

Red Heat (1988, C, 106m, R)
Soviet cop and his Chicago counterpart team
up to catch a Russian drug dealer on the lam
in the Windy City. Arnold Schwarzenegger
and Jim Belushi star. Walter Hill directed.
Both director and star have done much better. **AC9, CO13, DT56, ST195, XT11**

Red House, The (1947, B&W, 100m, NR)
Melodrama of simple farmer (Edward G. Robinson) and his fear of a certain house and its
mysterious occupants. With Lon McAllister,
Allene Roberts, Judith Anderson, Rory Calhoun, and Julie London. Overwrought; Calhoun and London are unintentionally
amusing as backwoods couple. **ST186**

Red Line 7000 (1965, C, 110m, NR)
Racing car drama from director Howard
Hawks stars James Caan, Laura Devon, Gail
Hire, and Charlene Holt. **AC10, DR22,
DT53**

Red Lion (1969, C, 115m, NR)
Toshiro Mifune stars in an action drama
about a soldier confronting the corrupt officials in his home town. **FF4, ST157**

Red Pony, The (1949, B&W, 89m, NR)
Drama of young boy's love for his horse and
the escape it offers him from family problems. Adapted from the John Steinbeck
novel. Robert Mitchum, Myrna Loy, and
Peter Miles star. **FA5, ST142, ST158, WR32**

Red Pony, The (1973, C, 101m, NR)
Latest version of the Steinbeck story, starring
Henry Fonda, Maureen O'Hara, Ben Johnson,
and Clint Howard. Originally made for TV.
FA5, ST71, ST167, WR32

Red River (1948, B&W, 133m, NR)
Classic cattle-drive story features John Wayne
and Montgomery Clift as a feuding father
and son. With Joanne Dru, Walter Brennan,
John Ireland, Noah Berry, Jr., Paul Fix, Harry
Carey, Sr., and Harry Carey, Jr. Borden Chase
and Charles Schnee adapted Schnee's story.
Directed by Howard Hawks. This video version includes footage restored from original
release. **CU10, DT53, ST32, ST224, WE1,
XT8,** *Essential, Recommended*

Red River Valley see *Man of the Frontier*

Red Scorpion (1989, C, 102m, R)
Dolph Lundgren plays a Russian special services officer assigned to kill the rebel leader
of an African freedom movement. **AC20,
AC25**

Red Shoes, The (1948, C, 133m, NR)
Ballerina must choose between her devoted
lover and a hard-driving impressario who
knows "what's best" for her career. Director
Michael Powell's film won Oscars for score
and art direction. Moira Shearer, Anton Walbrook, and Marius Goring star in this cult
favorite. **CL6, CL7, CL9, DT100, MU3**

Red Sonja (1985, C, 89m, PG-13)
Arnold Schwarzenegger and Brigitte Nielsen
team up as warriors in a land of sacred talis-
mans and magic. **AC18, ST167**

Red Sun (1972, C, 112m, R)
Western about a gunslinger and a samurai
joining forces features United Nations casting: Charles Bronson, Toshiro Mifune, and
Ursula Andress. **ST19, ST134**

Red Tent, The (1971, C, 121m, G)
Based on a true story, this adventure saga
dramatizes an ill-fated 1928 expedition to the
frozen Arctic led by General Nobile (Peter
Finch). Sean Connery costars. **AC12, AC24,
ST31**

Reds (1981, C, 200m, PG)
Epic story of John Reed, American journalist
and adventurer who chronicled the Mexican
and Russian Revolutions. Star Warren Beatty
won an Oscar for his direction; Diane Keaton, Jack Nicholson (as Eugene O'Neill),
Gene Hackman, and Oscar winner Maureen
Stapleton head the supporting cast. Narrative
is interspersed with interviews with "witnesses," contemporaries of Reed who offer
their impressions of him. Photography by
Vittorio Storaro. Beatty is more successful at
creating the ambience of the times than in
figuring out his central character. Still, this
would have been a top choice for Best Picture Oscar. **DR4, ST10, ST96, ST121,
ST163, WR25, XT5, XT6, XT28,**
Recommended

Reefer Madness (1936, B&W, 67m, NR)
Cheaply made melodrama warning audience

of the dangers of marijuana "addiction." A cult favorite at midnight showings in the 1960s. **CU1, CU11**

Reflecting Skin, The (1990, C, 106m, NR) Horror tale, set in the postwar 1940s, of young farm boy who believes mysterious neighbor woman is a vampire, even after his older brother begins an affair with her. Jeremy Cooper and Lindsay Duncan star. Cult film written and directed by Philip Ridley. **CU4, HO5, HO14**

Reflections in a Golden Eye (1967, C, 108m, NR) The dark side of life on a Southern military base, adapted from Carson McCullers novel. Marlon Brando and Elizabeth Taylor star, with Brian Keith, Julie Harris, and Robert Forster. John Huston directed. Brando's very good; everyone else is a cartoon. Interesting use of color may be lost on video. **DR3, DR19, DT60, ST18, ST212**

Reflections of Murder (1974, C, 100m, NR) Remake of French thriller *Diabolique*, about a neglected wife and scorned mistress conspiring to murder a schoolteacher. Tuesday Weld, Joan Hackett, and Sam Waterston star. Written by Carol Sobieski; originally made for TV. **FF8, MY14**

Regarding Henry (1991, C, 107m, PG-13) Harrison Ford plays a hard-driving Manhattan attorney whose life is turned inside out when a bullet wound triggers amnesia. With Annette Bening, Bill Nunn, and Mikki Allen. Directed by Mike Nichols. **DR2, DR8, DT91, ST12, ST74**

Regina (1983, C, 86m, NR) Ava Gardner stars in this drama of a smothering mom whose thirtysomething son is about to marry for the first time. With Anthony Quinn, Ray Sharkey, and Anna Karina. **ST79**

Rehearsal for Murder (1982, C, 100m, NR) Backstage mystery: star of new Broadway show is killed on opening night. Robert Preston and Lynn Redgrave star, with Patrick Macnee, Jeff Goldblum, and William Daniels. Written by William Levinson and Richard Link; originally made for TV. **MY12, ST90**

Reivers, The (1969, C, 107m, PG) Comedy set in turn-of-the-century Mississippi about a young boy's friendship with his family's ne'er-do-well chauffeur. Steve McQueen stars in this adaptation of the William Faulkner novel. With Rupert Crosse, Sharon Farrell, Will Geer, and Mitch Vogel.

Enjoyable, with one of McQueen's more relaxed performances. **ST146, WR7**

Relentless (1989, C, 92m, R) Judd Nelson stars in this thriller about a psychotic known as the Sunset Killer. With Leo Rossi and Robert Loggia. **MY13**

Reluctant Debutante, The (1958, C, 94m, NR) Comedy of proper parents (Rex Harrison and Kay Kendall) presenting their rebellious daughter to society. With Angela Lansbury, John Saxon, and Sandra Dee. Directed by Vincente Minnelli. **DT88, ST131**

Rembrandt (1936, B&W, 84m, NR) Charles Laughton plays the famous Dutch painter in this British production. With Elsa Lanchester, Gertrude Lawrence, and Roger Livesey. Directed by Alexander Korda. **CL2, ST132**

Remembrance of Love see *Holocaust Survivors . . . Remembrance of Love*

Rendez-vous (1985, C, 82m, R) French drama of stage actress (Juliette Binoche) involved with a man (Lambert Wilson) who performs in a live sex act. With Jean-Louis Trintignant. Directed by André Téchiné. Available in letterboxed format. **CU6, CU19, FF1**

Renegade Ranger (1938, B&W, 60m, NR) Rita Hayworth plays a lady outlaw in this Western, one of her early screen appearances. George O'Brien stars, with Tim Holt. **ST101, WE8**

Renegades (1989, C, 106m, R) A cop on the trail of stolen diamonds joins forces with a Native American after the same man, who stole a spear sacred to his tribe. Kiefer Sutherland and Lou Diamond Phillips star. **AC9**

Rent-a-Cop (1988, C, 95m, R) Burt Reynolds is the title character, Liza Minnelli the prostitute he's protecting from a serial killer. **MY3, ST183**

Repentance (1987, C, 151m, NR) Soviet parable, an indictment of Stalin's repression, concerns a corpse in a cemetery in a village in Georgia. **FF7**

Repo Man (1984, C, 92m, R) Offbeat comedy, with sci-fi undertones, about a punked-out kid falling in with a band of car repossessors in Los Angeles and learning the "repo" way of life. Emilio Estevez stars, with Harry Dean Stanton, Vonetta McGee, Sy Richardson, and Tracey Walter. Directed by Alex Cox. Unique, wryly funny;

a great showcase for Stanton. **CO2, CO12, CU5, ST205, XT10,** *Recommended*

Report to the Commissioner
(1975, C, 112m, PG)
Rookie New York cop mistakenly kills undercover female policeman, gets involved in department coverup. Michael Moriarty stars, with Yaphet Kotto, Susan Blakely, Hector Elizondo, Tony King, and in a small role, Richard Gere (his screen debut). Overheated, although there's one great standoff scene in an elevator. **AC9, ST84**

Repossessed (1990, C, 84m, PG-13)
Horror spoof of *Exorcist*-style films, starring Linda Blair as a housewife with a familiar problem. With Ned Beatty and Leslie Nielsen. **CO7, HO8, HO24**

Repulsion (1965, B&W, 105m, NR)
An unstable young woman, left alone in her sister's apartment, descends into madness. Catherine Deneuve stars in this disturbing psychological study from director Roman Polanski. **DT97, ST50,** *Recommended*

Rescue, The (1988, C, 98m, PG)
A band of teens whose U.S. Navy fathers are being held captive in North Korea launch a mission to bring them home. Kevin Dillon, Marc Price, and Kristina Harnos star. **AC20**

Rescuers, The (1977, C, 76m, G)
Animated film from Disney about all-mouse Rescue Aid Society, headed by Bernard and Bianca (voices by Bob Newhart and Eva Gabor). Additional voices by Geraldine Page, Joe Flynn, and Jeanette Nolan. **FA2**

Rescuers Down Under, The
(1990, C, 76m, G)
Sequel to Disney's 1977 animated feature about Bernard and Bianca, two mice in the Rescue Aid Society. Here they're in Australia to come to the aid of a young boy. Voice characterizations by Bob Newhart and Eva Gabor, with George C. Scott as a villainous hunter and John Candy as a friendly albatross. Discontinued from manufacture in April 1993; copies may be hard to find. **CO14, FA2, ST196**

Reservoir Dogs (1992, C, 105m, R)
Harrowing crime thriller about aftermath of botched jewelry heist and violent dissent among gang members. Harvey Keitel, Tim Roth, Steve Buscemi, and Michael Madsen are standouts as the gang, with Lawrence Tierney and Chris Penn as their bosses and the voice of Steven Wright as a deejay. Written and directed by Quentin Tarantino, who has a small role. Well-crafted story, nervy performances. Notorious torture scene is

more powerful for what it *suggests.* **CU7, DR16, MY2, MY18,** *Recommended*

Resurrection (1980, C, 103m, PG)
Ellen Burstyn plays a woman who recovers from an auto accident to learn that she has been endowed with powers of healing. With Sam Shepard, Richard Farnsworth, Roberts Blossom, and Eva LeGallienne. **DR2, DR10**

Retreat, Hell! (1952, B&W, 95m, NR)
Korean War drama about U.S. withdrawal from the Changjin Reservoir, starring Frank Lovejoy, Richard Carlson, and Russ Tamblyn. **AC3**

Return Engagement (1978, C, 76m, NR)
A lonely professor (Elizabeth Taylor) falls in love with one of her students (Joseph Bottoms). **DR3, ST212**

Return From the Past see *Dr. Terror's Gallery of Horrors*

Return From Witch Mountain
(1978, C, 93m, G)
Bette Davis and Christopher Lee play kidnappers in this family adventure from the Disney studios. Sequel to *Escape to Witch Mountain.* **FA1, FA15, ST44, ST135**

Return of a Man Called Horse, The
(1976, C, 129m, PG)
In this sequel to *A Man Called Horse*, Richard Harris again stars as the aristocrat who learns the ways of the Sioux Indians. With Gale Sondergaard and Geoffrey Lewis. Directed by Irvin Kershner. **WE8**

Return of Captain Invincible, The
(1983, C, 90m, PG)
A superhero who has turned into a broken-down drunk is persuaded to don his costume once again to save the world. Bizarre comedy, with musical numbers, stars Alan Arkin and Christopher Lee. **CO12, ST135**

Return of Chandu (The Magician)
(1934, B&W, 206m, NR)
Serial starring Bela Lugosi as a mysterious magician who uses his powers to rescue a maiden from a cat-worshipping cult. **ST143**

Return of Frank James, The
(1940, C, 92m, NR)
Henry Fonda plays the outlaw Jesse James's brother, looking to avenge his brother's murder. With Gene Tierney. Fritz Lang directed. **DT70, ST71, ST214, WE5**

Return of Martin Guerre, The
(1982, C, 111m, PG-13)
French peasant disappears; years later a man (Gérard Depardieu) turns up, claiming to be the missing man. Nathalie Baye costars in

this mystery based on a true story. Handsome, well-acted by the leads, but no big deal. U.S. remake: *Sommersby*. **FF1, FF8, ST52**

Return of Superfly (1990, C, 95m, R)
After an eighteen-year layoff, the cool dude is back, with Nathan Purdee recreating the role Ron O'Neal played in the original. Curtis Mayfield again supplies the music. **AC8, DR14, DR16**

Return of the Ape Man
(1944, B&W, 51m, NR)
Horror tale of mad doc Bela Lugosi planting John Carradine's brain into the head of an ape. **ST143**

Return of the Badmen
(1948, B&W, 90m, NR)
Randolph Scott has his hands full with outlaws including Billy the Kid (Dean White), The Sundance Kid (Robert Ryan), and The Dalton Gang. **HF1, ST193, ST197**

Return of the Dragon (1973, C, 91m, R)
Bruce Lee and Chuck Norris match kicks in this action drama about a Chinese in Rome protecting his family from mobsters. **ST134, ST165**

Return of the Fly, The
(1959, B&W, 80m, NR)
Sequel to *The Fly* has son following in his father's footsteps to duplicate dangerous experiment, with dire results. Vincent Price stars. **HO20, ST179**

Return of the Jedi (1983, C, 133m, PG)
The third in the *Star Wars* trilogy finds Luke Skywalker, Han Solo, and Princess Leia teaming with the Ewoks to do battle with Darth Vader and his minions. Harrison Ford, Mark Hamill, and Carrie Fisher star, with Billy Dee Williams, Alec Guinness, and James Earl Jones as the voice of Darth Vader. Good idea to give this series a rest. **FA8, SF11, SF13, SF23, ST74, ST95, ST118, ST227**

Return of the Living Dead, The
(1985, C, 91m, R)
Horror spoof, with plenty of gore, about zombies terrorizing group of people trapped in a mortuary. Clu Gulager and James Karen star. Very funny—if you're not averse to a little blood and guts. **HO6, HO18, HO24,** *Recommended*

Return of the Pink Panther, The
(1975, C, 113m, G)
The fourth installment in the comedy series about the bumbling Inspector Clouseau (Peter Sellers), as he matches what few wits he has with a master thief (Christopher

Plummer). Directed by Blake Edwards. **DT40, ST198**

Return of the Secaucus Seven
(1980, C, 100m, NR)
A reunion of 1960s pals who once got arrested in New Jersey on their way to a protest rally is the framework for this entertaining, insightful comedy-drama. John Sayles wrote, directed, and plays a small role. Superior film, except for no-name cast, to *The Big Chill*. **DR7, DT112,** *Recommended*

Return of the Seven (1966, C, 96m, NR)
Sequel to *The Magnificent Seven* has Yul Brynner rounding up a new collection of cowboys (including Warren Oates, Robert Fuller, and Jordan Christopher) to fight more Mexican bandits. **ST166**

Return of the Soldier, The
(1981, C, 101m, NR)
Alan Bates stars as a World War I veteran trying to put the pieces of his life back together. Glenda Jackson, Julie Christie, and Ann-Margret are the women who offer to help him. **DR5, ST9, ST30, ST117**

Return of the Vampire, The
(1943, B&W, 69m, NR)
Bela Lugosi plays a Rumanian vampire who's dead and buried in London—until German bombs disturb his grave. Then he's back to work, with the help of a werewolf assistant. **HO5, ST143**

Return to Macon County
(1975, C, 90m, PG)
Action and suspense down in Dixie, with two young hotheads ready for hot rod thrills. Don Johnson and Nick Nolte (in his film debut) star. **AC10, ST164**

Return to Oz (1985, C, 110m, PG)
Dorothy, the brave heroine of the Oz tales, goes back to the magic kingdom for a new set of adventures. Fairuza Balk stars, with Nicol Williamson, Jean Marsh, and Piper Laurie. Imaginative special effects; dark cast to story will turn off some viewers. **FA4, SF13**

Return to Salem's Lot, A
(1987, C, 96m, R)
More action in that Maine town of vampires made famous by Stephen King. Michael Moriarty stars, with Ricky Addison Reed, Samuel Fuller, Andrew Duggan, Evelyn Keyes, June Havoc, and Ronnee Blakely. Directed by Larry Cohen. **DT28, DT49, HO5, WR15**

Return to Snowy River, Part II
(1988, C, 97m, PG)
Sequel to *The Man From Snowy River*, with same young stars (Tom Burlinson, Sigrid

Thornton), same great wild horse action and lovely Australian scenery. **AC12, FF5**

Reuben, Reuben (1983, C, 101m, R) Tom Conti stars in this wry comedy about a lecherous poet who finds true, if temporary, love with a young woman (Kelly McGillis). Adapted from the Peter DeVries novel by Julius Epstein. Conti's best performance carries this one; McGillis makes strong impression. **CO1, DR19,** *Recommended*

Reunion (1989, C, 110m, PG-13) Jason Robards plays an elderly American Jew who journeys back to Stuttgart, Germany, to find a friend he left behind in 1933. With Christian Anholt, Samuel West, and Françoise Fabian. **DR1, ST185**

Reunion in France (1942, B&W, 104m, NR) Drama starring John Wayne and Joan Crawford, as they try to escape Nazi-occupied France. With Ava Gardner in a small role. **ST39, ST79, ST224**

Revenge (1971, C, 78m, NR) A vengeful mother (Shelley Winters) imprisons her daughter's rapist in a cage in her home. Originally made for TV. **ST232**

Revenge (1990, C, 124m, R) Kevin Costner plays an ex-Navy pilot who falls in love with the young wife (Madeleine Stowe) of an old buddy (Anthony Quinn). The buddy's henchmen take violent action, and our hero comes back for retribution. **AC19, ST38, ST209**

Revenge of the Dead (1960, B&W, 69m, NR) A "bad" horror movie classic, directed by the legendary Ed Wood, Jr. Narrated by the psychic Criswell—from a coffin. And that's just for starters. Also known as *Night of the Ghouls*. **CU11, DT141**

Revenge of the Nerds (1984, C, 90m, R) Social outcasts at a university get revenge on the snooty fraternity that runs the school. Robert Carradine stars, with Anthony Edwards, Julie Montgomery, and Curtis Armstrong. **CO4, CO18**

Revenge of the Pink Panther (1978, C, 99m, PG) Peter Sellers's final film as Inspector Clouseau has him in Hong Kong investigating his own murder. With Dyan Cannon, Herbert Lom, and Robert Webber. Directed by Blake Edwards. **DT40, ST198**

Revenge of the Zombies (1943, B&W, 61m, NR) Low-budget horror film about a mad doctor

(John Carradine), his zombie wife, and Nazis lurking in the background. **HO6**

Reversal of Fortune (1990, C, 120m, R) True, chilling story of Claus von Bulow, wealthy denizen of Newport, Rhode Island, accused of murdering his drug-addicted wife, Sunny. Jeremy Irons won a well-deserved Oscar for his crafty performance as von Bulow, with Glenn Close as Sunny (narrating the film from a coma!), Ron Silver as Alan Dershowitz (Claus's attorney), Fisher Stevens, and Annabella Sciorra. Nicholas Kazan adapted Dershowitz's book; directed by Barbet Schroeder. Ghoulish humor, real suspense, never less than fascinating. **DR6, DR8, DR17, ST33, ST116, XT2,** *Recommended*

Revolt of Job, The (1983, C, 97m, NR) In Hungary, a Jewish couple adopt a Gentile boy in the shadow of the Holocaust. **FF7**

Revolution (1985, C, 123m, PG) A lavishly produced drama about the American colonists' fight for independence from the British. Al Pacino, Nastassja Kinski, and Donald Sutherland star. **AC6, DR5, ST170**

Rhapsody (1954, C, 115m, NR) Three-cornered romance, featuring rich girl (Elizabeth Taylor) pursued by two classical musicians (Vittorio Gassman and John Ericson). Written by Fay and Michael Kanin. **ST212**

Rhapsody in Blue (1945, B&W, 139m, NR) Robert Alda plays American composer supreme George Gershwin. With Joan Leslie and Alexis Smith, and Oscar Levant playing the title tune. **MU5**

Rhinestone (1984, C, 111m, PG) Sylvester Stallone and Dolly Parton star in this comedy about a country singer's bet that she can turn a New York cabbie into a singing sensation. **CO8, ST204**

Rich and Famous (1981, C, 117m, R) Jacqueline Bisset and Candice Bergen play friends/rivals over a twenty-year period in this modern soap opera. With David Selby, Hart Bochner, Steven Hill, Meg Ryan, and Matt Lattanzi. Directed by George Cukor, his last film (sadly). **DR10, DT32**

Rich and Strange (1932, B&W, 92m, NR) Early Hitchcock drama, produced in Great Britain, concerning a couple whose boredom is alleviated by a sudden inheritance. Henry Kendall and Joan Barry star. **DT57**

Rich in Love (1993, C, 105m, PG-13) Comedy-drama about South Carolina family whose mom deserts her husband after long marriage, and how it affects their teen-age daughter. Albert Finney and Kathryn Erbe star, with Jill Clayburgh, Kyle MacLachlan, Piper Laurie, Ethan Hawke, Suzy Amis, and Alfre Woodard. Alfred Uhry adapted Josephine Humphreys's novel, Bruce Beresford directed. Finney's delightful, but the story suffers from poky exposition and a rushed wrap-up. **DR8, DR9, DR19, ST31, ST68**

Rich Kids (1979, C, 101m, PG)
Two teen-agers from wealthy New York families find comfort in their friendship as their parents' marriages break up. Trini Alvarado, Jeremy Levy, and John Lithgow star in this comedy-drama. Directed by Robert M. Young. **CO4, XT9**

Rich, Young and Pretty
(1951, C, 95m, NR)
MGM musical starring Jane Powell as gal on the loose in Paris, reuniting with her mom (Danielle Darrieux). With Wendell Corey, Vic Damone, and Fernando Lamas. **MU1**

Richard Lewis: "I'm in Pain"
(1985, C, 51m, NR)
Standup comedy from the comedian who makes misery funny. Guest stars: Billy Crystal, Robin Williams, Harold Ramis, and Rob Reiner. **CO13, CO14, CO16, DT103, ST228**

Richard Pryor (concert films)
Live and Smokin' (1971, C, 47m, NR)
Richard Pryor Is Back Live in Concert
(1979, C, 78m, R)
Richard Pryor Live on the Sunset Strip
(1982, C, 82m, R)
Richard Pryor Here and Now
(1983, C, 83m, R)
Pryor's no-holds-barred monologues on race, sex, and life's crazy moments. **ST180**

Richard II (1979, C, 157m, NR)
Shakespeare's drama of the fourteenth-century rebellion against the British crown, starring Derek Jacobi, Jon Finch, and John Gielgud. Originally part of TV series "The Shakespeare Plays." **ST86, WR28**

Richard III (1956, C, 155m, NR)
Laurence Olivier directed and stars in this version of Shakespeare's tragedy of the misshapen British monarch and his political problems. With John Gielgud, Ralph Richardson, and Claire Bloom. This full-length version contains 16 minutes of newly restored footage. **CU10, ST86, ST184, WR28,** *Recommended*

Richard's Things (1980, C, 104m, R)
Liv Ullmann plays a widow who is seduced by her late husband's girlfriend. English-language film shot in Great Britain. **ST220**

Ricochet (1991, C, 97m, R)
Revenge drama of rookie cop (Denzel Washington) putting away baddie (John Lithgow) who years later comes looking to ruin the man in a deadly game of cat and mouse. With Ice-T, Kevin Pollak, and Lindsay Wagner. **AC9, AC19, MY9, ST223**

Ride 'Em Cowboy (1942, B&W, 86m, NR)
Abbott and Costello open a hot-dog stand on the frontier. With Dick Foran, Anne Gwynne, and Johnny Mack Brown. Ella Fitzgerald sings "A Tisket, A Tasket." **ST1, WE14**

Ride in the Whirlwind
(1965, C, 83m, NR)
A case of mistaken identity has three cowboys fleeing from the law in this cult Western. Jack Nicholson and Harry Dean Stanton star. Monte Hellman directed. **ST163, ST205, WE15**

Ride Lonesome (1959, C, 73m, NR)
Randolph Scott stars in a Western drama of a man holding an outlaw captive in the hopes of smoking out the man's brother—the man he really wants to kill for revenge. With Karen Steele, Pernell Roberts, James Best, Lee Van Cleef, and James Coburn (his debut). Written by Burt Kennedy, directed by Budd Boetticher. Solid effort from the Scott-Kennedy-Boetticher series. Widescreen cinematography will be lost on video. **CU20, DT14, ST197, ST221, WE5,** *Recommended*

Ride, Ranger, Ride (1936, B&W, 56m, NR)
Gene Autry joins the cavalry and prevents an Indian war. **ST5**

Ride the High Country
(1962, C, 94m, NR)
Two aging gunfighters agree to bring a shipment of gold from a mountain camp; one plans to persuade his buddy to steal it. Sam Peckinpah directed this elegiac Western starring Joel McCrea and Randolph Scott (in his last movie), with Mariette Hartley, R.G. Armstrong, and Warren Oates. Widescreen photography will be lost on video. For anyone who thinks Peckinpah only did blood-soaked Westerns . . . this one's for you. **CU20, DT95, ST144, ST166, ST197, WE11, XT22,** *Essential, Highly Recommended*

Rider on the Rain (1970, C, 115m, PG)
A woman is attacked by a mysterious stranger, whom she manages to kill—but there's another man following her, too. Charles Bronson stars in this thriller made in France. **FF1, MY3, ST20**

Riders of Death Valley
(1941, B&W, 195m, NR)
Western serial about a trio of peacemakers

patrolling a crime-riddled mining area. Buck Jones, Dick Foran, and Leo Carrillo star; Lon Chaney, Jr., heads the supporting cast. **ST27**

Riders of the Storm (1986, C, 92m, R)
A pair of loony Vietnam veterans (Dennis Hopper and Michael J. Pollard) run a pirate TV station from their vintage aircraft in this satirical comedy. **CO12, ST110**

Riders of the Whistling Pines
(1949, B&W, 70m, NR)
Gene Autry rescues a girl about to be swindled out of her land. With Jason Robards, Sr., and Clayton Moore (TV's Lone Ranger). **ST5**

Ridin' Down the Canyon
(1942, B&W, 62m, NR)
Roy Rogers thwarts a band of horse rustlers who are gumming up the war effort. With Gabby Hayes. **ST188**

Ridin' on a Rainbow
(1941, B&W, 79m, NR)
In this Western, Gene Autry spends almost as much time singing on a showboat as he does riding the range to nab some outlaws. **ST5**

Riffraff (1935, B&W, 89m, NR)
Spencer Tracy and Jean Harlow star in this comedy-drama of a couple angling for a good living in the fishing business, falling into trouble with the law. With Una Merkel, Joseph Calleia, and Mickey Rooney. **ST98, ST189, ST217**

Rififi (1954, B&W, 115m, NR)
Four French jewel thieves decide to pull off the ultimate caper, but there is immediate mistrust and suspicion in the gang. Directed by Jules Dassin. **FF1, MY16, MY18, XT26**

Right of Way (1983, C, 106m, NR)
Bette Davis and James Stewart play an elderly couple who decide to end their lives rather than suffer the indignities of age and illness. Originally made for cable TV. **DR11, ST44, ST207**

Right Stuff, The (1983, C, 193m, PG)
Epic saga of the first Americans in space, adapted from the Tom Wolfe bestseller. Sam Shepard stars as Colonel Chuck Yeager; the large cast also includes Dennis Quaid, Scott Glenn, Ed Harris, Kim Stanley, Barbara Hershey, Fred Ward, Levon Helm, Pamela Reed, Veronica Cartwright, and Jeff Goldblum. Photographed by Caleb Deschanel; directed by Philip Kaufman. Glorious widescreen visuals won't work without letterboxing but there's still a lot to like, especially in the performances. **AC11, CU20, DR6, DT64, MU12, ST90, ST104,** *Recommended*

Rikisha-Man (1958, B&W, 105m, NR)
From Japanese director Hiroshi Inagaki, a drama of urban life starring Toshiro Mifune. **FF4, ST157**

Rikky and Pete (1988, C, 107m, R)
Australian comedy about brother and sister misfits and their adventures in an isolated mining town. Directed by Nadia Tass; written and photographed by her husband, David Parker, who also designed Pete's wacky inventions. **FF5**

Rim of the Canyon (1949, B&W, 70m, NR)
Gene Autry takes on a dual role, as himself and his old man; he's on the trail of some baddies Dad put behind bars. **ST5**

Ring, The (1927, B&W, 73m, NR)
Hitchcock silent drama of two boxers vying for the same woman. Carl Brisson, Ian Hunter, and Lillian Hall-Davies star. **DT57**

Ring of Bright Water (1969, C, 107m, G)
Family adventure about a man's friendship with his pet sea otter. Bill Travers and Virginia McKenna star. **FA4**

Rink, The/The Immigrant
(1917, B&W, 79m, NR)
Two Charlie Chaplin shorts. In the first, he plays a waiter in a wacky restaurant; in the second, he's a friendly immigrant who meets a young mother and her child on a boat to America. **DT24**

Rio Bravo (1959, C, 141m, NR)
A cult favorite of Westerns fans, starring John Wayne, Dean Martin, and Ricky Nelson as a trio trying to uphold the law in a small town. With Walter Brennan, Angie Dickinson, Ward Bond, John Russell, Claude Akins, and Bob Steele. Directed by Howard Hawks. The alleged charms of this one escape me. **CL14, CU13, DT53, MU12, ST149, ST224, WE15**

Rio Grande (1950, B&W, 105m, NR)
Life in a cavalry outpost in the days after the Civil War. John Wayne stars, with Maureen O'Hara, Ben Johnson, Harry Carey, Jr., and Victor McLaglen. John Ford directed. **DT44, ST167, ST224, WE4**

Rio Lobo (1970, C, 114m, G)
For Civil War veteran John Wayne, the war isn't over until he's dealt out his own brand of justice. With Jorge Rivero, Jennifer O'Neill, Jack Elam, Chris Mitchum, and Sherry Lansing. Director Howard Hawks's last film. **DT53, ST224**

Rio Rita (1942, B&W, 91m, NR)
Broadway musical given update by Abbott and Costello, who have their dude ranch

invaded by Nazis. With Kathryn Grayson, John Carroll, amd Tom Conway. **MU2, ST1**

Riot in Cell Block 11
(1954, B&W, 80m, NR)
Classic prison drama of convicts taking over, using the press to convey their demands. Neville Brand stars. Don Siegel directed. Didn't invent all the clichés of the genre, but did perfect them. **DR18, DT116,** *Recommended*

Rip Van Winkle (1985, C, 48m, NR)
The classic tale of the world's greatest sleeper, presented by Faerie Tale Theatre. Harry Dean Stanton stars. Francis Ford Coppola directed. **DT29, FA12, ST205**

Ripping Yarns (series)
(1979, C, 90m each, NR)
Three volumes (*Ripping Yarns, More Ripping Yarns,* and *Even More Yarns*) of parodies of schoolboy adventure tales, created by Monty Python's Michael Palin and Terry Jones. **CO15**

Rise and Fall of Legs Diamond, The
(1960, B&W, 101m, NR)
Gangster saga of title character who crossed the Mob once too often. Ray Danton stars, with Karen Steele, Jesse White, Warren Oates, and Dyan Cannon. Directed by Budd Boetticher. **AC22, DT14, ST166**

Rise of Louis XIV, The (1966, C, 100m, NR)
Roberto Rossellini's portrait of the Sun King, starring Jean-Marie Patte and Raymond Jourdon. Originally made for French TV. Lovely visuals defeated by intentionally static narrative. **DT109, FF1**

Risky Business (1983, C, 96m, R)
Suburban Chicago high school student, left alone by traveling parents, becomes involved with call girl and her nasty pimp. Tom Cruise and Rebecca De Mornay star in this comedy with real bite. With Curtis Armstrong, Bronson Pinchot, Raphael Sbarge, Joe Pantoliano, and Richard Masur. Written and directed by Paul Brickman. Outstanding musical score by Tangerine Dream, with songs by Bob Seger, Muddy Waters, Prince, and others. **CO4, ST41, XT11,** *Highly Recommended*

Rita, Sue and Bob Too (1986, C, 95m, R)
Raunchy British comedy about two teen babysitters involved in a ménage à trois with the husband of the couple they work for. Siobhan Finneran, Michelle Holmes, and George Costigan star. **CO4, CO17**

Ritz, The (1976, C, 91m, R)
Farce about a man on the run hiding out in gay baths. Jack Weston, Rita Moreno, and

Jerry Stiller star. Richard Lester directed. **CO20, DT74**

River, The (1951, C, 99m, NR)
Drama, adapted from a Rumer Godden novel, of English children growing up in India. Directed by Jean Renoir, with superb Technicolor cinematography by Claude Renoir. Patricia Walters, Nora Swinburne, and Adrienne Cori star. **CL9, DT104**

River, The (1984, C, 122m, PG-13)
A contemporary farm couple fight to save their land from developers, led by the woman's ex-boyfriend. Sissy Spacek, Mel Gibson, and Scott Glenn star. Directed by Mark Rydell. **DR7, ST85, ST202**

River Niger, The (1976, C, 105m, R)
The intertwined lives of a black family living in Harlem are dramatized in this film version of the award-winning play. James Earl Jones, Cicely Tyson, Glynn Turman, and Louis Gossett, Jr., star. **DR8, DR14, DR20, ST118**

River of No Return (1954, C, 91m, NR)
Western drama has Robert Mitchum caring for abandoned Marilyn Monroe in Indian-infested wilderness. With Tommy Rettig and Rory Calhoun. Directed by Otto Preminger. Widescreen will be lost on home video. Stars never quite mesh; director on unfamiliar ground. **CU20, DT100, ST158, ST159, WE8**

River Runs Through It, A
(1992, C, 123m, PG)
Adaptation of famed Norman Maclean novella of Montana family's love of trout fishing and the divergent paths in life its two sons take. Craig Sheffer and Brad Pitt star, with Tom Skerritt and Emily Lloyd. Set between 1910 and 1935. Director Robert Redford also narrated. A worthy try but comes up short of capturing book's marvelously evocative mood. **DR8, DR19, ST181**

River's Edge (1987, C, 99m, R)
True-life drama about a group of alienated high school kids, one of whom murders his girlfriend, none of whom will report the crime. Crispin Glover, Keanu Reeves, Roxana Zal, and Ione Skye Leitch star, with Daniel Roebuck, Jim Metzler, and Dennis Hopper. Directed by Tim Hunter. Harrowing stuff. Glover's over-the-top performance has been unfairly used to drag down the entire film. **DR7, DR9, ST110,** *Recommended*

Road Games (1981, C, 100m, PG)
A trucker and a lovely hitchhiker join forces to solve murders occurring on lonesome highways in the Australian outback. Stacy Keach and Jamie Lee Curtis star. **MY16, ST42, XT18**

Road House (1948, B&W, 95m, NR)
Film noir about two rivals, a roadhouse owner (Richard Widmark) and a parolee (Cornel Wilde). With Ida Lupino as the woman in the middle. **MY1**

Road House (1989, C, 114m, R)
Patrick Swayze plays a bouncer in the title location; Ben Gazzara is the town baddie. With Kelly Lynch and Sam Elliott. **AC25**

Road Runner vs. Wile E. Coyote: The Classic Chase (1985, C, 54m, NR)
A collection of superb cartoons, directed by Chuck Jones, about that lovable roadrunner and his inept adversary. **FA11,** *Recommended*

Road to Bali (1952, C, 90m, NR)
Bing Crosby and Bob Hope hit the highway for the Far East, with Dorothy Lamour along for laughs and songs. **CL15, ST40, ST108**

Road to Eternity see *Human Condition, Part II, The*

Road to Hong Kong, The
(1962, B&W, 91m, NR)
Last *Road* picture has Hope and Crosby involved with spies and space travel. With Joan Collins, Dorothy Lamour (in a bit as herself), Robert Morley, and a cameo by Peter Sellers. **CL15, ST40, ST108, ST198**

Road to Morocco (1942, B&W, 83m, NR)
Bob Hope-Bing Crosby comedy has Bing selling Bob to a slave trader. With Dorothy Lamour, Anthony Quinn, and Yvonne De Carlo. Bing sings "Moonlight Becomes You." **CL15, ST40, ST108**

Road to Rio (1947, B&W, 100m, NR)
Bob Hope and Bing Crosby are out to rescue Dorothy Lamour from her evil aunt (Gale Sondergaard). The Andrews Sisters show up for one number. **CL15, ST40, ST108**

Road to Salina (1971, C, 96m, R)
Drifter returns home to mother, proceeds to begin an affair with young girl who may be his sister. Offbeat thriller starring Robert Walker, Jr., Mimsy Farmer, and Rita Hayworth. **MY14, ST101**

Road to Singapore (1940, B&W, 84m, NR)
Bob Hope and Bing Crosby decide to give up women. With Dorothy Lamour, Anthony Quinn, and Charles Coburn. **CL15, ST40, ST108**

Road to Utopia (1945, B&W, 90m, NR)
Bob Hope and Bing Crosby travel to Alaska in search of gold and Dorothy Lamour, not necessarily in that order. Robert Benchley offers color commentary. **CL15, ST40, ST108**

Road to Yesterday, The
(1925, B&W, 136m, NR)
Cecil B. DeMille offers two romantic triangle stories, one present-day, the other from the seventeenth century, in this silent drama. **DT34**

Road to Zanzibar (1941, B&W, 92m, NR)
Bob Hope and Bing Crosby are circus performers looking to quit the big top when they learn of a diamond mine. With Dorothy Lamour, Una Merkel, and Eric Blore. **CL15, ST40, ST108**

Road Warrior, The (1982, C, 94m, R)
The second *Mad Max* adventure takes place in a post-apocalypse world where fuel is the most valuable commodity. Mel Gibson stars, with Bruce Spence as the Gyro Captain, Vernon Wells as the baddest heavy, Mike Preston, Emil Minty, and Kjell Nilsson as the lead baddie, Humongous, "the Ayatollah of rock 'n' rollah." Directed by George Miller. Outrageous costumes, hairdos, stunts; the final chase sequence is an action-picture classic. Also known as *Mad Max 2*. **AC10, AC24, AC25, FF5, ST85, XT18,** *Highly Recommended*

Roadie (1980, C, 105m, PG)
A Texas beer truck driver goes on the road in search of his rock 'n' idol, Alice Cooper, in this zany comedy from director Alan Rudolph. Meat Loaf stars, with Kaki Hunter and Art Carney. Appearances by music stars Debby Harry and Blondie, Roy Orbison, Asleep at the Wheel, Hank Williams, Jr., and Mr. Cooper. Has to be seen to be believed. Suggest you watch it with plenty of Shiner beer on hand. **CO8, DT110, MU9, MU12, XT18,** *Recommended*

Roadside Prophets (1992, C, 96m, R)
Road adventure of two cyclists (John Doe, Adam Horovitz) riding into Nevada desert in search of legendary El Dorado Casino. Mind-altering supporting cast headed by David Carradine, Timothy Leary, Arlo Guthrie, and John Cusack. **MU12, XT18**

Roaring Twenties, The
(1939, B&W, 104m, NR)
James Cagney and Humphrey Bogart trade punches and bullets in this classic saga of Prohibition and the gangsters who profited from it. With Priscilla Lane, Gladys George, Frank McHugh, and Joe Sawyer. Directed by Raoul Walsh. Zesty stuff. **AC22, DT131, ST15, ST24,** *Recommended*

Robbery (1967, C, 114m, NR)
Dramatic account of famous Great Train Robbery in 1963 Britain, starring Stanley Baker and Joanna Pettet. **MY8, MY15, MY18**

Robe, The (1953, C, 135m, NR)
Epic religious drama about the Roman centurion who carried out the execution of Christ. Richard Burton and Victor Mature star, with Jean Simmons, Michael Rennie, Richard Boone, Jay Robinson, and Dean Jagger. Widescreen will be lost on video. **CL13, ST22**

Robert et Robert (1978, C, 105m, NR)
French comedy of friendship struck up by traffic cop and taxi driver while waiting for their respective computer dates. Charles Denner and Jacques Villeret star. Directed by Claude Lelouch. **FF1**

Robert Klein: Child of the '60s, Man of the '80s (1984, C, 60m, NR)
Comic monologues from the comedian who waxes nostalgic about those golden days of protest. **CO16**

Robert Klein on Broadway
(1986, C, 60m, NR)
More comic observations about modern life from the stand-up comic. **CO16**

Roberta (1935, B&W, 85m, NR)
Fred Astaire and Ginger Rogers sparkle in this musical which features "Smoke Gets In Your Eyes" and "I Won't Dance." Irene Dunne and Randolph Scott costar. **CL15, ST4, ST62, ST187, ST197**

Robin and Marian (1976, C, 112m, PG)
The Robin Hood-Maid Marian story, continued: an aging Robin and Little John return from the Crusades to find that Marian has joined a convent. Sean Connery and Audrey Hepburn star, with Nicol Williamson as Little John, Robert Shaw as the Sheriff of Nottingham, and Richard Harris as King Richard. Richard Lester directed this bittersweet romance, written by James Goldman. Robin Hood for adults who don't mind a less heroic cast to the tale. **AC14, AC15, DR1, DT74, HF15, ST36, ST102,** *Highly Recommended*

Robin and the Seven Hoods
(1964, B&W, 103m, NR)
Gangster spoof starring Frank Sinatra and his Rat Pack pals (Dean Martin, Sammy Davis, Jr., et al.), plus Bing Crosby. Frank sings "My Kind of Town." Look fast for Edward G. Robinson. **CO7, ST40, ST149, ST186, ST199**

Robin Hood (1973, C, 83m, G)
Disney animated version of the classic tale, with animals playing the parts. **FA2, HF15**

Robin Hood (1991, C, 116m, NR)
Patrick Bergin stars in this made-for-TV version of the familiar story, with Uma Thurman as Maid Marian, Jeroen Krabbe, Jurgen Prochnow, and Edward Fox. Original running time: 150 minutes. **AC15, HF15**

Robin Hood and the Sorcerer
(1983, C, 115m, NR)
Michael Praed stars as the legendary bandit of Sherwood Forest; here, his opponent is not the Sheriff of Nottingham, but a wicked magician. **AC18, HF15**

Robin Hood of Texas
(1947, B&W, 71m, NR)
Gene Autry is accused of bank robbery and must clear his name to avoid the law. **ST5**

Robin Hood of the Pecos
(1941, B&W, 56m, NR)
Roy Rogers plays a Confederate veteran battling Northern politicians. **ST188**

Robin Hood: Prince of Thieves
(1991, C, 138m, PG-13)
Big-budget retelling of the legend stars Kevin Costner, with Morgan Freeman, Mary Elizabeth Mastrantonio, Christian Slater, Alan Rickman as a memorable Sheriff of Nottingham, and Sean Connery in a bit part. Directed by Kevin Reynolds. Sturdy, acceptable version with Costner somewhat less than dashing. **AC15, HF15, ST36, ST38, ST76, ST200**

Robin Williams Live (1986, C, 65m, NR)
From the famed stage of New York's Metropolitan Opera House comes this fast-paced, free-wheeling comic monologue from one of the funniest men alive. **CO16, ST228,** *Highly Recommended*

RoboCop (1987, C, 103m, R)
In the Detroit of the future, a critically wounded policeman is transformed into an impervious robot, who goes after the crooks who assaulted him. Peter Weller and Kurtwood Smith star, with Nancy Allen, Ronny Cox, and Miguel Ferrer. Directed by Paul Verhoeven. Exciting special effects (especially in the animation of Robo's robot nemesis) can't disguise yahoo-pleasing violence. **AC9, AC25**

RoboCop 2 (1990, C, 117m, R)
Peter Weller and Nancy Allen return to fight more adventures as Robo and his faithful female companion. With Daniel O'Herlihy, Belinda Bauer, Tom Noonan, and Patricia Charbonneau. **AC9, AC25**

Robot Carnival (1991, C, 91m, NR)
Animated Japanese science fiction adventure contains eight stories about various types of man-made machines, ranging from a romance to a Frankenstein story. **FF4, HF10, SF6, SF18**

Robot Monster (1953, B&W, 63m, NR)
Cult "bad" movie about an alien (actually, a gorilla with a diving helmet) terrorizing the last remaining family on Earth. **CU11**

Rocco and His Brothers
(1960, B&W, 170m, NR)
Episodic account of the trials and tribulations of a poor family living in contemporary Milan, from director Luchino Visconti. The cast is headed by Alain Delon, Renato Salvatori, Claudia Cardinale, and Annie Girardot. Video version restores footage to film's original length. Masterful study of contemporary urban life, with stunning cinematography by Giuseppe Rotunno. **CU10, DT127,** *Recommended*

Rock-a-Doodle (1992, C, 77m, G)
Animated story of a singing rooster making it in Vegas as an Elvis-style rocker. Several live-action scenes. Voices by Glen Campbell, Ellen Greene, Christopher Plummer, and Charles Nelson Reilly. **FA10**

Rock All Night (1957, B&W, 63m, NR)
Early Roger Corman no-budget tale of two hoods holding hostages at a restaurant. Dick Miller, Russell Johnson, Jonathan Haze, and Abby Dalton star, with musical appearances by the Platters, Nora Hayes, and the Blockbusters. **DT30**

Rock Music With the Muppets
(1985, C, 54m, NR)
The Muppets get down with Alice Cooper, Debbie Harry, Paul Simon, Linda Ronstadt, and Helen Reddy. **FA14**

Rock 'n' Roll High School
(1979, C, 93m, PG)
Riff Randell, a student at Vince Lombardi High, would rather listen to punk group The Ramones than attend classes. This spoof of teen exploitation movies, directed by Allan Arkush, has become a midnight movie staple. P.J. Soles, Paul Bartel, Mary Woronov, Dey Young, Vincent Van Patten, and Clint Howard star. Amusingly grungy; demands enormous tolerance for brain-damaging music of Ramones. **CO7, CO18, CU1, DT6, DT8, MU9**

Rock, Pretty Baby (1956, B&W, 89m, NR)
High-school rock band competes in a talent contest in this early rock musical. Sal Mineo, John Saxon, Rod McKuen, and Fay Wray star. **MU9**

Rock, Rock, Rock (1956, B&W, 83m, NR)
Tuesday Weld tries to raise money to buy a prom dress, but the story's a flimsy excuse to showcase a long list of rock and pop performers. Chuck Berry, Frankie Lymon and the Teenagers, and LaVern Baker headline. **MU9**

Rocket Gibraltar (1988, C, 100m, PG)
Family drama centering on the seventy-seventh birthday celebration of a patriarch (Burt Lancaster). With Suzy Amis, Patricia Clarkson, Frances Conroy, Sinead Cusack, John Glover, and Macaulay Culkin. **DR8, ST129**

Rocket Ship X-M (1950, B&W, 77m, NR)
A spaceship is struck by a meteor and forced to land on Mars, where astronauts find a planet ravaged by nuclear war and inhabited by mutant monsters. One of the first postwar sci-fi films. Lloyd Bridges and Hugh O'Brian star. **SF1, SF3**

Rocket to the Moon (1986, C, 118m, NR)
Clifford Odets story about a thirty-year-old New York dentist and his life crisis. John Malkovich and Judy Davis star, with Eli Wallach. Originally made for public TV. **ST46, ST147**

Rocketeer, The (1991, C, 108m, PG)
Comic-book hero exploits, set in late 1930s Hollywood, of daring flier who straps rocket pack to his back and gets mixed up with a Nazi spy ring headed by a major movie star. Bill Campbell and Jennifer Connelly star in this Disney adventure, with Alan Arkin, Timothy Dalton (as that star, based on Errol Flynn), Paul Sorvino, and Terry O'Quinn as Howard Hughes. Great period re-creation; but typical problem of recent films of this type: leads are sappy in extreme, villains wonderful. Fine for kids. **AC17, FA1**

Rocking Horse Winner, The
(1950, B&W, 91m, NR)
D.H. Lawrence tale of boy who can predict outcome of horse races. With Valerie Hobson, John Howard Davies, and John Mills. **DR9, WR17**

Rockula (1990, C, 87m, PG-13)
Teen virgin vampire (who's really four hundred years old) tries to meet girl of his dreams. Imagine his classified ad. Dean Cameron stars, with Tawny Fere, Toni Basil, Thomas Dolby, Susan Tyrrell, and Bo Diddley. **HO5**

Rocky (series)
Rocky (1976, C, 119m, PG)
Rocky II (1979, C, 119m, PG)
Rocky III (1982, C, 99m, PG)
Rocky IV (1985, C, 91m, PG)
Rocky V (1990, C, 104m, PG-13)
Sylvester Stallone plays Rocky Balboa, the prizefighter who rises from obscurity to the heavyweight championship in these five dramas. Talia Shire and Burt Young appear in all five as his wife and brother-in-law. In last film, Stallone's son Sage plays Rocky's boy. First installment won Best Picture and Director (John G. Avildsen) Oscars. **DR22,**

ST204, XT1, XT6, XT8 (*Rocky* only for **XT1** and **XT6**; *Rocky V* only for **XT8**), *Essential* (*Rocky* only)

Rocky Horror Picture Show, The (1975, C, 95m, R)
Midnight movie favorite, a rock musical spoof of mad scientist movies. Tim Curry stars, with Susan Sarandon and Barry Bostwick. **CO7, CO12, CU1, CU5, MU9, MU16, ST194**

Rocky Mountain Mystery (1936, B&W, 62m, NR)
Early Randolph Scott Western has him investigating murders at a radium mine. **ST197**

Rodan (1957, C, 70m, NR)
Fire-breathing creature threatens to incinerate Tokyo. **FF4, SF18**

Roe vs. Wade (1989, C, 100m, NR)
Holly Hunter and Amy Madigan star in this drama about the famous court case that legalized abortion. Originally made for TV. Both stars are superb. **DR6, DR10, ST113,** *Recommended*

Roger & Me (1989, C, 90m, NR)
Documentary from filmmaker Michael Moore about the effect on his hometown of Flint, Michigan, of a General Motors plant closing. Title refers to his efforts to reach GM chairman Roger Smith. Smarmy and smug; one of the most overrated films of recent years. **CU16**

Roger Corman: Hollywood's Wild Angel (1978, C, 58m, NR)
Documentary about the producer/director/ talent maven who gave career starts to many great directors and made scores of low-budget classics. Includes appearances by Corman alumni Martin Scorsese, Jonathan Demme, Allan Arkush, and Joe Dante. **CU16, DT6, DT30, DT33, DT35, DT114,** *Recommended*

Roll of Thunder, Hear My Cry (1978, C, 150m, NR)
Depresssion-era drama set in Mississippi about black family as seen through the eyes of an eleven-year-old girl. Claudia McNeil, Janet MacLachlan, Robert Christian, Larry Scott, Morgan Freeman, and Lark Ruffin star. Adapted from novels by Mildred D. Taylor. Originally made for TV. **DR9, DR14, ST76**

Roll on Texas Moon (1946, B&W, 68m, NR)
Roy Rogers tries to make peace betwen feuding sheepherders and cattle men. **ST188**

Rollerball (1975, C, 128m, R)
In the near future, a corporate dictatorship puts on brutal "games" for the masses, and one contestant decides to defy the system. James Caan and John Houseman star, with Maud Adams, John Beck, Moses Gunn, and Ralph Richardson. Directed by Norman Jewison. Numbingly downbeat. **DT63, SF11, ST184**

Rollercoaster (1977, C, 119m, PG)
Madman threatens to destroy popular amusement park ride. George Segal, Timothy Bottoms, Richard Widmark, and Henry Fonda star, with Harry Guardino, Susan Strasberg, Helen Hunt, and Dorothy Tristan. Standard stuff. **AC23, ST71**

Rolling Thunder (1977, C, 99m, R)
Vietnam veteran swears revenge on the thugs who killed his family and mutilated him. William Devane and Tommy Lee Jones star in this violent action drama. Written by Paul Schrader; directed by John Flynn. Has cult following which gives more weight to film's intentions than results. **AC19**

Rolling Vengeance (1987, C, 92m, R)
Young trucker uses his monster rig to gain revenge on the slimeballs who killed his family and brutalized his girlfriend. Don Michael Paul and Ned Beatty star. **AC10, AC19**

Rollover (1981, C, 118m, R)
When a multimillionaire is murdered, his widow and a financial troubleshooter sort out the financial conspiracy that caused his death. Jane Fonda and Kris Kristofferson star, with Hume Cronyn, Josef Sommer, and Martha Plimpton. Directed by Alan J. Pakula. **DR24, DT94, MU12, ST72**

Roman Holiday (1953, B&W, 119m, NR)
Audrey Hepburn won an Oscar for her first starring role, as a princess on the run from stuffy royal life, in love with an American reporter (Gregory Peck). Directed by William Wyler. **DT142, ST102, ST171, XT3, XT17, XT21**

Roman Scandals (1933, B&W, 92m, NR)
Eddie Cantor dreams he's back in ancient Rome in this musical romp. Choreography by Busby Berkeley. **DT12**

Roman Spring of Mrs. Stone, The (1961, C, 104m, NR)
A middle-aged American actress in Rome falls in love with a young Don Juan in this adaptation of a Tennessee Williams short novel. Vivien Leigh and Warren Beatty star, with Lotte Lenya and Jill St. John. **DR1, ST10, ST137, WR38, XT17**

Romance (1930, B&W, 76m, NR)
Greta Garbo plays an Italian opera singer involved with a young priest (Gavin Gordon). Directed by Clarence Brown. **ST78**

Romance and Riches see *Amazing Adventure*

Romance in Manhattan
(1934, B&W, 78m, NR)
Chorus girl (Ginger Rogers) romances illegal alien (Francis Lederer) in this comedy. **ST187**

Romance on the High Seas
(1948, C, 99m, NR)
Doris Day's debut has her involved in shipboard romance. MGM musical also features Jack Carson, Janis Paige, Don DeFore, and Oscar Levant. **MU1, ST47, XT21**

Romance on the Orient Express
(1985, C, 100m, NR)
American magazine editor (Cheryl Ladd) and old British flame (Stuart Wilson) renew romance aboard the famed train. With John Gielgud. Originally made for TV. **DR1, ST86, XT19**

Romance on the Range
(1942, B&W, 54m, NR)
Roy Rogers captures a gang of fur thieves as well as the heart of a lovely lady. **ST188**

Romancing the Stone
(1984, C, 105m, PG)
A romance writer finds herself living out one of her stories when her sister is kidnapped in South America. Kathleen Turner and Michael Douglas star in this rousing romantic adventure. With Danny DeVito and Zack Norman. Directed by Robert Zemeckis; written by Diane Thomas. Lots of fun—just don't think about it too long afterwards. **AC14, AC21, DT143, ST54, ST59, ST218,** *Recommended*

Romantic Comedy (1983, C, 103m, PG)
Dudley Moore and Mary Steenburgen are a playwright team with a good professional relationship—but he's looking to get personal. **CO1, CO8, ST160**

Romantic Englishwoman, The
(1975, C, 115m, R)
Romantic triangle involving a British novelist, his restless wife, and a German houseguest. Michael Caine, Glenda Jackson, and Helmut Berger star. Joseph Losey directed; written by Tom Stoppard and Thomas Wiseman. Comedy-drama is always intriguing. **DR1, DR23, ST25, ST117,** *Recommended*

Rome Adventure (1962, C, 119m, NR)
Glossy romance of American schoolteacher (Suzanne Pleshette) in the Eternal City to find Mr. Right. With Rosanno Brazzi and Troy Donahue as her suitors, and Angie Dickinson, Constance Ford, and Al Hirt. Directed by Delmer Daves. **DR1, XT17**

Romeo and Juliet (1936, B&W, 126m, NR)
Classic Hollywood production of the Shakespeare tragedy, with Norma Shearer and Leslie Howard starring. John Barrymore heads the supporting cast. Directed by George Cukor. **DR3, DT32, ST8, WR28**

Romeo and Juliet (1954, C, 140m, NR)
Laurence Harvey and Susan Shentall play Shakespeare's doomed lovers. With Flora Robson; introduced by John Gielgud. **DR3, ST86, WR28**

Romeo and Juliet (1968, C, 138m, PG)
Director Franco Zeffirelli's version of Shakespeare's classic love story, with Leonard Whiting and Olivia Hussey the doomed young lovers. **DR3, WR28**

Romeo and Juliet (1979, C, 167m, NR)
Patrick Ryecart and Rebecca Saire star in this version of the Shakespearean tragedy. With John Gielgud. Produced as part of the TV series "The Shakespeare Plays." **DR3, ST86, WR28**

Romero (1989, C, 105m, PG-13)
Raul Julia plays El Salvador Archbishop Oscar Romero, whose outspoken stand against repression earned him a martyr's death. With Richard Jordan. **DR4, DR7**

Romola (1925, B&W, 120m, NR)
Silent melodrama, set in Italy during the Renaissance, of young man escaping pirates with jewels to ransom his captured father, instead leading dissolute life in Florence. William Powell stars, with Lillian and Dorothy Gish, and Ronald Colman. Based on the George Eliot novel. **CL1, CL12, ST35, ST87, ST176, XT8**

Roof, The (1956, B&W, 98m, NR)
Italian drama from director Vittorio De Sica about a couple in postwar Rome looking for a home. **DT37, XT17**

Rooftops (1989, C, 95m, R)
Drama of contemporary gangs in New York living on the tops of buildings. Jason Gedrick stars. Directed by Robert Wise. **DT140, XT9**

Rookie, The (1990, C, 121m, R)
Clint Eastwood's back on the beat in this cop drama of a veteran and his newcomer partner (Charlie Sheen). With Raul Julia, Sonia Braga, Tom Skerritt, and Lara Flynn Boyle. Eastwood directed. **AC9, ST17, ST64**

Room, The (1987, C, 48m, NR)
A woman and her husband are threatened by the arrival of a strange couple who have been given their room. Linda Hunt stars, with Annie Lennox, Julian Sands, and Donald Pleasence. Written by Harold Pinter;

directed by Robert Altman. **DT4, MU12, WR26**

Room Service (1938, B&W, 78m, NR)
The Marx Brothers play a trio of penniless producers trying to stay one step ahead of their creditors and their hotel management, which wants them evicted. With Lucille Ball, Ann Miller, and Frank Albertson. Groucho plus Lucy don't quite add up to big laughs. **CO8, ST152**

Room With a View, A (1985, C, 115m, NR)
In the early 1900s, a young Englishwoman visits Florence, and despite her chaperone's best efforts, falls in love with a dashing Englishman. This adaptation of the E.M. Forster novel stars Helena Bonham Carter, Maggie Smith, Julian Sands, Denholm Elliott, and Daniel Day-Lewis. Directed by James Ivory; produced by Ismail Merchant. Engaging, literate, if a bit protracted. **DR1, DR23, DT61, ST48, WR9,** *Recommended*

Rooster Cogburn (1975, C, 107m, PG)
John Wayne recreates his Oscar-winning role from *True Grit* in this Western romp with Katharine Hepburn. **ST103, ST224, WE2, WE8**

Rootin' Tootin' Rhythm
(1938, B&W, 55m, NR)
Gene Autry and Smiley Burnette settle a range war before things get out of hand. **ST5**

Rope (1948, C, 80m, PG)
Hitchcock drama of two murderers who brazenly throw a party in the room where they've hidden the corpse. James Stewart plays the guest who unravels the crime. Farley Granger and John Dall costar. Stunt of shooting film all in one shot (no cutting to closeups, etc.) adds to stagebound flavor. Dahl and Granger good. **DT57, MY9, MY11, ST207,** *Recommended*

Rosalie Goes Shopping
(1990, C, 94m, PG)
The star (Marianne Sägebrecht) and director (Percy Adlon) of *Bagdad Cafe* and *Sugarbaby* reunite for this comedy of a housewife who lives to shop. **CO2**

Rose, The (1979, C, 134m, R)
Bette Midler plays a rock singer whose hard-living lifestyle starts to catch up with her. With Alan Bates, Frederic Forrest, and Harry Dean Stanton. Directed by Mark Rydell. Loud, overinsistent; the story has nowhere to go but downhill from the very start. Midler throws herself into the role but she's no rock 'n' roll singer. **DR12, MU4, MU9, ST9, ST156, ST205**

Rose Garden, The (1989, C, 111m, PG-13)
Liv Ullmann stars as a lawyer defending a man (Maximilian Schell) who attacked another he recognized as a commander of concentration camp where his family died. **DR17, ST220**

Rose Marie (1936, B&W, 110m, NR)
An opera singer (Jeanette MacDonald) searches for her brother (James Stewart) who is also being pursued by a Mountie (Nelson Eddy). The singer and the Mountie fall in love and sing "Indian Love Call." **CL15, MU1, ST207**

Rose Tattoo, The (1955, B&W, 117m, NR)
Oscar winner Anna Magnani plays a widow who's courted by a truck driver (Burt Lancaster) in this Tennessee Williams drama. Directed by Daniel Mann. Magnani is wonderful, Lancaster less so. **CL4, ST129, WR38, XT3**

Roseanne Barr see *HBO Comedy Club*

Rosebud Beach Hotel, The
(1984, C, 87m, R)
Anything-for-a-laugh comedy about schnook (Peter Scolari) and his girlfriend (Colleen Camp) running a resort whose bellgirls service the male clientele. With Christopher Lee, Fran Drescher, Chuck McCann, and Eddie Deezen. **ST135**

Roseland (1977, C, 103m, PG)
Trio of stories set in New York's famed dance hall. Teresa Wright, Lou Jacobi, Geraldine Chaplin, and Christopher Walken are among the stars. Directed by James Ivory; produced by Ismail Merchant. **DR15, DT61, ST222, XT9**

Rosemary's Baby (1968, C, 136m, R)
The wife of a New York actor suspects that her pregnancy may not be normal. Mia Farrow, John Cassavetes, and Oscar winner Ruth Gordon star in this modern horror classic from director Roman Polanski. With Ralph Bellamy, Maurice Evans, and in a small part, Charles Grodin. Adapted from the Ira Levin bestseller. Filmed in part at New York's famed Dakota apartment building. **DT97, HO10, HO11, HO19, ST65, ST94, XT5, XT9,** *Highly Recommended*

Rosencrantz and Guildenstern Are Dead (1990, C, 118m, PG)
Tom Stoppard's comedy of two minor characters in *Hamlet* trying to figure out what's going on. Gary Oldman and Tim Roth star, with Richard Dreyfuss and Iain Glen. Stoppard adapted his play and directed. Maybe it works better on the stage. **CO12, DR20, ST60, WR28**

Rough Cut (1980, C, 112m, R)
A jewel thief and a female agent from Scotland Yard fall in love in this caper comedy. Burt Reynolds and Lesley-Anne Down star. Directed by Don Siegel. **CO10, DT118, ST183**

Rough Riders' Roundup
(1939, B&W, 58m, NR)
Early Roy Rogers Western, with plenty of action and some singing as well. Raymond Hatton plays Roy's sidekick. **ST188**

'Round Midnight (1986, C, 130m, R)
In the 1950s, an American jazz musician moves to Paris, hoping to find peace and respect. Based loosely on the lives of jazz greats Bud Powell and Lester Young, this drama stars saxophonist Dexter Gordon. Martin Scorsese has a small role. Directed by Bertrand Tavernier. Musical score supervised by Herbie Hancock. Melancholy, with wonderful "performance" by Gordon and marvelous music on the soundtrack. Purists may scoff but it's not likely to get much better than this. **DR12, DR27, DT114, DT123, XT16,** *Recommended*

Round-up Time in Texas
(1937, B&W, 58m, NR)
One of Gene Autry's early films, featuring sidekick Smiley Burnette and the usual singing and light gunplay. **ST5**

Roustabout (1964, C, 101m, NR)
Elvis Presley musical has The King going to work in a carnival run by Barbara Stanwyck. **ST178, ST206**

Rowlf's Rhapsodies With the Muppets
(1985, C, 56m, NR)
Bloopers from the popular TV show, with guests stars Steve Martin, Peter Sellers, Marisa Berenson, and George Burns. **FA14, ST150, ST198**

Roxanne (1987, C, 107m, PG)
In this modern remake of *Cyrano de Bergerac,* Steve Martin plays a small-town fire chief with two problems: a large nose and unrequited love for visiting astronomer Daryl Hannah. With Shelley Duvall and Rick Rossovich. Directed by Fred Schepisi. Widescreen will be lost on video. Martin's wonderful and the movie's charm never wears thin. **CO1, CU20, ST150,** *Recommended*

Royal Flash (1975, C, 98m, PG)
George MacDonald Fraser's dashing fictional hero comes to the screen in this adventure-comedy starring Malcolm McDowell. He's pretending to be a Prussian nobleman. With Alan Bates, Florinda Bolkan, Oliver Reed, Britt Ekland, and Bob Hoskins in a small

role. Fraser adapted his own novel. Directed by Richard Lester. **DT74, ST9, ST111**

Royal Wedding (1951, C, 93m, NR)
A brother and sister dance team (Fred Astaire and Jane Powell) perform in London during the wedding festivities of Princess Elizabeth and Prince Phillip. Directed by Stanley Donen. **DT38, MU1, ST4**

Ruby (1992, C, 110m, R)
Danny Aiello plays the Dallas nightclub owner who killed accused JFK assassin Lee Harvey Oswald. This drama speculates on Ruby's ties to organized crime and the CIA. With Sherilyn Fenn and Arliss Howard. **DR5, MY6**

Ruby Gentry (1952, B&W, 82m, NR)
Jennifer Jones plays a Southern temptress who marries an older man to spite her real love (Charlton Heston) in this melodrama. Directed by King Vidor. Heavy going at times, with Jones redeeming, Heston a drawback. **CL5, DT126**

Rude Awakening (1989, C, 100m, R)
Cheech Marin and Eric Roberts play a couple of refugees from the 1960s who are, like, stuck out of time in the greedy 1980s. With Julie Hagerty, Robert Carradine, and Andrea Martin. **CO14, CO20, ST28**

Rude Boy (1980, C, 133m, NR)
Documentary-style drama of an English lad working as a roadie for rock band The Clash. Plenty of concert footage in this midnight movie favorite. **CU1, DR12**

Ruggles of Red Gap
(1935, B&W, 92m, NR)
A butler finds that he has been won in poker game by a rude rancher in this comedy Western. Charles Laughton stars, with Mary Boland, Charlie Ruggles, ZaSu Pitts, and Roland Young. Directed by Leo McCarey. **DT80, ST132, WE14**

Rules of the Game (1939, B&W, 105m, NR)
Director Jean Renoir's classic study of the subtle relationship of the aristocratic class and their servants during a weekend in the country. Marcel Dalio, Nora Gregor, and Renoir star. **DT104,** *Essential*

Ruling Class, The (1972, C, 154m, PG)
Zany British comedy about a wacky heir to British lordship (Peter O'Toole) who's convinced that he's Jesus Christ. With Alastair Sim, Arthur Lowe, Harry Andrews, and Coral Browne. Directed by Peter Medak. Irreverent, to say the least, with a cult following. One major problem: overlength. **CO17, CU5, HF17, ST169**

Rumble Fish (1983, B&W/C, 94m, R)
Matt Dillon stars as a restless teen, coping with his alcoholic father (Dennis Hopper), and idolizing his older brother (Mickey Rourke). With Diane Lane, Diana Scarwid, Vincent Spano, Nicolas Cage, Christopher Penn, Tom Waits, and Sofia Coppola. Moody, stylized drama from director Francis Ford Coppola, based on a novel by S.E. Hinton. Stephen Burum's b&w cinematography is the best thing about it. Performances vary. **DR9, DR19, DT29, MU12, ST56, ST110, ST190**

Rumpelstiltskin (1985, C, 60m, NR)
A Faerie Tale Theatre presentation of the classic story of a dwarf who forces a young maiden to spin gold out of straw. Shelley Duvall and Herve Villechaize star. **FA12**

Rumor Mill, The see *Malice in Wonderland*

Run (1990, C, 91m, R)
On-the-run thriller of student who accidentally kills the son of a gangster. Patrick Dempsey stars, with Kelly Preston and Ken Pogue. **MY7**

Run of the Arrow (1957, C, 86m, NR)
A Confederate veteran decides to throw in with the Sioux Indians after the Civil War. Rod Steiger and Charles Bronson star. Samuel Fuller directed. **DT49, ST20, WE6, WE7**

Run Silent, Run Deep
(1958, B&W, 93m, NR)
Submarine action during World War II, starring Clark Gable and Burt Lancaster as clashing officers. Directed by Robert Wise. **AC1, DT140, ST77, ST129**

Runaway (1984, C, 99m, PG-13)
Futuristic cops-and-robbers story about a mad inventor unleashing deadly robots on an unsuspecting policeman. Tom Selleck and Gene Simmons star, with Cynthia Rhodes and Kirstie Alley. **MU12, SF6, SF17**

Runaway Barge, The (1975, C, 78m, NR)
A trio of hard-living guys try to eke out a living as riverboat men in modern society. Bo Hopkins, Tim Matheson, and Nick Nolte star. Originally made for TV. **ST164**

Runaway Train (1985, C, 111m, R)
Two escaped convicts (Jon Voight and Eric Roberts) are trapped aboard a speeding train whose engineer has died of a heart attack. Shot on location in the Alaskan wilderness. With Rebecca De Mornay. Directed by Andrei Konchalovsky. Voight and Roberts are directed to act like dum-dums. **AC24, XT19**

Runestone, The (1992, C, 105m, R)
Horror tale of ancient Norse stone uncovered in rural Pennsylvania, brought to New York,

where it unleashes a monster. Peter Riegert and Joan Severance star, with William Hickey, Tim Ryan, Chris Young, Alexander Gudonov, and Lawrence Tierney. Some clever moments (especially the references to Carl Dreyer) but feels awfully padded. **HO16**

Runner Stumbles, The (1979, C, 99m, PG)
A middle-aged priest is attracted to a young nun, who winds up murdered. Dick Van Dyke and Kathleen Quinlan star. **DR3, DT67**

Running Away (1989, C, 101m, PG-13)
Sophia Loren and Sydney Penny star as a mother and daughter fleeing Rome during the last days of World War II. **ST141**

Running Brave (1983, C, 105m, PG)
True story of Billy Mills, the Native American who ran for a Gold Medal in the 1964 Olympics. Robby Benson stars. **DR22**

Running Man, The (1987, C, 101m, R)
Arnold Schwarzenegger plays a cop of the future who's sentenced by the dictatorship to be a contestant on a deadly quiz show—a test of skill only the strongest survive. With Richard Dawson, Maria Conchita Alonso, Yaphet Kotto, Jim Brown, Jesse Ventura, and Mick Fleetwood. **MU12, SF11, ST195**

Running on Empty (1988, C, 116m, PG)
A teen-ager with ambitions to become a music student is torn by loyalty to his fugitive parents, former antiwar activists still pursued by the FBI. River Phoenix stars, with Christine Lahti, Judd Hirsch, and Martha Plimpton. Directed by Sidney Lumet. Gets points for tackling tough subject matter; loses points for clumsy execution of same. **DR7, DR8, DT78**

Running Out of Luck (1986, C, 88m, R)
Mick Jagger stars in this musical adventure, based on songs from his album, *She's the Boss*. Shot in South America, it's about a rock star abandoned and left for dead. With Dennis Hopper, Jerry Hall, and Rae Dawn Chong. Directed by Julien Temple. **MU9, ST110**

Running Scared (1986, C, 106m, R)
Chicago cops Billy Crystal and Gregory Hines are ready to retire to Florida—but they'd like to nab just one more scumbag in this action comedy. With Steven Bauer, Darlanne Fluegel, Joe Pantoliano, and Dan Hedaya. Directed by Peter Hyams. **AC9, CO3, CO9, CO13, XT11**

Running Wild (1927, B&W, 68m, NR)
Silent comedy starring W.C. Fields as his usual put-upon family man. **CL11, ST67**

Rush (1991, C, 120m, R)
True story set in 1970s of female and male narcotics officers, partners and lovers, who get hooked on drugs. Jennifer Jason Leigh and Jason Patric star, with Sam Elliott, Max Perlich, and Gregg Allman. Directed by Lili Fini Zanuck; Pete Dexter adapted Kim Wozencraft's book. Music by Eric Clapton. One of those films with absolutely no surprises, despite earnest performance from Leigh and strong presence of Allman. Patric is a cypher as an actor. **DR6, DR16, MU12, ST136**

Russia House, The (1990, C, 123m, R)
John Le Carré's espionage tale of a book publisher (Sean Connery) turned spy and his involvement with a lovely Soviet translator (Michelle Pfeiffer). With Roy Scheider, James Fox, John Mahoney, and Ken Russell. Adapted by Tom Stoppard; directed by Fred Schepisi. Location scenes films in Moscow, Leningrad, and Portugal. Widescreen will be lost on video. Enjoyable without ever being thrilling—maybe because the chill has gone out of the Cold War. **CU20, DT111, MY6, MY16, ST36, ST173, WR18**

Russians Are Coming! The Russians Are Coming!, The (1966, C, 120m, NR)
When a Russian submarine runs aground off the New England coast, the locals are thrown into total panic. Satirical comedy about the Cold War stars Alan Arkin, Brian Keith, Carl Reiner, and Jonathan Winters. Directed by Norman Jewison. Very mixed bag; Arkin and Winters are hilarious. **CO2, DT63**

Rust Never Sleeps (1979, C, 103m, NR)
Concert film featuring rocker Neil Young and his band, Crazy Horse. Songs include "Down by the River" and "My, My, Hey, Hey." **MU10**

Rustler's Rhapsody (1985, C, 88m, PG)
Tom Berenger stars as Rex O'Herlihan, the last of the singing cowboys in this spoof. With Andy Griffith, Marilu Henner, Fernando Rey, Sela Ward, and Patrick Wayne. **CO7, WE14**

Ruthless Four, The (1968, C, 96m, NR)
Western drama about four partners in a gold mine, starring Van Heflin, Gilbert Roland, Klaus Kinski, and George Hilton. **ST126**

Ruthless People (1986, C, 93m, R)
Desperate couple kidnaps a wealthy businessman's wife just as he's about to bump her off so that he can run off with his mistress, who is two-timing him. Frantic comedy starring Bette Midler and Danny DeVito, with Judge Reinhold, Helen Slater, Anita Morris, and Bill Pullman. Wearying after a while but has some genuinely hilarious moments; Pullman steals the show as the rock-headed boyfriend. **CO10, ST54, ST156**

Rutles, The see *All You Need Is Cash*

Ryan's Daughter (1970, C, 176m, R)
In Northern Ireland, a young woman trapped in a loveless marriage to a middle-aged schoolteacher embarks on a scandalous affair with a British soldier. Sarah Miles, Robert Mitchum, and Christopher Jones star, with Oscar winner John Mills and Trevor Howard. Directed by David Lean; photographed by Fred A. Young. Best thing about film—the stunning visuals—won't matter much on video. What's left feels overinflated, with Mitchum sadly miscast. **DR3, DT71, ST158, XT4**

S.O.B. (1981, C, 121m, R)
Broad lampoon of modern Hollywood, with frantic director (Richard Mulligan) trying to talk his actress wife (Julie Andrews) into doing a nude scene to rescue his latest bomb. With William Holden (in his last film), Robert Preston, Shelley Winters, Robert Vaughn, Loretta Swit, Larry Hagman, Robert Webber, Stuart Margolin, Robert Loggia, and in small roles, Rosanna Arquette and Jennifer Edwards. Blake Edwards (Jennifer's dad) wrote and directed, reportedly basing much of his script on experiences he has suffered over the years in Hollywood, especially on *Darling Lili*. Anyone the least familiar with the filmmaking scene knows that little in this film is exaggerated. **CO8, DT40, ST2, ST106, ST232, XT22, XT26, XT30, XT31,** *Highly Recommended*

S.O.S. Coastguard (1937, B&W, 195m, NR)
Serial adventure about a Coast Guard commander who must stop a mad scientist (Bela Lugosi) from delivering a disintegrating gas to enemies of America. **ST143**

Sabaka (1955, C, 81m, NR)
Boris Karloff stars in a spooky tale of a cult, set in India. With Reginald Denny and Victor Jory. **ST119**

Sabotage (1936, B&W, 76m, NR)
Early Alfred Hitchcock thriller has a woman suspecting that her husband is secretly a mad bomber terrorizing London. Sylvia Sidney and Oscar Homolka star. **DT57, MY6, MY15**

Saboteur (1942, B&W, 108m, NR)
Robert Cummings plays the typical Alfred Hitchcock hero: the man accused of a crime he didn't commit, in this case, sabotage in the munitions industry. With Priscilla Lane and Norman Lloyd. Classic finale atop the Statue of Liberty. Screenplay cowritten by Dorothy Parker. Good fun, although Cum-

mings is a notch below Hitchcock's usual leading man. **DT57, MY6, MY7, XT9, XT18**

Saboteur: Code Name Morituri see *Morituri*

Sabrina (1954, B&W, 113m, NR)
Audrey Hepburn is a chauffeur's daughter romanced by two brothers, played by Humphrey Bogart and William Holden. Sparkling comedy directed by Billy Wilder. **CL4, DT139, ST15, ST102, ST106,** *Recommended*

Sacco and Vanzetti (1971, C, 120m, PG)
The story of the infamous trial of two Italian anarchists in the 1920s, with the worldwide protests that arose over their conviction and execution. Gian Maria Volonte stars. **FF2**

Sacketts, The (1979, C, 200m, NR)
Western drama, adapted from two novels by Louis L'Amour, about a trio of brothers (Sam Elliott, Tom Selleck, and Jeff Osterhage) making their fortunes on the post–Civil War frontier. Originally made for TV. **WR16**

Sacrifice, The (1986, C, 145m, NR)
Soviet director Andrei Tarkovsky's final film, produced in Sweden, deals with nuclear annihilation and the choices it forces on an aging intellectual. Erland Josephson stars. **FF7**

Sad Sack, The (1957, B&W, 98m, NR)
Jerry Lewis stars in this service comedy as the comic strip character created by George Baker. With Phyllis Kirk, David Wayne, Peter Lorre, and Gene Evans. **CO21, ST139**

Sadie McKee (1934, B&W, 90m, NR)
Joan Crawford plays a working girl balancing three men in her life (Franchot Tone, Gene Raymond, and Edward Arnold). **CL5, ST39**

Sadie Thompson (1928, B&W, 97m, NR)
Silent version of W. Somerset Maugham's story, "Rain," with Gloria Swanson as the woman of ill repute, Lionel Barrymore as the upright minister. Written, directed, and co-starring Raoul Walsh. **CL12, DT131, WR23**

Safari 3000 (1982, C, 91m, PG)
Action in the wilds of Africa, as an ex-stuntman tries to win an international car race. David Carradine stars, with Stockard Channing and Christopher Lee. **AC10, ST135**

Safety Last see *Harold Lloyd*

Saga of Death Valley
(1939, B&W, 56m, NR)
Roy Rogers battles an outlaw with a hidden identity. With Gabby Hayes and Don "Red" Barry. **ST188**

Saga of the Vagabonds, The
(1959, C, 115m, NR)
Japanese adventure drama of a band of bandits distributing money to overtaxed peasants. Toshiro Mifune stars. **FF4, ST157**

Saginaw Trail (1953, B&W, 56m, NR)
Gene Autry and old pal Smiley Burnette are reunited for this tuneful Western. **ST5**

Sahara (1943, B&W, 97m, NR)
During World War II, an Allied battalion is stranded in the desert without supplies or hope of reinforcements. Humphrey Bogart and Dan Duryea star. **AC1, ST15**

Saigon: Year of the Cat
(1987, C, 106m, NR)
Drama of three men—an American diplomat, a CIA operative, and a British bank clerk—trying to get out of Saigon in the final days of the war. Frederic Forrest, E.G. Marshall, and Judi Dench star. Directed by Stephen Frears. Originally made for British TV. **AC4, DT48**

The Saint (series)
The Saint in New York
(1938, B&W, 71m, NR)
The Saint in London
(1939, B&W, 72m, NR)
The Saint Strikes Back
(1939, B&W, 67m, NR)
The Saint Takes Over
(1940, B&W, 69m, NR)
The Saint's Vacation
(1941, B&W, 60m, NR)
Series of detective films based on the debonair sleuth created by Leslie Charteris. Louis Hayward plays the lead in *New York*, Hugh Sinclair in *Vacation*; George Sanders stars in the other films. Note: *The Saint Strikes Back* is packaged with a second feature, *Criminal Court*; see separate entry. **HF21**

Saint Joan (1957, B&W, 110m, NR)
The life of the French martyr (Jean Seberg), adapted from the George Bernard Shaw play. With John Gielgud, Richard Widmark, and Anton Walbrook. Written by Graham Greene; directed by Otto Preminger. **DR4, DT100, ST86, WR11, WR29**

Sakharov (1984, C, 118m, NR)
Drama about the Soviet scientist and dissident who was imprisoned for many years for defying authorities. Jason Robards and Glenda Jackson star. Originally made for cable TV. **DR6, ST117, ST185**

Salaam Bombay! (1988, C, 113m, NR)
Drama of a ten-year-old orphan living by his wits on the streets of Bombay. Directed by Mira Nair. **FF7**

Salamander, The (1981, C, 101m, NR)
Political intrigue in Italy, as a band of neo-Fascists plot a coup. Franco Nero stars, with Anthony Quinn, Martin Balsam, Christopher Lee, and Claudia Cardinale. Based on Morris West's novel. **ST135, MY6**

Salem's Lot (1979, C, 112m, PG)
A sinister antiques dealer (James Mason) is the protector of a vampire who takes over a small New England village. It is up to a writer (David Soul) and a teen-ager (Lance Kerwin) to stop him. Based on the Stephen King novel; directed by Tobe Hooper. A shorter version of the movie made originally for TV, with violent scenes added. **CU10, HO5, ST153, WR15**

Salesman (1969, B&W, 88m, NR)
Influential documentary, shot in cinema verite style, about a group of bible salesmen. Directed by Albert and David Maysles. **CU16,** *Essential, Recommended*

Sally of the Sawdust
(1925, B&W, 91m, NR)
Silent comedy starring W.C. Fields as a con man with a soft heart for a young girl who is an outcast of polite society. Directed by D.W. Griffith. **DT52, ST67**

Salome (1953, C, 103m, NR)
Biblical drama with Rita Hayworth as the title dancer, Stewart Granger as John the Baptist. With Charles Laughton and Judith Anderson. **CL13, ST101, ST132**

Salome's Last Dance (1988, C, 90m, R)
Outrageous depiction of imagined night in the life of notorious playwright Oscar Wilde, as a theatrical troupe performs the title play in a brothel before its author. Glenda Jackson stars, with Nickolas Grace as Wilde. Directed by Ken Russell. **DR4, DT111, ST117**

Salt of the Earth (1953, B&W, 94m, NR)
Cult drama of New Mexico miners' strike, made when the director and major stars were blacklisted in Hollywood during the Red Scare. Will Geer stars. Herbert Biberman directed. **CU9**

Salut l'Artiste (1974, C, 102m, NR)
French comedy of a pair of mediocre actors (Marcello Mastroianni and Jean Rochefort) and their misadventures. **FF1, ST154**

Salute to Chuck Jones, A
(1985, C, 57m, NR)
The Oscar-winning creator of Wile E. Coyote, the Road Runner, and Pepe LePew is showcased in eight cartoons, including the classics *For Scent-imental Reasons, One Froggy Evening,* and *What's Opera, Doc?* **FA11,** *Highly Recommended*

Salute to Friz Freleng, A
(1985, C, 57m, NR)
The veteran animator, winner of six Academy Awards, is represented here by eight of his major Warner Brothers cartoons, including *Birds Anonymous, Speedy Gonzales,* and *Knighty Knight Bugs.* **FA11**

Salute to Mel Blanc, A (1985, C, 58m, NR)
Mel, the man of more than four hundred voices, is at his most vocal in the eight cartoons in this compilation, including Robin Hood Daffy, Bad Ol' Putty Tat, and The Rabbit of Seville. **FA11,** *Recommended*

Salvador (1985, C, 123m, R)
American journalist and his wacked-out buddy travel to El Salvador in search of a story and cheap thrills; they get both as they witness the horrors of civil war raging there. Powerful performance by James Woods, with James Belushi, Michael Murphy, John Savage, Cindy (Cynthia) Gibb, and John Doe. Written and directed by Oliver Stone. **CO13, DR7, DR27, DT120, MU12, ST233,** *Recommended*

Salvation (1986, C, 80m, R)
Offbeat, timely comedy about a lustful preacher (Stephen McHattie) whose financial empire is threatened by blackmailers. Directed by Beth B. **CO12**

Sam Kinison: Live! (1988, C, 60m, NR)
Stand-up comedy from the man whose bellowing, outrageous style created controversy. Recorded at the Roxy Theater in Los Angeles. **CO16**

Samantha (1991, C, 101m, PG)
Comedy of young woman who turns twenty-one, only to find out she's adopted, embarks on search for her real parents. Martha Plimpton stars, with Dermot Mulroney, Ione Skye, Hector Elizondo, and Mary Kay Place. **CO1, CO4**

Sammy and Rosie Get Laid
(1987, C, 100m, NR)
Drama set in contemporary London about a Pakistani whose son and daughter-in-law are caught up in political and sexual escapades. Shashi Kapoor, Frances Barber, Claire Bloom, and Ayub Khan Din star. Written by Hanif Kureishi; directed by Stephen Frears. **DR23, DT48, XT15**

Sam's Song see *The Swap*

Samson and Delilah (1949, C, 128m, NR)
Cecil B. DeMille's Biblical spectacular about the strongman and his downfall at the hands of a temptress. Victor Mature and Hedy Lamarr star, with George Sanders, Angela

Lansbury, and Henry Wilcoxon. Spectacular finale but pretty rough going until then. **CL13, DT34, ST131**

Samurai see *The Seven Samurai*

Samurai Saga (1959, C, 112m, NR)
Swordplay and a romantic triangle are the ingredients of this Japanese action drama, starring Toshiro Mifune and Yoko Tsukasa. Hiroshi Inagaki directed. **FF4, ST157**

Samurai Trilogy, The
Samurai I (1954, C, 92m, NR)
Samurai II (1954, C, 102m, NR)
Samurai III (1955, C, 102m, NR)
Epic adventure story of Musashi Miyamoto, a warrior who must come to grips with defeat before he can taste true victory. Toshiro Mifune stars. Hiroshi Inagaki directed. **FF4, ST157**

San Antonio (1945, C, 111m, NR)
Errol Flynn Western has him romancing dance hall girl Alexis Smith. **ST69, WE8**

San Fernando Valley
(1944, B&W, 54m, NR)
Roy Rogers plays a lawman trying to keep the peace in a bad man's town. With Dale Evans. **ST188**

San Francisco (1936, B&W, 115m, NR)
Clark Gable, Spencer Tracy, and Jeanette MacDonald star in this lavish portrait of early twentieth-century San Francisco. Highlight is re-creation of the infamous earthquake of 1906. **AC13, AC23, CL3, ST77, ST217**

Sand Pebbles, The (1966, C, 179m, NR)
Steve McQueen is an American sailor assigned to a U.S. gunboat anchored in the Yangtze River during the 1926 Chinese Revolution. With Candice Bergen, Richard Crenna, Mako, and Richard Attenborough. Directed by Robert Wise. Absorbing, with strong lead performance by McQueen. **AC6, DT140, ST146**, *Recommended*

Sandpiper, The (1965, C, 116m, NR)
A free-spirited artist (Elizabeth Taylor) and married minister (Richard Burton) have an affair. Theme song "The Shadow of Your Smile" won an Oscar. With Eva Marie Saint and Charles Bronson. Directed by Vincente Minnelli. **CL15, DR3, DT88, ST20, ST22, ST212**

Sands of Iwo Jima, The
(1949, B&W, 110m, NR)
John Wayne earned an Oscar nomination for his portrayal of a tough Marine sergeant whose men are responsible for the recapturing of a strategic island during World War II. **AC1, ST224**

Sanjuro (1962, B&W, 96m, NR)
Sequel to *Yojimbo* follows further adventures of scruffy samurai sword-for-hire (Toshiro Mifune). Akira Kurosawa directed. **DT69, ST157**

SanShiro Sugata (1943, B&W, 82m, NR)
Debut of Japanese director Akira Kurosawa, with the story of a youth trained in the art of judo matched against a jujitsu master. Reveals a master filmmaker in the making. Not to be missed by Kurosawa faithful. **DT69**, *Recommended*

Sansho the Bailiff (1954, B&W, 125m, NR)
Classic drama of Japanese family broken up by a feudal lord and how the son and daughter struggle for survival in a slave labor camp. Directed by Kenji Mizoguchi. **FF4**

Santa Claus—The Movie
(1985, C, 112m, PG)
This comedy about St. Nick has an evil toymaker out to steal away his business. David Huddleston plays the title role; John Lithgow and Dudley Moore costar. **FA13, ST160**

Santa Fe Trail (1940, B&W, 110m, NR)
Civil War Western dramatizing the pursuit of fanatic John Brown, played by Raymond Massey. Errol Flynn and Olivia de Havilland star, with Ronald Reagan as George Armstrong Custer and Charles Middleton as Abraham Lincoln. **HF6, HF18, ST49, ST69, WE6**

Santa Sangre (1989, C, 124m, NC-17)
Bizarre, violent tale from Mexican director Alejandro Jodorowsky about a man who serves as an "armed killer" for his armless mother. Also available in an 118-minute, R-rated version. **CU1, CU7, CU10**

Saps at Sea (1940, B&W, 57m, NR)
Laurel and Hardy comedy, with Ollie trying to relax on a boat trip, Stanley making his life miserable. **ST133**

Sarafina! (1992, C, 115m, PG-13)
Drama with music of black South African girl's struggles with apartheid. Leleti Khumalo stars, with Whoopi Goldberg and Miriam Makeba. Adapted from the stage play. **DR7, DR14, DR20, MU12, ST89**

Sarah, Plain and Tall (1991, C, 100m, NR)
Family drama, set in 1910, stars Glenn Close as single woman who travels from Maine to Kansas to answer ad placed by widowed farmer in need of a woman to care for his children. With Christopher Walken, Lexi Randall, Margaret Sophie Stein, and Jon Devries. Adapted from Patricia MacLachlan's

children's book. Originally made for TV. Nicely observed but don't look for any surprises or true grit. **DR8, ST33, ST222**

Saratoga (1937, B&W, 94m, NR) Clark Gable is a bookie, Jean Harlow the granddaughter of a horsebreeder in this period drama set at New York's famed track. With Lionel Barrymore, Frank Morgan, Walter Pidgeon, Una Merkel, and Hattie McDaniel. **ST77, ST98, XT22**

Satan Met a Lady (1936, B&W, 75m, NR) Early screen version of Dashiell Hammett's *The Maltese Falcon* has ram's horn as central object. Bette Davis stars, with Warren William, Arthur Treacher, and Alison Skipworth. **ST44, MY10, WR12**

Satanic Rites of Dracula see *Count Dracula and His Vampire Bride*

Saturday Night Fever (1977, C, 119m, R) A working class Brooklyn youth (John Travolta) becomes the dancing king at the local disco on Saturday nights. With Karen Lynn Gorney, Barry Miller, and Donna Pescow. Also available in a PG-rated version. The ultimate disco film with bestselling soundtrack of all time has lost some of its luster. **DR15, MU3, XT9,** *Essential*

Saturn 3 (1980, C, 88m, R) Two research scientists (Farrah Fawcett and Kirk Douglas) create a Garden of Eden on their outer-space outpost. Their ideal life is threatened when a strange man (Harvey Keitel) and his killer robot arrive. Directed by Stanley Donen. **DT38, SF3, SF6, ST57**

Satyricon (1969, C, 129m, R) Director Federico Fellini's lavish look at the decadence of ancient Rome, starring Martin Potter and Hiram Keller as a pair of pleasure-seeking young men. Also known as *Fellini Satyricon*. Available in a letterboxed edition. **CU19, DT43**

Savage Is Loose, The (1974, C, 114m, NR) Drama of man, wife, and son stranded on desert island for years, contemplating the unthinkable—to procreate. George C. Scott stars, with Trish Van Devere and John David Carson. Scott directed. **AC24, DR3, ST196**

Savage Sam (1963, C, 103m, NR) In this sequel to *Old Yeller*, two brothers are kidnapped by Indians and their father sets out to rescue them. Brian Keith and Tommy Kirk star. **FA1**

Savage Streets (1984, C, 93m, R) A nice high school girl turns vigilante to avenge the rape of her sister. Linda Blair stars. Standard exploitation fare. **AC8, AC19**

Savages (1972, C, 106m, NR) Allegory focusing on group of primitives who discover a Long Island mansion and begin to take on trappings of civilization. Lewis J. Stadlen, Anne Francine, Thayer David, Salmone Jens, Susan Blakely, and Sam Waterston star. Written and directed by James Ivory, produced by Ismail Merchant. **DT61**

Savannah Smiles (1982, C, 107m, PG) A little runaway hooks up with two criminals and through her love she reforms them. Mark Miller and Donovan Scott star. **FA7**

Save the Tiger (1973, C, 101m, R) Oscar-winning performance by Jack Lemmon highlights this drama of a dress manufacturer disillusioned with his life, longing for the sweet pleasures of his youth. With Jack Gilford. Written by Steve Shagan; directed by John Avildsen. Lemmon is fine but script spends a whole lotta time noodling on The Way We Live Now. **DR24, ST138, XT2**

Sawdust and Tinsel (1953, B&W, 92m, NR) A romantic triangle, set in a traveling circus, is the basis for director Ingmar Bergman's observations on life and love. Also known as *The Naked Night*. **DT7**

Say Amen, Somebody (1983, C, 100m, G) Moving documentary celebrating gospel music and its two guiding lights, Thomas Dorsey and Willie Mae Ford Smith. **CU16,** *Recommended*

Say Anything (1989, C, 100m, PG-13) Romantic comedy-drama of an energetic high school senior (John Cusack) who woos the class valedictorian (Ione Skye), despite the misgivings of her father (John Mahoney). With Lili Taylor, Amy Brooks, Jason Gould, Bebe Neuwirth, and Joan Cusack, John's real-life sister as his screen sibling. Written and directed by Cameron Crowe. Refreshingly honest look at subject of so many bad films. **CO1, CO4, XT8,** *Recommended*

Say Goodbye, Maggie Cole (1972, C, 73m, NR) Susan Hayward's last film has her playing a widowed doctor taking up practice in a Chicago slum. With Darren McGavin, Michael Constantine, Dane Clark, and Beverly Garland. Originally made for TV. **DR10, ST100**

Sayonara (1957, C, 147m, NR) Romance blossoms between an Air Force pilot and a Japanese entertainer in this version of James Michener's novel. Marlon Brando and Miiko Taka star, with Oscar winners Red Buttons and Miyoshi Umeki,

Ricardo Montalban, and James Garner. **ST18, ST82, XT4, XT5**

Scalpel (1976, C, 96m, R)
A plastic surgeon, desperate for a family inheritance, transforms a young woman into the image of his late daughter. Robert Lansing stars. **MY14**

Scalphunters, The (1968, C, 102m, NR)
Comic Western about a rascal (Burt Lancaster) and his educated slave (Ossie Davis). With Telly Savalas and Shelley Winters. Directed by Sydney Pollack. **DT98, ST129, ST232, WE14**

Scandal (1989, C, 105m, R)
True-life story of the John Profumo-Christine Keeler affair which rocked 1963 Britain and helped bring down that country's Conservative government. John Hurt, Joanne Whalley-Kilmer, Bridget Fonda, and Ian McKellen star. Also available in an unrated version; running time: 115 minutes. Less titillating, more intelligent than expected, given subject matter. **CU10, DR5, DR21, DR23, ST70,** *Recommended*

Scandalous (1983, C, 93m, PG)
Comic thriller starring Robert Hays as a nosy reporter up to his ears in spies and skullduggery. Pamela Stephenson and John Gielgud costar. **MY17, ST86**

Scanners (1981, C, 102m, R)
A small group of people have the ability to read minds; one uses his power for evil and kills innocent people by making their heads explode. A good scanner tracks the evil one to stop him. Cult horror film directed by David Cronenberg. Aside from special effects, pretty forgettable. **CU4, CU7, DT31, HO7**

Scanners II: The New Order
(1991, C, 104m, R)
Followup to cult horror classic sees unscrupulous politician (Yvan Ponton) turning scanners into drug addicts. With David Hewlet and Deborah Raffin. **HO7**

Scaramouche (1952, C, 118m, NR)
Swashbuckler classic, with Stewart Granger as the eighteenth-century swordsman memorably dueling with villainous Mel Ferrer. With Eleanor Parker and Janet Leigh. **AC13, FA4**

Scarecrow (1973, C, 115m, R)
Gene Hackman and Al Pacino play a pair of drifters in this episodic comedy-drama with Dorothy Tristan, Eileen Brennan, and Ann Wedgeworth. Directed by Jerry Schatzberg; cinematography by Vilmos Zsigmond. Uneven script, strong performances. **ST96, ST170, XT18**

Scared Stiff (1953, B&W, 108m, NR)
Remake of Bob Hope horror comedy, *The Ghost Breakers,* starring Dean Martin and Jerry Lewis. They're stuck on a Caribbean island with Lizabeth Scott and Carmen Miranda. **CL15, HO2, HO3, HO19, HO24, ST139, ST149**

Scared to Death (1947, C, 65m, NR)
All those who accuse a woman (Joyce Compton) of murder wind up dead. Bela Lugosi stars. **ST143**

Scarface (1932, B&W, 90m, NR)
Paul Muni stars as a gangster whose career is loosely based on Al Capone. With Boris Karloff, George Raft, and Ann Dvorak. Ben Hecht cowrote and Howard Hawks directed. One of the very best of the early gangster stories, artfully told. **AC22, DT53, ST119,** *Essential, Highly Recommended*

Scarface (1983, C, 170m, R)
Remake and updating of classic gangster drama, with Al Pacino a Cuban immigrant rising to the top of the Miami drug trade. With Michelle Pfeiffer, Steven Bauer, Mary Elizabeth Mastrantonio, F. Murray Abraham, and Robert Loggia. Exceptionally violent film directed by Brian De Palma. Cult reputation ill-deserved; a numbing mess. **AC22, CU7, CU18, DT36, ST170, ST173**

Scarlet and the Black, The
(1983, C, 155m, NR)
During World War II, a Vatican official (Gregory Peck) tries to protect POWs from a sadistic Nazi commandant (Christopher Plummer). With John Gielgud. Originally made for TV. **ST86, ST171**

Scarlet Car, The (1917, B&W, 50m, NR)
Silent melodrama of embezzlers who think they've murdered a bank teller, only to have him survive. Lon Chaney stars. **ST26**

Scarlet Claw, The (1944, B&W, 74m, NR)
Sherlock Holmes mystery set in Canada, involving the gruesome murder of a noblewoman. Basil Rathbone and Nigel Bruce star. **HF14**

Scarlet Clue, The (1945, B&W, 65m, NR)
Charlie Chan wartime mystery has him tangling with spies who possess vital radar plans. Sidney Toler stars, with Benson Fong and Mantan Moreland. **HF4**

Scarlet Empress, The
(1934, B&W, 110m, NR)
Marvelous collaboration of Marlene Dietrich and director Josef von Sternberg is lavish tale of Russia's Catherine the Great and her rise to power. With John Lodge, Louise Dresser,

Sam Jaffe, and C. Aubrey Smith. Dazzling costumes, sets, gorgeous cinematography. UNAVAILABLE ON VIDEO. **XT29**

Scarlet Letter, The (1973, C, 90m, NR)
German director Wim Wenders's version of the classic Hawthorne tale of sin and redemption. **DT136**

Scarlet Pimpernel, The
(1934, B&W, 95m, NR)
A British aristocrat becomes the savior of French royalty during the French Revolution. Leslie Howard and Merle Oberon star. **AC13, FA4**

Scarlet Street (1945, B&W, 103m, NR)
Meek, middle-aged man is seduced into a life of crime by a shady lady and her no-good boyfriend. Edward G. Robinson, Joan Bennett, and Dan Duryea star. Fritz Lang directed this classic thriller. **DT70, MY1, MY4, ST186,** *Recommended*

Scars of Dracula (1970, C, 94m, R)
A man and woman must fight the legendary Dracula (Christopher Lee) while searching for the man's missing brother. **HF7, HO5, HO26, ST135**

Scavenger Hunt (1979, C, 117m, PG)
Frenetic comedy of disparate group of fortune hunters tipped off to trove by dying man (Vincent Price). The cast includes Richard Benjamin, James Coco, Scatman Crothers, Ruth Gordon, Cloris Leachman, Cleavon Little, Roddy McDowall, Robert Morley, Richard Mulligan, and in a bit part, Arnold Schwarzenegger. **CO9, ST179, ST195**

Scene of the Crime (1986, C, 90m, NR)
An escaped convict kidnaps a young boy and forces the child's mother to help him hide from the police. Catherine Deneuve stars in this French-made thriller. **FF1, ST50**

Scenes From a Mall (1991, C, 87m, R)
Teaming of Woody Allen and Bette Midler in comedy of bickering husband and wife shopping at Los Angeles shopping arena on their sixteenth anniversary. Written by Paul Mazursky and Roger Simon; directed by Mazursky. **CO2, CO3, DT2, DT87, ST156, XT10**

Scenes From a Marriage
(1973, C, 168m, NR)
Director Ingmar Bergman's portrait of a marriage in crisis, starring Liv Ullmann and Erland Josephson. Originally made for Swedish TV and edited into a theatrical film by the director. **DT11, ST220, XT30**

Scenes From the Class Struggle in Beverly Hills (1989, C, 102m, R)
Comedy from cult director Paul Bartel con-

cerning the sexual appetites of the filthy rich and their servants in a Southern California community. Jacqueline Bisset, Ray Sharkey, Robert Beltran, and Mary Woronov star, with Ed Begley, Jr., Wallace Shawn, Paul Mazursky, and Bartel. **CO2, DT8, DT87**

Scent of a Woman (1992, C, 157m, R)
Leisurely paced drama of prep school student acting as Thanksgiving weekend companion to blind and embittered veteran, who whisks him off to a lavish holiday in New York. Subplot involves student's implication in campus practical joke that could get him expelled. Oscar winner Al Pacino and Chris O'Donnell star, with James Rebhorn and Gabrielle Anwar. Written by Bo Goldman, directed by Martin Brest. Engrossing, but ultimately doesn't justify its length, which in turn magnifies some credibility problems. **DR9, DR15, DR25, ST170, XT2, XT9**

Schizoid (1980, C, 91m, R)
A psychiatrist's female patients are being killed. The killer tells an advice columnist of the murders and threatens her. Klaus Kinski and Marianna Hill star. **HO9, ST126**

School Daze (1988, C, 114m, R)
One-of-a-kind film, set in an all-black college, combines comedy and drama with musical numbers to cover variety of subjects, mainly racial identity. Spike Lee wrote and directed and stars as a young fraternity pledge. With Larry Fishburne, Giancarlo Esposito, Tisha Campbell, Kyme, Joe Seneca, Art Evans, Ossie Davis, Branford Marsalis, Kadeem Hardison, Joie Lee, and Jasmine Guy. Uneven, but rewarding for its best segments. **CO2, CO18, DR14, DT72, XT8,** *Recommended*

School Ties (1992, C, 107m, PG-13)
Prep school drama set in 1955 of Jewish student trying to hide his identity. Brendan Fraser stars, with Matt Damon, Chris O'Donnell, and Amy Locane. Directed by Robert Mandel. **DR7, DR9, DR25**

Scorpio (1973, C, 114m, PG)
Espionage thriller starring Burt Lancaster and Alain Delon as an aging CIA operative and a hit man looking to go straight. With Gayle Hunnicutt, Paul Schofield, and J.D. Cannon. Some scenes shot in Washington, D.C. **MY6, ST129, XT12**

Scott of the Antarctic
(1948, C, 110m, NR)
An account of the fateful Robert Scott expedition to the South Pole. John Mills stars, with Derek Bond and Christopher Lee. **CL3, ST135**

Scoumoune (1972, C, 87m, NR)
Jean-Paul Belmondo stars in this French
crime drama as a local "fixer" who's in a fix
himself when police heat comes down. With
Claudia Cardinale. **ST11**

Scream and Scream Again
(1970, C, 95m, PG)
A mad scientist attempts to create a master
race of unemotional beings. Vincent Price,
Christopher Lee, and Peter Cushing star.
HO20, HO26, ST43, ST135, ST179

Scream of Fear (1961, B&W, 81m, NR)
A wheelchair-bound young woman (Susan
Strasberg) visits her father's Riviera villa, only
to be told he's away. When she catches
glimpses of his corpse, she begins to suspect
her stepmother (Ann Todd) of foul play. British thriller costars Christopher Lee. **MY3,
MY15, ST135**

Screamers (1980, C, 89m, R)
A group of convicts escapes to an island
that's inhabited by a mad scientist who has
created sub-human creatures. Barbara Bach
and Joseph Cotten star. **HO20**

Scrooge (1935, B&W, 61m, NR)
British-produced version of Dickens's *A
Christmas Carol* stars Seymour Hicks as title
character, with Maurice Evans, Donald Cal-
throp, and Philip Front. **FA13, WR5**

Scrooge (1970, C, 118m, G)
A musical adaptation of *A Christmas Carol*.
Albert Finney stars, with Alec Guinness,
Edith Evans, and Kenneth More. **FA13,
MU14, ST68, ST95, WR5**

Scrooged (1988, C, 101m, PG-13)
Contemporary version of Dickens's *A
Christmas Carol*, with Bill Murray a callous
TV executive brought to his senses by a series
of wacky angels. With Carol Kane, John For-
sythe, Karen Allen, John Glover, Bobcat
Goldthwait, David Johansen, Robert Mit-
chum, and Alfre Woodard. **CO2, CO13,
FA13, MU12, ST158, WR5**

Scruffy (1985, C, 72m, NR)
An orphaned puppy searches for a home and
is befriended by a stray. **FA10**

Sea Chase, The (1955, C, 117m, NR)
John Wayne plays a German captain whose
World War II ship contains strange cargo and
a passenger list that includes Lana Turner,
Tab Hunter, James Arness, and Claude Akins.
AC1, ST219, ST224

Sea Devils (1953, C, 91m, NR)
British spy yarn set in the Napoleonic era,
starring Yvonne De Carlo and a young Rock

Hudson. Directed by Raoul Walsh. **DT131,
ST112**

Sea Gypsies, The (1978, C, 101m, G)
A man, his daughters, a journalist, and a
runaway go on a sailing expedition and learn
survival techniques when they are shipwrecked. **FA4**

Sea Hawk, The (1940, B&W, 127m, NR)
A buccaneer is given approval by Queen Eliz-
abeth I to wreak havoc on the Spanish fleet
and their cities in the New World. Errol
Flynn and Flora Robson star. Directed by
Michael Curtiz. Home video version contains
restored footage of scenes intended to boost
British wartime morale. **AC13, CU10, ST69**

Sea of Grass, The (1947, B&W, 131m, NR)
Katharine Hepburn-Spencer Tracy drama of
New Mexico grasslands conflict. With Robert
Walker, Melvyn Douglas, and Phyllis Thaxter.
Directed by Elia Kazan. **CL15, DT65, ST58,
ST103, ST217**

Sea of Love (1989, C, 112m, R)
A broken-down cop falls for a woman who
may be the serial killer he's seeking. Al
Pacino and Ellen Barkin star, with John
Goodman. Written by Richard Price. Red
herring aspect of story grows tiresome.
MY4, MY5, ST7, ST170

Sea Shall Not Have Them, The
(1954, B&W, 91m, NR)
World War II drama of downed British
bomber and a rescue attempt. Michael Redgrave and Dirk Bogarde star. **AC1, AC24,
ST14**

Sea Wife (1957, C, 82m, NR)
Richard Burton and Joan Collins star in a
World War II drama of survivors of a torpedo
attack; he falls in love with her, not knowing
she's a nun. **AC24, ST22**

Sea Wolf, The (1941, B&W, 90m, NR)
Jack London adventure tale of vicious cap-
tain dominating his crew and stowaways.
Edward G. Robinson stars, with John Gar-
field, Ida Lupino, Alexander Knox, Gene
Lockhart, and Barry Fitzgerald. **AC13, CL1,
ST80, ST186**

Sea Wolves, The (1980, C, 120m, PG)
Two British intelligence officers recruit a
retired fighting unit for a top-secret mission
against the Nazis. Roger Moore, Gregory
Peck, and David Niven star. **AC1, ST171**

Séance on a Wet Afternoon
(1964, B&W, 115m, NR)
Suspense drama about a shady medium and
her husband bilking a couple. Kim Stanley,
Richard Attenborough, and Patrick Magee

star. Directed by Bryan Forbes. Stanley is terrific. **DR23, MY15**

Search see *Probe*

Search, The (1948, C, 105m, NR)
Drama set in postwar Berlin starring Montgomery Clift as a G.I. looking out for a young concentration camp survivor (Ivan Jandl, who won a special Oscar for his performance). Directed by Fred Zinnemann. **DT144, ST32**

Search for Bridey Murphy, The (1956, B&W, 84m, NR)
Drama based on bestseller about true story of woman revealing under hypnosis that she lived a prior life. Teresa Wright stars, with Louis Hayward, Nancy Gates, and Kenneth Tobey. **DR6**

Search for Signs of Intelligent Life in the Universe, The (1991, C, 106m, NR)
Lily Tomlin's one-woman stage show, in which she plays a wide variety of characters. **CO16, ST215**

Searchers, The (1956, C, 119m, NR)
John Wayne spends years tracking down the Indians who kidnapped his niece (Natalie Wood). With Jeffrey Hunter, Vera Miles, Ward Bond, and Lana Wood. John Ford directed this cult favorite, more appreciated in the years since its initial release. **CL14, CU13, DT44, ST224, WE5, WE7, WE15, XT8,** *Essential, Recommended*

Season of the Witch (1972, C, 89m, R)
A housewife develops an interest in witchcraft and joins a coven. Directed by George Romero. **DT108, HO11**

Sebastian (1968, C, 100m, NR)
Spy drama starring Dirk Bogarde as expert code cracker. With Susannah York, Lilli Palmer, and John Gielgud. **MY6, ST14, ST86**

Second Chance (1953, C, 81m, NR)
Melodrama of boxer and gambler's moll meeting on the lam in Mexico. Robert Mitchum and Linda Darnell star, with Jack Palance. **ST158**

Second Chorus (1940, B&W, 83m, NR)
Fred Astaire and Burgess Meredith compete for Paulette Goddard in this musical featuring Artie Shaw and His Orchestra. **ST4**

Second Coming of Suzanne (1974, C, 90m, NR)
Early role for Richard Dreyfuss in story of young actress (Sondra Locke) and her encounter with a persuasive film director. **ST60**

Second Sight (1989, C, 85m, PG)
Comedy of a wacky crime-fighting team: a

straight-arrow private eye (John Larroquette) and a zany psychic (Bronson Pinchot). **CO10, CO11**

Seconds (1966, B&W, 106m, NR)
Old man is given second chance to start his life over when he agrees to operation that provides him with young body and face. Rock Hudson stars in this original thriller, with Salome Jens, John Randolph, Will Geer, Jeff Corey, and Murray Hamilton. Screenplay by Lewis John Carlino, directed by John Frankenheimer. Outstanding cinematography by James Wong Howe. One of the greatest final shots in film history. UNAVAILABLE ON VIDEO. **XT29**

Secret Agent, The (1936, B&W, 86m, NR)
Madeleine Carroll and John Gielgud are spies posing as man and wife to track down an enemy agent in Switzerland. Adapted from the W. Somerset Maugham story, "Ashenden." Directed by Alfred Hitchcock. **DT57, MY6, MY15, ST86, WR23**

Secret Beyond the Door (1948, B&W, 98m, NR)
Joan Bennett stars in this thriller as a woman who suspects that her husband is a killer. With Michael Redgrave. Fritz Lang directed. **DT70, MY3**

Secret Ceremony (1968, C, 109m, R)
A woman who grieves over her dead daughter forms a strange relationship with a girl whose mother is dead. Elizabeth Taylor and Mia Farrow star in this offbeat drama, with Robert Mitchum. Directed by Joseph Losey. **MY14, ST65, ST158, ST212**

Secret Diary of Sigmund Freud, The (1984, C, 129m, PG)
Comedy about the early days of the world's first therapist, starring Bud Cort, Carol Kane, Klaus Kinski, and Carroll Baker. **CO6, ST126**

Secret Garden, The (1949, B&W, 92m, NR)
Frances Hodgson Burnett story of girl finding run-down garden and bringing it to life. Margaret O'Brien stars, with Herbert Marshall, Dean Stockwell, Gladys Cooper, and Elsa Lanchester. **FA3, ST208**

Secret Honor (1984, C, 90m, NR)
Philip Baker Hall stars in this one-man show as Richard Nixon in all his paranoid glory. Directed by Robert Altman; originally made for cable TV. Level of Nixon fascination will determine your reaction. **DT4**

Secret Life of an American Wife, The (1968, C, 92m, NR)
Comedy of a neglected wife who poses as a

prostitute. Anne Jackson, Walter Matthau, and Patrick O'Neal star. **ST155**

Secret Life of Walter Mitty, The
(1947, C, 105m, NR)
A timid man (Danny Kaye) escapes his dull job and nagging mother through elaborate fantasies. Boris Karloff costars in this adaptation of the James Thurber story. **ST119, ST120**

Secret Obsessions (1988, C, 82m, NR)
Drama set in 1955 North Africa of triangle: father, illegitimate son, the woman they both love. Julie Christie, Ben Gazzara, and Patrick Bruel star. **ST30**

Secret of My Success, The
(1987, C, 110m, PG-13)
An ambitious young man from Iowa climbs the corporate ladder in a New York firm run by his uncle, whose wife has romantic designs on her nephew. Michael J. Fox stars in this comedy, with Richard Jordan, Margaret Whitton, and Helen Slater. **CO2, CO20**

Secret of NIMH, The (1982, C, 82m, G)
Animated adventure about a widowed mouse who seeks help in keeping her home and comes across a secret society of rats. Featuring the voices of Elizabeth Hartman, Derek Jacobi, and Peter Strauss. **FA10**

Secret Policeman's Other Ball, The
(1982, C, 91m, R)
Concert film, derived from two London benefits for Amnesty International. Featured are members of the Monty Python troupe doing some of their best routines, plus musical performances by Eric Clapton, Pete Townshend, Jeff Beck, and other British rock stars. **CO15,** *Recommended*

Secret Policeman's Private Parts, The
(1984, C, 77m, R)
Concert footage from an Amnesty International benefit show starring members of Monty Python, plus Peter Cook and singers Phil Collins, Pete Townshend, and Donovan. **CO15**

Secret Service, The (1944, B&W, 64m, NR)
Charlie Chan looks into the murder of an inventor who was working on a device to sink German U-boats. Sidney Toler stars, with Benson Fong. **HF4**

Secret War of Harry Frigg, The
(1968, C, 110m, NR)
Paul Newman stars as an Army hustler in this World War II comedy about a plot to free five kidnapped U.S. generals. **CO21, ST162**

Secret Weapons (1985, C, 100m, NR)
Russia trains a team of lovely women as KGB agents. Linda Hamilton and Sally Kellerman star, with Viveca Lindfors, Christopher Atkins, and Geena Davis. Originally made for TV. **ST45**

Secrets of Life (1956, C, 75m, NR)
This Disney documentary, part of the True-Life Adventure series, looks at natural wonders and sea, plant, and insect life. **FA1**

Secrets of Women
(1952, B&W, 114m, PG-13)
Three wives at a summer house compare notes on their relationships with their husbands in this comedy-drama from director Ingmar Bergman. **DT11**

Seduced and Abandoned
(1964, B&W, 118m, NR)
Italian comedy about a quirk in the law which allows a man who has seduced and abandoned a young girl to avoid prosecution if he marries her. Saro Urzi and Stefania Sandrelli star. **FF2**

Seduction of Joe Tynan, The
(1979, C, 107m, PG)
United States senator tries his best to resist temptations of political corruption, is less successful at resisting an affair. Alan Alda stars, with Meryl Streep, Barbara Harris, Rip Torn, and Melvyn Douglas. Torn and Douglas steal the show from Alda. **DR21, ST58, ST210, ST216**

Seduction of Mimi, The (1974, C, 89m, R)
Italian comedy of a working-class man (Giancarlo Giannini) and his problems, especially with women. Lina Wertmuller directed. Remade in the U.S. as *Which Way Is Up?* **DT137, FF8**

See How She Runs (1978, C, 100m, NR)
Joanne Woodward won an Emmy for her performance as a housewife who decides to run in the Boston Marathon. With John Considine and Lissy Newman (Woodward's real-life daughter). Originally made for TV. **DR10, ST234, XT8**

See No Evil (1971, C, 89m, PG)
A blind woman is stalked by a mad killer, who has already murdered her entire family at a secluded farm. Mia Farrow stars. **MY3, ST65**

See No Evil, Hear No Evil
(1989, C, 103m, R)
Richard Pryor (as a blind man) and Gene Wilder (as a deaf man) team up in this comedy of mistaken identity: they're accused of a murder and must find the real culprit. **CO3, CO10, ST180**

See You in the Morning
(1989, C, 115m, PG-13)
Drama of a second marriage and how the husband's ties to his first wife and set of children complicate his life. Jeff Bridges stars, with Alice Krige and Farrah Fawcett. Written and directed by Alan J. Pakula. **DR8, DT94, ST19**

Seems Like Old Times (1980, C, 121m, PG)
Neil Simon comedy about a well-meaning lawyer (Goldie Hawn) whose first husband (Chevy Chase) keeps popping up in her life, much to the annoyance of Husband Two (Charles Grodin). **CO13, ST94, ST99, WR30**

Seize the Day (1986, C, 93m, NR)
Saul Bellow's novel about a loser (Robin Williams) desperately trying to stay out of debt and in his father's good graces. With Joseph Wiseman, Jerry Stiller, Glenne Headly, Tony Roberts, Jo Van Fleet, and William Hickey. Directed by Fielder Cook. Williams is first-rate in this sleeper. **DR19, ST228,** *Recommended*

Seizure (1974, C, 93m, R)
Horror tale of a novelist plagued by a trio of evildoers who put him and his family through hellish tortures—although they may exist only in his imagination. Jonathan Frid stars, with Martine Beswick, Troy Donahue, Herve Villechaize, and Mary Woronov. Written and directed by Oliver Stone. **DT120, HO14**

Semi-Tough (1977, C, 108m, R)
Comedy poking fun at professional sports and self-help groups, among other modern institutions, starring Burt Reynolds, Jill Clayburgh, and Kris Kristofferson. With Robert Preston, Bert Convy, Lotte Lenya, and Roger E. Mosley. Based on Dan Jenkins's novel; directed by Michael Ritchie. Some funny moments, especially with Convy's Werner Erhard spoof, but the romantic tension is awkwardly handled. **CO2, CO19, MU12, ST31, ST183**

Senator Was Indiscreet, The
(1947, B&W, 81m, NR)
The revelations in a lawmaker's diary are the cause for much scandal in this satiric comedy starring William Powell and Ella Raines. Playwright George S. Kaufman directed, his only stint behind the camera. **CL10, CU15, ST176**

Send Me No Flowers (1964, C, 100m, NR)
Rock Hudson-Doris Day comedy of a man who thinks he's dying, assigns his pal (Tony Randall) to find his wife a new husband. Directed by Norman Jewison. **DT63, ST47, ST112**

Senior Trip (1981, C, 100m, NR)
Comic adventures of Midwestern high school kids in the Big Apple, starring Scott Baio, Fay Grant, Vincent Spano, Robert Townshend, and Mickey Rooney as himself. Originally made for TV. **ST189, XT9**

Sense of Loss, A (1972, C, 135m, NR)
Documentary detailing the terrible toll that the Catholic-Protestant conflict in Northern Ireland takes on citizens. Directed by Marcel Ophuls. **CU16, DT92**

Senso (1954, C, 90m, NR)
An aristocratic woman takes a young, poor man for her lover, with tragic consequences. Classic story of infidelity and obsession, directed by Luchino Visconti. Also known as *The Wanton Contessa*. **DT127**

Sentinel, The (1977, C, 93m, R)
New York horror tale of model renting apartment in building that proves to be chock-full of demons. Cristina Raines stars, with Ava Gardner, Chris Sarandon, Burgess Meredith, Sylvia Miles, José Ferrer, Arthur Kennedy, John Carradine, Christopher Walken, and Jeff Goldblum. **ST79, ST90, ST222**

Separate but Equal (1991, C, 200m, NR)
Drama detailing landmark civil rights case before Supreme Court, Brown vs. Board of Education. Sidney Poitier (as Thurgood Marshall) and Burt Lancaster (as John W. Davis) play opposing attorneys, with Richard Kiley as Earl Warren. Written and directed by George Stevens, Jr. Originally made for TV. **DR5, ST129, ST174**

Separate Peace, A (1972, C, 104m, PG)
Screen version of John Knowles's popular novel about friendship between two prep school students during the 1940s. Parker Stevenson and William Roerick star. **DR9, DR19, DR25**

Separate Tables (1958, B&W, 99m, NR)
All-star drama set at English resort, with intertwining stories of guests. Burt Lancaster, Rita Hayworth, David Niven, Deborah Kerr, and Wendy Hiller are the featured players; Niven and Hiller won Oscars. Based on Terence Rattigan's plays. **DR20, ST101, ST125, ST129, XT2, XT5**

Separate Tables (1983, C, 108m, PG)
Made-for-cable-TV version of the Terence Rattigan dramas of life at a seaside resort. Alan Bates, Julie Christie, and Claire Bloom star. Directed by John Schlesinger. **DR20, DR23, DT113, ST9, ST30**

September (1987, C, 82m, PG)
Woody Allen directed this somber drama about a faded movie actress, her daughter, and their tangled lives. Elaine Stritch and Mia Farrow star, with Denholm Elliott, Dianne Wiest, Sam Waterston, and Jack Warden. **DR8, DT2, ST65, XT30**

September Affair (1950, B&W, 104m, NR)
Romance between married man (Joseph Cotten) and pianist (Joan Fontaine) is allowed to continue after they're both listed as dead in a plane crash. With Françoise Rosey, Jessica Tandy, and Robert Arthur. **ST73**

Sgt. Pepper's Lonely Hearts Club Band (1978, C, 111m, PG)
Peter Frampton and the Bee Gees create a fantasy world from the songs on the Beatles album of the same name. With Steve Martin. **MU8, MU16, ST150**

Sergeant Rutledge (1960, C, 118m, NR)
Western drama set around court-martial of black cavalry officer (Woody Strode) accused of rape and murder. With Jeffrey Hunter, Constance Towers, Billie Burke, and Juano Hernandez. Directed by John Ford. **DR17, DT44, WE4**

Sergeant Ryker (1968, C, 85m, NR)
Lee Marvin plays a soldier on trial for treason during the Korean War. With Bradford Dillman and Vera Miles. **AC3, DR17, ST151**

Sergeant York (1941, B&W, 134m, NR)
Gary Cooper won an Oscar for his portrayal of World War I hero Alvin York. With Walter Brennan and Joan Leslie. Howard Hawks directed. **AC2, CL2, DT53, ST37, XT2**

Serial (1980, C, 86m, R)
Comedy about an affluent California suburb which embraces each new trend as it comes along. Martin Mull and Tuesday Weld star, with Sally Kellerman, Tom Smothers, Bill Macy, and Christopher Lee. Based on Cyra McFadden's novel. Occasional chuckle, but doesn't capture deadpan tone of source material. Lee is very funny. **CO2, ST135**

Serpent and the Rainbow, The (1988, C, 98m, R)
An American scientist travels to Haiti to investigate voodoo drugs and rituals that turn humans into zombies. Bill Pullman, Cathy Tyson, and Paul Winfield star. Directed by Wes Craven. **HO6, ST230**

Serpent's Egg, The (1978, C, 120m, R)
Director Ingmar Bergman's grim drama of Jews in pre-World War II Germany and the humiliation they suffer in order to survive. David Carradine and Liv Ullmann star. **DT11, ST220, XT30**

Serpico (1973, C, 129m, R)
True story of undercover New York cop who blew the whistle on corruption in the department and was nearly murdered for his honesty. Al Pacino stars, with John Randolph, Jack Kehoe, Tony Roberts, M. Emmet Walsh, and F. Murray Abraham. Sidney Lumet directed. Starmaking performance by Pacino makes this one worth seeing. **DR6, DR16, DT78, ST170, XT9, XT26,** *Recommended*

Servant, The (1963, B&W, 115m, NR)
From writer Harold Pinter and director Joseph Losey, the contemporary tale of a manservant (Dirk Bogarde) turning the tables on his decadent master (James Fox). With Sarah Miles and Wendy Craig. Symbolic of larger malaise in Britain subsequently submerged by Swingin' '60s scene. **DR23, MY19, ST14, WR26,** *Essential, Recommended*

Sesame Street Presents Follow That Bird see *Follow That Bird*

Set-Up, The (1949, B&W, 72m, NR)
Gritty drama of a faded boxer (Robert Ryan) asked to take a fall for gamblers but defying them at the last minute. Robert Wise directed. Compact, brutal, first-rate. **DR22, DT140, MY1, ST193,** *Essential, Recommended*

Seven Beauties (1976, C, 115m, R)
Breakthrough film from Italian director Lina Wertmuller (it got her an Oscar nomination), the tragicomic story of a man who will do anything to survive in a prisoner-of-war camp during World War II. Giancarlo Giannini stars. **DT137,** *Essential*

Seven Brides For Seven Brothers (1954, C, 103m, G)
When Howard Keel weds Jane Powell, his six brothers decide to follow suit by kidnapping six townsgirls. Rousing musical Western based on Stephen Vincent Benet's *Sobbin' Women.* Directed by Stanley Donen; outstanding choreography by Michael Kidd. **DT38, MU1, MU3, MU6, XT20**

Seven Brothers Meet Dracula, The (1974, C, 72m, R)
Horror-karate saga takes place in nineteenth-century China, where Van Helsing is in pursuit of the legendary count. Peter Cushing stars in this British production. **AC26, HF7, HO5, HO26, ST43**

Seven Chances (1925, B&W, 69m, NR)
Sidesplitting Buster Keaton comedy has him portraying a young man who on his twenty-seventh birthday will inherit $7 million if he's married by 7 P.M. The trouble really starts when he places a classified ad explain-

ing his plight. UNAVAILABLE ON VIDEO.
XT29

Seven Days in May (1964, B&W, 118m, NR)
U.S. President is threatened when one of his
high-ranking generals plots a coup. Burt Lancaster and Kirk Douglas star, with Fredric
March, Ava Gardner, Edmond O'Brien, and
John Houseman. Written by Rod Serling;
directed by John Frankenheimer. First-rate
political thriller. Discontinued from manufacturer; copies may be hard to find. **DR21,
ST57, ST79, ST129, ST148,** *Recommended*

Seven Dials Mystery, The
(1981, C, 100m, NR)
Agatha Christie whodunit focuses on a group
spending the weekend at a country home,
where a practical joke turns tragic. Cheryl
Campbell, Harry Andrews, and John Gielgud
star. **MY12, MY15, ST86, WR3**

7 Faces of Dr. Lao, The
(1964, C, 100m, NR)
Traveling circus weaves magic and stories to
show inhabitants of a Western town truly
important things in life. Tony Randall stars.
Directed by George Pal. **FA8, SF13, XT27**

Seven Little Foys, The (1955, C, 95m, NR)
When Eddie Foy's wife dies, he is left alone
to take care of his seven children. He adds
them to his vaudeville act and they become
stars. Bob Hope stars, with a special appearance by James Cagney as George M. Cohan.
CL7, MU5, ST24, ST108

Seven Miles From Alcatraz
(1942, B&W, 62m, NR)
Two escaped cons run into a band of Nazi
spies and must make a fateful decision. James
Craig and Frank Jenks star. **DR18**

Seven Percent Solution, The
(1976, C, 113m, PG)
Sherlock Holmes tale, with the famous detective traveling to Vienna for treatment by a
certain Dr. Freud for a drug habit. Sounds
spoofy, but it's played straight, with a superb
cast including Nicol Williamson, Robert
Duvall (as Watson), Alan Arkin, Vanessa Redgrave, and Laurence Olivier. **HF14, ST63,
ST168, ST182,** *Recommended*

Seven Samurai, The
(1954, B&W, 208m, NR)
A diverse collection of swordsmen come to
the aid of villagers who are being ravaged by
bandits. Takashi Shimura and Toshiro Mifune
star. Akira Kurosawa directed. Oscar winner
for Best Foreign Language Film under the
title *Samurai*. Also available in a 155-minute
version. U.S. remake: *The Magnificent Seven*.
Arguably the greatest action film of all time.

AC13, DT69, FF8, ST157, XT7, *Essential,
Highly Recommended*

Seven Sinners (1940, B&W, 87m, NR)
Marlene Dietrich is a South Seas chanteuse,
John Wayne her smitten protector in this
melodrama. **ST55, ST224**

Seven Thieves (1960, B&W, 102m, NR)
Monte Carlo is the scene for this heist thril-
ler, starring Edward G. Robinson, Rod Steiger,
Joan Collins, Eli Wallach, and Alexander
Scourby. **MY18, ST186**

Seven Year Itch, The (1955, C, 105m, NR)
A married man, with his wife and kids out of
town for the summer, gets ideas about a
beautiful blonde who has rented the apartment above his. Marilyn Monroe and Tom
Ewell star. Directed by Billy Wilder. Widescreen will be lost on video. One of Monroe's
signature roles but not one of Wilder's better
films. **CL10, CU20, DT139, ST159**

1776 (1972, C, 141m, G)
John Adams, Benjamin Franklin, and the rest
of the first American Congress sing and
dance their way to independence. William
Daniels and Howard da Silva recreate their
Broadway roles. **FA9, MU2, MU16**

Seventh Cavalry (1956, C, 75m, NR)
Randolph Scott Western set in aftermath of
Battle of Little Big Horn, about a soldier
accused of cowardice who heads the burial
detail. With Barbara Hale, Jay C. Flippen, and
Jeanette Nolan. **ST197**

Seventh Cross, The
(1944, B&W, 110m, NR)
Spencer Tracy stars in this drama about seven
escapees from a concentration camp pursued
by Nazis. With Signe Hasso, Hume Cronyn,
and Jessica Tandy. Directed by Fred Zinnemann. **DT144, ST217**

Seventh Seal, The (1956, B&W, 96m, NR)
Classic allegory from director Ingmar Bergman of medieval knight (Max von Sydow)
and his search for truth and beauty. With
Bibi Andersson. Somber and slow but rewarding. **DT13,** *Essential, Recommended*

Seventh Veil, The (1945, B&W, 95m, NR)
A young woman (Ann Todd) is victimized by
a neurotic cousin (James Mason) until a hypnotist (Herbert Lom) helps her out. **ST153**

Seventh Victim, The
(1943, B&W, 71m, NR)
Spooky thriller about young woman in New
York falling in with a group of devil worship-
pers. Kim Hunter (in her debut) stars, with
Tom Conway and Jean Brooks. Produced by
Val Lewton; directed by Mark Robson. Eerie,

first-rate Lewton. **HO10, HO11, HO27,**
Recommended

7th Voyage of Sinbad, The
(1958, C, 87m, G)
Sinbad must accomplish several tasks to save
a princess who has been miniaturized by an
evil magician. Kerwin Mathews and Kathryn
Grant are the leads, but the real star is Ray
Harryhausen and his special effects. The kind
of film that makes you feel like a kid again.
AC18, FA8, SF13, *Highly Recommended*

Seven-Ups, The (1973, C, 103m, PG)
Roy Scheider heads a special police task force
against mobsters that is brutally efficient.
Follow-up to *The French Connection.* **AC9**

Severed Ties (1992, C, 96m, R)
Horror story of evil mom (Elke Sommer) who
forces her imprisoned son to continue her
late husband's experiments with regenera-
tion. With Oliver Reed, Billy Morrisette, and
Garrett Morris. **HO14, HO20, HO21**

Sex and the College Girl
(1964, C, 100m, NR)
Drama of campus playboy starring John Gabriel, with Julie Sommers, Charles Grodin (his
debut), Richard Arlen, and Luana Anders.
ST94

Sex and the Single Girl
(1964, C, 114m, NR)
Romantic comedy borrows title of Helen
Gurley Brown's how-to manual for story of
psychologist (Natalie Wood) pursued by skin
magazine editor (Tony Curtis). With Lauren
Bacall, Henry Fonda, and Mel Ferrer. **CO1,
CO2, ST71**

Sex, Drugs, Rock & Roll (1991, C, 96m, R)
Eric Bogosian's one-man play in which he
presents ten characters commenting directly
and indirectly on a variety of contemporary
ills. **DR7, DR20**

sex, lies, and videotape
(1989, C, 104m, R)
Four-character drama: a young couple whose
marriage is on the rocks, a visiting buddy of
the husband, and the wife's sister, who's having an affair with her brother-in-law. James
Spader, Andie MacDowell, Peter Gallagher,
and Laura San Giacomo star. Written and
directed by Steven Soderbergh. MacDowell
and San Giacomo carry the film over some
mopey moments. **DR1, DR10, ST203,**
Recommended

Sex With a Smile (1976, C, 100m, R)
Five episodes in this Italian comedy demon-
strate how funny good, clean sex can be.
Marty Feldman stars. **FF2**

Sextette (1978, C, 91m, R)
Mae West's last film, based on her play,
about a woman's eventful honeymoon—her
ex-husbands keep making appearances. With
Tony Curtis, Ringo Starr, Dom DeLuise, Timothy Dalton, George Hamilton, Alice Cooper,
Keith Moon, Walter Pidgeon, and George
Raft. A movie with "camp" written all over
it. **CU2, ST226**

Shack Out on 101
(1955, B&W, 80m, NR)
Mind-blowing melodrama set in a hash
house on California's coastal highway, about
espionage and thwarted romance. Lee Marvin
is the cook named Slob who's really a Russian spy, Terry Moore is the lusted-after waitress, Frank Lovejoy is the professor working
on a top-secret project. A camp classic. **CU2,
MY1, ST151,** *Recommended*

Shadow Box, The (1980, C, 100m, NR)
Dramatic story of a trio of terminally ill patients at a rural California hospice, adapted
by Michael Cristofer from his play. Paul Newman directed. Joanne Woodward, Christopher Plummer, and James Broderick star.
Originally made for TV. Stunning performances, excellent writing. **DR7, DR20,
ST162, ST234, XT30,** *Recommended*

Shadow of a Doubt
(1943, B&W, 108m, NR)
Hitchcock thriller set in a small town, where
a young girl (Teresa Wright) suspects her
kindly uncle (Joseph Cotten) of murder.
With Macdonald Carey, Patricia Collinge,
and Hume Cronyn. Screenplay cowritten
by Thornton Wilder. **DR26, DT57, MY14,
MY19,** *Essential, Recommended*

Shadow of the Thin Man
(1941, B&W, 97m, NR)
Fourth *Thin Man* mystery, with sleuthing
couple Nick and Nora Charles at the racetrack, betting on losers but picking the right
murder suspect. William Powell and Myrna
Loy star. **CL15, HF5, MY17, ST142, ST176,
WR12**

Shadows (1922, B&W, 85m, NR)
A woman, who believes her nasty first hus-
band is dead, remarries and starts a family.
Soon after, she starts receiving blackmail
threats from her first husband. Lon Chaney,
Sr., stars in this silent drama. **ST26**

Shadows (1960, B&W, 87m, NR)
Director John Cassavetes's groundbreaking
independent film about an interracial romance, starring Hugh Hurd, Lelia Goldoni,
and Rupert Crosse. **DR3, DR14**

Shadows and Fog (1992, B&W, 86m, PG-13)
Strange Woody Allen comedy-drama, set in European village, with Woody as Kafkaesque clerk involved with vigilantes roaming night-time streets in search of serial killer. With an eye-popping cast that includes Mia Farrow, John Malkovich, and Madonna as circus per-formers, Kathy Bates, Jodie Foster, and Lily Tomlin as prostitutes, John Cusack as a uni-versity student, plus Fred Gwynne, Julie Kavner, Kenneth Mars, Kate Nelligan, Donald Pleasence, and Wallace Shawn. Thanks in part to stilted writing, the casting comes off like a stunt; only Cusack seems to be playing a real person. Woody's resemblance here to Stan Laurel may be unintentional but it's dis-arming. **CU17, DT2, MU12, ST65, ST75, ST147, ST215, XT30**

Shadows of Forgotten Ancestors
(1964, B&W, 99m, NR)
Drama set in rural Russia of the early twen-tieth century, about the trials and tribula-tions of a peasant (Ivan Nikolaychuk). **FF7**

Shaft (1971, C, 100m, R)
Debut of black private eye John Shaft (Rich-ard Roundtree), as he looks into abduction of a gangster's daughter. With Moses Gunn, Charles Cioffi, Drew Bundini Brown, Law-rence Pressman, and Antonio Fargas. Written by Ernest Tidyman, directed by Gordon Parks. Music by Isaac Hayes. Once you get past the novelty of a black hero, it's the same old story. **AC8, MY10**

Shaft's Big Score! (1972, C, 104m, R)
Second film about black private eye has him investigating friend's murder, getting caught up in gang wars. Richard Roundtree stars with Moses Gunn and Drew Bundini Brown. Written by Ernest Tidyman; directed by Gor-don Parks, who also wrote the music. **AC8, MY10**

Shag (1989, C, 98m, PG)
Four girls travel to Myrtle Beach, South Caro-lina, in 1963 for a last fling before one gets married. Phoebe Cates, Bridget Fonda, Anna-beth Gish, and Page Hannah star in this comedy. **CO6, ST70**

Shaggy D.A., The (1976, C, 91m, G)
In this sequel to *The Shaggy Dog*, a lawyer (Dean Jones) who's just been elected District Attorney turns into a sheepdog when an ancient spell is read. Suzanne Pleshette and Tim Conway costar. **FA1**

Shaggy Dog, The (1959, B&W, 104m, G)
A young boy whose father hates dogs dis-covers his older brother turns into a sheep-dog when an ancient spell is read. Fred

MacMurray and Tommy Kirk star in this classic Disney comedy. **FA1**

Shaka Zulu (1985, C, 300m, NR)
The true story of Shaka, a tribal leader who united the Zulu nation against the British in Africa during the 1900s. Trevor Howard and Chistopher Lee star. Originally made for TV. **DR5, ST135**

Shake, Rattle and Rock
(1956, B&W, 72m, NR)
Early rock musical with familiar story of adults battling kids over the new music. Touch (Mike) Connors stars, with Lisa Gaye, Sterling Holloway, and Margaret Dumont, with musical appearances by Fats Domino and Joe Turner. **MU9**

Shakedown (1988, C, 90m, R)
A crusading lawyer (Peter Weller) and an un-dercover cop (Sam Elliott) team to clean up the New York Police Department of corrup-tion. With Patricia Charbonneau. Plenty of wild chases. **AC9**

Shakes the Clown (1991, C, 83m, R)
Strange comedy with cult following about an alcoholic clown (Bobcat Goldthwait, who also directed) framed on a murder charge. With Julie Brown, Adam Sandler, Paul Doo-ley, Florence Henderson, and Robin Williams in a bit part as a music teacher. **CO12, CU5, CU12, ST228, XT23**

Shakespeare Wallah
(1965, B&W, 115m, NR)
Drama revolving around English theatrical troupe touring India; one actress becomes involved with an Indian playboy who already has a mistress-actress. Shashi Kapoor and Felicity Kendal star, with Geoffrey Ken-dal and Madhur Jaffrey. Produced by Ismail Merchant, directed by James Ivory, written by Ruth Prawer Jhabvala. **DR12, DR23, DR27, DT61**

Shalako (1968, C, 113m, NR)
Western drama about a hunting party of Europeans in New Mexico being attacked by Apaches. Sean Connery and Brigitte Bardot star. **ST6, ST36**

Shall We Dance (1937, B&W, 116m, NR)
A Russian ballet dancer (Fred Astaire) and an American musical performer (Ginger Rogers) marry as a publicity stunt and end up falling in love. **CL15, ST4, ST187,** *Recommended*

Shame (1961, B&W, 80m, NR)
Low-budget melodrama from director Roger Corman about a bigot (William Shatner) traveling the South, stirring up racial hatred. Also known as *The Intruder* or *I Hate Your Guts*. **DR7, DT30**

Shame (1968, B&W, 103m, R)
Superb Ingmar Bergman drama of two musicians living on island isolated from a civil war, which spreads to their retreat. Liv Ullmann and Max von Sydow star, with Gunnar Bjornstrand. Shot by Sven Nykvist. One of Bergman's best, with Ullmann radiant. **DT11, ST220, XT30,** *Highly Recommended*

Shame (1988, C, 95m, R)
Australian drama set in a small town which holds a terrible secret: a gang of young men have been attacking women without fear of interference from the community or its law officers. A female barrister, stranded in the town, tries to persuade one of the victims to press charges. **DR26, FF5**

Shampoo (1975, C, 112m, R)
A Beverly Hills hairdresser tries to satisfy his customers in the shop and after hours. Warren Beatty stars, with Julie Christie, Goldie Hawn, Jack Warden, Tony Bill, Carrie Fisher, and Oscar winner Lee Grant in this satiric comedy, set around the 1968 presidential election. Written by Beatty and Robert Towne; directed by Hal Ashby. **C01, C02, ST10, ST30, ST99, XT5, XT10,** *Essential, Recommended*

Shamus (1973, C, 106m, R)
Burt Reynolds plays a private eye with some offbeat detection methods in this mystery. Dyan Cannon costars. **MY10, ST183**

Shane (1953, C, 118m, NR)
Alan Ladd plays the lone gunman squared off against evil Jack Palance in this classic Western. With Van Heflin, Jean Arthur (in her last film), Brandon de Wilde, and Elisha Cook, Jr. Directed by George Stevens. Self-consciously mythic but still enjoyable. **DT119, ST3, ST128, WE2, XT22,** *Essential, Recommended*

Shanghai Cobra, The
(1945, B&W, 64m, NR)
Charlie Chan investigates series of murders by cobra venom. Sidney Toler stars, with Benson Fong and Mantan Moreland. Directed by Phil Karlson. **HF4**

Shanghai Express (1932, B&W, 80m, NR)
Delirious collaboration between star Marlene Dietrich and her mentor, director Josef von Sternberg. She's Shanghai Lily, woman of mystery, traveling on title train through war-torn China. With Anna May Wong, Warner Oland, Clive Brook, and Eugene Pallette. Exquisite Oscar-winning cinematography by Lee Garmes. **DT128, ST55, XT18,** *Recommended*

Shanghai Gesture, The
(1941, B&W, 106m, NR)
Josef von Sternberg directed this murky tale of a man who discovers his daughter working in an Oriental den of iniquity. Walter Huston, Gene Tierney, and Victor Mature star. **DT128, ST214**

Shanghai Surprise
(1986, C, 97m, PG-13)
Pop star Madonna plays a missionary in 1930s China. Sean Penn plays a soldier of fortune who helps her out of a tight spot. **AC21, MU12**

Sharad of Atlantis see *Undersea Kingdom*

Shark! (1969, C, 92m, PG)
Burt Reynolds stars in this underwater adventure of treasure divers encountering toothy creatures of the deep. Directed by Samuel Fuller. **AC12, DT49, ST183**

Sharky's Machine (1981, C, 119m, R)
An Atlanta cop's vendetta against a mobster gets personal when he becomes romantically involved with one of the crime boss's working girls. Burt Reynolds and Rachel Ward star, with Vittorio Gassman, Brian Keith, Bernie Casey, and Charles Durning. Good cast wasted on usual genre hijinks. **AC9, ST183**

Shattered (1972, C, 100m, NR)
British drama of middle-aged couple whose marriage is falling apart, starring Shelley Winters and Peter Finch. Also known as *Something To Hide*. **DR23, ST232**

Shattered (1991, C, 98m, R)
After suffering disfiguring injuries in a car accident, a man tries to rebuild his life—but flashbacks to a strange past keep haunting him. A private eye tries to help him sort it all out. Tom Berenger stars, with Bob Hoskins, Greta Scacchi, Joanne Whalley-Kilmer, Corbin Bernsen, and Theodore Bikel. Shot in and around San Francisco. **MY2, MY4, MY10, ST111, XT13**

She (1985, C, 90m, NR)
A warrior woman must stop an expedition that is searching for the Flame of Eternal Life. Based on a novel by H. Rider Haggard. Sandahl Bergman stars. **AC18**

She Couldn't Say No
(1954, B&W, 89m, NR)
Jean Simmons plays a rich young woman who decides to share her wealth with the citizens of a small town in Arkansas. With Robert Mitchum, Arthur Hunnicutt, Edgar Buchanan, and Wallace Ford. **DR26, ST158**

She Done Him Wrong
(1933, B&W, 66m, NR)
Mae West is Diamond Lil; she invites Cary
Grant to come up sometime and see her.
ST92, ST226

She Gods of Shark Reef
(1958, B&W, 63m, NR)
Low-budget adventure from director Roger
Corman about two men shipwrecked on an
island full of beautiful women. Bill Cord and
Don Durant star, with Lisa Montell and
Carol Lindsay. **DT30**

She Wore a Yellow Ribbon
(1949, C, 103m, NR)
John Wayne is a retiring cavalry officer with
one more Indian battle to fight. With Joanne
Dru, John Agar, Ben Johnson, and Ward
Bond. Directed by John Ford. Second and
best film in Ford's celebrated cavalry trilogy.
AC5, DT44, ST224, WE4, *Essential,*
Recommended

She-Devil (1989, C, 99m, PG-13)
Zany, contemporary comedy of a dumpy
housewife (Roseanne Barr) seeking vengenace
on her faithless husband (Ed Begley, Jr.) and
his lover (Meryl Streep), a lovely author.
With Linda Hunt and Sylvia Miles. Based on
Fay Weldon's novel; directed by Susan Seidelman. **CO2, DR10, ST210**

Sheena (1984, C, 117m, PG)
A white orphan raised by an African tribe has
the ability to communicate with animals.
Tanya Roberts stars in this adventure tale.
AC17

Sheik, The (1921, B&W, 80m, NR)
Starmaking vehicle for Rudolph Valentino in
this silent melodrama costarring Agnes Ayres.
Pretty creaky, though it's not hard to see
Rudy's appeal. **CL4, CL12,** *Essential*

Sheltering Sky, The (1990, C, 137m, R)
Adaptation of Paul Bowles's celebrated novel
of alienation in North Africa, as American
couple wanders from desert town to town.
Debra Winger and John Malkovich star, with
Campbell Scott and Bowles as a storyteller.
Directed by Bernardo Bertolucci. Valiant
attempt to film what may well be unfilm-
able. Vittorio Storaro's camera work is peerless. **DR19, DR27, DT13, ST147, ST231**

Shenandoah (1965, C, 105m, NR)
A Virginia farmer tries to stay neutral during
the Civil War, but his family soon drags him
into the fray. James Stewart stars, with Doug
McClure, Glenn Corbett, Patrick Wayne,
Rosemary Forsyth, and Katharine Ross. **AC5,
ST207, WE6**

Sheriff of Fractured Jaw, The
(1959, C, 103m, NR)
Western spoof has Britisher (Kenneth More)
out to tame a lawless town. With Jayne
Mansfield, Henry Hull, Bruce Cabot, and
Robert Morley. Directed by Raoul Walsh.
DT131, WE14

Sheriff of Tombstone
(1941, B&W, 60m, NR)
Roy Rogers sits in on a high-stakes poker
game. **ST188**

**Sherlock Holmes and the Incident at
Victoria Falls** (1991, C, 120m, NR)
Holmes (Christopher Lee) and Watson
(Patrick Macnee) promise to help King
George safeguard the Star of Africa diamond.
With Joss Ackland. Originally the first in a
series of Holmes adventures made for British
TV. **HF14, ST135**

**Sherlock Holmes and the Secret
Weapon** (1942, B&W, 68m, NR)
Basil Rathbone and Nigel Bruce star in this
contemporary Holmes case set during World
War II, involving the disappearance of an
inventor and his important discovery. With
Lionel Atwill as Professor Moriarty. **HF14**

**Sherlock Holmes and the Spider
Woman** see *Spider Woman*

**Sherlock Holmes and the Voice of Ter-
ror** (1942, B&W, 65m, NR)
More Holmes detection updated, with the
detective battling Nazis who make their terrorist demands over the airwaves. Basil Rathbone and Nigel Bruce star. **HF14**

Sherlock Holmes Faces Death
(1943, B&W, 68m, NR)
Basil Rathbone and Nigel Bruce are back for
more deducing, this time to solve what
appears to be a ritual murder. **HF14**

Sherlock Holmes in Washington
(1943, B&W, 71m, NR)
Further adventures of the great detective in
the World War II era, this time chasing spies
in the nation's capital. Basil Rathbone and
Nigel Bruce star. **HF14, XT12**

Sherman's March (1986, C, 155m, NR)
Unique film, a documentary record of a film-
maker (Ross McElwee) doing research on
Civil War general, winding up recording his
impressions of women in the contemporary
South. Quite rewarding and very funny.
CU16, XT18, XT31, *Recommended*

She's Gotta Have It
(1986, C/B&W, 84m, R)
Sexy comedy from director Spike Lee (who
also stars as hip messenger boy Mars Black-

mon) about a free-spirited woman (Tracy Camilla Johns) with three lovers and no qualms about keeping all of them. **CO1, CO2, CU6, DR14, DT72,** *Recommended*

She's Having a Baby
(1988, C, 106m, PG-13)
Comedy-drama from writer-director John Hughes, about the second thoughts of a young husband and father-to-be. Kevin Bacon and Elizabeth McGovern star. **CO1, DT59**

She's in the Army Now
(1981, C, 100m, NR)
Comedy of female recruits in today's Army, starring Kathleen Quinlan, Jamie Lee Curtis, and Melanie Griffith. **CO21, ST42, ST93**

She's Out of Control (1989, C, 97m, PG)
An overprotective father (Tony Danza) is driven to distraction when his teen-age daughter (Ami Dolenz) begins showing a healthy interest in boys. **CO5**

Shinbone Alley (1971, C, 85m, G)
Animated adventures of an independent alley cat and a poet cockroach who strike up an unusual friendship. Featuring the voices of Eddie Bracken, Carol Channing, and John Carradine. **FA10**

Shine On, Harvest Moon
(1938, B&W, 60m, NR)
Roy Rogers preserves the peace in the Old West against a gang of desperadoes. **ST188**

Shining, The (1980, C, 142m, R)
Writer agrees to stay at a deserted hotel for the winter with his wife and son, but the solitude (and other forces) prove too much for him. Jack Nicholson stars in this version of Stephen King's novel, directed by Stanley Kubrick. With Shelley Duvall, Scatman Crothers, and Danny Lloyd. Mechanical, with only a few good jolts, and ultimately much too long. **DT68, HO2, HO3, ST163, WR15**

Shining Hour, The (1938, B&W, 80m, NR)
Joan Crawford soap opera of family entanglements, with Margaret Sullavan, Robert Young, and Melvyn Douglas. Directed by Frank Borzage. **ST39, ST58**

Shining Season, A (1979, C, 100m, NR)
True story of college track athlete leading a ragtag girls' team to a championship. Timothy Bottoms stars, with Allyn Ann McLerie and Rip Torn. Originally made for TV. **DR6, DR22, ST216**

Shining Through (1992, C, 132m, R)
World War II espionage drama about an American secretary fluent in German, re-cruited for dangerous mission. Melanie Griffith and Michael Douglas star, with Liam Neeson, Joely Richardson, and John Gielgud. Based on Susan Isaacs's novel. **MY3, MY5, MY6, ST59, ST86, ST93**

Ship Ahoy (1942, B&W, 95m, NR)
MGM musical comedy stars Red Skelton as boob who mistakes U.S. agent for enemy spy. Eleanor Powell costars, with Virginia O'Brien, Bert Lahr, and the Tommy Dorsey Orchestra, featuring Frank Sinatra, Jo Stafford, and Buddy Rich. **MU1, ST199**

Ship of Fools (1965, B&W, 149m, NR)
Drama set aboard an ocean liner in the dark days just before World War II, with international assortment of characters. Based on Katherine Anne Porter's bestseller. Lee Marvin, Vivien Leigh, Oskar Werner, Simone Signoret, George Segal, Elizabeth Ashley, and Michael Dunne star. Directed by Stanley Kramer. Great cast but heavy hand of director spoils fun. **DR5, DR19, DT67, ST137, ST151**

Shipwrecked (1991, C, 93m, PG)
Disney adventure set in the nineteenth century of a fourteen-year-old Norwegian boy encountering pirates. **FA1, FA15**

Shirley Valentine (1989, C, 108m, R)
Pauline Collins re-creates her comic stage role as a bored working-class British housewife who runs off to Greece for a change of scenery. With Tom Conti. **CO1, CO17, DR10, DR20**

Shoah (1986, C, 570m, NR)
Monumental documentary about the effects of the Holocaust on its survivors and the townspeople who lived near the death camps. Relies almost exclusively on interview material, with almost no footage of the atrocities themselves. Directed by Claude Lanzmann. **CU16,** *Recommended*

Shock, The (1923, B&W, 96m, NR)
A mobster sends a hired gun to a small town to kill a rival banker. The gunman falls in love with a sweet young girl and decides to reform. Lon Chaney, Sr., stars in this silent drama. **ST26**

Shock (1946, B&W, 70m, NR)
Vincent Price and his gang plan to kill a girl who witnessed one of their crimes. **ST179**

Shock Corridor (1963, C/B&W, 101m, NR)
Enterprising reporter gets himself committed to insane asylum to expose conditions there and can't get out. Entertaining melodrama from writer-director Samuel Fuller stars Peter Breck, with Constance Towers, Gene Evans,

James Best, and Hari Rhodes. One dream sequence in color. Available in letterboxed edition. Watch out for those nymphos! **CU19, DT49,** *Recommended*

Shock to the System, A (1990, C, 89m, R)
Michael Caine stars in this black comedy as a man who's passed up for a promotion, triggering a vendetta against all his enemies. With Elizabeth McGovern, Peter Riegert, Swoosie Kurtz, and Will Patton. **CO2, CO12, ST25**

Shock Waves (1977, C, 86m, PG)
A Nazi scientist creates androids to man the Fuehrer's submarines. Peter Cushing stars. Also known as *Death Corps.* **ST43**

Shocker (1989, C, 110m, R)
An executed killer (Mitch Pileggi) is revived through TV waves to continue his nastiness in this horror film. **HO9**

Shoes of the Fisherman, The
(1968, C, 157m, G)
A drama about the election of the first Russian Pope and its effect on world peace. Anthony Quinn and Laurence Olivier star, with Vittorio De Sica, Oskar Werner, David Janssen, John Gielgud, and Leo McKern. **DR21, DT35, ST86, ST168**

Shoeshine (1946, B&W, 93m, NR)
Postwar Italian drama from director Vittorio De Sica about two youngsters living by their wits on the streets. Rinaldo Smerdoni and Franco Interlinghi star. Landmark film in Italy's neorealism movement is also heartbreakingly good. **DT37,** *Essential, Highly Recommended*

Shogun (1980, C, 550m, NR)
TV miniseries based on James Clavell novel of shipwrecked Englishman who became Japan's first foreign-born shogun. Richard Chamberlain stars, with Toshiro Mifune and Yoko Shimada. Also available in severely truncated two-hour version. **DR5, DR19, DR27, ST157**

Shogun Assassin (1981, C, 90m, R)
A swordsman travels the Japanese countryside, wheeling his son in a baby carriage, taking on all comers in this extremely violent action saga. Video version of this cult favorite is dubbed in English. **CU7, FF4**

Shoot Loud, Louder . . . I Don't Understand (1966, C, 100m, NR)
Crazy-quilt comedy from Italy about an antiques dealer (Marcello Mastroianni) and his loony adventures with a lovely woman (Raquel Welch) and some bumbling gunmen. **FF2, ST154**

Shoot the Living, Pray for the Dead
(1973, C, 90m, NR)
Klaus Kinski stars in a Western drama about a killer who promises his guide a share in stolen gold. **ST126**

Shoot the Moon (1982, C, 123m, R)
A husband's infidelity leads to the painful breakup of his marriage, with a devastating effect on his three daughters. Albert Finney and Diane Keaton star, with Peter Weller and Karen Allen. Written by Bo Goldman; Alan Parker directed. Painfully uninvolving. **DR8, ST68, ST121**

Shoot the Piano Player
(1962, B&W, 85m, NR)
A Parisian musician is torn between his musical ambitions and his relationships with gangsters. Moving drama from director François Truffaut, starring Charles Aznavour. Available in letterboxed format. One of the most notable early films of the French New Wave. **CU19, DT125, XT16,** *Essential, Recommended*

Shoot the Sun Down (1981, C, 93m, PG)
Western drama of disparate group of people—lone gunfighter, scalphunter, and indentured servant—on a quest for gold. Margot Kidder, Geoffrey Lewis, A Martinez, and Christopher Walken star. **ST222**

Shoot To Kill (1988, C, 110m, R)
An FBI agent (Sidney Poitier) and mountain guide (Tom Berenger) team to track a fugitive killer who has kidnapped the guide's girlfriend (Kirstie Alley). **AC12, ST174**

Shooting, The (1967, C, 82m, NR)
Cult Western starring Jack Nicholson and Warren Oates in a convoluted tale of revenge. With Millie Perkins and Will Hutchins. Directed by Monte Hellman, who made this and *Ride in the Whirlwind* at the same time. **ST163, ST166, WE15**

Shooting Elizabeth (1992, C, 96m, PG-13)
Jeff Goldblum plays a harried husband who decides to do away with his wife (Mimi Rogers)—except that she disappears first and he's charged with her murder. **ST90**

Shooting Party, The (1984, C, 108m, NR)
Weekend in the British countryside in 1913, with various personalities, class conflicts, and romantic entanglements. James Mason, Dorothy Tutin, Edward Fox, and John Gielgud star. **DR23, ST86, ST153**

Shootist, The (1976, C, 99m, PG)
In his last film, John Wayne plays a once-famous gunfighter who finds that he has cancer. With Lauren Bacall, James Stewart,

Ron Howard, Richard Boone, and Hugh O'Brian. Directed by Don Siegel. Film isn't really much, but it's a fine adios for the Duke. **DT58, DT116, ST207, ST224, WE2, WE11, XT22**

Shop Around the Corner, The
(1940, B&W, 97m, NR)
Classic romantic comedy of two shopworkers (James Stewart and Margaret Sullavan) who become unwitting lovers through correspondence. Directed by Ernst Lubitsch; written by Samson Raphaelson. **CL4, DT76, ST207, Essential**

Shop on Main Street, The
(1965, B&W, 128m, NR)
Oscar-winning drama from Czechoslovakia about the relationship between an elderly Jewish woman and the man who takes over her business during World War II. Directed by Jan Kadar. **FF7, XT7**

Short Circuit (1986, C, 98m, PG)
A robot escapes from its military keepers and is taken in by a lovely young animal lover. Gentle comedy with special effects humor, starring Ally Sheedy, Steve Guttenberg, and Austin Pendleton. **CO11, FA6**

Short Circuit 2 (1988, C, 110m, PG)
More adventures of Johnny Five, the playful robot. Fisher Stevens, Michael McKean, and Cynthia Gibb are the human costars. **CO11, FA6**

Short Eyes (1977, C, 104m, R)
Prison drama of a child molester's fate at the hands of fellow cons. Bruce Davison, Jose Perez, and Miguel Pinero star. Based on Pinero's play. Directed by Robert M. Young. Not for faint of heart; rewarding, realistic slice of dark side of life. **DR18, Recommended**

Short Films of D.W. Griffith: Volume 1, The (1911–12, B&W, 59m, NR)
Three early short films directed by D.W. Griffith. *The Battle* is a Civil War tale about a boy who shows signs of cowardice, then becomes a hero; Charles West and Blanche Sweet star. *The Female of the Species (A Psychological Tragedy)* is a tale of three women who become friends after facing a series of hardships. Mary Pickford stars. *The New York Hat* is about small town hypocrisy and the damage of gossip; Mary Pickford stars. **DT52**

Short Films of D.W. Griffith: Volume 2, The (1909–13, B&W, 112m, NR)
Five early films from the American cinema's first great director: *A Corner in Wheat, The Revenue Man and His Girl, The Musketeers of Pig Alley, A Girl and Her Trust,* and *The Battle*

of Elderbush Gulch. Among the stars: Lillian Gish, Bobby Harron, Mae Marsh, Lionel Barrymore, Dorothy Gish, Henry B. Walthall, and Harry Carey, Sr. **DT52, ST87, XT8**

Short Fuse (1987, C, 91m, R)
A Washington, D.C., journalist (Art Garfunkel) investigates a murder in the funky "go-go" clubs of the nation's capital. Plenty of music from Chuck Brown and the Soul Searchers, Trouble Funk, and other groups. Released theatrically as *Good to Go.* **AC8, MU12, XT12**

Short Time (1990, C, 97m, PG-13)
Darkly comic story of a police detective who mistakenly thinks he has a terminal illness, tries to get killed in the line of duty so his family can collect a big insurance check. Dabney Coleman stars, with Matt Frewer and Teri Garr. **CO10, CO12**

Shot in the Dark, A (1964, C, 101m, NR)
Second (and arguably funniest) *Pink Panther* adventure has Inspector Clouseau trying to prove that a lovely young woman is innocent of murder. Peter Sellers is in top form, as is Elke Sommer; Herbert Lom, George Sanders, and Bert Kwouk are all hilarious. Directed by Blake Edwards. **DT40, ST198, XT26, Essential, Highly Recommended**

Shout (1991, C, 89m, PG)
Rock musical set in small Texas town in the 1950s, when music teacher at boys' orphanage turns on his charges to that new beat. John Travolta stars, with Linda Fiorentino, Heather Graham, and Richard Jordan. **DR9, DR25, DR26, MU9**

Shout, The (1979, C, 87m, R)
A man who believes he can kill people by shouting terrorizes a young couple. Alan Bates, John Hurt, and Susannah York star in this strange drama directed by Jerzy Skolimowski. Pretty heavy going, even for fans of the director. **HO7, ST9**

Shout at the Devil (1976, C, 119m, PG)
Action drama, set in pre–World War I Africa, about a poacher recruiting an Englishman in a plot to blow up a German ship. Lee Marvin and Roger Moore star. **AC12, ST151**

Show Boat (1936, B&W, 113m, NR)
The Jerome Kern-Oscar Hammerstein musical of life on the old Mississippi, starring Irene Dunne, Allan Jones, Paul Robeson, and Helen Morgan. Directed by James Whale. **DT138, MU2, MU4, MU6, ST62**

Show Boat (1951, C, 107m, NR)
Second screen version of musical about the naive daughter (Kathryn Grayson) of the

owners of a show boat falling in love with a gambler (Howard Keel). With Ava Gardner, Joe E. Brown, Marge and Gower Champion, and William Warfield. **MU1, MU2, MU4, MU6, ST79**

Show of Force, A (1990, C, 93m, R)
Political thriller set in 1978 Puerto Rico, based on true events surrounding mysterious deaths of two alleged terrorists seeking independence from the U.S. Amy Irving stars, with Lou Diamond Phillips, Kevin Spacey, and in small roles, Robert Duvall and Andy Garcia. **MY6, ST63**

Show People (1928, B&W, 81m, NR)
Silent comedy set in Hollywood, with Marion Davies as an actress who lets success go to her head. Watch for cameos by Charlie Chaplin, Douglas Fairbanks, and other Movie Town notables of the period. Directed by King Vidor. Carl Davis composed a musical score for the video version. **CL7, CL11, DT24, DT126,** *Essential, Recommended*

Show Them No Mercy
(1935, B&W, 76m, NR)
Gangsters kidnap a couple and their baby, but run into stalwart G-Men. Rochelle Hudson, Cesar Romero, Bruce Cabot, and Edward Norris star. **AC22**

Showdown (1973, C, 99m, PG)
Familiar Western drama of former pals now on opposite sides of the law, fighting for same woman. Rock Hudson and Dean Martin star, with Susan Clark. **ST112, ST149**

Showdown at Boot Hill
(1958, B&W, 76m, NR)
Charles Bronson is a bounty hunter out to collect his money in this Western drama. **ST20**

Shriek in the Night, A
(1933, B&W, 66m, NR)
Suspense drama starring Ginger Rogers and Lyle Talbot as reporters out to trap a killer. **ST187**

Shy People (1988, C, 118m, R)
A New York journalist (Jill Clayburgh) travels with her daughter to the Louisiana bayou to meet a cousin (Barbara Hershey) as a subject for a story. With Martha Plimpton and Mare Winningham. **DR8, DR10, DR27, ST31, ST104**

Sibling Rivalry (1990, C, 88m, PG-13)
Dark comedy of shy wife (Kirstie Alley) whose one-night stand results in fatal heart attack for her partner (Sam Elliott), spinning off comic misunderstandings among her family. With Bill Pullman, Carrie Fisher, Jami

Gertz, Scott Bakula, and Ed O'Neill. Directed by Carl Reiner. **CO5**

Sicilian, The (1987, C, 146m, NR)
True story of Salvatore Giuliano, the Sicilian bandit who defied the wealthy landowners and gave the peasants a hero to look up to. This is the European cut with footage unseen in the American release. The 115-minute American version is also available. Christopher Lambert stars, with Terence Stamp, Barbara Sukowa, Joss Ackland, John Turturro, and Ray McAnally. Directed by Michael Cimino. **AC16, CU10, DR5**

Sid & Nancy (1986, C, 111m, R)
The heartbreaking story of English punk rocker Sid Vicious and Nancy Spungen, his American lover and partner in drug addiction. An instant midnight movie classic with stunning performances by Gary Oldman and Chloe Webb. Directed by Alex Cox. **CU1, DR6, DR12,** *Recommended*

Side Out (1990, C, 100m, PG-13)
The beach volleyball scene in Southern California is the backdrop for this drama. C. Thomas Howell and Peter Horton star. **DR22**

Sidewalk Stories (1989, B&W, 97m, R)
Silent comedy about a homeless street artist. Written, produced, directed by, and starring Charles Lane. **CO2**

Sidewalks of London
(1938, B&W, 84m, NR)
Charles Laughton plays a street entertainer, Vivien Leigh his ambitious protégée, in this British drama. With Rex Harrison. **CL7, DR23, ST132, ST137**

Sidney Sheldon's Bloodline
(1979, C, 116m, R)
Audrey Hepburn stars in this sudsy thriller about a woman who inherits a cosmetics company and is immediately plunged into danger and mystery. With Ben Gazzara, James Mason, Michelle Phillips, Omar Sharif, and Romy Schneider. Also known as *Bloodline*. **MY3, ST102, ST153**

Siege of Firebase Gloria, The
(1988, C, 95m, R)
Vietnam War drama centering on combat action at the time of the 1968 Tet Offensive. Wings Hauser and Lee Ermey star. **AC4**

Siegfried (1924, B&W, 100m, NR)
Fritz Lang directed this silent classic, based on the Teutonic legends. Sequel: *Kriemhide's Revenge.* **DT70, FF3**

Siesta (1987, C, 97m, R)
Convoluted tale of female stunt pilot (Ellen

Barkin) and her fragmented personal affairs. With Gabriel Byrne, Jodie Foster, Martin Sheen, Grace Jones, Julian Sands, and Isabella Rossellini. Music by Miles Davis. Pretentious nonsense. **DR10, MU12, ST7, ST75**

Sign O' the Times (1987, C, 85m, PG-13)
Concert film of controversial rock star Prince also features Sheila E. and Sheena Easton. **MU10**

Signal 7 (1983, C, 92m, NR)
Low-key drama about cabdrivers in San Francisco. Director Rob Nilsson encouraged his actors to improvise their dialogue. **DR15, XT13**

Signs of Life (1989, C, 91m, PG-13)
Drama set in a seaside Maine village, where a boat builder is going out of business. Arthur Kennedy stars, with Kevin J. O'Connor, Vincent D'Onofrio, and Michael Lewis. **DR26**

Silence, The (1963, B&W, 95m, NR)
Landmark drama from director Ingmar Bergman about two sisters, one a lesbian, the other a sexually promiscuous mother. Ingrid Thulin and Gunnel Lindblom star. **DT11,** *Essential*

Silence Like Glass (1990, C, 102m, R)
Heart-wrenching drama of young woman (Jami Gertz) diagnosed with a terminal illness. With Martha Plimpton, George Peppard, and Rip Torn. **DR2, ST216**

Silence of the Lambs, The
(1991, C, 118m, R)
White-knuckle thriller about young FBI trainee assigned to case of gruesome serial killer nicknamed Buffalo Bill; to figure him out, she interviews imprisoned madman, Dr. Hannibal Lecter (nicknamed The Cannibal). Oscar winners Jodie Foster and Anthony Hopkins star, with Scott Glenn, Ted Levine, Diane Baker, Charles Napier, and in small roles, Roger Corman and George Romero. Directed by Jonathan Demme, operating at full throttle. Ted Tally adapted Thomas Harris's novel, a sequel of sorts to his *Red Dragon*, filmed as *Manhunter*. Oscars for Best Picture, Director, and Adapted Screenplay. **DR10, DR19, DT30, DT35, DT108, MY2, MY3, MY9, MY13, ST75, ST109, XT1, XT2, XT3, XT6,** *Highly Recommended*

Silent Movie (1976, C, 86m, PG)
Mel Brooks's tribute to the early days of film comedy: a movie with no dialogue, only music and sound effects. Mel's costars are Marty Feldman, Dom DeLuise, and Sid Caesar; watch for guest cameos from Paul Newman, Anne Bancroft, and Burt Reynolds. Gives in to one of Brooks's worst impulses,

the tendency to overplay. **CO7, CO12, DT17, ST162, ST183**

Silent Night, Deadly Night
(1984, C, 79m, R)
A man becomes a homicidal maniac when forced to wear a Santa suit. **HO9**

Silent Night, Deadly Night 5:
The Toymaker (1991, C, 90m, R)
Name-only entry in series that kicked off with horror story of Santa Claus killer; this one focuses on evil toy manufacturer whose products kill their owners. Mickey Rooney stars, with Jake Higginson, William Thorne, and Tracy Fraim. **ST189**

Silent Night, Lonely Night
(1969, C, 98m, NR)
Love story of middle-aged couple meeting at a New England resort, starring Lloyd Bridges and Shirley Jones. With Carrie Snodgress, Cloris Leachman, and Jeff Bridges. Originally made for TV. **DR1, ST19, XT8**

Silent Partner, The (1978, C, 103m, R)
Thriller about a bank clerk who's tipped off in advance to a robbery and neatly transfers the "stolen" money into his own account. Then the robber comes after him, and things get very nasty. Elliott Gould and Christopher Plummer star. With Susannah York, Celine Lomez, and John Candy. Directed by Daryl Duke. Made in Canada. Plummer's terrific, and Gould's what-me-worry style is well used. **CO14, MY9,** *Recommended*

Silent Rage (1982, C, 105m, R)
Chuck Norris battles a killer who has been rendered virtually indestructible by a scientific experiment. **ST165**

Silent Running (1972, C, 90m, G)
By the twenty-first century pollution has killed off all the vegetation on Earth. On a specially designed spacecraft, the only botanical specimens left are carefully tended in hopes that one day they can be replanted on Earth. Bruce Dern stars in this science fiction drama directed by Douglas Trumbull. **SF3**

Silent Scream (1984, C, 60m, NR)
A former commandant of a concentration camp collects a variety of animals, including humans. Peter Cushing stars. **ST43**

Silhouette (1990, C, 100m, NR)
Faye Dunaway stars in this thriller of businesswoman stranded in small Texas town, pursued by killer after she witnesses one of his crimes. Originally made for TV. **MY3, ST61**

Silk Stockings (1957, C, 117m, NR)
A cold Russian emissary (Cyd Charisse) visiting Paris warms up to the attentions of a

playboy (Fred Astaire). Rouben Mamoulian directed this musical remake of *Ninotchka*. **CU18, DT83, MU1, MU14, ST4**

Silkwood (1983, C, 128m, R)
Meryl Streep plays Karen Silkwood, the factory worker who tried to expose safety practices in her nuclear plant and died in a mysterious car accident. With Kurt Russell, Cher, Craig T. Nelson, Fred Ward, Ron Silver, David Strathairn, Sudie Bond, and Tess Harper. Written by Nora Ephron and Alice Arlen; Mike Nichols directed. Superbly acted, shrewdly written. **DR6, DT91, ST29, ST191, ST210, XT26,** *Recommended*

Silver Bears (1978, C, 113m, PG)
Comedy-drama of shady dealings in the international silver market, starring Michael Caine and Cybill Shepherd, with Louis Jourdan and Martin Balsam. Based on Paul Erdman's novel. Amusing. **CO2, DR24, ST25**

Silver Blaze, The (1937, B&W, 60m, NR)
Arthur Wontner stars as Sherlock Holmes in this mystery about a missing racehorse. Also titled *Murder at the Baskervilles*. **HF14**

Silver Bullet (1985, C, 95m, R)
A deranged killer is terrorizing a small town and only a crippled boy (Corey Haim) and his irresponsible uncle (Gary Busey) realize the killer is really a werewolf. Based on a Stephen King novella. Directed by Dan Attias. Busey's a howl, but the rest is ordinary shocker stuff. **HO4, WR15**

Silver Chalice, The (1954, C, 144m, NR)
Drama of ancient Greece, about a sculptor who fashions cup for the Last Supper. Paul Newman's film debut; Virginia Mayo, Pier Angeli, and Jack Palance star. **CL13, ST162**

Silver River (1948, B&W, 110m, NR)
Errol Flynn Western has him playing good guy turned bad. With Ann Sheridan, Thomas Mitchell, Bruce Bennett, Tom D'Andrea, and Barton MacLane. Directed by Raoul Walsh. **DT131, ST69**

Silver Spurs (1943, B&W, 54m, NR)
A ranch foreman (Roy Rogers) rides to stop a villainous landgrabber (John Carradine). **ST188**

Silver Streak (1976, C, 113m, PG)
Comic thriller, set aboard a speeding train, with innocent editor (Gene Wilder) becoming involved with murder plot and lovely passenger (Jill Clayburgh). With Richard Pryor and Patrick McGoohan. Pryor and Wilder's best film. **CO3, CO10, ST31, ST180, XT19,** *Recommended*

Silverado (1985, C, 132m, PG-13)
A trio of cowboys ride out to protect the persecuted settlers of a prairie town. Kevin Kline, Scott Glenn, and Danny Glover star. The supporting cast includes Brian Dennehy, Linda Hunt, Rosanna Arquette, Jeff Goldblum, and John Cleese. Written and directed by Lawrence Kasdan. Tries hard for classic feel but falls well short of the mark. **CO15, ST38, ST88, ST90, ST127, WE1**

Simba (1955, C, 99m, NR)
Drama of relations in Kenya between British and the Mau Maus. Dirk Bogarde stars, with Virginia McKenna and Basil Sydney. **DR27, ST14**

Simon (1980, C, 97m, PG)
A group of scientists brainwash a man into believing he is an alien. Alan Arkin and Madeline Kahn star in this comedy written and directed by Marshall Brickman. Arkin's very good, but the film's a bit arid. **CO20, SF21**

Simon and Garfunkel: The Concert in Central Park (1982, C, 87m, NR)
Paul Simon and Art Garfunkel sing together for the first time in eleven years. **MU10**

Simon of the Desert
(1965, B&W, 45m, NR)
Director Luis Buñuel's sly comedy about a real-life holy man who supposedly spent many years perched on top of a pillar. Claudio Brook and Silvia Pinal star. **DT19,** *Recommended*

Simple Men (1992, C, 106m, R)
Offbeat drama from director Hal Hartley about two brothers in search of their father, an anarchist on the run from the law. Robert Burke and William Sage star, with Karen Sillas and Martin Donovan. **DR9**

Simple Story, A (1978, C, 110m, NR)
Romy Schneider is a woman at the crossroads of her life in this French drama. **FF1**

Sin of Harold Diddlebock, The
(1947, B&W, 90m, NR)
Harold Lloyd stars in his last sound comedy, about a timid bookkeeper and his first brush with alcohol. Directed by Preston Sturges. **DT121**

Sin of Madelon Claudet, The
(1931, B&W, 73m, NR)
Helen Hayes won an Oscar for her performance in this tearjerker about a woman who gives up everything to ensure her illegitimate son's happiness. With Lewis Stone, Neil Hamilton, Robert Young, and Jean Hersholt. **CL5, CL6, XT3**

Sinatra (1992, C, 220m, NR)
Philip Chasnoff plays the extraordinary
entertainer; story stretches from his youth
into the 1960s. With Olympia Dukakis as
Dolly Sinatra, Rod Steiger as Sam Giancana,
and Marcia Gaye Harden as Ava Gardner.
Originally a TV miniseries. Sinatra's original
vocals are used on the soundtrack. **MU5,
ST79, ST199**

Sinbad and the Eye of the Tiger
(1977, C, 113m, G)
Sinbad goes on another adventure with a
beautiful princess and an evil witch. Special
effects by Ray Harryhausen. Patrick Wayne
and Jane Seymour star. **FA8**

Sinbad the Sailor (1947, C, 117m, NR)
Colorful swashbuckler starring Douglas Fair-
banks, Jr., as the legendary adventurer, with
Maureen O'Hara, Anthony Quinn, Walter
Slezak, and Jane Greer. **AC15, ST167**

Since You Went Away
(1944, B&W, 172m, NR)
Epic, heart-wrenching story of homefront
America during World War II, produced by
David O. Selznick. Claudette Colbert, Jennifer
Jones, Joseph Cotten, and Shirley Temple
star, with Robert Walker, Monty Woolley,
Agnes Moorehead, and Hattie McDaniel.
CL5, CL6, ST34, ST213, *Recommended*

Sincerely, Charlotte (1986, C, 92m, NR)
A singer is a suspect in her boyfriend's mur-
der and flees from the police with the help
of an old lover. Isabelle Huppert stars in this
French thriller; her sister Caroline directed.
FF1, MY16

Sincerely Yours (1955, C, 115m, NR)
Liberace stars as a pianist whose music is an
inspiration to all around him. Written by
Irving Wallace. As bad as it sounds—but re-
vered by fans of campy movies. **CU2**

Sing (1989, C, 99m, PG-13)
A Brooklyn high school musical competition
between seniors and underclassman forms
the basis for this drama. Lorraine Bracco,
Peter Dobson, Louise Lasser, and Patti LaBelle
star. **DR12, DR25**

Singer Not the Song, The
(1961, C, 129m, NR)
Small town in Mexico is setting for this British drama of priest's and bandit's struggle for
control of citizens' hearts and minds. Dirk
Bogarde, John Mills, and Mylene Demongeot
star. **DR23, ST14**

Singin' in the Rain (1952, C, 102m, G)
Grand musical comedy set at the time when
sound pictures came to Hollywood. Gene

Kelly, Debbie Reynolds, and Donald O'Con-
nor star, with Jean Hagen and Cyd Charisse.
Directed by Kelly and Stanley Donen. Many
musical highlights, including Kelly's title
tune dance, and O'Connor's "Make 'Em
Laugh." Never a dull moment. **DT38, FA9,
MU1, MU4, ST123,** *Essential, Highly
Recommended*

Singing Nun, The (1966, C, 98m, NR)
Debbie Reynolds plays the Belgian sister
Souer Sourire, whose hit record, "Domini-
que," earned her a brief brush with fame.
With Ricardo Montalban, Greer Garson,
Agnes Moorehead, Katharine Ross, and Ed
Sullivan as himself. **MU5, ST83**

Single Standard, The
(1929, B&W, 73m, NR)
Silent drama with Greta Garbo as a San Francisco debutante having a scandalous affair
with an artist (Nils Asther). **CL12, ST78**

Single White Female (1992, C, 107m, R)
Contemporary thriller of New York woman
taking in roommate who turns out to be
homicidal maniac. Bridget Fonda and Jennifer Jason Leigh star, with Steve Weber,
Peter Friedman, and Stephen Tobolowsky.
Directed by Barbet Schroeder. Shows promise
of being an interesting psychological thriller
but eventually gives way to violence all too
common to this mini-genre. Both actresses
very good. **MY3, MY9, MY19, ST70,
ST136, XT9**

Singles (1992, C, 99m, PG-13)
Life among twentysomethings in Seattle is
basis for this sweet, engaging romantic comedy. Featured in the cast are Bridget Fonda,
Campbell Scott, Kyra Sedgwick, Sheila Kelley,
Jim True, and Matt Dillon, with Bill Pullman,
James LeGros, and Tim Burton as a clerk at a
video dating service. Written and directed by
Cameron Crowe. A real time-capsule movie
in many ways; if Fonda becomes a big star,
this may be regarded as her breakthrough
performance. **CO1, CO2, CO4, DT20, ST56,
ST70,** *Recommended*

Sinister Invasion (1970, C, 95m, NR)
A crazed scientist (Boris Karloff) creates a
death ray. Also known as *Incredible Invasion.*
ST119

Sinister Urge, The (1961, B&W, 75m, NR)
A pair of cops set out to break up a porno
movie ring in this low-budget, brain-dead
drama from director Ed Wood, Jr. **DT141**

Sink the Bismarck! (1960, B&W, 97m, NR)
Action in the North Atlantic, as British forces
try to destroy a seemingly impregnable Ger-

man battleship. Kenneth More and Dana Wynter star. **AC1**

Sinners in Paradise (1938, B&W, 65m, NR) Drama of plane crash survivors on tropical island who discover a recluse living there. John Boles stars, with Madge Evans, Bruce Cabot, Gene Lockhart, and Milburn Stone. Directed by James Whale. **DT138**

Sioux City Sue (1946, B&W, 69m, NR) Gene Autry is in Hollywood to try his hand at show business, but there are rustlers even in the Hills of Beverly. **ST5**

Sirocco (1951, B&W, 98m, NR) Humphrey Bogart plays a gunrunner during the 1920s. Lee J. Cobb and Zero Mostel costar in this thriller. **ST15**

Sister Act (1992, C, 100m, PG) Whoopi Goldberg comedy has her playing a Reno lounge singer hiding out from her mobster boyfriend in a convent. With Harvey Keitel, Maggie Smith, Kathy Najimy, Wendy Makkena, Mary Wickes, and Bill Nunn. Directed by Emile Ardolino. **CO20, ST89**

Sister Kenny (1946, B&W, 116m, NR) True-life story of courageous nurse and her fight against polio. Rosalind Russell stars, with Alexander Knox, Dean Jagger, and Beulah Bondi. **CL2, ST192**

Sister, Sister (1987, C, 91m, R) Horror tale of two siblings living in their late parents' mansion, which they've converted into a guest house for unsuspecting travelers. Judith Ivey and Jennifer Jason Leigh star, with Eric Stoltz. **HO14, ST136**

Sisters, The (1938, B&W, 98m, NR) Drama set around time of San Francisco earthquake, starring Bette Davis and Errol Flynn. She and her siblings (Anita Louise, Jane Bryan) have the usual troubles with men. **CL5, ST44, ST69**

Sisters (1973, C, 93m, R) Thriller about Siamese twins surgically separated at birth, one growing up to become a homicidal maniac (Margot Kidder). With Jennifer Salt as a nosy reporter, William Finley as a possessive doctor, Charles Durning as a private eye. Brian De Palma directed; outstanding musical score by Bernard Herrmann. De Palma scores big with this shocker; rarely effective use of split-screen. **DT36, HO15, MY11, MY13, XT27,** *Recommended*

633 Squadron (1964, C, 101m, NR) World War II action with Allied bombers pouring it on a German installation in Nor-

way. Cliff Robertson and George Chakiris star. **AC1, AC11**

Six Weeks (1982, C, 107m, PG) Tearjerker about a politician's friendship with a little girl, dying of cancer, and her mother. Dudley Moore, Mary Tyler Moore, and Katherine Healy star. Directed by Tony Bill. **DR2, ST160, XT23**

Sixteen Candles (1984, C, 93m, PG) A girl's sixteenth birthday is nearly ruined by her family's distractions over her older sister's wedding and her inability to get the attention of a special boy. Molly Ringwald stars, with Anthony Michael Hall as The Geek, Michael Schoeffling as her Dream Date, Paul Dooley, Justin Henry, Blanche Baker, John Cusack, and Joan Cusack. John Hughes wrote and directed. Ringwald's refreshingly unglamorous, Hall amusing. **CO4, DT59, XT8, XT20**

Sixteen Fathoms Deep (1934, B&W, 57m, NR) Adventure saga of sponge fishermen battling a moneylender, starring Creighton (Lon) Chaney (Jr.), Sally O'Neil, and George Rogers. **ST27**

Ski Patrol (1990, C, 91m, PG) Comedy focusing on the antics of young ski enthusiasts who are fighting a greedy developer (Martin Mull) and his plans to take over their resort. With Roger Rose, Corby Timbrook, T.K. Carter, and Ray Walston. **CO19**

Skin Deep (1989, C, 101m, R) The comic dilemmas of a compulsive ladies' man (John Ritter) in contemporary Los Angeles. With Vincent Gardenia, Alyson Reed, Joel Brooks, Julianne Phillips, Denise Crosby, and Michael Kidd. Written and directed by Blake Edwards. **CO1, DT40**

Skin Game, The (1931, B&W, 87m, NR) Early Hitchcock film about a family resorting to blackmail to thwart a neighbor's plans. Edmund Gwenn stars. **DT57**

Skin Game, The (1971, C, 102m, PG) Amiable, witty comedy about a pair of con men—one black, the other white—traveling through the Civil War South. James Garner and Louis Gossett, Jr., star, with Susan Clark, Ed Asner, Brenda Sykes, and Andrew Duggan. **CO6, ST82, WE6, WE15,** *Recommended*

Skirts Ahoy! (1952, C, 109m, NR) Esther Williams, Vivian Blane, and Joan Evans play WAVEs in this service musical. With Barry Sullivan, Keefe Brasselle, Debbie Reynolds, Bobby Van, and Billy Eckstine. **MU1**

Skokie (1981, C, 125m, NR)
True-life drama set in 1977 in a Chicago suburb, where Nazis wanted to stage a march and local Jewish residents tried to prevent it. Danny Kaye stars, with John Rubenstein, Carl Reiner, Kim Hunter, Eli Wallach, Lee Strasberg, and Brian Dennehy. Originally made for TV. **DR6, DR7, ST120**

Skull, The (1965, C, 83m, NR)
British horror story of the skull of the Marquis de Sade possessing evil powers. Peter Cushing stars, with Patrick Wymark, Christopher Lee, Nigel Green, and Jill Bennett. **HO26, ST43, ST135**

Skullduggery (1970, C, 105m, PG)
Adventure tale of scientists finding group of primitive people in New Guinea, taking them to court to prevent their slaughter by developers. Burt Reynolds and Susan Clark star. **AC12, ST183**

Sky Above, The Mud Below, The
(1961, C, 90m, NR)
Oscar-winning documentary on expedition into jungles of Dutch New Guinea. **CU16**

Sky Is Gray, The (1980, C, 46m, G)
Drama of black child in rural South and his first encounters with racial injustices, based on a story by Ernest Gaines. Olivia Cole, James Bond III, and Cleavon Little star. Originally made for TV. **DR14**

Sky's the Limit, The
(1943, B&W, 89m, NR)
A photographer (Joan Leslie) wants to meet a heroic pilot (Fred Astaire). Complications arise when she does meet him, but doesn't recognize him, as he is out of uniform. With Robert Benchley and Robert Ryan. Astaire sings "One For My Baby." **ST4, ST193**

Skyscraper Souls
(1932, B&W, 99m, NR)
Melodrama of stop-at-nothing businessman and his attempts to gain control of 100-story building. Warren William stars, with Maureen O'Sullivan, Gregory Ratoff, Anita Page, Jean Hersholt, Wallace Ford, and Hedda Hopper. Directed by Edgar Selwyn. Potent stuff that's surprisingly racy; made before Production Code was strictly enforced. **DR24,**
Recommended

Slamdance (1987, C, 100m, R)
A Los Angeles cartoonist is wrongly accused of murder, takes to the streets to prove his innocence. Tom Hulce stars, with Mary Elizabeth Mastrantonio, Virginia Madsen, and Harry Dean Stanton. Directed by Wayne Wang. **MY7, ST205, XT10**

Slap Shot (1977, C, 122m, R)
Broad, profane comedy about minor-league hockey team and its aging player-coach. Paul Newman stars, with Michael Ontkean, Lindsay Crouse, Jennifer Warren, Melinda Dillon, and Strother Martin. Directed by George Roy Hill; written by Nancy Dowd. Crowd-pleasing stuff with good performance by Newman. **CO19, DT55, ST162,**
Recommended

Slapstick (Of Another Kind)
(1984, C, 82m, PG)
Jerry Lewis comedy, based on Kurt Vonnegut, Jr., novel about deformed twins who are really aliens with the solutions to the world's problems. Madeline Kahn costars, with Marty Feldman, Samuel Fuller, and Jim Backus. **DR19, DT49, ST139**

Slaughter (1972, C, 92m, R)
Jim Brown plays an ex-Green Beret out to avenge his parents' deaths at the hands of organized crime. With Stella Stevens and Rip Torn. **AC19, ST216**

Slaughter in San Francisco
(1981, C, 87m, R)
Chuck Norris, in an early role, plays a killer who is being sought by the police. Originally filmed in 1973. **ST165**

Slaughterhouse (1987, C, 85m, R)
An old man with a retarded son doesn't want to sell his slaughterhouse. Soon after the offer is made, people begin to die. **HO24**

Slaughterhouse Five (1971, C, 104m, R)
Kurt Vonnegut, Jr.'s novel of a man unstuck in time, existing where the past, present, and future occur in random order. His most vivid memory of the past is the firebombing of Dresden during World War II, which he and other American POWs survived. Michael Sacks, Valerie Perrine, and Ron Leibman star. Directed by George Roy Hill; edited by Dede Allen. Improbably successful adaptation of difficult book. **CU4, DR19, DT55, SF4,**
Recommended

Slave of Love, A (1978, C, 94m, NR)
Russian drama, set during the Revolution, of a love affair between a silent film actress and her cameraman. **FF7**

Slaves of New York (1989, C, 125m, R)
Tama Janowitz's collection of stories about the contemporary art scene in New York was adapted by the writer, concentrating on Eleanor (Bernadette Peters), a hat designer with a heartless painter (Adam Coleman Howard) for a lover. Also in the cast: Chris Sarandon, Mary Beth Hurt, and Mercedes Ruehl. Di-

rected by James Ivory; produced by Ismail Merchant. **DR15, DR19, DT61, XT9**

Sleepaway Camp (1983, C, 90m, R)
A psychotic killer is brutally murdering the campers of Camp Arawat. **HO12**

Sleeper (1973, C, 88m, PG)
Woody Allen comedy about a man who is cryogenically frozen and revived two hundred years later to a vastly changed world. With Diane Keaton and John Beck. Sweet but undernourished; Keaton's Brando impression is memorable. **CO7, DT2, SF4, SF21, ST121, XT30**

Sleeping Beauty (1959, C, 75m, G)
An evil witch places a curse on a princess, and it is up to her true love to save her. A classic of Disney animation. Widescreen will be lost on video. **CU20, FA2**

Sleeping Beauty (1985, C, 60m, NR)
From the Faerie Tale Theatre series, the tale about a princess who is cursed and her true love who can free her. Christopher Reeve, Bernadette Peters, and Beverly D'Angelo star. **FA12**

Sleeping Dogs (1977, C, 107m, R)
From New Zealand, a political drama of a workers' strike and one man caught between both sides. Sam Neill stars, with Warren Oates. **FF5, ST166**

Sleeping Tiger, The (1954, B&W, 89m, NR)
British drama of triangle: Alexis Smith is married to Alexander Knox, a doctor who's treating Dirk Bogarde, a paroled criminal. Directed by Joseph Losey under the pseudonym Terence Hanbury. **DR23, ST14**

Sleeping With the Enemy
(1991, C, 98m, R)
Woman escapes marriage to psychotic by pretending to drown, escapes to small Iowa town, where her ex tracks her down. Julia Roberts stars, with Patrick Bergin and Kevin Anderson. **MY3**

Sleepwalkers (1992, C, 91m, R)
Stephen King wrote the script for this horror tale of a mother and son who are monstrous shape-changers living off the life force of teen-age virgins. Brian Krause and Alice Krige star, with Madchen Amick, Jim Haynie, Cindy Pickett, and cameo appearances by Joe Dante, John Landis, Clive Barker, Tobe Hooper, and Mr. King himself. Directed by Mick Garris. Also known as *Stephen King's Sleepwalkers*. **DT33, HO12, HO14, WR15**

Slender Thread, The (1965, B&W, 98m, NR)
Race-against-the-clock drama of student volunteer at suicide hot line talking with depressed woman while authorities try to locate her. Sidney Poitier and Anne Bancroft star, with Telly Savalas, Steven Hill, Edward Asner, and Dabney Coleman. Written by Stirling Silliphant, directed by Sydney Pollack. **DR10, DT98, ST174**

Sleuth (1972, C, 138m, PG)
A vindictive mystery novelist lures his wife's lover into a deadly cat-and-mouse game at a deserted country house. Laurence Olivier and Michael Caine star. Joseph L. Mankiewicz directed; Anthony Shaffer adapted his play. Goes on a bit long but two stars in top form. **DR20, DT84, MY9, MY15, ST25, ST168,** *Recommended*

Slightly Pregnant Man, A
(1973, C, 92m, NR)
Marcello Mastroianni plays a man suffering from morning sickness in this comedy co-starring Catherine Deneuve. **ST50, ST154**

Slightly Scarlet (1956, C, 99m, NR)
Thriller about political corruption involving a mayor's secretary and a gangster's secret affair. John Payne, Arlene Dahl, and Rhonda Fleming star. Based on a James M. Cain novel. **MY1, WR1**

Slipstream (1989, C, 92m, PG-13)
Science fiction cop drama of a lawman up against a bounty hunter and his prisoner. Mark Hamill, Ben Kingsley, and F. Murray Abraham star. **SF17**

Slither (1973, C, 97m, PG)
Cult comedy of group of eccentrics on road trip looking for a stash of money. James Caan and Sally Kellerman star, with Peter Boyle, Louise Lasser, Allen Garfield, and Richard B. Shull. Directed by Howard Zieff. Agreeably wacky. **CO10, CU5, XT18,** *Recommended*

Slithis (1979, C, 86m, PG)
Radiation leaks into the ocean and causes marine life to mutate, creating a horrifying monster. **HO21**

Slugger's Wife, The
(1985, C, 105m, PG-13)
Portrait of a modern romance between a baseball star and a pop singer, whose separate careers threaten to ruin their new marriage. Michael O'Keefe and Rebecca De Mornay star, with Randy Quaid and Martin Ritt. Written by Neil Simon, directed by Hal Ashby. Great possibilities, awful results. **DR1, DT105, WR30**

Slumber Party '57 (1977, C, 89m, R)
A group of sorority sisters gather to reveal how each lost her virginity. Noelle North, Bridget Hollman, and Debra Winger (in her debut) star. **ST231**

Slumber Party Massacre
(1982, C, 78m, R)
Teen-age girls are menaced by a killer with a power drill. Written by Rita Mae Brown; directed by Amy Jones. **HO9**

Small Back Room, The
(1949, B&W, 106m, NR)
British drama of World War II munitions worker trying to deal with his physical infirmity and the bureaucracy. David Farrar stars, with Jack Hawkins and Kathleen Byron. Directed by Michael Powell and Emeric Pressburger. **DT99**

Small Change (1976, C, 104m, PG)
Director François Truffaut's loving tribute to children is a loosely connected series of episodes in the lives of youngsters in a French village. **DT125,** *Recommended*

Small Town Girl
(1953, C, 93m, NR)
MGM musical about title character (Jane Powell) falling for a playboy (Farley Granger). With Ann Miller, Bobby Van, and Nat King Cole. Choreography by Busby Berkeley. **DT12, MU1**

Smallest Show on Earth, The
(1957, B&W, 80m, NR)
British comedy of couple (Bill Travers and Virginia McKenna) inheriting broken-down movie house and its three decrepit employees (Margaret Rutherford, Peter Sellers, and Bernard Miles). **CO17, ST198**

Smash-Up, The Story of a Woman
(1947, B&W, 103m, NR)
Susan Hayward plays a singer who decides to give up her career for marriage, descends gradually into alcoholism. With Lee Bowman, Marsha Hunt, and Eddie Albert. **CL5, CL7, ST100**

Smile (1975, C, 113m, PG)
Satiric look at a small-town beauty pageant, written by Jerry Belson. Bruce Dern stars, with Barbara Feldon, Michael Kidd, Geoffrey Lewis, Annette O'Toole, and Melanie Griffith. Directed by Michael Ritchie; written by Jerry Belson. Sharp satire. **CO2, CO8, ST93,** *Recommended*

Smile, Jenny, You're Dead
(1974, C, 100m, NR)
David Janssen plays a gumshoe investigating the murder of a young man, getting involved with his widow—who's the prime suspect. With John Anderson, Howard da Silva, Martin Gabel, Clu Gulager, Jodie Foster, and Andrea Marcovicci. The pilot film for the "Harry O" TV series. **MY10, ST75**

Smiles of a Summer Night
(1955, B&W, 108m, NR)
A weekend at a Swedish country estate is the setting for Ingmar Bergman's peerless romantic comedy. **DT11,** *Essential, Recommended*

Smith! (1969, C, 101m, G)
In this Disney Western, a farmer stands up for the rights of an Indian accused of murder. Glenn Ford stars, with Warren Oates. **FA1, ST166, WE7**

Smithereens (1982, C, 90m, R)
Zany story about a New York hustler whose ambition is to manage a punk rock band. Susan Berman, Brad Rinn, and Richard Hell star. Susan Seidelman directed. **DR15, XT9**

Smokescreen (1990, C, 91m, R)
Romantic triangle drama of a young ad executive, a gangster, and the woman they both love. Matt Craven, Dean Stockwell, and Kim Cattrall star. **ST208**

Smokey and the Bandit
(1977, C, 96m, PG)
Burt Reynolds's most popular good ol' boy comedy, about a bootlegger who delights in outwitting a numbskull sheriff (Jackie Gleason). With Sally Field, Jerry Reed, Paul Williams, and Pat McCormick. Directed by Hal Needham. Ham-handed. **CO9, ST66, ST183, XT18**

Smokey and the Bandit II
(1980, C, 104m, PG)
Follow-up to first *Smokey* film has Burt Reynolds and Sally Field transporting a pregnant elephant across the South, with sheriff Jackie Gleason in pursuit. **CO9, ST66, ST183, XT18**

Smokey and the Bandit 3
(1983, C, 98m, PG)
Third go-round for the action comedy series, with Jerry Reed now the good ol' boy foil for sheriff Jackie Gleason. Burt Reynolds puts in a brief appearance. **CO9, ST183, XT18**

Smooth Talk (1985, C, 92m, PG13)
A flirtatious adolescent (Laura Dern) meets a slick older man (Treat Williams). With Levon Helm and Mary Kay Place. Based on a short story by Joyce Carol Oates. Originally made for public TV. **DR9, MU12, ST53**

Smorgasbord see *Cracking Up*

Snake People (1968, C, 90m, NR)
A policeman investigates a series of murders on an island inhabited by a sect of voodoo snake worshipers. Boris Karloff stars. **ST119**

Snake Pit, The (1948, B&W, 108m, NR)
Harrowing tale of woman mistakenly diag-

nosed with serious mental disease, placed in hellish hospital. Olivia de Havilland stars, with Mark Stevens, Leon Genn, Celeste Holm, Glenn Langan, Leif Erickson, and Buelah Bondi. Directed by Anatole Litvak. **CL8, ST49**

Sneakers (1992, C, 125m, PG-13)
Caper film with comic touches about maverick group of electronics security experts taking on job for federal government under threat of blackmail against their leader (as a college student in the 1960s he and a buddy played a practical joke on the Pentagon's computers, but he was never caught). Robert Redford, Dan Aykroyd, Sidney Poitier, River Phoenix, and David Strathairn play the team; with Ben Kingsley as their adversary, and Mary McDonnell, Timothy Busfield, George Hearn, and James Earl Jones. Filmed in and around San Francisco. Directed and cowritten by Phil Alden Robinson. Clever, fairly entertaining, but meanders and overstays its welcome. **CO13, MY18, ST118, ST174, ST181, XT13**

Sniper (1993, C, 98m, R)
Action drama of Marine sniper (Tom Berenger) on assignment in Panama, showing his companion (Billy Zane) the ropes. **AC20**

Snoopy, Come Home (1972, C, 80m, G)
Snoopy runs away from home and the entire "Peanuts" gang searches for him in this animated feature. **FA10**

Snow Queen (1983, C, 60m, NR)
From the Faerie Tale Theatre series, the story of a queen who teaches a young boy about love and friendship and saves him from a cold curse. Lee Remick, Lance Kerwin, and Melissa Gilbert star. **FA12**

Snow White and the Seven Dwarfs
(1983, C, 60m, NR)
Brothers Grimm tale about a beautiful princess helped by seven dwarfs and a handsome prince after her jealous stepmother tries to kill her. Elizabeth McGovern, Vanessa Redgrave, Vincent Price, and Rex Smith star in this Faerie Tale Theatre production. **FA12, ST179, ST182**

Snowball Express (1972, C, 99m, G)
An accountant (Dean Jones) inherits a hotel in Colorado and tries to turn it into a ski resort. Harry Morgan and Keenan Wynn costar in this Disney comedy. **FA1**

Snows of Kilimanjaro, The
(1952, C, 117m, NR)
Hemingway tale of a writer in Africa assessing his life as he lies dying. Gregory Peck

stars, with Susan Hayward and Ava Gardner. **ST79, ST100, ST171, WR13**

So Dear to My Heart (1948, C, 84m, NR)
A young boy tames a wild black sheep in hopes of winning a blue ribbon at the state fair. This Disney film incorporates some animation with live-action sequences. Burl Ives and Bobby Driscoll star. **FA1**

So Ends Our Night (1941, B&W, 117m, NR)
Fredric March stars in this drama of a German rejecting the Nazi regime, fleeing Germany with agents in pursuit. With Margaret Sullavan, Frances Dee, Glenn Ford, and Erich Von Stroheim. Based on a novel by Erich Maria Remarque. **CL8, DT129, ST148**

So This Is Paris (1926, B&W, 68m, NR)
Silent comedy from director Ernst Lubitsch about a couple who are bored with each other. Monte Blue and Patsy Ruth Miller star, with Myrna Loy. Delightful preview of good things to come from this incomparable filmmaker. **CL11, DT76, ST142, Recommended**

Soapdish (1991, C, 95m, PG-13)
Behind-the-scenes comedy at a network soap opera centering on fading star (Sally Field), her ex-husband and new costar (Kevin Kline), ambitious niece (Elisabeth Shue), and jealous costar (Cathy Moriarty), pal writer (Whoopi Goldberg), and scheming producer (Robert Downey, Jr.). With Carrie Fisher and Garry Marshall. Written by Robert Harling and Andrew Bergman. Up-and-down with zaniness and goopiness alternating. Kline's dinner-theater scene is terrific. **CO8, ST66, ST89, ST127**

Sodom and Gomorrah
(1963, C, 154m, NR)
Biblical spectacle of the twin cities of evil and their destruction. Stewart Granger stars, with Pier Angeli, Stanley Baker, and Anouk Aimee. Directed by Robert Aldrich. **CL13, DT1**

Soft Skin, The (1964, B&W, 120m, NR)
A married French businessman finds himself drawn into an affair with a stewardess in this drama from director François Truffaut. Françoise Dorleac stars. **DT125**

Sois Belle et Tais-Toi
(1958, B&W, 110m, NR)
Lighthearted French thriller of police detective tracking jewel thieves. Henri Vidal stars, with Mylene Demongeot, Jean-Paul Belmondo, and Alain Delon. **FF1, ST11**

Soldier, The (1982, C, 96m, R)
A special agent is dispatched to the Middle East when Soviets hijack a truck packed with deadly plutonium. Ken Wahl and Klaus

Kinski star. James Glickenhaus directed. **AC25, ST126**

Soldier Blue (1970, C, 112m, R)
Violent and controversial Western focusing on the brutal massacre of an entire Indian village by U.S. cavalry soldiers. Candice Bergen and Peter Strauss star. Directed by Ralph Nelson. Overblown and badly acted, unfortunately in a good cause. **WE4, WE7**

Soldier in the Rain (1963, B&W, 88m, NR)
Conniving master sergeant (Jackie Gleason) takes advantage of the G.I. (Steve McQueen) who worships him. Comedy-drama costars Tuesday Weld and Tony Bill. Blake Edwards and Maurice Richlin adapted William Goldman's novel. Directed by Ralph Nelson. Shifting tone is asset for a while, finally liability; McQueen and Gleason are very good. **CO21, ST146**

Soldier of Fortune (1955, C, 96m, NR)
Clark Gable stars in the title role, as he's off to Hong Kong to bring back the kidnapped husband of a lovely woman. With Susan Hayward, Gene Barry, and Michael Rennie. **AC21, ST77, ST100**

Soldier of Orange (1979, C, 165m, R)
Epic story of six Dutch university students who enlist when the Nazis invade their homeland. Rutger Hauer and Jeroen Krabbe star. Directed by Paul Verhoeven. **AC1**

Soldiers of Fortune (1970, C, 97m, PG)
Action in war-torn Turkey of the 1920s, with Charles Bronson and Tony Curtis as mercenaries. Original title: *You Can't Win 'Em All.* **AC6, AC21, ST20**

Soldier's Prayer, A see *Human Condition, Part III, The*

Soldier's Story, A (1984, C, 102m, PG)
On a segregated Army base during World War II, an unpopular black officer is murdered, and another black officer is called in to investigate. Howard E. Rollins, Adolph Caesar, and Denzel Washington star, with Dennis Lipscomb, Art Evans, Larry Riley, David Alan Grier, Robert Townsend, Patti LaBelle, Wings Hauser, and Trey Wilson. Charles Fuller adapted his play. Directed by Norman Jewison. Overpraised drama with a great performance by Caesar. **DR14, DR20, DT63, ST223**

Sole Survivor (1984, C, 85m, R)
The only survivor of a plane crash is haunted by the victims of that disaster. **HO2**

Solid Gold Cadillac, The
(1956, C/B&W, 99m, NR)
Comedy set in the world of big business,

with Judy Holliday as a heroic stockholder taking on the greedy board of a big corporation. With Paul Douglas, Fred Clark, and John Williams; narrated by George Burns. Last scene in color. **ST107**

Solomon and Sheba (1959, C, 120m, NR)
Biblical spectacle starring Yul Brynner and Gina Lollobrigida in the title roles. With George Sanders. Directed by King Vidor. **CL13, DT126**

Some Call It Loving (1973, C, 103m, R)
Adult fantasy transplants Sleeping Beauty story to contemporary Los Angeles. Zalman King and Tisa Farrow star, with Carol White and Richard Pryor. **ST180**

Some Came Running (1958, C, 136m, NR)
James Jones story set in a small town in Indiana, with characters whose lives are going nowhere fast. Frank Sinatra, Shirley MacLaine, and Dean Martin star, with Arthur Kennedy and Martha Hyer. Directed by Vincente Minnelli. Widescreen will be lost on video. Fans of director and stars swear by it; others will be less enthralled. **DR19, DR26, DT88, ST145, ST149, ST199**

Some Kind of Hero (1982, C, 97m, R)
Comedy-drama about a Vietnam veteran who gets a few surprises when he comes home after six years' captivity as a POW. Richard Pryor stars. **DR7, ST180**

Some Kind of Wonderful
(1987, C, 93m, PG-13)
Teen triangle of guy who loves rich girl, is counseled by his best friend, a girl who loves him. Eric Stoltz, Lea Thompson, and Mary Stuart Masterson star. Written and produced by John Hughes. **CO4, DT59**

Some Like It Hot (1959, B&W, 119m, NR)
Hilarious comedy about a pair of musicians, on the lam from Al Capone, dressing up like women to join an all-girl jazz band. Jack Lemmon, Tony Curtis, and Marilyn Monroe star, with Joe E. Brown, George Raft, and Pat O'Brien. Written by Billy Wilder and I.A.L. Diamond; directed by Wilder, who should have won the Oscar that year. If you can find a funnier movie, rent it. **CL10, CO10, DT139, ST138, ST159, XT26, XT28,** *Essential, Highly Recommended*

Somebody Up There Likes Me
(1956, B&W, 113m, NR)
Bio of boxer Rocky Graziano, who worked his way from the New York slums and a criminal youth to become middleweight champion. Paul Newman stars, with Pier Angeli, Everett Sloane, Sal Mineo, and Robert Loggia. Watch for Steve McQueen in a small

role. Directed by Robert Wise. Good for its time but Newman was still some years away from assurance on screen. **DR4, DR22, DT140, ST146, ST162**

Someone Behind the Door
(1971, C, 97m, PG)
A psychiatrist (Anthony Perkins) discovers that his amnesia patient (Charles Bronson) is a killer and sets him up to kill the psychiatrist's unfaithful wife. **ST20**

Someone To Love (1987, C, 111m, R)
Filmmaker Henry Jaglom invites friends to a Valentine's Day party and records their responses to his questions about romance. Among the guests: Orson Welles, Sally Kellerman, Michael Emil, and Andrea Marcovicci. **CO1, DT134**

Someone To Watch Over Me
(1987, C, 106m, R)
Cop from Queens, New York, is assigned to protect Manhattan socialite threatened by murder suspect, and romance develops. Tom Berenger, Mimi Rogers, and Lorraine Bracco star. Ridley Scott directed. Stretches plausibility beyond breaking point. **DR3, DR15, DT115, MY3, MY5, XT9**

Something for Everyone
(1970, C, 112m, R)
Cult comedy about manipulative young man who sexually takes over the house of a poor noblewoman. Michael York and Angela Lansbury star. Harold Prince directed. **CU5, CU6, ST131**

Something of Value
(1957, B&W, 113m, NR)
Drama set in Kenya during vicious Mau Mau uprising. Rock Hudson, Sidney Poitier, and Wendy Hiller star. **DR14, ST112, ST174**

Something Short of Paradise
(1979, C, 91m, PG)
Romantic comedy pairing a movie-mad projectionist (David Steinberg) and journalist (Susan Sarandon). **CO1, ST194, XT31**

Something To Hide see *Shattered* (1972)

Something To Sing About
(1937, C, 82m, NR)
A bandleader goes Hollywood. James Cagney and William Frawley star. Original running time: 93 minutes. **ST24**

Something Wicked This Way Comes
(1983, C, 94m, PG)
The mysterious Mr. Dark and his Pandemonium Circus promise to make everyone's wishes come true—for a very high price. It's up to two small boys and an elderly man to stop him. Jason Robards and Jonathan Pryce

star in this version of Ray Bradbury's story. **FA8, HO19, SF13, ST185**

Something Wild (1986, C, 113m, R)
Unique comedy-drama about an investment analyst "kidnapped" by a free-spirited woman, who drags him off to her high school reunion, where they run into her ex-husband. Jeff Daniels, Melanie Griffith, and Ray Liotta star, with Margaret Colin, Tracey Walter, and, in cameo roles, directors John Waters (as a car salesman) and John Sayles (as a motorcycle cop). Jonathan Demme directed; written by Max Frye. Outstanding use of rock music, including several versions of "Wild Thing." Full of surprises; terrific performances by three leads, inventive direction. **CO2, CO12, CU1, DT35, DT112, DT132, ST93, XT18,** *Highly Recommended*

Sometimes a Great Notion
(1971, C, 114m, PG)
Drama of logging family in the Pacific Northwest, adapted from Ken Kesey's novel, starring Paul Newman (who also directed), Henry Fonda, Lee Remick, Michael Sarrazin, and Richard Jaeckel. Enjoyable without ever really getting off the ground dramatically. Jaeckel has one terrific scene. **DR8, DR19, ST71, ST162**

Sometimes They Come Back
(1991, C, 100m, NR)
Stephen King story of dead gang of punks who return as zombies to haunt the brother of a schoolteacher they killed many years ago. Tim Matheson and Brooke Adams star. Originally made for TV. **HO6, WR15**

Somewhere in Time (1980, C, 103m, PG)
Time-travel romance about a man so enthralled by a dead woman's portrait that he wills himself into the past and into her life. Christopher Reeve and Jane Seymour star. Has small but devoted cult following. **DR1, SF4**

Somewhere Tomorrow
(1983, C, 87m, NR)
Teen-age girl bumps her head and believes she's seeing the ghost of a boy killed in a plane crash. Family drama stars Sarah Jessica Parker. **FA7**

Sommersby (1993, C, 112m, PG-13)
Remake of French drama *The Return of Martin Guerre* switches setting to post–Civil War period, with tale of veteran returning to wife as gentleman he never was, her beginning to suspect he might be an impersonator. Richard Gere and Jodie Foster star, with Larry Flaherty, Wendell Wellman, Bill Pullman, and James Earl Jones. Directed by John Amiel.

DR1, DR2, DR5, FF8, ST75, ST84, ST118, *Recommended*

Son of Dracula (1943, B&W, 78m, NR)
Classic horror tale with misleading title; it's about the count himself. He's traveling through the American South. Lon Chaney, Jr., stars, with Louise Allbritton and Robert Paige. Directed by Robert Siodmak. **HF7, HO1, HO5, ST27**

Son of Flubber (1963, B&W, 100m, G)
Sequel to *The Absent-Minded Professor*, with more inventions and trouble. Fred MacMurray and Keenan Wynn star. **FA1**

Son of Frankenstein
(1939, B&W, 99m, NR)
The offspring of the famed scientist resurrects his father's creation, with the usual catastrophic results. Basil Rathbone stars, with Boris Karloff as The Monster and Bela Lugosi as Ygor. **HF10, HO1, HO20, ST119, ST143**

Son of Lassie (1945, C, 102m, NR)
The plucky collie's offspring does a stint in World War II in this drama costarring Peter Lawford, Donald Crisp, June Lockhart, Nigel Bruce, and Helen Koford (Terry Moore). **FA5**

Son of Paleface (1952, C, 95m, NR)
Follow-up to *Paleface* finds Bob Hope reunited with Jane Russell. Roy Rogers joins in the fun in this Western comedy. **ST108, ST188, WE14**

Son of Sinbad (1955, C, 88m, NR)
Sinbad's son carries on his father's legacy of adventure and romance. Dale Robertson stars, with Sally Forrest, Lili St. Cyr, and Vincent Price. **AC15, ST179**

Son of the Morning Star
(1991, C, 186m, PG-13)
The story of America's most notorious Indian battle, the June 1876 encounter on the banks of the Little Big Horn. Gary Cole stars as George Armstrong Custer, with Rosanna Arquette as his wife, Terry O'Quinn, David Strathairn, Dean Stockwell, George American Horse, and Rodney A. Grant. Adapted from the magnificent nonfiction work by Evan Connell. Originally made for TV. Decent dramatization but no match for the book's peerless narrative. **HF6, ST208, WE1, WE4**

Song of Arizona (1946, B&W, 67m, NR)
An outlaw entrusts his son with stolen money, and his gang sets out after the boy; only Roy Rogers can save the day. **ST188**

Song Is Born, A (1948, C, 113m, NR)
Musical remake of comedy classic *Ball of Fire*, about attempts by professor to learn more about jazz with help of burlesque dancer.

Danny Kaye and Virginia Mayo star, with Hugh Herbert, musical guest stars Benny Goodman, Louis Armstrong, Charlie Barnet, Lionel Hampton, Tommy Dorsey. Directed by Howard Hawks. **DT53, MU14, ST120**

Song of Bernadette
(1943, B&W, 156m, NR)
Jennifer Jones won an Oscar for her portrayal of the young French girl who saw a vision in Lourdes and was ostracized by her village, only to be vindicated years later by sainthood. With William Eythe, Charles Bickford, and Vincent Price. **CL13, DR4, ST179, XT3**

Song of Love (1947, B&W, 119m, NR)
Katharine Hepburn plays pianist Clara Schumann; Paul Henreid, her composer husband Robert in this standard Hollywood biography. With Robert Walker as Brahms. **MU5, ST103**

Song of Nevada (1944, B&W, 75m, NR)
Roy Rogers and friends come to the aid of a girl who's being terrorized by outlaws. Dale Evans and Bob Nolan and the Sons of the Pioneers costar. **ST188**

Song of Norway (1970, C, 142m, G)
The life of Norwegian composer Edvard Grieg, starring Florence Henderson, Toralv Maurstad, and Edward G. Robinson. **MU5, ST186**

Song of Texas (1953, B&W, 54m, NR)
Roy Rogers helps an alcoholic cowboy sober up and regain his pride. Bob Nolan and the Sons of the Pioneers vocalize. **ST188**

Song of the Islands, (1942, C, 75m, NR)
Betty Grable musical has her welcoming Victor Mature as a newcomer to her island paradise. With Jack Oakie and Thomas Mitchell. **ST91**

Song of the Thin Man
(1947, B&W, 86m, NR)
Sixth (and last) *Thin Man* film has Nick and Nora Charles aboard a gambling ship when a murder is committed. William Powell and Myrna Loy star, with Dean Stockwell (as Nick, Jr.), Keenan Wynn, and Gloria Grahame. **CL15, HF5, MY17, ST142, ST176, ST208, WR12,** *Recommended*

Song Remains the Same, The
(1976, C, 136m, NR)
Led Zeppelin's "home movie" mixes concert footage with fantasy sequences. **MU11**

Song to Remember, A (1945, C, 113m, NR)
Cornel Wilde plays Frederic Chopin in this biography costarring Paul Muni and Merle Oberon (as George Sand). **MU5**

Song Without End (1960, C, 141m, NR)
Lavish bio of composer-pianist Franz Liszt,
starring Dirk Bogarde, with Capucine,
Genevieve Page, and Patricia Morison. Co-
directed by Charles Vidor (who died during
production) and George Cukor. **DT32, MU5,
ST14**

Songwriter (1984, C, 94m, R)
Two country singers plot to "sting" a greedy
promoter in this amiable comedy starring
Willie Nelson and Kris Kristofferson. With
Lesley Anne Warren and Rip Torn. Directed
by Alan Rudolph. Plenty of fine music from
both leads, some zingers on music business.
CO8, DT110, ST216, *Recommended*

Sons of Katie Elder, The
(1965, C, 122m, NR)
Four brothers set out to avenge their mother's
death in this spirited Western starring John
Wayne and Dean Martin, with Martha Hyer,
Michael Anderson, Jr., George Kennedy, and
Dennis Hopper. Directed by Henry Hathaway.
ST110, ST149, ST224, WE5

Sons of the Desert (1933, B&W, 69m, NR)
Classic Laurel and Hardy comedy, with the
boys off to a convention for their lodge, then
concocting a coverup story for their wives.
CL10, ST133, *Essential, Highly Recommended*

Sons of the Pioneers
(1942, B&W, 61m, NR)
Roy Rogers is hired by a sheriff to help exterminate a particularly verminous band of outlaws. **ST188**

Sophia Loren: Her Own Story
(1980, C, 150m, NR)
The international star plays herself (and her
mother) in this biographical drama, costar-
ring John Gavin as Cary Grant, Rip Torn as
Carlo Ponti, and Edmund Purdom as Vittorio
De Sica. Originally made for TV. **DR4,
DT37, ST141, ST216**

Sophie's Choice (1982, C, 157m, R)
Intense drama, highlighted by Meryl Streep's
Oscar-winning performance as a concentra-
tion camp survivor living in postwar Brook-
lyn. Kevin Kline and Peter MacNicol play the
two men in her life. Adapted from William
Styron's novel. Directed by Alan J. Pakula.
Streep's sensational but movie tries to copy
book's excessive length to no good end.
**DR1, DR2, DR19, DT94, ST127, ST210,
XT3, XT9**

Sophie's Place see *Crooks and Coronets*

Sorcerer (1977, C, 122m, PG)
Remake of classic French adventure thriller
Wages of Fear, about quartet of men driving

trucks loaded with nitroglycerine over treach-
erous mountain roads in South America. Roy
Scheider, Bruno Cremer, Francisco Rabal, and
Amidou star. Directed by William Friedkin.
Atmospheric music by Tangerine Dream.
Underrated; if not up to impossibly high
standards of original, it does have its own
virtues. **AC12, AC24, FF8,** *Recommended*

Sorcerers, The (1967, C, 87m, NR)
British horror film stars Boris Karloff and
Catherine Lacey as husband-and-wife team
trying to experiment with domination of
will. With Ian Ogilvy and Susan George.
Directed by Michael Reeves, who picked up
cult following for his short career. **CU4,
HO20, ST119**

Sorority House Massacre
(1986, C, 74m, R)
A madman preys on the snobby sisters of
Theta Omega Theta, but his focus is on the
newest pledge, an orphan who suffers from
nightmares. **HO12**

Sorrow and the Pity, The
(1970, B&W, 260m, PG)
Epic documentary portrait of France during
the German Occupation and the aftershocks
still felt today. Marcel Ophuls directed.
CU16, DT92, *Essential, Highly Recommended*

Sorrowful Jones
(1949, B&W, 88m, NR)
Oft-filmed Damon Runyon story of Little
Miss Marker, the orphan left with a racetrack
hustler. Bob Hope stars, with Lucille Ball and
William Demarest. **ST108**

Sorrows of Satan, The
(1926, B&W, 111m, NR)
Silent drama from director D.W. Griffith
about two writers in love; he gives in to the
blandishments of the devil (in disguise).
Ricardo Cortez and Carol Dempster star, with
Adolphe Menjou. **DT52, HO10**

Sorry, Wrong Number
(1948, B&W, 89m, NR)
Barbara Stanwyck stars in this classic thriller
about a woman who overhears her own murder being plotted but can't get anyone to
believe her. Burt Lancaster costars. **MY1,
MY3, ST129, ST206,** *Essential, Recommended*

Sotto, Sotto (1984, C, 105m, NR)
Italian comedy from director Lina
Wertmuller of a woman (Veronica Lario) who
falls in love with a longtime woman friend
(Luisa de Santis). When her husband finds
out, he goes berserk. **DT137**

Soul Man (1986, C, 101m, PG-13)
Prospective law school student ups his

chances for admission to Harvard when he poses as a black. C. Thomas Howell stars, with Rae Dawn Chong and James Earl Jones. **CO2, CO18, CO20, ST118**

Soul to Soul (1971, C, 95m, NR)
A gathering of soul, jazz, and gospel stars to celebrate the fourteenth anniversary of Ghanian independence. Performers include Wilson Pickett, Roberta Flack, and Ike and Tina Turner. **MU10**

Sound of Music, The (1965, C, 174m, G)
A novice becomes the governess for the Von Trapp children and teaches them and their widowed father the value of love. This film adaptation of the hit Broadway musical won five Academy Awards, including Best Picture and Director (Robert Wise). Julie Andrews and Christopher Plummer star. Shamelessly and aggressively heart-tugging. My two viewings will last me a lifetime. **DT140, FA9, MU2, MU5, MU7, ST2, XT1, XT6**

Sounder (1972, C, 105m, G)
Drama of a black family's struggle in the rural South to survive hardships and injustice, starring Paul Winfield, Cicely Tyson, and Kevin Hooks. Directed by Martin Ritt. Moving, simple story. **DR14, DT105, ST230,** *Recommended*

South Central (1992, C, 99m, R)
Urban drama of ex-black gang member released from prison, trying to set his son on the right path. Bryon Keith Minns stars, with La Rita Shelby and Christian Coleman. Written and directed by Steve Anderson. **DR7, DR14, DR15**

South of St. Louis (1949, C, 88m, NR)
Western tale of three parties in land dispute. Joel McCrea, Zachary Scott, and Douglas Kennedy star, with Alexis Smith and Dorothy Malone. **ST144, WE6**

South of Santa Fe (1942, B&W, 54m, NR)
Roy Rogers falls in love with a young woman who owns a gold mine. **ST188**

South of the Border
(1939, B&W, 71m, NR)
Gene Autry and Smiley Burnette head off to Mexico for adventure and a few tunes, too. Duncan Renaldo (TV's Cisco Kid) costars. **ST5**

South Pacific (1958, C, 171m, NR)
Rodgers and Hammerstein's Broadway smash about Navy nurses on the Pacific Islands during World War II. Mitzi Gaynor and Rossano Brazzi star, with John Kerr, Ray Walston, and Juanita Hall. Directed by Joshua Logan. Comes on strong—way strong. Fast-forward

to musical numbers, especially Gaynor's. **FA9, MU2**

Southern Comfort (1981, C, 106m, R)
Survival adventure of a Louisiana National Guard troop on weekend maneuvers, lost in the swamps, harassed by vengeful Cajuns. Powers Boothe and Keith Carradine star, with Fred Ward and Peter Coyote. Walter Hill directed; music by Ry Cooder. Expert direction builds tension to breaking point. **AC24, DR27, DT56, XT26,** *Highly Recommended*

Southerner, The (1945, B&W, 91m, NR)
Jean Renoir directed this drama of an American farm family struggling against all odds to make a living. Zachary Scott, Betty Field, and Beulah Bondi star. **DT104**

Southward Ho! (1939, B&W, 54m, NR)
Roy Rogers plays a cowpoke with an itchin' for the warmer climes. **ST188**

Soylent Green (1973, C, 97m, PG)
In the year 2022, a policeman (Charlton Heston) investigates the death of an executive whose company makes soylent green, the only foodstuff left on earth. Edward G. Robinson (in his last film) costars. **SF8, ST186**

Space Rage (1986, C, 78m, R)
A gang of convicts on a penitentiary planet stage a revolt. Skilled weapons specialists are called in to quell the disturbance. Richard Farnsworth and Michael Paré star. **SF17**

Space Raiders (1983, C, 82m, PG)
A young boy and a band of mercenaries battle an evil intergalactic dictator. Vince Edwards stars. **SF13**

Spaceballs (1987, C, 96m, PG13)
Mel Brooks parody of *Star Wars* and other science fiction films has evil dictator plotting to steal the atmosphere of a neighboring planet. Brooks stars in two roles, with Daphne Zuniga, Bill Pullman, John Candy, and Rick Moranis. Some laughs but this isn't exactly a genre that needed ridicule. **CO7, CO14, DT17, SF21**

SpaceCamp (1986, C, 107m, PG)
At an astronaut training school, a group of young students and their instructor are accidentally launched into space. Kate Capshaw and Lea Thompson star. **SF3**

Spaced Invaders (1990, C, 100m, PG)
Five aliens, mistaking an Earth radio station broadcast of "War of the Worlds" as an invitation, invade a small town in the Midwest. Family sci-fi comedy stars Douglas Barr and Royal Dano. **FA8, SF13**

Spacehunter: Adventures in the Forbidden Zone (1983, C, 90m, PG)
Science fiction adventure, starring Peter Strauss and Molly Ringwald, who rescue three beautiful women from the vicious half man/half machine, Overdog (Michael Ironside). **SF3, SF13**

Spalding Gray: Terrors of Pleasure (1988, C, 60m, NR)
Comic monologue from the man who loves to talk about himself, this one about his dream of owning land. Originally made for cable TV. **CO16**

Spanish Gardener, The (1956, C, 96m, NR)
British drama of diplomat's son becoming attached to domestic worker, with his father's jealousy provoking a frameup. Dirk Bogarde stars, with Maureen Swanson, Jon Whiteley, and Cyril Cusack. Adapted from the A.J. Cronin novel. **DR23, ST14**

Spanish Main, The (1945, C, 100m, NR)
Swashbuckler features Paul Henreid as dashing pirate, with Maureen O'Hara, Walter Slezak, and Binnie Barnes. **AC15, ST167**

Sparkle (1976, C, 100m, PG)
Three friends form a singing trio in this fictional story based on the early career of The Supremes. Irene Cara and Philip Michael Thomas star. **DR12, DR14, MU4**

Sparrows (1926, B&W, 84m, NR)
Silent melodrama starring Mary Pickford as the protector of a group of orphans. **CL12**

Spartacus (1960, C, 185m, NR)
Epic tale of the Roman gladiator who led a slave revolt and paid a dear price. Kirk Douglas stars, with Jean Simmons, Laurence Olivier, Peter Ustinov (an Oscar winner), Charles Laughton, Tony Curtis, and Woody Strode. Stanley Kubrick directed; Dalton Trumbo adapted Howard Fast's book. Video version contains footage restored for 1991 theatrical rerelease; for controversial bath scene between Olivier and Curtis, Anthony Hopkins dubbed the late Olivier's lines. Available in letterboxed format. Solid spectacle, with Olivier, Laughton, and Ustinov providing delightfully hammy counterpoint to Douglas's usual square-jawed heroics. **CU19, DR5, DT68, ST57, ST132, ST168, XT4**, *Recommended*

Spawning, The see *Piranha II: The Spawning*

Speak Easily (1932, B&W, 82m, NR)
Buster Keaton plays a professor tangled up with an acting troupe in this comedy. Jimmy Durante costars, with Thelma Todd, Hedda Hopper, and Sidney Toler. **CL7, DT66**

Special Bulletin (1983, C, 105m, NR)
Riveting drama, presented like a real TV news story with two studio anchors doing running commentary about radicals engaged in dangerous protest against nuclear weapons. Ed Flanders, Kathryn Walker, Roxanne Hart, and Christopher Allport star. Originally made for TV. The reality-bending frame lifts this one above the ordinary. **DR7**, *Recommended*

Special Day, A (1977, C, 106m, NR)
Sophia Loren and Marcello Mastroianni star in this bittersweet story; a housewife and a homosexual have a chance encounter on a day when virtually everyone else in Rome is attending a parade celebrating Hitler's visit. Stars are fine but drama seems forced. **FF2, ST141, ST154** .

Special Delivery (1976, C, 99m, PG)
Action comedy of bank robber and nutty artist teaming up to recover loot and elude killers. Bo Svenson and Cybill Shepherd star, with Michael Gwynne, Tom Atkins, Sorrell Booke, and Jeff Goldblum. **CO10, ST90**

Special Effects (1984, C, 106m, R)
A desperate movie producer intends to use footage from a real murder in his latest production, but the dead actress's husband is out for revenge. Zoe Tamerlis and Eric Bogosian star. Larry Cohen directed. **DT28**

Speckled Band, The (1931, B&W, 90m, NR)
Raymond Massey plays Sherlock Holmes, as the famed sleuth helps a girl whose sister has been murdered. Angela Baddeley costars. **HF14**

Speed Zone (1989, C, 95m, PG)
In the grand tradition of the *Cannnonball Run* action comedies, here's more cross-country racing with an all-star cast. John Candy, Eugene Levy, Joe Flaherty, Tim Matheson, and Peter Boyle star, with cameo appearances from Brooke Shields (as herself), The Smothers Brothers, Carl Lewis, Michael Spinks, and Lee Van Cleef. **CO9, CO14, ST221**

Speedway (1968, C, 94m, NR)
Elvis Presley plays a singing race car driver who tries to romance his tax auditor (Nancy Sinatra). **ST178**

Spellbound (1945, B&W, 111m, NR)
A psychiatrist (Ingrid Bergman) and her patient (Gregory Peck) fall in love in this Alfred Hitchcock blend of suspense and romance. With Leo G. Carroll. Salvador Dali contributed sketches for several dream sequences. Peck's stiffness detracts from romantic angle. **DT57, MY5, ST13, ST171**

Spetters (1980, C, 115m, R)
From Holland, a contemporary drama of aimless youth, with Rutger Hauer as a motorcycle racing champion. Paul Verhoeven directed. **FF7**

Sphinx (1981, C, 117m, PG)
Adventure of British woman (Lesley-Anne Down) exploring an Egyptian tomb, encountering usual blend of menace and romance. With Frank Langella, Maurice Ronet, and John Gielgud. Directed by Franklin Schaffner. Predictable to a fault. **ST86**

Spider Baby (1964, B&W, 80m, NR)
Lon Chaney, Jr., stars as the chauffeur for a family of cannibals in this horror tale. Lon warbles the title tune, too. **ST27**

Spider Woman (1944, B&W, 62m, NR)
Sherlock Holmes (Basil Rathbone) and Dr. Watson (Nigel Bruce) take on a wily adversary, a woman (Gale Sondergaard) whose gang poisons wealthy businessmen and disguises the crimes as suicides. Also known as *Sherlock Holmes and the Spider Woman*. **HF14**

Spiders (1919, B&W/C, 137m, NR)
Silent film from German director Fritz Lang about a criminal organization. Color tinted. **DT70, FF3**

Spider's Strategem, The
(1970, C, 100m, NR)
Italian drama of young man returning to town where his father, an anti-Fascist, was assassinated thirty years before. Directed by Bernardo Bertolucci; photographed by Vittorio Storaro. Adapted from a story by Jorge Luis Borges. **DT13**

Spies (1928, B&W, 90m, NR)
A silent film classic from German director Fritz Lang, about a government agent on the trail of a master spy and his gang. **DT70, FF3**

Spies Like Us (1985, C, 103m, PG)
Chevy Chase and Dan Aykroyd star as two bumblers sent by the State Department on a diversionary mission. Features many cameo appearances from such directors as Costa-Gavras, Joel Coen, Martin Brest, and Terry Gilliam, as well as a special appearance by Bob Hope. **CO13, CO15, CU17, DT27, ST108**

Spike of Bensonhurst (1988, C, 101m, R)
Comic tale of a Brooklyn Romeo whose exploits with two young ladies land him in trouble with the local Mob boss. Sasha Mitchell and Ernest Borgnine star, with Sylvia Miles, Maria Pitillo and Talisa Soto. Directed by Paul Morrissey. Low-rent laughs. **DT90**

Spinout (1966, C, 90m, NR)
Elvis Presley at the racetrack, singing and shifting gears (and women). Shelley Fabares and Diane McBain costar. **ST178**

Spiral Staircase, The
(1946, B&W, 83m, NR)
Dorothy McGuire plays a mute servant who is sure there's a killer hiding in her house but can't get anyone to believe her. Directed by Robert Siodmak. **MY3**

Spirit of Tattoo see *Irezumi*

Spirit of St. Louis, The
(1957, C, 138m, NR)
James Stewart plays Charles A. Lindbergh in this drama which focuses on his historic transatlantic solo flight. Billy Wilder directed. Widescreen will be lost on video. Stewart's good but film is finally too static. **AC11, CL2, CU20, DT139, ST207**

Spirit of the Beehive, The
(1973, C, 95m, NR)
Spanish drama of a little girl (Ana Torrent) fascinated by the Frankestein monster after she sees the original Boris Karloff film. **FF7, HF10**

Spite Marriage (1929, B&W, 89m, NR)
Buster Keaton's last silent film has him playing a pants presser who adores an actress. With Dorothy Sebastian and Edward Earle. **CL11, DT66**

Spitfire (1934, B&W, 88m, NR)
Early Katharine Hepburn film has her playing a naive girl in love with a married man (Robert Young). **ST103**

Splash (1984, C, 111m, PG)
A mermaid falls for a young boy, contrives to meet him (on land) when they're a bit older and really ready for love. Daryl Hannah, Tom Hanks, John Candy, and Eugene Levy star. Directed by Ron Howard on location in New York City. Sweet comedy buoyed by strong leads. **CO1, CO14, CO20, DT58, ST97, XT9,** *Recommended*

Splendor in the Grass (1961, C, 124m, NR)
Tragic tale, set in a small town in the 1920s Midwest, about a thwarted love affair that shatters the life of a young girl. Natalie Wood and Warren Beatty (his film debut) star, with Pat Hingle, Sandy Dennis, Phyllis Diller, and Barbara Loden. Elia Kazan directed; written by Oscar winner William Inge. Intensely felt, if a bit long. **DR1, DR9, DR26, DT65, ST10, XT21,** *Recommended*

Split Decisions (1988, C, 95m, R)
Gene Hackman plays an ex-boxer with two sons in the fight game: one has been ordered

by the Mob to throw a big fight, while the other wants to go to college and try out for the Olympics. **DR22, ST96**

Split Image (1982, C, 111m, R)
When an impressionable college athlete joins a commune-like cult, his parents have him kidnapped by a ruthless deprogrammer. Michael O'Keefe, Karen Allen, Brian Dennehy, James Woods, Peter Fonda, and Elizabeth Ashley star. Good intentions but only extraordinary thing is Woods's performance as deprogrammer. **DR7, DR8, ST233**

Split Second (1953, B&W, 85m, NR)
An escaped convict (Stephen McNally) holds a group of people hostage in a Nevada town—unaware that it's a nuclear bomb test site. With Alexis Smith, Jan Sterling, and Keith Andes. Directed by Dick Powell. **MY1, ST175**

Split Second (1992, C, 90m, R)
Futuristic cops and robbers story set in 2008 London, starring Rutger Hauer as a policeman in search of a monster who killed his partner. With Kim Cattrall, Neil Duncan, and Michael J. Pollard. **SF17**

Spoilers, The (1942, B&W, 87m, NR)
Action on the Yukon frontier, with prospectors John Wayne and Randolph Scott tussling over dancehall girl Marlene Dietrich. **ST55, ST197, ST224, WE10**

Spontaneous Combustion
(1989, C, 97m, R)
Horror tale of a man whose parents were subjected to a radiation experiment in the 1950s; he has grown up with extraordinary powers (see title). Directed by Tobe Hooper. **SF5**

Spooks Run Wild (1941, B&W, 69m, NR)
The East Side Kids spend the night in a haunted mansion and run into Bela Lugosi. **ST143**

Spotswood (1992, C, 97m, NR)
Australian comedy about an efficiency expert giving the white-glove treatment to a moccasin factory. Anthony Hopkins stars, with Ben Mendelsohn and Bruno Lawrence. Also known as *The Efficiency Expert.* **FF5, ST109**

Springtime in the Rockies
(1937, B&W, 60m, NR)
Gene Autry is foreman on a ranch that switches from cattle to sheep. **ST5**

Springtime in the Rockies
(1942, C, 91m, NR)
Colorful musical about a Broadway couple's marital and professional ups and downs. Betty Grable and John Payne star, with Car-

men Miranda, Cesar Romero, Jackie Gleason, and Harry James and His Band. **MU4, ST91**

Springtime in the Sierras
(1947, B&W, 75m, NR)
Roy Rogers battles villainous big-game poachers. Andy Devine provides the laughs. **ST188**

Spy in Black, The (1939, B&W, 82m, NR)
Espionage drama set in World War I Scotland, starring Conrad Veidt as a devious German. Directed by Michael Powell; written by Emeric Pressburger. **DT99, MY6, MY15**

Spy Who Came in From the Cold, The
(1965, B&W, 112m, NR)
John Le Carré's story of a Cold Warrior trapped betwen duty and his conscience, starring Richard Burton, with Claire Bloom and Oskar Werner. Directed by Martin Ritt. One of Burton's best performances; it should have won him an Oscar. **DT105, MY6, ST22, WR18, XT28,** *Recommended*

Spy Who Loved Me, The
(1977, C, 125m, PG)
James Bond (Roger Moore) and a sexy Russian agent (Barbara Bach) must join forces to stop a mad mastermind (Curt Jurgens) from destroying the world. Spectacular stunts, especially in the opening sequence. **HF2,** *Recommended*

Square Dance (1987, C, 112m, PG-13)
A teen-ager leaves her granddaddy's Texas farm and strikes out for Ft. Worth and a reunion with her estranged mother. Winona Ryder, Jane Alexander, Rob Lowe, and Jason Robards star. Also known as *Home Is Where The Heart Is.* **DR8, DR9, ST185**

Squeeze, The (1980, C, 100m, R)
Lee Van Cleef plays a retired New York thief who decides to crack one more safe. With Karen Black, Edward Albert, and Lionel Stander. **ST221**

Squeeze, The (1987, C, 101m, R)
A con man and a debt collector team to solve a murder case involving the New York State lottery. Michael Keaton and Rae Dawn Chong star in this comic mystery. **MY11, MY17, ST122**

Squirm (1976, C, 92m, PG)
During a storm, a high voltage tower falls to the ground and turns the worms into voracious eating machines who devour everything in their path, including humans. **HO16**

Squizzy Taylor (1982, C, 89m, NR)
True saga of an Australian gangster who rose to fame in 1920s Melbourne. David Atkins stars. **AC22, FF5**

Stacking (1987, C, 109m, PG)
Coming-of-age drama set in the rural West of
the 1950s, starring Megan Follows, Christine
Lahti, and Frederic Forrest. **DR9**

Stacy's Knights (1983, C, 95m, PG)
Young woman (Andra Millian) addicted to
gambling is out for revenge when her teacher
(Kevin Costner) is killed by crooked casino
boss's henchmen. **AC19, ST38**

Stage Door (1937, B&W, 92m, NR)
A New York boardinghouse is the scene for
this comedy-drama about young women
with show-biz ambitions. Katharine Hep-
burn, Ginger Rogers, Lucille Ball, and Eve
Arden star. Morrie Ryskind and Anthony
Veiller adapted the Edna Ferber-George S.
Kaufman play. Directed by Gregory La Cava.
Witty, with first-rate performances all
around. **CL7, DR20, ST103, ST187,**
Recommended

Stage Door Canteen
(1943, B&W, 132m, NR)
Fictional story of a romance between a G.I.
and a hostess at the famous Stage Door Canteen is really an excuse to showcase a variety
of stars, including Katharine Hepburn, Harpo
Marx, Benny Goodman, Count Basie, Tallulah Bankhead, Edgar Bergen, Ethel Waters,
Gertrude Lawrence, Ethel Merman, and
many more. **MU15, ST103, ST152**

Stage Fright (1950, B&W, 110m, NR)
An actress's husband is dead, and suspicion
falls on a young drama student. Alfred Hitchcock thriller starring Jane Wyman and Marlene Dietrich. **DT57, ST55**

Stage Struck (1936, B&W, 86m, NR)
Busby Berkeley musical starring Dick Powell
and Joan Blondell in a story about life behind the scenes of a big show. **DT12,
ST175**

Stage Struck (1958, C, 95m, NR)
Remake of *Morning Glory*, with Susan Strasberg playing Katharine Hepburn's role of the
impressionable young actress. With Henry
Fonda, Joan Greenwood, Christopher Plummer, and Herbert Marshall. Sidney Lumet
directed. **CL7, CU18, DT78, ST71**

Stagecoach (1939, B&W, 96m, NR)
Legendary Western, starring John Wayne as
the Ringo Kid, the outlaw who comes to the
aid of a stagecoach in peril. With Claire
Trevor, Andy Devine, John Carradine, Oscar
winner Thomas Mitchell, Louise Platt,
George Bancroft, Donald Meek, Tim Holt,
and Tom Tyler. Directed by John Ford.
Wayne's breakthrough role, and Ford's first

Western shot in Monument Valley. **DT44,
ST224, WE3, XT4,** *Essential, Recommended*

Stakeout (1987, C, 115m, R)
Crime comedy-thriller about two cops
assigned to watch a waitress whose escaped
con boyfriend may show up, with one cop
falling in love with her. Richard Dreyfuss,
Emilio Estevez, Madeleine Stowe, and Aidan
Quinn star. Directed by John Badham. Dreyfuss and Stowe are terrific. **CO10, MY3,
ST60, ST209,** *Recommended*

Stalag 17 (1953, B&W, 120m, NR)
William Holden won an Academy Award for
his portrayal of a cynical sergeant in a World
War II POW camp. Outstanding supporting
cast includes Don Taylor, Otto Preminger,
Robert Strauss, Harvey Lembeck, and Peter
Graves. Billy Wilder directed. Deft blend of
low comedy and high drama; quintessential
Holden role. **AC7, DT100, DT139, ST106,
XT2,** *Essential, Highly Recommended*

Stalin (1992, C, 173m, NR)
Robert Duvall plays the Soviet tyrant in this
biographical drama. With Julia Ormand, Jeroen Krabbe, Joan Plowright, and Maximilian
Schell as Lenin. Directed by Ivan Passer. Originally made for cable TV. **DR4, ST63**

Stalking Moon, The (1969, C, 109m, G)
In the Old West, a woman who has been a
captive of the Apaches escapes with her half-
breed son and seeks protection from an
Army scout. Eva Marie Saint and Gregory
Peck star. **ST171, WE8**

Stand and Deliver (1988, C, 105m, PG)
True-life drama of Los Angeles high school
math teacher who inspired his underprivileged
kids to study hard and perform beyond expectations on standardized tests. Edward James
Olmos stars, with Lou Diamond Phillips, Andy
Garcia, and Rosana de Soto. Originally made
for public TV. Olmos is good; dramatics are
pretty standard. **DR6, DR15, DR25**

Stand by Me (1986, C, 87m, R)
Comedy-drama of four small-town pals (Wil
Wheaton, River Phoenix, Corey Feldman,
and Jerry O'Connell) who strike out on an
adventure to find a missing boy. With Kiefer
Sutherland, Casey Siemaszko, and John
Cusack; narrated by Richard Dreyfuss. Based
on a story by Stephen King; directed by Rob
Reiner. The loose-limbed comedy works bet-
ter than the self-conscious drama. **DR9,
DR26, DT103, ST60, WR15**

Stand Easy see *Down Among the Z-Men*

Stand Up and Cheer (1934, B&W, 80m, NR)
Shirley Temple does her part to chase away

the Depression blues in this musical comedy starring Warner Baxter, Madge Evans, and James Dunn. **ST213**

Stand-In (1937, B&W, 91m, NR)
Comedy poking fun at Hollywood, with Leslie Howard as a lawyer investigating Colossal Pictures, Joan Blondell as a perky stand-in, and Humphrey Bogart as a producer. **CL7, ST15**

Stanley & Iris (1990, C, 102m, PG-13)
Romantic drama involving an illiterate cook (Robert De Niro) and the factory worker (Jane Fonda) who teaches him to read. With Swoosie Kurtz and Martha Plimpton. Directed by Martin Ritt. **DR1, DT105, ST51, ST72**

Stanley and Livingstone
(1939, B&W, 101m, NR)
Historical drama of British explorer (Spencer Tracy) searching for famed missionary (Cedric Hardwicke) in the heart of uncharted Africa. With Richard Greene, Nancy Kelly, and Walter Brennan. **AC12, CL3, ST217**

Star, The (1952, B&W, 89m, NR)
Bette Davis drama of fading film star, with Sterling Hayden and Natalie Wood. **CL7, ST44**

Star Chamber, The (1983, C, 109m, R)
Young judge learns of secret tribunal that dispenses its own justice to criminals who beat the legal system. Michael Douglas, Hal Holbrook, and Yaphet Kotto star in this drama. **DR16, ST59**

Star Crystal (1985, C, 93m, R)
A group of scientist astronauts unknowingly pick up a new lifeform which begins to stalk them. **SF20**

STAR 80 (1983, C, 102m, R)
True story of model Dorothy Stratten and her murder by her manager-boyfriend. Mariel Hemingway and Eric Roberts star, with Cliff Robertson and Roger Rees. Bob Fosse directed. Same story dramatized in *Death of a Centerfold*. Director can't bring his usual artistry to bear on tabloid-style material. **DR6, DR13, DT47**

Star Is Born, A (1937, C, 111m, NR)
Classic tale of Hollywood marriage between fading star (Fredric March) and rising one (Janet Gaynor). Cowritten by Dorothy Parker; directed by William Wellman. **CL7, DR13, DT135, ST148**

Star Is Born, A (1954, C, 170m, G)
Judy Garland and James Mason star in this musical remake of the 1937 classic. Many outstanding numbers, including "The Man

That Got Away." With Jack Carson, Charles Bickford, and Tom Noonan. Directed by George Cukor. This version contains recently restored footage. A 154-minute version is also available. Longer version is must-see for crucial dramatic development, Judy's "Born in a Trunk" extravaganza. Widescreen is lost in either version. Both leads very strong in the best version of this story. **CL7, CU20, DR13, DT32, MU4, MU14, ST81, ST153,** *Essential, Highly Recommended*

Star Is Born, A (1976, C, 140m, R)
A rock 'n' roll remake of the familiar story. Kris Kristofferson plays a rock idol who marries Barbra Streisand, a promising singer, with tragic results. With Gary Busey, Paul Mazursky, Marta Heflin, Sally Kirkland, and Robert Englund. Oscar-winning song "Evergreen" is highlight of drab remake. **CU18, DT87, MU4, MU9, ST211**

Star of Midnight
(1935, B&W, 90m, NR)
Light-hearted mystery starring William Powell as a lawyer accused of murder, forced to prove his innocence. Ginger Rogers costars. **MY7, MY17, ST176, ST187**

Star Spangled Girl (1971, C, 92m, G)
Neil Simon comedy of squeaky-clean girl involved with two leftist college students. Sandy Duncan stars, with Tony Roberts and Tod Susman. **CO1, CO18, WR30**

Star Trek: The Motion Picture
(1979, C, 132m, G)
The *Enterprise* crew is brought back together to battle a strange force field before it can reach Earth. William Shatner and Leonard Nimoy star. Directed by Robert Wise. Video version adds twelve minutes of new footage. **CU10, DT140, FA8, SF3, SF13, SF23**

Star Trek II: The Wrath of Khan
(1982, C, 113m, PG)
Khan, a character introduced in the TV series, escapes from exile, looking to destroy Kirk and the rest of the universe. William Shatner and Ricardo Montalban star. Directed by Nicholas Meyer. **FA8, SF3, SF13, SF23**

Star Trek III: The Search for Spock
(1984, C, 105m, PG)
Kirk and his crew head out to find Spock (who "died" at the end of *Star Trek II*) so they can restore him with the essence held in Dr. McCoy's body. Meanwhile, the Klingons decide to get revenge against Kirk by capturing his son. William Shatner and DeForest Kelley star. Directed by Leonard Nimoy. **FA8, SF3, SF13, SF23, XT23**

Star Trek IV: The Voyage Home
(1986, C, 119m, PG)
A strange probe, which drains all energy, heads to Earth in search of whales, which are now extinct. Kirk and his crew decide to travel back to 1986 to retrieve a pair of whales, in order to save the Earth of their century. William Shatner and Leonard Nimoy (who directed) star. **FA8, SF3, SF4, SF13, SF23, XT23**

Star Trek V: The Final Frontier
(1989, C, 106m, PG)
A Vulcan (Laurence Luckinbill) forces the *Enterprise* to journey to a distant planet in this installment of the sci-fi series. Directed by William Shatner. **FA8, SF3, SF13, SF23, XT23**

Star Trek VI: The Undiscovered Country (1991, C, 109m, PG)
The Klingons try to make peace with Kirk and his crew in what is billed as the last *Star Trek* to feature the original veteran cast of the TV series. With Kim Cattrall, David Warner, Christopher Plummer, and in a small role, Christian Slater. Directed by Nicholas Meyer. **FA8, SF3, SF13, SF23, ST200**

Star Wars (1977, C, 121m, PG)
Landmark science fiction adventure about a young man (Mark Hamill) who helps rescue a rebel princess (Carrie Fisher) from the clutches of the Empire and goes on to become a general in the rebel forces. With Harrison Ford, Alec Guinness, Peter Cushing, and, as the voice of Darth Vader, James Earl Jones. Directed by George Lucas. Oscar winner for special effects. Two sequels: *The Empire Strikes Back* and *Return of the Jedi*. **DT77, FA8, SF11, SF13, SF15, SF16, SF23, ST43, ST74, ST95, ST118,** *Essential, Recommended*

Starchaser: The Legend of Orin
(1985, C, 107m, PG)
An animated tale about a young boy who leads a rebellion against an evil dictator. **FA10, SF13**

Stardust Memories (1980, B&W, 91m, PG)
Woody Allen comedy with very dark overtones, about a filmmaker who's frustrated with the demands of his fans, colleagues, and family. Echoes of 8½ and other Fellini movies abound. Charlotte Rampling, Jessica Harper, Marie-Christine Barrault, Tony Roberts, and Daniel Stern head the very large supporting cast. With Laraine Newman and Louise Lasser in small roles. Underrated film, criticized for its self-pitying tone, is actually more dramatically persuasive than most of Allen's recent work. **CO8, DT2, XT31,** *Recommended*

Stark (1985, C, 100m, NR)
Wichita cop in Vegas takes on the Mob in this action drama made as a pilot for a TV series. Marilu Henner and Nicolas Surovy star, with Pat Corley and Dennis Hopper. **AC9, ST110**

Starman (1984, C, 115m, PG)
An alien crash-lands in Wisconsin and retreats to a farm, where he transforms himself to look like a young widow's late husband. Karen Allen and Jeff Bridges star. John Carpenter directed. Likable romance stretched too far. **DR1, DR27, DT23, SF9, ST19**

Stars and Bars (1988, C, 94m, R)
British satire of contemporary art scene and American eccentrics, with English gallery representative trying to track down a valuable painting purchased by a nouveau riche American. Daniel Day-Lewis and Harry Dean Stanton head the cast. **CO2, CO17, ST48, ST205**

Stars and Stripes Forever
(1952, C, 89m, NR)
Clifton Webb plays American march music composer John Philip Sousa. With Robert Wagner, Ruth Hussey, and Debra Paget. **MU5, MU6**

Starstruck (1982, C, 95m, PG)
Australian musical comedy about a waitress (Jo Kennedy) with ambitions to be a famous singer. Directed by Gillian Armstrong. **DT7, FF5, MU4, MU9**

Start the Revolution Without Me
(1970, C, 98m, PG)
Wild comedy set during the French Revolution involving two mismatched sets of twins (Gene Wilder and Donald Sutherland). With Hugh Griffith, Jack MacGowran, Billie Whitelaw, Victor Spinetti, and Ewa Aulin; Orson Welles narrates. Directed by Bud Yorkin. Silly and irresistibly funny. **CO5, DT134, XT27,** *Recommended*

Starting Over (1979, C, 106m, R)
A newly divorced man falls in love with a vulnerable single woman, although he has trouble shaking his obnoxious ex-wife. Burt Reynolds, Jill Clayburgh, and Candice Bergen star in this romantic comedy. Alan J. Pakula directed. **CO1, DT94, ST31, ST183,** *Recommended*

State Fair (1945, C, 100m, NR)
Musical version of drama filmed in 1933, about a family's adventures at title event. Songs by Rodgers and Hammerstein. Jeanne Crain, Dana Andrews, Dick Haymes, and Viv-

ian Blaine star. Also known as *It Happened One Summer*. **FA9, MU6**

State Fair (1962, C, 118m, NR)
The second musical about an Iowa family's experiences at the title event. Pat Boone stars, with Bobby Darin, Pamela Tiffin, Ann-Margret, and Alice Faye. **FA9, MU6**

State of Grace (1990, C, 134m, R)
Violent urban crime melodrama starring Sean Penn as an undercover cop palling around with Irish-American thugs from old New York neighborhood. With Ed Harris, Gary Oldman, Robin Wright, John Turturro, and Burgess Meredith. Directed by Phil Joanou. Stylistic flourishes can't hide Penn's off-putting performance or elevate unsympathetic characters. Wright is easy on the eyes. **AC9, DR15, DR16, XT9**

State of Siege (1973, C, 120m, NR)
Based on a true story, this French-language political thriller concerns the kidnapping of an American diplomat (Yves Montand) in Latin America by guerrillas opposed to U.S. support of the country's secret police. Costa-Gavras directed. Wears its politics proudly but is dramatically wan. **FF1**

State of the Union (1948, B&W, 124m, NR)
Katharine Hepburn-Spencer Tracy comedy about a Presidential candidate and his fiercely independent wife. With Angela Lansbury and Van Johnson. Directed by Frank Capra. **CL15, DT22, ST103, ST131, ST217**

State of Things, The
(1982, B&W, 120m, NR)
Moody drama about a film crew on location in Portugal remaking the low-budget cult film, *The Day the World Ended*. Pointed behind-the-scenes look at today's filmmakers and their pretensions, directed by Wim Wenders, shot in English. Patrick Bauchau stars, with Sam Fuller, Allen Goorwitz, Paul Getty III, and, in a small role, Roger Corman. Recommended for people who can't get enough about the movies; others may find it studied and pretentious. **DR13, DT30, DT49, DT136**

State's Attorney (1932, B&W, 79m, NR)
John Barrymore plays the title role, a man in love with a woman and the bottle. With Helen Twelvetrees, William "Stage" Boyd, and Ralph Ince. **ST8**

Station West (1948, B&W, 92m, NR)
Western drama of undercover military officer investigating series of gold robberies. Dick Powell stars, with Jane Greer, Tom Powers, Steve Brodie, Raymond Burr, Agnes Moorehead, and Burl Ives. **ST175**

Statue, The (1971, C, 84m, R)
David Niven stars in this British comedy as a man who's the model for a seventy-foot statue with an inordinately large penis. With Virna Lisi, Robert Vaughn, and John Cleese. **CO15, CO17**

Stavisky (1974, C, 117m, PG)
Lavish drama about notorious French swindler of the 1930s, starring Jean-Paul Belmondo and Charles Boyer, with François Perier, Anny Duperey, Michel Lonsdale, and Gérard Depardieu in a bit part. Directed by Alain Resnais, with photography by Sacha Vierney and music by Stephen Sondheim. Lush trappings, but drama is a bit too muted. **FF1, ST11, ST16, ST52**

Stay As You Are (1978, C, 95m, NR)
Middle-aged man romances a teen-ager, who may be his illegitimate daughter. Marcello Mastroianni and Nastassja Kinski star. **ST154**

Stay Away, Joe (1968, C, 102m, NR)
Elvis Presley plays a Native American in this musical drama, with Burgess Meredith, Joan Blondell, and L.Q. Jones. **ST178**

Stay Hungry (1976, C, 103m, R)
Good ol' boy of the New South is torn between a career in real estate and his affection for a loony group of bodybuilders. Jeff Bridges, Sally Field, and Arnold Schwarzenegger star in this offbeat, engaging comedy. With R.G. Armstrong, Robert Englund, Helena Kallianiotes, Roger Mosley, Scatman Crothers, Fannie Flagg, Joanna Cassidy, and Ed Begley, Jr. Directed by Bob Rafelson. **CO2, ST19, ST66, ST195,** *Recommended*

Stay Tuned (1992, C, 87m, PG)
John Ritter and Pam Dawber star in this comedy about a married suburban couple trapped in their own TV, which is hooked up to a literal living hell of 666 channels run by ol' Lucifer himself (Jeffrey Jones). With David Tom, Heather McComb, and Eugene Levy. Lots of spoofs of TV shows and movies, with a six-minute animated sequence directed by Chuck Jones. **CO2, CO8, CO14, CO20, HO10**

Staying Alive (1983, C, 96m, PG)
This sequel to *Saturday Night Fever* has John Travolta trying to make it as a Broadway dancer. Directed by Sylvester Stallone. **DR12, MU4, ST204**

Staying Together (1989, C, 91m, R)
Three brothers in a small South Carolina town try to keep their family business from being sold off. Sean Astin, Tim Quill, and Dermot Mulroney star, with Stockard Channing, Melinda Dillon, and Levon Helm.

Directed by Lee Grant. **DR8, DR26, MU12, XT23**

Stealing Heaven (1988, C, 108m, R)
The Abelard and Heloise story, a forbidden affair between a teacher and his lovely young pupil, with Derek de Lint and Kim Thomson. An unrated version is also available: running time is 115 minutes. **CU10, DR3**

Stealing Home (1988, C, 98m, PG-13)
A former big-league pitcher recalls his youth when he hears of his babysitter's suicide. Mark Harmon stars, with Jodie Foster, Harold Ramis, and Blair Brown. **CO14, ST75**

Steamboat Bill, Jr. (1928, B&W, 71m, NR)
Buster Keaton plays a young man who has to prove himself to his father, a riverboat captain, in this silent classic. Finale, with cyclone destroying a town, is a highlight. **CL11, DT66,** *Essential, Recommended*

Steaming (1985, C, 95m, R)
The setting is a London steam bath for women, and the conversation is frank and revealing. Vanessa Redgrave, Sarah Miles, and Diana Dors star. Director Joseph Losey's last film. **DR23, ST182**

Steel Cowboy (1978, C, 100m, NR)
Trucker drama of independent misled into hauling rustled cattle. James Brolin stars, with Rip Torn, Strother Martin, and Jennifer Warren. Originally made for TV. **ST216**

Steel Helmet, The (1951, B&W, 84m, NR)
An American sergeant (Gene Evans) survives a massacre in North Korea and joins up with some other soldiers who have been cut off from their unit. Samuel Fuller directed. **AC3, DT49**

Steel Magnolias (1989, C, 118m, PG)
The intertwined lives of a group of women in a small Southern town are examined in this comedy-drama. Sally Field, Shirley MacLaine, Dolly Parton, Daryl Hannah, Olympia Dukakis, and Julia Roberts star, with Tom Skerritt and Sam Shepard. Based on the play by Robert Harling. **CO2, DR2, DR10, DR20, DR26, MU12, ST66, ST145**

Steele Justice (1987, C, 95m, R)
A Vietnam vet (Martin Kove) seeks revenge against a druglord who was a Vietcong general and the killer of the vet's best friend. Ronny Cox costars. **AC19**

Steelyard Blues (1973, C, 93m, PG)
Episodic comedy about a group of anti-establishment types and their pranks, starring Jane Fonda, Donald Sutherland, and Peter Boyle. **CO2, ST72**

Stella (1990, C, 106m, PG-13)
Updated version of *Stella Dallas*, the story of a woman who sacrifices for her illegitimate daughter. Bette Midler stars, with Trini Alvarado, John Goodman, Stephen Collins, and Marsha Mason. **CU18, DR2, DR10, ST156**

Stella Dallas (1937, B&W, 106m, NR)
Barbara Stanwyck stars in the classic soap opera of a woman who gives up everything for her daughter's happiness. Directed by King Vidor. **CL5, CL6, DT126, ST206,** *Essential*

St. Elmo's Fire (1985, C, 110m, R)
Melodramatic look at a group of friends fresh out of Georgetown University, trying to get on with their lives. Andrew McCarthy, Ally Sheedy, Rob Lowe, Demi Moore, Judd Nelson, Emilio Estevez, and Mare Winningham star. **DR7, XT12**

Step Lively (1944, B&W, 88m, NR)
Musical remake of *Room Service*, starring George Murphy as a wheeler-dealer producer. With Frank Sinatra, Adolphe Menjou, and Gloria DeHaven. **MU4, MU14, ST199**

Stepfather, The (1987, C, 89m, R)
A teen-age girl suspects her mother's new husband isn't entirely on the level, and she's right—he's a serial killer who sheds families and identities every few years. Terry O'Quinn and Jill Schoelen star, with Shelley Hack. **MY13, MY14,** *Recommended*

Stepfather II (1989, C, 86m, R)
Terry O'Quinn returns as the not-so-dear ol' dad, as he assumes a new identity and picks up with his murderous ways. With Meg Foster and Caroline Williams. **MY13, MY14**

Stephen King's Golden Years
(1991, C, 232m, NR)
Elderly janitor is exposed to chemicals in a laboratory, giving him new lease on life—and some very interested agents of the government on his tail. Keith Szarabajka and Frances Sternhagen star in this original screenplay from Stephen King. Originally made for TV. **HO20, WR15**

Stephen King's It (1990, C, 192m, NR)
In a small New England town lurks a malevolent force that takes the shape of a clown. A group of kids successfully fight it off, only to have it reappear thirty years later. John Ritter, Harry Anderson, Richard Thomas, Tim Curry, Annette O'Toole, and Tim Reid star in this adaptation of the King bestseller. Originally made for TV. **DR26, WR15**

Stephen King's Sleepwalkers see
Sleepwalkers

Steppenwolf (1974, C, 105m, R)
Moody drama of a suicidal writer and his involvement with a mysterious woman, based on Herman Hesse's cult novel. Max von Sydow, Dominique Sanda, and Pierre Clementi star. **DR19**

Stepping Out (1991, C, 106m, PG)
Buffalo dance teacher whips group of amateur hoofers into shape for a show. Liza Minnelli stars, with Shelley Winters, Ellen Greene, Julie Walters, and Andrea Martin. Screenplay by Richard Harris, adapted from his play. **CO14, DR12, ST232**

Sterile Cuckoo, The (1969, C, 107m, PG)
Story of young college boy's first romance, with a girl in desperate need of real affection. Liza Minnelli's film debut; Wendell Burton costars. Directed by Alan J. Pakula; adapted from John Nichols's novel. Modest drama with similar returns. **DR1, DR19, DT94**

Steve Martin Live (1986, C, 60m, NR)
Footage from a 1979 concert, plus some of his classic bits, including "King Tut" and his Oscar-nominated short film, *The Absent-Minded Waiter*. **CO16, ST150**

Steven Wright Live (1985, C, 53m, NR)
The poker-faced comedian in concert. **CO16**

Stevie (1978, C, 102m, PG)
Glenda Jackson plays eccentric, reclusive British poet Stevie Smith in this unusual film biography. Mona Washbourne costars as Smith's addled aunt. **DR4, DR23, ST117**

Stick (1985, C, 109m, R)
Burt Reynolds is an ex-con who gets mixed up in the Miami drug-dealing scene to avenge a friend's death. With Candice Bergen, George Segal, Charles Durning, and Dar Robinson. Based on Elmore Leonard's novel. Can't catch the flavor of Leonard's prose or characters. **AC9, ST183, WR19**

Still of the Night (1982, C, 91m, PG)
Thriller borrowing heavily from Hitchcock has psychiatrist (Roy Scheider) and the girlfriend of his murdered patient (Meryl Streep) falling in love. Robert Benton wrote and directed. **DT9, MY5, ST210**

Still Smokin' (1983, C, 91m, R)
Two-part Cheech and Chong comedy has them running wild at an Amsterdam film festival, plus extended concert footage. **ST28**

Sting, The (1973, C, 129m, PG)
Oscar-winning comedy about two Prohibition-era sharpies out to fleece a nasty gambler. Paul Newman and Robert Redford star, with Robert Shaw, Charles Durning, Ray Walston, Eileen Brennan, and Harold Gould.

Fine use of Scott Joplin music. Directed by Oscar winner George Roy Hill. Call me a Scrooge but . . . it's slick, smug, and only mildly amusing. **CO6, CO10, DT55, ST162, ST181, XT1, XT6**

Stir Crazy (1980, C, 111m, R)
A pair of inept bank robbers (Richard Pryor and Gene Wilder) make the most of their stay behind bars by joining the prison rodeo. With Georg Stanford Brown, JoBeth Williams, Craig T. Nelson, Barry Corbin, and Erland van Lidth de Jeude. Sidney Poitier directed. **CO3, CO10, ST174, ST180**

St. Ives (1976, C, 94m, PG)
A writer (Charles Bronson) becomes a pawn in a millionaire's international conspiracy plot. With John Houseman and Jacqueline Bisset. **MY6, ST20**

Stolen Kisses (1968, C, 90m, NR)
The third in the Antoine Doinel series of films from star Jean-Pierre Leaud and director François Truffaut finds our hero getting his first taste of real romance. **DT125**

Stolen Life, A (1946, B&W, 107m, NR)
Bette Davis stars in this psychological drama as twin sisters; one takes over with her sister's husband (Glenn Ford). **ST44**

Stone Boy, The (1984, C, 93m, PG)
Montana family is torn apart when one son accidentally shoots and kills his brother. Robert Duvall, Jason Presson, and Glenn Close star, with Wilford Brimley and Frederic Forrest. Finely drawn characters, sensitive performances. **DR8, ST33, ST63,** *Recommended*

Stone Cold (1991, C, 90m, R)
Renegade cop goes undercover to join cycle gang. Former football star Brian Bosworth makes his motion picture debut; with Lance Henriksen as Chains and William Forsythe as Ice. **AC25**

Stone Killer, The (1973, C, 95m, R)
A dedicated cop (Charles Bronson) works to solve a string of murders linked to organized crime. **AC9, ST20**

Stop Making Sense (1984, C, 99m, NR)
This Talking Heads concert film captures the essence of the band, thanks to director Jonathan Demme and his brilliant crew. Three songs added for video version. **CU10, DT35, MU10,** *Highly Recommended*

Stop! Or My Mom Will Shoot
(1992, C, 87m, PG)
Comedy of tough big-city cop being humiliated by visiting mother. Sylvester Stallone and Estelle Getty star, with JoBeth Williams

and Roger Rees. Directed by Roger Spottiswoode. **CO5, CO9, ST204**

Storm Boy (1976, C, 90m, NR)
From Australia, a family drama about a young boy learning about life from an elderly aboriginine. **FF5**

Storm in a Teacup (1937, B&W, 87m, NR)
British comedy starring Vivien Leigh and Rex Harrison as legal antagonists in a case of a little old lady and a dog license. **CO17, ST137**

Storm Over Asia (1928, B&W, 102m, NR)
Silent Soviet historical drama of a Mongolian fur trader leading a fight against occupying British troops in Central Asia. Directed by V.I. Pudovkin. Also known as *The Heir to Genghis Khan*. **FF7**

Stormy Monday (1988, C, 93m, R)
Moody thriller set in English town of Newcastle, where an American developer (Tommy Lee Jones) puts the squeeze on a club owner (Sting). With Melanie Griffith and Sean Bean. Written and directed by Mike Figgis, who also composed the music. Good atmosphere, with Jones superb as villain. **DR23, MU12, MY2, MY15, ST93,** *Recommended*

Stormy Weather (1943, B&W, 77m, NR)
Musical with thin story line as showcase for many of the top black entertainers of the 1940s. Lena Horne, Bill Robinson, Fats Waller, Cab Calloway, and The Nicholas Brothers star. **MU3, MU4, MU13,** *Recommended*

Story of a Love Story (1973, C, 110m, NR)
Alan Bates plays a writer who has a love affair—or is it part of his active imagination? With Dominique Sanda and Evans Evans. Directed by John Frankenheimer. **ST9**

Story of Adele H, The (1975, C, 97m, PG)
True tale of the daughter of French novelist Victor Hugo and her obsession with a young soldier. Francois Truffaut directed Isabelle Adjani in the title role. **DT125**

Story of Ruth, The (1960, C, 132m, NR)
Biblical tale of faithful daughter-in-law of Naomi, starring Elana Eden, Stuart Whitman, and Tom Tryon. **CL13**

Story of Seabiscuit, The
(1949, C, 93m, NR)
Horseracing drama starring an adolescent Shirley Temple, with Barry Fitzgerald and Lon McCallister. **FA5, ST213**

Story of Vernon and Irene Castle, The
(1939, B&W, 93m, NR)
Fred Astaire and Ginger Rogers play the real-life husband and wife dance team in this musical biography. **CL15, MU4, MU5, ST4, ST187**

Story of Women (1988, C, 110m, NR)
Intense drama starring Isabelle Huppert as an abortionist in wartime France, being ostracized by a hypocritical community. Directed by Claude Chabrol. **FF1**

Storyville (1992, C, 112m, R)
Political/courtroom melodrama set in New Orleans about aspiring politician on the hot seat: he's defending a one-night stand lover on charges she murdered her father. *And* he's slowly unraveling a mystery that would solve the suicide of his politician father. James Spader stars, with Joanne Whalley-Kilmer, Jason Robards, Charlotte Lewis, Michael Warren, Michael Parks, Charles Haid, Piper Laurie, and Woody Strode. Directed and cowritten by Mark Frost, who cocreated TV's "Twin Peaks" and tries for same effects here but generally fails, although courtroom finale is a jaw-dropper. May be worth checking out for cast, who all seem to be having fun. **DR17, DR21, ST185, ST203, XT14**

Stowaway (1936, B&W, 86m, NR)
A cute little stowaway on a cruise ship helps a young couple find romance. Shirley Temple, Alice Faye, and Robert Young star. **ST213**

Straight Out of Brooklyn
(1991, C, 91m, R)
Urban drama of black family living in housing project, with abusive father, son who decides to become a robber. George T. Odom, Ann D. Sanders, Lawrence Gilliard, Jr., and Barbara Sanon star. Written and directed by Matty Rich. **DR7, DR14, DR15, XT9**

Straight Shootin' (1917, B&W, 53m, NR)
Silent Western, one of director John Ford's first films, stars Hoot Gibson and Harry Carey, Sr. **DT44**

Straight Talk (1992, C, 91m, PG)
Dolly Parton comedy of woman mistaken for psychologist, taking over a radio talk show and dispensing down-home advice to Chicago listeners. With James Woods, Griffin Dunne, Michael Madsen, John Sayles, Spalding Gray, Charles Fleischer, and Jay Thomas. **CO2, CO20, DT112, MU12, ST233, XT11**

Straight Time (1978, C, 114m, R)
Ex-con tries to go straight, but is drawn inevitably into old bad habits. Dustin Hoffman stars, with Theresa Russell, Gary Busey, Harry Dean Stanton, and M. Emmet Walsh in this underrated drama. Based on novel by Edward Bunker, real-life convict when he wrote it. **DR16, ST105, ST205,** *Recommended*

Straight to Hell (1987, C, 86m, R)
The last word in Western spoofs, with a hip cast that includes Dennis Hopper, Jim Jarmusch, and rock stars Elvis Costello, Dick Rude, Grace Jones, and Joe Strummer. Directed by Alex Cox. **DT62, MU12, ST110, WE14**

Strait-Jacket (1964, B&W, 89m, NR)
Instant camp classic stars Joan Crawford as a just-released convict who served twenty years for ax-murdering her husband and his girlfriend in front of her baby daughter. After she moves in with her grown daughter, a series of similar murders occur. **CU2, HO19, ST39**

Strange Brew (1983, C, 90m, PG)
Rick Moranis and Dave Thomas expand their McKenzie Brothers bit from "SCTV" into a feature-length comedy about those Canadian stooges and their search for the perfect beer. Pretty flat. **CO14**

Strange Cargo (1940, B&W, 105m, NR)
Allegory of prisoners escaping from Devil's Island in a boat carrying a Christ-like character. Joan Crawford and Clark Gable star, with Ian Hunter and Peter Lorre. **ST39, ST77**

Strange Case of Dr. Jekyll & Mr. Hyde (1989, C, 60m, NR)
Anthony Andrews and Laura Dern star in this version of the Robert Louis Stevenson tale. Originally made for TV. **ST53, WR33**

Strange Case of Madeleine see *Madeleine*

Strange Interlude (1932, B&W, 110m, NR)
Eugene O'Neill drama of a married woman's lack of fulfillment, with characters' thoughts supplied in voiceovers. Norma Shearer stars, with Clark Gable, May Robson, Maureen O'Sullivan, and Robert Young. **ST77, WR25**

Strange Interlude (1988, C, 190m, NR)
Eugene O'Neill drama of a neurotic woman who manipulates the men in her life. Glenda Jackson stars, with José Ferrer, David Dukes, and Ken Howard. Originally made for public TV. **ST117, WR25**

Strange Invaders (1983, C, 94m, PG)
Paul LeMat and Nancy Allen star in this gentle spoof of '50s sci-fi movies. An alien force is ready to return home after being on Earth for twenty-five years, and they want to take the pre-teen daughter of an alien-human union with them. Directed by Michael Laughlin. Fans of genre will want to check it out; others beware. **SF9, SF21**

Strange Love of Martha Ivers, The (1946, B&W, 117m, NR)
Barbara Stanwyck plays a woman with a past

that haunts her in this classic *film noir*, co-starring Van Heflin and Kirk Douglas. **MY1, ST57, ST206**

Strange Skirts see *When Ladies Meet*

Stranger, The (1946, B&W, 95m, NR)
Ex-Nazi (Orson Welles) lives a second life in New England town until he's tracked down by a relentless pursuer. With Loretta Young and Edward G. Robinson. Welles directed this first-rate thriller. **DT134, MY1, MY6, ST186,** *Recommended*

Stranger, The (1967, C, 105m, NR)
Adaptation of Albert Camus's classic novel of alienation, starring Marcello Mastroianni as the man whose impulsive act of violence costs him dearly. With Anna Karina and Bernard Blier. Directed by Luchino Visconti. Everything you could hope for in a screen version of an important literary work. UNAVAILABLE ON VIDEO. **XT29**

Stranger Among Us, A (1992, C, 111m, R)
Melanie Griffith plays a police detective investigating the murder of a jewelry merchant in New York's Hassidic Jewish community. With Eric Thal, John Pankow, Tracey Pollan, Lee Richardson, Mia Sara, and Jamey Sheridan. Directed by Sidney Lumet. **DR15, DR27, DT78, MY3, ST93, XT9**

Stranger and the Gunfighter, The (1976, C, 107m, PG)
A martial arts spaghetti Western. Lee Van Cleef teams with Lo Lieh to track down a killer. **ST221, WE13**

Stranger Is Watching, A (1982, C, 92m, R)
A New York newscaster (Kate Mulgrew) and her daughter are abducted by a madman (Rip Torn). **MY3, ST216, XT9**

Stranger on the Third Floor, The (1940, B&W, 64m, NR)
A reporter's testimony helps convict an innocent man, but the journalist has second thoughts and decides to find the real killer. Peter Lorre stars. **MY7**

Stranger Than Paradise (1984, B&W, 90m, R)
Poker-faced comedy from director Jim Jarmusch about two New York goofs and a sixteen-year-old Hungarian girl. They sit around in New York apartments, they walk around in the snow in Cleveland, they drive to Florida. John Lurie, Richard Edson, and Eszter Balint star. Demands a lot of patience. **CO12, CU1, DT62, MU12**

Stranger Wore a Gun, The
(1953, C, 83m, NR)
Randolph Scott Western has him falling in
with a bandit, involved against his will in a
holdup. With Claire Trevor, Joan Weldon,
George Macready, Lee Marvin, and Ernest
Borgnine. **ST151, ST197, WE3**

Strangers see *Voyage to Italy*

Strangers Kiss (1984, C, 94m, R)
Drama about the making of a low-budget
film whose director tries to encourage a
behind-the-scenes romance between his stars
to pump up their love scenes on camera.
Peter Coyote, Blaine Novak, and Victoria
Tennant star, with Richard Romanus. Of
interest to viewers fascinated with politics of
moviemaking. Based on making of early
Stanley Kubrick film, *Killer's Kiss.* **DR13,
XT26**

Strangers on a Train
(1951, B&W, 101m, NR)
Alfred Hitchcock classic about a psychotic
(Robert Walker) trying to talk a tennis pro
(Farley Granger) into a murder swap, then
carrying out his end of the bargain. With
Ruth Roman, Leo G. Carroll, Patricia Hitch-
cock (the director's daughter), and Marion
Lorne as Walker's ditsy mom. Lots of chills,
even on repeated viewings; Walker is superb.
DT57, MY9, MY13, MY19, XT19, *Essential,
Highly Recommended*

**Strangers: The Story of a Mother and
Daughter** (1979, C, 100m, NR)
Bette Davis won an Emmy for her role as a
widow whose daughter (Gena Rowlands)
comes to visit after twenty years of separation. Originally made for TV. **DR8, ST44**

Strangers When We Meet
(1960, B&W, 117m, NR)
Glossy romantic drama of an affair between a
married man and woman, starring Kirk Douglas, Kim Novak, Ernie Kovacs, Barbara Rush,
and Walter Matthau. **DR1, ST57, ST155**

Strapless (1989, C, 103m, R)
British drama of relationship between sisters,
one an American doctor living in London
and turning forty, the other a twenty-five-
year-old visiting from the U.S. Blair Brown
and Bridget Fonda star, with Bruno Ganz and
Alan Howard. **DR10, DR23, ST70**

Strategic Air Command
(1955, C, 114m, NR)
James Stewart is a baseball player who puts
away his mitt when he's called into the Air
Force. With June Allyson, Frank Lovejoy, and
Barry Sullivan. Anthony Mann directed.
AC11, DT85, ST207

Straw Dogs (1971, C, 113m, R)
American academic visiting in rural England
is harassed by local toughs and finally fights
back in a violent confrontation. Dustin Hoffman stars, with Susan George, Peter Vaughan,
T.P. McKenna, and David Warner. Sam Peckinpah directed. Tough to like, easier to
admire; called by one critic a "fascist masterpiece." **DT95, ST105**, *Essential, Recommended*

Strawberry Blonde, The
(1941, B&W, 97m, NR)
A dentist (James Cagney) is infatuated with a
golddigger (Rita Hayworth) but marries a
woman (Olivia de Havilland) who really
loves him. Directed by Raoul Walsh. **DT131,
ST24, ST49, ST101**

Stray Dog (1949, B&W, 122m, NR)
In postwar Tokyo, a police detective's gun is
stolen, leading him on a strange odyssey.
Toshiro Mifune and Takashi Shimura star.
Akira Kurosawa directed. Superb blend of sus-
pense and social realism. **DT69, ST157**,
Recommended

Streamers (1983, C, 118m, R)
Intense drama set in an Army barracks at the
start of the Vietnam War, starring Matthew
Modine, Michael Wright, and Mitchell
Lichtenstein. Directed by Robert Altman;
screenplay by David Rabe, from his own
play. **DR7, DR20, DT4**

Street of Shame (1956, B&W, 96m, NR)
Japanese drama from director Kenji Mizoguchi (his last completed film), about prostitutes in a Tokyo brothel called Dreamland.
Machiko Kyo stars. **FF4**

Street Scene (1931, B&W, 80m, NR)
Drama of life in the New York tenements,
starring Sylvia Sidney and William Collier, Jr.
Directed by King Vidor. **CL8, DT126**

Street Smart (1987, C, 97m, R)
Hotshot New York reporter, on a tight deadline, concocts story about black pimp; the
details happen to match a real pimp who's
on trial for murder. Christopher Reeve and
Morgan Freeman star in this story of contemporary ethics and life in the media spotlight.
With Kathy Baker and Andre Gregory. Interesting premise not well handled, with weak
lead performance. Freeman is magnetic.
DR7, DR15, ST76, XT9

Street With No Name, The
(1948, B&W, 91m, NR)
Film noir based on true story of urban crime
boss's exposure and capture by the FBI. Mark
Stevens, Richard Widmark, and Lloyd Nolan
star. **AC22, MY1**

Streetcar Named Desire, A
(1951, B&W, 122m, NR)
Tennessee Williams play of brutal Stanley
Kowalski (Marlon Brando), his tough wife
Stella (Kim Hunter), and her fragile sister
Blanche DuBois (Vivien Leigh). Both actresses
and Karl Malden won Oscars. Elia Kazan di-
rected. Powerful film perfectly captures
essence of Williams's play and art. Brando
also deserved an Oscar. **DT65, ST18, ST137,
WR38, XT3, XT4, XT5, XT28,** *Essential,
Highly Recommended*

Streets of Fire (1984, C, 93m, PG)
Rock singer is kidnapped by the leader of a
biker gang, and her ex-boyfriend, a soldier of
fortune, sets out to rescue her. Diane Lane,
Willem Dafoe, and Michael Paré star in this
self-proclaimed "rock 'n' roll fable" with
music by Ry Cooder, The Blasters, and
others. With Rick Moranis and Amy Madigan. Directed by Walter Hill. Great-looking
sets; Paré and Lane are minuses, Dafoe and
most of the music a plus. Lane's vocals
dubbed. **AC8, AC25, CO14, DT56**

Streets of Gold (1986, C, 95m, R)
Russian boxing coach defects to America,
finds two fighters to train for international
competition against you-know-who. Klaus
Maria Brandauer stars, with Adrian Pasdar
and Wesley Snipes. **DR22, ST201**

Streets of L.A., The (1979, C, 100m, NR)
Joanne Woodward plays a middle-class
housewife who travels into barrio neighborhood to find the punks who slashed the tires
of her car. With Robert Webber, Michael C.
Gwynne, and Fernando Allende. Originally
made for TV. **DR15, ST234, XT10**

Streetwise (1985, C, 92m, NR)
Moving, uncompromising documentary portrait of homeless children in Seattle is a searing look at discarded youth. Directed by
Martin Bell. **CU16, XT26** *Recommended*

Strictly Business (1991, C, 84m, PG-13)
Modern comedy of relationship between two
black men working in real estate firm: mailroom clerk (Tommy Davidson) and executive
(Joseph C. Phillips). With Anne Marie Johnson, Halle Berry, and David Marshall Grant.
CO2, CO20, DR14

Strike (1924, B&W, 82m, NR)
Director Sergei Eisenstein's dramatic account
of a 1912 workers' clash with government
police. Silent classic of political filmmaking.
CU9, DT41

Strike Force (1975, C, 78m, NR)
Policemen and federal agents team up to
bring down a drug ring. Cliff Gorman stars,

with Donald Blakely, Richard Gere, and Joe
Spinell. Also known as *Crack*. **AC9, ST84**

Strike It Rich (1990, C, 87m, PG)
British comedy, adapted from Graham
Greene novella *Loser Takes All*, of couple
honeymooning beyond their means. Robert
Lindsay and Molly Ringwald star, with John
Gielgud. **CO17, ST86, WR11**

Strike Up the Band
(1940, B&W, 120m, NR)
A high school band schemes to compete in a
radio contest. Mickey Rooney and Judy Garland star. Busby Berkeley directed. **CL15,
DT12, MU1, MU4, ST81, ST189**

Stripes (1981, C, 105m, R)
Old-fashioned service comedy with brand-
new cast of comedians, featuring Bill Murray,
Harold Ramis, and John Candy as the lovable
losers, Warren Oates as their perplexed sergeant, and in small roles, Joe Flaherty and
Dave Thomas. **CO13, CO14, CO21, ST166**

Stripper, The (1963, B&W, 95m, NR)
Drama of a no-win love affair between an
aging stripper (Joanne Woodward) and a
teen-ager (Richard Beymer). Based on a play
by William Inge. **DR3, ST234**

Stroker Ace (1983, C, 96m, PG)
Burt Reynolds vehicle has him once again
playing the good ol' boy of the car racing circuit. Loni Anderson, Ned Beatty, and Jim
Nabors costar. **CO19, ST183**

Stromboli (1950, B&W, 107m, NR)
Ingrid Bergman stars in this drama of a
woman and her loveless marriage to an Italian fishermmn. Directed by Roberto Rossellini, then her husband. New video version
restores footage from 81 minutes to original
running time. **CU10, DT109, FF2, ST13,
XT30**

Strong Man, The (1926, B&W, 78m, NR)
Silent comedy featuring Harry Langdon as a
World War I soldier who returns to the U.S.
to claim the love of a woman who wrote to
him during the war. Directed by Frank Capra.
CL11, DT22

Stroszek (1977, C, 108m, NR)
Odd trio of Germans (ex-mental patient,
prostitute, and eccentric old man) travel to
American Midwest to find a new life. Bruno
S., Eva Mattes, and Clemens Scheitz star.
Directed by Werner Herzog. Dialogue in Ger-
man and English. **DR27, DT54**

Student Prince, The (1954, C, 107m, NR)
Sigmund Romberg's operetta of heir to
throne off on one last fling. Edmund Purdom

stars (his voice supplied by Mario Lanza), with Ann Blyth and John Ericson. **MU1**

Student Prince in Old Heidelberg, The (1927, B&W, 105m, NR)
Silent drama from director Ernst Lubitsch, a love story of a prince (Ramon Novarro) and a barmaid (Norma Shearer). **CL12, DT76**

Studs Lonigan (1960, B&W, 95m, NR)
Drama of aimless Chicago youth in 1920s and his inevitable fate. Based on James T. Farrell's novel, starring Christopher Knight, Frank Gorshin, and (in a small, early role) Jack Nicholson. **DR15, DR19, ST163**

Study in Scarlet, A (1933, B&W, 70m, NR)
Sherlock Holmes mystery which has nothing to do with the story which introduced the famed detective. Reginald Owen stars. **HF14**

Study in Terror, A (1965, C, 94m, NR)
Sherlock Holmes (John Neville) takes on Jack the Ripper in this British-made mystery. Donald Houston costars as Dr. Watson. **HF14**

Stuff, The (1985, C, 93m, R)
A popular new dessert is killing people. A spoof of 1950s sci-fi/horror films. Michael Moriarty and Garrett Morris star. Larry Cohen directed. **CO13, DT28, HO24**

Stunt Man, The (1980, C, 129m, R)
Comedy-drama about filmmaker who offers a fugitive the most dangerous job in movies after the film's stunt man is killed in an accident. Peter O'Toole, Steve Railsback, and Barbara Hershey star in this dazzling look at the way movies create the illusion of reality. Directed by Richard Rush. O'Toole has the time of his life with this role, and you will, too. **DR13, ST104, ST169, XT26, XT31,** *Recommended*

Stunts (1977, C, 89m, PG)
When a stunt man is killed during filming, his brother suspects foul play and decides to investigate on his own. Robert Forster stars. **DR13, MY11**

Stuntwoman (1984, C, 95m, NR)
Raquel Welch plays the title character, a woman whose work keeps messing up her love life. With Jean-Paul Belmondo. **ST11**

St. Valentine's Day Massacre, The (1967, C, 100m, NR)
Jason Robards portrays Al Capone in this re-creation of the events leading up to the famous gangster massacre. With George Segal. Roger Corman directed. **AC22, DT30, ST185**

Suburban Commando (1991, C, 90m, PG)
Wrestler Hulk Hogan plays an alien fugitive hiding out in typical suburban family's home in this comedy. With Christopher Lloyd and Shelley Duvall. **CO5, FA6, SF9**

Suburbia (1983, C, 96m, R)
No-holds-barred drama of society's castoffs, kids living in deserted tract houses, stealing for food, drinking, and getting high. Chris Pederson, Bill Coyne, Jennifer Clay, and Timothy Eric O'Brien star. Directed by Penelope Spheeris. Also known as *The Wild Side*. **CU12, DR9,** *Recommended*

Subway to the Stars (1987, C, 103m, R)
Brazilian drama of a musician (Guilherme Fontes) in search of his missing girlfriend on the streets of Rio de Janeiro. Directed by Carlos Diegues. **FF6**

Succubus see *The Devil's Nightmare*

Such Good Friends (1971, C, 100m, R)
Wicked comedy from writer Elaine May and director Otto Preminger, about a woman whose husband is hospitalized for major surgery when she discovers that he has been systematically cheating on her. Dyan Cannon stars, with James Coco, Jennifer O'Neill, Ken Howard, Laurence Luckinbill, Louise Lasser, and Burgess Meredith. Adapted from Lois Gould's novel. May insisted a pseudonym be substituted for her name in the credits, but her biting wit is still much in evidence. UNAVAILABLE ON VIDEO. **XT29**

Sudden Impact (1983, C, 117m, R)
Dirty Harry entry about a woman who is, one by one, killing the people responsible for the gang rape she and her sister suffered. Clint Eastwood and Sondra Locke star. Confused look at vigilantism. **AC9, AC19, ST64**

Suddenly (1954, B&W, 77m, NR)
Thriller about a gang of thugs planning to assassinate the President as he passes through a small town. Frank Sinatra stars. **DR16, MY1, ST199**

Suddenly, Last Summer (1959, B&W, 114m, NR)
Tennessee Williams drama of a young girl's breakdown and her aunt's manipulative attempts to cure her. Elizabeth Taylor, Katharine Hepburn, and Montgomery Clift star. Adapted by Gore Vidal; directed by Joseph L. Mankiewicz. **DR8, DT84, ST32, ST103, ST212, WR38**

Sugar Cane Alley (1984, C, 107m, NR)
French drama set in 1930s Martinique, centering on the hopes and dreams of a ten-year-old boy (Garry Cadenat). Directed by Euzhan Palcy. **FF1**

Sugarbaby (1985, C, 87m, R)
An odd-couple comedy from Germany about a romance between a plump mortuary attendant and a wimpy subway conductor. Marianne Sägebrecht stars. Percy Adlon directed. **FF3**

Sugarland Express, The
(1974, C, 109m, PG)
Comedy-drama, based on a true story, about a fugitive couple, their baby, and a hostage state trooper pursued across Texas by a small army of law enforcement agents. Goldie Hawn, William Atherton, and Michael Sacks star, with Ben Johnson. Directed by Steven Spielberg. Widescreen will be lost on video. Perpetual motion; one of the director's most enjoyable films. **CU20, DR6, DT118, ST99, XT18,** *Recommended*

Suicide Run see *Too Late the Hero*

Sullivans, The see *Fighting Sullivans, The*

Sullivan's Travels (1941, B&W, 91m, NR)
Writer-director Preston Sturges's satire about a Hollywood director (Joel McCrea) who sets out to make a "serious" film by bumming around the country. Veronica Lake, William Demarest, and Eric Blore head the supporting cast. Superbly written, with McCrea sensational in lead. **CL10, CO20, DT121, ST144, XT18,** *Essential, Highly Recommended*

Summer (1986, C, 98m, R)
From French director Eric Rohmer, a comedy about a Parisian secretary's attempts to escape the city during August. Marie Riviere stars. **DT107**

Summer and Smoke (1961, C, 118m, NR)
Tennessee Williams drama of spinster in love with a young man. Geraldine Page and Laurence Harvey star, with Una Merkel, John McIntire, Pamela Tiffin, and Rita Moreno. **WR38**

Summer Camp Nightmare
(1987, C, 87m, PG-13)
At a summer camp run by a strict counselor, the kids stage a revolt and imprison all the adults. **HO12**

Summer City (1976, C, 83m, NR)
A quartet of teens are out for a good-times weekend at a seaside resort but run into trouble with resentful locals. Mel Gibson stars in this Australian drama. **FF5, ST85**

Summer Holiday (1948, C, 92m, NR)
Musical remake of Eugene O'Neill's *Ah, Wilderness*, about a young man's coming of age in a small town. Mickey Rooney stars (he played the younger brother in the earlier film), with Walter Huston, Frank Morgan,

and Agnes Moorehead. Directed by Rouben Mamoulian. Superb color photography by Charles Schoenbaum. **CL9, DT83, MU14, ST189, WR25**

Summer Interlude (1951, B&W, 90m, NR)
Early Ingmar Bergman drama about a woman sorting out the details of her relationship with a now-dead lover. Also known as *Illicit Interlude*. **DT11**

Summer Lovers (1982, C, 98m, R)
A young man and two attractive women enjoy a summer fling on a Greek island in this sexy movie with a cult following. Peter Gallagher, Daryl Hannah, and Valerie Quennessen star. **CU6, DR3**

Summer Magic (1963, C, 100m, NR)
Disney comedy-drama about a Maine widow raising her family on a meager income. Dorothy McGuire and Hayley Mills star. **FA1**

Summer Night (1987, C, 94m, R)
A rich businesswoman (Mariangela Melato) holds a terrorist captive on an island in this comedy from Italian director Lina Wertmuller. Full title: *Summer Night, With Greek Profile, Almond Eyes and Scent of Basil*. **DT137**

Summer Place, A (1959, C, 130m, NR)
Quintessential 1950s romantic drama, set on the coast of Maine, focusing on older couple (Richard Egan and Dorothy McGuire) and younger (Sandra Dee and Troy Donahue). **DR1**

Summer Rental (1985, C, 88m, PG)
John Candy stars in this comedy about an air traffic controller's disastrous summer at the beach. With Rip Torn and Richard Crenna. **CO14, ST216**

Summer School (1987, C, 98m, PG-13)
A laid-back physical education teacher is roped into teaching a summer course in history to a class of misfits. Mark Harmon stars with Kirstie Alley in this comedy. **CO18**

Summer Solstice (1981, C, 75m, NR)
An aging couple (Henry Fonda and Myrna Loy) return to the beach where they first met fifty years ago. With Lindsay Crouse and Stephen Collins. Originally made for TV. **DR11, ST71, ST142**

Summer Stock (1950, C, 109m, NR)
Gene Kelly and his troupe invade Judy Garland's farm in order to rehearse their Broadway show. When the female star of the show leaves, Judy fills in. Gene dances with newspapers and Judy sings "Get Happy." With Eddie Bracken, Marjorie Main, Gloria De Haven, Phil Silvers, and Hans Conried. **MU4, ST81, ST123**

Summer Wishes, Winter Dreams
(1973, C, 93m, PG)
Joanne Woodward plays a New York woman whose emotional distance from everyone around her frustrates her. With Martin Balsam and Sylvia Sidney. **DR10, ST234**

Summer With Monika
(1952, B&W, 96m, NR)
Ingmar Bergman drama of couple whose affair leads to pregnancy and marriage. Harriet Andersson and Lars Ekborg star. Also known as *Monika*. **DT11**

Summertime (1958, C, 99m, NR)
Tearjerker about a spinster (Katharine Hepburn) from Ohio visiting Venice, falling in love with a married man (Rossano Brazzi). David Lean directed. **CL4, CL6, DT71, ST103**

Summertree (1971, C, 88m, PG)
Michael Douglas plays a student at odds with his parents over the Vietnam War. With Jack Warden, Brenda Vaccaro, and Barbara Bel Geddes. **DR8, ST59**

Sun Shines Bright, The
(1953, B&W, 92m, NR)
Director John Ford's remake of his own *Judge Priest*, about political election in a small Southern town. Charles Winninger stars, with Arleen Whelan, John Russell, Stepin Fetchit, Milburn Stone, Slim Pickens, and Mae Marsh. Video and TV versions contain footage not seen in original release. Reportedly the director's favorite of his films. **CU10, CU18, DR26, DT44**

Sun Valley Serenade
(1941, B&W, 86m, NR)
Former Olympic skating star Sonja Henie stars in this musical about a war refugee traveling with the Glenn Miller Orchestra. With John Payne, Milton Berle, Joan Davis, and Dorothy Dandridge. **MU4**

Sunburn (1979, C, 94m, PG)
An insurance investigator (Charles Grodin) is joined by a lovely blonde (Farrah Fawcett) in Mexico to investigate a murder/suicide. With Art Carney, Joan Collins, and William Daniels. **MY10, ST94**

Sunday Bloody Sunday (1971, C, 110m, R)
Romantic triangle drama, with middle-aged man and young woman competing for the same man. British drama stars Peter Finch, Glenda Jackson, and Murray Head. Look for Daniel Day-Lewis in a small role. Screenplay by Penelope Gilliatt; directed by John Schlesinger. **DR3, DR23, DT113, ST48, ST117,** *Recommended*

Sunday in the Country, A
(1984, C, 94m, G)
An aging painter invites his loved ones to spend a day at his rural estate. Bertrand Tavernier directed this French drama. **DT123**

Sundays and Cybèle
(1962, B&W, 110m, NR)
A war veteran suffering from shell-shock finds comfort in the friendship of a young girl. Hardy Krüger and Nicole Courcel star. Oscar winner for Best Foreign Language Film. **FF1, XT7**

Sundown (1941, B&W, 90m, NR)
Gene Tierney plays a native girl in this World War II drama of British troops stationed in Africa. With Bruce Cabot, George Sanders, Harry Carey, and Dorothy Dandridge. **AC1, ST214**

Sundowners, The (1960, C, 113m, NR)
Drama of Australian sheepherding family, starring Robert Mitchum, Deborah Kerr, and Peter Ustinov. Directed by Fred Zinnemann. Kerr deserved an Oscar; film is pleasant but nothing special. **DT144, ST125, ST158, XT28**

Sunrise at Campobello
(1960, C, 143m, NR)
Ralph Bellamy's famed portrait of Franklin D. Roosevelt, adapted from the Dore Schary stage hit. Greer Garson plays Eleanor; Hume Cronyn and Jean Hagen costar. **DR4, ST83**

Sunset (1988, C, 107m, PG-13)
In 1920s Hollywood, former Western lawman Wyatt Earp and cowboy movie star Tom Mix team to solve a murder mystery. James Garner and Bruce Willis star, with Malcolm McDowell, Mariel Hemingway, Jennifer Edwards, Kathleen Quinlan, M. Emmet Walsh, and Joe Dallesandro. Blake Edwards directed this nostalgic comedy, with plenty of detail about Hollywood in the Jazz Age. **CO6, CO8, DT40, MY17, ST82, ST229**

Sunset Boulevard (1950, B&W, 110m, NR)
Legendary look at the seamy underside of Hollywood, with reclusive former star (Gloria Swanson) taking in young screenwriter (William Holden). With Erich von Stroheim, Nancy Olson, Jack Webb, and Buster Keaton and Cecil B. DeMille in bit parts. Billy Wilder directed. Mordant, cynical, and absolutely fascinating. **CL7, DR13, DT34, DT66, DT129, DT139, MY1, ST106, XT26,** *Essential, Highly Recommended*

Sunset in El Dorado
(1944, B&W, 56m, NR)
Roy Rogers and Dale Evans ride to the aid of farmers who are being defrauded. **ST188**

Sunset in the West (1950, B&W, 67m, NR)
A deputy sheriff (Roy Rogers) battles gunrunners. **ST188**

Sunset Limousine (1983, C, 100m, NR)
Comedy of stand-up comic/limo driver mixed up with hit men. John Ritter stars, with Susan Dey, Lainie Kazan, Martin Mull, Paul Reiser, George Kirby, and Martin Short. Originally made for TV. **CO14**

Sunset on the Desert
(1942, B&W, 53m, NR)
Roy Rogers action, with a man returning to his home-town to help his late father's partner out of a jam. **ST188**

Sunset Serenade (1942, B&W, 58m, NR)
Roy Rogers and Gabby Hayes step in the way of some dastardly villains intent on murder and thievery. Bob Nolan and the Sons of the Pioneers add some harmonizing. **ST188**

Sunshine Boys, The (1975, C, 111m, PG)
A pair of ex-vaudeville partners, not on speaking terms, are persuaded to reteam for a TV special. Neil Simon comedy stars Walter Matthau and Oscar winner George Burns. With Richard Benjamin, Lee Meredith, and Howard Hesseman. Directed by Herbert Ross. **CO3, CO8, ST155, WR30, XT4**

Super, The (1991, C, 86m, R)
Joe Pesci plays a slumlord who's sentenced by a judge to do time—in one of his own buildings. Comedy also features Vincent Gardenia, Madolyn Smith Osborne, Rubén Blades, and Stacey Travis. **CO2, CO20, MU12, ST172**

Superdad (1974, C, 96m, G)
A father (Bob Crane) challenges his daughter's fiancé (Kurt Russell) to various competitions to test his worthiness in this Disney comedy. **FA1, ST191**

Superfly (1972, C, 96m, R)
Ron O'Neal stars in landmark urban drama as Priest, the drug dealer with style to burn. Music by Curtis Mayfield. Belated sequel: *Return of Superfly.* **AC8, DR14, DR16**

Supergirl (1984, C, 114m, PG)
Supergirl, cousin to Superman, is sent to Earth to recover the Omegahedron, a source of unlimited power, which has fallen into the hands of an evil witch. Helen Slater stars, with Faye Dunaway, Mia Farrow, and Peter O'Toole. **AC17, FA4, ST61, ST65, ST169**

Superman (1978, C, 143m, PG)
The history of Superman, from Krypton to Metropolis. Christopher Reeve stars, with Margot Kidder, Gene Hackman, Ned Beatty, Marlon Brando, Susannah York, and Marc

McClure. Directed by Richard Donner. The special effects won a special Academy Award. Helped to launch cycle of big-budget special effects extravaganzas. Some thrills, with Reeve a fine superhero, but lumbering direction. **AC17, FA4, SF15, ST18, ST96,** *Essential*

Superman II (1980, C, 127m, PG)
Three villains from Krypton come to Earth with plans to rule the world. Christopher Reeve, Margot Kidder, Gene Hackman, and Terence Stamp star. Directed by Richard Lester. Widescreen will be lost on video. Improvement over the first entry, thanks to Lester's adroit direction. **AC17, CU20, DT74, FA4, ST96**

Superman III (1983, C, 123m, PG)
A master villain cons a computer genius into splitting Superman's personalities, one good, one bad. Christopher Reeve, Richard Pryor, and Robert Vaughn star. Richard Lester directed. Series begins to show wear and tear. **AC17, DT74, FA4, ST180**

Superman IV: The Quest for Peace
(1987, C, 90m, PG)
Lex Luthor creates a monster to battle Superman, who has just rid the world of nuclear weapons. Christopher Reeve and Gene Hackman star. **AC17, FA4, ST96**

Supernaturals, The (1986, C, 85m, R)
A troop of new recruits on manuevers end up fighting for their lives when a ghost army of Confederate soldiers come to life seeking revenge. Maxwell Caulfield, LeVar Burton, and Nichelle Nichols star. **HO2**

Superstar: The Life and Times of Andy Warhol (1991, C, 87m, NR)
Fascinating documentary on pop artist/ filmmaker includes commentary by wide range of Warhol friends and associates: Paul Morrissey, Tom Wolfe, Sylvia Miles, David Hockney, Taylor Mead, Dennis Hopper, Viva, and Ultra-Violet. Directed by Chuck Workman. **CU16, DT90, ST110,** *Recommended*

Support Your Local Sheriff!
(1969, C, 93m, PG)
Amiable Western comedy, with James Garner as a peaceable lawman who has to bring in the bad guys without benefit of a six-shooter. **ST82, WE14**

Sure Thing, The (1985, C, 94m, PG-13)
Road comedy about two mismatched college students finding romance as they hitchhike cross-country. John Cusack and Daphne Zuniga star. Directed by Rob Reiner. Modest, consistently entertaining, thanks to engaging

leads. Reiner's best film. **CO1, DT103, XT18,** *Recommended*

Surrender (1987, C, 95m, PG)
A much-divorced novelist and a struggling artist find romance. Michael Caine, Sally Field, and Steve Guttenberg star in this comedy, with Peter Boyle, Jackie Cooper, Julie Kavner, Louise Lasser, and Iman. **CO1, ST25, ST66**

Surviving Desire (1991, C, 86m, NR)
Wry comedy from director Hal Hartley about a professor teaching *The Brothers Karamazov*, falling in love with one of his students. Martin Donovan and May Ward star, with Matt Malloy and Rebecca Nelson. Also on this tape are two early Hartley short films, *Theory of Achievement* (about drifting New Yorkers) and *Ambition* (a philosophical talkfest). Originally shown on public TV. The feature has some funny moments, most of them thanks to Donovan's performance. **CO1**

Survivors, The (1983, C, 102m, R)
Two unemployed men are fingered by the same hit man and flee for their lives to a survivalist commune. Comedy starring Walter Matthau and Robin Williams, with Jerry Reed and John Goodman. Directed by Michael Ritchie. **CO2, CO3, ST155, ST228**

Susan and God (1940, B&W, 115m, NR)
Joan Crawford melodrama of devout woman whose obsessions turn her away from her family. With Fredric March, Ruth Hussey, and Rita Hayworth. Adapted by Anita Loos from Rachel Crothers's play. Directed by George Cukor. **DR20, DT32, ST39, ST101, ST148**

Susan Lennox: Her Fall and Rise (1931, B&W, 76m, NR)
Teaming of Greta Garbo and Clark Gable in tale of woman fleeing from arranged marriage. **CL5, ST77, ST78**

Susan Slept Here (1954, C, 98m, NR)
Comedy of songwriter (Dick Powell) forced to keep an eye on rambunctious teen (Debbie Reynolds). With Anne Francis and Glenda Farrell. Directed by Frank Tashlin. **ST175**

Susana (1951, B&W, 82m, NR)
Director Luis Buñuel's study of a vagrant girl's alluring hold over a respectable Spanish family. Rosita Quintana stars, with Fernando Soler. **DT21**

Susanna Pass (1949, C, 67m, NR)
Roy Rogers and Dale Evans team up with Cuban star Estelita Rodriguez for Western action and plenty of songs. **ST188**

Susannah of the Mounties (1939, B&W, 78m, NR)
Shirley Temple goes West in this sentimental tale of a Mountie (Randolph Scott) who adopts a girl orphaned in an Indian raid. **ST197, ST213**

Suspect (1987, C, 101m, R)
Drama set in Washington, D.C., about a public defender (Cher) whose client is accused of murder and a juror (Dennis Quaid) on the case who uncovers evidence that he decides to share with her. With Liam Neeson, John Mahoney, Joe Mantegna, and Philip Bosco. **DR17, ST29, XT12**

Suspicion (1941, B&W, 99m, NR)
Shy young woman is pursued by charming playboy and marries him, then immediately begins to suspect he's targeted her for murder. Classic Alfred Hitchcock suspense starring Oscar winner Joan Fontaine and Cary Grant. Grant good in relatively unsympathetic role. **DT57, MY3, MY5, ST73, ST92, XT3**

Suspicion (1987, C, 97m, NR)
Remake of the Alfred Hitchcock thriller about a woman who suspects her playboy husband of wanting to murder her, starring Jane Curtin and Anthony Andrews. Originally made for cable TV. **CO13, CU18, MY3, MY5**

Suspiria (1977, C, 92m, R)
Horror tale with cult following, about an American girl who learns that her European dance school is really a coven for witches. Jessica Harper stars. Also available in an unrated version; running time: 97 minutes. Has some scary moments. Overbearing rock score is a real minus. **CU4, CU10, HO12**

Suzy (1936, B&W, 99m, NR)
World War I spy drama starring Jean Harlow, Cary Grant as French flier, with Franchot Tone and Lewis Stone. **AC2, ST92, ST98**

Svengali (1931, B&W, 81m, NR)
John Barrymore plays the famed mesmerizer, with Marion Marsh as Trilby, his singer protégée. **ST8**

Svengali (1983, C, 100m, NR)
The classic tale of a young woman's rise to fame and her manipulative benefactor, updated to star Jodie Foster as a rock singer and Peter O'Toole in the title role. With Elizabeth Ashley and in a small role, Holly Hunter. Originally made for TV. **ST75, ST113, ST169**

Swamp Diamonds (1955, C, 73m, NR)
Four female convicts escape, go looking for treasure amid the muck. Michael Connors,

Marie Windsor, and Beverly Garland star. Also known as *Swamp Women*. Directed by Roger Corman. **DT30**

Swamp Thing (1982, C, 91m, PG)
A research scientist who discovers a potion to end world hunger is covered with the substance and becomes a human vegetable. Adrienne Barbeau and Louis Jourdan star. Directed by Wes Craven. **HO16**

Swamp Women see *Swamp Diamonds*

Swan, The (1956, C, 112m, NR)
Grace Kelly, in a preview of her future career, plays a princess set to wed Alec Guinness but attracted to Louis Jourdan. With Agnes Moorehead, Jessie Royce Landis, Brian Aherne, and Leo G. Carroll. Comedy based on 1920 play by Ferenc Molnàr. **DR20, ST95, ST124**

Swann in Love (1984, C, 110m, R)
A French aristocrat finds himself drawn to a woman of less than impeccable breeding in this adaptation of Marcel Proust's classic novel. Jeremy Irons and Ornella Muti star. Directed by Volker Schlondorff. **DR19, FF1, ST116**

Swap, The (1969, C, 92m, R)
Drama about a film editor's search for the killers of his brother, starring Robert De Niro in an early screen appearance. Originally released in different form as *Sam's Song*; this version adds several new characters. **ST51**

Swarm, The (1978, C, 116m, PG)
Deadly killer bees buzz all-star cast which includes Michael Caine, Katharine Ross, Henry Fonda, Olivia de Havilland, and Richard Chamberlain. **HO16, SF7, ST25, ST49, ST71**

Swashbuckler (1976, C, 101m, PG)
Lavish attempt at classic pirate film stars Robert Shaw, James Earl Jones, Genevieve Bujold, Peter Boyle, Beau Bridges, and Anjelica Huston in a small role. Stick with Errol Flynn and Stewart Granger. **AC15, ST115, ST118**

Swashbuckler, The (1984, C, 100m, NR)
French adventure saga set during that country's Revolution, starring Jean-Paul Belmondo, with Marlene Jobert and Laura Antonelli. **AC15, FF1, ST11**

Swedenhielms (1935, B&W, 88m, NR)
Ingrid Bergman stars in this drama, made in Sweden before her emergence as a star in Hollywood. She's the girlfriend of a young man whose impoverished family is counting on their patriarch to win the Nobel Prize. **FF7, ST13**

Sweeney Todd (1984, C, 139m, NR)
Filmed record of Stephen Sondheim Broadway musical about murderous barber and his assistant. Sara Woods, Angela Lansbury, and George Hearn star. **MU2, ST131**

Sweet Adeline (1935, B&W, 87m, NR)
Jerome Kern-Oscar Hammerstein operetta, a spy chase, starring Irene Dunne, Donald Woods, and Hugh Herbert. **MU1, ST62**

Sweet Bird of Youth
(1962, C, 120m, NR)
Tennessee Williams drama of fading star and her fling with youthful lover. Geraldine Page and Paul Newman star, with Rip Torn and Oscar winner Ed Begley. **ST162, ST216, WR38, XT4**

Sweet Charity (1969, C, 153m, G)
A dancehall hostess wants a traditional wedding and marriage, but keeps falling in love with ne'er-do-wells who only want her money. The directorial debut of Bob Fosse. Shirley MacLaine stars, with Chita Rivera and Sammy Davis, Jr. Video version adds twenty minutes of footage. **CU10, DT47, MU2, MU3, MU14, ST145**

Sweet Dreams (1985, C, 115m, PG-13)
Jessica Lange portrays legendary country singer Patsy Cline. With Ed Harris and Ann Wedgeworth. Cline's voice was used on the soundtrack recordings. Reasonably accurate and entertaining; music is sublime. **DR2, DR12, MU5, ST130, XT26**, *Recommended*

Sweet Hearts' Dance
(1988, C, 101m, R)
A small Vermont town is the setting for this romantic comedy about a couple (Don Johnson and Susan Sarandon) whose shaky marriage isn't helped by his best buddy (Jeff Daniels). **CO1, ST194**

Sweet Liberty (1986, C, 107m, PG)
The author of a bestselling book on the American Revolution is appalled when a movie crew arrives in his hometown and begins filming a very loose adaptation of his work. Alan Alda stars, with Michael Caine, Michelle Pfeiffer, Bob Hoskins, and Lillian Gish. Alda also wrote and directed. **CO8, ST25, ST87, ST111, ST173**

Sweet Movie (1975, C, 97m, NR)
Unique film from director Dusan Makavejev about sexuality. Two stories parallel: in one, the winner of a Miss Virginity contest marries a crass Texan; in the second, a female ship's captain and a Soviet sailor have a murderous sexual encounter. Recommended only for the very adventurous. **CU6**

Sweet 16 (1981, C, 90m, R)
As beautiful and promiscuous Melissa approaches her sixteenth birthday, her boy-friends start to die. Susan Strasberg and Bo Hopkins star. **HO7**

Sweet Smell of Success
(1957, B&W, 96m, NR)
A ruthless New York gossip columnist (Burt Lancaster) uses his power to destroy anyone who doesn't curry favor with him. Tony Curtis costars as a sycophantic press agent. With Martin Milner and Susan Harrison. Superb screenplay by Ernest Lehman and Clifford Odets, juicy performances by Curtis and Lancaster. **CL7, MY1, ST129** *Essential, Highly Recommended*

Sweet Sweetback's Baadasssss Song
(1971, C, 97m, R)
A black man kills two racist cops and flees for his life. Written and directed by Melvin Van Peebles, who also stars. **AC8, DR14**

Sweethearts (1938, C, 120m, NR)
Colorful show-biz saga of a Broadway couple (Nelson Eddy and Jeanette MacDonald) whose partnership is threatened when Holly-wood beckons. **CL7, CL15**

Sweetie (1990, C, 100m, NR)
Australian story of two sisters (Karen Col-ston, Genevieve Lemon) and their bizarre relationship. Directed by Jane Campion. **FF5**

Swept Away (1975, C, 116m, R)
An Italian comedy-drama about a ship-wrecked odd couple—a snooty rich woman and a lusty sailor. Giancarlo Giannini and Mariangela Melato star; Lina Wertmuller directed. **DT137**

Swimmer, The (1968, C, 94m, PG)
Burt Lancaster stars in this drama about a suburbanite who swims through his neigh-bors' pools on his way home, recalling past experiences along the way. With Janet Land-gard, Janice Rule, Marge Champion, Kim Hunter, and Joan Rivers. Based on a John Cheever story. Directed by Frank Perry. **ST129**

Swimming to Cambodia
(1987, C, 100m, NR)
Actor/monologist Spalding Gray recounts his experiences on location in Thailand for *The Killing Fields* in this mesmerizing one-man show. Directed by Jonathan Demme. **CO12, CO16, DT35**, *Recommended*

Swindle, The see *Il Bidone*

Swing High, Swing Low
(1937, B&W, 95m, NR)
Fred MacMurray is a trumpet player whose career hits every note on the scale. Carole Lombard costars. **CL7, ST140**

Swing Kids (1993, C, 112m, PG-13)
Drama set in Nazi Germany of young trio of friends who love American swing music, strictly *verboten* by their repressive govern-ment. Robert Sean Leonard, Christian Bale, and Frank Whaley star, with Barbara Hershey and Kenneth Branagh (uncredited). **DR5, DR9, ST104**

Swing Shift (1984, C, 100m, PG)
Goldie Hawn goes to work in a factory when her husband goes to fight in World War II. Christine Lahti, Kurt Russell, and Ed Harris star, with Fred Ward, Sudie Bond, Holly Hunter, and in small roles, Roger Corman and Belinda Carlisle. Directed by Jonathan Demme. Seriously compromised when star ordered reshooting and additional scenes not approved by director. Result is not a mess, just flawed. **DR3, DR5, DR10, DT30, DT35, ST99, ST113, ST191**

Swing Time (1936, B&W, 103m, NR)
Fred Astaire-Ginger Rogers musical about a gambler who falls in love with a dance teacher, even though he is engaged to another woman. George Stevens directed this classic musical. **CL15, DT119, MU4, ST4, ST187** *Essential, Highly Recommended*

Swiss Family Robinson
(1960, C, 128m, G)
A shipwrecked family learns to survive on a deserted island. John Mills and Dorothy McGuire star in Disney's version of the fam-ily adventure classic. **FA1**

Swiss Miss (1938, B&W, 72m, NR)
Laurel and Hardy comedy, set in the Alps, with Ollie a love-smitten yodeler. **ST133**

Switch (1991, C, 114m, R)
A notorious ladies' man is shot and killed by three of his girlfriends and his spirit surfaces in the body of a woman. Ellen Barkin stars in this comedy, with Jimmy Smits, JoBeth Wil-liams, Lorraine Bracco, Tony Roberts, and Perry King. Written and directed by Blake Edwards. Potential minefield of material explodes in everyone's face. **CO20, DT40, ST7, XT24**

Switchblade Sisters (1975, C, 91m, R)
Urban action drama centering on the exploits of a female street gang. Robbie Lee, Joanne Nail, and Kitty Bruce star. **AC8**

Switching Channels (1988, C, 105m, PG)
Romantic comedy triangle composed of a TV news producer (Burt Reynolds), his star re-porter and ex-wife (Kathleen Turner), and her

fiancé (Christopher Reeve). A loose remake of *The Front Page* and *His Girl Friday*. Weakest of all versions—yet. **CO1, CU18, ST183, ST218**

Swoon (1992, B&W, 90m, R)
Stylized take on the notorious Crime of the Century, the 1924 Leopold-Loeb case, focusing on the antisemitic and homophobic atmosphere surrounding their trial. Craig Chester and Daniel Schlachet star. Written and directed by Tom Kalin. **DR3, DR5, MY8**

Sword and the Rose, The
(1953, C, 93m, NR)
Mary Tudor works her charms on a knight, incurs the wrath of a duke, and is noticed by Henry VIII. Disney version of *When Knighthood Was in Flower*, starring Glynis Johns and Richard Todd. **FA1**

Sword in the Stone, The
(1963, C, 75m, G)
Disney animated feature about a young boy who is destined to be king of England and is helped by the wizard Merlin. **FA2**

Sword of Doom (1967, B&W, 120m, NR)
Tatsuya Nakadai stars in this adventure film as a samurai whose lust for action alienates even his own family. Toshiro Mifune appears in a small supporting role. **FF4, ST157**

Sword of Sherwood Forest
(1961, C, 80m, NR)
Richard Greene stars as Robin Hood in this costume adventure, with Peter Cushing. **AC15, HF15, ST43**

Sword of the Valiant (1982, C, 101m, PG)
In order to become a knight, Gawain (Miles O'Keeffe) must battle the Green Knight (Sean Connery) and solve a riddle. Trevor Howard and Peter Cushing costar. **FA4, ST36, ST43**

Sybil (1976, C, 132m, NR)
Famous case of woman with multiple personalities and the therapist who helped cure her. Sally Field stars, with Joanne Woodward. Originally made for TV with a running time of 198m. **DR6, ST66, ST234**

Sylvester (1985, C, 104m, PG)
Young woman trains her favorite show horse for competition. Melissa Gilbert stars. **DR22, FA5**

Sylvia and the Phantom
(1945, B&W, 97m, NR)
French comedy of a teen-aged girl's infatuation with the painting of a long-dead nobleman. Odette Joyeux stars, with Jacques Tati. **DT122**

Sylvia Scarlett (1935, B&W, 94m, NR)
Katharine Hepburn and Cary Grant star in this offbeat story of a traveling troupe of players; she's disguised as a boy and he doesn't suspect a thing—for a while. Directed by George Cukor; underappreciated until recent rediscovery. **CL14, DT32, ST92, ST103,** *Highly Recommended*

Sympathy for the Devil
(1970, C, 92m, NR)
French director Jean-Luc Godard alternates political rhetoric with shots of the Rolling Stones recording the title song. Curio for fans of director and group only. **CU9, DT50**

THX 1138 (1971, C, 88m, PG)
In the future, computers keep the humans drugged so they cannot think and feel for themselves. One man (Robert Duvall) and his roommate (Maggie McOmie) decide to stop taking the drugs and begin to feel human emotions. Director George Lucas's debut feature. **DT77, SF11, ST63**

T-Men (1947, B&W, 96m, NR)
Undercover government agents try to expose a counterfeit ring. Suspenseful drama from director Anthony Mann, starring Dennis O'Keefe. **DT85, MY1**

T.N.T. Jackson (1974, C, 73m, R)
A female karate expert (Jeanne Bell) searches for her missing brother. **AC26**

Table for Five (1983, C, 122m, PG)
Tearjerker of divorced father (Jon Voight) trying to make up for lost time by taking three children on European cruise. With Richard Crenna, Marie-Christine Barrault, Millie Perkins, Roxana Zal, Robby Kiger, Son Hoang Bui, and in a small role, Kevin Costner. **DR2, DR8, ST33**

Tabu (1931, B&W, 82m, NR)
Unusual romantic drama, shot documentary-style by director F.W. Murnau on location in Tahiti. A young fisherman (Matahi) falls in love with a woman (Anna Chevalier) considered taboo to all men by superstition. Documentary pioneer Robert Flaherty began filming as Murnau's partner but left production because of disagreements. **CL4**

Tai-Pan (1986, C, 127m, R)
Historical drama about the founding of modern Hong Kong, based on James Clavell's epic novel. Bryan Brown and Joan Chen star. **DR5**

Take a Hard Ride (1975, C, 103m, PG)
Jim Brown, Lee Van Cleef, and Fred Williamson head the cast of this Western drama about a cowboy carrying a payroll shipment across the Mexico border. **ST221, WE9**

Take Me Out to the Ball Game
(1949, C, 93m, NR)
Busby Berkeley musical about a woman

(Esther Williams) who takes over a winning baseball team. Gene Kelly and Frank Sinatra are her star players, who sing and dance better than they hit and field. Colorful stuff, although Kelly and Sinatra are better in other films of time. **DT12, MU1, MU6, ST123, ST199**

Take the Money and Run
(1969, C, 85m, PG)
Woody Allen's tale of an inept bank robber spoofs documentaries, crime movies, love stories—you name it. Janet Margolin costars; narrated by Jackson Beck. Allen's debut as writer-director-star is occasionally funny, more often just amusing. **CO7, CO10, DT2**

Take This Job and Shove it
(1981, C, 100m, PG)
Hometown boy returns to modernize his conglomerate's brewery, has a change of mind when he sees how it affects workers. Comedy-drama stars Robert Hays, with Barbara Hershey, David Keith, and Martin Mull. **CO2, ST104**

Taking Care of Business
(1990, C, 107m, R)
Comedy of mistaken identity when escaped con (Jim Belushi) finds organizer of busy ad executive (Charles Grodin) and assumes his lifestyle. **CO13, CO20, ST94**

Taking of Pelham One Two Three, The
(1974, C, 104m, PG)
A gang of hijackers hold the passengers of a New York subway car hostage. Walter Matthau is the cop on the case, Robert Shaw the lead baddie. With Martin Balsam, Hector Elizondo, Jerry Stiller, and Tony Roberts. Shaw's very good; refreshingly non-violent. **AC9, ST155, XT9, XT19**

Tale of the Frog Prince, The
(1985, C, 60m, NR)
A spoiled princess is forced to tend a talented frog who turns out to be a cursed prince. Robin Williams and Teri Garr star in this presentation from Faerie Tale Theatre. **FA12, ST228**

Tale of Two Cities, A
(1935, B&W, 121m, NR)
Charles Dickens's classic story of the French Revolution and one man's sacrifice for another on the guillotine. Ronald Colman, Elizabeth Allan, and Edna May Oliver star. **CL3, ST35, WR5,** *Recommended*

Tale of Two Cities, A
(1958, B&W, 117m, NR)
The Dickens classic of life during the French Revolution, with Dirk Bogarde as Sidney Carton, and Dorothy Tutin, Cecil Parker, Step-

hen Murray, and Christopher Lee. **CL3, ST14, ST135, WR5**

Talent for the Game (1991, C, 91m, PG)
Tale of Los Angeles Angels baseball scout given one last chance by new team owner, landing small-town prospect his bosses then try to rush into the big leagues. Edward James Olmos stars, with Lorraine Bracco, Jamey Sheridan, Terry Kirney, and Jeff Corbett. Even baseball fans may not make it to the last inning of this snoozer. **DR22**

Tales From The Crypt (1972, C, 92m, PG)
Five criminally minded people are trapped in catacombs with a mind-reading monk. He shows them the consequences if they carry out the crimes they are plotting. Joan Collins and Peter Cushing star, with Ralph Richardson. **HO23, HO26, ST43, ST184**

Tales From the Crypt (1989, C, 81m, NR)
Three-part horror film from directors Walter Hill, Robert Zemeckis, and Richard Donner, based on the old E.C. comics stories. **DT56, DT143, HO23**

Tales From the Darkside: The Movie
(1990, C, 93m, R)
Anthology horror film based on stories by Stephen King, Arthur Conan Doyle, and Michael McDowell. Among the stars: Deborah Harry, Christian Slater, David Johansen, William Hickey, James Remar, and Rae Dawn Chong. **HO23, MU12, ST200, WR15**

Tales of Hoffmann (1951, C, 138m, NR)
Opera by Jacques Offenbach of student fantasies, filmed in dazzling color by Michael Powell and Emeric Pressburger. Moira Shearer and Robert Ronnseville star. Video restores film to full running time. **CL9, CU10, DT99, MU8**

Tales of Ordinary Madness
(1983, C, 107m, NR)
Drama of hard-drinking poet who meets unusual assortment of women in his travels. Ben Gazzara, Ornella Muti, and Susan Tyrrell star. Based on stories by Charles Bukowski. **CU6**

Tales of Terror (1962, C, 90m, NR)
Three stories based on Edgar Allen Poe; *The Black Cat, Morella,* and *The Case of M. Valdemar.* Vincent Price and Peter Lorre star. Directed by Roger Corman. **DT30, HO23, ST179, WR27**

Talk of the Town, The
(1942, B&W, 118m, NR)
Comedy-drama with Cary Grant a fugitive hiding out in boardinghouse run by Jean Arthur, debating fellow boarder Ronald Col-

man on the justice system. Directed by George Stevens. **CL10, DT119, ST3, ST92**

Talk Radio (1988, C, 110m, R)
Eric Bogosian plays a smart-mouthed radio talk show host whose personal life matches the turmoil he creates on the air. Oliver Stone directed; based on Bogosian's play and true incidents in the life of Alan Berg, a host who was assassinated by white supremacists. **DR6, DR7, DR12, DR20, DT120**

Tall Blond Man With One Black Shoe, The (1972, C, 90m, PG)
French spy spoof starring Pierre Richard as a man caught in the middle of a battle between espionage agents. U.S. remake: *The Man With One Red Shoe*. **FF1, FF8**

Tall Guy, The (1989, C, 90m, R)
Jeff Goldblum stars in an amusing comedy about an American actor in London stage musical version of *The Elephant Man*, romancing a no-nonsense nurse. With Emma Thompson, Rowan Atkinson, and Geraldine James. **CO8, CO17, ST90, XT15,** *Recommended*

Tall Men, The (1955, C, 122m, NR)
After the Civil War, two Rebs sign on a cattle drive from Texas to Montana. Clark Gable and Robert Ryan star, with Jane Russell. Directed by Raoul Walsh. **DT131, ST63, ST165**

Tall Story (1960, B&W, 91m, NR)
Romantic comedy of basketball player and the young woman who puts a full-court press on him. Anthony Perkins and Jane Fonda (her film debut) star, with Ray Walston, Anne Jackson, and Murray Hamilton. Based on a play by Howard Lindsay and Russel Crouse. **CO1, CO19, DR20, ST72**

Tall T, The (1957, C, 78m, NR)
Cult Western starring Randolph Scott and Maureen O'Sullivan; they're kidnapped by outlaws and plot their escape. With Richard Boone, Arthur Hunnicutt, Skip Homeier, and Henry Silva. Adapted by Burt Kennedy from an Elmore Leonard story, directed by Budd Boetticher. Among the best of the Scott-Boetticher-Kennedy collaborations. **DT14, ST197, WE15, WR19,** *Recommended*

Tamarind Seed, The (1974, C, 123m, PG)
Blake Edwards directed this story of romance and espionage, starring Omar Sharif and Julie Andrews. He's a Russian agent trying to recruit her at a Caribbean resort, but love intervenes. With Anthony Quayle, Daniel O'Herlihy, Sylvia Sims, and Oscar Homolka. **DT40, MY5, MY6, ST2, XT30**

Taming of the Shrew, The (1967, C, 126m, NR)
Elizabeth Taylor-Richard Burton version of Shakespeare's classic comedy of a headstrong woman and her equally stubborn suitor. Franco Zeffirelli directed. **CL15, ST22, ST212, WR28,** *Recommended*

Tampopo (1987, C, 114m, NR)
Japanese comedy centering on a widow's attempts to open her own noodle restaurant, with a gruff truck driver coming to her rescue. Numerous subplots and sight gags revolve around the subject of food. Directed, with great gusto, by Juzo Itami. **FF4,** *Recommended*

Tango and Cash (1989, C, 98m, R)
Sylvester Stallone and Kurt Russell play rival L.A. cops who team up to bring down an illegal drug organization. With Teri Hatcher, Jack Palance, and Brion James. **AC9, ST191, ST204**

Tank (1984, C, 113m, PG)
A teen-ager is arrested on trumped-up charges by a bigoted sheriff and his father decides to use a surplus tank to free him. James Garner, C. Thomas Howell, G.D. Spradlin, and Shirley Jones star. **DR8, ST82**

Tanner (1988, C, 352m, NR)
Witty look at contemporary politics, with fictional Presidential candidate slogging through 1988 primaries, dealing with ever-present media. Michael Murphy and Pamela Reed star, with appearances by many political and entertainment personalities playing themselves. Written by Garry Trudeau; directed by Robert Altman. Originally made for cable TV. A condensed, 120m. version is also available under the title *Tanner '88*. **CO2, DT4, XT18, XT26,** *Recommended*

Tap (1989, C, 111m, PG-13)
Just out of jail, an ex-dancer is torn between continuing his life of crime and returning to his love of the stage. Gregory Hines stars, with Sammy Davis, Jr. and a host of exponents of old-time tap dancing. **DR12, MU3**

Tapeheads (1988, C, 97m, R)
Comedy about a pair of clumsy but with-it guys (Tim Robbins and John Cusack) trying to make it big in the rock music video biz. With Mary Crosby, Doug McClure, Connie Stevens, and real-life rockers Sam Moore and Junior Walker as a singing duo called The Swanky Modes. Robbins and Cusack are engaging, and the show-biz satire is on target. **CO8, MU9,** *Recommended*

Taps (1981, C, 118m, R)
Timothy Hutton and George C. Scott star in this drama about a rebellious military school

student and his commanding officer. With Tom Cruise and Sean Penn. **DR9, DR25, ST41, ST196**

Target (1985, C, 117m, R)
When a businessman's wife is kidnapped on a trip to Paris, he's forced to admit to his son his association with the CIA. Gene Hackman and Matt Dillon star in this thriller directed by Arthur Penn. **DT96, MY6, ST56, ST96, XT16**

Targets (1968, C, 90m, PG)
Twin stories, which eventually intersect, about an aging horror film star (Boris Karloff) about to retire and a mad sniper. With Tim O'Kelly, Nancy Hsueh, and Peter Bogdanovich, who made his directing debut. Uncredited executive producer: Roger Corman; scenes from his Karloff film, *The Terror*, are used. Great finale at drive-in theater. **CU14, DR13, MY13, ST119**

Tarzan and His Mate
(1934, B&W, 93m, NR)
Second teaming of Johnny Weissmuller and Maureen O'Sullivan as jungle man and his woman is cult favorite, mainly for long-censored footage of stars in skimpy attire. Story is about ivory poachers and T's battle with them. With Jack Conway and Neil Hamilton. Video version contains restored footage—but it's still suitable for kids. **CU10, FA4, HF22,** *Recommended*

Tarzan and the Green Goddess
(1938, B&W, 72m, NR)
Feature film version of serial *The New Adventures of Tarzan*, starring Herman Brix (aka Bruce Bennett). **HF22**

Tarzan and the Trappers
(1958, B&W, 74m, NR)
Gordon Scott plays the Lord of the Apes in this collection of three pilots for an unsold TV series. **FA4, HF22**

Tarzan Escapes (1936, B&W, 95m, NR)
Tarzan is captured by a hunter who wants to turn him into a sideshow freak. Johnny Weissmuller and Maureen O'Sullivan star. **FA4, HF22**

Tarzan Finds a Son!
(1939, B&W, 90m, NR)
The first appearance of Boy in the series; he's a baby adopted by Tarzan and Jane after his parents are killed in a plane crash. Johnny Weissmuller and Maureen O'Sullivan star, with Ian Hunter and Laraine Day. Originally intended as O'Sullivan's swan song as Jane but ending was reshot so she could return. **FA4, HF22**

Tarzan of the Apes
(1918, B&W, 130m, NR)
Elmo Lincoln stars as the screen's first Tarzan. This one's a silent film, so don't listen for that famous yell. **HF22**

Tarzan, the Ape Man
(1932, B&W, 99m, G)
Johnny Weissmuller's debut as the jungle hero. Maureen O'Sullivan costars. **FA4, HF22,** *Essential*

Tarzan, the Ape Man (1981, C, 112m, R)
An adult version of the famous story, with Miles O'Keeffe as the swingin' jungle man and Bo Derek as a frequently unclad Jane. With Richard Harris. Directed by John Derek. Cult following more for its sheer ineptness than sexiness. **CU11, HF22**

Tarzan the Fearless (1933, B&W, 85m, NR)
Buster Crabbe puts on the loincloth for this feature version of a Tarzan serial. **FA4, HF22**

Tarzan's New York Adventure
(1942, B&W, 72m, NR)
Circus owners kidnap Boy and take him to the Big Apple, with Tarzan and Jane in pursuit. Johnny Weissmuller and Maureen O'Sullivan star, with Johnny Sheffield. O'Sullivan's last appearance as Jane. Weissmuller looks great in a double-breasted suit. **DR27, FA4, HF22**

Tarzan's Revenge (1938, B&W, 70m, NR)
Olympic athletes Glenn Morris and Eleanor Holm play Tarzan and Jane in this installment of the long-running adventure series. **FA4, HF22**

Tarzan's Secret Treasure
(1941, B&W, 81m, NR)
Gold prospectors enlist Tarzan's help. Johnny Weissmuller, Maureen O'Sullivan, and Johnny Sheffield star. **FA4, HF22**

Taste of Honey, A (1961, B&W, 100m, NR)
British drama starring Rita Tushingham as a young woman left pregnant by a black sailor, taken in by a gay friend. Adapted from Shelagh Delaney's play. **DR3, DR20, DR23**

Taxi Blues (1990, C, 110m, NR)
Soviet comedy-drama set in Moscow follows relationship of bigoted cabbie and alcoholic Jewish musician. Pyotr Mamonov and Vladimir Kachpour star. Directed by Pavel Lounguine. **FF7**

Taxi Driver (1976, C, 113m, R)
Riveting drama of a paranoid New York cab driver getting involved with a twelve-year-old prostitute, whom he tries to "save" from the evils of the streets. Robert De Niro stars, with Cybill Shepherd, Jodie Foster, Albert Brooks,

and Harvey Keitel. Written by Paul Schrader; directed by Martin Scorsese. Violent finale nearly got the film an "X" rating. Music by Bernard Herrmann, his last film score. **CU7, DR15, DT12, DT114, MY2, ST51, ST75, XT9, XT26,** *Essential, Highly Recommended*

Taxing Woman, A (1988, C, 127m, NR)
Japanese comedy of a female tax collector who has to battle the prejudices of her male colleagues and the deceit of taxpayers. Directed by Juzo Itami. **FF4**

Tea and Sympathy (1956, C, 122m, NR)
Adaptation of Robert Anderson's play about scandalous affair between student (John Kerr) and teacher's wife (Deborah Kerr). With Leif Erickson, Edward Andrews, and Darryl Hickman. Directed by Vincente Minnelli. **DR2, DR3, DR20, DT88, ST125**

Tea for Two (1950, C, 98m, NR)
Doris Day musical loosely based on *No, No Nanette,* about young woman who bets her uncle that for one weekend she can answer every question with the word "no". With Gordon MacRae, Gene Nelson, Eve Arden, and S.Z. Sakall. **ST47**

Teachers (1984, C, 106m, R)
Life at a big-city high school, where the students don't care and most of the teachers are just collecting a paycheck. Nick Nolte stars, with JoBeth Williams, Ralph Macchio, and Richard Mulligan. Look for Conra Dern in a small role. Blows opportunity to explore urgent issue with broad comedy and fumbling dramatics. **DR25, ST53, ST164**

Teacher's Pet (1958, B&W, 120m, NR)
The editor of a newspaper (Clark Gable) enrolls in a night school class in journalism to make time with the teacher (Doris Day). With Gig Young. **CO18, ST47, ST77**

Teahouse of the August Moon, The (1956, C, 123m, NR)
Service comedy set in postwar Okinawa, with occupying Americans clashing with Japanese. Marlon Brando and Glenn Ford star, with Machiko Kyo and Eddie Albert. **CO21, ST18**

Teddy Ruxpin: Teddy Outsmarts M.A.V.O. (1987, C, 75m, NR)
Animated adventure of Teddy and his friends pursued by the villainous members of M.A.V.O., who want a special crystal Teddy is carrying. **FA10**

Teen Wolf (1985, C, 91m, PG)
A teen-ager (Michael J. Fox) discovers he is descended from a family of werewolves and becomes popular at school when his classmates find out. **CO4, CO11, HO4**

Teenage Mutant Ninja Turtles (1990, C, 93m, PG)
The popular superheroes—Raphael, Michelangelo, Donatello, and Leonardo—debut in their first live-action feature. **AC17, FA4**

Teenage Mutant Ninja Turtles II: The Secret of The Ooze (1991, C, 88m, PG)
Those pizza-lovin' turtles return for another adventure against their nemesis, the evil Shredder. With Paige Turco and David Warner. **AC17, FA4**

Teenage Mutant Ninja Turtles III: The Turtles Are Back . . . in Time (1993, C, 95m, PG)
In this installment of the series, the turtles and their pal April are transported back to seventeenth-century Japan, taking the place of five samurai warriors. Elias Koteas and Paige Turco star. **AC17, FA4, SF4**

Telefon (1977, C, 102m, PG)
Charles Bronson plays a Russian agent teaming up with the CIA to prevent an unhinged Soviet spy from unleashing a lethal army of hypnotized bombers. With Lee Remick. Don Siegel directed. **DT116, MY6, ST20**

Telephone, The (1988, C, 82m, R)
Whoopi Goldberg stars in a strange tale of an unemployed actress coming unraveled. With Severn Darden, Amy Wright, Elliott Gould, and John Heard. Written by Harry Nilsson and Terry Southern, directed by Rip Torn. **ST89, ST216, XT23**

Tell Me a Riddle (1980, C, 90m, PG)
Adaptation of Tillie Olsen novella of dying woman recalling her marriage of forty years. Melvyn Douglas and Lila Kedrova star, with Brooke Adams. Directed by Lee Grant. **DR8, DR11, DR19, ST58, XT23**

Tell Them Willy Boy Is Here (1969, C, 96m, G)
True story set in American West of 1910s about Native American (Robert Blake) who killed a man in self-defense and was pursued by a large posse to his death. Robert Redford plays the sheriff with mixed emotions about the politically motivated manhunt. With Katharine Ross, Susan Clark, Barry Sullivan, Charles McGraw, and John Vernon. Directed by Abraham Polonsky. **ST181, WE3, WE7, WE11**

Temp, The (1993, C, 95m, R)
Thriller about a temporary secretary who takes over her young boss's life, creating major problems at his office. Timothy Hutton and Lara Flynn Boyle star, with Dwight Schultz, Oliver Platt, and Faye Dunaway. **DR24, MY4, MY19, ST61**

Tempest (1928, B&W, 102m, NR)
Drama of the Russian Revolution starring John Barrymore as peasant turned sergeant. With Camilla Horn and Louis Wolheim. **CL3, ST8**

Tempest (1982, C, 140m, PG)
Mid-life crisis drama of New Yorker (John Cassavetes) who escapes to Greek island with teen-aged daughter (Molly Ringwald). With Gena Rowlands, Susan Sarandon, Vittorio Gassman, and Raul Julia. Written and directed by Paul Mazursky, who also has a small role. Any resemblance to Shakespeare's play is intentional. **DT87, ST194, WR28**

Tempest, The (1963, C, 76m, NR)
Shakespeare's classic, starring Maurice Evans, Richard Burton, Roddy McDowall, and Lee Remick. **ST21, WR22**

10 (1979, C, 122m, R)
Comedy about middle-aged man who can't decide between marriage to his charming but predictable girlfriend and a wild fling with woman of his dreams. Dudley Moore, Julie Andrews, and Bo Derek star, with Brian Dennehy, Robert Webber, and Dee Wallace. Blake Edwards directed. Widescreen will be lost on video. Career booster for Derek and Ravel, composer of "Bolero." **CO1, CU20, DT40, ST2, ST160, XT30**, *Essential*

Ten Commandments, The
(1923, B&W, 146m, NR)
Cecil B. DeMille's silent classic, combining a modern tale of sin and redemption with the the story of Moses and the famous tablets. Theodore Roberts, Richard Dix, and Rod La Rocque star. **CL12, CL13, DT34**, *Essential*

Ten Commandments, The
(1956, C, 220m, G)
Biblical epic about the life of Moses, from birth to his leading the Jews out of Egypt. Charlton Heston stars, with Yul Brynner as Ramses, Anne Baxter, Debra Paget, Edward G. Robinson, Vincent Price, and John Derek. Directed by Cecil B. DeMille; his last film. Available in letterboxed edition. Rousing entertainment; only DeMille can make the Bible this much fun. Should have won the Oscar for Best Picture. **CL9, CL13, CU19, DT34, ST179, ST186, XT28**, *Essential, Highly Recommended*

Ten Days That Shook the World/October (1927, B&W, 104m, NR)
From director Sergei Eisenstein, a documentary of the events surrounding the 1917 Russian Revolution. **CU9, CU16, DT41**

Ten Days Wonder (1972, C, 101m, PG)
Offbeat story of young man having an affair with his stepmother. Anthony Perkins and Marlene Jobert star, with Orson Welles and Michel Piccoli. Based on a novel by Ellery Queen. Directed by Claude Chabrol; dialogue in English. **DR3, DT134**

Ten From Your Show of Shows
(1973, B&W, 92m, NR)
Classic bits from the legendary TV show of the early 1950s, starring Sid Caesar, Imogene Coca, Carl Reiner, and Howard Morris. Sketch comedy at its absolute best. **CO16**, *Highly Recommended*

Ten Little Indians (1975, C, 98m, PG)
Latest version of Agatha Christie's classic whodunit, with setting switched to a hotel in Iranian desert. Oliver Reed, Elke Sommer, and Herbert Lom head the list of victims/suspects. **MY12, WR3**

Ten North Frederick
(1958, B&W, 102m, NR)
John O'Hara story of man pushed into politics by ambitious wife. Gary Cooper and Geraldine Fitzgerald star, with Diane Varsi, Suzy Parker, and Tom Tully. **DR21, ST37, WR24**

10 Rillington Place (1971, C, 111m, PG)
True story of the infamous John Christie murders in Britain, and how the real killer's testimony helped send the wrong man to the gallows. Richard Attenborough and John Hurt star. **DR16, MY7, MY8, MY15**

Ten to Midnight (1983, C, 100m, R)
Charles Bronson stars as a police detective tracking a psycho killer who has made the big mistake of harassing Bronson's daughter. **MY13, ST20**

Ten Wanted Men (1955, C, 80m, NR)
Randolph Scott Western, costars Richard Boone as a rival rancher who resorts to intimidation to get his way. With Lee Van Cleef. **ST197, ST221**

Ten Who Dared (1960, C, 92m, NR)
Disney adventure, based on the exploits of Major John Wesley Powell (Brian Keith), who explored the uncharted Colorado River in 1869. With Ben Johnson, R.G. Armstrong, and L.Q. Jones. **FA1**

Tenant, The (1976, C, 125m, R)
Disturbed man moves into the Parisian apartment of a suicide victim, begins to assume her identity. Director Roman Polanski stars in this psychological drama, with Isabelle Adjani, Shelley Winters, and Melvyn Douglas. Polanski's last great film. **DT97, ST58, ST232**, *Recommended*

Tender Comrade (1943, C, 102m, NR)
World War II homefront drama of group of women living together commune-style. Gin-

ger Rogers and Robert Ryan star, with Ruth Hussey and Kim Hunter. Directed by Edward Dmytryk. **CL8, ST187, ST193**

Tender Mercies (1983, C, 93m, PG)
A down-and-out country singer finds redemption in the love of a farm widow and her son. Oscar winner Robert Duvall stars, with Tess Harper, Ellen Barkin, and Betty Buckley as the women in his life. Directed by Bruce Beresford. Duvall is magnificent but story feels undernourished. **DR1, DR2, DR12, DT10, ST7, ST63, XT2**

Tender Trap, The (1955, C, 111m, NR)
Romantic comedy of confirmed New York bachelor (Frank Sinatra) landed by determined young woman (Debbie Reynolds). With Celeste Holm, David Wayne, Carolyn Jones, and Lola Albright. Frank sings title tune, written by Sammy Cahn and Jimmy Van Heusen. **CO1, ST199**

Tentacles (1977, C, 90m, PG)
A giant octopus terrorizes a seaside community. John Huston, Henry Fonda, Bo Hopkins, and Shelley Winters star. **DT60, ST71, ST232**

Tenth Anniversary Young Comedians Special see *HBO Comedy Club*

Tenth Man, The (1988, C, 94m, NR)
Drama of Frenchman, held captive by Nazis, bargaining away his property to fellow prisoner, who takes his place in front of firing squad. After the war, he returns incognito to his home, where he falls in love with the dead man's sister. Anthony Hopkins stars, with Kristin Scott Thomas, Derek Jacobi, and Cyril Cusack. Based on a Graham Greene novella. **ST109, WR11**

Tenth Victim, The (1965, B&W, 92m, NR)
In a future society, killing humans is legal, with organized hunting. A science fiction spoof from Italy, starring Marcello Mastroianni and Ursula Andress. **FF2, SF21, ST154**

Teorema (1968, C, 98m, NR)
Allegorical tale from Italian director Paolo Pasolini describes series of events precipitated by visit to family of wealthy industrialist by a mysterious stranger (Terence Stamp). With Silvana Mangano, Massimo Girotti, Anna Wiazemsky, and Laura Betti. **FF2**

Tequila Sunrise (1988, C, 116m, R)
Romantic triangle involving an ex-drug dealer, a narcotics cop (who is also the ex-dealer's best friend), and the lovell owner of a posh Italian restaurant. Mel Gibson, Kurt Russell, and Michelle Pfeiffer star. With Raul

Julia and in a small part, Budd Boetticher. Written and directed by Robert Towne. Attractive leads carry familiar tale; Gibson almost makes drug dealer sympathetic. **DR1, DT10, MY2, ST85, ST173, ST191,** *Recommended*

Teresa Venerdi (1941, B&W, 90m, NR)
Italian director Vittorio De Sica stars in this comedy of a doctor at an orphanage who's involved with three women. Anna Magnani costars. **DT37**

Terminal Choice (1985, C, 97m, R)
A series of mysterious deaths at a computerized hospital is the basis for this horror film. Joe Spano, Diane Venora, David McCallum, and Ellen Barkin star. **HO20, ST7**

Terminal Man, The (1974, C, 104m, PG)
A mini-computer is created to help control a person's psychopathic tendencies. When the computer is implanted in the brain of a test subject, it fails and turns him homicidal. George Segal stars, with Joan Hackett, Richard Dysart, Jill Clayburgh, and James B. Sikking. Directed by Michael Hodges. Based on the novel by Michael Crichton. **HO20, SF4, ST31**

Terminal Station see *Indiscretion of an American Wife, The*

Terminator, The (1984, C, 108m, R)
Cyborg assassin from the year 2029 is sent to 1984 to kill the woman who will give birth to his opposition's leader. Arnold Schwarzenegger, Michael Biehn, and Linda Hamilton star, with Paul Winfield. Written and directed by James Cameron, who breathes new life into familiar material. **AC25, DT21, SF4, SF6, ST195, ST230,** *Recommended*

Terminator 2: Judgment Day
(1991, C, 136m, R)
Return of murderous cyborg from the future, now sent to help female target of first adventure and her young son. Arnold Schwarzenegger stars, with Linda Hamilton, Edward Furlong, Robert Patrick as the shape-shifting bad cyborg, and Joe Morton. Co-written and directed by James Cameron. Tons of money went into Oscar winning special effects but humor and speed of first film were lost in process. Enough, enough! **AC25, DR21, DT21, SF4, SF6, SF15, ST195**

Terms of Endearment
(1983, C, 132m, PG)
Shirley MacLaine and Debra Winger play a mother and daughter whose relationship virtually defines the phrase "love-hate" in this Ossar-winning drama. With Jack Nicholson, Jeff Daniels, John Lithgow, and Danny

DeVito. MacLaine and Nicholson, writer-director James L. Brooks also won Oscars. Based on Larry McMurtry's novel. Get out your handkerchiefs. **DR2, DR8, DR19, ST54, ST145, ST163, ST231, XT1, XT3, XT4, XT6,** *Highly Recommended*

Terror, The (1963, C, 81m, NR)
A soldier in Napoleon's army (Jack Nicholson) follows a mysterious woman (Sandra Knight) to a castle owned by a sinister man (Boris Karloff). Directed by Roger Corman. Footage from this film appears in *Targets.* **DT30, ST119, ST163**

Terror at the Red Wolf Inn
(1972, C, 90m, NR)
A student on vacation stays at an inn run by two very nice old people who have a retarded grandson. When several guests disappear, she discovers that the proprietors are cannibals. **HO24**

Terror by Night (1946, B&W, 60m, NR)
Sherlock Holmes mystery starring Basil Rathbone and Nigel Bruce, set aboard a train, concerning a famous jewel and murders. **HF14**

Terror Castle see *Horror Castle*

Terror Circus see *Nightmare Circus*

Terror House see *Night Has Eyes, The*

Terror in the Wax Museum
(1973, C, 93m, PG)
A girl inherits a wax museum where a grisly murder took place. When she moves into the apartment above the museum, she is terrorized by the wax figures of famous criminals. Ray Milland and Elsa Lanchester star. **HO26**

Terror of Mechagodzilla
(1978, C, 79m, NR)
Aliens who want to invade Japan create a robot Godzilla monster to battle the real Godzilla, now the protector of Japan. **FF4, SF18**

Terror of Tiny Town, The
(1938, B&W, 63m, NR)
A one-of-a-kind Western drama, with an all-midget cast! This one has to be seen to be believed. **CU11, WE15**

Terror Squad (1987, C, 92m, NR)
Small-town sheriff (Chuck Connors) leads an ad-hoc army against a band of terrorists who have taken over a nuclear plant. **AC20**

Terror Train (1980, C, 97m, R)
Fraternity party aboard train is plagued by mad killer. Jamie Lee Curtis, Hart Bochner,

Ben Johnson, and David Copperfield star. **HO12, ST42, XT19**

Terror Vision (1986, C, 85m, R)
An alien emerges from a family's television set and wreaks havoc. **SF20**

Terrorists, The (1975, C, 97m, PG)
Sean Connery plays a hostage negotiator in this thriller about an airline hijacking. **ST36**

Terry Fox Story, The (1983, C, 97m, NR)
True, heartfelt tale of a young Canadian runner who loses a leg to cancer and undertakes a cross-country run to raise funds to research his disease. Real-life amputee Eric Fryer stars, with Robert Duvall. Originally made for cable TV. **DR6, ST63**

Tess (1979, C, 170m, PG)
Literate adaptation of the Thomas Hardy novel of a young girl (Nastassja Kinski) twice wronged in love. With Peter Firth, John Bett, and Tom Chadbon. Roman Polanski directed. Oscar winning Cinematography, Art Direction, and Costumes. Stately, elegant, with only Kinski's uncertain performance a debit. **DR19, DT97,** *Recommended*

Test Pilot (1938, C, 118m, NR)
Saga of daredevil pilots, starring Clark Gable, Spencer Tracy, and Myrna Loy, with Lionel Barrymore and Marjorie Main. **AC11, ST77, ST142, ST217**

Testament (1983, C, 89m, PG)
Jane Alexander tries to hold her family together after a nuclear attack, as they wait for the radiation approaching their small town. With William Devane, Rebecca De Mornay, and in a small role, Kevin Costner. **DR7, DR10, DR26, SF12, ST38**

Testament of Dr. Cordelier, The
(1959, C, 95m, NR)
Jean Renoir directed this fantasy of a Jekyll-Hyde character stalking the streets of Paris. **DT104, XT16**

Testament of Dr. Mabuse, The
(1933, B&W, 120m, NR)
A criminal kingpin controls his operations even while he's locked up in an insane asylum. Classic crime drama, with touches of the supernatural, from German director Fritz Lang. **DT70, FF3, SF2**

Testament of Orpheus
(1960, B&W, 80m, NR)
Director Jean Cocteau's last film takes a fanciful journey through his life and times. Cocteau appears, with Maria Casares, Jean-Pierre Léaud, Yul Brynner, Brigitte Bardot, Jean Marais, Pablo Picasso, and Charles Aznavour. **DT26, ST6**

Tetsuo: The Iron Man
(1992, B&W, 67m, NR)
Violent Japanese science fiction fantasy, with
cult following, of people turning into metal
creatures. Tomoroh Taguchi and Kei Fujiwara
star. Produced, written, and directed by
Shinya Tsukamoto, who also has a small role.
Feels like a 1950s underground film gone
high-tech; worth a look for those with strong
stomachs and admiring of brilliant filmmaking technique. Also on the same tape: *Drum
Struck* (1991, B&W, 25m, NR), about a lethal
audition competition for a rock band,
directed and cowritten by Greg Nickson.
CU1, CU7, FF4, HO17, SF6

Tex (1982, C, 103m, PG)
Well-meaning but mischievous teen-ager
(Matt Dillon) is raised by his older brother
after their mother dies and father deserts
them. With Jim Metzler, Meg Tilly, Bill
McKinney, Ben Johnson, and Emilio Estevez.
Based on S.E. Hinton's novel. Modest
rewards. **DR9, DR19, ST56**

Texas (1941, B&W, 93m, NR)
William Holden and Glenn Ford play saddle
pals competing for the same woman (Claire
Trevor) in this Western drama. **ST106**

Texas Carnival (1951, C, 77m, NR)
Esther Williams and Red Skelton star in this
musical of carnival performers mistaken for a
couple of Lone Star State millionaires. With
Howard Keel, Ann Miller, Keenan Wynn, and
Red Norvo. **MU1, MU6**

Texas Chainsaw Massacre, The
(1974, C, 83m, R)
A group of teen-agers stumble onto a family
of cannibals. Cult horror directed by Tobe
Hooper. Set new standards for gore in more
or less mainstream films. **CU1, CU4, CU7,
HO12, HO14,** *Essential*

Texas Chainsaw Massacre 2, The
(1986, C, 95m, NR)
An ex-lawman (Dennis Hopper) swears
revenge on the cannibal family who use
human meat in their prize-winning chili.
This sequel to *The Texas Chainsaw Massacre*
was also directed by Tobe Hooper. **HO14,
ST110**

Texas Lady (1955, C, 86m, NR)
Claudette Colbert stars in this low-key Western about a newspaper editor battling injustice on the frontier. **ST34, WE8**

Texas Legionnaires (1943, B&W, 71m, NR)
Roy Rogers referees another feud between
sheepherders and cattlemen. With the Sons
of the Pioneers. **ST188**

Texasville (1990, C, 123m, R)
Sequel to *The Last Picture Show* picks up characters twenty-five-plus years later, during
1984 oil bust. Virtually all the stars from the
pre-vious film return: Jeff Bridges, Cybill
Shepherd, Timothy Bottoms, Cloris Leachman, Randy Quaid, and Eileen Brennan; with
Annie Potts. Based on Larry McMurtry's
novel. Directed by Peter Bogdanovich. **DR7,
DR19, DR26, ST19**

Thank God, It's Friday
(1978, C, 90m, PG)
Musical comedy centering on characters who
hang out at a disco, starring Donna Summer
and The Commodores, and featuring early
screen appearances by Debra Winger and Jeff
Goldblum. **MU9, ST90, ST231**

Thank Your Lucky Stars
(1943, B&W, 127m, NR)
Eddie Cantor puts on a show to support the
war effort and has many of Warner Brothers'
dramatic stars doing musical and comedy
sketches. Highlights include Bette Davis singing "They're Either Too Young or Too Old."
Other appearances include Humphrey Bogart,
Errol Flynn, John Garfield, and Olivia de
Havilland. **MU15, ST15, ST44, ST49, ST69,
ST80**

That Certain Woman
(1937, B&W, 93m, NR)
Bette Davis plays a gangster's widow who
falls in love with a straight-arrow guy (Henry
Fonda). With Donald Crisp, Ian Hunter, and
Sidney Toler. **CL5, ST44, ST71**

That Certain Thing
(1928, B&W, 65m, NR)
Silent comedy, directed by Frank Capra, of a
man who loses his inheritance but marries
for love. Viola Dana, Ralph Graves, and Burr
McIntosh star. **DT22**

That Championship Season
(1982, C, 110m, R)
A high school basketball team reunites years
later with their coach in this drama based on
Jason Miller's play. Robert Mitchum stars,
with Bruce Dern, Stacy Keach, Martin Sheen,
and Paul Sorvino. Directed by Miller. Great
cast can't deliver cliches; Mitchum seems
out of position as coach. **DR20, DR22,
ST158**

That Cold Day in the Park
(1969, C, 113m, R)
Suspense drama about a spinster who takes
in a young man and holds him prisoner.
Sandy Dennis and Michael Burns star.
Directed by Robert Altman. **DT4**

That Darn Cat (1965, C, 116m, G)
A pet cat leads the FBI to a gang of kidnappers. Hayley Mills and Dean Jones star in this Disney comedy. **FA1**

That Forsyte Woman (1949, C, 114m, NR)
John Galsworthy's novel of a marital betrayal, with Greer Garson the woman attracted to her niece's fiancé. Errol Flynn costars, with Walter Pidgeon, Robert Young, and Janet Leigh. **DR19, ST69, ST83**

That Hamilton Woman
(1941, B&W, 128m, NR)
Classic love story, based on historical events, of affair between Lord Nelson and Lady Hamilton. Laurence Olivier and Vivien Leigh star. Directed by Alexander Korda. **CL3, CL5, ST137, ST168**

That Lucky Touch (1975, C, 93m, PG)
Romantic comedy of arms dealer and inquisitive journalist stars Roger Moore and Susannah York, with Shelley Winters and Lee J. Cobb. **CO1, ST232**

That Midnight Kiss (1949, C, 96m, NR)
Mario Lanza's screen debut has him playing an unknown talent romancing a big singing star (Kathryn Grayson). With José Iturbi, Ethel Barrymore, and Keenan Wynn. **MU1, MU4**

That Naughty Girl (1958, C, 77m, NR)
Brigitte Bardot plays the title role, the bored daughter of a nightclub owner. **ST6**

That Obscure Object of Desire
(1977, C, 103m, R)
A wealthy man with unconventional sexual ideas falls in love with a maid who accommodatingly teases him. Fernando Rey stars; Carole Bouquet and Angela Molina play the maid. Last film from director Luis Buñuel; it should have won Oscar for Best Foreign Language Film. **DT21, XT28**

That Sinking Feeling (1979, C, 92m, PG)
Comedy set in Glasgow, Scotland, about a group of bored youths who turn to stealing sinks to pass the time. Directed by Bill Forsyth. **CO17, DT46**

That Touch of Mink (1962, C, 99m, NR)
Doris Day-Cary Grant romantic fluff about a playboy pursuing a determined woman of virtue. With Gig Young, John Astin, Audrey Meadows, and Dick Sargent. **CO1, ST47, ST92**

That Uncertain Feeling
(1941, B&W, 84m, NR)
Romantic comedy from director Ernst Lubitsch about a married couple (Merle Oberon and Melvyn Douglas) and their zany musician friend (Burgess Meredith). **DT76, ST58**

That Was Rock (1984, B&W, 92m, NR)
Compilation of rock and R&B performances from two films, *The T.A.M.I. Show* (1964) and *The Big T.N.T Show* (1966). Performers include Chuck Berry, James Brown, The Supremes, The Rolling Stones, and many more. Also known as *Born to Rock.* **MU10**

That Was Then, This Is Now
(1985, C, 102m, R)
Drama about relationship between stepbrothers, one of whom is jealous of his brother's new girlfriend. Emilio Estevez stars; he also wrote the screenplay, based on an S.E. Hinton novel. With Craig Sheffer, Kim Delaney, and in a small role, Morgan Freeman. **DR9, ST76**

That'll Be the Day (1974, C, 90m, PG)
British working class youth in the 1950s decides to become a rock star. David Essex stars, with Ringo Starr and Keith Moon. **MU4, MU9**

That's Adequate (1990, C, 82m, R)
Comic look at fictional Hollywood studio, Adequate Pictures, and its output. Among the stars: Tony Randall, Robert Downey, Jr., Bruce Willis, Robert Townsend, Peter Riegert, and Susan Dey. **CO8, ST229**

That's Dancing! (1985, C/B&W, 105m, G)
A compilation of fifty years of dance numbers from MGM musicals, including a Ray Bolger/Scarecrow dance number that was cut from the final version of *The Wizard of Oz.* Includes Fred Astaire and Ginger Rogers, *West Side Story*, and more. Astaire, John Travolta, Gene Kelly, Liza Minnelli, and Sammy Davis, Jr., host. **MU3, MU15, ST4, ST123, ST187**

That's Entertainment! (1974, C, 132m, G)
To mark its fiftieth anniversary, MGM produced this compilation of scenes from one hundred of their musicals. Among the stars featured: Fred Astaire, Gene Kelly, Bing Crosby, Clark Gable, Judy Garland, and Frank Sinatra. **MU1, MU15, ST4, ST40, ST77, ST81, ST123, ST199,** *Recommended*

That's Entertainment, Part 2
(1976, C, 133m, G)
A sequel to *That's Entertainment!*, this time including scenes from non-musical films (featuring Katharine Hepburn and Spencer Tracy, plus the Marx Brothers) as well as more classic MGM numbers. **MU1, MU15, ST4, ST40, ST77, ST81, ST103, ST123, ST152, ST199, ST217**

That's Life! (1986, C, 102m, R)
Jack Lemmon and Julie Andrews play a middle-aged couple preoccupied with their individual problems, less considerate of each other and their children. Drama from director Blake Edwards. Members of Lemmon's and Andrews's and Edwards's families play small roles. **DR8, DT40, ST2, ST138, XT8, XT30**

Theatre of Blood (1973, C, 104m, R)
Shakespearean actor begins to kill off all his critics with methods from various Shakespeare plays. Vincent Price at his campy best. With Diana Rigg, Coral Browne, and Robert Morley. **CU4, HO24, HO26, ST179**

Theatre of Death (1967, C, 90m, NR)
The deaths on a Grand Guignol stage are no longer fake. Christopher Lee stars in this British mystery. **MY15, ST135**

Thelma & Louise (1991, C, 128m, R)
Two women, out for weekend of fun on their own, find themselves fugitives when they kill a would-be rapist. Road comedy-drama stars Susan Sarandon and Geena Davis, with Harvey Keitel, Michael Madsen, Christopher McDonald, and Brad Pitt. Written by Callie Khouri; directed by Ridley Scott. One of the few films in recent memory that really matters, even with its faults. **DR10, DR16, DT115, ST45, ST194, XT18,** *Recommended*

Thelonius Monk: Straight, No Chaser (1989, C/B&W, 90m, PG-13)
Incisive, if incomplete, documentary portrait of pioneering jazz pianist. Directed by Charlotte Zwerin; material from the 1960s shot by Christian Blackwood. **CU16,** *Recommended*

Them! (1954, B&W, 94m, NR)
Classic 1950s science fiction thriller about giant ants, mutated by radiation. James Whitmore and James Arness star. **CU4, SF1, SF10, SF16,** *Recommended*

There Was a Crooked Man (1970, C, 123m, R)
Darkly comic tale, set in the Old West, of convict (Kirk Douglas) who breaks out of prison and is pursued by greedy warden (Henry Fonda) to a cache of stolen money. With John Randolph, Hume Cronyn, and Warren Oates. Written by Robert Benton and David Newman; directed by Joseph L. Mankiewicz. Sharp script performed with gusto by veteran cast. **DR18, DT84, ST57, ST71, ST166, WE3, WE14, WE15,** *Recommended*

There's a Girl in My Soup (1970, C, 95m, R)
Middle-aged businessman falls for flower child in this comedy starring Peter Sellers and Goldie Hawn. **ST99, ST198**

There's No Business Like Show Business (1954, C, 117m, NR)
A husband and wife vaudeville team return to the stage with their three children now in the act. Ethel Merman, Dan Dailey, Donald O'Connor, and Marilyn Monroe star. **MU4, ST159**

There's Nothing Out There (1990, C, 91m, NR)
Spoof of the popular Teens in Peril genre of horror films, about seven young people at a secluded cabin watching horror films on TV. Craig Peck and Wendy Bednarz star. **CO7, HO12, HO24**

Therese (1986, C, 96m, NR)
True-life drama from French director Alain Cavalier about Therese Martin, a young nun whose devotion and patient suffering resulted in sainthood. **FF1**

These Three (1936, B&W, 93m NR)
Two teachers and a doctor have their professional and personal reputations ruined by the malicious stories of a spoiled little girl. Miriam Hopkins, Merle Oberon, Joel McCrea, and Bonita Granville star. Based on Lillian Hellman's play, *The Children's Hour;* directed by William Wyler. Remade by Wyler under play's title. **DR20, DT142, ST144**

They All Laughed (1981, C, 115m, PG)
Amiable comedy about three New York private eyes and their various love lives. Ben Gazzara, John Ritter, and Blaine Novak are the gumshoes. With Audrey Hepburn, Dorothy Stratten, Colleen Camp, and Patti Hansen. Directed by Peter Bogdanovich. **CO10, ST102, XT9,** *Recommended*

They Call Me MISTER Tibbs! (1970, C, 108m, PG)
Sidney Poitier plays his *In the Heat of the Night* character, Virgil Tibbs, in this crime drama set in San Francisco. With Barbara McNair and Martin Landau. **AC9, ST174**

They Call Me Trinity (1971, C, 109m, PG)
In this Western spoof, Terence Hill and Bud Spencer play cowboys who agree to protect settlers from a band of Mexican marauders. **WE13, WE14**

They Came From Within (1975, C, 87m, R)
David Cronenberg directed this horrific tale of parasites who take over the residents of a high-rise apartment building. **DT31**

They Came to Cordura (1959, B&W, 123m, NR)
Gary Cooper stars in this Western set in 1916 Mexico, about an officer accused of cowar-

dice and determined to regain his pride. With Rita Hayworth, Van Heflin, and Tab Hunter. **ST37, ST101, WE9**

They Died With Their Boots On
(1941, B&W, 138m, NR)
The story of George Armstrong Custer and his infamous Last Stand, with Errol Flynn as the notorious general. Olivia de Havilland costars, with Charles Middleton as Abraham Lincoln. Directed by Raoul Walsh. **HF6, HF18, DT131, ST49, ST69, WE4**

They Drive By Night
(1940, B&W, 93m, NR)
A pair of brothers battle the crooked bosses running the trucking industry. Humphrey Bogart, George Raft, and Ann Sheridan star. Directed by Raoul Walsh. **CL8, DT131, ST15**

They Got Me Covered
(1943, B&W, 95m, NR)
Wartime spy comedy set in Washington, D.C., starring Bob Hope, Dorothy Lamour, and Otto Preminger. **DT100, ST108**

They Knew What They Wanted
(1940, B&W, 96m, NR)
Romance by correspondence, as an Italian grape grower (Charles Laughton) falls in love with a lonely waitress (Carole Lombard). Garson Kanin directed. **ST132, ST140**

They Live (1988, C, 95m, R)
Aliens are taking over Earth, cleverly disguised and only detected through specially-made sunglasses. Roddy Piper stars. John Carpenter directed this low-budget science fiction drama. **DT23, SF9**

They Live by Night (1949, B&W, 95m, NR)
Depression-era tale of young lovers turned outlaws, starring Farley Granger and Cathy O'Donnell. Cult favorite, directed by Nicholas Ray. **DT101, MY1, XT18,** *Essential*

They Made Me a Criminal
(1939, B&W, 92m, NR)
John Garfield stars in this thriller about a man on the run from the law for a crime he didn't commit. Claude Rains, May Robson, and the Dead End Kids costar. Directed by Busby Berkeley, in a rare non-musical outing. **DT12, MY7, ST80**

They Might Be Giants (1971, C, 98m, PG)
Gentle comedy of a man who believes he's Sherlock Holmes and his female shrink, named Dr. Watson. George C. Scott and Joanne Woodward star. **HF14, ST196, ST234**

They Only Kill Their Masters
(1972, C, 97m, PG)
Whodunit set in small California town about sheriff looking into murder of woman; the prime suspect is her Doberman. James Garner stars, with Katharine Ross, Hal Holbrook, Harry Guardino, June Allyson, Tom Ewell, Peter Lawford, Christopher Connelly, and Edmond O'Brien. **MY12, ST82**

They Saved Hitler's Brain
(1963, B&W, 74m, NR)
Classic "bad" movie about Nazi cult controlled by Der Führer's still-living head. **CU11**

They Shall Have Music
(1939, B&W, 101m, NR)
Classical violinist gives concert to benefit poor children. Jascha Heifetz stars, with Joel McCrea, Andrea Leeds, and Walter Brennan. **ST144**

They Shoot Horses, Don't They?
(1969, C, 121m, PG)
Grim drama centering on Depression marathon dance contest. Jane Fonda stars, with Michael Sarrazin, Susannah York, Red Buttons, Bruce Dern, Bonnie Bedelia, and Oscar winner Gig Young. Adapted from Horace McCoy's cult novel; directed by Sydney Pollack. One of Fonda's best performances; good direction by Pollack. **DR19, DT98, ST72, XT4,** *Recommended*

They Went That-A-Way and That-A-Way (1978, C, 95m, PG)
Two amateur comedians, whose specialty is doing Laurel and Hardy impersonations, escape from prison. Tim Conway and Chuck McCann star. **FA6**

They Were Expendable
(1945, B&W, 135m, NR)
American PT boats in the Pacific engage Japanese cruisers in battle. John Wayne and Robert Montgomery star. Directed by John Ford. **AC1, DT44, ST224**

They Who Step on the Tiger's Tail see *Men Who Tread on the Tiger's Tail, The*

They Won't Believe Me
(1947, B&W, 79m, NR)
On trial for murder, a man tries to explain the twisted circumstances which brought him to his fate. Robert Young plays the philandering man on the witness stand; Susan Hayward, Jane Greer, and Rita Johnson costar. Gripping if occasionally implausible story. **DR17, MY1, MY7, ST100,** *Recommended*

They Won't Forget (1937, B&W, 95m, NR)
Murder of teen-ager in small Southern town results in sensational murder trial. Based loosely on the famed Leo Frank case. Claude Rains, Gloria Dickson, and Otto Kruger star, with Lana Turner playing the girl, in her first important role. **CL8, DR17, DR26, ST219**

They're Playing With Fire
(1984, C, 96m, R)
A sexy teacher and her naive student lover
plot a murder in this thriller starring Eric
Brown and Sybil Danning. **MY5**

Thief (1981, C, 122m, R)
Drama about the world of a professional
thief, starring James Caan and Tuesday Weld,
with Robert Prosky and Willie Nelson.
Directed by Michael Mann; music by Tangerine Dream. Mannered, with dull lead performance. **AC8, DR16, MU12**

Thief of Bagdad, The
(1924, B&W, 132m, NR)
Silent film version of the Arabian Nights tale
of a professional thief who saves the Princess
of Bagdad from an evil Mongol prince. Douglas Fairbanks stars. Directed by Raoul Walsh.
AC13, CL12, DT131, SF2, *Essential*

Thief of Bagdad, The (1940, C, 106m, NR)
Colorful fantasy from the Arabian Nights,
with a plucky native boy and a prince duel-
ing a wicked sorcerer. Oscar winner for pho-
tography and special effects. Sabu, John
Justin, and Conrad Veidt star. Co-directed by
Michael Powell. **AC13, CL9, DT99, FA4,
FA8,** *Essential*

Thief of Hearts (1984, C, 100m, NR)
A burglar's haul includes a married woman's
diary, which contains her secret sexual fantasies. The thief conspires to meet the woman
and a romance soon develops. Steven Bauer
and Barbara Williams star. Some additional
scenes were added for the home video version. **CU6, CU10, MY5**

Thief Who Came to Dinner, The
(1973, C, 105m, PG)
Computer programmer turns to life of crime
as a jewel thief in this comedy starring Ryan
O'Neal, with Jacqueline Bisset, Warren Oates,
Jill Clayburgh, and Ned Beatty. **CO10, ST31,
ST166**

Thieves Like Us (1974, C, 123m, R)
Director Robert Altman's beautifully realized
remake of cult classic *They Live by Night,*
about Depression-era couple on the run from
the law. Keith Carradine and Shelley Duvall
star, with John Schuck, Bert Remsen, Louise
Fletcher, and Tom Skerritt. Altman, Calder
Willingham, and Joan Tewksbury wrote the
screenplay. One of the director's great
neglected films. UNAVAILABLE ON VIDEO.
XT29

Thieves of Fortune (1989, C, 100m, R)
Adventure tale of $28 million fortune hunt,
starring former Miss Universe Shawn Weath-

erly, with Michael Nouri and Lee Van Cleef.
ST221

Thin Blue Line, The (1988, C, 106m, NR)
Mesmerizing documentary study of a 1976
Dallas, Texas, murder case, for which the
wrong man (Randall Dale Adams) was convicted and nearly executed. This film helped
to reopen the case and eventually set Adams
free. Directed by Errol Morris; music by Philip Glass. **CU16, DT89, MY8,** *Highly
Recommended*

Thin Man, The (1934, B&W, 93m, NR)
First in the series of films about high society
detectives Nick and Nora Charles, created by
Dashiell Hammett. William Powell and
Myrna Loy mix martinis and murder in a
uniquely sophisticated kind of mystery. (For
other series titles, see HF5.) **CL10, CL15,
HF5, MY17, ST142, ST176, WR12,** *Essential, Highly Recommended*

Thin Man Goes Home, The
(1944, B&W, 100m, NR)
Fifth in the Nick and Nora Charles series has
the high society duo returning to Nick's
hometown with baby Nick, Jr., and solving a
murder case. William Powell and Myrna Loy
star. **CL15, HF5, MY17, ST142, ST176,
WR12**

Thing, The (1982, C, 108m, R)
A group of researchers in the Antarctic are
terrorized by an alien creature who can transform itself into any living organism. Kirk
Russell stars in this explicitly gory remake of
the 1951 classic. John Carpenter directed. For
fans of the genre only. **CU18, DT17, HO17,
SF9, SF20, ST191**

Thing (From Another World), The
(1951, B&W, 87m, NR)
A U.S. outpost at the North Pole finds a
crashed spaceship and manages to save its
pilot. The alien is made of vegetable matter,
feeds on blood, and intends to destroy the
humans. Kenneth Tobey stars, with James
Arness as the alien. **CU4, SF1, SF9,** *Essential,
Recommended*

Things Are Tough All Over
(1982, C, 92m, R)
Cheech and Chong comedy, with the boys
driving around around in a car with $5 mil-
lion hidden in it. C&C also play two Arab
brothers. **ST28**

Things Change (1988, C, 105m, PG)
Comic yarn of an elderly shoemaker (Don
Ameche) persuaded to serve a short jail term
for a crime boss he resembles. He and his
"guard," a Mob flunky (Joe Mantegna), take
off for one last fling in Lake Tahoe. David

Mamet directed; he and Shel Silverstein wrote the screenplay. Ingratiating comedy with Ameche and Mantegna a funny team. **CO10, CO20,** *Recommended*

Things To Come (1936, B&W, 91m, NR) H.G. Wells wrote this science fiction drama about a war which nearly destroys the world and how the survivors try to construct a utopian society. Raymond Massey, Ralph Richardson, and Cedric Hardwicke star. **SF2, SF12, SF14, ST184, WR37**

Think Big (1990, C, 86m, PG-13) Action comedy featuring a pair of dim-witted, muscular truckers (Peter and David Paul, real-life brothers) hauling toxic waste and a teen stowaway across the country. With Ari Meyers, Martin Mull, David Carradine, and Richard Kiel. **CO9, XT8, XT18**

Third Man, The (1949, B&W, 104m, NR) Classic Graham Greene thriller set in postwar Vienna, with good guy writer (Joseph Cotten) finding out his old friend Harry Lime (Orson Welles) is working for the bad guys. With Trevor Howard and Valli. Carol Reed directed. Welles steals the film; adeptly captures postwar mood in Europe. **MY6, DT134, WR11,** *Essential, Highly Recommended*

Third Man on the Mountain (1959, C, 105m, NR) A young man (James MacArthur) learns about life while attempting to climb the Matterhorn. Drama from the Disney studios. **FA1**

13 Ghosts (1960, B&W, 88m, NR) A family inherits a haunted house and must solve several mysterious deaths in order to free the spirits. **HO2, HO3, HO19**

13 Rue Madeleine (1946, B&W, 95m, NR) An Allied agent tries to locate a German missile site in World War II France. James Cagney stars. **AC1, ST24**

Thirteenth Guest, The (1932, B&W, 69m, NR) A dinner party is held thirteen years after same company saw their host drop dead— and leave his estate to a mystery guest. Ginger Rogers and Lyle Talbot star. **MY12, ST187**

30 Is a Dangerous Age, Cynthia (1968, C, 98m, NR) Dudley Moore plays a young man whose approaching thirtieth birthday is driving him loony with anxiety. Moore also co-wrote the screenplay and composed the music for this British comedy. **CO17, ST160**

Thirty Seconds Over Tokyo (1944, B&W, 138m, NR) Drama of America's first air raid on Japan during World War II. Van Johnson, Robert Walker, and Spencer Tracy star, with Robert Mitchum in a small role. **AC1, ST158, ST217**

39 Steps, The (1935, B&W, 87m, NR) One of Alfred Hitchcock's best: innocent man Robert Donat becomes enmeshed in elaborate mystery involving spies and saboteurs. Madeleine Carroll is the woman he's handcuffed to. Many classic moments, including finale with "Mr. Memory." **DT57, MY6, MY7, MY15, XT18,** *Essential, Highly Recommended*

39 Steps, The (1978, C, 102m, PG) Remake of the Alfred Hitchcock classic, starring Robert Powell, David Warner, and Karen Dotrice. **CU18, MY6, MY7, XT18**

This Boy's Life (1993, C, 115m, R) Writer Tobias Wolff's memoir of his teen years, growing up in the 1950s in a small Washington town under the thumb of a repressive stepfather. Robert De Niro, Ellen Barkin, and Leonardo DiCaprio star. Robert Getchell adapted Wolff's marvelous book; Michael Caton-Jones directed. **DR4, DR8, DR9, ST7, ST51**

This Gun for Hire (1942, B&W, 80m, NR) Alan Ladd's first starring role, as the ruthless gunman of Graham Greene's novel. With Veronica Lake, Robert Preston, and Laird Cregar. Adaptation by Albert Maltz and W.R. Burnett. Excellent character study. **MY1, ST128, WR11, XT21,** *Recommended*

This Happy Breed (1944, B&W, 114m, NR) Drama adapted from Noel Coward's play about life of British family between the world wars. Robert Newton and Celia Johnson star, with John Mills, Kay Walsh, and Stanley Holloway. Directed by David Lean. **DR23, DT71, WR4**

This Happy Feeling (1958, C, 92m, NR) Debbie Reynolds plays a woman smitten by a vain actor (Curt Jurgens) and courted by an earnest young man (John Saxon). Comedy from director Blake Edwards. **DT40**

This Is Elvis (1981, C/B&W, 144m, PG) Portrait of The King combining documentary footage with recreated scenes from his life. Video version adds nearly forty-five minutes of footage to theatrical release. Sensational assemblage of performance highlights. **CU10, MU5, MU11, ST178,** *Recommended*

This Is Korea/December 7th (1951/1943, C/B&W, 85m, NR) John Ford directed these two propaganda documentaries for the Navy. *This Is Korea* praises the U.S. military effort in that conflict. *December 7th* recreates the bombing of Pearl Harbor and won an Academy Award for Best Documentary. *December 7th* now available in full-length version; see separate entry. **AC1, AC3, CU16, DT44**

This Is My Life (1992, C, 105m, R)
Divorced New Jersey mother of two daughters (ages sixteen and ten) decides on a sea change: she wants to become a stand-up comic. Julie Kavner stars, with Samantha Mathis, Gaby Hoffman, Carrie Fisher, and Dan Aykroyd. Nora Ephron directed; she and her sister Delia adapted Meg Wolitzer's comic novel. **CO5, CO8, CO13**

This Is Spinal Tap (1984, C, 82m, R)
A British heavy metal group that's beginning to show some signs of rust tours America. Christopher Guest, Michael McKean, and Harry Shearer star in this hilarious parody of rock documentaries. Directed by Rob Reiner, who also plays the pretentious director making a film about the band. Cameo appearances by Paul Shaffer, Billy Crystal, many others. **CO7, CO13, DT103, MU11, XT26,** *Recommended*

This Island Earth (1954, C, 86m, NR)
Inhabitants from Metaluna come to Earth hoping our scientists can help them find a new energy source before their home is destroyed. Jeff Morrow and Rex Reason star. **SF1, SF3, SF9**

This Land Is Mine (1943, B&W, 103m, NR)
Charles Laughton stars as a French schoolteacher who rises to acts of heroism under Nazi Occupation. With Maureen O'Hara, George Sanders, and Walter Slezak. Directed by Jean Renoir. **DT104, ST132, ST167**

This Man Must Die (1970, C, 115m, PG)
A man's son is killed by a hit-and-run driver and he becomes obsessed with exacting his own justice. French thriller from director Claude Chabrol. **FF1**

This Property Is Condemned
(1966, C, 109m, NR)
Tennessee Williams play about a young woman (Natalie Wood) falling for a drifter (Robert Redford) who is staying at her mother's boarding house. With Charles Bronson, Kate Reid, Mary Badham, and Robert Blake. Sydney Pollack directed. **DT98, ST20, ST181, WR38**

This Sporting Life (1963, B&W, 129m, NR)
Powerful, no-holds-barred drama of British rugby player (Richard Harris) whose star rises and falls quickly. With Rachel Roberts.

Directed by Lindsay Anderson. Still one of the best of the British Angry Young Man movies of the late 50s and early 60s. **DR22, DR23,** *Essential, Recommended*

Thomas Crown Affair, The
(1968, C, 102m, R)
A bored millionaire playboy (Steve McQueen) plots the perfect bank robbery. An insurance investigator (Faye Dunaway) is on the case, but she falls in love with her quarry. With Paul Burke, Jack Weston, and Yaphet Kotto. Directed by Norman Jewison. Slick, occasionally entertaining but split-screen technique dates badly. **DT63, MY5, MY18, ST61, ST146**

Thompson's Last Run
(1986, C, 100m, NR)
Western saga of boyhood pals now on oppostie sides of the law as old men. Robert Mitchum and Wilford Brimley star. Originally made for TV. **ST158**

Thorn Birds, The (1983, C, 486m, NR)
TV miniseries about the lives and loves of a handsome priest (Richard Chamberlain). With Rachel Ward and Barbara Stanwyck. Based on Colleen McCullough's novel. **DR1, DR3, ST206**

Thoroughbreds Don't Cry
(1937, B&W, 80m, NR)
First pairing of Mickey Rooney and Judy Garland in this tale of shady dealings at a racetrack. With Sophie Tucker, C. Aubrey Smith, and Frankie Darrow. **CL15, ST81, ST189**

Thoroughly Modern Millie
(1967, C, 138m, NR)
Musical farce set in Roaring Twenties, with flappers and flivvers, speakeasies and wild parties, and a gang of white slavers. Julie Andrews stars, with James Fox, Mary Tyler Moore, Carol Channing, Beatrice Lillie, John Gavin, and Pat Morita. Directed by George Roy Hill. Some original tunes mix with period songs. **DT55, MU6, ST2**

Those Calloways (1965, C, 131m, NR)
Eccentric New England family wants to build a bird sanctuary on some land near a lake and must battle some shady developers who want the land as a hunting resort. Brian Keith and Vera Miles star in this Disney film. **FA1**

Those Daring Young Men in Their Jaunty Jalopies (1969, C, 93m, G)
Family comedy of 1920s road race ending in Monte Carlo. Tony Curtis and Susan Hampshire star, with Terry-Thomas, Gert Frobe,

Peter Cook, and Dudley Moore. **CO6, CO9, FA6, ST160**

Those Lips, Those Eyes (1980, C, 107m, R) Young man working behind the scenes at a summer theater in Cleveland during the 1950s learns about show biz and love from two of the company's performers. Thomas Hulce, Frank Langella, and Glynnis O'Connor star. Langella's most ingratiating performance; O'Connor a real asset. **CO6, CO8**

Those Magnificent Men in Their Flying Machines (1965, C, 132m, NR) The early days of aviation races are the subject for this knockabout comedy starring Stuart Whitman, Sarah Miles, and James Fox. **CO6, CO9, FA6**

Thousand Clowns, A (1965, B&W, 118m, NR) A full-time nonconformist and part-time TV writer has his life turned upside down when social workers try to wrest his nephew from his custody. Jason Robards stars, with Barbara Harris, William Daniels, Barry Gordon, Gene Saks, and Oscar winner Martin Balsam. Shot on location in New York City. Terrific ensemble acting. **CO5, ST185, XT4, XT9,** *Recommended*

Thousand Eyes of Dr. Mabuse, The (1960, B&W, 103m, NR) Director Fritz Lang's last film, reuniting him with one of his great silent-film characters, the arch-criminal Mabuse, now reincarnated in Berlin. Dawn Addams, Peter Van Eyck, and Gert Frobe star. **DT70, FF3**

Thousand Pieces of Gold (1991, C, 105m, NR) Western drama based on true story of Chinese woman emigrating to 1880s Idaho, overcoming prejudice. Rosalind Chao stars, with Chris Cooper and Dennis Dun. Directed by Nancy Kelly. **WE8**

Thousands Cheer (1943, C, 126m, NR) A commander's daughter (Kathryn Grayson) falls in love with a private (Gene Kelly) and they decide to put on an all-star show for the troops. Mickey Rooney and Judy Garland costar, with appearances by many MGM musical stars. **MU15, ST81, ST123, ST189**

Thrashin' (1986, C, 90m, PG-13) Drama about competitive downhill skateboarding, with Josh Brolin as the young contender for the championship. **DR22**

Threads (1984, C, 110m, NR) The devastating aftermath of a nuclear attack and its effects on the lives of working-class people in Sheffield, England, are dramatized in this British equivalent of *The Day After.* **SF12, SF19**

Three Ages, The (1923, B&W, 59m, NR) Buster Keaton comedy spoofing historical epics (and especially D.W. Griffith's *Intolerance*), with segments taking place in prehistoric days, ancient Rome, and modern times. **CL11, DT66**

¡Three Amigos! (1986, C, 105m, PG) Trio of out-of-work movie actors in 1920s Hollywood are summoned to a Mexican village, which mistakenly thinks they are real cowboys, for a rescue mission. Steve Martin, Chevy Chase, and Martin Short star. Cowritten by Randy Newman, who also wrote the songs and supplied the voice for a talking bush. **CO3, CO13, CO14, ST150**

Three Broadway Girls (1932, B&W, 79m, NR) Familiar comedy of gold-digging girls at work in the Big Apple. Joan Blondell, Ina Claire, and Madge Evans star. Watch quickly for Betty Grable. Directed by Lowell Sherman. Also known as *The Greeks Had a Word for Them.* **ST91**

Three Brothers (1980, C, 113m, PG) Italian brothers return to their village for their mother's funeral, sparking many memories. Philippe Noiret stars. Directed by Francesco Rosi. **FF2**

Three Caballeros, The (1945, C, 70m, NR) Disney trip to Latin America mixes animation and live action, with Donald Duck hosting. Great fun. **FA2,** *Recommended*

Three Came Home (1950, B&W, 106m, NR) Drama of British and American families interned in World War II Japanese prison on Borneo. Claudette Colbert and Sessue Hayakawa star. Based on a true story. **ST34**

Three Comrades (1938, B&W, 98m, NR) Drama set in post-World War I Germany, about trio of pals in love with the same woman, with rise of Nazism lurking in background. Robert Taylor, Franchot Tone, Robert Young, and Margaret Sullavan star. Cowritten by F. Scott Fitzgerald, directed by Frank Borzage. **CL8, WR8**

Three Days of the Condor (1975, C, 117m, R) A CIA researcher in New York survives an assassination attack which decimates his entire office, goes on the lam with almost no help from Washington. Robert Reddord and Faye Dunaway star, with Max von Sydow, Cliff Robertson, and John Houseman. Sydney Pollack directed. Entertaining, sometimes farfetched. **DT98, MY6, MY7, ST61, ST181**

Three Faces of Eve, The
(1957, B&W, 91m, NR)
Joanne Woodward won an Oscar for her portrayal of a woman with three distinct personalities. With Lee J. Cobb and David Wayne; narrated by Alistair Cooke. Written and directed by Nunnally Johnson; based on a true story. **DR6, DR10, ST234, XT3**

Three Faces West (1940, B&W, 79m, NR)
Unusual John Wayne vehicle has The Duke leading a group of Austrian refugees to Oregon during World War II. **ST224, WE12**

Three Fugitives (1989, C, 96m, PG-13)
Nick Nolte stars in this chase comedy as an ex-con who's kidnapped by a loony bank robber (Martin Short). With Sarah Rowland Doroff and James Earl Jones. **CO10, CO14, ST118, ST164, XT18**

3 Godfathers (1948, C, 105m, NR)
Western drama of three outlaws (John Wayne, Pedro Armendariz, and Harry Carey, Jr.) who find an infant abandoned in the desert. With Ward Bond, Mae Marsh, Jane Darwell, and Ben Johnson. Directed by John Ford. **DT44, ST224, WE3**

Three Little Pigs, The (1985, C, 60m, NR)
From the Faerie Tale Theatre series, a look at three pigs who each build their own home and the wolf who wants to have them for dinner. Billy Crystal, Jeff Goldblum, Valerie Perrine, and Stephen Furst star. **CO13, FA12, ST90**

Three Little Words (1950, C, 102m, NR)
Film biography of songwriters Bert Kalmar and Harry Ruby. Fred Astaire, Red Skelton, Vera-Ellen, and Arlene Dahl star. **MU1, MU5, ST4**

Three Lives of Thomasina, The
(1964, C, 97m, NR)
A mysterious woman brings Thomasina, a cat owned by a veterinarian's daughter, back from the dead. Patrick McGoohan stars in this Disney fantasy. **FA1**

Three Men and a Baby
(1987, C, 102m, PG)
Tom Selleck, Ted Danson, and Steve Guttenberg star as three bachelor roommates with a baby on their hands. American remake of *Three Men and a Cradle*. Directed by Leonard Nimoy. **CO2, FA6, FF8, XT23**

Three Men and a Cradle
(1985, C, 100m, PG-13)
French comedy about a trio of bachelors who find themselves caring for an infant whom one of them has fathered. U.S. remake: *Three Men and a Baby*. **FF1, FF8**

Three Men and a Little Lady
(1990, C, 100m, PG)
Ted Danson, Tom Selleck, and Steve Guttenberg return as those lovable bachelor fathers. The baby is now a little girl whose mother is planning a wedding to a stuffy British actor. With Nancy Travis, Robin Weisman, Christopher Cazenove, and Fiona Shaw. By the numbers. **CO2, FA6, XT20**

Three Musketeers, The
(1948, C, 125m, NR)
The Dumas tale of a farm boy (Gene Kelly) who wants to be a musketeer and gets caught up in court intrigues. With Lana Turner, June Allyson, Van Heflin, Angela Lansbury, Vincent Price, Keenan Wynn, and Gig Young. **AC13, ST123, ST131, ST179, ST219**

Three Musketeers, The
(1974, C, 105m, PG)
Swashbuckling adventure, romance, and splastick are brilliantly mixed in this adaptation of the Dumas tale. Oliver Reed, Richard Chamberlain, Frank Finlay, and Michael York star, with Faye Dunaway, Christopher Lee, Raquel Welch, Charlton Heston, Geraldine Chaplin, and Roy Kinnear. Directed by Richard Lester; followed by sequel, *The Four Musketeers*. Breathes new life into genre. **AC15, DT74, ST61, ST135,** *Highly Recommended*

3 Ninjas (1992, C, 84m, PG)
Action comedy of trio of brothers trained in martial arts by their Oriental grandfather. They swing into action when taken hostage by an arms dealer. Michael Treanor, Max Elliott Slade, and Chad Power star. **AC26, CO9, FA6**

Three on a Match (1932, B&W, 64m, NR)
Three women, childhood pals, meet by accident and renew their friendship. Joan Blondell, Bette Davis, and Ann Dvorak star. With Humphrey Bogart, Lyle Talbot, and Glenda Farrell. **CL5, ST15, ST44**

Three Sovereigns for Sarah
(1985, C, 180m, NR)
Saga of Salem witch trials, starring Vanessa Redgrave, Phyllis Thaxter, and Kim Hunter. Originally made for public TV. **DR5, ST182**

Three Strange Loves
(1949, B&W, 84m, NR)
Early drama from director Ingmar Bergman examines the lives of a trio of ballerinas. **DT11**

Threepenny Opera, The
(1931, B&W, 112m, NR)
Film version of the famous Kurt Weill-Bertolt Brecht musical play about a gangster and his

cronies. Rudolph Forster and Lotte Lenya star. **FF3**

3:10 to Yuma (1957, B&W, 92m, NR)
A farmer tries to hold an outlaw captive until a prison train arrives. Western suspense starring Glenn Ford and Van Heflin. Based on a novel by Elmore Leonard. Solid suspense, with Ford good as the baddie. **WE15, WR19,** *Recommended*

Threshold (1981, C, 97m, PG)
Drama of the first artificial heart transplant stars Donald Sutherland, with John Marley, Mare Winningham, and Jeff Goldblum. **ST73**

Thrill of a Romance (1945, C, 105m, NR)
Esther Williams musical set amid the scenic splendors of Yosemite National Park. With Van Johnson, Frances Gifford, Henry Travers, Spring Byington, and Tommy Dorsey. **MU1**

Thrill of It All, The (1963, C, 108m, NR)
Domestic comedy with Doris Day a housewife who suddenly becomes a TV commercials star, much to the dismay of her husband (James Garner). Directed by Norman Jewison. **DT63, ST47, ST82**

Throne of Blood (1957, B&W, 105m, NR)
Japanese version of *Macbeth*, starring Toshiro Mifune as the ambitious nobleman. Stunning direction by Akira Kurosawa. **DT69, ST134, WR22,** *Highly Recommended*

Through a Glass, Darkly
(1962, B&W, 91m, NR)
Ingmar Bergman's study of a woman recently released from a mental hospital and her relationships with her husband, father, and brother. Harriet Andersson stars in this Oscar-winning film. **DT11, XT7**

Throw Momma from the Train
(1987, C, 88m, PG-13)
Comedy teaming Billy Crystal as a writing teacher with a grudge against his wife and Danny DeVito as his student with a monster for a mother (Anne Ramsey). DeVito hits on a "murder swap" scheme after seeing Hitchcock's *Strangers on a Train*. **CO3, CO10, CO13, ST45**

Thumbelina (1983, C, 60m, NR)
From the Faerie Tale Theatre series, a tale about a beautiful and kind princess who is only the size of a human thumb. Carrie Fisher, William Katt, and Burgess Meredith star. **FA12**

Thunder Bay (1953, C, 102m, NR)
Louisiana shrimp fisherman and oil drillers battle over Gulf waters. James Stewart stars, with Joanne Dru, Gilbert Roland, and Dan Duryea. Anthony Mann directed. **DT85, ST177**

Thunder in the City
(1937, B&W, 86m, NR)
Edward G. Robinson plays a brash American promoter who takes London by storm with a newly discovered mineral. With Ralph Richardson. **DR23, ST184, ST186**

Thunder Road (1958, B&W, 92m, NR)
Hot-rodding action with a family of moonshiners (Robert and Jim Mitchum, playing brothers; in real life they're father and son) outrunning the feds and gangsters. The elder Mitchum sings the title tune. **AC10, ST158, XT8**

Thunderball (1965, C, 129m, PG)
James Bond (Sean Connery) battles a villain who wants to destroy Miami in this underwater adventure. With Claudine Auger and Adolfo Celi; plenty of underwater action. Remade as *Never Say Never Again*. **AC12, HF2, ST36**

Thunderbolt and Lightfoot
(1974, C, 114m, R)
A professional thief (Clint Eastwood) takes on an apprentice (Jeff Bridges) and, together with the thief's old partners, set out to recover money from a previous heist. With George Kennedy and Geoffrey Lewis. Directed by Michael Cimino. Nasty violence; Bridges is terrific. **AC9, MY18, ST19, ST64**

Thunderheart (1992, C, 118m, R)
Mystery-drama set in late 1970s on an Oglala Sioux reservation in South Dakota where a part-Indian FBI agent is investigating murders. Val Kilmer stars, with Sam Shepard, Graham Greene, Fred Ward, Fred Dalton Thompson, and Sheila Tousey. Directed by Michael Apted, coproduced by Robert De Niro. Companion piece to Apted's documentary *Incident at Oglala*. **DR7, DR27**

Ticket to Heaven (1981, C, 107m, PG)
Canadian drama of young man lulled into joining a cult and his subsequent deprogramming experience. Nick Mancuso, Saul Rubinek, and R.H. Thomson star. **DR9**

Tickle Me (1965, C, 90m, NR)
A rodeo star (Elvis Presley) gets a job at an all-girl dude ranch, goes on a gold hunt, and finds love. **ST178**

Tie Me Up! Tie Me Down!
(1990, C, 101m, NC-17)
Spanish director Pedro Almodovar's comedy of a sex-film star kidnapped by an adoring fan. Victoria Abril and Antonio Banderas star. Originally rated X but released theatrically

unrated. Rerated for video with new designation. **CU6, DT3**

Tiger Bay (1959, B&W, 105m, NR)
Hayley Mills stars as a child who witnesses a murder and is kidnapped by the killer (Horst Buchholz) in this classic British thriller. **FA7, MY15**

Tiger Town (1983, C, 95m, NR)
Young boy idolizes Detroit Tiger ballplayer, tries to help him through a slump. Justin Henry and Roy Scheider star. Originally made for cable TV. **DR22, FA7**

Tiger Walks, A (1964, C, 91m, NR)
Disney drama of a girl who tries to protect a runaway tiger from small-town politicians and bigots. Pamela Franklin stars, with Brian Keith, Vera Miles, Sabu, and Kevin Corcoran. **DR26, FA1**

Tight Little Island see *Whisky Galore*

Tightrope (1984, C, 114m, R)
A New Orleans cop (Clint Eastwood) is searching for a sex murderer and uncovers some nasty truths about himself. With Genevieve Bujold and Alison Eastwood (Clint's real-life daughter). Give Clint some points for trying something different with this genre. **AC9, ST64, XT8, XT14**

Till the Clouds Roll By
(1946, C, 137m, NR)
Robert Walker plays songwriter Jerome Kern in this biography that's really a series of musical numbers. Songs performed by a variety of MGM's stable of stars, including Frank Sinatra, Judy Garland, Angela Lansbury, Lena Horne, Tony Martin, Dinah Shore, and Cyd Charisse. **MU1, MU5, ST81, ST131, ST199**

Till the End of Time
(1946, B&W, 100m, NR)
A trio of World War II veterans find heartbreak and frustration back in the States.Guy Madison, Robert Mitchum, and Bill Williams star, with Dorothy McGuire. Overlooked, partly because of immense success of *The Best Years of Our Lives*. **CL8, ST158,** *Recommended*

Tillie's Punctured Romance
(1914, B&W, 73m, NR)
First feature-length comedy, starring Charlie Chaplin as a swindler, Marie Dressler as his victim. Mabel Normand costars. Mack Sennet directed this silent film. **DT24**

Tim (1979, C, 108m, PG)
Australian drama of the friendship between a slightly retarded man (Mel Gibson) and an older woman (Piper Laurie). Based on a novel by Colleen McCullough. **FF5, ST85**

Time After Time (1979, C, 112m, PG)
H.G. Wells (Malcolm McDowell) invents a time machine that Jack the Ripper (David Warner) uses in order to escape from the police. Wells follows him to modern-day San Francisco where, with the help of a bank teller (Mary Steenburgen), he tries to stop the Ripper from launching another killing spree. Adapted from elements in several H.G. Wells stories. Clever idea nicely executed. **AC14, SF4, WR37, XT13,** *Recommended*

Time Bandits (1981, C, 110m, PG)
Six dwarfs and a British schoolboy in possession of a time map tratvel through history in an effort to escape the map's evil owner. Written by Terry Gilliam and Michael Palin; directed by Gilliam. With Sean Connery as Agamemnon, John Cleese as Robin Hood, Michael Palin, Shelley Duvall, Ralph Richardson, David Warner, and Ian Holm as Napoleon. Inventive and amusing. **CO15, FA8, FA15, HF15, HF19, SF4, ST36, ST184,** *Recommended*

Time for Dying, A (1971, C, 87m, PG)
Audie Murphy stars in his last film, a Western drama from director Budd Boetticher. **DT14**

Time Guardian, The (1987, C, 105m, PG)
Australian time-travel drama has entire city moving from 4037 to 1987, fleeing murderous cyborgs. Tom Burlinson stars, with Nikki Coghill, Dean Stockwell, and Carrie Fisher. **FF5, SF4, ST208**

Time Machine, The (1960, C, 103m, G)
H.G. Wells yarn of inventor constructing title contraption and, after stopping at various intervals, ends up in the year 802701. Rod Taylor and Yvette Mimieux star. George Pal produced and directed this Oscar winner for special effects. **FA8, SF4, SF13, SF15, WR37**

Time of Destiny, A (1988, C, 118m, PG-13)
Old-fashioned melodrama of revenge, with William Hurt as a World War II soldier pursuing fellow G.I. Timothy Hutton, whom Hurt blames for his father's death. With Melissa Leo, Stockard Channing, Megan Follows, and Francisco Rabal. Written by Gregory Nava and Anna Thomas; Thomas produced and Nava directed. Rocky going, even for fans of the actors. **ST114**

Time of Indifference
(1964, B&W, 84m, NR)
Social drama of a poor Italian family's struggles during the 1920s. Rod Steiger, Shelley Winters, Claudia Cardinale, and Paulette Goddard star. **FF2, ST232**

Time of Their Lives, The
(1946, B&W, 82m, NR)
Abbott and Costello comedy, with Lou and
Marjorie Reynolds as ghosts from the eighteenth century who are haunting a home
inhabited by Bud and his pals. **ST1, XT24**

Time of Your Life, The
(1948, B&W, 109m, NR)
William Saroyan's play about the diverse
characters who hang out at a waterfront
saloon. James Cagney stars. **DR20, ST24**

Time Stands Still (1981, C/B&W, 99m, NR)
Drama set in Hungary in the early 1960s
about a group of bored, rebellious, and angry
young men who idolize American pop culture heroes like Elvis Presley. **FF7**

Time To Kill (1989, C, 110m, R)
Nicolas Cage plays a soldier stationed in
North Africa who rapes and murders a
woman, has to deal with his conscience.
With Giancarlo Giannini. **ST23**

Time to Love and a Time to Die, A
(1958, C, 132m, NR)
Drama about German soldier who must
return to battle after brief romance. John
Gavin stars; Klaus Kinski has a small role.
Directed by Douglas Sirk. Widescreen will be
lost on video. **CU20, DT117, ST219**

Time Warp see *The Day Time Ended*

Timerider (1983, C, 93m, PG)
A motocross rider is caught in a government
experiment and gets sent back in time to
1877. Fred Ward stars, with Belinda Bauer,
Peter Coyote, Ed Lauter, Richard Masur,
Tracey Walter, and L. Q. Jones. **SF4**

Times of Harvey Milk, The
(1984, C, 87m, NR)
Moving documentary about San Francisco's
first gay public official and his assassination.
Oscar winner directed by Robert Epstein.
Narrated by Harvey Fierstein; haunting music
by Mark Isham. **CU16,** *Recommended*

Times Square (1980, C, 111m, R)
Two runaways in New York get a helping
hand from a deejay (Tim Curry) who makes
them stars. **DR15, MU9, XT9**

Tin Drum, The (1979, C, 142m, R)
Adapted from Gunter Grass's bestselling
novel, this German drama traces a boy's
bizarre adventures during the years of the
Third Reich. Oscar winner for Best Foreign
Language Film. David Bennent stars. Directed
by Volker Schlondorff. Landmark work of
New German Cinema is sensational adapta-
tion of difficult book. **DR19, FF3, XT7,**
Essential, Recommended

Tin Men (1987, C, 110m, R)
Comic feud between two Baltimore
aluminum-siding salesmen in the early 1960s
spills over into competition for woman married to one of them. Richard Dreyfuss and
Danny DeVito star, with Barbara Hershey,
Bruno Kirby, John Mahoney, Jackie Gayle,
and Michael Tucker. Written and directed by
Barry Levinson. Male characters' relationships with Hershey provide unsettling dramatic counterpoint. **CO3, CO6, DT75,
ST54, ST60, ST104**

Tin Star, The (1957, B&W, 93m, NR)
A tenderfoot sheriff calls on a veteran bounty
hunter for help. Anthony Perkins and Henry
Fonda star, with Betsy Palmer, Neville Brand,
and Lee Van Cleef. Anthony Mann directed.
DT85, ST71, ST221, WE2

Tingler, The (1959, C/B&W, 82m, NR)
Horror tale of a scientist (Vincent Price) who
discovers a growth on people's spines that
can be cured only by screaming. One
sequence in color. **ST179**

Tip Off, The (1931, B&W, 75m, NR)
Gangster's girl (Ginger Rogers) romances a
naive young man. With Eddie Quillan and
Robert Armstrong. **ST187**

To Be or Not To Be (1942, B&W, 99m, NR)
Bold comedy, considering when it was released, about a troupe of Polish actors defying Nazis with elaborate plan to protect a
downed flier. Jack Benny and Carole Lombard (in her last film) star, with Robert Stack
and Tom Dugan playing Hitler. Ernst
Lubitsch directed; one of tte best films from
a great director. Remake released in 1983.
**CL10, CL14, CU5, DT76, HF12, ST140,
XT22,** *Highly Recommended*

To Be or Not To Be (1983, C, 108m, PG)
Remake of the Lubitsch classic, with Mel
Brooks and Anne Bancroft in the Benny and
Lombard roles. With Tim Matheson, José Fer-
rer, and Roy Goldman as Hitler. Directed by
Alan Johnson. **CU18, DT17, HF12**

To Catch a Spy see *Catch Me a Spy*

To Catch a Thief (1955, C, 103m, NR)
Colorful Alfred Hitchcock thriller, set on the
French Riviera, about a suave cat burglar
(Cary Grant) and the woman he intends to
victimize (Grace Kelly). Widescreen will be
lost on video. Stars can't be beat; story never
seems to gather urgency. **CU20, DT57,
MY5, ST92, ST124**

To Have and Have Not
(1944, B&W, 100m, NR)
First teaming of Humphrey Bogart and Lau-

ren Bacall (her debut) in this loose adaptation of the Hemingway story about the French Resistance. With Walter Brennan, Hoagy Carmichael, and Dan Seymour. Directed by Howard Hawks; co-written by William Faulkner. **CL15, DT53, MY4, ST15, WR13, XT21**

To Hell and Back (1955, C, 106m, NR)
Audie Murphy, America's most decorated World War II veteran, plays himself in this film based on his autobiography. **AC1, CL2**

To Joy (1949, B&W, 95m, NR)
Early film from director Ingmar Bergman, the story of a marriage falling apart. Stig Olin, Maj-Britt Nilsson, and Victor Sjöström star. **DT11**

To Kill a Mockingbird
(1962, B&W, 129m, NR)
Small-town Southern lawyer (Gregory Peck, an Oscar winner) defends an innocent black man accused of rape. Each night, he tries to explain the case to his young children. With Brock Peters, Mary Badham, Philip Alford, and Robert Duvall. Written by Horton Foote; directed by Robert Mulligan. **CL8, DR17, DR26, ST63, ST171, XT2,** *Recommended*

To Live and Die in L.A. (1985, C, 116m, R)
Counterfeiter kills a Secret Service agent and the agent's partner does everything he can to get revenge. William L. Petersen, John Pankow, and Willem Dafoe star, with Debra Feuer, Darlanne Fluegel, and Dean Stockwell. Directed by William Friedkin on location in Los Angeles. Jazzy and gritty; Dafoe makes memorable villain. **AC9, MY2, ST208, XT10,** *Recommended*

To Paris With Love (1955, C, 78m, NR)
Alec Guinness stars in this British comedy of a father taking his son to France for a liberal education. **ST78**

To Sir, With Love (1967, C, 105m, NR)
Sidney Poitier plays a new teacher in London's East End who earns the respect of his rowdy class and teaches them how to get along in the world. Pop singers Lulu and Michael Des Barres play two of his students. **DR25, MU12, ST174**

To Sleep With a Vampire
(1993, C, 76m, R)
Remake of cult horror film *Dance of the Damned,* story of one-night stand between a vampire (Scott Valentine) and a suicidal stripper (Charlie Spradling). **HO5**

To Sleep With Anger (1990, C, 102m, PG)
Drama of contemporary urban black family whose lives are disrupted by a visiting story-teller (Danny Glover). With Paul Butler, Mary Alice, Carl Lumbly, and Vonetta McGee. Written and directed by Charles Burnett. **DR8, DR14, ST88**

To the Devil, a Daughter
(1976, C, 95m, R)
A satanist (Christopher Lee) and his followers pursue a young woman (Natassja Kinski) to force her to mate with the Devil. Her only hope for escape is an occult expert (Richard Widmark). **HO10, HO26, ST135**

To the Last Man (1933, B&W, 74m, NR)
A family feud in Kentucky spills over to the frontier West. Randolph Scott stars in this drama; Shirley Temple has a small role. **ST197, ST213**

To the Shores of Tripoli
(1942, C, 86m, NR)
Marine action in World War II, with John Payne the soft, rich kid learning the ropes. With Randolph Scott and Maureen O'Hara. **AC1, ST167, ST224**

Toast of New York, The
(1937, B&W, 109m, NR)
Colorful tale of turn-of-the-century businessman Jim Fiske, played by Edward Arnold, with Cary Grant as his partner. Frances Farmer costars. **CL2, ST92**

Tobruk (1967, C, 110m, NR)
World War II drama, as Allies battle Rommel in the African desert. Rock Hudson stars, with George Peppard and Nigel Green. **AC1, ST112**

Toby Tyler (1960, C, 96m, NR)
At the turn of the century, a young boy runs away from home and joins the circus. Kevin Corcoran stars in this Disney drama. **FA1**

Tokyo Joe (1949, B&W, 88m, NR)
Humphrey Bogart plays a World War II veteran in search of his ex-wife and her child in postwar Japan. Sessue Hayakawa stars as a villainous Secret Service agent. **ST15**

Tokyo Olympiad (1966, C, 170m, NR)
Superb documentary of the 1964 Olympic Games, directed by Kon Ichikawa. This is the full-length version in letterboxed format. **CU16, CU19,** *Essential, Recommended*

Tokyo Story (1953, B&W, 134m, NR)
Drama from influential Japanese director Yasujiro Ozu of an elderly couple visiting their children in Tokyo. **FF4,** *Essential*

Tokyo-Ga (1983, C, 92m, NR)
German director Wim Wenders's documentary impressions of Japan, which he had only known through the films of Yasujiro Ozu. **CU16, DT136**

Tom Brown's School Days
(1940, B&W, 86m, NR)
A look into life at a boys' school during the Victorian era. Cedric Hardwicke and Freddie Bartholomew star. **FA2**

Tom, Dick and Harry
(1941, B&W, 86m, NR)
Ginger Rogers comedy has her choosing from a trio of men: George Murphy, Alan Marshal, and Burgess Meredith. **ST187**

Tom Horn (1980, C, 98m, R)
Steve McQueen plays the legendary Wyoming outlaw and bounty hunter who was framed by men who hired him. With Linda Evans, Richard Farnsworth, Billy "Green" Bush, Slim Pickens, and Elisha Cook. Low-key to the point of silence. **ST146, WE3, WE11**

Tom Jones (1963, C, 122m, NR)
Oscar-winning comedy about a young British rake lusting his way through the eighteenth-century countryside. Albert Finney stars, with Hugh Griffith, Edith Evans, Susannah York, Joyce Redmond, Diane Cilento, Peter Bull, and David Warner in fine support. Based on the Henry Fielding novel; directed by Tony Richardson. New video version (film was out of circulation for many years) is seven minutes shorter than original film, as per director's editing. **CL1, CO17, ST68, XT1, XT6,** *Essential*

Tom Sawyer (1973, C, 104m, G)
Musical version of Mark Twain's classic story, with Johnnie Whitaker, Celeste Holm, Warren Oates, and Jodie Foster. **FA3, ST75, ST166, WR35**

tom thumb (1958, C, 98m, NR)
Children's musical fantasy of a tiny lad (Russ Tamblyn) who's taken in by a kindly couple, then exploited by a pair of crooks (Terry-Thomas and Peter Sellers). Special effects won an Oscar. **FA8, SF15, ST198**

Tomb of Ligeia (1965, C, 81m, NR)
Edgar Allan Poe tale about a man's dead wife who comes back to haunt him when he remarries. Vincent Price stars, with Elizabeth Shepherd. Roger Corman directed; written by Robert Towne. **DT30, ST179, WR27**

Tommy (1975, C, 111m, PG)
The Who's rock opera about a deaf, dumb, and blind boy's adventures. Roger Daltrey, Oliver Reed, and Ann-Margret star, with special appearances by Elton John, Tina Turner, Eric Clapton, Keith Moon, and Jack Nicholson. Directed by Ken Russell. If someone had to do this, Russell probably was a good choice but it's all better left to the imagination. **DT111, MU8, MU9, ST163**

Tomorrow (1972, C, 103m, PG)
William Faulkner story of farmer who takes in abandoned pregnant woman and learns to love her. Robert Duvall stars. Written by Horton Foote. **ST63, WR7**

Tomorrow Is Forever
(1946, B&W, 105m, NR)
Sentimental drama of man thought dead in the war, turning up to find his wife has remarried. Orson Welles and Claudette Colbert star, with George Brent, Lucile Watson, and Natalie Wood. **CL6, DT134, ST34**

Toni (1934, B&W, 90m, NR)
Early film from director Jean Renoir is a realistic drama set in a French village involving love, jealousy, and murder. **DT104**

Tonight and Every Night
(1945, C, 92m, NR)
As their contribution to the war effort, the London's Music Box Revue never misses a performance, not even for an air raid or personal tragedy. Rita Hayworth stars in this musical. **MU4, ST101**

Tonight for Sure
(1961, B&W, 66m, NR)
Two men recall their various sexual experiences in this "nudie" film directed by a young Francis Ford Coppola. **DT29**

Tonio Kroger (1965, B&W, 92m, NR)
German drama about a young writer's loves and struggles to find his identity as a man and an artist. Based on a novel by Thomas Mann. **FF3**

Tony Rome (1967, C, 110m, NR)
Frank Sinatra plays a private investigator who's hired by a rich man to look into his daughter's less-than-perfect lifestyle. With Jill St. John, Richard Conte, Sue Lyon, and Gena Rowlands. **MY10, ST199**

Too Beautiful for You (1990, C, 91m, R)
French comedy has Gérard Depardieu playing a businessman who unaccountably cheats on his lovely wife (Carole Bouquet) for a pudgy secretary (Josiane Balasko). **FF1, ST52**

Too Hot to Handle
(1938, B&W, 105m, NR)
Comedy of two newsreel photographers (Clark Gable and Walter Pidgeon) competing for the same aviatrix (Myrna Loy). **CL12, ST77, ST142**

Too Late for Tears see *Killer Bait*

Too Late the Hero (1970, C, 133m, PG)
Two soldiers are sent on a suicide mission in the South Pacific during World War II. Michael Caine, Cliff Robertson, and Henry Fonda star. Directed by Robert Aldrich. Also known as *Suicide Run*. **AC1, DT1, ST25, ST71**

Too Much Sun (1991, C, 110m, R)
Comedy of gay brother and sister racing to be first to produce an offspring and collect whopping inheritance. Robert Downey, Jr., and Laura Ernst star, with Jim Haynie, Eric Idle, Ralph Macchio, and Andrea Martin. Directed by Robert Downey. **CO5, CO14, CO15**

Tootsie (1983, C, 116m, PG)
Desperate for a job, an actor dresses up in drag and lands a part on a soap opera, where he becomes an overnight sensation. Dustin Hoffman stars in this smashing modern comedy, with Oscar winner Jessica Lange, Bill Murray (wonderful), Teri Garr, Charles Durning, George Gaynes, and in a small role, Geena Davis. Directed by Sydney Pollack, who also plays Hoffman's agent; he should have won the Oscar for orchestrating this marvelous film. **CO2, CO8, CO13, DT98, ST45, ST105, ST130, XT5, XT26, XT28,** *Highly Recommended*

Top Gun (1986, C, 109m, PG)
Hotshot student pilot enrolls in a Naval flying school, where he must compete with other pilots as skilled as he is. Tom Cruise, Kelly McGillis, and Val Kilmer star. Directed by Tony Scott; produced by Don Simpson and Gerry Bruckheimer. *Wings* with rock 'n' roll—except *Wings* is better, much better. **AC11, ST41**

Top Hat (1935, B&W, 99m, NR)
Fred Astaire falls for divorcée Ginger Rogers, who hates most men, particularly him. Then she dances with him. . . . With Edward Everett Horton, Eric Blore, and in a small role, Lucille Ball. **CL15, ST4, ST187,** *Essential, Highly Recommended*

Top Secret! (1984, C, 90m, PG)
American rock singer touring East Germany ends up helping the French Resistance battle some neo-Nazis. A spy spoof by the makers of *Airplane!* Val Kilmer stars, with Omar Sharif and Peter Cushing. **CO7, ST43**

Topaz (1969, C, 127m, PG)
Alfred Hitchcock Cold War thriller, with American and French spies hunting down a deadly double agent. John Forsythe stars. **DT57, MY6**

Topaze (1933, B&W, 78m, NR)
John Barrymore stars in this version of Marcel Pagnol's story of an honest but naive teacher duped by an aristocrat. With Myrna Loy and Albert Conti. **ST8, ST142**

Topkapi (1964, C, 120m, NR)
Elaborate heist story featuring an odd assortment of crooks assembled to steal a jeweled sword from a Turkish museum. Melina Mercouri and Maximilian Schell star, with Oscar winner Peter Ustinov as the gang's designated bumbler. **MY16, MY18, XT4, XT26,** *Recommended*

Topper (1937, B&W, 97m, NR)
Put-upon businessman is haunted by two delightful ghosts in this comedy classic. Roland Young stars, with Cary Grant and Constance Bennett the playful spirits. **SF2, ST92**

Tora! Tora! Tora! (1970, C, 143m, G)
Dramatic recreation of the events that led up to the attack on Pearl Harbor, as seen from both the American and Japanese points of view. Oscar-winning special effects. Martin Balsam, Jason Robards, and E.G. Marshall star. **AC1, ST185**

Torch Song (1953, C, 90m, NR)
Joan Crawford vehicle has her playing a tough Broadway star who falls for a blind pianist (Michael Wilding). **CL7, ST39**

Torch Song Trilogy (1988, C, 120m, R)
Harvey Fierstein stars in this adaptation of his play about a gay man whose mother (Anne Bancroft) won't accept his lifestyle. With Matthew Broderick and Brian Kerwin. **DR3, DR20**

Torment (1986, C, 85m, R)
A mild-mannered man on the surface, he's a killer with a hair-trigger temper beneath. Taylor Gilbert stars in this suspense movie about a man who has even his wife and daughter intimidated by his bizarre behavior. **MY14**

Torn Curtain (1966, C, 128m, NR)
Alfred Hitchcock thriller about an American scientist pretending to be a defector in Berlin. Paul Newman and Julie Andrews star. Mild. **DT57, MY6, ST2, ST162**

Tornado (1983, C, 90m, NR)
American soldiers fighting in Vietnam are pushed to the limit by a sadistic sergeant. **AC4**

Torpedo Alley (1953, B&W, 84m, NR)
Drama of submarine action during the Korean War, starring Dorothy Malone, Mark Stevens, and Bill Williams. **AC3**

Tortilla Flat (1942, B&W, 105m, NR)
John Steinbeck's tale of life in a California fishing community, starring Spencer Tracy, Hedy Lamarr, and John Garfield, with Frank Morgan, and Akim Tamiroff. Directed by Victor Fleming. **DR26, ST6, ST217, WR32**

Torture Chamber of Dr. Sadism, The (1967, C, 90m, NR)
A mysterious man (Christopher Lee) lures a couple to his castle and takes his revenge by torturing them. Based on Edgar Allan Poe's *The Pit and the Pendulum.* **ST135, WR27**

Torture Garden (1968, C, 93m, NR)
A carnival sideshow mystic offers customers a look into their futures. Jack Palance and Peter Cushing star. **HO23, ST43**

Total Recall (1990, C, 109m, R)
Arnold Schwarzenegger sci-fi adventure set in the twenty-first century, about a man sent to Mars to discover his true identity, winding up in fight against evil dictator. With Rachel Ticotin, Sharon Stone, Ronny Cox, and Michael Ironside. Oscar-winning special effects. Directed by Paul Verhoeven. Enough action and special effects for three movies, but it just doesn't know when to stop. **AC25, SF11, SF15, ST195**

Toto le Heros (1991, C, 90m, PG-13)
French drama depicting various stages of one man's life, starting with his boyhood when he dreams of becoming a superhero named Toto. Michel Bouquet stars. Written and directed by Jaco Van Dormael. **FF1**

Touch and Go (1980, C, 92m, R)
A group of respectable ladies resort to burglary to save their local kindergarten. Wendy Hughes stars in this comedy from Australia. **FF5**

Touch and Go (1986, C, 101m, R)
Michael Keaton plays a hockey star whose self-centered attitude is challenged when he falls in love with the mother of a troubled boy who tried to rob him. Maria Conchita Alonso costars. **ST122**

Touch of Class, A (1973, C, 105m, PG)
Married man is determined to have a carefree affair, even if it nearly kills him. Romantic comedy starring George Segal and Oscar winner Glenda Jackson. Directed by Melvin Frank. Good chemistry between leads. **CO1, ST117, XT3**

Touch of Evil (1958, B&W, 108m, NR)
Stylized thriller from Orson Welles, with the director playing a crooked border cop at odds with a Mexican police detective (Charlton Heston) over a car bombing. With Janet Leigh,

Akim Tamiroff, Marlene Dietrich, Dennis Weaver, and Mercedes McCambridge. Music by Henry Mancini. Video version restores 15 minutes cut from original release. Welles's last truly great film. **CL14, CU10, DT134, MY1, ST55**, *Essential, Highly Recommended*

Tough Enough (1983, C, 106m, R)
An aspiring country singer (Dennis Quaid) turns to amateur boxing in Tough Man competitions. With Carlene Watkins, Stan Shaw, Pam Grier, and Warren Oates. **DR22, ST166**

Tough Guys (1986, C, 103m, PG)
Two train robbers, released after thirty years in prison, try to adjust to life in the 1980s in this comedy pairing Burt Lancaster and Kirk Douglas. With Charles Durning, Alexis Smith, Dana Carvey, Darlanne Fluegel, and Eli Wallach. Pretty strained, although the stars do seem to be having fun. **CO3, CO10, CO20, DR11, ST57, ST129**

Tough Guys Don't Dance (1987, C, 110m, R)
Norman Mailer's twisted tale of a failed writer returning home to Provincetown, Massachusetts, getting involved with series of grisly murders. Ryan O'Neal stars, with Isabella Rossellini, Debra Sandlund, Wings Hauser, Lawrence Tierney, John Bedford Lloyd, and Clarence Williams III. Mailer adapted his novel and directed. Full of bizarre characters and touches; O'Neal, Tierney (as his father), and Hauser (as an unhinged lawman) are good but the female characters are unbelievable and not well portrayed. Nice feel for wintertime resort town. Worth a look for fans of the offbeat. **DR19, DR26, MY2, MY4**

Tougher Than Leather (1988, C, 92m, R)
Urban action drama of murder and revenge, featuring the rap music group Run-DMC in dramatic roles, with some musical interludes. **AC8**

Tournament (1929, B&W, 90m, NR)
Silent drama from director Jean Renoir, set in time of Catherine de Medici, dramatizing clash of Catholics and Protestants. **DT104**

Tous les Matins du Monde (1992, C, 114m, NR)
French drama of composer Marin Marais, who specialized in works for seventeenth-century stringed instrument the viola da gamba. Gérard Depardieu stars, with his real-life son Guillaume as young Marais. Directed by Alain Corneau. **FF1, XT8**

Tower of London (1939, B&W, 92m, NR)
Historical drama of Richard III (Basil Rathbone) and his executioner Mord (Boris

Karloff). With Barbara O'Neil, Ian Hunter, and Vincent Price, who plays Richard in the 1962 remake. **CL3, ST119, ST179**

Tower of London (1962, B&W, 79m, NR) Political skullduggery with Richard III (Vincent Price) out to eliminate his enemies. Remake of 1939 film, in which Basil Rathbone played Richard and Price had a supporting role. Directed by Roger Corman. **DT30, ST179**

Towering Inferno, The
(1974, C, 165m, PG)
All-star disaster film about a fire that engulfs the world's largest skyscraper. Steve McQueen and Paul Newman star, with William Holden, Faye Dunaway, Fred Astaire, Richard Chamberlain, Susan Blakely, Jennifer Jones, and O. J. Simpson. Foremost example of short-lived early '70s genre has dazzling special effects but stars are confined in two-dimensional characters. **AC23, ST4, ST61, ST106, ST146, ST162,** *Essential*

Town Like Alice, A (1980, C, 301m, NR) Epic drama, based on Nevil Shute novel, of couple meeting in a World War II POW camp and reunited later to face a different set of hardships in the Australian outback. Bryan Brown and Helen Morse star. Originally a TV miniseries. **DR5, FF5**

Toxic Avenger (1985, C, 100m, R) Harassed nerd falls into a vat of nuclear waste and becomes a mutated superhero. Gory spoof of horror films spawned several sequels. Acceptable if your standards are low enough. **HO21, HO24**

Toy, The (1982, C, 99m, PG) Rich man's son who has everything insists on "owning" a man he sees in a toy store, and Dad obliges. Richard Pryor and Jackie Gleason star. **CO5, ST180**

Toy Soldiers (1984, C, 91m, R) Two mercenaries (Cleavon Little and Jason Miller) rescue a group of students from a Central American country in the midst of a revolution. **AC20**

Toy Soldiers (1991, C, 112m, R) Military school students fight back when their academy is taken over by terrorists. Sean Astin, Wil Wheaton, and Keith Coogan star, with Andrew Divoff and Louis Gossett, Jr. **AC20, DR25**

Toys (1992, C, 121m, PG-13) Comedy of toy manufacturer whose death initiates struggle over company between heirs, one of whom wants to make war toys. Robin Williams stars, with Michael Gambon,

Joan Cusack, Robin Wright, LL Cool J, Donald O'Connor, and Jack Warden. Written by Valerie Curtin and Barry Levinson, directed by Levinson. **CO2, CO12, DT75, MU12, ST228**

Toys in the Attic (1963, B&W, 90m, NR) Lillian Hellman's play about New Orleans man returning home with young bride. Dean Martin stars, with Geraldine Page, Yvette Mimieux, Wendy Hiller, and Gene Tierney. Directed by George Roy Hill. **DR8, DR20, DT55, ST149, ST214**

Traces of Red (1992, C, 104m, R) Whodunit set in ritzy Palm Beach, Florida, involving murder of a prostitute and investigation by a cop who suspects everyone he meets. James Belushi stars, with Lorraine Bracco, Tony Goldwyn, William Russ and Faye Grant. **CO13, MY12**

Track 29 (1988, C, 90m, R) Bizarre drama from director Nicolas Roeg, starring Theresa Russell as a woman trapped in a loveless marriage, obsessed with the child she had to give up for adoption when she was raped as a teen-ager. With Gary Oldman, Christopher Lloyd, and Sandra Bernhard. Written by Dennis Potter. Star isn't able to bring difficult role to life. **DT106, XT30**

Tracks (1977, C, 90m, R) Dennis Hopper stars as a Vietnam veteran whose cross-country train ride with the body of a fallen comrade proves to be too much for his fragile state of mind. With Taryn Power, Dean Stockwell, Zack Norman, and Michael Emil. Directed by Henry Jaglom. Pretentious; Norman and Emil provide much-needed comic relief. **ST110, ST208, XT19**

Trading Places (1983, C, 106m, R) Pair of wealthy brothers make a bet and force a black street hustler and white stockbroker to switch positions. Eddie Murphy, Dan Aykroyd, Ralph Bellamy, and Don Ameche star in this comedy from director John Landis. With Jamie Lee Curtis and Denholm Elliott. Directed by John Landis. Four leads are terrific; they keep thin premise cooking right along. **CO3, CO13, CO20, ST42,** *Recommended*

Tragedy of a Ridiculous Man
(1981, C, 116m, PG)
Italian drama of businessman (Ugo Tognazzi) trying to deal with his son's kidnapping by political terrorists. Directed by Bernardo Bertolucci. **DT13**

Trail of Robin Hood
(1950, B&W, 67m, NR)
Roy Rogers hooks up with a collection of famous Western stars to aid cowboy actor

Jack Holt in delivering Christmas trees to orphans. Rex Allen heads the supporting cast. **ST188**

Trail of the Pink Panther
(1982, C, 97m, PG)
The very last *Pink Panther* movie, made after the death of Peter Sellers, has a reporter doing a story on Inspector Clouseau—an excuse to show footage from previous films. David Niven, Herbert Lom, and Burt Kwouk costar. Directed by Blake Edwards. **DT40, ST198**

Trail Street (1947, B&W, 84m, NR)
Randolph Scott plays Bat Masterson, as the lawman tries to clean up a corrupt town. With Robert Ryan, Anne Jeffreys, and George "Gabby" Hayes. **ST193, ST197**

Train, The (1965, B&W, 113m, NR)
French Resistance fighters rush to waylay a Nazi train loaded with art treasures. Burt Lancaster and Jeanne Moreau star. Directed by John Frankenheimer. **AC1, ST129, ST161, XT19**

Train Robbers, The (1973, C, 92m, PG)
John Wayne and buddies try to help out a lovely widow (Ann-Margret) in this Western drama. With Rod Taylor, Ben Johnson, Ricardo Montalban, and Bobby Vinton. **ST224, XT19**

Tramp, The/A Woman
(1915, B&W, 57m, NR)
Two early shorts from Charlie Chaplin. The first is considered to be his first short masterpiece. In the second, he does a hilarious bit in drag. **DT24,** *Recommended*

Trancers (1985, C, 85m, PG13)
In the year 2285 an evil cult leader wants to rule the world. His plan is to travel back to 1985 to alter the future to his advantage. It's up to Jack Deth (Tim Thomerson) to follow and destroy him. With Helen Hunt. **SF17**

Transatlantic Tunnel
(1935, B&W, 70m, NR)
The trials and tribulations of building a tunnel under the Atlantic Ocean. Spectacularly convincing sets. **SF14**

Transformers: The Movie
(1986, C, 86m, PG)
A feature-length film starring the television/toy superheroes battling an evil planet (voice provided by Orson Welles). **DT134, FA10, SF13**

Transmutations (1985, C, 103m, R)
A doctor (Denholm Elliott) creates a drug that mutates its users. Originally titled *Underworld*. **HO21**

Transylvania 6-5000 (1985, C, 93m, PG)
Horror movie spoof, with Jeff Goldblum and Ed Begley, Jr., as reporters snooping around a mad doctor's laboratory in modern-day Transylvania. With Joseph Bologna, Carol Kane, Geena Davis, John Byner, and Petar Buntic as the Frankenstein Monster. **C07, HF10, ST45, ST90**

Transylvania Twist (1990, C, 82m, PG-13)
Horror comedy with Robert Vaughan as Byron Orlock, a vampire, and comic Steve Altman as his sidekick. With Teri Copley and Boris Karloff (in clips from some of his old films). Executive producer: Roger Corman. **HO24, ST119**

Trapeze (1956, C, 105m, NR)
Romantic triangle among circus performers, starring Burt Lancaster, Gina Lollobrigida, and Tony Curtis. Directed by Carol Reed. Widescreen visuals will be lost on video. **CL7, CU20, ST129**

Trash (1970, C, 110m, NR)
From director Paul Morrissey and producer Andy Warhol, the story of Joe (Joe Dallesandro) and Holly (Holly Woodlawn) and their Lower East Side adventures in the world of drug addiction and trash-can rummaging. **CU12, DT90**

Travelling North (1988, C, 97m, PG-13)
Australian drama of a May-September romance between a retiree (Leo McKern) and a younger woman (Julia Blake). **FF5**

Treasure Island (1934, B&W, 105m, NR)
Adaptation of Robert Louis Stevenson's story about a young boy who travels with pirates in search of treasure. Wallace Beery and Jackie Cooper star. **AC13, FA3, FA4, FA15, WR33**

Treasure Island (1950, C, 96m, G)
Disney version of the Robert Louis Stevenson tale about a young boy's adventures with pirates. Bobby Driscoll and Robert Newton star. **FA1, FA4, FA15, WR33**

Treasure Island (1990, C, 131m, NR)
Charlton Heston plays Long John Silver in this new version of the Stevenson tale. With Christian Bale, Richard Johnson, Oliver Reed, and Christopher Lee. Written and directed by Frazier Heston, Chuck's son. Originally made for cable TV. **FA3, FA4, FA15, ST135, WR33**

Treasure of Pancho Villa, The
(1955, C, 96m, NR)
Western action south of the border, with Glenn Ford, Shelley Winters, and Gilbert Rowland. **ST232, WE9**

Treasure of the Four Crowns
(1983, C, 97m, PG)
A soldier of fortune is hired to recover an ancient treasure, the source of mystical powers. Tony Anthony stars. **AC21**

Treasure of the Sierra Madre, The
(1948, B&W, 124m, NR)
Three men in search of gold in Mexico form an uneasy partnership. Humphrey Bogart, Walter Huston (an Oscar winner), and Tim Holt star in this classic version of B. Traven's novel. With Barton MacLane, Bruce Bennett, Bobby (Robert) Blake, and the inimitable Alfonso Bedoya. Written and directed by Oscar winner John Huston, who also appears in a small role. Durably entertaining. **AC12, AC13, AC24, DR27, DT60, ST15, XT4, XT6, XT8, XT26,** *Essential, Highly Recommended*

Tree Grows in Brooklyn, A
(1945, B&W, 128m, NR)
Warm drama of a young girl's coming of age in turn-of-the-century New York. Dorothy McGuire and Peggy Ann Garner star, with Oscar winner James Dunn. Directed by Elia Kazan. **DT65, XT4,** *Essential, Recommended*

Tree of the Wooden Clogs, The
(1978, C, 185m, NR)
Epic Italian drama of a year in the daily lives of peasants in a northern village, set at the turn of the century. Directed by Ermanno Olmi. **FF2**

Tremors (1990, C, 96m, PG-13)
Tongue-in-cheek sci-fi monster movie about large worms wreaking havoc in a desert town. Kevin Bacon and Fred Ward star, with Finn Carter, Michael Gross, and Reba McIntire. Fun, if you're not in a demanding mood. **HO16, HO21, HO24, MU12**

Trespass (1992, C, 101m, R)
Urban action tale of two white firemen looking for stash of precious religious objects hidden in ruins of factory in East St. Louis ghetto neighborhood, encountering a rubout by black drug dealers. Bill Paxton, William Sadler, Ice T, and Ice Cube star, with Art Evans and De'voreaux White. Written by Robert Zemeckis and Bob Gale, directed by Walter Hill. Music by Ry Cooder. Nifty variation on *Treasure of Sierra Madre* is Hill's best film in years. **AC8, AC24, DT56, MU12, XT26,** *Recommended*

Trespasser, The (1985, C, 90m, NR)
D.H. Lawrence story of painter's affair with a young woman ruining his family. Alan Bates stars, with Dinah Stabb and Pauline Morgan. **ST9, WR17**

Trial, The (1963, B&W, 118m, NR)
Franz Kafka story of a man accused of a crime he doesn't know by people he can never see, directed by Orson Welles. Anthony Perkins stars, with Welles, Jeanne Moreau, and Romy Schneider. Some flashes of Welles genius. **DR19, DT134, ST161**

Tribute (1980, C, 121m, PG)
Drama of a man dying with cancer who tries for reunion with his long-estranged son. Jack Lemmon and Robby Benson star. **DR8, ST138**

Trigger, Jr. (1950, C, 68m, NR)
Roy Rogers and his famous horse help to teach a young boy not to be afraid of animals—with the help of Trigger's son. Dale Evans costars. **ST188**

Trilogy of Terror (1975, C, 78m, NR)
Karen Black plays four different characters in three suspenseful tales. The best story is the third, in which a tiny warrior doll comes to life and tries to kill her. **HO23**

Trinity Is STILL My Name!
(1972, C, 117m, PG)
Sequel to *My Name Is Trinity* features more Western spoofing by Terence Hill and Bud Spencer. **WE13, WE14**

Trio (1950, B&W, 91m, NR)
Sequel to *Quartet* (1949) offers three more W. Somerset Maugham stories, starring Harold French, James Hayter, Michael Rennie, and Jean Simmons. **DR23, WR23**

Trip, The (1967, C, 85m, NR)
TV director decides to experiment with LSD, and the results are both beautiful and horrifying. Peter Fonda, Bruce Dern, and Susan Strasberg star, with Dennis Hopper. Roger Corman directed; Jack Nicholson wrote the screenplay. **CU3, DT30, ST110**

Trip to Bountiful, The
(1985, C, 106m, PG)
Geraldine Page won an Oscar for her performance as a lonely widow who returns to her small Texas hometown to find that it's completely deserted. With John Heard, Carlin Glynn, and Rebecca De Mornay. Written by Horton Foote; directed by Peter Masterson. Page is wonderful; story wanders to no great effect. **DR11, XT3**

Triple Echo, The (1973, C, 90m, R)
British drama of World War II army deserter persuaded by farm woman to pose as her sister. Glenda Jackson stars, with Brian Deacon and Oliver Reed. Directed by Michael Apted. **DR23, ST117**

Tristan and Isolde see *Lovespell*

Tristana (1970, C, 98m, PG)
Director Luis Buñuel's tale of a young woman (Catherine Deneuve) who becomes the love object of her elderly guardian and a young man. With Fernando Rey and Franco Nero. **DT19, ST49, XT28**

Triumph of Sherlock Holmes, The (1935, B&W, 75m, NR)
Arthur Wontner stars as the legendary detective in this screen version of Arthur Conan Doyle's *Valley of Fear* tale. **HF14**

Triumph of the Spirit (1989, C, 120m, R)
Fact-based drama of a Greek boxing champ consigned to Nazi death camp, forced to fight for his captors. Willem Dafoe stars, with Edward James Olmos and Robert Loggia. **DR5**

Triumph of the Will (1935, B&W, 110m, PG-13)
Infamous documentary, filmed at Hitler's behest, dramatizes the Nazi appeal to German people at 1934 Nuremberg rally. Directed by Leni Riefenstahl. Chilling content, but a stunning historical document nonetheless. **CU16,** *Essential, Recommended*

Triumphs of a Man Called Horse (1983, C, 86m, PG)
The third installment in the *Man Called Horse* trilogy has Richard Harris and his half-breed Indian son battling for Indian rights. **WE7**

Trojan Women, The (1972, C, 105m, PG)
Classic Greek tragedy of the effects of war on the women of Troy, starring Katharine Hepburn, Irene Papas, Genevieve Bujold, and Vanessa Redgrave. **DR20, ST103, ST182**

Troll (1986, C, 86m, PG13)
An evil troll possesses the body of a little girl and sets out to transform her apartment building into a troll kingdom. Shelley Hack, Michael Moriarty, and Sonny Bono star. **HO16**

Tron (1982, C, 96m, PG)
The designer of a vast computer system is pulled into the computer and forced into a videogame competition with the computerized beings who want to overthrow the program that controls their lives. Jeff Bridges and Bruce Boxleitner star. Widescreen visuals will be lost on video. Groundbreaking use of computer animation overwhelms human element. **CU20, FA1, SF11, SF13, SF16, ST19**

Troop Beverly Hills (1989, C, 105m, PG)
A spoiled Southern California woman finds herself the leader of a Girl Scout troop in this comedy. Shelley Long stars, with Craig T. Nelson. **CO20**

Tropical Snow (1988, C, 87m, R)
Action drama of impoverished American couple so desperate to get out of Colombia they decide to get involved with the drug trade. Madeleine Stowe and Nick Corri star, with David Carradine. **ST209**

Trouble Along the Way (1953, B&W, 110m, NR)
John Wayne plays a divorced dad who takes up coaching a Catholic school football team to keep custody of his young daughter (Sherry Jackson). **DR2, ST224**

Trouble in Mind (1985, C, 111m, R)
Ex-cop just released from prison gets caught up with a naive girl and her hustler boyfriend. Kris Kristofferson stars, with Keith Carradine, Lori Singer, Genevieve Bujold, and Divine. Alan Rudolph directed. Moody and often funny (watch Carradine's hairstyles), with rare performance by Divine as male character. Set in fictional Rain City (Seattle). **DR1, DT110, MU12,** *Recommended*

Trouble in Texas (1937, B&W, 65m, NR)
Tex Ritter Western has him thwarting outlaws involved in a rodeo robbery. With Rita Cansino (Hayworth) nd Yakima Canutt. **ST101**

Trouble With Angels, The (1966, C, 112m, NR)
Two students at a convent school create havoc with the Mother Superior. Hayley Mills, June Harding, and Rosalind Russell star in this Disney comedy. Directed by Ida Lupino. **CO18, FA1, ST192, XT23**

Trouble With Girls, The (1969, C, 104m, G)
Elvis Presley musical set in the 1920s, has El in charge of a Chautauqua company, a traveling medicine and educational show. With Marlyn Mason, Sheree North, Vincent Price, and John Carradine. **ST178, ST179**

Trouble With Harry, The (1955, C, 99m, PG)
The good folks of a New England village aren't sure just what to do with a dead body found in the woods. John Forsythe and Shirley MacLaine (her debut) star in this darkly comic mystery from Alfred Hitchcock. With Edmund Gwenn, Mildred Natwick, Mildred Dunnock, Jerry Mathers, and Royal Dano. **CL14, CO10, CO12, DT57, MY17, ST145, XT21**

Trout, The see *La Truite*

True Believer (1989, C, 103m, R)
Lawyer, former anti-war radical in the 1960s, now defends drug dealers. He gets a chance

for redemption when he defends a convict on a jail murder charge and soon realizes it's a frame and part of a large-scale political conspiracy. James Woods stars, with Robert Downey, Jr., and Kurtwood Smith. Woods's energy isn't enough to carry film over preposterous plot points. **MY2, MY11, ST233**

True Colors (1991, C, 111m, R)
Fellow law students go on to work in Washington, one (John Cusack) as an ambitious political aide, the other (James Spader) as a Justice Department attorney. With Imogen Stubbs, Mandy Patinkin, and Richard Widmark. Directed by Herbert Ross. Intended as sharp commentary on contemporary politics but falls well short, with Cusack's character not believable. **DR7, DR21, ST203, XT12**

True Confessions (1981, C, 108m, R)
A pair of brothers, one a priest (Robert De Niro), the other a police detective (Robert Duvall), become enmeshed in a murder case in 1940s Los Angeles. With Charles Durning, Burgess Meredith, Ed Flanders, Kenneth McMillan, and Dan Hedaya. Written by John Gregory Dunne and Joan Didion, based on Dunne's novel. Effective contemporary *film noir* with both leads in good form. **DR16, MY2, MY14, ST51, ST63, XT10, Recommended**

True Grit (1969, C, 128m, G)
John Wayne won his only Oscar for his portrayal of Rooster Cogburn, the one-eyed sheriff on the trail of a gang of desperadoes. Glen Campbell and Kim Darby costar, with Robert Duvall and Dennis Hopper. Directed by Henry Hathaway. Wayne's a hoot; the story is pure corn. **MU12, ST63, ST110, ST224, WE2, XT2**

True Heart Susie (1919, B&W, 93m, NR)
A plain farm girl raises the money to send her true love to college, where he repays her by falling in love with a beautiful and cruel city woman. Lillian Gish stars in this silent drama directed by D.W. Griffith. **DT52, ST87**

True Identity (1991, C, 93m, R)
Black actor with hit man on his trail disguises himself as white man. Comedy stars Lenny Henry, with Frank Langella, J.T. Walsh, Anne-Marie Johnson, and Charles Lane, who directed. **CO10, CO20**

True Love (1989, C, 104m, R)
Comedy set before, during, and after an Italian wedding in the Bronx. Ron Eldard and Annabella Sciorra star. Directed by Nancy Savoca. **CO1, CO5, XT20**

True West (1986, C, 110m, NR)
Sam Shepard's powerful drama about two brothers, one a petty thief, the other a respectable screenwriter, starring John Malkovich and Gary Sinise. Originally shown on public TV. **DR8, DR20, ST147, Recommended**

Truly, Madly, Deeply (1991, C, 107m, NR)
Romantic drama of British woman whose dead lover keeps popping up with his ghostly friends. Juliet Stevenson and Alan Rickman star, with Bill Paterson and Michael Maloney. **DR1, DR23, XT24**

Trumps see *Enormous Changes*

Trust (1990, C, 90m, R)
Comedy-drama of aimless young man (Martin Donovan) who befriends pregnant high school student (Adrienne Shelly). With Merritt Nelson and John MacKay. Written and directed by Hal Hartley, whose deliberate pacing yields mixed results. **CO2, CO5, CO12**

Truth or Dare (1991, B&W/C, 118m, R)
Pop singer and media darling Madonna on tour, with plenty of backstage trauma and comedy, both high and low. With appearances by Warren Beatty, Sandra Bernhard, and Kevin Costner. Musical performances filmed in color. Directed by Alek Keshishian. Available in letterboxed edition. Prime example of self-mythmaking; always fascinating. **CU19, MU11, ST10, ST38, XT26, Recommended**

Try and Get Me (1951, B&W, 85m, NR)
Hard-luck World War II veteran falls into a life of crime; he and his partner accidentally kill a kidnap victim. Frank Lovejoy and Lloyd Bridges star. Also known as *The Sound of Fury*. **MY1**

Tuck Everlasting (1980, C, 100m, NR)
Natalie Babbitt's novel about a magical family who never age or die. **FA8**

Tucker: The Man and His Dream (1988, C, 111m, PG)
The true story of Preston Tucker, the automobile creator who challenged Detroit's Big Three carmakers with his revolutionary designs. Jeff Bridges stars, with Martin Landau, Joan Allen, Frederic Forrest, Mako, Dean Stockwell (as Howard Hughes), Christian Slater, and Lloyd Bridges. Inventively directed by Francis Ford Coppola. **DR4, DR24, DT29, ST19, ST200, ST208, XT8, Recommended**

Tuff Turf (1985, C, 112m, R)
Familiar tale of suburban youth in turmoil, set in San Fernando Valley. James Spader

stars, with Kim Richards, Paul Mones, Matt Clark, and Robert Downey, Jr. **DR9, ST203**

Tulsa (1949, C, 90m, NR)
Susan Hayward plays a tough Oklahoma oil-woman in this drama with Robert Preston, Pedro Armendariz, Chill Wills, and Ed Begley. **ST100**

Tune in Tomorrow . ..
(1990, C, 102m, PG-13)
New Orleans in 1951 is the setting for this two-tiered comedy, about a thirtysomething woman's affair with her twenty-one-year-old nephew by marriage, and a wacky writer's incorporating the story into his radio soap opera. Barbara Hershey, Keanu Reeves, and Peter Falk star. Adapted from Mario Vargas Llosa's *Aunt Julia and the Scriptwriter*, which was set in South America. Directed by Jon Amiel; music by Wynton Marsalis. **CO1, CO5, CO8, ST104, XT14**

Tunes of Glory (1960, C, 106m, NR)
British army drama about the conflict between crusty officer and his replacement. Alec Guinness and John Mills star, with Susannah York. **ST95**

Tunnel of Love, The
(1958, B&W, 98m, NR)
Doris Day comedy of couple overcoming obstacles on their way toward adopting a baby. With Richard Widmark, Gig Young, and Gia Scala. Based on the Joseph Fields-Peter De Vries play, in turn based on De Vries's novel. **ST47**

Tunnelvision (1976, C, 67m, R)
Parody of TV's future is series of skits featuring Phil Procter, Howard Hesseman, Ernie Anderson, Gerrit Graham, Betty Thomas, Chevy Chase, Al Franken, Tom Davis, and Laraine Newman. **CO8, CO13**

Turk 182 (1985, C, 96m, PG-13)
New York fireman is injured on the job but can't collect compensation, so his younger brother, a graffiti artist, decides to use his talent to dramatize the predicament. Timothy Hutton and Robert Urich star in this drama. **DR15, XT9**

Turkish Delight (1974, C, 96m, NR)
Dutch drama starring Rutger Hauer as an artist with a very free and easy lifestyle. Directed by Paul Verhoeven. **FF7**

Turn of the Screw (1974, C, 120m, NR)
Governess (Lynn Redgrave) tries to save her two charges from the ghosts of their former governess and her lover. Based on a story by Henry James. **HO2, HO19, HO26, WR14**

Turner and Hooch (1989, C, 100m, PG)
Comedy of friendship between a cop and his slobbering but resourceful dog. Tom Hanks stars, with Mare Winningham and Craig T. Nelson. **CO10, ST97**

Turning Point, The (1977, C, 119m, PG)
Shirley MacLaine and Anne Bancroft play former dance colleagues whose lives have gone in opposite directions. With Tom Skerritt, Leslie Browne, and Mikhail Baryshnikov. Directed by Herbert Ross. Intermittently successful updating of elements of classic women's melodramas. **DR10, DR12, ST145,** *Essential*

Turtle Beach (1992, C, 85m, R)
Australian drama of plight of Vietnamese boat people in Malaysia, focusing on relationship between journalist and one refugee. Greta Scacchi and Joan Chen star, with Jack Thompson, Art Malik, and Norman Kaye. **DR7, FF5**

Turtle Diary (1985, C, 97m, PG)
Unusual love story of two lonely souls in London who unite in a common cause: to kidnap a pair of giant sea turtles from a zoo and return them to their home in the sea. Glenda Jackson and Ben Kingsley star, with Richard Johnson, Michael Gambon, and Eleanor Bron. Original screenplay by Harold Pinter, who also has a small role. Quietly rewarding, with superb lead performances. **DR1, DR23, ST117, WR26, XT15,** *Recommended*

Tuttles of Tahiti, The
(1942, B&W, 91m, NR)
Charles Laughton stars in this comedy of a nonconformist and his brood living the good life on a South Seas isle. With Jon Hall, Peggy Drake, and Florence Bates. **ST132**

12 Angry Men (1957, B&W, 95m, NR)
Classic courtroom drama of lone juror holding out for acquittal of murder suspect. Henry Fonda stars; Lee J. Cobb, Jack Warden, Jack Klugman, and E.G. Marshall are among the other deliberators. Directed by Sidney Lumet. **CL8, DR17, DT78, ST71,** *Essential, Recommended*

Twelve Chairs, The (1970, C, 94m, G)
Mel Brooks comedy based on Russian story about the race to find one of a set of dining room chairs with a fortune hidden in the seat. Ron Moody, Dom DeLuise, and Frank Langella star, with Brooks hilarious as an idiot servant. **CO6, DT17**

Twelve O'Clock High
(1949, B&W, 132m, NR)
American bomber pilots stationed in Great Britain get a new commander (Gregory Peck), who nearly cracks under the responsibility.

With Gary Merrill and Oscar winner Dean Jagger. **AC1, AC11, ST171, XT4**

Twentieth Century (1934, B&W, 91m, NR)
Slam-bang comedy, set aboard the title train, involving a Broadway producer (John Barrymore) and the girl he makes a star (Carole Lombard). Both leads are outstanding under Howard Hawks's direction. Adapted by Ben Hecht and Charles MacArthur from their play. **CL7, CL10, DT53, ST8, ST140, XT19,** *Essential, Highly Recommended*

20,000 Leagues Under the Sea
(1954, C, 127m, G)
The Jules Verne tale about Captain Nemo (James Mason), a nineteenth-century inventor who builds a nuclear-powered submarine which he uses to sink warships. Kirk Douglas, Paul Lukas, and Peter Lorre costar. The special effects in this Disney film won an Academy Award. Lots of fun, even for grownups. **FA1, FA3, SF3, SF13, SF15, ST57, ST153, WR36,** *Recommended*

25 x 5: The Continuing History of the Rolling Stones (1990, C, 130m, NR)
Career retrospective of self-proclaimed world's great rock 'n' roll band, with plenty of performance clips and interviews with all the current members of the group. **MU11,** *Recommended*

29th Street (1991, C, 101m, R)
True story of Frank Pesce, winner of first New York lottery in 1976, and the effect his wealth had on his Italian-American family. Anthony LaPaglia stars in this comedy, with Danny Aiello, Lainie Kazan, and the real Pesce as his own brother. **CO2, CO5**

Twenty-One (1991, C, 101m, R)
Contemporary tale of young girl who leaves London for new life in New York. Patsy Kensit stars, with Jack Shepherd, Patrick Ryecart, and Sophie Thompson. **DR10**

21 Hours at Munich (1976, C, 100m, NR)
Thriller set during 1972 Olympics stars William Holden as German police chief attempting to negotiate freedom of Israeli hostages. With Shirley Knight, Franco Nero, and Anthony Quayle. Originally made for TV. **DR6, ST106**

Twice Dead (1988, C, 85m, R)
Haunted house story, with spirit of a dead movie star helping a family fend off a gang of punkers. Tom Breznahan and Jill Whitlow star. **HO3**

Twice in a Lifetime (1985, C, 117m, R)
A long-time marriage crumbles when the husband meets an attractive barmaid, leaving

his wife confused and one of his grown daughters embittered. Gene Hackman, Ellen Burstyn, Ann-Margret, Amy Madigan, and Ally Sheedy star. Earnest, scores some good points. **DR8, ST96**

Twice-Told Tales (1963, C, 119m, NR)
Three suspense stories based on works by Nathaniel Hawthorne; *Dr. Heidegger's Experiment, Rapaccini's Daughter,* and *The House of the Seven Gables.* Vincent Price stars. **HO23, ST179**

Twilight in the Sierras
(1950, C, 67m, NR)
Roy Rogers comes to the rescue of a reformed outlaw. With Dale Evans and Pat Brady. **ST188**

Twilight on the Rio Grande
(1941, B&W, 54m, NR)
Gene Autry gets mixed up with a female knife-thrower and jewel smugglers. **ST5**

Twilight Zone—The Movie
(1983, C, 102m, PG)
Four tales of terror patterned after the famous TV show. Dan Aykroyd and Albert Brooks star in a witty prologue; among the segment stars are Vic Morrow (in his last film), Scatman Crothers, Kathleen Quinlan, Jeremy Licht, and John Lithgow. Individual segments directed by John Landis, Steven Spielberg, Joe Dante, and George Miller. Last story, of terrified plane passenger who thinks he sees something on the wing, is only truly satisfying segment. **CO13, DT16, DT33, DT118, HO23**

Twilight's Last Gleaming
(1977, C, 146m, R)
Renegade American general seizes nuclear warhead facility, threatens to start World War III if his demands aren't met. Burt Lancaster, Paul Winfield, Richard Widmark, and Melvyn Douglas star. Directed by Robert Aldrich. **DR7, DT1, ST58, ST129, ST230**

Twin Peaks (1991, C, 120m, NR)
Reworking of original episode of cult TV series about murder of high school girl in small Pacific Northwest town. Kyle MacLachlan stars, with Michael Ontkean, Piper Laurie, Richard Beymer, Lara Flynn Boyle, Sherilyn Fenn, Peggy Lipton, and Russ Tamblyn. Directed by David Lynch. Video version offers new footage that "solves" the murder. **CU10, DR26, DT79, MY2,** *Recommended*

Twin Peaks: Fire Walk With Me
(1992, C, 135m, R)
Prequel of sorts to cult TV series, detailing the last days of small-town high school student's life. Many of the show's cast members

reprise their roles: Sheryl Lee stars as Laura Palmer, and Ray Wise as her father, Kyle MacLachlan as Special Agent Dale Cooper, Dana Ashbrook, Peggy Lipton, James Marshall, Grace Zabriskie, Madchen Amick, and Miguel Ferrer. Moira Kelly subs for Lara Flynn Boyle as Donna, with David Bowie, Chris Isaak, Harry Dean Stanton, and Kiefer Sutherland as new characters. Cowritten and directed by David Lynch, who plays Gordon Cole. Drops the humor (where are you, Lucy and Andy?) that leavened the weirdness of the show. Lee gives a terrific performance, but even the most devout fans would admit Lynch has overplayed his hand with this material. **DR9, DR26, DT79, MU12, MY2, ST205**

Twinky see *Lola*

Twins (1988, C, 107m, PG)
Comedy of long-lost brothers reunited, one a gentle giant (Arnold Schwarzenegger), the other a pint-sized hustler (Danny DeVito). With Kelly Preston, Chloe Webb, and Trey Wilson. It sounded good on paper . . . **CO3, CO5, ST54, ST195**

Twins of Evil (1972, C, 85m, R)
One of a set of beautiful twins (Mary and Madeleine Collinson) is a vampire. Peter Cushing costars. **HO15, ST43**

Twisted (1992, C, 82m, R)
Christian Slater stars in this thriller about a warped teen killer harrassing an unstable babysitter. With Lois Smith, Tandy Cronyn, and Brooke Tracy. Made in 1986 and released only after Slater's rise to fame. **ST200**

Twisted Obsession (1990, C, 109m, R)
Jeff Goldblum plays a screenwriter fascinated by the sister of a director. With Miranda Richardson. **ST90**

Twister (1988, C, 94m, PG-13)
Comic story set in Kansas about an odd family featuring a loony patriarch (Harry Dean Stanton) and his son and daughter (Crispin Glover, Suzy Amis). They're entertaining various relatives and friends during a storm. Adapted from Mary Robison's novel, *Oh!* **CO5, DR19, ST205**

Twitch of the Death Nerve
(1971, C, 90m, R)
Italian horror film from director Mario Bava that predates the recent slasher trend; at an isolated house a mad killer knocks victims off one by one. Claudine Auger, Claudio Volonte, and Luigi Pistilli star. **CU7, FF2, HO9**

Two by Scorsese
(1967–74, B&W/ C, 55m, NR)
Two early short films from Martin Scorsese,

The Big Shave, about a man's bloody grooming experience, and *Italianamerican*, a loving portrait of the filmmaker's parents which includes his mother's recipe for spaghetti sauce. **DT114,** *Recommended*

Two Daughters (1961, B&W, 114m, NR)
From India, a drama in two parts: in *The Postmaster*, a young servant girl learns obedience to her employer; in *The Conclusion*, a new bride flees an arranged marriage but later returns. Directed by Satyajit Ray. **DT102**

Two English Girls (1972, C, 130m, NR)
French director François Truffaut's study of a romantic triangle involving a Frenchman and two very different British sisters. Jean-Pierre Léaud, Kika Markham, and Stacey Tendeter star. Based on a novel by Henri Roche, also the source author of Truffaut's *Jules and Jim*. Video version includes footage restored by the director in 1984. Intensely felt, very moving. **CU10, DT125, XT26,** *Recommended*

Two Evil Eyes (1990, C, 115m, R)
A pair of tales from Edgar Allan Poe. *The Facts in the Case of Mr. Valdemar* stars Adrienne Barbeau, Ramy Zada, and E.G. Marshall in a story of a greedy wife and a doctor who leave her husband in limbo between life and death. In *The Black Cat*, a man's perfect crime is betrayed by the cat he despises. Harvey Keitel, Madeline Potter, John Amos, Sally Kirkland, and Kim Hunter star. Directed by George Romero and Dario Argento. **DT108, WR27**

Two for the Road (1967, C, 112m, NR)
Literate comedy-drama of romance, marriage, and breakup of an attractive couple (Albert Finney and Audrey Hepburn). Written by Frederic Raphael; directed by Stanley Donen. **DR1, DT38, ST68, ST102, XT18,** *Recommended*

Two for the Seesaw (1962, B&W, 102m, NR)
Romantic comedy-drama set in New York, starring Robert Mitchum as a lawyer new in town and Shirley MacLaine as a zany woman attracted to him. Adapted from William Gibson's play, directed by Robert Wise. **DR1, DR20, DT140, ST145, ST158**

Two Girls and a Sailor
(1944, B&W, 124m, NR)
MGM musical features romantic title triangle (June Allyson, Gloria DeHaven, and Van Johnson). With Jimmy Durante, Jose Iturbi, Lena Horne, and Harry James. **MU1**

200 Motels (1971, C, 98m, R)
Frank Zappa and the Mothers of Invention satirize suburban America. Ringo Starr, disguised as Zappa, narrates. **CU1, CU3, MU9**

Two Jakes, The (1990, C, 137m, R)
Sequel to *Chinatown*, set in 1948 Los Angeles, has private eye Jake Gittes (Jack Nicholson) investigating suspicious murder involving real estate developer Jake Berman (Harvey Keitel) and his wife (Meg Tilly). With Madeleine Stowe, Eli Wallach, Rubén Blades, Frederic Forrest, David Keith, Richard Farnsworth, Tracey Walter, Tom Waits, and the voice of Faye Dunaway. Written by Robert Towne; directed by Nicholson. Despite overlength, delivers absorbing story with colorful characters. **MU12, MY2, MY10, ST61, ST162, ST209, XT10,** *Recommended*

Two Moon Junction (1988, C, 104m, R)
Steamy trash, with engaged modern Southern belle attracted to an often shirtless carnival worker, causing tongues in her small town to wag. Sherilyn Fenn and Richard Tyson star, with Louise Fletcher, Burl Ives, and Kristy McNichol. **CU6, DR3, DR26**

Two Mrs. Carrolls, The
(1947, B&W, 99m, NR)
Rare later-career villainous role for Humphrey Bogart as a mad artist who paints women's portraits, then murders them. With Barbara Stanwyck as his latest victim. **MY3, ST15, ST206**

Two Mules for Sister Sara
(1970, C, 105m, PG)
A prostitute disguised as a nun is befriended by an unsuspecting cowboy. Western action stars Clint Eastwood and Shirley MacLaine. Directed by Don Siegel. **DT116, ST64, ST145, WE8**

Two Rode Together (1961, C, 109m, NR)
James Stewart and Richard Widmark ride off to rescue settlers captured by Indians in this Western directed by John Ford. **DT44, ST207**

2000 Maniacs (1964, C, 75m, NR)
Legendary film from director Herschell Gordon Lewis, who pioneered the splatter genre of horror films. A century after Union renegades overran their town, the ghosts of a Southern town rise to lure a group of Yankee tourists to their gruesome doom. **CU7**

2001: A Space Odyssey(1968, C, 139m, G)
Stanley Kubrick's landmark science fiction epic about the search for the aliens that have been helping humans develop throughout time. Keir Dullea, Gary Lockwood, and a computer named HAL 9000 star. Special effects supervised by Douglas Trumbull won an Oscar. For a time, cult following as a "head" movie. Now available in letterboxed format; still better seen on the big screen.

CU3, CU4, CU19, DT68, SF3, SF6, SF15, SF16, *Essential, Recommended*

2010: The Year We Make Contact
(1984, C, 114m, PG)
An American and Soviet space crew journey towards Jupiter in hopes of unraveling the mystery that began in *2001: A Space Odyssey*. Roy Scheider stars. **SF3**

Two Way Stretch (1960, B&W, 87m, NR)
Classic British comedy starring Peter Sellers as a convict who leads his cellmates on a robbery expedition outside the prison. **CO10, CO17, ST198**

Two Weeks in Another Town
(1962, C, 107m, NR)
Movie-set melodrama starring Kirk Douglas and Edward G. Robinson as director and producer trying for comeback on location in Rome. With Cyd Charisse, George Hamilton, and Claire Trevor. Directed by Vincente Minnelli. Companion piece to his *The Bad and the Beautiful*; uses footage from that film. **CL7, DT88, ST57, ST186**

Two Weeks With Love (1950, C, 92m, NR)
MGM musical of young girl on vacation in Catskills resort who tries to prove to her parents she's a grownup. Debbie Reynolds stars, with Jane Powell, Richardo Montalban, and Louis Calhern. **MU1**

Two Women (1961, B&W, 99m, NR)
Sophia Loren won an Oscar for her performance as a woman who is brutally attacked, along with her daughter, by soldiers during World War II. With Jean-Paul Belmondo. Directed by Vittorio De Sica. **DT37, ST11, ST141, XT3**

Two-Faced Woman (1941, B&W, 94m, NR)
Greta Garbo's last film, a comedy of mistaken identity, with Melvyn Douglas and Constance Bennett. Directed by George Cukor. **DT32, ST58, ST78**

Tycoon (1947, C, 128m, NR)
John Wayne stars in this drama about railroad builders. With Laraine Day, Cedric Hardwicke, and Judith Anderson. **ST224**

UFOria (1985, C, 100m, PG)
Offbeat comedy about a grocery store clerk who is sure that aliens have contacted her. Cindy Williams stars, with Harry Dean Stanton, Fred Ward, and Harry Carey, Jr. Made in 1980. **CO12, ST175**

UHF (1989, C, 96m, PG13)
Al Yankovic stars as a wacky cable TV programmer in this spoof of TV and movies. With Victoria Jackson and Kevin McCarthy. **CO8**

U2 Live at Red Rocks: Under A Blood Red Sky (1983, C, 55m, NR)
This Irish band in concert at a natural outdoor amphitheatre in Colorado. **MU10**

U2: Rattle and Hum
(1988, B&W/ C, 99m, PG-13)
Documentary focusing on the popular Irish rock band and their travels in America. One concert segment in color; the rest of the film was shot in B&W. **MU11**

Ugetsu (1953, B&W, 96m, NR)
From Japan, a classic drama of two peasants seeking their fortunes—one as a businessman in the city, the other as a samurai—and bringing disaster upon their families. Directed by Kenji Mizoguchi. **FF4**, *Essential, Recommended*

Ugly American, The (1963, C, 120m, NR)
American diplomat in Southeast Asia is caught in political turmoil created by communist elements; he spearheads disastrous official reaction to those events. Marlon Brando stars in this adaptation of the Eugene Burdick novel. **DR7, DR21, DR27, ST18**

Ultimate Solution of Grace Quigley, The see *Grace Quigley*

Ulysses (1955, C, 104m, NR)
The classic Greek myth of the warrior who is destined to travel for seven years after the Trojan War before he can return home. Kirk Douglas stars. **AC18, ST57**

Ulysses (1967, B&W, 140m, NR)
Valiant attempt to adapt James Joyce's monumental novel of one day in the life of several Dubliners, starring Barbara Jefford as Molly Bloom, Milo O'Shea as Leopold Bloom, Maurice Roeves as Stephen Daedelus, and T.P. McKenna, Martin Dempsey, and Sheila O'Sullivan. Voiceover readings from text dominate imagery, which can't keep up. **DR19, DR23**

Ulzana's Raid (1972, C, 103m, R)
The U.S. Cavalry and a band of Indian marauders battle it out in this violent Western tale with cult following. Burt Lancaster stars, with Bruce Davison, Jorge Lake, and Richard Jaeckel. Directed by Robert Aldrich. Written by Alan Sharp. Typical no-win situations from director in one of his better films. **DT1, ST129, WE4, WE7, WE15,** *Recommended*

Umberto D (1952, B&W, 89m, NR)
Italian director Vittorio De Sica's acclaimed study of a retired bureaucrat (Carlo Battisti) and his struggle to maintain his dignity. **DT37,** *Essential*

Umbrellas of Cherbourg, The
(1964, C, 91m, NR)
Musical drama (all the dialogue is sung) about two sisters and their umbrella shop in a French seaside resort. Catherine Deneuve stars. **FF1, MU16, ST50**

Un Chien Andalou (1928, B&W, 20m, NR)
Surrealistic film, directed by Luis Buñuel and Salvador Dali, is a series of memorable images. A preview of things to come from both artists. **DT19,** *Essential, Recommended*

Un Singe en Hiver (1962, B&W, 105m, NR)
An aging alcoholic gets a new lease on life when a young stranger enters his world. Jean Gabin and Jean-Paul Belmondo star in this French drama. **ST11**

Unbearable Lightness of Being, The
(1988, C, 172m, R)
Adaptation of Milan Kundera's novel of romance and betrayal set against the backdrop of the Czech reforms of 1968 and the Russian invasion of Prague. Daniel Day-Lewis, Lena Olin, and Juliette Binoche star. Directed by Philip Kaufman. Fine moments; ultimately too long for amount of ground it covers. **CU6, DR1, DR7, DR19, DT64, ST48**

Unbelievable Truth, The
(1990, C, 90m, R)
Dark comedy about young man's return from prison to small town on Long Island. Adrienne Shelly and Robert Burke star. Directed by Hal Hartley. **CO12, DR26**

Uncanny, The (1977, C, 85m, NR)
Peter Cushing introduces a trio of horror stories to support the notion that household cats are responsible for evil. With Ray Milland, Susan Penhaligon, Alexandra Stewart, Donald Pleasence, and Samantha Eggar. **HO16, HO23, ST43**

Uncle Buck (1989, C, 100m, PG)
John Candy comedy, as he plays an irrepressible relative who provides an unlikely role model for his little relatives. Directed by John Hughes. **CO5, CO14, DT59**

Uncommon Valor (1983, C, 105m, R)
A retired colonel recruits some Vietnam vets to help him find his MIA son in Laos. Gene Hackman stars, with Robert Stack, Patrick Swayze, and Fred Ward. **AC4, AC20**

Undead, The (1957, B&W, 75m, NR)
Early low-budget effort from director Roger Corman is time travel tale of scientist experimenting with reincarnation, taking trip to the Dark Ages. Richard Garland stars, with Pamela Duncan, Mel Welles, and Billy Barty. **DT30, SF4**

Undefeated, The (1969, C, 119m, G)
Western drama set in the aftermath of the
Civil War, starring John Wayne and Rock
Hudson as opposing colonels who must find
a way to live in peace. **ST112, ST224, WE6**

Under California Stars
(1948, B&W, 71m, NR)
When the famous stallion Trigger is kidnapped, Roy Rogers swings into action. With
Andy Devine and Bob Nolan and the Sons of
the Pioneers. **ST188**

Under Capricorn (1949, C, 117m, NR)
Ingrid Bergman plays the weak wife of Australian pioneer Joseph Cotten in this rare
costume drama from Alfred Hitchcock.
DT57, ST13

Under Cover (1987, C, 94m, R)
Action drama about male-female cop team
busting a narcotics ring. David Neidorf and
Jennifer Jason Leigh star, with Barry Corbin
and Kathleen Wilhoite. **AC9, ST136**

Under Fire (1983, C, 128m, R)
A trio of American journalists covering the
downfall of the dictator Somoza in Nicaragua
get personally involved in a story. Powerful
drama starring Nick Nolte, Gene Hackman,
and Joanna Cassidy. Co-written by Ron Shelton; directed by Roger Spottiswoode. Music
by Jerry Goldsmith, played by Pat Metheny.
DR7, DR21, ST96, ST164, *Recommended*

Under Milk Wood (1973, C, 90m, PG)
Dylan Thomas play about the lives of people
in a mythical Welsh town. Elizabeth Taylor,
Richard Burton, and Peter O'Toole star.
CL15, ST22, ST169, ST212

Under Nevada Skies
(1944, B&W, 68m, NR)
Roy Rogers leads a band of friendly Indians
against a gang of claim jumpers. **ST188**

Under Satan's Sun (1987, C, 97m, NR)
French drama of country priest, starring Gér-
ard Depardieu, with Sandrine Bonnaire and
Maurice Pialat, who also directed. **FF1, ST52**

Under Siege (1992, C, 102m, R)
One-man army saga of ex-Navy SEAL working undercover as cook aboard battleship
about to be decommissioned, when a terrorist gang takes it over. Steven Seagal stars,
with Tommy Lee Jones, Gary Busey, Erika
Eleniak, and Patrick O'Neal. Directed by
Andrew Davis. Very good of its kind, thanks
in large part to Jones and Busey's florid performances as villains. **AC24, AC25,**
Recommended

Under Suspicion (1992, C, 99m, R)
British mystery set in 1959 Brighton, about a
seedy private eye accused of murder he
didn't commit. Liam Neeson stars, with
Laura San Giacomo and Kenneth Cranham.
Directed by Simon Moore. **MY7, MY10,
MY15**

Under the Gun (1989, C, 89m, R)
Cop (Sam Jones) and lovely lawyer (Vanessa
Williams) form a team to avenge the death
of his brother. With John Russell. **AC9**

Under the Rainbow (1981, C, 98m, PG)
Farce set in a hotel during the making of *The
Wizard of Oz*, involving that film's midget
actors, spies, and secret agents. Chevy Chase,
Carrie Fisher, Eve Arden, and Billy Barty star.
CO8, CO13

Under the Roofs of Paris
(1930, B&W, 92m, NR)
This early sound film from France employs
song and mime to tell the comic tale of a
romantic triangle. Directed by René Clair.
DT25, FF1

Under the Volcano (1984, C, 109m, R)
Somber drama, set in 1930s Mexico, of alcoholic British diplomat's final days. Albert Finney, Jacqueline Bisset, and Anthony Andrews
star in this adaptation of the famed Malcolm
Lowry novel. Directed by John Huston. Finney's very good; the novel's dense meditative
prose doesn't translate. **DR19, DT60, ST68**

Under Western Stars
(1945, B&W, 83m, NR)
Roy Rogers stars in this tuneful Western with
his faithful steed Trigger and Smiley Burnette.
ST188

Undercurrent (1946, B&W, 116m, NR)
Katharine Hepburn melodrama of woman
who discovers she's married a killer. With
Robert Taylor and Robert Mitchum. Directed
by Vincente Minnelli. **DT88, MY1, MY3,
ST103, ST158**

Underground (1976, C, 88m, NR)
Documentary portrait of leftist activists in
hiding from government, a series of inter-
views with subjects. Directed by Emile De
Antonio, Mary Lampson, and Haskell Wexler.
CU16

Underground Aces (1980, C, 93m, PG)
Episodic comedy of parking lot attendants
and their zany antics. Dirk Benedict, Melanie
Griffith, and Audrey Landers star. **ST93**

Undersea Kingdom
(1936, B&W, 223m, NR)
Serial about adventurers finding the lost
kingdom of Atlantis. With Lon Chaney, Jr.
Also known as *Sharad of Atlantis.* **AC12,
ST27**

Underworld see *Transmutations*

Underworld Story, The
(1950, B&W, 90m, NR)
Small-town reporter uncovers mob corruption in this drama starring Gale Storm, Dan Duryea, and Herbert Marshall. **AC22, DR26**

Underworld, U.S.A. (1961, B&W, 99m, NR)
Young man (Cliff Robertson) swears revenge on the Mob after his father is murdered. Samuel Fuller directed. **AC19, DT49**

Unfaithfully Yours
(1948, B&W, 105m, NR)
Orchestra conductor, convinced that his lovely young wife is cheating on him with a musician, plots to do away with both of them. Classic comedy starring Rex Harrison, Linda Darnell, and Kurt Kreuger. Written and directed by Preston Sturges. Not top-drawer Sturges. **CL10, DT121**

Unfaithfully Yours (1984, C, 96m, PG)
Remake of the Preston Sturges classic, with Dudley Moore, Nastassja Kinski, and Armand Assante the points of the triangle. With Albert Brooks. **CU18, DT16, ST160**

Unforgiven, The (1960, C, 125m, NR)
Feuding in frontier Texas between two families and an Indian tribe, which claims a young woman (Audrey Hepburn) as one of theirs. Burt Lancaster stars, with Audie Murphy, Lillian Gish, and Charles Bickford. John Huston directed. **DT60, ST87, ST102, ST129, WE1, WE7, WE8**

Unforgiven (1992, C, 130m, R)
Western drama of ex-outlaw, now a widowed and struggling farmer, hired by group of prostitutes to kill a pair of ranch hands who disfigured one of their girls. Clint Eastwood stars, with Gene Hackman, Morgan Freeman, Richard Harris, Jaimz Woolvett, Saul Rubinek, Frances Fisher, and Anna Thompson. Screenplay by David Webb Peoples, directed by Eastwood. Oscar winner for Best Picture, Director, and Supporting Actor (Hackman). Superb in every way, further proof that Eastwood is an underrated filmmaker. **ST64, ST76, ST96, WE3, WE5, XT1, XT4, XT6,** *Recommended*

Unholy, The (1988, C, 100m, R)
A priest in New Orleans investigates the murders of two fellow clerics—and comes up with a surprising revelation about himself. Horror story stars Ben Cross, Hal Holbrook, Trevor Howard, and Ned Beatty. **HO10**

Unholy Three, The (1925, B&W, 86m, NR)
Silent melodrama starring Lon Chaney as a circus performer who teams up with a strong man and midget to pull off a robbery. With Mae Busch, Matt Moore, Victor McLaglan, and Harry Earles. Directed by Tod Browning. **CL12, DT18, ST26**

Unholy Three, The (1930, B&W, 72m, NR)
Sound remake of 1925 melodrama of circus performers pulling off a robbery. Lon Chaney and Harry Earles reprise their roles. Pretty stiff, although Chaney, in his last film, showed he could make the transition to sound. **ST26, XT22**

Unidentified Flying Oddball
(1979, C, 92m, G)
Disney version of *A Connecticut Yankee In King Arthur's Court.* A man gets sent back to medieval times. Dennis Dugan and Jim Dale star. **FA1, WR35**

Uninvited, The (1944, B&W, 98m, NR)
Classic ghost story of spirit of dead mother haunting her daughter. Gail Russell, Ray Milland, and Ruth Hussey star. Directed by Lewis Allen. **HO1, HO2, HO19**

Union City (1980, C, 87m, PG)
Debby Harry plays a housewife in this thriller about paranoia and murder. **MU12, MY2**

Union Station (1950, B&W, 80m, NR)
A madman (Lyle Bettger) kidnaps a blind woman (Allene Roberts) and a police detective (William Holden) heads the manhunt. **MY1, ST106**

Universal Soldier (1992, C, 104m, R)
Jean-Claude Van Damme and Dolph Lundgren square off in this tale of Vietnam vets whose corpses are frozen, brought back to life twenty-five years later as part of government antiterrorism unit. The problem: the programming on one goes haywire and he becomes an unstoppable killing machine. With Ally Walker, Ed O'Ross, and Jerry Orbach. **AC20, AC25**

Unknown, The (1927, B&W, 60m, NR)
Lon Chaney melodrama of man on the lam from police, hiding out in circus where he pretends to be armless wonder, falls for girl who can't stand touch of any man. Directed by Tod Browning. **DT18, ST26**

Unknown Chaplin
(1983, B&W/C, 180m, NR)
Trio of programs, originally made for British TV, on the cinema's greatest genius. *My Happiest Years* details Chaplin's time at the Mutual Studios in late 1910s. *The Great Director* demonstrates his emergence as a filmmaker in total control of his work, with extensive footage devoted to the making of *City Lights. Hidden Treasures* presents outtakes and

recently discovered footage never seen before. Contains interviews with several Chaplin associates still alive when the film was produced; made with the cooperation of Chaplin's widow. Directed by Kevin Brownlow and David Gill. Almost too good to be true: a magnificently rich portrait of a key figure in the history of film. **CU16, DT24,** *Highly Recommended*

Unlawful Entry (1992, C, 111m, R)
Thriller of L.A. cop who makes life hell for couple when he becomes romantically obsessed with the wife. Ray Liotta, Madeleine Stowe, and Kurt Russell star, with Robert E. Mosley, Ken Lerner, and Deborah Offner. Directed by Jonathan Kaplan. Expert handling of familiar material but the climax just pushes violence too hard and too far. **MY3, MY9, MY19, ST191, ST209**

Unmarried Woman, An
(1978, C, 124m, R)
Middle-class Manhattan wife and mother picks up the pieces after her husband leaves her for another woman. Jill Clayburgh stars, with Michael Murphy and Alan Bates. Written and directed by Paul Mazursky, who plays a small role. Of the films nominated that year, the most worthy Oscar winner for Best Picture and Actress. **DR10, DT87, ST9, ST31, XT9, XT28,** *Recommended*

Unnatural Causes (1986, C, 100m, NR)
True story of Veterans Administration benefits counselor helping Vietnam vet in fight for attention to victims of Agent Orange. Alfre Woodard and John Ritter star, with Patti LaBelle and John Sayles (who wrote the screenplay). Originally made for TV. **DR6, DR7, DT112, MU12**

Unremarkable Life, An
(1989, C, 92m, PG)
Drama of two aging sisters living together, one wooed by Japanese-American. Shelley Winters and Patricia Neal star, with Mako. **DR8, ST232**

Unsinkable Molly Brown, The
(1964, C, 128m, NR)
Debbie Reynolds plays a poor miner's daughter who becomes a millionairess and a heroine of the Titanic disaster in this musical. Based on a true story. Harve Presnell costars. **MU1, MU6**

Unsuitable Job for a Woman, An
(1981, C, 94m, NR)
British private eye story with a twist: the gumshoe's a woman (Pippa Guard) who's investigating the suicide of her boss. Based on a novel by P.D. James. **MY10, MY15**

Untamed Heart (1993, C, 102m, PG-13)
Sentimental romantic drama of plain waitress (Marisa Tomei) and shy busboy (Christian Slater); the latter believes a boyhood transplant operation gave him a baboon heart. With Rosie Perez and Kyle Secor. Directed by Tony Bill. **DR1, DR2, ST200, XT23**

Until September (1984, C, 95m, R)
Love story set in Paris involving an American woman (Karen Allen) and a married French banker (Thierry Lhermitte). **DR1**

Until They Sail (1957, B&W, 95m, NR)
Drama involving four sisters in World War II New Zealand with usual quota of love and betrayal, winding up with big trial scene. Joan Fontaine, Jean Simmons, Sandra Dee, and Piper Laurie star, with Paul Newman. Based on a James Michener story. **CL5, DR17, ST73, ST162**

Untouchables, The (1987, C, 119m, R)
In Prohibition-era Chicago, Al Capone rules over all—until a determined government agent named Eliot Ness arrives in town. Kevin Costner stars, with Oscar winner Sean Connery, Robert De Niro as Al Capone, Charles Martin Smith, Andy Garcia, and Billy Drago as Frank Nitti. Written by David Mamet; Brian De Palma directed. Some bravura sequences and great turn by Connery offset by dead center of lead character. **AC22, DT36, ST36, ST38, ST51, XT4**

Up in Arms (1944, C, 106m, NR)
A hypochondriac (Danny Kaye, in his film debut) wreaks havoc on the Army. Constance Dowling and Dinah Shore costar. **CO21, ST120**

Up in Smoke (1978, C, 87m, R)
The movie debut of Cheech and Chong, those stoned L.A. hipsters. **CU3, ST28**

Up the Creek (1958, B&W, 83m, NR)
British service comedy set aboard a mothballed ship, with the emphasis on slapstick humor. David Tomlinson, Wilfrid Hyde-White, and Peter Sellers star. **CO21, ST198**

Up the Sandbox (1972, C, 97m, R)
Comedy-drama of a young New York wife and mother whose overactive imagination results in some bizarre fantasies. Barbra Streisand stars, with David Selby. Directed by Irvin Kershner. Not always successful, but worth seeing for fans of genre or star. **DR10, ST211**

Uptown Saturday Night
(1974, C, 104m, PG)
Comedy starring Sidney Poitier and Bill Cosby as a couple of screw-ups who are after

a valuable lottery ticket. With Harry Belafonte and Richard Pryor. Poitier directed. **ST174, ST180**

Uranus (1991, C, 99m, NR)
Drama of political strife in small town in postwar France. Gérard Depardieu and Philippe Noiret star. Directed by Claude Berri. **FF1, ST52**

Urban Cowboy (1980, C, 135m, R)
Set in contemporary Houston, this drama centers on the life and loves of a young hard-hat who hangs around the mammoth honky-tonk bar, Gilley's. John Travolta and Debra Winger star, with Scott Glenn. Winger and Glenn steal the show from the lead. **DR15, ST231, WE12**

Urge To Kill (1984, C, 96m, NR)
A convicted killer is released from a mental institution and has problems readjusting to the outside world. Karl Malden stars, with Holly Hunter, Alex McArthur, and Paul Sorvino. Originally made for TV. **ST113**

Used Cars (1980, C, 111m, R)
Wild comedy with cult following about twin car dealer brothers (both played by Jack Warden), one honest, the other totally unscrupulous. Kurt Russell stars in this contemporary slapstick classic, with Gerrit Graham, Frank McRae, Deborah Harmon, David L. Lander, Michael McKean, and Joseph P. (Joe) Flaherty. Written by Bob Gale and Robert Zemeckis; directed by Zemeckis. **CO12, CO14, CU5, DT143, ST191, XT27,** *Recommended*

Used People (1992, C, 115m, PG-13)
Comedy-drama set in 1969 Queens, New York, involving recently widowed Jewish woman (Shirley MacLaine) her dotty mom (Jessica Tandy), her two daughters (Kathy Bates, Marcia Gay Harden) and her new Italian-American suitor (Marcello Mastroianni). With Sylvia Sidney and Joe Pantoliano. Screenplay by Todd Graff, directed by Beeban Kidron. **DR1, DR8, ST145, ST154**

Users, The (1978, C, 125m, NR)
Trashy tale of small-town girl managing comeback of fading film star. Jaclyn Smith stars, with Tony Curtis, Joan Fontaine, Red Buttons, George Hamilton, John Forsythe, Darren McGavin, and Michelle Phillips. Originally made for TV. **DR13, ST73**

Utah (1945, B&W, 54m, NR)
Roy Rogers tries to talk a young woman (Dale Evans) who has inherited a ranch out of selling it. **ST188**

Utopia see *Atoll K*

V.I.P.s, The (1963, C, 119m, NR)
Glossy melodrama set in international airport, focusing on intersecting lives of the rich and famous. Elizabeth Taylor and Richard Burton star in their first film after *Cleopatra*; with Louis Jourdan, Margaret Rutherford (Oscar winner for Best Supporting Actress), Rod Taylor, Maggie Smith, and Orson Welles. Written by Terence Ratigan. **CL15, DT134, ST22, ST212, XT5**

V.I. Warshawski (1991, C, 89m, R)
Kathleen Turner plays the title character, a no-nonsense Chicago private eye, in this mystery. With Charles Durning and Jay O. Sanders. Based on a character created by Sara Peretsky. **MY4, MY10, ST218, XT11**

Vagabond (1985, C, 105m, R)
Moody, stylized story of a young woman (Sandrine Bonnaire) and her aimless wandering through the French countryside. Agnes Varda directed. **DR10, FF1,** *Recommended*

Valley Girl (1983, C, 95m, R)
Romance blossoms between a San Fernando Valley mall rat and a punked-out dude from Los Angeles. Deborah Foreman and Nicolas Cage star, with Frederic Forrest, Colleen Camp, and Elizabeth Daily. Martha Coolidge directed. Clever; skirts obvious situations. **CO2, CO4, ST23,** *Recommended*

Valley of Fire (1951, B&W, 63m, NR)
Gene Autry plays matchmaker for a lonely gang of prospectors. **ST5**

Valley of the Dolls (1967, C, 123m, NR)
The Jacqueline Susann story of three young women enmeshed in the seamier side of show biz. Barbara Parkins, Patty Duke, and Sharon Tate star with Susan Hayward, Paul Burke, Tony Scotti, Lee Grant, Martin Milner, Joey Bishop, and George Jessel. Look quickly for Richard Dreyfuss. Sinks to level of book; long regarded a camp classic. **CU2, DR12, DR19, ST60, ST100**

Valmont (1989, C, 137m, R)
Director Milos Forman's version of the *Les-Liaisons Dangereuses* story of love and intrigue in eighteenth-century France, filmed before under its original title and as *Dangerous Liaisons*. Colin Firth and Annette Bening star as the schemers, with Meg Tilly, Fairuza Balk, Sian Phillips, Jeffrey Jones, and Henry Thomas. **DR1, DR5, DT45, ST12**

Vamp (1986, C, 94m, R)
Four college frat boys decide to hire a hooker for their party. They get more than they paid for when they hire a vampire. Grace Jones plays the prostitute with a taste for blood. **HO5, HO24, MU12**

Vampire Bat, The (1933, B&W, 71m, NR)
Mad doctor opus starring Lionel Atwill as a man in search of "blood substitute." With Melvyn Douglas, Fay Wray, and Dwight Frye. **HO20, ST58**

Vampire Lovers, The (1971, C, 88m, R)
An erotic thriller from Britain's Hammer Studios about lesbian vampires. Peter Cushing stars. **HO5, HO25, ST43**

Vampire Over London
(1952, B&W, 74m, NR)
British horror tale featuring comic Old Mother Riley character (actor Arthur Lucan in drag). She's involved with man who's sure he's a vampire—not surprising, since he's played by Bela Lugosi. Also known as *My Son, the Vampire*. **HO5, HO26, ST143**

Vampire's Kiss (1989, C, 103m, R)
Delirious tale of modern Manhattan vampire (Nicolas Cage), who's a literary agent and womanizer. With Jennifer Beals. **HO5, ST23**

Vampyr (1932, B&W, 60m, NR)
Danish director Carl Dreyer's classic horror tale may strike contemporary audiences as stodgy but has its own virtues: rich imagery and atmosphere. **DT39, HO5**

Van, The (1976, C, 92m, R)
Shy guy finds new way to attract women—with his new customized van. Stuart Getz stars, with Deborah White, Danny DeVito, and Harry Moses. **ST54**

Vanina Vanini (1961, B&W, 113m, NR)
Roberto Rossellini directed this story of an affair between an aristocrat's daughter and a fugitive soldier. Set in 1824; based on a story by Stendahl. **DT109**

Vanishing, The (1988, C, 105m, NR)
Thriller from Holland about woman's strange disappearance while on holiday with her husband. To give away more than that wouldn't be fair. Gene Bervoets, Johanna ter Steege, and Bernard-Pierre Donnadieu star. Directed by George Sluizer, who remade the story in the U.S. in 1993. Genuinely disturbing without a smidgen of violence; ending will knock you out. **FF7, FF8, MY3, MY9, Recommended**

Vanishing, The (1993, C, 110m, R)
American remake of Dutch thriller about young woman who disappears during trip with her boyfriend, his attempts to track her down. Kiefer Sutherland, Jeff Bridges, and Nancy Travis star, with Sandra Bullock, Park Overall, and Lisa Eichorn. Screenplay by Todd Graff, directed by George Sluizer, who made the original. **FF8, MY3, MY9, ST19**

Vanishing American, The
(1925, B&W, 148m, NR)
Classic silent Western about the mistreatment of Indians, based on a novel by Zane Grey. **WE7**

Vanishing Point (1971, C, 107m, PG)
Hired to drive a car from Denver to San Francisco, a young man decides to see if he can make the trip in fifteen hours without stopping for anything, especially the police. Barry Newman and Cleavon Little star in this cult adventure. **AC10**

Vanishing Prairie, The (1954, C, 75m, G)
This Disney documentary, part of the True-Life Adventure series, won an Academy Award for its look at animal life on the Great Plains. **FA1**

Vanity Fair (1932, B&W, 73m, NR)
Myrna Loy stars in an updated version of the William Thackeray novel about a young social climber. **CL1, ST142**

Variety (1925, B&W, 79m, NR)
Classic silent German drama about a love triangle in a circus mirroring the decadence of 1920s Germany. Emil Jannings stars. **CL12, FF3**

Variety Lights (1950, B&W, 93m, NR)
First feature by Federico Fellini (co-directed with Alberto Lattuada) is a comedy about a touring company of actors. Giulietta Masina, Peppino De Filippo, and Carla Del Poggio star. Marvelous taste of great films to come. **DT43, XT30, *Recommended***

Vegas Strip Wars, The
(1984, C, 100m, NR)
Rock Hudson plays a casino owner battling some new sleazy competition in this TV movie. With James Earl Jones, Pat "Noriyuki" Morita, and Sharon Stone. **ST112, ST118**

Velvet Touch, The (1948, B&W, 97m, NR)
Rosalind Russell plays a stage actress who turns detective to solve a murder. With Leo Genn, Claire Trevor, and Sydney Greenstreet. **MY11, ST192**

Vengeance Valley (1951, C, 83m, NR)
Western drama about feuding brothers and their women, starring Burt Lancaster and Robert Walker. **ST129**

Venom (1982, C, 98m, R)
A black mamba, the world's deadliest snake, is loose in a London home whose residentsare being held hostage by kidnappers. Klaus Kinski, Oliver Reed, and Nicol Williamson star. Not quite bad enough to be a classic. **HO16, ST126**

Vera Cruz (1954, C, 94m, NR)
In 1860s Mexico, two American cowboys become involved in revolutionary politics. Gary Cooper and Burt Lancaster star, with Denise Darcel, George Macready, Cesar Romero, Ernest Borgnine, and Charles Bronson. Directed by Robert Aldrich. Good, clean fun. **DT1, ST20, ST37, ST129, WE9,** *Recommended*

Verboten! (1959, B&W, 93m, NR)
Romantic drama of American G.I. and German girl, set in occupied Berlin. James Best and Susan Cummings star. Directed by Samuel Fuller. **DR1, DR3, DT49**

Verdict, The (1982, C, 129m, R)
Broken-down defense lawyer tries to rise to the occasion when he's involved in a complicated malpractice case against a skilled and well-funded legal team. Paul Newman stars, with James Mason, Charlotte Rampling, Jack Warden, and Lindsay Crouse. Sidney Lumet directed; David Mamet adapted Barry Reed's novel. One of Newman's best late-career performances. **DR17, DT78, ST153, ST162,** *Recommended*

Vernon, Florida (1981, C, 60m, NR)
Documentary by Errol Morris depicts the lives of folk in a small town in Florida which seems to contain a high proportion of eccentrics. **CU16, DR26, DT89,** *Recommended*

Veronika Voss (1982, B&W, 105m, R)
Rainer Werner Fassbinder drama of 1940s movie actress, allegedly a friend of Goebbels, whose career takes a turn for the worse. Rosel Zech stars. **DT42**

Vertigo (1958, C, 128m, PG)
Classic Alfred Hitchcock film, regarded by a growing cult as his best, about one man's obsession with a woman he thinks has died in a tragic fall. James Stewart and Kim Novak star. Shot on location in San Francisco. Music by Bernard Herrmann. Widescreen visuals will be lost on video. **CL14, CU13, CU20, DT57, MY5, ST177, XT13, XT27,** *Essential, Highly Recommended*

Very Curious Girl, A (1969, C, 105m, R)
From France, a comedy about a peasant girl who enjoys making love with the men in her village so much she decides to charge for her services. **FF1**

Very Edge, The (1963, B&W, 82m, NR)
British thriller about a pregnant woman (Anne Heywood) harassed by a sex criminal (Jeremy Brett). **MY3**

Very Private Affair, A (1962, C, 95m, NR)
Marcello Mastroianni and Brigitte Bardot star in this romantic drama in which a theater director gives shelter to a high-strung movie star. Directed by Louis Malle. **DT82, ST6, ST154**

Vibes (1988, C, 99m, PG)
Jeff Goldblum and Cyndi Lauper play a pair of psychics in this adventure comedy about a treasure hunt in Peru. Peter Falk costars. **CO2, CO3, MU12, ST90**

Vice Squad (1982, C, 97m, R)
A man is mutilating prostitutes in Los Angeles, and a hooker helps a cop solve the case. Gary Swanson and Season Hubley star, with Wings Hauser as the memorable villain. **AC9, XT10**

Vice Versa (1988, C, 97m, PG)
A department store executive and his young son find their minds switched through the spell of a magic totem. Judge Reinhold and Fred Savage star. **CO5, CO20**

Victim (1961, B&W, 100m, NR)
British drama of lawyer (Dirk Bogarde) being blackmailed by men who killed his gay former lover. With Sylvia Sims, Dennis Price, and Nigel Stock. One of the first films to confront the subject of homosexuality openly. **DR3, DR23, ST14**

Victor/Victoria (1982, C, 133m, PG)
Farce of misunderstanding and sexual confusion, as a Paris nightclub singer (Julie Andrews) pretends to be a man impersonating a woman, much to the consternation of an American gangster (James Garner). With Robert Preston, Lesley Anne Warren, and Alex Karras. Blake Edwards directed. Preston's wonderful; film just goes on too long. **CO1, DT40, ST2, ST82, XT30**

Victory (1981, C, 110m, PG)
Allied personnel in a German POW camp challenge a Third Reich soccer team to a game. Michael Caine, Sylvester Stallone, and Pele star. Directed by John Huston. Except for Pele's big kick near the film's end, a snooze. **DR22, DT60, ST25, ST204**

Videodrome (1983, C, 88m, R)
James Woods plays a cable TV programmer who stumbles onto a show that seduces and then ultimately controls its audience. Debbie Harry plays a kinky woman looking for the ultimate sexual thrill. Directed by David Cronenberg. Disturbing imagery; story isn't always coherently told. **DT31, HO11, HO22, MU12, ST233**

Vietnam: In the Year of the Pig
(1968, B&W, 115m, NR)
Director Emile de Antonio's documentary of the controversial war paints a bleak portrait of American policy and conduct. **CU16**

View to a Kill, A (1985, C, 131m, PG)
In this last James Bond film starring Roger Moore, 007 is up against a pair of villains (Christopher Walken and Grace Jones) who intend to create a devastating earthquake in Silicon Valley. Moore didn't quit too soon. **HF2, MU12, ST222, XT13**

Vigilante (1982, C, 90m, R)
Ex-cop joins a gang of vigilantes to avenge the brutal assault of his wife and child. Robert Forster and Fred Williamson star. **AC19**

Vikings, The (1958, C, 114m, NR)
Kirk Douglas and Tony Curtis terrorize the countryside as a pair of nasty Norsemen. With Janet Leigh and Ernest Borgnine; narrated by Orson Welles. Great kiddie stuff. **AC13, DT134, ST57**

Villa Rides (1968, C, 125m, PG)
Yul Brynner stars as the Mexican bandit and reolutionary, Pancho Villa. Robert Mitchum and Charles Bronson lead the supporting cast. **ST20, ST158, WE9**

Village of the Damned
(1960, B&W, 78m, NR)
A strange mist covers an English village and everyone is rendered unconscious until the mist clears. Later, twelve woman discover they are pregnant and give birth to look-alike children with telepathic powers. George Sanders stars. **HO13, HO26, SF9, SF19**

Village of the Giants (1965, C, 80m, NR)
H.G. Wells story, updated with teen-aged protagonists growing to mammoth size. Tommy Kirk, Johnny Crawford, Beau Bridges, and Ronny Howard star. **DT58, WR37**

Villain, The (1979, C, 89m, PG)
Slapstick Western starring Kirk Douglas, Ann-Margret, and Arnold Schwarzenegger, with Paul Lynde, Foster Brooks, Ruth Buzzi, Jack Elam, and Strother Martin. **ST57, ST195, WE14**

Vincent & Theo (1990, C, 138m, PG-13)
Dramatization of relationship between Vincent van Gogh and his brother, who often acted as his agent. Tim Roth and Paul Rhys star. Robert Altman directed. Originally a four-hour miniseries made for European TV. Slow going; some dazzling imagery. **DR4, DT4**

Vincent, François, Paul and the Others
(1974, C, 113m, NR)
French drama centering on the friendship of three middle-aged men (Yves Montand, Michel Piccoli and Serge Reggiani). With Gérard Depardieu. Directed by Claude Sautet. **FF1, ST52**

Vincent: The Life and Death of Vincent Van Gogh (1987, C, 99m, NR)
Documentary focusing on the Dutch painter, directed by Paul Cox, narrated by John Hurt. **CU16**

Violent Men, The (1955, C, 96m, NR)
Western drama starring Edward G. Robinson as ruthless rancher, Barbara Stanwyck as his suffering wife. With Glenn Ford, Brian Keith, and Richard Jaeckel. **ST186, ST206, WE8**

Violent Years, The (1956, B&W, 60m, NR)
The king of no-budget trash, Ed Wood, Jr., strikes again with this drama of spoiled debutantes turning to robbery and rape. **DT141**

Violets Are Blue . . . (1986, C, 88m, PG-13)
Successful photographer returns to her hometown and picks up with an old high school flame who's now married. Sissy Spacek and Kevin Kline star, with Bonnie Bedelia. **DR1, ST127, ST202**

Virgin and the Gypsy, The
(1970, C, 92m, R)
D.H. Lawrence story of the daughter of a strict priest and her sexual awakening. Joanna Shimkus and Franco Nero star. **DR1, WR17**

Virgin Queen, The (1955, C, 92m, NR)
Bette Davis plays Queen Elizabeth I in this historical drama about her relationship with Sir Walter Raleigh. Richard Todd and Joan Collins costar. **CL3, ST44**

Virgin Spring, The (1959, B&W, 88m, NR)
Oscar-winning drama from director Ingmar Bergman: a woodsman seeks revenge on the men who raped and murdered his daughter. U.S. horror remake: *Last House on the Left.* **DT11, FF8, XT7**

Virginia City (1940, B&W, 121m, NR)
Civil War Western, a sequel to events dramatized in *Dodge City,* starring Errol Flynn, Humphrey Bogart, and Randolph Scott, with Miriam Hopkins as a Rebel spy. **ST15, ST69, ST197, WE6, WE8**

Virginian, The (1929, B&W, 90m, NR)
Gary Cooper stars in one of his first Westerns, based on the classic Owen Wister novel. With Richard Arlen, Walter Huston, Mary Brian, and Eugene Pallette. Directed by Victor Fleming. **ST37**

Viridiana (1961, B&W, 90m, NR)
Controversial drama, banned for years in its native Spain, about a nun (Silvia Pinal) whois constantly thwarted in her attempts to dogood in a world full of sinners. Luis Buñuel directed. Audacious; one of the director's

great achievements. **CU8, DT19,** *Essential, Highly Recommended*

Virus (1980, C, 155m, PG)
A deadly manmade virus is accidentally unleashed, sparking a worldwide epidemic. The survivors (858 men and eight women) must then try to restore civilization. Madein Japan, with a partly American cast that includes Chuck Connors, Glenn Ford, Olivia Hussey, and George Kennedy. **SF12, SF18**

Vision, The (1987, C, 100m, NR)
British thriller about TV evangelists trying to control peoples' minds. Lee Remick and Dirk Bogarde star, with Helena Bonham Carter. **ST14**

Vision Quest (1985, C, 107m, R)
High school wrestler (Matthew Modine) embarks on ambitious training program for upcoming match, is distracted by the new female boarder (Linda Fiorentino) in his house. Modine is very good. **DR9,DR22**

Visitor, The (1979, C, 90m, R)
Horror tale of doctor and his wife involved with devil worshippers in order to conceive a devil child. Mel Ferrer and Glenn Ford star, with a crazy supporting cast: Lance Henriksen, directors John Huston and Sam Peckinpah, and Shelley Winters. **DT60, DT95, HO10, ST232**

Vital Signs (1990, C, 103m, R)
Drama of first-year medical students, staring Adrian Pasdar, Diane Lane, Jimmy Smits, and Norma Aleandro. **DR25**

Viva Knievel! (1977, C, 106m, PG)
Film bio of stunt driver Evel Knievel, with Evel playing himself. With Gene Kelly,Lauren Hutton, Marjoe Gortner, Red Buttons, Leslie Nielsen, and Frank Gifford.**DR4, ST123**

Viva Las Vegas (1964, C, 86m, NR)
Ann-Margret thinks Elvis Presley spends too much time with his sports car and sets out to win him over. **ST178**

Viva Villa! (1934, B&W, 115m, NR)
Wallace Beery plays the Mexican bandit/revolutionary. With Leo Carillo, Fay Wray, Donald Cook, and Stuart Erwin. Written by Ben Hecht, directed by Jack Conway. **CL2, WE9**

Viva Zapata! (1952, B&W, 113m, NR)
Marlon Brando plays the legendary Mexican bandit who rose to political power. With Oscar winner Anthony Quinn, Jean Peters, Joseph Wiseman, Margo, and Mildred Dunnock. Screenplay by John Steinbeck; directed by Elia Kazan. **DT65, ST18, WE9, WR32, XT4**

Vivacious Lady (1938, B&W, 90m, NR)
A professor (James Stewart) marries a funloving nightclub singer (Ginger Rogers), which takes his conservative family and his fiancée by surprise. Directed by George Stevens. **DT119, ST187, ST207**

Voices of Sarafina! (1989, C, 85m, NR)
Documentary follows behind-the-scenes activities of young black South African actors performing in musical show *Sarafina*, about the 1976 Soweto uprising. **CU16**

Volpone (1939, B&W, 80m, NR)
French-language version of Ben Jonson's play of a man (Harry Baur) who pretends to be dying to play off his heirs against one another. Directed by Maurice Tourneur. **DR20, FF1**

Volunteers (1985, C, 106m, R)
An Ivy League student with gambling debts joins the Peace Corps to escape his creditors and winds up paired with a gung-ho boob. Tom Hanks and John Candy star. Lame, with off-putting performance by Hanks. **CO3, CO14, ST97**

Von Ryan's Express (1965, C, 117m, NR)
World War II drama starring Frank Sinatra asa POW who commandeers a train in a bold escape plan. **AC7, ST171**

Voulez-Vous Danser Avec Moi?
(1959, C, 90m, NR)
Brigitte Bardot stars in this comedy/mystery about a woman trying to clear her dance-instructor husband of a murder charge. **ST6**

Voyage of the Damned
(1976, C, 134m, PG)
Shipload of Jewish refugees fleeing Germany is denied permission to dock and forced to return to Germany. Drama, based on fact, starsFaye Dunaway, Max von Sydow, Oskar Werner, James Mason, and Orson Welles. **DR5, DT134, ST61, ST153**

Voyage 'Round My Father, A
(1989, C, 85m, NR)
Laurence Olivier stars in this British drama of an elderly man whose longtime blindness hasn't dampened his spirit. With Alan Bates. Written by John Mortimer, based on experiences with his own father. **DR8, DR23, ST9, ST168**

Voyage to Italy (1953, B&W, 75m, NR)
A married couple (Ingrid Bergman and George Sanders) travels to Italy in an attempt to patch up their differences. Directed by Roberto Rossellini, then Bergman's husband. Also known as *Strangers*. Original running time: 97m. **DT109, ST13, XT30**

Voyage to the Bottom of the Sea
(1961, C, 105m, NR)
An atomic powered submarine is on its
maiden voyage beneath the Antarctic, when
it is discovered that the polar cap is melting.
Only the sub can save the Earth from
destruction. Directed by Irwin Allen. Walter
Pidgeon and Joan Fontaine star, with Robert
Sterling, Barbara Eden, Michael Ansara, Peter
Lorre, and Frankie Avalon. **MU12, SF3, ST73**

Voyager (1991, C, 117m, PG-13)
Sam Shepard plays an American drifting
through 1950s Europe, looking for some connection to his pre–World War II student
days, becoming involved with a German
woman. With Julie Delpy and Barbara Sukowa. Based on Max Frisch's novel, *Homo
Faber*. Directed by Volker Schlondorff. Dialogue in English. **DR19, DR27**

W (1974, C, 95m, NR)
Drama of people trying to survive in a post-
holocaust world. **SF8**

W.C. Fields Comedy Bag
(1930/1932/1933, B&W, 56m, NR)
Three classic Fields shorts: *The Gold Specialist,
The Dentist,* and *A Fatal Glass of Beer.* **ST67**

W.C. Fields Festival (1930, B&W, 56m, NR)
Further evidence of W.C. Fields's comic
genius in this collection of his early short
films. **ST67**

WR—Mysteries of the Organism
(1971, C, 84m, NR)
Yugoslavian director Dusan Makavejev's
exploration of the sexual theories of Wilhelm
Reich, paralleling a dramatic story of a liber-
ated woman and her Soviet lover. **FF7**

Wackiest Ship in the Army, The
(1960, C, 99m, NR)
Service comedy has Army rigging up schoo-
ner as a Japanese fishing boat to rescue a spy.
Jack Lemmon and Ricky Nelson star. **CO21,
MU12, ST138**

Wages of Fear, The (1952, B&W, 105m, NR)
French thriller about a quartet of desperate
men who volunteer to drive two trucks
loaded with explosives over dangerous
mountain roads. Yves Montand stars, with
Charles Vanel, Peter Van Eyck, Vera Clouzot,
and Folco Lulli. Directed by Henri-Georges
Clouzot. U.S. remake: *Sorcerer*. Heart-
pounding thrills, with star-making performance by Montand. **AC13, FF1, FF8,** *Essential, Highly Recommended*

Wagner (1983, C, 300m, NR)
The life and times of the famed composer,
Richard Wagner. Richard Burton and Vanessa

Redgrave star, with Ralph Richardson, Laurence Olivier, and John Gielgud. Also available in a 540-minute version. Originally
made for British TV. **MU5, ST22, ST86,
ST168, ST182, ST184**

Wagon Wheels (1934, B&W, 54m, NR)
Randolph Scott Western focusing on wagon
train beset by Indian raids. With Gail Patrick
and Billy Lee. **ST197**

Wagonmaster (1950, B&W, 86m, NR)
Two cowboys join a group of pioneer Mormons and help them on their way to the
promised land. Ben Johnson, Ward Bond,
and Harry Carey, Jr., star, with Joanne Dru,
Jane Darwell, and James Arness. Directed by
John Ford. **DT44**

Wait Until Dark (1967, C, 108m, NR)
Blind woman unknowingly possesses a doll
stuffed with smuggled drugs, and a trio of
nasty thugs harass her to get it back. Audrey
Hepburn stars, with Alan Arkin, Richard
Crenna, and Jack Weston. Sensational thrills,
with Arkin memorable sadist. Hepburn's performance should have won an Oscar. **MY3,
ST102,** *Recommended*

Wait Until Spring, Bandini
(1990, C, 104m, PG)
Drama of laborer's scandalous affair with
wealthy widow, set in 1930s California, based
on autobiographical novel by John Fante. Joe
Mantegna and Faye Dunaway star, with
Ornella Muti. **DR8, DR19, ST61**

Waiting for the Light (1990, C, 90m, PG)
Shirley MacLaine plays an ex-magician with
an impressionable grand-niece and nephew;
one of her "tricks" stirs up a small town during the 1962 Cuban missile crisis. With Teri
Garr, Vincent Schiavelli, Colin Baumgartner,
and Hillary Wolf. **CO5, ST145**

Wake of the Red Witch
(1948, B&W, 106m, NR)
Adventure in the East Indies, starring John
Wayne, Gail Russell, Luther Adler, and Gig
Young. **ST224**

Walk, Don't Run (1966, C, 114m, NR)
In his last film, Cary Grant plays match-
maker to Samantha Eggar and Jim Hutton as
the three share cramped quarters during the
Tokyo Olympics. Remake of *The More the
Merrier*. **CO20, CU18, ST92, XT22**

Walk in the Spring Rain, A
(1970, C, 100m, PG)
Ingrid Bergman and Anthony Quinn star in
this romantic drama of a married woman's
unexpected love affair. **DR1, ST13**

Walk in the Sun, A
(1945, B&W, 117m, NR)
Combat drama about an American infantry unit that is attacking a German stronghold in Italy. Dana Andrews stars. **AC1**

Walk Into Hell (1957, C, 93m, NR)
Adventure tale of an oil mining engineer and his lovely companion stranded in the New Guinea jungle. Chips Rafferty stars in this Australian film. **FF5**

Walk on the Wild Side
(1962, B&W, 114m, NR)
Bordello in 1930s New Orleans is the setting for this drama of a drifter seeking his lost love. Laurence Harvey stars, with Barbara Stanwyck as the madam, and Capucine and Jane Fonda among her employees. Based on a novel by Nelson Algren; directed by Edward Dmytryk. **DR19, ST72, ST206**

Walk Softly, Stranger
(1950, B&W, 81m, NR)
Love story of cardsharp on the lam from a big robbery, falling in love with crippled daughter of small-town business tycoon. Joseph Cotten and Valli star, with Spring Byington, Paul Stewart, and Jack Paar. Written by Frank Genton, directed by Robert Stevenson. A sleeper that benefits from solid script and good lead performances. **CL4,** *Recommended*

Walk With Destiny see *Gathering Storm*

Walkabout (1971, C, 95m, PG)
Beautifully filmed adventure of Australian teenager and her younger brother stranded in outback, led on odyssey to safety by young aborigine. Jenny Agutter, Lucien John, and David Gulpilil star. Directed by Nicholas Roeg. One of this erratic filmmaker's very best works. UNAVAILABLE ON VIDEO. **XT29**

Walking Tall (1973, C, 125m, R)
Joe Don Baker plays real-life Tennessee sheriff Buford Pusser, who took on local corruption with a baseball bat. Directed by Phil Karlson. With Elizabeth Hartman, Gene Evans, and Noah Beery. Over-the-top violence mars what might have been inspiring story. **AC9, AC25**

Walking Tall, Part Two
(1975, C, 109m, PG)
Walking Tall: The Final Chapter
(1977, C, 113m, R)
Bo Svenson takes over the role of Tennessee sheriff Buford Pusser in these two sequels to *Walking Tall.* **AC9, AC25**

Wall Street (1987, C, 124m, R)
Greed and manipulation in the stock market are the subjects of this topical drama, starring Oscar winner Michael Douglas and Charlie Sheen. With Daryl Hannah, Martin Sheen, James Spader, and Sean Young. Written and directed by Oliver Stone. Ripe subject is well-served by Douglas's performance but not by either Sheen's. **DR7, DR24, DT120, ST59, ST203, XT2, XT8, XT9**

Wall Street Cowboy
(1939, B&W, 54m, NR)
Roy Rogers takes to the streets of the big city to protect his land interests. **ST188**

Walpurgis Night (1941, B&W, 82m, NR)
Swedish drama featuring Ingrid Bergman in supporting role, in tale of blackmailed wife of businessman. Lars Hanson and Karin Carlsson-Pavil star. **ST13**

Waltz of the Toreadors
(1962, C, 105m, NR)
Peter Sellers stars as a retired military officer with an eye for the ladies in this British comedy classic. With Margaret Leighton. **CO17, ST198**

Wanda Nevada (1979, C, 105m, PG)
Western about prospector (Peter Fonda, who directed) winning young girl (Brooke Shields) in a poker game. With Fiona Lewis, Luke Askew, Paul Fix, and in a small role, Henry Fonda. **ST71, XT8, XT23**

Wanderers, The (1979, C, 113m, R)
Life on the Bronx streets, 1963, with four tough guys who name their mini-gang after the Dion song. Comedy-drama stars Ken Wahl, with John Friedrich, Karen Allen, Linda Manz, Toni Kalem, Erland van Lidth de Jeude, and Olympia Dukakis. Philip Kaufman directed and adapted Richard Price's novel. Adroitly captures novel's grit and surrealism. **DR15, DT64,** *Recommended*

Wannsee Conference, The
(1984, C, 87m, NR)
German drama, based on actual meeting in January 1942, in which Nazi officials discussed plans for the Final Solution. Directed by Heinz Schirk. Chilling docudrama. **FF3,** *Recommended*

Wanted: Dead or Alive (1987, C, 104m, R)
Rutger Hauer plays a high-tech bounty hunter who must stop an international terrorist, played by Gene Simmons. **AC25, MU12**

Wanton Contessa, The see *Senso*

War and Peace (1956, C, 208m, NR)
Leo Tolstoy's epic story of Russian society during the struggle against Napoleon, starring Henry Fonda, Audrey Hepburn, and Mel Ferrer, with Herbert Lom as Napoleon.

Directed by King Vidor. **CL1, CL3, DT126, HF19, ST71, ST102**

War and Peace (1968, C, 373m, NR)
Mammoth, Russian-produced version of the Tolstoy classic, directed by Sergei Bondarchuk, who also is in the supporting cast. Lyudmila Savelyeva and Vyacheslav Tihonov star, with Vladislav Strzhelchik as Napoleon. Winner of Oscar as Best Foreign Language Film. Video is English-language dubbed version. **CL1, CL3, FF7, HF19, XT7**

War and Remembrance
(1988, C, 1440m, NR)
Mammoth TV miniseries based on Herman Wouk novel of World War II, sequel to his *Winds of War*. Robert Mitchum stars, with John Gielgud, Jane Seymour, Victoria Tenant, and Hart Bochner. Available in one seven-seven set and one five-tape set titled *War and Remembrance: The Final Chapter*. **AC1, DR19, ST86, ST158**

War Game, The (1967, B&W, 47m, NR)
Oscar-winning docudrama about the effect on Britain of a nuclear attack. Directed by Peter Watkins. Originally made for British TV but banned there for its horrific scenes of violence. Amazingly influential film that still packs a punch. **CU8, CU9, DR23, XT25,** *Essential; Recommended*

War Lord, The (1965, C, 123m, NR)
Historical drama set in eleventh-century Normandy, about title character exercising right to visit another man's wife on her wedding night. Charlton Heston stars, with Rosemary Forsyth, Richard Boone, Maurice Evans, Guy Stockwell, and Michael Conrad. Directed by Franklin Schaffner. Widescreen cinematography will be lost on video. **AC16, CU20**

War Lover, The (1962, B&W, 105m, NR)
While in the air, a hotshot World War II combat pilot (Steve McQueen) is considered a good luck charm to the rest of the squad. On the ground, he antagonizes everyone, including his co-pilot (Robert Wagner). Based on a novel by John Hersey. **AC1, AC11, DR19, ST146**

War of the Roses, The
(1989, C, 116m, R)
Domestic comedy starring Michael Douglas and Kathleen Turner as longtime couple whose marital breakup involves custody of their dream home. Director Danny DeVito costars as Douglas's attorney. Broad, to say the least, with a cruel streak that's hard to like. Give it credit for an uncompromising ending. **CO1, CO2, ST54 ST59, ST218**

War of the Wildcats
(1943, B&W, 102m, NR)
John Wayne is an oil wildcatter in frontier Oklahoma. With Martha Scott, Albert Dekker, Gabby Hayes, and Dale Evans. **ST224**

War of the Worlds (1953, C, 85m, G)
Martian war machines invade Earth, intent on destroying all humans. Based on the H.G. Wells novel. Produced by George Pal; Academy Award winner for special effects. Gene Barry stars. Great kid stuff. **FA8, SF1, SF7, SF9, SF13, WR37**

War Party (1988, C, 100m, R)
In a Montana town, a historical reenactment of an Indian massacre sets off a Blackfoot Indian, who murders a local white man and in turn is pursued by a posse. Billy Wirth and Kevin Dillon star, with M. Emmet Walsh and Dennis Banks. **WE7, WE12**

War Wagon, The (1967, C, 101m, NR)
John Wayne and Kirk Douglas pull off a gold heist in this light-hearted Western. **ST57, ST224, WE14**

WarGames (1983, C, 110m, PG)
Computer whiz (Matthew Broderick) accidentally taps into Pentagon system and precipitates a serious war exercise. With Ally Sheedy, Dabney Coleman, and John Wood. Directed by John Badham. Far-fetched; Broderick is engaging. **DR7, SF5**

Warlock (1959, C, 121m, NR)
Henry Fonda is the gunfighter, Anthony Quinn the gambler, and Richard Widmark the sheriff in this Western drama that concentrates on character rather than action. Directed by Edward Dmytryk. **ST71, WE2**

Warlords of the 21st Century
(1982, C, 91m, PG)
During an oil shortage after World War III an ex-commando decides to take a stand against an evil dictator. **SF8**

Warm Nights on a Slow Moving Train
(1987, C, 90m, R)
Offbeat Australian drama about a schoolteacher (Wendy Hughes) who moonlights as a prostitute on trains to support her brother's morphine addiction. With Colin Friels. **FF5, XT19**

Warriors, The (1955, C, 85m, NR)
A British prince (Errol Flynn) defends a French village from marauders. With Peter Finch, Joanne Dru, and Christopher Lee. Flynn's last swashbuckling film. **ST69, ST135**

Warriors, The (1979, C, 90m, R)
A New York City gang is falsely accused of murder and must fight its way across its rivals'

turfs to get to safety. Michael Beck and James Remar star, with Thomas Waites, Dorsey Wright, and Deborah Van Valkenburgh. Walter Hill directed this controversial film which allegedly sparked violence in several theaters. Thrilling, stylized action. **AC8, CU7, DR15, DT56, XT9,** *Essential, Recommended*

Warriors of the Wasteland
(1983, C, 87m, R)
In a post-holocaust world three adventurers protect a band of settlers against the Templars, a gang of very nasty people. **SF8**

Warriors of the Wind (1985, C, 95m, PG)
An animated futuristic fantasy. **AC18**

Warrior's Rest see *Le Repos du Guerrier*

Wasn't That a Time! (1982, C, 78m, PG)
Loving documentary about the 1980 reunion of The Weavers, folk-singing group who were blacklisted during the McCarthy era. Lee Hays, Pete Seeger, Ronnie Gilbert, and Fred Hellerman offer wonderful harmonizing. Also known as *The Weavers: Wasn't That a Time!* **MU4,** *Recommended*

Wasp Woman, The (1960, B&W, 66m, NR)
Low-budget horror tale from director Roger Corman about a cosmetic maker who uses ingredients from wasp venom with predictable results. Susan Cabot stars, with Fred (Anthony) Eisley and Barboura Morris. **DT30, HO21**

Watch on the Rhine
(1943, B&W, 114m, NR)
Nazi agents harass a German (Paul Lukas, in an Oscar-winning performance) and his American wife (Bette Davis) who now live in Washington D.C. With Geraldine Fitzgerald. Dashiell Hammett adapted Lillian Hellman's play. **DR20, ST44, WR12, XT2**

Watcher in the Woods, The
(1980, C, 84m, PG)
An American family moves into an English country house and the two children see visions of a missing girl. Bette Davis stars in this Disney horror film. With Carroll Baker, David McCallum, Lynn-Holly Johnson, and Kyle Richards. **FA1, FA8, HO2, HO3, HO26, SF13, ST44**

Watchers (1988, C, 92m, R)
A government experiment goes haywire and unleashes a monster named Oxcom and a super-intelligent dog on an unsuspecting populace. Corey Haim stars, with Michael Ironside and Barbara Williams. **HO20**

Water (1985, C 95m, PG-13)
Michael Caine stars in this comedy as the governor of a Caribbean island, where discovery of a valuable mineral water turns things upside-down. With Brenda Vacarro, Leonard Rossiter, and Valerie Perrine. **ST25**

Water Babies, The (1978, C, 92m, NR)
This underrea adventure mixes live action and animation. James Mason stars. **FA8, ST153**

Waterdance, The (1992, C, 106m, R)
Eric Stoltz plays a young man paralyzed from the waist down in a hiking accident, forced to adjust to a new life in a convalescent hospital. With Helen Hunt, William Forsythe, Wesley Snipes, and Elizabeth Pena. Written by Neal Jiminez, based in part on his own experiences; directed by Jiminez and Michael Steinberg. **DR6, ST201**

Waterhole #3 (1967, C, 95m, NR)
Comic Western about a trio of robbers concealing their loot in the title location. James Coburn stars, with Carroll O'Connor, Claude Akins, and Bruce Dern. **WE14**

Waterland (1992, C, 95m, R)
Jeremy Irons plays a British schoolteacher working in Pittsburgh, relating his boyhood experiences to his students. With Ethan Hawke, Sinead Cusack, and John Heard. Based on Graham Swift's novel, directed by Stephen Gyllenhaal. **DR19, DR23, DR25, ST116**

Waterloo (1971, C, 123m, G)
Rod Steiger plays Napoleon in this big-budget drama of his comeuppance. With Christopher Plummer, Orson Welles, and Jack Hawkins. **DR5, DT134, HF19**

Waterloo Bridge (1940, B&W, 103m, NR)
Vivien Leigh and Robert Taylor star in the classic romance about a ballet dancer and soldier falling in love during an air raid. **CL4, ST137**

Watership Down (1978, C, 92m, PG)
In this animated adventure, a warren of rabbits pursue freedom in the face of threats from humans, cats, dogs, and their own kind. Featuring the voices of John Hurt, Ralph Richardson, and Denholm Elliott. **FA10**

Wavelength (1983, C, 87m, PG)
A rock star (Robert Carradine) stumbles onto a government cover-up of aliens who crashlanded in California. **SF9**

Way Ahead, The see *Immortal Battalion, The*

Way Back Home (1932, B&W, 81m, NR)
Drama of orphan boy in clutches of an evil guardian is notable mainly for early appear-

ance of Bette Davis in small role. Phillips Lord and Frank Albertson star. **ST44**

Way Down East (1920, B&W, 119m, NR) Classic silent melodrama, starring Lillian Gish, of a woman shunned because of her illegitimate baby. With Richard Barthelmess and Lowell Sherman. D.W. Griffith directed. Finale on the ice floes is breathtaking. **CL12, DT52, ST87,** *Essential, Recommended*

Way Out West (1937, B&W, 65m, NR) Laurel and Hardy star in this delightful comedy set in the Old West. **ST133, WE14,** *Recommended*

Way We Were, The (1973, C, 118m, PG) Romantic drama about a Jewish political activist and WASP-y writer, following their lives from college in the 1930s to Hollywood and the blacklist in the 1950s. Barbra Streisand and Robert Redford star, with Bradford Dillman, Patrick O'Neal, Lois Chiles, and in a small role, James Woods. Directed by Sydney Pollack. Touchstone romance tries to cover too many bases. **DR1, DR13, DT80, ST181, ST211, ST233,** *Essential*

Way West, The (1967, C, 122m, NR) A.B. Guthrie's classic novel of pioneers in the Old West. Kirk Douglas, Robert Mitchum, and Richard Widmark star, with Sally Field in a small role. **ST57, ST66, ST158, WE1**

Wayne's World (1992, C, 95m, PG-13) Affably dopey comedy based on "Saturday Night Live" skit of two Midwestern airheads with their own public-access TV show. Mike Myers and Dana Carvey star as Wayne Campbell and Garth Algar. With Rob Lowe, Tia Carrere, Brian Doyle-Murray, Lara Flynn Boyle, Alice Cooper as himself, Ed O'Neill, and Meat Loaf. Directed by Penelope Spheeris. Surprisingly inventive and sweet-natured look at suburban subculture. **CO4, CO8, MU12,** *Recommended*

We All Loved Each Other So Much (1977, C, 124m, NR) From Italy, a comic story of friendship and love, about three pals who all lust for the same woman over a thirty-year span. Federico Fellini and Marcello Mastroianni appear in bit parts as themselves. **DT43, FF2, ST154**

We of the Never Never (1983, C, 132m, G) Visually rich adventure of first white woman to explore the Australian outback. Angela Punch McGregor and Arthur Dignam star. **AC12, FF5**

We Think the World of You (1989, C, 91m, R) British comedy of a pair of male lovers (Alan

Bates and Gary Oldman) who are separated when one goes to prison and the other has to care for his friend's dog. **CO17, ST9**

Weavers: Wasn't That a Time!, The see *Wasn't That a Time!*

Wedding, A (1978, C, 125m, PG) Comedy about variety of oddball family members and guests who show up at a suburban Chicago wedding. Robert Altman directed a diverse cast, including Carol Burnett, Desi Arnaz, Jr., Pat McCormick, Mia Farrow, Viveca Lindfors, Paul Dooley, Lillian Gish, Lauren Hutton, Howard Duff, and Vittorio Gassman. Widescreen will be lost on video. One of Altman's funniest comedies, with a near-perfect cast. Not recommended for prospective brides or grooms. **CO5, CU17, CU20, DT4, ST65, ST87, XT20,** *Recommended*

Wedding in Blood (1973, C, 98m, PG) Two lovers make plans to murder their respective spouses. French thriller from director Claude Chabrol, starring Stephane Audran. **FF1, MY16**

Wedding in White (1972, C, 106m, NR) Canadian drama of young girl (Carol Kane) made pregnant by older man, a friend of her father's, and the resulting family crisis. Donald Pleasence costars. **DR8, XT20**

Wedding March, The (1928, B&W/C, 113m, NR) Erich Von Stroheim directed this silent drama of depravity set in pre-World War I Vienna. One sequence in color. Footage restored for home video. **CL12, CU10, DT129, XT20,** *Recommended*

Wedding Party, The (1969, B&W, 92m, NR) Comedy about preparations for marriage, starring Jill Clayburgh and Robert De Niro, both in their first film. Brian De Palma co-directed, with Cynthia Munroe and Wilford Leach. **DT36, ST31, ST51, XT20**

Wedlock see *Deadlock*

Wee Willie Winkie (1937, B&W, 100m, NR) Rudyard Kipling tale of a British regiment in India and their mascot (Shirley Temple). Victor McLaglen stars. John Ford directed. **DT44, FA4, ST213**

Weeds (1987, C, 115m, R) Nick Nolte stars in this drama based on fact, about a ex-con playwright who takes a troupe of his fellow former prisoners on the road with his plays. With Rita Taggart, Lane

Smith, and William Forsythe. **DR6, DR18, ST164**

Weekend (1967, C, 103m, NR)
Director Jean-Luc Godard's masterful dissection of bourgeois life, about a couple's harrowing trip in the French countryside. Mireille Darc and Jean Yanne star. Political polemics and the damnedest traffic jam you've ever seen. For the adventurous. **DT50, XT18,** *Essential, Recommended*

Weekend at Bernie's
(1989, C, 97m, PG-13)
Knockabout comedy of two young men spending the weekend at their boss's Long Island digs, arriving to discover he's dead, trying to cover up the fact. Andrew McCarthy and Jonathan Silverman star, with Terry Kiser as the corpse. **CO9**

Weekend of Shadows (1977, C, 94m, NR)
Australian drama of a Polish immigrant accused of murder, chased by an angry mob. John Waters and Melissa Jaffer star. **FF5**

Weird Science (1985, C, 94m, PG-13)
Pair of teen nerds create a lovely woman in their basement laboratory in this comedy. Anthony Michael Hall, Ilan Mitchell-Smith, and Kelly LeBrock star. Written and directed by John Hughes. **CO11, DT59**

Welcome Home (1989, C, 90m, R)
Returning Vietnam veteran, missing in action for many years, finds that his wife has remarried. Kris Kristofferson stars, with JoBeth Williams and Sam Waterston. **DR7, MU12**

Welcome Home, Roxy Carmichael
(1990, C, 98m, PG-13)
Drama of small-town Ohio girl (Winona Ryder) who fantasizes that movie star returning to her hometown is her mother. With Jeff Daniels and Laila Robins. **DR9, DR26**

Welcome to L.A. (1977, C, 106m, R)
Episodic drama about contemporary Californians and their aimless lives. Keith Carradine, Sally Kellerman, Geraldine Chaplin, Sissy Spacek, and Harvey Keitel star. Alan Rudolph directed. Stultifying. **DT110, ST202, XT10**

We're No Angels (1955, C, 106m, NR)
Three convicts escape from Devil's Island, hide out with a kind and understanding family, and get themselves into mischief. Humphrey Bogart stars in a rare comedy role, with Peter Ustinov and Basil Rathbone. Remake released in 1989. **ST15**

We're No Angels (1989, C, 108m, PG-13)
Loose remake of the Bogart comedy about escaped cons; this time, there are two (Robert De Niro and Sean Penn), who masquerade as priests in a small town. With Demi Moore and Hoyt Axton. Written by David Mamet. **CO20, CU18, ST51**

We're Not Married (1952, B&W, 85m, NR)
Comedy of six couples who learn that their marriages are invalid, adjusting to possibility of starting over again. Ginger Rogers, Fred Allen, Victor Moore, Marilyn Monroe, Paul Douglas, David Wayne, Eve Arden, and Zsa Zsa Gabor star. **ST159, ST187**

Werewolf of London
(1935, B&W, 75m, NR)
First film about werewolves star Henry Hull as scientist studying lycanthropy. With Warner Oland and Valerie Hobson. **HO1, HO4, HO20**

Werewolf of Washington, The
(1973, C, 90m, PG)
Personal friend of the President (Dean Stockwell) is bitten by a werewolf while in Budapest. When he returns to Washington as a werewolf, he begins to kill off all opponents of the administration. **HO4, ST208**

Werner Herzog Eats His Shoe
(1980, C, 20m, NR)
The German director makes good on a bet involving colleague Errol Morris's ability to finish a film. Directed by Les Blank. **DT54**

West of Zanzibar (1928, B&W, 63m, NR)
Lon Chaney plays the crippled king of a jungle kingdom who's bent on revenge against the man who ruined his life. With Lionel Barrymore, Mary Noland, and Warner Baxter. Directed by Tod Browning. **DT18, ST26**

West Point Story, The
(1950, B&W, 113m, NR)
Broadway producer decides to put on a show at the United States Military Academy. James Cagney and Doris Day star, with Virginia Mayo, Gordon MacRae, and Gene Nelson. **MU6, ST24, ST47**

West Side Story (1961, C, 151m, G)
Broadway hit musical from Leonard Bernstein and Stephen Sondheim is Romeo and Juliet story set in contemporary New York, with fighting gangs rather than feuding families. Natalie Wood, Richard Beymer, and Russ Tamblyn star. Winner of ten Oscars, including Best Picture, Supporting Actor and Actress (George Chakiris and Rita Moreno), and Director (Robert Wise). Wise and choreographer Jerome Robbins directed; Robbins was awarded a special Oscar. Widescreen will be sorely missed on video, especially during dazzling dance numbers. **CU20, DT140, FA9, MU2, MU3, MU6, MU7, MU14, XT1,**

XT4, XT5, XT6, XT9, *Essential,*
Recommended

Western Union (1941, C, 94m, NR)
Drama of the Old West and the establish-
ment of telegraph lines between Omaha and
Salt Lake City. Robert Young and Randolph
Scott star, with Dean Jagger and John Car-
radine. Fritz Lang directed. **DT70, ST197**

Westerner, The (1940, B&W, 100m, NR)
Gary Cooper gets involved in land feuds in
this Western, with Oscar winner Walter Brennan as Judge Roy Bean. Directed by William
Wyler. **DT142, ST37, WE2, XT4**

Westfront 1918 (1930, B&W, 90m, NR)
Classic antiwar drama from German director
G.W. Pabst, his first sound picture. **FF3,
XT25**

Westworld (1973, C, 88m, PG)
Amusement park for the rich is populated by
robots who look and act human. One day
the robots rebel and slaughter all the human
tourists—except one, who desperately tries to
escape. Yul Brynner and Richard Benjamin
star. **SF6**

Wetherby (1985, C, 97m, R)
British drama of stranger at a Yorkshire home
committing suicide, leaving his hosts and
others to sort it all out. Vanessa Redgrave,
Joely Richardson, Judi Dench, and Ian Holm
star. Written and directed by David Hare.
DR23, ST182

Whales of August, The
(1987, C, 90m, NR)
Screen legends Lillian Gish and Bette Davis
star in this drama of two elderly sisters
spending a summer on the coast of Maine.
With Vincent Price, Ann Sothern, and Harry
Carey, Jr. Directed by Lindsay Anderson.
DR8, DR11, ST44, ST87, ST179

What? see *Diary of Forbidden Dreams*

What About Bob? (1991, C, 99m, PG)
Richard Dreyfuss and Bill Murray team in
this comedy about a psychiatrist on family
vacation and his obsessive patient who joins
him. With Julie Hagerty and Charlie Korsmo.
CO2, CO3, CO5, CO13, ST60

**What Did You Do During the War,
Daddy?** (1966, C, 119m, NR)
Service comedy about loosely organized out-
fit of Americans attempting to take over vil-
lage of Italian eccentrics during World War II.
James Coburn stars, with Dick Shawn, Sergio
Fantoni, Aldo Ray, Harry Morgan, and Car-
roll O'Connor. Written by William Peter
Blatty, directed by Blake Edwards. **CO21,
DT40**

What Ever Happened to Baby Jane?
(1962, B&W, 132m, NR)
Unbalanced ex-child star, Baby Jane Hudson
(Bette Davis), terrorizes her crippled sister
(Joan Crawford), a former movie idol. With
Victor Buono. A camp classic directed by
Robert Aldrich. Spun off cycle of similar films
with veteran female stars. **CU2, DR13, DT1,
HO14, ST39, ST44,** *Essential*

What Have I Done to Deserve This!
(1984, C, 100m, NR)
Comedy from Spanish director Pedro Almodóvar about a frantic housewife running a
wild working-class family. Carmen Maura
stars. **DT3**

What! No Beer? (1933, B&W, 66m, NR)
Comedy starring Buster Keaton and Jimmy
Durante as a pair of bootleggers. With Roscoe
Ates and Phyllis Barry. Directed by Edward
Sedgwick. **DT66**

What Price Glory? (1952, C, 111m, NR)
James Cagney, Dan Dailey, and Robert Wagner are fighting in the French trenches during World War I. Directed by John Ford.
AC2, DT44, ST24

What Price Hollywood?
(1932, B&W, 88m, NR)
Fascinating look at early sound movies, with
Constance Bennett as the Brown Derby waitress who gets a break from tipsy director
Lowell Sherman, then leaves him broken-
hearted for another man. With Neil Hamilton and Gregory Ratoff. Directed by George
Cukor. First version of the *Star Is Born* story;
Cukor directed the outstanding Judy Gar-
land-James Mason variation twenty years
later. **CL7, DT32,** *Recommended*

What's New, Pussycat?
(1965, C, 108m, NR)
Woman-crazy man consults loony shrink for
help, which only makes his problems worse.
Zany comedy starring Peter O'Toole and
Peter Sellers, with Woody Allen (who wrote
the screenplay), Romy Schneider, Capucine,
Paula Prentiss, and Ursula Andress. Tom
Jones sings the title tune. **CO1, DT2, ST169,
ST198,** *Recommended*

What's the Matter With Helen?
(1971, C, 101m, PG)
Hollywood in the 1930s is the setting for this
tongue-in-cheek tale of two women who set
up a school for gifted children to conceal
their sordid past. Debbie Reynolds and Shelley Winters star. **MY4, ST232**

What's Up, Doc? (1972, C, 94m, G)
Modern screwball comedy, set in San Francisco, with a free spirit (Barbra Streisand), a

straight arrow (Ryan O'Neal), his uptight fiancee (Madeline Kahn), and assorted jewel thieves and other characters. With Kenneth Mars, Austin Pendleton, Sorrell Booke, Michael Murphy, John Hillerman, and M. Emmet Walsh. Written by Robert Benton and David Newman; directed by Peter Bogdanovich. Mildly enjoyable but more often has air of strained casual nuttiness. **ST211, XT13**

What's Up, Tiger Lily? (1966, C, 80m, NR) Unique comic film co-written and "directed" by Woody Allen, who took a Grade B Japanese spy thriller called *Key of Keys* and dubbed in hilarious English dialogue. Silly fun. **CO7, DT2,** *Recommended*

Wheel of Fortune (1941, B&W, 83m, NR) John Wayne plays a country lawyer out to put a crooked politician behind bars—even though he loves the man's daughter. With Frances Dee. Also known as *A Man Betrayed.* **ST224**

Wheeler Dealers, The (1963, C, 105m, NR) Broad comedy set in the business world of Texas millionaires. James Garner and Lee Remick star, with Jim Backus, Phil Harris, Shelley Berman, and Chill Wills. **ST82**

Wheels of Fire (1985, C, 81m, R) A look into the future shows Earth as a wasteland and a car gang terrorizing the populace. **AC10**

When a Woman Ascends the Stairs (1960, B&W, 111m, NR) Japanese drama of widow working as madam in Ginza district bar, facing her thirtieth birthday. Hideko Takamine stars. Directed by Mikio Naruse. Available in letterboxed format. **CU19, FF4**

When Comedy Was King (1960, B&W, 81m, NR) Compilation of silent comedy clips featuring Charlie Chaplin, Buster Keaton, Laurel and Hardy, and Fatty Arbuckle. **CL11, DT24, DT66, ST133**

When Father Was Away on Business (1985, C, 144m, R) Drama of Yugoslavian family trying to get by when head of household is sent away to a labor camp for innocent indiscretion. Morena D'E Bartolli stars as the six-year-old son, through whose eyes we see the story. Directed by Emir Kusturica. **FF7**

When Harry Met Sally . . . (1989, C, 95m, R) Comedy of a couple who get acquainted as college students moving to New York, strike

up a friendship over the years, and eventually fall in love. Billy Crystal and Meg Ryan star, with Carrie Fisher and Bruno Kirby. Written by Nora Ephron; directed by Rob Reiner. Songs sung by Harry Connick, Jr. Lightly likable without amounting to much. Apparent disparity in stars' ages is distraction. **CO1, CO13, DT103, XT9**

When He's Not a Stranger (1989, C, 100m, NR) Drama of date rape set at a college campus, starring Annabeth Gish and John Terlesky, with Kevin Dillon. Originally made for TV. **DR7, DT10, DR25**

When It Was a Game (1992, C/B&W, 57m, NR) Evocative, moving collection of amateur movies, shot by fans, of baseball players and games taken between 1934 and 1957. Originally shown on cable TV. Fresh glimpse at familiar chapter of sports history. **CU16,** *Highly Recommended*

When Ladies Meet (1941, B&W, 108m, NR) Joan Crawford melodrama of writer in love with a married man (Herbert Marshall) also comments on women's rights. With Greer Garson and Robert Taylor. Based on play by Rachel Crothers; made once before in 1933. Also known as *Strange Skirts.* **CL5, DR20, ST39, ST83**

When Michael Calls (1971, C, 73m, NR) Thriller of mother receiving mysterious phone calls from her dead son. Elizabeth Ashley, Ben Gazzara, and Michael Douglas star. Originally made for TV. Also known as *Shattered Silence.* **MY3, ST59**

When the Legends Die (1972, C, 105m, PG) Richard Widmark and Frederic Forrest star as a rodeo cowboy and his young Indian friend in this contemporary Western. **WE7, WE12**

When the North Wind Blows (1974, C, 113m, G) Trapper in Siberia tries to protect snow tigers. Henry Brandon stars. **FA4**

When the Whales Came (1989, C, 100m, PG) British drama set on a remote island off the southwest coast, where a local legend involving a beached whale and a curse seems to be coming true. Paul Scofield stars, with Helen Mirren, David Threlfall, David Suchet, and Helen Pearce. **DR23**

When Time Ran Out . . . (1980, C, 144m, PG) Posh resort on a Polynesian island and its guests are in danger when a long-dormant volcano erupts. Video version has 20 minutes of additional footage not seen in the theatrical release. Paul Newman, William Holden, and Jacqueline Bisset head the cast. **AC23, CU10, ST87, ST106, ST162**

When Wolves Cry see *Christmas Tree, The*

When Worlds Collide (1951, C, 81m, G)
Small band of scientists and students who believe the Earth is on a collision course with a star race against time to build a space ark. Special effects won an Oscar; produced by George Pal. **SF1, SF7**

Where Angels Fear To Tread
(1991, C, 112m, NR)
E.M. Forster story of British widow (Helen Mirren) on a trip to Italy meeting and marrying a younger Italian man, much to the chagrin of her stuffy in-laws. With Helena Bonham Carter, Judy Davis, Rupert Graves, and Giovanni Guidelli. Directed by Charles Sturridge. Not quite up to the standards set by *Room With a View* and *Howards End,* but lots to like, including Carter and Davis's performances. **DR23, ST46, WR9,** *Recommended*

Where Are the Children?
(1982, C, 97m, R)
Jill Clayburgh plays a woman under suspicion when children from her second marriage disappear (she was accused of murdering two children from a previous marriage but found innocent). Frederic Forrest costars in this thriller. **MY14, ST31**

Where Eagles Dare (1968, C, 158m, PG)
Richard Burton and Clint Eastwood go undercover to rescue a kidnapped general from a Nazi stronghold. **AC1, ST22, ST64**

Where Love Has Gone
(1964, C, 114m, NR)
Melodrama of three generations of women: domineering grandmother (Bette Davis), her daughter (Susan Hayward), and granddaughter (Joey Heatherton), the latter accused of killing her mom's lover. With Michael Connors and Jane Greer. Directed by Edward Dmytryk. **CL5, ST44**

Where Sleeping Dogs Lie
(1992, C, 89m, R)
Cat-and-mouse thriller of aspiring novelist living in deserted mansion, encountering an intruder. Dylan McDermott and Tom Sizemore star, with Sharon Stone. **MY9**

Where the Buffalo Roam
(1980, C, 96m, R)
The life and very hard times of gonzo journalist Hunter S. Thompson, portrayed by Bill Murray. Excruciatingly unfunny; highlight is Neil Young singing "Home on the Range" over opening credits. **CO2, CO13**

Where the Day Takes You
(1992, C, 92m, R)
Drama of young runaways hanging out around Hollywood Boulevard, featuring Dermot Mulroney, Lara Flynn Boyle, Balthazar Getty, Sean Astin, James LeGros, Will Smith, and Ricki Lake, with Kyle MacLachlan, Laura San Giacomo, and Christian Slater in a bit role. **DR7, DR9, DR15, MU12, ST200, XT10**

Where the Green Ants Dream
(1984, C, 100m, NR)
An Australian uranium mining company comes into conflict with a local aborigine tribe when drilling begins on sacred tribal grounds. Bruce Spence stars. Werner Herzog directed. **DT54**

Where the Heart Is (1990, C, 94m, R)
Whimsical comedy of a New York wrecking company tycoon (Dabney Coleman) and his live-in children (Uma Thurman, Suzy Amis, and David Hewlett). He gives them a condemned (but historically protected) house to live in, to start their own lives. With Joanna Cassidy, Crispin Glover, and Christopher Plummer. Directed by John Boorman. Delightful, unappreciated film. **CO2, CO5, CU5, DT15, XT9,** *Recommended*

Where the Hot Wind Blows
(1958, B&W, 120m, NR)
Drama, set in an Italian seaport, about a lusty young girl's many liaisons with the men of the village. Gina Lollobrigida, Marcello Mastroianni, Melina Mercouri, and Yves Montand star. **ST154**

Where the Lilies Bloom (1974, C, 96m, G)
Family drama of four kids living in rural Appalachia who cover up their father's death to avoid being split up by welfare authorities. Julie Gholson stars, with Jan Smithers, Matthew Burril, Helen Harmon, Harry Dean Stanton, and Rance Howard. Screenplay by Earl Hamner, Jr. Solid, unheralded film from the creator of "The Waltons". **FA7, FA15, ST205,** *Recommended*

Where the Red Fern Grows
(1974, C, 90m, NR)
Family drama set in Depression-era Oklahoma, about a farm boy's devotion to two hunting dogs. James Whitmore, Beverly Garland, and Jack Ging star. **FA5**

Where the Red Fern Grows, Part Two
(1992, C, 105m, G)
Continuation of story set in rural Oklahoma during the Depression about a teen's devo-

tion to his hound and her puppies. Doug McKeon stars, with Lisa Whelchel, Chad McQueen, and Wilford Brimley. **FA5**

Where the River Runs Black
(1986, C, 100m, PG)
Young white boy reared in the Amazon jungle swears revenge on the hunters who killed his mother. Charles Durning, Alessandro Rabelo, Marcello Rabelo, and Conchata Ferrell star. **DR9, FA7**

Where Time Began (1978, C, 86m, G)
Group of adventurers travel to the center ofthe Earth and encounter a time warp. Loosely based on Jules Verne's *Journey To The Center of the Earth*. Kenneth More stars. **SF4, WR36**

Where Were You When the Lights Went Out? (1968, C, 94m, PG)
Smirky comedy of New Yorkers' catastrophes during November 9, 1965, blackout. Doris Day stars, with Robert Morse, Terry-Thomas, Steve Allen, Lola Albright, Jim Backus, Pat Paulsen, and Earl Wilson as himself. **CO2, ST47, XT9**

Where's Picone? (1984, C, 122m, NR)
Italian comedy about a tailor living on his wits in modern-day Naples. Giancarlo Giannini stars. **FF2**

Where's Poppa? (1970, C, 82m, R)
Comedy, with cult following for its outrageous humor, about a senile woman whose son is trying to scare her to death. Ruth Gordon and George Segal star, with Trish Van Devere, Ron Liebman, and in a small role, Rob Reiner. Carl Reiner directed. Stretches the limits of bad taste; crude direction doesn't help. **CO5, CO12, CU5, CU12, DT103**

Which Way Is Up? (1977, C, 94m, R)
Richard Pryor plays three roles in this comedy about a farm worker mixed up in politics and woman troubles. Remake of Italian film *The Seduction of Mimi*. **FF8, ST180, XT27**

Which Way to the Front?
(1970, C, 96m, G)
Jerry Lewis plays a World War II draftee who's declared 4-F but enlists a bunch of similar misfits to fight the Germans. Jan Murray, John Wood, Kaye Ballard, and Sidney Miller as Adolf Hitler. Lewis directed. **CO21, HF12, ST139**

While the City Sleeps
(1956, B&W, 100m, NR)
Fritz Lang directed this suspenseful tale of policemen and reporters looking for a serial killer. Dana Andrews, Ida Lupino, and Vin-

cent Price star. **DT70, MY1, ST179,** *Recommended*

Whisky Galore (1949, B&W, 82m, NR)
Classic British comedy about the efforts of island folk to recover booze from a sunken World War II ship. Basil Radford and Joan Greenwood star. Alexander Mackendrick directed. Also known as *Tight Little Island*. **CO17**

Whispers (1990, C, 96m, R)
Thriller of woman twice attacked by same man; she kills him and he then reappears. Victoria Tennant and Jean Leclerc star, with Chris Sarandon and Peter MacNeill. Based on a novel by Dean Koontz. Produced in Canada. **MY3**

Whispers in the Dark (1992, C, 102m, R)
Thriller of psychiatrist involved with her female patient's lover, later suspected in patient's murder. Annabella Sciorra stars, with Jamey Sheridan, Anthony LaPaglia, Jill Clayburgh, Alan Alda, and Deborah Unger. Written and directed by Christopher Crowe. **MY3, MY19, ST31**

Whistle Blower, The (1987, C, 100m, PG)
Michael Caine stars in this British thriller as a former intelligence agent with an idealistic son in a sensitive government job. With Nigel Havers, Edward Fox, and John Gielgud. **MY6, MY15, ST25, ST86**

Whistle Down the Wind
(1961, B&W, 99m, NR)
Three children find a murderer hiding in their barn and think he is Christ. Hayley Mills and Alan Bates star. **FA7, HF17, ST9**

Whistle Stop (1946, B&W, 85m, NR)
Melodrama of woman caught between two no-good men, a drifter and a nightclub owner. Ava Gardner, George Raft, and Tom Conway star. **ST79**

Whistling in Brooklyn
(1943, B&W, 87m, NR)
Third in comic mystery series about radio criminologist (Red Skelton), known to his listeners as "The Fox." This time he's a suspect in a series of murders. With Ann Rutherford, Jean Rogers, "Rags" Ragland, Ray Collins, and William Frawley. **MY17**

Whistling in the Dark
(1941, B&W, 77m, NR)
Comic mystery starring Red Skelton as "The Fox," a radio crime expert who gets involved with a fiendish cult out to murder an heiress for her money. With Ann Rutherford, Conrad Veidt, "Rags" Ragland, Virginia Grey, and Eve Arden. Followed by two sequels. **MY17**

White Buffalo, The (1977, C, 97m, PG)
Charles Bronson plays Wild Bill Hickok in this drama about the gunslinger's premonitions of death. With Jack Warden, Will Sampson, Kim Novak, Slim Pickens, and John Carradine. Based on a novel by Richard Sale. **HF11, ST20, WE2**

White Christmas (1954, C, 120m, NR)
Two army buddies team up and become famous as a song and dance act. With the assistance of two singing sisters, they help out their old army commander, whose hotel is in financial trouble. Bing Crosby, Danny Kaye, Vera-Ellen, and Rosemary Clooney star. **MU4, MU6, ST40, ST120**

White Cliffs of Dover, The
(1944, B&W, 126m, NR)
Love story of American woman who marries Briton while visiting abroad, only to lose him in World War I, then watch her son grow up to serve in World War II. Irene Dunne stars, with Alan Marshal, Van Johnson, Frank Morgan, C. Aubrey Smith, Dame May Whitty, Roddy McDowall, and Elizabeth Taylor in a bit part. **CL4, ST62, ST212**

White Dawn, The (1974, C, 109m, PG)
Three whalers stranded in the Arctic take advantage of the Eskimos who rescue them. Warren Oates, Timothy Bottoms, and Louis Gossett, Jr., star. Directed by Philip Kaufman. Worth a look for genre fans. **AC12, AC24, DR27, DT64, ST166**

White Fang (1991, C, 107m, PG)
Disney version of the Jack London story, set during the Alaskan Gold Rush of 1898, about a courageous dog. Ethan Hawke stars, with Klaus Maria Brandauer. **FA1, FA5**

White Heat (1949, B&W, 114m, NR)
James Cagney plays Cody Jarrett, the gangster with a mother fixation, in this crime drama with the explosive "Top of the World" ending. With Edmond O'Brien, Virginia Mayo, Steve Cochran, and Margaret Wycherly as "Ma." Directed by Raoul Walsh. **AC22, DT131, MY1, ST24,** *Essential, Highly Recommended*

White Hunter, Black Heart
(1990, C, 112m, PG)
Clint Eastwood plays an obsessive film director on location in Africa, more interested in big-game hunting than in filming. With Jeff Fahey, George Dzundza, Alun Armstrong, and Marisa Berenson. Based on the Peter Viertel novel, in turn based on John Huston's exploits during the filming of *The African Queen.* Eastwood directed. Interesting for the most part, thanks to good script by Viertel,

James Bridges, and Burt Kennedy. Eastwood takes a different approach as an actor, and it mostly works. **DR13, ST64,** *Recommended*

White Lightning (1973, C, 101m, PG)
Moonshiner Burt Reynolds gets revenge on the lawman who killed his brother. **AC19, ST183**

White Mama (1980, C, 105m, NR)
A poor widow (Bette Davis) and a streetwise black kid (Ernest Harden) form an alliance for their mutual survival. Originally made for TV. **DR11, ST44**

White Men Can't Jump (1992, C, 114m, R)
Engaging comedy of two hustlers, played by Woody Harrelson and Wesley Snipes, working scams on the outdoor basketball courts of Los Angeles. With Rosie Perez and Tyra Ferrell. Written and directed with great gusto by Ron Shelton. Does almost as much for street ball as Shelton did for minor league hardball in *Bull Durham*—can a football movie be next? **CO2, CO3, CO19, ST201, XT10,** *Recommended*

White Mischief (1988, C, 100m, R)
British colony in 1940s Africa is rocked by scandal: the public affair between the young wife of a diplomat and an army officer, and the officer's mysterious murder. Based on real events, this drama stars Greta Scacchi and Charles Dance as the lovers, with Sarah Miles, Joss Ackland, and John Hurt. Has some fine moments, just not enough of them. **DR5, DR23**

White Nights (1957, B&W, 94m, NR)
Luchino Visconti directed this story of a love affair, based on a Dostoevsky tale. Maria Schell and Jean Marais star, with Marcello Mastroianni. **DT127, ST154**

White Nights (1985, C, 135m, PG-13)
Airplane carrying an expatriate Soviet dancer crashes in Siberia, and the Russians hold the man in detention, using a black American defector as his guardian. Mikhail Baryshnikov and Gregory Hines are the dancers (and they do dance!). With Jerzy Skolimowski, Isabella Rossellini, Helen Mirren, and Geraldine Page. Directed by Taylor Hackford. If the story were up to the level of the hoofing . . . **DR21**

White of the Eye (1988, C, 113m, R)
Thriller set in Arizona, where a woman suspects her loving husband of being a vicious serial killer. Stylish drama, starring Cathy Moriarty and David Keith, directed by Donald Cammell. **MY13, MY14,** *Recommended*

White Palace (1990, C, 103m, R)
Love story of twenty-seven-year-old Jewish man (James Spader) and forty-three-year-old waitress (Susan Sarandon) defying family and friends. With Jason Alexander, Kathy Bates, Eileen Brennan, and Steven Hill. Directed by Luis Mandoki; based on Glen Savan's novel. **DR1, ST194, ST203**

White Rose, The (1923, B&W, 120m, NR)
Silent drama from director D.W. Griffith about an aspiring minister who seduces and abandons a young woman. Although he later becomes engaged, he admits to his indiscretion when he meets the woman and their child. Mae Marsh, Carol Dempster, and Ivor Novello star. **DT52**

White Rose, The (1983, C, 108m, NR)
German drama about a small group of youths who defy Hitler. Lena Stolze and Martin Benrath star. Directed by Michael Verhoeven. **FF3**

White Sands (1992, C, 101m, R)
Tangled thriller set in New Mexico about small-town lawman taking on identity of murdered man found with briefcase full of money, getting involved with rogue FBI agents, narcotics and drug dealers. Willem Dafoe stars, with Mary Elizabeth Mastrantonio, Mickey Rourke, Samuel L. Jackson, M. Emmet Walsh, and Mimi Rogers. Directed by Roger Donaldson. Never as clever as it aspires to be. Dafoe is less interesting in more or less straight role. **MY2, MY9, ST190**

White Sheik, The (1951, B&W, 88m, NR)
Italian comedy about a couple on their honeymoon in Rome and the wife's adventures with a cartoon hero called The White Sheik. Alberto Sordi, Brunella Bava, and Leopoldo Trieste star, with Giulietta Masina. Federico Fellini directed. **DT43, XT17, XT30**

White Sister, The (1923, B&W, 108m, NR)
Silent melodrama of woman who takes to a convent, thinking her lover dead, only to see him turn up alive. Lillian Gish and Ronald Colman star. **ST35, ST87**

White Wilderness (1958, C, 73m, G)
This Disney documentary, part of the True-Life Adventure series, goes to the Arctic to examine the animal and plant life there. **FA1**

White Zombie (1932, B&W, 73m, NR)
The owner of a sugar mill in Haiti cuts down on labor costs by creating an army of zombies. Bela Lugosi stars. **HO1, HO6, ST143**

Who Am I This Time? (1982, C, 60m, NR)
Charming comedy about a troupe of amateur actors in a small town and their bold, talented star—who's a painfully shy nerd offstage. Christopher Walken and Susan Sarandon star. Directed by Jonathan Demme. Originally made for public TV. Stars at top of their form. **CO1, DT35, ST194, ST222,** *Highly Recommended*

Who Done It? (1942, B&W, 75m, NR)
Abbott and Costello comedy has the boys pretending to be detectives when they're really a couple of radio scriptwriters. With William Bendix and Mary Wickes. **MY17, ST1**

Who Framed Roger Rabbit
(1988, C, 103m, PG)
Mind-boggling combination of live action and animation in the story of a flesh-and-blood 1930s private eye (Bob Hoskins) investigating the murder of a movie studio executive, allegedly by one of his cartoon stars. Christopher Lloyd and Joanna Cassidy head the supporting cast, but the real stars are the cartoon characters, including many familiar faces in "cameo" appearances. Kathleen Turner supplied the voice of Jessica Rabbit. Directed by Robert Zemeckis; animation supervised by Richard Williams. **CO8, CO10, CO11, DT143, FA6, ST111, ST218,** *Highly Recommended*

Who Killed Baby Azaria
(1983, C, 96m, NR)
Australian drama based on the famous Lindy Chamberlain case, of a mother accused of murdering her baby girl. A better-known version of the same events is *A Cry in the Dark.* **FF5**

Who Slew Auntie Roo? (1971, C, 89m, R)
Shelley Winters stars in this horror version of the Hansel and Gretel tale. With Mark Lester, Chloe Franks, and Ralph Richardson. **ST184, ST232**

Who'll Stop the Rain? (1978, C, 126m, R)
American journalist in Vietnam persuades a Marine buddy to smuggle some heroin back to the States, where all hell breaks loose. Nick Nolte, Tuesday Weld, and Michael Moriarty star, with Anthony Zerbe, Richard Masur, Ray Sharkey, and Charles Haid. Based on Robert Stone's novel, *Dog Soldiers.* Directed by Karel Reisz. Powerful thriller, with underlying commentary on effects of the war. One of Nolte's best performances. Only flaw: overuse of title tune. **DR7, DR19, MY2, ST164,** *Highly Recommended*

Wholly Moses (1980, C, 109m, R)
Irreverent comedy about a nerd (Dudley Moore) who thinks God has picked him to lead the Jews to the Promised Land. With

Richard Pryor, Laraine Newman, Madeline Kahn, James Coco, Dom DeLuise, and John Houseman. **CO13, ST160, ST180**

Whoopi Goldberg: Fontaine . . . Why Am I Straight? (1989, C, 51m, NR) Comedienne Whoopi Goldberg assumes the role a street-smart junkie, just "cured" by the Betty Ford Center. **CO16, ST89**

Whoopi Goldberg Live (1986, C, 75m, NR) The stage show that launched Goldberg's film career, as she plays a wide variety of characters in a tour-de-force performance. Directed by Mike Nichols. **CO16, DT91, ST89**

Whoops Apocalypse (1981, C, 137m, NR) British satire lampoons world politics and the news media, as the events leading up to World War III are chronicled. John Barron, John Cleese, and Richard Griffiths star. **CO2, CO15, CO17**

Who's Afraid of Virginia Woolf? (1966, B&W, 129m, NR) Elizabeth Taylor and Richard Burton in their best film, an adaptation of Edward Albee's play about a battlefield of a marriage. With George Segal and Sandy Dennis costar. Adapted by Ernest Lehman; Mike Nichols directed. Taylor and Dennis won Oscars. **CL15, DR8, DR20, DT91, ST22, ST212, XT3, XT5,** *Essential, Recommended*

Who's Harry Crumb? (1989, C, 87m, PG-13) John Candy plays a private eye who resorts to highly unorthodox methods to rescue a kidnap victim. With Jeffrey Jones, Annie Potts, and Barry Corbin. **CO10, CO14**

Who's That Girl (1987, C, 94m, PG) Madonna plays a kook just released from prison for a crime she didn't commit. She involves an innocent lawyer (Griffin Dunne) in her zany schemes. **MU12**

Who's That Knocking at My Door? (1968, B&W, 90m, R) Debut feature for director Martin Scorsese, about young layabout in New York Italian neighborhood and his romance with a "nice" girl. Harvey Keitel and Zina Bethune star. Director's mother Catherine appears in film's prologue. Also known as *J.R.* Suggests themes elaborated on in later Scorsese films; terrific use of rock 'n' roll on soundtrack. **DR1, DR15, DT114, XT9,** *Recommended*

Whore (1991, C, 85m, NC-17) Theresa Russell plays a Los Angeles prostitute who's quite vocal about her life—even talk-

ing directly to the camera. With Benjamin Mouton and Antonio Fargas. Ken Russell directed; he also plays a small role. Available in three other versions: unrated, with seven minutes of additional footage; R-rated, with eighty-minute running time; and R-rated version titled *If You Can't Say It, Just See It.* If you're confused, so is your video store. **CU10, DR10, DT111**

Whose Life Is It Anyway? (1981, C, 118m, R) An artist, paralyzed from the neck down in a car accident, insists that he be allowed to end his life, against the wishes of his girl-friend and doctor. Richard Dreyfuss stars in this version of Brian Clark's play, with Christine Lahti and John Cassavetes. **DR7, DR20, ST60**

Why Didn't They Ask Evans? (1980, C, 180m, NR) Agatha Christie mystery featuring amateur sleuthing team of Lady Derwent and Bobby Jones, as they try to solve riddle posed by dying explorer's inquiry. Francesca Annis and James Warwick star, and Eric Porter and John Gielgud. Originally produced for British TV. **MY11, MY15, ST86, WR3**

Why Shoot the Teacher? (1977, C, 101m, PG) Canadian drama, set during the Depression, about a young schoolteacher's experiences in a small town. Bud Cort and Samantha Eggar star. **DR25, DR26**

Wichita (1955, C, 81m, NR) Joel McCrea plays Wyatt Earp, as he tries to clean up the proverbial dirty Western town. With Vera Miles, Lloyd Bridges, and Peter Graves. Directed by Jacques Tourneur. **DT124, HF9, ST123**

Wicked Lady, The (1945, B&W, 104m, NR) British adventure tale of female outlaw (Margaret Lockwood) and her exploits with a handsome accomplice (James Mason). Remake released in 1983. **ST153**

Wicked Lady, The (1983, C, 98m, R) Campy version of the old highwaywoman tale, starring Faye Dunaway as the robber. With Alan Bates and John Gielgud. **CU2, ST9, ST61, ST86**

Wicked Stepmother (1989, C, 92m, PG-13) Bette Davis's last film, in which she plays a witch who shrinks people. With Barbara Carrera, Colleen Camp, and Lionel Stander. Davis and writer-director Larry Cohen had a falling-out during shooting, and she left the production; her character disappears about halfway through the story. **DT28, ST44**

Wicker Man, The (1973, C, 95m, R)
While investigating the disappearance of a
child, a policeman travels to a remote Scottish island and discovers pagan cultists.
Edward Woodward, Christopher Lee, and
Britt Ekland star in this thriller with its own
cult following. **CU4, HO11, ST135**

Wife vs. Secretary (1936, B&W, 88m, NR)
Drama described in title, with Clark Gable
caught between Myrna Loy and Jean Harlow.
With May Robson and James Stewart.
Directed by Clarence Brown. **ST77, ST98,
ST142, ST207**

Wifemistress (1977, C, 110m, R)
A young woman's husband disappears and
she discovers evidence that he has been less
than faithful to her. Laura Antonelli and
Marcello Mastroianni star in this Italian comedy. **FF2, ST154**

Wilby Conspiracy, The (1975, C, 101m, R)
Chase thriller set in Africa, where a black
political activist (Sidney Poitier) is on the lam
with a reluctant white journalist (Michael
Caine). With Nicol Williamson. **DR21,
ST25, ST174**

Wild Angels, The (1966, C, 93m, NR)
Director Roger Corman's low-budget biker
classic, about the baddest set of dudes ever.
Peter Fonda stars, with Nancy Sinatra, Bruce
Dern, Michael J. Pollard, Diane Ladd, and
Gayle Hunnicutt. **AC10, DT30**

Wild at Heart (1990, C, 127m, R)
Outrageous road movie of Sailor (Nicolas
Cage), an ex-con, and Lula (Laura Dern), the
girl of his dreams, fleeing her witchy mother
(Diane Ladd, Dern's real-life mom). With
Willem Dafoe as a villain with bad overbite,
Harry Dean Stanton, Isabella Rossellini,
Crispin Glover, and in small roles, Jack
Nance, Sherilyn Fenn, and Sheryl Lee. Written and directed by David Lynch; based
loosely on Barry Gifford's novel. The two
leads are sensational. So determinedly weird
it often descends into self-parody. Thumbs
up on the Elvis motif; thumbs down on the
Wizard of Oz references. Just don't say you
weren't warned. **CU1, DT79, MY2, ST23,
ST53, ST205, XT8, XT18**

Wild Boys of the Road
(1933, B&W, 68m, NR)
Fascinating drama with documentary feel
about depression-era kids wandering America. Frankie Darro stars, with Rochelle Hudson, Dorothy Coonan, and Edwin Phillips.
Directed by William Wellman. Great timecapsule glimpse of 1930s. UNAVAILABLE ON
VIDEO. **XT29**

Wild Bunch, The (1969, C, 143m, R)
Aging band of outlaws is pursued along the
Tex-Mex border by a ragged band of bounty
hunters. Director Sam Peckinpah's masterful
and violent tale of the last days of the frontier stars William Holden and Robert Ryan,
with Warren Oates, Ben Johnson, Jaime Sanchez, Edmond O'Brien, Albert Dekker, Emilio
Fernandez, Bo Hopkins, Strother Martin, and
L.Q. Jones. Widescreen cinematography by
Lucien Ballard will be lost on video. Video
version has two key flashback scenes
restored. Arguably the greatest Western ever
made; certainly one of the most controversial. **CU7, CU20, DT95, ST106, ST166,
ST193, WE3, WE9, WE11,** *Essential, Highly
Recommended*

Wild Child, The (1969, B&W, 85m, G)
François Truffaut's moving drama, based on
true incident of Wild Boy of Aveyron, youngster in eighteenth-century France found living in the forest, brought to doctor who tries
to teach him the ways of civilization.
Truffaut plays the physician, Jean-Pierre Cargol the boy. Lovely cinematography by Nestor Almendros; evocative use of Vivaldi on
the soundtrack. My personal favorite of
Truffaut's many great films. **DT125,** *Highly
Recommended*

Wild Country, The (1971, C, 92m, G)
Disney frontier adventure of a family who
moves in the 1880s from Pittsburgh to Wyoming. Steve Forrest and Vera Miles star, with
Ronny Howard, Jack Elam, and Clint Howard. **DT58, FA1, XT8**

Wild Duck, The (1983, C, 96m, PG)
Updating of Henrik Ibsen play about a couple and their struggle to raise a blind child.
Liv Ullmann and Jeremy Irons star. Produced
in Australia. **DR20, FF5, ST116, ST220**

Wild for Kicks (1962, B&W, 92m, NR)
British teen rebels get involved with murder.
David Farrar stars, with Noelle Adam, Christopher Lee, Shirley Anne Field, and Oliver
Reed. **ST135**

Wild Geese, The (1978, C, 134m, R)
Action saga of a band of mercenaries who set
out to free a captured African leader, starring
Richard Burton, Roger Moore, and Richard
Harris, with Hardy Kruger and Stewart
Granger. **AC20, ST22**

Wild Geese II (1985, C, 125m, R)
Mercenaries are hired to break Nazi Rudolph
Hess out of Spandau Prison. Scott Glenn,
Barbara Carrera, and Laurence Olivier star.
AC20, ST168

Wild Hearts Can't Be Broken
(1991, C, 88m, G)
Disney tale, set in the 1930s, of girl who
joins circus to star in diving act atop a horse,
and is blinded in an accident. Based on a
true story. Gabrielle Anwan stars, with Michael Schoeffling and Cliff Robertson. **DR2,
FA1, FA5**

Wild in the Country (1961, C, 114m, NR)
Backwoods boy (Elvis Presley) gets in trouble
with the law; under a psychiatrist's care he is
encouraged to write. Script by Clifford Odets.
ST178

Wild in the Streets (1968, C, 97m, PG)
Satiric look at contemporary youth culture
has a rock star elected President when the
voting age is lowered to fourteen. Christopher Jones stars, with Shelley Winters, Diane
Varsi, Hal Holbrook, and Richard Pryor. **CO2,
ST180, ST232**

Wild Life, The (1984, C, 96m, R)
High school graduate gets his first apartment
and taste of freedom in this comedy about
partying hearty. Christopher Penn, Ilan
Mitchell-Smith, and Eric Stoltz star, with
Jenny Wright, Lea Thompson, Rick Moranis,
Hart Bochner, Sherilyn Fenn, and Lee Ving.
CO14

Wild One, The (1954, B&W, 79m, NR)
Biker Marlon Brando and his gang (including
Lee Marvin) roar into a small California town
and terrorize the locals. Fifties scare movie
that has since become a camp classic.
Directed by Laslo Benedek. **CU2, DR26,
ST18, ST151,** *Essential*

Wild Orchid (1990, C, 117m, NR)
Steamy story of the sexual awakening of a
lovely young lawyer. Mickey Rourke and
Carre Otis star, with Jacqueline Bisset. Also
available in tamer, R-rated version with 111m.
running time. **CU6, CU10, DR3, ST190**

Wild Orchid II: Two Shades of Blue
(1992, C, 107m, R)
Writer-director Zalman King offers this name-
only sequel to his Mickey Rourke-Carre Otis
skinfest. Nina Siemaszko and Brent Fraser are
the young lovers this time around; she's a
young thing forced into prostitution after
her father's death, he's a boy she once met
and still thinks about. With Wendy Hughes,
Tom Skerritt, and Joe Dallesandro. Also available in an unrated version with additional
footage, I presume, not of Ms. Hughes and
Mr. Skerritt. **CU6, CU10**

Wild Orchids (1929, B&W, 102m, NR)
A married woman falls in love with another
man while on a holiday. Greta Garbo, Lewis

Stone, and Nils Asther star in this silent soap
opera. **ST78**

Wild Party, The (1929, B&W, 76m, NR)
Jazz Age drama of the relationship between a
professor (Fredric March) and a perky student
(Clara Bow). Directed by Dorothy Arzner.
ST148

Wild Party, The (1975, C, 95m, R)
Hollywood drama about fading film star trying to revive his career with major-league
wing-ding. James Coco and Raquel Welch
star. James Ivory directed. **DR13, DT61**

Wild Ride, The (1960, B&W, 63m, NR)
Early Jack Nicholson film has him playing an
amoral hotrodder not above murder or stealing his best buddy's girl. **ST163**

Wild Rovers (1971, C, 138m, PG)
William Holden and Ryan O'Neal star as saddle pals in this cult Western drama from
director Blake Edwards. With Karl Malden,
Lynn Carlin, Tom Skerritt, Joe Don Baker,
Rachel Roberts, and Moses Gunn. The video
version contains 29 minutes of footage not
included in the theatrical release. **CU10,
DT40, ST106, WE15**

Wild Side, The see *Suburbia*

Wild Strawberries (1957, B&W, 90m, NR)
An elderly professor (Victor Sjöström), on his
way to receive an honorary degree, recalls his
past, especially his disappointments. One of
director Ingmar Bergman's great achievements. **DT11,** *Essential, Recommended*

Wild Style (1982, C, 82m, R)
A rappin' musical about a graffiti artist in
New York City. Lee Quinones stars. **MU9**

Wild Times (1980, C, 200m, NR)
Saga of dime-novel hero turned Western
showman, starring Sam Elliott, with Ben
Johnson, Bruce Boxleitner, Dennis Hopper,
Cameron Mitchell, and Harry Carey, Jr. Based
on a novel by Brian Garfield. Originally
made for TV. **ST110, WE11**

Wildcats (1986, C, 107m, R)
Divorced mother badly in need of a job
agrees to coach an inner-city high school
football team. Goldie Hawn stars in this
comedy, with James Keach, Swoosie Kurtz,
and Nipsey Russell. **CO19, ST99**

Wilderness Family Part 2, The
(1978, C, 105m, G)
The family who left the city behind in *The
Adventures of the Wilderness Family* continue
their lives in this sequel. Robert Logan stars.
FA4

Wildflower (1991, C, 94m, NR)
Drama set in 1930s of rural teen-agers
befriending an epileptic girl whose unthink-
ing father has confined her to a cage. Beau
Bridges, Susan Blakely, William McNamara,
Patricia Arquette, and Reese Witherspoon
star. Directed by Diane Keaton. Originally
made for TV. **DR9, FA15, ST121**

Will Penny (1968, C, 108m, NR)
Western with deserved cult following features
Charlton Heston as an aging saddlehand
befriending a settler (Joan Hackett) and her
young son. With Donald Pleasence, Lee
Majors, Bruce Dern, Ben Johnson, Anthony
Zerbe, and G.D. Spradlin. Directed by Tom
Gries. **WE15,** *Recommended*

Willard (1971, C, 95m, PG)
Disturbed young man (Bruce Davison) trains
his pet rats to attack all his enemies. With
Sondra Locke and Ernest Borgnine. **HO16**

Willie and Phil (1980, C, 115m, R)
American remake of François Truffaut's mas-
terful *Jules and Jim,* about romantic triangle
involving two good friends and an impet-
uous young woman. Michael Ontkean, Ray
Sharkey, and Margot Kidder star. Directed by
Paul Mazursky. Disappointingly flat. **DR1,
DT87, FF8**

**Willie Wonka and the Chocolate Fac-
tory** (1971, C, 100m, G)
Musical adaptation of Roald Dahl's story,
Charlie and the Chocolate Factory. Charlie wins
a trip to a chocolate factory owned by a mysterious man. Gene Wilder stars. **FA8, FA9**

Willow (1988, C, 126m, PG)
Lavish fantasy adventure revolving around
the efforts of a brave dwarf (Warwick Davis)
to protect an infant from the clutches of an
evil witch. Val Kilmer, Joanne Whalley, and
Jean Marsh costar. Produced by George
Lucas; directed by Ron Howard. Entertaining
only in fits and starts. **AC18, DT58, FA8,
SF13**

Wilma (1977, C, 100m, NR)
True story of Wilma Rudolph, childhood
polio victim who went on to become an
Olympic track medalist. Shirley Jo Finney
stars, with Cicely Tyson and Denzel Washington. Originally made for TV. **DR4, DR22,
ST223**

Wilson (1944, C, 154m, NR)
Large-scale bio of U.S. president who led the
nation through World War I and attempted
to forge a postwar new world order. Alexander Knox stars, with Charles Coburn, Geraldine Fitzgerald, Thomas Mitchell, Cedric

Hardwicke, and Vincent Price. **CL2, DR21,
ST179**

Win, Place or Steal (1975, C, 75m, PG)
Russ Tamblyn and Alex Karras star in this
comedy as a pair of bumblers trying to pull
of a caper at a racetrack. With Dean Stockwell and McLean Stevenson. Also known as
The Big Payoff. **CO10, ST208**

Winchester '73 (1950, B&W, 92m, NR)
James Stewart stars in this classic Western
drama of a man in search of his stolen gun.
Anthony Mann directed. With Rock Hudson,
Shelley Winters, and Will Geer as Wyatt
Earp. **DT85, HF9, ST112, ST207, ST232,**
Essential, Recommended

Wind, The (1928, B&W, 82m, NR)
Lillian Gish gives one of her finest performances in this silent drama of a young innocent and her hard life on the prairie. Excellent direction by Victor Sjöström. Video version features a new musical score by Carl
Davis. **CL5, CL12, ST87,** *Essential,
Recommended*

Wind (1992, C, 125m, PG-13)
Drama centered around sailing's big event,
the America's Cup race. Matthew Modine
and Jennifer Gray star, with Rebecca Miller
and Cliff Robertson. Directed by Carroll Ballard. **AC12, DR22**

Wind and the Lion, The
(1975, C, 119m, PG)
An American diplomat's wife (Candice
Bergen) and her son are kidnapped by a
Moroccan bandit (Sean Connery), and a
romance develops. Based on true events.
With Brian Keith (as Theodore Roosevelt)
and John Huston. Directed by John Milius.
Connery's good, if you can forgive a Moroc-
can with a Scotch accent, and Keith's a bully
Teddy, but Bergen's weak. **AC12, AC14,
AC16, DT60, ST36**

Wind in the Willows, The
(1982, C, 47m, G)
Kenneth Grahame's story about the tale of
four gentlemen friends, Mr. Badger, Mr.
Mole, Mr. Ratty, and Mr. Toad. Originally
part of the 1950 Disney animated feature,
Adventures of Ichabod and Mr. Toad. **FA2**

Window, The (1949, B&W, 73m, NR)
Thriller focusing on a young boy (Bobby
Driscoll) who witnesses a murder in his New
York tenement but can't get anyone to
believe his story. With Barbara Hale, Arthur
Kennedy, Paul Stewart, and Ruth Roman.
Based on a story by Cornell Woolrich. **MY1,
WR39**

Winds of War, The (1983, C, 840m, NR)
Epic TV miniseries based on Herman Wouk novel about days leading up to World War II. Robert Mitchum stars, with Ali MacGraw, Jan-Michael Vincent, Victoria Tenant, and John Houseman. Sequel: *War and Remembrance*. **DR5, DR19, ST158**

Windwalker (1980, C, 108m, PG)
An Indian patriarch returns to his tribe to prevent an act of revenge by his long-lost brother. Trevor Howard stars in this offbeat Western. **WE7**

Windy City (1984, C, 103m, R)
A reunion of old neighborhood chums in Chicago dramatizes their successes and failures as adults. John Shea, Kate Capshaw, and Josh Mostel star. **DR7, XT11**

Wing and A Prayer (1944, B&W, 97m, NR)
Drama set on aircraft carrier during World War II. Don Ameche and Dana Andrews star, with William Eythe, Richard Jaeckel, and Charles Bickford. **AC1**

Wings (1927, B&W, 139m, NR)
When the U.S. enters World War I, two friends in love with the same girl enlist in the Army Air Corps. This silent classic won the first Academy Award for Best Picture. Clara Bow, Buddy Rogers, and Richard Arlen star, with Gary Cooper. Directed by William Wellman. **AC2, AC11, CL12, DT135, ST37, XT1**, *Essential*

Wings of Desire (1988, B&W/C, 130m, NR)
From German director Wim Wenders, a captivating fantasy-drama focusing on the adventures of a pair of angels in contemporary Berlin. Bruno Ganz stars, with Otto Sander, Solveig Dommartin, and Peter Falk. Wenders and Peter Handke wrote the screenplay, inspired in part by poetry of Rainer Maria Rilke. Even better on repeated viewings. **DT136, XT24**, *Recommended*

Wings of Eagles, The (1957, C, 110m, NR)
John Wayne stars as Frank "Spig" Wead, real-life aviator turned screenwriter. With Maureen O'Hara, Dan Dailey, and Ward Bond. Directed by John Ford. **AC11, CL7, DT44, ST167, ST224**

Wings of the Morning (1937, C, 89m, NR)
Henry Fonda falls in love with a Gypsy while training a racehorse. With Annabella, John McCormack, and Leslie Banks. The first British film shot in Technicolor. **ST71**

Winning (1969, C, 123m, PG)
Paul Newman plays a race car driver who's driven to become the best in this drama co-starring Joanne Woodward and Robert Wagner. Pedestrian. **DR22, ST162, ST234**

Winning of the West
(1953, B&W, 57m, NR)
Gene Autry and Smiley Burnette ride together to help a crusading newspaper publisher in the Old West. **ST5**

Winning Team, The
(1952, B&W, 98m, NR)
Ronald Reagan plays baseball pitcher Grover Cleveland Alexander, who overcame problems with the bottle to pitch his way into the Hall of Fame. With Doris Day, Frank Lovejoy, Eve Miller, Russ Tamblyn, and real-life ballplayers Bob Lemon, Gene Mauch, Hank Sauer, and others. **DR22, ST47**

Winter Kills (1979, C, 97m, R)
Wild political thriller about the brother of a slain President searching for the killers and uncovering a massive conspiracy. Jeff Bridges stars, with John Huston, Toshiro Mifune, Anthony Perkins, Belinda Bauer, Richard Boone, Sterling Hayden, Eli Wallach, and in a brief role, Elizabeth Taylor. Based on Richard Condon's novel; directed by William Richert. Once-outrageous plot seems less so since release of *JFK*. **CU9, CU17, DR19, DR21, DT60, MY6, MY14, ST19, ST157, ST212**

Winter Light (1962, B&W, 80m, NR)
Priest in a Swedish village wrestles with problems of faith in this Ingmar Bergman drama. Ingrid Thulin and Gunnar Björnstrand star. **DT11**

Winter Meeting (1948, B&W, 104m, NR)
Bette Davis vehicle has her playing a writer in love with a war hero. With James (Jim) Davis, Janis Paige, and John Hoyt. **ST44**

Winter of Our Dreams, The
(1981, C, 90m, R)
Married bookstore owner becomes involved with an embittered prostitute. Australian drama starring Bryan Brown and Judy Davis. **FF5, ST46**

Winter People (1989, C, 110m, PG-13)
In the 1934 North Carolina backwoods, romance blossoms between an unwed mother (Kelly McGillis) and a visiting widower (Kurt Russell). With Lloyd Bridges. **DR1, ST191**

Winter Rates see *Out of Season*

Wired (1989, C, 112m, R)
Stylized bio of comic John Belushi, starring Michael Chiklis, with Ray Sharkey, J.T. Walsh as Bob Woodward, and Patti D'Arbanville as Cathy Smith. **DR4, DR12**

Wisdom (1986, C, 109m, R)
Emilio Estevez wrote, directed, and stars in this drama of a young man and his girlfriend

who take to robbing banks and redistributing the money to needy farmers. With Demi Moore. **DR16**

Wise Blood (1979, C, 108m, PG)
Bizarre, fascinating drama, populated by various Southern grotesques, including a young man claiming to be a preacher for The Church Without Christ. Brad Dourif stars, with Daniel Shor, Amy Wright, Harry Dean Stanton, and Ned Beatty. John Huston directed. Based on Flannery O'Connor's novel. O'Connor fans may never see a better realization of her work; others may find it just weird. **DR19, DT60, ST205,** *Recommended*

Wise Guys (1986, C, 92m, R)
A pair of bumbling hit men are assigned to knock each other off in this comedy starring Joe Piscopo and Danny DeVito. Brian De Palma directed. **CO3, CO10, CO13, DT36, ST54**

Wisecracks (1991, C, 90m, NR)
Astute documentary on women who practice stand-up comedy for a living, including generous clips and incisive interviews. Features Phyllis Diller, Whoopi Goldberg, Jenny Jones, and Paula Poundstone. Directed by Gail Singer. **CU16, ST89,** *Recommended*

Wish You Were Here (1987, C, 92m, R)
British comedy-drama about a teen-ager (Emily Lloyd) growing up in a stuffy small town in the 1950s, defying the locals with her sexy behavior. With Tom Bell, Clare Clifford, and Barbara Durkin. Written and directed by David Leland. Character grew up to be central figure in film *Personal Services*, which Leland wrote. Lloyd is very good; story meanders. **CO17**

Wistful Widow of Wagon Gap, The
(1947, B&W, 78m, NR)
Abbott and Costello Western comedy has Lou caring for ornery widow (Marjorie Main) and her seven kids after he accidentally kills her husband. **ST1, WE14**

Witchcraft Through the Ages
(1921, B&W, 120m, NR)
Notorious silent film, made in Sweden, banned in several countries for its explicit scenes purporting to explore the dark side of human nature. Available in several versions; above running time is for the full-length version. Also known as *Häxan*. **CU8, FF7**

Witches, The (1990, C, 92m, PG)
Little boy at resort hotel stumbles onto a meeting of witches, and when he is transformed into a mouse, he and his grandmother plot revenge. Jasen Fisher, Mai

Zetterling, and Anjelica Huston star. Directed by Nicolas Roeg, who's more restrained than usual. Charming story; Huston is very good. **DT106, FA8, ST115,** *Recommended*

Witches' Brew (1980, C, 99m, PG)
Horror spoof, featuring Teri Garr as a professor's wife who uses witchcraft to help her hubby's career. With Lana Turner and Richard Benjamin. **HO24, ST219**

Witches of Eastwick, The
(1987, C, 118m, R)
New England village becomes a battleground when three contemporary witches collide with a mysterious newcomer. Jack Nicholson, Cher, Michelle Pfeiffer, and Susan Sarandon star. George Miller directed this adaptation of John Updike's novel. Nicholson's bravura turn shifts story emphasis and elaborate special effects finally overwhelm all. **DR10, DR19, DR26, ST29, ST163, ST173, ST194**

Witching, The see *Necromancy*

Witchtrap (1989, C, 90m, R)
Paranormal experts are called in to exorcise the spirit of a man whose house has been inherited by his nephew. James W. Quinn and Kathleen Bailey star. **HO3**

With Six You Get Eggroll
(1968, C, 95m, G)
Comedy of widow and widower marrying, combining large broods of children. Doris Day and Brian Keith star, with Barbara Hershey, George Carlin, and Pat Carroll. **CO4, ST47, ST104**

Withnail & I (1987, C, 110m, R)
Two unemployed actors in 1969 London decide to take a holiday in the country, with nearly disastrous results. Dark comedy starring Richard E. Grant, Paul McGann, and Richard Griffiths. Written and directed by Bruce Robinson. **CO17**

Without a Clue (1988, C, 107m, PG)
Sherlock Holmes played for laughs, with the famed detective (Michael Caine) a bungler and Dr. Watson (Ben Kingsley) the real brains of the operation. **HF14, MY17, ST25**

Without a Trace (1983, C, 120m, PG)
True story of a woman whose young son disappears in New York City and her frantic efforts to find him. Kate Nelligan and Judd Hirsch star. **MY8, MY14, XT9**

Without Love (1945, B&W, 111m, NR)
Spencer Tracy and Katharine Hepburn drama of an inventor and widow who discover romance only after they marry. With Lucille Ball and Keenan Wynn. **CL4, CL15, ST103, ST217**

Without Reservations
(1946, B&W, 107m, NR)
The author of a successful novel discovers the perfect man to play her hero in the movies. Claudette Colbert and John Wayne star in this romantic comedy, with cameos by several stars, including Cary Grant. **ST34, ST92, ST224**

Without You I'm Nothing
(1990, C, 94m, R)
Sandra Bernhard presents her unusual concept of comedy, a virtually one-woman show that lampoons show business celebrities and questions assumptions about contemporary life, particularly sexual mores. **CO16**

Witness (1985, C, 112m, R)
Drama of Amish boy witnessing murder on a visit to Philadelphia and the cop who befriends him and his mother. Harrison Ford, Kelly McGillis, and Lukas Haas star, with Danny Glover and Alexander Godunov. Peter Weir directed. Suspense just doesn't build, and romance falls flat. **DR16, DR27, DT133, ST74, ST88**

Witness for the Prosecution
(1957, B&W, 114m, NR)
Agatha Christie courtroom drama, with Charles Laughton defending Tyrone Power on murder charge. Marlene Dietrich costars as Power's wife; with Elsa Lanchester and John Williams. Directed by Billy Wilder. Superbly played and directed. Lanchester's nominated performance should have won the Oscar. **DR17, DT139, ST55, ST132, ST177, WR3, XT28,** *Recommended*

Wives Under Suspicion
(1938, B&W, 69m, NR)
District attorney decides to investigate his own wife, whom he suspects is cheating on him. Warren William and Gail Patrick star. Directed by James Whale; a remake of his earlier film, *The Kiss Before the Mirror.* **DT138**

Wiz, The (1978, C, 133m, G)
Update of *The Wizard of Oz,* based on the Broadway musical hit. Diana Ross stars, with Richard Pryor, Michael Jackson, Nipsey Russell, Ted Ross, Mabel King, and Lena Horne. Directed by Sidney Lumet. Only occasionally graceful; Ross is badly miscast. **DT78, FA9, MU2, MU8, MU13, ST180**

Wizard, The (1989, C, 100m, PG)
Family drama of young video-game whiz traveling across country with his brother to compete in a big tournament. Fred Savage and Luke Edwards star, with Beau Bridges and Christian Slater. **FA7, FA15, ST200, XT18**

Wizard of Loneliness, The
(1988, C, 110m, PG-13)
During World War II, a young boy is sent to live with his kindly but eccentric grandparents in a Vermont village. Lukas Haas stars in this drama, with Lea Thompson. Based on a novel by John Nichols. **DR9, DR19, DR26**

Wizard of Oz, The (1925, B&W, 93m, NR)
Silent version of the L. Frank Baum classic tale, starring Dorothy Dwan, with Oliver Hardy as the Tin Woodsman. **ST133**

Wizard of Oz, The
(1939, C/B&W, 101m, G)
Girl from Kansas discovers the power of friendship and love in a strange land over the rainbow. Judy Garland stars, with Ray Bolger, Bert Lahr, Jack Haley, Margaret Hamilton, and Frank Morgan. Available in a limited edition celebrating the fiftieth anniversary of the film's release, containing footage not used in the original release. **CU10, FA9, MU8, SF13, ST81,** *Essential, Highly Recommended*

Wizard of Oz, The (1982, C, 78m, NR)
Animated adaptation of Frank L. Baum's classic story about a little girl and her dog and their adventures in the land over the rainbow. **FA10**

Wizards (1977, C, 80m, PG)
Animated adventure set in a world of magic. A good wizard rules his kingdom with kindness. His evil brother sets out to conquer the rest of the planet. **SF13**

Wizards of the Lost Kingdom
(1985, C, 76m, PG)
Bo Svenson stars in this futuristic fantasy with plenty of swordplay. **AC18**

Wolf at the Door (1987, C, 90m, NR)
French-produced bio of painter Paul Gauguin, focusing on his middle years, when he returned from Tahiti to Paris to make money. Donald Sutherland stars. **DR4**

Wolf Man, The (1941, B&W, 70m, NR)
Lawrence Talbot (Lon Chaney, Jr.) is bitten by a werewolf (Bela Lugosi) and lives to carry on the curse. A horror classic. **HO1, HO4, HO17, ST27, ST143,** *Recommended*

Wolfen (1981, C, 115m, R)
New York police detective (Albert Finney) discovers a race of wolf men living in the slums of the South Bronx. With Gregory Hines, Diane Venora, and Edward James Olmos. Spooky, offbeat thriller which effectively uses real locations. Directed by Michael Wadleigh. **HO4, HO16, ST68, XT9,** *Recommended*

Woman Called Golda, A
(1982, C, 200m, NR)
The life of former Israeli prime minister,
Golda Meir. Ingrid Bergman won an Emmy
for her portrayal of this courageous leader.
With Judy Davis, Leonard Nimoy, Anne Jackson, and Ned Beatty. Originally made for TV.
DR4, ST13, ST46

Woman in Flames, A (1982, C, 106m, R)
A housewife deserts her husband and falls
into a life of prostitution in this contemporary German drama. Gudrun Landgrebe stars.
Robert Van Ackeren directed. **FF3**

Woman in Green, The
(1945, B&W, 68m, NR)
Sherlock Holmes and Dr. Watson battle the
nefarious Professor Moriarty in this tale of a
murderer whose trademark is leaving corpses
with one thumb missing. Basil Rathbone and
Nigel Bruce star. **HF14**

Woman in Red, The (1984, C, 87m, PG-13)
Romantic comedy starring Gene Wilder as
happily married man with hang-up on lovely
woman he glimpsed one day in a parking
garage. Kelly LeBrock costars, with Gilda
Radner, Charles Grodin, and Judith Ivey. Wilder directed. Remake of French film, *Pardon
Mon Affaire*. Forced and mostly just not funny.
LeBrock is nice too look at, not so nice to listen to. **CO1, CO13, FF8, ST94, XT23**

Woman in the Dark see *Woman in the
Shadows*

Woman in the Dunes
(1964, B&W, 123m, NR)
Japanese scientist becomes trapped in a sandpit with a strange woman who lives there. Offbeat drama, with cult following, directed by
Hiroshi Teshigahara. Should have won Best
Foreign Language Film Oscar. **FF4, XT28**

Woman in the Moon, The
(1929, B&W, 146m, NR)
Fritz Lang directed this silent science fiction
tale about the first expedition to the moon.
DT70

Woman in the Shadows
(1934, B&W, 70m, NR)
Melodrama of ex-con trying to find peace in
woodsy cabin, meeting up with wayward
woman and her brutal lover. Ralph Bellamy,
Fay Wray, and Melvyn Douglas star. Based on
a story by Dashiell Hammett. Originally
titled *Woman in the Dark*. **ST58, WR12**

Woman Is A Woman, A
(1960, C, 83m, NR)
From director Jean-Luc Godard, a drama of a
stripper who wants to have a baby by her

bookseller boyfriend, although his best friend
seems more interested in accommodating her
wishes. Jean-Paul Belmondo, Jean-Claude
Brialy, Anna Karina, and Jeanne Moreau star.
DT50, ST11, ST161

Woman Next Door, The
(1981, C, 106m, NR)
Married man's new neighbor, also married, is
his ex-lover, and they resume their relationship. French drama from François Truffaut,
starring Gérard Depardieu and Fanny Ardant.
DT125, ST52

Woman of Affairs, A
(1928, B&W, 96m, NR)
Early Greta Garbo talkie has her playing a
socialite covering up her husband's thievery.
With John Gilbert, Lewis Stone, John Mack
Brown, and Douglas Fairbanks, Jr. Based on
Michael Arlen's novel *The Green Hat*. Directed
by Clarence Brown. **DR19, ST78**

Woman of Distinction, A
(1950, B&W, 85m, NR)
Campus comedy of visiting professor (Ray
Milland) getting strait-laced dean (Rosalind
Russell) involved in a scandal. **CO18, ST192**

Woman of Paris, A (1923, B&W, 81m, NR)
This silent drama is about a woman pledged
to marry who becomes a wealthy man's mistress through a series of misunderstandings.
Edna Purviance, Adolphe Menjou, and Carl
Miller star. A rare dramatic outing for director Charlie Chaplin, who has only a bit part
as a railway porter. **CL12, DT24**

Woman of Substance, A
(1984, C, 300m, NR)
TV miniseries about the rise of an impoverished girl (Jenny Seagrove) to become a
respectable businesswoman (Deborah Kerr).
With Barry Bostwick and Barry Morse. **DR10,
ST125**

Woman of the Year
(1942, B&W, 112m, NR)
First pairing of Katharine Hepburn and
Spencer Tracy has her playing a political
commentator, him a sportswriter. Written by
Ring Lardner, Jr., and Michael Kanin (Oscar
winners); directed by George Stevens. Sheer
joy. **CL10, CL15, DT119, ST103, ST217,**
Essential, Highly Recommended

Woman Rebels, A (1936, B&W, 88m, NR)
Katharine Hepburn stars as a crusader for
woman's rights in Victorian England. **CL5,
ST103**

Woman Times Seven (1967, C, 99m, NR)
Shirley MacLaine plays seven roles in this
series of comic sketches costarring Peter Sel-

lers, Rossano Brazzi, Michael Caine, Alan Arkin, and Vittorio Gassman. Directed by Vittorio De Sica. **DT37, ST25, ST145, ST198, XT27**

Woman Under the Influence, A
(1974, C, 155m, NR)
Intense drama from director John Cassavetes about a wife suffering mental collapse and her blue-collar husband and their family's inability to help her. Gena Rowlands and Peter Falk star, with Katherine Cassavetes (the director's mother) and Lady Rowlands (the star's mother). Harrowing stuff, with Rowlands giving the performance of her career. **DR8, DR10, XT8, XT23, XT30,** *Recommended*

Woman Without Love, A
(1951, C, 91m, NR)
Director Luis Buñuel's drama of infidelity, adapted from a Guy de Maupassant story. **DT19**

Woman's Face, A (1938, B&W, 100m, NR)
Ingrid Bergman stars in this Swedish drama of a woman whose life is transformed after she undergoes plastic surgery. **FF7, ST13**

Woman's Face, A (1941, B&W, 105m, NR)
Woman with a disfigured face has plastic surgery which transforms her life. Joan Crawford and Melvyn Douglas star. Directed by George Cukor. **CL5, DT32, ST39, ST58**

Woman's Secret, A (1949, B&W, 85m, NR)
Drama of two women and their relationship, one a singer, the other her mentor. Maureen O'Hara and Gloria Grahame star, with Melvyn Douglas. **CL7, DT101, ST58, ST167**

Woman's Tale, A (1991, C, 93m, PG-13)
Australian drama of seventy-eight-year-old woman with cancer trying to die with dignity. Notable for lead performance by Sheila Florance, who was really ill during filming and died after the film was completed. With Gosia Dobrowolska and Norman Kaye. Directed by Paul Cox. **DR11, FF5**

Women, The (1939, B&W, 132m, NR)
Witty comedy about a group of female friends and their love lives, adapted from the Clare Boothe play. Rosalind Russell, Joan Crawford, Norma Shearer, Paulette Goddard, and Joan Fontaine head the all-female cast. George Cukor directed. Regarded in some circles as campy fun—but it's certainly possible to take it straight, too. **CL5, CU2, DT32, ST39, ST73, ST192,** *Highly Recommended*

Women, The (1969, C, 86m, NR)
Brigitte Bardot plays a secretary who seduces a disenchanted writer (Maurice Ronet). **ST6**

Women & Men: Stories of Seduction
(1990, C, 90m, NR)
Trio of stories: Mary McCarthy's *The Man in the Brooks Brothers Suit*, Dorothy Parker's *Dusk Before Fireworks*, and Ernest Hemingway's *Hills Like White Elephants*. The stars include Beau Bridges, Elizabeth McGovern, Molly Ringwald, Peter Weller, James Woods, and Melanie Griffith. The directors: Frederic Raphael, Ken Russell, and Tony Richardson. **DR1, DR19, DT111, ST93, ST233, WR13**

Women & Men: Stores of Seduction, Part 2 (1991, C, 90m, NR)
Trio of stories; *Return to Kansas City,* Irwin Shaw's tale of New York boxer (Matt Dillon) and his wife (Kyra Sedgwick), who yearns for her home in the Midwest; Carson McCullers's *A Domestic Dilemma*, about a young alcoholic wife (Andie MacDowell) and her forgiving husband (Ray Liotta); and Henry Miller's *Mara*, about a writer (Scott Glenn) in Paris and his relationship with a prostitute (Juliette Binoche). Originally made for cable TV. Each story moderately successful but not much more. **DR1, DR19, ST56**

Women in Love (1970, C, 129m, R)
D.H. Lawrence story of two love affairs, starring Alan Bates, Glenda Jackson (an Oscar winner), Oliver Reed, and Jennie Linden. Vigorous direction by Ken Russell. Prequel: *The Rainbow*. **DR1, DR23, DT111, ST9, ST117, WR17, XT3,** *Recommended*

Women of Valor (1986, C, 100m, NR)
World War II drama of nurses taken prisoner by Japanese, starring Susan Sarandon and Kristy McNichol. Originally made for TV. **AC7, ST194**

Women on the Verge of a Nervous Breakdown (1988, C, 88m, NR)
Spanish comedy from director Pedro Almodóvar, featuring an actress (Carmen Maura) who's trying to learn of her lover's infidelity. Zany look at how popular culture infects our lives. **DT3,** *Recommended*

Wonder Man (1945, C, 98m, NR)
Danny Kaye plays twins, one a nightclub singer and one a scholar. The singer gets killed and his ghost pushes his brother into solving the murder. With Virginia Mayo. **MU4, ST120**

Wonderful World of the Brothers Grimm, The (1962, C, 129m, NR)
The lives of the famous German storytellers, with dramatizations of many of their best-loved tales. Laurence Harvey and Karl Boehm star in this family fantasy. **FA8**

Wonderland (1989, C, 107m, R)
British drama, set in Liverpool, of relationship between two young gay men, one (Emile Charles) a mama's boy and movie fan, the other (Tony Forsyth) a hard-nosed punk. Directed by Philip Saville. **DR3, DR23**

Woodstock (1970, C, 184m, R)
Oscar-winning documentary about three days of peace, love, and music in August 1969. Among the musical highlights: The Who, Ritchie Havens, Joe Cocker, Santana, Sly and the Family Stone, and Jimi Hendrix performing "The Star-Spangled Banner." An exceptional filmmaking achievement, directed by Michael Wadleigh; Martin Scorsese was among the editors. Now available in an edition which letterboxes key musical sequences. **CU19, MU10, XT26,** *Essential, Highly Recommended*

Words and Music (1948, C, 119m, NR)
This biography of songwriters Richard Rodgers and Lorenz Hart is really a showcase for thirty-six of their best songs. Mickey Rooney and Tom Drake star, with cameo appearances from many MGM musical stars, including Judy Garland, plus Gene Kelly and Vera-Ellen in an eight-minute ballet. **MU1, MU5, ST81, ST123, ST189**

Work/Police (1915/1916. B&W, 81m, NR)
Two early Charlie Chaplin short films. In the first, he's an inept paper hanger; in the second, he's an ex-con with a penchant for trouble. **DT24**

Working Girl (1988, C, 113m, R)
With her female boss laid up by a skiing injury, a bright, ambitious Wall Street secretary takes over a major deal—and falls in love with a handsome colleague. Melanie Griffith, Harrison Ford, and Sigourney Weaver star in this contemporary romantic comedy. With Joan Cusack and Alec Baldwin. Mike Nichols directed. Enjoyable fairy tale with solid performances. **CO1, CO2, DR10, DT91, ST74, ST93, ST225, XT9,** *Recommended*

Working Girls (1987, C, 90m, NR)
Vivid, sometimes comic portrait of everyday lives of several New York prostitutes, directed by Lizzie Borden. **DR10,** *Recommended*

World According to Garp, The
(1982, C, 136m, R)
Seriocomic adventures of a college professor and his family, adapted from the John Irving bestseller. Robin Williams stars, with Mary Beth Hurt, Glenn Close, John Lithgow, Hume Cronyn, and Jessica Tandy. Directed by George Roy Hill. Mixed bag of performances; exposes some of the novel's more pretentious features. **DR8, DR19, DT55, ST33, ST228**

World Apart, A (1988, C, 112m, PG)
South Africa is the setting for this drama of a young white girl whose mother neglects her to work in the anti-apartheid movement. Barbara Hershey and Jodhi May star. Shawn Slovo's script was based on her own experiences. **DR6, DR7, DR8, ST104**

World of Apu, The
(1959, B&W, 103m, NR)
The concluding film in Indian director Satyajit Ray's classic *Apu* trilogy finds the young hero finally marrying and becoming a father. **DT102,** *Essential*

World of Henry Orient, The
(1964, C, 106m, NR)
Two New York teen-agers with a crush on a concert pianist make his life miserable by following him everywhere. Peter Sellers, Tippy Walker, and Merrie Spaeth star, with Angela Lansbury and Paula Prentiss. Directed by George Roy Hill. **CO4, DT55, ST131, ST198, XT9**

World of Suzie Wong, The
(1960, C, 129m, NR)
An American artist living in Hong Kong falls in love with an Asian prostitute. William Holden and Nancy Kwan star. **DR27, ST106**

World War III (1982, C, 200m, NR)
Russian forces seize the Alaskan pipeline in retaliation for grain embargo in this drama set in 1987. Rock Hudson and David Soul stars, with Brian Keith, Cathy Lee Crosby, and Jeroen Krabbe. Originally made for TV. **MY6, ST112**

World's Greatest Athlete, The
(1973, C, 93m, G)
Coach (John Amos) visiting Africa discovers a teen-aged Tarzan (Jan-Michael Vincent) who's a super athlete, and takes him to America. Tim Conway costars in this Disney comedy. **FA1**

World's Greatest Lover, The
(1977, C, 89m, PG)
Comedy set in 1920s Hollywood, starring Gene Wilder as an actor auditioning for a Valentino-like role. His neglected wife (Carol Kane) leaves him for the real Rudy. With Dom DeLuise and Fritz Feld. Directed by Wilder; inspired by Fellini's *The White Sheik.* **CO6, CO8, XT23**

Worth Winning (1989, C, 102m, PG-13)
Philadelphia TV weatherman bets his buddies that he can successfully propose to three women—all on videotape. Mark Harmon stars

in this comedy, with Madeleine Stowe, Lesley Ann Warren, Maria Holvoe, Mark Blum, and Andrea Martin. **CO1, CO14, ST209**

Woyzeck (1978, C, 82m, NR) German drama of soldier driven to insanity and murder, based on the Georg Büchner play. Klaus Kinski stars, with Eva Mattes and Wolfgang Reichmann. Directed by Werner Herzog. **DT54, ST216**

Wraith, The (1986, C, 91m, PG-13) Mysterious car begins to terrorize a group of teen-agers. Charlie Sheen, Nick Cassavetes, and Randy Quaid star. **AC10**

Wreck of the Mary Deare, The (1959, C, 105m, NR) Drama of ship's captain accused of negligence in title event, undergoing inquest. Gary Cooper and Charlton Heston star, with Michael Redgrave, Emlyn Williams, and Richard Harris. **AC12, DR17, ST37**

Written on the Wind (1956, C, 99m, NR) From director Douglas Sirk, a lush melodrama about an irresponsible playboy (Robert Stack) and his sexually promiscuous sister (Oscar winner Dorothy Malone) and their wasted lives. Rock Hudson and Lauren Bacall costar. Sirk fans will love it; others may consider it ordinary soap opera. Stack deserved an Oscar. **CL6, DT117, ST112, XT5, XT28**

Wrong Arm of the Law, The (1962, B&W, 94m, NR) A trio of robbers find themselves pursued by crooks and cops in this British comic romp starring Peter Sellers. **CO17, ST198**

Wrong Box, The (1966, C, 105m, NR) Zany British comedy, set in Victorian England, featuring skullduggery over immense inheritance. Great cast includes Ralph Richardson, John Mills, Dudley Moore, Peter Cook, Michael Caine, Nanette Newman, and Peter Sellers. Based on a story by Robert Louis Stevenson. **CO17, ST25, ST160, ST184, ST198, WR33,** *Recommended*

Wrong Is Right (1982, C, 117m, R) Satirical look at how modern news media shape political events, with Sean Connery hopscotching the world for news. Written for the screen and directed by Richard Brooks. With George Grizzard, Katharine Ross, Robert Conrad, Henry Silva, Dean Stockwell, Leslie Nielsen, and Jennifer Jason Leigh in a small role. **CO2, ST36, ST136, ST208**

Wrong Man, The (1956, B&W, 105m, NR) Henry Fonda stars in this low-key Hitchcock thriller about a musician falsely accused of

robbery, trying to overcome the system to prove he's innocent. Based on a true case. **DT57, MY7, MY8, ST71**

Wrong Move (1975, C, 103m, NR) German drama of a young writer's odyssey toward self-discovery and experience. Directed by Wim Wenders. Rudiger Vogler, Hanna Schygulla, and Nastassja Kinski star. **DT136**

Wuthering Heights (1939, B&W, 103m, NR) Laurence Olivier and Merle Oberon star in this version of the Brontë novel. William Wyler directed this classic romantic drama, photographed by Gregg Toland. **CL1, CL4, CL6, DT142, ST168,** *Essential, Recommended*

Wuthering Heights (1954, B&W, 90m, NR) Director Luis Buñuel's version of the Brontë classic, filmed in Mexico, starring Iraseme Dilian and Jorge Mistral. **CL1, DT19**

X: The Man With the X-Ray Eyes (1963, C, 80m, NR) Ray Milland invents eye drops to give him X-ray vision, which eventually leads to madness. Directed by Roger Corman. **DT30, SF5**

X: The Unheard Music (1985, C, 87m, R) A documentary of the L.A.-based punk/country band, filmed between 1980 and 1985. **MU11**

X, Y and Zee (1972, C, 110m, PG) Drama of three-way relationship between a woman (Elizabeth Taylor), her husband (Michael Caine), and his mistress (Susannah York). **DR3, ST23, ST181**

Xanadu (1980, C, 88m, PG) An angel tries to help a roller-boogie boy achieve stardom. Olivia Newton-John stars, with a special appearance by Gene Kelly. **MU8, ST123**

Xtro (1983, C, 82m, R) A man disappears and three years later returns to his son. It is then revealed that the man is an alien and that he intends to take his son to his home at any cost. **SF20**

Yakuza, The (1975, C, 112m, R) Robert Mitchum returns to Japan to rescue Brian Keith's daughter from the Yakuza, the Japanese Mafia. With Takakura Ken. Directed by Sydney Pollack; co-written by Paul Schrader. Solid drama with interesting cross-cultural touches. **AC22, DR27, DT98, ST158** *Recommended*

Yank in the RAF, A (1941, B&W, 98m, NR) Tyrone Power plays an American airman who signs up with the Brits to be near a London-based singer (Betty Grable). **AC1, ST91, ST177**

Yankee Doodle Dandy
(1942, B&W, 126m, NR)
James Cagney won an Oscar for his irresistible portrayal of songwriter George M. Cohan. With Joan Leslie, Walter Huston, and Jeanne Cagney (the star's real-life sister). Directed by Michael Curtiz. **FA9, MU5, MU6, MU7, ST24, XT2, XT8,** *Essential, Recommended*

Yanks (1979, C, 139m, R)
Drama of American servicemen stationed in Britain during World War II and their affairs with the native lasses. Richard Gere, Vanessa Redgrave, William Devane, Lisa Eichhorn, Rachel Roberts, and Chick Vennera star. Directed by John Schlesinger. Handsome looking; drama lacks urgency. **DR1, DR5, DR27, DT113, ST84, ST182**

Year My Voice Broke, The
(1987, C, 103m, PG-13)
Australian coming-of-age drama set in early 1960s about a teen-aged boy's friendship with a troubled girl. Noah Taylor stars, with Loene Carmen, Ben Mendelsohn, and Graeme Blundell. Written and directed by John Duigan. Sequel: *Flirting.* **DR9, FF5**

Year of Living Dangerously, The
(1983, C, 115m, PG)
Romantic drama, set in turbulent Indonesia during the mid-1960s, about a naive Australian reporter (Mel Gibson) and a British embassy aide (Sigourney Weaver). Linda Hunt won an Oscar for her portrayal of a male photographer. Peter Weir directed. Hunt does steal the show from less than believable leads. **DR21, DT133, ST85, ST225, XT5**

Year of the Comet (1992, CV, 89m, PG-13)
Romantic comedy-adventure stars Penelope Ann Miller as a wine auctioneer's daughter and Timothy Daly as troubleshooter for a millionaire. They're on the trail of fabulously valuable bottle of wine and up against some unscrupulous types. With Louis Jourdan. Written by William Goldman, directed by Peter Yates. **AC14, CO1**

Year of the Dragon, The
(1985, C, 136m, R)
Cynical police captain intrudes on gang warfare in New York's Chinatown. Mickey Rourke, Ariane, and John Lone star. Directed by Michael Cimino; Oliver Stone adapted Robert Daley's novel. Pretentious as only Cimino can be. **AC9, ST190**

Year of the Gun (1991, C, 111m, R)
Thriller set in 1978 about American writer whose book on the Red Brigades terrorist organization puts him in jeopardy. Andrew

McCarthy stars, with Valeria Golino, Sharon Stone, and John Pankow. Directed by John Frankenheimer; based on Michael Mewshaw's novel. **DR27, MY6, MY7, MY16**

Year of the Jellyfish, The see *L'Annee des Meduses*

Year of the Quiet Sun, A
(1985, C, 106m, PG)
Drama set in postwar Germany about an affair between an American soldier and a Polish war widow. Directed by Krzysztof Zanussi. **FF7**

Yearling, The (1946, C, 128m, NR)
Family living in the Florida swamps during the Depression finds an injured fawn and adopts it. Warm adaptation of the Marjorie Kinnan Rawlings book, starring Gregory Peck, Jane Wyman, and Claude Jarman, Jr. Oscar winner for lovely color photography. **CL9, FA5, ST171**

Yellow Cab Man, The
(1950, B&W, 85m, NR)
Red Skelton comedy about inventor of unbreakable glass involved with gangsters and crooked businessmen. With Gloria De Haven, Walter Slezak, Edward Arnold, and James Gleason. **CL10**

Yellow Rose of Texas, The
(1944, B&W, 55m, NR)
Roy Rogers goes undercover to catch some outlaws. Dale Evans costars, with vocal support from Bob Nolan and the Sons of the Pioneers. **ST188**

Yellow Submarine (1968, C, 85m, G)
The Beatles star in this surreal, animated tale about a band who set out to save Pepperland from the Blue Meanies. **CU3, MU8, MU9,** *Recommended*

Yellowbeard (1983, C, 101m, PG)
Comic pirate movie with a boatload of stars, including Graham Chapman, Cheech and Chong, Marty Feldman, James Mason, Peter Cook, and Eric Idle. Written by Chapman and Cook. **CO7, CO15, ST28, ST153**

Yentl (1983, C, 134m, PG)
Barbra Streisand plays a Jewish woman living in nineteenth-century Eastern Europe who disguises herself as a male to obtain an education. The star, who also directed and co-wrote the script for this comedy-drama, sings a dozen soliloquy songs. With Mandy Patinkin, Amy Irving, and Steven Hill. The songs don't always mix well with the rest of the film, which is well done. **CO20, ST211**

Yesterday, Today and Tomorrow
(1964, C, 119m, NR)
Oscar-winning comedy from Italy, a trio of

tales about sex and money, starring Sophia Loren and Marcello Mastroianni. Vittorio De Sica directed. **DT37, ST141, ST154, XT7**

Yin and Yang of Mr. Go, The
(1971, C, 89m, R)
Espionage drama, set in Hong Kong, with a CIA agent out to retrieve stolen military plans. Jeff Bridges stars, with James Mason, Burgess Meredith, and Broderick Crawford. **MY6, ST19, ST153**

Yodelin' Kid From Pine Ridge
(1937, B&W, 59m, NR)
Gene Autry finds himself in Georgia, refereeing a feud between cattlemen and lumbermen. With Smiley Burnette and Betty Bronson. **ST5**

Yojimbo (1961, B&W, 110m, NR)
Classic samurai adventure, exaggerated for comic effect, about a lone swordsman (Toshiro Mifune) playing off two feuding families against one another. Akira Kurosawa directed. Loosely remade as *A Fistful of Dollars*. **AC13, DT69, FF8, ST157,** *Essential, Recommended*

Yolanda and the Thief
(1945, C, 108m, NR)
Con man tries to convince an heiress that he is her guardian angel. Fred Astaire stars in this colorful musical fantasy directed by Vincente Minnelli. **CL9, MU8, DT88, ST4**

You Can't Cheat an Honest Man
(1939, B&W, 76m, NR)
W.C. Fields costars with Edgar Bergen and Charlie McCarthy in this comedy set in a circus. **CL10, ST67**

You Can't Hurry Love (1988, C, 92m, R)
Comedy of Los Angeles singles scene, featuring David Packer, Scott McGinnis, and Bridget Fonda, with David Leisure, Sally Kellerman, Kristy McNichol, and Charles Grodin in a small role. **CO4, ST70, ST94**

You Can't Take It With You
(1938, B&W, 127m, NR)
The George S. Kaufman-Moss Hart play about a zany family, directed for the screen by Frank Capra. James Stewart and Jean Arthur star, with Lionel Barrymore, Edward Arnold, Mischa Auer, and Ann Miller. Oscar winner for Best Picture and Director. **CL10, DR20, DT22, ST3, ST207, XT1, XT6**

You Can't Take It With You
(1984, C, 116m, NR)
Videotaped live performance of the George S. Kaufman-Moss Hart comedy of a determinedly wacky family, starring Colleen Dewhurst, James Coco, Jason Robards, Elizabeth Wilson, and George Rose. **CO8, DR20, ST185**

You Can't Win 'em All see *Soldiers of Fortune*

You Only Live Once (1937, B&W, 86m, NR)
Henry Fonda and Sylvia Sidney are a couple on the run in this superb crime drama from director Fritz Lang. **DT70, MY1, ST71, XT18, XT26,** *Essential, Recommended*

You Only Live Twice (1967, C, 116m, PG)
James Bond (Sean Connery) must outsmart Ernst Stavro Blofeld (Donald Pleasence) before the villain can cause the superpowers to go to war. **HF2, ST36**

You Were Never Lovelier
(1942, B&W, 97m, NR)
Hotel owner (Adolphe Menjou) allows a gambler (Fred Astaire) to work off his debts by trying to tame the man's headstrong daughter (Rita Hayworth). **ST4, ST101**

You'll Find Out (1940, B&W, 97m, NR)
Kay Kyser and His Orchestra spend the night at a haunted house. Boris Karloff, Bela Lugosi, and Peter Lorre costar in this comic horror story. **HO3, HO24, ST119, ST143**

You'll Never Get Rich
(1941, B&W, 88m, NR)
Choreographer (Fred Astaire) starts to romance a chorus girl (Rita Hayworth), then he's drafted. He is able to continue the romance when he arranges to put on a show at his base featuring her. **MU4, ST4, ST101**

Young and Innocent
(1937, B&W, 80m, NR)
A fugitive from justice is aided by a young girl in proving his innocence. Directed by Alfred Hitchcock. Derrick de Marney and Nova Pilbeam star. One of Hitchcock's best British films. **DT57, MY7, MY15,** *Recommended*

Young and Willing (1943, B&W, 82m, NR)
Screen version of stage comedy *Out of the Frying Pan*, about the wacky world of show-biz hopefuls, starring William Holden, Eddie Bracken, Susan Hayward, and Barbara Britton. **CL7, DR20, ST100, ST106**

Young at Heart (1954, C, 117m, NR)
Frank Sinatra romances Doris Day in this musical about small-town life. With Gig Young, Ethel Barrymore, and Dorothy Malone. Remake of *Four Daughters*. **DR26, MU14, ST47, ST199**

Young Bill Hickok (1940, B&W, 54m, NR)
Roy Rogers plays the legendary Western scout, as Hickok matches wits with a pair of crafty outlaws. **HF11, ST188**

Young Buffalo Bill (1940, B&W, 54m, NR)
The Legend of the Plains is portrayed by Roy

Rogers, who helps the U.S. Army put down an Indian uprising. **HF3, ST188**

Young Catherine (1991, C, 186m, NR)
Epic drama of Russia's notorious monarch, Catherine the Great, and her rise to power. Vanessa Redgrave, Christopher Plummer, Marthe Keller, Franco Nero, and Julia Ormond star. Originally made for cable TV. Also available in a 165 minute version. **DR4, ST182**

Young Doctors in Love (1982, C, 95m, R)
Comedy set in a hospital where anything goes, starring Michael McKean, Sean Young, Harry Dean Stanton, Dabney Coleman, Pamela Reed, many others. Directed by Garry Marshall. **ST205**

Young Einstein (1988, C, 90m, PG)
Wacky Australian comedy which purports to tell the story of how Albert Einstein, with the help of rock 'n' roll and Madame Curie, formulated the theory of relativity. Written and directed by Yahoo Serious, who also stars in the title role. **CO12, FF5**

Young Frankenstein
(1974, B&W, 105m, PG)
Mel Brooks's parody of the great black-and-white monster movies from the 1930s, with Gene Wilder as the mad doctor, Peter Boyle as his creation, plus Marty Feldman, Teri Garr, Cloris Leachman, and (in a hilarious cameo) Gene Hackman. Brooks's best film. **CO7, DT17, HF10, ST96,** *Essential, Highly Recommended*

Young Guns (1988, C, 107m, R)
Western tale of a youthful band of ruffians, led by Billy the Kid, out for revenge when their kindly rancher friend is murdered. Emilio Estevez stars as Billy, with Charlie Sheen, Kiefer Sutherland, Lou Diamond Phillips, Jack Palance, and Terence Stamp. **HF1, WE5, XT8**

Young Guns II (1990, C, 103m, PG)
Return of three lost boys from the first adventure, including Emilio Estevez as Billy the Kid, with Kiefer Sutherland and Lou Diamond Phillips, plus Christian Slater, James Coburn, and William Peterson as Pat Garrett. The gang is off to Mexico to hide out. **HF1, ST200, WE9**

Young Lions, The (1958, B&W, 167m, NR)
In this World War II drama, Marlon Brando plays a sensitive Nazi officer who questions the morality of his orders; Montgomery Clift is an American Jewish soldier contending with anti-Semitism within his unit. Dean Martin costars in this adaptation of Irwin Shaw's novel, with Hope Lange, Barbara

Rush, Maximilian Schell, and Lee Van Cleef. Directed by Edward Dmytryk. A bit long, with a surprisingly sympathetic interpretation by Brando; Clift and Martin very good. **AC1, DR19, ST18, ST32, ST149, ST221,** *Recommended*

Young Magician, The (1987, C, 99m, NR)
Family comic fantasy of a young boy who has to learn to control his magical powers. **FA6**

Young Man With a Horn
(1950, B&W, 112m, NR)
A talented trumpet player who dreams of the big time heads for destruction when he marries a socialite. Kirk Douglas, Lauren Bacall, and Doris Day star. **MU4, ST47, ST57**

Young Mr. Lincoln
(1939, B&W, 100m, NR)
Henry Fonda plays the future President as a struggling lawyer in this classic directed by John Ford. With Alice Brady, Marjorie Weaver, Donald Meek, and Richard Cromwell. **CL2, DT44, HF18, ST71,** *Essential, Recommended*

Young Philadelphians, The
(1959, B&W, 136m, NR)
Soap opera about an ambitious lawyer (Paul Newman) hoping to crack Philadelphia society with a socialite (Barbara Rush). With Alexis Smith, Brian Keith, and Robert Vaughn. **ST162**

Young Scarface see *Brighton Rock*

Young Sherlock Holmes
(1985, C, 109m, PG-13)
The movie that asks the question, What if Holmes and Watson had really met as prep school students? Nicholas Rowe and Alan Cox star as the future detective and his sidekick in this fanciful detective story. With Sophie Ward and Anthony Higgins. Directed by Barry Levinson. The heavy hand of executive producer Steven Spielberg is all too obvious, with over-emphasis on special effects. Still, there are some delights, including a rip-snorting last shot at the end of the final credits. **DT75, FA4, HF14**

Young Winston (1972, C, 145m, PG)
The early days of Winston Churchill, from his schooling up to his first election to Parliament. Simon Ward, Anne Bancroft, Robert Shaw, and John Mills star, with Anthony Hopkins. Richard Attenborough directed. **DR4, DR23, ST109, XT23**

Youngblood (1986, C, 110m, R)
Brash hockey player has a lot to prove to hard-driving coach, especially when he falls

in love with the man's daughter. Rob Lowe stars, with Patrick Swayze, Ed Lauter, and Cynthia Gibb. **DR22**

Your Favorite Laughs From an Evening at the Improve (1986, C, 59m, NR)
Highlights of stand-up routines by Billy Crystal, Harry Anderson, Sandra Bernhard, Michael Keaton, and Steven Wright. **CO13, CO16, ST122**

Your Past Is Showing see *The Naked Truth*

Your Ticket Is No Longer Valid (1979, C, 91m, R)
Melodrama of an impotent businessman (Richard Harris) and the Parisian madam (Jeanne Moreau) who tries to cure his problem. **ST138**

You're a Big Boy Now (1966,C, 96m, NR)
New York youth falls for a hard-hearted actress, against the wishes of his overbearing parents. Sweet, offbeat comedy from director Francis Ford Coppola, starring Peter Kastner, with Tony Bill, Elizabeth Hartman, Rip Torn, and Geraldine Page. Songs by the Lovin' Spoonful. Torn and Page are very funny; central characters are a drag. **CO4, CO12, DT29, ST216, XT9**

You're Telling Me (1934, B&W, 67m, NR)
W.C. Fields comedy of a small-town inventor with nagging wife, daughter in love with son of town snob, etc. Remake of Fields's silent *So's Your Old Man* is one of his best, with hilarious climactic golf game. UNAVAILABLE ON VIDEO. **XT29**

Yours, Mine and Ours (1968, C, 111m, G)
Comedy, based on true story of what happens when a widow (Lucille Ball) with eight children marries a widower (Henry Fonda) with ten. **CO5, FA6, ST58**

Z (1969, C, 127m, PG)
Yves Montand stars as a popular politician whose murder by right-wing thugs sets off a major social movement in his country. With Irene Papas, Jean-Louis Trintignant, and Charles Denner. Oscar winner for Best Foreign Language Picture; directed by Costa-Gavras. Exciting blend of suspense and political commentary. **FF1, MY16, XT7,** *Essential, Recommended*

Zabriskie Point (1970, C, 112m, R)
Italian director Michelangelo Antonioni's impressions of life in late-1960s America (and particularly Los Angeles) are wrapped around the story of a campus demonstrator on the run after shooting a policeman. Mark Frechette and Daria Halprin star, with Rod Taylor, Paul Fix, and in a small role, Harrison

Ford. Music by Pink Floyd, The Grateful Dead, Patti Page, and others. Widescreen will be lost on video. May not convert you to Antonioni Fan Club but it is a real time-capsule film with stunning visuals. **CU3, CU20, DR7, DT5, ST74, XT10,** *Essential, Recommended*

Zandalee (1991, C, 100m, R)
New Orleans is the setting for this romantic triangle involving a free-spirited woman (Erika Anderson), her straight-arrow hubbie (Judge Reinhold), and his lusty pal (Nicolas Cage). With Joe Pantoliano, Viveca Lindfors, Aaron Neville, and Marisa Tomei. Also available in unrated version with extra footage. **CU6, CU10, DR3, MU12, ST23**

Zandy's Bride (1974, C, 116m, PG)
Gene Hackman and Liv Ullmann star in a Western drama about a pioneer and his feisty mail-order bride. With Harry Dean Stanton, Susan Tyrrell, and Sam Bottoms. **ST96, ST205, ST220, WE8**

Zardoz (1974, C, 105m, R)
In the year 2293, the Brutals and the Exterminators are constantly at war, spurred on by the "god" Zardoz. Sean Connery stars, with Charlotte Rampling. John Boorman directed. **CU4, DT15, SF8, SF19, ST36**

Zatoichi vs. Yojimbo (1970, C, 116m, NR)
Showdown between the fabled blind swordsman and mercenary in this action drama, starring Toshiro Mifune. **FF4, ST157**

Zazie dans le Metro (1960, C, 88m, NR)
Slapstick comedy of Parisian girl wreaking havoc, written and directed by Louis Malle. Catherine Demongeot and Philippe Noiret star. **DT82, FF1, XT16**

Zebra in the Kitchen (1965, C, 93m, NR)
Jay North plays a kid who loves to keep wild pets, decides to take on restrictive zoo and its policies. With Martin Milner, Andy Devine, Joyce Meadows, and Jim Davis. **FA5**

Zebrahead (1992, C, 100m, R)
High school drama of romance between white boy (Michael Rappoport) and black girl (N'Bushe Wright). With Paul Butler, DeShonn Castle, Candy Ann Brown, Ray Sharkey, and Helen Shaver. **DR3, DR9, DR14, DR25**

Zed & Two Noughts, A (1985, C, 115m, NR)
British director Peter Greenaway offers yet another of his unique cinematic puzzles, about a woman (Andrea Ferreol) and two brothers (Brian & Eric Deacon) affected by the same car crash. **DT51, XT8**

Zelig (1983, C/B&W, 79m, PG)
Woody Allen spoofs newsreels and documentaries with his tale of the fictional Leonard Zelig, the man who knew every celebrity in the twentieth century, from Babe Ruth to Adolf Hitler. Marvelous use of actual newsreel footage with Allen's character inserted. With Mia Farrow; Susan Sontag and Saul Bellow are among the "experts" to offer running commentary. **C07, C012, DT2, HF12, ST65, XT30,** *Recommended*

Zelly and Me (1988, C, 87m, PG)
Drama set in 1950s Virginia about a young orphan girl's relationship with her nanny. Alexandra Johnes is the little girl, Isabella Rossellini her nanny. With Glynis Johns, Joe Morton, and David Lynch. **DR9, DT79**

Zentropa (1991, B&W/C, 114m, R)
Unusual drama of American working as railroad conductor in occupied Germany immediately following the war, involved with mystery woman and her family. Jean-Marc Barr stars, with Barbara Sukowa, Eddie Constantine, and Udo Kier; narrated by Max von Sydow. Directed by Lars Von Trier, a Dane; dialogue in English and German. Color used occasionally for dramatic effect; widescreen will be lost on video. Original title: *Europa*. Fascinating, if occasionally slow-moving, glimpse at little explored subject. Perhaps the ultimate in train movies. **CU1, DR27, FF3, XT19,** *Recommended*

Zeppelin (1971, C, 101m, G)
World War I tale of British aviator born in Germany, with torn loyalties. Michael York and Elke Sommer star. **AC2, AC11**

Zero for Conduct
(1933, B&W, 44m, NR)
Hilarious, surreal comedy about life in a boys' boarding school from French director Jean Vigo. **C018, FF1,** *Essential, Highly Recommended*

Ziegfeld Follies (1946, C, 110m, NR)
Musical revue showcasing such talents as Judy Garland, Fred Astaire, Gene Kelly, Lena Horne, Esther Williams, and many more. William Powell opens the show as Flo Ziegfeld in heaven. Directed by Vincente Minnelli. **DT88, MU1, MU4, ST4, ST81, ST123, ST176, XT30**

Ziegfeld Girl (1941, B&W, 131m, NR)
MGM musical about the ups and downs of a trio of show-biz hopefuls (Judy Garland, Lana Turner and Hedy Lamarr). James Stewart stars. Choreography by Busby Berkeley. **DT12, MU1, ST81, ST207, ST219**

Ziggy Stardust and the Spiders From Mars (1983, C, 91m, PG)
An early David Bowie alter ego, Ziggy Stardust, filmed at a 1973 performance. **MU10**

Zombie (1979, C, 91m, NR)
The island of Matool is the setting for a zombie epidemic. **H06, H018**

Zombie High (1987, C, 91m, R)
All the students are well mannered and obedient at this school. A curious transfer student discovers why. Virginia Madsen stars. **H012**

Zombie Island Massacre
(1984, C, 95m, NR)
A group of tourists commit a sacrilege when they witness an ancient voodoo ceremony. They are then hunted and killed by the island inhabitants. Rita Jenrette plays one of the victims. A ripe candidate for one of the great "bad" movies of them all. **CU11, H06**

Zombies on Broadway
(1945, B&W, 68m, NR)
Comedy of two press agents looking for zombies to appear in a stage act. Wally Brown and Alan Carney star, with Bela Lugosi. **ST143**

Zoot Suit (1981, C, 103m, R)
Filmed performance of musical drama about Sleepy Lagoon murder case in 1942 Los Angeles, when young Mexican-Americans were wrongly charged with murder. Daniel Valdez and Edward James Olmos star, with Charles Aidman and Tyne Daly. Written and directed by Luis Valdez. Moments of real power; shots of audience break the spell too often. **DR5, DR15, MU6**

Zorba the Greek (1964, B&W, 146m, NR)
Anthony Quinn plays the title role, a peasant who teaches a visiting Britisher (Alan Bates) a thing or two about living. Lila Kedrova won an Oscar for her performance as a fatally ill prostitute. **DR27, ST9, XT5**

Zou Zou (1934, B&W, 92m, NR)
Josephine Baker stars in this French musical about a Creole laundress who becomes a stage sensation. **FF1**

Zulu (1964, C, 138m, NR)
British soldiers hold off 4,000 Zulu warriors in this true story about the 1879 battle in Natal, South Africa. Michael Caine and Stanley Baker star. **AC6, ST25**

Zulu Dawn (1979, C, 121m, PG)
This follow-up to *Zulu* is actually about the events leading up to battle between the British Forces and the Zulu nation for control of Natal, South Africa. Peter O'Toole and Burt Lancaster star. **AC6, ST129, ST169**

Check List Index